CBSE IX 2020

Chapter and Topic-Wise
Question Bank

Mathematics

CL MEDIA (P) LTD.

Edition : 2020

Administrative and Production Offices

Published by : CL Media (P) Ltd.

A-45, Mohan Cooperative Industrial Area,
Near Mohan Estate Metro Station,
New Delhi - 110044

Marketed by : G.K. Publications (P) Ltd.

A-45, Mohan Cooperative Industrial Area,
Near Mohan Estate Metro Station,
New Delhi - 110044

ISBN 978-93-89718-01-0

Typeset by : CL Media DTP Unit

For product information :
Visit :- **www.gkpublications.com**
or
Email :- **gkp@gkpublications.com**

CONTENTS

UNIT I: NUMBER SYSTEMS

UNIT II: ALGEBRA

UNIT III: COORDINATE GEOMETRY

UNIT IV: GEOMETRY

UNIT V: MENSURATION

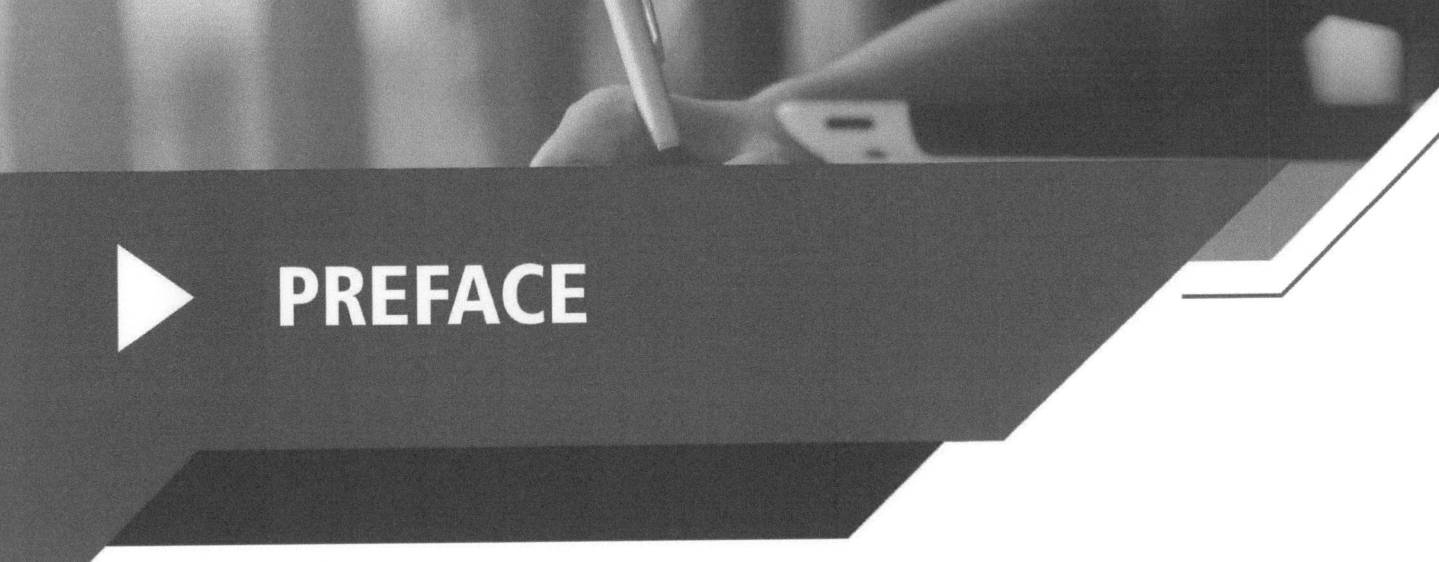

PREFACE

Class IX Exams are very important in lying a strong foundation for Class X Board Exams. You must know how to manage time efficiently if you want to ace your exams. Our Chapter and Topic-Wise Question Bank for Mathematics have been designed to help you become acquainted with the exam pattern and hone your time management skills, both at the same time.

Exclusively designed for the students of CBSE Class IX by highly experienced teachers, the book follows a three-pronged approach to make your study more focused. The questions are arranged Chapter-wise so that you can begin your preparation with the areas that demand more attention. These are further segmented topic-wise and eventually the break-down is as per the marking scheme. This division will equip you with the ability to gauge which questions require more emphasis and answer accordingly. Apart from this, several value-based questions have also   been included.

We hope the book provides the right exposure to Class IX students so that you not only ace your Exams but mold a better future for yourself. And as always, Career Launcher's school team is behind you with its experienced gurus to help your career take wings.

Wishing you all the best,
Team CL

Blueprint & Marks Distribution

Units	Unit Name	Marks
I	Number Systems	08
II	Algebra	17
III	Coordinate Geometry	04
IV	Geometry	28
V	Mensuration	13
VI	Statistics & Probability	10
	Total	80

UNIT I: NUMBER SYSTEMS

1. REAL NUMBERS

(16) Periods

1. Review of representation of natural numbers, integers, rational numbers on the number line. Representation of terminating / non-terminating recurring decimals on the number line through successive magnification. Rational numbers as recurring/terminating decimals. Operations on real numbers.

2. Examples of non-recurring/non-terminating decimals. Existence of non-rational numbers (irrational numbers) such as $\sqrt{2}, \sqrt{3}$, and their representation on the number line. Explaining that every real number is represented by a unique point on the number line and conversely, viz. every point on the number line represents a unique real number.

3. Definition of nth root of a real number.

4. Rationalization (with precise meaning) of real numbers of the type $\dfrac{1}{a + b\sqrt{x}}$ and $\dfrac{1}{\sqrt{x} + \sqrt{y}}$ and (and their combinations) where x and y are natural number and a and b are integers.

5. Recall of laws of exponents with integral powers. Rational exponents with positive real bases (to be done by particular cases, allowing learner to arrive at the general laws.)

UNIT II: ALGEBRA

1. POLYNOMIALS

(23) Periods

Definition of a polynomial in one variable, with examples and counter examples. Coefficients of a polynomial, terms of a polynomial and zero polynomial. Degree of a polynomial. Constant, linear, quadratic and cubic polynomials. Monomials, binomials, trinomials. Factors and multiples. Zeros of a polynomial. Motivate and State the Remainder Theorem with examples.

Statement and proof of the Factor Theorem. Factorization of $ax^2 + bx + c$, $a \neq 0$ where a, b and c are real numbers, and of cubic polynomials using the Factor Theorem.

Recall of algebraic expressions and identities. Verification of identities:

$$\left(x + y + z\right)^2 = x^2 + y^2 + z^2 + 2xy + 2yz + 2zx$$

$$\left(x \pm y\right)^3 = x^3 \pm y^3 \pm 3xy\left(x \pm y\right)$$

$$x^3 \pm y^3 = \left(x \pm y\right)\left(x^2 \mp xy + y^2\right)$$

$$x^3 + y^3 + z^3 - 3xyz = \left(x + y + z\right)\left(x^2 + y^2 + z^2 - xy - yz - zx\right)$$

and their use in factorization of polynomials.

2.   **LINEAR EQUATIONS IN TWO VARIABLES**   **(14) Periods**

Recall of linear equations in one variable. Introduction to the equation in two variables . Focus on linear equations of the type $ax + by + c = 0$. Explain that a linear equation in two variables has infinitely many solutions and justify their being written as ordered pairs of real numbers, plotting them and showing that they lie on a line. Graph of linear equations in two variables. Examples, problems from real life, including problems on Ratio and Proportion and with algebraic and graphical solutions being done simultaneously.

UNIT III: COORDINATE GEOMETRY

COORDINATE GEOMETRY   **(6) Periods**

The Cartesian plane, coordinates of a point, names and terms associated with the coordinate plane, notations, plotting points in the plane.

UNIT IV: GEOMETRY

1.   **INTRODUCTION TO EUCLID'S GEOMETRY (Not for assessment)**   **(6) Periods**

History - Geometry in India and Euclid's geometry. Euclid's method of formalizing observed phenomenon into rigorous Mathematics with definitions, common/obvious notions, axioms/postulates and theorems. The five postulates of Euclid. Equivalent versions of the fifth postulate. Showing the relationship between axiom and theorem, for example:

(Axiom) 1. Given two distinct points, there exists one and only one line through them. (Theorem) 2. (Prove) Two distinct lines cannot have more than one point in common.

2.   **LINES AND ANGLES**   **(13) Periods**

  1.   (Motivate) If a ray stands on a line, then the sum of the two adjacent angles so formed is 180° and the converse.
  2.   (Prove) If two lines intersect, vertically opposite angles are equal.
  3.   (Motivate) Results on corresponding angles, alternate angles, interior angles when a transversal intersects two parallel lines.
  4.   (Motivate) Lines which are parallel to a given line are parallel.
  5.   (Prove) The sum of the angles of a triangle is 180°.
  6.   (Motivate) If a side of a triangle is produced, the exterior angle so formed is equal to the sum of the two interior opposite angles.

3.   **TRIANGLES**   **(20) Periods**

  1.   (Motivate) Two triangles are congruent if any two sides and the included angle of one triangle is equal to any two sides and the included angle of the other triangle (SAS Congruence).

2.   (Prove) Two triangles are congruent if any two angles and the included side of one triangle is equal to any two angles and the included side of the other triangle (ASA Congruence).

3.   (Motivate) Two triangles are congruent if the three sides of one triangle are equal to three sides of the other triangle (SSS Congruence).

4.   (Motivate) Two right triangles are congruent if the hypotenuse and a side of one triangle are equal (respectively) to the hypotenuse and a side of the other triangle. (RHS Congruence)

5.   (Prove) The angles opposite to equal sides of a triangle are equal.

6.   (Motivate) The sides opposite to equal angles of a triangle are equal.

7.   (Motivate) Triangle inequalities and relation between 'angle and facing side' inequalities in triangles.

4.   QUADRILATERALS (10) Periods

1.   (Prove) The diagonal divides a parallelogram into two congruent triangles.

2.   (Motivate) In a parallelogram opposite sides are equal, and conversely.

3.   (Motivate) In a parallelogram opposite angles are equal, and conversely.

4.   (Motivate) A quadrilateral is a parallelogram if a pair of its opposite sides is parallel and equal.

5.   (Motivate) In a parallelogram, the diagonals bisect each other and conversely.

6.   (Motivate) In a triangle, the line segment joining the mid points of any two sides is parallel to the third side and in half of it and (motivate) its converse.

5.   AREA (7) Periods

Review concept of area, recall area of a rectangle.

1.   (Prove) Parallelograms on the same base and between the same parallels have equal area.

2.   (Motivate) Triangles on the same base (or equal bases) and between the same parallels are equal in area.

6.   CIRCLES (15) Periods

Through examples, arrive at definition of circle and related concepts-radius, circumference, diameter, chord, arc, secant, sector, segment, subtended angle.

1.   (Prove) Equal chords of a circle subtend equal angles at the center and (motivate) its converse.

2.   (Motivate) The perpendicular from the center of a circle to a chord bisects the chord and conversely, the line drawn through the center of a circle to bisect a chord is perpendicular to the chord.

3.   (Motivate) There is one and only one circle passing through three given non-collinear points.

4.   (Motivate) Equal chords of a circle (or of congruent circles) are equidistant from the center (or their respective centers) and conversely.

5.   (Prove) The angle subtended by an arc at the center is double the angle subtended by it at any point on the remaining part of the circle.

6.   (Motivate) Angles in the same segment of a circle are equal.

7.   (Motivate) If a line segment joining two points subtends equal angle at two other points lying on the same side of the line containing the segment, the four points lie on a circle.

8.   (Motivate) The sum of either of the pair of the opposite angles of a cyclic quadrilateral is 180° and its converse.

7.   CONSTRUCTIONS   (10) Periods

1.   Construction of bisectors of line segments and angles of measure 60°, 90°, 45° etc., equilateral triangles.

2.   Construction of a triangle given its base, sum/difference of the other two sides and one base angle.

3.   Construction of a triangle of given perimeter and base angles.

UNIT V: MENSURATION

1.   AREAS   (4) Periods

Area of a triangle using Heron's formula (without proof) and its application in finding the area of a quadrilateral.

2.   SURFACE AREAS AND VOLUMES   (12) Periods

Surface areas and volumes of cubes, cuboids, spheres (including hemispheres) and right circular cylinders/cones .

UNIT VI: STATISTICS & PROBABILITY

1.   STATISTICS   (13) Periods

Introduction to Statistics: Collection of data, presentation of data — tabular form, ungrouped /grouped, bar graphs, histograms (with varying base lengths), frequency polygons. Mean, median and mode of ungrouped data.

2.   PROBABILITY   (9) Periods

History, Repeated experiments and observed frequency approach to probability.

Focus is on empirical probability. (A large amount of time to be devoted to group and to individual activities to motivate the concept; the experiments to be drawn from real - life situations, and from examples used in the chapter on statistics).

MATHEMATICS

Question Paper Design

CLASS – IX (2019-20)

Time: 3 Hrs.   *Max. Marks: 80*

S. No.	Typology of Questions	Very Short Answer-Objective Type (VSA) (1 Mark)	Short Answer-I (SA) (2 Marks)	Short Answer-II (SA) (3 Marks)	Long Answer (LA) (4 Marks)	Total Marks	% Weightage (approx.)
1	**Remembering:** Exhibit memory of previously learned material by recalling facts, terms, basic concepts, and answers.	6	2	2	1	20	25
2	**Understanding:** Demonstrate understanding of facts and ideas by organizing, comparing, translating, interpreting, giving descriptions, and stating main ideas	6	1	1	3	23	29
3	**Applying:** Solve problems to new situations by applying acquired knowledge, facts, techniques and rules in a different way.	5	2	2	1	19	24

S. No.	Typology of Questions	Very Short Answer-Objective Type (VSA) (1 Mark)	Short Answer-I (SA) (2 Marks)	Short Answer-II (SA) (3 Marks)	Long Answer (LA) (4 Marks)	Total Marks	% Weightage (approx.)
4	**Analysing :** Examine and break information into parts by identifying motives or causes. Make inferences and find evidence to support generalizations **Evaluating:** Present and defend opinions by making judgments about information, validity of ideas, or quality of work based on a set of criteria. **Creating:** Compile information together in a different way by combining elements in a new pattern or proposing alternative solutions	3	1	3	1	18	22
	Total	20×1 =20	6×2 =12	8×3=24	6×4=24	80	100

Internal Assessment	20 Marks
Pen Paper Test and Multiple Assessment (5+5)	10 Marks
Portfolio	05 Marks
Lab Practical (Lab activities to be done from the prescribed books)	05 Marks

UNIT I
Number Systems

CHAPTER 1

Real Numbers

Real Numbers

- Review of representation of natural numbers, integers, rational numbers on the number line.
- Representation of terminating/non-terminating recurring decimals on the number line through successive magnification.
- Rational numbers as recurring/terminating decimals. Operation on real numbers.
- Examples of non-recurring/ non-terminating decimals.
- Existence of non-rational numbers (irrational numbers) such as $\sqrt{2}, \sqrt{3}$ and their representation on the number line.

- Explaining that every real number is represented by a unique point on the number line and conversely. viz. every point on the number line represents a unique real number.
- Definition of nth root of a real number.
- Rationalization (with precise meaning) of real numbers of the type $\dfrac{1}{a + b\sqrt{x}}$ and $\dfrac{1}{\sqrt{x} + \sqrt{y}}$ (and their combinations) where x and y are natural numbers and a and b are integers.
- Recall of laws of exponents with integral powers.
- Rational exponents with positive real bases (to be done by particular cases, allowing learner to arrive at the general laws)

A Flow Chart on Basic Concepts of Number System:-

Real Numbers
A collection of rational and irrational numbers

Rational Numbers

A number is called a rational number if it can be written in the form $\frac{p}{q}$, where p and q are integers and $q \neq 0$.

Irrational Numbers

A number is called an irrational number, if it cannot be written in the form $\frac{p}{q}$, where p and q are integers and $q \neq 0$.

The decimal expansion of a rational number is either terminating or non-terminating, recurring, conversely. A number whose decimal expansion is terminating or non-terminating recurring is rational number.

A number whose decimal expansion is non-terminating and non-recurring is irrational number.

Natural Numbers (N):
The counting numbers 1, 2, 3,.....etc. are called natural numbers

Natural Numbers (W):
Natural numbers 0, 1, 2, 3, ... etc. are called whole numbers.

Integers (Z) :
The rest of natural numbers, zero and zero and negative of natural numbers, are called integers.

If r is a rational number and s is an irrational number then $(R + s)$ and $(R - s)$ are irrational numbers, $(r \times s)$ and $\left(\frac{r}{s}\right)$ are also irrational numbers, where $r \neq 0$

There is a unique real number corresponding to every point on the number line. Morever, corresponding to each real number, there is a unique point on the number line.

Let $a > 0$ be a real number and n be a positive integer. Then $\sqrt[n]{a} = b$, if $b^n = a$ and $b > 0$. The symbol '$\sqrt{\ }$' used in $\sqrt[n]{a}$, is called the radical sign.

If a, b are positive real numbers and m, n are rational numbers. Then, we have,

(i) $a^{-m} = \frac{1}{a^m}$

(ii) $(a^m)^n = a^{mn}$

(iii) $a^m \times a^n = a^{m+n}$

(iv) $\frac{a^m}{a^n} = a^{m-n}$

(v) $\frac{a^m}{b^m} = \left(\frac{a}{b}\right)^m$

(vi) $a^m b^m = (ab)^m$

(vii) $(a^m)^{\frac{1}{n}} = \left(a^{\frac{1}{n}}\right)^m$

(viii) $\sqrt[n]{a^m} = (\sqrt[n]{a})^m = a^{\frac{m}{n}}$

If a and b are positive integers, then

(i) Rationalising factor of $\frac{1}{\sqrt{a}}$ is $\sqrt{a}$.

(ii) Rationalising factor of $\frac{1}{a \pm \sqrt{b}}$ is $(a \pm \sqrt{b})$

(iii) Rationalising factor of $\frac{1}{\sqrt{a} \pm \sqrt{b}}$ is $(\sqrt{a} \mp \sqrt{b})$

[Topic-1] Rational Numbers

Points to be Remembered

- The numbers of the form $\dfrac{p}{q}$, where p and q are integers and $q \neq 0$, are called rational numbers.

- Every rational number can be expressed as decimal. If the decimal expression of $\dfrac{p}{q}$ terminates, then it is called a terminating decimal.

- A rational number $\dfrac{p}{q}$ is said to be in simple form, if p and q $(q \neq 0)$ are integers having no common factor other than 1.

- A decimal in which a digit or a group of digits repeats periodically, is called a recurring decimal.

- The decimal expression of a rational number is either terminating or non-terminating recurring.

- If $\dfrac{p}{q}$ and $\dfrac{r}{s}$ are any two rational numbers such that $\dfrac{p}{q} < \dfrac{r}{s}$, then $\dfrac{p+q}{r+s}$ is a rational number, such that $\dfrac{p}{q} < \left(\dfrac{p+q}{r+s}\right) < \dfrac{r}{s}$.

- If a rational number $\dfrac{p}{q}$, $(q \neq 0)$ can be expressed in the form $\dfrac{P}{2^m \times 5^n}$, where $P \in Z$ and $(m, n) \in W$, then the rational number will have a terminating decimals. Otherwise, the rational number will have a non-terminating repeating (recurring) decimal.

- Every integer is a rational number. e.g, -2, -1, $+1$, $+2$.

- There are infinite rational numbers between any two given rational numbers.

- If x and y are any two rational numbers, then we get
  (i) $(x + y)$ is a rational number
  (ii) $(x - y)$ is a rational number
  (iii) $(x \times y)$ is a rational number
  (iv) $(x \div y)$ is a rational number, where $y \neq 0$.

PREVIOUS YEARS' EXAMINATION QUESTIONS

TOPIC 1

Multiple Choice Questions

(1 Mark Each)

1. Every rational number is **[NCERT Exemp.]**
   (a) a natural number (b) an integer
   (c) a real number (d) a whole number

Sol. (c) Rational and irrational numbers taken together are known as real numbers. Therefore, every rational number is a real number. Hence option
(c) is correct.

2. All the rational and irrational numbers make up the collection of **[NCERT Exemp.]**
   (a) whole numbers (b) natural numbers
   (c) real numbers (d) integers

Sol. (c) All the rational and irrational numbers make up the collection of real numbers.

3. Decimal representaiton of a rational number cannot be **[NCERT Exemp.]**
   (a) terminating
   (b) non-terminating
   (c) non-terminating/repeating
   (d) non-terminating/non-repeating

Sol. (d) The decimal representation of a rational number cannot be non-terminating and non-repeating. Hence, option (d) is correct.

4. Between two rational numbers **[NCERT Exemp.]**
   (a) there is no rational numbers
   (b) there is exactly one rational number
   (c) there are infinitely many rational numbers
   (d) there are only rational numbers and no irrational numbers

Sol. (c) Between two rational numbers there are infinite rational numbers, for example, between 5 and 6 there are 5.1, 5.2, 5.22, 5.3 ...... rational numbers.

5. $0.\overline{45}$ as a fraction in simplest form, can be written as

[NCERT Exemp.]

(a) $\dfrac{45}{90}$ (b) $\dfrac{41}{99}$

(c) $\dfrac{45}{100}$ (d) $\dfrac{5}{11}$

Sol. (d) Let $x = 0.\overline{45} = 0.45454545....$

$\Rightarrow \quad 100x = 45.4545 ....$

$\Rightarrow \quad 100x - x = (45.4545 ....) - (0.4545 ....)$

$\Rightarrow \quad 99x = 45$

$\therefore \ x = \dfrac{45}{99} = \dfrac{5}{11}$

6. The value of 1.999 .... in the form of $\dfrac{p}{q}$ where p and q are integers and is

(a) $\dfrac{19}{10}$ (b) $\dfrac{1,999}{1,000}$

(c) 2 (d) $\dfrac{1}{9}$

[NCERT Exemp.]

Sol. (c) Let $x = 1.999999.... = 1.\overline{9}$ ...(1)

Then, $10x = 19.9999... = 19.\overline{9}$ ....(2)

On Subtracting (1) from (2), we get

$$\begin{array}{r} 10x = 19.9999.... \\ x = \ \ 1.9999.... \\ \hline 9x = 18 \end{array}$$

$\therefore \ x = \dfrac{18}{9} = 2$

Hence, the value of 1.999... in the $\dfrac{p}{q}$ form is 2 or $\dfrac{2}{1}$.

7. A rational number between $\sqrt{2}$ and $\sqrt{3}$ is

(a) $\dfrac{\sqrt{2} + \sqrt{3}}{2}$

(b) $\dfrac{\sqrt{2} - \sqrt{3}}{2}$

(c) 1.5

(d) 1.8

Sol. (c) We know that

$\sqrt{2} = 1.4142135...$ and $\sqrt{3} = 1.732050807$

Clearly 1.5 is a rational number which lies between 1.4142135..... and 1.732050807

Very Short Answer Type Questions (1 Mark Each)

1. Write the following in decimal form and say what kind of decimal expansion each has

(a) $\dfrac{36}{100}$ (b) $\dfrac{1}{11}$

(c) $\dfrac{33}{8}$ (d) $\dfrac{3}{13}$

(e) $\dfrac{2}{11}$ (f) $\dfrac{329}{400}$

[NCERT EXEMPLAR]

Sol. (a) $\dfrac{36}{100} = 0.36$ [Terminating decimal]

(b) $\dfrac{1}{11} = 0.\overline{09}$ [Non-terminating and recurring decimal]

(c) $\dfrac{33}{8} = 4.125$ [Terminating decimal]

(d) $\dfrac{3}{13} = 0.0\overline{230769}$ [Non-terminating and recurring decimal]

(e) $\dfrac{2}{11} = 0.\overline{18}$ [Non-terminating and recurring decimal]

(f) $\dfrac{329}{400} = 0.8225$ [Terminating decimal]

2. Express the rational number $0.\overline{9}$ in the form $\dfrac{p}{q}$, where p and q are integers and $q \neq 0$.

[NCERT][BOARD TERM I, 2014]

Sol. Let $x = 0.999...$ ....(i)

Then, $10x = 0.999$ ....(ii)

On subtracting (i) from (ii), we get

$\therefore \ 10x - x = (9.999...) - (0.999)$

$\Rightarrow 9x = 9$

$\therefore \ x = 1$

Hence, the required rational number $= \dfrac{1}{1}$

3. Find the decimal expansion of $\dfrac{58}{1000}$.

[BOARD TERM I, 2015, SET 20UIYN]

Sol. $\dfrac{58}{1000} = 0.058$ (Decimal point is shifted three places to the left)

4. Find two rational numbers between 4 and 5.

[BOARD TERM I, 2016, SET JQ22L5C]

Sol. $4 = \dfrac{4}{5} \times 5$ and $5 = \dfrac{5}{5} \times 5$

i.e, $4 = \dfrac{20}{5}$ and $5 = \dfrac{25}{5}$

Hence, required numbers are $\dfrac{21}{5}$ and $\dfrac{22}{5}$ between 4 and 5. rational.

5. Insert three rational numbers between $-\dfrac{1}{3}$ and $-\dfrac{2}{3}$.

[BOARD TERM I, 2016, SET JQ22L5C]

Sol. $-\dfrac{1}{3} = -\dfrac{1 \times 4}{3 \times 4} = -\dfrac{4}{12}$ and $-\dfrac{2}{3} = -\dfrac{2 \times 4}{3 \times 4} = -\dfrac{8}{12}$

Hence, three rational numbers are

$-\dfrac{5}{12}, -\dfrac{6}{12}$ and $-\dfrac{7}{12}$.

6. Write a real number which has terminating decimal expansion.

Sol. Required real number is as follows:

$$\dfrac{37}{125} = 0.296$$

7. Calculate the decimal which represents the fraction $\dfrac{7}{8}$.

Sol. $\dfrac{7}{8} = 0.875$.

Hence, the decimal expansion = 0.875

8. Write the decimal form of $\dfrac{3}{11}$.

Sol. Decimal form of $\dfrac{3}{11}$ is 0.27

```
      0.2727
  11)3.0000
     22
     ──
      80
      77
      ──
       30
       22
       ──
        80
        77
        ──
         3
```

9. Write the simplest form of a rational number $\dfrac{177}{413}$.

Sol. $\dfrac{177}{413} = \dfrac{177 \div 59}{413 \div 59} = \dfrac{3}{7}$.

Hence, the simplest form is $\dfrac{3}{7}$.

10. Calculate the value of $2.\overline{9}$ in the form of $\dfrac{p}{q}$, where p and q are integers and $q \neq 0$.

Sol. Let, $x = 2.\overline{9} = 2.9999$ ...(i)

Then, $10x = 29.999$ ...(ii)

On subtracting (i) from (ii), we get,

$\Rightarrow 10x - x = (29.999...) - (2.999 ....)$

$\Rightarrow 9x = 27$

$\therefore \quad x = \dfrac{27}{9} = 3$

Hence, required rational number $= \dfrac{3}{1}$

11. Is $\dfrac{\sqrt{98}}{\sqrt{2}}$ a rational number or not?

Sol. $\dfrac{\sqrt{98}}{\sqrt{2}} = \sqrt{\dfrac{98}{2}} = \sqrt{49} = 7$

Hence, it is a rational number.

12. Calculate the $\dfrac{p}{q}$ from of 0.777, where p and q are integers and $q \neq 0$.

Sol. Let, $x = 0.777$ ...(i)

Then $10x = 7.777$ ...(ii)

On Subtracting (i) from (ii) we get,

$10x - x = (7.777 ...) - (0.777...) \Rightarrow 9x = 7$

$\therefore \quad x = \dfrac{7}{9}$

Hence, required rational number $= \dfrac{7}{9}$

13. Find a rational number lying between 3 and 4.

Sol. Here, $4 > 3$

We know that, if x and y are two numbers such that $y > x$.

Then, $\dfrac{x + y}{2}$ is a rational number between x and y.

Hence, a rational number between 3 and 4

$= \dfrac{3 + 4}{2} = \dfrac{7}{2}$.

14. Write the sum of $0.\overline{3}$ and $0.\overline{4}$.

Sol. $0.\overline{3} + 0.\overline{4} = (0.333...) + (0.444...) = 0.777....$

Let $x = 0.777....$ ...(i)

Then $10x = 7.777....$ ...(ii)

On subtracting (i) from (ii), we get,

$10 - x = (7.777....) - (0.777 ....)$

$\Rightarrow 9x = 7.0$

$\therefore\ x = \dfrac{7}{9}$

Hence, required sum = $\dfrac{7}{9}$

15. Is the number $\left(3 - \sqrt{7}\right)\left(3 + \sqrt{7}\right)$ rational or irrational?

Sol. $\left(3 - \sqrt{7}\right)\left(3 + \sqrt{7}\right) = (3)^2 - \left(\sqrt{7}\right)^2 = 9 - 7 = 2$

Hence, given number is a rational number.

Short Answer Type Questions I
(2 Marks Each)

1. Express $0.\overline{6}$ in the form of $\dfrac{p}{q}$, where p and q are integers and $q \neq 0$.

[BOARD TERM–I, 2013], [NCERT]

Sol. Let $x = 0.\overline{6}$

and $x = 0.6666.....$ ....(i)

On multiplying by 10 on both the sides, we get,

$10x = 6.6666$ ...(ii)

From (ii) − (i), we get,

$9x = 6.0$

$\therefore\ x = \dfrac{6}{9} = \dfrac{2}{3}$

Hence Required rational number is $\dfrac{2}{3}$

2. $\dfrac{\sqrt{147}}{\sqrt{75}}$ is not a rational number as $\sqrt{147}$ and $\sqrt{75}$ are not rational. State whether it is true or false. Justify your answer.

[BOARD TERM I, 2012, SET 39]

Sol. Given statement is false.

Justification : $\dfrac{\sqrt{147}}{\sqrt{75}} = \sqrt{\dfrac{147}{75}} = \sqrt{\dfrac{49}{25}} = \dfrac{7}{5}$

which is a rational number.

Since, $\sqrt{147}$ and $\sqrt{75}$ are not rational but

$\dfrac{\sqrt{147}}{\sqrt{75}} = \dfrac{7}{5}$ is a rational number.

3. Express the decimal number $2.2\overline{18}$ in the form of $\dfrac{p}{q}$, where p and q are integers and $q \neq 0$.

[BOARD TERM I, 2012, SET 41]

Sol. Let $x = 2.2\overline{18} = 2.218181818$ ....(i)

Then, $10x = 22.18181818$ ....(ii)

and $1000x = 2218.181818$ ....(iii)

On subtracting (ii) from (iii), we get,

$1000x - 10x = (2218.181818....) - (22.181818...)$

$\Rightarrow 990x = 2196.00$

$\therefore\ x = \dfrac{2196}{990} = \dfrac{2 \times 3 \times 3 \times 122}{2 \times 3 \times 3 \times 55} = \dfrac{122}{55}$

Hence, required rational number = $\dfrac{122}{55}$

4. If $7x = 1$, then find the decimal expansion of x.

[BOARD TERM I, 2012, SET 18]

Sol. Given $7x = 1$

$\Rightarrow x = \dfrac{1}{7}$

$$7\overline{)10.0000}\,\,0.142857$$

```
        0.142857
  7)10.0000
     7
     ──
     30
     28
     ──
     20
     14
     ──
     60
     56
     ──
     40
     35
     ──
     50
     49
     ──
      1
```

$\therefore x = 0.\overline{142857}$

Hence, required decimal expansion of

$x = 0.\overline{142857}$

5. Represent $0.\overline{237}$ in the form of $\dfrac{p}{q}$, where p and q are integers and $q \neq 0$.

[BOARD TERM I, 2012, SET 38]

Sol. Let $x = 0.\overline{237} = 0.237237237237....$ ...(i)

then $1000x = 237.237237....$ ...(ii)

On subtracting (i) from (ii), we get,

$1000x - x \,(237.237237....) - (0.237237....)$

$\Rightarrow 999x = 237$

$\therefore\ x = \dfrac{237}{999}.$

Hence, required rational number = $\dfrac{237}{999}.$

6. Insert three rational numbers between $\dfrac{3}{5}$ and $\dfrac{5}{7}$.

[BOARD TERM I, 2012, SET 60]

Sol. LCM of 5 and 7 = 5 × 7 = 35

$$\frac{3}{5} = \frac{3}{5} \times \frac{7}{7} = \frac{21}{35}$$

and $\dfrac{5}{7} = \dfrac{5}{7} \times \dfrac{5}{5} = \dfrac{25}{35}$

so, $\dfrac{21}{35} < \dfrac{22}{35} < \dfrac{23}{35} < \dfrac{24}{35} < \dfrac{25}{35}$

Hence, required three rational numbers are $\dfrac{22}{35}, \dfrac{23}{35}$ and $\dfrac{24}{35}$.

7. Express $\dfrac{2157}{625}$ in the decimal form and state whether it is terminating or not.

[BOARD TERM I, 2012, SET 40]

Sol. Given = $\dfrac{2157}{625}$

$$
\begin{array}{r}
3.4512 \\
625\overline{)2157} \\
-1875 \\ \hline
2820 \\
-2500 \\ \hline
3200 \\
-3125 \\ \hline
750 \\
-625 \\ \hline
1250 \\
1250 \\ \hline
\times \\ \hline
\end{array}
$$

$\therefore \dfrac{2157}{625} = 3.4512$

Hence, decimal expansion of $\dfrac{2157}{625}$ is terminating.

8. Is zero (0) a rational number? Justify your answer.

[BOARD TERM I, 2015, SET 2]

Sol. Yes, zero is a rational number.

Zero can be expressed as $\dfrac{0}{5}, \dfrac{0}{26}, \dfrac{0}{100}$ etc,

Which are in the form of $\dfrac{p}{q}$, where p and q are integers and q $\neq$ 0.

9. Find two rational numbers between 0.121221222 122221... and 0.141441444144441... in the form of $\dfrac{p}{q}$, where p and q are integers and q $\neq$ 0..

[BOARD TERM I, 2016, SET BQS6 IZK]

Sol. Two rational numbers between 0.1212212221 .... and 0.141441444144441 ... are 0.13 and 0.14

i.e. $\dfrac{13}{100}$ and $\dfrac{14}{100}$

or $\dfrac{13}{100}$ and $\dfrac{7}{50}$.

Hence, required two rational numbers are $\dfrac{13}{100}$ and $\dfrac{7}{50}$.

10. Express −0.00875 in the form of $\dfrac{p}{q}$, where p and q are integers and q $\neq$ 0..

[BOARD TERM I, 2016, SET 20C NJE9]

Sol. Given, $-0.00875 = -\dfrac{875}{100000} = \dfrac{-35}{4000} = \dfrac{-7}{800}$

Hence, $\dfrac{p}{q}$ form of = 0.00875 = $\dfrac{-7}{800}$.

Short Answer Type Questions II
(3 Marks Each)

1. Find six rational numbers between 3 and 4.

[NCERT] [BOARD TERM I, 2014,]

Sol. Let a = 3 and b = 4

Now, we find six rational numbers, i.e., n = 6

$$\therefore \ d = \frac{b-a}{n+1} = \frac{4-3}{6+1} = \frac{1}{7}$$

First rational number = a + d = 3 + $\dfrac{1}{7}$ = $\dfrac{22}{7}$

Second rational number = a + 2d = 3 + $\dfrac{2}{7}$ = $\dfrac{23}{7}$

Third rational number = a + 3d = 3 + $\dfrac{3}{7}$ = $\dfrac{24}{7}$

Fourth rational number = a + 4d = 3 + $\dfrac{4}{7}$ = $\dfrac{25}{7}$

Fifth rational number = a + 5d = 3 + $\dfrac{5}{7}$ = $\dfrac{26}{7}$

Sixth rational number = a + 6d = 3 + $\dfrac{6}{7}$ = $\dfrac{27}{7}$

Hence, required six rational numbers are $\dfrac{22}{7}, \dfrac{23}{7}, \dfrac{24}{7}, \dfrac{25}{7}, \dfrac{26}{7}$ and $\dfrac{27}{7}$

2. Express $0.3\overline{28}$ in the form of $\dfrac{p}{q}$, which are integers and $q \neq 0$.

[BOARD TERM I, 2012, SET 49]

Sol. Let $x = 0.3\overline{28} = 0.3282828....$ ...(i)

Then, $10x = 3.282828 ....$ ...(ii)

and $1000x = 328.282828....$ ...(iii)

On subtracting (ii) from (iii), we get,

$1000x - 10x = 328.2828 ... - 32828$

$990x = 325.000$

$x = \dfrac{325}{900} = \dfrac{65}{198}$

Hence, required rational number in the form of $\dfrac{p}{q}$ is $\dfrac{65}{198}$.

3. Find four rational numbers between $\dfrac{1}{5}$ and $\dfrac{1}{6}$.

[BOARD TERM, I, 2012, SET 78]

Sol. LCM of 5 and 6 = $2 \times 3 \times 5 = 30$

$\therefore \dfrac{1}{6} = \dfrac{1}{6} \times \dfrac{5}{5} = \dfrac{5}{30} \times \dfrac{5}{5} = \dfrac{25}{150}$

and $\dfrac{1}{5} = \dfrac{1}{5} \times \dfrac{6}{6} = \dfrac{6}{30} \times \dfrac{5}{5} = \dfrac{30}{150}$

Hence, four rational numbers between $\dfrac{1}{6}$ and $\dfrac{1}{5}$ are $\dfrac{26}{150}, \dfrac{27}{150}, \dfrac{28}{150}, \dfrac{29}{150}$

4. Find three rational numbers between $\dfrac{5}{7}$ and $\dfrac{9}{11}$.

[BOARD TERM, I, 2014]

Sol. LCM of 7 and 11 = $7 \times 11 = 77$

$\therefore \dfrac{5}{7} = \dfrac{5}{7} \times \dfrac{11}{11} = \dfrac{55}{77}$ and $\dfrac{9}{11} = \dfrac{9}{11} \times \dfrac{7}{7} = \dfrac{63}{77}$

Hence, three rational numbers between $\dfrac{5}{7}$ and $\dfrac{9}{11}$ are $\dfrac{56}{77}, \dfrac{57}{77}, \dfrac{58}{77}$

5. Express $32.12\overline{35}$ in the form of $\dfrac{p}{q}$.

Sol. Let $x = 32.12353535...$

Then, $100x = 3212.3535...$ ...(i)

and $10000x = 321235.3535...$ ...(ii)

On subtracting (i) from (ii), we get

$10000x - 100x = (321235.3535...) - (3212.353535...)$

$\Rightarrow 9900x = 318023$

$\therefore x = \dfrac{318023}{9900}$

Hence, required rational number in the form of $\dfrac{p}{q}$ is $\dfrac{318023}{9900}$

Long Answer Type Questions
(4 Marks Each)

1. Express $0.6 + 0.\overline{7} + 0.4\overline{7}$ In the form of $\dfrac{p}{q}$, where p, q are integers and $q \neq 0$.

[NCERT EXEMPLAR]

Sol. Let $x = 0.\overline{7} = 0.777$ ...(i)

On multiplying (i) by 10, we get

$10x = 7.777$ ....(ii)

On subtracting (i) from (ii), we get

$10x - x = (7.777)..... - (0.777....)$

$\Rightarrow 9x = 7$

$\therefore x = \dfrac{7}{9}$

Again, let $y = 0.4\overline{7} = 0.4777$ ....(iii)

On multiplying eq. (iii) by 10, we get

$10y = 4.777$ ....(iv)

and $100y = 47.777$ ....(v)

Now, on subtracting (iv) from (v), we get,

$100y - 10y = (47.777....) - (4.777....)$

$\Rightarrow 90y = 43$

$\therefore y = \dfrac{43}{90}$

Now, given expression = $0.6 + 0.\overline{7} + 0.4\overline{7}$

$= \dfrac{6}{10} + \dfrac{7}{9} + \dfrac{43}{90} = \dfrac{54 + 70 + 43}{90} = \dfrac{167}{90}$

2. Arrange in descending order $\sqrt[3]{2}$, $\sqrt[4]{5}$, $\sqrt[6]{7}$ and $\sqrt[12]{3}$

[BOARD TERM I, 2012, SET 57]

Sol. LCM of 3, 4, 6 and 12

$\sqrt[3]{2} = 2^{\frac{1}{3}} = 2^{\frac{4}{12}} = \sqrt[12]{16}$

$\sqrt[4]{5} = 5^{\frac{1}{4}} = 5^{\frac{3}{12}} = \sqrt[12]{125}$

$\sqrt[6]{7} = 7^{\frac{1}{6}} = 7^{\frac{2}{12}} = \sqrt[12]{49}$

$\sqrt[12]{3} = 3^{\frac{1}{12}} = \sqrt[12]{3}$

Now, on arranging in descending order.

$\sqrt[12]{125} > \sqrt[12]{49} > \sqrt[12]{16} > \sqrt[12]{3}$

i.e. $\sqrt[4]{5} > \sqrt[6]{7} < \sqrt[3]{2} > \sqrt[12]{3}$.

3. Express $1.3\bar{2} + 0.\overline{35}$ in the form $\frac{p}{q}$, where p and q are integers and $q \neq 0$.

[Board Term I, 2012, Set-37]

Sol. Let,

$x = 1.3\bar{2} = 1.32222......$ ...(i)

Then, $10x = 13.222......$ ...(ii)

and $100x = 132.222......$ ...(iii)

On subtracting (ii) from (iii), we get,

$100x - 10x = (132.222.....) - (13.222....)$

$\Rightarrow \quad 90x = 119.00$

$x = \frac{119}{90}$

Again, let $y = 0.\overline{35} = 0.353535......$ ...(iv)

Then, $100y = 35.3535......$ ...(v)

On subtracting (iv) from (v), we get,

$100y - y = (35.3535.....) - (0.3535......)$

$\Rightarrow \quad 99y = 35$

$\therefore \quad y = \frac{35}{99}$

$\therefore$ Given expression $= 1.3\bar{2} + 0.\overline{35} = x + y$

$= \frac{119}{90} + \frac{35}{99}$

$= \frac{119 \times 11 + 35 \times 10}{990}$

$= \frac{1309 + 350}{990}$

$= \frac{1659}{990}$

4. Give two rational numbers whose

(i) difference is a rational number,

(ii) sum is a rational number,

(iii) product is a rational number,

(iv) division is a rational number, Justify also,

[BOARD TERM I, 2015, SET 2]

Sol. Let $m = \frac{3}{5}$, $n = \frac{7}{2}$

(i) Difference $= \frac{7}{2} - \frac{3}{5} = \frac{35 - 6}{10} = \frac{29}{10}$

[Rational Number]

(ii) Sum $= \frac{3}{5} + \frac{7}{2} = \frac{6 + 35}{10} = \frac{41}{10}$

[Rational Number]

(iii) Product $= \frac{3}{5} \times \frac{7}{2} = \frac{21}{10}$

[Rational Number]

(iv) Division $= \frac{7}{2} \div \frac{3}{5} = \frac{7}{2} \times \frac{5}{3} = \frac{35}{6}$

[Rational Number]

5. In a survey, it was found that 9 out of every 11 households are donating some amount of their income to an orphanage or old age home or institutions for physically handicapped.

(i) What fraction of households are not donating?

(ii) Write it in decimal form and find what type of decimal expansion it has?

(iii) What values of society are depicted in this question?

Sol. (i) Total households = 11

and Donating households = 9

Not donating households = $11 - 9 = 2$

$\therefore$ Fraction of households

Households, which are not donating $= \frac{2}{11}$

$\begin{array}{r}) \,2.0\,(0.1818 \\ \underline{11} \\ 90 \\ \underline{88} \\ 20 \\ \underline{11} \\ 90 \\ \underline{88} \\ 2 \end{array}$

(ii) We have, $\frac{2}{11} \Rightarrow \frac{2}{11} = 0.\overline{18}$

Thus, $\frac{2}{11}$ has non-terminating repeating decimal expansion.

(iii) People are becoming more social, helpful and cooperative.

[Topic 2] Irrational Numbers

Points to be Remembered

- An irrational number is a number that cannot be expressed as the ratio of two integers.

- An irrational number is a non-terminating and non-recurring decimal. i.e. it cannot be written in form $\dfrac{p}{q}$ where p and q are both integers and $q \neq 0$. For example:-
$\sqrt{2}, \sqrt{3}, \sqrt{5}, \sqrt{2} + \sqrt{5}, \pi$ etc. are all irrational numbers.

- If a real number is not rational number, then it must be an irrational number.

- The sum or difference of a rational number and an irrational number is always an irrational number.

- The product or quotient of non-zero rational number and an irrational number is also an irrational number.

- The sum, difference, product or quotient of two irrational numbers need not to be irrational. The result may be rational or irrational.

PREVIOUS YEARS' EXAMINATION QUESTIONS
TOPIC 2

Multiple Choice Questions
(1 Mark Each)

1. A number which cannot be written in the form of $\dfrac{p}{q}$, where p and q are integers and $q \neq 0$ is called: **[NCERT Exemp.]**
   (a) positive integer
   (b) rational number
   (c) irrational number
   (d) negative integer

Sol. (c) A number which cannot be written in the form of $\dfrac{p}{q}$ where p and q are integers and $q \neq 0$, is called irrational number.

2. The decimal expansion of the number $\sqrt{2}$ is
   (a) a finite decimal **[NCERT Exemp.]**
   (b) 1.41421
   (c) non-terminating recurring
   (d) non-terminating/non-recurring

Sol. (d) The decimal expansion of the number $\sqrt{2}$ is 1.41421 ...... which is non-terminating non-recurring.

3. The product of any two irrational number is **[NCERT Exemp.]**
   (a) always an irrational number
   (b) always a rational number
   (c) always an integer
   (d) sometimes rational, sometimes irrational

Sol. (d) The product of any two irrational numbers is sometimes rational and sometimes irrational. For example-
$$\sqrt{2} \times \sqrt{2} = 2 \,(\text{Rational number})$$
and $\sqrt{2} \times \sqrt{3} = \sqrt{6}$ (Irrational number)

4. Which of the following is irrational? **[NCERT Exemp.]**
   (a) 0.14
   (b) $0.14\overline{16}$
   (c) $0.\overline{1416}$
   (d) 0.4014001400014....

Sol. (d) A number is irrational if and only if its decimal representation is non-terminating and non-recurring.
   (a) 0.14 is a terminating decimal and therefore it cannot be an irrational number.
   (b) $0.14\overline{16}$ is a non-terminating and recurring decimal and therefore it cannot be irrational.
   (c) $0.\overline{1416}$ is a non-terminating and recurring decimal and therefore it cannot be irrational.
   (d) 0.4014001400014.... is a non-terminating and non-recurring decimal and therefore it is an irrational number.

5. Which of the following is irrational? **[NCERT Exemp.]**
   (a) $\dfrac{\sqrt{4}}{9}$
   (b) $\dfrac{\sqrt{12}}{\sqrt{3}}$
   (c) $\sqrt{7}$
   (d) $\sqrt{81}$

Sol. (c) A number whose decimal expansion is non-terminating and non-recurring is irrational number.

(a) $\dfrac{\sqrt{4}}{9} = \dfrac{2}{3} = 0.\overline{6}$ (Rational Number)

(b) $\dfrac{\sqrt{12}}{\sqrt{3}} = \dfrac{\sqrt{4} \times \sqrt{3}}{\sqrt{3}} = 2$ (Rational Number)

(c) $\sqrt{7} = 2.6457513$ (Irrational Number)

(d) $\sqrt{81} = 9$ (Rational Number)

6. $\left(\sqrt{12} + \sqrt{10} - \sqrt{2}\right)$ is

(a) a positive rational number

(b) equal to zero

(c) an irrational number

(d) a negative integer

Sol. (c) $\left(\sqrt{12} + \sqrt{10} - \sqrt{2}\right) = \left(2\sqrt{3} + \sqrt{10} - \sqrt{2}\right)$

Hence, given number is an irrational number.

7. Which of the following numbers is an irrational number that lies between the fractions $\dfrac{2}{7}$ and $\dfrac{3}{7}$?

(a) 0.150151152....

(b) 0.286286....

(c) 0.35363738....

(d) 0.42714271....

Sol. (c) An irrational number 0.35363738... lies between the fractions $\dfrac{2}{7}$ and $\dfrac{3}{7}$.

8. State whether the following statements are true or false.

[NCERT Exemp.]

(i) $\dfrac{\sqrt{15}}{\sqrt{3}}$ is written in the form $\dfrac{p}{q}$ where $q \neq 0$ and so it is a rational number.

(ii) $\dfrac{\sqrt{2}}{3}$ is a rational number

(iii) There are infinitely many integers between any two integers.

(iv) Number of rational numbers between 15 and 18 is finite.

(v) The square of an irrational number is always rational.

(vi) $\dfrac{\sqrt{12}}{\sqrt{3}}$ is not a rational number as $\sqrt{12}$ and $\sqrt{3}$ are not integers.

(vii) There are numbers which can not be written in the form $\dfrac{p}{q}$, $q \neq 0$, p, q both are not integers.

Sol. (i) Clearly given statement is false since, $\dfrac{\sqrt{15}}{\sqrt{3}} = \sqrt{\dfrac{15}{3}} = \sqrt{5} = \dfrac{\sqrt{5}}{1}$, where $p = \sqrt{5}$ is irrational number. It is not necessary that any number written in the form $\dfrac{p}{q}$ is rational.

(ii) Clearly the given statement is false since $\dfrac{\sqrt{2}}{3}$ is of the form $\dfrac{p}{q}$ but $p = \sqrt{2}$ is not an integer

(iii) Clearly, the given statement is false. Consider two integers 8 and 9. There are no integers between 8 and 9.

(iv) Clearly, the given statement is false. There are infinite rational numbers between any two rational numbers.

(v) Clearly. the given statement is false. Consider an irrational number $\sqrt[4]{5}$ then, its square $\left(\sqrt[4]{5}\right)^2 = \sqrt{5}$, which is not a rational number.

(vi) Clearly, the given statement is false. $\dfrac{\sqrt{12}}{\sqrt{3}} = \sqrt{\dfrac{12}{3}} = \sqrt{4} = 2$, which is a rational number.

(vii) Clearly, the given statement is true. For example, $\dfrac{\sqrt{5}}{\sqrt{7}}$ is of the form $\dfrac{p}{q}$ but $p = \sqrt{5}$ and $q = \sqrt{7}$ are not integers.

Very Short Answer Type Questions

(1 Mark Each)

1. Find two irrational numbers between $\dfrac{1}{7}$ and $\dfrac{2}{7}$, when it is given that $\dfrac{1}{7} = 0.142857142857...$

[NCERT EXEMPLAR]

Sol. We have $\dfrac{1}{7} = 0.\overline{142857}$ and $\dfrac{2}{7} = 0.\overline{285714}$

Above irrational number have non-terminating non-repeating decimals.

Hence, two irrational numbers between $\dfrac{1}{7}$ and $\dfrac{2}{7}$ may be

2. Identify an irrational number among the following numbers :

$$0.13, 0.13\overline{15}, 0.\overline{1315}, 0.3013001300013...$$

Sol. 0.13 is a terminating number. Therefore, it is not an irrational number.

$0.13\overline{15} = 0.131515...$, is repeating, continuously. Therefore, it is not an irrational number.

$0.\overline{1315} = 0.13151315$ is repeating continuously, Therefore, it is not an irrational number.

$0.3013001300013....$, is non-terminating and non-recurring decimal. Therefore, it is an irrational number.

Hence only 0.3013001300013 is an irrational number.

3. Simplify the number $\left(\sqrt{2}+5\right)^2$.

Sol.
$$\left(\sqrt{2}+5\right)^2 = \left(\sqrt{2}\right)^2 + \left(\sqrt{5}\right)^2 + 2\times\sqrt{2}\times\sqrt{5}$$
$$= 2+5+2\sqrt{10}$$
$$= 7+2\sqrt{10}$$

4. Is the product of two irrational numbers always an irrational number?

Sol. No, it may be rational or irrational.

for example:-
$$\sqrt{2}\times\sqrt{3} = \sqrt{6}$$

Which is an irrational number.

5. Calculate the irrational number between 2 and 2.5.

Sol. Since, $\sqrt{5} = 2.236$

Hence, the irrational number between 2 and 2.5 is $\sqrt{5}$.

6. Write the sum $2\sqrt{5}$ and $3\sqrt{7}$.

Sol. Sum of $2\sqrt{5}$ and $3\sqrt{7} = 2\sqrt{5} + 3\sqrt{7}$.

Short Answer Type Questions I

(2 Marks Each)

1. Let x and y be rational and irrational numbers, respectively. Is (x + y) necessarily an irrational number? Give an example in support of your answer.

Sol. Yes, (x + y) is necessarily an irrational number.

For example

Let $x = 5$ and $y = \sqrt{3}$

Then, $x + y = 5 + \sqrt{3}$

If possible. let $x + y = 5 + \sqrt{3}$ be a rational number.

Consider,

$$a = 5 + \sqrt{3}$$

On squaring both sides, we get

$$a^2 = \left(5+\sqrt{3}\right)^2$$
$$\Rightarrow a^2 = 5^2 + \left(\sqrt{3}\right)^2 + 2(5).\left(\sqrt{3}\right)$$
$$= 25 + 3 + 10\sqrt{3} = 28 + 10\sqrt{3} = \frac{a^2-28}{10} = \sqrt{3}$$

Since, a is a rational number.

So, $\dfrac{a^2-28}{10}$ will also rational and

Here, $= \dfrac{a^2-28}{10}$ is rational and $\sqrt{3}$ is irrational.

$\because$ Rational number cannot equal to irrational number.

$\therefore$ This is contradict of our assumption.

Thus, our assumption is wrong.

Hence, (x + y) is an irrational number.

2. Find any two irrational numbers between 0.5 and 0.55.

Sol. $0.5101001000100001...$ and $0.502002000200002...$ are two irrational numbers between 0.5 and 0.55.

3. Find an irrational number between $\dfrac{1}{7}$ and $\dfrac{2}{7}$, when it is given that $\dfrac{1}{7} = 0.\overline{142857}$

Sol. Given,
$$\frac{1}{7} = 0.142857142857.......$$
$$\text{and } \frac{2}{7} = (0.142857142857......)\times 2$$
$$= 0.285714285714.........$$

Hence, required number can be $0.160160016000...$ between $\dfrac{1}{7}$ and $\dfrac{2}{7}$

4. Find any two irrational numbers between 0.1 and 0.12

[BOARD TERM I, 2014]

Sol. Required two irrational numbers are

0.101100100010000..... and

0.10200200020000..... between 0.1 and 0.12

Short Answer Type Questions II

(3 Marks Each)

1. Represent $\sqrt{9.3}$ on the number line.?

[NCERT] [Delhi Board 2013 Board Term I, 2011, Set-12; 2010, Set B1 2012, Set-50]

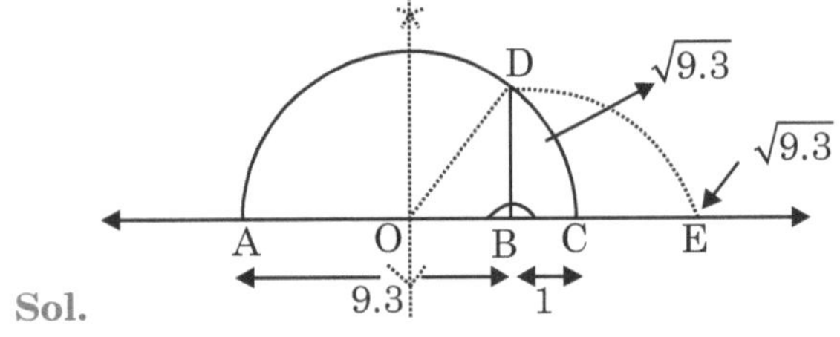

Sol.

Consider the distance 9.3 units from a fixed point A on a given line to obtain a point B such that AB = 9.3 units. From B, take a distance of 1 unit and mark the new points as C. Find the mid-point of AC and mark that point as O. Now Draw a semi-circle with centre O and radius OC and draw a line perpendicular to AC passing through B and intersecting the semi-circle at D.

Then, BD = $\sqrt{9.3}$

To represent $\sqrt{9.3}$ on the number line, let us consider the line BC as the number line, with B as zero C as 1, and so on.

Draw an arc with centre B and radius BD, which intersects the number line at E.

Hence, point E represents $\sqrt{9.3}$ on the number line.

2. Represent $\sqrt{5}$ on the number line.

[NCERT EXAMPLAR, BOARD TERM I, 2014, BQS61ZK], [NCERT]

Sol. We know that, $\sqrt{5}, = \sqrt{4+1} = \sqrt{2^2 + 1^2}$

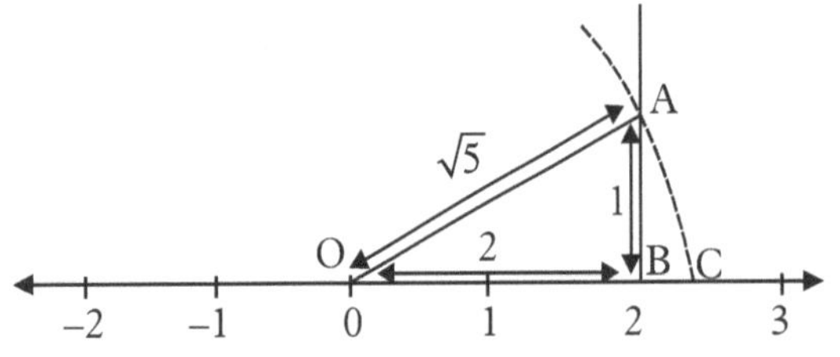

Therefore, Draw right angled $\triangle$OBA, such that OB = 2, units, AB = 1 unit and $\angle$OBA = 90°

By Pythagoras theorem, we have

$OA^2 = OB^2 + AB^2 = 2^2 + 1^2$

$\therefore$ OA = $\sqrt{4+1}$ = $\sqrt{5}$

Now take O as centre, OA = $\sqrt{5}$ as radius, draw an arc which intersects the line at point C.

Hence, the point C represents $\sqrt{5}$ on the number line.

3. Find three irrational numbers between $\frac{5}{7}$ and $\frac{9}{11}$.

[BOARD TERM, I, 2016, SET 7 AEDLQR, NCERT]

Sol. Given, $\frac{5}{7} = 0.\overline{714285}$

and $\frac{9}{11} = 0.\overline{81}$

Hence, three irrational numbers between $\frac{5}{7}$ and $\frac{9}{11}$ will be as follows:

(i) 0.727227222....

(ii) 0.737337333....

(iii) 0.747447444....

4. Represent $\sqrt{4.5}$ on the number line.

[BOARD TERM, I, 2014]

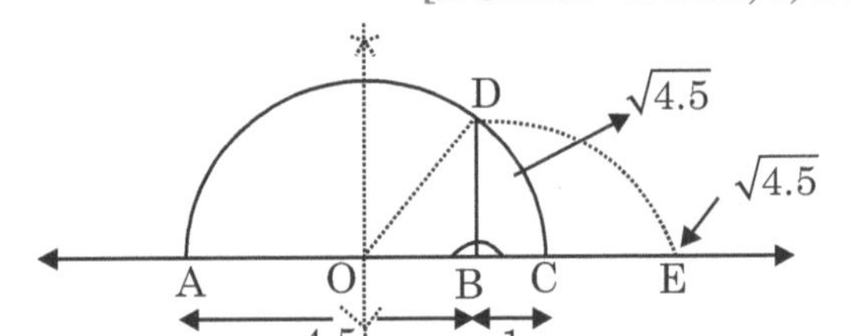

Sol.

Consider a line segment AB = 4.5 units. Extend AB upto point C such that BC = 1 unit.

$\therefore$ AC = 4.5 + 1 = 5.5 units. Now mark O as the midpoint of AC. With O as centre and radius OC draw a semicircle. Draw perpendicular BD on AC which intersect the semicircle at D.

This length BD = $\sqrt{4.5}$ units.

To show BD on the number line, consider line ABC as number line with point B as zero. Therefore,

BC = 1 unit.

With B as centre and radius BD draw an arc which intersects number line ABC at E. So this portion represents $\sqrt{4.5}$ on number line.

AB = 4.5 units

BC = 1 unit

$\therefore$ BD = BE = $\sqrt{4.5}$ units

5. Represent $\sqrt{9.5}$ on the number line.?

[Board Term I, 2016, Set-20CNJE9]

Sol.

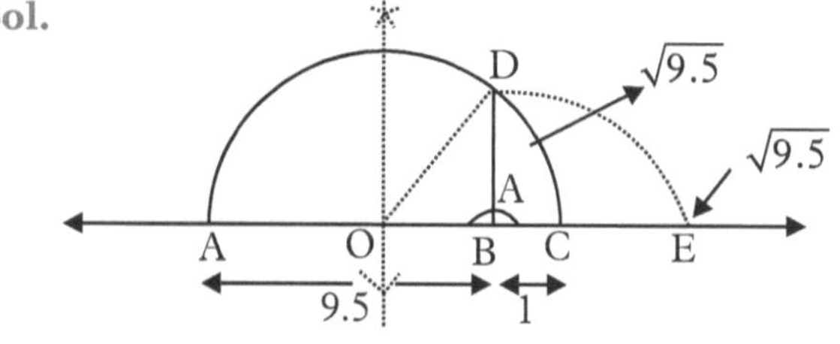

Consider the distance 9.5 units from a fixed point A on a given line to obtain a point B such that AB = 9.5 units. From B, consider a distance of 1 unit and mark a new points as C. Find the mid-point of AC and mark that point as O. Now Draw a semi-circle with centre O and radius OC and draw a line perpendicular to AC passing through B and intersecting the semi-circle at D.

Then, BD = $\sqrt{9.5}$

To represent $\sqrt{9.5}$ on the number line, let us consider the line BC as the number line, with B as zero C as 1, and so on.

Now draw an arc with centre B and radius BD, which intersects the number line at E.

Therefore, point E represents $\sqrt{9.5}$ on the number line.

6. Examine whether $\sqrt{2}$ is rational or irrational.

[Board Term I, 2016, Set-QGL21FS]

Sol. Let $\sqrt{2}$ be rational and its simplest form is $\dfrac{p}{q}$ where p and q are integers having no common factor other than 1 and $q \neq 0$

Now, $\sqrt{2} = \dfrac{p}{q}$ or, $2 = \dfrac{p^2}{q^2}$ [on squaring both sides]

or, $2q^2 = p^2$ ....(i)

or, 2 divides p^2 [$\because$ 2 divides $2q^2$]

or 2 divides p [$\because$ 2 is prime and divide p^2]

Let p = 2r for some integer r

Putting a = 2r in (i) we get

$2q^2 = 4r^2$ or, $q^2 = 2r^2$

$\Rightarrow$ 2 divides q^2 [$\because$ 2 divide $2c^2$]

$\Rightarrow$ 2 divides q [2 is prime and 2 divides q^2 or, 2 divides q]

Thus 2 is a common factor of p and q

But this contradicts the fact that p and q have no common factor other than 1.

The contradiction arises by assuming that $\sqrt{2}$ is rational number.

Hence, $\sqrt{2}$ is irrational.

7. Represent $\sqrt{3}$ on the number line.

[Board Term I, 2013]

Sol.

Let AB = BC = 1 unit length

By Pythagoras theorem, we have,

$OC = \sqrt{1^2 + 1^2} = \sqrt{2}$

Construct CD = 1 unit length perpendicular to OC, then by Pythagoras theorem, we have

$OD = \sqrt{\left(\sqrt{2}\right)^2 + 1^2} = \sqrt{3}$

Using a compass with centre O and radius OD, draw an arc which intersects the number line at the point Q, then Q corresponds to $\sqrt{3}$

Hence, point Q represents $\sqrt{3}$ on the number line.

Long Answer Type Questions

(4 Marks Each)

1. Give an example of two irrational numbers whose:

    (i)   difference is a irrational number,

    (ii) sum is a irrational number,

    (iii) product is an irrational number,

    (iv) division is an irrational number. Justify also.

[BOARD TERM I, 2015, SET - 20UIGYH]

Sol. Let two irrational numbers are $\sqrt{15}$ and $\sqrt{3}$

    (i) $\sqrt{15} - \sqrt{3}$

          = Difference is an irrational number.

    (ii) $\sqrt{15} + \sqrt{3}$

          = sum is an irrational number.

    (iii) $\sqrt{15} \times \sqrt{3} = \sqrt{45} = 3\sqrt{5}$ = Product is an irrational number

    (iv) $\dfrac{\sqrt{15}}{\sqrt{3}} = \sqrt{\dfrac{15}{3}} = \sqrt{5}$

          = division is an irrational number.

[Topic 3] n^{th} Root of a Real Number

Points to be Remembered

- If $a^n = b$, where a and b are real numbers and n is a positive integer, then

  (i) a is n^{th} root of b.

  (ii) It is can be written as $\sqrt[n]{b} = a$

  (iii) also known as radical.

- Second root of a number is square root.

- Third root of a number is cube root.

- Some other properties of nth root are as follows-

  (i) $\sqrt{a} \times \sqrt{a} = a$

  (ii) $\sqrt[3]{a} \times \sqrt[3]{a} \times \sqrt[3]{a} = a$

  (iii) $\sqrt[n]{a} \times \sqrt[n]{a} \times \dots\dots n$ times $= a$

  (iv) $\sqrt[n]{rs} = \sqrt[n]{r} \cdot \sqrt[n]{s}$

(v) $\sqrt[n]{\dfrac{r}{s}} = \dfrac{\sqrt[n]{r}}{\sqrt[n]{s}}$

(vi) $\left(\sqrt{r} + \sqrt{s}\right)\left(\sqrt{r} - \sqrt{s}\right) = (r - s)$

(vii) $\left(r + \sqrt{s}\right)\left(r - \sqrt{s}\right) = r^2 - s$

(viii) $\left(\sqrt{r} - \sqrt{s}\right)^2 r - 2\sqrt{r}\sqrt{s} + s$

(ix) $\sqrt[n]{a^n} = a$

(x) $\sqrt[m]{\sqrt[n]{a}} = \sqrt[n]{\sqrt[m]{a}}$

(xi) $\dfrac{\sqrt[p]{a^n}}{\sqrt[p]{a^m}} = \sqrt[p]{a^{n-m}}$

(xii) $\sqrt[p]{a^n} \times a^m = \sqrt[p]{a^{n+m}}$

(xiii) $\sqrt[p]{\left(a^n\right)^m} = \sqrt[p]{a^{nm}}$

PREVIOUS YEARS'
EXAMINATION QUESTIONS
TOPIC 3

Multiple Choice Questions
(1 Mark Each)

1. What is the value of the expression $\dfrac{3^{\frac{9}{4}}.3^{\frac{3}{4}}}{3^3}$?

    [NCERT Exemp.]

    (a) $\dfrac{1}{9}$ (b) $\dfrac{1}{3}$

    (c) 1   (d) 3

    Sol. (c) Given expression

    $$\dfrac{3^{\frac{9}{4}}.3^{\frac{3}{4}}}{3^3} = \dfrac{3^{\left(\frac{9}{4}+\frac{3}{4}\right)}}{3^3} = \dfrac{3^{\frac{12}{4}}}{3^3} = \dfrac{3^3}{3^3} = 1$$

2. The value of $\dfrac{\sqrt{32} + \sqrt{48}}{\sqrt{8} + \sqrt{12}}$ is equal to

    [NCERT Exemp.]

    (a) $\sqrt{2}$ (b) 2

    (c) 4   (d) 8

    Sol. (b) Given expression

    $$\dfrac{\sqrt{32} + \sqrt{48}}{\sqrt{8} + \sqrt{12}} = \dfrac{\sqrt{4 \times 4 \times 2} + \sqrt{4 \times 4 \times 3}}{\sqrt{2 \times 2 \times 2} + \sqrt{2 \times 2 \times 3}}$$

    $$= \dfrac{4\sqrt{2} + 4\sqrt{3}}{2\sqrt{2} + 2\sqrt{3}} = \dfrac{4\left(\sqrt{2} + \sqrt{3}\right)}{2\left(\sqrt{2} + \sqrt{3}\right)} = \dfrac{4}{2} = 2$$

3. The number obtained on rationalising the denominator of $\dfrac{1}{\sqrt{7} - 2}$ is

    [NCERT Exemp.]

    (a) $\dfrac{\sqrt{7} + 2}{3}$ (b) $\dfrac{\sqrt{7} - 2}{3}$

    (c) $\dfrac{\sqrt{7} + 2}{5}$ (d) $\dfrac{\sqrt{7} + 2}{45}$

Sol. (a) Given expression $= \dfrac{1}{\sqrt{7}-2}$

On rationalizing the denominator.

$$= \dfrac{1}{\sqrt{7}-2} \times \dfrac{\sqrt{7}+2}{\sqrt{7}+2} = \dfrac{\sqrt{7}+2}{7-4} = \dfrac{\sqrt{7}+2}{3}$$

4. $2\sqrt{3}+\sqrt{3}$ is equal to   [NCERT Exemp.]

(a) $2\sqrt{6}$ (b) 6

(c) $3\sqrt{3}$ (d) $4\sqrt{6}$

Sol. (c) $2\sqrt{3}+\sqrt{3} = \sqrt{3}(2+1) = 3\sqrt{3}$

5.   After rationalising the denominator of $\dfrac{7}{3\sqrt{3}-2\sqrt{2}}$, we get the denominator as

[NCERT Exemp.]

(a) 13   (b) 19

(c) 5   (d) 35

Sol. (b) Given expression $= \dfrac{7}{3\sqrt{3}-2\sqrt{2}}$

On rationalizing the denominator,

$$= \dfrac{7}{3\sqrt{3}-2\sqrt{2}} \times \dfrac{\left(3\sqrt{3}+2\sqrt{2}\right)}{3\sqrt{3}+2\sqrt{2}}$$

$$= \dfrac{3\sqrt{3}+2\sqrt{2}}{27-8} = \dfrac{3\sqrt{3}+2\sqrt{2}}{19}$$

Therefore, required denominator is 19.

6. $\sqrt{10} \times \sqrt{15}$ is equal to   [NCERT Exemp.]

(a) $6\sqrt{5}$ (b) $5\sqrt{6}$

(c) $\sqrt{25}$ (d) $10\sqrt{5}$

Sol. (b) We have $\sqrt{10} \times \sqrt{15} = \sqrt{10 \times 15} = \sqrt{2 \times 5 \times 3 \times 5}$

$$= 5\sqrt{2 \times 3} = 5\sqrt{6}$$

7. $\dfrac{1}{\sqrt{9}-\sqrt{8}}$ is equal to   [NCERT Exemp.]

(a) $\dfrac{1}{2}\left(3-2\sqrt{2}\right)$

(b) $\dfrac{1}{3+2\sqrt{2}}$

(c) $3-2\sqrt{2}$

(d) $3+2\sqrt{2}$

Sol. (d) Given expression $= \dfrac{1}{\sqrt{9}-\sqrt{8}} = \dfrac{1}{3-\sqrt{8}}$

On rationalizing the denominator,

$$= \dfrac{1}{3-\sqrt{8}} = \dfrac{1}{3-\sqrt{8}} \times \dfrac{3+\sqrt{8}}{3+\sqrt{8}} = \dfrac{3+\sqrt{8}}{9-8}$$

$$= 3+\sqrt{2\times4} = 3+2\sqrt{2}$$

8.   The simplest form of

$$\left(\dfrac{81}{16}\right)^{-\frac{3}{4}} \times \left[\left(\dfrac{25}{9}\right)^{-\frac{3}{2}} \div \left(\dfrac{5}{2}\right)^{-3}\right] \text{ is}$$

[NCERT Exemp.]

(a) $\dfrac{5}{3}$ (b) $\dfrac{3}{5}$

(c) $\dfrac{3}{2}$ (d) 1

Sol. (d) Given expression

$$= \left(\dfrac{81}{16}\right)^{-\frac{3}{4}} \times \left[\left(\dfrac{25}{9}\right)^{-\frac{3}{2}} \div \left(\dfrac{5}{2}\right)^{-3}\right]$$

$$= \left(\dfrac{16}{81}\right)^{\frac{3}{4}} \times \left[\left(\dfrac{9}{25}\right)^{\frac{3}{2}} \div \left(\dfrac{2}{5}\right)^{3}\right]$$

$$= \left(\dfrac{2}{3}\right)^{3} \times \left[\left(\dfrac{3}{5}\right)^{3} \div \dfrac{8}{125}\right]$$

$$= \dfrac{8}{27} \times \left[\dfrac{27}{125} \times \dfrac{125}{8}\right] = \dfrac{8}{27} \times \dfrac{27}{8} = 1$$

Very Short Answer Type Questions
(1 Mark Each)

1.   Simplify : $\left(5+\sqrt{5}\right)\left(5-\sqrt{5}\right)$

[BORD TERM I, 2014] [NCERT]

Sol. Given expression $\left(5+\sqrt{5}\right)\left(5-\sqrt{5}\right)$

$$= \left[5^{2}-\left(\sqrt{5}\right)^{2}\right]$$

$$= (25-5)$$

$$= 20$$

2.   Simplify : $\sqrt{72}+\sqrt{800}-\sqrt{18}$.

[BOARD TERM I, 2016]

Sol. given expression $= \sqrt{72}+\sqrt{800}-\sqrt{18}$.

$$= \sqrt{36\times2}+\sqrt{400\times2}-\sqrt{9\times2}$$

$$= 6\sqrt{2}+20\sqrt{2}-3\sqrt{2}$$

$$= 26\sqrt{2}-3\sqrt{2} = 23\sqrt{2}$$

3. Write the equivalent of $\sqrt{12} \times \sqrt{8}$.

Sol. Given expression $\sqrt{12} \times \sqrt{8}$

$$= \sqrt{4 \times 3} \times \sqrt{4 \times 2}$$

$$= 2\sqrt{3} \times 2\sqrt{2} = 4\sqrt{3 \times 2} = 4\sqrt{6}$$

4. Write the equivalent $\left(a + \sqrt{b}\right)\left(a - \sqrt{b}\right)$

Sol. Given expression $= \left(a + \sqrt{b}\right)\left(a - \sqrt{b}\right)$

$$= (a)^2 - \left(\sqrt{b}\right)^2 = a^2 - b$$

5. Calculate the value of $4\sqrt{28} \div 3\sqrt{7}$.

Sol. Given expression $= 4\sqrt{28} \div 3\sqrt{7}$

$$= 4\sqrt{4 \times 7} \div 3\sqrt{7}$$

$$4 \times 2\sqrt{7} \div 3\sqrt{7} = \frac{8\sqrt{7}}{3\sqrt{7}} = \frac{8}{3}$$

6. If $b > 0$ and $b^2 = a$, then find the value of $\sqrt{a}$.

Sol. Given, $b^2 = a$ $(b > 0)$

$$\therefore \ \sqrt{a} = b$$

7. Find the value of $\dfrac{(0.6)^0 - (0.1)^{-1}}{\left(\frac{3}{8}\right)^{-1}\left(\frac{3}{2}\right)^3 + \left(-\frac{1}{3}\right)^{-1}}$.

Sol. Given expression $= \dfrac{(0.6)^0 - (0.1)^{-1}}{\left(\frac{3}{8}\right)^{-1}\left(\frac{3}{2}\right)^3 + \left(-\frac{1}{3}\right)^{-1}}$

$$= \frac{1 - \dfrac{1}{0.1}}{\dfrac{8}{3} \times \dfrac{27}{8} + (-3)}$$

$$= \frac{1 - 10}{9 - 3} = \frac{-9}{6} = -\frac{2}{3}$$

8. Find the value of $\sqrt[4]{(64)^{-2}}$.

Sol. Given expression $= \sqrt[4]{(64)^{-2}} = \left[(64)^{-2}\right]^{\frac{1}{4}}$

$$= (64)^{-2 \times \frac{1}{4}} = (64)^{-\frac{1}{2}}$$

$$= \left(8^2\right)^{-\frac{1}{2}} = (8)^{2 \times \left(-\frac{1}{2}\right)} = 8^{-1} = \frac{1}{8}$$

Short Answer Type Questions I
(2 Marks Each)

1. Find the product of $5\sqrt{2}\left(3 + \sqrt{2}\right)\left(5 + \sqrt{2}\right)$.

[BOARD TERM I, 2012, SET 62]

Sol. Given expression

$$= 5\sqrt{2}\left(3 + \sqrt{2}\right)\left(5 + \sqrt{2}\right)$$

$$= 5\sqrt{2}\left(3 \times 5 + 3\sqrt{2} + 5\sqrt{2} + \sqrt{2} \times \sqrt{2}\right)$$

$$= 5\sqrt{2}\left(15 + 3\sqrt{2} + 5\sqrt{2} + 2\right)$$

$$= 5\sqrt{2}\left(17 + 8\sqrt{2}\right)$$

$$= 5\sqrt{2} \times 17 + 5\sqrt{2} \times 8\sqrt{2}$$

$$= 85\sqrt{2} + 40 \times 2 = 85\sqrt{2} + 80$$

2. Multiply : $2\sqrt[3]{3}$ by $3\sqrt{2}$.

[BOARD TERM I, 2012, SET 58]

Sol. LCM of 2 and 3 = 2 × 3 = 6

$$\therefore \ 2\sqrt[3]{3} = 2(3)^{\frac{1}{3} \times \frac{2}{2}} = 2\sqrt[6]{3^2} = 2\sqrt[6]{9}$$

and $3\sqrt{2} = 3(2)^{\frac{1}{2} \times \frac{3}{3}} = 3\sqrt[6]{2^3} = 3\sqrt[6]{8}$

Now, given expression

$$= 2\sqrt[3]{3} \times 3\sqrt{2} = 2\sqrt[6]{9} \times 3\sqrt[6]{8} = 6\sqrt[6]{9 \times 8}$$

$$= 6\sqrt[6]{72}$$

3. Simplify : $\sqrt{50} - \sqrt{98} + \sqrt{162}$.

[BOARD TERM I, 2012, SET 46]

Sol. Given expression

$$= \sqrt{50} - \sqrt{98} + \sqrt{162}$$

$$= \sqrt{5 \times 5 \times 2} - \sqrt{7 \times 7 \times 2} + \sqrt{3 \times 3 \times 3 \times 3 \times 2}$$

$$= 5\sqrt{2} - 7\sqrt{2} + 9\sqrt{2}$$

$$= 7\sqrt{2}$$

4. Simplify : $3\sqrt[3]{40} - 4\sqrt[3]{320} - \sqrt[3]{5}$.

[BOARD TERM I, 2012, SET 20]

Sol. Ist term $= \sqrt[3]{40} = \sqrt[3]{2 \times 2 \times 2 \times 5} = 2\sqrt[3]{5}$

IInd term $= \sqrt[3]{320} = \sqrt[3]{2 \times 2 \times 2 \times 2 \times 2 \times 2 \times 5}$

$$= 2 \times 2\sqrt[3]{5} = 4\sqrt[3]{5}$$

Now, given expression $= 3\sqrt[3]{40} - 4\sqrt[3]{320} - \sqrt[3]{5}$

$$= 3 \times 2\sqrt[3]{5} - 4 \times 4\sqrt[3]{5} - \sqrt[3]{5}$$

$$= 6\sqrt[3]{5} - 16\sqrt[3]{5} - \sqrt[3]{5} = -17\sqrt[3]{5} + 6\sqrt[3]{5} = -11\sqrt[3]{5}$$

5. Simplify : $\left(4\sqrt{3} - 3\sqrt{5}\right)^2$.

[BOARD TERM I, 2012, SET 43]

Sol. Given expression = $\left(4\sqrt{3} - 3\sqrt{5}\right)^2$

$\left(4\sqrt{3}\right)^2 + \left(3\sqrt{5}\right)^2 - 2 \times 4\sqrt{3} \times 3\sqrt{5}$

$[\because (a - b)^2 = a^2 + b^2 - 2ab]$

$= 16 \times 3 + 9 \times 5 - 24\sqrt{3 \times 5}$

$= 48 + 45 - 24\sqrt{15}$

$= 93 - 24\sqrt{15}$

$= 3\left(31 - 8\sqrt{15}\right)$

6. Simplify the product: $\left(4\sqrt{3} + 3\sqrt{2}\right) \times \left(4\sqrt{3} - 3\sqrt{2}\right)$

[BOARD TERM 2013 BOARD TERM I, 2012, SET 49]

Sol. Given expression = $\left(4\sqrt{3} + 3\sqrt{2}\right) \times \left(4\sqrt{3} - 3\sqrt{2}\right)$

$= \left(4\sqrt{3}\right)^2 - \left(3\sqrt{2}\right)^2 = 16 \times 3 - 9 \times 2$

$= 48 - 18$

$= 30.$

7. Simplify : $2\sqrt{50} \times 3\sqrt{32} \times 4\sqrt{18}$.

[BOARD TERM I, 2014]

Sol. Given expression = $2\sqrt{50} \times 3\sqrt{32} \times 4\sqrt{18}$

$= 2\sqrt{5 \times 5 \times 2} \times 3\sqrt{4 \times 4 \times 2} \times 4\sqrt{3 \times 3 \times 2}$

$= 10\sqrt{2} \times 12\sqrt{2} \times 12\sqrt{2}$

$= 2880\sqrt{2}$

8. Simplify : $\sqrt[4]{16} - 6\sqrt[3]{343} + 18\sqrt[5]{243} - \sqrt{196}$.

[BOARD TERM I, 2014]

Sol. I^{st} term = $\sqrt[4]{16} = \sqrt[4]{2 \times 2 \times 2 \times 2} = 2$

IInd term = $\sqrt[3]{343} = \sqrt[3]{7 \times 7 \times 7} = 7$

IIIrd term = $\sqrt[5]{243} = \sqrt[5]{3 \times 3 \times 3 \times 3 \times 3} = 3$

IV^{rth} term = $\sqrt{196} = 14$

Now, Given expression

$= \sqrt[4]{16} - 6\sqrt[3]{343} + 18\sqrt[5]{243} - \sqrt{196}$

$= 2 - 6 \times 7 + 18 \times 3 - 14$

$= 2 - 42 + 54 - 14$

$= 56 - 56 = 0.$

9. Simplify : $8\sqrt{3} - 2\sqrt{3} + 4\sqrt{3}$.

[BOARD TERM I, 2015, SET 20UI6YH]

Sol. Given expression = $8\sqrt{3} - 2\sqrt{3} + 4\sqrt{3}$

$= 12\sqrt{3} - 2\sqrt{3}$

$= 10\sqrt{3}$

10. Simplify : $\sqrt{m^2 n^2} \times \sqrt[6]{m^2 n^2} \times \sqrt[3]{m^2 n^2}$.

Sol. Given expression = $\sqrt{m^2 n^2} \times \sqrt[6]{m^2 n^2} \times \sqrt[3]{m^2 n^2}$

$= \left(m^2 n^2\right)^{\frac{1}{2}} \times \left(m^2 n^2\right)^{\frac{1}{6}} \times \left(m^2 n^2\right)^{\frac{1}{3}}$

$= \left(m^2 n^2\right)^{\frac{1}{2} + \frac{1}{6} + \frac{1}{3}}$ $\qquad [\because (a)^m \times (a)^n = (a)^{m+n}]$

$= \left(m^2 n^2\right)^{\frac{3+1+2}{6}} = \left(m^2 n^2\right)^{\frac{6}{6}} = m^2 n^2$

11. Simplify : $\sqrt{a^3 b^4} \cdot \sqrt[3]{a^4 b^3}$.

Sol. Given expression = $\sqrt{a^3 b^4} \cdot \sqrt[3]{a^4 b^3}$

$= \sqrt{\left(ab^2\right)^2 a} \cdot \sqrt[3]{(ab)^3 a}$

$\left[\left(ab^2\right)^2\right]^{\frac{1}{2}} (a)^{\frac{1}{2}} \times \left[(ab)^3\right]^{\frac{1}{3}} (a)^{\frac{1}{3}}$

$= ab^2 a^{\frac{1}{2}} \times aba^{\frac{1}{3}}$

$= a^2 b^3 a^{\frac{1}{2}} \times a^{\frac{1}{3}}$

$= a^2 b^3 \cdot a^{\frac{1}{2} + \frac{1}{3}}$ $\qquad [\because a^m \times a^n = a^{m+n}]$

$= a^2 b^3 (a)^{\frac{5}{6}} = a^{\left(2 + \frac{5}{6}\right)} b^3 = a^{\frac{12+5}{6}} b^3 = a^{\frac{17}{6}} \cdot b^3$

Alternate method

$\sqrt{a^3 b^4} \cdot \sqrt[3]{a^4 b^3} = \left(a^3 b^4\right)^{1/2} \cdot \left(a^4 b^3\right)^{1/3}$

$= a^{3/2} b^2 \cdot a^{4/3} \cdot b = a^{\left(\frac{3}{2} + \frac{4}{3}\right)} \cdot b^{(2+1)} = a^{\frac{17}{6}} \cdot b^3$

12. Simplify $3\sqrt{48} - \dfrac{5}{2}\sqrt{\dfrac{1}{3}} + 4\sqrt{3}$.

Sol. Given expression = $3\sqrt{48} - \dfrac{5}{2}\sqrt{\dfrac{1}{3}} + 4\sqrt{3}$

$= 3\sqrt{2 \times 2 \times 2 \times 2 \times 3} - \dfrac{5}{2}\sqrt{\dfrac{1}{3}} + 4\sqrt{3}$

$= 3\sqrt{2^2 \times 2^2 \times 3} - \dfrac{5}{2}\sqrt{\dfrac{1}{3}} + 4\sqrt{3}$

$= 12\sqrt{3} - \dfrac{5}{2\sqrt{3}} + 4\sqrt{3}$

$= \dfrac{24 \times 3 - 5 + 8 \times 3}{2\sqrt{3}} = \dfrac{72 - 5 + 24}{2\sqrt{3}} = \dfrac{96 - 5}{2\sqrt{3}} = \dfrac{91}{2\sqrt{3}}$

On rationalizing the denominator by multiplying numerator and denominator by $\sqrt{3}$, we get,

$= \dfrac{91}{2\sqrt{3}} \times \dfrac{\sqrt{3}}{\sqrt{3}} = \dfrac{91\sqrt{3}}{6}$

Short Answer Type Questions II
(3 Marks Each)

1. Evaluate: $\sqrt{5+2\sqrt{6}} + \sqrt{8-2\sqrt{15}}$.

[BOARD TERM I, 2012, SET48]

Sol. I^{st} term $= \sqrt{5+2\sqrt{6}} = \sqrt{3+2+2\sqrt{6}}$

$= \sqrt{\left(\sqrt{3}+\sqrt{2}\right)^2} = \sqrt{3}+\sqrt{2}$

and IInd term $= \sqrt{8-2\sqrt{15}} = \sqrt{5+3-2\sqrt{15}}$

$= \sqrt{\left(\sqrt{5}-\sqrt{3}\right)^2} = \sqrt{5}-\sqrt{3}$

Given expression $= \sqrt{5+2\sqrt{6}} + \sqrt{8-2\sqrt{15}}$

$= \sqrt{3}+\sqrt{2}+\sqrt{5}-\sqrt{3} = \sqrt{2}+\sqrt{5}$

Alternate Method:

Given expression $= \sqrt{5+2\sqrt{6}} + \sqrt{8-2\sqrt{15}}$

$= \sqrt{3+2+2\sqrt{3\times 2}} + \sqrt{5+3-2\sqrt{5\times 3}}$

$= \sqrt{\left(\sqrt{3}\right)^2+\left(\sqrt{2}\right)^2+2\times\sqrt{3}\times\sqrt{2}} + \sqrt{(5)^2+\left(\sqrt{3}\right)^2-2.\sqrt{5}\sqrt{3}}$

$= \sqrt{\left(\sqrt{3}+\sqrt{2}\right)^2} + \sqrt{\left(\sqrt{5}-\sqrt{3}\right)^2}$

$[\because a^2+b^2+2ab = (a+b)^2 \ \& \ a^2+b^2-2ab = (a-b)^2]$

$= \sqrt{3}+\sqrt{2}+\sqrt{5}-\sqrt{3} = \sqrt{2}+\sqrt{5}$

2. Find the value of $(729)^{\frac{-1}{6}}$.

[BOARD TERM I, 2012, SET 14]

Sol. Given expression $(729)^{\frac{-1}{6}} = \left(3^6\right)^{-\frac{1}{6}}$

$3^{6\times\left(\frac{-1}{6}\right)} = (3)^{-1} = \frac{1}{3}$

3. Simplify : $3\sqrt{45} - \sqrt{125} + \sqrt{200} - \sqrt{50}$.

[BOARD TERM, I, 2014]

Sol. Given expression $= 3\sqrt{45} - \sqrt{125} + \sqrt{200} - \sqrt{50}$

$= 3\sqrt{3\times 3\times 5} - \sqrt{5\times 5\times 5} + \sqrt{10\times 10\times 2} - \sqrt{5\times 5\times 2}$

$= 9\sqrt{5} - 5\sqrt{5} + 10\sqrt{2} - 5\sqrt{2} = 4\sqrt{5} + 5\sqrt{2}$

4. Simplify $\dfrac{\sqrt{25}}{\sqrt[3]{64}} + \left(\dfrac{256}{625}\right)^{-\frac{1}{4}} + \dfrac{1}{\left(\dfrac{64}{125}\right)^{\frac{2}{3}}}$.

Sol. Given expression $= \dfrac{\sqrt{25}}{\sqrt[3]{64}} + \left(\dfrac{256}{625}\right)^{-\frac{1}{4}} + \dfrac{1}{\left(\dfrac{64}{125}\right)^{\frac{2}{3}}}$

$= \dfrac{\sqrt{5\times 5}}{\sqrt[3]{4\times 4\times 4}} + \left(\dfrac{625}{256}\right)^{\frac{1}{4}} + \left(\dfrac{125}{64}\right)^{\frac{2}{3}}$

$\left[\because (a)^{-m} = \dfrac{1}{(a)^m}\right]$

$= \dfrac{5}{4} + \left(\dfrac{5\times 5\times 5\times 5}{4\times 4\times 4\times 4}\right)^{\frac{1}{4}} + \left(\dfrac{5\times 5\times 5}{4\times 4\times 4}\right)^{\frac{2}{3}}$

$= \dfrac{5}{4} + \left(\dfrac{5^4}{4^4}\right)^{\frac{1}{4}} + \left(\dfrac{5^3}{4^3}\right)^{\frac{2}{3}}$

$= \dfrac{5}{4} + \left(\dfrac{5}{4}\right)^{4\times\frac{1}{4}} + \left(\dfrac{5}{4}\right)^{3\times\frac{2}{3}} \quad \left[\because \left(a^m\right)^n = a^{mn}\right]$

$= \dfrac{5}{4} + \dfrac{5}{4} + \left(\dfrac{5}{4}\right)^2$

$= \dfrac{5}{4} + \dfrac{5}{4} + \dfrac{25}{16}$

$= \dfrac{20+20+25}{16} = \dfrac{65}{16}$

5. Show that $\dfrac{x^{a(b-c)}}{x^{b(a-c)}} \div \left(\dfrac{x^b}{x^a}\right)^c = 1$.

Sol. Given, $\dfrac{x^{a(b-c)}}{x^{b(a-c)}} \div \left(\dfrac{x^b}{x^a}\right)^c = 1$.

By taking L. H. S,

LHS $= \dfrac{x^{a(b-c)}}{x^{b(a-c)}} \div \left(\dfrac{x^b}{x^a}\right)^c$

$= \dfrac{(x)^{ab-ac}}{(x)^{ab-bc}} \div \dfrac{(x)^{bc}}{(x)^{ac}} \quad \left[\because \left(a^m\right)^n = a^{mn}\right]$

$= (x)^{ab-ac-ab+bc} \div (x)^{bc-ac} \quad \left[\because \dfrac{a^m}{a^n} = a^{m-n}\right]$

$= (x)^{bc-ac} \div (x)^{bc-ac}$

$= (x)^{bc-ac-bc+ac}$

$= (x)^0 = 1 \quad\quad [\because (a)^m \div (a)^n = (a)^{m-n}]$

$[\because a^0 = 1]$

L.H.S = R.H.S

Hence proved.

Long Answer Type Questions

(4 Marks Each)

1. Find the value of :

$$\frac{4}{(216)^{-\frac{2}{3}}} + \frac{1}{(256)^{-\frac{3}{4}}} + \frac{2}{(243)^{-\frac{1}{5}}}$$

Sol. Given expression $= \dfrac{4}{(216)^{-\frac{2}{3}}} + \dfrac{1}{(256)^{-\frac{3}{4}}} + \dfrac{2}{(243)^{-\frac{1}{5}}}$

$= 4 \times (216)^{\frac{2}{3}} + (256)^{\frac{3}{4}} + 2 \times (243)^{\frac{1}{5}} \quad \left[\because \dfrac{1}{(a)^{-m}} = a^m \right]$

$= 4 \times (6 \times 6 \times 6)^{\frac{2}{3}} + (4 \times 4 \times 4 \times 4)^{\frac{3}{4}}$

$\qquad + 2(3 \times 3 \times 3 \times 3 \times 3)^{\frac{1}{5}}$

$= 4 \times \left(6^3\right)^{\frac{2}{3}} + \left(4^4\right)^{\frac{3}{4}} + 2 \times \left(3^5\right)^{\frac{1}{5}}$

$= 4 \times (6)^{3 \times \frac{2}{3}} + (4)^{4 \times \frac{3}{4}} + 2 \times (3)^{5 \times \frac{1}{5}}$

$= 4 \times (6)^2 + (4)^3 + 2 \times (3)^1 \qquad [\because (a^{\,m})^n = a^{mn}]$

$= 4 \times 36 + 64 + 6$

$= 144 + 64 + 6$

$= 214$

2. If $2^a = 3^b = 6^c$, then show that.

$$c = \frac{ab}{a+b}$$

[**BOARD TERM I, 2012, SET 57**]

Sol. Let $2^a = 3^b = 6^c = k$

$\therefore 2 = k^{1/a}$, $3 = k^{1/b}$ and $6 = k^{1/c}$

Now, $6 = k^{1/c}$

$\Rightarrow 2 \times 3 = k^{1/c} \Rightarrow k^{1/a} \times k^{1/b} = k^{1/c}$

$\qquad\qquad [\because 2 = k^{1/a}$ and $3 = k^{1/b}]$

$\Rightarrow k^{1/a\,+\,1/b} = k^{1/c} \Rightarrow k^{b+a/ab} = k^{1/c}$

On equating the power of k from both sides, we get

$\Rightarrow \dfrac{b+a}{ab} = \dfrac{1}{c} \quad \therefore \ c = \dfrac{ab}{a+b}$

[Topic 4] Laws of Exponents with Integral Powers

Points to be Remembered

- Some properties of exponents with integral powers if $a > 0$ be a real number and 'm' and 'n' be rational number, then

(i) $a^m \cdot a^n = a^{m+n}$.

(ii) $(a^m)^n = a^{mn}$.

(iii) $\dfrac{a^m}{a^n} = a^{m-n}$ where $m > n$

(iv) $\dfrac{a^m}{b^m} = \left(\dfrac{a}{b}\right)^m$

(v) $\dfrac{1}{a^m} = a^{-m}$ or $a^m = \dfrac{1}{a^{-m}}$

(vi) $a^m \cdot b^m = (ab)^m$.

(vii) $\left(\dfrac{a}{b}\right)^{-m} = \left(\dfrac{b}{a}\right)^m$

(viii) $(a)^{\frac{m}{n}} = \left(a^{\frac{1}{n}}\right)^m = \left(a^m\right)^{\frac{1}{n}}$

(ix) $a^0 = 1$

PREVIOUS YEARS'
EXAMINATION QUESTIONS
TOPIC 4
Multiple Choice Questions

(1 Mark Each)

1. If $\sqrt{2} = 1.4142...$ then is $\sqrt{\dfrac{\sqrt{2}-1}{\sqrt{2}+1}}$ equal to

   (a) 2.4142   (b) 5.8282

   (c) 0.4142   (d) 0.1718

   [NCERT Exemp.]

Sol. (c) After rationalisation, we get

$\qquad \sqrt{2} - 1 = 1.4142 - 1$

$\qquad\qquad = 0.4142$

2. Value of $256^{0.16} \times 256^{0.09}$ is

   (a) 4

   (b) 16

   (c) 64

   (d) 256.25

   [NCERT Exemp.]

Sol. (a) $256^{0.16} \times 256^{0.09} = 256^{0.16+0.09} = 256^{0.25}$.

$256^{\frac{1}{4}} = 4^{4\frac{1}{4}} = 4^{4 \times \frac{1}{4}} = 4$

3. The product $\sqrt[3]{2} \cdot \sqrt[4]{2} \cdot \sqrt[12]{32}$ equals.

(a) $\sqrt{2}$ (b) 2

(c) $\sqrt[12]{2}$ (d) $\sqrt[12]{32}$

[NCERT Exemp.]

Sol. (b) We have,

$$\sqrt[3]{2} \cdot \sqrt[4]{2} \cdot \sqrt[12]{32} = 2^{\frac{1}{3}} \cdot 2^{\frac{1}{4}} \cdot 2^{\frac{5}{12}} = 2^{\frac{1}{3}+\frac{1}{4}+\frac{5}{12}} = 2^{\frac{12}{12}} = 2$$

4. $\sqrt[4]{\sqrt[3]{2^2}}$ equal

(a) $2^{\frac{-1}{6}}$ (b) 2^{-6}

(c) $2^{\frac{1}{6}}$ (d) 2^6 [NCERT Exemp.]

Sol. (c) $\sqrt[4]{\sqrt[3]{2^2}} = \sqrt[4]{\left(2^2\right)^{\frac{1}{3}}} = 2^{\frac{2^{\frac{1}{4}}}{3}} = 2^{\frac{2}{3}\times\frac{1}{4}} = 2^{\frac{1}{6}}$

5. Value of $\sqrt[4]{81^{-2}}$ is

(a) $\dfrac{1}{9}$ (b) $\dfrac{1}{3}$

(c) 9 (d) $\dfrac{1}{81}$

[NCERT Exemp.]

Sol. (a) $\sqrt[4]{81^{-2}} = \dfrac{1}{9^{\frac{2^{\frac{1}{4}}}{}}} = \dfrac{1}{9^{4\times\frac{1}{4}}} = \dfrac{1}{9}$

6. Which of the following is equal to x?

(a) $x^{\frac{12}{7}} - \dfrac{5}{x^7}$ (b) $\sqrt[12]{x^{4\frac{1}{3}}}$

(c) $\sqrt{x^3}^{\frac{2}{3}}$ (d) $x^{\frac{12}{7}} \times x^{\frac{7}{12}}$

[NCERT Exemp.]

Sol. (c) (a) $x^{\frac{12}{7}} \times x^{\frac{5}{7}} \neq x$

(b) $\sqrt[12]{x^{4\frac{1}{3}}} = x^{\frac{4}{3}\times\frac{1}{12}} - x^{\frac{1}{9}} \not\neq x$

(c) $\sqrt{x^3}^{\frac{2}{3}} = x^{\frac{2}{3}\times\frac{2}{3}} = x$

(d) $x^{\frac{12}{7}} \times x^{\frac{7}{12}} = x^{\frac{12}{7}+\frac{7}{12}} = x^{\frac{193}{84}}$

7. What is the value of x in $2^{x-6} \times 5^{x-5} = 500$?

(a) 5

(b) 6

(c) 7

(d) 8 [NCERT Exemp.]

Sol. (d) According to the question,

$2^{x-6} \times 5^{x-5} = 500$

$\Rightarrow \quad 2^{x-6} \times 5^{x-5} = 2 \times 2 \times 5 \times 5 \times 5 = 2^2 \times 5^3$

On equating the power of 2 from both sides, we get

$x - 6 = 2$

$\therefore \quad x = 2 + 6 = 8$

8. Which of the following is equivalent to the expression $\dfrac{16\times 2^{n+1} - 4\times 2^n}{16\times 2^{n+2} - 2\times 2^{n+2}}$

(a) $\dfrac{1}{4}$ (b) $\dfrac{1}{2}$

(c) $\dfrac{1}{8}$ (d) $\dfrac{1}{16}$

[NCERT Exemp.]

Sol. (b) Given expression $= \dfrac{16\times 2^{n+1} - 4\times 2^n}{16\times 2^{n+2} - 2\times 2^{n+2}}$

$$= \dfrac{2^4 \times 2^{n+1} - 2^2 \times 2^n}{2^4 \times 2^{n+2} - 2\times 2^{n+2}}$$

$$= \dfrac{2^{n+5} - 2^{n+2}}{2^{n+6} - 2^{n+3}}$$

$$= \dfrac{2^n\left(2^5 - 2^2\right)}{2^n\left(2^6 - 2^3\right)} = \dfrac{32-4}{64-8}$$

$$= \dfrac{28}{56} = \dfrac{1}{2}$$

Very Short Answer Type Questions

(1 Mark Each)

1. Find the value of $(256)^{0.16} \times (256)^{0.09}$.

[NCERT Exemp.]

Sol. Given expression $= (256)^{0.16} \times (256)^{0.09} . = (256)^{0.16+0.09}$

$$= (256)^{0.25} = (256)^{\frac{1}{4}} = \left(4^4\right)^{\frac{1}{4}} = 4$$

2. Find the value of $\left[(16)^{\frac{1}{2}}\right]^{\frac{1}{2}}$

[BOARD TERM I, 2014]

Sol. Given expression $= \left[(16)^{\frac{1}{2}}\right]^{\frac{1}{2}} = \left[4^{2\times\frac{1}{2}}\right]^{\frac{1}{2}} = \left[4^{2\times\frac{1}{2}}\right]^{\frac{1}{2}}$

$$= [4]^{\frac{1}{2}} = \sqrt{4} = 2$$

3. Find the value of $\sqrt[4]{625^{-2}}$

[BOARD TERM I, 2016, SET QGL21F5]

Sol. Given expression $= \sqrt[4]{625^{-2}}$

$$= (625^{-2})^{\frac{1}{4}} = \left(625^{-2\times\frac{1}{4}}\right)$$

$$= \left(625^{-\frac{1}{2}}\right)$$

$$= \left(\frac{1}{625}\right)^{\frac{1}{2}} = \frac{1}{\sqrt{625}} = \frac{1}{25}$$

4. Simplify : $\sqrt[4]{\left(\dfrac{132}{143}\right)^{-2}}$

[BOARD TERM I, 2016, SET BQS6IZK]

Sol. Given expression $= \sqrt[4]{\left(\dfrac{132}{143}\right)^{-2}} = \sqrt{\left(\dfrac{143}{132}\right)^{2}}$

$$= \sqrt[4]{\left(\frac{13\times11}{11\times12}\right)^{2}} = \left[\left(\frac{13}{12}\right)^{2}\right]^{\frac{1}{4}} = \left(\frac{13}{12}\right)^{2\times\frac{1}{4}}$$

$$= \left(\frac{13}{12}\right)^{\frac{1}{2}} = \frac{\sqrt{13}}{\sqrt{12}}$$

$$= \frac{\sqrt{13}}{2\sqrt{3}} \times \frac{\sqrt{3}}{\sqrt{3}} = \frac{1}{6}\sqrt{39}$$

5. If p = 3, q = 5, then find the value of $\left(\dfrac{1}{p}+\dfrac{1}{q}\right)^{p}$.

Sol. On putting the value of p & q, $\left(\dfrac{1}{p}+\dfrac{1}{q}\right)^{p} = \left(\dfrac{1}{3}+\dfrac{1}{5}\right)^{3}$

$$= \left(\frac{5+3}{15}\right)^{3} = \left(\frac{8}{15}\right)^{3} = \frac{512}{3375}.$$

6. Calculate the value of $\dfrac{16^{\frac{3}{4}}}{16^{-\frac{1}{4}}}$

Sol. Given, expression $= \dfrac{16^{\frac{3}{4}}}{16^{-\frac{1}{4}}}$

$$= (16)^{\frac{3}{4}+\frac{1}{4}} = (16)^{\frac{4}{4}} = (16)^{1} = 16$$

7. Calculate the quotient obtained when $\sqrt{1500}$ is divided by $2\sqrt{15}$.

Sol. According to the question,

$$\sqrt{1500} \div 2\sqrt{15} = \frac{\sqrt{1500}}{2\sqrt{15}} = \frac{1}{2}\times\sqrt{\frac{1500}{15}}$$

$$= \frac{1}{2}\times\sqrt{100} = \frac{10}{2} = 5$$

8. Calculate the value of $\left[\left\{(81)^{\frac{-1}{2}}\right\}^{\frac{-1}{4}}\right]^{2}$.

Sol. Given expression $= \left[\left\{(81)^{\frac{-1}{2}}\right\}^{\frac{-1}{4}}\right]^{2}$

$$= \left[(81)^{\frac{-1}{2}}\right]^{\frac{-1}{2}} = (81)^{\left(-\frac{1}{2}\right)\times\left(-\frac{1}{2}\right)}$$

$$= (81)^{\frac{1}{4}} = (3^{4})^{\frac{1}{4}} = (3)^{3\times\frac{1}{4}}$$

$$= 3.$$

9. Find the value of $\sqrt[3]{\dfrac{54}{250}}$.

Sol. Given expression $= \sqrt[3]{\dfrac{54}{250}}$

$$\left[\frac{54}{250}\right]^{\frac{1}{3}} = \left[\frac{27}{125}\right]^{\frac{1}{3}} = \left[\frac{3^{3}}{5^{3}}\right]^{\frac{1}{3}}$$

$$= \left[\left(\frac{3}{5}\right)^{3}\right]^{\frac{1}{3}} = \left(\frac{3}{5}\right)^{3\times\frac{1}{3}} = \frac{3}{5}$$

10. Simplify : $\left[7\left(81^{\frac{1}{4}}+256^{\frac{1}{4}}\right)^{\frac{1}{4}}\right]^{4}$.

Sol. Given expression $= \left[7\left(81^{\frac{1}{4}}+256^{\frac{1}{4}}\right)^{\frac{1}{4}}\right]^{4}$

$$= \left[7(3+4)^{\frac{1}{4}}\right]^{4}$$

$$= \left[7.7^{\frac{1}{4}}\right]^{4} = \left[7^{1+\frac{1}{4}}\right]^{4}$$

$$= \left[7^{\frac{5}{4}}\right]^{4} = 7^{5}$$

Short Answer Type Questions I
(2 Marks Each)

1. Simplify : $\left[5\left[8^{\frac{1}{3}}+27^{\frac{1}{3}}\right]^{3}\right]^{\frac{1}{4}}$.

[BOARD TERM I, 2012, SET 66], [NCERT EXEMPLAR]

Sol. Given expression = $\left[5\left[8^{\frac{1}{3}}+27^{\frac{1}{3}}\right]^{3}\right]^{\frac{1}{4}}$

$= \left[5\left(2^{3\times\frac{1}{3}}+3^{3\times\frac{1}{3}}\right)^{3}\right]^{\frac{1}{4}} = \left[5(2+3)^{3}\right]^{\frac{1}{4}}$

$= \left[5(5)^{3}\right]^{\frac{1}{4}} = (5^{4})^{\frac{1}{4}} = 5^{4\times\frac{1}{4}} = 5$

2. If a = 2 and b = 3, then find the value of $a^{b} + b^{a}$.

[BOARD TERM I, 2012, SET 47]

Sol. Given a = 2 and b = 3.

$a^{b} + b^{a} = 2^{3} + 3^{2}$

$= 8 + 9 = 17$

3. Simplify : $\left(\dfrac{81}{16}\right)^{-\frac{5}{4}} \times \left(\dfrac{25}{9}\right)^{-\frac{5}{2}}$.

[BOARD TERM I, 2012, SET 55]

Sol. Given expression = $\left(\dfrac{81}{16}\right)^{-\frac{5}{4}} \times \left(\dfrac{25}{9}\right)^{-\frac{5}{2}}$

$= \left[\left(\dfrac{3}{2}\right)^{4}\right]^{-\frac{5}{4}} \times \left[\left(\dfrac{5}{3}\right)^{2}\right]^{-\frac{5}{2}}$

$= \left(\dfrac{3}{2}\right)^{4\times\left(\frac{-5}{4}\right)} \times \left(\dfrac{5}{3}\right)^{2\times\left(\frac{-5}{2}\right)}$

$= \left(\dfrac{3}{2}\right)^{-5} \times \left(\dfrac{5}{3}\right)^{-5}$

$= \left(\dfrac{2}{3}\right)^{5} \times \left(\dfrac{3}{5}\right)^{5} = \dfrac{2^{5}}{3^{5}} \times \dfrac{3^{5}}{5^{5}}$

$= \dfrac{2^{5}}{5^{5}}$

4. Find the value of $\left(1^{3} + 2^{3} + 3^{3}\right)^{-\frac{3}{2}}$.

[BOARD TERM I, 2012, SET 56]

Sol. Given expression = $\left(1^{3} + 2^{3} + 3^{3}\right)^{-\frac{3}{2}}$

$= (1 + 8 + 27)^{-\frac{3}{2}}$

$= (36)^{-\frac{3}{2}}$

$= \left[(6)^{2}\right]^{-\frac{3}{2}} = 6^{-3}$

$= \dfrac{1}{6^{3}} = \dfrac{1}{216}$

5. If a = 2, and b = 3, then find the value of:
   (i) $(a^{b} + b^{a})^{-1}$
   (ii) $(a^{a} + b^{b})^{-1}$

[BOARD TERM I, 2012, SET 51]

Sol. Given, a = 2 and b = 3.

(i) $(a^{b} + b^{a})-1 = (2^{3} + 3^{2})-1$

$= \dfrac{1}{(2^{3} + 3^{2})} = \dfrac{1}{8+9} = \dfrac{1}{17}$

(ii) $(a^{a} + b^{b})^{-1} = (2^{2} + 3^{3})^{-1}$.

$= \dfrac{1}{(2^{2} + 3^{3})} = \dfrac{1}{4+27} = \dfrac{1}{31}$

6. Simplify : $\dfrac{16\times 2^{n+1} - 4\times 2^{n}}{16\times 2^{n+2} - 2\times 2^{n+2}}$.

[BOARD TERM I, 2014]

Sol. Given expression = $\dfrac{16\times 2^{n+1} - 4\times 2^{n}}{16\times 2^{n+2} - 2\times 2^{n+2}}$

$= \dfrac{2^{4}\times 2^{n+1} - 2^{2}\times 2^{n}}{2^{4}\times 2^{n+2} - 2\times 2^{n+2}}$

$= \dfrac{2^{n+5} - 2^{n+2}}{2^{n+6} - 2^{n+3}} = \dfrac{2^{n+5} - 2^{n+2}}{2.2^{n+5} - 2.2^{n+2}}$

$= \dfrac{2^{n+5} - 2^{n+2}}{2(2^{n+5} - 2^{n+2})} = \dfrac{1}{2}$

7. If $125^{x} = \dfrac{25}{5^{x}}$, then find the value of x.

Sol. According to the question, $125^{x} = \dfrac{25}{5^{x}}$

$\Rightarrow (5^{3})^{x} = \dfrac{5^{2}}{5^{x}}$

On equating power from both sides, we get,

$3x = 2 - x \Rightarrow 4x = 2$

$\therefore \quad x = \dfrac{2}{4} = \dfrac{1}{2}$

Short Answer Type Questions II
(3 Marks Each)

1. Find the value of $\dfrac{4}{(216)^{-\frac{2}{3}}} - \dfrac{1}{(256)^{-\frac{3}{4}}}$.

[BOARD TERM I, 2012, SET 46; 2011, SET 17, 19]

Sol. Given expression $= \dfrac{4}{(216)^{-\frac{2}{3}}} - \dfrac{1}{(256)^{-\frac{3}{4}}}$

$= \dfrac{4}{\left(6^3\right)^{-\frac{2}{3}}} - \dfrac{1}{\left(4^4\right)^{-\frac{3}{4}}} = \dfrac{4}{(6)^{-2}} - \dfrac{1}{(4)^{-3}}$

$= 4 \times 6^2 - 4^3 = 144 - 64 = 80$

2. Simplify : $\left(2\sqrt{2} - 5\right)^2 + \left(3\sqrt{2} + \sqrt{3}\right)^2 - \left(\sqrt{2} - 1\right)^2$.

[BOARD TERM I, 2012, SET 63]

Sol. Given expression

$= \left(2\sqrt{2} - 5\right)^2 + \left(3\sqrt{2} + \sqrt{3}\right)^2 - \left(\sqrt{2} - 1\right)^2$

$= \left(2\sqrt{2}\right)^2 - 2\left(2\sqrt{2}\right)(5) + (5)^2 + \left(3\sqrt{2}\right)^2 + 2\left(3\sqrt{2}\right)$

$\left(\sqrt{3}\right) + \left(\sqrt{3}\right)^2 - \left(\sqrt{2}\right)^2 - (1)^2 + 2\left(\sqrt{2}\right)(1)$

$[\because (a - b)^2 = a^2 + b^2 - 2ab \ \& \ (a + b)^2$
$= a^2 + b^2 + 2ab]$

$= 8 + 25 - 20\sqrt{2} + 18 + 3 + 6\sqrt{6} - 2 - 1 + 2\sqrt{2}$

$= 54 - 3 - 18\sqrt{2} + 6\sqrt{6}$

$= 51 - 18\sqrt{2} + 6\sqrt{6}$

3. Simplify : $\left(\dfrac{5^{-1} \times 7^2}{5^2 \times 7^{-4}}\right)^{\frac{7}{2}} \times \left(\dfrac{5^{-2} \times 7^3}{5^3 \times 7^{-5}}\right)^{-\frac{5}{2}}$.

[BOARD TERM, I, 2012, SET 43]

Sol. Given expression $= \left(\dfrac{5^{-1} \times 7^2}{5^2 \times 7^{-4}}\right)^{\frac{7}{2}} \times \left(\dfrac{5^{-2} \times 7^3}{5^3 \times 7^{-5}}\right)^{-\frac{5}{2}}$

$= \left(\dfrac{7^4 \times 7^2}{5^2 \times 5^1}\right)^{7/2} \times \left(\dfrac{7^5 \times 7^3}{5^3 \times 5^2}\right)^{-5/2}$

$= \left(\dfrac{7^6}{5^3}\right)^{\frac{7}{2}} \times \left(\dfrac{7^8}{5^5}\right)^{\frac{-5}{2}} = \left(\dfrac{7^{42}}{5^{21}}\right)^{\frac{1}{2}} \times \left(\dfrac{7^{40}}{5^{25}}\right)^{-\frac{1}{2}}$

$= \left(\dfrac{7^{42}}{5^{21}}\right)^{\frac{1}{2}} \times \left(\dfrac{5^{25}}{7^{40}}\right)^{\frac{1}{2}} = \left(\dfrac{7^{42}}{5^{21}} \times \dfrac{5^{25}}{7^{40}}\right)^{\frac{1}{2}}$

$= \left(7^2 \times 5^4\right)^{\frac{1}{2}} = 7^{2 \times \frac{1}{2}} \times 5^{4 \times \frac{1}{2}}$

$= 7 \times 5^2 = 7 \times 25 = 175$

4. Simplify $\left(\sqrt{x}\right)^{-\frac{2}{3}} \sqrt{y^4} \div \sqrt{(xy)^{-\frac{1}{2}}}$.

[BOARD TERM I, 2012, SET15]

Sol. Given expression

$= \dfrac{\left(x^{\frac{1}{2}}\right)^{\frac{-2}{3}} \left(y^4\right)^{\frac{1}{2}}}{x^{\frac{-1}{4}} y^{\frac{-1}{4}}} = x^{\frac{-1}{3}} \cdot y^2 \cdot x^{\frac{1}{4}} \cdot y^{\frac{1}{4}}$

$= x^{\left(-\frac{1}{3} + \frac{1}{4}\right)} \cdot y^{\left(2 + \frac{1}{4}\right)} = x^{\frac{-1}{12}} \cdot y^{\frac{9}{4}} = \dfrac{y^{\frac{9}{4}}}{x^{\frac{1}{12}}}$

Alternate Method:

$\left(\sqrt{x}\right)^{-\frac{2}{3}} \sqrt{y^4} \div \sqrt{(xy)^{-\frac{1}{2}}} = \left(x^{\frac{1}{2}}\right)^{-\frac{2}{3}} \cdot \left(y^4\right)^{\frac{1}{2}} \div \left[(xy)^{-\frac{1}{2}}\right]^{\frac{1}{2}}$

$= x^{\frac{-1}{3}} \cdot y^2 \div (xy)^{-\frac{1}{4}} = x^{-\frac{1}{3}} \cdot y^2 \div \left(\dfrac{1}{xy}\right)^{-\frac{1}{4}}$

$= x^{\frac{-1}{3}} \cdot y^2 \times (xy)^{\frac{1}{4}}$

$= x^{\frac{-1}{3} + \frac{1}{4}} \cdot y^{2 + \frac{1}{4}}$

$= x^{\frac{-1}{12}} \cdot y^{\frac{9}{4}} = \dfrac{y^{\frac{9}{4}}}{x^{\frac{1}{12}}}$

5. If $x^a = y$, $y^b = z$ and $z^c = x$, then prove that abc = 1.

[BOARD TERM, I, 2012, SET 20]

Sol. Given, $x^a = y$, $y^b = z$ and $z^c = x$, then

$x^{abc} = (x^a)^{bc} = (y)^{bc} = (y^b)^c = (z)^c = x$

$\Rightarrow x^{abc} = x^1$

On equating the power of x from both sides, we get

$\therefore$ abc = 1

6. Show that : $(x^{a-b})^{a+b} (x^{b-c})^{b+c} \cdot (x^{c-a})^{c+a} = 1$.

[BOARD TERM, I, 2012, SET-49]

Sol. Given, $(x^{a-b})^{a+b} (x^{b-c})^{b+c} \cdot (x^{c-a})^{c+a} = 1$

on taking L.H.S.

L.H.S $= (x^{a-b})^{a+b} (x^{b-c})^{b+c} \cdot (x^{c-a})^{c+a}$

$= x^{a^2 - b^2} \cdot x^{b^2 - c^2} \cdot x^{c^2 - a^2}$

$= x^{a^2 - b^2 + b^2 - c^2 + c^2 - a^2}$

$= x^0 = 1$

(Any number to the power 0 is 1)

$\therefore$ L.H.S = R.H.S

Hence proved.

7. Find x, if $\left(\dfrac{2}{3}\right)^{x} \cdot \left(\dfrac{3}{2}\right)^{2x} = \dfrac{81}{16}$.

[BOARD TERM, I, 2012, SET-46]

Sol. According to the question, $\left(\dfrac{2}{3}\right)^{x} \cdot \left(\dfrac{3}{2}\right)^{2x} = \dfrac{81}{16}$

$$\Rightarrow \frac{2^x}{3^x} \cdot \frac{3^{2x}}{2^{2x}} = \frac{3^4}{2^4}$$

$\Rightarrow 2^{x-2x} \cdot 3^{2x-x} = 3^4 \cdot 2^{-4}$

On equating the power of 2 from both sides, we get

$\Rightarrow x - 2x = -4$

$\Rightarrow -x = -4$

$\therefore x = 4$

Alternate Method:

$$\left(\frac{2}{3}\right)^{x} \cdot \left(\frac{3}{2}\right)^{2x} = \frac{81}{16}$$

$\Rightarrow \left(\dfrac{2}{3}\right)^{x} \cdot \left(\dfrac{2}{3}\right)^{-2x} = \left(\dfrac{3}{2}\right)^{4} \Rightarrow \left(\dfrac{2}{3}\right)^{x-2x} = \left(\dfrac{2}{3}\right)^{-4}$

On comparing the exponents we get

$\Rightarrow x - 2x = -4$

$\Rightarrow -x = -4$

$\Rightarrow x = 4.$

8. If $x = 5$ and $y = 2$, then find the value of:

(i) $(x^y + y^x)^{-1}$

(ii) $(x^x + y^y)^{-1}$

[BOARD TERM, I, 2012, SET-38]

Sol. Given $x = 5$ and $y = 2$

(i) $(x^y + y^x)^{-1} = (5^2 + 2^5)^{-1} = (25 + 32)^{-1} = (57)^{-1} = \dfrac{1}{57}$

(ii) $(x^x + y^y)^{-1} = (5^5 + 2^2)^{-1} = (3125 + 4)^{-1}$

$$= (3129)^{-1} = \frac{1}{3129}$$

9. If $\left(\dfrac{a}{b}\right)^{x-1} = \left(\dfrac{b}{a}\right)^{2x-8}$, then find the value of x.

[BOARD TERM, I, 2012, SET-20]

Sol. Given $\left(\dfrac{a}{b}\right)^{x-1} = \left(\dfrac{b}{a}\right)^{2x-8}$

$$\Rightarrow \left(\frac{a}{b}\right)^{x-1} = \left(\frac{a}{b}\right)^{-[2x-8]}$$

On equating the power of $\left(\dfrac{a}{b}\right)$

From the both sides, we get

$\Rightarrow x - 1 = -[2x - 8]$

$\Rightarrow 3x = 9$

$\therefore x = 3$

10. If $2^x \times 4^x = (8)^{\frac{1}{3}} \times (32)^{\frac{1}{5}}$

[BOARD TERM, I, 2012, SET-62]

Sol. Given,

$$2^x \times 4^x = (8)^{\frac{1}{3}} \times (32)^{\frac{1}{5}}$$

$$\Rightarrow 2^x \times (2^2)^x = (2^3)^{\frac{1}{3}} \times (2^5)^{\frac{1}{5}}$$

$\Rightarrow 2^x \cdot 2^{2x} = 2^1 \times 2^1$

$\Rightarrow 2^{x+2x} = 2^{1+1}$

$2^{3x} = 2^2$

On comparing the power of both sides, we get

$3x = 2$

$$\therefore \quad x = \frac{2}{3}$$

11. Write $\sqrt[3]{4}, \sqrt{3}, \sqrt[4]{6}$ in ascending order.

[BOARD TERM, I, 2012, SET-52]

Sol. $3^{\frac{1}{2}}, 4^{\frac{1}{3}}, 6^{\frac{1}{4}} = 3^{\frac{6}{12}}, 4^{\frac{4}{12}}, 6^{\frac{3}{12}}$

$$(3^6)^{\frac{1}{12}}, (4^4)^{\frac{1}{12}}, (6^3)^{\frac{1}{12}}$$

$$729^{\frac{1}{12}}, 256^{\frac{1}{12}}, 216^{\frac{1}{12}}$$

On arranging in ascending order,

$$(216)^{\frac{1}{12}} < (256)^{\frac{1}{12}} < (729)^{\frac{1}{12}}$$

i.e. $\sqrt[4]{6} < \sqrt[3]{4} < \sqrt{3}$.

Alternate Method:

Since LCM of 2, 3, 4 = 2 × 2 × 3 = 12

$\therefore \sqrt[3]{4}, \sqrt{3}, \sqrt[4]{6} = 4^{\frac{1}{3}}, 3^{\frac{1}{2}}, 6^{\frac{1}{4}}$

$= 4^{\frac{1}{3} \times \frac{4}{4}}, 3^{\frac{1}{2} \times \frac{6}{6}}, 6^{\frac{1}{4} \times \frac{3}{3}}$

$= 4^{4 \times \frac{4}{12}}, 3^{6 \times \frac{1}{12}}, 6^{3 \times \frac{1}{12}}$

$$256^{\frac{1}{12}}, 729^{\frac{1}{12}}, 216^{\frac{1}{12}}$$

Arranging in ascending order,

$$(216)^{\frac{1}{12}} < (256)^{\frac{1}{12}} < (729)^{\frac{1}{12}}$$

i.e. $\sqrt[4]{6} < \sqrt[3]{4} < \sqrt{3}$.

12. Prove that : $\dfrac{a^{-1}}{a^{-1}+b^{-1}}+\dfrac{a^{-1}}{a^{-1}-b^{-1}}=\dfrac{-(2b^2)}{a^2-b^2}$.

[BOARD TERM, I, 2012, SET 51]

Sol. On taking L.H.S of the given expression,

$$\text{L.H.S} = \frac{a^{-1}}{a^{-1}+b^{-1}}+\frac{a^{-1}}{a^{-1}-b^{-1}} = \frac{\dfrac{1}{a}}{\dfrac{1}{a}+\dfrac{1}{b}}+\frac{\dfrac{1}{a}}{\dfrac{1}{a}-\dfrac{1}{b}}$$

$$= \frac{\dfrac{1}{a}}{\dfrac{a+b}{ab}}+\frac{\dfrac{1}{a}}{\dfrac{b-a}{ab}}$$

$$= \frac{b}{a+b}+\frac{b}{b-a}$$

$$= \frac{b(b-a)+b(b+a)}{(b+a)(b-a)}$$

$$= \frac{b^2-ab+b^2+ab}{b^2-a^2}$$

$$= \frac{2b^2}{-(a^2-b^2)}=\frac{-2b^2}{a^2-b^2}$$

$\therefore$ L.H.S = R.H.S

Hence Proved.

13. Evaluate $\dfrac{(243)^{\frac{n}{5}}.3^{2n+1}}{9^n\times 3^{n-1}}$.

Sol. Given expression $= \dfrac{(243)^{\frac{n}{5}}.3^{2n+1}}{9^n\times 3^{n-1}}$

$$= \frac{(3\times3\times3\times3\times3)^{\frac{n}{5}}.(3)^{2n+1}}{(3^2)^n\times(3)^{n-1}}$$

$$= \frac{(3^5)^{\frac{n}{5}}\times(3)^{2n+1}}{(3^2)^n\times(3)^{n-1}} = \frac{3^n\times(3)^{2n+1}}{3^{2n}\times(3)^{n-1}}$$

$$= \frac{(3)^{3n+1}}{(3)^{3n-1}} \qquad [\because a^m\times a^n = a^{m+n}]$$

$$= (3)^{3n+1-(3n-1)} \qquad [\because a^m\div a^n = a^{m-n}]$$

$$= (3)^2 = 9$$

14. If x, y and z are positive real numbers, then show that $\sqrt{x^{-1}y}\cdot\sqrt{y^{-1}z}\cdot\sqrt{z^{-1}x}=1$.

Sol. On taking L.H.S of the given expression,

$$\text{L.H.S} = \sqrt{x^{-1}y}\cdot\sqrt{y^{-1}z}\cdot\sqrt{z^{-1}x}$$

$$= \sqrt{\frac{y}{x}}\cdot\sqrt{\frac{z}{y}}\cdot\sqrt{\frac{x}{z}} \qquad \left[\because a^{-m}=\frac{1}{a^m}\right]$$

$$= \left(\frac{y}{x}\right)^{\frac{1}{2}}\left(\frac{z}{y}\right)^{\frac{1}{2}}\left(\frac{x}{z}\right)^{\frac{1}{2}}$$

$$= \frac{(y)^{\frac{1}{2}}}{(x)^{\frac{1}{2}}}\cdot\frac{(z)^{\frac{1}{2}}}{(y)^{\frac{1}{2}}}\cdot\frac{(x)^{\frac{1}{2}}}{(z)^{\frac{1}{2}}}=1$$

$\therefore$ L.H.S = R.H.S

Hence proved

15. Find the value of x, if $2^{7x}\div 2^{2x}=\sqrt[5]{2^{15}}$.

Sol. Given, $2^{7x}\div 2^{2x}=\sqrt[5]{2^{15}}$

$$\Rightarrow (2)^{7x-2x}=\sqrt[5]{2^{15}} \qquad [\because a^m\div a^n = (a)^{m-n}]$$

$$\Rightarrow (2)^{5x}=(2)^{15\times\frac{1}{5}} \qquad [\because (a^m)^n = a^{mn}]$$

$$\Rightarrow 2^{5x} = 2^3$$

On comparing the power of 2 from both sides, we get

$$5x = 3 \quad \therefore \quad x = \frac{3}{5}$$

Long Answer Type Questions
(4 Marks Each)

1. Prove that : $\left(\dfrac{x^a}{x^b}\right)^{\frac{1}{ab}}\cdot\left(\dfrac{x^b}{x^c}\right)^{\frac{1}{bc}}\cdot\left(\dfrac{x^c}{x^a}\right)^{\frac{1}{ca}}=1$

[BOARD TERM I, 2012, SET-67]

Sol. On taking the L.H.S of the given expression

$$\text{L.H.S} = \left(x^{a-b}\right)^{\frac{1}{ab}}\cdot\left(x^{b-c}\right)^{\frac{1}{bc}}\cdot\left(x^{c-a}\right)^{\frac{1}{ca}}$$

$$= x^{\frac{a-b}{ab}+\frac{b-c}{x^{bc}}+\frac{c-a}{x^{ca}}}$$

$$= x^{\frac{a-b}{ab}+\frac{b-c}{bc}+\frac{c-a}{ca}}$$

$$= x^{\frac{ac-bc+ab-ca+bc-ab}{abc}} = x^{\frac{0}{abc}}$$

$$= x^0$$

$$= 1$$

$\therefore$ L.H.S = R.H.S

Hence Proved.

2. Show that : $\dfrac{\left[x^{(a+b)}\right]^2 . \left[x^{(b+c)}\right]^2 . \left[x^{(c+a)}\right]^2}{\left(x^a x^b x^c\right)^4} = 1$

[BOARD TERM I, 2012, SET-46]

Sol. On taking the L.H.S of the given expression,

$$\text{L.H.S} = \dfrac{\left[x^{(a+b)}\right]^2 . \left[x^{(b+c)}\right]^2 . \left[x^{(c+a)}\right]^2}{\left(x^a x^b x^c\right)^4}$$

$$= \dfrac{x^{2a+2b} . x^{2b+2c} . x^{2c+2a}}{x^{4a} . x^{4b} . x^{4c}}$$

$$= \dfrac{x^{2a+2b+2b+2c+2c+2a}}{x^{4a+4b+4c}}$$

$$= \dfrac{x^{4a+4b+4c}}{x^{4a+4b+4c}}$$

$$= 1$$

$\therefore$ L.H.S = R.H.S

Hence proved

3. Evaluate : $\dfrac{4}{(2187)^{-\frac{3}{7}}} - \dfrac{5}{(256)^{-\frac{1}{4}}} + \dfrac{2}{\left(1331^2\right)^{-\frac{1}{3}}}$

[BOARD TERM I, 2012, SET-43]

Sol. Given expression

$$= \dfrac{4}{(2187)^{-\frac{3}{7}}} - \dfrac{5}{(256)^{-\frac{1}{4}}} + \dfrac{2}{\left(1331^2\right)^{-\frac{1}{3}}}$$

$$= 4 \times (2187)^{\frac{3}{7}} - 5 \times (256)^{\frac{1}{4}} + 2 \times \left(1331^2\right)^{\frac{1}{3}}$$

$$= 4 \times \left(2187^{\frac{1}{7}}\right)^3 - 5 \times 256^{\frac{1}{4}} + 2 \times \left(1331^{\frac{1}{3}}\right)^2$$

$$= 4 \times \left((3^7)^{\frac{1}{7}}\right)^3 - 5 \times (4^4)^{\frac{1}{4}} + 2 \times \left((11^3)^{\frac{1}{3}}\right)^2$$

$$= 4 \times 27 - 5 \times 4 + 2 \times 121$$

$$= 108 - 20 + 242 = 330$$

4. Simplify : $\left(\dfrac{2^{-1} \times 3^2}{2^2 \times 3^{-4}}\right)^{\frac{7}{2}} \times \left(\dfrac{2^{-2} \times 3^3}{2^3 \times 3^{-5}}\right)^{-\frac{5}{2}}.$

[BOARD TERM I, 2012, SET 47]

Sol. Given expression $= \left(\dfrac{2^{-1} \times 3^2}{2^2 \times 3^{-4}}\right)^{\frac{7}{2}} \times \left(\dfrac{2^{-2} \times 3^3}{2^3 \times 3^{-5}}\right)^{-\frac{5}{2}}$

$$= \left(\dfrac{3^{2+4}}{2^{2+1}}\right)^{\frac{7}{2}} \times \left(\dfrac{3^{3+5}}{2^{3+2}}\right)^{-\frac{5}{2}}$$

$$= \left(\dfrac{3^6}{2^3}\right)^{\frac{7}{2}} \times \left(\dfrac{3^8}{2^5}\right)^{-\frac{5}{2}}$$

$$= \dfrac{3^{6 \times \frac{7}{2}}}{2^{3 \times \frac{7}{2}}} \times \dfrac{3^{8 \times \left(-\frac{5}{2}\right)}}{2^{5 \times \left(-\frac{5}{2}\right)}} = \dfrac{3^{21}}{2^{\frac{21}{2}}} \times \dfrac{3^{-20}}{2^{-\frac{25}{2}}}$$

$$= \dfrac{3^{21}}{2^{\frac{21}{2}}} \times \dfrac{2^{\frac{25}{2}}}{3^{20}}$$

$$= 3 \times 2^2 = 3 \times 4 = 12$$

5. If $5^{2x-1} - 25^{x-1} = 2500$, then find the value of x.

[BOARD TERM I, 2012, SET-56]

Sol. Given, $5^{2x-1} - (5^2)^{x-1} = 2500$

$$\Rightarrow 5^{2x-1} - 5^{2x-2} = 2500$$

$$\Rightarrow 5^{2x-2} (5 - 1) = 2500$$

$$\Rightarrow 5^{2x-2} = \dfrac{2500}{4} = 625 = 5^4$$

On equating the power of 5 from both sides, we get.

$$\Rightarrow 2x - 2 = 4 \Rightarrow x = 3$$

6. If $xyz = 1$, then show that $(1 + x + y^{-1})^{-1} + (1 + y + z^{-1})^{-1} + (1 + z + x^{-1})^{-1} = 1$.

[BOARD TERM I, 2012, SET-52]

Sol. On taking L.H.S of the given expression, we have

$$\text{LHS} = \dfrac{1}{\dfrac{y + xy + 1}{y}} + \dfrac{1}{1 + y + xy} + \dfrac{1}{1 + \dfrac{1}{xy} + \dfrac{1}{x}}$$

$$\left(\because \ xyz = 1 \text{ or}, \dfrac{1}{z} = xy\right)$$

$$= \dfrac{y}{xy + y + 1} + \dfrac{1}{xy + 1 + y} + \dfrac{xy}{xy + y + 1}$$

$$= \dfrac{y + 1 + xy}{xy + y + 1} = 1$$

$\therefore$ L.H.S = R.H.S

Hence Proved.

7. If x is positive real number and exponents are rational number then simplify :

$$\left[\dfrac{x^b}{x^c}\right]^{b+c-a} \times \left[\dfrac{x^c}{x^a}\right]^{c+a-b} \times \left[\dfrac{x^a}{x^b}\right]^{a+b-c}$$

[BOARD TERM I, 2016, SET 7AEDLQR]

Sol. Given expression

$$= \left[\dfrac{x^b}{x^c}\right]^{b+c-a} \times \left[\dfrac{x^c}{x^a}\right]^{c+a-b} \times \left[\dfrac{x^a}{x^b}\right]^{a+b-c}$$

$$= \left[x^{b-c}\right]^{b+c-a} \times \left[x^{c-a}\right]^{c+a-b} \times \left[x^{a-b}\right]^{a+b-c}$$

$$\left[\because \ \dfrac{a^m}{a^n} = a^{m-n}\right]$$

$$= x^{b^2-c^2-ab+ac} \times x^{c^2-a^2-bc+ab} \times x^{a^2-b^2-ac+bc}$$

$$= x^{b^2-c^2-ab+ac+c^2-a^2-bc+ab+a^2-b^2-ac+bc}$$

$$= x^0 = 1$$

8. Evaluate : $\left(\dfrac{81}{16}\right)^{\frac{-3}{4}} \times \left[\left(\dfrac{9}{25}\right)^{\frac{3}{2}} \div \left(\dfrac{5}{2}\right)^{-3}\right]$

[BOARD TERM I, 2016, BQS6JZK]

Sol. Given expression = $\left(\dfrac{81}{16}\right)^{\frac{-3}{4}} \times \left[\left(\dfrac{9}{25}\right)^{\frac{3}{2}} \div \left(\dfrac{5}{2}\right)^{-3}\right]$

$$= \left(\dfrac{16}{81}\right)^{\frac{3}{4}} \times \left[\left(\dfrac{9}{25}\right)^{\frac{3}{2}} \div \left(\dfrac{2}{5}\right)^{3}\right]$$

$$= \left(\dfrac{2^4}{3^4}\right)^{\frac{3}{4}} \times \left[\left(\dfrac{3^2}{5^2}\right)^{\frac{3}{2}} \times \left(\dfrac{5}{2}\right)^{3}\right]$$

$$= \left[\left(\dfrac{2}{3}\right)^{4}\right]^{\frac{3}{4}} \times \left[\left[\left(\dfrac{3}{5}\right)^{2}\right]^{\frac{3}{2}} \times \left(\dfrac{5}{2}\right)^{3}\right]$$

$$\left(\dfrac{2}{3}\right)^{4 \times \frac{3}{4}} \times \left[\left(\dfrac{3}{5}\right)^{2 \times \frac{3}{2}} \times \left(\dfrac{5}{2}\right)^{3}\right]$$

$$= \left(\dfrac{2}{3}\right)^{3} \times \left[\left(\dfrac{3}{5}\right)^{3} \times \left(\dfrac{5}{2}\right)^{3}\right]$$

$$= \dfrac{2^3}{3^3} \times \left[\left(\dfrac{3^3}{5^3}\right) \times \dfrac{5^3}{2^3}\right] = \dfrac{2^3}{2^3} \times \dfrac{3^3}{5^3} \times \dfrac{5^3}{2^3} = 1$$

9. Simplify : $2\sqrt[4]{81} - 8\sqrt[3]{216} + 15\sqrt[5]{32} + \sqrt{225} - \sqrt[4]{16}$

[BOARD TERM I, 2016]

Sol. Given expression

$$= 2\sqrt[4]{81} - 8\sqrt[3]{216} + 15\sqrt[5]{32} + \sqrt{225} - \sqrt[4]{16}$$

$$= 2\left(3^4\right)^{\frac{1}{4}} - 8\left(6^3\right)^{\frac{1}{3}} + 15\left(2^5\right)^{\frac{1}{5}} + 15 - \left(2^4\right)^{\frac{1}{4}}$$

$$= 2 \times 3 - 8 \times 6 + 15 \times 2 + 15 - 2$$

$$= 6 - 48 + 30 + 15 - 2 = 51 - 50 = 1$$

10. If $a = \dfrac{2^{x-1}}{2^{x-2}}, b = \dfrac{2^{-x}}{2^{x+1}}$ and $a - b = 0$, find the value of x.

[BOARD TERM I, 2016]

Sol. Given $a = \dfrac{2^{x-1}}{2^{x-2}}$ and $b = \dfrac{2^{-x}}{2^{x+1}}$

$$\therefore \quad a - b = 0$$

$$\Rightarrow \dfrac{2^{x-1}}{2^{x-2}} - \dfrac{2^{-x}}{2^{x+1}} = 0$$

$$\Rightarrow 2^{x-1-(x-2)} - 2^{-x-(x+1)} = 0$$

$$\Rightarrow 2^{x-1-x+2} - 2^{-x-x-1} = 0$$

$$\Rightarrow 2^1 - 2^{-2x-1} = 0$$

$$\Rightarrow 2^{-2x-1} = 2^1$$

$$\Rightarrow -2x - 1 = 1$$

$$\Rightarrow -2x = 2$$

$$x = -\dfrac{2}{2} = -1$$

[Topic 5] Rationalization of Real Numbers

Points to be Remembered

- The process of converting the irrational denominator of a number by multiplying its numerator and denominator by a suitable number, is called rationalization.
- To rationalize the denominator of the expression given in the form of $\dfrac{1}{\sqrt{r}+s}$, we multiply this by $\dfrac{\sqrt{r}-s}{\sqrt{r}-s}$, where r and s are integers.

For example:-

$$\dfrac{1}{\sqrt{7}-\sqrt{6}} = \dfrac{1}{\sqrt{7}-\sqrt{6}} \times \dfrac{\sqrt{7}+\sqrt{6}}{\sqrt{7}+\sqrt{6}}$$

[On rationalizing the denominator]

$$= \dfrac{\sqrt{7}+\sqrt{6}}{\left(\sqrt{7}\right)^2 - \left(\sqrt{6}\right)^2} = \dfrac{\sqrt{7}+\sqrt{6}}{7-6} = \sqrt{7}+\sqrt{6}$$

PREVIOUS YEARS' EXAMINATION QUESTIONS

TOPIC 5

Multiple Choice Questions

(1 Mark Each)

1. $\dfrac{28}{\sqrt{28}-\sqrt{7}}$ is equal to:

   (a) $4\sqrt{7}$
   (b) $\dfrac{4}{\sqrt{7}}$
   (c) $\dfrac{4\sqrt{7}}{3}$
   (d) $\dfrac{4}{\sqrt{3}}$

Sol. (a) Given expression $= \dfrac{28}{\sqrt{28}-\sqrt{7}}$

On rationalizing,

$$= \frac{28}{\sqrt{28}-\sqrt{7}} \times \frac{\sqrt{28}+\sqrt{7}}{\sqrt{28}+\sqrt{7}}$$

$$= \frac{28\left(2\sqrt{7}+\sqrt{7}\right)}{28-7} = \frac{28\times3\sqrt{7}}{21} = 4\sqrt{7}$$

2. The value of $\dfrac{1}{\sqrt{10}}$, when $\sqrt{10}=3.162$ is:

   (a) 0.3162
   (b) 31.62
   (c) 0.03162
   (d) 316.2

Sol. (a) $\dfrac{1}{\sqrt{10}} = \dfrac{1}{\sqrt{10}} \times \dfrac{\sqrt{10}}{\sqrt{10}} = \dfrac{\sqrt{10}}{10} = \dfrac{3.162}{10} = 0.3162$

3. $\dfrac{30}{\sqrt{20}+\sqrt{5}}$ is equal to:

   (a) $\dfrac{10}{3\sqrt{5}}$
   (b) $\dfrac{30}{\sqrt{5}}$
   (c) $\dfrac{10}{\sqrt{5}}$
   (d) $2\sqrt{5}$

Sol. (c) Given expression $= \dfrac{30}{\sqrt{20}+\sqrt{5}}$

$$= \frac{30}{2\sqrt{5}+\sqrt{5}} = \frac{30}{3\sqrt{5}} = \frac{10}{\sqrt{5}}$$

4. What is the simplified form of the expression
   $7\sqrt{3}-2\sqrt{7}+8\sqrt{2}+9\sqrt{7}+\sqrt{7}+11\sqrt{3}-2\sqrt{2}$?

   (a) $18\sqrt{3}+6\sqrt{7}+8\sqrt{2}$
   (b) $8\sqrt{3}+18\sqrt{7}+6\sqrt{2}$
   (c) $18\sqrt{2}+6\sqrt{7}+6\sqrt{3}$
   (d) $18\sqrt{3}+8\sqrt{7}+6\sqrt{2}$

Sol. (d) $7\sqrt{3}-2\sqrt{7}+8\sqrt{2}+9\sqrt{7}+\sqrt{7}+11\sqrt{3}-2\sqrt{2}$

$$= 18\sqrt{3}+8\sqrt{7}+6\sqrt{2}$$

5. $\left(7+\sqrt{7}\right)\left(7-\sqrt{7}\right)$ is equal to:

   (a) 49
   (b) 14
   (c) 42
   (d) $49\sqrt{7}$

Sol. (c) $\left(7+\sqrt{7}\right)\left(7-\sqrt{7}\right) = (7)^2 - \left(\sqrt{7}\right)^2$

$$= 49 - 7 = 42$$

Very Short Answer Type Questions

(1 Mark Each)

1. If $\sqrt{2}=1.4142$, then find the value of
   $$\sqrt{\frac{\sqrt{2}-1}{\sqrt{2}+1}}$$

   [NCERT Exemp.]

Sol. $\because \sqrt{2} = 1.4142$

Now, Given expression $= \sqrt{\dfrac{\sqrt{2}-1}{\sqrt{2}+1}}$

$$= \sqrt{\frac{\left(\sqrt{2}-1\right)}{\left(\sqrt{2}+1\right)} \times \frac{\left(\sqrt{2}-1\right)}{\left(\sqrt{2}-1\right)}}$$

[by rationalizing the denominator]

$$= \sqrt{\frac{\left(\sqrt{2}-1\right)^2}{2-1}} = \frac{\sqrt{\left(\sqrt{2}-1\right)^2}}{1}$$

$\because \sqrt{2}-1 = 1.4142 - 1 = 0.4142$

2. Write the rationalizing factor of $\dfrac{1}{\sqrt{50}}$

Sol. $\dfrac{1}{\sqrt{50}} = \dfrac{1}{\sqrt{5\times5\times2}} = \dfrac{1}{5\sqrt{2}} = \dfrac{1}{5\sqrt{2}} \times \dfrac{\sqrt{2}}{\sqrt{2}} = \dfrac{\sqrt{2}}{10}$

Hence, rationalizing factor is $\sqrt{2}$.

3. Simplify the expression $\dfrac{3}{\sqrt{48}-\sqrt{75}}$.

Sol. $\dfrac{3}{\sqrt{48}-\sqrt{75}}$

$$= \frac{3}{4\sqrt{3}-5\sqrt{3}} = \frac{3}{\sqrt{3}\left(4-5\right)}$$

$$= \frac{3}{-\sqrt{3}} \times \frac{\sqrt{3}}{\sqrt{3}} = \frac{3\sqrt{3}}{-3} = -\sqrt{3}$$

[by rationalizing the denominator]

4. Simplify : $\dfrac{2\sqrt{3}}{3} - \dfrac{\sqrt{3}}{6}$.

Sol. Given expression $= \dfrac{2\sqrt{3}}{3} - \dfrac{\sqrt{3}}{6}$

$$= \dfrac{4\sqrt{3} - \sqrt{3}}{6} = \dfrac{3\sqrt{3}}{6} = \dfrac{\sqrt{3}}{2}$$

5. Write the value of $\dfrac{1}{\sqrt{5} - \sqrt{4}}$.

Sol. Given expression $= \dfrac{1}{\sqrt{5} - \sqrt{4}} = \dfrac{1}{\sqrt{5} - 2} \times \dfrac{\sqrt{5} + 2}{\sqrt{5} + 2}$

[by rationalizing the denominator]

$$= \dfrac{\sqrt{5} + 2}{\left(\sqrt{5}\right)^2 - (2)^2} = \dfrac{\sqrt{5} + 2}{5 - 4} = 2 + \sqrt{5}$$

Short Answer Type Questions I
(2 Marks Each)

1. Find the value of $\dfrac{6}{\sqrt{5} - \sqrt{3}}$,

If $\sqrt{3} = 1.732$ and $\sqrt{5} = 2.236$

$\qquad\qquad$ **[NCERT EXEMPLAR]**

Sol. $\because\ \sqrt{3} = 1.732$ and $\sqrt{5} = 2.236$

Given expression $= \dfrac{6}{\sqrt{5} - \sqrt{3}} = \dfrac{6}{\sqrt{5} - \sqrt{3}} \times \dfrac{\sqrt{5} + \sqrt{3}}{\sqrt{5} + \sqrt{3}}$

[by rationalizing the denominator]

$$= \dfrac{6\left(\sqrt{5} + \sqrt{3}\right)}{\left(\sqrt{5}\right)^2 - \left(\sqrt{3}\right)^2} \qquad \left[\because (a - b)(a + b) = a^2 - b^2\right]$$

$$= \dfrac{6\left(\sqrt{5} + \sqrt{3}\right)}{5 - 3} = \dfrac{6\left(\sqrt{5} + \sqrt{3}\right)}{2} = 3\left(\sqrt{5} + \sqrt{3}\right)$$

$$= 3(2.236 + 1.732) = 3(3.968) = 11.904$$

2. If $\sqrt{2} = 1.414$ and $\sqrt{3} = 1.732$, then find the value of $\dfrac{4}{3\sqrt{3} - 2\sqrt{2}} + \dfrac{3}{3\sqrt{3} + 2\sqrt{2}}$.

$\qquad\qquad$ **[NCERT EXEMPLAR]**

Sol. $\because\ \sqrt{2} = 1.414$ and $\sqrt{3} = 1.732$,

Given expression $= \dfrac{4}{3\sqrt{3} - 2\sqrt{2}} + \dfrac{3}{3\sqrt{3} + 2\sqrt{2}}$

$$= \dfrac{4\left(3\sqrt{3} + 2\sqrt{2}\right) + 3\left(3\sqrt{3} - 2\sqrt{2}\right)}{\left(3\sqrt{3} - 2\sqrt{2}\right)\left(3\sqrt{3} + 2\sqrt{2}\right)}$$

$$= \dfrac{12\sqrt{3} + 8\sqrt{2} + 9\sqrt{3} - 6\sqrt{2}}{\left(3\sqrt{3}\right)^2 - \left(2\sqrt{2}\right)^2}$$

$\qquad\qquad\qquad \left[\because (a + b)(a - b) = a^2 - b^2\right]$

$$= \dfrac{21\sqrt{3} + 2\sqrt{2}}{27 - 8} = \dfrac{21\sqrt{3} + 2\sqrt{2}}{19}$$

$$= \dfrac{21 \times 1.732 + 2 \times 1.414}{19}$$

$$= \dfrac{36.372 + 2.828}{19} = \dfrac{39.2}{19} = 2.06316$$

3. If $\sqrt{2} = 1.414$, then find the value of $\dfrac{1}{\sqrt{2} + 1}$.

$\qquad\qquad$ **[BOARD TERM I, 2012, SET 36]**

Sol. $\because\ \sqrt{2} = 1.414$

Given expression $= \dfrac{1}{\sqrt{2} + 1} = \dfrac{1}{\sqrt{2} + 1} \times \dfrac{\left(\sqrt{2} - 1\right)}{\left(\sqrt{2} - 1\right)}$

[by rationalizing the denominator]

$$= \dfrac{\left(\sqrt{2} - 1\right)}{\left(\sqrt{2}\right)^2 - (1)^2}$$

$$= \dfrac{\sqrt{2} - 1}{2 - 1} = \dfrac{1.414 - 1}{1} = 0.414$$

4. Taking $\sqrt{2} = 1.414$ and $\pi = 3.141$, evaluate $\dfrac{1}{\sqrt{2}} + \pi$ upto three places of decimal.

$\qquad\qquad$ **[BOARD TERM I, 2012, SET 19]**

Sol. $\dfrac{1}{\sqrt{2}} = \dfrac{1}{\sqrt{2}} \times \dfrac{\sqrt{2}}{\sqrt{2}}$

$\qquad\qquad$ [rationalizing the denominator]

$$\dfrac{\sqrt{2}}{2} = \dfrac{1.414}{2} = 0.707$$

Given expression $= \dfrac{1}{\sqrt{2}} + \pi = 0.707 + 3.141$

$\qquad\qquad \left[\because \sqrt{2} = 1.414 \text{ and } \pi = 3.141\right]$

$$= 3.848.$$

5. Simplify: $\dfrac{6 - 4\sqrt{3}}{6 + 4\sqrt{3}}$ by rationalizing the denominator. $\qquad$ **[BOARD TERM I, 2014]**

Sol. Given expression $= \dfrac{6 - 4\sqrt{3}}{6 + 4\sqrt{3}} = \dfrac{6 - 4\sqrt{3}}{6 + 4\sqrt{3}} \times \dfrac{6 - 4\sqrt{3}}{6 - 4\sqrt{3}}$

[by rationalizing the denominator]

$$= \dfrac{\left(6 - 4\sqrt{3}\right)^2}{(6)^2 - \left(4\sqrt{3}\right)^2}$$

$$= \dfrac{\left(6 - 4\sqrt{3}\right)^2}{36 - 48}$$

$$= \dfrac{36 + 48 - 48\sqrt{3}}{-12}$$

$$= \dfrac{84 - 48\sqrt{3}}{-12} = -\left(7 - 4\sqrt{3}\right) = 4\sqrt{3} - 7$$

6. If $x = 3 - 2\sqrt{2}$, find the value of $\sqrt{x} + \dfrac{1}{\sqrt{x}}$.

[**BOARD TERM I, 2014**]

Sol. $\because \; x = 3 - 2\sqrt{2}$

$= 1 + 2 - 2\sqrt{2}$

$= \left(\sqrt{2} - 1\right)^2$

$\Rightarrow \sqrt{x} = \sqrt{2} - 1$

and $\dfrac{1}{\sqrt{x}} = \dfrac{1}{\sqrt{2} - 1} \times \dfrac{\sqrt{2} + 1}{\sqrt{2} + 1}$

[On rationalizing the denominator]

$= \dfrac{\left(1 + \sqrt{2}\right)}{\left(\sqrt{2}\right)^2 - (1)^2} = \dfrac{\left(1 + \sqrt{2}\right)}{2 - 1} = \left(\sqrt{2} + 1\right)$

$\therefore$ Given expression $= \sqrt{x} + \dfrac{1}{\sqrt{x}}$

$= \sqrt{2} - 1 + \sqrt{2} + 1$

$= 2\sqrt{2}$

7. Rationalise the denominator of $\dfrac{4}{2 + \sqrt{3} + \sqrt{7}}$

Sol. Given expression $= \dfrac{4}{2 + \sqrt{3} + \sqrt{7}}$

$= \dfrac{4}{\left(2 + \sqrt{3}\right) + \sqrt{7}} \times \dfrac{\left(2 + \sqrt{3}\right) - \sqrt{7}}{\left(2 + \sqrt{3}\right) - \sqrt{7}}$

[by rationalizing the denominator]

$= \dfrac{8 + 4\sqrt{3} - 4\sqrt{7}}{\left(2 + \sqrt{3}\right)^2 - \left(\sqrt{7}\right)^2}$ $\quad [\because a^2 - b^2 = (a + b)\,(a - b)]$

$= \dfrac{8 + 4\sqrt{3} - 4\sqrt{7}}{4 + 3 + 4\sqrt{3} - 7}$ $\quad [\because (a + b)^2 = a^2 + b^2 + 2ab]$

$= \dfrac{8 + 4\sqrt{3} - 4\sqrt{7}}{7 + 4\sqrt{3} - 7}$

$= \dfrac{8 + 4\sqrt{3} - 4\sqrt{7}}{4\sqrt{3}} \times \dfrac{\sqrt{3}}{\sqrt{3}}$

[Again rationalizing the denominator]

$= \dfrac{8\sqrt{3} + 12 - 4\sqrt{21}}{12}$

$= \dfrac{8\sqrt{3}}{12} + \dfrac{12}{12} - \dfrac{4\sqrt{21}}{12}$

$= \dfrac{2\sqrt{3}}{3} + 1 - \dfrac{\sqrt{21}}{3}$

Short Answer Type Questions II

(3 Marks Each)

1. Simplify: $\dfrac{\sqrt{6}}{\sqrt{2} + \sqrt{3}} + \dfrac{3\sqrt{2}}{\sqrt{6} + \sqrt{3}} - \dfrac{4\sqrt{3}}{\sqrt{6} + \sqrt{2}}$.

[**BOARD TERM I, 2010, SET B, 2012, SET 51**]

Sol. I^{st} term $= \dfrac{\sqrt{6}}{\sqrt{2} + \sqrt{3}} = \sqrt{18} - \sqrt{12} = 3\sqrt{2} - 2\sqrt{3}$

IInd term $= \dfrac{3\sqrt{2}}{\sqrt{6} + \sqrt{3}} = \sqrt{12} - \sqrt{6} = 2\sqrt{3} - \sqrt{6}$

and IIIrd term $= \dfrac{4\sqrt{3}}{\sqrt{6} + \sqrt{2}} = \sqrt{18} - \sqrt{6} = 3\sqrt{2} - \sqrt{6}$

$\therefore$ Given expression

$= 3\sqrt{2} - 2\sqrt{3} + 2\sqrt{3} - \sqrt{6} - 3\sqrt{2} + \sqrt{6}$

$= 0$

Alternate Method:

Given expression

$= \dfrac{\sqrt{6}}{\sqrt{2} + \sqrt{3}} + \dfrac{3\sqrt{2}}{\sqrt{6} + \sqrt{3}} - \dfrac{4\sqrt{3}}{\sqrt{6} + \sqrt{2}}$

$= \dfrac{\sqrt{6}}{\sqrt{2} + \sqrt{3}} \times \dfrac{\left(\sqrt{3} - \sqrt{2}\right)}{\left(\sqrt{3} - \sqrt{2}\right)} + \dfrac{\left(3\sqrt{2}\right)}{\left(\sqrt{6} + \sqrt{3}\right)} \times \dfrac{\left(\sqrt{6} - \sqrt{3}\right)}{\left(\sqrt{6} - \sqrt{3}\right)}$

$\qquad - \dfrac{4\sqrt{3}}{\left(\sqrt{6} + \sqrt{2}\right)} \times \dfrac{\left(\sqrt{6} - \sqrt{2}\right)}{\left(\sqrt{6} - \sqrt{2}\right)}$

[by rationalizing the denominator]

$= \dfrac{\sqrt{18} - \sqrt{12}}{3 - 2} + \dfrac{3\sqrt{12} - 3\sqrt{6}}{6 - 3} - \dfrac{4\sqrt{18} - 4\sqrt{6}}{6 - 2}$

$= \sqrt{18} - \sqrt{12} + \dfrac{3\left(\sqrt{12} - \sqrt{6}\right)}{3} - \dfrac{4\left(\sqrt{18} - \sqrt{6}\right)}{4}$

$= \sqrt{18} - \sqrt{12} + \sqrt{12} - \sqrt{6} - \sqrt{18} + \sqrt{6} = 0$

2. Simplify : $\dfrac{1}{1 + \sqrt{2}} + \dfrac{1}{\sqrt{2} + \sqrt{3}} + \dfrac{2}{\sqrt{3} + \sqrt{5}}$.

[**BOARD TERM I, 2012, SET-45**]

Sol. Given expression $= \dfrac{1}{1 + \sqrt{2}} + \dfrac{1}{\sqrt{2} + \sqrt{3}} + \dfrac{2}{\sqrt{3} + \sqrt{5}}$

$= \dfrac{1}{\left(\sqrt{2} + 1\right)} \times \dfrac{\left(\sqrt{2} - 1\right)}{\left(\sqrt{2} - 1\right)} + \dfrac{1}{\left(\sqrt{3} + \sqrt{2}\right)} \times \dfrac{\left(\sqrt{3} - \sqrt{2}\right)}{\left(\sqrt{3} - \sqrt{2}\right)}$

$\qquad + \dfrac{2}{\left(\sqrt{5} + \sqrt{3}\right)} \times \dfrac{\left(\sqrt{5} - \sqrt{3}\right)}{\left(\sqrt{5} - \sqrt{3}\right)}$

[by rationalizing the denominator]

$= \dfrac{\left(\sqrt{2} - 1\right)}{2 - 1} + \dfrac{\left(\sqrt{3} - \sqrt{2}\right)}{3 - 2} + \dfrac{2\left(\sqrt{5} - \sqrt{3}\right)}{5 - 3}$

$= \sqrt{2} - 1 + \sqrt{3} - \sqrt{2} + \sqrt{5} - \sqrt{3} = \sqrt{5} - 1$

3. Simplify : $\dfrac{5+\sqrt{3}}{7-4\sqrt{3}} \times \dfrac{5+\sqrt{3}}{7+4\sqrt{3}}$.

[BOARD TERM, I, 2012, SET-42]

Sol. First term = $\dfrac{5+\sqrt{3}}{7-4\sqrt{3}}$

On rationalizing the denominator

$\dfrac{5+\sqrt{3}}{7-4\sqrt{3}} \times \dfrac{7+4\sqrt{3}}{7+4\sqrt{3}} = \dfrac{35+20\sqrt{3}+7\sqrt{3}+12}{49-48}$

$= \dfrac{47+27\sqrt{3}}{1}$ and

Second term $= \dfrac{5+\sqrt{3}}{7+4\sqrt{3}} = \dfrac{(5+\sqrt{3})(7-4\sqrt{3})}{(7+4\sqrt{3})(7-4\sqrt{3})}$

$= \dfrac{35-20\sqrt{3}+7\sqrt{3}-12}{(7)^2-(4\sqrt{3})^2} = \dfrac{23-13\sqrt{3}}{1}$

Given expression

$= \dfrac{5+\sqrt{3}}{7-4\sqrt{3}} - \dfrac{5+\sqrt{3}}{7+4\sqrt{3}} = (47+27\sqrt{3})-(23-13\sqrt{3})$

$= 24+40\sqrt{3} = 8(3+5\sqrt{3})$

Alternate Method ;

Given expression $= \dfrac{5+\sqrt{3}}{7-4\sqrt{3}} \times \dfrac{5+\sqrt{3}}{7+4\sqrt{3}}$

$= \dfrac{(5+\sqrt{3})(7+4\sqrt{3})-(5+\sqrt{3})(7-4\sqrt{3})}{(7-4\sqrt{3})(7+4\sqrt{3})}$

$= \dfrac{35+20\sqrt{3}+7\sqrt{3}+12-35+20\sqrt{3}-7\sqrt{3}+12}{49-48}$

$= \dfrac{40\sqrt{3}+24}{1} = 24+40\sqrt{3} = 8(3+5\sqrt{3})$

4. Rationalize the denominator of $\dfrac{30}{5\sqrt{3}-3\sqrt{5}}$.

[BOARD TERM I, 2012, SET 49]

Sol. Given expression

$= \dfrac{30}{5\sqrt{3}-3\sqrt{5}} = \dfrac{30}{(5\sqrt{3}-3\sqrt{5})} \times \dfrac{(5\sqrt{3}+3\sqrt{5})}{(5\sqrt{3}+3\sqrt{5})}$

[On rationalizing the denominator]

$= \dfrac{30(5\sqrt{3}+3\sqrt{5})}{(5\sqrt{3})^2-(3\sqrt{5})^2} = \dfrac{30(5\sqrt{3}+3\sqrt{5})}{25\times3-9\times5}$

$= \dfrac{30(5\sqrt{3}+3\sqrt{5})}{75-45} = \dfrac{30(5\sqrt{3}+3\sqrt{5})}{30}$

$= 5\sqrt{3}+3\sqrt{5}$

5. If $\sqrt{2}=1.414$ and $\sqrt{3}=1.732$, then calculate $\dfrac{4}{3\sqrt{3}-2\sqrt{2}}+\dfrac{3}{3\sqrt{3}+2\sqrt{2}}$.

[BOARD TERM, I, 2012, SET-50][NCERT EXEMPLAR]

Sol. $\because$ $\sqrt{2}=1.414$ and $\sqrt{3}=1.732$

Given expression $= \dfrac{4}{3\sqrt{3}-2\sqrt{2}}+\dfrac{3}{3\sqrt{3}+2\sqrt{2}}$

$= \dfrac{4(3\sqrt{3}+2\sqrt{2})+3(3\sqrt{3}-2\sqrt{2})}{(3\sqrt{3}-2\sqrt{2})(3\sqrt{3}+2\sqrt{2})}$

$= \dfrac{12\sqrt{3}+8\sqrt{2}+9\sqrt{3}-6\sqrt{2}}{27-8}$

$= \dfrac{21\sqrt{3}+2\sqrt{2}}{19}$

$= \dfrac{21\times1.732+2\times1.414}{19}$

$= \dfrac{36.372+2.828}{19} = \dfrac{39.2}{19} = 2.063$

6. Simplify : $(\sqrt{3}+1)(1-\sqrt{12})+\dfrac{9}{(\sqrt{3}+\sqrt{12})}$

[BOARD TERM, I, 2012, SET-58]

Sol. Given expression

$= (\sqrt{3}+1)(1-\sqrt{12})+\dfrac{9}{(\sqrt{3}+\sqrt{12})}$

$= (\sqrt{3}-6+1-\sqrt{12})+\dfrac{9}{(\sqrt{12}+\sqrt{3})} \times \dfrac{(\sqrt{12}-\sqrt{3})}{(\sqrt{12}-\sqrt{3})}$

[On rationalizing the denominator]

$= (\sqrt{3}-6+1-\sqrt{12})+\dfrac{(9\sqrt{12}-\sqrt{3})}{(\sqrt{12})^2-(\sqrt{3})^2}$

$= (\sqrt{3}-6+1-\sqrt{12})+\dfrac{9(\sqrt{12}-\sqrt{3})}{12-3}$

$= \sqrt{3}-5-\sqrt{12}+\sqrt{12}-\sqrt{3} = -5.$

7. If $p=5+2\sqrt{6}$ and $x=\dfrac{1}{p}$, then what will be the value of p^2+x^2?

[BOARD TERM, I, 2012, SET 50]

Sol. Given, $p=5+2\sqrt{6}$

$\therefore$ $x=\dfrac{1}{p}=\dfrac{1}{5+2\sqrt{6}}$

$= \dfrac{1}{5+2\sqrt{6}} \times \dfrac{(5-2\sqrt{6})}{(5-2\sqrt{6})}$

[On rationalizing the denominator]

$$= \frac{5 - 2\sqrt{6}}{(5)^2 - (2\sqrt{6})^2} = \frac{5 - 2\sqrt{6}}{25 - 24} = 5 - 2\sqrt{6}$$

$\therefore$ Expression $= p^2 + x^2 = \left(5 + 2\sqrt{6}\right)^2 + \left(5 - 2\sqrt{6}\right)^2$

$$= (5)^2 + (2\sqrt{6})^2 + 2 \times 5 \times 2\sqrt{6} + (5)^2 + (2\sqrt{6})^2$$
$$- 2 \times 5 \times 2\sqrt{6}$$

$$= 25 + 24 + 20\sqrt{6} + 25 + 24 - 20\sqrt{6}$$
$$= 98.$$

8. Evaluate : $\dfrac{\sqrt{5} + \sqrt{2}}{\sqrt{5} - \sqrt{2}}$, given that $\sqrt{10} = 3.162$.

   [BOARD TERM, I, 2012, SET-67]

Sol. Given expression $= \dfrac{\sqrt{5} + \sqrt{2}}{\sqrt{5} - \sqrt{2}}$

$$= \frac{\sqrt{5} + \sqrt{2}}{\sqrt{5} - \sqrt{2}} \times \frac{\sqrt{5} + \sqrt{2}}{\sqrt{5} + \sqrt{2}}$$

[On rationalizing the denominator]

$$= \frac{\left(\sqrt{5}\right)^2 + \left(\sqrt{2}\right)^2 + 2 \times \sqrt{5} \times \sqrt{2}}{\left(\sqrt{5}\right)^2 - \left(\sqrt{2}\right)^2}$$

$$= \frac{5 + 2 + 2\sqrt{10}}{5 - 2} = \frac{7 + 2\sqrt{10}}{3}$$

$$= \frac{7 + 2 \times 3.162}{3} \left[\because \sqrt{10} = 3.162 \, (\text{given}) \right]$$

$$= \frac{7 + 6.324}{3} = \frac{13.324}{3}$$

$$= 4.441 \, (\text{approx})$$

9. Find the value of $\left(x - \dfrac{1}{x}\right)^3$, if $x = 1 + \sqrt{2}$.

   [BOARD TERM, I, 2012, SET-44]

Sol. $\because x = 1 + \sqrt{2}$

and $\dfrac{1}{x} = \dfrac{1}{1 + \sqrt{2}} \times \dfrac{1 - \sqrt{2}}{1 - \sqrt{2}}$

   [On rationalizing the denominator]

$$= \frac{1 - \sqrt{2}}{1 - 2} = \sqrt{2} - 1$$

$\therefore$ Given expression

$$= \left(x - \frac{1}{x}\right)^3 = \left[(1 + \sqrt{2}) - (\sqrt{2} - 1)\right]^3$$

$$= \left[1 + \sqrt{2} - \sqrt{2} + 1\right]^3 = 2^3 = 8$$

10. If $x = 9 + 4\sqrt{5}$, then find the value of $\sqrt{x} - \dfrac{1}{\sqrt{x}}$.

    [BOARD TERM, I, 2012, SET-45]

Sol. $\because x = 9 + 4\sqrt{5} = 5 + 4 + 4\sqrt{5}$

$$x = \left(\sqrt{5} + 2\right)^2$$

Taking square root of both sides, we get

$$\sqrt{x} = \sqrt{5} - 2 \text{ and } \frac{1}{\sqrt{x}} = \sqrt{5} - 2$$

$\therefore$ Expression $= \sqrt{x} - \dfrac{1}{\sqrt{x}} = \sqrt{5} + 2 - \left(\sqrt{5} - 2\right)$

$$= \sqrt{5} + 2 - \sqrt{5} + 2 = 4.$$

11. Find the values of a and b, when $a + b\sqrt{15}$
$= \dfrac{\sqrt{5} + \sqrt{3}}{\sqrt{5} - \sqrt{3}}$.

    [BOARD TERM, I, 2012, SET-14]

Sol. R.H.S $= \dfrac{\sqrt{5} + \sqrt{3}}{\sqrt{5} - \sqrt{3}}$

$$= \frac{\sqrt{5} + \sqrt{3}}{\sqrt{5} - \sqrt{3}} \times \frac{\sqrt{5} + \sqrt{3}}{\sqrt{5} + \sqrt{3}}$$

[On rationalizing the denominator]

$$= \frac{5 + 3 + 2 \times \sqrt{5} \times \sqrt{3}}{5 - 3}$$

$$= \frac{8 + 2\sqrt{15}}{2} = \frac{2\left(4 + \sqrt{15}\right)}{2} = 4 + \sqrt{15}$$

Now, $a + b\sqrt{15} = 4 + \sqrt{15}$

On comparing both sides, we get

$a = 4, b = 1.$

12. If $x = \dfrac{\sqrt{p + 2q} + \sqrt{p - 2q}}{\sqrt{p + 2q} - \sqrt{p - 2q}}$, then show that:

    $qx^2 - px + q = 0.$

    [BOARD TERM, I, 2012, SET-52]

Sol. $\because \; x = \dfrac{\sqrt{p + 2q} + \sqrt{p - 2q}}{\sqrt{p + 2q} - \sqrt{p - 2q}}$

$$= \frac{\sqrt{p + 2q} + \sqrt{p - 2q}}{\sqrt{p + 2q} - \sqrt{p - 2q}} \times \frac{\sqrt{p + 2q} + \sqrt{p - 2q}}{\sqrt{p + 2q} + \sqrt{p - 2q}}$$

[On rationalizing the denominator]

$$= \frac{(p + 2q) + (p - 2q) + 2 \times \sqrt{p + 2q} \times \sqrt{p - 2q}}{(p + 2q) - (p - 2q)}$$

$$= \frac{2p + 2\sqrt{p^2 - 4q^2}}{p + 2q - p + 2q}$$

$$\therefore \quad x = \frac{2\left(p + 2\sqrt{p^2 - 4q^2}\right)}{4q}$$

$$\text{and } 2qx = \frac{2q \times 2\left(p + 2\sqrt{p^2 - 4q^2}\right)}{4q}$$

$$= p + 2\sqrt{p^2 - 4q^2}$$

$$\Rightarrow 2qx - p = 2\sqrt{p^2 - 4q^2}$$

On squaring both sides, we get

$$\Rightarrow 4q^2x^2 + p^2 - 4pqx = p^2 - 4q^2$$
$$\Rightarrow 4q(qx^2 - px) = -4q^2 \Rightarrow (qx^2 - px) = -q$$
$$\therefore qx^2 - px + q = 0.$$

13. Simplify : $\dfrac{\sqrt{2}}{\sqrt{5}+2} - \dfrac{2}{\sqrt{10}-2\sqrt{2}} + \dfrac{8}{\sqrt{2}}$

[BOARD TERM, I, 2013]

Sol. Given expression $= \dfrac{\sqrt{2}}{\sqrt{5}+2} - \dfrac{2}{\sqrt{10}-2\sqrt{2}} + \dfrac{8}{\sqrt{2}}$

$$= \frac{\sqrt{2}\left(\sqrt{5}-2\right)}{5-4} - \frac{2\left(\sqrt{10}+2\sqrt{2}\right)}{10-8} + \frac{8\sqrt{2}}{2}$$

$$= \frac{\sqrt{10}-2\sqrt{2}}{1} - \left(\sqrt{10}+2\sqrt{2}\right) + 4\sqrt{2}$$

$$= \sqrt{10} - 2\sqrt{2} - \sqrt{10} - 2\sqrt{2} + 4\sqrt{2} = 0.$$

14. If $\dfrac{3}{4\sqrt{5}-\sqrt{3}} + \dfrac{2}{4\sqrt{5}+\sqrt{3}} = a\sqrt{5} + b\sqrt{3}$, then find the values of a and b.

[BOARD TERM, I, 2013]

Sol. Given, $\dfrac{3}{4\sqrt{5}-\sqrt{3}} + \dfrac{2}{4\sqrt{5}+\sqrt{3}} = a\sqrt{5} + b\sqrt{3}$ ...(i)

$$\text{L.H.S} = \frac{3}{4\sqrt{5}-\sqrt{3}} + \frac{2}{4\sqrt{5}+\sqrt{3}}$$

$$= \frac{3\left(4\sqrt{5}+\sqrt{3}\right) + 2\left(4\sqrt{5}-\sqrt{3}\right)}{\left(4\sqrt{5}-\sqrt{3}\right)\left(4\sqrt{5}+\sqrt{3}\right)}$$

$$= \frac{12\sqrt{5}+3\sqrt{3}+8\sqrt{5}-2\sqrt{3}}{\left(4\sqrt{5}\right)^2 - \left(\sqrt{3}\right)^2}$$

$$= \frac{12\sqrt{5}+3\sqrt{3}+8\sqrt{5}-2\sqrt{3}}{80-3}$$

$$= \frac{20\sqrt{5}+\sqrt{3}}{77} = \frac{20\sqrt{5}}{77} + \frac{\sqrt{3}}{77}$$

From eq. (i)

$$\frac{20\sqrt{5}}{77} + \frac{\sqrt{3}}{77} = a\sqrt{5} + b\sqrt{3}$$

On Comparing both sides, we get

$$a = \frac{20}{77} \text{ and } b = \frac{1}{77}$$

15. Find the values of 'a' and 'b' when

$$\frac{5+\sqrt{6}}{5-\sqrt{6}} = a + b\sqrt{6}$$

[BOARD TERM, I, 2014]

Sol. Given, $a + b\sqrt{6} = \dfrac{5+\sqrt{6}}{5-\sqrt{6}}$

$$= \frac{5+\sqrt{6}}{5-\sqrt{6}} \times \frac{5+\sqrt{6}}{5+\sqrt{6}}$$

[On rationalizing the denominator]

$$= \frac{\left(5+\sqrt{6}\right)^2}{(5)^2 - \left(\sqrt{6}\right)^2}$$

$$= \frac{25+6+10\sqrt{6}}{25-6}$$

$$= \frac{31+10\sqrt{6}}{19}$$

$$\therefore a + b\sqrt{6} = \frac{31}{19} + \frac{10}{19}\sqrt{6}$$

On comparing the rational and irrational parts of both sides, we get

$$a = \frac{31}{19} \text{ and } b = \frac{10}{19}$$

16. If $x = \dfrac{1}{3-2\sqrt{2}}$ and $y = \dfrac{1}{3+2\sqrt{2}}$, then find the value of x + y + xy.

[BOARD TERM, I, 2014]

Sol. Given, $x = \dfrac{1}{3-2\sqrt{2}}$

$$= \frac{1}{3-2\sqrt{2}} \times \frac{3+2\sqrt{2}}{3+2\sqrt{2}}$$

[On rationalizing the denominator]

$$= \frac{3+2\sqrt{2}}{9-8} = 3 + 2\sqrt{2}$$

$$\text{and } y = \frac{1}{3+2\sqrt{2}}$$

$$= \frac{1}{3+2\sqrt{2}} \times \frac{3-2\sqrt{2}}{3-2\sqrt{2}}$$

[On rationalizing the denominator]

$$= \frac{3-2\sqrt{2}}{9-8} = 3 - 2\sqrt{2}$$

$$\therefore \text{ Expression} = x + y + xy$$

$$= 3 + 2\sqrt{2} + 3 - 2\sqrt{2} + \left(3+2\sqrt{2}\right)\left(3-2\sqrt{2}\right)$$

$$= 6 + 9 - 4 \times 2$$

$$= 6 + 9 - 8 = 7$$

17. If $x = \sqrt{2} - 1$, then find the value of $\left(x - \dfrac{1}{x}\right)^3$.

[BOARD TERM, I, 2014]

Sol. Given, $x = \sqrt{2} - 1$

$$\therefore \quad \frac{1}{x} = \frac{1}{\sqrt{2} - 1} \times \frac{\sqrt{2} + 1}{\sqrt{2} + 1}$$

[On rationalizing the denominator]

$$= \frac{\sqrt{2} + 1}{2 - 1} = \sqrt{2} + 1$$

$$\therefore \text{ Expression} = \left(x - \frac{1}{x}\right)^3 = \left(\sqrt{2} - 1 - \sqrt{2} - 1\right)^3$$

$$= (-2)^3 = -8$$

18. Rationalize the denominator : $\dfrac{1}{2\sqrt{7} + 3\sqrt{3}}$.

[BOARD TERM, I, 2014]

Sol. Given expression $= \dfrac{1}{2\sqrt{7} + 3\sqrt{3}}$

$$= \frac{1}{2\sqrt{7} + 3\sqrt{3}} \times \frac{\left(2\sqrt{7} - 3\sqrt{3}\right)}{\left(2\sqrt{7} - 3\sqrt{3}\right)}$$

[On rationalizing the denominator]

$$= \frac{2\sqrt{7} - 3\sqrt{3}}{\left(2\sqrt{7}\right)^2 - \left(3\sqrt{3}\right)^2}$$

$$= \frac{2\sqrt{7} - 3\sqrt{3}}{4 \times 7 - 9 \times 3} = \frac{2\sqrt{7} - 3\sqrt{3}}{28 - 27} = \frac{2\sqrt{7} - 3\sqrt{3}}{1}$$

$$= 2\sqrt{7} - 3\sqrt{3}$$

19. If $x = 2 + \sqrt{3}$, then find the value of $x^2 + \dfrac{1}{x^2}$.

[BOARD TERM, I, 2015 SET-2]

Sol. Given, $x = 2 + \sqrt{3}$ $\qquad$ ....(i)

$$\therefore \frac{1}{x} = \frac{1}{2 + \sqrt{3}} = \frac{1}{2 + \sqrt{3}} \times \frac{2 - \sqrt{3}}{2 - \sqrt{3}}$$

[On rationalizing the denominator]

$$\frac{1}{x} = \frac{2 - \sqrt{3}}{4 - 3} = 2 - \sqrt{3} \qquad ...(ii)$$

On adding equation (i) and (ii),

$$\therefore \quad x + \frac{1}{x} = 4$$

On squaring, both sides, we get

$$x^2 + \frac{1}{x^2} + 2 = 16$$

$$\therefore \quad x^2 + \frac{1}{x^2} = 16 - 2 = 14$$

20. Rationalize the denominator of $\dfrac{\sqrt{3} + \sqrt{2}}{5 + \sqrt{2}}$.

[BOARD TERM, I, 2015, SET-2]

Sol. Given expression $= \dfrac{\sqrt{3} + \sqrt{2}}{5 + \sqrt{2}}$.

$$= \frac{\sqrt{3} + \sqrt{2}}{5 + \sqrt{2}} \times \frac{5 - \sqrt{2}}{5 - \sqrt{2}}$$

[On rationalizing the denominator]

$$= \frac{5\sqrt{3} + 5\sqrt{2} - \sqrt{6} - 2}{25 - 2}$$

$$= \frac{5\sqrt{3} + 5\sqrt{2} - \sqrt{6} - 2}{23}$$

21. Simplify:

$$\frac{1}{\sqrt{3} + \sqrt{2}} - \frac{2}{\sqrt{5} - \sqrt{3}} - \frac{3}{\sqrt{2} - \sqrt{5}}.$$

[BOARD TERM, I, 2016, SET QGL21FS]

Sol. Given expression

$$= \frac{1}{\sqrt{3} + \sqrt{2}} - \frac{2}{\sqrt{5} - \sqrt{3}} - \frac{3}{\sqrt{2} - \sqrt{5}}$$

$$= \frac{\sqrt{3} - \sqrt{2}}{3 - 2} - \frac{2\left(\sqrt{5} + \sqrt{3}\right)}{5 - 3} - \frac{\left(3\sqrt{2} - \sqrt{5}\right)}{2 - 5}$$

$$= \sqrt{3} - \sqrt{2} - \frac{2\left(\sqrt{5} + \sqrt{3}\right)}{2} + \frac{3\left(\sqrt{2} - \sqrt{5}\right)}{3}$$

$$= \sqrt{3} - \sqrt{2} - \sqrt{5} - \sqrt{3} + \sqrt{2} - \sqrt{5}$$

$$= -2\sqrt{5}$$

22. Find the value of a and b if $\dfrac{\sqrt{2} + 1}{\sqrt{2} - 1} - \dfrac{\sqrt{2} - 1}{\sqrt{2} + 1} = a + \sqrt{2}b$

[BOARD TERM, I, 2016, SET BQ56LZK]

Sol. Given $\dfrac{\sqrt{2} + 1}{\sqrt{2} - 1} - \dfrac{\sqrt{2} - 1}{\sqrt{2} + 1} = a + \sqrt{2}b$

$$\Rightarrow \frac{\left(\sqrt{2} + 1\right)^2 - \left(\sqrt{2} - 1\right)^2}{\left(\sqrt{2} - 1\right)\left(\sqrt{2} + 1\right)} = a + \sqrt{2}b$$

$$\Rightarrow \frac{2 + 1 + 2\sqrt{2} - 2 - 1 + 2\sqrt{2}}{2 - 1} = a + \sqrt{2}b$$

$$\Rightarrow 4\sqrt{2} = a + \sqrt{2}b$$

On comparing both sides, we get

$$a = 0, \; b = 4$$

23. If $a = 2 + \sqrt{5}$ and $b = \dfrac{1}{a}$, find $a^2 + b^2$.

[BOARD TERM, I, 2016 SET 5Q22L5C]

Sol. Given, $a = 2 + \sqrt{5}$

$\therefore \quad b = \dfrac{1}{a}$

$= \dfrac{1}{2 + \sqrt{5}}$

$= \dfrac{1}{2 + \sqrt{5}} \times \dfrac{2 - \sqrt{5}}{2 - \sqrt{5}}$

[On rationalizing the denominator]

$= \dfrac{2 - \sqrt{5}}{-1} = -2 + \sqrt{5}$

$\therefore \quad a^2 = \left(2 + \sqrt{5}\right)^2 = 9 + 4\sqrt{5}$

and $b^2 = \left(-2 + \sqrt{5}\right)^2 = 9 - 4\sqrt{5}$

Hence, $a^2 + b^2 = 9 + 4\sqrt{5} + 9 - 4\sqrt{5} = 18$

24. If $\dfrac{30}{4\sqrt{3} + 3\sqrt{2}} = 4\sqrt{3} - a\sqrt{2}$ find the value of a.

[BOARD TERM, I, 2016, SET-JQ22L5C]

Sol. According to the question,

$\dfrac{30}{4\sqrt{3} + 3\sqrt{2}} = 4\sqrt{3} - a\sqrt{2}$

$\Rightarrow \dfrac{30}{4\sqrt{3} + 3\sqrt{2}} \times \dfrac{4\sqrt{3} - 3\sqrt{2}}{4\sqrt{3} - 3\sqrt{2}} = 4\sqrt{3} - a\sqrt{2}$

[On rationalizing the denominator]

$\Rightarrow \dfrac{30\left(4\sqrt{3} - 3\sqrt{2}\right)}{\left(4\sqrt{3}\right)^2 - \left(3\sqrt{2}\right)^2} = \dfrac{30\left(4\sqrt{3} - 3\sqrt{2}\right)}{48 - 18}$

$\Rightarrow \dfrac{30\left(4\sqrt{3} - 3\sqrt{2}\right)}{30} = 4\sqrt{3} - a\sqrt{2}$

$\Rightarrow 4\sqrt{3} - 3\sqrt{2} = 4\sqrt{3} - a\sqrt{2}$

On comparing both sides, we have,

$a = 3$

25. Find a and b if $\dfrac{1 - \sqrt{3}}{1 + \sqrt{3}} = a + b\sqrt{3}$.

[BOARD TERM, I, 2016, SET-14]

Sol. According to the question,

$a + b\sqrt{3} = \dfrac{1 - \sqrt{3}}{1 + \sqrt{3}}$

$= \dfrac{1 - \sqrt{3}}{1 + \sqrt{3}} \times \dfrac{1 - \sqrt{3}}{1 - \sqrt{3}}$

[On rationalizing the denominator]

$= \dfrac{\left(1 - \sqrt{3}\right)^2}{1 - 3}$

$= \dfrac{1 + 3 - 2\sqrt{3}}{-2}$

$= \dfrac{4 - 2\sqrt{3}}{-2} = \dfrac{2\left(2 - \sqrt{3}\right)}{-2}$

$\Rightarrow a + b\sqrt{3} = -2 + \sqrt{3}$

On comparing both sides, we get

$a = -2$ and $b = 1$

Long Answer Type Questions
(4 Marks Each)

1. If $a = \dfrac{2 - \sqrt{5}}{2 + \sqrt{5}}$, $b = \dfrac{2 + \sqrt{5}}{2 - \sqrt{5}}$, then find $(a + b)^3$.

[BOARD TERM I, 2012, SET 42]

Sol. Given $a = \dfrac{2 - \sqrt{5}}{2 + \sqrt{5}}$

$= \dfrac{2 - \sqrt{5}}{2 + \sqrt{5}} \times \dfrac{2 - \sqrt{5}}{2 - \sqrt{5}} = \dfrac{\left(2 - \sqrt{5}\right)^2}{-1} = -\left(4 - 4\sqrt{5} + 5\right)$

$= 4\sqrt{5} - 9$

and

$b = \dfrac{2 + \sqrt{5}}{2 - \sqrt{5}} \times \dfrac{2 + \sqrt{5}}{2 + \sqrt{5}} = \dfrac{\left(2 + \sqrt{5}\right)^2}{-1}$

$= -\left(4 + 4\sqrt{5} + 5\right)$

$= -9 - 4\sqrt{5}$

$\therefore$ Expression $= (a + b)^3$

$= \left[4\sqrt{5} - 9 - 9 - 4\sqrt{5}\right]^3$

$= (-18)^3 = -5832$

Alternate Method:

$\therefore \quad a + b = \dfrac{2 - \sqrt{5}}{2 + \sqrt{5}} + \dfrac{2 + \sqrt{5}}{2 - \sqrt{5}}$

$= \dfrac{\left(2 - \sqrt{5}\right)^2 + \left(2 + \sqrt{5}\right)^2}{\left(2 + \sqrt{5}\right)\left(2 - \sqrt{5}\right)}$

$= \dfrac{4 + 5 - 4\sqrt{5} + 4 + 5 + 4\sqrt{5}}{4 - 5}$

$= \dfrac{18}{-1} = -18$

Hence, $(a + b)^3 = (-18)^3 = -5832$

2. If $x = \dfrac{\sqrt{3}+1}{\sqrt{3}-1}, y = \dfrac{\sqrt{3}-1}{\sqrt{3}+1}$, then find the value of $x^2 + y^2 + xy$. **[BOARD TERM I, 2012]**

Sol. Given $x = \dfrac{\sqrt{3}+1}{\sqrt{3}-1} = \dfrac{\sqrt{3}+1}{\sqrt{3}-1} \times \dfrac{\sqrt{3}+1}{\sqrt{3}+1}$

$= \dfrac{4+2\sqrt{3}}{2} = \dfrac{2(2+\sqrt{3})}{2} = 2+\sqrt{3}$

and $y = \dfrac{\sqrt{3}-1}{\sqrt{3}+1} = \dfrac{\sqrt{3}-1}{\sqrt{3}+1} \times \dfrac{\sqrt{3}-1}{\sqrt{3}-1}$

$= \dfrac{4-2\sqrt{3}}{2} = \dfrac{2(2-\sqrt{3})}{2} = 2-\sqrt{3}$

Now,

$xy = \dfrac{\sqrt{3}+1}{\sqrt{3}-1} \times \dfrac{\sqrt{3}-1}{\sqrt{3}+1} = 1$

$\therefore$ Expression

$= x^2 + y^2 + xy = (2+\sqrt{3})^2 + (2-\sqrt{3})^2 + 1$

$= 4 + 3 + 4\sqrt{3} + 4 + 3 - 4\sqrt{3} + 1$

$= 15$

3. Evaluate : $\dfrac{15}{\sqrt{10}+\sqrt{20}+\sqrt{40}-\sqrt{5}-\sqrt{80}}$, given that $\sqrt{5} = 2.2$ and $\sqrt{10} = 3.2$

[BOARD TERM I, 2012, SET 44]

Sol. Given expression $= \dfrac{15}{\sqrt{10}+\sqrt{20}+\sqrt{40}-\sqrt{5}-\sqrt{80}}$

$= \dfrac{15}{\sqrt{10}+\sqrt{4\times 5}+\sqrt{4\times 10}-\sqrt{5}-\sqrt{16\times 5}}$

$= \dfrac{15}{\sqrt{10}+2\sqrt{5}+2\sqrt{10}-\sqrt{5}-4\sqrt{5}}$

$= \dfrac{5}{\sqrt{10}-\sqrt{5}}$

$= \dfrac{5}{\sqrt{10}-\sqrt{5}} \times \dfrac{(\sqrt{10}+\sqrt{5})}{(\sqrt{10}+\sqrt{5})}$

$= \dfrac{5\times(\sqrt{10}+\sqrt{5})}{10-5}$

$= \dfrac{5(3.2+2.2)}{5}$ $\qquad [\because \sqrt{5} = 2.2 \text{ and } \sqrt{10} = 3.2]$

$= 3.2 + 2.2$

$= 5.4$

4. Find the values of a and b in $\dfrac{3-\sqrt{5}}{3+2\sqrt{5}} = a\sqrt{5} - \dfrac{b}{11}$

[BOARD TERM I, 2012]

Sol. Given, $a\sqrt{5} - \dfrac{b}{11} = \dfrac{3-\sqrt{5}}{3+2\sqrt{5}}$

$\Rightarrow a\sqrt{5} - \dfrac{b}{11} = \dfrac{(3-\sqrt{5})}{(3+2\sqrt{5})} \times \dfrac{(3-2\sqrt{5})}{(3-2\sqrt{5})}$

[On rationalizing the denominator]

$\Rightarrow a\sqrt{5} - \dfrac{b}{11} = \dfrac{9-6\sqrt{5}-3\sqrt{5}+2\times 5}{(3)^2-(2\sqrt{5})^2}$

$\Rightarrow a\sqrt{5} - \dfrac{b}{11} = \dfrac{9-9\sqrt{5}+10}{9-20}$

$\Rightarrow a\sqrt{5} - \dfrac{b}{11} = \dfrac{19-9\sqrt{5}}{-11}$

$\Rightarrow a\sqrt{5} - \dfrac{b}{11} = \dfrac{19}{-11} - \dfrac{9\sqrt{5}}{-11} = \dfrac{9\sqrt{5}}{11} - \dfrac{19}{11}$

$\Rightarrow a\sqrt{5} - \dfrac{b}{11} = \dfrac{9}{11}\sqrt{5} - \dfrac{19}{11}$

On comparing both sides, we get

$a = \dfrac{9}{11}$ and $b = 19$

5. If $x = 3 - 2\sqrt{2}$ then find the value of $x^4 - \dfrac{1}{x^4}$.

[BOARD TERM I, 2012, SET 52]

Sol. Given, $x = 3 - 2\sqrt{2}$

$\therefore \dfrac{1}{x} = \dfrac{1}{(3-2\sqrt{2})} \times \dfrac{(3+2\sqrt{2})}{(3+2\sqrt{2})}$

[On rationalizing the denominator]

$= \dfrac{(3+2\sqrt{2})}{9-8} = 3+2\sqrt{2}$

Now, $\dfrac{1}{x^2} = (3+2\sqrt{2})^2 = 9+8+12\sqrt{2} = 17+12\sqrt{2}$

and $x^2 = (3-2\sqrt{2})^2 = 9+8-12\sqrt{2} = 17-12\sqrt{2}$

$\therefore$ Given expression

$= x^4 - \dfrac{1}{x^4} = \left(x^2 - \dfrac{1}{x^2}\right)\left(x^2 + \dfrac{1}{x^2}\right)$

$= \left[(17-12\sqrt{2}) - (17+12\sqrt{2})\right]$

$\qquad \left[(17-12\sqrt{2}) + (17+12\sqrt{2})\right]$

$= (17-12\sqrt{2}-17-12\sqrt{2})(17-12\sqrt{2}+17+12\sqrt{2})$

$= (-24\sqrt{2}) \times 34 = -816\sqrt{2}$

6. If $x = \dfrac{1}{2-\sqrt{3}}$, then find the value of $x^3 - 2x^2 - 7x + 5$.

[BOARD TERM I, 2012, SET-44]

Sol. Given, $x = \dfrac{1}{2-\sqrt{3}}$

$= \dfrac{1}{2-\sqrt{3}} \times \dfrac{\left(2+\sqrt{3}\right)}{\left(2+\sqrt{3}\right)}$

[On rationalizing the denominator]

$= \dfrac{2+\sqrt{3}}{4-3} = 2+\sqrt{3}$

$\Rightarrow (x-2) = \left(\sqrt{3}\right)$

On squaring both sides,

$\Rightarrow (x-2)^2 = \left(\sqrt{3}\right)^2 = 3$

$\Rightarrow x^2 - 4x + 4 = 3$

$\Rightarrow x^2 - 4x + 4 - 3 = 0$

$\Rightarrow x^2 - 4x + 1 = 0$

Given expression $= x^3 - 2x^2 - 7x + 5$

$= x(x^2 - 4x + 1) + 2(x^2 - 4x + 1) + 3$

$= x \times 0 + 2 \times 0 + 3 = 3$

7. Find a and b, if $\dfrac{2\sqrt{5}+\sqrt{3}}{2\sqrt{5}-\sqrt{3}} + \dfrac{2\sqrt{5}-\sqrt{3}}{2\sqrt{5}+\sqrt{3}} = a + \sqrt{15}b$

[BOARD TERM I, 2013]

Sol. Given, $\dfrac{2\sqrt{5}+\sqrt{3}}{2\sqrt{5}-\sqrt{3}} + \dfrac{2\sqrt{5}-\sqrt{3}}{2\sqrt{5}+\sqrt{3}} = a + \sqrt{15}b$

$\Rightarrow \dfrac{\left(2\sqrt{5}+\sqrt{3}\right)^2 + \left(2\sqrt{5}-\sqrt{3}\right)^2}{\left(2\sqrt{5}-\sqrt{3}\right)\left(2\sqrt{5}+\sqrt{3}\right)} = a + \sqrt{15}b$

$\Rightarrow \dfrac{4\times5+3+2\times2\sqrt{5}\times\sqrt{3}+4\times5+3-2\times2\sqrt{5}\times\sqrt{3}}{\left(2\sqrt{5}\right)^2 - \left(\sqrt{3}\right)^2}$

$= a + \sqrt{15}b$

$\Rightarrow \dfrac{20+3+4\sqrt{15}+20+3-4\sqrt{15}}{20-3} = a + \sqrt{15}b$

$\Rightarrow \dfrac{46}{17} = a + \sqrt{15}b$

$\Rightarrow \dfrac{46}{17} + \sqrt{15}(0) = a + \sqrt{15}b$

On comparing both sides, we get

$a = \dfrac{46}{17}$ and $b = 0$

8. Rationalize the denominator of $\dfrac{1}{\left(\sqrt{2}+\sqrt{3}\right)-\sqrt{4}}$.

[BOARD TERM I, 2014]

Sol. Given expression $= \dfrac{1}{\left(\sqrt{2}+\sqrt{3}\right)-\sqrt{4}}$

$= \dfrac{1}{\left(\sqrt{2}+\sqrt{3}\right)-\sqrt{4}} \times \dfrac{\left(\sqrt{2}+\sqrt{3}\right)+\sqrt{4}}{\left(\sqrt{2}+\sqrt{3}\right)+\sqrt{4}}$

[On rationalizing the denominator]

$= \dfrac{\sqrt{2}+\sqrt{3}+\sqrt{4}}{\left(\sqrt{2}+\sqrt{3}\right)^2 - 4} = \dfrac{\sqrt{2}+\sqrt{3}+\sqrt{4}}{\left(2+3+2\sqrt{6}\right)-4}$

$= \dfrac{\sqrt{2}+\sqrt{3}+\sqrt{4}}{1+2\sqrt{6}} \times \dfrac{\left(1-2\sqrt{6}\right)}{\left(1-2\sqrt{6}\right)}$

[Again on rationalizing the denominator]

$= \dfrac{\sqrt{2}+\sqrt{3}+\sqrt{4}-2\sqrt{12}-2\sqrt{18}-4\sqrt{6}}{1^2 - \left(2\sqrt{6}\right)^2}$

$= \dfrac{\sqrt{2}+\sqrt{3}+\sqrt{4}-4\sqrt{3}-6\sqrt{2}-4\sqrt{6}}{1-24}$

$= \dfrac{-5\sqrt{2}-3\sqrt{3}+2-4\sqrt{6}}{-23}$

$= \dfrac{+5\sqrt{2}+3\sqrt{3}+4\sqrt{6}-2}{23}$

9. Prove that

$$\dfrac{1}{3+\sqrt{7}} + \dfrac{1}{\sqrt{7}+\sqrt{5}} + \dfrac{1}{\sqrt{5}+\sqrt{3}} + \dfrac{1}{\sqrt{3}+1} = 1$$

[BOARD TERM I, 2014]

Sol. Ist term $= \dfrac{1}{3+\sqrt{7}} = \dfrac{1}{3+\sqrt{7}} \times \dfrac{3-\sqrt{7}}{3-\sqrt{7}}$

$= \dfrac{3-\sqrt{7}}{(3)^2 - \left(\sqrt{7}\right)^2} = \dfrac{3-\sqrt{7}}{9-7} = \dfrac{3-\sqrt{7}}{2}$

IInd term $= \dfrac{1}{\sqrt{7}+\sqrt{5}}$

$= \dfrac{1}{\sqrt{7}+\sqrt{5}} \times \dfrac{\sqrt{7}-\sqrt{5}}{\sqrt{7}-\sqrt{5}} = \dfrac{\sqrt{7}-\sqrt{5}}{\left(\sqrt{7}\right)^2 - \left(\sqrt{5}\right)^2}$

$= \dfrac{\sqrt{7}-\sqrt{5}}{7-5} = \dfrac{\sqrt{7}-\sqrt{5}}{2}$

IIIrd term $= \dfrac{1}{\sqrt{5} + \sqrt{3}}$

$= \dfrac{1}{\sqrt{5} + \sqrt{3}} \times \dfrac{\sqrt{5} - \sqrt{3}}{\sqrt{5} - \sqrt{3}} = \dfrac{\sqrt{5} - \sqrt{3}}{\left(\sqrt{5}\right)^2 - \left(\sqrt{3}\right)^2}$

$= \dfrac{\sqrt{5} - \sqrt{3}}{5 - 3} = \dfrac{\sqrt{5} - \sqrt{3}}{2}$

and IVth term $= \dfrac{1}{\sqrt{3} + 1}$

$= \dfrac{1}{\sqrt{3} + 1} \times \dfrac{\sqrt{3} - 1}{\sqrt{3} - 1} = \dfrac{\sqrt{3} - 1}{\left(\sqrt{3}\right)^2 - 1} = \dfrac{\sqrt{3} - 1}{3 - 1}$

$= \dfrac{\sqrt{3} - 1}{2}$

Now,

$\text{L.H.S} = \dfrac{3 - \sqrt{7}}{2} + \dfrac{\sqrt{7} - \sqrt{5}}{2} + \dfrac{\sqrt{5} - \sqrt{3}}{2} + \dfrac{\sqrt{3} - 1}{2}$

$= \dfrac{3 - \sqrt{7} + \sqrt{7} - \sqrt{5} + \sqrt{5} - \sqrt{3} + \sqrt{3} - 1}{2}$

$= \dfrac{3 - 1}{2}$

$= \dfrac{2}{2} = 1$

$\therefore$ L.H.S = R.H.S

Hence proved.

10. If $x = 4 - \sqrt{15}$, then find the value of $\left(x + \dfrac{1}{x}\right)^2$.

[BOARD TERM I, 2014]

Sol. Given, $x = 4 - \sqrt{15}$

$\therefore \quad \dfrac{1}{x} = \dfrac{1}{4 - \sqrt{15}} \times \dfrac{4 + \sqrt{15}}{4 + \sqrt{15}}$

[On rationalizing the denominator]

$= \dfrac{4 + \sqrt{15}}{16 - 15}$

$= 4 + \sqrt{15}$

$\therefore$ Given expression $= \left(x + \dfrac{1}{x}\right)^2$

$= \left(4 - \sqrt{15} + 4 + \sqrt{15}\right)^2$

$= (8)^2$

$= 64$

11. Prove that:

$$\dfrac{1}{3 - \sqrt{8}} - \dfrac{1}{\sqrt{8} - \sqrt{7}} + \dfrac{1}{\sqrt{7} - \sqrt{6}} - \dfrac{1}{\sqrt{6} - \sqrt{5}} + \dfrac{1}{\sqrt{5} - 2} = 5$$

[BOARD TERM I, 2014]

Sol. On taking the L.H. S of the given expression,

$\text{L.H.S.} = \dfrac{1}{3 - \sqrt{8}} - \dfrac{1}{\sqrt{8} - \sqrt{7}} + \dfrac{1}{\sqrt{7} - \sqrt{6}}$

$\qquad - \dfrac{1}{\sqrt{6} - \sqrt{5}} + \dfrac{1}{\sqrt{5} - 1}$

$= \dfrac{3 + \sqrt{8}}{(3)^2 - \left(\sqrt{8}\right)^2} - \dfrac{\sqrt{8} + \sqrt{7}}{\left(\sqrt{8}\right)^2 - \left(\sqrt{7}\right)^2} + \dfrac{\left(\sqrt{7} + \sqrt{6}\right)}{\left(\sqrt{7}\right)^2 - \left(\sqrt{6}\right)^2}$

$\qquad - \dfrac{\left(\sqrt{6} + \sqrt{5}\right)}{\left(\sqrt{6}\right)^2 - \left(\sqrt{5}\right)^2} + \dfrac{\left(\sqrt{5} + 2\right)}{\left(\sqrt{5}\right)^2 - (2)^2}$

On rationalizing the denominator of each term.

$= \dfrac{\sqrt{5} + 2}{5 - 4} + \dfrac{3 + \sqrt{8}}{9 - 8} - \dfrac{\left(\sqrt{8} + \sqrt{7}\right)}{8 - 7} + \dfrac{\left(\sqrt{7} + \sqrt{6}\right)}{7 - 6} - \dfrac{\left(\sqrt{6} + \sqrt{5}\right)}{6 - 5}$

$= 3 + \sqrt{8} - \sqrt{8} - \sqrt{7} + \sqrt{7} + \sqrt{6} - \sqrt{6} - \sqrt{5} + 2 + \sqrt{5}$

$= 5 = \text{R.H.S.}$

12. If $x = \dfrac{\sqrt{3} + \sqrt{2}}{\sqrt{3} - \sqrt{2}}$ and $y = \dfrac{\sqrt{3} - \sqrt{2}}{\sqrt{3} + \sqrt{2}}$, then find $x^2 + y^2$.

[BOARD TERM I, 2014]

Sol. Given, $x = \dfrac{\sqrt{3} + \sqrt{2}}{\sqrt{3} - \sqrt{2}}$

and $y = \dfrac{\sqrt{3} - \sqrt{2}}{\sqrt{3} + \sqrt{2}}$

Now, $x^2 + y^2 = \left(\dfrac{\sqrt{3} + \sqrt{2}}{\sqrt{3} - \sqrt{2}}\right)^2 + \left(\dfrac{\sqrt{3} - \sqrt{2}}{\sqrt{3} + \sqrt{2}}\right)^2$

$= \dfrac{\left(\sqrt{3} + \sqrt{2}\right)^2}{\left(\sqrt{3} - \sqrt{2}\right)^2} + \dfrac{\left(\sqrt{3} - \sqrt{2}\right)^2}{\left(\sqrt{3} + \sqrt{2}\right)^2}$

$= \left(\dfrac{3 + 2 + 2\sqrt{6}}{3 + 2 - 2\sqrt{6}}\right) + \left(\dfrac{3 + 2 - 2\sqrt{6}}{3 + 2 + 2\sqrt{6}}\right)$

$= \dfrac{5 + 2\sqrt{6}}{5 - 2\sqrt{6}} + \dfrac{5 - 2\sqrt{6}}{5 + 2\sqrt{6}}$

$= \dfrac{\left(5 + 2\sqrt{6}\right)^2 + \left(5 - 2\sqrt{6}\right)^2}{(5)^2 - \left(2\sqrt{6}\right)^2}$

$= \dfrac{25 + 24 + 20\sqrt{6} + 25 + 24 - 20\sqrt{6}}{25 - 24}$

$= 98$

13. If $x = \dfrac{\sqrt{2}-1}{\sqrt{2}+1}$ and $y = \dfrac{\sqrt{2}+1}{\sqrt{2}-1}$ then find the value of $x^2 + 5xy + y^2$.

[BOARD TERM I, 2016, SET B Q56IZK]

Sol. Given expression $= x^2 + 5xy + y^2 = (x + y)^2 + 3xy$

$$= \left[\frac{\sqrt{2}-1}{\sqrt{2}+1} + \frac{\sqrt{2}+1}{\sqrt{2}-1}\right]^2 + 3\left(\frac{\sqrt{2}-1}{\sqrt{2}+1}\right)\times\left(\frac{\sqrt{2}+1}{\sqrt{2}-1}\right)$$

$$\left[\because x = \frac{\sqrt{2}-1}{\sqrt{2}+1} \text{ and } y = \frac{\sqrt{2}+1}{\sqrt{2}-1}\right]$$

$$= \frac{\left(\sqrt{2}-1\right)^2 + \left(\sqrt{2}+1\right)^2}{\left(\sqrt{2}+1\right)\left(\sqrt{2}-1\right)}$$

$$= \left(\frac{2+1-2\sqrt{2}+2+1+2\sqrt{2}}{2-1}\right)^2 + 3$$

$$= (6)^2 + 3$$

$$= 36 + 3 = 39$$

14. If $a = \dfrac{1}{7-4\sqrt{3}}$ and $b = \dfrac{1}{7+4\sqrt{3}}$, then find the values of the following :

(i) $a^2 + b^2$

(ii) $a^3 + b^3$

Sol. Given $a = \dfrac{1}{7-4\sqrt{3}} = \dfrac{1}{7-4\sqrt{3}}\times\dfrac{7+4\sqrt{3}}{7+4\sqrt{3}}$

[by rationalizing the denominator]

$$= \frac{7+4\sqrt{3}}{(7)^2 - \left(4\sqrt{3}\right)^2} \qquad [\because a^2 - b^2 = (a-b)(a+b)]$$

$$= \frac{7+4\sqrt{3}}{49-48} = 7+4\sqrt{3}$$

and $b = \dfrac{1}{7+4\sqrt{3}} = \dfrac{1}{7+4\sqrt{3}}\times\dfrac{7-4\sqrt{3}}{7-4\sqrt{3}}$

[by rationalizing the denominator]

$$= \frac{7-4\sqrt{3}}{(7)^2 - \left(4\sqrt{3}\right)^2} = \frac{7-4\sqrt{3}}{49-48} = 7-4\sqrt{3}$$

$$\therefore \ a + b = 7+4\sqrt{3} + 7-4\sqrt{3} = 14$$

and $ab = \left(7+4\sqrt{3}\right)\left(7-4\sqrt{3}\right)$

$$= (7)^2 - \left(4\sqrt{3}\right)^2 = 49 - 16\times 3 = 49 - 48 = 1$$

$$[\because (a-b)(a+b) = a^2 - b^2]$$

(i) $\because (a+b)^2 = a^2 + b^2 + 2ab$

$\Rightarrow (14)^2 = a^2 + b^2 + 2$

$\therefore a^2 + b^2 = 196 - 2 = 194$

(ii) $\because (a+b)^3 = a^3 + b^3 + 3ab\,(a+b)$

$\therefore a^3 + b^3 = (a+b)^3 - 3ab\,(a+b)$

$(14)^3 - 3\times 1 \times 14$

$= 2744 - 42 = 2702$

15. If $x = \dfrac{\sqrt{5}+1}{\sqrt{5}-1}$ and $y = \dfrac{\sqrt{5}-1}{\sqrt{5}+1}$ then find the value of $x^2 + y^2$.

Sol. Given, $x = \dfrac{\sqrt{5}+1}{\sqrt{5}-1}$

$$\therefore x^2 = \left[\frac{\sqrt{5}+1}{\sqrt{5}-1}\right]^2 = \frac{\left(\sqrt{5}+1\right)^2}{\left(\sqrt{5}-1\right)^2} = \frac{5+1+2\sqrt{5}}{5+1-2\sqrt{5}}$$

$$= \frac{6+2\sqrt{5}}{6-2\sqrt{5}} = \frac{3+\sqrt{5}}{3-\sqrt{5}}$$

and $y = \dfrac{\sqrt{5}-1}{\sqrt{5}+1}$

$$\therefore y^2 = \left[\frac{\sqrt{5}-1}{\sqrt{5}+1}\right]^2 = \frac{\left(\sqrt{5}-1\right)^2}{\left(\sqrt{5}+1\right)^2} = \frac{5+1-2\sqrt{5}}{5+1+2\sqrt{5}}$$

$$= \frac{6-2\sqrt{5}}{6+2\sqrt{5}} = \frac{3-\sqrt{5}}{3+\sqrt{5}}$$

Now, $x^2 + y^2 = \dfrac{3+\sqrt{5}}{3-\sqrt{5}} + \dfrac{3-\sqrt{5}}{3+\sqrt{5}}$

$$\therefore \quad \frac{\left(3+\sqrt{5}\right)^2 + \left(3-\sqrt{5}\right)^2}{\left(3-\sqrt{5}\right)\left(3+\sqrt{5}\right)}$$

$$= 2\left[(3)^2 + \left(\sqrt{5}\right)^2\right]$$

$$= \frac{9+5+6\sqrt{5}+9+5-6\sqrt{5}}{9-5}$$

$$= \frac{28}{4} = 7$$

16. Prove that:

$$\frac{1}{\sqrt{4}+\sqrt{5}} + \frac{1}{\sqrt{5}+\sqrt{6}} + \frac{1}{\sqrt{6}+\sqrt{7}} + \frac{1}{\sqrt{7}+\sqrt{8}} + \frac{1}{\sqrt{8}+\sqrt{9}}$$

$$= 1$$

Sol. Ist term $= \dfrac{1}{\sqrt{4}+\sqrt{5}} = \dfrac{1}{\left(\sqrt{5}+\sqrt{4}\right)}\times\dfrac{\left(\sqrt{5}-\sqrt{4}\right)}{\sqrt{5}-\sqrt{4}}$

[On rationalizing the denominator]

$$= \frac{\sqrt{5}-\sqrt{4}}{5-4} = \sqrt{5}-\sqrt{4}$$

IInd term $= \dfrac{1}{\sqrt{5}+\sqrt{6}} = \dfrac{1}{(\sqrt{6}+\sqrt{5})} \times \dfrac{(\sqrt{6}-\sqrt{5})}{(\sqrt{6}-\sqrt{5})}$

[On rationalizing the denominator]

$= \dfrac{\sqrt{6}-\sqrt{5}}{6-5} = \sqrt{6}-\sqrt{5}$

IIIrd term

$= \dfrac{1}{\sqrt{6}+\sqrt{7}} = \dfrac{1}{(\sqrt{7}+\sqrt{6})} \times \dfrac{(\sqrt{7}-\sqrt{6})}{(\sqrt{7}-\sqrt{6})} = \dfrac{\sqrt{7}-\sqrt{6}}{7-6}$

[On rationalizing the denominator]

$= \sqrt{7}-\sqrt{6}$

IVth term

$= \dfrac{1}{\sqrt{7}+\sqrt{8}} = \dfrac{1}{(\sqrt{8}+\sqrt{7})} \times \left(\dfrac{\sqrt{8}-\sqrt{7}}{\sqrt{8}-\sqrt{7}}\right) = \dfrac{(\sqrt{8}-\sqrt{7})}{8-7}$

[On rationalizing the denominator]

$= \sqrt{8}-\sqrt{7}$

V^{th} term

$= \dfrac{1}{\sqrt{8}+\sqrt{9}} = \dfrac{1}{(\sqrt{9}+\sqrt{8})} \times \dfrac{(\sqrt{9}-\sqrt{8})}{(\sqrt{9}-\sqrt{8})} = \dfrac{\sqrt{9}-\sqrt{8}}{9-8}$

$= \sqrt{9}-\sqrt{8}$

[On rationalizing the denominator]

Now, LHS

$= \dfrac{1}{\sqrt{4}+\sqrt{5}} + \dfrac{1}{\sqrt{5}+\sqrt{6}} + \dfrac{1}{\sqrt{6}+\sqrt{7}} + \dfrac{1}{\sqrt{7}+\sqrt{8}} + \dfrac{1}{\sqrt{8}+\sqrt{9}}$

$= \sqrt{5}-\sqrt{4}+\sqrt{6}-\sqrt{5}+\sqrt{7}-\sqrt{6}+\sqrt{8}$
$\qquad\qquad -\sqrt{7}+\sqrt{9}-\sqrt{8}$

$= -\sqrt{4}+\sqrt{9}$

$= -2+3 = 1$

$\therefore$ L.H.S = R.H.S.

Hence proved.

17. If $x = (5+2\sqrt{6})$, then show that

$$\sqrt{x} + \dfrac{1}{\sqrt{x}} = 2\sqrt{3}$$

Sol. We have, $x = 5+2\sqrt{6}$

Now, $\dfrac{1}{x} = \dfrac{1}{5+2\sqrt{6}} \times \dfrac{5-2\sqrt{6}}{5-2\sqrt{6}}$

[by rationalizing the denominator]

$= \dfrac{5-2\sqrt{6}}{(5)^2 - (2\sqrt{6})^2}$ $\qquad [\because a^2 - b^2 = (a-b)\,(a+b)]$

$= \dfrac{5-2\sqrt{6}}{25-24} = 5-2\sqrt{6}$

$\therefore$ $x + \dfrac{1}{x} = 5+2\sqrt{6}+5-2\sqrt{6} = 10$

$\Rightarrow x + \dfrac{1}{x} + 2 = 12$

[adding 2 on both sides]

$\Rightarrow \left[(\sqrt{x})^2 + \left(\dfrac{1}{\sqrt{x}}\right)^2 + 2.\sqrt{x}.\dfrac{1}{\sqrt{x}}\right]$

$\Rightarrow \left(\sqrt{x} + \dfrac{1}{\sqrt{x}}\right)^2 = (2\sqrt{3})^2$

$$\left[\because \left(\sqrt{a} + \dfrac{1}{\sqrt{a}}\right)^2 = a + \dfrac{1}{a} + 2\right]$$

On taking square root, we get

$$\sqrt{x} + \dfrac{1}{\sqrt{x}} = 2\sqrt{3}$$

Since, $\sqrt{x}$ is always a positive value, so $\sqrt{x} + \dfrac{1}{\sqrt{x}}$ is always a positive value.

18. If $a = \dfrac{\sqrt{5}+\sqrt{2}}{\sqrt{5}-\sqrt{2}}$ and $b = \dfrac{\sqrt{5}-\sqrt{2}}{\sqrt{5}+\sqrt{2}}$. Find the value

of $\dfrac{a^2 + ab + b^2}{a^2 - ab + b^2}$

Sol. $\because a = \dfrac{\sqrt{5}+\sqrt{2}}{\sqrt{5}-\sqrt{2}}$

$= \dfrac{\sqrt{5}+\sqrt{2}}{\sqrt{5}-\sqrt{2}} \times \dfrac{\sqrt{5}+\sqrt{2}}{\sqrt{5}+\sqrt{2}}$

[On rationalizing the denominator]

$= \dfrac{(\sqrt{5}+\sqrt{2})^2}{(\sqrt{5})^2 - (\sqrt{2})^2} = \dfrac{(\sqrt{5}+\sqrt{2})^2}{5-2}$

$= \dfrac{5+2+2\sqrt{10}}{3} = \dfrac{7+2\sqrt{10}}{3}$

and $b = \dfrac{\sqrt{5}-\sqrt{2}}{\sqrt{5}+\sqrt{2}}$

$= \dfrac{\sqrt{5}-\sqrt{2}}{\sqrt{5}+\sqrt{2}} \times \dfrac{\sqrt{5}-\sqrt{2}}{\sqrt{5}-\sqrt{2}}$

[On rationalizing the denominator]

$$= \frac{(\sqrt{5} - \sqrt{2})^2}{(\sqrt{5})^2 - (\sqrt{2})^2}$$

$$= \frac{5 + 2 - 2\sqrt{10}}{5 - 2}$$

$$= \frac{7 - 2\sqrt{10}}{3}$$

Now, Numerator $= a^2 + ab + b^2$

$$= (a+b)^2 - ab = \left(\frac{7 + 2\sqrt{10}}{3} + \frac{7 - 2\sqrt{10}}{3}\right)^2$$

$$- \left(\frac{7 + 2\sqrt{10}}{3}\right)\left(\frac{7 - 2\sqrt{10}}{3}\right)$$

$$= \left(\frac{14}{3}\right)^2 - \left(\frac{49 - 40}{9}\right)$$

$$= \frac{196}{9} - \frac{9}{9} = \frac{196 - 9}{9}$$

$$= \frac{187}{9}$$

and denominator $= a^2 - ab + b^2$

$$= (a-b)^2 + ab = \left(\frac{7 + 2\sqrt{10}}{3} - \frac{7 - 2\sqrt{10}}{3}\right)^2$$

$$+ \left(\frac{7 + 2\sqrt{10}}{3}\right)\left(\frac{7 - 2\sqrt{10}}{3}\right)$$

$$= \left(\frac{4\sqrt{10}}{3}\right)^2 + \frac{49 - 40}{9}$$

$$= \frac{160}{9} + \frac{9}{9} = \frac{169}{9}$$

Hence, given expression

$$= \frac{a^2 + ab + b^2}{a^2 - ab + b^2} = \frac{(a+b)^2 - ab}{(a-b)^2 + ab}$$

$$= \frac{\dfrac{187}{9}}{\dfrac{169}{9}} = \frac{187}{9} \times \frac{9}{169}$$

$$= \frac{187}{169}$$

UNIT II
Algebra

CHAPTER 2

Polynomials

- Defination of a polynomial in one variable, with examples and counter examples.
- Coefficients of a polynomial, terms of a polynomial and zero polynomial. Degree of a polynomial.
- Constant, linear, quadratic and cubic polynomials. Monomials, binomials, trinomials. Factors and multiples.
- Zeros of a polynomial. Motivate and state the remainder theorem with examples.
- Statement and proof of the factor theorem.
- Factorization of $ax^2 + bx + c$, $a \neq 0$ where a, b and c are real numbers, and of cubic polynomials using the factor theorem.
- Recall of algebraic expressions and identities. Verification of identities.

$(x + y + z)^2 = x^2 + y^2 + z^2 + 2xy + 2yz + 2zx$

$(x \pm y)^3 = x^3 \pm y^3 \pm 3xy(x \pm y)$

$x^3 \pm y^3 = (x \pm y) (x^2 \mp xy + y^2)$

$$x^3 + y^3 + z^3 - 3xyz = (x + y + z) (x^2 + y^2 + z^2 - xy - yz - zx)$$

and their use in factorization of polynomials

Example

1. Which of the following is/are polynomial?

(a) $\dfrac{x^3}{2} - \dfrac{2}{x^3}$ $\qquad$ (b) $\sqrt{5x} - 4$

(c) $x^2 + \dfrac{3x^{3/2}}{x^{-1/2}}$

Sol. (c) $x^2 + \dfrac{3x^{3/2}}{x^{-1/2}} = x^2 + \dfrac{3x^{3/2}}{x^{-1/2}} = x^2 + 3x^{\left(\frac{3}{2}+\frac{1}{2}\right)}$

$= x^2 + 3x^{\frac{4}{2}}$

$= x^2 + 3x^2 = 4x^2$

Hence, only (c) is a polynomial.

[Topic 1] Polynomials

Points to be Remembered

- An algebraic expression of the form $p(x) - a_n x^n + a_{n-1}x^{n-1} + \ldots + a_2 x^2 + a_1 x + a_0$ is called polynomial in one variable x of degree 'n' where a_0, a_1, a_2, ... a_n are constants $(a_n \neq 0)$ and n is a whole number.
- In a polynomial of one variable, the highest power of the variable is called the degree of a polynomial.
- Types of polynomials

(i) Polynomial on the basis of number of terms	
Monomial	A polynomial having one term is called a monomial.
	Examples : 5, 8 m, 13 ab
Binomial	A polynomial having two terms is called a binomial.
	Examples : 4x + 3, 4a − 3, 13 p + 1
Trinomial	A polynomial having three terms is called a trinomial.
	Examples : $4x^2 + 8x - 13$, $2a^2 + 3a + 9$

(ii) Polynomial based on degree	
Constant	A polynomial of degree zero is called constant polynomial. **Examples :** $4, -3, \dfrac{1}{3}, \sqrt{5}$
Linear	A polynomial of degree one is called linear polynomial. **Examples :** $41x - 3,\ 3a + 4$
Quadratic	A polynomial of degree two is called quadratic polynomial. **Examples :** $3\sqrt{5}x^2 + 8x - 4,\ 2x^2 + 4x + 5$
Cubic	A polynomial of degree three is called cubic polynomial. **Examples :** $13y^3,\ 4x^3 + 3x^2 + 4x + 5,\ 6m^3 + 7m + 4$

PREVIOUS YEARS'
EXAMINATION QUESTIONS
TOPIC 1

Multiple Choice Questions
(1 Mark Each)

1. Which of the following expressions is polynomial?

   (a) $t^2 - \sqrt{3} + \sqrt{7}t$ (b) $4\sqrt{x} + 7$

   (c) $y + \dfrac{5}{y} + 9$ (d) $\sqrt[3]{x} + 2$

Sol. (a) $(t^2 - \sqrt{3} + \sqrt{7}t)$ is a polynomial

2. The value of the polynomial $5x - 4x^2 + 3$, when $x = -1$ is

   (a) -6 (b) 6

   (c) 2 (d) -2 [NCERT Exemp.]

Sol. (a) Let $f(x) = 5x - 4x^2 + 3$

   On putting $x = -1$ in given polynomial, we get

   $f(-1) = 5(-1) - 4(-1)^2 + 3$

   $\qquad = -5 - 4 + 3$

   $\qquad = -9 + 3 = -6$

3. If $p(x) = x^2 - 2\sqrt{2}x + 1$, then $p(2\sqrt{2})$ is equal to

   (a) 0 (b) 1

   (c) $4\sqrt{2}$ (d) $8\sqrt{2} + 1$

   [NCERT Exemp.]

Sol. (b) Given, $p(x) = x^2 - 2\sqrt{2}x + 1$

   On putting $x = 2\sqrt{2}$, we get

   $p(x) = x^2 - 2\sqrt{2}x + 1$

   $\therefore\ p(2\sqrt{2}) = (2\sqrt{2})^2 - 2\sqrt{2} \times 2\sqrt{2} + 1$

   $\qquad = 4 \times 2 - 4 \times 2 + 1 = 1$

4. Which one of the following is a polynomial?

   (a) $\dfrac{x^2}{2} - \dfrac{2}{x^2}$ (b) $\sqrt{2x} - 1$

   (c) $x^2 + \dfrac{3x^{\frac{3}{2}}}{\sqrt{x}}$ (d) $\dfrac{x-1}{x+1}$ [NCERT Exemp.]

Sol. (c) We know that the degree of polynomial is whole number, then

   $$x^2 + \frac{3x^{3/2}}{x^{1/2}} = x^2 + 3x^{\frac{3}{2} - \frac{1}{2}}$$

   $$= x^2 + 3x^{\frac{3-1}{2}} = x^2 + 3x$$

   Hence, $x^2 + \dfrac{3x^{3/2}}{\sqrt{x}}$ is a polynomial.

5. Zero of the polynomial $p(x) = 2x + 5$ is

   (a) $-\dfrac{2}{5}$ (b) $-\dfrac{5}{2}$

   (c) $\dfrac{2}{5}$ (d) $\dfrac{5}{2}$ [NCERT Exemp.]

Sol. (b) Given $p(x) = 2x + 5$

   On putting $p(x) = 0$, we get

   $\qquad 2x + 5 = 0$

   $\Rightarrow \qquad 2x = 0 - 5$

   $\Rightarrow \qquad 2x = -5$

   $\therefore \qquad x = -\dfrac{5}{2}$

6. Degree of the zero polynomial is

   (a) 0

   (b) 1

   (c) any natural number

   (d) not defined   [NCERT Exemp.]

Sol. (d) In zero polynomial, we cannot determine the degree of the polynomial because the coefficient of any variable is zero polynomial is zero.

7. $\sqrt{2}$ is a polynomial of degree
   (a) 2
   (b) 0
   (c) 1
   (d) $\dfrac{1}{2}$ [NCERT Exemp.]

Sol. (b) $\sqrt{2} = \sqrt{2}x^0$

∵ Exponent of x is 0.

Hence, the degree of polynomial $\sqrt{2}$ is 0.

8. Zero of the polynomial $p(x)$, where $p(x) = ax + 1$, $a \neq 0$, is :
   (a) 1
   (b) $-a$
   (c) 0
   (d) $-\dfrac{1}{a}$ [NCERT Exemp.]

Sol. (d) Given, $p(x) = ax + 1$ (where $a \neq 0$)

On putting $p(x) = 0$, we get
$$ax + 1 = 0$$
$$\Rightarrow \quad ax = -1$$
$$\therefore \quad x = \dfrac{-1}{a}$$

9. If $p(x) = x + 3$, then $p(x) + p(-x)$ is equal to
   (a) 3
   (b) $2x$
   (c) 0
   (d) 6   [NCERT Exemp.]

Sol. (d) Given $p(x) = x + 3$
$$\therefore \quad p(x) + p(-x) = x + 3 + (-x + 3)$$
$$= x + 3 - x + 3 = 6$$

10. Degree of the polynomial $4x^4 + 0x^3 + 0x^5 + 5x + 7$ is
   (a) 4
   (b) 5
   (c) 3
   (d) 7   [NCERT Exemp.]

Sol. (a) Given polynomial $= 4x^4 + 0x^3 + 0x^5 + 5x + 7$

Highest power of variable x is 4. Hence, degree of the polynomial is 4.

11. One of the zeros of the polynomial $2x^2 + 7x - 4$ is
   (a) 2
   (b) $\dfrac{1}{2}$
   (c) $-\dfrac{1}{2}$
   (d) -2 [NCERT Exemp.]

Sol. (b) Given polynomial $= 2x^2 + 7x - 4$

By splitting the middle term,
$$2x^2 + 7x - 4 = 2x^2 + (8x - x) - 4$$
$$= 2x^2 + 8x - x - 4$$
$$= 2x(x + 4) - 1(x + 4)$$
$$= (x + 4)(2x - 1)$$

On putting the factors equal to 0. We get zeroes of the polynomial.

Now, $(x + 4)(2x - 1) = 0$

If $\qquad (x + 4) = 0$

∴ $\qquad x = -4$ and if $(2x - 1) = 0$

$\Rightarrow \qquad 2x = 1$

∴ $\qquad x = \dfrac{1}{2}$

12. Zero of the zero polynomial is
   (a) 0
   (b) 1
   (c) any real number
   (d) not defined   [NCERT Exemp.]

Sol. (c) We know that in zero polynomial $0(x - k)$ where k is a real number. For determining the zero of the given polynomial.

Now, $(x - k) = 0$

∴ $x = k$ (Any real number)

Write True or False

1. Verify whether the following are True or False :
   (a) $-\dfrac{1}{3}$ is a zero of $3x + 1$
   (b) 0 and 2 are the zeros of $t^2 - 2t$
   (c) $\dfrac{-4}{5}$ is a zero of $4 - 5y$
   (d) -3 is a zero of $x - 3$
   (e) -3 is a zero of $y^2 + y - 6$ [NCERT Exemp.]

Sol. (a) Given statement is True.

On putting $(3x + 1) = 0$, we get
$$\Rightarrow \quad 3x = -1$$
$$\therefore \quad x = \dfrac{-1}{3}$$

(b) Given statement is True.
$$\because \quad t^2 - 2t = 0$$
$$\Rightarrow \quad t(t - 2) = 0$$
$$\therefore \quad t = 0 \text{ and } t = 2$$

(c) Given statement is False.

On putting $(4 - 5y) = 0$, we get
$$4 - 5y = 0$$
$$\Rightarrow \quad 5y = 4$$
$$\therefore \quad y = \dfrac{4}{5}$$

(d) Given statement is False.

∵ Zero of $x - 3$ is 3.
$$\Rightarrow \quad x - 3 = 0$$
$$\therefore \quad x = 3$$

(e) Given statement is True.
$$\because \quad y^2 + y - 6 = 0$$
$$\Rightarrow \quad y^2 + 3y - 2y - 6 = 0$$
$$\Rightarrow \quad y(y + 3)(y - 2) = 0$$
$$\Rightarrow \quad y + 3 = 0 \text{ and } y - 2 = 0$$
$$\therefore \quad y = -3 \text{ and } y = 2.$$

Very Short Answer Type Questions
(1 Mark Each)

1. Which of the following expressions are polynomials in one variable and which are not?

   (i) $4x^2 - 3x + 7$ (ii) $y^2 + \sqrt{2}$

   (iii) $3\sqrt{t} + t\sqrt{2}$ (iv) $y + \dfrac{2}{y}$

   (v) $x^{10} + y^3 + t^{50}$ [NCERT]

Sol. Here, (i) and (ii) are the polynomials in one variable, (v) is a polynomial in three variables and (iii) and (iv) are not polynomials, because in each of these exponents of the variable is not a whole number.

2. If -4 is a zero of the polynomial $p(x) = x^2 + 11x + k$, then calculate the value of k.

Sol. Given, $p(x) = x^2 + 11x + k$

   Since -4 is a zero of polynomial

   Now, on putting $x = -4$, $p(x) = 0$,

   $\Rightarrow \qquad p(-4) = 0$

   $\Rightarrow \qquad (-4)^2 + 11 \times (-4) + k = 0$

   $\Rightarrow \qquad 16 - 44 + k = 0 \Rightarrow -28 + k = 0$

   $\therefore \qquad\qquad k = 28$

3. Write the expression which represents a polynomial.

Sol. Examples of a polynomials are $\sqrt{2}x^2 + x - 1$, $x^3 + x^2 + x + 3$ etc.

4. What is the degree of the polynomial $(x^3 + 5)$ $(4 - x^5)$?

Sol. We know that highest power of polynomial is the degree of that polynomial.

   Degree of $(x^3 + 5) = 3$

   and Degree of $(4 - x^5) = 5$

   Hence, Degree of $(x^3 - 5)(4 - x^5) = 3 + 5 = 8$.

5. Find $p(0)$ if $p(y) = y^2 - y + 1$. [Board Term I, 2014]

Sol. Given, $p(y) = y^2 - y + 1$

   Now, putting $y = 0$

   $\therefore p(0) = 0^2 - 0 + 1 = 1$

6. What is the degree of a zero polynomial?

Sol. The degree of a zero polynomial is not defined.

7. Write the number of zeros in a cubic polynomial.

Sol. Total number of zeros in a cubic polynomial = 3.

8. Name of the polynomial on the basis of degree $-3x + 2$.

Sol. The degree of a given polynomial $(-3x + 2)$ is 1. Therefore it is a linear polynomial.

9. Write the zeros of the polynomial $p(x) = x(x - 2)$ $(x - 3)$.

Sol. Given $p(x) = x(x - 2)(x - 3)$

   On putting $p(x) = 0$, we get

   $x(x - 2)(x - 3) = 0$

   then, $x = 0, 2$ and 3

10. What is the zero of the zero polynomial?

Sol. Every real number is a zero of the zero polynomial.

11. In the expression $x^2 + \dfrac{\pi}{2}x - 7$, what is the coefficient of x?

Sol. Co-efficient of x in the given expression $x^2 + \dfrac{\pi}{2}x - 7$ is $\dfrac{\pi}{2}$.

12. What is $x + \dfrac{1}{x}$?

Sol. Given $x + \dfrac{1}{x} = \dfrac{x^2 + 1}{x}$

   Therefore, given expression is not a polynomial.

13. What is the degree of polynomial $\sqrt{3}$?

Sol. The degree of the given polynomial is 0.

14. Write any polynomial in one variable.

Sol. Polynomials in one variable are. $\sqrt{3}x^2 + 2x + 3$ or $\sqrt{5}y^2 + 2y$.

15. Name the polynomial containing two non-zero terms.

Sol. The polynomial containing two non-zero terms is called binomial.

16. If $p(x) = x^3 - 3x + 2$, then what is the value of $p(0) + p(2)$?

Sol. Given $p(x) = x^2 - 3x + 2$

   On putting $x = 0$, we get

   $p(0) = 0 - 3 \times 0 + 2 = 2$

   Again, putting, $x = 2$, we get

   $p(2) = 2^2 - 3 \times 2 + 2$

   $\qquad = 4 - 6 + 2 = 0$

   Thus, $p(0) + p(2) = 2 + 0 = 2$.

17. Write an example of a constant polynomial.

Sol. Constant polynomial is 9.

18. If $p(x) = x^2 - 2\sqrt{2}x + 1$, then find the value of $p(2\sqrt{2})$.

Sol. Given, $p(x) = x^2 - 2\sqrt{2}x + 1$

   On putting $x = 2\sqrt{2}$, we get

   $\therefore p(2\sqrt{2}) = (2\sqrt{2})^2 - 2\sqrt{2}(2\sqrt{2}) + 1 = 1$

Short Answer Type Questions I

(2 Marks Each)

1. Verify that whether -2 and 3 are zeros of the polynomial $x^2 - x - 6$.

Sol. Let given polynomial be

$$p(x) = x^2 - x - 6 \qquad \text{...(i)}$$

On putting $x = -2$ in eq. (i), we get

$$p(-2) = (-2)^2 - (-2) - 6 = 4 + 2 - 6 = 0$$

Again, on putting $x = 3$ in eq. (i), we get

$$p(3) = (3)^2 - (3) - 6 = 9 - 3 - 6 = 0$$

Here, $p(-2) = 0$ and $p(3) = 0$

Hence, $x = -2$ and $x = 3$ are zeros of the given polynomial.

2. Classify the following as linear, quadratic and cubic polynomials : [Board Term I, 2013]

  (a) $x^2 + x$ (b) $x - x^3$

  (c) $1 + x$ (d) $7x^3$

Sol. (a) $x^2 + x$ [Quadratic polynomial, degree = 2]

  (b) $x - x^3$ [Cubic polynomial, degree = 3]

  (c) $1 + x$ [Linear polynomial, degree = 1]

  (d) $7x^3$ [cubic polynomial, degree = 3]

3. Find the value of the polynomial $p(x) = x^3 - 3x^2 - 2x + 6$ at $x = \sqrt{2}$

    [Board Term I, 2014]

Sol. Given, $p(x) = x^3 - 3x^2 - 2x + 6$

On putting $x = \sqrt{2}$, we get

Then, $p(\sqrt{2}) = (\sqrt{2})^3 - 3(\sqrt{2})^2 - 2(\sqrt{2}) + 6$

$$= 2\sqrt{2} - 6 - 2\sqrt{2} + 6$$

$$= 0$$

4. If $y = 2$ and $y = 0$ are the zeros of the polynomial $f(y) = 2y^3 - 5y^2 + ay + b$ find the value of a and b.

    [Board Term I, 2016, Set-20CNJE9]

Sol. Given, $\qquad f(y) = 2y^3 - 5y^2 + ay + b$

On putting, $\quad y = 2, f(2) = 0$, we get

$\therefore \qquad f(2) = 2(2)^3 - 5(2)^2 + a(2) + b = 0$

$\Rightarrow \qquad 16 - 20 + 2a + b = 0$

$\Rightarrow \qquad 2a + b = 4 \qquad \text{...(i)}$

$\therefore \qquad f(0) = b = 0$

From (i), $2a + 0 = 4$

or, $\qquad a = 2$

$\therefore \qquad a = 2, b = 0$

Short Answer Type Questions II

(3 Marks Each)

1. What are the possible expressions for the dimensions of the cuboids whose volumes are given below?

  (i) Volume $= 3x^2 - 12x$

  (ii) Volume $= 12ky^2 + 8ky - 20k$.   [NCERT]

Sol. (i) We have,

Volume of cuboid $= 3x^2 - 12x = 3x(x - 4)$

Hence, the possible expressions for the dimensions of the cuboids are 3, x and $x - 4$.

[$\because$ volume of cuboid = length × breadth × height]

(ii) We have,

Volume of cuboid $= 12ky^2 + 8ky - 20k$

$$= 12ky^2 + (20 - 12)ky - 20k$$

[by splitting the middle term]

$$= 12ky^2 + 20ky - 12ky - 20k$$

$$= 4ky(3y + 5) - 4k(3y + 5)$$

$$= (3y + 5)(4ky - 4k)$$

$$= (3y + 5)\, 4k(y - 1)$$

$$= 4k(3y + 5)(y - 1)$$

Hence, the possible expressions for the dimensions of the cuboid are $4k$, $3y + 5$ and $y - 1$.

2. If $f(x) = x^3 - 3x^2 + 3x - 4$, find $f(2) + f(-2) + f(0)$.

    [Board Term I, 2016, BQS6IZK 9]

Sol. Given, $f(x) = x^3 - 3x^2 + 3x - 4$

On putting $x = 2$, we get

$\Rightarrow \qquad f(2) = (2)^3 - 3(2)^2 + 3(2) - 4$

$$= 8 - 12 + 6 - 4 = 14 - 16$$

$\therefore \qquad f(2) = -2$

Again, on putting $x = -2$, we get

$\qquad f(-2) = (-2)^3 - 3(-2)^2 + 3(-2) - 4$

$$= -8 - 12 - 6 - 4$$

$\therefore f(-2) = -30$

and on putting $x = 0$, we get

$\qquad f(0) = -4$

$\therefore$ Give expression $= f(2) + f(-2) + f(0)$

$$= -2 - 30 - 4 = -36$$

3. If $f(x) = x^4 - 4x^3 + 3x^2 - 2x + 1$, then find whether $f(0) \times f(-1) = f(2)$. [Board Term I, 2016, Set-20CNJE9]

Sol. Given, $f(x) = x^4 - 4x^3 + 3x^2 - 2x + 1$

On putting $x = 0$, we get

$\therefore \qquad f(0) = 1$

Again, on putting $x = -1$, we get

$\qquad f(-1) = (-1)^4 - 4(-1)^3 + 3(-1)^2 - 2(-1)$

$$= 1 + 4 + 3 + 2 + 1 = 11$$

and on putting $x = 2$, we get

$f(2) = (2)^4 - 4(2)^3 + 3(2)^2 - 2(2) + 1$

$= 16 - 32 + 12 - 4 + 1$

$= 29 - 36 = -7$

$\therefore$ Given expression $= f(0) \times f(-1) = 11 \neq f(2)$

4. If $f(x) = 5x^2 - 4x + 5$, find $f(1) + f(-1) + f(0)$.
[Board Term I, 2016, Set-20 Q4L2IF59]

Sol. Given, $f(x) = 5x^2 - 4x + 5$

On putting $x = 1$, we get

$f(1) = 5 - 4 + 5 = 6$

Again, on putting $x = -1$, we get

$f(-1) = 5(-1)^2 - 4(-1) + 5$

$= 5 + 4 + 5 = 14$

and on putting $x = 0$, we get

$f(0) = 5$

$\therefore$ Given expression $= f(1) + f(-1) + f(0)$

$= 6 + 14 + 5 = 25$

5. Find the value of the polynomial $x^2 - 3x + 6$ at

(i) $x = \sqrt{2}$,   (ii) $x = 3$.

Sol. Given, $p(x) = x^2 - 3x + 6$

(i) When $x = \sqrt{2}$, then we get

$\therefore$ $p(\sqrt{2}) = (\sqrt{2})^2 - 3 \times \sqrt{2} + 6$

$= 2 - 3\sqrt{2} + 6$

$= 8 - 3\sqrt{2}$

(ii) When $x = 3$, then we get

$\therefore$ $p(3) = 3^2 - 3 \times 3 + 6$

$= 9 - 9 + 6 = 6$

6. If $f(x) = 3x + 5$, evaluate $f(7) - f(5)$.

Sol. Given, $f(x) = 3x + 5$

On putting $x = 7$, we get

$f(7) = 3 \times 7 + 5 = 26$

On putting $x = 5$, we get

$f(5) = 3 \times 5 + 5 = 20$

$\therefore$ Given expression $= f(7) - f(5) = 26 - 20 = 6$.

Long Answer Type Questions

(4 Marks Each)

1. One-fourth of a herd of camels was seen in the forest. Twice the square root of the herd had gone to mountains and the remaining 15 camels were seen on the bank of a river. Find the total number of camels.   [NCERT Exmp.]

Sol. Let the total number of camels be x.

Then, number of herds of camels seen in the forest

$= \dfrac{x}{4}$

Number of camels gone to mountains $= 2\sqrt{x}$

Number of camels on the bank of river $= 15$

According to the question,

$\therefore$ Total number of camels $= \dfrac{x}{4} + 2\sqrt{x} + 15$

$\Rightarrow$ $x = \dfrac{x}{4} + 2\sqrt{x} + 15$

$\Rightarrow$ $x - \dfrac{x}{4} - 2\sqrt{x} - 15 = 0$

$\Rightarrow$ $\dfrac{4x - x - 8\sqrt{x} - 15 \times 4}{4} = 0$

$\Rightarrow$ $3x - 8\sqrt{x} - 60 = 0$ ...(i)

Let $\sqrt{x} = y$, then we get

$3y^2 - 8y - 60 = 0$

$\Rightarrow$ $3y^2 - (18 - 10)y - 60 = 0$

[by splitting the middle term]

$\Rightarrow$ $3y^2 - 18y + 10y - 60 = 0$

$\Rightarrow$ $3y(y - 6) + 10(y - 6) = 0$

$\Rightarrow$ $(3y + 10)(y - 6) = 0$

$\Rightarrow$ $3y + 10 = 0$ and $y - 6 = 0$ $\therefore y = 6$

$\Rightarrow$ $3y = -10$

$\therefore$ $y = \dfrac{-10}{3}$

Now, $y = \dfrac{-10}{3}$, $\therefore \sqrt{x} = \dfrac{-10}{3}$

which is not possible [put $y = \sqrt{x}$] and $y = 6$

$\Rightarrow$ $\sqrt{x} = 6$ [put $y = \sqrt{x}$]

On squaring both sides,

$\therefore$ $x = 6^2 = 36$

Hence, the number of camels is 36.

2. If $p(x) = x^3 + 3x^2 - 2x + 4$, then find the value of $p(2) + p(-2) - p(0)$.   [Board Term I, 2012, Set-45]

Sol. Given, $p(x) = x^3 + 3x^2 - 2x + 4$

On putting $x = 2$, we get

$\therefore$ $p(2) = (2)^3 + 3(2)^2 - 2(2) + 4$

$= 8 + 12 - 4 + 4 = 20$

On putting $x = -2$, we get

$\therefore$ $p(-2) = (-2)^3 + 3(-2)^2 - 2(-2) + 4$

$= -8 + 12 + 4 + 4 = 12$

On putting $x = 0$, we get

$\therefore$ $p(0) = 4$

$\therefore$ Given expression $= p(2) + p(-2) - p(0)$

$= 20 + 12 - 4 = 32 - 4 = 28$

3. If $f(x) = x^2 - 5x + 7$, evaluate $f(2) - f(-1) + f\left(\dfrac{1}{3}\right)$.

[Board Term I, 2014]

Sol. Given, $f(x) = x^2 - 5x + 7$

On putting $x = 2$, we get

$f(2) = 2^2 - 5 \times 2 + 7 = 1$

Again, on putting $x = -1$, we get

$f(-1) = (-1)^2 - 5(-1) + 7 = 13$

and on putting $x = \dfrac{1}{3}$, we get

$f\left(\dfrac{1}{3}\right) = \left(\dfrac{1}{3}\right)^2 - 5\left(\dfrac{1}{3}\right) + 7 = \dfrac{49}{9}$

$\therefore$ Given expression =

$f(2) - f(-1) + f\left(\dfrac{1}{3}\right) = 1 - 13 + \dfrac{49}{9} = \dfrac{-59}{9}$

4. During assembly election in a constituency of 18 lakh people, 'x' number of people voted for candidate A, while $\sqrt{16}$ times of x people voted for candidate B and 10 lakh people did not go for voting at all.

(i) Find the value of x, using above information.

(ii) What values are shown by the people, casting their votes for either candidate A or B none of them? **(Value Based Question)**

Sol. (i) Given, total number of people for voting

$= 1800000$

Also, given people voting for person A = x

People voting for person B = $\sqrt{16}x$ = 4x and people did not go for voting = 1000000

According to the question,

By using all the above information, we get

$18000000 = x + 4x + 1000000$

$\Rightarrow \qquad 800000 = 5x$

$\therefore \qquad x = \dfrac{800000}{5} = 160000$

(ii) People who have casted their vote, know the value of vote and their duties for the democracy. While the other group who did not cast the vote, is not aware about the value of vote and their duties towards democracy and nation.

[Topic 2] Remainder Theorem

Points to be Remembered

- If a polynomial $p(x)$ of degree greater than or equal to one is divided by a linear polynomial $(x - a)$ then the remainder is $p(a)$, where a is only real number.
- If $p(x)$ is divided by $(x + a)$, then the remainder is $p(-a)$.
- If $p(x)$ is divided by $(ax - b)$, then the remainder is $p\left(\dfrac{b}{a}\right)$.
- If $p(x)$ is divided by $(ax + b)$, then the remainder is $p\left(-\dfrac{b}{a}\right)$.

- Division algorithm for polynomials: If $p(x)$ and $g(x)$ are two polynomials with $g(x) \neq 0$, then we can find $q(x)$ and $r(x)$ such that

$p(x) = g(x) \times q(x) + r(x)$, in the simple words:

Dividend = Divisor $\times$ Quotient + Remainder

Example : Find the remainder when,

$f(x) = x^3 - ax^2 + 6x - a$ is divided by $(x - a)$.

Sol. We have

$$f(x) = x^3 - ax^2 + 6x - a$$

On putting $x = a$, we get

$f(a) = a^3 - a(a)^2 + 6a - a$

$\qquad = a^3 - a^3 + 5a = 5a$

Hence, the required remainder is 5a

Sol. (b) Let assume $(x + 1)$ is a factor of $x^3 + x^2 + x + 1$.

$\therefore \quad -1$ is zero of $x^3 + x^2 + x + 1$

On putting $x = -1$, we get

$(-1)^3 + (-1)^2 + (-1) + 1 = -1 + 1 - 1 + 1$

$\qquad\qquad = 2 - 2 = 0$

2. If $x + 1$ is a factor of the polynomial $2x^2 + kx$, then the value of k is

(a) -3

(b) 4

(c) 2

(d) -2

[NCERT Exemp.]

PREVIOUS YEARS'

EXAMINATION QUESTIONS

TOPIC 2

Multiple Choice Questions

(1 Mark Each)

1. x + 1 is a factor of the polynomial

(a) $x^3 + x^2 - x + 1$ (b) $x^3 + x^2 + x + 1$

(c) $x^4 + x^3 + x^2 + 1$ (d) $x^4 + 3x^3 + 3x^2 + x + 1$.

Sol. (c) Given, $f(x) = 2x^2 + kx$

On putting $x = -1$ in given polynomial, we get

$f(x) = 0$

$\Rightarrow \quad 2x^2 + kx = 0$

$\Rightarrow \quad 2(-1)^2 + k(1) = 0$

$\Rightarrow \quad 2 + (-k) = 0$

$\Rightarrow \quad 2 = 0 + k$

$\therefore \quad k = 2$

3. If $x^{51} + 51$ is divided by $x + 1$, then remainder is

   (a) 0   (b) 1

   (c) 49   (d) 50   [NCERT Exemp.]

Ans. (d)

Sol. Let $p(x) = x^{51} - 51$

$\because$ it is divided by $(x + 1)$

On putting $x = -1$, we get

$\therefore \quad p(-1) = (-1)^{51} + 51$

$\qquad\qquad = -1 + 51$

$\qquad\qquad = 50$

Hence, the required remainder = 50

Very Short Answer Type Questions

(1 Mark Each)

1. Find the remainder and the quotient when $4x^3 + 20x^2 + 33x + 18$ is divided by $2x + 3$.

Sol. By long division method,

$$\begin{array}{r}
2x^2 + 7x + 6 \\
2x + 3 \overline{\smash{)}\ 4x^3 + 20x^2 + 33x + 18} \\
\underline{4x^3 + 6x^2} \qquad\qquad\qquad \\
14x^2 + 33x \qquad \\
\underline{14x^2 + 21x} \qquad \\
12x + 18 \\
\underline{12x + 18} \\
0
\end{array}$$

Thus, we get

$4x^3 + 20x^2 + 33x + 18 = (2x + 3) \times (2x^2 + 7x + 6) + 0$

Hence, quotient $= 2x^2 + 7x + 6$ and remainder $= 0$.

2. If $x^{11} + 101$ is divided by $x + 1$, then what remainder do we get?

Sol. Let, $f(x) = x^{11} + 101$

$\because$ It is divided by $(x + 1)$

$\therefore \quad x + 1 = 0$

$\therefore \quad x = -1$

On putting $x = -1$, we get

$f(-1) = (-1)^{11} + 101$

$\qquad = -1 + 101 = 100$

Hence, required remainder = 100

3. Find the remainder, when $f(x) = x^2 + 2x + 1$ is divided by $(x + 2)$.

Sol. Given, $f(x) = x^2 + 2x + 1$

Put $x + 2 = 0 \Rightarrow x = -2$

Then $f(-2) = (-2)^2 + 2(-2) + 1$

$\qquad\qquad = 4 - 4 + 1 = 1$

Hence, required remainder = 1

4. On dividing $5y^3 - 2y^2 - 7y + 1$ by y, what remainder do we get ?

Sol. Let, $p(y) = 5y^3 - 2y^2 - 7y + 1$,

On putting $y = 0$, we get

$\qquad p(0) = 0 - 0 - 0 + 1 = 1.$

Hence, required remainder = 1

Short Answer Type Questions I

(2 Marks Each)

1. Find the remainder when $x^3 + 6x - ax^2 - a$ is divided by $x - a$.   [NCERT]

Sol. Given, $p(x) = x^3 - ax^2 + 6x - a$,

and the zero of $x - a$ is a.

$\therefore$ On putting $x = a$, we get

$\qquad p(a) = a^3 - a.a^2 + 6a - a = 5a.$

Hence, by the remainder theorem 5a is the remainder when $x^3 - ax^2 + 6x - a$, is divided by $x - a$.

2. Find the remainder when $x^3 + x^2 + x + 1$ is divided by $x - \dfrac{1}{2}$, using remainder theorem.

[Board Term I, 2012, Set-53]

Sol. Given, $p(x) = x^3 + x^2 + x + 1$

$\because p(x) = x^3 + x^2 + x + 1$ is divided by $x - \dfrac{1}{2}$.

$\Rightarrow \qquad x - \dfrac{1}{2} = 0$

$\therefore \qquad x = \dfrac{1}{2}$

Now, on putting $x = \dfrac{1}{2}$, we get

$\therefore\ p\left(\dfrac{1}{2}\right) = \left(\dfrac{1}{2}\right)^3 + \left(\dfrac{1}{2}\right)^2 + \left(\dfrac{1}{2}\right) + 1$

$= \dfrac{1}{8} + \dfrac{1}{4} + \dfrac{1}{2} + 1 = \dfrac{1 + 2 + 4 + 8}{8} = \dfrac{15}{8}.$

Hence, by the remainder theorem $\dfrac{15}{8}$ is the remainder when $x^3 + x^2 + x + 1$ is divided by $\left(x - \dfrac{1}{2}\right)$.

3. Find the remainder when the polynomial

    $f(x) = 4x^3 - 12x^2 + 14x - 3$ is divided by $(2x - 1)$
    [Board Term I, 2016, Set-BQS61ZK]

Sol. Given, $f(x) = 4x^3 - 12x^2 + 14x - 3$

$\because$ $f(x)$ is divided by $(2x - 1)$

$\therefore \quad 2x - 1 = 0$

$\Rightarrow \quad 2x = 1$

$\therefore \quad x = \dfrac{1}{2}$

By remainder theorem, if $f(x)$ is divided by $2x - 1$,

the remainder is $f\left(\dfrac{1}{2}\right)$

$\therefore\ f\left(\dfrac{1}{2}\right) = 4\left(\dfrac{1}{2}\right)^3 - 12\left(\dfrac{1}{2}\right)^2 + 14\left(\dfrac{1}{2}\right) - 3$

$= 4 \times \dfrac{1}{8} - 12 \times \dfrac{1}{4} + 14 \times \dfrac{1}{2} - 3$

$= \dfrac{1}{2} - 3 + 7 - 3$

$= \dfrac{1}{2} + 1$

$= \dfrac{3}{2}$

Hence required remainder is $\dfrac{3}{2}$.

4. If the polynomials $ax^3 + 3x^2 + 5x - 4$ and $x^3 - 4x + a$ leaves the same remainder, when divided by $(x - 2)$, then find the value of a.

Sol. Let $p_1(x) = ax^3 + 3x^2 + 5x - 4$,

and $p_2(x) = x^3 - 4x + a$ and $g(x) = x - 2$

For finding the zero of $g(x)$, put $g(x) = 0$

$\Rightarrow \quad x - 2 = 0 \therefore x = 2$

So, $x = 2$ is the zero of $g(x)$.

On putting $x = 2$ in both $p_1(x)$ and $p_2(x)$ respectively, we get the remainders

$p_1(2) = a(2)^3 + 3(2)^2 + 5(2) - 4$

$\qquad = 8a + 12 + 10 - 4 = 8a + 18$

and $\quad p_2(2) = (2)^3 - 4(2) + a$

$\qquad = 8 - 8 + a = a$

According to the question,

$p_1(2) = p_2(2) \Rightarrow 8a + 18 = a$

$\Rightarrow \quad 8a - a = -18 \Rightarrow 7a = -18$

$\therefore \quad a = \dfrac{-18}{7}$

Hence, required value of a $= \dfrac{-18}{7}$.

5. By actual division, find the quotient and remainder when $p(x) = 2x^3 + 3x^2 - 9x + 4$ is divided by $2x - 1$.

Sol. Given, $p(x) = 2x^3 + 3x^2 - 9x + 4$

$$
\begin{array}{r}
x^2 + 2x - \dfrac{7}{2} \\[4pt]
2x - 1 \overline{)\, 2x^3 + 3x^2 - 9x + 4} \\
\underline{-2x^3 \mp x^2} \\
4x^2 + 9x \\
\underline{-4x^2 \mp 2x} \\
-7x + 4 \\
\underline{-7x + \dfrac{7}{2}} \\
\dfrac{1}{2}\ \text{(Remainder)}
\end{array}
$$

Hence, Quotient $= x^2 + 2x - \dfrac{7}{2}$

and Remainder $= \dfrac{1}{2}$

6. Divide $p(x)$ by $g(x)$,

    when $p(x) = 4x^3 - 3x^2 + 2x - 1$ and $g(x) = x - 3$.

Sol. Given, $p(x) = 4x^3 - 3x^2 + 2x - 1$

and $\quad g(x) = x - 3$

By long division, we have

$$
\begin{array}{r}
4x^2 + 9x + 29 \\[4pt]
x - 3 \overline{)\, 4x^3 - 3x^2 + 2x - 1} \\
\underline{-4x^3 + 12x^2} \\
9x^2 + 2x \\
\underline{-9x^2 \mp 27x} \\
29x - 1 \\
\underline{29x - 87} \\
86
\end{array}
$$

Thus,

$4x^3 - 3x^2 + 2x - 1 = (x - 3)(4x^2 + 9x + 29) + 86$

Hence, quotient $= 4x^2 + 9x + 29$

and remainder $= 86$.

Short Answer Type Questions II

(3 Marks Each)

1. Polynomial $3x^3 - 5x^2 + kx - 2$ and $-x^3 - x^2 + 7x + k$ leave the same remainder when divided by $x + 2$. Find the value at k. **[Board Term I, 2013]**

Sol. Let, $p(x) = 3x^3 - 5x^2 + kx - 2$,

and $q(x) = -x^3 - x^2 + 7x + k$

$\because$ $p(x)$ and $q(x)$ is divided by $(x + 2)$.

$\therefore \quad x + 2 = 0$

$\therefore \quad x = -2$

On putting $x = -2$, we get

$p(-2) = 3(-2)^3 - 5(-2)^2 + k(-2) - 2$

$\qquad = -24 - 20 - 2k - 2 = -2k - 46$

and $q(-2) = -(-2)^3 - (-2)^2 + 7(-2) + k$

$$= 8 - 4 - 14 + k$$
$$= -10 + k$$

$\because$ $p(x)$ and $q(x)$ leave the same remainder when divided by $x + 2$.

According to the question,

$\therefore -2k - 46 = k - 10$

$\Rightarrow \qquad -3k = 36$

$\therefore \qquad k = \dfrac{-36}{3} = -12$

2. Using remainder theorem, factorize:

   $6x^3 - 25x^2 + 32x - 12$. **[Board Term I, 2013]**

Sol. Given, $p(x) = 6x^3 - 25x^2 + 32x - 12$

Factors of $12 = (\pm 1, \pm 2, \pm 3, \pm 4, \pm 6, \pm 12)$

On putting $x = 2$, we get

$$p(2) = 6(2)^3 - 25(2)^2 + 32 \times 2 - 12$$
$$= 48 - 100 + 64 - 12$$
$$= 112 - 112 = 0$$

$\therefore \qquad x = 2$ is a zero of $p(x)$

or $(x - 2)$ is a factor of $p(x)$.

So, $6x^3 - 25x^2 + 32x - 12$

$$= 6x^2(x - 2) - 13x(x - 2) + 6(x - 2)$$
$$= (x - 2)(6x^2 - 13x + 6)$$
$$= (x - 2)(6x^2 - 9x - 4x + 6)$$
$$= (x - 2)[3x(2x - 3) - 2(2x - 3)]$$
$$= (x - 2)(2x - 3)(3x - 2).$$

Hence, required factors are $(x - 2)(2x - 3)(3x - 2)$

3. The polynomial

   $p(x) = x^4 - 2x^3 + 3x^2 - ax + 3a - 7$, when divided by $(x + 1)$, leaves the remainder 19.

   Find the value of a. Also, find the remainder, when $p(x)$ is divided by $x + 2$.

Sol. Given, $p(x) = x^4 - 2x^3 + 3x^2 - ax + 3a - 7$

$\because$ $p(x)$ is divided by $(x + 1)$, then it leaves the remainder $p(-1)$.

According to the question,

$\therefore \quad p(-1) = 19$

$\Rightarrow \quad (-1)^4 - 2(-1)^3 + 3(-1)^2 - a(-1) + 3a - 7 = 19$

$\Rightarrow \quad 1 + 2 + 3 + a + 3a - 7 = 19$

$\Rightarrow \quad 4a - 1 = 19$

$\Rightarrow \qquad 4a = 20$

$\therefore \qquad a = 5$

Now, on putting $a = 5$ in the given expression, we get

$\therefore p(x) = x^4 - 2x^3 + 3x^2 - 5x + 15 - 7$ [Put $a = 5$]

$$= x^4 - 2x^3 + 3x^2 - 5x + 8$$

If $p(x)$ is divided by $(x + 2)$, then

$\therefore p(-2) = (-2)^4 - 2(-2)^3 + 3(-2)^2 - 5(-2) + 8$

$$= 16 + 16 + 12 + 10 + 8 = 62$$

Hence, required remainder $= 62$.

4. The polynomials $bx^3 + 3x^2 - 3$ and $2x^3 - 5x + b$, when divided by $(x - 4)$ leave the remainder r_1 and r_2, respectively. Find the value of b, if $2r_1 - r_2 = 0$.

Sol. Let $f(x) = bx^3 + 3x^2 - 3$

and $g(x) = 2x^3 - 5x + b$

Here, the zero of $(x - 4)$ is $x = 4$.

$$[\because x - 4 = 0 \therefore x = 4]$$

$\because$ $f(x)$ and $g(x)$ are divided by $(x - 4)$, then we get

$\therefore \qquad f(4) = b(4)^3 + 3(4)^2 - 3 = r_1$ [given]

$\Rightarrow \quad 64b + 48 - 3 = r_1$

$\Rightarrow \qquad 64b + 45 = r^1$ \qquad ...(i)

and $\qquad g(4) = 2(4)^3 - 5 \times 4 + b = r_2$

$\Rightarrow \quad 128 - 20 + b = r_2$

$\Rightarrow \qquad 108 + b = r_2$ \qquad ...(ii)

It is given that, $2r_1 - r_2 = 0$ \qquad ...(iii)

Now, on putting the value of r_1 and r_2 in eqⁿ (iii), we have

$$2(64b + 45) - (108 + b) = 0$$

$\Rightarrow \quad 128b + 90 - 108 - b = 0$

$\Rightarrow \qquad 127b - 18 = 0$

$\therefore \qquad b = \dfrac{18}{127}$

Long Answer Type Questions
(4 Marks Each)

1. Without actual division, prove that $2x^4 - 5x^3 + 2x^2 - x + 2$ is divisible by $x^2 - 3x + 2$.

   [NCERT Exemplar]

Sol. Let $\qquad p(x) = 2x^4 - 5x^3 + 2x^2 - x + 2$

and $x^2 - 3x + 2 = x^2 - 2x - x + 2$

$\qquad$ [by splitting the middle term]

$$= x(x - 2) - 1(x - 2)$$
$$= (x - 1)(x - 2)$$

$\therefore \qquad x = 1, 2$

Hence, zeros of $x^2 - 3x + 2$ are 1 and 2.

Now, we have to prove that $2x^4 - 5x^3 + 2x^2 - x + 2$ is divisible $x^2 - 3x + 2$,

$\therefore \qquad p(1) = 0$ and $p(2) = 0$.

Now, $\quad p(1) = 2(1)^4 - 5(1)^3 + 2(1)^2 - 1 + 2$

$$= 2 - 5 + 2 - 1 + 2 = 6 - 6 = 0$$

and $\quad p(2) = 2(2)^4 - 5(2)^3 + 2(2)^2 - 2 + 2$

$\qquad = 2 \times 16 - 5 \times 8 + 2 \times 4 + 0$

$\qquad = 32 - 40 + 8 = 40 - 40 = 0$

Hence, $p(x) = 2x^4 + 5x^3 + 2x^2 - x + 2$ is divisible by $x^2 - 3x + 2$.

2. If the polynomial $ax^3 + 4x^2 + 3x - 4$ and $x^3 - 4x + a$ leave the same remainder when divided by $(x - 3)$. Find the value of a.

[Board Term I, 2012, Set 65], [NCERT Exemplar]

Sol. Let $p(x) = ax^3 + 4x^2 + 3x - 4$

and $q(x) = x^3 - 4x + a$

$\because$ $p(x)$ is divided by $(x - 3)$,

$\Rightarrow \qquad x - 3 = 0$

$\therefore \qquad x = 3$

On putting the value, we have

$\therefore \qquad p(3) = a(3)^3 + 4(3)^2 + 3 \times 3 - 4$

$\qquad = 27a + 36 + 9 - 4 = 27a + 41$

Again, in $q(x)$,

$\qquad q(3) = (3)^3 - 4(3) + a$

$\qquad = 27 - 12 + a = 15 + a$

Now, According to the question,

$\qquad p(3) = q(3)$

$\Rightarrow \quad 27a + 41 = 15 + a$

$\Rightarrow \quad 27a - a = 15 - 41$

$\Rightarrow \qquad 26a = - 26$

$\therefore \qquad a = \dfrac{-26}{26} = -1$

3. The polynomials $ax^3 - 3x^2 + 4$ and $2x^3 - 5x + a$ when divided by $(x - 2)$ leave the remainders p and q respectively. If $p - 2q = 4$, find the value of a.

[Board Term I, 2011, Set-14; 2010, Set C1]

Sol. Let, $\quad f(x) = ax^3 - 3x^2 + 4$

and $\quad g(x) = 2x^3 - 5x + a$

when divided by $(x - 2)$, we get

$\qquad f(2) = p$

$\Rightarrow \qquad f(2) = a \times 2^3 - 3 \times 2^2 + 4$

$\Rightarrow \qquad p = 8a - 12 + 4$

$\Rightarrow \qquad p = 8a - 8 \qquad$ ...(i)

Again, $g(2) = q \Rightarrow g(2) = 2 \times 2^3 - 5 \times 2 + a$

$\Rightarrow \qquad q = 16 - 10 + a$

$\Rightarrow \qquad q = 6 + a \qquad$ ...(ii)

According to the question,

$\qquad p - 2q = 4,$

$\Rightarrow \quad 8a - 8 - 12 - 2a = 4$

$\Rightarrow \quad 6a - 20 = 4 \Rightarrow 6a = 4 + 20 = 24$

$\therefore \qquad a = \dfrac{24}{6} = 4$

4. Divide $3x^3 - 8x^2 + 3x + 2$ by $x^2 - 3x + 2$ and verify the division algorithm.

[Board Term I, 2012, Set-63]

Sol. Let $f(x) = 3x^3 - 8x^2 + 3x + 2$

and $g(x) = x^2 - 3x + 2$

Now, by long division method.

$$
\begin{array}{r}
3x + 1 \\
x^2 - 3x + 2 \overline{\smash{\big)}\ 3x^3 - 8x^2 + 3x + 2} \\
\underline{-3x^3 \mp 9x^2 \pm 6x} \\
x^2 - 3x + 2 \\
\underline{x^2 - 3x + 2} \\
0
\end{array}
$$

We have

Quotient = $3x + 1$ and remainder = 0

Verification :

Divisor × Quotient + Remainder

$\qquad = (x^2 - 3x + 2)(3x + 1) + 0$

$\qquad = 3x^3 - 8x^2 + 3x + 2$

$\therefore$ Dividend = Divisor × Quotient + Remainder (Division algorithm)

5. What must be subtracted from $x^4 + 1$ so that $x^4 + 1$ is exactly divisible by $(x - 1)$. Write the resultant polynomial which is exactly divisible by $(x - 1)$. [Board Term I, 2012, Set-51]

Sol. Let $\quad p(x) = x^4 + 1$

$\therefore$ $p(x)$ is divided by $(x - 1)$,

$\therefore \qquad x - 1 = 0$

$\therefore \qquad x = 1$

On putting $x = 1$, we have

$\qquad p(1) = (1)^4 + 1 = 1 + 1 = 2$

Hence, 2 must be subtracted from $x^4 + 1$ so that it is exactly divisible by $(x - 1)$.

and resultant polynomial to be divisible by $(x - 1)$

$\qquad = x^4 + 1 - 2$

$\qquad = x^4 - 1.$

6. Divide $x^3 + 4x^2 - 3x - 10$ by $x + 1$ and verify your remainder by remainder theorem.

[Board Term I, 2012, Set-50]

Sol. Let $f(x) = x^3 + 4x^2 - 3x - 10$

and $g(x) = x + 1$

Now, by long division method,

$$
\begin{array}{r}
x^2 + 3x - 6 \\
x + 1 \overline{\smash{\big)}\ x^3 + 4x^2 - 3x - 10} \\
\underline{x^3 + x^2} \\
3x^2 - 3x \\
\underline{3x^2 + 3x} \\
-6x - 10 \\
\underline{-6x - 6} \\
-4
\end{array}
$$

Thus, we have

Quotient = $x^2 + 3x - 6$

and remainder = -4

Verification:

Let, $f(x) = x^3 + 4x^2 - 3x - 10$

By remainder theorem, remainder

$f(-1) = (-1)^3 + 4(-1)^2 - 3(-1) - 10$

$= -1 + 4 + 3 - 10 = -4.$

7. Find the quotient when $p(x) = x^3 + 3x^2 + 3x + 5$ is divided by $g(x) = x + 2$. Also, find the remainder.

[Board Term I, 2013]

Sol. Given $p(x) = x^3 + 3x^2 + 3x + 5$

and $g(x) = x + 2$

Now, by long division method,

$$\begin{array}{r} x^2 + x + 1 \\ x + 2 \overline{\smash{\big)}\ x^3 + 3x^2 + 3x + 5} \\ \underline{x^3 + 2x^2} \\ x^2 + 3x \\ \underline{x^2 + 2x} \\ x + 5 \\ \underline{x + 2} \\ 3 \end{array}$$

we have,

$\therefore$ Quotient = $x^2 + x + 1$

and Remainder = 3.

Hence, required remainder = 3.

8. Find the value of 'a' if remainder is same when polynomial $p(x) = x^3 + 8x^2 + 17x + ax$ is divided by $(x + 2)$ and $(x + 1)$.   [Board Term I, 2014]

Sol. Given, $p(x) = x^3 + 8x^2 + 17x + ax$

$\because$ $p(x)$ leave the same remainder when divided by $(x + 2)$ and $(x + 1)$.

On putting $x = -2$, we have

$\therefore p(-2) = (-2)^3 + 8(-2)^2 + 17(-2) + a \times (-2)$

$= -8 + 32 - 34 - 2a$

$= -10 - 2a$

On putting $x = -1$, we have

Again $p(-1) = (-1)^3 + 8(-1)^2 + 17(-1) + a(-1)$

$= -1 + 8 - 17 - a$

$= -10 - a$

According to the question,

$\because$ Remainder are equal

So, $-10 - 2a = -10 - a$

$\Rightarrow$ $-10 + 10 = -a + 2a$

$\therefore$ $a = 0$

9. Find the quotient and remainder obtained on dividing $p(x) = 4x^4 + 11x^3 + 2x^2 - 11x + 6$ by $x^2 + 2x + 2$ and verify the remainder by using division algorithm.   [Board Term I, 2014]

Sol. Given, $p(x) = 4x^4 + 11x^3 + 2x^2 - 11x + 6$

Now, by long division method.

$$\begin{array}{r} (4x^2 + 3x - 12) \\ x^2+2x + 2 \overline{\smash{\big)}\ 4x^4 + 11x^3 + 2x^2 - 11x + 6} \\ \underline{4x^4 + 8x^3 + 8x^2} \\ 3x^3 - 6x^2 - 11x + 6 \\ \underline{3x^3 + 6x^2 + 6x} \\ -12x^2 - 17x + 6 \\ \underline{-12x^2 - 24x - 24} \\ 7x + 30 \end{array}$$

Thus, quotient = $4x^2 + 3x - 12$

and remainder = $7x + 30$

Verification:

Now, By Remainder theorem,

Dividend = (Divisor $\times$ Quotient) + Remainder

$\therefore$ $4x^4 + 11x^3 + 2x^2 - 11x + 6$

$= [(x^2 + 2x + 2) \times (4x^2 + 3x - 12)] + (7x + 30)$

$= [4x^4 + 8x^3 + 8x^2 + 3x^3 - 6x^2 + 6x - 12x^2$

$\qquad\qquad\qquad - 24x - 24] + 7x + 30$

$= 4x^4 + 11x^3 + 2x^2 - 11x + 6$

10. The polynomials $ax^3 + 3x^2 - 13$ and $2x^3 - 5x + a$ leave the same remainder in each case, when divided by $(x - 2)$. Find the value of a.

[Board Term I, 2014]

Sol. Let $p(x) = ax^3 + 3x^2 - 13$

and $g(x) = 2x^3 - 5x + a$

Remainder $R_1 = p(2)$

and remainder $R_2 = g(2)$

Now, $p(2) = a(2)^3 + 3(2)^2 - 13$

$\therefore$ $R_1 = 8a + 12 - 13$

$= 8a - 1$ ...(i)

and $R_2 = 2(2)^3 - 5(2) + a$

$= 16 - 10 + a$

$\therefore$ $R_2 = 6 + a$ ...(ii)

Now, according to the question,

$\therefore$ $R_1 = R_2$

$\Rightarrow$ $8a - 1 = 6 + a$

or, $\Rightarrow$ $7a = 7$

$\therefore$ $a = 1$

11. Find what must be subtracted from the polynomial $4y^4 + 12y^3 + 6y^2 + 50y + 26$ so that the obtained polynomial is exactly divisible by $y^2 + 4y + 2$.

[Board Term I, 2015 Set 20UIOH]

Sol. Let $f(x) = 4y^4 + 12y^3 + 6y^2 + 50y + 26$

and $g(x) = y^2 + 4y + 2$

Now, by long division method,

$$
\begin{array}{r}
4y^2 + 4y + 14 \\
y^2 + 4y + 2 \overline{)\, 4y^4 + 12y^3 + 6y^2 + 50y + 26} \\
4y^4 + 16y^3 + 8y^2 \\
\hline
-4y^3 - 2y^2 - 50y \\
-4y^3 - 16y^2 - 8y \\
\hline
-14y^3 + 58y + 26 \\
-14y^2 + 56y + 28 \\
\hline
2y - 2
\end{array}
$$

Hence, $2y - 2$ must be subtract from $4y^4 + 12y^3 + 6y^2 + 50y + 26$.

12. Divide polynomial $p(x) = 2x^4 + 3x^3 - 2x^2 - 9x - 2$ by $q(x) = x^2 - 3$ and find what should be subtracted from $p(x)$ so that it is divisible by $q(x)$.

[Board Term I, 2016 Set-7AEDLQR]

Sol. Given, $p(x) = 2x^4 + 3x^3 - 2x^2 - 9x - 2$

and $q(x) = x^2 - 3$

By long division method,

$$
\begin{array}{r}
2x^2 + 3x + 4 \\
x^2 - 3 \overline{)\, 2x^4 + 3x^3 - 2x^2 - 9x - 2} \\
4x^4 \qquad - 6x^2 \\
\hline
3x^3 + 4x^2 - 9x \\
3x^3 \qquad - 9x \\
\hline
4x^2 - 2 \\
4x^2 - 12 \\
\hline
10
\end{array}
$$

Then, we have

quotient $= 2x^2 + 3x + 4$ and remainder $= 10$

Hence, 10 should be subtracted from $p(x)$.

13. Divide the polynomial $3x^4 + 2x^2 - 3$ by $x + 1$ and find quotient and remainder.

[Board Term I, 2016 Set 7 AEDLQR]

Sol. Let $f(x) = 3x^4 + 2x^2 - 3$

and $g(x) = (x + 1)$

Now, by long division method,

$$
\begin{array}{r}
3x^3 - 3x^2 + 5x - 5 \\
x + 1 \overline{)\, 3x^4 + 2x^2 - 3} \\
4x^4 + 3x^3 \\
\hline
-3x^3 + 4x^2 \\
-3x^3 - 3x^2 \\
\hline
5x^2 - 3 \\
5x^2 - 5x \\
\hline
-5x - 3 \\
-5x - 5 \\
\hline
2
\end{array}
$$

we have

$\therefore$ Quotient $= 3x^3 - 3x^2 + 5x - 5$ and remainder $= 2$

Hence, required remainder $= 2$.

14. Divide polynomial $p(x) = x^4 - 4x^3 + 4x^2 - 3x + 4$ by $q(x) = x - 1$ and find what should be added in $p(x)$, so that it is divisible by $q(x)$.

[Board Term I, 2016 Set-20CNJE9]

Sol. Given $p(x) = x^4 - 4x^3 + 4x^2 - 3x + 4$

and $q(x) = x - 1$

Now, by long division method,

$$
\begin{array}{r}
x^3 - 3x^2 + x - 2 \\
x - 1 \overline{)\, x^4 - 4x^3 + 4x^2 - 3x + 4} \\
x^4 - x^3 \\
\hline
-3x^3 + 4x^2 \\
-3x^3 + 3x^2 \\
\hline
x^2 - 3x \\
x^2 - x \\
\hline
-2x + 4 \\
-2x + 2 \\
\hline
2
\end{array}
$$

we have

$\therefore$ Quotient $= x^3 - 3x^2 + x - 2$

and Remainder $= 2$

Hence, -2 should be added in $p(x)$.

So that is completely divisible by $q(x)$.

15. By long division find the remainder when the polynomial $4x^4 - 6x^3 + 6x^2 - 1$ is divided by $2x^2 - 3$.

[Board Term I, 2016 Set-JQ22L5C]

Sol. Let $f(x) = 4x^4 - 6x^3 + 6x^2 - 1$

and $g(x) = 2x^2 - 3$

Now, by long division method.

$$2x^2 - 3\overline{)\,4x^4 - 6x^3 + 6x^2 - 1\,}\;\; 2x^2 - 3x + 6$$

we have

$\therefore$ Quotient $= 2x^2 - 3x + 6$

and Remainder $= -9x + 17$

Hence, required remainder $= -9x + 17$

16. If $f(x) = x^4 - 2x^3 + 3x^2 - ax + b$ is a polynomial such that when it is divided by $x - 1$ and $x + 1$, the remainders are 5 and 19 respectively. Determine the remainder when $f(x)$ is divided by $x - 2$.

Sol. Given, $f(x) = x^4 - 2x^3 + 3x^2 - ax + b$

$\because f(x) = x^4 - 2x^3 + 3x^2 - ax + b$ is divided by $(x - 1)$,

$\therefore x - 1 = 0$

$\therefore x = 1$

On putting $x = 1$ in $f(x)$, we get

$f(1) = (1)^4 - 2(1)^3 + 3(1)^2 - a \times 1 + b$

$\Rightarrow 5 = 1 - 2 + 3 - a + b$

$\Rightarrow 5 = 2 - a + b$

$\Rightarrow a - b = 2 - 5$

$\Rightarrow a - b = -3$ ...(1)

$\because f(x) = x^4 - 2x^3 + 3x^2 - ax + b$ is divided by $(x + 1)$,

$\therefore x + 1 = 0$

$\therefore x = -1$

On putting $x = -1$ in $f(x)$, we get

$f(-1) = (-1)^4 - 2(-1)^3 + 3(-1)^2 - a(-1) + b$

$\Rightarrow 19 = 1 + 2 + 3 + a + b$

$\Rightarrow 19 - 6 = a + b$

$\Rightarrow a + b = 13$ ...(2)

Adding equations (1) and (2),

$2a = 10$

$\therefore a = 5$

By equation (2),

$5 + b = 13$

$\therefore b = 8$

$f(x) = x^4 - 2x^3 + 3x^2 - 5x + 8$

Again put, $x - 2 = 0$ or $x = 2$ in $f(x)$

$\therefore f(2) = (2)^4 - 2(2)^3 + 3(2)^2 - 5 \times 2 + 8$

$= 16 - 16 + 12 - 10 + 8 = 20 - 10 = 10$

Hence, required remainder $= 10$

17. Without actual division, prove that $(2x^4 - 6x^3 + 3x^2 + 3x - 2)$ is exactly divisible by $(x^2 - 3x + 2)$.

HOTS

Sol. Let $f(x) = 2x^4 - 6x^3 + 3x^2 + 3x - 2$

and $g(x) = x^2 - 3x + 2 = x^2 - 2x - x + 2$

[by splitting the middle term]

$= x(x - 2) - 1(x - 2)$

$= (x - 2)(x - 1)$

Now, $f(x)$ will be exactly divisible by $g(x)$, if it is exactly divisible by $(x - 2)$ as well as $(x - 1)$.

$x = 2$ and 1

for this, we must have $f(2) = 0$ and $f(1) = 0$,

Now, $f(2) = 2 \times 2^4 - 6 \times 2^3 + 3 \times 2^2 + 3 \times 2 - 2$

$= 32 - 48 + 12 + 6 - 2 = 0$

and $f(1) = 2 \times 1^4 - 6 \times 1^3 + 3 \times 1^2 + 3 \times 1 - 2$

$= 2 - 6 + 3 + 3 - 2 = 0$

Thus, $f(x)$ is exactly divisible by $(x - 2)$ as well as $(x - 1)$.

$\therefore f(x)$ is exactly divisible by

$(x - 2)(x - 1)$.

Hence, $f(x) = 2x^4 - 6x^3 + 3x^2 + 3x - 2$ is exactly divisible by

$(x^2 - 3x + 2)$.

18. Find the quotient and remainder when $6x^4 + 11x^3 + 13x^2 - 3x + 27$ is divided by $3x + 4$. Also check the remainder obtained by using remainder theorem.

Sol. Let $f(x) = 6x^4 + 11x^3 + 13x^2 - 3x + 27$

$$3x + 4\overline{)\,6x^4 + 11x^3 - 13x^2 - 3x + 27\,}\;\; 2x^3 + x^2 + 3x - 5 \text{ (quotient)}$$

Thus, quotient $= 2x^3 + x^2 + 3x - 5$ and remainder $= 47$

$\therefore f(x) = 6x^4 + 11x^3 + 13x^2 - 3x + 27$

Then, zero of $(3x + 4)$ is, $3x + 4 = 0$

$\Rightarrow 3x = -4$

$\therefore x = \dfrac{-4}{3}$

By remainder theorem,

$$f\left(\dfrac{-4}{3}\right) = 6\left(\dfrac{-4}{3}\right)^4 + 11\left(\dfrac{-4}{3}\right)^3 + 13\left(\dfrac{-4}{3}\right)^2 -3\left(\dfrac{-4}{3}\right) + 27$$

$$= \dfrac{512}{27} + \left(\dfrac{-704}{27}\right) + \dfrac{208}{9} + 4 + 27$$

$$= \dfrac{512 - 704 + 624}{27} + 31$$

$$= 16 + 31$$

$$= 47.$$

Hence, required remainder = 47.

[Topic 3] Factor Theorem

Points to be Remembered

- If $P(x)$ is a polynomial of degree $n \geq 1$ and a is any real number, then

(i) $(x - a)$ is a factor of $P(x)$, if $P(a) = 0$

(ii) $P(a) = 0$, if $(x - a)$ is a factor of $P(x)$.

Factorization of a Polynomial:

(i) Let a quadratic polynomial be $x^2 + lx + m$, where l and m are constants. Now, factorize the polynomial by splitting the middle term lx as $(ax + bx)$, so that $ab = m$. Then, we get

$x^2 + lx + m = x^2 + (ax + bx) + ab$

$= x(x + a) + b(x + a) = (x + a)(x + b)$

(ii) Consider a quadratic polynomial $ax^2 + bx + c$, where a, b and c are constants. It has two factors $(x - \alpha)$ and $(x - \beta)$

$\therefore$ $ax^2 + bx + c = a(x - \alpha)(x + \beta)$

$= ax^2 - a(\alpha + \beta)x + a\alpha\beta$

Now, $\alpha + \beta = \dfrac{-b}{a}$ and $\alpha\beta = \dfrac{c}{a}$

Example: Write the factors of a polynomial given below $x^2 + 5\sqrt{2}\,x + 12$

Sol. $x^2 + 5\sqrt{2}\,x + 12 = x^2 + 3\sqrt{2}\,x + 2\sqrt{2}\,x + 12$

$= x(x + 3\sqrt{2}) + 2\sqrt{2}(x + 3\sqrt{2})$

$= (x + 3\sqrt{2})(x + 2\sqrt{2})$

Hence, required factors are $(x + 3\sqrt{2})$ and $(x + 2\sqrt{2})$

PREVIOUS YEARS' EXAMINATION QUESTIONS TOPIC 3

Multiple Choice Questions

(1 Mark Each)

1. $9x^2 + 12xy$ can be factorized as:

    (a) $3x(3x + 4y)$ (b) $3(3x + 4y)$

    (c) $3x(4x + 3y)$ (d) $3x(3x - 4y)$

    [NCERT Exemp.]

Sol. (a) Given expression $= 9x^2 + 12xy = 3x(3x + 4y)$

2. One of the factors of $(25x^2 - 1) + (1 + 5x)^2$ is

    (a) $5 + x$.   (b) $5 - x$.

    (c) $5x - 1$.   (d) $10x$.   [NCERT Exemp.]

Sol. (d) Given expression $= (25x^2 - 1) + (1 + 5x)^2$

$= [(5x)^2 - (1)^2] + (1 + 5x)^2$

[Using identity $a^2 - b^2 = (a + b)(a - b)$]

$= [(1 + 5x)(5x - 1)] + (1 + 5x)^2$

$= (1 + 5x)[5x - 1 + 1 + 5x]$

$= (1 + 5x)(10x)$

Hence, One of the factors $= 10x$

3. $x^2 + xy - 2xz - 2yz$ is equal to:

    (a) $(x + y)(x - 2z)$ (b) $(x - y)(x + 2z)$

    (c) $(x + y)(x + 2z)$ (d) $(x - y)(x - 2z)$

    [NCERT Exemp.]

Sol. (a) Given expression $= x^2 + xy - 2xz - 2yz$

$= x(x + y) - 2z(x + y)$

$= (x + y)(x - 2z)$

4. The factorisation of $4x^2 + 8x + 3$ is
   (a) $(x + 1)(x + 3)$.   (b) $(2x + 1)(2x + 3)$.
   (c) $(2x + 2)(2x + 5)$. (d) $(2x - 1)(2x - 3)$.
   [NCERT Exemp.]

Sol. (b) Given expression $= 4x^2 + 8x + 3$ (By splitting the middle term)
$4x^2 + (6x + 2x) + 3$
$2x(2x + 3) + 1(2x + 3) = (2x + 1)(2x + 3)$

5. $a(a - 1) - b(b - 1)$ can be factorised as:
   (a) $(a + b)(a + b - 1)$
   (b) $(a - b)(a + b - 1)$
   (c) $(a - b)(a - b - 1)$
   (d) $(a - b)(a + b + 1)$ [NCERT Exemp.]

Sol. (b) Given expression $= a(a - 1) - b(b - 1)$
$$= a^2 - a - b^2 + b$$
$$= a^2 - b^2 - a + b$$
$$= (a - b)(a + b) - 1(a - b)$$
$$= (a - b)(a + b - 1)$$

Very Short Answer Type Questions

(1 Mark Each)

1. Factorize : $12a^2b - 6ab^2$.   [Board Term I, 2014]

Sol. $12a^2b - 6ab^2 = 6ab(2a - b)$

2. Factorize : $x^2 - 3x$.   [Board Term I, 2014]

Sol. Given expression $= x^2 - 3x = x(x - 3)$

3. Find the value of k, if $2x - 1$ is a factor of the polynomial $6x^2 + kx - 2$.
   [Board Term I, 2015, Set-20 UI6YH]

Sol. Given, $p(x) = 6x^2 + kx - 2$
$\because (2x - 1)$ is a factor of $p(x)$.
$\therefore 2x - 1 = 0$
$\Rightarrow 2x = 1$
$\therefore \quad x = \dfrac{1}{2}$
On putting $x = \dfrac{1}{2}$, we have
$\Rightarrow \quad p\left(\dfrac{1}{2}\right) = 0$
$\Rightarrow \quad 6 \times \dfrac{1}{4} + k \times \dfrac{1}{2} - 2 = 0$
$\Rightarrow \quad \dfrac{3}{2} + \dfrac{k}{2} - 2 = 0$
$\Rightarrow \quad \dfrac{k}{2} = 2 - \dfrac{3}{2}$
$\therefore \quad k = \dfrac{1}{2} \times 2 = 1$

4. Find the value of m, if $x + 4$ is a factor of the polynomial $x^2 + 3x + m$.
   [Board Term I, 2015, Set-2]

Sol. Let $x^2 + 3x + m = p(x)$
$\because (x + 4)$ is a factor of $p(x)$.
$\therefore x + 4 = 0$
$\therefore x = -4$
On putting $x = -4$, we have
$\Rightarrow \quad p(-4) = 0$
$\Rightarrow \quad 16 - 12 + m = 0$
$\Rightarrow \quad 4 + m = 0$
$\therefore \quad m = -4$

5. Factorize : $8y^3 - 125x^3$.
   [Board Term I, 2016, Set BUS6IZK; Set-JQ22L5C]

Sol. Given expression $= 8y^3 - 125x^3 = (2y)^3 - (5x)^3$
$$= (2y - 5x)(4y^2 + 10xy + 25x^2)$$

6. Factorize : $20x^2 - 9x + 1$.
   [Board Term I, 2016, Set-7AEOLQR]

Sol. Given expression $= 20x^2 - 9x + 1$
$$= 20x^2 - 5x - 4x + 1$$
$$= 5x(4x - 1) - 1(4x - 1)$$
$$= (4x - 1)(5x - 1)$$

7. Factorize : $6 - x + x^2$.
   [Board Term I, 2016, Set 20-CNJE9]

Sol. Given expression $= 6 - x - x^2 = 6 - 3x + 2x - x^2$
$$= 3(2 - x) + x(2 - x)$$
$$= (2 - x)(3 + x)$$

8. Write the factors of the polynomial :
   $x^2 + 5\sqrt{2}\,x + 12$.

Sol. Given expression $= x^2 + 5\sqrt{2}\,x + 12$
$$= x^2 + 3\sqrt{2}\,x + 2\sqrt{2}\,x + 12$$
$$= x(x + 3\sqrt{2}) + 2\sqrt{2}(x + 3\sqrt{2})$$
$$= (x + 3\sqrt{2})(x + 2\sqrt{2}).$$
Hence, Factors are $x + 3\sqrt{2}$ and $x + 2\sqrt{2}$.

9. Find the value of k, if $x - 2$ is a factor of $p(x) = 2x^2 + 3x - k$.

Sol. Given, $p(x) = 2x^2 + 3x - k$
$\because (x - 2)$ is a factor of $p(x)$.
$\Rightarrow \quad x - 2 = 0$
$\therefore \quad x = 2$
On putting $x = 2$, we have
Then $\quad p(2) = 0$
$\Rightarrow \quad p(2) = 2 \times (2)^2 + 3 \times 2 - k = 0$
$\Rightarrow \quad 8 + 6 - k = 0$
$\Rightarrow \quad 14 - k = 0$
$\quad\quad k = 14.$

10. Find the value of k, if $(x - 1)$ is a factor of
$$p(x) = 4x^3 + 3x^2 - 4x + k.$$

Sol. Given, $p(x) = 4x^3 + 3x^2 - 4x + k$

$\because$ $(x - 1)$ is a factor of $p(x)$.

$\Rightarrow$ $\quad x - 1 = 0$

$\therefore$ $\quad\quad x = 1$

On putting $x = 1$, we have

$\therefore$ $\quad p(1) = 0$

$\Rightarrow$ $\quad 4(1)^3 + 3(1)^2 - 4(1) + k = 0$

$\Rightarrow$ $\quad 4 + 3 - 4 + k = 0 \Rightarrow k = -3.$

11. Write the factors of polynomial
$$4x^2 + y^2 + 4xy + 8x + 4y + 4.$$

Sol. Given expression $= 4x^2 + y^2 + 4xy + 8x + 4y + 4$

$= (2x)^2 + (y)^2 + (2)^2 + 2 \times 2x \times y + 2$
$$\times\, 2x \times 2 + 2 \times y \times 2$$

$= (2x + y + 2)^2.$

Hence, Factor is $(2x + y + 2)$

12. If $f(x)$ be a polynomial such that $f\left(-\dfrac{1}{3}\right) = 0$, then calculate one factor of $f(x)$.

Sol. Since, $\quad f\left(-\dfrac{1}{3}\right) = 0$

$\therefore$ $-\dfrac{1}{3}$ is a zero of polynomial $f(x)$

Hence, $\left(x + \dfrac{1}{3}\right)$ or $(3x + 1)$ is a factor of $f(x)$.

13. Write the factors of $a^7 + ab^6$.

Sol. Given expression $= a^7 + ab^6 = a(a^6 + b^6)$

Therefore, factors are a and $(a^6 + b^6)$.

14. Write one factor of $(x + 1)^3 - (x + 1)$.

Sol. Given expression $= (x + 1)^3 - (x + 1)$

$= (x + 1)\,[(x + 1)^2 - 1]$

Hence, One factor of $(x + 1)^3 - (x + 1)$ is $(x + 1)$.

15. Write the factors of $a^3 - 1$.

Sol. Given expression $= a^3 - 1 = (a - 1)(a^2 + 1 + a \times 1)$

Then factors of $(a^3 - 1)$ are $(a - 1)$ and $(a^2 + 1 + a)$.

Short Answer Type Questions I

(2 Marks Each)

1. Give possible expressions for the length and the breadth of each of the following rectangles, in which their areas are given.

(i) Area $= 25a^2 - 35a + 12$

(ii) Area $= 35y^2 + 13y - 12.$ [NCERT]

Sol. (i)

$\therefore$ Area of rectangle $= 25a^2 - 35a + 12$

$= 25a^2 - (20 + 15)a + 12$

[by splitting the middle term]

$= 25a^2 - 20a - 15a + 12$

$= 5a(5a - 4) - 3(5a - 4)$

$= (5a - 4)\,(5a - 3)$

Hence, possible expression for length $= (5a - 3)$ and possible expression for breadth $= (5a - 4)$.

(ii) $\because$ Area of rectangle $= 35y^2 + 13y - 12$

$= 35y^2 + 28y - 15y - 12$

$= 7y\,(5y + 4) - 3(5y + 4)$

$= (5y + 4)(7y - 3)$

Hence, possible expression for length $= (5y + 4)$ and breadth $= (7y - 3)$.

2. Check, whether $(7 + 3x)$ is a factor of $3x^3 + 7x$.

   [NCERT]

Sol. Let $f(x) = 3x^3 + 7x$ and $g(x) = 7 + 3x$

On putting $g(x) = 0$, we get

$\quad 7 + 3x = 0$

$\Rightarrow$ $\quad 3x = -7$ $\quad \therefore x = \dfrac{-7}{3}$

Thus, zero of $g(x)$ is $x = \dfrac{-7}{3}$.

Again, on putting $x \neq -\dfrac{7}{3}$ in $f(x)$, we get

$$f\left(\frac{-7}{3}\right) = 3\left(\frac{-7}{3}\right)^3 + 7\left(\frac{-7}{3}\right) = 3\left(-\frac{343}{27}\right) - \frac{49}{3}$$

$$= -\frac{343}{9} - \frac{49}{3} = \frac{-343 - 147}{9} = \frac{-490}{9}$$

Here, $f\left(\dfrac{-7}{3}\right) = 0$ $i.e.$, the remainder obtained on dividing $f(x)$ by $7 + 3x$ is not zero.

Hence, $g(x) = 7 + 3x$ is not factor of

$\quad f(x) = 3x^3 - 7x.$

$\quad f(x) = 3x^3 - 7x.$

3. Show that $(x - 1)$ is a factor of the polynomial $f(x) = 2x^3 - 3x^2 + 7x - 6$.

   [Board Term I, 2012, Set-41]

Sol. Given, $\quad f(x) = 2x^3 - 3x^2 + 7x - 6$

$\therefore$ $(x - 1)$ is a factor of $f(x)$.

$\Rightarrow$ $\quad x - 1 = 0$

$\therefore$ $\quad\quad x = 1$

On putting $x = 1$, we get

Thus, $f(1) = 2 \times 1^3 - 3 \times 1^2 + 7 \times 1 - 6$

$= 2 - 3 + 7 - 6 = 0$

Hence, $(x - 1)$ is a factor of $f(x)$.

4. For what value of k, $(x + 1)$ is a factor of $p(x) = kx^2 - x - 4$?   [Board Term I, 2012, Set-43]

Sol. Given, $p(x) = kx^2 - x - 4$

$\because$ $(x + 1)$ is a factor of $p(x)$, then

$\therefore$ $x + 1 = 0$

$\therefore$ $x = -1$

On putting $x = -1$, we have

$\therefore$ $p(-1) = 0$

$\therefore$ $k(-1)^2 - (-1) - 4 = 0$

$\therefore$ $k + 1 - 4 = 0 \Rightarrow k - 3 = 0$

$k = 3$

5. Find the value of 'k' if $(x - 1)$ is a factor of $p(x) = 2x^2 + kx + \sqrt{2}$ [Board Term I, 2014]

Sol. Given, $p(x) = 2x^2 + kx + \sqrt{2}$

$\because$ $(x - 1)$ is a factor of $p(x)$, then

$\therefore$ $x - 1 = 0$

$\therefore$ $x = 1$

On putting $x = 1$, we have

$\therefore$ $p(1) = 0$

$\Rightarrow$ $2(1)^2 + k(1) + \sqrt{2} = 0$

$\Rightarrow$ $2 + k + \sqrt{2} = 0$

$\therefore$ $k = -2 - \sqrt{2}$

6. For what value of k, is the polynomial $p(x) = 2x^3 - kx^2 + 3x + 10$ exactly divisible by $(x + 2)$?   [Board Term I, 2014]

Sol. Given, $p(x) = 2x^3 - kx^2 + 3x + 10$

$\therefore$ $(x + 2)$ is a factor of $p(x)$.

$\therefore$ $x + 2 = 0$

$\therefore$ $x = -2$

On putting $x = -2$, we have

$\therefore$ $p(-2) = 0$

$\Rightarrow$ $2(-2)^3 - k(-2)^2 + 3(-2) + 10 = 0$

$\Rightarrow$ $-16 - 4k - 6 + 10 = 0$

$\Rightarrow$ $-4k - 12 = 0$

$\Rightarrow$ $4k = -12$

$\therefore$ $k = \dfrac{-12}{4} = -3$

7. Find the value of 'a' for which $(x - 1)$ is a factor of the polynomial $a^2x^3 - 4ax + 4a - 1$.

[Board Term I, 2016, Set-QGL21F5]

Sol. Given, $f(x) = a^2x^3 - 4ax + 4a - 1$

$\because$ $(x - 1)$ is a factor of $f(x)$.

$\therefore$ $x - 1 = 0$

$\therefore$ $x = 1$

On putting $x = 1$, we have

$f(1) = 0$

$\Rightarrow$ $a^2(1)^3 - 4a(1) + 4a - 1 = 0$

$\Rightarrow$ $a^2 - 4a + 4a - 1 = 0$

$\Rightarrow$ $a^2 - 1 = 0$

$\therefore$ $a = \pm 1$

8. Find the value of k, if $x - 2$ is a factor of $p(x) = x^2 + kx + 2k$.

[Board Term I, 2016, Set-JQ22L5C]

Sol. Given, $f(x) = x^2 + kx + 2k$

$\because$ $(x - 2)$ is a factor of $f(x)$.

$\therefore$ $x - 2 = 0$

$\therefore$ $x = 2$

$\therefore$ $f(2) = 0$

$\Rightarrow$ $(2)^2 + k(2) + 2k = 0$

$\Rightarrow$ $4 + 2k + 2k = 0$

$\Rightarrow$ $4 + 4k = 0$

$\Rightarrow$ $4k = -4$

$\therefore$ $k = \dfrac{-4}{4} = -1$

9. Find the value of k, so that polynomial $x^3 + 3x^2 - kx - 3$ has one factor as $x + 3$.

[Board Term I, 2016, Set-7AEDLQR]

Sol. Given, $f(x) = x^3 + 3x^2 - kx - 3$

$\because$ $(x + 3)$ is a factor of $f(x) = x^3 + 3x^2 - kx - 3$

$\therefore$ $x + 3 = 0$

$\therefore$ $x = -3$

On putting $x = -3$, we have

Now, $f(-3) = 0$

$\Rightarrow$ $(-3)^3 + 3(-3)^2 - k(-3) - 3 = 0$

$\Rightarrow$ $-27 + 27 + 3k - 3 = 0$

$\Rightarrow$ $3k - 3 = 0$

$\therefore$ $k = 1$

Short Answer Type Questions II

(3 Marks Each)

1. If $(x - 2)$ and $\left(x - \dfrac{1}{2}\right)$ are factors of $px^2 + 5x + r$, then show that $p = r$.

[Board Term I, 2012, Set 18], [NCERT Exemplar]

Sol. Let $f(x) = px^2 + 5x + r$

$\therefore$ $(x - 2)$ and $\left(x - \dfrac{1}{2}\right)$ are the factors of $f(x)$.

$\therefore x = 2, \dfrac{1}{2}$

Now, $f(2) = 0$ and $F\left(\dfrac{1}{2}\right) = 0$

$f(2) = 0 \Rightarrow 4p + 10 + r = 0$

$\Rightarrow \quad 4p + r = -10$ ...(1)

$f\left(\dfrac{1}{2}\right) = 0$ or, $\dfrac{p}{4} + \dfrac{5}{2} + r = 0$

$\Rightarrow \quad p + 10 + 4r = 0$

$\Rightarrow \quad p + 4r = -10$ ...(2)

According to the question,

Equations (1) = (2) as both are equal to –10.

$p + 4r = 4p + r$

$\Rightarrow \qquad 4r - r = 4p - p$

$\Rightarrow \qquad\qquad 3r = 3p$

$\Rightarrow \qquad\qquad r = p$

Hence proud

2. If $x - a$ is the factor of $3x^2 - mx - nx$, then prove that $a = \dfrac{m + n}{3}$.   [Board Term I, 2012, Set-19]

Sol. Given, $p(x) = 3x^2 - mx - nx$

$\therefore$ $(x - a)$ is a factor of $p(x)$, then

$\therefore$ $x - a = 0$

$\therefore$ $x = a$

On putting $x = a$, we have

$\therefore$ $p(a) = 0$

$\Rightarrow 3(a)^2 - m \times a - n \times a = 0$

$\Rightarrow a[3a - m - n] = 0, a \neq 0$

$\Rightarrow 3a - m - n = 0 \Rightarrow 3a = m + n$

$\therefore$ $a = \dfrac{m + n}{3}$.

3. If $(3x - 2)$ is a factor of $3x^3 + x^2 - 20x + 12$, find other factors.   [Board Term I, 2012, Set-66]

Sol. Let, $p(x) = 3x^3 + x^2 - 20x + 12$

Given $(3x - 2)$ is a factor of $p(x)$.

Now, by long division method,

$$
\begin{array}{r}
x^2 + x - 6 \\
3x - 2 \overline{) 3x^3 + x^2 - 20x + 12} \\
\underline{3x^3 - 2x^2} \\
3x^2 - 20x + 12 \\
\underline{3x^2 - 2x} \\
18x + 12 \\
\underline{18x + 12} \\
0
\end{array}
$$

and $x^2 + x - 6 = x^2 + 3x - 2x - 6$

$\qquad\qquad = x(x + 3) - 2(x + 3)$

$\qquad\qquad = (x + 3)(x - 2)$

Hence, the other factors are $(x - 2)$ and $(x + 3)$.

4. Find the value of a for which $(x - a)$ is a factor of the polynomial $x^6 - ax^5 + x^4 - ax^3 + 3x - a + 2$.

[Board Term I, 2012, Set-46]

Sol. $\because$ Let $p(x) = x^6 - ax^5 + x^4 - ax^3 + 3x - a + 2$

$\therefore$ $(x - a)$ is a factor of the polynomial $p(x)$, then

$x - a = 0$

$\therefore$ $x = a$

On putting $x = a$, we get

$p(a) = 0$

$\Rightarrow \quad a^6 - a \times a^5 + a^4 - a \times a^3 + 3 \times a - a + 2 = 0$

$\Rightarrow \quad a^6 - a^6 + a^4 + 3a - a + 2 = 0$

$\Rightarrow \quad 2a = 2 \therefore a = -1.$

5. Factorize : $x^3 - 3x^2 - 9x - 5$.

[Board Term I, 2012, 2014 Set-42], NCERT

Sol. Let, $p(x) = x^3 - 3x^2 - 9x - 5$,

On putting $x = -1$, we get

$p(-1) = -1 - 3 + 9 - 5 = 0$

Since, $(x + 1)$ is a factor of $x^3 - 3x^2 - 9x - 5$

$\therefore$ $(x^3 - 3x^2 - 9x - 5) = (x + 1)(x^2 - 4x - 5)$

[by splitting the middle term]

$x^2 - 4x - 5 = x^2 - 5x + x - 5$

$\qquad\qquad = x(x - 5) + 1(x - 5)$

$\qquad\qquad = (x + 1)(x - 5)$

Hence, other factors are : $(x + 1)$ and $(x - 5)$

6. Check whether $p(x)$ is a multiple of $g(x)$ or not.

$p(x) = x^4 - 2x^3 + 3x^2 + 4x$ and $g(x) = x - 1$

Sol. Given, $\qquad p(x) = x^4 - 2x^3 + 3x^2 + 4x$

and $\qquad\qquad g(x) = x - 1$

We have, $g(x) = x - 1$

For the zero of $g(x)$, put $g(x) = 0$

$\therefore$ $x - 1 = 0 \therefore x = 1$

On putting $x = 1$ in $p(x)$, we get

$p(1) = 1 - 2 + 3 + 4 = 6 \neq 0$

i.e., the remainder obtained on dividing $p(x)$ by $g(x)$ is not zero. Hence, $g(x)$ is not a factor of $p(x)$. i.e., $p(x)$ is not a multiple of $g(x)$.

7. Find k, if $x^{51} + 2x^{60} + 3x + k$ is divisible by $x + 1$.

Sol. Let $p(x) = x^{51} + 2x^{60} + 3x + k$

Given that, $p(x)$ is divisible by $(x + 1)$

$\therefore$ $x + 1 = 0$

$\therefore$ $x = -1$

On putting $x = -1$, we get

$\therefore \quad p(-1) = 0$

$\Rightarrow \quad (-1)^{51} + 2(-1)^{60} + 3(-1) + k = 0$

$\Rightarrow \quad -1 + 2 - 3 + k = 0 \Rightarrow k - 4 + 2 = 0$

$\Rightarrow \quad k - 2 = 0 \qquad \therefore k = 2$

8. Find m and n, if $(x + 2)$ and $(x + 1)$ are the factors of $x^3 + 3x^2 - 2mx + n$.

Sol. Let $f(x) = x^3 + 3x^2 - 2mx + n$

Since, $(x + 2)$ and $(x + 1)$ are the factors of $f(x)$.

$\therefore x = -2$ and -1

Then, $f(-2) = 0$

$\Rightarrow (-2)^3 + 3(-2)^2 - 2m(-2) + n = 0$

$\Rightarrow -8 + 12 + 4m + n = 0$

$\Rightarrow 4m + n = -4 \qquad\qquad ...(i)$

and $f(-1) = 0$

$\Rightarrow (-1)^3 + 3(-1)^2 - 2m(-1) + n = 0$

$\Rightarrow -1 + 3 + 2m + n = 0$

$\Rightarrow 2m + n = -2 \qquad\qquad ...(ii)$

On multiplying eq. (ii) by 2 and then subtracting eq. (i) from eq. (ii), we get

$4m + n - (4m + 2n) = -4 - (-4)$

$4m + n - 4m - 2n = 0 \therefore n = 0$

Put $n = 0$ from equation (ii) we get

$2m + 0 = -2 \therefore m = -1$

Long Answer Type Questions

(4 Marks Each)

1. Without actual division, show that $f(x) = 2x^4 - 6x^3 + 3x^2 + 3x - 2$ is exactly divisible by $x^2 - 3x + 2$.

[Board Term I, 2013, 2012, Set-48; 2011, Set-13], [NCERT Exemplar]

Sol. Let, $g(x) = x^2 - 3x + 2$

[By splitting the middle term]

$= x^2 - 2x - x + 2$

$= x(x - 2) - 1(x - 2)$

$= (x - 2)(x - 1)$

Zero of $x - 2$ is 2, as $x - 2 = 0 \therefore x = 2$

Zero of $x - 1$ is 1, as $x - 1 = 0 \therefore x = 1$

Now, $f(x) = 2x^4 - 6x^3 + 3x^2 + 3x - 2$

$f(2) = 2(2^4) - 6(2^3) + 3(2^2) + 3(2) - 2$

$= 32 - 48 + 12 + 6 - 2 = 0$

and $f(1) = 2(1)^4 - 6(1)^3 + 3(1)^2 + 3(1) - 2$

$= 2 - 6 + 3 + 3 - 2 = 0$

$\therefore (x - 1)$ and $(x - 2)$ are the factors of $f(x)$.

Hence, $f(x)$ is exactly divisible by $g(x)$.

2. Using factor theorem, factorize $x^3 - 2x^2 - 5x + 6$.

[Board Term I, 2012, Set-69]

Sol. Let, $p(x) = x^3 - 2x^2 - 5x + 6$

On putting $x = 1$, we have

$p(1) = (1)^3 - 2(1)^2 - 5 \times 1 + 6$

$= 1 - 2 - 5 + 6 = 0$

Hence, $(x - 1)$ is a factor of $p(x)$, then

$x^3 - 2x^2 - 5x + 6 = x^2(x - 1) - x(x - 1) - 6(x - 1)$

$= (x - 1)(x^2 - x - 6)$

[By splitting the middle term]

$= (x - 1)(x^2 - 3x + 2x - 6)$

$= (x - 1)[x(x - 3) + 2(x + 3)]$

$= (x - 1)(x - 3)(x + 2)$.

3. Verify that $(x - 1)$, $(x - 2)$ and $(2x + 1)$ are the factors of the polynomial $2x^3 - 5x^2 + x + 2$.

[Board Term I, 2012, Set-58]

Sol. Let, $p(x) = 2x^3 - 5x^2 + x + 2$

On putting $x = 1$, we have

$p(1) = 2(1)^3 - 5(1)^2 + 1 + 2$

$= 2 - 5 + 1 + 2 = 0$

Hence, $(x - 1)$ is a factor of $p(x)$.

Again, On putting $x = 2$, we have

$p(2) = 2(2)^3 - 5(2)^2 + 2 + 2$

$= 16 - 20 + 2 + 2 = 0$

Hence, $(x - 2)$ is also a factor of $p(x)$.

and on putting $x = -\dfrac{1}{2}$ in $p(x)$

$\therefore \; p\left(-\dfrac{1}{2}\right) = 2\times\left(-\dfrac{1}{2}\right)^3 - 5\left(-\dfrac{1}{2}\right)^2 + \left(-\dfrac{1}{2}\right) + 2$

$= 2\times\left(-\dfrac{1}{8}\right) - 5\times\dfrac{1}{4} - \dfrac{1}{2} + \dfrac{2}{1}$

$= \dfrac{-1 - 5 - 2 + 8}{4} = \dfrac{0}{4} = 0$

Hence, $\left(x + \dfrac{1}{2}\right)$ or $(2x + 1)$ is a factor of $p(x)$.

4. Factorize: $2x^3 - 9x^2 + x + 12$.

[Board Term I, 2013]

Sol. Let, $p(x) = 2x^3 - 9x^2 + x + 12$

On putting $x = -1$ in $p(x)$, we have

$p(-1) = 2 \times (-1)^3 - 9(-1)^2 + (-1) + 12$

$= -2 - 9 - 1 + 12$

$= -12 + 12 = 0$

Hence, $(x + 1)$ is a factor of $p(x)$, then we have

$2x^3 - 9x^2 + x + 12$

$$= 2x^2 (x + 1) - 11x (x + 1) + 12 (x + 1)$$

$$= (x + 1) (2x^2 - 11x + 12)$$

[By splitting the middle term]

$$= (x + 1) [2x^2 - 8x - 3x + 12]$$

$$= (x + 1)[2x (x - 4) - 3 (x - 4)]$$

$$= (x + 1) (x - 4) (2x - 3)$$

Hence, required factors are $(x + 1) (x - 4)$ and $(2x - 3)$.

5. Show by long divisoin method that $x - 3$ is a factor of $2x^4 + 3x^3 - 26x^2 - 5x + 6$.

[Board Term I, 2014]

Sol. Let, $p(x) = 2x^4 + 3x^3 - 26x^2 - 5x + 6$,

$\because$ $(x - 3)$ is a factor of $p(x)$.

then it completely divide $p(x)$

By long division method,

$$
\begin{array}{r}
2x^3 + 9x^2 + x - 2 \\
x - 3 \overline{)\, 2x^4 + 3x^3 - 26x^2 - 5x + 6} \\
\underline{2x^4 - 6x^3} \\
9x^3 - 26x^2 \\
\underline{9x^3 - 27x^2} \\
x^2 - 5x \\
\underline{x^2 - 3x} \\
- 2x + 6 \\
\underline{- 2x + 6} \\
2
\end{array}
$$

$\therefore$ Quotient $= 2x^3 + 9x^2 + x - 2$

and $\therefore$ remainder $= 0$.

Hence, $(x - 3)$ is a factor of $p(x)$.

6. Factorize: $x^3 + 13x^2 + 32x + 20$.

[Board Term I, 2014]

Sol. Let $p(x) = x^3 + 13x^2 + 32x + 20$

On putting $x = - 2$ in $p(x)$, we have

$$p(-2) = (-2)^3 + 13(-2)^2 + 32(-2) + 20$$

$$= - 8 + 52 - 64 + 20 = 0$$

Hence, $(x + 2)$ is factor of $p(x)$.

$$x^3 + 13x^2 + 32x + 20 = (x + 2) (x^2 + 11x + 10)$$

or, $x^2 + 11x + 10 = x^2 + 10x + x + 10$

$$= x(x + 10) + 1(x + 10)$$

$$= (x + 1) (x + 10)$$

Hence, factors are $(x + 2) (x + 1)$ and $(x + 10)$

Alternate method :

Factors of $20 = (\pm 1, \pm 2, \pm 4, \pm 5, \pm 10, \pm 20)$

$$p(x) = x^3 + 13x^2 + 32x + 20$$

On putting $x = -1$, we have

$$p(-1) = (-1)^3 + 13(-1)^2 + 32(-1) + 20$$

$$= -1 + 13 - 32 + 20$$

$$= 33 - 33 = 0$$

$\therefore$ $x = - 1$ is a zero of $p(x)$, and $(x + 1)$ is a factor of $p(x)$

Then, $x^3 + 13x^2 + 32x + 20$

$$= x^2(x + 1) + 12x(x + 1) + 20(x + 1)$$

$$= (x + 1) (x^2 + 12x + 20)$$

[By splitting the middle term]

$$= (x + 1) [x(x + 10) + 2(x + 10)]$$

$$= (x + 1) (x + 2) (x + 10)$$

7. Using factor theorem, find the value if 'a' if $2x^4 - ax^3 + 4x^2 - x + 2$ is divisible by $2x + 1$.

[Board Term I, 2014]

Sol. Let $p(x) = 2x^4 - ax^3 + 4x^2 - x + 2$

If $(2x + 1)$ is a factor of $p(x)$, then $2x + 1 = 0$

$\therefore$ $x = \dfrac{-1}{2}$ is a zero of the polynomial $p(x)$.

$\therefore$ $p\left(\dfrac{-1}{2}\right) = 0$

$\Rightarrow p\left(\dfrac{-1}{2}\right) = 2 \times \left(\dfrac{-1}{2}\right)^4 - a\left(\dfrac{-1}{2}\right)^3 + 4\left(\dfrac{-1}{2}\right)^2 - \left(\dfrac{-1}{2}\right) + 2$

$\Rightarrow 2 \times \dfrac{1}{16} + a \times \dfrac{1}{8} + 4 \times \dfrac{1}{4} + \dfrac{1}{2} + 2 = 0$

$\Rightarrow \dfrac{1}{8} + \dfrac{a}{8} + 1 + \dfrac{1}{2} + 2 = 0$

$\Rightarrow \dfrac{29}{8} + \dfrac{a}{8} = 0$

$\Rightarrow \dfrac{29 + a}{8} = 0 \Rightarrow 29 + a = 0$

$\therefore$ $a = - 29$

8. Factorize : $x^3 - 12x^2 + 47x - 60$.

[Board Term I, 2014]

Sol. Let $p(x) = x^3 - 12x^2 + 47x - 60$

On putting $x = 3$ in $p(x)$, we have

$$p(3) = (3)^3 - 12(3)^2 + 47(3) - 60$$

$$= 27 - 12 \times 9 + 141 - 60$$

$$= 27 - 108 + 141 - 60$$

$$= 168 - 168 = 0$$

$\therefore$ $(x - 3)$ is a factor of $p(x)$.

Now, $x^3 - 12x^2 + 47x - 60$

$$= x^2(x - 3) - 9x(x - 3) + 20(x - 3)$$

$$= (x - 3) (x^2 - 9x + 20)$$

$$= (x - 3) (x^2 - 5x - 4x + 20)$$

$$= (x - 3) [x(x - 5) - 4(x - 5)]$$

$$= (x - 3) (x - 4) (x - 5)$$

9. Find the value of p for which the polynomial $x^3 + 4x^2 - px + 8$ is exactly divisible by $x - 2$. Hence factorize the polynomial.

[Board Term I, 2014]

Sol. Let $f(x) = x^3 + 4x^2 - px + 8$

$p(x)$ is exactly divisible by $x - 2$.

On putting $x = 2$, we have

$\therefore \qquad f(2) = 0$

$\Rightarrow \qquad f(2) = (2)^3 + 4(2)^2 - p(2) + 8 = 0$

$\Rightarrow \qquad 8 + 16 - 2p + 8 = 0$

$\Rightarrow \qquad 32 - 2p = 0$

$\therefore \qquad p = 16$

$\therefore \qquad f(x) = x^3 + 4x^2 - 16x + 8$

Then,

$x^3 + 4x^2 - 16x + 8 = x^2(x - 2) + 6x(x - 2) - 4(x - 2)$

$= (x - 2)(x^2 + 6x - 4)$

10. Using factor theorem, show that $(m - n)$, $(n - p)$ and $(p - m)$ are factors of

$m(n^2 - p^2) + n(p^2 - m^2) + p(m^2 - n^2)$.

[Board Term I, 2015, Set-20UIXH]

Sol. Let $f = m(n^2 - p^2) + n(p^2 - m^2 + p(m^2 - n^2)$

Now, using factor theorem,

$f(m = n) = n(n^2 - p^2) + n(p^2 - n^2) + p(n^2 - n^2)$

$= n(n^2 - p^2) - n(n^2 - p^2) + 0$

$= 0$

$m - n$ is a factor of f

Similarly $f(n = p)$ 0 & $f(p = m) = 0$

$n - p$ is a factor of f.

and $p - m$ is a factor of f.

11. Verify if 1 and -3 are zeroes of the polynomial $3x^3 + 5x^2 - 11x + 3$. If yes, then factorize the polynomial.

[Board Term I, 2015, Set-20UI6YH]

Sol. Let $p(x) = 3x^3 + 5x^2 - 11x + 3$

On putting $x = 1$, we have

$p(1) = 3 + 5 - 11 + 3 = 0$

$\therefore$ 1 is a zero of $p(x)$

Again, on putting $x = -3$, we have

$p(-3) = -81 + 45 + 33 + 3 = 0$

$\therefore$ -3 is a zero of $p(x)$

Hence, $(x - 1)(x + 3) = x^2 + 2x - 3$ is a factor of $p(x)$

Now, $\dfrac{p(x)}{x^2 + 2x - 3} = 3x - 1$, when we divide

physically

Hence, required factors are $(x - 1)$, $(x + 3)$ and $(3x - 1)$.

12. State factor theorem. Using factor theorem factories $x^3 - 3x^2 - x + 3$.

[Board Term I, 2015, Set-2]

Sol. Factor theorem : If $p(x)$ is a polynomial of degree $n \geq 1$ and a is any real number, then

(i) $(x - a)$ is a factor of $p(x)$, if $p(a) = 0$

(ii) $p(a) = 0$, if $(x - a)$ is a factor of $p(x)$.

Let $p(x) = x^3 - 3x^2 - x + 3$

The factors of the constant term 3 are ± 1, ± 3

$p(1) = 1^3 - 3(1)^2 - 1 + 3 = 0$

$\therefore$ $(x - 1)$ is a factor of $p(x)$.

Again, $p(-1) = (-1)^3 - 3(-1)^2 - (-1) + 3 = 0$

$\therefore$ $(x + 1)$ is a factor of $p(x)$.

and $p(3) = 3^3 - 3(3)^2 - 3 + 3 = 0$

$\therefore$ $(x - 3)$ is a factor of $p(x)$

Hence, $(x - 1)$, $(x + 1)$ and $(x - 3)$ are the factors of $p(x)$.

13. If $x + 4$ is a factor of the polynomial $x^3 - x^2 - 14x + 24$ find its other factors.

[Board Term I, 2016, Set-JQ22LC]

Sol. Let $p(x) = x^3 - x^2 - 14x + 24$

$\because$ $x + 4$ is a factor the polynomial $x^3 - x^2 - 14x + 24$

To get other factors, dividing $p(x)$ by $(x + 4)$,

By long division method

$$
\begin{array}{r}
x^2 - 5x + 6 \\
x + 4 \overline{)\, x^3 - x^2 - 14x + 24} \\
\underline{x^3 + 4x^2} \qquad\qquad \\
-5x^2 + 14x \qquad \\
\underline{-5x^3 - 20x} \qquad \\
6x + 24 \\
\underline{6x + 24} \\
0
\end{array}
$$

$\therefore$ $x^2 - 5x + 6 = x^2 - 3x - 2x + 6$

$= x(x - 3) - 2(x - 3) = (x - 3)(x - 2)$

Hence, the other factors are $(x - 3)$ and $(x - 2)$.

14. Verify if -2 and 3 are zeroes of the polynomial $2x^3 - 3x^2 - 11x + 6$. If yes, factorize the polynomials.

[Board Term I, 2016, Set-7AEDLQR]

Sol. Let $p(x) = 2x^3 - 3x^2 - 11x + 6$

for $x = -2$, we have

$p(-2) = 2(-2)^3 - 3(-2)^2 - 11(-2) + 6$

$= -16 - 12 + 22 + 6 = -28 + 28 = 0$

and for $x = 3$, we have

$p(3) = 2(3)^3 - 3(3)^2 - 11(3) + 6$

$= 54 - 27 - 33 + 6 = 60 - 60 = 0$

$\therefore$ -2 and 3 are zeroes of the given polynomial

Now, $p(x) = 2x^3 - 3x^2 - 11x + 6$

$\therefore (x + 2)(x - 3) = x^2 - x - 6$ is a factor of $p(x)$

Now, by division method,

$$
\begin{array}{r}
2x - 1 \\
x^2 - x - 6\,\overline{\smash{)}\,2x^3 - 3x^2 - 11x + 6} \\
\underline{2x^3 - 2x^2 - 12x} \\
-x^2 + x + 6 \\
\underline{-x^3 + x + 6} \\
0
\end{array}
$$

$\therefore \dfrac{p(x)}{x^2 - x - 6} = 2x - 1$

Hence, $p(x) = (2x - 1)(x^2 - x - 6)$

$= (2x - 1)(x^2 - 3x + 2x - 6)$

$= (2x - 1)[x(x - 3) + 2(x - 3)]$

$= (2x - 1)(x - 3)(x + 2)$

15. Factorize : $9x^3 - 3x^2 - 5x - 1$.

[Board Term I, 2016, Set-20CNJE9]

Sol. Let $p(x) = 9x^3 - 3x^2 - 5x - 1$

On putting $x = 1$, in $p(x)$ we have

$p(1) = 9 - 3 - 5 - 1 = 0$

$\therefore x - 1$ is a factor of $p(x)$

Now, $9x^3 - 3x^2 - 5x - 1 = 9x^2(x - 1) + 6x(x - 1) + 1(x - 1)$

$= (x - 1)(9x^2 + 6x + 1) = (x - 1)(3x + 1)^2$

Hence, $p(x) = (x - 1)(3x + 1)(3x + 1)$

16. If $2x^3 + ax^2 + bx - 6$ has $(x - 1)$ as a factor and leaves a remainder 2 when divided by $x - 2$, find the relation between a and b.

[Board Term I, 2016, Set-BQ56IZK]

Sol. Let $f(x) = 2x^3 + ax^2 + bx - 6$ ...(i)

$\because (x - 1)$ is a factor of $f(x)$, then by factor theorem

$f(1) = 0$ ...(ii)

On putting $x = 1$ in (1) we get

$f(1) = 2 + a + b - 6 = 0$

$\Rightarrow \quad a + b - 4 = 0 \Rightarrow a + b = 4$ ...(iii)

When $f(x)$ is divided by $(x - 2)$ it leaves remainder

$\therefore$ By remainder theorem $f(2) = 2$ ...(iv)

On putting $x = 2$ in (i) and using (4), we get

$f(2) = 2(2)^3 + a(2)^2 + b(2) - 6 = 2$

$\Rightarrow \quad 16 + 4a + 2b - 6 = 2$

$\Rightarrow \quad 4a + 2b + 8 = 0$

$\Rightarrow \quad 2a + b + 4 = 0$

$\Rightarrow \quad -2a - b = 4$ ...(v)

From (iii) and (v),

$a + b = -2a - b$

$\Rightarrow \quad 2a + b + a + b = 0$

$\Rightarrow \quad 3a + 2b = 0$

$\Rightarrow \quad 3a = -2b$

$\therefore \quad a = \dfrac{-2}{3}b$

17. Using long division method, show that the polynomial $p(x) = x^3 + 1$ is divisible by $q(x) = x + 1$. Verify result using factor theorem.

[Board Term I, 2016, Set-QGL21F5]

Sol. Given $p(x) = x^3 + 1$

and $q(x) = x + 1$

Now, by division method,

$$
\begin{array}{r}
x^2 - x + 1 \\
x + 1\,\overline{\smash{)}\,x^3 + 1} \\
\underline{x^3 + x^2} \\
-x^2 + 1 \\
\underline{-x^2 \mp x} \\
x + 1 \\
\underline{x + 1} \\
0
\end{array}
$$

$\therefore$ Remainder = 0 and Quotient = $x^2 - x + 1$

Now, $p(x)$ is divisible by $q(x)$, where

$p(x) = x^3 + 1$, $q(x) = x + 1$

$p(-1) = (-1)^3 + 1 = -1 + 1 = 0$

Hence, $x + 1$ is a factor of $p(x)$ by factor theorem.

18. Factorize $x^3 + 2x^2 - 5x - 6$.

[Board Term I, 2016, Set-7AEDLQR]

Sol. Factor of $6 = (\pm 1, \pm 2, \pm 3, \pm 6)$

Given, $p(x) = x^3 + 2x^2 - 5x - 6$

On putting $x = -1$, we have

$p(-1) = (-1)^3 + 2(-1)^2 - 5(-1) - 6$

$= -1 + 2 + 5 - 6 = 7 - 7 = 0$

$\because x = -1$ is zero of $p(x)$ of $(x + 1)$ is a factor of $p(x)$

Now, $x^3 + 2x^2 - 5x - 6$

$= x^2(x + 1) + x(x + 1) - 6(x + 1)$

$= (x + 1)[x^2 + x - 6]$

[By splitting the middle term]

$= (x + 1)[x^2 + 3x - 2x - 6]$

$= (x + 1)[x(x + 3) - 2(x + 3)]$

$= (x + 1)(x + 3)(x - 2)$

19. Factorize $2x^4 + x^3 - 14x^2 - 19x - 6$.

[Board Term I, 2016, Set-JQ22LC]

Sol. Let $f(x) = 2x^4 + x^3 - 14x^2 - 19x - 6$

The factors of the constant term are ± 1, ± 2, ± 3 and ± 6, The factor of coefficient of x^4 is 2

$\therefore$ possible rational factors are ± 1, ± 2, ± 3, $\pm \dfrac{1}{2}, \pm \dfrac{3}{2}$

On putting $x = -1$, we have
$f(-1) = 2(-1)^4 + (-1)^3 - 14(-1)^2 - 19(-1) - 6$
$\qquad = 2 - 1 - 14 + 19 - 6$
$\qquad = 21 - 21 = 0$
and on putting $x = -2$, we have
$\qquad f(-2) = 2(-2)^4 + (-2)^3 - 14(-2)^2 - 19(-2) - 6$
$\qquad = 32 - 8 - 56 + 38 - 6$
$\qquad = 70 - 70 = 0$
$\therefore$ $(x + 1)$ and $(x + 2)$ are factors of f(x).
$\Rightarrow x^2 + 3x + 2$ is a factor of f(x).
Now, divide $f(x) = 2x^4 + x^3 + 14x^2 - 19x - 6$ by $x^2 + 3x + 2$, we have

$$
\begin{array}{r}
2x^3 - 5x - 3 \\
x^2 + 3x + 2 \overline{)\, 2x^4 + x^3 - 14x^2 - 19x - 6} \\
2x^4 + 6x^3 + 4x^2 \\
\hline
-5x^3 - 18x^2 - 19x \\
-5x^3 - 15x^2 - 10x \\
\hline
-3x^2 - 9x - 6 \\
-3x^2 - 9x - 6 \\
\hline
0
\end{array}
$$

$\therefore$ $2x^4 + x^3 - 14x^2 + 9x - 6$
$\qquad = (x^2 + 3x + 2)\,(2x^2 - 5x - 3)$
$\qquad = (x + 1)\,(x + 2)\,(2x^2 - 6x + x - 3)$
$\qquad = (x + 1)\,(x + 2)[2x(x - 3) + 1(x - 3)]$
$\qquad = (x + 1)(x + 2)\,(x - 3)\,(2x + 1)$
Hence, required factors are $(x + 1)$, $(x + 2)$, $(x - 3)$ and $(2x - 1)$.

20. Show by long division that $2x + 3$ is a factor of $p(x) = 4x^4 + 8x^3 + 5x^2 + x - 3$.

[Board Term I, 2016, Set-BQS61ZK]

Sol. Given $p(x) = 4x^4 + 8x^3 + 5x^2 + x - 3$
and $(2x + 3)$ is factor of p(x).
Now, divide p(x) by $(2x + 3)$,

$$
\begin{array}{r}
2x^3 + 9x^2 + x - 2 \\
2x + 3 \overline{)\, 4x^4 + 8x^3 + 5x^2 + x - 3} \\
4x^4 + 6x^3 \\
\hline
2x^3 - 5x^2 \\
2x^3 + 3x^2 \\
\hline
2x^2 + x \\
2x^2 + 3x \\
\hline
-2x - 3 \\
-2x - 3 \\
\hline
0
\end{array}
$$

$\therefore$ Quotient $= 2x^3 + x^2 + x - 1$ and remainder $= 0$
Hence, $(2x + 3)$ is a factor of
$p(x) = 4x^4 + 8x^3 + 5x^2 + x - 3$

21. If $x - 3$ and $x - \dfrac{1}{3}$ are factors of the polynomial $px^2 + 3x + r$, show that $p = r$.

Sol. Let $f(x) = px^2 + 3x + r$
If $(x - 3)$ is the factor of f(x).
Then, putting $x = 3$ in f(x), we get
$p(3)^2 + 3(3) + r = 0$
$\Rightarrow 9p + 9 + r = 0 \Rightarrow 9p + r = -9$ $\qquad$ ...(i)
Again, $\left(x - \dfrac{1}{3} \right)$ is the factor of f(x).

On putting $x = \dfrac{1}{3}$ in f(x), we get

$p\left(\dfrac{1}{3}\right)^2 + 3\left(\dfrac{1}{3}\right) + r = 0$

$\Rightarrow \dfrac{p}{9} + 1 + r = 0$

$\Rightarrow p + 9 + 9r = 0$

$\Rightarrow p + 9r = -9$ $\qquad$ ...(ii)
From eqs. (i) and (ii),
$9p + r = p + 9r$
$\Rightarrow 8p = 8r$
$\therefore$ $p = r$

22. If the polynomial $2x^3 + ax^2 + 7x - 6$ is exactly divisible by $2x - 1$, then find the value of a. Hence factorize the polynomial.

Sol. Let $p(x) = 2x^3 + ax^2 + 7x - 6$
$\because$ p(x) is divisible by $2x - 1$
$\therefore$ $2x - 1 = 0$
$\therefore$ $x = \dfrac{1}{2}$
On putting $x = \dfrac{1}{2}$, we have
$\therefore$ $p\left(\dfrac{1}{2}\right) = 0$

$\Rightarrow p\left(\dfrac{1}{2}\right) = 2\left(\dfrac{1}{2}\right)^3 + a\left(\dfrac{1}{2}\right)^2 + 7\left(\dfrac{1}{2}\right) - 6 = 0$

$\Rightarrow 2 \times \left(\dfrac{1}{8}\right) + a\left(\dfrac{1}{4}\right) + 7\left(\dfrac{1}{2}\right) - 6 = 0$

$\Rightarrow \dfrac{1}{4} + \dfrac{a}{4} + \dfrac{7}{2} - 6 = 0$

$\Rightarrow \dfrac{a}{4} - \dfrac{9}{4} = 0 \Rightarrow \dfrac{a - 9}{4} = 0 \Rightarrow a - 9 = 0$

$\therefore$ $a = 9$

Now, divide $p(x) = 2x^3 + 9x^2 + 7x - 6$ by $(2x - 1)$, we have

$$\require{enclose}\begin{array}{r} x^2 + 5x + 6 \\ 2x - 1 \overline{\smash{)}\; 2x^3 + 9x^2 + 7x - 3} \\ \underline{2x^3 - x^2} \\ 10x^2 - 7x \\ \underline{10x^2 - 5x} \\ 12x - 6 \\ \underline{12x - 6} \\ 0 \end{array}$$

$\therefore\ x^2 + 5x + 6 = x^2 + 3x + 2x + 6$
$\qquad = x(x + 3) + 2(x + 3)$
$\qquad = (x + 3)\ (x + 2)$

Hence, $\quad p(x) = (2x - 1)\ (x + 2)\ (x + 3)$

23. If $(x + a)$ is a factor of the polynomials $x^2 + px + q$ and $x^2 + mx + n$, then prove that $a = \dfrac{n - q}{m - p}$

Sol. Let $\quad f(x) = x^2 + px + q$

and $g(x) = x^2 + mx + n$

When $(x + a)$ divides $f(x)$, then the remainder is $f(- a)$. When $(x + a)$ divides $g(x)$ then the remainder is $g(-a)$.

Now, $f(-a) = (-a)^2 + p(-a) + q = a^2 - ap + q$

and $g(-a) = (-a)^2 + m(-a) + n = a^2 - ma + n$

Now, according to the question,

$\qquad f(-a) = g(-a)$

$\therefore \qquad a^2 - ap + q = a^2 - ma + n$

$\Rightarrow \quad -ap + ma = n - q$

$\Rightarrow \quad a(m - p) = n - q$

Hence, $a = \dfrac{n - q}{m - p}$

24. Find the values of a and b, if $x^2 - 4$ is a factor of $ax^4 + 2x^3 - 3x^2 + bx - 4$ and hence factorize if completely.

Sol. Let $p(x) = ax^4 + 2x^3 - 3x^2 + bx - 4$

$\because\ x^2 - 4$ or $(x - 2)\ (x + 2)$ is a factor of $p(x)$, then

On putting $x = 2$ in $p(x)$, we have

$\therefore\quad p(2) = a(2)^4 + 2(2)^3 - 3(2)^2 + b \times 2 - 4 = 0$

$\Rightarrow\ 16a + 16 - 12 + 2b - 4 = 0$

$\Rightarrow\ 16a + 2b = 0$

$\Rightarrow\ 8a + b = 0 \qquad\qquad$ ...(i)

On putting $x = - 2$ in $p(x)$ we have

$\therefore\ p(-2) = a(-2)^4 + 2(-2)^3 - 3(-2)^2 + b \times - 2 - 4 = 0$

$\Rightarrow\ 16a - 16 - 12 - 2b - 4 = 0$

$\Rightarrow\ 16a - 2b = 32$

$\Rightarrow\ 8a - b = 16 \qquad\qquad$ ...(ii)

On adding eqn. (i) and (ii)

$$\begin{array}{r} 8a + b = 0 \\ 8a - b = 16 \\ \hline 16a = 16 \end{array}$$

$\therefore \qquad a = 1$

From equation (1),

$8 \times 1 + b = 0 \therefore b = - 8$

$$\require{enclose}\begin{array}{r} x^2 + 2x + 1 \\ x^2 - 4 \overline{\smash{)}\; x^4 + 2x^3 - 3x^2 - 8x - 4} \\ \underline{x^4 \qquad\ - 4x^2} \\ 2x^3 + x^2 - 8x - 4 \\ \underline{2x^3 \qquad\quad - 8x} \\ x^2 \qquad\ - 4 \\ \underline{x^2 \qquad\ - 4} \\ 0 \end{array}$$

$\therefore\ p(x) = x^4 + 2x^3 - 3x^2 - 8x - 4$
$\qquad = (x^2 - 4)\ (x^2 + 2x + 1)$
$\qquad = (x - 2)\ (x + 2)\ (x + 1)^2.$

[Topic 4] Algebraic Identities

Points to be Remembered

- An algebraic identity is an algebraic equation that is true for all values of the variables occurring in it.
- Some useful algebraic identities are given below :

(i) $(x + y)^2 = x^2 + y^2 + 2xy$

(ii) $(x - y)^2 = x^2 - 2xy + y^2$

(iii) $x^2 - y^2 = (x + y)\ (x - y)$

(iv) $(x + y)^3 = x^3 + y^3 + 3xy(x + y)$

(v) $(x - y)^3 = x^3 - y^3 - 3xy(x - y)$

(vi) $x^3 + y^3 = (x + y)\ (x^2 - xy + y^2)$

(vii) $x^3 - y^3 = (x - y)\ (x^2 + xy + y^2)$

(viii) $(x + y + z)^2 = x^2 + y^2 + z^2 + 2xy + 2yz + 2zx$

(ix) $(x + a)\ (x + b) = x^2 + (a + b)x + ab$

(x) $x^3 + y^3 + z^3 - 3xyz = (x + y + z)\ (x^2 + y^2 + z^2 - xy - yz - zx)$

$\qquad$ or $= \dfrac{1}{2}(x + y + z)\ [(x - y)^2 + (y - z)^2 + (z - x)^2]$

PREVIOUS YEARS'
EXAMINATION QUESTIONS
TOPIC 4

Multiple Choice Questions
(1 Mark Each)

1. If $(a + b + c) = 5$ and $ab + bc + ca = 12$, then the value of $a^2 + b^2 + c^2$ is :
    (a) 49 (b) 1
    (c) 0 (d) −1   [NCERT Exemp.]

Sol. (b) We know that

$(a + b + c)^2 = a^2 + b^2 + c^2 + 2ab + 2bc + 2ca$

$\Rightarrow (a + b + c)^2 = a^2 + b^2 + c^2 + 2(ab + bc + ca)$

$[\because a + b + c = 5 \text{ and } ab + bc + ca = 12]$

$\Rightarrow (5)^2 = a^2 + b^2 + c^2 + 2(12)$

$\therefore a^2 + b^2 + c^2 = 25 − 24 = 1$

2. The coefficient of x in the expansion of $(x + 3)^3$ is
    (a) 1 (b) 9
    (c) 18 (d) 27   [NCERT Exemp.]

Sol. (d) $(x + 3)^3 = (x)^3 + (3)^3 + 3 \times x \times 3 \times (x + 3)$

$= x^3 + 27 + 9x(x + 3)$

$= x^3 + 27 + 9x^2 + 27x$

Hence, Co-efficient of $x = 27$

3. which of the following is a factor of $(x + y)^3 − (x^3 + y^3)$?
    (a) $x^2 + y^2 + 2xy$ (b) $x^2 + y^2 − xy$
    (c) xy^2 (d) $3xy$ [NCERT Exemp.]

Sol. (d) Given expression $= (x + y)^3 − (x^3 + y^3)$

[Using identity $a^3 + b^3 = (a + b) (a^2 + b^2 − 2ab)$]

$= (x + y)^3 − [(x + y) (x^2 + y^2 − xy)]$

$= (x + y) [(x + y)^2 − (x^2 + y^2 − xy)]$

$= (x + y) [x^2 + y^2 + 2xy − x^2 − y^2 + xy]$

[Using identity $(a + b)^2 = a^2 + b^2 + 2ab$]

$= (x + y) (3xy)$

Hence, one of the factor of given polynomial is $3xy$.

4. The value of $249^2 − 248^2$ is
    (a) 1^2 (b) 477
    (c) 487 (d) 497   [NCERT Exemp.]

Sol. (d) Given expression

$249^2 − 248^2 = (249 + 248) (249 − 248)$

$= 497 \times 1 = 497$

5. If $\dfrac{x}{y} + \dfrac{y}{x} = -1$ (x, y ≠ 0) the value of $x^3 − y^3$ is
    (a) 1 (b) −1
    (c) 0 (d) $\dfrac{1}{2}$ [NCERT Exemp.]

Sol. (c) $\because \dfrac{x}{y} + \dfrac{y}{x} = -1$

$\Rightarrow \dfrac{x^2 + y^2}{xy} = -1$

$\Rightarrow x^2 + y^2 = −xy$

$\Rightarrow x^2 + y^2 + xy = 0$ ...(i)

$\therefore$ Given expression $= x^3 − y^3$

$= (x − y) (x^2 + y^2 + xy)$

$= (x − y) (0)$ [Using equation (i)]

$= 0$

6. If $49x^2 − b = \left(7x + \dfrac{1}{2} \right)\left(7x − \dfrac{1}{2} \right)$

    Then the value of b is

    (a) 0 (b) $\dfrac{1}{\sqrt{2}}$

    (c) $\dfrac{1}{4}$ (d) $\dfrac{1}{2}$ [NCERT Exemp.]

Sol. (d) Given, $49x^2 − (\sqrt{b})^2 = \left[(7x)^2 − \left(\dfrac{1}{2} \right)^2 \right]$

[Using identity $a^2 − b^2 = (a + b) (a − b)$]

$\Rightarrow 49x^2 − (\sqrt{b})^2 = 49x^2 − \dfrac{1}{4}$

On comparing both the sides,

$\Rightarrow −(\sqrt{b})^2 = −\dfrac{1}{4}$

$\Rightarrow (\sqrt{b})^2 = \dfrac{1}{4}$

$\therefore b = \dfrac{1}{4}$

7. If $a + b + c = 0$, then $a^3 + b^3 + c^3$ is equal to
    (a) 0 (b) abc
    (c) 3abc (d) 2abc   [NCERT Exemp.]

Sol. (c) Given, $a + b + c = 0$

$\Rightarrow a + b = −c$ ...(i)

On cubing both the sides of equation (i), we get

$(a + b)^3 = (−c)^3$

$\Rightarrow a^3 + b^3 + 3ab(a + b) = (−c)^3$

[By using identity $(a + b)^3 = a^3 + b^3 + 3ab(a + b)$]

$\Rightarrow \quad a^3 + b^3 + 3ab(-c) = (-c)^3$

[By using equation (i)]

$\Rightarrow \quad a^3 + b^3 - 3abc = (-c)^3$

$\therefore \quad a^3 + b^3 + c^3 = 3abc$

8. If $x + \dfrac{1}{2} = 2$, then the value of $x^3 + \dfrac{1}{x^3}$ is

 (a) 1   (b) 2

 (c) 14   (d) 8

Sol. (b) Given, $x + \dfrac{1}{x} = 2$

On cubing both sides,

$$\left(x + \frac{1}{x}\right)^3 = (2)^3$$

$$\Rightarrow \quad x^3 + \frac{1}{x^3} + 3 \times x \times \frac{1}{x}\left(x + \frac{1}{x}\right) = 8$$

$$\Rightarrow \quad x^3 + \frac{1}{x^3} + 3(2) = 8$$

$$\therefore \quad x^3 + \frac{1}{x^3} = 8 - 6 = 2$$

9. If $(a - b) = 5$ and $ab = 28$, then the value of $a^3 - b^3$ is :

 (a) 500   (b) 420

 (c) 545   (d) 454

Sol. (c) We know that

$\therefore \quad a^3 - b^3 = (a - b)\,(a^2 + b^2 + ab)$

Given, $(a - b) = 5$

On squaring both sides, we have

$\quad a^2 + b^2 - 2ab = 25 \Rightarrow a^2 + b^2 - 2 \times 28 = 25$

$\Rightarrow \quad a^2 + b^2 = 25 + 56 = 81$

$\therefore \quad a^3 - b^3 = 5(81 + 28) = 5 \times 109 = 545$

10. If $x + \dfrac{1}{x} = 8$, then the value of $x^2 + \dfrac{1}{x^2}$ is equal to :

 (a) 64   (b) 62

 (c) 66   (d) 60

Sol. (b) Given, $x + \dfrac{1}{x} = 8$

On squaring both sides,

$$\left(x + \frac{1}{x}\right)^2 = (8)^2 \Rightarrow x^2 + \frac{1}{x^2} + 2 = 64$$

$$\therefore \quad x^2 + \frac{1}{x^2} = 64 - 2 = 62$$

Very Short Answer Type Questions
(1 Mark Each)

1. Using appropriate identify factorize $4x^2 - \dfrac{y^2}{9}$.

[Board Term I, 2012, Set QGL21F5]

Sol. Given expression $= 4x^2 - \dfrac{y^2}{9} = (2x)^2 - \left(\dfrac{y}{3}\right)^2$

$$= \left(2x + \frac{y}{3}\right)\left(2x - \frac{y}{3}\right)$$

2. If $\dfrac{x}{y} + \dfrac{y}{x} = -1$, $(x \neq y,\ y \neq 0,\ x \neq 0)$, then what is the value of $x^3 - y^3$.

Sol. Given, $\dfrac{x}{y} + \dfrac{y}{x} - 1 \Rightarrow \dfrac{x^2 + y^2}{xy} = -1$

$\Rightarrow \quad x^2 + y^2 = -xy$

$\Rightarrow \quad x^2 + y^2 + xy = 0$ ...(i)

$\therefore \quad$ Given expression $= x^3 - y^3$

$= (x - y)\,(x^2 + y^2 + xy)$

$= (x - y) \times 0$ [From equation (i)]

$= 0$

3. Simplify : $\left(x + \dfrac{1}{2}\right)\left(x + \dfrac{3}{2}\right)$.

Sol. Given expression

$$= \left(x + \frac{1}{2}\right)\left(x + \frac{3}{2}\right) = x^2 + \frac{3}{2}x + \frac{1}{2}x + \frac{3}{4}$$

$$= x^2 + \frac{3x + x}{2} + \frac{3}{4}$$

$$= x^2 + 2x + \frac{3}{4}.$$

4. if $x + y + z = 0$, then find the value of $x^3 + y^3 + z^3$.

Sol. We know that

$x^3 + y^3 + z^3 - 3xyz$

$= (x + y + z)\,(x^2 + y^2 + z^2 - xy - yz - zx)$

Now, if $x + y + z = 0$, then

$\quad x^3 + y^3 + z^3 - 3xyz = 0$

$\Rightarrow \quad x^3 + y^3 + z^3 = 3xyz.$

5. Write the co-efficient of x^2 in the expansion of $(x - 2)^3$.

Sol. Given, $(x - 2)^3 = (x)^3 - (2)^3 - 3 \times x \times 2(x - 2)$

$\qquad\qquad = x^3 - 8 - 6x^2 + 12x$

Hence, the co-efficient of x^2 in the expansion of $(x - 2)^3 = 6$

6. Calculate the value of $\dfrac{83^3 + 17^3}{83^2 - 83 \times 17 + 17^2}$.

Sol. Given expression $= \dfrac{83^3 + 17^3}{83^2 - 83 \times 17 \times 17^2}$

$= \dfrac{(83 + 17)\,(83^2 - 83 \times 17 + 17^2)^2}{(83^2 - 83 \times 17 + 17^2)}$

$$[\because\ a^3 + b^3 = (a + b)\,(a^2 + b^2 - ab)]$$

$= 83 + 17 = 100.$

7. If $x^2 + px - 30 = (x - 5)\,(x + 6)$, $\forall x$, then find the value of p.

Sol. We have, $x^2 + px - 30 = (x - 5)\,(x + 6)$

On multiplying the factors of RHS, we get

$$x^2 + px - 30 = x^2 + x - 30$$

On comparing the coefficients of x from both sides, we get p = 1.

8. If $x + \dfrac{1}{x} = 4$, then calculate the value of

$x^2 + \dfrac{1}{x^2}.$

Sol. We know that $x + \dfrac{1}{x} = 4$

On squaring both sides, we have

$$\left(x + \dfrac{1}{x} \right)^2 = (4)^2$$

$\Rightarrow\quad x^2 + \dfrac{1}{x^2} + 2 = 16$

$\therefore\quad x^2 + \dfrac{1}{x^2} = 16 - 2 = 14$

9. Find the value of 104×96.

Sol. Given expression $= 104 \times 96 = (100 + 4)\,(100 - 4)$

$= (100)^2 - (4)^2 = 10000 - 16$

$$[\because\ (a + b)\,(a - b) = a^2 - b^2]$$

$= 9984$

Short Answer Type Questions I

(2 Marks Each)

1. Without finding the cubes, factorise $(x - 2y)^3 + (2y - 3z)^3 + (3z - x)^3$. [NCERT Exemplar]

Sol. We know that,

$a^3 + b^3 + c^3 - 3abc$

$\qquad = (a + b + c)\,(a^2 + b^2 + c^2 - ab - bc - ca)$

We know that if $a + b + c = 0$,

then $a^3 + b^3 + c^3 = 3abc$

Now, $(x - 2y) + (2y - 3z) + (3z - x)$

$\qquad = x - 2y + 2y - 3z + 3z - x = 0$

Therefore, $(x - 2y)^3 + (2y - 3z)^3 + (3z - x)^3$

$\qquad = 3(x - 2y)\,(2y - 3z)\,(3z - x).$

2. Evaluate the following using suitable Identities.
   (i) $(102)^3$ (ii) $(998)^3$
   (iii) $(99)^3$ [NCERT]

Sol. (i) $(102)^3 = (100 + 2)^3$

$= (100)^3 + (2)^3 + 3 \times 100 \times 2(100 + 2)$

$$[\because\ (a + b)^3 = a^3 + b^3 + 3ab(a + b)]$$

$= 1000000 + 8 + 600(102)$

$= 1000000 + 8 + 61200 = 1061208$

(ii) $(998)^3 = (1000 - 2)^3$

$= (1000)^3 - (2)^3 - 3 \times 1000 \times 2(1000 - 2)$

$= 1000000000 - 8 - 6000 \times 998$

$= 1000000000 - 8 - 5988000 = 994011992$

(iii) $(99)^3 = (100 - 1)^3$

$= (100)^3 - (1)^3 - 3 \times 100 \times 1\,(100 - 1)$

$$[\because\ (a - b)^3 = a^3 - b^3 - 3ab(a - b)]$$

$= 1000000 - 1 - 300(100 - 1)$

$= 1000000 - 1 - 300 \times 99$

$= 1000000 - 29701 = 970299$

3. Without actually calculating the cubes, find the value of each of the following.
   (i) $(-12)^3 + (7)^3 + (5)^3$
   (ii) $(28)^3 + (-15)^3 + (-13)^3$. [NCERT]

Sol. (i) We know that, $x^3 + y^3 + z^3 - 3xyz$

$= (x + y + z)\,(x^2 + y^2 + z^2 - xy - yz - zx)$

Also, we know that, if

$$x + y + z = 0$$

Then, $\quad x^3 + y^3 + z^3 = 3xyz$

$\therefore$ Given expression $= (-12)^3 + (7)^3 + (5)^3$

$\because\quad -12 + 7 + 5 = 0$

$\therefore (-12)^3 + (7)^3 + (5)^3 = 3 \times (-12) \times 7 \times 5 = -1260$

(ii) We know that $x^3 + y^3 + z^3 - 3xyz$

$= (x + y + z)\,(x^2 + y^2 + z^2 - xy - yz - zx)$

Also we know that,

if $\quad x + y + z = 0$

then $x^3 + y^3 + z^3 = 3xyz$

$\therefore$ Given expression $= (28)^3 + (-15)^3 + (-13)^3$

$\because\ 28 - 15 - 13 = 0$

$\therefore (28)^3 + (-15)^3 + (-13)^3 = 3 \times (28) \times (-15) \times (-13)$

$= 16380$

4. If a, b, c are all non-zero and $a + b + c = 0$, prove $\dfrac{a^2}{bc} + \dfrac{b^2}{ac} + \dfrac{c^2}{ab} = 3$

[Board Term I, 2012, Set-39] [NCERT Exemplar]

Sol. Given, $a + b + c = 0$

To prove $\dfrac{a^2}{bc} + \dfrac{b^2}{ac} + \dfrac{c^2}{ab} = 3$

$$\text{L.H.S.} = \frac{a^2}{bc} + \frac{b^2}{ac} + \frac{c^2}{ab} = \frac{a^3 + b^3 + c^3}{abc}$$

$$= \frac{3abc}{abc} \qquad \left(\begin{array}{l} \because a + b + c = 0 \\ \therefore a^3 + b^3 + c^3 = 3abc \end{array} \right)$$

5. Using suitable identity evaluate $(103)^3$.

[Board Term I, 2012, Set-14], [NCERT Exemplar]

Sol. Given expression, $103^3 = (100 + 3)^3$

[By using identity $(a + b)^3 = a^3 + b^3 + 3abc(a + b)$]

$$= 100^3 + 3^3 + 3 \times 100 \times 3 \ (100 + 3)$$
$$= 1000000 + 27 + 900 \times 103$$
$$= 1000000 + 27 + 92700 = 1092727$$

6. Give possible expression for the length and breadth of a rectangle whose area is given by $25a^2 - 35a + 12$.

[Board Term I, 2012 Set-38], [NCERT]

Sol. Given, area of rectangle $= 25a^2 - 35a + 12$

[By splitting middle term]

$$= 25a^2 - 20a - 15a + 12$$
$$= 5a(5a - 4) - 3(5a - 4)$$
$$= (5a - 3) \ (5a - 4) = \text{length} \times \text{breadth}$$

Hence, length and breadth are $(5a - 3)$ and $(5a - 4)$ respectively.

7. Factorize : $64a^3 - 27b^3 - 144a^2b + 108ab^2$

[Board Term I, 2014], [NCERT]

Sol. Given expression $= 64a^3 - 27b^3 - 144a^2b + 108ab^2$

$$= (4a)^3 - (3b)^3 - 3 \times (4a)^2 \times (3b) \times 3 \times (4a) \times (3b)^2$$
$$= (4a)^3 - (3b)^3 - 3 \times 4a \times 3b \ (4a - 3b)$$
$$= (4a - 3b)^3 \qquad [\because a^3 - b^3 - 3ab(a - b) = (a - b)^3]$$

8. Find the value of $x^2 + \dfrac{1}{x^2}$, if $x - \dfrac{1}{x} = \sqrt{3}$.

[Board Term I, 2011, Set-17]

Sol. Given, $x - \dfrac{1}{x} = \sqrt{3}$

On squaring both sides, we get

$$\left(x - \frac{1}{x} \right)^2 = \left(\sqrt{3} \right)^2$$

$$\Rightarrow \quad x^2 + \frac{1}{x^2} - 2 \times x \times \frac{1}{x} = 3$$

$$\Rightarrow \quad x^2 + \frac{1}{x^2} - 2 = 3$$

$$\therefore \quad x^2 + \frac{1}{x^2} = 3 + 2 = 5.$$

9. Simplify: $\left(x + \dfrac{1}{x} \right)\left(x - \dfrac{1}{x} \right)\left(x^2 + \dfrac{1}{x^2} \right)\left(x^4 + \dfrac{1}{x^4} \right)$

[Board Term I, 2012, Set-48; 2011, Set-15]

Sol. Given expression

$$= \left(x + \frac{1}{x} \right)\left(x - \frac{1}{x} \right)\left(x^2 + \frac{1}{x^2} \right)\left(x^4 + \frac{1}{x^4} \right)$$

$$= \left(x^2 - \frac{1}{x^2} \right)\left(x^2 + \frac{1}{x^2} \right)\left(x^4 + \frac{1}{x^4} \right)$$

[Using identity $(a + b) \ (a - b) = a^2 - b^2$]

$$= \left(x^4 - \frac{1}{x^4} \right)\left(x^4 + \frac{1}{x^4} \right) = \left(x^8 - \frac{1}{x^8} \right)$$

10. Factorize : $64x^3 + \sqrt{125}y^3$.

[Board Term I, 2012, Set-47]

Sol. Given expression

$$64x^3 + \sqrt{125}y^3 = (4x)^3 + (\sqrt{5}y)^3$$

$$= (4x + \sqrt{5}y)\left[(4x)^2 + (\sqrt{5}y)^2 - 4x \times \sqrt{5}y \right]$$

[By using identity $a^3 + b^3 = (a + b) \ (a^2 + b^2 - ab)$]

$$= (4x + \sqrt{5}y) \left[16x^2 + 5y^2 - 4\sqrt{5}xy \right]$$

11. Find the value of the polynomial $x^2 - 9$, for $x = 97$.

[Board Term I, 2012, Set-18]

Sol. Given expression $= x^2 - 9 = (97)^2 - (3)^2$

$$= (97 + 3) \ (97 - 3)$$

[By using identity $a^2 - b^2 = (a + b) \ (a - b)$]

$$= 100 \times 94 = 9400.$$

12. Expand $\left(\dfrac{a}{4} - \dfrac{b}{2} + 1 \right)^2$ using identity.

[Board Term I, 2012, Set-36]

Sol. Given expression

$$= \left(\frac{a}{4} - \frac{b}{2} + 1 \right)^2 = \left[\frac{a}{4} + \left(-\frac{b}{2} \right) + 1 \right]^2$$

$$= \left(\frac{a}{4} \right)^2 + \left(-\frac{b}{2} \right)^2 + (1)^2 + 2 \times \frac{a}{4} \times \left(-\frac{b}{2} \right) + 2$$

$$\times \left(\frac{-b}{2} \right) \times (1) + 2 \times \left(\frac{a}{4} \right) \times (1)$$

[By using identity $(a + b + c)^2 = a^2 + b^2 + c^2 + 2ab + 2bc + 2ca$]

$$= \frac{a^2}{16} + \frac{b^2}{4} + 1 - \frac{ab}{1} - b + \frac{a}{2}.$$

13. Factorize : $x^4 - y^4$. [Board Term I, 2012, Set-45]

Sol. Given expression $= x^4 - y^4 = (x^2)^2 - (y^2)^2$

$$= (x^2 - y^2) \ (x^2 + y^2)$$
$$= (x - y) \ (x + y) \ (x^2 + y^2)$$

[By using identity $a^2 - b^2 = (a + b) \ (a - b)$]

14. Factorize : $2y^3 + y^2 - 2y - 1$.

[**Board Term I, 2012, Set-14**]

Sol. Given expression

$$2y^3 + y^2 - 2y - 1 = 2y^3 - 2 + y^2 - 2y + 1$$
$$= 2(y^3 - 1) + y^2 - 2y + 1$$
$$= 2(y - 1)(y^2 + y + 1) + (y - 1)^2$$
$$= (y - 1)(2y^2 + 2y + 2) + (y - 1)^2$$
$$= (y - 1)[2y^2 + 2y + 2 + y - 1]$$
$$= (y - 1)[2y^2 + 3y + 1]$$
$$= (y - 1)[2y^2 + 2y + y + 1]$$
$$= (y - 1)[2y(y + 1) + 1(y + 1)]$$
$$= (y - 1)(y + 1)(2y + 1)$$

15. Evaluate : 249×251 by using an identity.

[**Board Term I, 2012, Set-58**]

Sol. Given expression $= 249 \times 251$
$$= (250 - 1)(250 + 1)$$
$$= (250)^2 - (1)^2$$

[By using identity $a^2 - b^2 = (a + b)(a - b)$]
$$= 62500 - 1 = 62499$$

16. If x and y are two positive real numbers such that $x^2 + 4y^2 = 17$ and $xy = 2$, then find the value of $(x + 2y)$. [**Board Term I, 2012, Set-19**]

Sol. $(x + 2y)^2 = x^2 + 4y^2 + 2 \times x \times 2y$
$$= 17 + 4 \times 2 \qquad [\because (a + b)^2 = a^2 + b^2 + 2ab]$$
$$= 17 + 8 = 25$$

Hence, $(x + 2y) = \pm\sqrt{25} = \pm 5$.

17. Find the value of $8x^3 + 27y^3$, if $2x + 3y = 8$ and $xy = 2$. [**Board Term I, 2012, Set-55**]

Sol. Given, $2x + 3y = 8$

On cubing both sides, we have
$$(2x + 3y)^3 = 8^3$$
$$\Rightarrow 8x^3 + 27y^3 + 3 \times 2x \times 3y(2x + 3y) = 512$$
$$\Rightarrow 8x^3 + 27y^3 + 18 \times 2 \times 8 = 512$$
$$\Rightarrow 8x^3 + 27y^3 = 512 - 288$$

Hence, $8x^3 + 27y^3 = 224$.

18. Factorize : $m(m - 1) - n(n - 1)$

[**Board Term I, 2012, Set-54**]

Sol. Given expression $= m(m - 1) - n(n - 1)$
$$= m^2 - m - n^2 + n$$
$$= m^2 - n^2 - m + n$$
$$= (m - n)(m + n) - (m - n)$$
$$= (m - n)(m + n - 1).$$

19. Factorize : $12(x^2 + 7)^2 - 8(x^2 + 7)(2x - 1) - 15(2x - 1)^2$. [**Board Term I, 2012, Set-66**]

Sol. Let, $x^2 + 7 = p$ and $2x - 1 = q$, then

Given expression $= 12p^2 - 8pq - 15q^2$

[By splitting middle term]
$$= 12p^2 - 18pq + 10pq - 15q^2$$
$$= 6p(2p - 3q) + 5q(2p - 3q)$$
$$= (2p - 3q)(6p + 5q)$$

Now, on putting the value of p and q, we have
$$= [2(x^2 + 7) - 3(2x - 1)][6(x^2 + 7) + 5(2x - 1)]$$
$$= (2x^2 + 14 - 6x + 3)(6x^2 + 42 + 10x - 5)$$
$$= (2x^2 - 6x + 17)(6x^2 + 10x + 37)$$

20. Factorize : $8 - 27a^3 - 36a + 54a^2$.

[**Board Term I, 2013, 2012, Set-52**]

Sol. Given expression $= 8 - 27a^3 - 36a + 54a^2$
$$= (2)^3 - (3a)^3 - 18a(2 - 3a)$$
$$= (2)^3 - (3a)^3 - 3 \times 2 \times 3a(2 - 3a) = (2 - 3a)^3.$$

[By using identity $(a - b)^3 = a^3 - b^3 - 3ab(a - b)$]

21. Without actually calculating the cubes. Evaluate $14^3 + 13^3 - 27^3$. [**Board Term I, 2012, Set-46**]

Sol. Let $14 = a$, $13 = b$, $-27 = c$

Now, $a + b + c = 14 + 13 - 27 = 0$

$$[\because a^3 + b^3 + c^3 = 3abc]$$

$\therefore$ Given expression
$$= (14)^3 + (13)^3 + (-27)^3 = 3 \times 14 \times 13 \times (-27)$$
$$= -14742.$$

22. Factorize : $x^4 - 125xy^3$. [**Board Term I, 2012, Set-35**]

Sol. Given expression $= x^4 - 125xy^3 = x(x^3 - 125y^3)$
$$= x[(x)^3 - (5y)^3] = x(x - 5y)[x^2 + (5y)^2 + x + 5y]$$
$$[\because a^3 + b^3 = (a - b)(a^2 + b^2 + ab)]$$
$$= x(x - 5y)(x^2 - 25y^2 + 5xy).$$

23. Expand using suitable identity $(2x - 3y + z)^2$.

[**Board Term I, 2012, Set-47**]

Sol. Given expression
$$= (2x - 3y + z)^2 = [2x + (-3y) + z]^2$$
$$= (2x)^2 + (-3y)^2 + z^2 + 2 \times 2x \times (-3y) + 2 \times (-3y) \times z + 2 \times 2x \times z$$
$$[\because (a + b + c)^2 = a^2 + b^2 + c^2 + 2ab + 2bc + 2ca]$$
$$= 4x^2 + 9y^2 + z^2 - 12xy - 6yz + 4xz.$$

24. Expand : $\left(\dfrac{1}{3}x - \dfrac{2}{3}y\right)^3$ [**Board Term I, 2013**]

Sol. Given expression $= \left(\dfrac{1}{3}x - \dfrac{2}{3}y\right)^3$

$$= \left(\dfrac{1}{3}x\right)^3 - \left(\dfrac{2}{3}y\right)^3 - 3 \times \dfrac{1}{3}x \times \dfrac{2}{3}y\left(\dfrac{1}{3}x - \dfrac{2y}{3}\right)$$

[By using identity $(a + b)^3 = a^3 + b^3 + 3ab(a + b)$]

$$= \dfrac{x^3}{27} - \dfrac{8y^3}{27} - \dfrac{2xy}{3}\left(\dfrac{x}{3} - \dfrac{2y}{3}\right)$$

$$= \dfrac{x^3}{27} - \dfrac{8y^3}{27} - \dfrac{2x^2y}{9} + \dfrac{4xy^2}{9}$$

25. Factorize : $8a^3 + 8b^3$. [Board Term I, 2014]

Sol. Given expression

$= 8a^3 + 8b^3 = (2a)^3 + (2b)^3$

$= (2a + 2b)\,[(2a)^2 + (2b)^2 - (2a) \times (2b)] = (2a + 2b)$

$[4a^2 + 4b^2 - 4ab]$

$[\because a^3 + b^3 = (a + b)\,(a^2 + b^2 - ab)]$

$= 2(a + b) \times 4(a^2 + b^2 - ab)$

$= 8(a + b)\,(a^2 + b^2 - ab)$

26. Expand by using identity $(2x - y + z)^2$.

[Board Term I, 2014]

Sol. By using the identity, $(a + b + c)^2$

$= a^2 + b^2 + c^2 + 2ab + 2bc + 2ca$

Given expression

$= [2x + (-y) + z]^2 = (2x)^2 + (-y)^2 + z^2 + 2(2x)\,(-y)$

$+ 2(-y)\,(z) + 2(z)\,(2x)$

$= 4x^2 + y^2 + z^2 - 4xy - 2yz + xz$

27. Factorize : $9x^2 + 6xy + y^2$. [Board Term I, 2014]

Sol. Given expression

$= 9x^2 + 6xy + y^2 = (3x)^2 + 2 \times (3x) \times y + y^2$

$= (3x + y)^2$ $[\because a^2 + 2ab + b^2 = (a + b)^2]$

28. Factorize : $8x^3 - (2x - y)^3$.

[Board Term I, 2015, Set-1]

Sol. Given expression

$= 8x^3 - (2x - y)^3 = (2x)^3 - (2x - y)^3$

$= [2x - (2x - y)]\,[(2x)^2 + (2x - y)^2 + 2x(2x - y)]$

$[\because (a^3 - b^3) = (a - b)\,(a^2 + b^2 + ab)]$

$= [2x - 2x + y]\,[4x^2 + 4x^2 + y^2 - 4xy + 4x^2 - 2xy]$

$= y[4x^2 + 4x^2 + y^2 - 4xy + 4x^2 - 2xy]$

$= y[12x^2 + y^2 - 6xy]$

29. Find the value of $27x^3 + 8y^3$, if $3x + 2y = 20$ and

$xy = \dfrac{11}{9}$.

Sol. Given, $3x + 2y = 20$

On cubing both sides, we get

$(3x + 2y)^3 = (20)^3$

$\Rightarrow$ $(3x)^3 + (2y)^3 + 3 \times 3x \times 2y(3x + 2y) = 8000$

$[\because (a + b)^3 = a^3 + b^3 + 3ab(a + b)]$

$\Rightarrow$ $27x^3 + 8y^3 + 18xy\,(3x + 2y) = 8000$

On putting $3x + 2y = 20$ and $xy = \dfrac{11}{9}$, we get

$27x^3 + 8y^3 + 18 \times \dfrac{11}{9} \times 20 = 8000$

$\Rightarrow$ $27x^3 + 8y^3 + 440 = 8000$

$\therefore$ $27x^3 + 8y^3 = 8000 - 440 = 7560$

30. Factorize the following $a^3(b - c)^3 + b^3(c - a)^3 + c^3(a - b)^3$.

Sol. Given expression

$= a^3(b - c)^3 + b^3(c - a)^3 + c^3(c - b)^3$

$= [a(b - c)]^3 + [b(c - a)]^3 + [c(a - b)]^3$

On putting $a(b - c) = x$, $b(c - a) = y$

and $c(a - b) = z$, we get

$[a(b - c)]^3 + [b(c - a)]^3 + [c(a - b)]^3$

$= x^3 + y^3 + z^3 = 3xyz$

$[\because x + y + z = a(b - c) + b(c - a) + c(a - b)$

$= ab - ac + bc - ba + ca - bc = 0]$

$= 3[a(b - c)]\,[b(c - a)]\,[c(a - b)]$

[On putting $x = a(b - c)$, $y = b(c - a)$

and $z = c(a - b)] = 3abc(a - b)\,(b - c)\,(c - a)$

Short Answer Type Questions II

(3 Marks Each)

1. Factorize : $27p^3 - \dfrac{1}{216} - \dfrac{9}{2}p^2 + \dfrac{1}{4}p$.

[Board Term I, 2012, 2010, Set-C1; 2011, Set-4; Set-14], [NCERT]

Sol. Given expression $= 27p^3 - \dfrac{1}{216} - \dfrac{9}{2}p^2 + \dfrac{1}{4}p$

$= (3p)^3 - \left(\dfrac{1}{6}\right)^3 - 3.(3p)^2 \dfrac{1}{6} + 3(3p)\left(\dfrac{1}{6}\right)^2$

$\left(3p - \dfrac{1}{6}\right)^3$ $[\because (a - b)^3 = a^3 - b^3 - 3ab(a - b)]$

$= \left(3p - \dfrac{1}{6}\right)\left(3p - \dfrac{1}{6}\right)\left(3p - \dfrac{1}{6}\right)$

2. If $x + y + z = 0$, show that $x^3 + y^3 + z^3 = 3xyz$.

[Board Term I, 2016, 2015, Set-1, JQ22L5C] [NCERT]

Sol. Given, $x + y + z = 0$

$\therefore$ $x + y = -z$

On cubing both sides, $(x + y)^3 = (-z)^3$

$\Rightarrow$ $x^3 + y^3 + 3xy(-z) = -z^3$

$\Rightarrow$ $x^3 + y^3 - 3xyz = -z^3$

$\Rightarrow$ $x^3 + y^3 + z^3 = 3xyz$

Hence proved.

3. Simplify : $\left(\dfrac{x}{3} + \dfrac{y}{5}\right)^3 - \left(\dfrac{x}{3} - \dfrac{y}{5}\right)^3$.

[Board Term I, 2011, Set-43]

Sol. Given expression

$$= \left(\frac{x}{3} + \frac{y}{5}\right)^3 - \left(\frac{x}{3} - \frac{y}{5}\right)^3 = \left[\frac{x}{3} + \frac{y}{5} - \frac{x}{3} + \frac{y}{5}\right]$$

$$\left[\left(\frac{x}{3} + \frac{y}{5}\right)^2 + \left(\frac{x}{3} - \frac{y}{5}\right)^2 + \left(\frac{x}{3} + \frac{y}{5}\right)\left(\frac{x}{3} - \frac{y}{5}\right)\right]$$

$$[\because a^3 - b^3 = (a - b)(a^2 + b^2 + ab)]$$

$$= \left(\frac{2y}{5}\right)\left[\frac{x^2}{9} + \frac{y^2}{25} + 2 \times \frac{x}{3} \times \frac{y}{5}\right.$$

$$\left. + \frac{x^2}{9} + \frac{y^2}{25} - 2 \times \frac{x}{3} \times \frac{y}{5} + \frac{x^2}{9} - \frac{y^2}{25}\right]$$

$$= \frac{2y}{5}\left[3 \times \frac{x^2}{9} + \frac{y^2}{25}\right] = \frac{2y}{5}\left(\frac{x^2}{3} + \frac{y^2}{25}\right)$$

4. If $a^2 + b^2 + c^2 = 280$ and $ab + bc + ca = \dfrac{9}{2}$, then find the value of $(a + b + c)^3$.

[Board Term I, 2012, Set-35]

Sol. We know that

$$(a + b + c)^2 = a^2 + b^2 + c^2 + 2(ab + bc + ca)$$

$$= 280 \times 2 \times \frac{9}{2}$$

$$\left[\because a^2 + b^2 + c^2 = 280 \text{ and } ab + bc + ca = \frac{9}{2}\right]$$

$$\Rightarrow \quad (a + b + c)^2 = 280 + 9 = 289$$

$$\Rightarrow \quad a + b + c = \sqrt{289} = 17$$

Hence, given expression

$$= (a + b + c)^3 = 17^3 = 4913.$$

5. Factorize :

(i) $x^2 + \dfrac{1}{x^2} + 2 - 2x - \dfrac{2}{x}$ (ii) $x^4 - y^4$.

[Board Term I, 2012, Set-67]

Sol. (i) Given expression $= x^2 + \dfrac{1}{x^2} + 2 - 2x - \dfrac{2}{x}$

$$= (x)^2 + \left(\frac{1}{x}\right)^2 + 2 \times x \times \frac{1}{x} - 2x - \frac{2}{x}$$

$$= \left(x + \frac{1}{x}\right)^2 - 2\left(x + \frac{1}{x}\right)$$

$$= \left(x + \frac{1}{x}\right)\left(x + \frac{1}{x} - 2\right)$$

(ii) Given expression

$$= x^4 - y^4 = (x^2)^2 - (y^2)^2 \ [\because a^2 - b^2 = (a - b)(a + b)]$$

$$= (x^2 - y^2)(x^2 + y^2)$$

$$= (x - y)(x + y)(x^2 + y^2).$$

6. Factorize : $3 - 12(a - b)^2$

[Board Term I, 2012, Set-46]

Sol. Given expression

$$3 - 12(a - b)^2 = 3[1 - 4(a - b)^2]$$

$$= 3[(1)^2 - \{2(a - b)\}^2]$$

$$= 3[1 + 2(a - b)] [1 - 2(a - b)]$$

$$[\because a^2 - b^2 = (a - b)(a + b)]$$

7. Factorize : $250x^3 - 432y^3$.

[Board Term I, 2012, Set-57]

Sol. Given expression

$$250x^3 - 432y^3 = 2[125x^3 - 216y^3]$$

$$= 2[(5x)^3 - (6y)^3]$$

$$= 2(5x - 6y)[(5x)^2 + (6y)^2 + 5x \times 6y]$$

$$[\because a^3 - b^3 = (a - b)(a^2 + b^2 + ab)]$$

$$= 2(5x - 6y)(25x^2 + 36y^2 + 30xy)$$

8. If $x + y + 4 = 0$, then find the value of $x^3 + y^3 - 12xy + 64$.

[Board Term I, 2012, Set-45]

Sol. Given, $x + y + 4 = 0$

If $a + b + c = 0$ then $a^3 + b^3 + c^3 = 3abc$

Now, $x^3 + y^3 + 4^3 = 3xy\ (4)$

i.e., $x^3 + y^2 - 12xy + 64 = 0$

9. Factorize : $a^6 - b^6$. [Board Term I, 2012, Set-14]

Sol. Given expression $= a^6 - b^6 = (a^3)^2 - (b^3)^2$

$$= (a^3 - b^3)(a^3 + b^3)$$

$$= (a - b)(a^2 + b^2 + ab)(a + b)(a^2 + b^2 - ab)$$

$$[\because a^3 - b^3 = (a - b)(a^2 + b^2 + ab)(a + b)(a^2 + b^2 - ab)]$$

$$= (a - b)(a + b)(a^2 + b^2 + ab)(a^2 + b^2 - ab)$$

10. Simplify : $\dfrac{(a^2 - b^2)^3 + (b^2 - c^2)^3 + (c^2 - a^2)^3}{(a - b)^3 + (b - c)^3 + (c - a)^3}$.

[Board Term I, 2012, Set-43]

Sol. Given expression

$$= \frac{(a^2 - b^2)^3 + (b^2 - c^2)^3 + (c^2 - a^2)^3}{(a - b)^3 + (b - c)^3 + (c - a)^3}$$

$\because$ Both numerator and denominator are of the form $a^3 + b^3 + c^3$

We know that if $a + b + c = 0$

then $a^3 + b^3 + c^3 = 3abc$

For numerator, $a^2 - b^2 + b^2 - c^2 + c^2 - a = 0$

and for denominator, $a - b + b - c + c - a = 0$

$$\therefore \quad \frac{(a^2 - b^2)^3 + (b^2 - c^2)^3 + (c^2 - a^2)^3}{(a - b)^3 + (b - c)^3 + (c - a)^3}$$

$$= \frac{3 \times (a^2 - b^2)(b^2 - c^2)(c^2 - a^2)}{3(a - b)(b - a)(b - c)}$$

$$= \frac{(a-b)(a+b)(b-c)(b+c)(c-a)(c+a)}{(a-b)(b-c)(c-a)}$$

$$= (a+b)(b+c)(c+a).$$

11. Factorize : $125x^3 - 27y^3 + z^3 + 45xyz.$

[*Board Term I, 2012, Set-44*]

Sol. Given expression

$= 125x^3 - 27y^3 + z^3 + 45xyz$

$= (5x)^3 + (-3y)^3 + (z)^3 - 3 \times (5x)(-3y)(z)$

$= (5x - 3y + z)[(5x)^2 + (-3y)^2 + (z)^2 - (5x)(-3y)$

$\qquad\qquad\qquad\qquad - (-3y)(z) - (5x)(z)]$

$\qquad\qquad\qquad [\because a^3 + b^3 + c^3 - 3abc]$

$= [(a+b+c)(a^2 + b^2 + c^2 - ab - bc - ca)]$

$= (5x - 3y + z)[25x^2 + 9y^2 + z^2 + 15xy + 3yz - 5xz]$

12. Factorize : $a^7 + ab^6.$ [*Board Term I, 2012, Set-50*]

Sol. Given expression

$= a^7 + ab^6 = a(a^6 + b^6)$

$= a[(a^2)^3 + (b^2)^3]$

$= a(a^2 + b^2)[(a^2)^2 + (b^2)^2 - a^2 \times b^2]$

$\qquad\qquad [\because x^3 + y^3 = (x+y)(x^2 + y^2 - xy)]$

$= a(a^2 + b^2)(a^4 + b^4 - a^2b^2)$

13. Find the value of $ab + bc + ca$, if $a + b + c = 9$ and $a^2 + b^2 + c^2 = 35.$ [*Board Term I, 2012, Set-71*]

Sol. Given, $a + b + c = 9$

On squaring both sides,

$(a + b + c)^2 = 9^2$

$\Rightarrow \quad a^2 + b^2 + c^2 + 2(ab + bc + ca) = 81$

$\qquad [\because (a+b+c)^2 = a^2 + b^2 + c^2 (ab + bc + ca)]$

$\Rightarrow \quad 35 + 2(ab + bc + ca) = 81$

$\qquad\qquad\qquad [\because a^2 + b^2 + c^2 = 35]$

$\Rightarrow \quad 2(ab + bc + ca) = 81 - 35 = 46$

$\therefore \quad ab + bc + ca = 46/2 = 23$

14. Factorize : $9x^2 + y^2 + z^2 - 6xy + 2yz - 6xz$. Hence, find its value when $x = 1$, $y = 2$ and $z = -1$.

[*Board Term I, 2012, Set-48*]

Sol. Given expression

$= 9x^2 + y^2 + z^2 - 6xy + 2yz - 6xz$

$= (-3x)^2 + (y)^2 + (z)^2 + 2 \times (-3x)(y) + 2 \times (y)(z)$

$\qquad\qquad\qquad\qquad + 2(-3x)(z)$

$= (-3x + y + z)^2$

$\qquad [\because (a+b+c)^2 = a^2 + b^2 + c^2 + 2ab + 2bc + 2ca]$

If $x = 1$, $y = 2$, $z = -1$, then

$(-3x + y + z)^2 = (-3 \times 1 + 2 - 1)^2$

$= (-3 + 2 - 1)^2 = 4.$

15. Simplify: $(a + 2b + 3c)^2 - (a - 2b - 3c)^2 - 6b^2 - 9bc.$

[*Board Term I, 2012, Set-37*]

Sol. Given expression

$= (a + 2b + 3c)^2 - (a - 2b - 3c)^2 - 6b^2 - 9bc$

$= (a + 2b + 3c + a - 2b - 3c)(a + 2b + 3c - a + 2b$

$\qquad\qquad\qquad\qquad + 3c) - 6b^2 - 9bc$

$\qquad\qquad [\because a^2 - b^2 = (a - b)(a + b)]$

$= 2a(4b + 6c) - 6b^2 - 9bc$

$= 2a \times 2(2b + 3c) - 3b(2b + 3c)$

$= (2b + 3c)(4a - 3b)$

16. Factorize : $(x^2 - 4x)(x^2 - 4x - 1) - 20.$

[*Board Term I, 2012*]

Sol. Let, $x^2 - 4x = a$

$\therefore$ Given expression $= (x^2 - 4x)(x^2 - 4x - 1) - 20$

$= a(a - 1) - 20$

$= a^2 - a - 20 = a^2 - 5a + 4a - 20$

$= a(a - 5) + 4(a - 5) = (a - 5)(a + 4)$

$= (x^2 - 4x - 5)(x^2 - 4x + 4)$

$= (x - 5)(x + 1)(x - 2)^2$

17. If $x = \dfrac{\sqrt{3} + \sqrt{2}}{\sqrt{3} - \sqrt{2}}$ and $y = \dfrac{\sqrt{3} - \sqrt{2}}{\sqrt{3} + \sqrt{2}}$, find the value of $x^2 - y^2 + xy$, if $\sqrt{6} = 2.4.$

[*Board Term I, 2012, Set-51*]

Sol. Given expression

$$= x^2 - y^2 + xy = \left(\frac{\sqrt{3} + \sqrt{2}}{\sqrt{3} - \sqrt{2}}\right)^2 - \left(\frac{\sqrt{3} - \sqrt{2}}{\sqrt{3} + \sqrt{2}}\right)^2$$

$$+ \left(\frac{\sqrt{3} + \sqrt{2}}{\sqrt{3} - \sqrt{2}}\right) \times \left(\frac{\sqrt{3} - \sqrt{2}}{\sqrt{3} + \sqrt{2}}\right)$$

$$\left[\because x = \frac{\sqrt{3} + \sqrt{2}}{\sqrt{3} - \sqrt{2}} \text{ and } y = \frac{\sqrt{3} - \sqrt{2}}{\sqrt{3} + \sqrt{2}}\right]$$

$$= \frac{3 + 2 + 2\sqrt{6}}{3 + 2 - 2\sqrt{6}} - \frac{3 + 2 - 2\sqrt{6}}{3 + 2 + 2\sqrt{6}} + 1$$

$$= \frac{5 + 2\sqrt{6}}{5 - 2\sqrt{6}} - \frac{5 - 2\sqrt{6}}{5 + 2\sqrt{6}} + 1$$

$$= \frac{\left(5 + 2\sqrt{6}\right)^2 - \left(5 - 2\sqrt{6}\right)^2}{\left(5 - 2\sqrt{6}\right)\left(5 + 2\sqrt{6}\right)} + 1$$

$$= \frac{25 + 24 + 20\sqrt{6} - 25 - 24 + 20\sqrt{6}}{25 - 24} + 1$$

$= 40\sqrt{6} + 1$

$= 40 \times 2.4 + 1 = 96 + 1 = 97.$

18. Find the value of $(x - a)^3 + (x - b)^3 + (x - c)^3 - 3(x - a)(x - b)(x - c)$, if $a + b + c = 3x.$

[*Board Term I, 2013; 2012, Set-52*]

Sol. Given, $a + b + c = 3x$

$\therefore 3x - a - b - c = 0$

$\therefore$ Given expression $= (x - a)^3 + (x - b)^3 + (x - c)^3$
$$- 3(x - a)(x - b)(x - c)$$
$$= [x - a + x - b + x - c][(x - a)^2 + (x - b)^2 + (x - c)^2$$
$$-(x - a)(x - b) - (x - b)(x - c) - (x - a)(x - c)]$$
$$= [3x - a - b - c][(x - a)^2 + (x - b)^2 + (x - c)^2$$
$$- (x - a)(x - b) - (x - b)(x - c) - (x - a)(x - c)]$$
$$[\because 3x - a - b - c = 0]$$
$$= 0 \times [(x - a)^2 + (x - b)^2 + (x - c)^2 - (x - a)(x - b)$$
$$-(x - b)(x - c) - (x - c)(x - a)] = 0.$$

19. Factorize : $p^3q^3 + \dfrac{343}{729}$.

[Board Term II, 2013, Set-66]

Sol. Given expression

$$= p^3q^3 + \frac{343}{729} = (pq)^3 + \left(\frac{7}{9}\right)^3$$

$$= \left(pq + \frac{7}{9}\right)\left((pq)^2 + \left(\frac{7}{9}\right)^2 - pq \times \frac{7}{9}\right)$$

$$[\because a^3 + b^3 = (a + b)(a^2 + b^2 - ab)]$$

$$= \left(pq + \frac{7}{9}\right)\left(p^2q^2 + \frac{49}{81} - \frac{7pq}{9}\right)$$

20. Find the product :

$(x + y + 2z)(x^2 + y^2 + 4z^2 - xy - 2yz - 2zx).$

[Board Term I, 2013, Set-66]

Sol. Given expression

$$= (x + y + 2z)(x^2 + y^2 + 4z^2 - xy - 2yz - 2zx)$$
$$= (x + y + 2z)[x^2 + y^2 + (2z)^2 - x \times y - y \times 2z$$
$$- x \times 2z]$$
$$[\because (a + b + c)(a^2 + b^2 + c^2 - ab - bc - ca)$$
$$= a^3 + b^3 + c^3 - 3bc]$$
$$\therefore (x + y + 2z)(x^2 + y^2 + (2z)^2 - x \times y - y \times 2z - x$$
$$\times 2z)$$
$$= (x)^3 + (y)^3 + (2z)^3 - 3 \times x \times y \times 2z$$
$$= x^3 + y^3 + 8z^3 - 6xyz.$$

21. Find the value of $x^3 + y^3 + 15xy - 125$, when $x + y = 5$.   [Board Term I, 2013]

Sol. Given, $x + y = 5$, then

Given expression $= x^3 + y^3 + 15xy - 125$
$$= x^3 + y^3 - 125 + 15xy$$
$$= (x)^3 + (y)^3 + (-5)^3 - 3 \times x \times y \times (-5)$$
$$= (x + y - 5)[(x)^2 + (y)^2 + (-5)^2$$
$$-x \times (-5) - y \times (-5) - x \times y)]$$
$$= (5 - 5)(x^2 + y^2 + 25 + 5x + 5y - xy)$$
$$= 0(x^2 + y^2 + 25 + 5x + 5y - xy) = 0$$

22. Evaluate : $(\sqrt{2} + \sqrt{3})^2 + (\sqrt{5} - \sqrt{2})^2$.

[Board Term I, 2013]

Sol. Given expression $=$

$$(\sqrt{2} + \sqrt{3})^2 + (\sqrt{5} - \sqrt{2})^2 = (\sqrt{2})^2 + (\sqrt{3})^2 + 2 \times \sqrt{2}$$
$$\times \sqrt{3} + (\sqrt{5})^2 + (\sqrt{2})^2 - 2 \times \sqrt{5} \times \sqrt{2}$$

$$[\because (a + b)^2 = a^2 + b^2 + 2ab \text{ and } (a - b)^2$$
$$= a^2 + b^2 - 2ab]$$

$$= 2 + 3 + 2\sqrt{6} + 5 + 2 - 2\sqrt{10}$$
$$= 12 + 2\sqrt{6} - 2\sqrt{10}$$
$$= 2(6 + \sqrt{6} - \sqrt{10})$$

23. Simplify : $(2a + 3b)^3 - (2a - 3b)^3$

[Board Term I, 2015, Set-20U16YH]

Sol. Given expression

$$= (2a + 3b)^3 - (2a - 3b)^3 = x^3 - y^3$$

Let $2a + 3b = x$ and $2a - 3b = y$

Now, $x^3 - y^3 = (x - y)(x^2 + xy + y^2)$
$$= [(2a + 3b) - (2a - 3b)][(2a + 3b)^2 + (2a + 3b)$$
$$(2a - 3b) + (2a - 3b)^2]$$
$$= 6b[(4a^2 + 12ab + 9b^2) + (4a^2 - 9b^2) + (4a^2 - 12ab$$
$$+ 9b^2)]$$
$$= 6b(12a^2 + 9b^2)$$
$$= 6b \times 3 \times (4a^2 + 3b^2)$$
$$= 18b(4a^2 \times 3b^2)$$

24. Factorize : $(x - y)^2 - 7(x^2 - y^2) + 12(x + y)^2$

[Board Term I, 2015, Set-2]

Sol. Given expression

$$= (x - y)^2 - 7(x + y)(x - y) + 12(x + y)^2$$
$$= (x - y)^2 - 4(x + y)(x - y) - 3(x + y)(x - y)$$
$$+ 12(x + y)^2$$
$$= (x - y)[x - y - 4x - 4y] - 3(x + y)[x - y - 4x - 4y]$$
$$= (x - y)[-5y - 3x] - 3(x + y)[-3x - 5y]$$
$$= (-5y + 3x)[x - y - 3(x + y)]$$
$$= -(5y + 3x)(-2x - 4y)$$
$$= (5y + 3x)(2x + 4y)$$
$$= 2(x + 2y)(5y + 3x)$$

25. Evaluate 111^3, using a suitable identity.

[Board Term I, 2015, Set-1]

Sol. $111^3 = (100 + 11)^3$

$$= (100)^3 + 3(100)^2(11) + 3(100)(11)^2 + (11)^3$$
$$[\because (a + b)^3 = a^3 + b^3 + 3ab(a + b)]$$
$$= 1000000 + 330000 + 300 \times 121 + 1331$$
$$= 1367631$$

26. If $z^2 + \dfrac{1}{z^2} = 14$, find the value $z^3 + \dfrac{1}{z^3}$ taking only positive value of $z + \dfrac{1}{z}$.

[Board Term I, 2016, Set-BQ56IZK]

Sol. We know that

$$\left(z + \frac{1}{z}\right)^2 = z^2 + \frac{1}{z^2} + 2$$

$$= 14 + 2 = 15 \qquad \left[\because z^2 + \frac{1}{z^2} = 14\right]$$

$\therefore$ Given expression

$$= z^3 + \frac{1}{z^3} = \left(z + \frac{1}{z}\right)^3 - \left(z + \frac{1}{z}\right)$$

$$= (4)^3 - 3(4)$$

$$= 64 - 12 = 52$$

27. If $x^2 + \dfrac{1}{x^2} = 98$, then find value of $x^3 + \dfrac{1}{x^3}$.

[Board Term I, 2016, Set-JQ22L5C]

Sol. Given, $x^2 + \dfrac{1}{x^2} = 98$

We know that

$$\left(x + \frac{1}{x}\right)^2 = x^2 + \frac{1}{x^2} + 2$$

$$= 98 + 2 = 100$$

$\therefore$ $x + \dfrac{1}{x} = 10$

$\therefore$ Expression

$$= x^3 + \frac{1}{x^3} = \left(x + \frac{1}{x}\right)\left(x^2 - x\frac{1}{x} + \frac{1}{x^2}\right)$$

$$= (10)\left(x^2 + \frac{1}{x^2} - 1\right)$$

$$= (10)(98 - 1)$$

$$= 10 \times 97 = 970$$

28. Using a suitable identity, find, $(98)^3$.

[Board Term I, 2016, Set-7AELQR]

Sol. Given expression

$$= (98)^3 = (100 - 2)^3$$

$$= (100)^3 - (2)^3 - 3 \times 100 \times 2(100 - 2)$$

$$\text{[using identify } (a - b)^3 = a^3 - b^3 - 3ab(a + b)]$$

$$= 1000000 - 8 - 600 \times 98$$

$$= 1000000 - 8 - 58800$$

$$= 1000000 - 58808 = 941192$$

29. Simplify : $(3a - 2b)(9a^2 + 6ab + 4b^2) - (2a + 3b)(4a^2 - 6ab + 9b^2)$.

[Board Term I, 2016, Set-]

Sol. Given expression $= (3a - 2b)(9a^2 + 6ab + 4b^2) - (2a+ 3b)(4a^2 - 6ab + ab^2)$

$$= [(3a)^3 - (2b)^3] - [(2a)^3 + (3b)^3]$$

$$[\because a^3 - b^3 = (a - b)(a^2 + b^2 + ab)]$$

$$= [27a^3 - 8b^3] - [8a^3 + 27b^3]$$

$$= 27a^3 - 8b^3 - 8a^3 - 27b^3$$

$$= 19a^3 - 35b^3$$

30. If $x^2 + \dfrac{1}{x^2} = 7$ Find the value of $x^3 + \dfrac{1}{x^3}$, taking only the positive value of $x + \dfrac{1}{x}$.

[Board Term I, 2016, Set-74ED2QR]

Sol. We know that

$$\left(x + \frac{1}{x}\right)^2 = x^2 + \frac{1}{x^2} + 2.x.\frac{1}{x}$$

$$= x^2 + \frac{1}{x^2} + 2 = 7 + 2 \left[\because x^2 + \frac{1}{x^2} = 7\right]$$

$$\Rightarrow \left(x + \frac{1}{x}\right)^2 = 9$$

$$\therefore \left(x + \frac{1}{x}\right) = \pm 3$$

$$x + \frac{1}{x} = 3 \text{ [on taking +ve value]}$$

Now, Given expression

$$= x^3 + \frac{1}{x^3} = \left(x + \frac{1}{x}\right)\left(x^2 + \frac{1}{x^2} - x \cdot \frac{1}{x}\right)$$

$$= \left(x + \frac{1}{x}\right)\left(x^2 + \frac{1}{x^2} - 1\right) = (3)(7 - 1) = 3 \times 6 = 18$$

31. Sunita donated ₹ $\left(x^3 + \dfrac{1}{x^3}\right)$ to an orphanage children. Her friend Anita wanted to know the amount donated by her.

Sunita did not disclose the amount but she gave a clue that $x + \dfrac{1}{x}$ ₹ 8.

(i) Find the amount donated by Sunita to orphanage children.

(ii) By donating amount to orphanage children, which value is depicted by Sunita?

Sol. (i) Given, $x + \dfrac{1}{x} = 8$ ...(i)

On cubing eq. (i) both sides, we get

$$\left(x + \frac{1}{x}\right)^3 = (8)^3$$

$$\Rightarrow x^3 + \frac{1}{x^3} + 3 \times x \times \frac{1}{x}\left(x + \frac{1}{x}\right) = 512$$

$$[\because (a + b)^3 = a^3 + b^3 + 3ab \,(a+b)]$$

$$\Rightarrow x^3 + \frac{1}{x^3} + 3(8) = 512 \qquad \text{[from eq. (i)]}$$

$$\therefore \ x^3 + \frac{1}{x^3} = 512 - 24 = 488$$

Hence, Sunita donated ₹488 to orphanage.

(ii) The value depicted by Sunita is to help poor and needy children.

Long Answer Type Questions
(4 Marks Each)

1. Prove that $(a + b + c)^3 - a^3 - b^3 - c^3 = 3(a + b)(b + c)(c + a)$. [NCERT Exemplar]

Sol. To prove,

$(a + b + c)^3 - a^3 - b^3 - c^3 = 3(a + b)(b + c)(c + a)$

LHS $= [(a + b + c)^3 - a^3] - (b^3 + c^3)$

$= (a + b + c - a)[(a + b + c)^2 + a^2 + a(a + b + c)]$
$\quad - [(b + c)(b^2 + c^2 - bc)]$

$[\because a^3 + b^3 = (a+ b)(a^2 + b^2 - ab) \text{ and } a^3 - b^3$
$\qquad\qquad = (a - b)(a^2 + b^2 + ab)]$

$= (b + c)[(a^2 + b^2 + c^2 + 2ab + 2bc +2ca) + a^2$
$\qquad\qquad + a^2 + ab + ac] - (b + c)(b^2 + c^2 - bc)$

$= (b + c)[(b^2 + c^2 + 3a^2 + 3ab + 3ac + 2bc)$
$\qquad\qquad\qquad\qquad - b^2 - c^2 + bc]$

$= (b + c)[3a^2 + 3ab + 3ac + 3bc]$

$= (b + c)[3(a^2 + ab + ac + bc)]$

$= 3(b + c)[a(a + b) + c(a + b)]$

$= 3(b + c)[(a + c)(a + b)]$

$= 3(a + b)(b + c)(c + a) = $ RHS

Hence proved.

2. Evaluate (by using identities).

(i) 103×107 (ii) $(102)^3$

[Board Term I, 2014, [NCERT]]

Sol. (i) $103 \times 107 = (100 + 3)(100 + 7)$

$= 100^2 + (3 + 7) \times 100 + 3 \times 7$

$= 10000 + 1000 + 21 = 11021$

(ii) $(102)^3 = (100 + 2)^3$

$= (100)^3 + 2^3 + 3 \times 100 \times 2 \,(100 + 2)$

$[\because (a + b)^3 = a^3 + b^3 +3ab \,(a + b)]$

$= 1000000 + 8 + 600 \times 102$

$= 1000000 + 8 + 61200$

$= 1061208$

3. Prove that $x^3 + y^3 + z^3 - 3xyz = \dfrac{1}{2}(x + y + z)$

$[(x - y)^2 + (y - z)^2 + (z - x)^2]$

[Board Term I, 2015, Set-1 [NCERT]]

Sol. To prove,

$$x^3 + y^3 + z^3 - 3xyz = \frac{1}{2}(x + y + z)$$

$$[(x - y)^2 + (y - z)^2 + (z - x)^2]$$

RHS. $= \dfrac{1}{2}(x + y + z) [(x - y)^2 + (y - z)^2 + (z - x)^2]$

$$= \frac{1}{2}(x + y + z)\begin{bmatrix} x^2 + y^2 - 2xy + y^2 + z^2 \\ -2yz + z^2 + x^2 - 2zx \end{bmatrix}$$

$$= \frac{1}{2}(x + y + z)\begin{bmatrix} 2x^2 + 2y^2 + 2z^2 \\ -2xy - 2yz - 2zx \end{bmatrix}$$

$$= \frac{1}{2}(x + y + z).2\begin{bmatrix} x^2 + y^2 + z^2 \\ -xy - yz - zx \end{bmatrix}$$

$= x^3 + y^3 + z^2 - 3xyz \qquad \text{[By identity]}$

$= $ LHS.

Hence Proved.

4. Factorize (i) $4a^2 - 9b^2 - 2a - 3b$

(ii) $a^2 + b^2 - 2(ab - ac + bc)$.

[Board Term I, 2011, Set-12]

Sol. (i) Given expression $= 4a^2 - 9b^2 - 2a - 3b$

$= (2a)^2 - (3b)^2 - (2a + 3b)$

$= (2a - 3b)(2a + 3b) - 1(2a + 3b)$

$[\because x^2 - y^2 = (x + y)(x - y)]$

$= (2a + 3b)(2a - 3b - 1)$

(ii) **Given Expression** $= a^2 + b^2 - 2(ab - ac + bc)$

$= a^2 + b^2 - 2ab + 2ac - 2bc$

$= (a - b)^2 + 2c(a - b) \quad [\because x^2 + y^2 - 2xy = (x - y)^2]$

$= (a - b)[(a - b) + 2c]$

$= (a - b)(a - b + 2c).$

5. If $a = 5 + 2\sqrt{6}$ and $b = \dfrac{1}{a}$ then what will be the value of $a^2 + b^2$ and $a^3 + b^3$.

[Board Term I, 2012, Set-36]

Sol. Given $a = 5 + 2\sqrt{6}$

$$b = \frac{1}{a} = \frac{1}{5 + 2\sqrt{6}} \times \frac{\left(5 - 2\sqrt{6}\right)}{\left(5 - 2\sqrt{6}\right)}$$

$$= \frac{\left(5 - 2\sqrt{6}\right)}{25 - 24} = 5 - 2\sqrt{6}$$

$\therefore \ a + b = 5 + 2\sqrt{6} + 5 - 2\sqrt{6} = 10$

Also, $b = \dfrac{1}{a} \Rightarrow ab = 1$

$\therefore \ a^2 + b^2 = (a + b)^2 - 2ab \ [\because a + b = 10 \text{ and } ab = 1]$

$= (10)^2 - 2 \times 1 = 100 - 2 = 98$

and $(a^3 + b^3) = (a + b)^3 - 3ab(a + b)$

$= (10)^3 - 3 \times 1 \times 10$

$[\because (a^3 + b^3) = (a + b)^3 - 3ab \,(a + b)]$

$= 1000 - 30 = 970.$

6. If x and y are two positive real numbers such that $8x^3 + 27y^3 = 730$ and $2x^2y + 3xy^2 = 15$, then evaluate $2x + 3y$. [Board Term I, 2012, Set-18]

Sol. $(2x + 3y)^3 = (2x)^3 + (3y)^3 + 3 \times 2x \times 3y(2x + 3y)$

$\qquad [\because (a + b)^3 = a^3 + b^3 + 3ab\,(a + b)]$

$= 8x^3 + 27y^3 + 18(2x^2y + 3xy^2)$

$= 730 + 18 \times 15$

$[\because 8x^3 + 27y^3 = 730$ and $2x^2y + 3xy^2 = 15$ (Given)]

$= 730 + 270$

or, $(2x + 3y)^3 = 1000$

$\therefore$ Given expression $= 2x + 3y = \sqrt[3]{1000} = 10$

7. If $a + b + c = 6$ and $ab + bc + ca = 11$, find the value of $a^3 + b^3 + c^3 - 3abc$.

$\qquad$ [Board Term I, 2012, Set-14]

Sol. Given, $a + b + c = 6$

and $ab + bc + ca = 11$

$(a + b + c)^2 = a^2 + b^2 + c^2 + 2(ab + bc + ca)$

$(6)^2 = a^2 + b^2 + c^2 + 2 \times 11$

$a^2 + b^2 + c^2 = 36 - 22 = 14$

Given expression $= a^3 + b^3 + c^3 - 3abc = (a + b + c)$

$\qquad [a^2 + b^2 + c^2 - (ab + bc + ca)]$

$= 6 \times (14 - 11) = 6 \times 3 = 18.$

8. Simplify and factorize $(a + b + c)^2 - (a - b - c)^2 + 4b^2 - 4c^2$. [Board Term I, 2012, Set-14]

Sol. Given expression

$= [(a + b + c)^2 - (a - b - c)^2] + [4b^2 - 4c^2]$

$= (a + b + c + a - b - c)\,(a + b + c - a + b + c)$

$\qquad\qquad + (2b)^2 - (2c)^2$

$\qquad\qquad [\because x^2 - y^2 = (x + y)\,(x - y)]$

$= 2a \times (2b + 2c) + (2b - 2c)\,(2b + 2c)$

$= (2b + 2c)\,(2a + 2b - 2c)$

$= 2(b + c) \times 2(a + b - c)$

$= 4(b + c)\,(a + b - c).$

9. Factorize: $(a^2 - 2a)^2 - 23(a^2 - 2a) + 120$.

$\qquad$ [Board Term I, 2012, Set-53]

Sol. Given expression $= (a^2 - 2a)^2 - 23(a^2 - 2a) + 120$

$= (a^2 - 2a)^2 - 15(a^2 - 2a) - 8(a^2 - 2a) + 120$

$\qquad$ [By splitting the middle term]

$= (a^2 - 2a)\,[a^2 - 2a - 15] - 8[a^2 - 2a - 15]$

$= (a^2 - 2a - 15)\,(a^2 - 2a - 8)$

$= (a^2 - 5a + 3a - 15)\,(a^2 - 4a + 2a - 8)$

$= [a(a - 5) + 3(a - 5)]\,[a(a - 4) + 2(a - 4)]$

$= (a - 5)\,(a + 3)\,(a - 4)\,(a + 2).$

10. If $x + y + z = 10$ and $x^2 + y^2 + z^2 = 40$. Find $xy + yz + zx$ and $x^3 + y^3 + z^3 - 3xyz$.

$\qquad$ [Board Term I, 2012, Set-57]

Sol. Given, $x + y + z = 10$

and $x^2 + y^2 + z^2 = 40$

Now, we know that

$(x + y + z)^2 = x^2 + y^2 + z^2 + 2(xy + yz + zx)$

$\Rightarrow (10)^2 = 40 + 2(xy + yz + zx)$

$\Rightarrow 100 = 40 + 2(xy + yz + zx)$

$\Rightarrow 100 - 40 = 2(xy + yz + zx)$

$\therefore xy + yz + zx = \dfrac{60}{2} = 30$

and $x^3 + y^3 + z^3 - 3xyz$

$= (x + y + z)\,[x^2 + y^2 + z^2 - (xy + yz + zx)]$

$= 10\,[40 - 30] = 10 \times 10 = 100.$

11. Simplify : $(a + b)^3 + (a - b)^3 + 6a(a^2 - b^2)$.

$\qquad$ [Board Term I, 2012, Set-51]

Sol. Given expression $= (a + b)^3 + (a - b)^3 + 6a(a^2 - b^2)$

$= (a + b)^3 + (a - b)^3 + 3 \times 2a(a - b)\,(a + b)$

On adding and subtraction b, we have

$= (a + b)^3 + (a - b)^3 + 3(a + b)\,(a - b)\,(a + b)$

$\qquad\qquad\qquad\qquad\qquad + (a - b)]$

$= [(a + b) + (a - b)]^3$

$\qquad\qquad [\because x^3 + y^3 + 3xy\,(x + y) = (x + y)^3]$

$= (2a)^3 = 8a^3$

12. Find the value of $p^3 - q^3$, if $p - q = \dfrac{10}{9}$ and $pq = \dfrac{5}{3}$. [Board Term I, 2012, Set-44]

Sol. Given $p - q = \dfrac{10}{9}$ and $pq = \dfrac{5}{3}$

Now, we know that

$(p - q)^3 = p^3 - q^3 - 3pq(p - q)$

$\Rightarrow \left(\dfrac{10}{9}\right)^3 = p^3 - q^3 - 3 \times \dfrac{5}{3} \times \dfrac{10}{9}$

$\therefore p^3 - q^3 = \dfrac{1000}{729} + \dfrac{50}{9} = \dfrac{1000 + 4050}{729} = \dfrac{5050}{729}.$

Alternate method :

$p^3 - q^3 = (p - q)\,(p^2 + q^2 + pq)$

$= (p - q)[(p - q)^2 + 3pq]$

$\qquad\qquad [\because a^3 - b^3 = (a - b)\,(a^2 + b^2 + ab)]$

$= \dfrac{10}{9}\left[\left(\dfrac{10}{9}\right)^2 + 3 \times \dfrac{5}{3}\right]$

$= \dfrac{10}{9}\left[\dfrac{100}{81} + 5\right]$

$= \dfrac{10}{9}\left[\dfrac{100 + 405}{81}\right] = \dfrac{10}{9} \times \dfrac{505}{81} = \dfrac{5050}{729}.$

13. Factorize: $(m + 2n)^2 + 101(m + 2n) + 100$.

[Board Term I, 2014]

Sol. Given expression $= (m + 2n)^2 + 101(m + 2n) + 100$

$= (m + 2n)^2 + (1 + 100)(m + 2n) + 100$

$= (m + 2n)^2 + (m + 2n) + 100(m + 2n) + 100$

$= (m + 2n)[(m + 2n) + 1] + 100[(m + 2n) + 1]$

$= (m + 2n + 1)[m + 2n + 100]$

14. Verify $x^3 - y^3 = (x - y)(x^2 + y^2 + xy)$. Hence factorize $216x^3 - 125y^3$.

[Board Term I, 2012, Set-35]

Sol. Given, $x^3 - y^3 = (x - y)(x^2 + y^2 + xy)$

RHS $= (x - y)(x^2 + y^2 + xy)$

$= x^3 + xy^2 + x^2y - x^2y - y^3 - xy^2$

$= x^3 - y^3 =$ LHS

Hence proved.

Now, Given expression

$216x^3 - 125y^3 = (6x)^3 - (5y)^3$

$= (6x - 5y)[(6x)^2 + (5y)^2 + 6x \times 5y]$

$= (6x - 5y)(36x^2 + 25y^2 + 30xy)$.

15. Factorize : $(x^2 - 3x)^2 - 8(x^2 - 3x) - 20$.

[Board Term I, 2012, Set-QGL2IF5]

Sol. Let $x^2 - 3x = y$, then

Given expression $= (x^2 - 3x)^2 - 8(x^2 - 3x) - 20$

$= y^2 - 8y - 20 = y^2 - 10y + 2y - 20$

[By splitting the middle term]

$= y(y - 10) + 2(y - 10)$

$= (y - 10)(y + 2)$

$= (x^2 - 3x - 10)(x^2 - 3x + 2)$

$= (x^2 - 5x + 2x - 10)(x^2 - 2x - x + 2)$

$= [x(x - 5) + 2(x - 5)][x(x - 2) - 1(x - 2)]$

$= [(x - 5)(x + 2)][(x - 1)(x - 2)]$

$= (x - 1)(x - 2)(x + 2)(x - 5)$

16. Find the value of $x^3 - 8y^3 - 36xy - 216$, when $x = 2y + 6$.

[Board Term I, 2012, Set-58]

Sol. Given expression $= x^3 - 8y^3 - 36xy - 216$

$= (x)^3 + (-2y)^3 + (-6)^3 - 3(x)(-2y)(-6)$

$= [x + (-2y) + (-6)][x^2 + (-2y)^2 + (-6)^2 - (x) - (-2y)$

$\qquad\qquad - (-2y)(-6) - (x)(-6)]$

$[\because a^3 + b^3 + c^3 = (a + b + c)(a^2 + b^2 + c^2 - ab - bc - ca)]$

$= (x - 2y - 6)(x^2 + 4y^2 + 36 + 2xy - 12y + 6x)$

$= 0 \times [x^2 + 4y^2 + 36 + 2xy - 12y + 6x]$,

$(\because x = 2y + 6 \text{ or } x - 2y - 6 = 0)$

$\therefore x^3 - 8y^3 - 36xy - 216 = 0$.

17. Factorize: $x^4 + 2x^3y - 2xy^3 - y^4$.

[Board Term I, 2012, Set-47]

Sol. Given expression $= x^4 + 2x^3y - 2xy^3 - y^4$

$= (x^2)^2 - (y^2)^2 + 2x^3y - 2xy^3$

$= (x^2 - y^2)(x^2 + y^2) + 2xy(x^2 - y^2)$

$[\because a^2 - b^2 = (a + b)(a - b)]$

$= (x^2 - y^2)(x^2 + y^2 + 2xy)$

$= (x - y)(x + y)(x + y)^2$

$= (x - y)(x + y)^3$.

18. Prove that $2x^3 + 2y^3 + 2z^3 - 6xyz = (x + y + z)[(x - y)^2 + (y - z)^2 + (z - x)^2]$.

Hence evaluate : $2(13)^3 + 2(14)^3 + 2(15)^3 - 6 \times 13 \times 14 \times 15$.

[Board Term I, 2013, 2012, Set-43, Set-64]

Sol. Given,

$2x^3 + 2y^3 + 2z^3 - 6xyz = (x + y + z)[(x - y)^2 + (y - z)^2 + (z - x)^2]$

L.H.S $= 2x^3 + 2y^3 + 2z^3 - 6xyz$

$= 2[x^3 + y^3 + z^3 - 3xyz]$

$= 2\left[\dfrac{1}{2}(x + y + z)\{(x - y)^2 + (y - z)^2 + (z - x)^2\}\right]$

$= (x + y + z)[(x - y)^2 + (y - z)^2 + (z - x)^2]$

Now, Given expression,

$= 2(13)^3 + 2(14)^3 + 2(15)^3 - 6 \times 13 \times 14 \times 15$

$= (13 + 14 + 15)[(13 - 14)^2 + (14 - 15)^2 + (15 - 13)^2]$

$= 42 \times [1 + 1 + 4] = 42 \times 6 = 252$.

19. prove that : $(x + y)^3 + (y + z)^3 + (z + x)^3 - 3(x + y)(y + z)(z + x) = 2(x^3 + y^3 + z^3 - 3xyz)$.

[Board Term I, 2016, Set-7ADLQR]

[Board Term I, 2012, Set-60]

Sol. L.H.S $= (x + y)^3 + (y + z)^3 + (z + x)^3 - 3(x + y)(y + z)(z + x)$

$[\because a^3 + b^3 + c^3 - 3abc = (a + b + c)(a^2 + b^2 + c^2 - ab - bc - ca)]$

$= (x + y + y + z + z + x)[(x + y)^2 + (y + z)^2 + (z + x)^2 - (x + y)(y + z) - (y + z)(z + x) - (x + y)(z + x)]$

$= 2(x + y + z)[x^2 + y^2 + 2xy + y^2 + z^2 + 2yz + z^2 + x^2 + 2zx - xy - xz - y^2 - yz - yz - xy - z^2 - zx - xz - x^2 - yz - xy]$

$= 2(x + y + z)[x^2 + y^2 + z^2 - xy - yz - zx]$

$= 2(x^3 + y^3 + z^3 - 3xyz)$.

$\therefore$ L.H.S = R.H.S

Hence proved.

20. If $x^2 + \dfrac{1}{x^2} = 7$, find the value of $x^3 + \dfrac{1}{x^3}$.

[Board Term I, 2016, Set-7AEDLQR]

[Board Term I, 2012, Set-41]

Sol. Given, $x^2 + \dfrac{1}{x^2} = 7$

On adding 2 both sides, we have

$x^2 + \dfrac{1}{x^2} + 2 = 7 + 2 = 9$

$\left(x + \dfrac{1}{x}\right)^2 = 9 \qquad [\because a^2 + b^2 + 2ab = (a+b)^2]$

$\Rightarrow x + \dfrac{1}{x} = \sqrt{9} = 3$

Now, we know that

$\left(x + \dfrac{1}{x}\right)^3 = x^3 + \dfrac{1}{x^3} + 3\left(x + \dfrac{1}{x}\right)$

$\Rightarrow 3^3 = x^3 + \dfrac{1}{x^3} + 3 \times 3 \Rightarrow 27 = x^3 + \dfrac{1}{x^3} + 9$

$\therefore x^3 + \dfrac{1}{x^3} = 27 - 9 = 18$

21. Factorize : $(p + q)^2 - 20\,(p + q) - 125$.

[Board Term I, 2013]

Sol. Let, $p + q = x$, then

Give expression $= (p + q)^2 - 20(p + q) - 125$

$= x^2 - 20x - 125 \qquad$ [By splitting middle term]

$= x^2 - 25x + 5x - 125$

$= x(x - 25) + 5(x - 25)$

$= (x - 25)\,(x + 5)$

$= (p + q - 25)\,(p + q + 5) \qquad [\because x = p + q]$

22. Factorize completely : $x^8 - y^8$.

[Board Term I, 2013]

Sol. Given expression $= x^8 - y^8 = (x^4)^2 - (y^4)^2$

$= (x^4 + y^4)\,(x^4 - y^4)$

$\qquad$ [By using identity $a^2 - b^2 = (a + b)\,(a - b)$]

$= (x^4 + y^4)\,[(x^2)^2 - (y^2)^2]$

$= (x^4 + y^4)\,(x^2 + y^2)\,(x^2 - y^2)$

$= (x^4 + y^4)\,(x^2 + y^2)\,(x + y)\,(x - y)$

23. Factorize : $\dfrac{1}{64}x^3 - 8y^3 + \dfrac{3}{16}x^2y - \dfrac{3}{2}xy^2$.

[Board Term I, 2014]

Sol. Given expression $= \dfrac{1}{64}x^3 - 8y^3 + \dfrac{3}{16}x^2y - \dfrac{3}{2}xy^2$

$= \left(\dfrac{1}{4}x\right)^3 - (2y)^3 + \dfrac{3}{4}xy\left[\dfrac{1}{4}x - 2y\right]$

$= \left(\dfrac{1}{4}x - 2y\right)\left[\left(\dfrac{1}{4}x\right)^2 + (2y)^2 + \dfrac{1}{4}x \times 2y\right]$
$\quad + \dfrac{3}{4}xy\left[\dfrac{1}{4}x - 2y\right]$

$\qquad [\because a^3 - b^3 = (a - b)\,(a^2 + b^2 + ab)]$

$= \left(\dfrac{1}{4}x - 2y\right)\left(\dfrac{1}{16}x^2 + 4y^2 + \dfrac{1}{2}xy + \dfrac{3}{4}xy\right)$

$= \left(\dfrac{1}{4}x - 2y\right)\left(\dfrac{x^2}{16} + 4y^2 + \dfrac{5}{4}xy\right)$

$= \left(\dfrac{x}{4} - 2y\right)\left(\dfrac{x^2}{16} + \dfrac{1}{4}xy + xy + 4y^2\right)$

$= \left(\dfrac{x}{4} - 2y\right)\left[\dfrac{x}{4}\left(\dfrac{x}{4} + y\right) + 4y\left(\dfrac{x}{4} + y\right)\right]$

$= \left(\dfrac{x}{4} - 2y\right)\left(\dfrac{x}{4} + y\right)\left(\dfrac{x}{4} + 4y\right)$

24. Factorize : $125a^3 - 27b^3 + 75a^2b - 45ab^2$.

[Board Term I, 2014]

Sol. Given expression $= 125a^3 - 27b^3 + 75a^2b - 45ab^2$

$= 125a^3 + 75a^2b - 45ab^2 + 27b^3$

$= 25a^2\,(5a + 3b) - 9b^2\,(5a + 3b)$

$= (5a + 3b)\,(25a^2 - 9b^2)$

$= (5a + 3b)\,[(5a)^2 - (3b)^2]$

$= (5a + 3b)\,(5a + 3b)\,(5a - 3b)$

$\qquad [\because a^2 - b^2 = (a - b)\,(a + b)]$

$= (5a + 3b)^2\,(5a + 3b)$

25. If $x + \dfrac{1}{x} = 5$, evaluate $x^2 + \dfrac{1}{x^2}$

[Board Term I, 2014]

Sol. Given, $x + \dfrac{1}{x} = 5$

On squaring both sides, we get

$\left(x + \dfrac{1}{x}\right)^2 = 5^2$

$\Rightarrow \quad x^2 + \left(\dfrac{1}{x}\right)^2 + 2 \times x + \dfrac{1}{x} = 25$

$\qquad [\because (a + b)^2 = a^2 + b^2 + 2ab]$

$\Rightarrow \quad x^2 + \dfrac{1}{x^2} + 2 = 25$

$\therefore \quad x^2 + \dfrac{1}{x^2} = 25 - 2 = 23$

26. If $x - \dfrac{1}{x} = 2$, find $x^4 + \dfrac{1}{x^4}$

[Board Term I, 2015, Set-2]

Sol. Given, $x - \dfrac{1}{x} = 2$

Now, $x^2 + \dfrac{1}{x^2} = \left(x - \dfrac{1}{x}\right)^2 + 2 = (2)^2 + 2$

$\qquad\qquad = 4 + 2 = 6$

On squaring both sides,

$\left(x^2 + \dfrac{1}{x^2}\right)^2 = \left(x^4 + \dfrac{1}{x^4}\right) + 2$

$$\Rightarrow \qquad (6)^2 = \left(x^4 + \frac{1}{x^4}\right) + 2$$

$$\Rightarrow \qquad 36 - 2 = x^4 + \frac{1}{x^4}$$

$$\therefore \qquad x^4 + \frac{1}{x^4} = 34$$

27. Prove that $(a^2 - b^2)^3 + (b^2 - c^2)^3 + (c^2 - a^2)^3 = 3(a + b)(b + c)(c + a)(a - b)(b - c)(c - a)$.

[Board Term I, 2016, Set-BQ56IZK]

Sol. Let $x = a^2 - b^2$, $y = b^2 - c^2$, $z = c^2 - a^2$

Now, $x + y + z = a^2 - b^2 + b^2 - c^2 + c^2 - a^2 = 0$

$\because \qquad x + y + z = 0$

$\therefore \qquad x^3 + y^3 + z^3 = 3xyz$

L.H.S $= (a^2 - b^2)^3 + (b^2 - c^2)^3 + (c^2 - a^2)^3$

$\qquad = 3(a^2 - b^2)(b^2 - c^2)(c^2 - a^2)$

$\qquad = 3(a + b)(a - b)(b + c)(b - c)(c + a)(c - a)$

$\qquad = 3(a + b)(b + c)(c + a)(a - b)(b - c)(c - a)$

$\therefore$ L.H.S = R.H.S

Hence proved

28. $ab + bc + ca = 0$, find the value of

$$\frac{1}{a^2 - bc} + \frac{1}{b^2 - ca} + \frac{1}{c^2 - ac}.$$

[Board Term I, 2016, Set-JQ22L5C]

Sol. Given, $ab + bc + ca = 0$

$\Rightarrow \qquad -bc = ab + ca \qquad \qquad$ ...(i)

$\qquad \quad - ca = ab + bc \qquad \qquad$ ...(ii)

and $\quad -cb = bc + ca \qquad \qquad$ ...(iii)

Now, Given expression

$$= \frac{1}{a^2 - bc} + \frac{1}{b^2 - ca} + \frac{1}{c^2 - ab}$$

$$= \frac{1}{a^2 + ab + ca} + \frac{1}{b^2 + ab + bc} + \frac{1}{c^2 + bc + ca}$$

$$= \frac{1}{a(a + b + c)} + \frac{1}{b(a + b + c)} + \frac{1}{c(a + b + c)}$$

$$= \frac{1}{(a + b + c)}\left[\frac{1}{a} + \frac{1}{b} + \frac{1}{c}\right]$$

$$= \frac{bc + ca + ab}{abc(a + b + c)}$$

$$= \frac{0}{abc(a + b + c)} \qquad [\because ab + bc + ca = 0]$$

$$= 0$$

29. If $x + \frac{1}{x} = \sqrt{3}$ evaluate $x^3 + \frac{1}{x^3}$.

[Board Term I, 2016, Set-20CNJE9]

Sol. Given, $\left(x + \frac{1}{x}\right) = \sqrt{3}$

On Cubing both sides, we get

$$\left(x + \frac{1}{x}\right)^3 = \left(\sqrt{3}\right)^3$$

$$\Rightarrow x^3 + \frac{1}{x^3} + 3x \cdot \frac{1}{x}\left(x + \frac{1}{x}\right) = 3\sqrt{3}$$

$$\Rightarrow x^3 + \frac{1}{x^3} + 3\left(\sqrt{3}\right) = 3\sqrt{3} \qquad \left[\because x + \frac{1}{x} = \sqrt{3}\right]$$

$$\therefore \quad x^3 + \frac{1}{x^3} = 0$$

30. If $a + b + c = 5$ and $ab + bc + ca = 15$, then find the value of $(a + b)^3 + (b + c)^3 + (a + c)^3 - 3(a + b)(b + c)(a + c)$. HOTS

Sol. Given, $a + b + c = 5$

On squaring both sides, we get

$(a + b + c)^2 = 25$

$\Rightarrow a^2 + b^2 + c^2 + 2ab + 2bc + 2ca = 25$

$\Rightarrow a^2 + b^2 + c^2 = 25 - 2 \times 15 = -5 \qquad$ ...(i)

$[\because ab + bc + ca = 15 \text{ (given)}]$

Now,

$\therefore$ Expression $= (a + b)^3 + (b + c)^3 + (a + c)^3$

$\qquad \qquad \qquad - 3(a + b)(b + c)(a + c)$

$= [(a + b) + (b + c) + (c + a)]\{(a + b)^2 + (b + c)^2$

$\qquad + (c + a)^2 - (a + b)(b + c) - (b + c)(c + a)$

$\qquad \qquad \qquad - (c + a)(a + b)\}$

$[\because x^3 + y^3 + z^3 - 3xyz = (x + y + z)(x^2 + y^2 + z^2$

$\qquad \qquad \qquad \qquad - xy - yz - zx)]$

$= 2(a + b + c)[a^2 + b^2 + 2ab + b^2 + c^2 + 2ab$

$\qquad + c^2 + a^2 + 2ac - ab - ac - b^2 - bc - bc$

$\qquad \qquad - ba - c^2 - ca - ca - cb - a^2 - ab]$

$= 2(a + b + c)\{a^2 + b^2 + c^2 - ab - bc - ac\}$

$\qquad [\because a + b + c = +5, a^2 + b^2 + c^2 = -5$

$\qquad \qquad \text{and } ab + bc + ca = 15 \text{ (Given]}$

$= 2 \times 5(-5 - 15)$

$= 10 \times (-20) = -200$

CHAPTER 3

Linear Equations in Two Variables

- Recall of linear equations in one variable. Introduction to the equation in two variables.
- Focus on linear equations of the type ax + by + c = 0. Prove that a linear equation in two variables has infinitely many solutions and justify their being written as ordered pairs of real numbers, plotting them and showing that they lie on a line.
- Graph of linear equations in two variables. Examples, problems from real life, including problems on Ratio and Proportion and with algebraic and graphical solutions being done simultaneously.

A flow chart on the basic concepts:

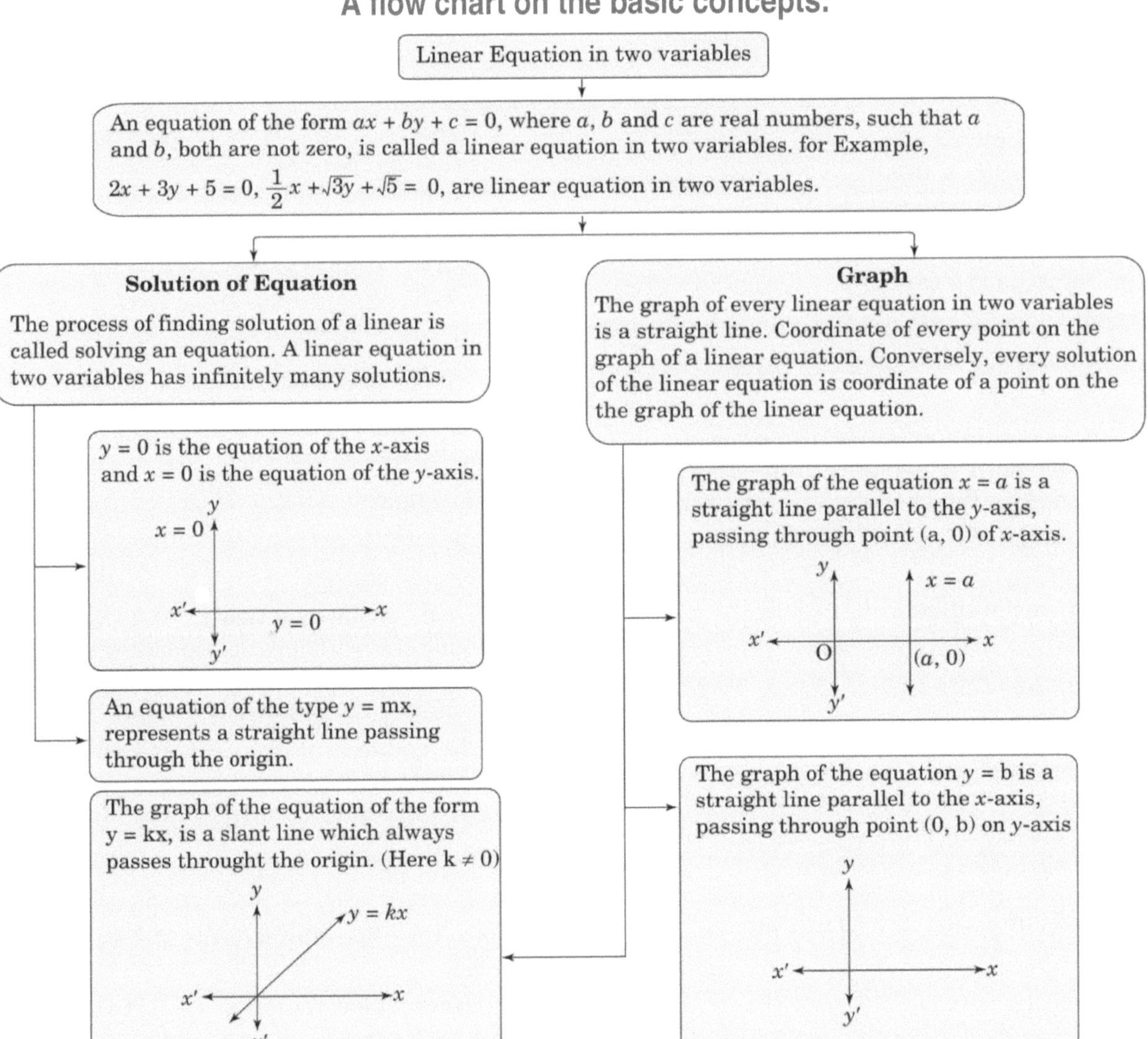

[Topic 1] Introduction of Linear Equation

Points to be Remembered

- An equation of the form ax + by + c = 0, where 'a', 'b' and 'c' are real numbers such that 'a' and 'b' are not both zero, is called a linear equation.
- A linear equation is an equation which involves linear polynomials.
- A value of the variable which makes the two sides of the equation equal is called the solution of the equation.
- There can be an infinite number of solution of a linear equation.

- **Linear equation in two variables :** An equation of the form ax + by + c = 0, where a, b and c are real numbers, such that a and b are both non zero, is called a linear equation in two variables. For example:

  x + y = 16, p + 3q = 9, $3 = \sqrt{7}\,x - y$ and 2l + m = 3

  All are linear equations in two variables.
- Any pair of values of x and y which satisfies the equation ax + by + c = 0, is called its solution. This solution can be written as an ordered pair (x, y), first writing value of x and then value of y.
- Linear equation in two variable has infinitely many solutions.

PREVIOUS YEARS'

EXAMINATION QUESTIONS
TOPIC 1

Multiple Choice Questions
(1 Mark Each)

1. If we multiply or divide both sides of a linear equation with a non-zero number, then the solution of the linear equation

   (a) changes

   (b) remains the same

   (c) changes in case of multiplication only

   (d) changes in case of division only.

   [NCERT Exemp.]

   Sol. (b) If we multiply or divide both sides of a linear equation with a non-zero number, then the solution of the linear equation remains the same.

2. The equation 2x + 5y = 7 has a unique solution, if x, y are

   (a) natural numbers

   (b) positive real numbers

   (c) real numbers

   (d) rational numbers   [NCERT Exemp.]

   Sol. (a) The equation 2x + 5y = 7 has a unique solution if x and y are natural numbers.

3. Any solution of the linear equation : 2x + 0y + 9 = 0 in two variables is of the form

   (a) $\left(-\dfrac{9}{2},\, m \right)$ (b) $\left(n, \dfrac{9}{2} \right)$

   (c) $\left(0, \dfrac{9}{2} \right)$ (d) (− 9, 0)

   [NCERT Exemp.]

   Sol. (a) According to the question,

   $$\Rightarrow \quad 2x + 0y + 9 = 0$$
   $$\Rightarrow \quad 2x + 9 = 0$$
   $$\Rightarrow \quad 2x = -9$$
   $$\therefore \quad x = -\frac{9}{2}$$

   And y can be any real number.

   Hence, $\left(-\dfrac{9}{2},\, m \right)$ is the required form of solution of the given linear equation:

   $$2x + 0y + 9 = 0$$

4. The equation of x-axis is of the form

   (a) x = 0   (b) y = 0

   (c) x + y = 0   (d) x = y [NCERT Exemp.]

   Sol. (b) The equation of x-axis is of the form y = 0.

5. The linear equation 2x − 5y = 7 has

   (a) a unique solution

   (b) two solutions

   (c) infinitely many solutions

   (d) no solution   [NCERT Exemp.]

   Sol. (c) In given equation 2x − 5y = 7, for every value of x, we get a corresponding value of y and vice-versa; therefore, the linear equation has infinitely many solutions.

6. The equation x = 7, in two variables, can be written as

   (a) 1.x + 1.y = 7   (b) 1.x + 0.y = 7

   (c) 0.x + 1.y = 7   (d) 0.x + 0.y = 7

   [NCERT Exemp.]

   Sol. (b) Co-efficient of y in the given equation x = 7 is 0.

   Hence, the equation x = 7 in two variables, is 1.x + 0.y = 7.

7. If $(2, 0)$ is a solution of the linear equation $2x + 3y = k$, then the value of k is

   (a) 4   *(b)* 6

   (c) 5   *(d)* 2   [NCERT Exemp.]

Sol. *(a)* $\because$ $(2, 0)$ is a solution of linear equation $2x + 3y = k$.

Put $x = 2, y = 0$ in the equation

$$2x + 3y = k$$
$$\Rightarrow \quad 2(2) + 3(0) = k$$
$$\Rightarrow \quad 4 + 0 = k$$

Hence, $\quad k = 4$

8. The positive solutions of the equation $ax + by + c = 0$ always lie in the

   (a) 1st quadrant   *(b)* 2nd quadrant

   (c) 3rd quadrant   *(d)* 4th quadrant

   [NCERT Exemp.]

Sol. *(a)* The positive solutions of the equation $ax + by + c = 0$, always lie in the 1st quadrant.

Because the coordinates of all points in the 1st quadrant are positive.

9. $x = 5, y = 2$ is a solution of the linear equation

   (a) $x + 2y = 7$ *(b)* $5x + 2y = 7$

   (c) $x + y = 7$ *(d)* $5x + y = 7$

   [NCERT Exemp.]

Sol. *(c)* Put $x = 5$ and $y = 2$ in equation $x + y = 7$, we have

$$\Rightarrow \quad x + y = 7$$
$$\Rightarrow \quad 5 + 2 = 7$$
$$\Rightarrow \quad 7 = 7$$

Hence, $(5, 2)$ is a solution of the given equation.

10. Any point on the line $y = x$ is of the form

    (a) (a, a) *(b)* $(0, a)$

    (c) $(a, 0)$ *(d)* $(a, -a)$

    [NCERT Exemp.]

Sol. *(a)* Every point on the line $y = x$ has same value of x and y coordinates, i.e., $x = a$ and $y = a$. Hence, (a, a) is the required form of the solution of given linear equation.

11. How many linear equations in x and y can be satisfied by $x = 1$ and $y = 2$?

    (a) only one

    (b) two

    (c) infinitely many

    (d) three   [NCERT Exemp.]

Sol. *(c)* Let the linear equation be $ax + by + c = 0$

On putting $x = 1$ and $y = 2$, we have

$$a + 2b + c = 0$$

where a, b and c are real numbers. So, different values of a, b and c satisfy $a + 2b + c = 0$. Hence, infinitely many linear equations in x and y can be satisfied by $x = 1$ and $y = 2$.

12. Any point on the x-axis is of the form

    (a) (x, y) *(b)* $(0, y)$

    (c) $(x, 0)$ *(d)* (x, x)

Sol. *(c)* Any point on the x-axis has its y-coordinates equal to zero, i.e., $y = 0$.

Hence, the point on x-axis is of $(x, 0)$ form.

13. Which one of the following options is true, and why? $y = 3x + 5$ has

    (a) a unique solution

    (b) only two solutions

    (c) infinitely many solutions [NCERT Exemp.]

Sol. *(c)* $y = 3x + 5$ is a linear equation in two variables and it has infinite possible solutions. For every value of x, there will be value of y which satisfying the given equation and vice-versa.

(a) $y = 3x + 5$ has a unique solution.   (False)

(b) $y = 3x + 5$ has only two solutions.   (False)

(c) $y = 3x + 5$ has infinitely many solutions.

(True)

14. The point of the form $(a, -a)$, where $a \neq 0$ lies on:

    (a) x-axis

    (b) y-axis

    (c) the line $y - x = 0$

    (d) the line $x + y = 0$ [NCERT Exemp.]

Sol. *(d)* The point of the form $(a, -a)$ lies on the line $x + y = 0$

15. If a linear equation has solutions $(-2, 2)$, $(0, 0)$ and $(2, -2)$, then it is of the form

    (a) $y - x = 0$ *(b)* $x + y = 0$

    (c) $-2x + y = 0$ *(d)* $-x + 2y = 0$

    [NCERT Exemp.]

Sol. *(b)* By putting all the solutions in equation $x + y = 0$

(i) $-2 + (2) = 0$ [On putting $(-2, 2)$]

(ii) $0 + 0 = 0$ [On putting $(0, 0)$]

(iii) $2 + (-2) = 0$ [On putting $(2, -2)$

Hence, $x + y = 0$ is the required form of the linear equation.

Very Short Answer Type Questions
(1 Mark Each)

1. If $(0, 2)$ is a solution of the linear equation $2x + 3y = k$, then find the value of k.
   [NCERT Exemplar Board, Term II, 2012, Set-20]

Sol. $\because$ $(0, 2)$ is the solution of given equation
$$2x + 3y = k$$
$\therefore$ It satisfies the equation
$$\therefore \quad 2(0) + 3(2) = k$$
$$\therefore \quad k = 0 \times 2 + 6 = 6$$

2. Any solution of linear equation $2x + 0y + 9 = 0$ in two variables is ....
   [NCERT Exemplar Board Term II, 2012, Set-8]

Sol. Given, $2x + 0y + 9 = 0$
$$\Rightarrow \quad 2x + 9 = 0$$
$$\Rightarrow \quad 2x = -9$$
$$\therefore \quad x = -\frac{9}{2}$$
For $x = -\frac{9}{2}$, y can be any real number.

Hence, $\left(-\dfrac{9}{2}, \text{m}\right)$ is the required form of solution.

3. If the linear equation has solutions $(-5, 5)$, $(0, 0)$, $(5 - 5)$, then the equation is ....
   [Board Term II, 2012, Set-25]

Sol. Linear equation $x + y = 0$, has solutions $(-5, 5)$, $(0, 0)$ and $(5, -5)$.

4. If x represent the present age of father and y represents the present age of the son, then the statement "present age of father is 5 more than 6 times of the age of son" in mathematical term equation is .... [Board Term II, 2012, Set-25]

Sol. According to the question,
$$x = 6y + 5$$
$$\Rightarrow \quad x - 6y = 5$$

5. The value of y at $x = -1$ in the equation $5y = 2$, is .... [Board Term II, 2012, Set-15]

Sol. Given equation,
$$5y = 2$$
$$\therefore \quad y = \frac{2}{5}$$

6. The equation $x = 7$ in two variables can be written as .... [Board Term II, 2012, Set-01]

Sol. The equation $x = 7$ in two variables can be written as $1.x + 0.y = 7$

7. The co-ordinates of the points where lines $ax = by$ and $ay = bx$ intersect, are ....
   [Board Term II, 2012, Set-01]

Sol. Both lines $ax = by$ and $ay = bx$ passing through origin.
$$\therefore \quad \text{Intersection point} = (0, 0)$$

8. The general form of linear equation in two variables is .... [Board Term II, 2012, Set-15]

Sol. The general form of linear equation in two variables is $ax + by + c = 0$, where a, b, c are real numbers and both a, $b \neq 0$.

9. If $x = 1$, $y = -1$ is a solution of equation $px - 2y = 10$, the value of p is ....
   [Board Term II, 2012, Set-30]

Sol. Given equation,
$$px - 2y = 10$$
On putting $x = 1$, $y = -1$, we have
$$p \times 1 - 2(-1) = 10$$
$$\Rightarrow \quad p + 2 = 10$$
$$\therefore \quad p = 10 - 2 = 8$$

10. Is $x = 4$, $y = 0$, the solution of $y - 4 = 0$?
    [Board Term II, 2012, Set-01]

Sol. No. ($\because$ $0 - 4 \neq 0$)
Because the solution of $y - 4 = 0$ is $(0, 4)$

11. Is $0x + 0y + c = 0$, a linear equation?
    [Board Term II, 2012, Set-43]

Sol. $\because$ a, $b \neq 0$ for a linear equation
$\therefore$ $0x + 0y + c = 0$ is not a linear equation.

12. If the point $(2, 3)$ lies on the line $4y = ax + 5$, then $a = $.......... [Board Term II, 2013]

Sol. Given point lies on the line
$$\text{i.e.,} \quad 4(3) = a(2) + 5$$
$$\text{or,} \quad 2a = 12 - 5 = 7$$
$$\text{or,} \quad a = \frac{7}{2}$$

13. If $\sqrt{3}x = \sqrt{2}x + 1$ then x is equal to :
    [Board Term II, 2013]

Sol. Given, $\sqrt{3}x = \sqrt{2}x + 1$
$$\Rightarrow \quad \sqrt{3}x - \sqrt{2}x = 1$$
$$\therefore \quad x(\sqrt{3} - \sqrt{2}) = 1$$
$$\therefore \quad x = \frac{1}{\sqrt{3} - \sqrt{2}} \times \frac{\sqrt{3} + \sqrt{2}}{\sqrt{3} + \sqrt{2}}$$
$$= \frac{\sqrt{3} + \sqrt{2}}{3 + 2} = \sqrt{3} + \sqrt{2}$$

14. Does the following equation $x = 5y$ represent a straight line passing through the point $(0, 0)$?
    [Board Term II, KVS 2014]

Sol. Given equation : $x = 5y$
The point $(0, 0)$ satisfies the given equation,
Hence, line $x = 5y$ represent a line passing through the point $(0, 0)$.

15. In a one day cricket match, Raina and Dhoni scored 198 runs. Express this as a linear equation in two variables. [Board Term II, 2014]

Sol. Let the runs scored by Raina and Dhoni are x and y respectively then,

According to the question, $x + y = 198$

16. Find the point where equation $3x + 2y = 12$ intersects y-axis. [Board Term II, 2014]

Sol. As the line intersects y-axis, put $x = 0$ in the given equation, we get

$$3(0) + 2y = 12$$
$$\Rightarrow \qquad 0 + 2y = 12$$
$$\Rightarrow \qquad y = \frac{12}{2} = 6$$

Hence, the required point is $(0, 6)$.

17. Total number of legs in a herd of goats and hens is 40. Represent this in the form of linear equation of two variables. [Board Term II, 2014]

Sol. Let the number of goats and hens in herd are x and y respectively then,

According to the question,

$$4x + 2y = 40$$

18. Express $\frac{x}{4} - 3y = 7$ in the form of $ax + by + c = 0$ [Board Term II, 2017, Set-Z6K408K]

Sol. Given, $\qquad \frac{x}{4} - 3y = 7$

$$\Rightarrow \qquad \frac{x - 12y}{4} = 7$$
$$\Rightarrow \qquad x - 12y = 28$$
$$\therefore \qquad x - 12y - 28 = 0$$

Hence, it is in the form of $ax + by + c = 0$

19. In $-2y + 3x = 14$, express y in terms of x. [Board Term II, 2017, Set-UAH4DQ7]

Sol. Given, $\quad -2y + 3x = 14$

$$\Rightarrow \qquad 3x - 14 = 2y$$
$$\therefore \qquad y = \frac{3x - 14}{2}$$

20. Find one solution of $y - 5 = 0$ in a cartesian frame. [Board Term II, 2017, Set-UAH4DQ7]

Sol. According to the question,

$$y - 5 = 0$$
$$y = 5$$

$\therefore$ $(0, 5), (1, 5), (2, 5)$ .... any one.

21. An equation of the form $ax + by + c = 0$ will be a linear equation in two variables, when $a \neq 0$, $b \neq 0$. It is True or False?

Sol. The given statement is true.

22. Find two solutions of the equation $3x + 4y = 24$

Sol. Given equation is $3x + 4y = 24$,

On putting $x = 0$ in the given equation, we have

$$0 + 4y = 24$$
$$\therefore \qquad y = \frac{24}{4} = 6$$

Now, on putting $y = 0$ in the given equation, we have

$$3x + 0 = 24$$
$$\therefore \qquad x = \frac{24}{3} = 8$$

Hence, the two solutions of the given equation are $(0, 6)$ and $(8, 0)$.

23. If $x = 2\alpha + 1$ and $y = \alpha - 1$ is a solution of the equation $2x - 3y + 5 = 0$, then find the value of α.

Sol. $\because$ $x = 2\alpha + 1$ and $y = \alpha - 1$ is a solution of the equation

$$2x - 3y + 5 = 0$$

So, it must satisfy the equation.

On putting $x = 2\alpha + 1$ and $y = \alpha - 1$ in the given equation, we get

$$2(2\alpha + 1) - 3(\alpha - 1) + 5 = 0$$
$$\Rightarrow \quad 4\alpha + 2 - 3\alpha + 3 + 5 = 0$$
$$\Rightarrow \qquad \alpha + 10 = 0$$
$$\therefore \qquad \alpha = -10$$

Short Answer Type Questions I
(2 Marks Each)

1. The point $(3, 4)$ lies on the graph of the equation $3y = ax + 7$. Find the value of 'a'.

[NCERT Exemplar Board Term II, Set-A1, 2011]

Sol. Given, $\qquad 3y = ax + 7$

If point $(3, 4)$ lies on, then

$$3y = ax + 7$$
$$\Rightarrow \qquad 3 \times 4 = 3a + 7$$
$$\Rightarrow \qquad 12 = 3a + 7$$
$$\Rightarrow \qquad 3a = 12 - 7 = 5$$
$$\therefore \qquad a = \frac{5}{3}$$

2. Express y in terms of x, given that $2x - 5y = 7$. Check whether the point $(-3, -2)$ is on the given line. [Board Term II, Set-A1, A2, 2011, 2010]

Sol. Given, $\qquad 2x - 5y = 7$

$$\Rightarrow \qquad 5y = 2x - 7$$
$$\Rightarrow \qquad y = \frac{2x - 7}{5}$$

Now, when $\qquad x = -3,$

$$y = \frac{2(-3) - 7}{5} = -\frac{13}{5} \neq -2$$

Therefore, the point $(-3, -2)$ does not lie on the given line.

3. Find the value of k so that $x = -1$ and $y = -1$ is a solution of the linear equation $9kx + 12ky = 63$.

[Board Term II, Set-A1, C1, 2011, 2010]

Sol. On substituting $x = -1$ and $y = -1$ in $9kx + 12ky = 63$, we get

$$\Rightarrow 9k(-1) + 12k(-1) = 63$$
$$\Rightarrow \quad -9k - 12k = 63$$
$$\Rightarrow \quad -21k = 63$$
$$\therefore \qquad k = -\frac{63}{21} = -3$$

4. After 5 years, the age of father will be two times the age of his son. Write a linear equation in two variables to represent this statement.

[Board Term II, Set-A1, B1, 2011, 2010]

Sol. Let father's present age = x years

and Son's present age = y years

After 5 years father's age will be = $(x + 5)$ years

After 5 years son's age will be = $(y + 5)$ years

According to the question,
$$x + 5 = 2(y + 5)$$
$$\Rightarrow \qquad x + 5 = 2y + 10$$
$$\Rightarrow \qquad x - 2y = 10 - 5$$
$$\therefore \qquad x - 2y = 5$$

5. Check which of the following is (are) the solution (s) of the equation $3y - 2x = 1$.

(i) $(4, 3)$ (ii) $(2\sqrt{2}, 3\sqrt{2})$

[Board Term II, Set-A1, 2011]

Sol. (i) On putting $(4, 3)$ in the given equation, we have
$$\therefore \qquad 3y - 2x = 3(3) - 2(4) = 1$$
Hence, $(4, 3)$ is the solution of the equation.

(ii) On putting $(2\sqrt{2}, 3\sqrt{2})$ in the given equation, we have
$$\therefore \qquad 3y - 2x = 3(3\sqrt{2}) - 2(2\sqrt{2})$$
$$= 5\sqrt{2} \neq 1$$
Hence, $(2\sqrt{2}, 3\sqrt{2})$ is not a solution of the given equation.

6. Find the co-ordinates of points where the graph of the equation $4x + 3y = 12$ intersects x-axis and y-axis.

[Board Term II, Set-A1 2011]

Sol. Given equation,
$$4x + 3y = 12$$
For intersection with x-axis,
put $\qquad y = 0$
$$4x + 3 \times 0 = 12$$
$$\Rightarrow \qquad 4x = 12$$
$$x = \frac{12}{4} = 3$$

Hence, co-ordinates are $(3, 0)$

For intersection with y-axis
$$x = 0$$
$$\therefore \qquad 3y = 12$$
or $\qquad y = 4$

Hence, co-ordinates are $(0, 4)$

7. A part of monthly expenses of a family on milk is fixed which is Rs. 700 and the remaining varies with the quantity of milk taken extra at the rate of Rs. 25 per litre. Taking the quantity of milk required extra as x litre and total expenditure on milk is Rs. y. Write a linear equation representing the above information.

[Board Term II, Set-A1, 2011]

Sol. According to the question,
$$700 + 25x = y$$
$$25x - y + 700 = 0$$
Hence, the above linear equation representing the value.

8. If the point $(2k - 3, k + 2)$ lies on the graph of the equation $2x + 3y + 15 = 0$, find value of k. [Board Term II, Set-A1, 2011]

Sol. On putting $x = 2k - 3$, $y = k + 2$ in $2x + 3y + 15 = 0$, we get
$$2(2k - 3) + 3(k + 2) + 15 = 0$$
$$\Rightarrow \quad 4k - 6 + 3k + 6 + 15 = 0$$
$$\Rightarrow \qquad 7k + 15 = 0$$
$$\Rightarrow \qquad 7k = -15$$
$$\therefore \qquad k = \frac{-15}{7}$$

9. If $x = 2$ and $y = 1$ is the solution of the linear equation $2x + 3y + k = 0$, find the value of k. [Board Term II, Set-A1, 2011]

Sol. Given, $2x + 3y + k = 0$

If $x = 2$, and $y = 1$ is the solution of the linear equation $2x + 3y + k = 0$ then

On putting $x = 2$ and $y = 1$,
$$2(2) + 3(1) + k = 0$$
$$\Rightarrow \qquad 4 + 3 + k = 0$$
$$\therefore \qquad k = -7$$

10. Express y in terms of x in equation $2x - 3y = 12$. Find the points where the line represented by this equation cuts x-axis and y-axis.

[Board Term II, 2012 Set-10, A1, 2011]

Sol. Given equation,
$$2x - 3y = 12$$
$$\Rightarrow \qquad 3y = 2x - 12$$
$$\therefore \qquad y = \frac{2x - 12}{3}$$

On x-axis $y = 0$

$\therefore$ $\dfrac{2x - 12}{3} = 0$

$\Rightarrow$ $2x - 12 = 0$

$\Rightarrow$ $2x = 12$

$\therefore$ $x = 6$

Hence, at point $(6, 0)$ the given line cuts the x-axis.

Now, on y-axis $x = 0$

$\therefore$ $y = \dfrac{2 \times 0 - 12}{3} = -4$

Hence at point $(0, -4)$ the given line cuts the y-axis.

11. Find three solutions of linear equation $7x - 5y = 35$ in two variables.   [Board Term II, 2014]

Sol. So, when

$$y = \dfrac{7x - 35}{5}$$

x	5	0	10
y	0	−7	7

Hence, three solutions are $(5, 0)$, $(0, -7)$ and $(10, 7)$

12. Find the value of k for which the point $(-1, 3)$ lies on the graph of the equation $2x - y + k = 0$.   [Board Term II, KVS 2016]

Sol. $(-1, 3)$ lies on the graph $2x - y + k = 0$

$\therefore$ $2(-1) - 3 + k = 0$

$\Rightarrow$ $-2 - 3 + k = 0$

$\therefore$ $k = 2 + 3 = 5$

13. Express y in terms of x from the equation $3x + 2y = 8$ and check whether the point $(4, -2)$ lies on the line.

Sol. Given, $3x + 2y = 8$

$\Rightarrow$ $2y = 8 - 3x$

$\therefore$ $y = \dfrac{8 - 3x}{2}$

For $x = 4$, we get

$$y = \dfrac{8 - 3 \times 4}{2}$$

$$= \dfrac{8 - 12}{2} = \dfrac{-4}{2} = -2$$

Hence, $(4, -2)$ lies on the line.

14. Find the point at which the equation $3x - 2y = 6$ meets the x-axis.

Sol. On x-axis, y co-ordinate is zero.

On putting $y = 0$ in $3x - 2y = 6$, we get

$\Rightarrow$ $3x - 0 = 6$

$\therefore$ $x = \dfrac{6}{3} = 2$

Hence $3x - 2y = 6$ meets the x-axis at $(2, 0)$.

15. Give equations of two lines on the same plane which are intersecting at point $(2, 3)$.

Sol. The equation of two lines on the same plane which are intersecting at point $(2, 3)$ are:

$$x + y = 5$$

and $y - x = 1$

16. Sum of the digits of a two-digit number is 14. If we add 18 to the original number, the digits interchange their places. Write two equations for these two statements.

Sol. Let the digit at unit place be x and the digit at ten's place be y.

$\therefore$ Original number $= x + 10y$

$\therefore$ Sum of the digit $= 14$

$\therefore$ $x + y = 14$ ...(i)

When the digit interchange, the new number $= y + 10x$

According to question,

$$x + 10y + 18 = y + 10x$$

$\Rightarrow$ $x + 10y + 18 - y - 10x = 0$

$\Rightarrow$ $-9x + 9y + 18 = 0$

Dividing throughout by -9, we have

$$x - y - 2 = 0$$

$\Rightarrow$ $x - y = 2$ ...(ii)

Hence, equations (i) and (ii) are required linear equations.

Short Answer Type Questions II
(3 Marks Each)

1. Determine the point on the graph of the linear equation $2x + 5y = 19$, whose ordinate is $1\dfrac{1}{2}$ times its abscissa.   [NCERT Exemplar]

Sol. Let x and y be the abscissa and ordinate, respectively of the point lie on given line

$$2x + 5y = 19 \qquad \text{...(i)}$$

Then, by given condition,

$$\text{Ordinate } (y) = 1\dfrac{1}{2}x \text{ (Abscissa)}$$

$\Rightarrow$ $y = \dfrac{3}{2}x$ ...(ii)

Now, On putting $y = \dfrac{3}{2}x$ in equation (i), we get

$$2x + 5\left(\dfrac{3}{2}\right)x = 19$$

$\Rightarrow$ $4x + 15x = 38$

$\Rightarrow$ $19x = 38$

$\therefore$ $x = 2$

On substituting the value of x in equation (ii), we get

$$\therefore \qquad y = \frac{3}{2} \times 2 = 3$$

Hence, the required point is (2, 3).

2. When 5 times the larger of the two numbers is divided by the smaller, the quotient and remainder are 2 and 9 respectively. Form a linear equation in two variables. Write it in standard form.   **[Board Term II, 2012, Set-25]**

Sol. Let larger number be x, then 5 times of larger number = 5x and smaller number be y

$$\therefore \qquad \text{Quotient} = 2 \text{ and remainder} = 9$$

According to the question,

$$5x = 2y + 9$$
$$\therefore \qquad 5x - 2y - 9 = 0$$

Hence, above equation is the required linear equation in two variables.

3. Find k in each case, if x = 2, y = 1 is a solution of the equations :

(i) $3x + 2y = k$ (ii) $2x - ky = 6$

(iii) $\dfrac{x}{4} + \dfrac{y}{3} = 5k$ **[Board Term II, 2012, Set-23]**

Sol. (i) Given, $3x + 2y = k$

On putting x = 2, y = 1, then we have

$$3(2) + 2(1) = k$$
$$\therefore \qquad k = 8$$

(ii) Given, $2x - ky = 6$

On putting x = 2, y = 1, then we have

$$2(2) - k(1) = 6$$
$$\text{or} \qquad 4 - k = 6$$
$$\therefore \qquad k = 4 - 6 = -2$$

(iii) Given, $\dfrac{x}{4} + \dfrac{y}{3} = 5k$

On putting x = 2, y = 1, then we have

$$\therefore \qquad \frac{2}{4} + \frac{1}{3} = 5k$$
$$\Rightarrow \qquad 5k = \frac{10}{12} = \frac{5}{6}$$
$$\therefore \qquad k = \frac{5}{6} \times \frac{1}{5} = \frac{1}{6}$$

4. If the point $(-1, -5)$ lies on the graph of $3x = ay + 7$, then find the value of 'a'.

[Board Term II, 2012, Set-20]

Sol. $\therefore$ Point $(-1, -5)$ lies on the graph of

$$3x = ay + 7$$

On putting x = -1 and y = -5,

$$\therefore \qquad 3(-1) = a \times (-5) + 7$$
$$\Rightarrow \qquad -3 = -5a + 7$$
$$\Rightarrow \qquad 5a = 10$$

5. Write the equation $y\sqrt{3} = 8x + \sqrt{3}$ in the form of ax + by + c = 0. Check whether $(0, -1)$ and $(\sqrt{3}, 9)$ are the solutions of this equation.

[Board Term II, 2012, Set-24]

Sol. Given, $\qquad y\sqrt{3} = 8x + \sqrt{3}$

$$\Rightarrow \quad 8x - y\sqrt{3} + \sqrt{3} = 0$$

On putting x = 0 and y = -1

$$8 \times 0 - (-1) \times \sqrt{3} + \sqrt{3} = 0$$
$$\text{or} \qquad \sqrt{3} + \sqrt{3} \neq 0$$

$\therefore$ $(0, -1)$ is not the solution of given equation.

On putting $x = \sqrt{3}, y = 9$

$$\text{or } 8\sqrt{3} - 9\sqrt{3} + \sqrt{3} = 0$$
$$\Rightarrow \qquad -\sqrt{3} + \sqrt{3} = 0$$
$$\Rightarrow \qquad 0 = 0$$

Hence, $(\sqrt{3}, 9)$ is a solution of the given equation.

6. Find the coordinates of the points where the line representing the equation $\dfrac{x}{4} = 1 - \dfrac{y}{6}$ cuts the x-axis and the y-axis.

[Board Term II, 2012, Set-30]

Sol. The standard form of equation

$$3x + 2y - 12 = 0$$

Now, on x-axis, y = 0, we have

$$3x + 2 \times 0 - 12 = 0$$
$$\Rightarrow \qquad 3x - 12 = 0$$
$$\Rightarrow \qquad 3x = 12$$
$$\therefore \qquad x = \frac{12}{3} = 4$$

Hence, point on the x-axis = (4, 0)

Again, on y-axis, x = 0, we have

$$\Rightarrow \qquad 2y - 12 = 0$$
$$\Rightarrow \qquad 2y = 12$$
$$\therefore \qquad y = 6$$

Hence, point on the y-axis = (0, 6).

7. Find three different solutions for the equation $3x + 2y = 1$.   **[Board Term II, 2012, Set-05]**

Sol. Given, $\qquad 3x + 2y = 1$

$$\frac{1 - 3x}{2} = y$$

(i) On putting x = 1, then

$$y = \frac{1 - 3(1)}{2} = \frac{-2}{2} = -1$$

(ii) On putting x = 3, then

$$y = \frac{1 - 3(3)}{2} = \frac{1 - 9}{2} = -4$$

(iii) On putting $x = 5$, then

$$y = \frac{1 - 3(5)}{2} = \frac{1 - 15}{2} = -7$$

Hence, three different solutions for the equation $3x + 2y = 1$.

x	1	3	5
y	−1	−4	−7

8. Give the equation of a line passing through (2, 14). How many more such lines are there? Write the equation in the form $ax + by + c = 0$.

[Board Term II, 2012, Set-6]

Sol. The line passing through (2, 14) is

$$2y = 14x$$
$$\Rightarrow \qquad y = 7x$$

∴ Infinitely many lines are there.

Hence, the equation in the form $ax + by + c = 0$ is

$$7x - y + 0 = 0$$

9. Determine the point on the graph of the linear equation $x + y = 6$, whose ordinate is 2 times its abscissa. [Board Term II, 2012, Set-20]

Sol. Given, $y = 2x$

On putting $y = 2x$ in the equation $x + y = 6$, we get

$$x + 2x = 6$$
$$\Rightarrow \qquad 3x = 6$$
$$\Rightarrow \qquad x = 2$$
$$\text{and} \qquad y = 2 \times 2 = 4$$

Hence required point is (2, 4).

10. Show that the points A(1, 2), B(− 1, − 16) and C(0, − 7) lie on the graph of the linear equation $y = 9x - 7$. [Board Term II, 2012, Set-8]

Sol. The given equation is

$$y = 9x - 7$$

Point A(1, 2); $\qquad 2 = 9(1) - 7$

$$2 = 2;$$

∴ Point A(1, 2) lies on the linear equation $y = 9x - 7$.

Point B(− 1, − 16);

$$-16 = 9(-1) - 7 = -9 - 7 = -16;$$

∴ Point B(− 1, − 16) lies on the linear equation $y = 9x - 7$.

Point C(0, − 7);

$$-7 = 9(0) - 7$$
$$= 0 - 7 = -7; \text{ True}$$

∴ Point C(0, − 7) lies on the linear equation $y = 9x - 7$.

11. If the point (3, 4) lie on the graph of the linear equation $3y = kx + 7$, then find the value of k.

[Board Term II, 2012, Set-8]

Sol. On putting (3, 4) in the equation of the line

$$3y = kx + 7$$
$$\Rightarrow \qquad 3(4) = k(3) + 7$$
$$\Rightarrow \qquad 12 = 3k + 7$$
$$\Rightarrow \qquad 3k = 5$$
$$\therefore \qquad k = \frac{5}{3}$$

12. Given the equation $2x + y = 7$,

(i) What is the value of x, when the value of y is 3?

(ii) What is the value of y, when the value of x is 4?

(iii) Find one more solution for the above equation.

[Board Term II, 2012, Set-23, KVS 2014]

Sol. (i) When $y = 3$, then

$$2x + 3 = 7$$
$$\Rightarrow \qquad 2x = 4$$
$$\therefore \qquad x = 2$$

(ii) When $x = 4$, then

$$2(4) + y = 7 \Rightarrow 8 + y = 7$$
$$\therefore \qquad y = 7 - 8 = -1$$

(iii) When $x = 1$, then

$$2 + y = 7 \therefore y = 5$$

Hence, required one more solution = (1, 5).

13. For what value of p; $x = 2$, $y = 3$ is a solution of $(p + 1)x - (2p + 3)y - 1 = 0$ and write the equation. [Board Term II, 2013]

Sol. Given, $(p + 1)x - (2p + 3)y - 1 = 0$ ...(i)

If $x = 2$, $y = 3$ is the solution of the equation (i), then $(p + 1)2 - (2p + 3) 3 - 1 = 0$

$$\Rightarrow \quad 2p + 2 - 6p - 9 - 1 = 0$$
$$\Rightarrow \quad -4p + 2 - 10 = 0$$
$$\Rightarrow \qquad -4p - 8 = 0$$
$$\therefore \qquad p = -2$$

On putting the value of p in the equation (i), then

$$-x + y - 1 = 0$$

Hence, $x - y + 1 = 0$, is the required equation.

14. For what value of k, the linear equation $2x + ky = 8$ has $x = 2$ and $y = 1$ as its solution?

If $x = 4$, then find the value of y.

[Board Term II, KVS 2014]

Sol. The linear equation is $2x + ky = 8$

At $x = 2$, $y = 1$,

$$2(2) + k(1) = 8$$
$$4 + k = 8$$
$$\Rightarrow \qquad k = 4$$

∴ Therefore, the value of $k = 4$

If $x = 4$, then

$$\text{or} \qquad 2(4) + 4y = 8$$
$$\Rightarrow \qquad 8 + 4y = 8$$
$$\Rightarrow \qquad 4y = 0$$
$$\therefore \qquad y = 0$$

Hence, the value of $y = 0$

15. ABCD is a square. Co-ordinates of A and C are $(-1, -1)$ and $(1, 1)$ respectively. Write the coordinates of B and D. Also write the equations of all the sides of square.   [Board Term II, 2014]

Sol. Given, $A(-1, -1)$ and $C(1, 1)$

Then, $B(1, -1)$ and $D(-1, 1)$

Therefore, equations of sides of square are,

Equation of line AB
$$Y = -1$$

Equation of line BC
$$X = 1$$

Equation of line CD
$$Y = 1$$

Equation of line DA
$$X = -1$$

16. Find the equations of any two lines passing through the point $(-1, 2)$. How many such lines can be here?   [Board Term II, 2017, Set-UAH4DQ7]

Sol. Equation of two lines passing through the point $(-1, 2)$ are
$$x + y = 1$$
and
$$2x + y = 0$$
We know that infinite number of lines can pass through the point $(-1, 2)$.

17. The point $(2, 3)$ lies on the graph of the linear equation $3x - (a - 1)y = 2a - 1$. If the same point also lies on the graph of the linear equation $5x + (1 - 2a)y = 3b$, then find the value of b.

Sol. Given, point $(2, 3)$ lies on the linear equation.
$$3x - (a - 1)y = 2a - 1 \qquad ...(i)$$
Hence, point $(2, 3)$ is the solution of equation we have
$$3 \times 2 - (a - 1) \times 3 = 2a - 1$$
$$\Rightarrow \qquad 6 - 3a + 3 = 2a - 1$$
$$\Rightarrow \qquad -3a - 2a = -1 - 9$$
$$\Rightarrow \qquad -5a = -10$$
$$\therefore \qquad a = 2$$
Also, $(2, 3)$ is the solution of equation $5x + (1 - 2a)y = 3b$
$$\therefore \quad 5 \times 2 + (1 - 2a) \times 3 = 3b$$
$$\Rightarrow \qquad 10 + 3 - 6a = 3b$$
$$\Rightarrow \qquad 13 - 6 \times 2 = 3b \qquad [\because a = 2]$$
$$\Rightarrow \qquad 1 = 3b$$
$$\therefore \qquad b = \frac{1}{3}$$

Hence, the value of b is $\frac{1}{3}$.

18. I am three times as old as my son. Five years later, I shall be two and half times as old as my son. Taking my age as x year and son's age as y year, write the linear equation so formed.

Sol. Given, my age is x year and son's age is y year.

Then, $\qquad x = 3y$

Now, according to the question,
$$x + 5 = \frac{5}{2}(y + 5)$$
$$\Rightarrow \qquad 2(x + 5) = 5y + 25$$
$$\Rightarrow \qquad 2x + 10 = 5y + 25 \Rightarrow 2x - 5y = 15$$
Hence, above equation is the required linear equations.

Long Answer Type Questions
(4 Marks Each)

1. A pharmacist needs to strengthen a 15% alcoholic solution to one of 32% alcohol. How much pure alcohol should be added to 800 ml of 15% solution?

Sol. Let x mL of pure alcohol be added to the 15% alcoholic solution to get 32% alcoholic solution.

$\therefore$ Total volume of alcoholic solution
$$= (800 + x)\text{ mL}$$
and quantity of pure alcohol in $(800 + x)$ ml solution

= Quantity of pure alcohol in 800 mL solution
$$+ \text{ x mL}$$
= 15% of 800 + x

According to the question,
$$\frac{32}{100} \times (800 + x) = \frac{15}{100} \times 800 + x$$
$$\Rightarrow \qquad 25600 + 32x = 12000 + 100x$$
$$\Rightarrow \qquad 100x - 32x = 25600 - 12000$$
$$\Rightarrow \qquad 68x = 13600$$
$$\therefore \qquad x = \frac{13600}{68} = 200$$

Hence, 200 mL of pure alcohol should be added. to 800 ml of 15% solution.

2. In a housing society, people decided to do rainwater harvesting. Rainwater is collected in the underground tank at the rate of 30 cm^3/s. Taking volume of water collected in x second as y cm^3.

(i) From a linear equation.

(ii) Write it in standard form as ax + by + c = 0.

(iii) Find the values of a, b and c in part (ii).

Sol. (i) Given, volume of water collected in x second
$$= y\text{ cm}^3$$
Now, According to the question,

y = 30x, which is required linear equation.

(ii) The standard form of linear equation y = 30x
$$30x - y = 0 \Rightarrow 30x - y + 0 = 0 \qquad ...(i)$$
(iii) On comparing eqn. (i) with
$$ax + by + c = 0,$$
we get, a = 30, b = −1 and c = 0

3. For the following pairs of linear equations, find solutions of the form x = a, y = 0 and x = 0, y = b.

(i) $3x + 2y = 6$ and $5x - 2y = 10$

(ii) $9x + 7y = 63$ and $x - y = 10$

Sol. (i) Given equation $3x + 2y = 6$ can be written

$$2y = 6 - 3x$$

$$\therefore \qquad y = \frac{6 - 3x}{2} \qquad\qquad ...(i)$$

When x = 2, then

$$y = \frac{6 - (3 \times 2)}{2} = \frac{6 - 6}{2} = 0$$

When x = 0, then $y = \dfrac{6 - (3 \times 0)}{2} = \dfrac{6}{2} = 3$

Also given equation $5x - 2y = 10$ can be written as

$$\Rightarrow \qquad 2y = 5x - 10$$

$$\therefore \qquad y = \frac{5x - 10}{2} \qquad\qquad ...(ii)$$

When x = 2, then

$$y = \frac{(5 \times 2) - 10}{2} = \frac{10 - 10}{2} = 0$$

When x = 0, then $y = \dfrac{(5 \times 0) - 10}{2} = -5$

Hence, required solutions are $(2, 0)$, $(0, 3)$ and $(2, 0)$, $(0, -5)$.

Yes, both equations have a common solution $(2, 0)$.

(ii) Given equation $9x + 7y = 63$ can be written as

$$7y = 63 - 9x$$

$$\therefore \qquad y = \frac{63 - 9x}{7} \qquad\qquad ...(i)$$

when x = 7, then

$$y = \frac{63 - 9 \times 7}{7} = \frac{63 - 63}{7} = 0$$

when x = 0, then

$$y = \frac{63 - 0}{7} = \frac{63}{7} = 9$$

Also given equations are $5x - 2y = 10$ can be written as

$$y = x - 10$$

when x = 10, then $y = 10 - 10 = 0$

when x = 0, then $y = 0 - 10 = -10$

Hence, the required solutions are $(7, 0)$, $(0, 9)$ and $(10, 0)$, $(0, -10)$. No, solution is common.

[Topic 2] Graphical Representation of Linear Equation in Two Variables

Points to be Remembered

- The graph of a linear equation in two variables is a straight line.
- Every point on the graph of a linear equation in two variables is a solution of the linear equation. On the other hand, every solution of a linear equation is a point of the graph of the linear equation.
- x = 0 is the equation of the y-axis.
- y = 0 is the equation of the x-axis.
- The graph of x = a is a straight line parallel to the y-axis.

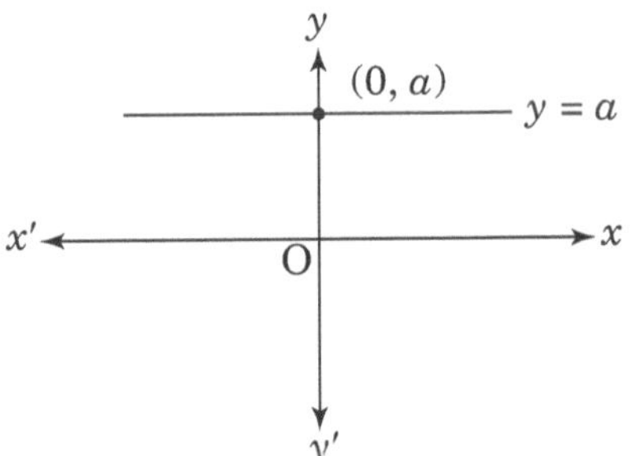

- The graph of y = a is a straight line parallel to the x-axis.

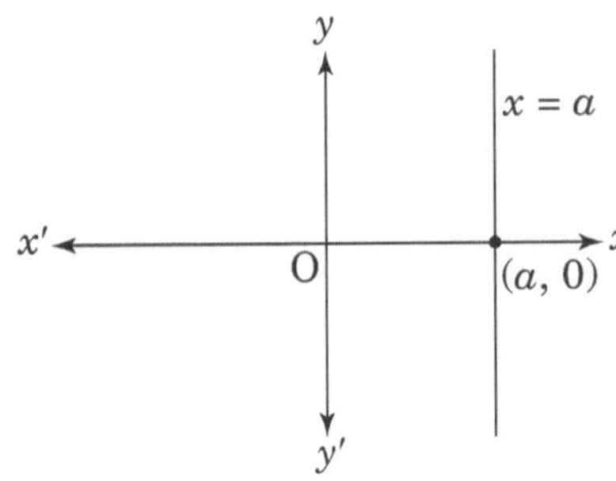

- An equation of the type y = mx, is a straight line passing through the origin.

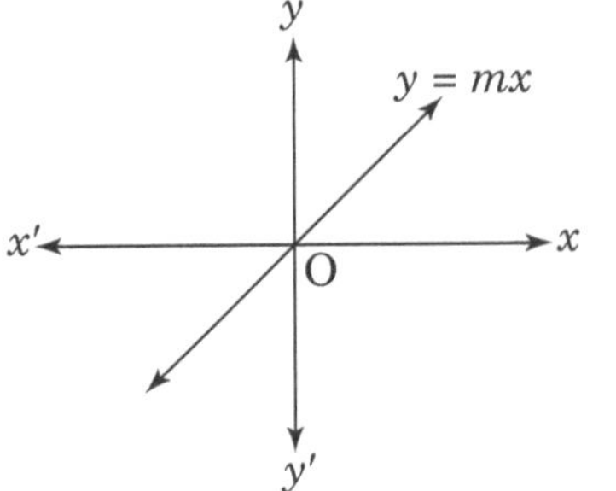

PREVIOUS YEARS'
EXAMINATION QUESTIONS
TOPIC 2

Multiple Choice Questions
(1 Mark Each)

1. The graph of the equation $y = -3$ is a line:

    [NCERT Exemp.]

    (a) parallel to x-axis, at a distance of 3 units from origin and below x-axis

    (b) parallel to x-axis, at a distance of 3 units from origin.

    (c) parallel to y-axis, at a distance of 3 units from origin to the left side of y-axis

    (d) cuts intercept of 6 units on both axes

    [NCERT Exemp.]

Sol. (a) The graph of the equation $y = -3$ is a line parallel to x-axis, at a distance of 3 units from origin and below x-axis.

2. The graph of the linear equation $2x + 3y = 6$ is a line which meets the x-axis at the point

    (a) (0, 2) (b) (2, 0)

    (c) (3, 0) (d) (0, 3) [NCERT Exemp.]

Sol. (c) Given equation $2x + 3y = 6$
On putting $y = 0$ in given equation

$\Rightarrow \qquad 2x + 3(0) = 6$

$\Rightarrow \qquad\qquad 2x = 6$

$\therefore \qquad\qquad x = 3$

Hence, the graph of equation $2x + 3y = 6$ is a line which meets the x-axis at the point (3, 0).

3. The graph of $y = 6$ is a line

    (a) parallel to x-axis at distance 6 units from the origin.

    (b) parallel to y-axis at distance 6 units from the origin.

    (c) making an intercept 6 on the x-axis

    (d) making an intercept 6 on both the axes.

    [NCERT Exemp.]

Sol. (a) Given equation $y = 6$ can be written as

$$0.x + 1.y = 6$$

When $x = 0$, then $y = 6$

When $x = 2$, then $y = 6$

x	0	2
y	6	6

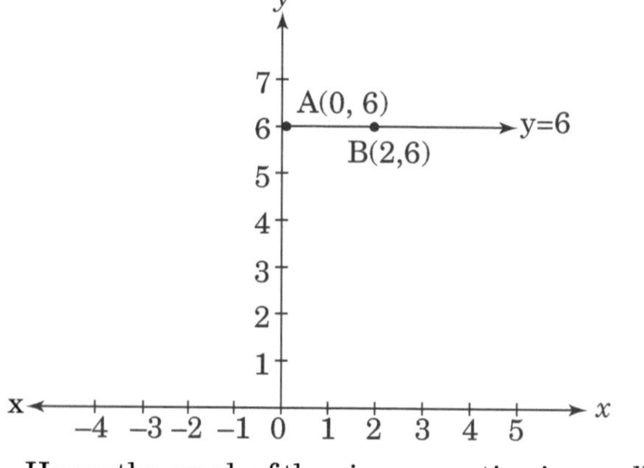

Hence the graph of the given equation is parallel to x-axis and at a distance of 6 units from the origin.

4. The point of the form $(a, -a)$ always lies on the line

    (a) $x = a$ (b) $y = -a$

    (c) $y = x$ (d) $x + y = 0$

    [NCERT Exemp.]

Sol. (d) On putting $x = a$ and $y = -a$, we have

$$x + y = a + (-a) = 0$$

Hence, the point $(a, -a)$ always lies on the line $x + y = 0$.

5. The point of the form (a, a) always lies on

    (a) x-axis (b) y-axis

    (c) On the line $y = x$

    (d) On the line $x + y = 0$ [NCERT Exemp.]

Sol. (c) Since, the given point (a, a) has same value of x and y co-ordinates. Therefore, the point (a, a) must be lie on the line $y = x$.

6. The graph of the linear equation $2x + 3y = 6$ cuts the y-axis at the point

    (a) (2, 0) (b) (0, 3)

    (c) (3, 0) (d) (0, 2)

Sol. (d) Given, $2x + 3y = 6$

Since the graph of linear equation $2x + 3y = 6$ cuts the y-axis.

On putting $x = 0$ in the given equation, we have

$$2x + 3y = 6$$

$\Rightarrow \qquad 2(0) + 3y = 6$

$\Rightarrow \qquad\qquad 0 + 3y = 6$

$\therefore \qquad\qquad\qquad y = 2$

Hence, at the point (0, 2) the given linear equation cuts the y-axis.

7. The graph of the linear equation $y = x$ passes through the point

(a) $\left(\dfrac{3}{2}, \dfrac{-3}{2}\right)$ (b) $\left(0, \dfrac{3}{2}\right)$

(c) $(1, 1)$ (d) $\left(\dfrac{-1}{2}, \dfrac{1}{2}\right)$

[NCERT Exemp.]

Sol. (c) The linear equation $y = x$ has the same value of x and y co-ordinates. Therefore, linear equation $y = x$ passes through the point $(1, 1)$.

8. $x = 5$, $y = -2$ is a solution of the linear equation:

(a) $2x + y = 9$ (b) $2x - y = 12$

(c) $x + 3y = 1$ (d) $x + 3y = 0$

Sol. (b) From option (b),

$$2x - y = 12$$

On putting $x = 5$ and $y = -2$,

$$2 \times 5 - (-2) = 12$$
$$\Rightarrow \quad 10 + 2 = 12$$
$$\Rightarrow \quad 12 = 12$$

Very Short Answer Type Questions
(1 Mark Each)

1. At what point, the graph of linear equation $2x + 3y = 6$ cuts the y-axis?   [NCERT Exemp.]

Sol. Since the graph of linear equation $2x + 3y = 6$ cuts the y-axis.

$\therefore$ At y-axis, $x = 0$

Now, on putting $x = 0$ in

$$2x + 3y = 6, \text{ we get}$$
$$\Rightarrow \quad 2(0) + 3y = 6$$
$$\Rightarrow \quad 3y = 6$$
$$\therefore \quad y = 2$$

Hence, $(0, 2)$ is the point at which the graph of linear equation cuts the y-axis.

2. The graph of $y = 6$ is a line .... to x-axis and at a distance of .... units from the origin.

[Board Term II, 2012, Set-02]

Sol. The graph of $y = 6$ is a line parallel to x-axis and at a distance of 6 units from the origin.

3. The equation of a line parallel to y-axis is ....

[Board Term II, 2012, Set-10]

Sol. The equation of a line parallel to y-axis is $x = k$ where k is any real number.

4. Draw the graph representing the equation of $x + y = 0$.   [Board Term II, 2012, Set-23]

Sol. Given, $x + y = 0$

$\therefore \quad y = -x$

when $x = 0$, then $y = 0$

when $x = 1$, then $y = -1$

when $x = -1$, then $y = 1$

x	0	1	−1
y	0	−1	1

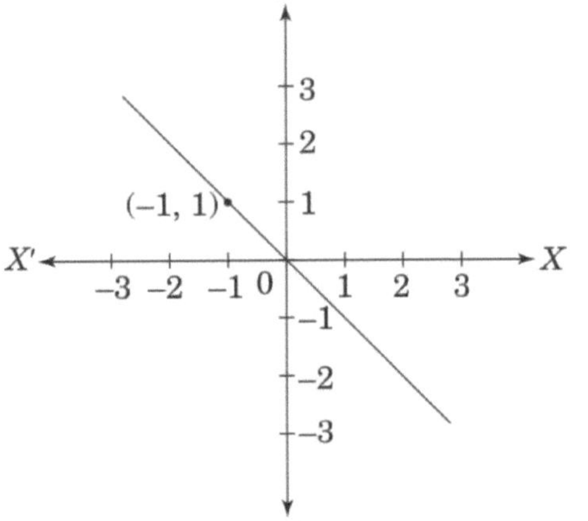

5. $x = 4$ is a line parallel to line ....

[Board Term II, 2012, Set-24]

Sol. $x = 4$ is a line parallel to the y-axis or $x = 0$.

6. The graph of the linear equation $3x + 5y = 15$ cuts the x-axis at the point ....

[Board Term II, 2012, Set-06]

Sol. Given,

$$3x + 5y = 15$$

On putting $y = 0$ at x-axis, we have

$$3x + 0 = 15$$
$$\therefore \quad x = \dfrac{15}{3} = 5$$

Hence, required point $= (5, 0)$

7. The maximum number of points that lie on a graph of the linear equation in two variables is ....

[Board Term II, 2012, Set-01]

Sol. There are infinite points that lie on a linear equation in two variable.

8. The graph of the linear equation $4x - 3y = 12$ cuts y-axis at ....

[Board Term II, 2013]

Sol. $\qquad 4x - 3y = 12$

$\therefore$ It cuts y-axis

$\therefore \qquad x = 0$

On putting $x = 0$ in given equation.

$$4(0) - 3y = 12$$
$$\Rightarrow \quad y = \dfrac{-12}{3} = -4$$

Hence, required point $= (0, -4)$

9. The graph of the equation $x + a = 0$ is a line parallel to y-axis and to the left of the y-axis if .... [Board Term II, 2013]

Sol. If $a > 0$, then the graph of $x + a = 0$ is a line parallel to y-axis and to the left of the y-axis.

10. If the graph of $2x + ky = 5$ passes through the point $(-2, 1)$, find k. [Board Term II, 2017, Set-Z6K408K]

Sol. Given, $2x + ky = 5$

On putting $x = -2, y = 1$

$$2(-2) + k(1) = 5$$
$$\Rightarrow \quad -4 + k = 5$$
$$\therefore \quad k = 5 + 4 = 9$$

11. What is the equation of a line parallel to x-axis?

Sol. $y = k$, is the equation of a line parallel to x-axis.

12. To which linear equation does the graph represent?

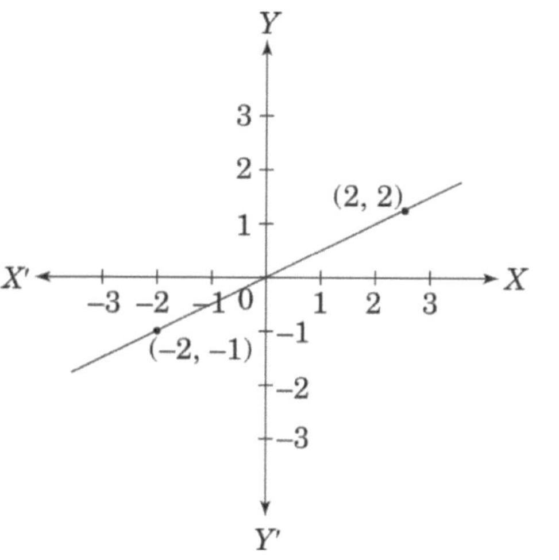

Sol. From the given graph, the linear equation is as follows:

$$3x - 4y + 2 = 0$$

Write whether the following statements are True or False? Justify your answer

(1 Mark Each)

1. The graph of every linear equation in two variables need not be a line? [NCERT Exemp.]

Sol. The given statement is false. Since, the graph of a linear equation in two variables always represents a line.

2. Every point on the graph of a linear equation in two variables does not represent a solution of the linear equation. [NCERT Exemp.]

Sol. The given statement is false. Since every point on the graph of the linear equation represents a solution.

Short Answer Type Questions-I

(2 Marks Each)

1. Write linear equation such that each point on its graph has ordinate 3 times its abscissa. [NCERT Exemp.]

Sol. Let the abscissa of the point be x and the ordinate of the point be y.

According to the question, $y = 3x$

When $x = 1$, then $y = 3 \times 1 = 3$

When $x = 2$, then $y = 3 \times 2 = 6$

When $x = 3$, then $y = 3 \times 3 = 9$

x	1	2	3
y	3	6	9

So, three points A(1, 3), B(2, 6) and C(3, 9).

Hence, we can see that any point on the line joining these points has an ordinate 3 times its abscissa.

2. How many solution(s) of the equation $2x + 1 = x - 3$ are there on the

(i) number line?   (ii) cartesian plane? [NCERT Exemp.]

Sol. Given equation is $2x + 1 = x - 3$

$$\Rightarrow \quad 2x - x = -3 - 1$$
$$\therefore \quad x = -4$$

(i) Number line represents the all real values of x on the x-axis. Therefore, $x = -4$ is exactly one point which lies on the number line.

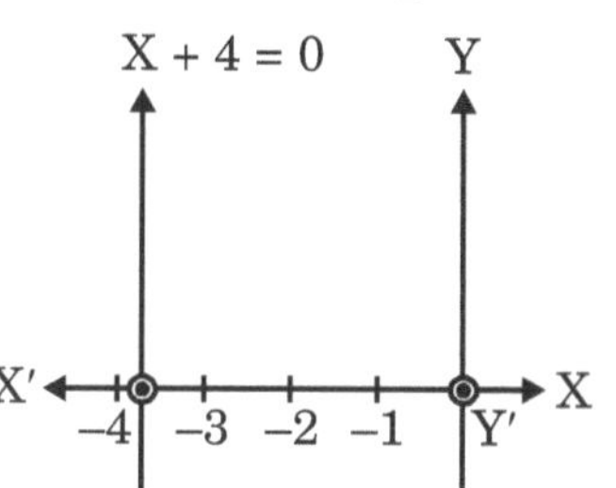

(ii) If we treated $x = -4$ as an equation in two variables, then it can be written as $1 \cdot x + 0 \cdot y = -4$, whereas the equation $x + 4 = 0$ represents a straight line parallel to Y-axis and infinitely many points lie on a line in the cartesian plane.

3. Find two different solutions of the equation $4x + 3y = 12$ from its graph. [Board Term II, 2012, Set-02]

Sol. Given equation, $4x + 3y = 12$

On putting $x = 0$, then $0 + 3y = 12$

$$\therefore \quad y = 4$$

Hence, point on y-axis is $(0, 4)$

Now, on putting y = 0, then
$$4x + 0 = 12$$
∴ $x = 3$
Hence, point on x-axis is (3, 0)

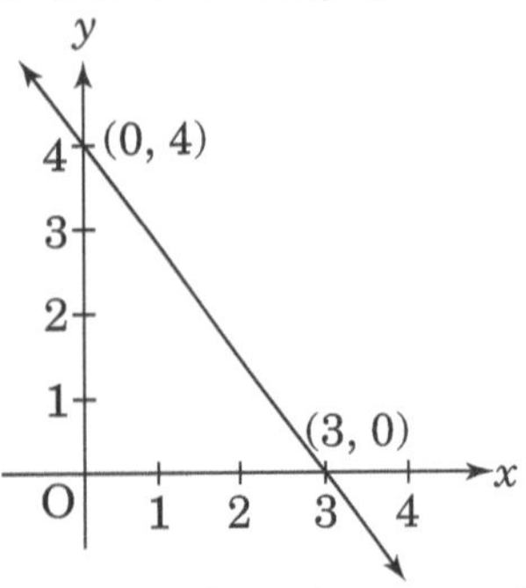

4. Give the equations of two lines passing through (2, 14). How many more such lines are there, and why?

Sol. Let $\quad 7x - y = 0$ ...(i)

and $\quad 2x + y = 18$ ...(ii)

are two linear equations.

On substituting x = 2 and y = 14 in eqn. (i), we have
$$7(2) - 14 = 14 - 14 = 0$$
∴ (2, 14) is the solution of eqn. (i).

and from equation (ii), we have
$$2(2) + 14 = 4 + 14 = 18$$

It is quite obvious that graphs of equations (i) and (ii) are two straight lines and the point (2, 14) lies on both the lines. Hence, the two lines pass through the point (2, 14).

Therefore, there are infinite straight lines which are passing through the point (2, 14).

5. A part of monthly expenses of a family on milk is fixed which is ₹ 500 and the remaining varies with the quantity of milk taken extra at the rate of ₹ 20 per liter. Taking the quantity of milk required extra as x L and the total expenditure on milk is ₹ y, write a linear equation for this information and draw its graph.

Sol. Let the quantity of milk required extra be x L and total expenditure on milk be ₹ y.

∴ Required equation is
$$y = 500 + 20x \qquad ...(i)$$
When x = 0, then
$$y = 500 + 20 \times 0 = 500$$
When x = 2, then
$$y = 500 + 20 \times 2$$
$$= 500 + 40 = 540$$
When x = 3, then
$$y = 500 + 20 \times 3$$
$$= 500 + 60 = 560$$

Now,

x	0	2	3
y	500	540	560

Now, plot the points (0, 500), (2, 540) and (3, 560) on a graph and join them by a line to get required graph.

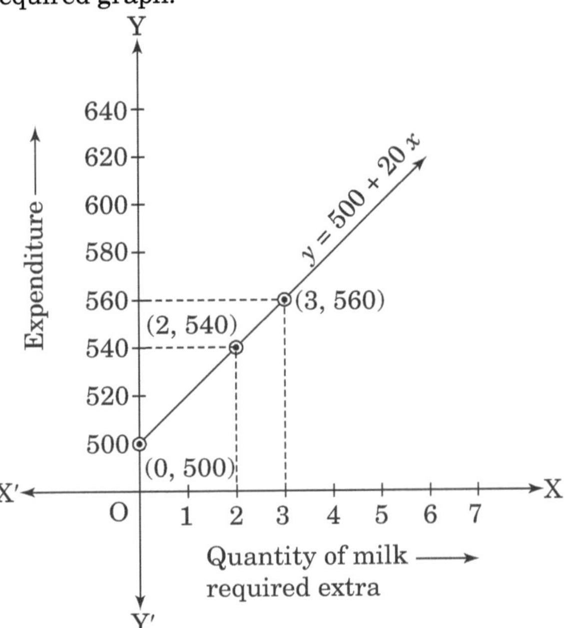

Short Answer Type Questions-II
(3 Marks Each)

1. Write three solutions of the equation 3x = y + 3. Draw its graph and find the points where the graph intersects the axes.

[**Board Term II, 2012, Set-12**]

Sol. Given, $\quad 3x = y + 3;$

when $\quad x = 1$, then y = ?

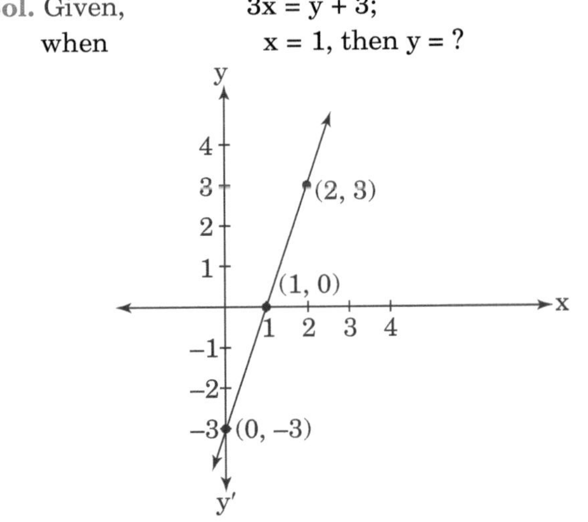

Hence, from graph it is clear that line meets x-axis at (1, 0) and y-axis at (0, − 3).

2. Draw a triangle whose sides are represented by $x = 0$, $y = 0$ and $x + y = 3$ in the Cartesian system. Also find the co-ordinates of its vertices.

[Board Term II, 2012, Set-15]

Sol. Given, $\qquad x + y = 3$

On the y-axis put $x = 0$ then we have

$$y = 3$$

Hence on the y-axis co-ordinate of B is $(0, 3)$

On the x-axis put $y = 0$ then we have

$$x = 3$$

Hence, on the x-axis co-ordinate of A is $(3, 0)$ and triangle whose sides are $x = 0$, $y = 0$, and $x + y = 3$ is as shown in figure.

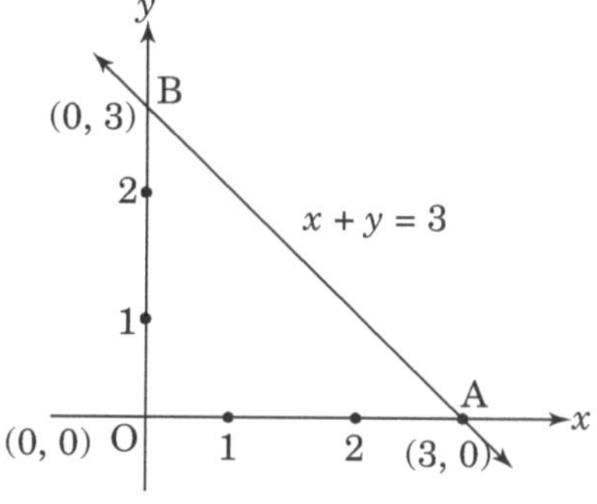

Hence, the vertices of triangle are A $(3, 0)$, B $(0, 3)$ and O$(0, 0)$.

3. Express x in terms of y, in the equation $7x - 3y = 15$. Check if the line represented by the equation intersects the y-axis $y = -5$.

[Board Term II, 2012, Set-01]

Sol. Given, $\qquad 7x - 3y = 15$

$$\Rightarrow \qquad x = \frac{15 + 3y}{7}$$

At y-axis $\qquad x = 0;$

$\therefore \qquad 7(0) - 3y = 15$

$\Rightarrow \qquad 0 - 3y = 15$

$\therefore \qquad y = \dfrac{15}{-3} = -5$

Hence, the line $7x - 3y = 15$ intersects the y-axis at $y = -5$.

4. Draw the graph of $2x - 3y - 12 = 0$ on the graph paper. [Board Term II, 2012, Set-05]

Sol. Given, $2x - 3y - 12 = 0$

$$\Rightarrow \qquad y = \frac{2x - 12}{3}$$

when $x = 6$, then $y = \dfrac{2 \times 6 - 12}{3} = \dfrac{12 - 12}{3} = 0$

when $x = 9$, then $y = \dfrac{2 \times 9 - 12}{3}$

$$= \frac{18 - 12}{3} = \frac{6}{3} = 2$$

when $x = 3$, then $y = \dfrac{2 \times 3 - 12}{3}$

$$= \frac{6 - 12}{3} = \frac{-6}{3} = -2$$

x	6	9	3
y	0	2	-2

5. Draw the graphs of the equations $3x + 4y = 7$ and $3x - 2y = 1$ and find their point of intersection of lines representing the equations.

[Board Term II, 2012, Set-01]

Sol. Given, $3x + 4y = 7$

$$\Rightarrow \qquad 4y = 7 - 3x$$

$$\Rightarrow \qquad y = \frac{7 - 3x}{4}$$

Now, when $x = 1$,

then $\qquad y = \dfrac{7 - 3}{4} = \dfrac{4}{4} = 1$

when $x = -3$,

then $\qquad y = \dfrac{7 - 3(-3)}{4}$

$$= \frac{7 + 9}{4} = \frac{16}{4} = 4$$

x	1	-3
y	1	4

and $\qquad 3x - 2y = 1$

$$\Rightarrow \qquad 2y = 3x - 1$$

$$\Rightarrow \qquad y = \frac{3x - 1}{2}$$

when $x = 1$,

then $\qquad y = \dfrac{3 \times 1 - 1}{2} = \dfrac{2}{2} = 1$

when $x = -1$ then

$$y = \frac{3(-1) - 1}{2} = \frac{-4}{2} = -2$$

x	1	−1
y	1	−2

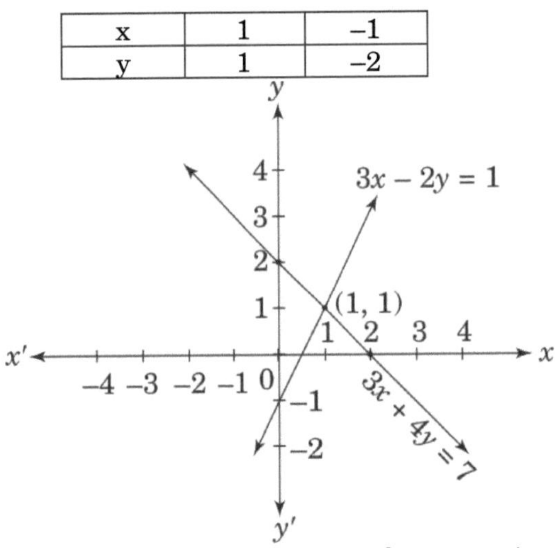

Hence, from the graph, point of intersection is (1, 1).

6. The cost of a toy elephant is the same as the cost of 3 balls. Express the statement as a linear equation in two variables and plot the equation on a graph paper. [Board Term II, 2012, Set-05]

Sol. Let the cost of a toy elephant = x and ball = y

$$\therefore \qquad 3y = x \Rightarrow y = \frac{x}{3}$$

when x = 3, then y = $\frac{3}{3}$ = 1

when x = 6, then y = $\frac{6}{3}$ = 2

when x = 9, then y = $\frac{9}{3}$ = 3

x	3	6	9
y	1	2	3

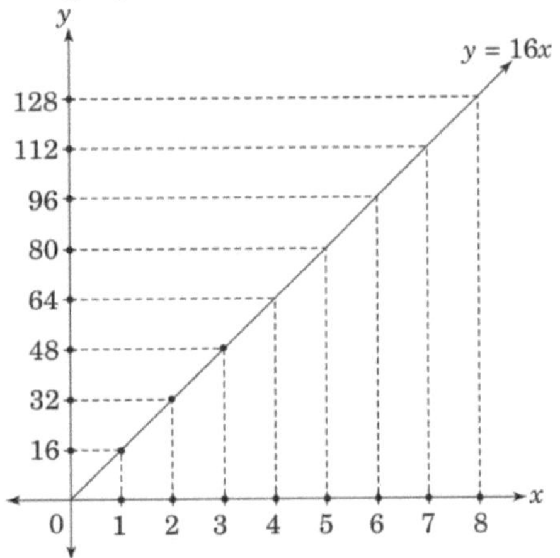

7. The cost of a pen is ₹ 16. Taking number of pens bought as x and total cost as y, form a linear equation in x and y and draw its graph. Find the cost of 6 pens from the graph.

[Board Term II, 2012, Set-08]

Sol. Total cost = value of pen × number of pens

$$\therefore \qquad y = 16x \qquad \qquad ...(i)$$

x	0	1	2	3	4	5	6
y	0	16	32	48	64	80	96

From the graph, cost of 6 pens = ₹ 96.

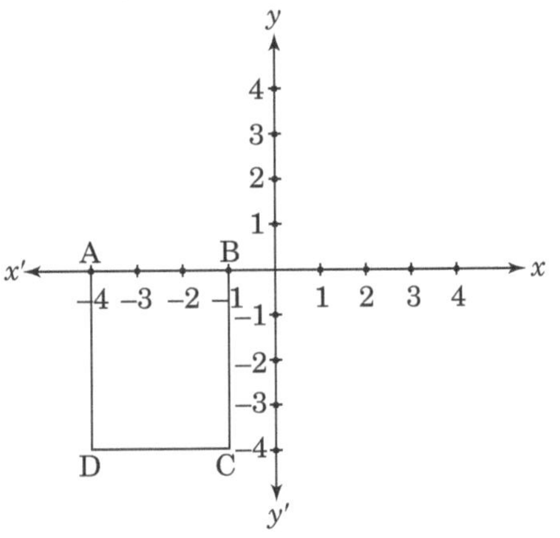

8. Solve the equation $\frac{x}{3} + 2 = 2x - 3$ and represent the solution on the Cartesian plane.

[Board Term II, 2012, Set-12]

Sol. Given, $\qquad \frac{x}{3} + 2 = 2x - 3$

$$\Rightarrow \qquad \frac{x}{3} - 2x = -3 - 2$$

$$\Rightarrow \qquad x - 6x = -5 \times 3$$

$$\Rightarrow \qquad -5x = -15$$

$$\therefore \qquad x = 3$$

Now, plot x = 3 on the cartesian plane

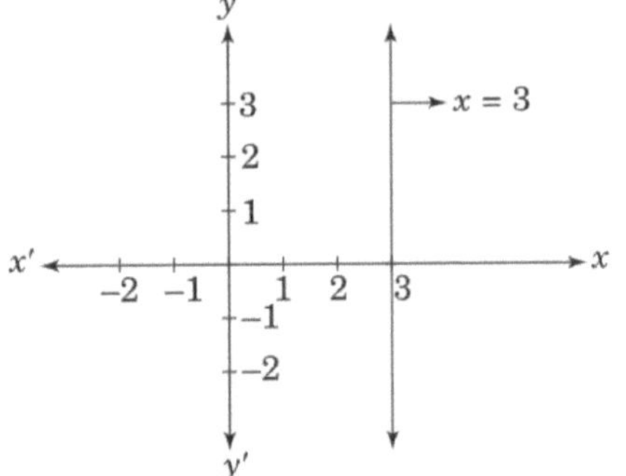

Hence, on cartesian plane, x = 3 is a line parallel to y-axis.

9. ABCD is a rectangle. Write the equation of its sides. Also, find its area. [Board Term II, 2014]

Sol. According to the graph,

Equation of line AB : $Y = 0$

Equation of line BC : $X = -1$

Equation of line CD : $Y = -4$

Equation of line DA : $X = -4$

Hence, area of rectangle ABCD = BC × AB

$$= 4 \times 3 = 12 \text{ sq. units}$$

10. Write the equation $\dfrac{x}{2} + \dfrac{3y}{5} = -1$ in standard form and draw the graph.   [Board Term II, 2014]

Sol. The given equation can be written as,

$$5x + 6y = -10$$

$$\Rightarrow \qquad -y = \frac{(5x+10)}{6}$$

when $x = -2$, then

$$y = \frac{-[5\times(-2)+10]}{6} = \frac{-[-10+10]}{6} = 0$$

when $x = 4$, then

$$y = \frac{-[5\times 4 + 10]}{6} = \frac{-30}{6} = -5$$

when $x = 10$, then

$$y = \frac{-[5\times 10 + 10]}{6}$$

$$= \frac{-[50+10]}{6} = \frac{-60}{6} = -10$$

x	−2	4	10
y	0	−5	−10

11. Write the equation $4x = 6(1-y) + 3x$ in the form $ax + by = c$ and also find the co-ordinate of the points where its graph cuts the two axes?

[Board Term II, 2017, Set-Z6K408K]

Sol. Given, $\qquad 4x = 6(1-y) + 3x$

$$\Rightarrow \qquad 4x = 6 - 6y + 3x$$

$$\Rightarrow \qquad x = 6 - 6y$$

$$\Rightarrow \qquad x + 6y = 6$$

The graph cuts x-axis at $y = 0$

$$\therefore \qquad x + 6 \times 0 = 6$$

$$\therefore \qquad x = 6$$

and the graph cuts y-axis at $x = 0$

$$\therefore \qquad 0 + 6y = 6$$

$$\therefore \qquad y = \frac{6}{6} = 1$$

Hence, the line cuts x-axis at $(6, 0)$ and y-axis at $(0, 1)$.

12. Draw the graphs of $y = x + 1$ and $x + y = 5$ on the same cartesian plane. Shade the triangle formed by these graphs and y-axis and also find its area.

[Board Term II, 2017, Set-UAH4DQ7]

Sol. Given, $\qquad y = x + 1$

when $x = 0$, then $y = 1$

when $x = 2$, then $y = 2 + 1 = 3$

x	0	2
y	1	3

and $x + y = 5$, $y = 5 - x$

when $x = 0$, then $y = 5 - 0 = 5$

when $x = 5$, then $y = 5 - 5 = 0$

x	0	5
y	5	0

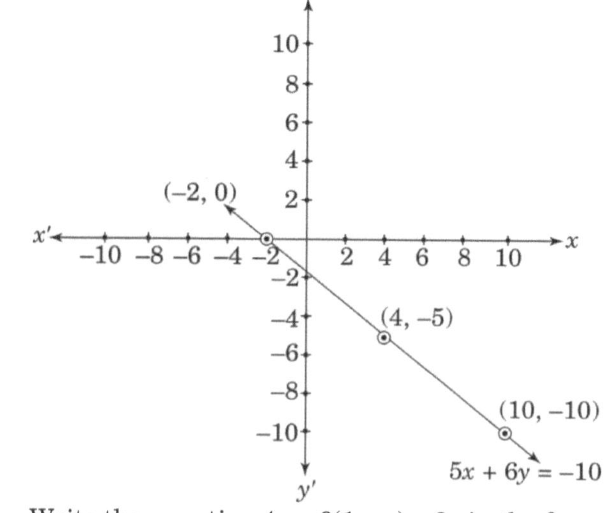

$$\therefore \quad \text{Area of } \Delta PQR = \frac{1}{2} \times \text{base} \times \text{height}$$

$$= \frac{1}{2} \times 4 \times 2 = 2 \times 2 = 4 \text{ sq. units}$$

13. Write $3x + 2y = 18$, in the form of $y = mx + c$. Draw its graph. [Board Term II, 2017, Set-Z6K408K]

Sol. Given equation,
$$3x + 2y = 18$$
$$\Rightarrow \quad 2y = 18 - 3x$$
$$\Rightarrow \quad y = \frac{18 - 3x}{2}$$

when x = 0, then
$$y = \frac{18 - 3 \times 0}{2} = \frac{18}{2} = 9$$

when x = 2, then
$$y = \frac{18 - 3 \times 2}{2} = \frac{12}{2} = 6$$

when x = 6, then
$$y = \frac{18 - 3 \times 6}{2} = \frac{18 - 18}{2} = 0$$

x	0	2	6
y	9	6	0

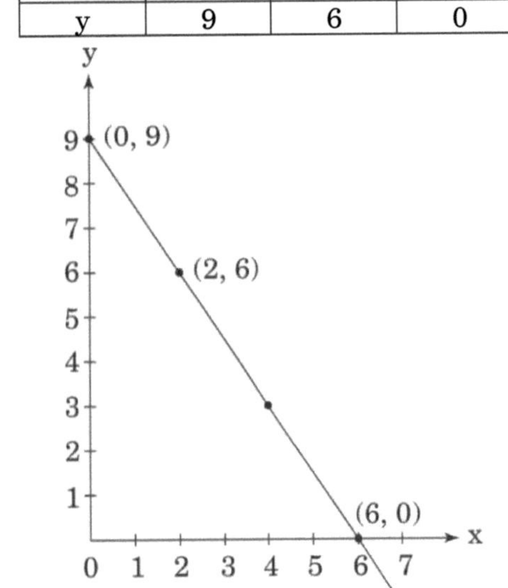

$$3x + 2y = 18$$
$$\Rightarrow \quad 2y = 18 - 3x$$
$$\Rightarrow \quad y = \frac{18 - 3x}{2}$$
$$\Rightarrow \quad y = 9 - \frac{3}{2}x$$

Hence, required equation is
$$y = \frac{-3}{2}x + 9$$

14. Draw the graph of the linear equation $3x - 5y - 15 = 0$. Write the coordinates of the points where the line intersects the two axes.

Sol. Given equation
$$3x - 5y - 15 = 0$$
$$\Rightarrow \quad 5y = 3x - 15$$
$$\Rightarrow \quad y = \frac{3x - 15}{5}$$
$$\Rightarrow \quad y = \frac{3}{5}(x - 5)$$

when x = 0, then
$$y = \frac{3}{5}(0 - 5) = \frac{3}{5}(-5) = -3$$

when x = 5, then
$$y = \frac{3}{5}(5 - 5) = \frac{3}{5} \times 0 = 0$$

	A	B	C
x	0	5	-5
y	-3	0	-6

To plot these points on graph paper, join these points. Hence the graph of the line intersects x-axis at (5, 0) and y-axis at (0, − 3).

Long Answer Type Questions
(4 Mark Each)

1. The following observed values of x and y are thought to satisfy a linear equation. Write the linear equation.

x	6	-6
y	-2	6

Draw the graph, using the values x and y as given in the above table. At what points, the graph of the linear equation.

(i) cuts the x-axis?

(ii) cuts the y-axis? [NCERT Exemp.]

Sol. Let the linear equation $y = mx + c$ satisfies the points $(6, -2)$ and $(-6, 6)$, then
$$\therefore \quad -2 = 6m + c \qquad \text{...(i)}$$
$$\text{and} \quad 6 = -6m + c \qquad \text{...(ii)}$$

On subtracting eqn. (ii) from eqn. (i), we get
$$6 = -6m + c$$
$$-2 = +6m + c$$
$$\underline{+ \quad\quad - \quad\quad -}$$
$$8 = -12m$$

$$12\,m = -8$$

$$\therefore \qquad m = -\frac{2}{3}$$

On putting the value of $m = -\dfrac{2}{3}$ in eqn. (i), we get

$$-2 = 6\left(\frac{-2}{3}\right) + c$$

$$\Rightarrow \qquad -2 = -4 + c$$

$$\therefore \qquad c = 4 - 2 = 2$$

Now, $\qquad y = -\dfrac{2}{3}x + 2$

$$\Rightarrow \qquad 3y = -2x + 6$$

$$\Rightarrow \qquad 3y + 2x = 6 \qquad\qquad ...(iii)$$

Hence, required linear equation is $2x + 3y = 6$

On putting $y = 0$ in eqn. (iii), we get

$$0 + 2x = 6$$

$$\therefore \qquad x = \frac{6}{2} = 3$$

Hence, $(3, 0)$ is a solution of the equation.

Again, putting $x = 0$ in eqn. (iii), we get

$$3y + 0 = 6$$

$$\therefore \qquad y = \frac{6}{3} = 2$$

Hence, $(0, 2)$ is a solution of the equation.

(i) The graph of the linear equation will cut x-axis at $(3, 0)$

(ii) The graph of the linear equation will cut y-axis at $(0, 2)$.

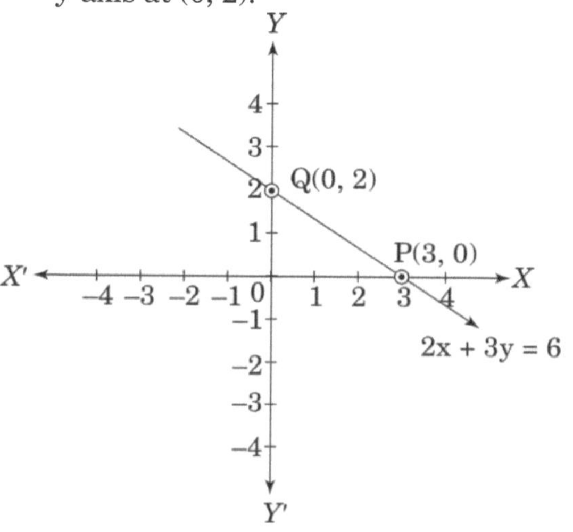

2. Draw the graph of $x = 3y - 4$. Find the :

(i) value of y, when $x = -1$

(ii) value of x, when $y = 5$.

[NCERT Board Term II, 2012, Set-69]

Sol. Given, $\qquad x = 3y - 4$

$$3y = x + 4$$

$$\Rightarrow \qquad y = \frac{x + 4}{3}$$

when $x = 2$, then

$$y = \frac{2 + 4}{3} = \frac{6}{3} = 2$$

when $x = 5$, then

$$y = \frac{5 + 4}{3} = \frac{9}{3} = 3$$

when $x = 8$, then

$$y = \frac{8 + 4}{3} = \frac{12}{3} = 4$$

x	2	5	8
y	2	3	4

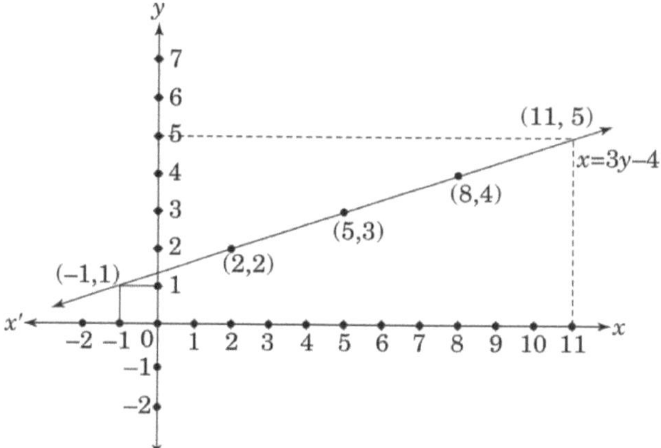

From the graph, it is clear that:

(i) when $x = -1$, then $y = 1$,

(ii) when $y = 5$, then $x = 11$

3. The auto rickshaw fare in a city is charged ₹ 10 for first kilometre and @ ₹ 4 per kilometre for subsequent distance covered. Write the linear equation to express the above statement. Draw the graph of the linear equation.

[Board Term II, KVS 2016][NCERT Exemplar]

Sol. Total distance covered = x km.

Total fare = ₹ y

Fare for the first kilometre = ₹ 10

Subsquent distance = $(x - 1)$ km

$\therefore$ Fare for the subsequent distance = ₹ $4(x - 1)$

According to question,

$$y = 10 + 4\,(x - 1)$$

$$y = 10 + 4x - 4$$

$$\Rightarrow \qquad y = 4x + 6 \qquad\qquad ...(i)$$

Now,

when $x = 0$, then $y = 4 \times 0 + 6 = 6$

when $x = 1$, then $y = 4 \times 1 + 6 = 10$

when $x = -1$, then $y = 4 \times (-1) + 6$

$$= -4 + 6 = 2$$

x	0	1	-1
y	6	10	2

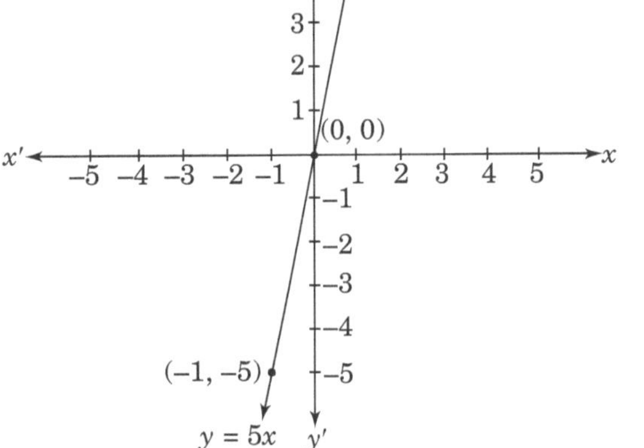

4. Force applied on a body is directly proportional to the acceleration produced in the body. Write an equation to express the situation and plot the graph of the equation taking the constant to be 5 units. [NCERT, Board Term II, 2012, Set-01]

Sol. Let F be the force applied and a be the acceleration produced

$$F \propto a$$
$$\Rightarrow \quad F = ka, \text{ where k is constant}$$

Now replace a by x and F by y.

$$\Rightarrow \quad y = k(x)$$
$$y = xk$$

Here, $\quad k = 5 \quad$ (Given)

$$\Rightarrow \quad y = 5x$$

Now, when $x = 0$, then $y = 5 \times 0 = 0$

when $x = 1$, then $y = 5 \times 1 = 5$

when $x = -1$, then $y = 5 \times (-1) = -5$

x	0	1	−1
y	0	5	−5

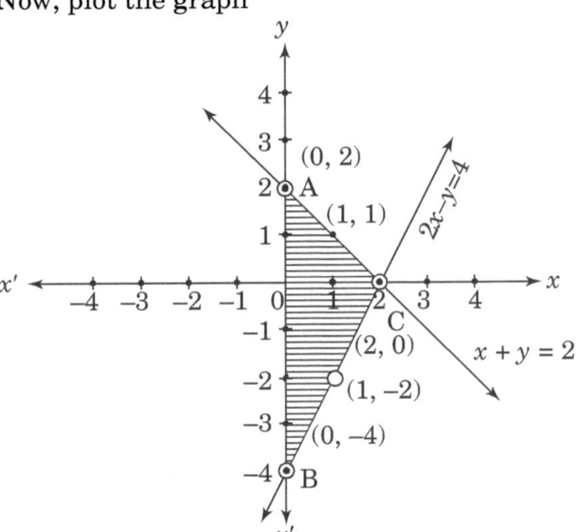

5. Shade the triangle formed by the graphs of $2x - y = 4$, $x + y = 2$ and the y-axis. Write the co-ordinates of vertices of the triangle.

[Board Term II, 2012, Set-01]

Sol. Given, $\quad 2x - y = 4$

$$\Rightarrow \quad y = 2x - 4$$

when $x = 0$, then $y = 2 \times 0 - 4 = -4$

when $x = 2$, then $y = 2 \times 2 - 4 = 0$

when $x = 1$, then $y = 2 \times 1 - 4$

$$= 2 - 4 = -2$$

x	0	2	1
y	−4	0	−2

and $\quad x + y = 2$

$$\Rightarrow \quad y = 2 - x$$

when $x = 0$, then $y = 2 - 0 = 2$

when $x = 2$, then $y = 2 - 2 = 0$

when $x = 1$, then $y = 2 - 1 = 1$

x	0	2	1
y	2	0	1

Now, plot the graph

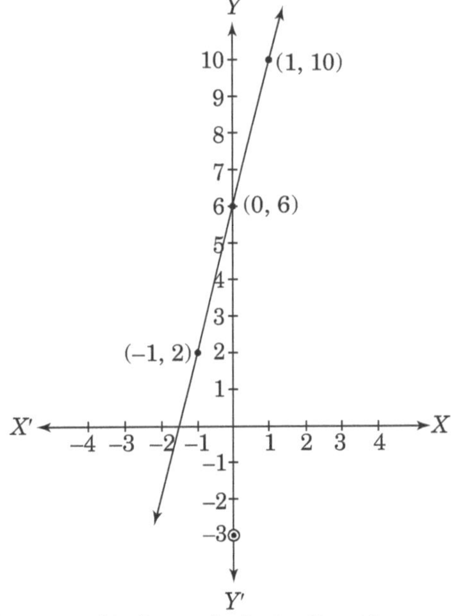

Hence, from the graph, ∆ABC is the required triangle and its vertices are A(0, 2), B(0, − 4) and C(2, 0).

6. Draw the graph of the linear equation $x + y = 7$. Verify from the graph that $(8, - 1)$ is a solution of the equation $x + y = 7$.

[Board Term II, 2012, Set-05]

Sol. Given linear equation,

$$x + y = 7$$

or, $\quad y = 7 - x$

when $x = 5$, then $y = 7 - 5 = 2$

when $x = 7$, then $y = 7 - 7 = 0$

when $x = 4$, then $y = 7 - 4 = 3$

x	5	7	4
y	2	0	3

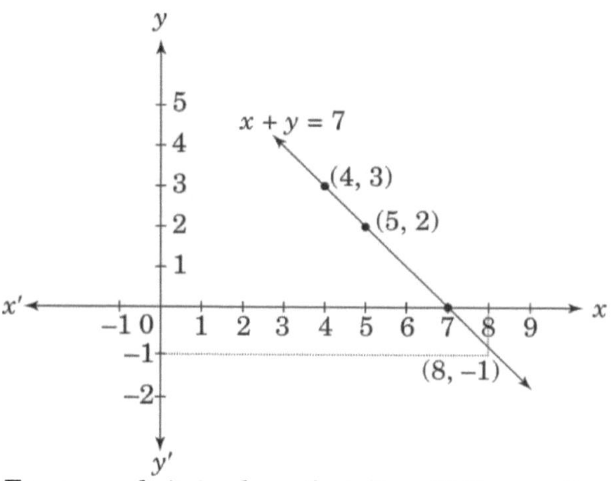

From graph it is clear that $(8, -1)$ lies on the line AB.

Hence, $(8, -1)$ is a solution of the given equation.

7. Draw the graph of linear equation $2x + y = 8$ on cartesian plane. Write the co-ordinates of the points where this line intersects x-axis and y-axis.   [Board Term II, 2012, Set-24]

Sol. Given linear equation,
$$2x + y = 8$$
$$\therefore \qquad y = -2x + 8$$
when $x = -1$, then $y = -2 \times (-1) + 8$
$$= 2 + 8 = 10$$
when $x = 0$, then $y = -2 \times 0 + 8 = 8$
when $x = 1$, then $y = -2 \times 1 + 8$
$$= -2 + 8 = 6$$

x	−1	0	1
y	10	8	6

Hence, from the graph it is clear that
Line intersects x-axis at $(4, 0)$
and y-axis at $(0, 8)$.

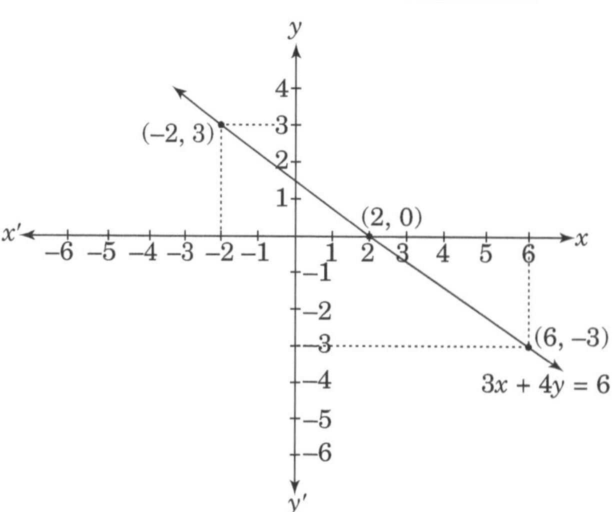

8. Draw the graph of the linear equation $3x + 4y = 6$. Find the points where the line representing the equation $3x + 4y = 6$ cuts the axes of x and y.

[Board Term II, 2012, Set-08]

Sol. Given linear equation is
$$3x + 4y = 6$$
(i) When it cuts x-axis then
put $y = 0$ i.e., $\quad 3x = 6$
or, $\qquad\qquad x = 2$
Hence point on x-axis is $(2, 0)$
(ii) when it cuts y-axis then
put $x = 0$ i.e., $\quad 4y = 6$
or $\qquad\qquad y = \dfrac{3}{2}$
Hence, point on y-axis is $\left(0, \dfrac{3}{2}\right)$
$$3x + 4y = 6$$
$$\therefore \qquad y = \frac{6 - 3x}{4}$$
when $x = 2$, then
$$y = \frac{6 - 3 \times 2}{4} = \frac{6 - 6}{4} = 0$$
when $x = -2$, then
$$y = \frac{6 + 3 \times 2}{4} = \frac{12}{4} = 3$$
when $x = 6$, then
$$y = \frac{6 - 3 \times 6}{4} = \frac{6 - 18}{4} = \frac{-12}{4} = -3$$

x	2	−2	6
y	0	3	−3

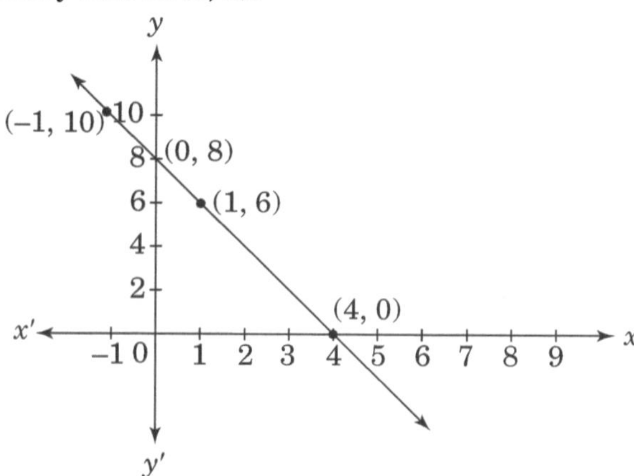

9. Draw the graph of $\dfrac{2}{3}x - y = 2$ and find the points where it cuts the co-ordinate axes.

[Board Term II, 2012, Set-12]

Sol.
$$\frac{2}{3}x - y = 2$$
$$\Rightarrow \qquad 2x - 3y = 6$$
$$\Rightarrow \qquad 2x = 3y + 6$$
$$\therefore \qquad x = \frac{3y + 6}{2}$$

(i) When the line cuts x-axis then put $y = 0$, we have

$$2x = 6$$
$$\therefore \quad x = 3$$

Hence, point is $(3, 0)$.

(ii) When the line cuts y-axis then put $x = 0$

$$3y + 6 = 0$$
$$\therefore \quad y = -2$$

Hence, point is $(0, -2)$

x	0	3	6
y	−2	0	2

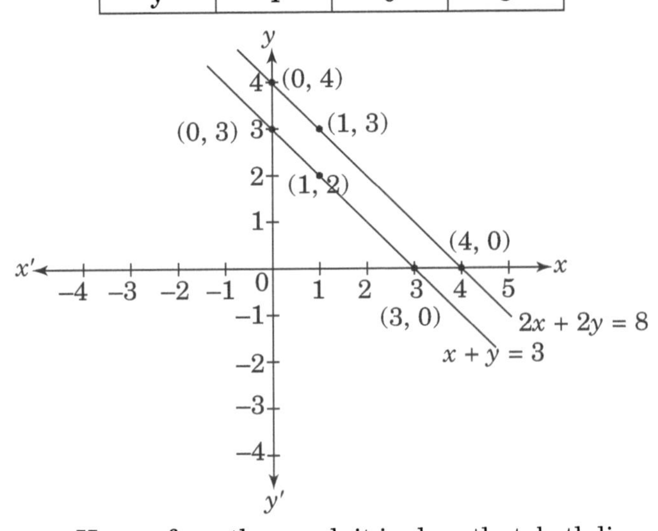

10. Ramesh is driving his car with a uniform speed of 90 km per hour. Draw the time-distance graph on the graph paper. From the graph, find the distance travelled by him in:

(i) $\dfrac{1}{2}$ hour   (ii) 2 hour

[Board Term II, 2012, Set-01]

Sol. Graph of equation $y = 90x$,

where x is time and y is distance]

Now, from the graph

(i) Total distance travelled in $\dfrac{1}{2}$ hour = 45 km

(ii) Total distance travelled in 2 hours = 180 km

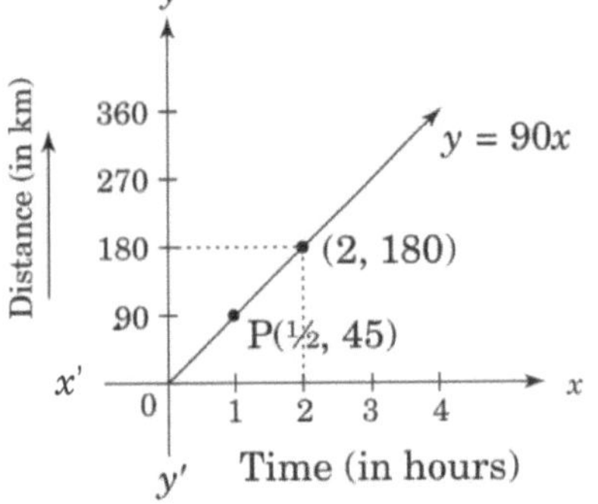

11. Draw the graph of $x + y = 3$ and $2x + 2y = 8$ on the same axes. What does the graph of these lines represent?

[Board Term II, 2012, Set-02]

Sol.

$$x + y = 3$$
$$\Rightarrow \quad y = 3 - x$$

when $x = 0$, then $y = 3 - 0 = 3$

when $x = 3$, then $y = 3 - 3 = 0$

when $x = 1$, then $y = 3 - 1 = 2$

x	0	3	1
y	3	0	2

and $\quad 2x + 2y = 8$

$$\Rightarrow \quad x + y = 4$$
$$\Rightarrow \quad y = 4 - x$$

when $x = 0$, then $y = 4 - 0 = 4$

when $x = 4$, then $y = 4 - 4 = 0$

when $x = 1$, then $y = 4 - 1 = 3$

x	0	4	1
y	4	0	3

Hence, from the graph it is clear that, both lines are parallel to each other.

12. Give the geometrical representation of the equation $3x + 15 = 0$ as an equation:

(i) In one variable.

(ii) In two variables. [Board Term II, 2012, Set-01]

Sol.

$$3x + 15 = 0$$
$$\Rightarrow \quad 3x = -15$$
$$\therefore \quad x = -5$$

(i) The geometric representation of the equation $3x + 15 = 0$ as an equation in one variable is as follows.

$\therefore$ A point P at a distance of 5 units to left of O on the number line.

(ii) The geometric representation of the equation $3x + 15 = 0$ as an equation in two variables is as follows. A line AB parallel to y-axis at a distance of 5 units to the left of y-axis.

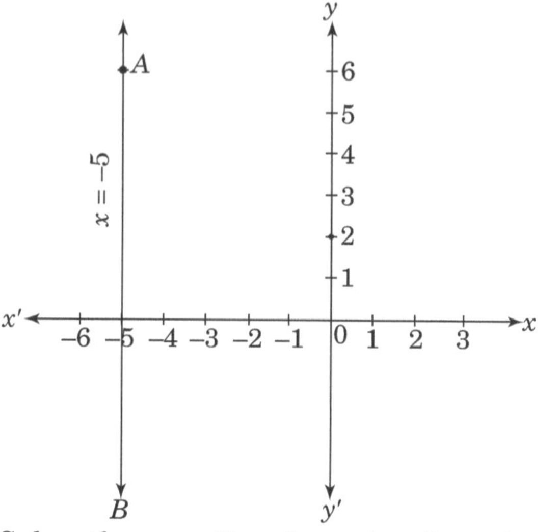

13. Solve the equation $3x + 4 = 5x + 8$ and represent the solution on (i) the number line (ii) the cartesian plane. What do you get as the representation of the solution on the cartesian plane? In cartesian planes, how many solutions this equation has?   [Board Term II, 2012, Set-13]

Sol. According to the question,
$$3x + 4 = 5x + 8$$
$$\Rightarrow \qquad 5x - 3x = 4 - 8$$
$$\Rightarrow \qquad 2x = -4$$
$$\therefore \qquad x = -2$$

(i) On the number line the point P(-2, 0) represent the solution

(ii) On the cartesian plane $x = -2$ is a line parallel to the y-axis at a distance of 2 units to left of it.

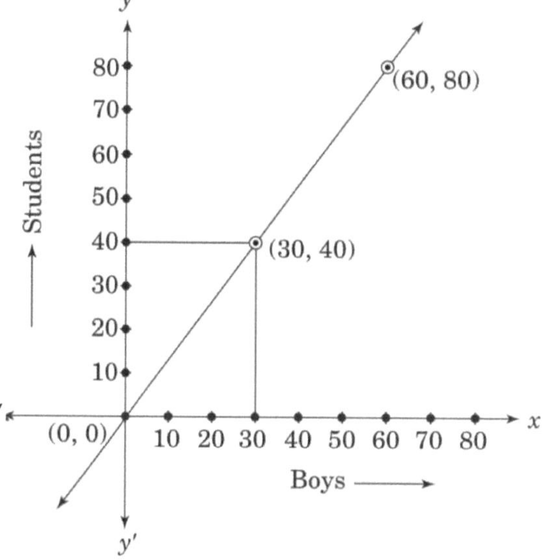

Therefore, in cartesian planes there are infinite solutions.

14. The ratio of girls and boys in a class is 1 : 3. Set up an equation between the students of a class and boys and then draw its graph. Also find the number of boys in a class of 40 students from the graph.   [Board Term II, 2012, Set-6]

Sol. Total students in the class = y

Let the boys in the class = x, then equation between the students and the boys
$$y = \frac{4}{3}x$$

when x = 0, then $y = \frac{4}{3} \times 0 = 0$

when x = 30, then $y = \frac{4}{3} \times 30 = 40$

when x = 60, then $y = \frac{4}{3} \times 60 = 80$

x	0	30	60
y	0	40	80

Now, draw a graph between these points.

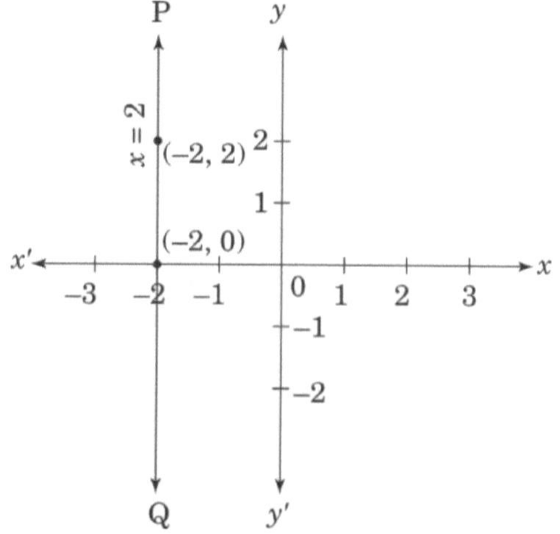

From the graph it is clear that there are 30 boys in a class of 40 students.

15. Solve $5x - 2 = 3x - 8$ and represent the solution
(i) on a number line
(ii) in the cartesian plane

[Board Term II, 2012, Set-05]

Sol. According to the question,
$$5x - 2 = 3x - 8$$
$$\Rightarrow \qquad 2x = -6$$
$$\therefore \qquad x = \frac{-6}{2} = -3$$

(i) Point P(-3, 0) represents the solution $x = -3$ on the number line.

(ii) Line AB represents the solution in the cartesian plane.

16. For the linear equation $3x - 5y - 15 = 0$, find the points where its graph intersects x and y axis. Using these, draw the graph of the equation. And find its area. [Board Term II, 2012, Set-06]

Sol. Given linear equation, $3x - 5y - 15 = 0$

On substituting $y = 0$ in the equation, we have
$$3x - 0 - 15 = 0 \Rightarrow 3x = 15$$
$$\therefore \qquad x = 5$$
Hence, the point on x-axis is $(5, 0)$
Again, when substituting $x = 0$ in the equation, we get
$$(3 \times 0) - 5y - 15 = 0$$
$$\therefore \qquad y = -3$$
Hence, point on y-axis is $(0, -3)$
Plotting $A(5, 0)$ and $B(0, -3)$, we get the triangle AOB.

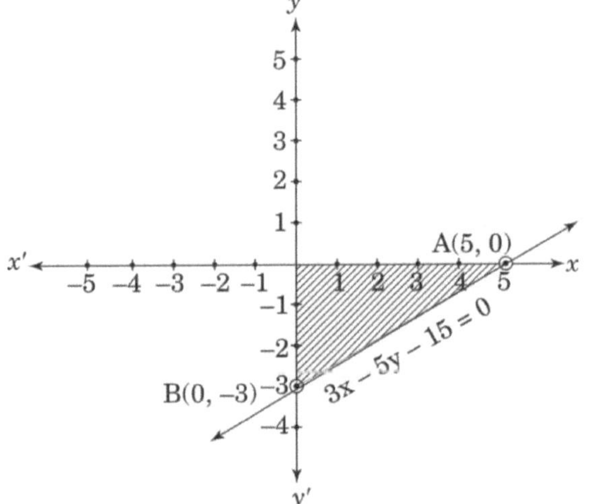

Since $OA = 5$ units and $OB = 3$ units

Hence, Area of $\triangle AOB = \dfrac{1}{2} \times OA \times OB = \dfrac{1}{2} \times 5 \times 3$

$$\dfrac{15}{2} = 7.5 \text{ sq. unit}$$

17. Two friends Sita and Gita, together contributed ₹ 200 towards Prime Minister's Relief Fund. Write a linear equation which satisfies this data. Draw the graph. [Board Term II, 2012, Set-69 KVS 2014]

Sol. Let Sita contribute = ₹ x and
Gita contribute = ₹ y, then
According to the question
$$x + y = 200 \Rightarrow y = 200 - x$$
when $x = 0$, then $y = 200 - 0 = 200$
when $x = 200$, then $y = 200 - 200 = 0$
when $x = 100$, then $y = 200 - 100 = 100$

x	0	200	100
y	200	0	100

18. A student Amit of class IX is unable to write in his examination, due to fracture in his arm. Akhil a student of class VI writes for him. The sum of their ages is 25 years.

(i) Write a linear equation for the above situation and represent it graphically.

(ii) Find the age of Akhil from the graph, when age of Amit is 14 years. [Board Term II, 2013, Set-261C]

Sol. Let, Age of Amit = x years
and Age of Akhil = y years
(i) According to the question, the linear equation for the above situation is
$$x + y = 25 \Rightarrow y = 25 - x \qquad ...(i)$$
when $x = 0$, then $y = 25 - 0 = 25$
when $x = 10$, then $y = 25 - 10 = 15$
when $x = 15$, then $y = 25 - 15 = 10$

x	0	10	15
y	25	15	10

(ii) From the graph when Amit's age = 14 years, then Akhil's age = 11 years.

19. Draw the graph of linear equations $x + y = 10$ and $2x - y = 5$ and find the point of intersection.

[Board Term II, 2013, Set-261C 2013]

Sol. Given $x + y = 10$

$\Rightarrow \qquad y = 10 - x \qquad$ ...(i)

when $x = 0$, then $y = 10 - 0 = 10$

when $x = 2$, then $y = 10 - 2 = 8$

when $x = 3$, then $y = 10 - 3 = 7$

when $x = 4$, then $y = 10 - 4 = 6$

when $x = 5$, then $y = 10 - 5 = 5$

x	0	2	3	4	5
y	10	8	7	6	5

and $2x - y = 5 \Rightarrow y = 2x - 5 \qquad$ ...(ii)

when $x = 0$, then $y = 2 \times 0 - 5 = 5$

when $x = 2$, then $y = 2 \times 2 - 5 = -1$

when $x = 5$, then $y = 2 \times 5 - 5 = 5$

x	0	2	5
y	-5	-1	5

Plot these points on the graph paper.

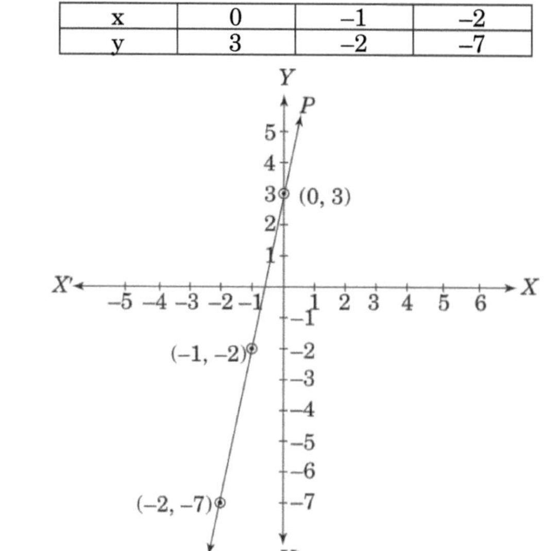

Hence, from graph it is clear that point of intersection is $(5, 5)$.

20. The taxi fare in a city is as follows: For the first kilometre, the fare is ₹ 8 and for the subsequent distance it is ₹ 5 per km. Taking distance covered as x km and the total fare as ₹ y. Write a linear equation for this information and draw its graph.

[NCERT Board Term II, 2014, 2012, Set-06]

Sol. The fare for first kilometer is ₹ 8.00

Let the total distance to be covered is x km and Fare for $(x - 1)$ kilometre at the rate of ₹ 5 per km $= 5 (x - 1)$

$\therefore \quad$ Total fare $\quad y = 5(x - 1) + 8$

$\qquad\qquad\qquad = 5x - 5 + 8 = 5x + 3$

$\therefore \qquad\qquad y = 5x + 3 \qquad$ ...(i)

when $x = 0$, then $y = 5 \times 0 + 3 = 3$

when $x = -1$, then $y = 5(-1) + 3 = -5 + 3 = -2$

when $x = -2$, then $y = 5(-2) + 3 = -10 + 3 = -7$

x	0	−1	−2
y	3	−2	−7

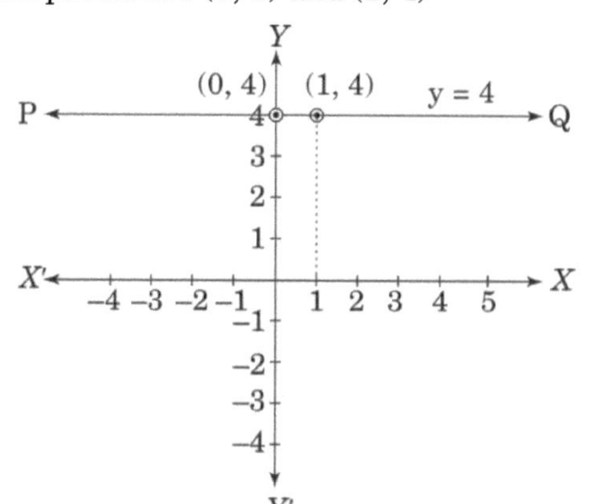

21. Give the geometric representation of $y = 4$ as an equation in : [Board Term II, 2014 KVS]

(i) One variable   (ii) Two variable

Sol. (i) The geometric representation of $y = 4$ as an equation in one variable is as follows:

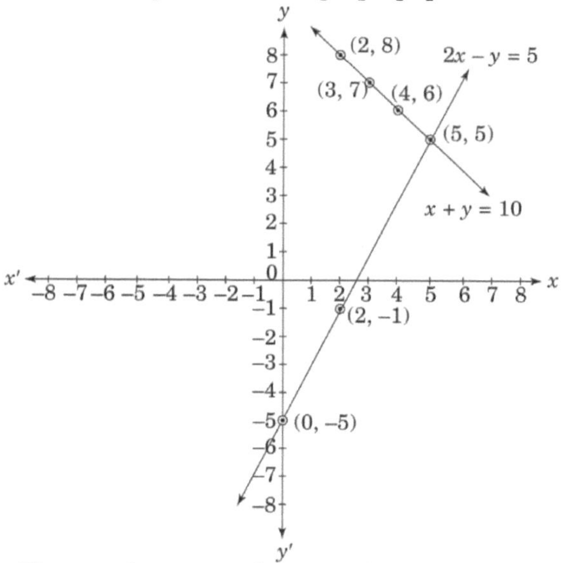

(ii) The geometric representation of $y = 4$ as an equation in two variables is as follows:

$\qquad\qquad 0x + y = 4$

$\Rightarrow \qquad\qquad y - 4 = 0$

$\therefore \qquad\qquad\qquad y = 4$

The points are $(0, 4)$ and $(1, 4)$

22. Fahrenheit (F) and Celsius (C) are two different units of temperature and the relation between them is given by $C = \dfrac{5}{9}(F - 32)$. Draw the graph for this relation, At what temperature both units read the same also find temperature °C, which is equal to 30 °F.

[Board Term II, 2014]

[Board Term II, 2017, Set-UAHYDQ7]

Sol. Given, $\qquad\qquad C = \dfrac{5}{9}(F - 32)$

Now, let $C = x$ and $F = y$

$$x = \frac{5}{9}(y - 32)$$

when y = 50, then $x = \frac{5}{9}(50 - 32) = \frac{5}{9}(18) = 10$

when y = – 40, then $x = \frac{5}{9}(-40 - 32)$

$$= \frac{5}{9}(-72) = -40$$

when y = 5, then $x = \frac{5}{9}(5 - 32) = \frac{5}{9}(-27) = -15$

x	10	–40	–15
y	50	–40	5

Let x = y = a

$\therefore$ $\qquad a = \frac{5}{9}(a - 32)$

or $\qquad 9a = 5a - 160$

or $\qquad a = -40$

$\therefore$ $\qquad -40°C = -40°F$

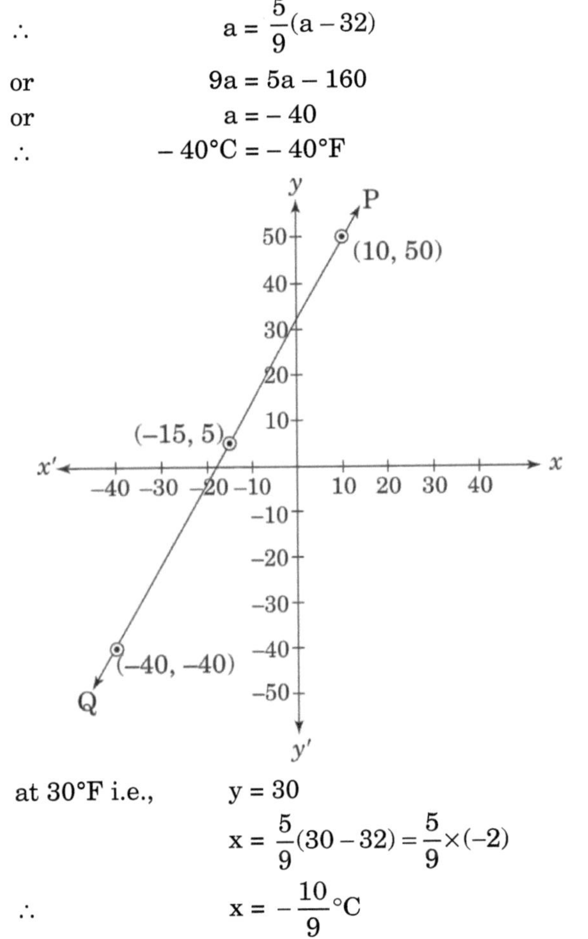

at 30°F i.e., $\qquad y = 30$

$$x = \frac{5}{9}(30 - 32) = \frac{5}{9} \times (-2)$$

$\therefore$ $\qquad x = -\frac{10}{9}°C$

Hence, $30°F = -\frac{10}{9}°C$

23. Draw the graphs of the following equations on same graph sheet : x = 0, y = 0, x + y = 3, also find the area enclosed between these lines.

[Board Term II, 2017, Set-UAH4DQ7]

Sol. x = 0, y = 0, x + y = 3

x	0	3
y	3	0

Area of $\triangle$AOB $= \frac{1}{2} \times$ base $\times$ height

$$= \frac{1}{2} \times 3 \times 3$$

$$= \frac{9}{2}$$

$$= 4.5 \text{ sq. units}$$

For drawing the graph plot the ordered pairs (0, 3) and (3, 0) on the graph paper.

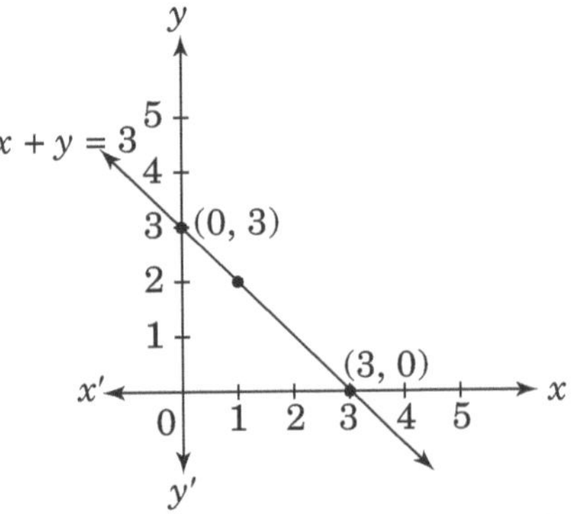

24. Write the equations of lines p and r in the given graph.

A student answered the equation of a line 'q' as x + y = 1. Did he answered correctly? Also, find the area of lines enclosed between p, q and r.

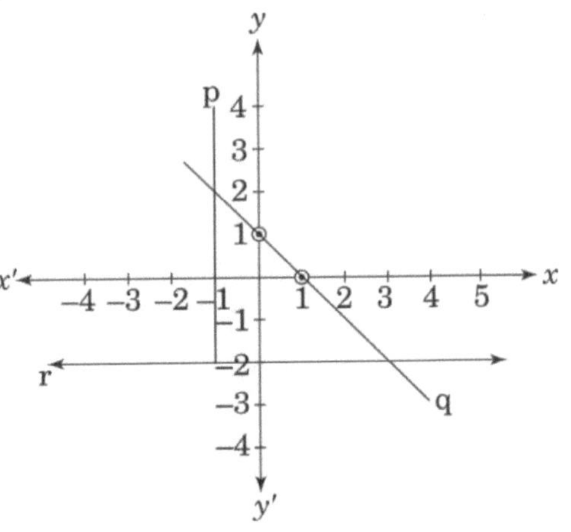

Sol. Equation of line p is

$$x = -1$$

Equation of line r is

$$y = -2$$

Now the equation of q is

$$x + y = 1$$

Therefore, the student answered correctly.

Hence, enclosed area between p, q and r.

$$= \frac{1}{2} \times 4 \times 4$$

$$= 8 \text{ sq. units}$$

25. Yamini and Fatima, two students, of class IX of a school, together contributed ₹ 100 towards the Prime Minister's Relief Fund to help the earthquake victims. Write a linear equation which satisfies the data. (You may take their contributions as ₹ x, and ₹ y). Draw the graph of the same.

Sol. Let the contributions of Yamini and Fatima towards the Prime Minister's Relief Fund to help the earthquake victims are ₹ x and ₹ y respectively, then

According to the question,

$$x + y = 100 \Rightarrow y = 100 - x$$

When x = 0, then y = 100 – 0 = 100

When x = 20 then y = 100 – 20 = 80

When x = 50, then y = 100 – 50 = 50

When x = 70 then y = 100 – 70 = 30

When x = 100, then y = 100 – 100 = 0

We get the following table

x	0	20	50	70	100
y	100	80	50	30	0

For drawing the graph, plot the ordered pairs (0, 100), (20, 80), (50, 50) (70, 30) and (100, 0) on a graph paper. Joining these points we get a line PQ.

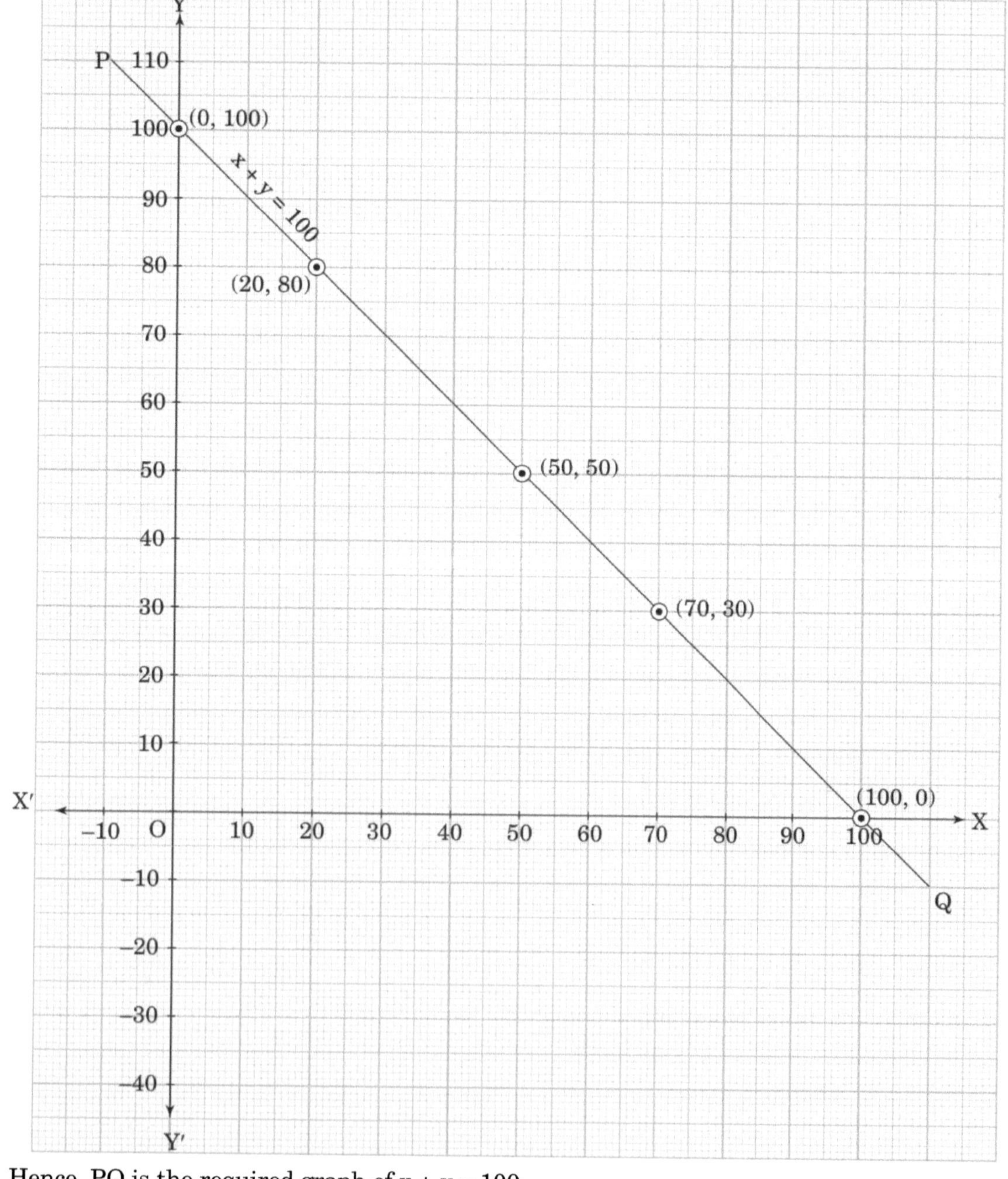

Hence, PQ is the required graph of x + y = 100.

UNIT III
Coordinate Geometry

CHAPTER 4

Coordinate Geometry

- The cartesian plane, co-ordinates of a point, names and terms associated with the coordinate plane, notations, plotting points in the plane.

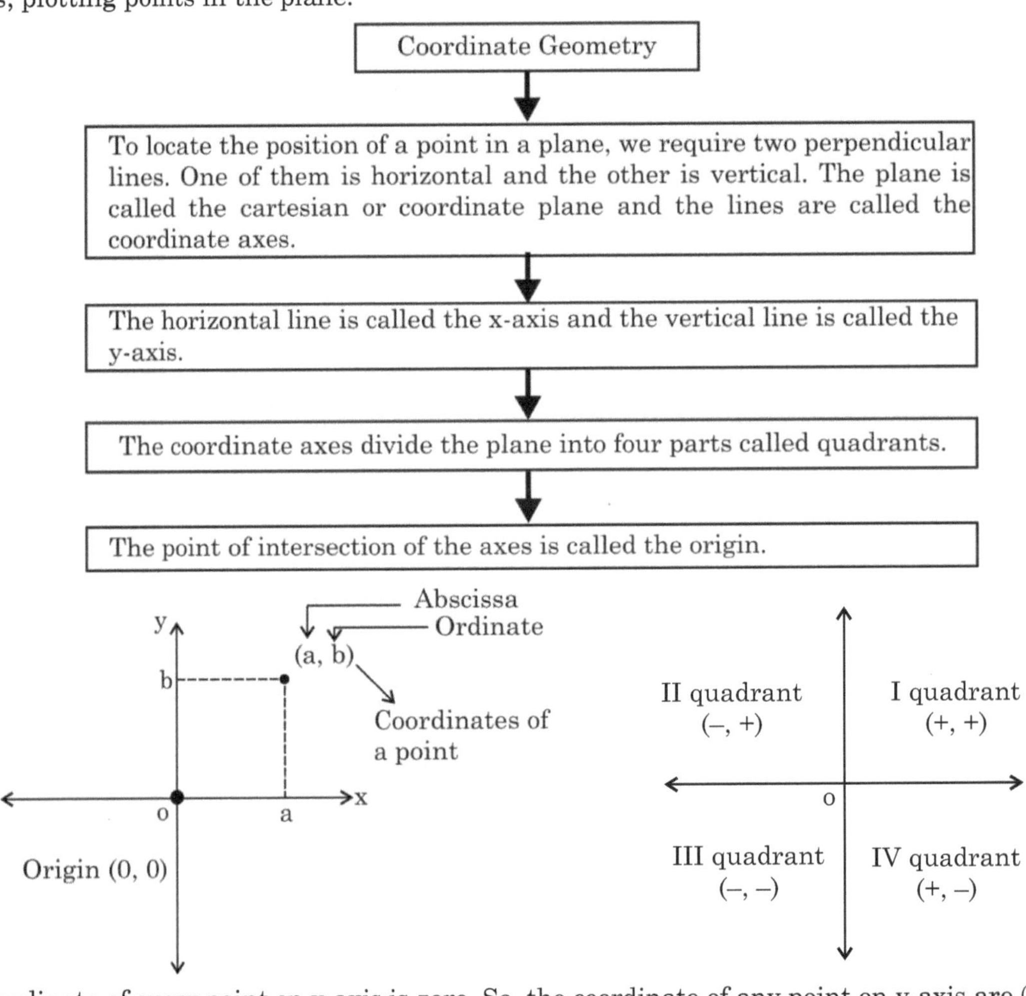

- The x-coordinate of every point on y-axis is zero. So, the coordinate of any point on y-axis are $(0, y)$.
- The y-coordinate of every point on x-axis is zero. So, the coordinate of any point on x-axis are $(x, 0)$
- An equation of the type $y = mx$ represents a straight line passing through the origin.
- The coordinate of origin is $(0, 0)$.

[Topic 1] Cartesian System

Points to be Remembered

- The system by which we can describe the position of a point in a plane is called cartesian system.

- The plane is called the cartesian or co-ordinate plane and the lines are called the co-ordinate axes.

- The co-ordinate axes divide the plane into four parts called quadrants numbered I, II, III and IV anti-clockwise from OX.

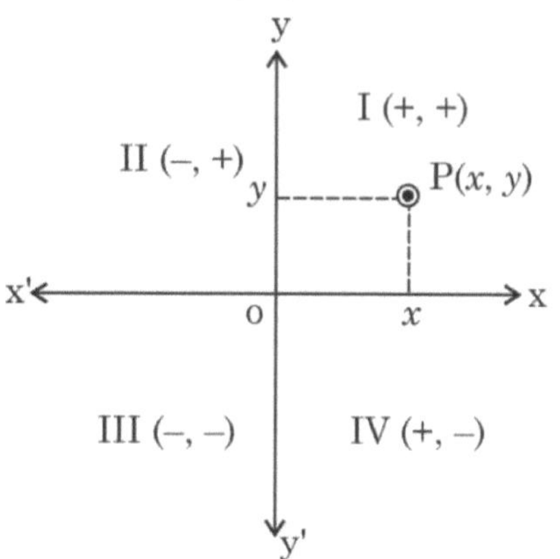

- The horizontal line is called the x-axis and the vertical line is called the y-axis.

- The x-coordinate of a point $P(x, y)$ is called the abscissa.

- The y-coordinate of a point $P(x, y)$ is called the ordinate.

- The coordinates of the origin are (0, 0).

- x is the perpendicular length of $P(x, y)$ from y-axis.

- y is the perpendicular length of $P(x, y)$ from x-axis.

- The abscissa of every point is 0 on the y-axis and the ordinate of every point is 0 on the x-axis.

PREVIOUS YEARS'
EXAMINATION QUESTIONS
TOPIC 1
Multiple Choice Questions
(1 Mark Each)

1. The abscissa of the point (−3, 4) is

   [NCERT Exemplar]

   (a) 3   (b) 4

   (c) − 3   (d) none of these

Sol. (c) We know that.

$$(x, y)$$

Abscissa   Ordinate

Hence required abscissa of point (−3, 4) = − 3

2. Signs of the abscissa and ordinate of a point in the second quadrant are respectively.

   [NCERT Exemplar]

   (a) +, +

   (b) −, −

   (c) −, +

   (d) +, −

Sol. (c) In second quadrant, x-axis in negative and y-axis is positive. Hence, sign of abscissa of a point is negative and sign of ordinate of a point is positive.

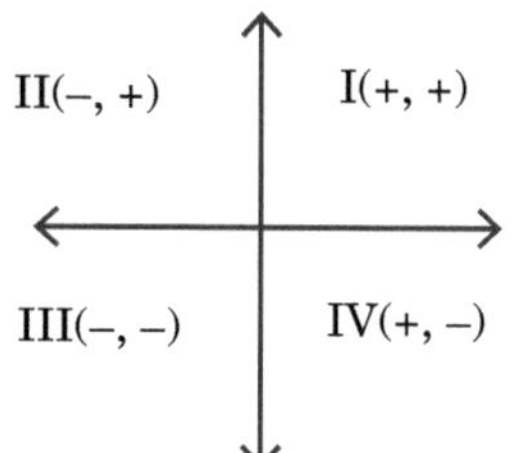

3. Abscissa of all the points on the x-axis is

   [NCERT Exemplar]

   (a) 0   (b) 1

   (c) 2   (d) any number

Sol. (d) Abscissa of all the points on the x-axis is any real number.

Because x-axis is a number line which contains many real numbers on it.

4. The point at which the two coordinate axes meet is called the   [NCERT Exemplar]

   (a) abscissa

   (b) ordinate

   (c) origin

   (d) quadrant

Sol. (c) It is the point at which both x-axis and y-axis meet and its co-ordinates are $(0, 0)$, is called the origin.

5. Point $(-3, 5)$ lies in the   [NCERT Exemplar]

   (a) first quadrant   (b) second quadrant

   (c) third quadrant   (d) fourth quadrant

Sol. (b) In point $(-3, 5)$, x-co-ordinate is negative and y-co-ordinate is positive. So, the point lies in second quadrant.

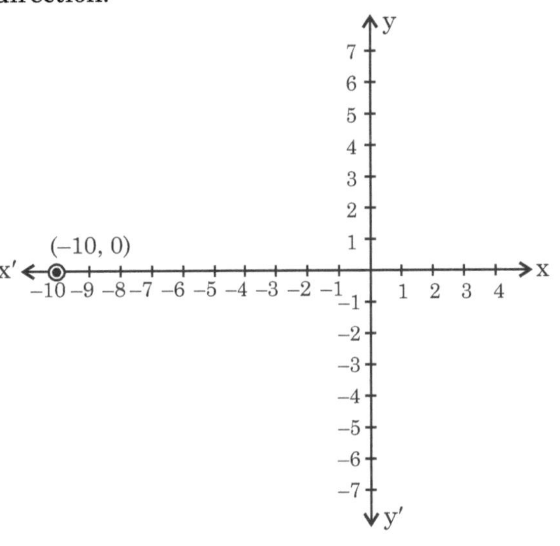

6. Point $(-10, 0)$ lies   [NCERT Exemplar]

   (a) on the negative direction of the x-axis

   (b) on the negative direction of the y-axis

   (c) in the third quadrant

   (d) in the fourth quadrant.

Sol. (a) In point $(-10, 0)$ y-co-ordinate is zero, so it lies on x-axis and x-co-ordinate is negative. Hence, the point $(-10, 0)$ lies on x-axis in the negative direction.

7. Ordinate of all points on the x-axis is

   (a) 0   (b) 1

   (c) -1 (d) any number

   [NCERT Exemplar]

Sol. (a) Because ordinate of a point is perpendicular distance of this point from the x-axis measured along the y-axis. If a point lies on x-axis, then the perpendicular distance of a point from x-axis will be zero, therefore, ordinate will be zero.

8. Point $(0, -7)$ lies

   (a) on the x-axis.

   (b) in the second quadrant.

   (c) on the y-axis

   (d) in the fourth quadrant

Sol. (c) In the point $(0, -7)$, x-co-ordinate is zero. So it lies on y-axis and y-co-ordinate is negative so the point lies on y-axis in the negative direction.

9. The points $(2, -1)$, $(6, -5)$ and $(-3, -2)$ will:

   (a) lies in the I quadrant

   (b) lies in the II quadrant

   (c) lies in the IV quadrant

   (d) do not lie in the same quadrant

Sol. (d)

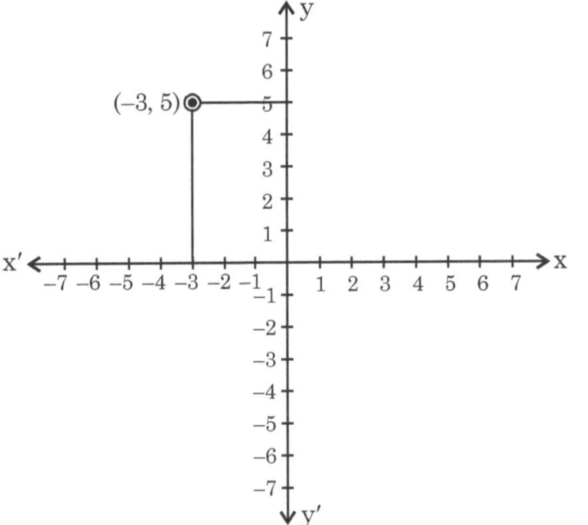

10. The point at which the two coordinates meet is called the:

    (a) abscissa

    (b) ordinate

    (c) origin

    (d) coordinate

Sol. (c) The point at which the two coordinates meet is called the origin.

Very Short Answer Type Questions
(1 Mark Each)

1. In which quadrant point $(-3, 5)$ lies?

    [NCERT Exemplar]

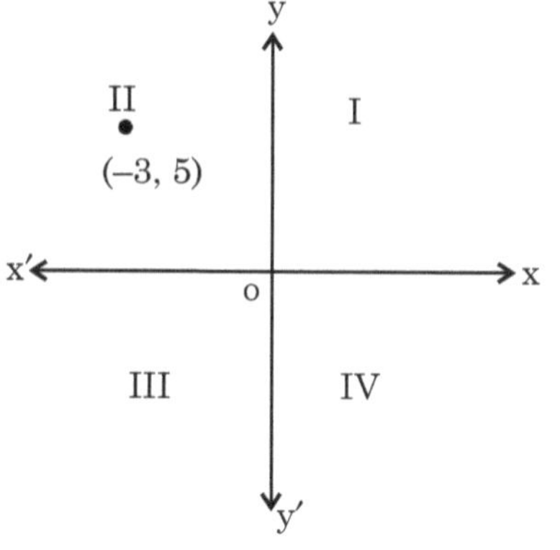

Sol. Hence, point $(-3, 5)$ lies in II quadrant.

2. What does the point at which the two co-ordinate axes meet is called?

    [NCERT EXEMPLAR]

Sol. The point at which the two co-ordinate axes meet is called origin.

3. Point P is on x-axis and is at a distance of 4 units from y-axis to its left. Write the co-ordinates of the point P.

    BOARD TERM I, 2014]

Sol. The P is on x-axis

$y = 0$

P is at a distance of 4 units from y-axis to its left.

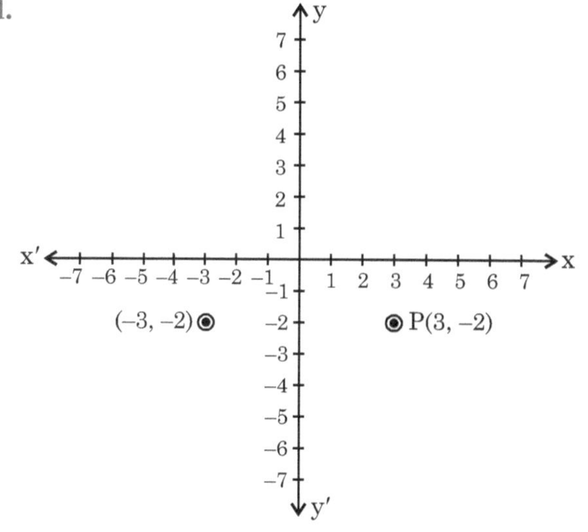

$\therefore$ In second quadrant, the co-ordinates of the point P $(-4, 0)$.

4. Write any two points lying on the negative direction of x-axis.   [BOARD TERM I, 2014]

Sol. In II quadrant, $x < 0$

Points $= (-4, 0), (-6, 0)$

5. What do you mean by abscissa of a point?

    [BOARD TERM I, 2014]

Sol. The distance of a point from the y-axis is called its abscissa.

6. Find the reflection of the points $(-3, -2)$ in y-axis.

    [BOARD TERM I, 2015, SET-1]

Sol.

Hence, point P is the reflection of point $(-3, -2)$ which is $(3, -2)$.

7. In which quadrants the point P $(2, -3)$ and Q$(-3, 2)$ lie?

    [BOARD TERM I, 2015, SET-2]

Sol. P$(2, -3)$ and Q$(-3, 2)$ lie in IV and II quadrants.

8. The points P(a, b) lies in the IV quadrant. Find which of a or b is greater?

    [BOARD TERM I, 2016, SET-20CNJE9, BQ56IZK]

Sol. Since P(a, b) lies in IV quadrant

$\therefore$ a is positive and b is negative

$\therefore$ a > 0, and b < 0

$\therefore$ a > b

9. If $(a, b) = (0, -2)$. Find the value of a and b.

    [BOARD TERM I, 2016, SET-7AEDLQR]

Sol. Given, $(a, b) = (0, -2)$

On comparing both sides,

$\therefore$ a = 0 and b = −2

10. Find one solution of $y - 5 = 0$ in a cartesian plane.
[BOARD TERM II, 2017, SET-UANYDQ7]

Sol. Given, $y - 5 = 0$

$\therefore y = 5$

Hence, $(0, 5)$ is the solution of $y - 5 = 0$.

11. Mention the co-ordinate of a point which is 7 units away from the x-axis and lies on the negative direction of the y-axis.

Sol.

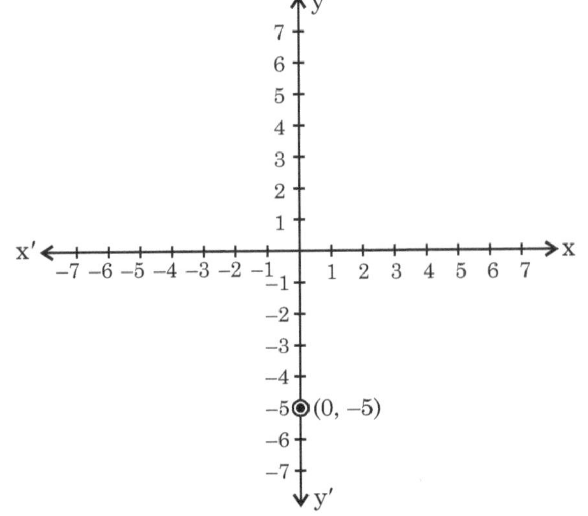

Hence, the co-ordinate of point is $(0, -7)$.

12. What is the x-coordinate of any point on the y-axis?

Sol. x-coordinate of any point on y-axis is zero.

13. What will be the ordinates of the point which lies in the fourth quadrant?

Sol. Negative ordinate i.e., $(x, -y)$

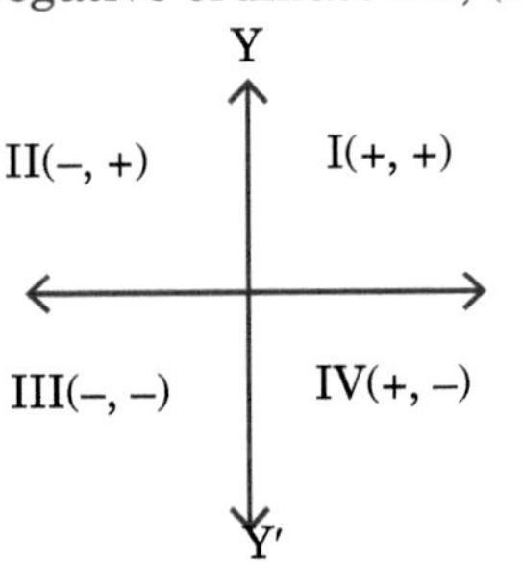

14. Write the abscissa of all the points on y-axis.

Sol. Abscissa of all points on y-axis will be 0 (zero).

15. Write a point which lies in the II quadrant.

Sol. The point $(-5, 2)$ lies in the II quadrant.

16. If $x \neq y$, then $(x, y) \neq (y, x)$. What is if $x = y$?

Sol. $(x, y) = (y, x)$

17. Find the distance of the points $(0, -5)$ from the origin.

Sol. 5 units

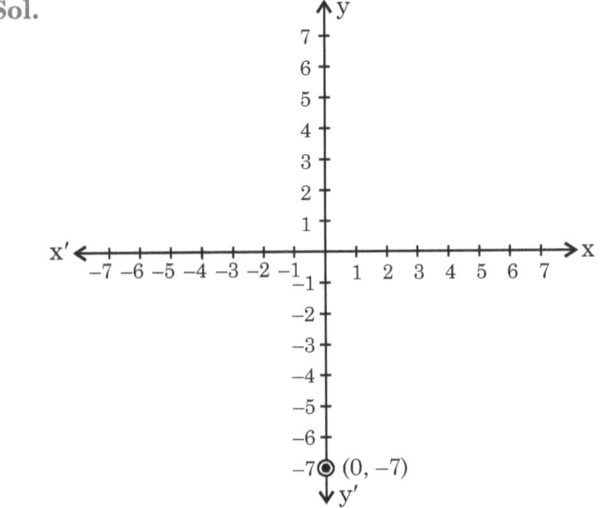

18. If the point A(2, 0), B(−6, 0) and C(3, a − 3) lie on x-axis then calculate the value of a.

Sol. Point C(3, a − 3) lie on x-axis

In x-axis $y = 0$,

$\therefore a - 3 = 0$

$\therefore a = 3$

19. Where do the points $(3, 0)$ and $(-3, 0)$ always lie?

Sol. $\because$ In both the points $y = 0$

$\therefore$ Both the points $(3, 0)$ and $(-3, 0)$ lie on x-axis.

20. What will be the perpendicular distance of the point $(7, 5)$ from y-axis.

Sol. The perpendicular distance of the point $(7, 5)$ from the y-axis $= 7$

21. A point $(-x, y)$ lies in the II quadrant. If the signs of x and y are interchanged, then in which quadrant the point lies?

Sol. If the signs of x and y are interchanged, then the point $(x, -y)$ lies in IV quadrant.

22. Write the co-ordinate of any point on the x-axis.

Sol. The co-ordinate on x-axis $= (x, 0)$

23. In which quadrant the points $(3, -5)$ and $(-5, 3)$ lies?

Sol. Point $(3, -5)$ lies in IV quadrant and point $(-5, 3)$ lies in II quadrant.

24. Mention the co-ordinate of a point whose ordinate is 6 and which lies on y-axis.

Sol. Hence, the required point $= (0, 6)$

25. Where does the point in which abscissa and ordinate have different sign will lie?

Sol. In II and IV quadrants, the point in which abscissa and ordinate have different signs will lie.

Short Answer Type Questions-I
(2 Marks Each)

1. Write the co-ordinate of A, B, C and D from the following figure :

   [BOARD TERM I, 2011, SET 17; 2010, SET-C1]

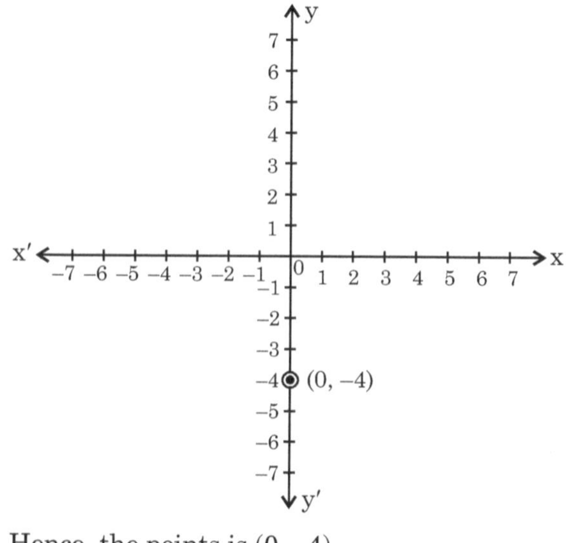

Sol. Co-ordinates of point A = (5, 0)

Co-ordinates of point B = (5, 3)

Co-ordinates of point C = (–2, 4)

Co-ordinates of point D = (0, –3).

2. Find the co-ordinate of the point which lies on y-axis at a distance of 4 units in negative direction of y-axis.

   (i) (–4, 0)   (ii) (4, 0)

   (iii)(0, –4)   (iv) (0, 4)

   [BOARD TERM I, 2011, SET 12]

Sol. The point on y-axis has x-coordinate 0.

Since it lies at a distance of 4 units in the negative direction of y-axis.

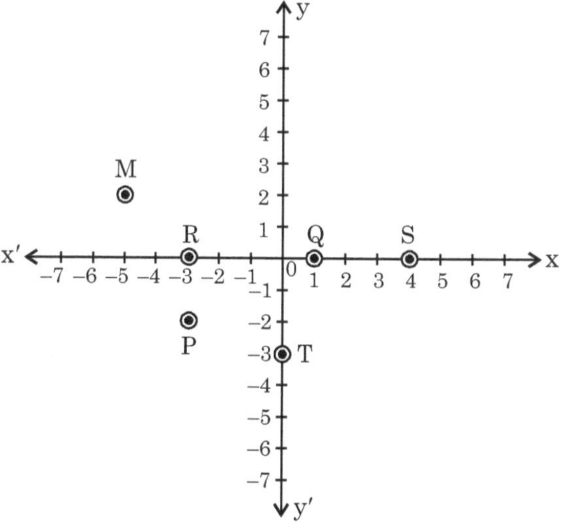

Hence, the points is (0, –4).

3. A point lies on x-axis at a distance of 9 units from y-axis. What are its co-ordinates? What will be the co-ordinates of a point if it lies on y-axis at a distance of –9 units from x-axis?

   [BOARD TERM I, 2011, SET 11]

Sol. *(i)* Since the point P lies on x-axis at a distance of 9 units from y-axis. Hence its co-ordinates are (9, 0).

(ii) According to the question, the required co-ordinates of R are (0, –9).

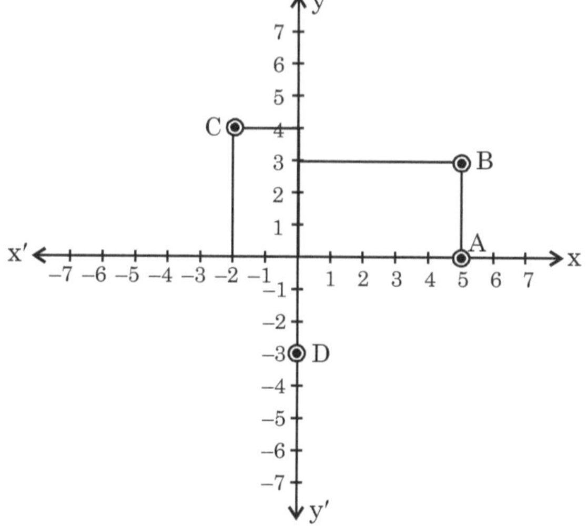

4. In which quadrant do the following points lie?

   (i) (–6, 2)   (ii) (–5, –4)

   (iii)(3, –2)   (iv) (9, 6)

   [BOARD TERM I, 2011, SET 19]

Sol. (i) (–6, 2) ⇒ II quadrant

(ii) (–5, –4) ⇒ III quadrant

(iii) (3, –2) ⇒ IV quadrant

(iv) (9, 6) ⇒ I quadrant

5. From the given figure, write the following :

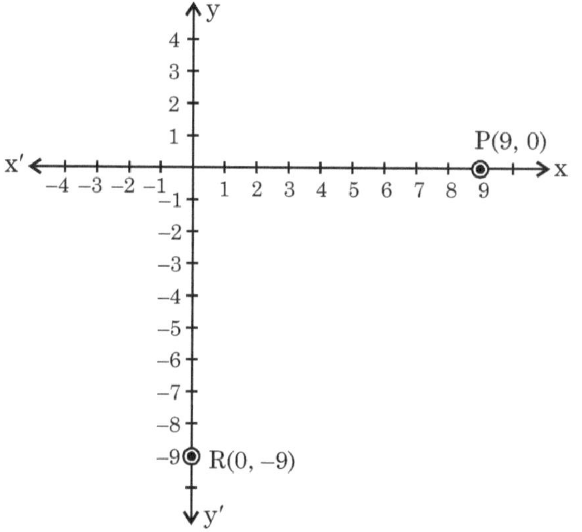

(i)   The co-ordinates of P.

(ii) The abscissa of the point Q.

(iii) The ordinates of the point R.

(iv) The points whose abscissa is 0.

[BOARD TERM I, 2011, SET 20]

Sol. (i) The co-ordinates of point P is (–3, –2)

(ii) The abscissa of the point Q = 0

(iii) The ordinates of the point R = 0

(iv) Points Q and T, whose abscissa is 0.

6.   Locate and write the co-ordinates of a point:
(i)   above x-axis lying on y-axis at a distance of 5 units from origin.

(ii) below x-axis lying on y-axis at a distance of 3 units from origin.

(iii) lying on x-axis to the right of origin at a distance of 5 units.

(iv) lying on x-axis to the left of origin at a distance of 2 units.

[BOARD TERM I, 2011, SET 2]

Sol. (i) Co-ordinates of P (0, 5)

(ii) Co-ordinates of Q(0, –3)

(iii) Co-ordinates of R (5, 0)

(iv) Co-ordinates of S (–2, 0)

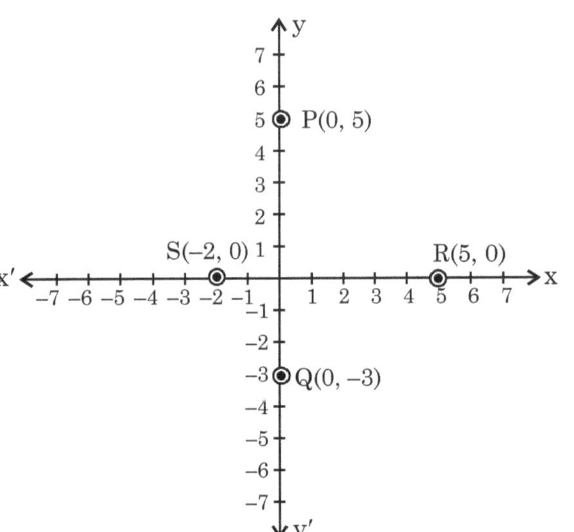

7.   Write ordinates of following points:

(3, 4), (4, 0), (0, 4), (5, –3)

[BOARD TERM I, 2015, SET 20UI6YH]

Sol. Ordinates of the points (3, 4), (4, 0), (0, 4), (5, –3) are 4, 0, 4, –3 respectively.

8.   Find distances of points C(–3, –2) and D(5, 2) from x-axis and y-axis.

[BOARD TERM I, 2016, SET JQ22L5CJ]

Sol. C(–3, –2), distance from x-axis = 2 units

and distance form y-axis = 3 units

D(5, 2) distance from x-axis = 2 units

and distance from y-axis = 5 units

9.   In which quadrant will the point lie, if:
(i)   the ordinate is 2 and the abscissa is –3?

(ii) the abscissa is –4 and the ordinate is –2?

(iii) the ordinate is 3 and the abscissa is 4?

(iv) the ordinate is 3 and the abscissa is –2?

Sol. (i) II quadrant (–3, 2). (ii) III quadrant (–4, –2).

(iii) I quadrant (4, 3). (iv) II quadrant (–2, 3).

10.   Name the quadrant in which the graph of point $P(x, y)$ lies when
(i) $x > 0$ and $y > 0$

(ii) $x < 0$ and $y < 0$

Sol. (i) Point P (X, Y) has X > 0 i.e. its abscissa is positive and Y > 0 i.e. its ordinate is positive.

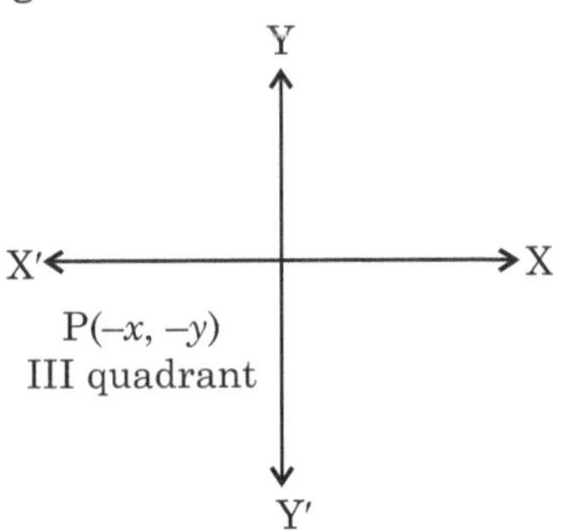

Thus, point $P(x, y)$ lies in the I quadrant.

(ii) Point $P(x, y)$ has $x < 0$ i.e its abscissa is negative and $y < 0$ i.e. its ordinate is negative.

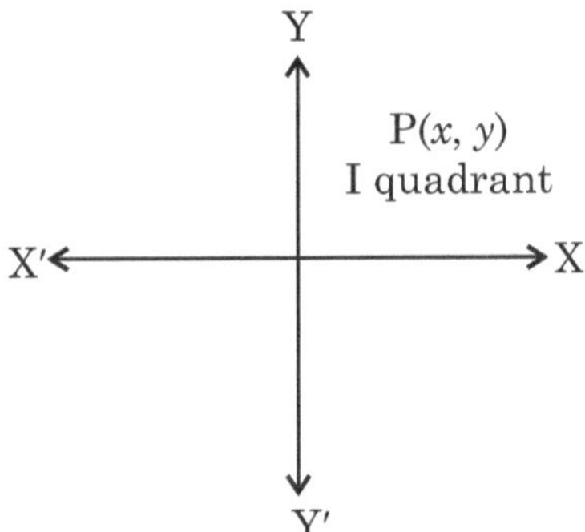

Thus, point $P(x, y)$ lies in the III quadrant.

Short Answer Type Questions II
(3 Marks Each)

1. In the given figure, LM is a line parallel to the Y-axis at a distance of 3 units.

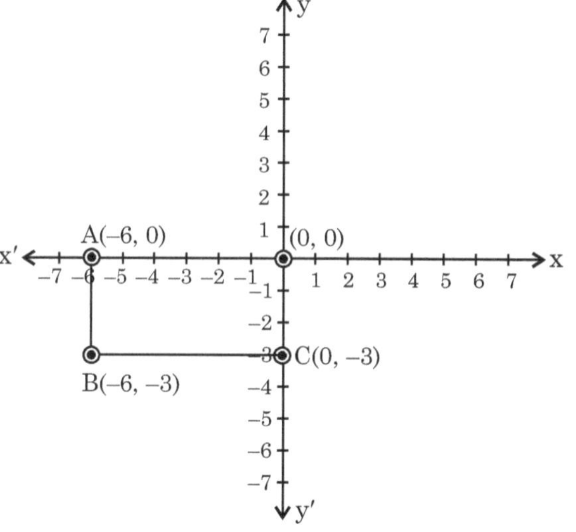

   (i) What are the coordinates of the point P, R and Q?

   (ii) What is the difference between the abscissa of the points L and M?

   [NCERT Exemplar]

   Sol. According to the graph, LM is a line parallel to the Y-axis and its perpendicular distance from Y-axis is 3 units.

   (i) Coordinates of point P = (3, 1)

   Coordinates of point Q = (3, −1)

   and Coordinates of point R = (3, 0)

   (ii) Abscissa of point L = 4, abscissa of points M = −3

   Hence required difference between abscissa of points L and M = 4 − (−3) = 4 + 3 = 7

2. Write the co-ordinates of each points P, Q, R, S, T and O from the figure given below.

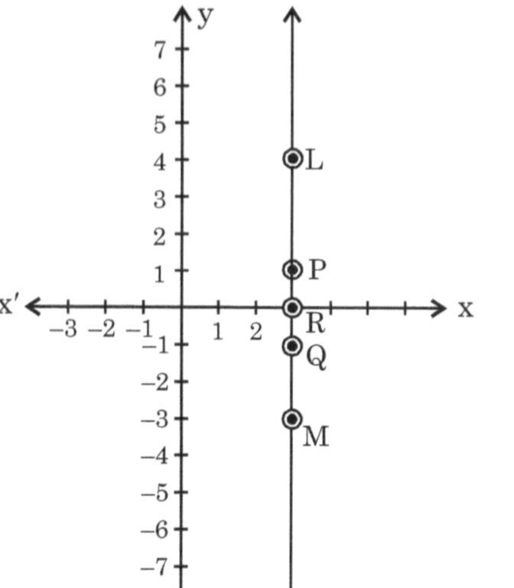

   [NCERT Exemplar]

Sol. Co-ordinates of point P = (1, 1).

Co-ordinates of point Q = (−3, 0)

Co-ordinates of point R = (−2, −3)

Co-ordinates of point S = (2, 1)

Co-ordinates of point T = (4, −2)

Co-ordinates of point O = (0, 0)

3. Find the co-ordinates of the point.

   (i) Which lies on x and y-axis, both

   (ii) whose abscissa is 5 and ordinate is 6.

   (iii) whose ordinate is 6 and which lies on y-axis

   (iv) whose ordinate is 3 and abscissa is −7.

   (v) whose abscissa is 3 and which lies on x-axis.

   (vi) whose abscissa is 4 and ordinate is 4.

   Sol. (i) A point which lies on x and y-axes is (0, 0) i.e., origin

   (ii) A point whose abscissa is 5 and ordinate is 6 is (5, 6).

   (iii) A point whose ordinate is 6 and lies on y-axis is (0, 6).

   (iv) A point whose ordinate is 3 and abscissa is −7 is (−7, 3).

   (v) A point whose abscissa is 3 and lies on x-axis is (3, 0)

   (vi) A point whose abscissa is 4 and ordinate is 4 is (4, 4)

4. Write the co-ordinates of the vertices of a rectangle whose length and breadth are 6 and 3 units respectively, one vertex at the origin, the longer side lies on the x-axis and one of the vertices lies in the III quadrant.

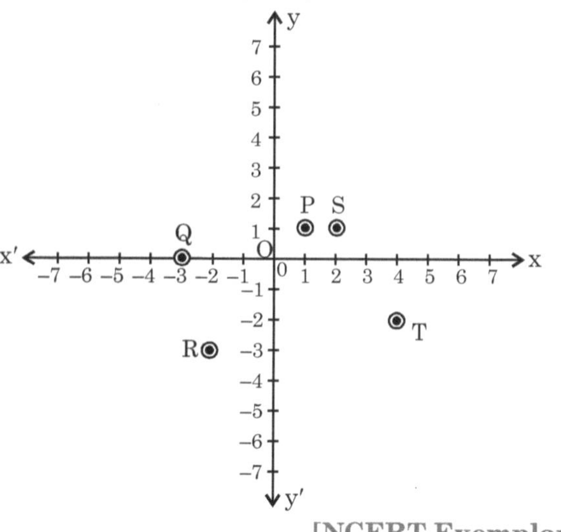

Sol. The vertices of the rectangle OABC are O(0, 0), A(−6, 0), B(−6, −3) and C(0, −3)

5. In which quadrant or on which axis does each of the following points lie

$(-5, 3), (4, -3), (5, 0), (6, 6), (-5, -4)$?

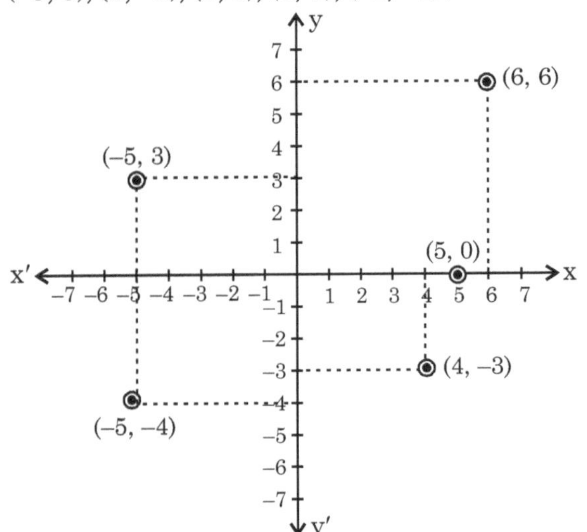

Sol. In a point $(-5, 3)$, $x < 0$ and $y > 0$

∴ Point $(-5, 3)$ lies in II quadrant.

In a point $(4, -3)$, $x > 0$ and $y < 0$

∴ Point $(4, -3)$ lies in IV quadrant.

In a point $(5, 0)$, $x > 0$ and $y = 0$.

∴ Point $(5, 0)$ lies on x-axis

In a point $(6, 6)$, $x > 0$ and $y > 0$

∴ Point $(6, 6)$ lies in I quadrant.

In a point $(-5, -4)$, $x < 0$ and $y < 0$.

∴ Point $(-5, -4)$ lies in III quadrant

Long Answer Type Questions

(4 Marks Each)

1. Write the quadrant in which each of the following points lie:

   (i) $(-3, -5)$

   (ii) $(2, -3)$

   (iii) $(-3, 5)$

   Also verify by locating them on the cartesian plane.

   [NCERT Exemplar, CBSE SQP I]

Sol. (i) Point $(-3, -5)$ lies in III quadrant, as $x < 0$ and $y < 0$

   (ii) Point $(2, -5)$ lies in IV quadrant, as $x > 0$ and $y < 0$.

   (iii) Point $-3, 5)$ lies in II quadrant, as $x < 0$ and $y > 0$.

Verification : The points $(-3, -5)$, $(2, -5)$ and $(-3, 5)$ are plotted as shown in figure :

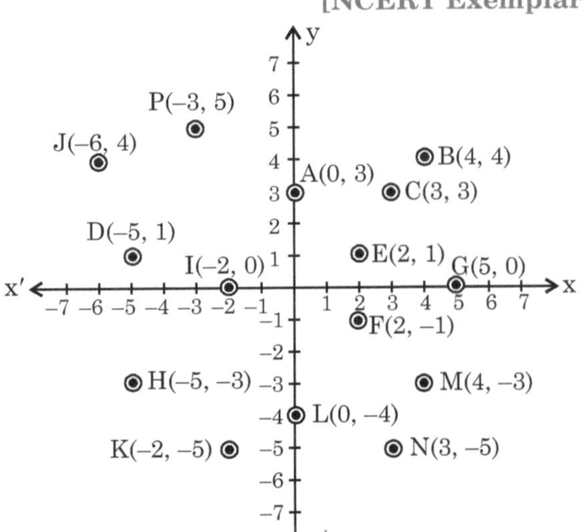

(i) Point $(-3, -5)$ lies in III quadrant.

(ii) $(2, -5)$ lies in IV quadrant.

(iii) $(-3, 5)$ lies in II quadrant.

2. From the given figure answer the following:

   (i) Write the points whose abscissa is 0.

   (ii) Write the points whose ordinate is 0.

   (iii) Write the points whose abscissa is -5.

   [NCERT Exemplar]

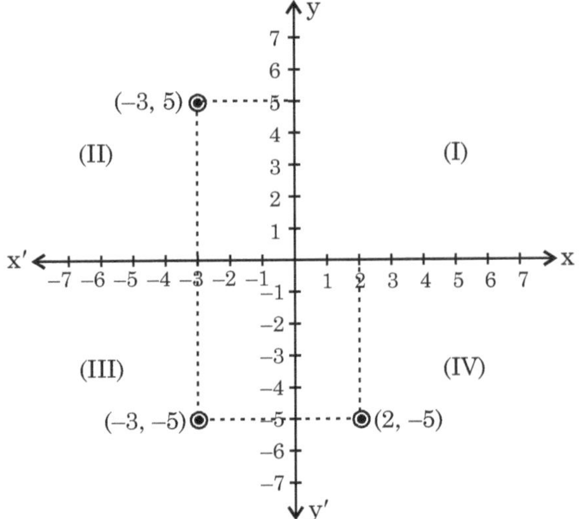

Sol. (i) Required points are A$(0, 3)$ and L$(0, -4)$; [whose abscissa is 0]

(ii) Required points are G$(5, 0)$ and I$(-2, 0)$; [whose ordinate is 0]

(iii) Required points are D$(-5, 1)$ and H$(-5, -3)$; [whose abscissa is -5]

3. If the co-ordinates of a point M are $(-2, 9)$ which can also be expressed as $(1 + x, y^2)$ and $y > 0$, then find in which quadrant do the following points lie :

P(y, x), Q$(2, x)$, R$(x^2, y - 1)$, S$(2x, - 3y)$.

[BOARD TERM I, 2011, SET-21]

Sol. According to the question,

$(-2, 9) = (1 + x, y^2)$

On comparing both sides, we get

$\therefore -2 = 1 + x$

$\therefore x = -3$

and $9 = y^2$.

$\therefore y = 3, (y > 0)$

So, Point $P(y, x) = P(3, -3)$,

which will be in IV quadrant.

Point $Q(2, x) = Q(2, -3)$,

which will be in IV quadrant.

Point $R(x^2, y - 1) = R(9, 2)$,

which will be in I quadrant.

Point $S(2x, -3y) = S(-6, -9)$,

which will be in III quadrant.

4. Observe the points plotted in the figure and find the following :

(i) The co-ordinates of E.

(ii) The point with the co-ordinates $(-4, -1)$.

(iii) The abscissa of A − abscissa of B.

(iv) The ordinate of C + ordinate of F.

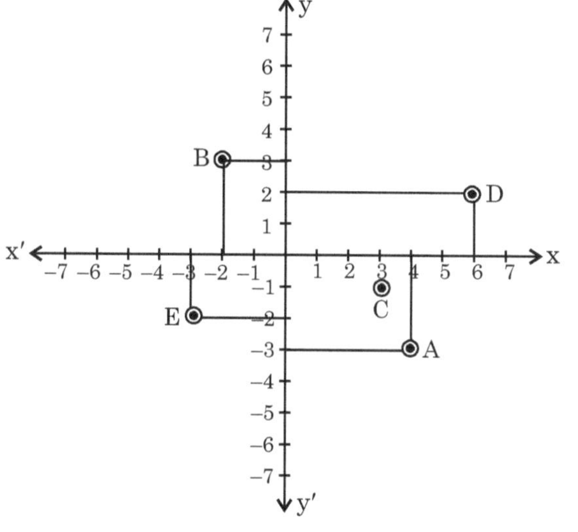

[BOARD TERM I, 2011, SET 19]

Sol. (i) The co-ordinates of E is $(-1, 2)$.

(ii) The point with the ordinates $(-4, -1)$ is D.

(iii) The co-ordinates of A = $(2, -2)$ co-ordinates of B = $(4, 1)$

$\therefore$ The abscissa of A − abscissa of B = $2 - 4$
$= -2$

(iv) The co-ordinates of C = $(3, 3)$ and co-ordinates of F = $(-1, -4)$

$\therefore$ The ordinate of C + ordinate of
$F = 3 + (-4) = -1$.

5. See figure and write the following :

(i) The co-ordinate of B.

(ii) The point identified by the coordinates $(-3, -2)$.

(iii) The abscissa of the point D.

(iv) The ordinate of the point C.

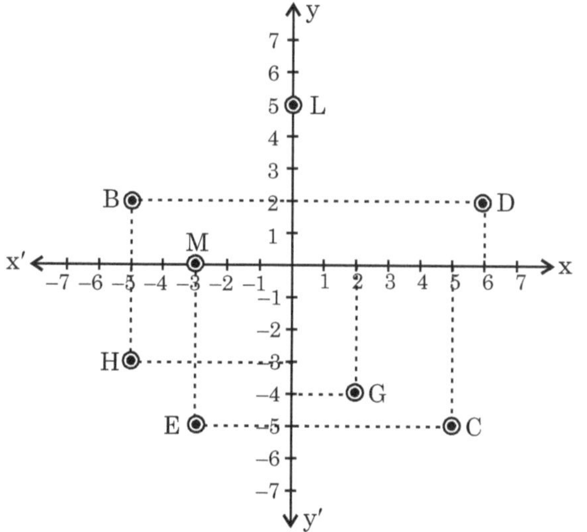

[BOARD TERM I, 2014]

Sol. (i) The co-ordinate of B = $(-2, 3)$

(ii) E is the point which is identified by the coordinates $(-3, -2)$

(iii) The co-ordinate of the point D is $(6, 2)$

$\therefore$ Abscissa of point D is 6.

(iv) The co-ordinate of the point C is $(3, -1)$

$\therefore$ Ordinate of point C is -1.

6. See figure and find the following:

(i) The coordinates of the point B.

(ii) The coordinates of the point C.

(iii) The point identified by the coordinates $(-3, -5)$.

(iv) The point identified by the coordinates $(2, -4)$.

(v) The abscissa of the point D.

(vi) The ordinate of the point H.

(vii) The coordinates of the point L.

(viii) The coordinates of the point M.

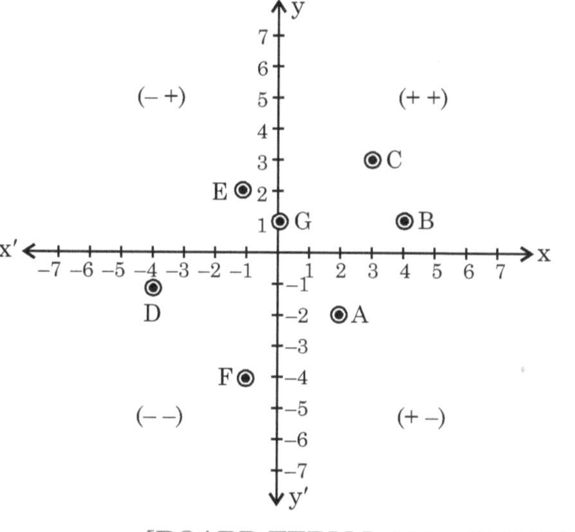

Sol. *(i)* Point B is at a distance of 5 units from the Y-axis in negative direction of X-axis and 2 units from the X-axis. Hence, the coordinates of the point B are (–5, 2).

(ii) Point C is at a distance of 5 units from Y-axis in positive direction of X-axis and 5 units from the x-axis in negative direction of y-axis.

Hence, the co-ordinates of point C are (5, –5).

(iii) Point, which has distance 3 units from the Y-axis in negative direction of X-axis and 5 units from the X-axis in negative direction Y-axis is E.

(iv) The point identified by the co-ordinates (2, –4) is G.

(v) Point D is at a distance of 6 units from the Y-axis. Hence, its abscissa is 6.

(vi) Point H is at a distance of 3 units from the X-axis in negative direction of Y-axis.

Hence, its ordinate is –3.

(vii) Point L is at a distance of 5 units from X-axis.

Hence, the co-ordinates of point L are (0, 5).

(viii) Point M is at a distance of 3 units from the Y-axis in negative direction of x-axis.

Hence, the coordinates of point M are (–3, 0)

[Topic 2] Plotting of a point (x, y) in xy-plane

Points to be Remembered

- We can represent a point in XY-plane. A point is an ordered pair of real numbers, called the coordinates of that point.

- The position of a point in a plane is determined with reference to two fixed mutually perpendicular lines, called the coordinate axes. The horizontal line is called the x-axis and the vertical line is called the y-axis.

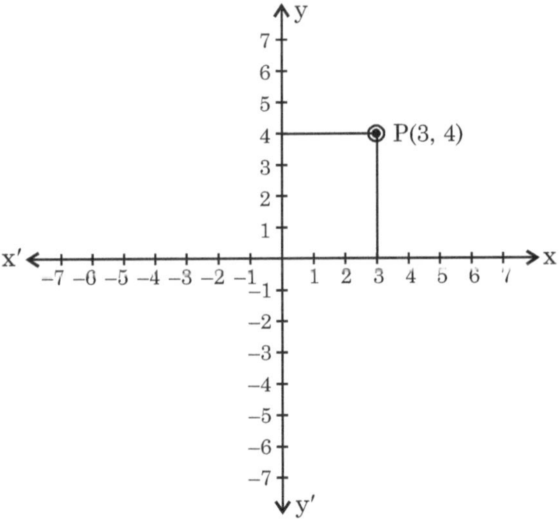

∴ Point P is the position of the point (3, 4) as distance of point P from y-axis is 3 units and distance from x-axis is 4 units.

PREVIOUS YEARS' EXAMINATION QUESTIONS
TOPIC 2

Multiple Choice Questions
(1 Mark Each)

1. Abscissa of a point is positive in
   (a) I and II quadrants   [NCERT Exemplar]
   (b) I and IV quadrants
   (c) I quadrant only
   (d) II quadrant only

Sol. (b) Abscissa of a point is positive in I and IV quadrants.

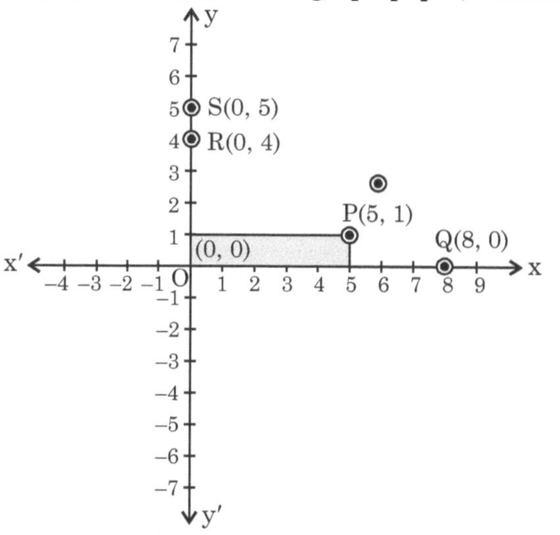

2. If the coordinates of the two points are P(−2, 3) and Q(−3, 5), then (abscissa of P) − (abscissa of Q) is   [NCERT Exemplar]
   (a) −5
   (b) 1
   (c) −1
   (d) −2

Sol. (b) Given, two points P(−2, 3) and Q(−3, 5)

Abscissa of P = −2

and Abscissa of Q = −3

According to the question,

(Abscissa of P) − (Abscissa of Q) = (−2) − (−3)

$\Rightarrow -2 + 3 = 1$

3. If P(−1, 1), Q(3, −4), R(1, −1), S(−2, −3) and T(−4, 4) are plotted on the graph paper, then the point(s) in the fourth quadrant are
   (a) P and T   [NCERT Exemplar]
   (b) Q and R
   (c) Only S
   (d) P and R

Sol. (b) On plotting the points

P(−1, 1), Q(3, −4), R(1, −1), S(−2, −3) and T(−4, 4)

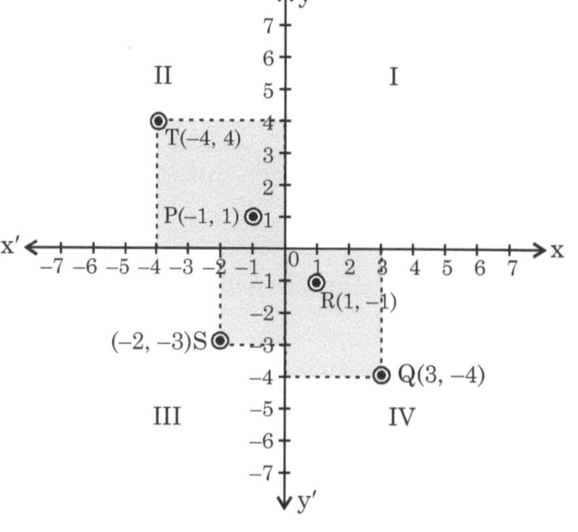

Hence, it is clear from the above graph. Point Q and R lie in the IV quadrant.

4. Points (1, −1), (2, −2), (4, −5), (−3, −4)
   (a) lie in II quadrant.   [NCERT Exemplar]
   (b) lie in III quadrant.
   (c) lie in IV quadrant.
   (d) do not lie in the same quadrant

Sol. (d) In points (1, −1), (2, −2) and (4, −5) x-co-ordinate is positive and y-co-ordinate is negative. So they all lie in IV quadrant. In point (−3, −4), x-co-ordinate and y-co-ordinate both are negative, so it lies in III quadrant. Hence, all the points do not lie in same quadrant.

5. If P(5, 1), Q(8, 0), R(0, 4), S(0, 5) and O(0, 0) are plotted on the graph paper, then the point(s) on the x-axis are   [NCERT Exemplar]
   (a) P and R   (b) R and S
   (c) Only Q   (d) Q and O

Sol. (d) On plotting the points P(5, 1), Q(8, 0), R(0, 4), S(0, 5) and O(0, 0) on the graph paper, we have

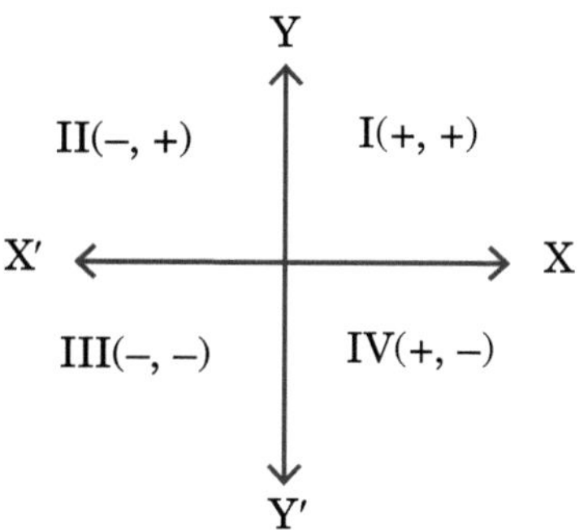

A point lies on x-axis, if its y-co-ordinate is zero. So, on plotting the given points on graph paper, we get Q and O lie on the x-axis.

6. A point both of whose coordinates are negative will lie in
   (a) I quadrant.
   (b) II quadrant.
   (c) III quadrant.
   (d) IV quadrant.

[NCERT Exemplar]

Sol. (c) A point both of whose co-ordinates are negative will lie in III quadrant because in III quadrant x-co-ordinate and y-co-ordinate both are negative.

7. On plotting the points O(0, 0), A(3, 0), B(3, 4), C(0, 4) and joining OA, AB, BC and CO which of the following figure is obtained?
   (a) Square
   (b) Rectangle
   (c) Trapezium
   (d) Rhombus

Sol. (b) On plotting the points O(0, 0), A(3, 0), B(3, 4) and C(0, 4) on the graph paper, we have

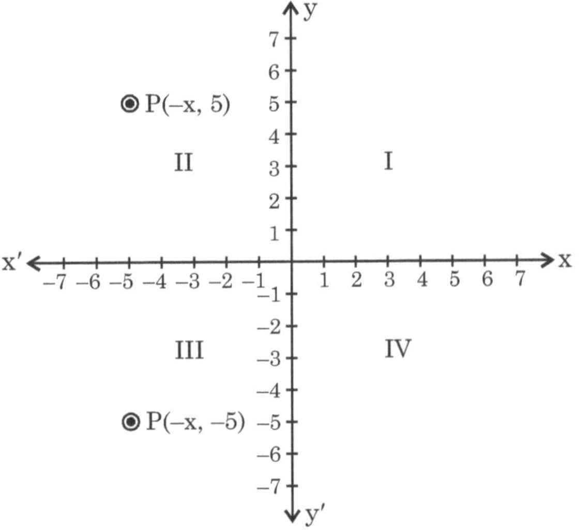

Hence, the obtained figure is a rectangle.

8. If the perpendicular distance of a point P from the x-axis is 5 units and the foot of the perpendicular lies on the negative direction of x-axis, then the point P has
   (a) x-co-ordinate = −5.
   (b) y-co-ordinate = 5 only
   (c) y-co-ordinate = −5 only
   (d) y-co-ordinate = 5 or −5

[NCERT Exemplar]

Sol. (d) According to the question,

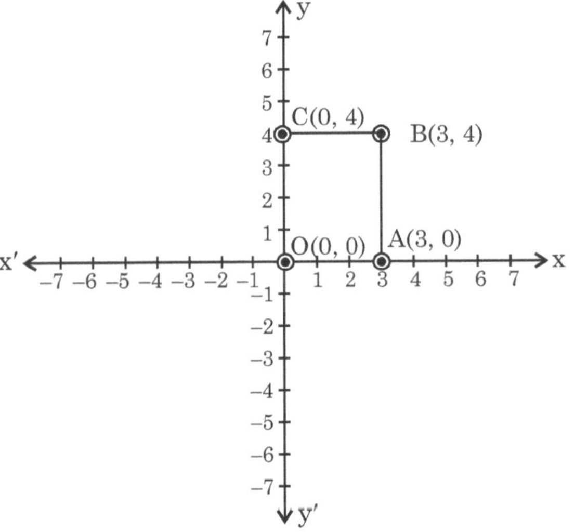

The perpendicular distance of a point from the x-axis gives y-co-ordinate of that point. The foot of the perpendicular lies on the negative direction of x-axis, so perpendicular distance can be measure in II or III quadrant. So the point P has y-co-ordinate = 5 or −5.

9. The points whose abscissa and ordinate have different signs will lie in [NCERT Exemplar]
   (a) I and II quadrants   (b) II and III quadrants
   (c) I and III quadrants   (d) II and IV quadrants

Sol. (d) The points whose abscissa and ordinate have different signs will be of the form (−x, y) or (x, −y) and these points will lie in II and IV quadrants.

10. If y co-ordinate of a point is zero, then this point always lies.   [NCERT Exemplar]
    (a) in I quadrant   (b) in II quadrant
    (c) on x-axis   (d) on y-axis

Sol. (c) If y co-ordinate of a point is zero, then this point always lies on x-axis.

Because perpendicular distance of the point from x-axis measured along y-axis is zero.

11. Which of the points P(0, 3), Q(1, 0), R(0, −1), S(−5, 0), T(1, 2) do not lie on the x-axis?

[NCERT Exemplar]

    (a) P and R only   (b) Q and S only
    (c) P, R and T   (d) Q, S and T

Sol. (c) If a point is of the form (x, 0), i.e, its y-co-ordinate is zero, then it will lie on x-axis. Here y-co-ordinates of point P(0, 3), R(0, −1), T(1, 2) are not zero, hence these points do not lie on x-axis.

12. The perpendicular distance of the point P(3, 4) from the y-axis is   [NCERT Exemplar]

(a) 3   (b) 4

(c) 5   (d) 7

Sol. (a) According to the question,

Abscissa or the x-coordinate of a point is its perpendicular distance from the y-axis. So the abscissa of point P = 3

13. The point whose ordinate is 4 and which lies on y-axis is   [NCERT Exemplar]

(a) (4, 0)   (b) (0, 4)

(c) (1, 4)   (d) (4, 2)

Sol. (b) According to the question,

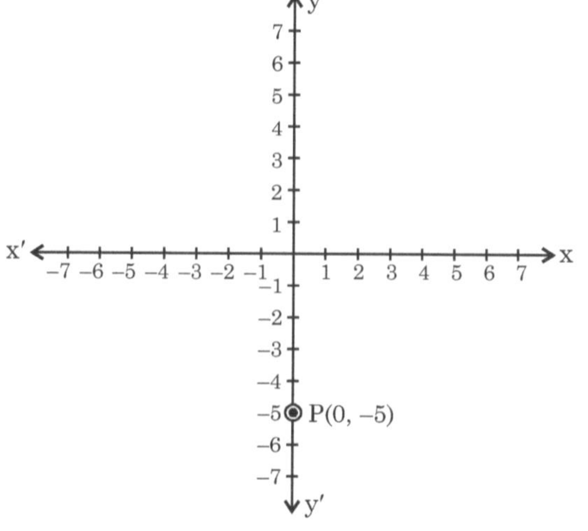

Ordinate of the point is 4 and the point lies on y-axis so its abscissa is zero. Hence, the required point is (0, 4).

14. The point which lies on y-axis at a distance of 5 units in the negative direction of y-axis is   [NCERT Exemplar]

(a) (0, 5)   (b) (5, 0)

(c) (0, −5)   (d) (−5, 0)

Sol. (c) According to the question,

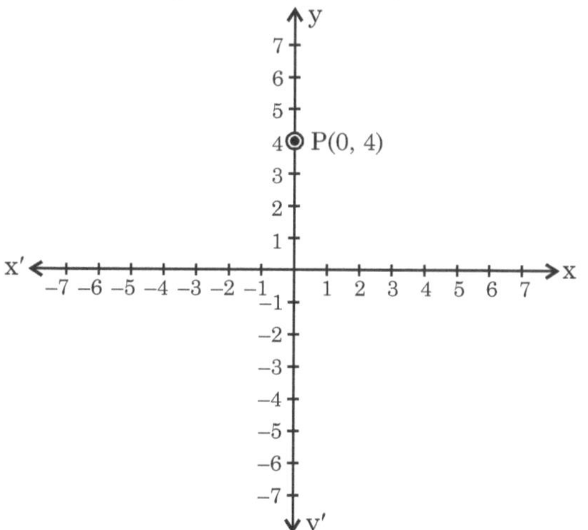

The point lies on y-axis it means its x-co-ordinate is zero. It is at a distance of 5 units in negative direction of y-axis, so its y-co-ordinate is negative.

15. If we join the points (−2, 0), (0, 1), (2, 0) and (0, −1), then name the figure formed is:

(a) square   (b) rectangle

(c) rhombus   (d) parallelogram

Sol. (c) On plotting the points (−2, 0), (0, 1), (2, 0) and (0, −1) on the graph, we have

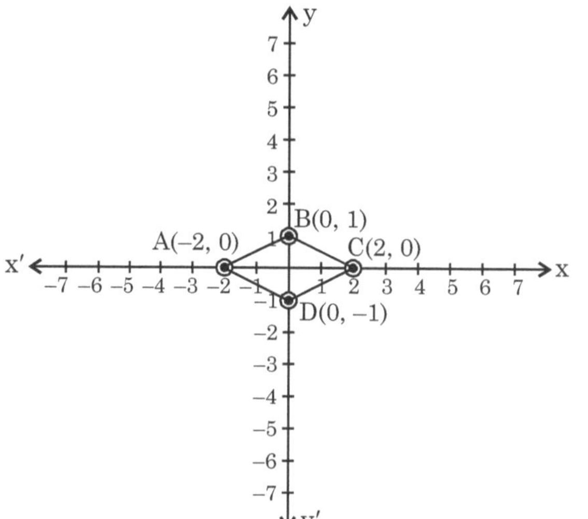

Hence, the obtained figure is a rhombus.

16. Write whether the following statements are True or False? Justify your answer.

[NCERT Exemplar]

(i) Points (1, −1) and (−1, 1) lie in the same quadrant.

(ii) Point (3, 0) lies in the first quadrant.

(iii) A point lies on y-axis at distance of 2 units from the x-axis. Its co-ordinates are (2, 0)

(iv) (−1, 7) is a point in the II quadrant.

(v) The co-ordinates of a point whose ordinate is $-\dfrac{1}{2}$ and abscissa is 1 are $-\dfrac{1}{2}$, 1.

Sol. (i) False, because in point (1, −1) x-co-ordinate is positive and y-co-ordinate is negative so it lies in IV quadrant and (−1, 1), x-co-ordinate is negative and y-co-ordinate is positive, so it lies in II quadrant.

(ii) False, since the ordinate of the point (3, 0) is zero. So, the point lies on x-axis.

(iii) False, because point (2, 0) lies on x-axis whose distance from y-axis is 2 units.

(iv) The given statement is True, because in a point (−1, 7) abscissa is negative and ordinate is positive.

(v) False, because abscissa comes first and then ordinate.

Very Short Answer Type Questions

(1 Mark Each)

1. Draw a quadrilateral ABCD, whose vertices are A(3, 2), B(2, 3), C(–4, 5) and D(5, –3).

[BOARD TERM I, 2011, SET-22]

Sol. On plotting the points, A(3, 2), B(2, 3), C(–4, 5) and D(5, –3). Joining AB, BC, CA, AD, we get a quadrilateral ABCD.

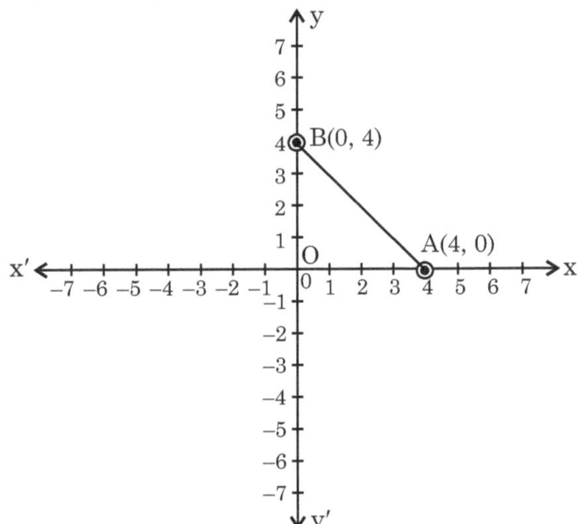

2. Plot the point P(2, –6) on a graph paper and from it draw PM and PN perpendiculars to x-axis and y-axis respectively. Write the co-ordinates of the points M and N.

[BOARD TERM I, 2011, SET-13, 14]

Sol. On plotting the point P(2, –6) we have,

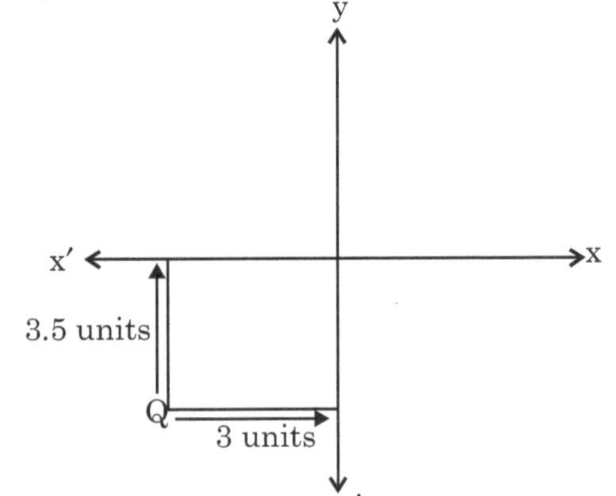

Hence, the co-ordinates of point M(2, 0) and co-ordinates of point N(0, –6).

3. Name the figure formed by joining the points (4, 0) and (0, 4) in a Cartesian plane.

[BOARD TERM I, 2014]

Sol. According to the question, on plotting the points (4, 0) and (0, 4), we have

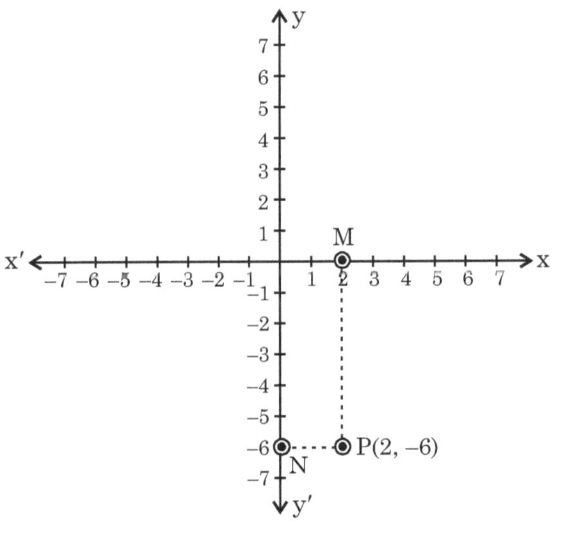

Hence, it is clear from the given graph, the obtained figure is a right-angled triangle.

4. From the figure given below find the c-ordinates of point Q.

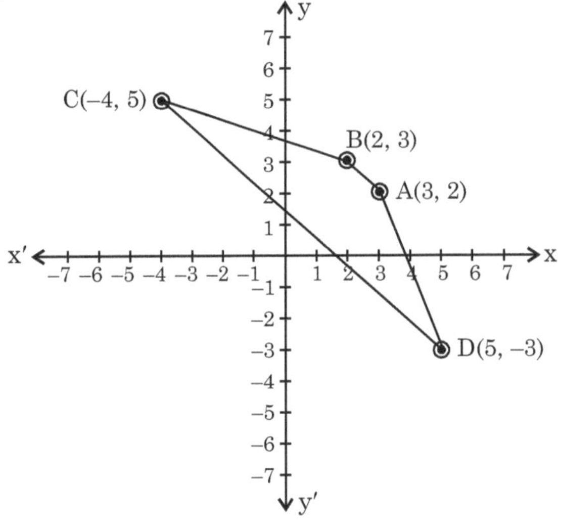

Sol. The co-ordinate of point Q = (–3, –3.5)

5. Write the shape of the quadrilateral formed by joining (1, 1), (6, 1) (4, 5) and (3, 5) on graph paper.

Sol. On plotting the points (1, 1), (6, 1), (4, 5) and (3, 5) on the graph paper, we have

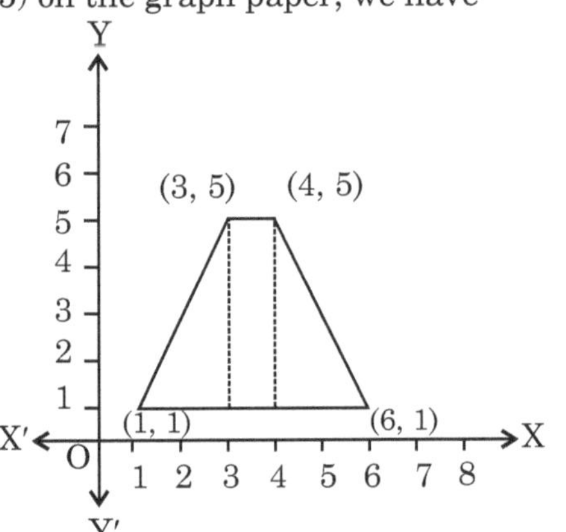

Hence, it is clear from the given figure, the obtained figure is a trapezium.

6. Find the point where line $3x + 6y - 4 = 0$ intersect the x-axis.

Sol. Given equation, $3x + 6y - 4 = 0$

∴ Line intersect the x-axis

∴ $y = 0$

$3x + 6 \times (0) - 4 = 0$

$\Rightarrow 3x + 0 - 4 = 0$

$\Rightarrow 3x = 4$

∴ $x = \dfrac{4}{3}$

Hence, the point where line intersect the x-axis is $(\dfrac{4}{3}, 0)$.

7. $y = a$ is a straight line parallel to ....

Sol. $y = a$ is a straight line parallel to x-axis.

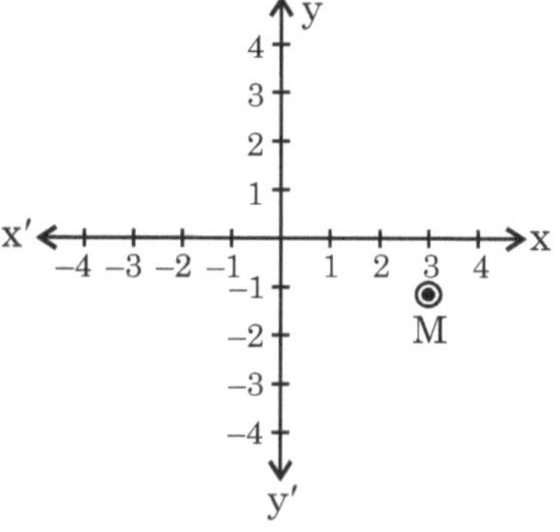

8. In the given figure, write the coordinates of the points M.

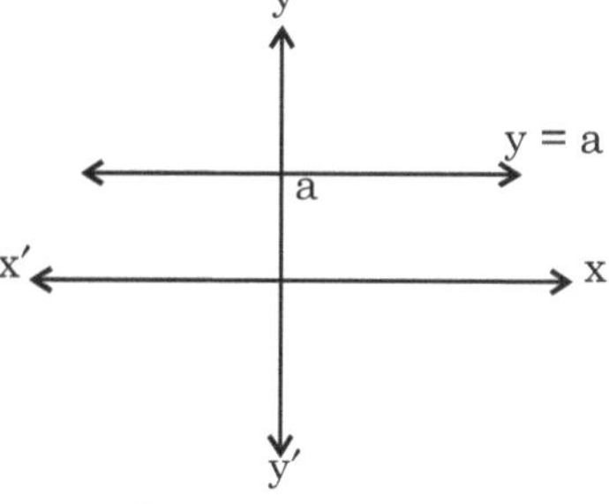

Sol. ∵ The perpendicular distance from point M to x-axis is 1 and to y-axis is 3 and point M lies in IV quadrant. Hence, the coordinates of the point M is $(3, -1)$.

9. Find the point on the line $y = 3x + 6$.

Sol. Given, $y = 3x + 6$

Put $x = 0$, we get $y = 3 \times 0 + 6 = 6$

∴ The point is $(0, 6)$

Similarly, $x = 1$, $y = 9$

Hence, points $(0, 6)$, $(1, 9)$ lies on the line $y = 3x + 6$.

10. Express the equation $2x + y - 4 = 0$ in the form of $y = mx + c$.

Sol. Given equation $2x + y - 4 = 0$

∴ $y = -2x + 4$ ....(i)

Hence, the above equation is in the form of $y = mx + c$.

11. A policeman and a thief are equidistant from the jewel box. Upon considering the jewel box as origin, the position of policeman is $(0, 5)$. If the ordinate of the position of thief is zero, then what will be the position of the thief?

Sol. According to the question, a policeman and a thief are equidistant from the jewel box.

Hence, position of thief is either $(-5, 0)$ or $(5, 0)$.

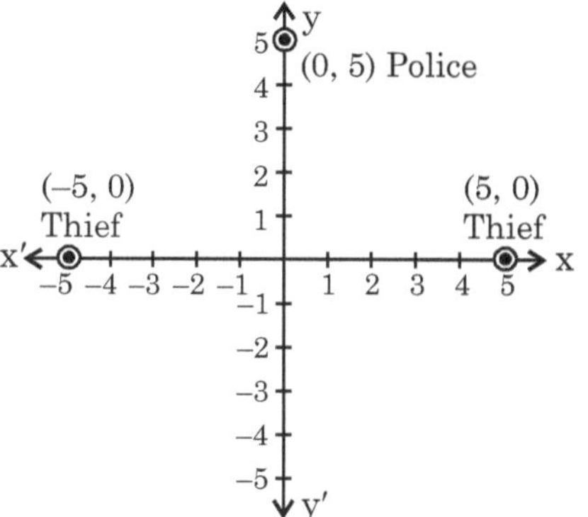

Short Answer Type Questions-I
(2 Marks Each)

1. Plot the points $A(1, -1)$ and $B(4, 5)$ on a Cartesian plane and draw a line segment joining these points. Now, write any one coordinate of a point on this line segment which lies between the points A and B.

[NCERT Exemplar]

Sol. On plotting the points $A(1, -1)$ and $B(4, 5)$ which is in IV and I quadrants respectively, then joining A and B.

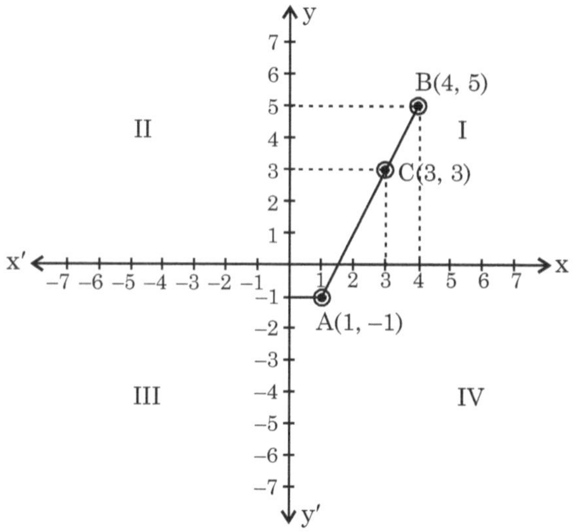

Hence, from the above figure, it is clear that, $C(3, 3)$ is a point, which lies between the points A and B.

2. In the following figure, identify the coordinate (–5, 3)

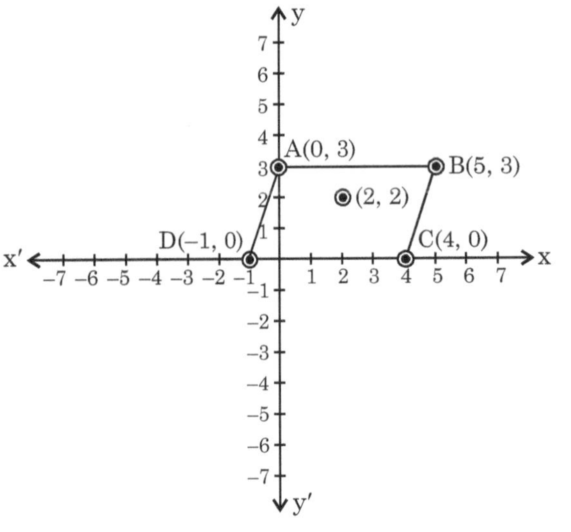

[NCERT Exemplar]

Sol. For the point (–5, 3), x-coordinate is negative and y-coordinate is positive. So, it will lie in II quadrant, whose perpendicular distance from Y-axis is 5 units and from X-axis is 3 units.

Hence the required point is L which has the coordinates (–5, 3).

3. Plot the points A(0, 3), B(5, 3), C(4, 0) and D(–1, 0) on the graph paper. Identify the figure ABCD and find whether the point (2, 2) lies inside the figure or not?

[BOARD TERM I, 2011, SET 15]

Sol. According to the question, plot the points A(0, 3), B(5, 3), C(4, 0) and D(–1, 0) on the graph paper.

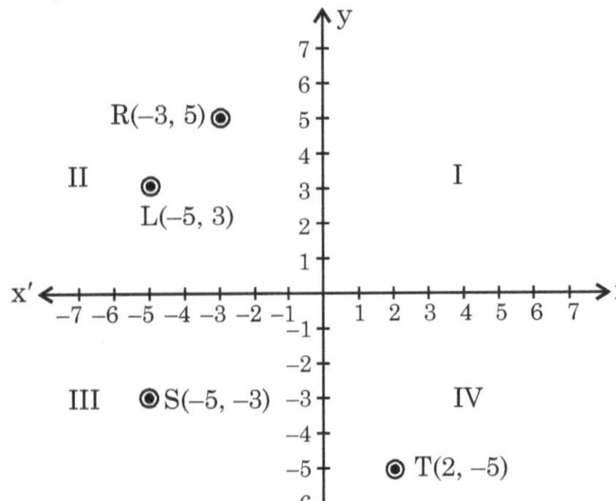

Now, from the figure, it is clear that the obtained figure is a parallelogram and the point (2, 2) lies inside the parallelogram.

4. Plot the following points on a graph sheet and join them in order :

B(–5, 3), E(–3, –2), S(4, –2), T(1, 3).

Also mention the quadrant in which the points lie.

[BOARD TERM I, 2012, SET 41]

Sol. On plotting the points B(–5, 3), E(–3, –2), S(4, –2) and T (1, 3) on the graph we have,

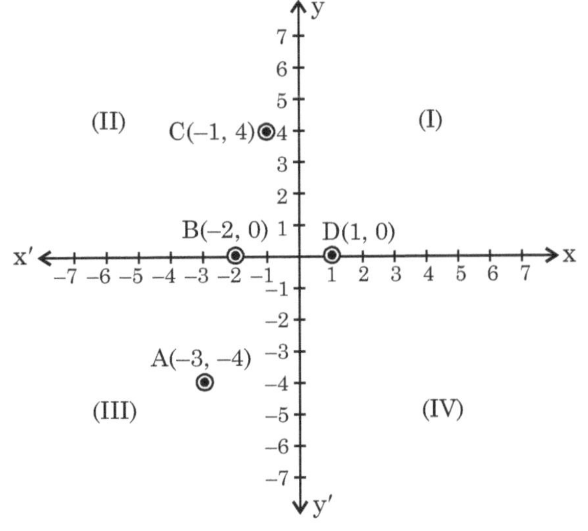

Point B lies in II quadrant.

Point E lies in III quadrant.

Point S lies in IV quadrant.

and point T lies in I quadrant.

5. Plot the following points on the graph sheet :

A(–3, –4), B(–2, 0), C(–1, 4), D(1, 0).

These points lie in which quadrant or axes?

[BOARD TERM I, 2012, SET 43]

Sol. On plotting the points

A(–3, –4), B(–2, 0), C(–1, 4) and D(1, 0) on the graph, we have

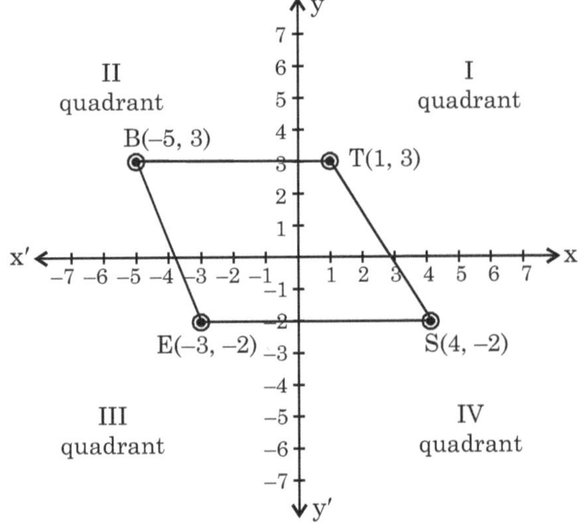

Point A(–3, –4) lies in III quadrant.

Point B(–2, 0) lies on x-axis.

Point C(–1, 4) lies in II quadrant.

and point D(1, 0) lies on x-axis.

6. In which quadrant or on which axis do the points (–2, –4), (2, 4), (0, –2) and (4, –6) lie? Verify your answer by locating them on the cartesian plane.

[BOARD TERM I, 2014]

Sol. The given points are :

(–2, –4) = A

(2, 4) = B

(0, –2) = C

and (4, –6) = D

The point A will lie in III quadrant

The point B will lie in I quadrant

The point C will lie in y-axis (i.e., x = 0)

The point D will lie in IV quadrant.

Verification :

On plotting the points (–2, –4), (2, 4), (0, –2) and (4, –6) on the graph, we have

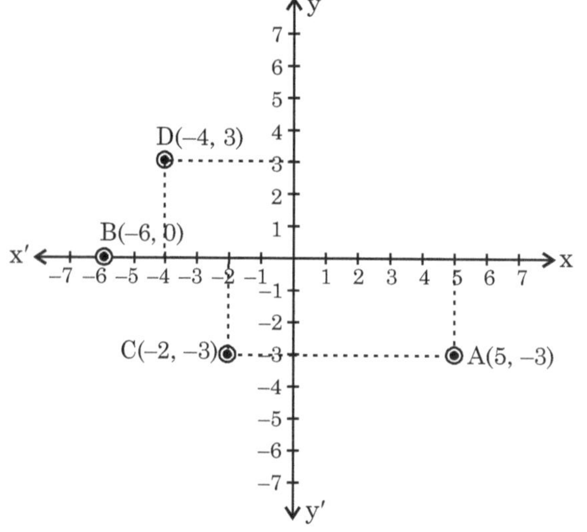

We find that point A is lying in III quadrant, B is lying in I quadrant, C is in the negative direction of y-axis and D is in IV quadrant.

Hence, result is verified.

7. Plot the points (5, –3), (–6, 0), (–2, –3) and (–4, 3) on the graph.

[BOARD TERM I, 2014]

Sol. For plotting a point A(5, –3), we will take a distance of –3 units in the negative direction of y-axis and a distance of 5 units in the positive direction of x-axis, which is shown in the figure given below. Similarly, we plot all the points i.e., B(–6, 0), C(–2, –3) and D(–4, 3).

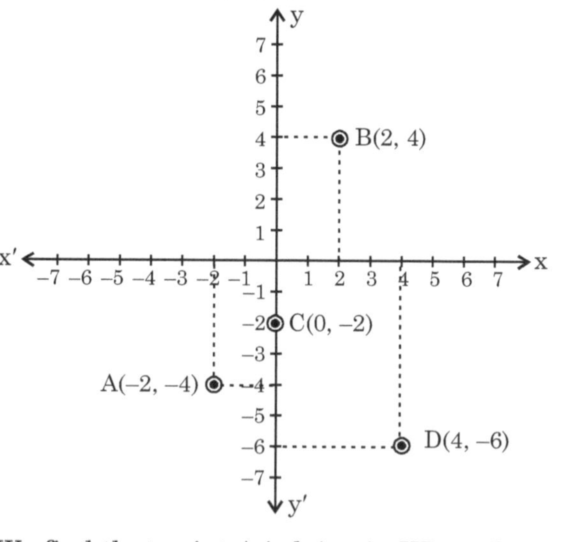

8. Plot the points A(3, 10), B(–3, 5) and C(–1, –6) on the graph paper. Join them in pairs and identify the figure so formed.

[BOARD TERM I, 2014]

Sol. On plotting the points A(3, 10), B(–3, 5) and C(–1, –6) on the graph paper.

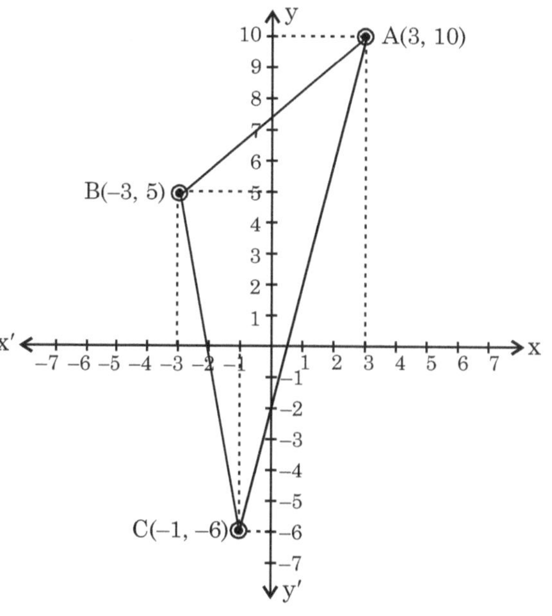

Hence, after joining the points the formed figure is a triangle.

9. In the co-ordinate plane, draw a square of side 3 units, taking origin as one vertex. Also, write the co-ordinates of its vertices.

[BOARD TERM I, 2015, SET 2]

Sol. On plotting the points of a square, we have

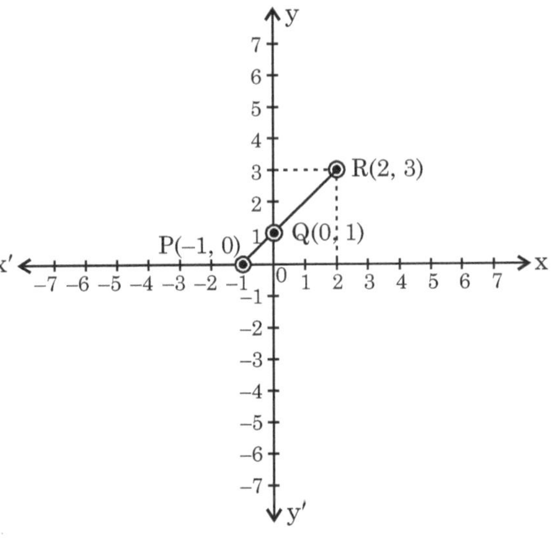

Hence, vertices are (0, 0), (3, 0), (3, 3) and (0, 3).

10. Plot the points P(–1, 0), Q(0, 1) and R(2, 3) on the graph paper and check whether they are collinear or not.

[BOARD TERM I, 2016, SET QGL21I5]

Sol. On plotting the points P(–1, 0), Q(0, 1) and R(2, 3) on the graph paper, we have

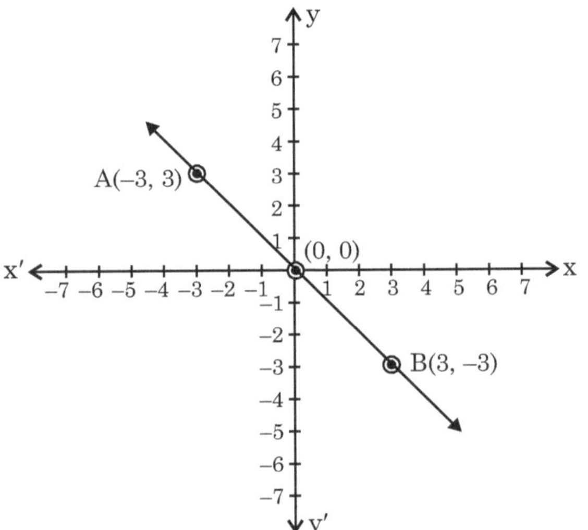

Hence it is clear from the graph, points P, Q and R are collinear.

11. Which of the following point lie (i) on x-axis? (ii) on y-axis?

A(0, 2), B(5, 6), C(23, 0), D(0, 23), E(0, 4), F(6, 0), G(3, 0)

[BOARD TERM I, 2016, SET 20 CNJE9]

Sol. Points lie on x-axis

= C(23, 0), F(6, 0) and G(3, 0)

Points lie on y-axis = A(0, 2), D(0, 23) and (0, 4)

12. Plot two points A(–3, 3) and B(3, –3) on the graph paper. Draw line segment AB and find its mid point.

[BOARD TERM I, 2016, SET BQS6IZK]

Sol. On plotting two points A(–3, 3) and B(3, –3) on the graph paper, we have

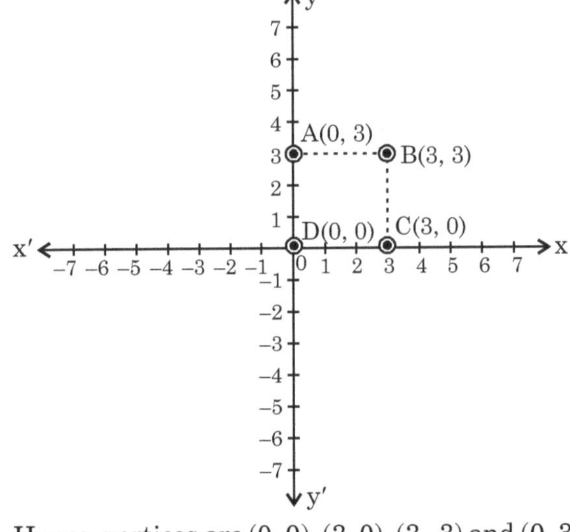

Hence, the mid point of the line segment AB is (0, 0).

Short Answer Type Questions-II

(3 Marks Each)

1. Plot the points A(–2, 3), B(–2, 0), C(2, 0) and D(2, 6) on the graph paper. Join them consecutively and find the length of BC and AB. Also find the area of ΔABC.

[NCERT Exemplar]

Sol. On plotting the A(–2, 3), B(–2, 0), C(2, 0) and D(2, 6), the graph is as follows:-

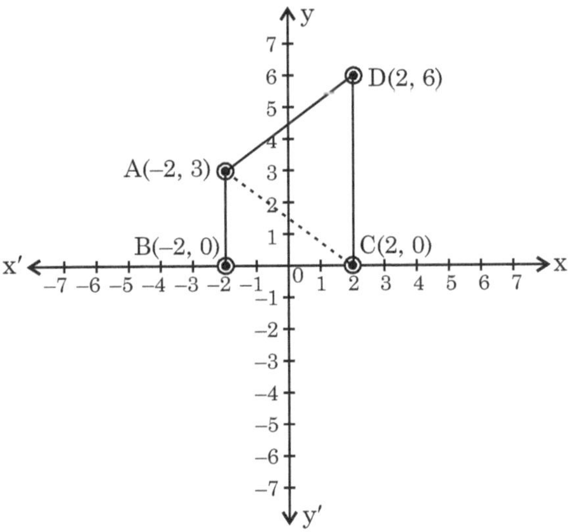

On joining AB, BC, CD and DA, the obtained trapezium ABCD.

From figure,

The length of BC = 2 − (−2)

$\qquad$ = 4 units

and The length of AB = 3 − 0

$\qquad$ = 3 units

Now, area of $\triangle$ABC = $\dfrac{1}{2}$ × BC × AB

$\qquad$ = $\dfrac{1}{2}$ × 4 × 3

$\qquad$ = 6 sq. units.

2. Plot the following points and write the name of the figure obtained by joining them in order.

   P(−3, 2), Q(−7, −3), R(6, −3), S(2, 2)

   [NCERT EXEMPLAR]

Sol. On plotting the given points P(−3, 2), (which is in II quadrant), Q(−7, −3) (which is in III quadrant), R(6, −3) (which is in IV quadrant) and S(2, 2) (which is in I quadrant) on the graph paper. Join all these points in order.

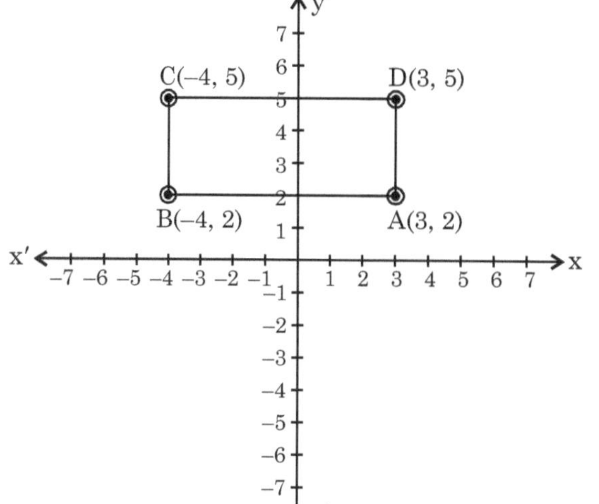

Here PS || OR, PQ and RS are two non-parallel lines. Hence, the obtained figure is a trapezium.

3. Three vertices of rectangle are (3, 2), (−4, 2) and (−4, 5). Plot these points and find the coordinates of the fourth vertex.

   [NCERT Exemplar]

Sol. On plotting the three vertices of rectangle as, A(3, 2), −(4, 2) and C(−4, 5), the graph is as follows:

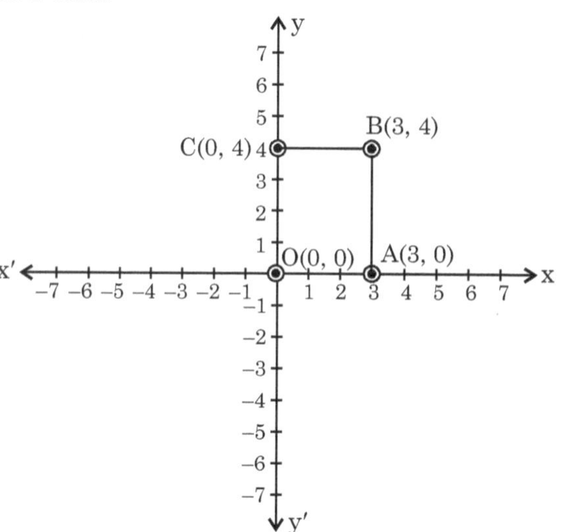

We have to find the coordinates of the fourth vertex D so that ABCD is a rectangle.

Because, the opposite sides of a rectangle are equal, so the abscissa of point D should be equal to abscissa of point A, i.e., 3 and ordinate of point D should be equal to the ordinate of point C i.e., 5.

Hence, the coordinate of D are (3, 5).

4. On plotting the points O(0, 0), A(3, 0), B(3, 4), C(0, 4) and joining OA, AB, BC and CO, which shape is obtained?

   [NCERT Exemplar]

Sol. Here, point O(0, 0) is the origin. A(3, 0) lies on positive direction of X-axis, B(3, 4) lies in I quadrant and C(0, 4) lies on positive direction of Y-axis.

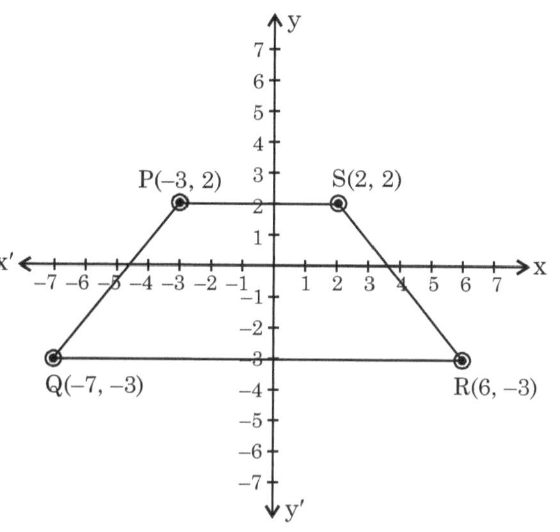

Hence, it is clear from the above diagram, on joining OA, AB, BC and CO the obtained figure is a rectangle.

5. Plot the following points in the cartesian plane:
A(5, 0), B(3, 2), C(0, –5), D(–6, 1), E(–4, –4),
F(2, –3).   [BOARD TERM I, 2010, SET-C1]

Sol. On plotting the points A(5, 0), B(3, 2), C(0, –5),
D(–6, 1), E(–4, –4) and F(2, –3), the graph is as
follows:-

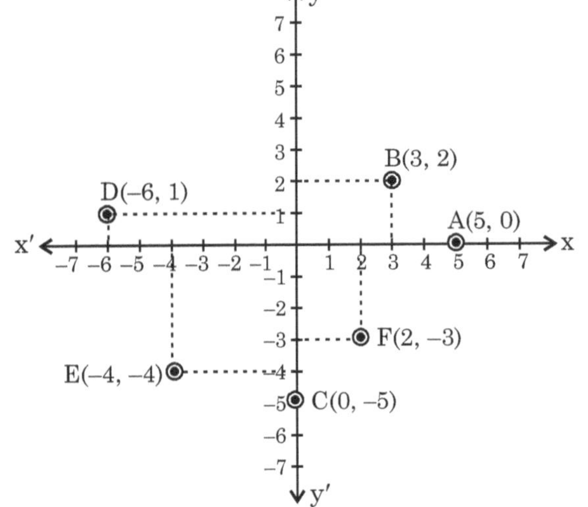

6. In figure, $\triangle ABC$ and $\triangle ADB$ are equilateral
triangles. Find the co-ordinates of point C and D.

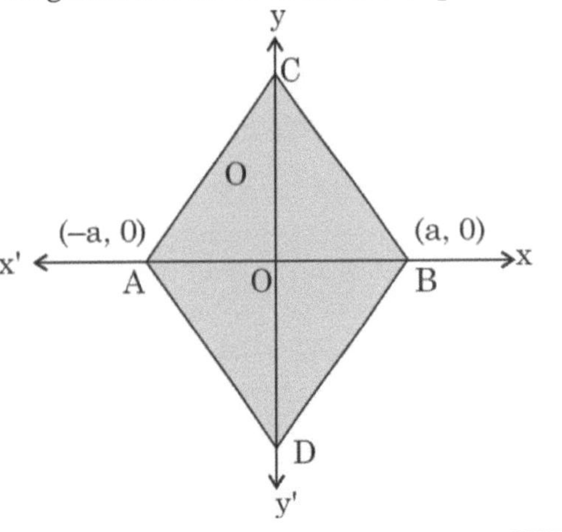

[BOARD TERM I, 2010, SET-A1]

Sol. According to the question,

OB = a, OA = a

or, AB = 2a

and AC = 2a   [∵ AB = AC]

By Pythagoras theorem in $\triangle COA$, we have

$$AC^2 = OA^2 + (OC)^2$$

$$\Rightarrow \quad (2a)^2 = a^2 + (OC)^2$$

$$(OC)^2 = 3a^2$$

Hence, ∴ OC = $a\sqrt{3}$

Hence, co-ordinates of point C are $(0,\ a\sqrt{3})$.

Similarly, co-ordinates of point D are $(0, -a\sqrt{3})$.

7. In figure, PQR is an equilateral triangle in
the co-ordinates of Q and R as (0, 4) and
(0, –4). Find the co-ordinates of the vertex P.

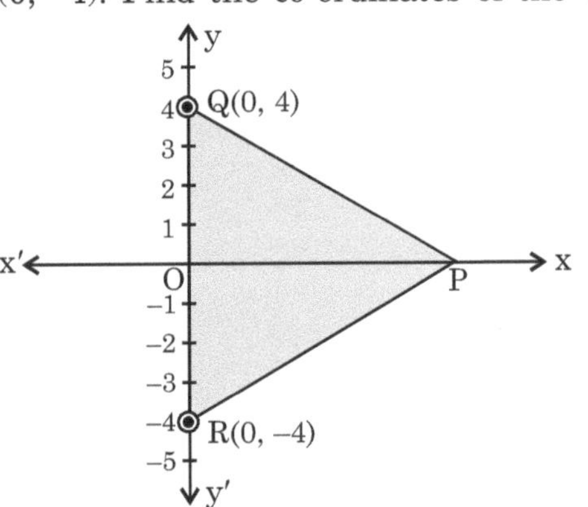

[BOARD TERM I, 2011, SET-16, 2010, SET-B1]

Sol. In $\triangle POQ$,

$$\Rightarrow \angle POQ = 90°$$

QR = 8 and OQ = 4

By Pythagoras theorem,

$$OP^2 + OQ^2 = PQ^2$$

$$\Rightarrow OP^2 + 4^2 = 8^2, (\because PQ = QR = RP)$$

$$\Rightarrow OP^2 = 48$$

$$\therefore\ OP = \sqrt{48} \text{ or } 4\sqrt{3}$$

Hence, the co-ordinates of P are $(\sqrt{48}, 0)$

8. Plot the points A(–3, –3), B(3, –3) C(3, 3),
D(–3, 3) in the cartesian plane. Also, find the
length of line segment AB.

[BOARD TERM I, 2011, SET-13]

Sol. On plotting the points A(–3, –3), B(3, –3),
C(3, 3), D(–3, 3) in the cartesian plane, we have

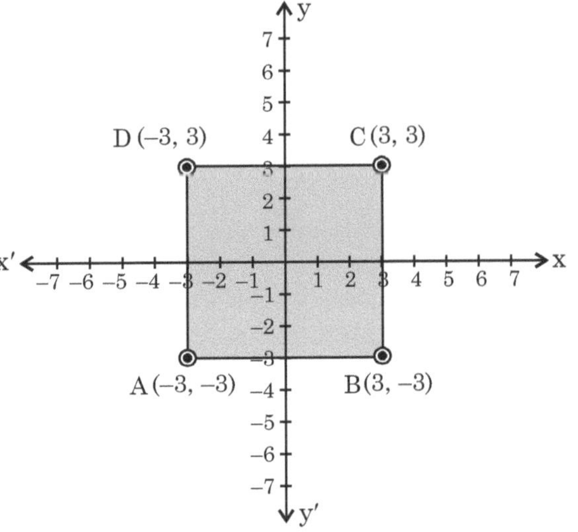

Hence, from figure length of line segment AB is
6 units.

9. Plot (–3, 0), (5, 0) and (0, 4) on cartesian plane. Name the figure formed by joining these points and find its area.

[BOARD TERM I, 2011, SET-24]

Sol. On plotting the points A(–3, 0), B(5, 0) and C(0, 4) can be plotted as shown below:

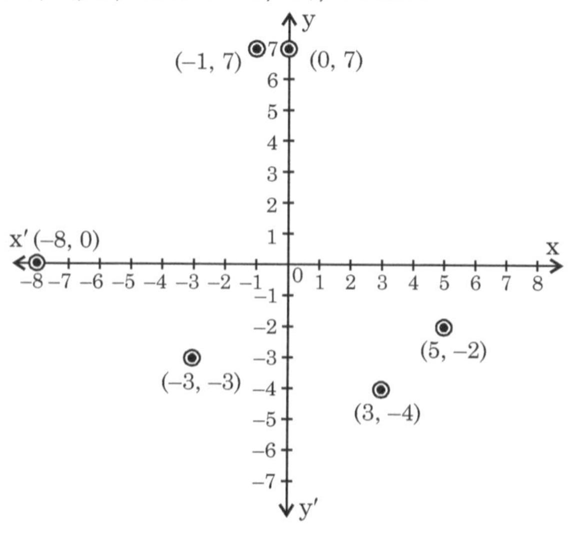

Figure formed is a triangle ABC.

Area of $\triangle ABC = \dfrac{1}{2} \times AB \times OC$

$$= \dfrac{1}{2} \times 8 \times 4 = 16 \text{ sq. units}$$

Hence, AB = 8 and OC = 4

10. Plot the points given in the table below in the cartesian plane:

x	–1	3	0	–8	5	–3
y	7	–4	7	0	–2	–3

[BOARD TERM I, 2011, SET-14]

Sol. On plotting the points (–1, 7) (3, –4), (0, 7), (–8, 0), (5, –2) and (–3, –3), we have

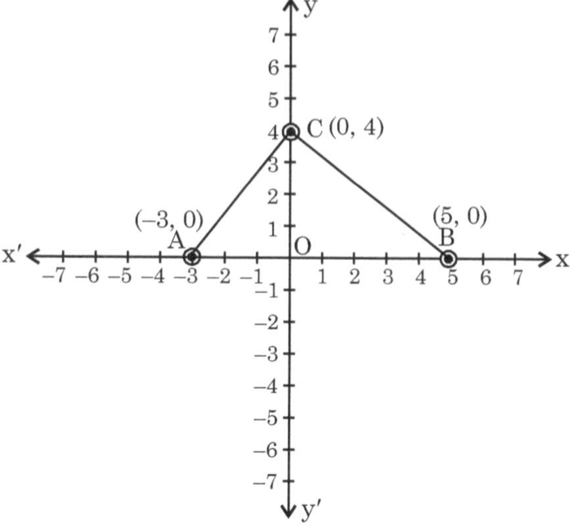

11. (i) Plot the points M(4, 3), N(4, 0), O(0, 0), P(0, 3).

(ii) Name the figure obtained by joining MNOP.

(iii) Find the perimeter of the figure.

[BOARD TERM I, 2011, SET-18]

Sol. (i) On plotting the points M(4, 3), N(4, 0), O(0, 0) and P(0, 3) on the graph paper is shown below :

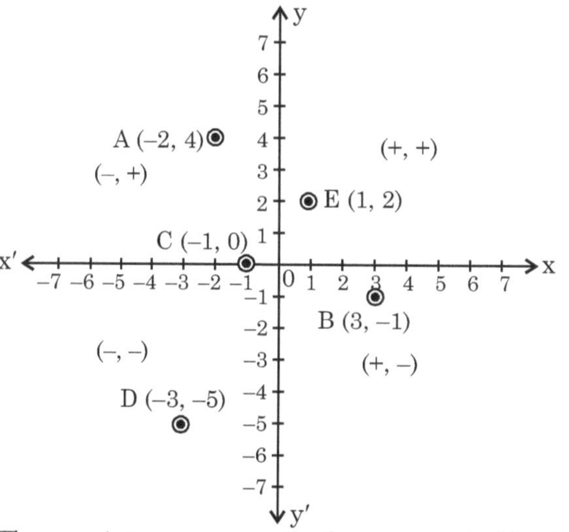

(ii) By joining MNOP, the figure so obtained will be rectangle.

(iii) Perimeter of rectangle = 2(l + b) = 2(ON + MN)

$$= 2(4 + 3) = 2 \times 7 = 14 \text{ units}$$

12. In which quadrant or on which axis do each of the points (–2, 4), (3, –1), (–1, 0), (–3, –5) and (1, 2) lie? Verify your answer by locating them on the cartesian plane.

[BOARD TERM I, 2011, SET-25]

Sol. (i) The point (–2, 4) lies in the II quadrant.

(ii) The point (3, –1) lies in the IV quadrant.

(iii) The point (–1, 0) lies on the negative x-axis.

(iv) The point (–3, –5) lies in the III quadrant.

(v) The point (1, 2) lies in the I quadrant.

Locations of these points are shown in the figure.

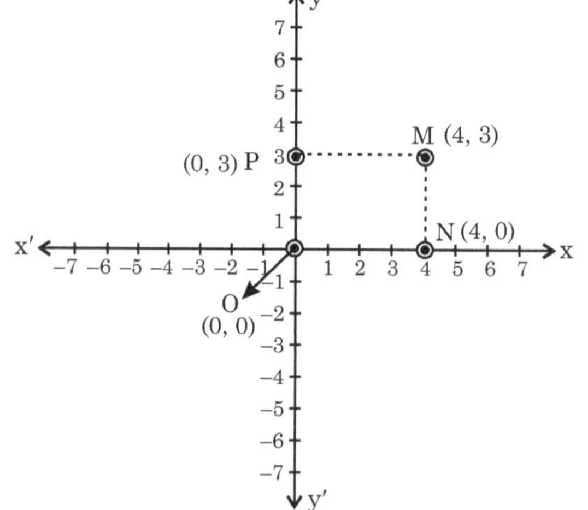

These points are respectively represented by A, B, C, D and E, which clearly verify their location.

13. Plot points A(4, 0) and B(0, 4). Join AB to the origin O. Find the area of $\triangle$AOB.

[BOARD TERM I, 2011, SET-11]

Sol. On plotting A(4, 0) and B(0, 4), we have

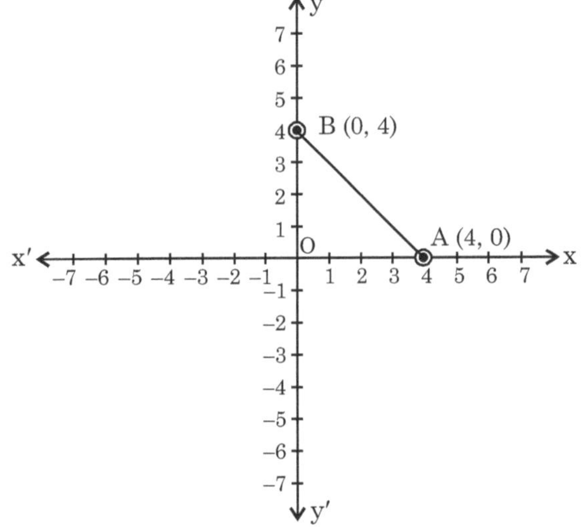

From above figure, OA = 4 units

and OB = 4 units

$\therefore$ Area of $\triangle$OAB $= \dfrac{1}{2} \times$ OA $\times$ OB

$= \dfrac{1}{2} \times 4 \times 4 = \dfrac{16}{2}$

$= 8$ square units.

14. (i) Plot the points A(0, 4), B(–3, 0), C(0, –4), D(3, 0)

(ii) Name the figure obtained by joining the points A, B, C, D.

(iii) Also name the quadrants in which sides AB and AD lie.

[BOARD TERM I, 2011, SET-17]

Sol. (i) On plotting the points A(0, 4), B(–3, 0), C(0, –4), D(3, 0), we have

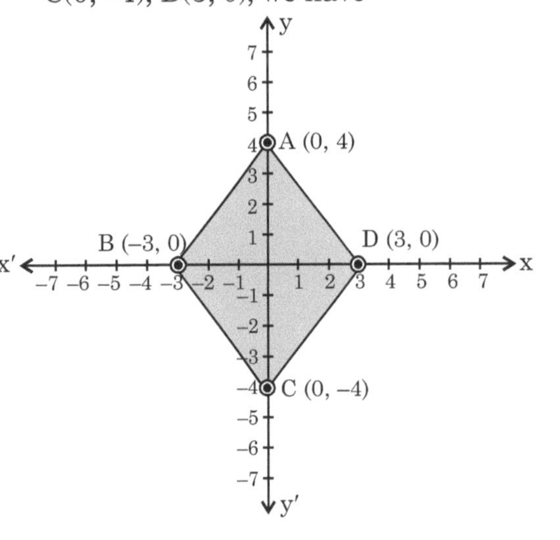

(ii) After joining the points A, B, C and D, the obtained figure is a Rhombus.

(iii) Sides AB lies in II quadrant and sides AD lies in I quadrant.

15. Plot the points (x, y) given in the following table on the cartesian plane, choosing suitable units of distance on the axes:

x	2	4	–4	–2	6	0
y	5	–3	3	5	–1	2.5

[BOARD TERM I, 2015, SET-II]

Sol. On plotting the points (2, 5), (4, –3), (–4, 3), (–2, 5), (6, –1) and (0, 2.5)

Now, we have

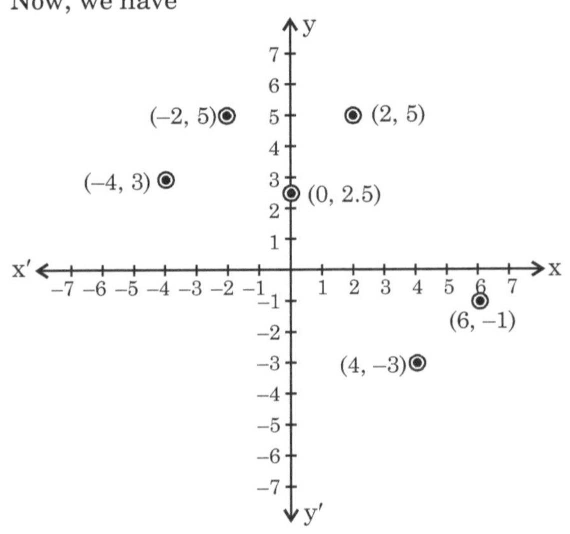

[Scale 1 unit = 1 cm]

16. Plot the points (–1, 0), (1, 0), (1, 1), (0, 2) and (–1, 1). Join them in order. What figure do you get?   [BOARD TERM I, 2015, SET-2]

Sol. On plotting the points (–1, 0), (1, 0), (1, 1), (0, 2) and (–1, 1) we have,

Hence, it is clear from the graph required figure is a pentagon.

17. Plot three points P(1, 5), Q(1, 1) and R(5, 1) on the graph paper. Now plot point S so that PQRS is a square. Give co-ordinate of point of intersection of diagonals.

[BOARD TERM I, 2016, SET-QGL21F5]

Sol. On plotting three points P(1, 5), Q(1, 1) and R(5, 1) on the graph paper, we have, point S = (5, 5)

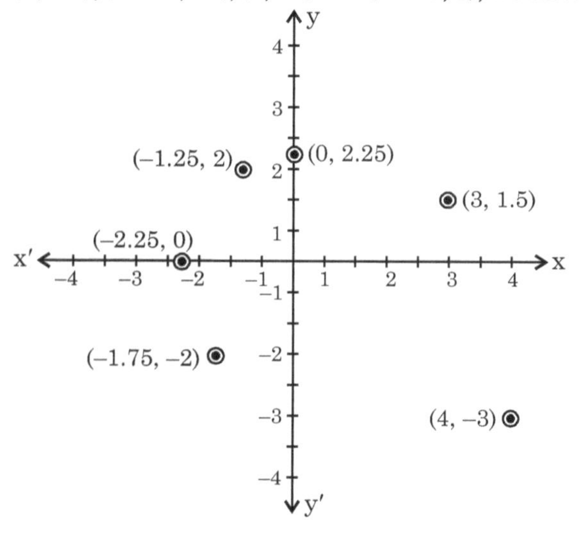

Now, the diagonals are PR and QS and the intersection of diagonals is point A(3, 3).

18. Plot the points (x, y) given in the following table on the cartesian plane, choosing suitable units of distance on the axes.

x	−1.25	0	3	−1.75	4	−2.25
y	2	2.25	1.5	−2	−3	0

[BOARD TERM I, 2016, SET-JQ22L5C]

Sol. On plotting the points (−1.25, 2), (0, 2.25), (3, 1.5), (−1.75, −2), (4, −3) and (−2.25, 0), we have

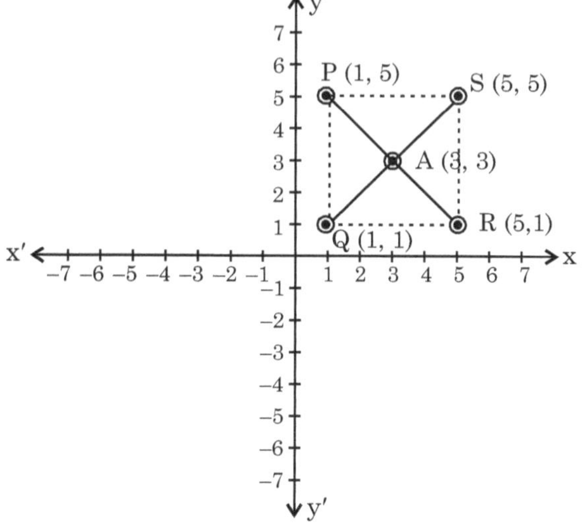

[Scale 1 unit = 0.5 cm]

19. Draw the quadrilateral ABCD whose vertices are A(0, 0), B(5, 0), C(3, 2) and D(0, 2).

[BOARD TERM I, 2016, SET-BQ56IZK]

Sol. On plotting the points A(0, 0), B(5, 0), C(3, 2) and D(0, 2), we have

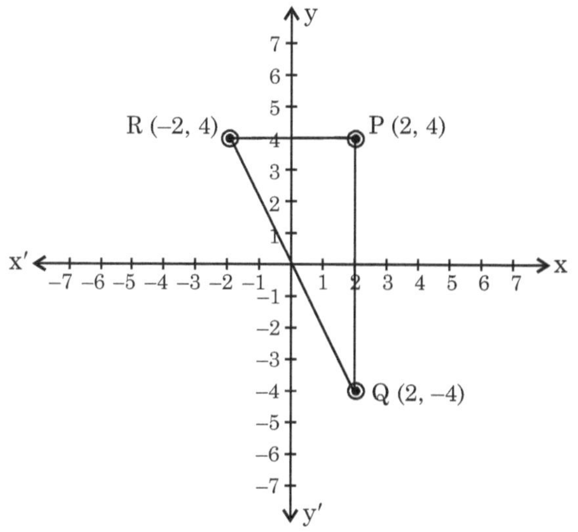

Hence, the required quadrilateral is ABCD.

20. Plot a point P(2, 4) on the graph paper. Now, plot reflections of p in x-axis and y-axis and denote them as Q and R respectively. Name the type of triangle PQR so formed.

[BOARD TERM I, 2016, SET-7AEDLQR]

Sol. On plotting the graph, we have,

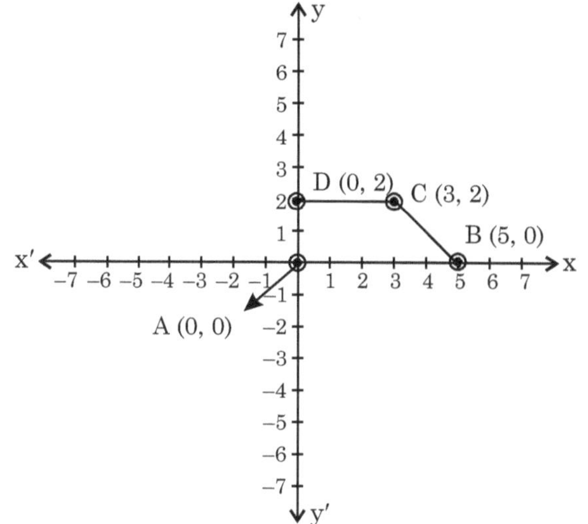

From the above graph,

PQ ⊥ PR

PR = 4, PQ = 8

Hence, the figure PQR is a right angle triangle.

21. Point A(4, 2), B(–1, 2) and D(4, –5) are three vertices of a square ABCD. Plot these points and hence find the vertex C.

[BOARD TERM I, 2016, SET-20CNJE9]

Sol. On plotting the points A(4, 2), B(–1, 2) and D(4, –5) of square ABCD. We have

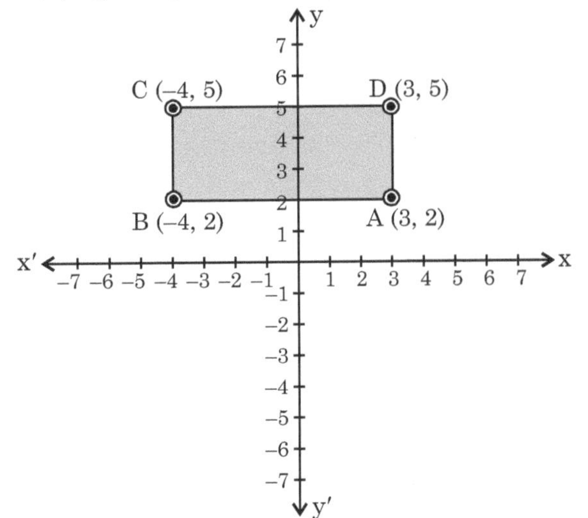

Hence, from the graph it is clear that the vertex c = (–1, –5)

22. Plot the following points and write the name of the figure, thus obtained.

A(3, 0), B(5, 0), C(5, 3) and D(3, 3).

Sol. Firstly, we plot all the points i.e.,

A(3, 0), B(5, 0), C(5, 3) and D(3, 3) on graph paper and join all these points.

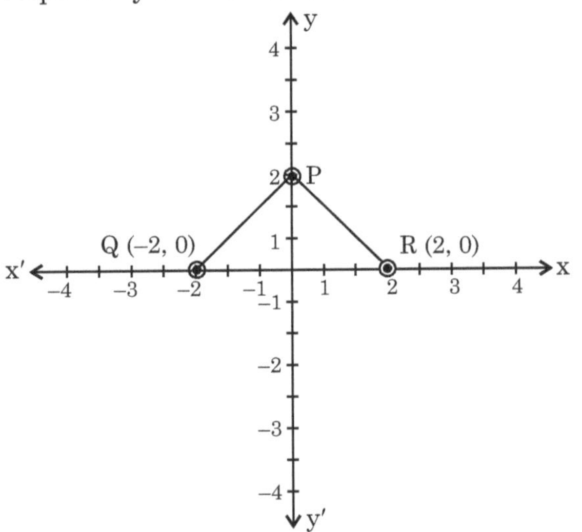

Here AB = CD = 2 and BC = DA = 3

and all lines are perpendicular to each other.

Hence, the obtained figure ABCD is a rectangle.

23. In the given figure, PQR is an equilateral triangle with co-ordinates of Q and R as (–2, 0) and (2, 0) respectively. Find the co-ordinates of the vertex P.

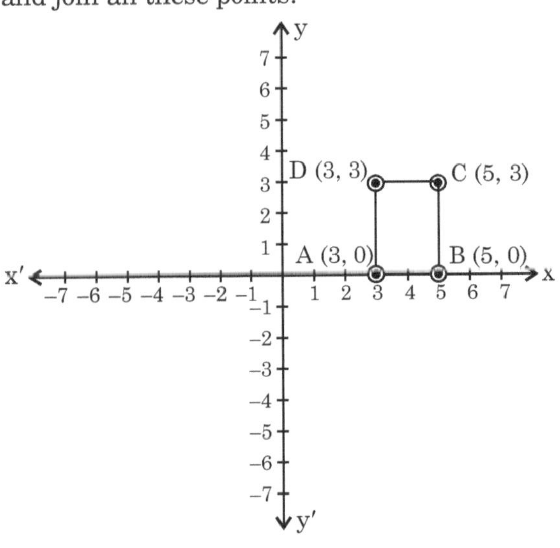

Sol. According to the graph.

QR = 2 + 2 = 4

∴ PQ = QR = RP = 4

Now, OR = 2

Now from right triangle OPR, by Pythagoras theorem,

$OP^2 = PR^2 - OR^2 = 4^2 - 2^2 = 16 - 4 = 12$

So, $OP = 2\sqrt{3}$

Hence, the co-ordinates of P are $(0, 2\sqrt{3})$.

Long Answer Type Questions
(4 Marks Each)

1. Three vertices of a rectangle are (3, 2), (–4, 2) and (–4, 5). Plot these points and find the co-ordinates of the fourth vertex.   [NCERT Exemplar]

Sol. On plotting three vertices of the rectangle as A(3, 2), B(–4, 2) and C(–4, 5).

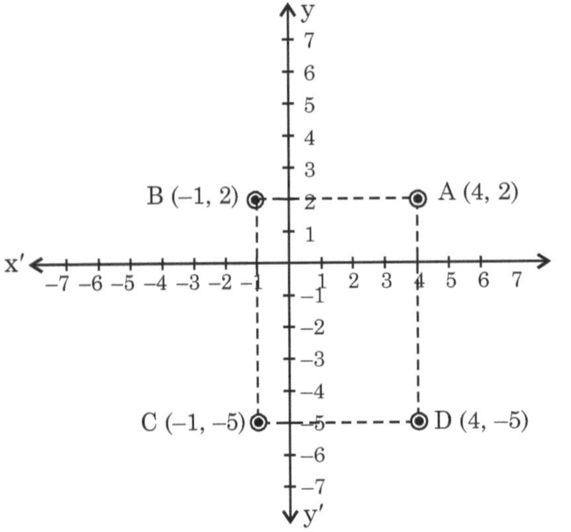

Now, we have to find the co-ordinates of the fourth vertex D. Since the opposite sides of a rectangle are equal, so the abscissa of D should be equal to abscissa of A, i.e., 3 and the ordinate of D should be equal to the ordinate of C, i.e., 5.

Hence, the co-ordinates of point D are (3, 5).

2. In the given figure, ΔABC and ΔADC are equilateral triangles on common base AC, each side of triangles being 2a units. Vertices A and C lies on x-axis, vertices B and D lies on y-axis. O is the mid-point of AC and BD. Find the co-ordinates of the point B. **[NCERT Exemplar]**

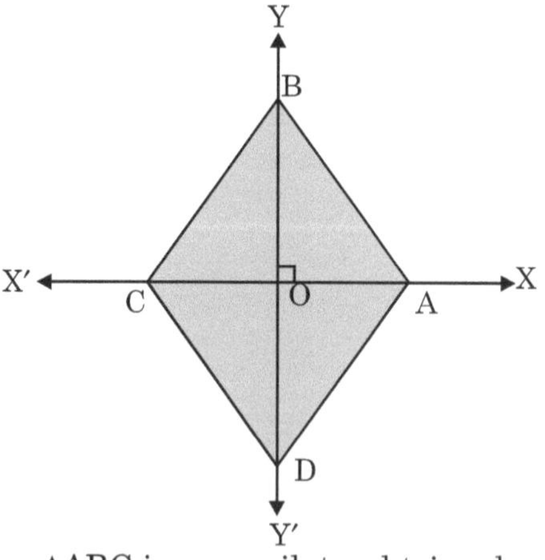

Sol. According to the question,

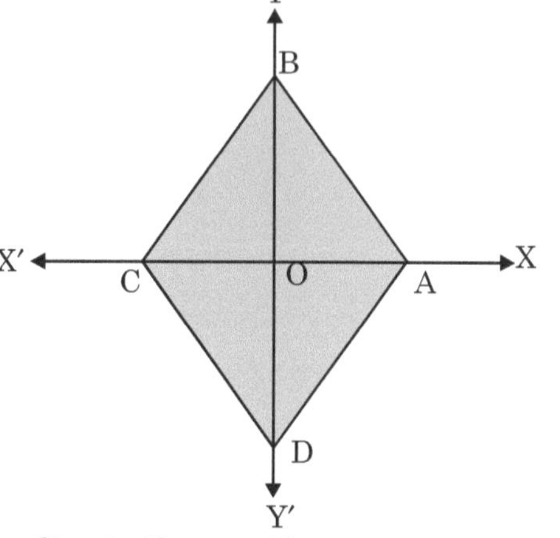

Since ΔABC is an equilateral triangle with side 2a units, therefore

AB = BC = CA = 2a units

∵   O is the mid-point of AC, then

$$OA = \frac{1}{2} AC = \frac{1}{2}(2a) = a \text{ units}$$

Now, in right angle triangle AOB, by Pythagoras theorem,

$$OB = \sqrt{AB^2 - OA^2} = \sqrt{(2a)^2 - a^2}$$
$$= \sqrt{4a^2 - a^2} = \sqrt{3a^2} = a\sqrt{3} \text{ units}$$

Hence, the co-ordinates of B are $\left(0, a\sqrt{3}\right)$

3. Find the co-ordinates of the vertices of a rectangle placed in III quadrant in the cartesian plane with length 'p' units on x-axis and breadth 'q' units on y-axis.
   [BOARD TERM I, 2011, SET-20]

Sol. According to the question,

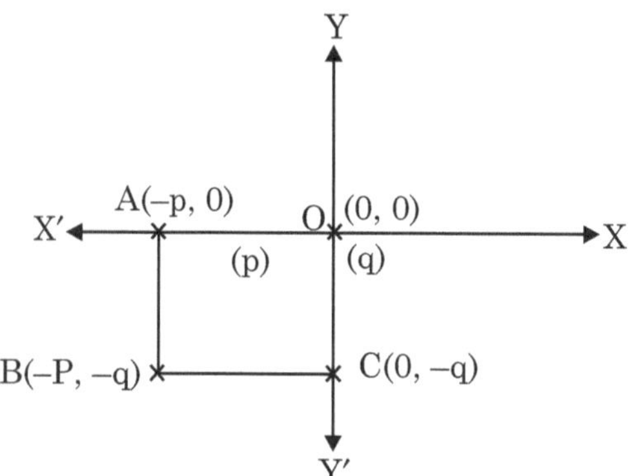

From figure the co-ordinate of vertices of a rectangle are:

Point O(0, 0)

Point A(–p, 0)

Point B(–p, –q)

and Point C(0, –q)

4. (i) Plot the points M(5, –3) and N(–3, –3).

   (ii) What is the length of MN?

   (iii)Find the co-ordinates of points A, B and C lying on MN, such that:
   [BOARD TERM I, 2011, SET 22]

Sol.(i) On plotting of points M(5, –3) and N(–3, –3) on the graph paper is shown in the diagram.

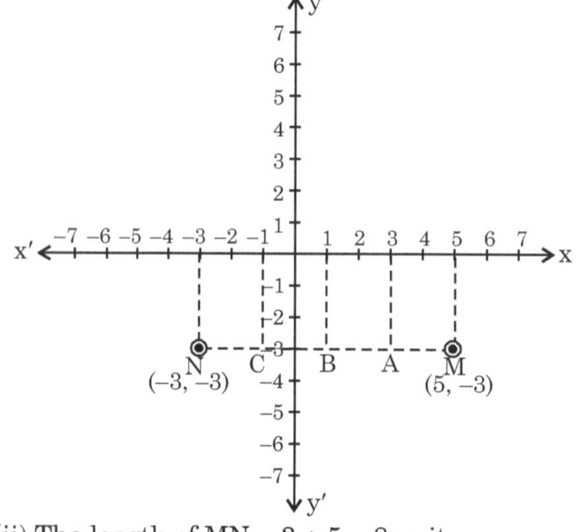

(ii) The length of MN = 3 + 5 = 8 units

(iii) From figure,

∵   MA = AB = BC = CN

A(3, –3), B(1, –3) and C(–1, –3)

5. In the given figure, PQR is an equilateral triangle. The coordinates of Q and R as (0, 6) and (0, –6). Find the coordinates of the vertex P.

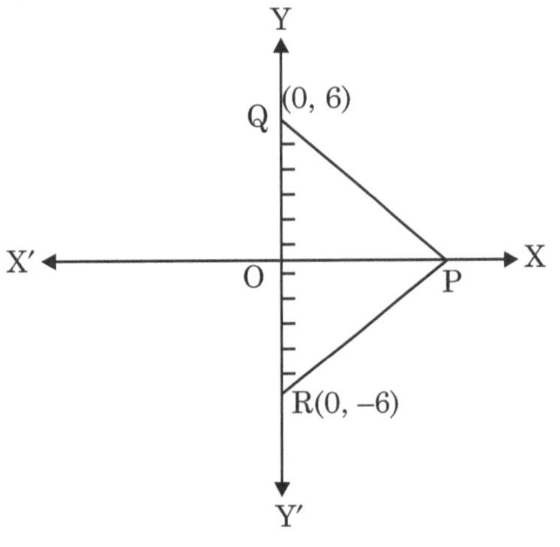

Sol. Here Q is (0, 6) and R is (0, –6)

QR = 6 – (–6) = 12 units

$\because$ ΔPQR is an equilateral triangle

$\therefore$ PQ = QR = PR = 12 units

$\because$ Now, in right angle triangle POQ.

PQ = 12 units and OQ = 6 units

Now, by Pythagoras theorem,

$$\therefore \quad OP = \sqrt{PQ^2 - OQ^2} = \sqrt{12^2 - 6^2}$$

$$= \sqrt{144 - 36} = \sqrt{108} = 6\sqrt{3} \text{ units}$$

$\therefore$ Abscissa of point P = $6\sqrt{3}$ and it lies on x-axis

$\therefore$ Its ordinate is 0.

Hence, the coordinates of point P are ($6\sqrt{3}$, 0)

UNIT IV
Geometry

CHAPTER 5

Introduction to Euclid's Geometry

- History – Geometry in India and Euclid's geometry. Euclid's method of formalizing observed phenomenon into rigorous Mathematics with definitions, common/obvious notions, axioms/postulates and theorems.
- The five postulates of Euclid. Equivalent versions of the fifth postulate.
- Showing the relationship between axiom and theorem, for example :

(Axiom) 1: Given two distinct points, there exists one and only one line through them.

(Theorem) 2. (Prove) Two distinct lines cannot have more than one point in common.

A flow chart on basic concepts:

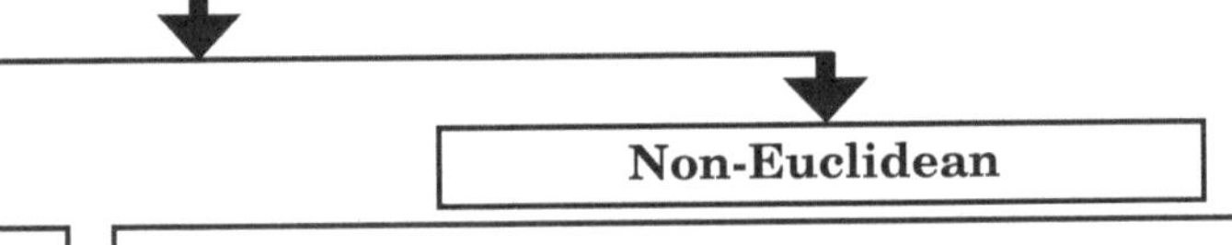

Some Euclid's Axioms

- Things which are equal to the same thing are equal to one another.
- If equals are added to equals, the wholes are equal.
- If equals are subtracted from equals, the remainders are equal.
- Things which coincide with one another are equal to one another.
- The whole is greater than the part.
- Things which are double of the same things are equal to one another.
- Things which are halves of the same things are equal to one anther.

Euclid's Postulates

- Postulate 1 : A straight line may be drawn from any one point to any other point.
- Postulate 2 : A terminated line can be produced indefinitely.
- Postulate 3 : A circle can be drawn with any centre and any radius.
- Postulate 4 : All right angles are equal to one another.
- Postulate 5 : If a straight line falling on two straight lines makes the interior angles on the same side of it, taken together less than two right angles, then the two straight lines, if produced indefinitely, meet on that side on which the sum of angles is less than two right angles.

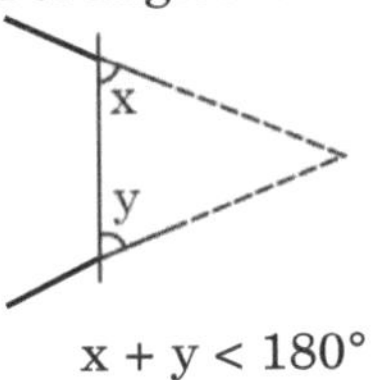

Points to be Remembered

- Two equivalent versions of Euclid's fifth postulates are:
  (i) "For every line l and for every point p not lying on l, there exists a unique line m passing through p and parallel to l." It is also called parallel axiom.
  (ii) Two distinct intersecting lines cannot be parallel to the same line.
- Axioms are the assumptions which are obvious universal truths. They are not proved.
- The basic facts which are taken for granted, without proof and which are specific to geometry are called postulates.
- Non-Euclidean geometries: All the attempts to prove the Euclid's fifth postulate using the first 4 postulates failed. But they led to the discovery of several other geometries, called non-Euclidean geometries.
- Theorems : Theorems are statements which are proved using definitions, axioms, previously proved statements and deductive reasoning.

PREVIOUS YEARS'

EXAMINATION QUESTIONS

Multiple Choice Questions

(1 Mark Each)

1. In ancient India, the shapes of altars used for household rituals were   [NCERT Exemp.]
   (a) squares and circles.
   (b) triangles and rectangles.
   (c) trapeziums and pyramids.
   (d) rectangles and squares.

Sol. (a) In Ancient India, the shapes of altars used for household rituals were squares and circles.

2. The side faces of a pyramid are   [NCERT Exemp.]
   (a) triangles
   (b) squares
   (c) polygons
   (d) trapeziums

Sol. (a) The side faces of pyramid are triangles.

3. The number of dimensions, a surface has   [NCERT Exemp.]
   (a) 1
   (b) 2
   (c) 3
   (d) 0

Sol. (b) A surface has length and breadth. Therefore, a surface has two dimensions.

4. The total number of propositions in "the Elements" is   [NCERT Exemp.]
   (a) 465
   (b) 460
   (c) 13
   (d) 55

Sol. (a) The total number of propositions in "the Elements" is 465.

5. Which of the following needs a proof?   [NCERT Exemp.]
   (a) Theorem
   (b) Axiom
   (c) Definition
   (d) Postulate

Sol. (a) Theorems need a proof.

6. Pythagoras was a student of
   (a) Thales
   (b) Euclid
   (c) both (a) and (b)
   (d) Archimedes   [NCERT Exemp.]

Sol. (a) Pythagoras was a student of Thales.

7. Boundaries of solids are   [NCERT Exemp.]
   (a) surfaces
   (b) curves
   (c) lines
   (d) points

Sol. (a) Boundaries of solids are surfaces.

8. Euclid belongs to the country   [NCERT Exemp.]
   (a) Babylonia
   (b) Egypt
   (c) Greece
   (d) India

Sol. (c) Euclid belongs to the Greece.

9. The number of dimension, a point has   [NCERT Exemp.]
   (a) 0
   (b) 1
   (c) 2
   (d) 3

Sol. (a) According to Euclid, a point is that which has no part, that is, no length, no breadth and no height. Therefore, it has no dimension.

10. Three steps from solids to points are   [NCERT Exemp.]
    (a) Solids - surfaces - lines - points.
    (b) Solids - lines - surfaces - points.
    (c) Lines - points - surfaces - solids.
    (d) Lines - surfaces - points - solids.

Sol. (a) The three steps are solids - surfaces - lines - points.

11. In Ancient India, Altars with combination of shapes like rectangles, triangles and trapeziums were used for **[NCERT Exemp.]**
    (a) public worship   (b) households rituals
    (c) both (a) and (b)   (d) none of (a), (b) and (c)

Sol. (a) In Ancient India, Altars with combination of shapes like rectangles, triangles and trapeziums were used for public worship.

12. Thales belongs to the country
    [NCERT Exemp.]
    (a) Babylonia   (b) Egypt
    (c) Greece   (d) Rome

Sol. (c) Thales belongs to the Greece.

13. It is known that if x + y = 10 then x + y + z = 10 + z. The Euclid's axiom that illustrates this statement is   **[NCERT Exemp.]**
    (a) First Axiom   (b) Second Axiom
    (c) Third Axiom   (d) Fourth Axiom

Sol. (b) If x + y = 10 and then x + y + z = 10 + z. The Euclid's second axiom states that if equals are added to equals, the wholes are equal.

14. The number of dimensions, a solid has
    (a) 1   (b) 2 **[NCERT Exemp.]**
    (c) 3   (d) 0

Sol. (c) A solid has three dimensions shape, size and position respectively, and can be moved from one place to another.

15. Greek's emphasised on   **[NCERT Exemp.]**
    (a) inductive reasoning
    (b) deductive reasoning
    (c) both (a) and (b)
    (d) practical use of geometry.

Sol. (b) The Greeks were interested in establishing the truth of the statements they discovered using deductive reasoning. A Greek mathematician, Thales is credited with giving the first known proof.

16. In Indus Valley Civilisation (about 3,000 B.C.), the bricks for construction work were having dimensions in the ratio.   **[NCERT Exemp.]**
    (a) 1 : 3 : 4.   (b) 4 : 2 : 1.
    (c) 4 : 4 : 1.   (d) 4 : 3 : 2.

Sol. (b) In Indus Valley Civilisation, the bricks used for construction work were having dimensions in the ratio are 4 : 2 : 1.

17. Euclid divided his famous treatise 'The Elements' into   **[NCERT Exemp.]**
    (a) 13 chapters   (b) 12 chapters
    (c) 11 chapters   (d) 9 chapters

Sol. (a) We know that Euclid divided his famous treatise "The Elements" into 13 chapters.

18. Boundaries of surfaces are **[NCERT Exemp.]**
    (a) surfaces   (b) curves
    (c) lines   (d) points

Sol. (b) Obviously, boundaries of surfaces are curves.

19. The number of inter-woven isosceles triangles in Sriyantra (in the Atharva Veda) is
    [NCERT Exemp.]
    (a) seven   (b) eight
    (c) nine   (d) eleven

Sol. (c) Clearly, the number of inter-woven isosceles triangle in Sriyantra (in Atharva Veda) is nine.

20. A pyramid is a solid figure, the base of which is
    [NCERT Exemp.]
    (a) only a triangle   (b) only a square
    (c) only a rectangle   (d) any polygon

Sol. (d) We know that a pyramid is a solid figure, the base of which is any polygon.

Very Short Answer Type Questions
(1 Mark Each)

1. Explain when a system of axioms is called consistent.
    [BOARD TERM I, 2015, SET-20UI6YH]

Sol. A system of axioms is called consistent, when it is impossible to deduce from these axioms, a statement that contradicts any axiom or previously proved statement.

2. Express in variables the things which are double of the same thing

Sol. Let, first thing = x = 2a
    and second thing = y = 2a
    then, According to the question, x = y

3. What does a theorem require?

Sol. Any theorem requires a proof.

4. Write the number of dimension(s) of a surface.

Sol. Dimension of Surface = Length and Breadth
    Hence, a surface has two dimensions.

5. Give any one example of a geometrical line from your surroundings.

Sol. An example of a geometrical line from our surroundings i.e., meeting place of two walls.

6. How many lines can be passed through two distinct points?

Sol. Obviously, only one line passes through two distinct points.

7. How can we identify parallel lines?

Sol. Lines are parallel if they do not intersect on being extended.

For example :

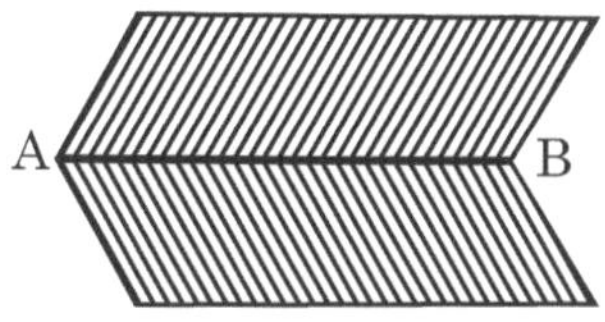

Therefore, $l \parallel m$ and $P \parallel Q$.

8. What is a surface?

Sol. A surface is that which has length and breadth, two dimensions.

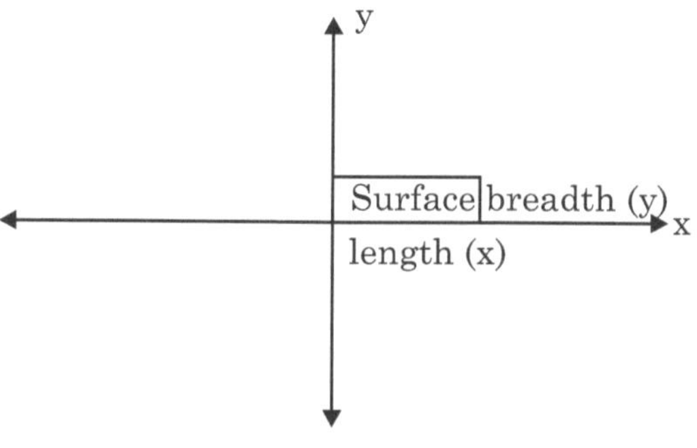

9. What is a straight line?

Sol. Two planes intersects each other to form a straight line.

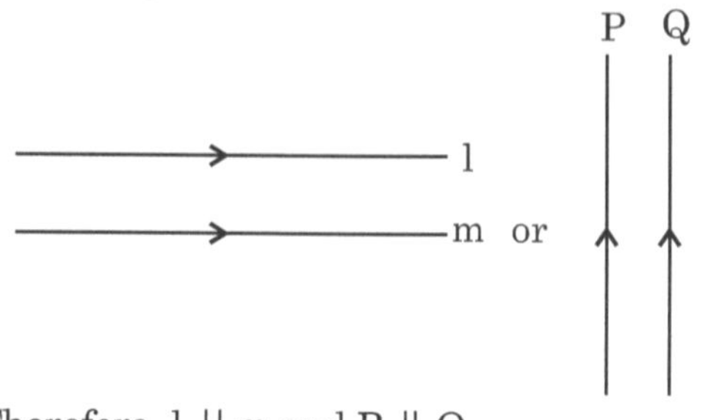

Hence, AB is a straight line.

Write whether the following statements are True or False? Justify your answer.

1. The things which are double of the same thing are equal to one another.   [NCERT Exemp.]

Sol. The given statement is true, since, it is one of the Euclid's axioms.

2. Euclidean geometry is valid only for curved surface.   [NCERT Exemp.]

Sol. The given statement is False, Euclidean geometry is valid only for the figures in the plane.

3. The statements that are proved are called axioms.

[NCERT Exemp.]

Sol. The given statement is false, the statements that are proved are called theorems.

4. The boundaries of the solids are curves.

[NCERT Exemp.]

Sol. The given statement is false, boundaries of solids are surfaces.

5. The edges of a surface are curves.

[NCERT Exemp.]

Sol. The given statement is false, the edges of surfaces are lines.

6. If a quantity B is a part of another quantity A, then A can be written as the sum of B and some third quantity C.

[NCERT Exemp.]

Sol. The given statement is true, it is one of Euclid's axioms.

7. (a) A terminated line can be produced indefinitely on both the sides.

(b) Only one line can pass through a single point.

(c) If two circles are equal, then their radii are equal.

(d) In the given figure, if $AB = BQ$ and $PQ = XY$, then $AB = XY$.

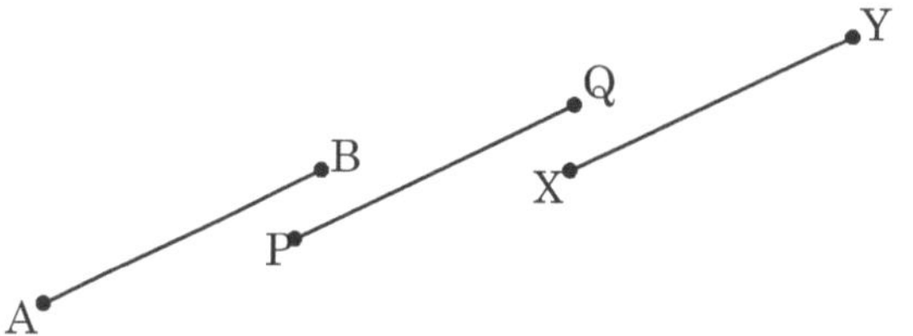

(e) There are an infinite number of lines, which pass through two distinct points.

[NCERT Exemp.]

Sol. (a) The given statement is True, since line segment is a part of line.

(b) The given statement is False, infinite number of lines can pass through a single point.

(c) The given statement is True, if their radii are equal then definitely they should be equal.

(d) The given statement is True, if one thing is equal to other and the same thing is equal to another, then the both things are equal to each other.

(e) The given statement is False, only one line can be drawn or pass through two distinct points.

Short Answer Type Questions I
(2 Marks Each)

1. Ram and Ravi have the same weight. If they each gain weight by 2 kg, how will their new weights be compared?

[NCERT EXEMPLAR PROBLEM]

Sol. Let x kg be the weight of Ram and Ravi each. Now, on gaining 2 kg, weight of Ram and Ravi will be (x + 2) kg each.

According to Euclid's second axiom, when equals are added to equals, the wholes are equal. Hence, weights of Ram and Ravi are again equal.

2. In the given figure, it is given that $\angle 1 = \angle 4$ and $\angle 3 = \angle 2$. By which Euclid's axiom, it can be shown that if $\angle 2 = \angle 4$, then $\angle 1 = \angle 3$.

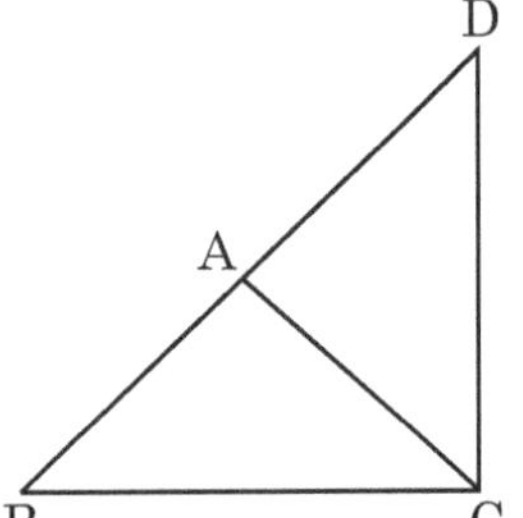

[BOARD TERM I, 2011, SET 22]

Sol. Given, $\angle 1 = \angle 4$ and $\angle 3 = \angle 2$

$\therefore \angle 2 = \angle 4$

Axiom : Things which are equal to the same or equal things are equal to one another.

$\therefore \angle 1 = \angle 3$.

3. In the given figure, we have $\angle 1 = \angle 2$, $\angle 3 = \angle 4$. Show that $\angle ABC = \angle DBC$. State the Euclid's axiom used.

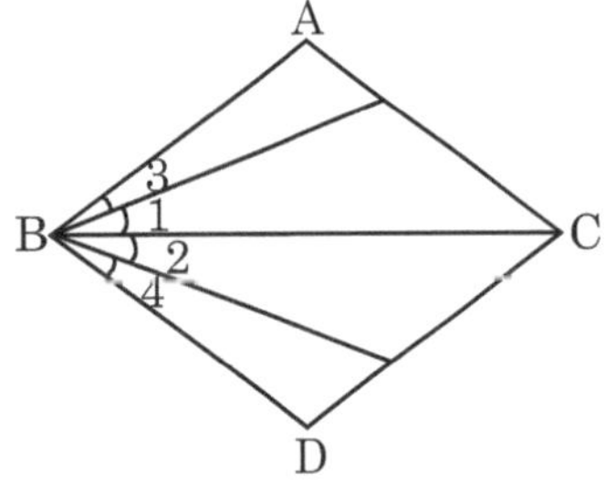

[BOARD TERM I, 2012, SET 46]

Sol. Given, $\angle 1 = \angle 2$, ...(1)

and $\angle 3 = \angle 4$. ...(2)

On adding (1) + (2), we get

$\angle 1 + \angle 3 = \angle 2 + \angle 4$

$\therefore \angle ABC = \angle DBC$

Euclid's axiom used : If equals are added to equals, then wholes are equal.

4. In the given figure, we have AB = AD and AC = AD. Prove that AB = AC. State the Euclid's axiom to support this.

[BOARD TERM I, 2012, SET 47]

Sol. According to the question,

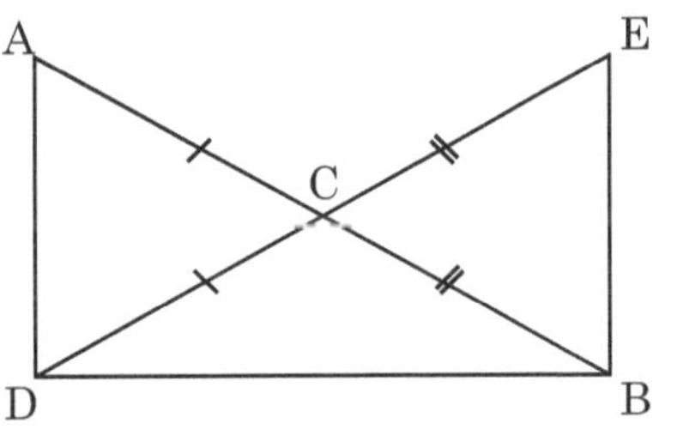

AB = AD

and AC = AD

$\therefore$ AB = AC

Euclid's axiom:

Things which are equal to the same thing are equal to one another.

5. Solve the equation x – 15 = 25 and state Euclid's axiom used here.

[BOARD TERM I, 2012, SET 69]

Sol. According to the question,

x – 15 = 25

On adding 15 on both sides,

$\Rightarrow$ x – 15 + 15 = 25 + 15

$\therefore$ x = 40

Euclid's axiom:

If equals are added to equals, the wholes are equal.

6. In the given figure, AC = DC, CB = CE, show that AB = DE.

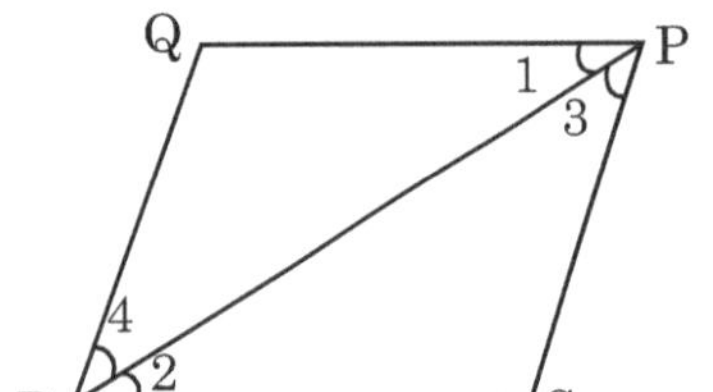

[BOARD TERM I, 2012, SET 48]

Sol. Given, AC = DC ...(i)

and CB = CE ...(ii)

On adding equation (i) and (ii), we have

AC + CB = DC + CE

$\therefore$ AB = DE

Euclid's axiom: If equals are added to equals, the wholes are equal.

7. State any two Euclid's axioms.

[BOARD TERM I, 2014, 2012 SET 41]

Sol. Euclid's axioms are as follows.

(i) Things which are equal to the same thing are equal to one another.

(ii) If equals are added to equals, the wholes are equal.

8. P and Q are the centres of two intersecting circles. Prove that PQ = QR = PR.

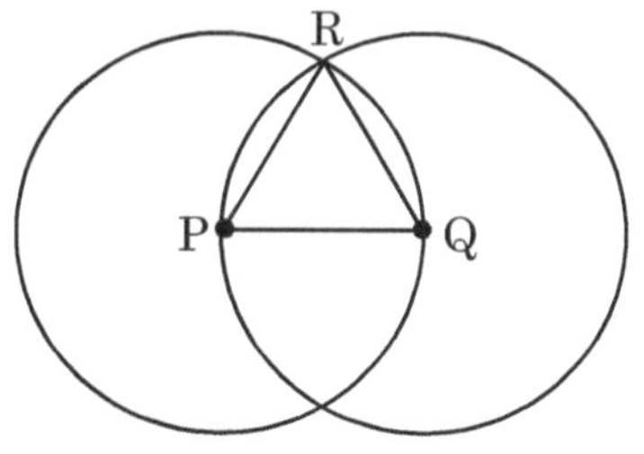

[BOARD TERM I, 2016; 2013; 2012, SET 20, QGL21RS]

Sol. According to the question,

In a circle having centre at P, we have

PR = PQ = radius

In a circle having centre at Q, we have

QR = QP = radius

Euclid's axiom : Things which are equal to the same thing are equal to one another.

$\therefore$ PR = PQ = QR.

Hence proved.

9. In triangle PQR, X and Y are the points on PQ and QR respectively. If PQ = QR and QX = QY, show that PX = RY.

[BOARD TERM I, 2016, SET JQ22L5C]

Sol. Given, PQ = QR and QX = QY

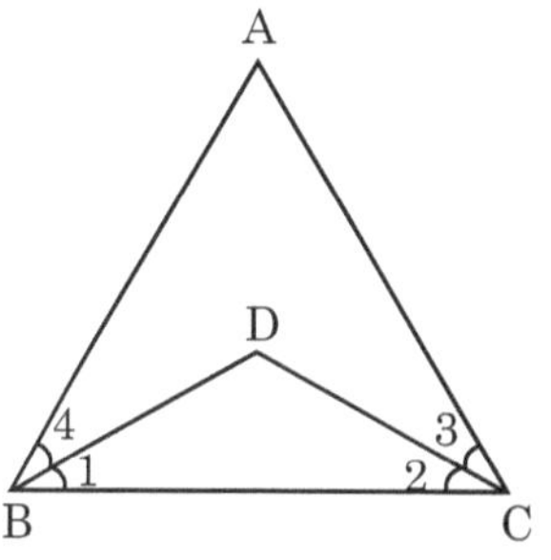

Euclid's axiom:

If equals are subtracted from equals, the remainders are also equal

We have

PQ − QX = QR − QY

PX = RY

Hence proved.

10. Solve the equation x + 4 = 10 and state Euclid's axiom used.

[BOARD TERM I, 2016, SET 7 AELQR]

Sol. According to the question, x + 4 = 10

On subtracting 4 in both sides,

$\Rightarrow$ x + 4 − 4 = 10 − 4

$\therefore$ x = 6

Euclid's axiom:

If equals are subtracted from equals, the remainder are equal.

Short Answer Type Questions II

(3 Marks Each)

1. In the given figure, we have $\angle ABC = \angle ACB$, $\angle 3 = \angle 4$. Show that $\angle 1 = \angle 2$.

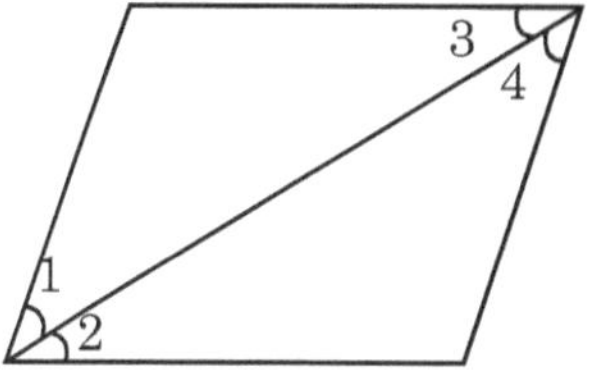

[NCERT EXEMPLAR]

Sol. Given, $\angle ABC = \angle ACB$

Now from the given figure,

$\angle 1 + \angle 4 = \angle 2 + \angle 3$

On subtracting $\angle 4$ from both sides,

$\Rightarrow \angle 1 + \angle 4 − \angle 4 = \angle 2 + \angle 3 − \angle 4$

(As, $\angle 3 = \angle 4$)

$\Rightarrow \angle 1 + \angle 4 − \angle 4 = \angle 2 + \angle 3 − \angle 3$

$\therefore \angle 1 = \angle 2$

Hence proved

2. In the given figure, if $\angle 1 = \angle 3$, $\angle 2 = \angle 4$ and $\angle 3 = \angle 4$, write the relation between $\angle 1$ and $\angle 2$, using Euclid's axiom.

[NCERT EXEMPLAR]

Sol. Given, $\angle 3 = \angle 4$ and $\angle 1 = \angle 3$ and $\angle 2 = \angle 4$. Euclid's first axiom says, the things which are equal to same things are equal to one another.

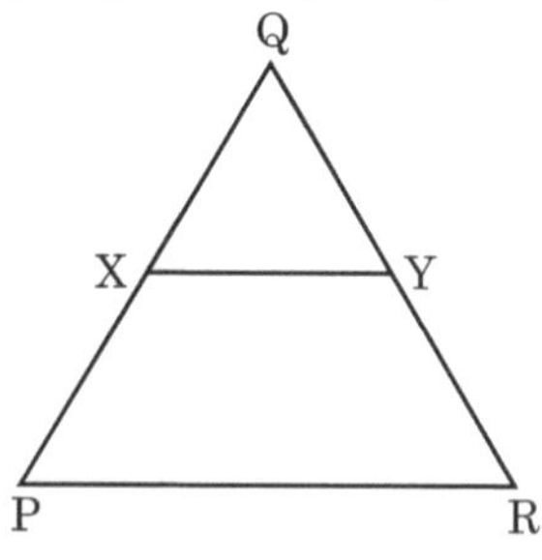

Hence, the relation between $\angle 1$ and $\angle 2$ is $\angle 1 = \angle 2$

3. In a triangle ABC, X and Y are the points on AB and BC such that BX = BY and AB = BC. Show that AX = CY. State the Euclid's Axiom used.

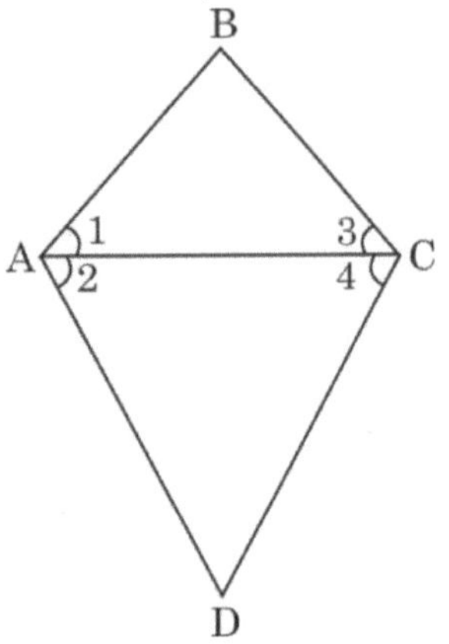

[BOARD TERM I, 2015, SET 2]

Sol. Given, AB = BC and BX = BY

Euclid's Axioms: If equals are subtracted from equals, then remains are also equal.

AB − BX = BC − BY

∴ AX = CY

Hence proved.

4. Show that of all the line segments drawn from a given point to a line, not on it, the perpendicular line segment is the shortest.

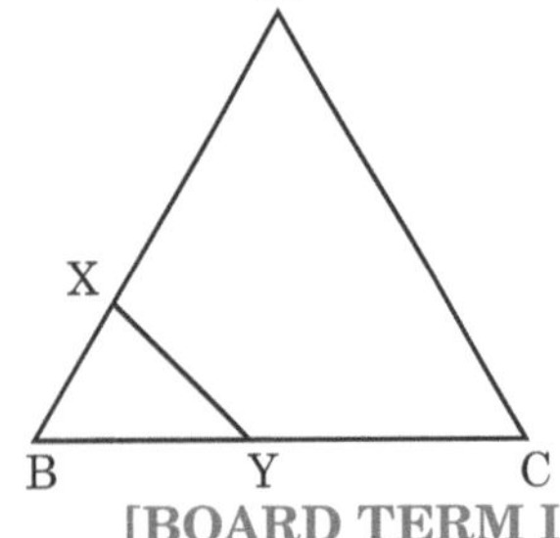

[BOARD TERM I, 2011, SET 16]

Sol. Let AB be perpendicular to a line l and AP is any other line segment.

Now, according to the question,

In right ΔABP,

$\angle B > \angle P$, ($\because \angle B = 90°$) or, AP > AB or AB < AP.

5. How many planes can be made to pass through:
   (i) Three collinear points.
   (ii) Three non-collinear points.

[BOARD TERM I, 2012, SET 49]

Sol. (i) Infinite planes can be made to pass through three collinear points

(ii) Only one planes can be made to pass through three non-collinear points.

6. State Playfair's axiom. Is it equivalent to one of the Euclid's postulate.

[BOARD TERM I, 2015, SET 2]

Sol. Playfair's Axiom (statement) : For every line l and for every point P not lying on l, there exists a unique line m passing through P and parallel to l. It is equivalent to Euclid's fifth postulate.

7. In the given figure, we have $\angle 1 = \angle 3$ and $\angle 2 = \angle 4$. Show that, $\angle A = \angle C$.

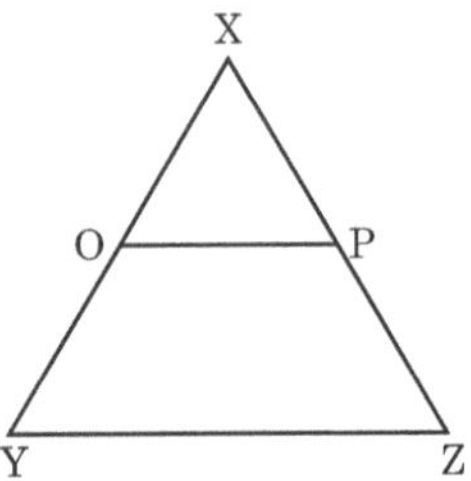

Sol. According to the question,

$\angle 1 = \angle 3$ ...(i)

and $\angle 2 = \angle 4$ ...(ii)

On adding both equations, we have

$\Rightarrow \angle BAD = \angle BCD$

$\therefore \angle A = \angle C$.

Hence proved.

Long Answer Type Questions
(4 Marks Each)

1. In the figure, if $OX = \frac{1}{2}XY$, $PX = \frac{1}{2}XZ$ and OX = PX, Show that XY = XZ. State which axiom you use here. Also give two more axioms other than the axiom used in the above situation.

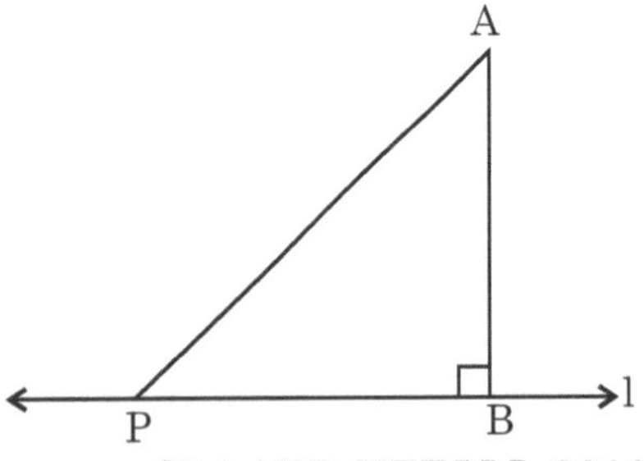

[BOARD TERM I, 2016, SET JQ22L5C]

Sol. According to the question,

$$OX = \frac{1}{2}XY$$

and $PX = \frac{1}{2}XZ$

Also, Ox = PX

or $\therefore \quad \frac{1}{2}XY = \frac{1}{2}XZ$

Hence, XY = XZ

Euclid's axiom:

Things equal to half of equals, are equal to one another.

Two another axioms are as follows:

Things coincide with one another are equal to one another.

e.g., If $\overline{AB}$ coincide with $\overline{XY}$, such that A falls on X and B falls on Y, then $\overline{AB} = \overline{XY}$

The whole is greater than the part.

e.g., if $m\angle 1 = m\angle 2 + m\angle 3$, then $m\angle 1 > m\angle 2$ and $m\angle 1 > m\angle 3$.

2. In the figure, we have $\angle 1 = \angle 3$ and $\angle 2 = \angle 4$. Show that $\angle A = \angle C$. State which axiom you use here. Also give two more axioms other than the axioms used in the above situation.

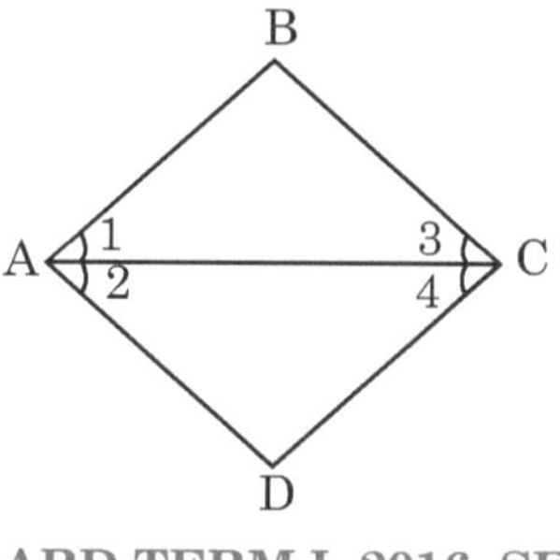

[BOARD TERM I, 2016, SET BQ56ICK]
[NCERT EXEMPLAR]

Sol. According to the question,

$\angle 1 = \angle 3$ ...(i)

and $\angle 2 = \angle 4$ ...(ii)

On adding both equations, we have

$\angle 1 + \angle 2 = \angle 3 + \angle 4$

$\Rightarrow \angle BAD = \angle BCD$

$\Rightarrow \angle A = \angle C$

If equals are added to equal the wholes are equal.

Two more axioms are as follows:

Things which are equal to the same thing are equal to one another e.g.,

$\overline{AB} = \overline{PQ}$ and $\overline{PQ} = \overline{XY}$, then $\overline{AB} = \overline{XY}$

If equals are subtracted from equals, the remainders are equal.

e.g, if $m\angle 1 = m\angle 2$ then

$m\angle 1 - m\angle 3 = m\angle 2 - m\angle 3$

3. Using Euclid's axiom, compare length AD and AF. State which axiom you used here. Also give two more axioms other than the axiom used in the above situation.

A   B   C   D   E   F   G   H

[BOARD TERM I, 2016, SET-QGL21F5]

Sol. According to the question, AD is part of AF

$\therefore$ AD < AF

As whole is greater than part

Two more axioms :

If equals are added to equals, the wholes are equal.

e.g., if $m\angle 1 = m\angle 2$, then

$m\angle 1 = m\angle 3 = m\angle 2 + m\angle 3$

If equals are subtracted from equals, the remainders are equal.

e.g., if $m\angle 1 = m\angle 2$, then

$m\angle 1 - m\angle 3 = m\angle 2 - m\angle 3$

4. It is known that if $a + b = 10$, then $a + b - c = 10 - c$. Write the Euclid's axiom that best illustrates this statement. Also give two more axioms other than the axiom used in the above situation.

[BOARD TERM I, 2015, SET-20UI6YH]

Sol. Axiom : If equals be subtracted from equals, the remainders are equal.

Two more axioms are:

(i) Things which are halves of the same thing are equal to one other.

(ii) The whole is greater than the part OR any of Euclid's Axioms can be stated.

5. A square is a polygon made up of fair line segments, out of which, length of three line segments are equal to the length of fourth of one and all its angles are right angles". Define the term used in this definition which have been highlighted/underlined.

[BOARD TERM I, 2016, SET-20CNJE9]

Sol. Polygon : A simple closed figure made up of three or more line segments.

Line Segment : Part of a line with two end points.

Angle : A figure formed by two rays with a common initial point.

Right angle : Angle whose measure is 90°.

CHAPTER 6

Lines and Angles

- (Motivate) If a ray stands on a line, then the sum of the two adjacent angles so formed is 180° and the converse.
- (Prove) If two lines intersect, vertically opposite angles are equal.
- (Motivate) results on corresponding angles, alternate angles interior angles when a transversal intersects two parallel lines.
- (Motivate) Lines which are parallel to a given line are parallel.
- (Prove) The sum of the angles of triangle is 180°.
- (Motivate) If a side of a triangle is produced, the exterior angle so formed is equal to the sum of the two interior opposite angles.

A flow chart on the basic concepts of Lines and Angles

Lines and Angles

Lines
- **Intersecting Line:** Two line are intersecting if they have a common point. The common point is called the point of intersection.
- **Concurrent Lines:** There or more lines intersecting at the same point are said to be concurrent.
- Line parallel to the same line are parallel to each other.

- If a transversal intersects tw parallel lines, then
- Each pair of corresponding angles is equal.

→ Each pair of alternate interior angles are equal.

→ Each pair of alternate exterior angles are equal.

→ Each pair of interior angles on the same side of transversal is supplementary.

→ If two lines intersect each other, then the vertically opposite angles are equal.

Angles
- Angle is formed by two rays with a common initial point
- Two congruent angles have same measure and conversely two angles of equal measure are congruent.

→ **Acute Angle:** An angle whose measure is less than 90°.

→ **Right Angle:** An angle whose measure is 90°.

→ **Obtuse Angle:** An angle whose measure is more than 90° but less than 180°

→ **Straight Angle:** An angle whose measure is 180°

→ **Reflex Angle:** An angle whose measure is more than 180°.

→ **Complementary Angles:** Two angles are said to be complementary, if the sum of their measure is 90°.

→ **Supplementary Angles:** Two angles are said to be supplementary, if the sum of their measure is 180°.

→ **Adjacent Angles:** Two angles having a common vertex and a common arm are called adjacent angles if their uncommon arms are on either side of the common arm.

[Topic 1] Different Types of Angles

Points to be Remembered

- Line is a collection of points which has only length neither breadth nor thickness.
- An angle is formed when two rays originate from the same end point. The rays making an angle are called the arms and the end point is called the vertex.
- **Different types of angles:**
  (i) An angle whose measure is more than $0°$ but less than $90°$ is called an **Acute Angle.**

where $(0° < θ° < 90°)$

  (ii) An angle whose measure is $90°$, is called **Right Angle.**

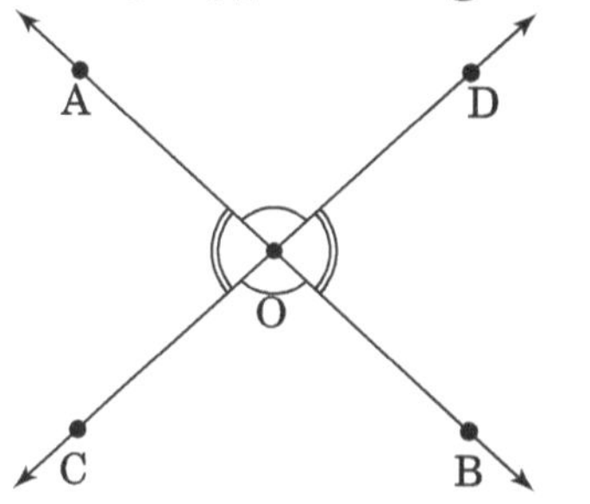

where $(θ = 90°)$

  (iii) An angle whose measure is more than $90°$, but less than $180°$ is called **Obtuse Angle.**

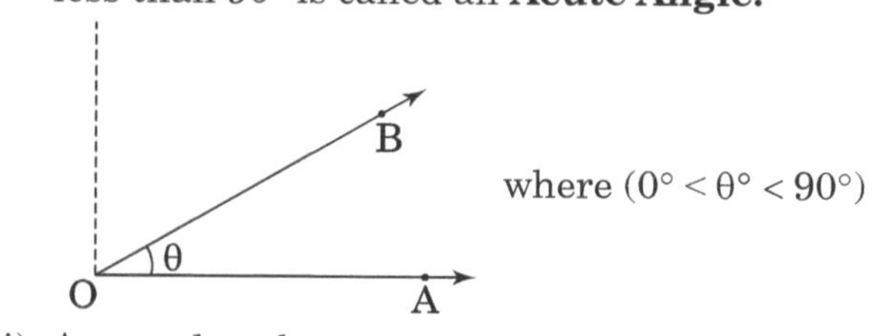

where $90° < θ < 180°$

  (iv) An angle whose measure is $180°$, is called a **Straight Angle.**

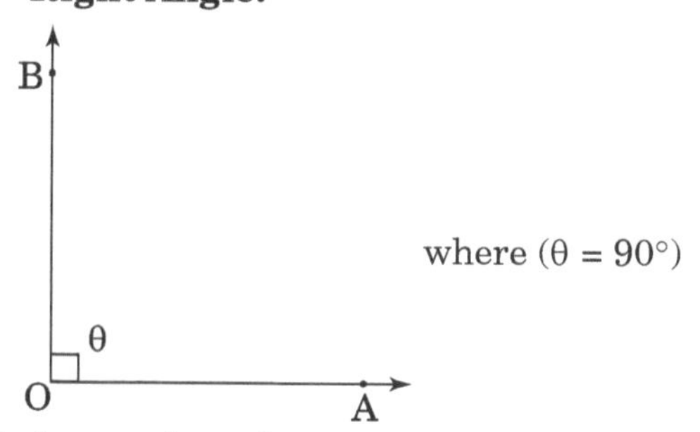

where $(θ = 180°)$

(v) An angle whose measure is $360°$, is called a **Complete Angle.**

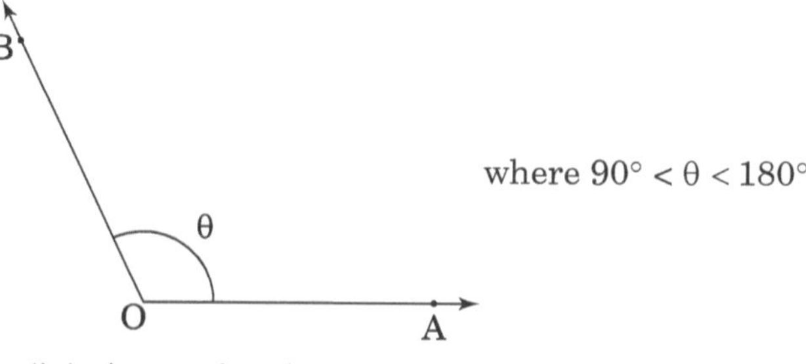

where $θ = 360°$

- Two angles whose sum is $90°$, are called complementary angles. For example : $40°$ and $50°$ are **complementary angles**.
- Two angles whose sum is $180°$ are called supplementary angles. For example : $60°$ and $120°$ are **supplementary angles**.
- When two straight lines intersect each other four angles are formed. the pair of angles which lie on the opposite sides of the point of intersection are called **Vertically Opposite Angles**

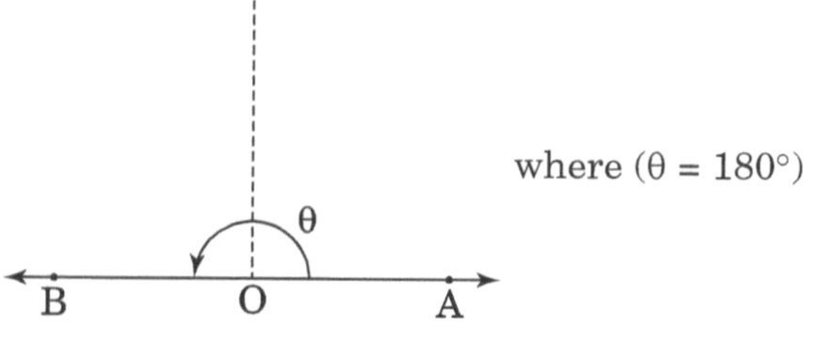

where $∠AOC = ∠BOD$ and $∠AOD = ∠BOC$

PREVIOUS YEARS' EXAMINATION QUESTIONS
TOPIC 1

Multiple Choice Questions
(1 Mark Each)

1. An exterior angle of a triangle is $105°$ and its two interior opposite angles are equal. Each of these equal angles is

   (a) $37\dfrac{1}{2}^{\circ}$ (b) $52\dfrac{1}{2}^{\circ}$

   (c) $72\dfrac{1}{2}^{\circ}$ (d) $75°$ [NCERT Exemp.]

Sol. (b) Let each interior, equal angle is x°, then

$$\text{exterior angle} = 105° \text{ (Given)}$$

According to the question,

$$\text{Sum of interior angles} = \text{Exterior angle}$$
$$x + x = 105°$$
$$\Rightarrow \quad 2x = 105°$$
$$\therefore \quad x = \frac{105°}{2} = 52.5°$$

2. In given figure, POQ is a line, The value of x is
   (a) 20°   (b) 25°
   (c) 30°   (d) 35°

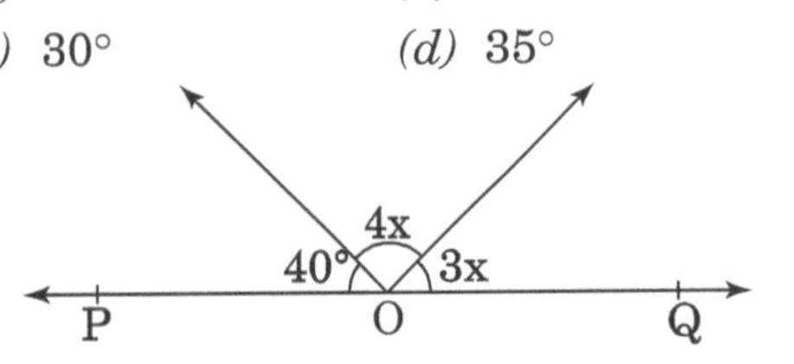

[NCERT Exemp.]

Sol. (a) According to the given figure,

$$40° + 4x + 3x = 180°$$

(∵ POQ is straight line)

$$\Rightarrow \quad 7x = 180° - 40°$$

$$\therefore \quad x = \frac{140°}{7} = 20°$$

3. The angles of triangle are in the ratio 5 : 3 : 7. The triangle is
   (a) An acute angled triangle
   (b) An obtuse angled triangle
   (c) a right triangle
   (d) an isosceles triangle   [NCERT Exemp.]

Sol. (a) Let the angles of a triangles are $5x°$, $3x°$ and $7x°$ respectively, then

According to question,

$$5x + 3x + 7x = 180° \text{ (angle sum property)}$$

$$\Rightarrow \quad 15x = 180°$$

$$\therefore \quad x = \frac{180°}{15} = 12°$$

$$\text{First angle} = 5 \times 12 = 60°$$

$$\text{Second angle} = 3 \times 12 = 36°$$

$$\text{and third angle} = 7 \times 12 = 84°$$

Hence, The triangle is an acute angled triangle.

4. If two complementary angles are in the ratio 13 : 5, then the angles are :
   (a) 65°, 35°   (b) 65°, 25°
   (c) 13x, 5x   (d) 25°, 65°

Sol. (b) Let two complementary angles are 13x and 5x, respectively.

According to the question.

$$13x + 5x = 90°$$

(Sum of complementary angle)

$$\Rightarrow \quad 18x = 90°$$

$$\therefore \quad x = \frac{90°}{18°} = 5°$$

Hence, required angles are

$$13 \times 5 = 65° \quad \text{and} \quad 5 \times 5 = 25°$$

5. In figure If x : y = 1 : 4, then values of x and y are respectively:
   (a) 36° and 144°   (b) 18° and 72°
   (c) 144° and 36°   (d) 72° and 18°

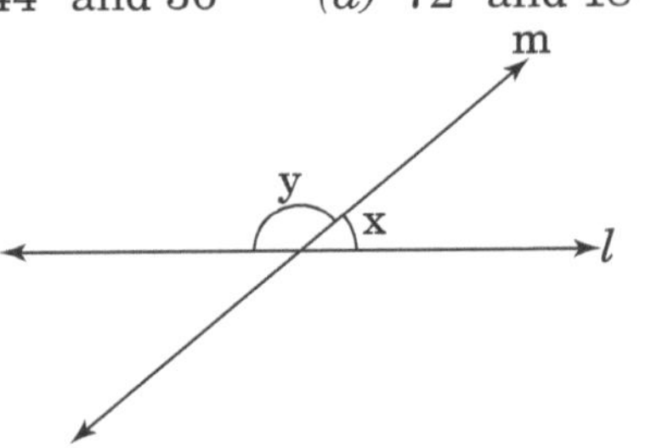

Sol. (d) 72° and 18°

6. If the difference between two complementary angles is 10°, then the angles are:
   (a) 50°, 60°   (b) 50°, 40°
   (c) 80°, 10°   (d) 35°, 45°

Sol. (b) From option (b),

$$50° + 40° = 90°$$

∵ Sum is 90° and difference is 10°

∴ Both angles are complementary angles.

Very Short Answer Type Questions
(1 Mark Each)

1. Two supplementary angles are in ratio 2 : 7. Find the measures of angles.

[Board Term I, 2016, Set-BQS6I2K]

Sol. Let the two supplementary angles are 2x and 7x, respectively, then

According to the question,

$$2x + 7x = 180° \quad \Rightarrow \quad 9x = 180°$$

$$\therefore \quad x = \frac{180°}{9} = 20°$$

Supplementary angles are

$$2x = 2 \times 20° = 40°$$

and

$$7x = 7 \times 20° = 140°$$

Hence, two angles are 40° and 140°.

2. If the measure of an angles is twice the measure of its supplementary angle, then find its measure.

Sol. Let the required angle be $x°$

∴ Its supplement angle = 180° − x

From the question,

we obtain

$$x = 2(180° - x)$$

$$\Rightarrow \quad x = 360° - 2x$$

$$\Rightarrow \quad 3x = 360°$$

$$\therefore \quad x = \frac{360°}{3} = 120°$$

Hence, the required angle is 120°.

3. Two angles measure $(55° + 3a)$ and $(115° - 2a)$. If each is supplement of the other, then calculate the value of a.

Sol. Angle $(55° + 3a)$ and $(115° - 2a)$ are supplement of each other, then,

According to the question,

$$\text{Sum of angles} = 180°$$
$$55° + 3a + 115° - 2a = 180°$$
$$\therefore \qquad a = 180° - 170°$$
$$= 10°$$

4. In the figure below, AOB is a straight line. Calculate the measure of $\angle COD$.

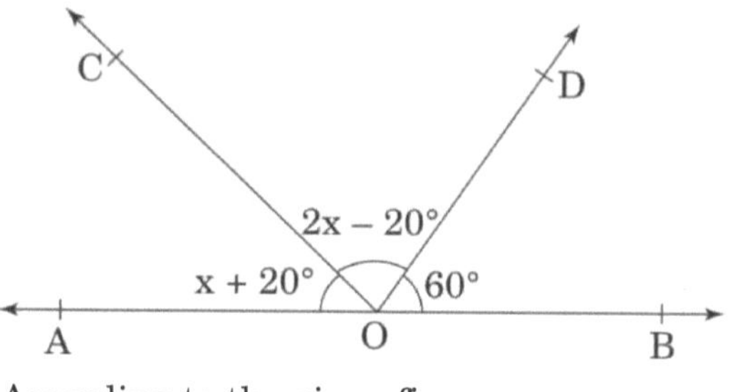

Sol. According to the given figure,

$$x + 20° + 2x - 20° + 60° = 180°$$

(∵   Straight line makes an angle 180°)

$$\Rightarrow \qquad 3x = 180° - 60° = 120°$$
$$\therefore \qquad x = \frac{120}{3} = 40°$$

Hence, $\angle COD = 2x - 20° = 80° - 20° = 60°$.

5. Find the supplement of $\dfrac{3}{5}$ of a right angle.

Sol. Given, angle $= \dfrac{3}{5}$ of a right angle

$$= \frac{3}{5} \times 90°$$
$$= 3 \times 18° = 54°$$

∴   Supplement of 54°
$$= \text{An angle of measure } (180° - 54°)$$
$$= \text{an angle of measure } 126°$$

Hence, the required angle is 126°

6. In figure below, calculate the value of angle q.

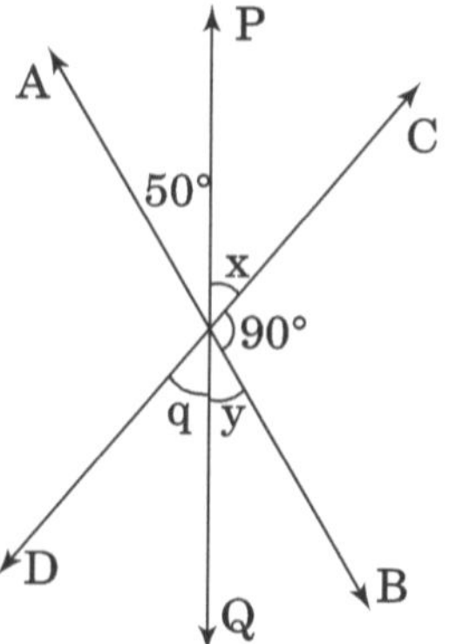

Sol. According to the given figure,

$$x + 50° + 90° = 180°$$
$$\Rightarrow \qquad q = x = 40°$$

(Vertically opposite angles)

7. Write the complement of $(90° - a)$.

Sol. Since, The sum of complementary angles is 90°.

The Complement of $(90° - a) = 90° - (90° - a)$
$$= 90° - 90° + a = a$$

8. Write the complementary angle of 65°.

Sol. Since, the sum of complementary angles is 90°.

Complementary angle of 65°
$$= 90° - 65° = 25°$$

9. Calculate the value of x in the figure given below.

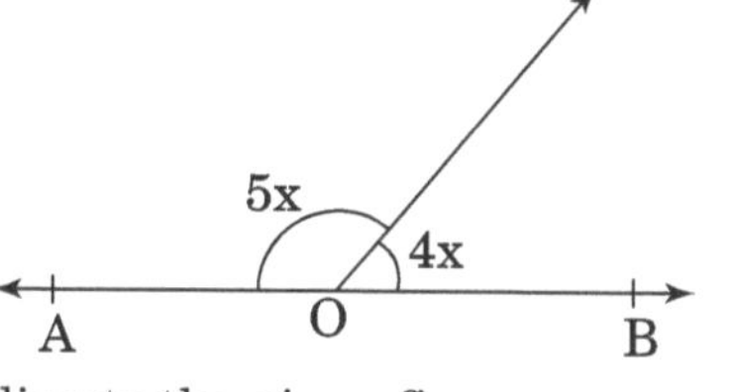

Sol. According to the given figure,

$$5x + 4x = 180°$$

(∵   Straight line makes an angle of 180°)

$$x = \frac{180°}{9}$$
$$= 20°$$

Hence, the measure of x = 20°.

10. In the figure below, calculate the value of y.

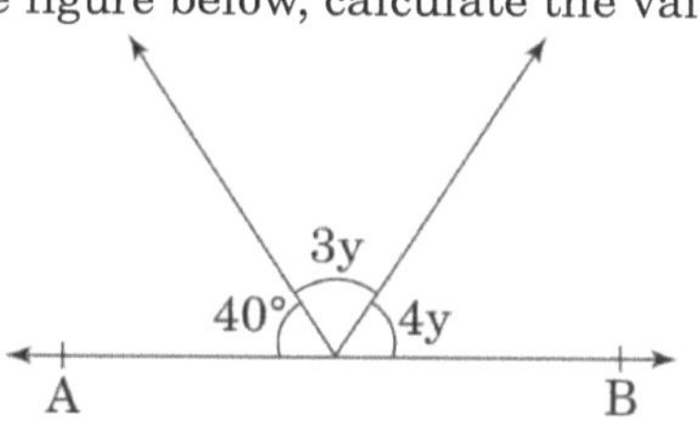

Sol. According to the given figure,

$$40° + 3y + 2y = 180°$$

(∵ Straight line makes an angle of 180°)

$$\Rightarrow \qquad 5y = 140°$$
$$\therefore \qquad y = \frac{140°}{5} = 28°$$

Hence, the measure of $y = 28°$.

11. In the given figure, AB‖CD, $\angle EAB = 50°$. If $\angle ECD = 60°$, then find $\angle AEB$.

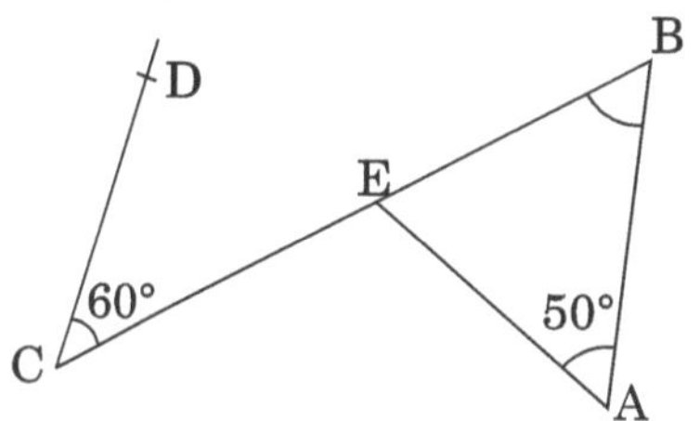

Sol. Given, AB ∥ CD and BC is a transversal.

∴ $\quad\quad$ ∠DCE = ∠EBA

[alternate interior angles]

⇒ $\quad\quad$ ∠EBA = 60°

[∵ ∠DCE = 60° (given)]

In ΔABE, we have

∠EBA + ∠EAB + ∠AEB = 180°

[since, sum of all the angles of a triangle is 180°]

⇒ $\quad$ 60° + 50° + ∠AEB = 180°

⇒ $\quad$ 110° + ∠AEB = 180°

∴ $\quad\quad$ ∠AEB = 180° − 110° − 70°

12. Two angles measure $(30° − a)$ and $(125° + 2a)$. If each one is the supplement of the other, then find the value of a.

Sol. Angles $(30° − a)$ and $(125° + 2a)$ are supplementary of each other, then

According to the question,

$30° − a + 125° + 2a = 180°$

∴ $\quad\quad$ $a = 180° − 155°$

$\quad\quad\quad = 25°.$

13. Write the angle which is one-fifth of its complement.

Sol. Let the angle be x, then

According to the question,

$$x = \frac{1}{5}(90° − x)$$

or $\quad\quad$ $6x = 90°$

$\quad\quad\quad$ $5x = 90° − x$

⇒ $\quad\quad$ $6x = 90°$

∴ $\quad\quad$ $x = \dfrac{90°}{6} = 15°$

14. What is the measure of an angle which is complement of itself?

Sol. Let the angle be x, then

According to the question,

$\quad\quad$ Angle x = Complement of x

⇒ $\quad\quad$ $x = 90° − x$

⇒ $\quad\quad$ $2x = 90°.$

∴ $\quad\quad$ $x = \dfrac{90°}{2}$

$\quad\quad\quad$ $x = 45°$

Hence, the required angle = 45°

Short Answer Type Questions I

(2 Marks Each)

1. If one angle of a triangle is equal to the sum of the other two angles, then show that the triangle is a right angled triangle.

[NCERT Examplar]

Sol. Let the angles of a ΔABC be ∠A, ∠B and ∠C.

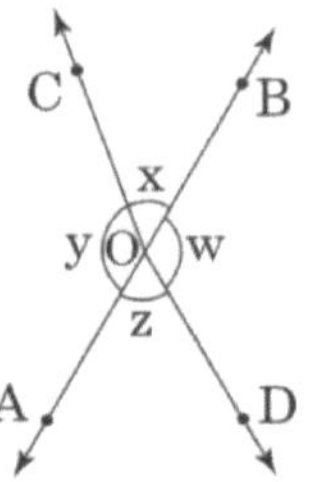

Given, $\quad\quad$ ∠A = ∠B + ∠C $\quad\quad$ ...(i)

In ΔABC, ∠A + ∠B + ∠C = 180° $\quad\quad$ ...(ii)

[Since, sum of all angles of a triangle is 180°]

According to the question

⇒ $\quad\quad$ ∠A + ∠A = 180° $\quad\quad$ [from eq. (i)]

⇒ $\quad\quad$ 2∠A = 180°

∴ $\quad\quad$ $∠A = \dfrac{180°}{2}$

$\quad\quad\quad = 90°$

∴ Hence, the triangle is a right angled triangle.

2. In the given figure, If $x + y = w + z$. then prove that AOB is a line. $\quad$ [NCERT]

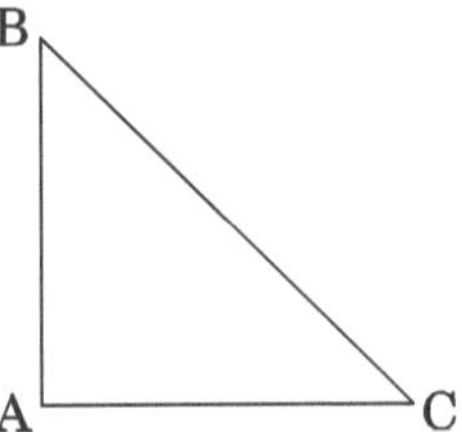

Sol. We know that, sum of all the angles around a point in 360°.

∴ $\quad$ $x + y + z + w = 360°$

⇒ $(x + y) + (z + w) = 360°$

∴ $\quad$ $(x + y) + (x + y) = 360°$

[∵ x + y = z + w, given]

⇒ $\quad\quad$ $2(x + y) = 360°$

⇒ $\quad\quad$ $(x + y) = \dfrac{360°}{2}$

∴ $\quad\quad$ $x + y = 180°$

Hence, AOB is a straight line.

3. In the given figure, $\angle AOC$ and $\angle BOC$ from a line AB. If $a - b = 80°$, find the values of a and b.

[Board Term I, 2012, Set-35; 2011, Set-12; 2010, Set-12]

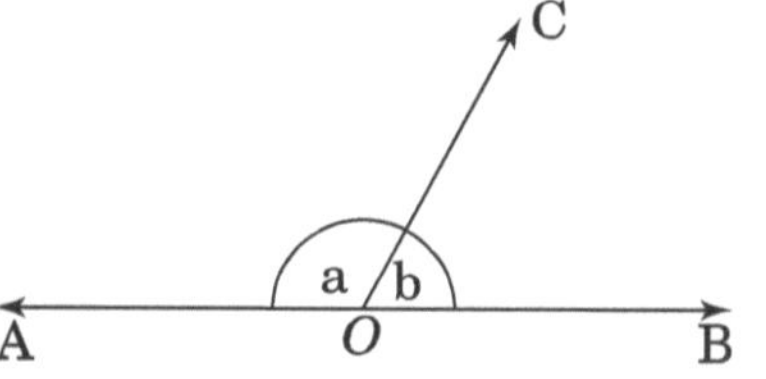

Sol. From the given figure,

$$a + b = 180° \qquad \text{... (i) (Linear pair)}$$

and $\qquad a - b = 80° \qquad$ ... (ii) (Given)

On adding equation (i) and (ii), we have

$$2a = 260°$$
$$a = 130°$$

and $\qquad b = 180° - a \;\Rightarrow\; 180° - 130°$
$$= 50°$$

4. In figure, $\angle DOB = 87°$ and $\angle COA = 82°$. If $\angle BOA = 35°$, then find $\angle COB$ and $\angle COD$.

[Board Term I, 2012, Set-20]

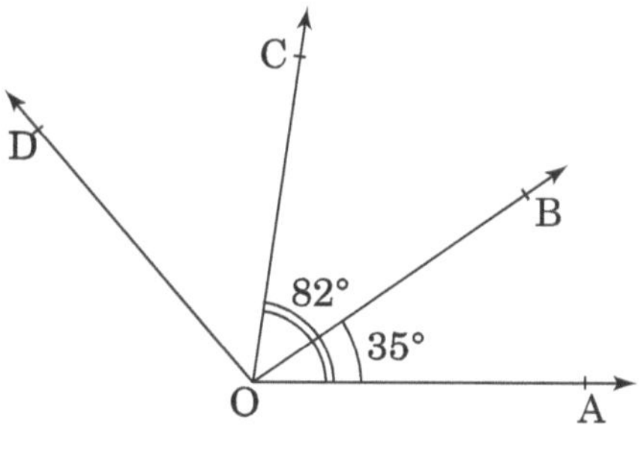

Sol. According to the given figure,

$$\angle COA = 82°$$
$$\Rightarrow \angle COB + \angle BOA = 82°$$
$$\Rightarrow \quad \angle COB + 35° = 82° \qquad (\because \angle BOA = 35°)$$
$$\therefore \qquad \angle COB = 82° - 35° = 47°$$

Similarly, $\quad \angle DOB = \angle DOC + \angle COB$
$$\Rightarrow \qquad 87° = \angle DOC + 47°$$
$$\therefore \qquad \angle DOC = 87° - 47° = 40°$$

5. In figure, prove that $\angle AOB + \angle BOC + \angle COD + \angle DOA = 360°$.

[Board Term I, 2012, Set-19]

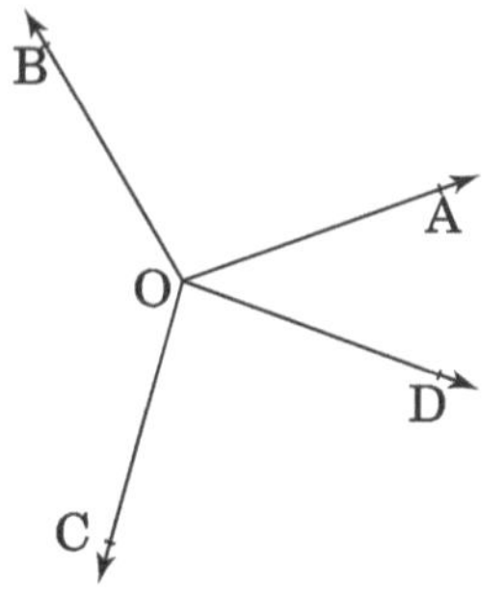

Sol. According to the question

Extend AO to E

$\therefore\; \angle AOB + \angle BOE = 180° \qquad$ (Linear pair) ...(i)

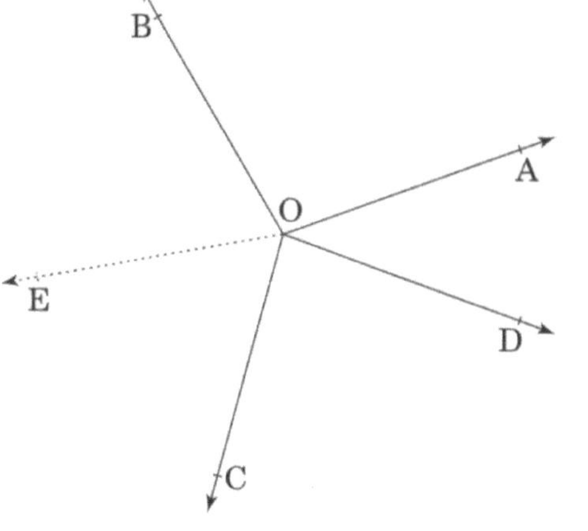

and $\qquad \angle EOC + \angle COD + \angle DOA = 180°$

(Adjacent angles) ...(ii)

On adding (i) and (ii), we have,

$$\angle AOB + \angle BOE + \angle EOC + \angle COD + \angle DOA$$
$$= 180° + 180°$$
$$= 360°$$

6. In the figure, lines XY and MN intersect at O. If $\angle POY = 90°$ and $a : b = 2 : 3$, find the value of c.

[Board Term I, 2012, Set-44]

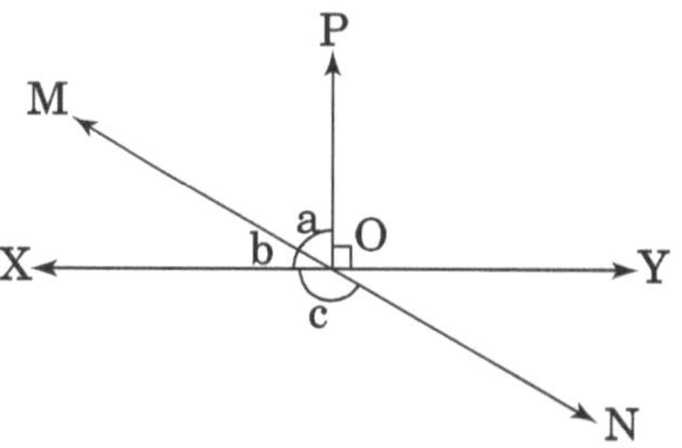

Sol. Let, $\qquad \angle a = 2x \quad$ and $\quad \angle b = 3x$

Then, According to the question,

$$\angle a + \angle b = 90°$$
$$\Rightarrow \qquad 2x + 3x = 90°$$
$$\Rightarrow \qquad 5x = 90°$$
$$\therefore \qquad x = \frac{90°}{5} = 18°$$
$$a = 2 \times 18° = 36°$$
$$b = 3 \times 18° = 54°$$

and $\qquad c = 180° - b = 180° - 54° = 126°$

Hence, the value of $c = 126°$

7. In the given figure, $\angle AOB : \angle BOC = 2 : 3$ if $\angle AOC = 75°$, then find the measure of $\angle AOB$ and $\angle OBC$.

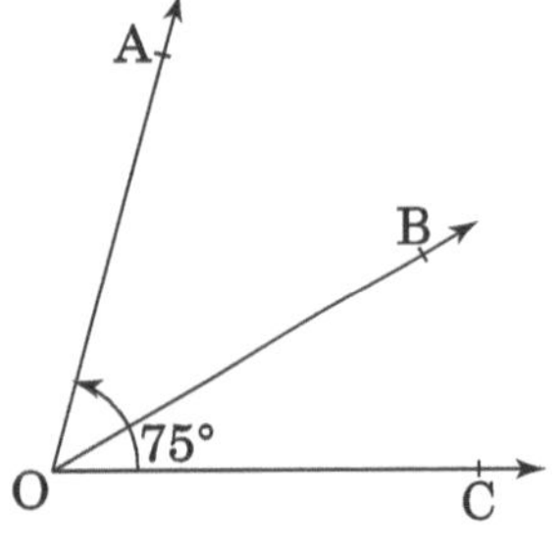

[Board Term I, 2012, Set-19]

Sol. Let, $\qquad \angle AOB = 2x$

$\qquad\qquad \angle BOC = 3x$

According to the question,

$\qquad \angle AOB + \angle BOC = \angle AOC$

$\Rightarrow \qquad 2x + 3x = 75° \quad \Rightarrow \quad 5x = 75°$

or $\qquad\qquad x = \dfrac{75°}{5} = 15°$

$\therefore \qquad \angle AOB = 2x = 2 \times 15° = 30°$

and $\qquad \angle BOC = 3x = 3 \times 15 = 45°$

8. Two supplementary angles are in the ratio $2 : 3$, find the angles.   [Board Term I, 2012, Set-51]

Sol. Let the two supplementary angles are $2x$ and $3x$ then, According to the question,

$\qquad\qquad 2x + 3x = 180°$

$\Rightarrow \qquad\qquad 5x = 180°$

$\Rightarrow \qquad\qquad x = \dfrac{180°}{5} = 36°$

Hence, the angles are $2x$ and $3x = 180°$

$\qquad\qquad 2x = 2 \times 36 = 72°$

and $\qquad\qquad 3x = 3 \times 36 = 108°$

9. If $\angle AOP = 5y$, $\angle QOD = 2y$ and $\angle BOC = 5y$ in the given figure , find the value of y.

[Board term I, 2015, Set-2, 2012, Set-50]

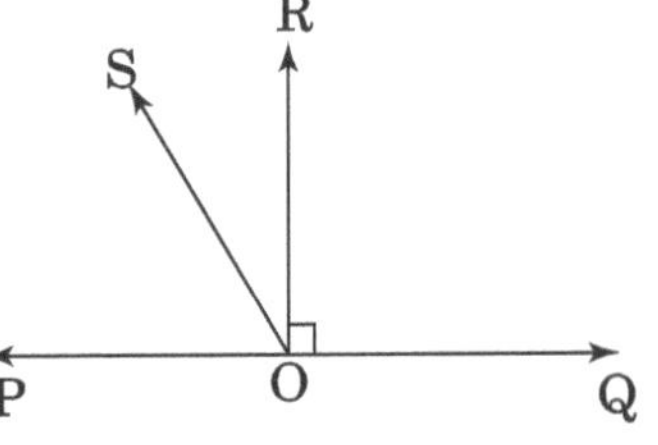

Sol. According to the given figure,

$\qquad \angle POC = 2y \quad$ and $\quad \angle AOD = 5y$

$\qquad\qquad$ (Vertically opp. angles)

$\therefore \qquad 5y + 2y + 5y = 180°$

$\Rightarrow \qquad\qquad 12y = 180°$

$\therefore \qquad\qquad y = \dfrac{180°}{12} = 15°$

10. If $(3x - 15°)$ and $(x + 5°)$ are complementary angles, find the angles.

[Board Term I, 2015, Set-2]

Sol. $\because$ $(3x - 15°)$ and $(x + 5°)$ are complementary angles.

$\therefore$ Sum of complementary angles is $90°$

$(3 - 15°) + (x + 5°) = 90°$

$\Rightarrow \qquad 4x = 90° + 10 = 100°$

$\therefore \qquad\qquad x = \dfrac{100°}{4} = 25°$

Hence, angles are

$\qquad (3x - 15°) = 3 \times 25 - 15°$

$\qquad\qquad = 75° - 15° = 60°$

and $\qquad (x + 5°) = 25° + 5° = 30°$

Short Answer Type Questions II

(3 Marks Each)

1. In figure, POQ is a line. Ray $OR \perp PQ$. OS is another ray lying between OP and OR.

Prove that : $\angle ROS = \dfrac{1}{2}[\angle QOS - \angle POS]$

[NCERT, Board Term I, 2012, Set-42; 2011, Set-17]

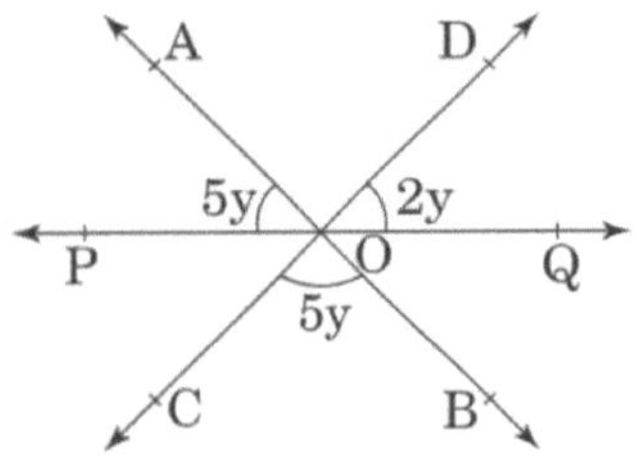

Sol. According to the question,

$\qquad\qquad \therefore OR \perp PQ$

$\qquad\qquad \angle POR = \angle ROQ = 90°$

$\qquad \angle POS + \angle ROS = 90°$

$\qquad\qquad \angle ROS = 90° - \angle POS$

On adding $\angle ROS$ on both sides, we have,

$\qquad \angle ROS + \angle ROS = 90° - \angle POS + \angle ROS$

$\Rightarrow \qquad 2\angle ROS = 90° + \angle ROS - \angle POS$

$\qquad\qquad 2\angle ROS = \angle QOS - \angle POS$

$\qquad\qquad\qquad (\because \quad 90° + \angle ROS = \angle QOS)$

$\therefore \qquad \angle ROS = \dfrac{1}{2}(\angle QOS - \angle POS)$

Hence Proved.

2. Lines PQ and RS intersect each other at O (see figure). IF $\angle POR : \angle ROQ = 5 : 7$, find all the angles a, b, c and d.

[Board Term I, 2012, Set-41, NCERT]

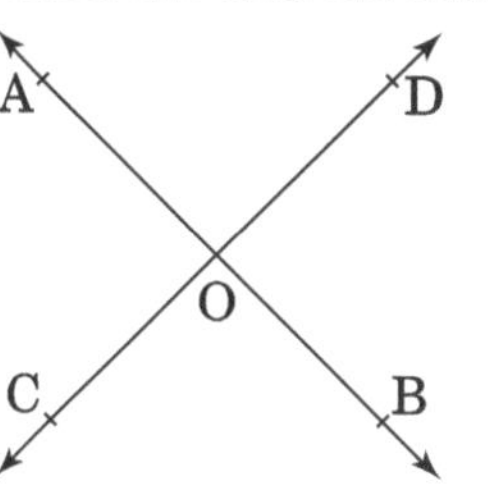

Sol. Let $\qquad \angle POR = 5x$
and $\qquad \angle ROQ = 7x$, then
According to the question,
$$5x + 7x = 180°$$
$$12x = 180°$$
$$x = \frac{180°}{12} = 15°$$
Hence, all the angles are
$$\angle POR = d = b = 5x = 5 \times 15° = 75°$$
$$\angle ROQ = c = a = 7x = 7 \times 15° = 105°.$$

3. In the figure, if $x + y = w + z$, then prove that AOB is a straight line.

[Board Term I, 2015, Set-2, NCERT]

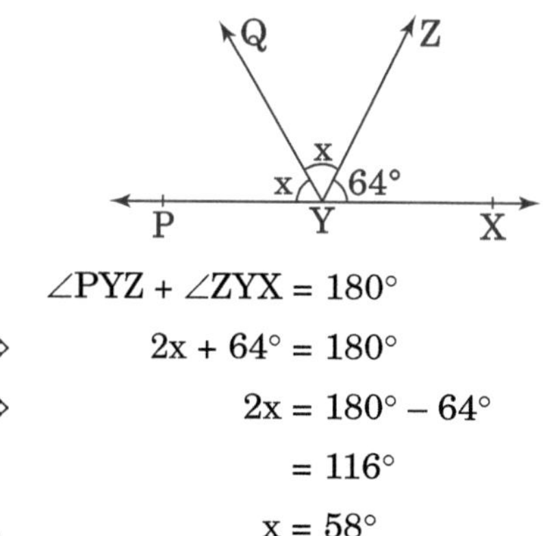

Sol. According to the question,

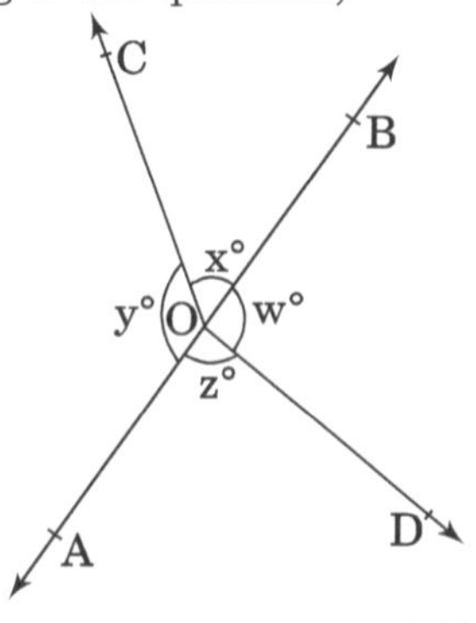

$$x + y + w + z = 360°$$
$$\Rightarrow \qquad 2(x + y) = 360° \qquad (\because x + y = w + z)$$
$$\Rightarrow \qquad x + y = 180°$$
Therefore, AOB is a straight line.

4. Prove that if two line intersect, vertically opposite angles are equal.

[Board Term I, 2016, Set-QGL21FS, NCERT Exemplar]

Sol. Given : Two lines AB and CD intersect a point O

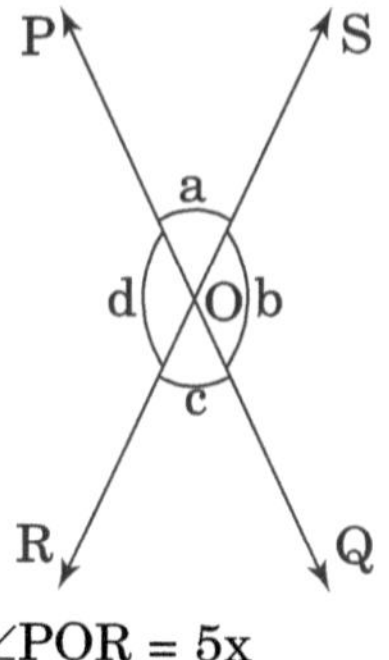

To Prove : Vertically opposite angles are equal.
(i) $\angle AOC = \angle BOD$
(ii) $\angle AOD = \angle BOC$
Proof $\therefore$ Ray OA stand on line CD
$$\angle AOC + \angle AOD = 180° \qquad …(i) \text{ [Linear pair]}$$
Again ray OD stand on line AB
$$\therefore \ \angle AOD + \angle BOD = 180° \qquad … (ii) \text{ [Linear pair]}$$
from eqn. (i) and (ii),
$$\angle AOC + \angle AOD = \angle AOD + \angle BOD$$
[Each equal to 180°]
$$\therefore \qquad \angle AOC = \angle BOD$$
Similarly $\angle AOD = \angle BOC$

Hence proved.

5. It is given that $\angle XYZ = 64°$ and XY is produced to a point P. Draw a figure from the given information. If ray YQ bisects $\angle ZYP$, find $\angle XYQ$ and reflex $\angle QYP$.

[Board Term I, 2012, Set-51]

Sol. According to the question,

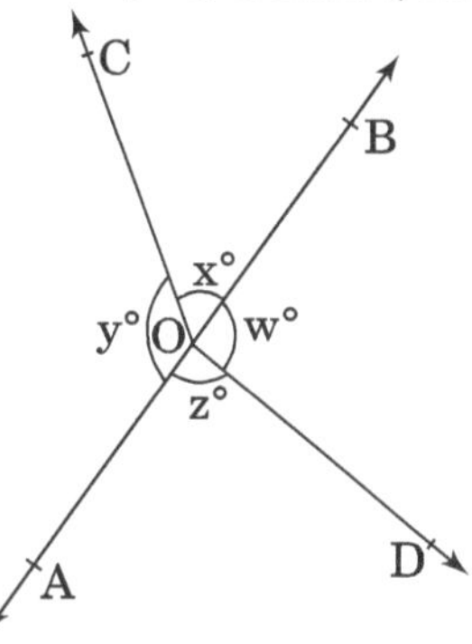

$$\angle PYZ + \angle ZYX = 180°$$
$$\Rightarrow \qquad 2x + 64° = 180°$$
$$\Rightarrow \qquad 2x = 180° - 64°$$
$$= 116°$$
$$\therefore \qquad x = 58°$$
Now, $\qquad \angle XYQ = 64° + 58° = 122°$
Reflex $\qquad \angle QYP = 360° - x$
$$= 360° - 58° = 302°.$$

6. In the given figure, PO $\perp$ AB. If x : y : z = 1 : 3 : 5, then find the degree measure of x, y and z.

[Board Term I, 2014, 2012, Set 18]

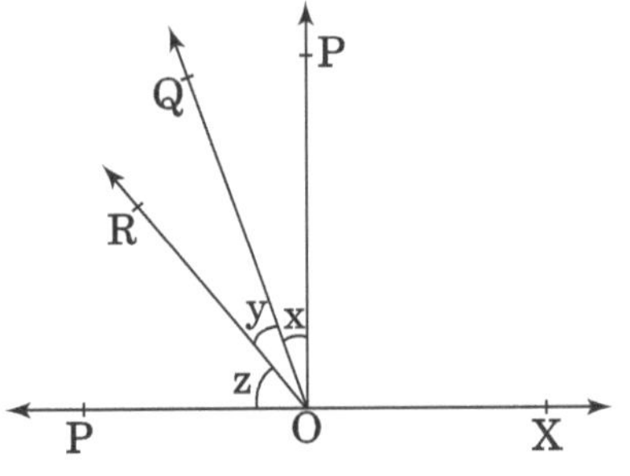

Sol.

$$OP \perp AB$$

or, $\angle POA = 90°$

Let $x = \angle POQ = a$

$\therefore$ $y = \angle QOR = 3a$

and $z = \angle ROA = 5a$

According to the figure,

$$a + 3a + 5a = 90°$$

$$9a = 90°$$

$\therefore$ $a = \dfrac{90°}{9} = 10°$

Hence, required angles are

$\therefore$ $x = 10°$

$y = 3 \times 10° = 30°$

and $z = 5 \times 10° = 50°$

7. In the figure, if AB $||$ CF and CD $||$ FE, then find the value of x.

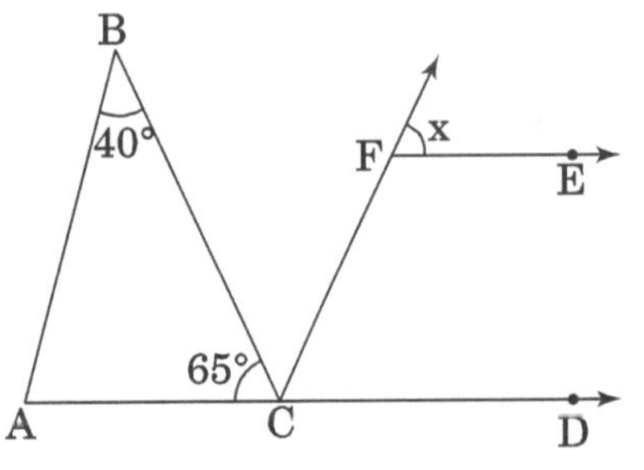

[Board Term I, 2014]

Sol. According to the question,

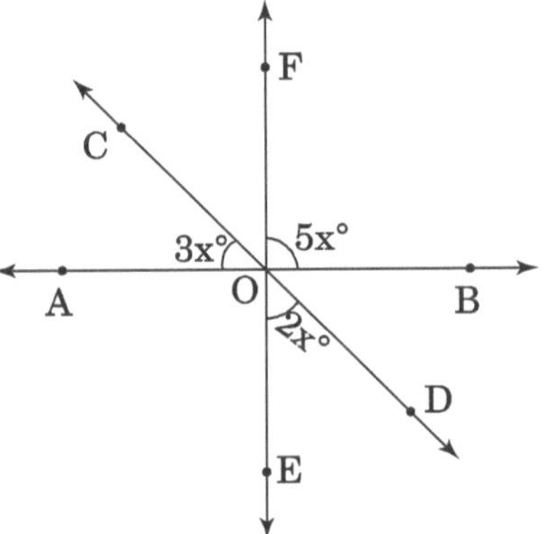

$\because$ AB $||$ CF

$\therefore$ $\angle ABC = \angle BCF$ [Alternate interior angle]

$$40° = \angle BCF$$

Now, $\angle ACB + \angle BCF + \angle FCD = 180°$ (Linear pair)

$\Rightarrow 65° + 40° + \angle FCD = 180°$

$\therefore$ $\angle FCD = 180° - 105° = 75°$

Now, FE $||$ CD

$\therefore$ $\angle FCD = \angle x$ (Corresponding angles)

$\therefore$ $\angle x = 75°$

Hence, the value of x = 75°

8. In the given figure, lines AB, CD and EF meet at O. Find the value of x, hence find all the three indicated angles.

[Board Term I, 2016, Set-BQ56IZK]

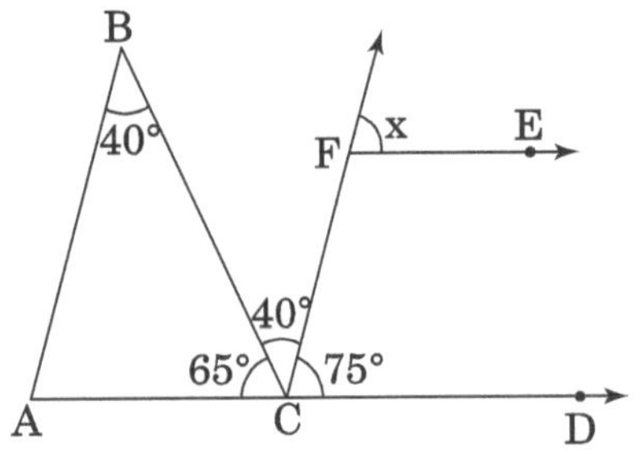

Sol. According to the question,

$$\angle COF = 2x°$$

(vertically opposite angles)

$\therefore$ $3x° + 2x° + 5x° = 180°$ (Linear Pair)

$\Rightarrow$ $10x° = 180° = x = 18°$

Hence, all three angles are

$$\angle AOC = 3x = 3 \times 18° = 54°$$

$$\angle BOF = 5x° = 5 \times 18° = 90°$$

$$\angle DOE = 2x = 2 \times 18° = 36°$$

9. Prove that bisectors of pair of vertically opposite angles are in the same straight line.

[Bozrd Term I, 2016, Set-7AEDLQR]

Sol. **Given:** Two lines AB and CD intersect at point O. Also, OM and ON are the bisectors of $\angle AOC$ and $\angle BOD$ respectively.

To prove: MON is a straight line.

Prove: Since the sum of all the angles around a point O is 360°, we have

$$\angle AOC + BOC + BOD + AOD = 360°$$
$$\Rightarrow\ 2\angle MOC + 2\angle BOC + 2\angle BON = 360°$$

$[\because \angle BOC = \angle AOD$ (vertically opposite angles) and OM is the bisector of $\angle AOC$; ON is the bisector of $\angle BOD]$

$$\Rightarrow\quad \angle MOC + \angle BOC + \angle BON = 180°$$
$$\therefore\quad \angle MON = 180°$$

Hence, MON is a straight line.

10. In the figure PQ and RS intersect each other at point O. If $\angle POR : \angle ROQ = 2 : 3$, Find $\angle POR$ and $\angle ROQ$.   Board Term I, 2016, Set-ZOCNJE9]

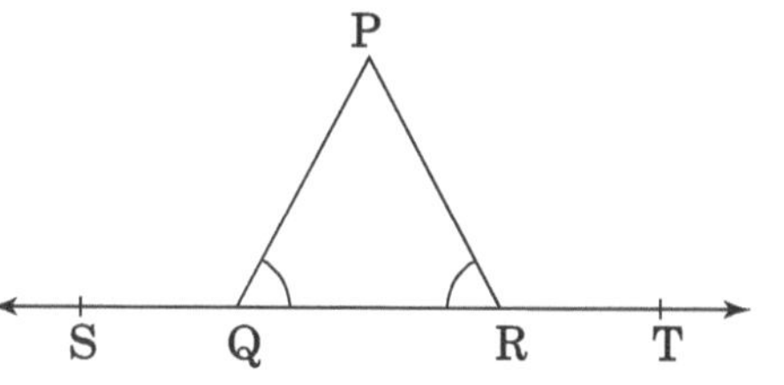

Sol. Let $\angle POR = 2x$ and $\angle ROQ = 3x$

then, According to the question,
$$\angle POR + \angle ROQ = 180°$$
$$\Rightarrow\qquad 2x + 3x = 180°\ \Rightarrow\ 5x = 180°$$
$$\therefore\qquad x = \frac{180}{5} = 36°$$

Hence, required angles are
$$\angle POR = 2x = 2 \times 36° = 72°$$
and $\qquad \angle ROQ = 3x = 3 \times 36° = 108°$

11. In the figure, two straight lines PQ and RS intersect each other at O. If $\angle POT = 75°$, find the values of a, b and c.

[Board Term I, 2016, Set-JQ22L5C]

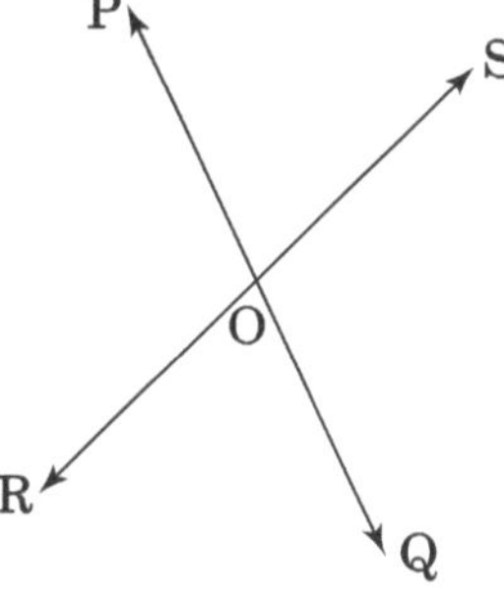

Sol. According to the question;
$$4b + 75 + b = 180°$$
$$\Rightarrow\qquad 5b + 75° = 180°$$
$$\Rightarrow\qquad 5b = 180° - 75° = 105°$$
$$\therefore\qquad b = \frac{105°}{5} = 21°$$

Now, $\qquad 4b = 4 \times 21° = 84°$

[Vertically opposite angle]

$$\therefore\qquad a = 4b = 4 \times 21 = 84°$$
$$2c = 180° - a = 180° - 84°$$
$$\therefore\qquad 2c = 96° \Rightarrow c = 48°$$

12. In the given figure $\angle PQR = \angle PRQ$, then prove that $\angle PQS = \angle PRT$.

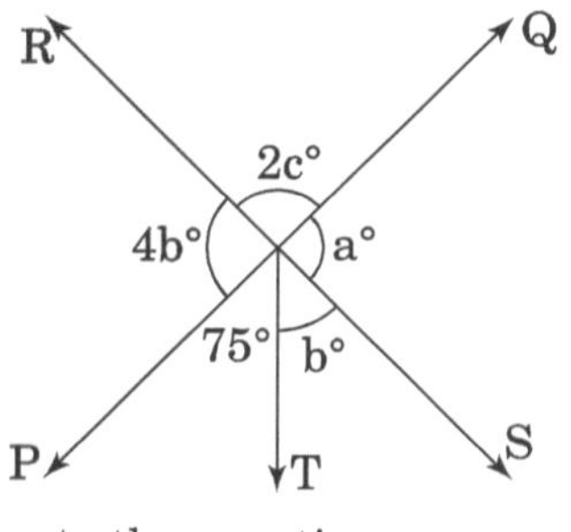

Sol. $\qquad \angle PQS + \angle PQR = 180°$ …(i) (linear pair)
$\qquad \angle PRT + \angle PRQ = 180°$ …(ii) (linear pair)

From eqs. (i) and (ii), we have
$$\angle PQS + \angle PQR = \angle PRT + \angle PRQ$$
$$\therefore\qquad \angle PQS = \angle PRT$$
$$[\because \angle PQR = \angle PRQ\ (\text{given})]$$

Hence proved.

13. The supplement of an angle is one-fifth of itself. Determine the angle and its supplement.

Sol. Let the angel is x and its supplementary angle is $(180° - x)$.

According to question
$$(180° - x) = \frac{1}{5} \times x$$
$$\Rightarrow\qquad 180 = \frac{1}{5}x + x$$
$$\Rightarrow\qquad 180 = \frac{x + 5x}{5}\ \Rightarrow\ \frac{6x}{5} = 180$$
$$\therefore\qquad x = \frac{180 \times 5}{6} = 150°$$

Supplementary angle $\angle x = (180° - 150°) = 30°$

Hence, required angle is 150° and its supplementary angle is 30°

14. Find the measure of an angle, if six times its complement is 12° less than twice its supplement.

Sol. Let the required angle be $x°$.

Then, its supplementary angle be $(180 - x)°$ and its complementary angle be $(90 - x)°$

According to the question,
$$6(90 - x) = 2(180 - x) - 12$$
$$\Rightarrow\qquad 540° - 6x = 360° - 2x - 12°$$
$$\Rightarrow\ 540° - 360° + 12° = 4x$$
$$\Rightarrow\qquad 4x = 192°\ \therefore\ x = 48°$$

Hence, the value of x is 48°.

Long Answer Type Questions
(4 Marks Each)

1. In figure, m and n are two plane mirrors perpendicular to each other, Show that incident ray CA is parallel to reflected ray BD.

   [Board Term I, 2016, Set-JQ22LSC, NCERT Exemplar]

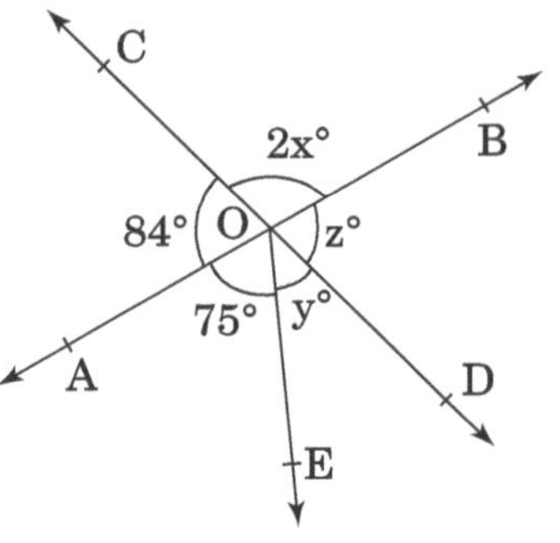

Sol. Let normals at A and B meet at P

then, According to the question

As mirrors are perpendicular at each other there fore BP || OA and AP || OB

So BP $\perp$ PA,

i.e., $\qquad \angle BPA = 90°$

Therefore $\angle 3 + \angle 2 = 90°$ $\qquad$ ...(i)

$\qquad\qquad$ (Angle sum property)

Also, $\qquad \angle 1 = \angle 2$ and $\angle 4 = \angle 3$

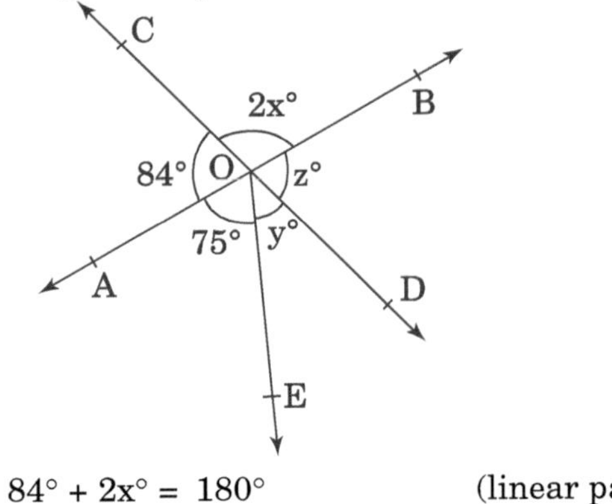

(Angle of incidence = angle of reflection)

Therefore, $\angle 1 + \angle 4 = 90°$ $\qquad$ ...(ii) [from (i)]

On adding eq^n (i) and (ii) we have,

$\Rightarrow \quad \angle 1 + \angle 2 + \angle 3 + \angle 4 = 180°$

$\Rightarrow \qquad \angle CAB + \angle DBA = 180°$

$\therefore$ Sum of interior angles is 180°

Hence $\qquad\qquad$ CA || BD

2. In the given figure, lines AB and CD intersect each other at O. Find the values of x, y and z.

   [Board Term I, 2014]

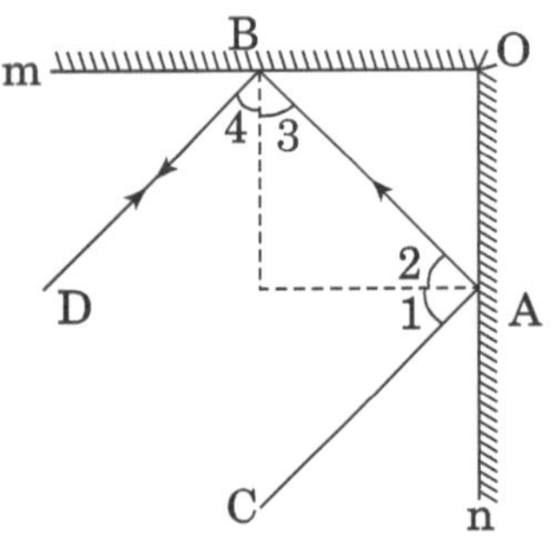

Sol. According to the question

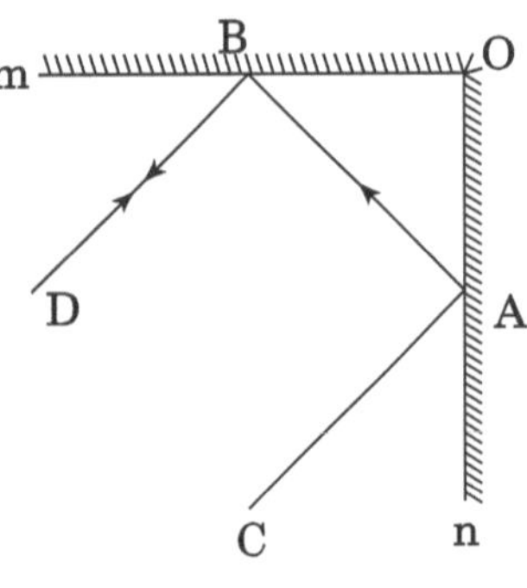

$\qquad 84° + 2x° = 180°$ $\qquad$ (linear pair)

$\Rightarrow \qquad 2x = 96°$

$\therefore \qquad x = \dfrac{96°}{2} = 48°$

Again, $\quad y + 75 = 2x$ (Vertically opposite angle)

or, $\qquad y = 2 \times 48° - 75°$

$\qquad\qquad = 96° - 75° = 21°$

and $\qquad z = 84°$ (Vertically opposite angle)

[Topic 2] Transversal Line
Points to be Remembered

I. A straight line which intersects two or more given lines at distinct points is called a transversal of the given lines.

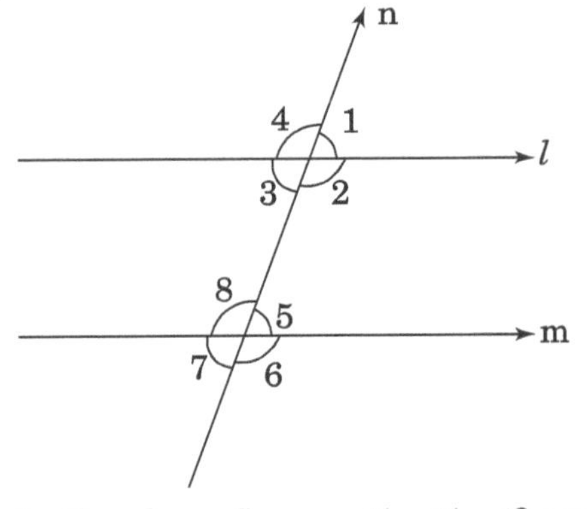

(i) In the above figure, $\angle 1$, $\angle 4$, $\angle 6$ and $\angle 7$ are exterior angles.

(ii) In the given figure, $\angle 2$, $\angle 3$, $\angle 5$ and $\angle 8$ are interior angles.

(iii) **Corresponding Angles :**

$\angle 1 = \angle 5$, $\angle 2 = \angle 6$, $\angle 3 = \angle 7$, $\angle 4 = \angle 8$

(iv) **Alternate Interior Angles:**

$\angle 2 = \angle 8$ and $\angle 3 = \angle 5$

(v) **Alternate Exterior Angles:**

$\angle 1 = \angle 7$ and $\angle 4 = \angle 6$

(vi) **Consecutive Interior Angles.**

$\angle 2 + \angle 5 = \angle 3 + \angle 8 = 180°$

Theorem 1: If a transversal intersects two parallel lines, then each pair of alternate interior angles is equal.

Given: AB || CD and PQ is a transversal line, α and β are alternate interior angles.

To Prove: $\alpha = \beta$

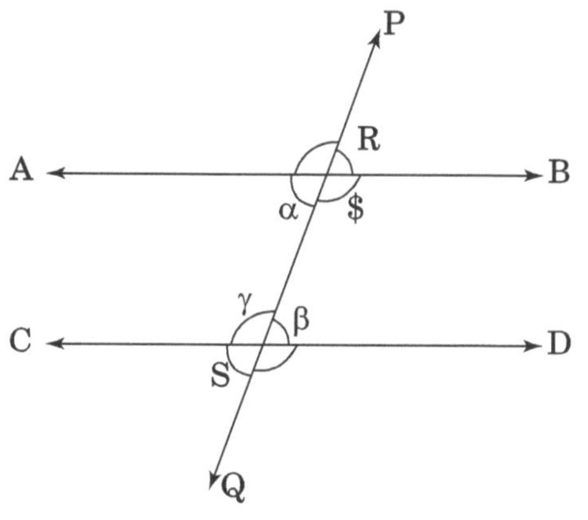

Proof: In the given figure.

$$\angle PRB = \angle RSD = \beta \qquad ...(i)$$
[Corresponding Angles]

and $\qquad \angle PRB = \angle ARS = \alpha \qquad ...(ii)$

[Vertically Opposite Angles]

From equation (i) and (ii), we get

$$\alpha = \beta$$

Similarly, $\qquad \gamma = \$$

Hence, alternate interior angles are equal.

Theorem 2. If a transversal intersects two lines such that a pair of alternate interior angles is equal, then the two lines are parallel.

Theorem 3. If a transversal intersects two lines such that a pair of interior angles on the same side of the transversal is supplementary, then the two lines are parallel.

Theorem 4. If a transversal intersects two parallel lines, then each pair of interior angles on the same side of the transversal is supplementary.

Theorem 5. Lines which are parallel to the same line are parallel to each other.

PREVIOUS YEARS' EXAMINATION QUESTIONS

Topic 2

Multiple Choice Questions (1 Mark Each)

1. In given figure, if OP || RS, $\angle OPQ = 110°$ and $\angle QRS = 130°$, then $\angle PQR$ is equal to

[Board Term I, 2014]

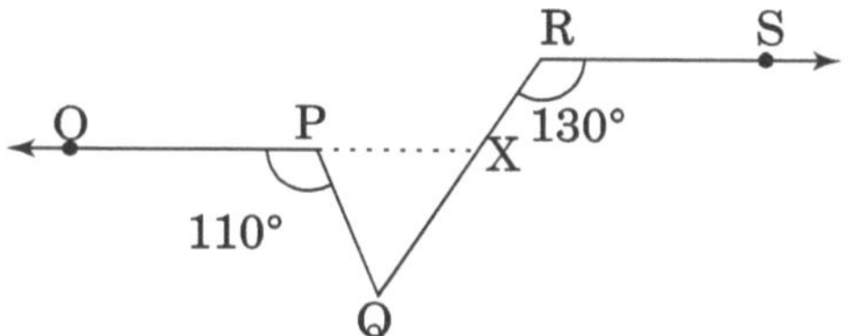

(a) 40° (b) 50°
(c) 60° (d) 70°

Sol. (c) Construction: Draw PX || RS

$\angle XRS = 130°$ (given)

$\angle RXP = 130°$ (alternate angle)

$\therefore \qquad \angle QPX = 180° - 110°$ (Linear pair)

$= 70°$

Now, in the given figure,

$\therefore \quad \angle QXP = 180° - \angle RXP = 180° - 130° = 50°$

In ΔPQX, $\angle QPX + \angle QXP + \angle PQR = 180°$

(angle sum property)

$\Rightarrow \qquad 70° + 50° + \angle PQR = 180°$

$\therefore \qquad \angle PQR = 180° - 120° = 60°$

2. In the given figure, L || M || N. Then value of x is:

(a) 40° (b) 50°
(c) 140° (d) 130°

Sol. (c) According to the given figure,

$\because \qquad L || M || N$

$\therefore \qquad \angle LOP = \angle MPQ = 40°$

[Corresponding Angles]

Now, $\angle MPQ + \angle PQN = 180°$
$\Rightarrow$ $40° + x = 180°$
$\therefore$ $x = 180° - 40° = 140°$

3. In given figure, if AB || CD || EF, PQ || RS, $\angle RQD = 25°$ and $\angle CQP = 60°$, then $\angle QRS$ is equal to

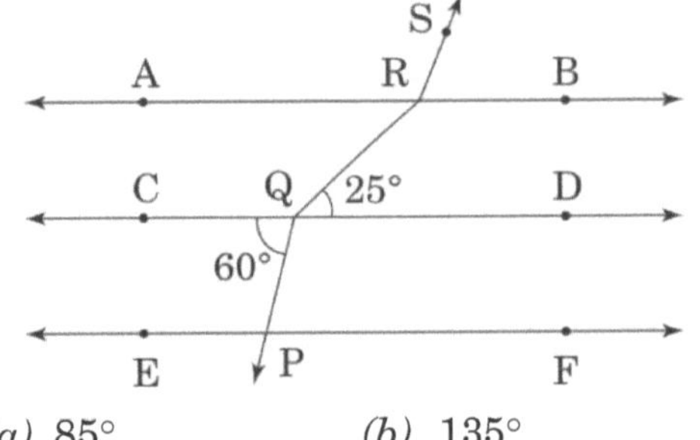

(a) 85° (b) 135°
(c) 145° (d) 110°

Sol. (c) According to the given figure,

PQ || RS

$\therefore$ $\angle BRS = \angle PQC = 60°$ (alternate exterior $\angle s$)

$\angle ARQ = \angle DQR = 25°$ (alternate interior $\angle s$)

$\angle ARS = 180° - \angle BRS$

$= 180° - 60° = 120°$ (linear pair)

Hence, $\angle QRS = \angle ARQ + \angle ARS$

$= 25° + 120° = 145°$

4. In the given figure, p || q. The value of x is:

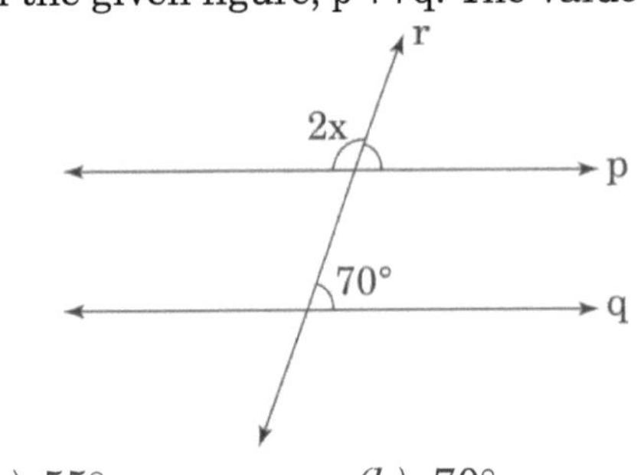

(a) 55° (b) 70°
(c) 35° (d) 110°

Sol. (a) According to the question,

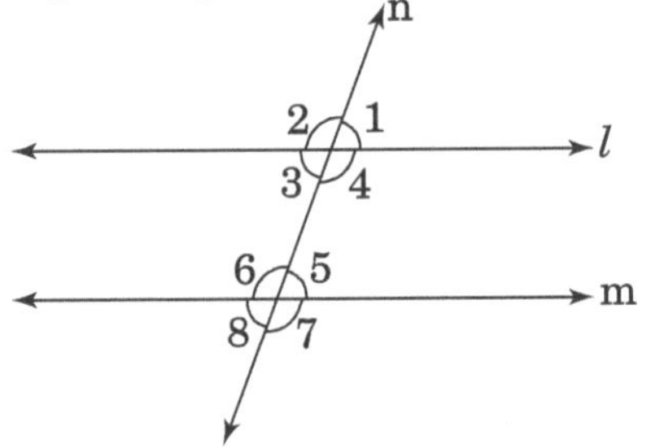

$\therefore$ $\angle QMN = \angle MNO$

(alternate interior angle)

$\therefore$ $y = 70°$

Now, $2x + y = 180°$ (linear pair)
$\Rightarrow$ $2x + 70° = 180°$
$\therefore$ $x = \dfrac{110°}{2} = 55°$

5. In the given figure, $\angle 4$ and $\angle 5$ are known as:

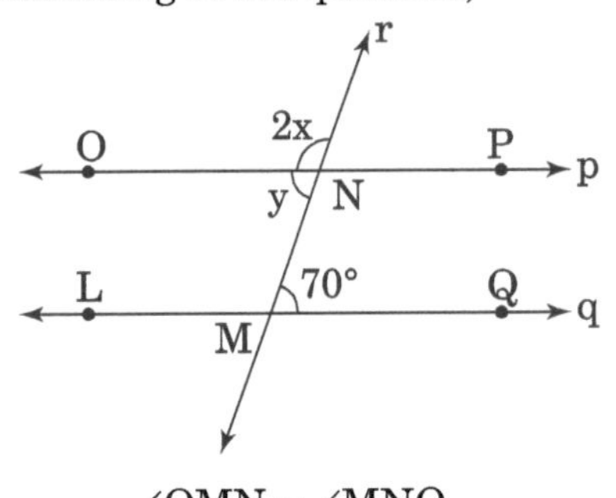

(a) interior angles
(b) alternate angles
(c) corresponding angles
(d) interior angles on the same side of transversal

Sol. (d) $\angle 4$ and $\angle 5$ are known as interior angles on the same side of transversal line

Very Short Answer Type Questions
(1 Mark Each)

1. In the given figure find the value of x for which the lines l and m are parallel.[NCERT Examplar]

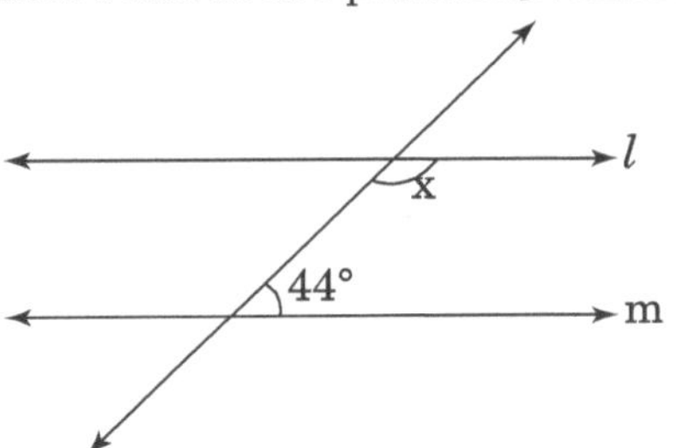

Sol. According to the question, l || m and we know that, if a transversal intersects two parallel lines, then sum of interior angles on the same side of a transversal is supplementary.

$\therefore$ $x + 44° = 180°$
$\Rightarrow$ $x = 180° - 44°$
$= 136°$

2. If a transversal intersects two parallel lines, then which of the pairs of angles is equal.

Sol. If a transversal intersects two parallel lines then pair of alternate interior angles.

3. A transversal l intersects two lines m and n such that a pair of alternate interior angles is equal. Then, what can you say about the lines m and n?

Sol. A transversal l intersects two lines m and n.

∵ Pair of alternate interior angles is equal.

Hence, m and n lines are parallel.

4. In the given figure, If l and m are parallel lines, then find $\angle x$.

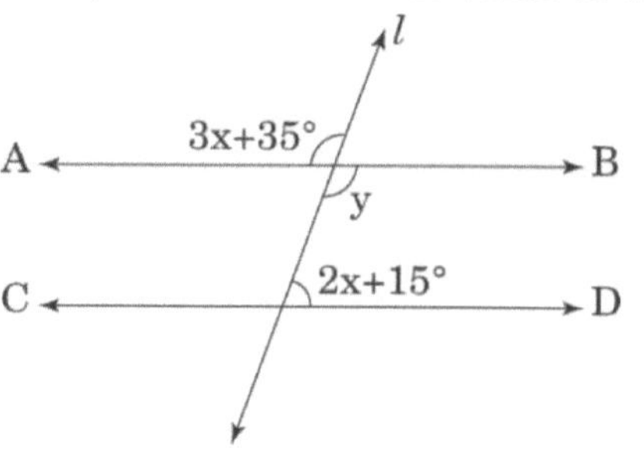

Sol. According to the given figure, $l \parallel m$ and AB is a transversal.

∴ $\angle EBC = 70°$ [by linear pair axiom]

Also EBD is a straight line and BC is a ray stands on it.

∴ $\angle EBC + \angle DBC = 180°$

[by linear pair axiom]

⇒ $70° + \angle DBC = 180°$

⇒ $\angle DBC = 180° - 70°$

$= 110°$

In $\triangle BCD$, we have

$\angle DBC + \angle BCD + \angle BDC = 180°$

[since, sum of all the angles of a triangle is $180°$]

⇒ $110° + 30° + x = 180°$

⇒ $140° + x = 180°$

⇒ $x = 180° - 140°$

∴ $= 40°$

5. In the given figure, PQ $\parallel$ RS and EF $\parallel$ QS. If $\angle PQS = 60°$, then what will be the measure of $\angle RFE$?

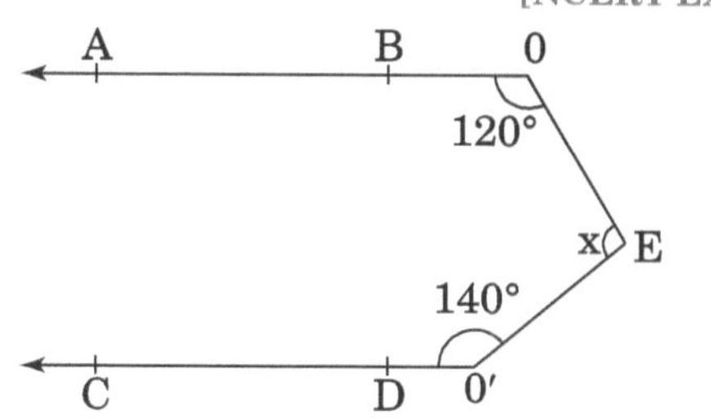

Sol. According to the given figure,

$\angle PQS + \angle QSF = 180°$

(angles on the same side of transversal)

⇒ $\angle PQS + \angle RFE = 180°$, as $\angle QSF = \angle EFR$

⇒ $60° + \angle RFE = 180°$

(Corresponding Angles)

$\angle RFE = 180° - 60°$

$= 120°$

6. In the given figure, AB $\parallel$ CD and 'l' is transversal, then calculate the value of 'x'

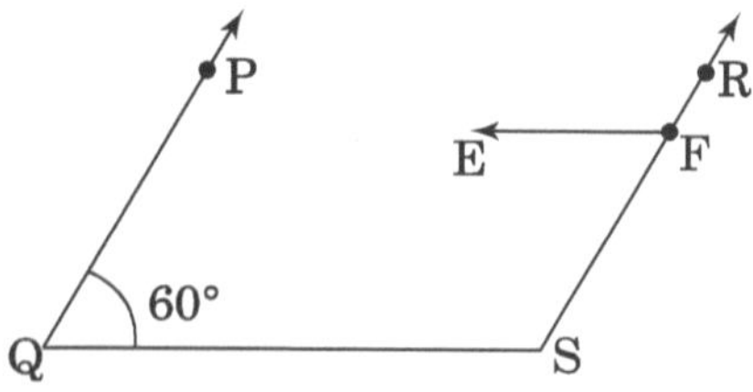

Sol. According to the question,

$y = 3x + 35°$

(Vertically Opposite Angles)

∴ $y + 2x + 15° = 180°$

(Corresponding Interior Angles)

⇒ $3x + 35° + 2x + 15° = 180°$

⇒ $5x + 50° = 180°$

⇒ $5x = 130°$

∴ $x = \dfrac{130°}{5} = 26°$

7. In the given figure AB and CD are parallel to each other, then calculate the value of x.

[NCERT Examplar]

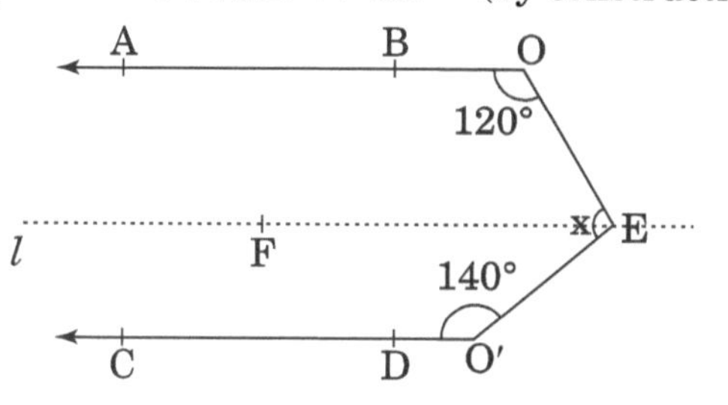

Sol. Let, $l \parallel$ AB $\parallel$ CD   (by construction)

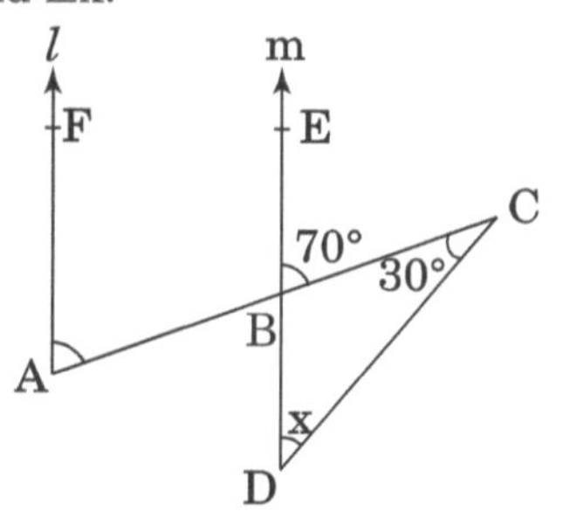

then, According to the given figure,

$\angle OEF + \angle BOE = 180°$

⇒ $\angle O'EF + \angle DO'E = 180°$

[Corresponding Interior Angles]

⇒ $\angle OEF + \angle O'EF + 120° + 140° = 360°$

⇒ $\angle OEO' = 360° - 260°$

∴ $x = 100°.$

8. In figure, if m | | n and $\angle a : \angle b = 2 : 3$, then what will be the measure of $\angle h$?

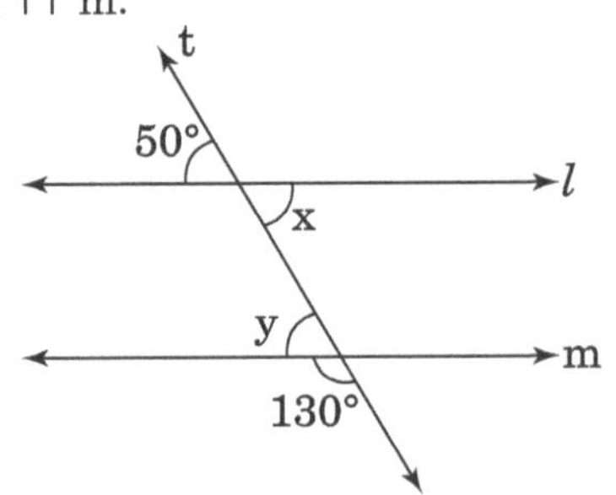

Sol. Let, $\qquad \angle a = 2x$ and $\angle b = 3x$

Then, According to the question,

$$2x + 3x = 180°$$
$$\Rightarrow \qquad 5x = 180°$$
$$\therefore \qquad x = \frac{180°}{5} = 36°$$
$$\therefore \qquad \angle a = 2x = 72°$$

Now, $\qquad \angle h + \angle a = 180°$

$$\therefore \qquad \angle h = 180° - \angle a$$

(Corresponding exterior angles)

$$= 180° - 72° = 108°.$$

Short Answer Type Questions I

(2 Marks Each)

1. In the given figure, if $PQ \perp PS$, PQ | | SR, $\angle SQR = 28°$ and $\angle QRT = 65°$ then find the values of x and y.

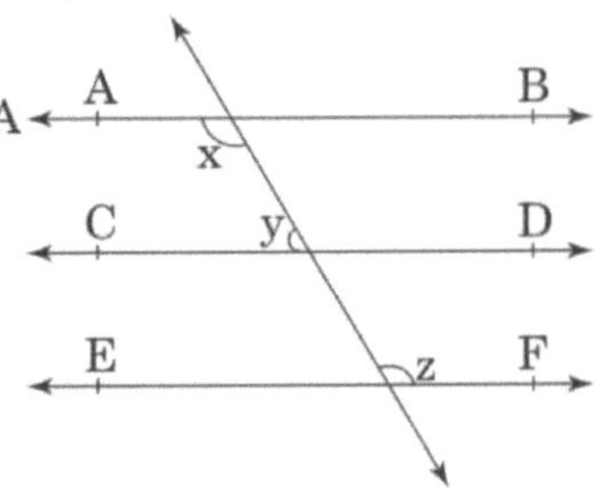

[NCERT]

Sol. For ΔQSR, $\angle QRT$ is an exterior angle.

So, $\qquad \angle QRT = \angle SQR + \angle QSR$

[∵ exterior angle = sum of interior opposite angles]

$$\Rightarrow \qquad 65° = 28° + \angle QSR$$

[∵ $\angle QRT = 65°$ and $\angle SQR = 28°$]

$$\Rightarrow \qquad \angle QSR = 65° - 28°$$
$$\therefore \qquad \angle QSR = 37°$$

Given PQ | | SR and SQ is the transversal which intersects PQ and ST at Q and S, respectively

$$\therefore \qquad \angle QSR = \angle PQS$$

[Alternate Interior angles]

$$\therefore \qquad x = 37°$$

Now, in ΔPQS

$$\angle SPQ + \angle PQS + \angle PSQ = 180°$$

[∵ sum of all the angles of a triangle is 180°]

$$\Rightarrow \qquad 90° + 37° + y = 180°$$

[∵ $PQ \perp PS \Rightarrow \angle SPQ = 90°$]

$$\Rightarrow \qquad 127° + y = 180°$$
$$\therefore \qquad y = 180° - 127° = 53°$$

Hence, x = 37° and y = 53°.

2. In the given figure, if AB | | CD, CD | | EF and $y : z = 3 : 7$, Then find the value of x.   [NCERT]

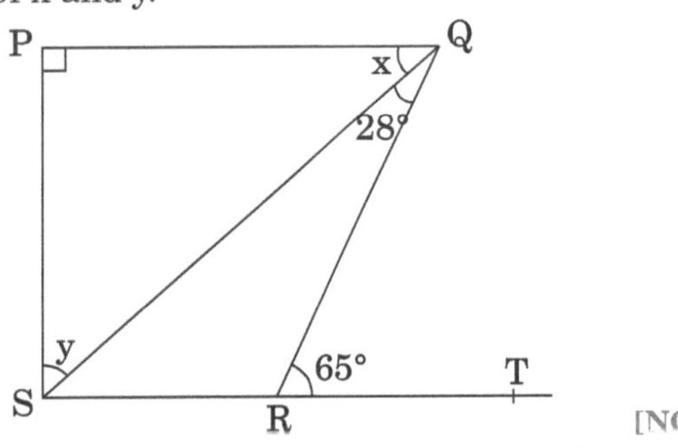

Sol. Given, AB | | CD and CD | | EF

$$\therefore \qquad AB \ | \ | \ EF$$

[∵ lines which are parallel to the same line, are parallel to each other]

Then, $\qquad \angle x = \angle z$ $\qquad$ ...(i)

[alternate interior angels]

Also, given that $y : z = 3 : 7$

$$\Rightarrow \qquad y : x = 3 : 7 \qquad \text{[from eq. (i)]} \ ...(ii)$$

Let $\angle y = 3a$ and $\angle x = 7a$, then

According to the question,

Now, AB | | CD

$$\therefore \qquad \angle x + \angle y = 180°$$

[∵ interior angles are supplementary]

$$\Rightarrow \qquad 7a + 3a = 180°$$
$$\Rightarrow \qquad 10a = 180°$$
$$\therefore \qquad a = \frac{180°}{10} = 18°$$
$$\therefore \qquad x = 7a$$
$$= (7 \times 18)° = 126°$$

Hence, the value of x = 126°.

3. In the given figure, find x and y and then show that l | | m.

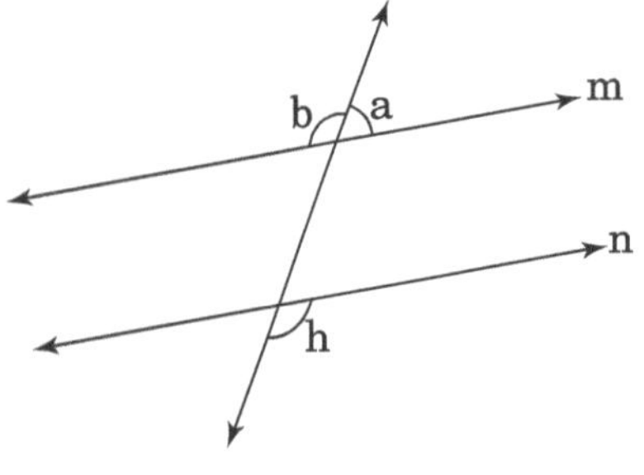

[Board Term I, 2012, Set-45; 2011, Set-30; 2010, Set-B1]

Sol. According to the question,

$$x = 50° \quad \text{(Vertically opposite angles)}$$

and $\quad y + 130° = 180° \quad$ (linear pair)

$$\therefore \quad y = 180° - 130°$$
$$= 50°$$
$$\therefore \quad x = y = 50°$$

But x and y are alternate angles and they are equal.

Hence, lines l and m are parallel.

4. In the figure, AB || DE, $\angle ABC = 140°$ and $\angle CDE = 100°$. Find $\angle BCD$.

[Board Term I, 2013; 2012, Set-54; 2011, Set- 30]

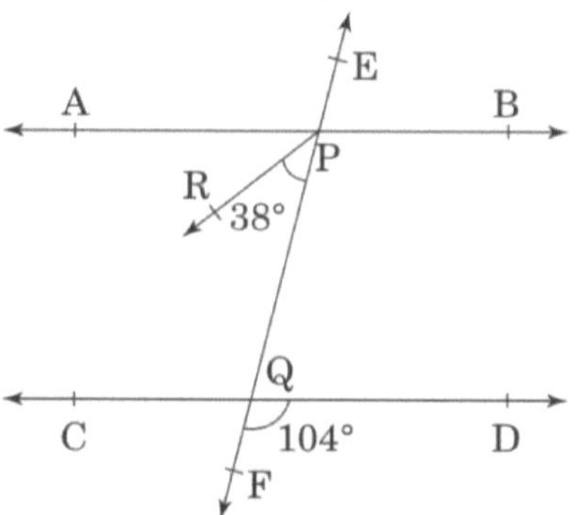

Sol. In the given figure, draw a line l parallel to line AB, then

$\because \qquad\qquad$ AB|| DE

$\therefore \qquad\qquad\ l$ || DE

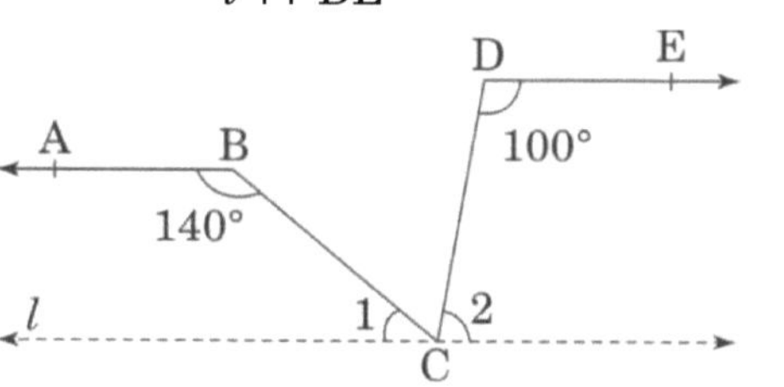

$$\angle 1 + \angle 140° = 180° \text{ (consecutive interior angles)}$$
$$\angle 1 = 180° - 140° = 40°$$

Similarly,

$$\angle 2 = 80°$$
$$\angle 1 + \angle BCD + \angle 2 = 180° \quad \text{(Linear pair)}$$
$$\Rightarrow \quad 40° + \angle BCD + 80° = 180$$
$$\therefore \angle BCD = 180° - 40° - 80° = 60°$$

5. In the figure PR is the angle bisector of $\angle APQ$. Prove that AB || CD. [Board Term I, 2012, Set-20]

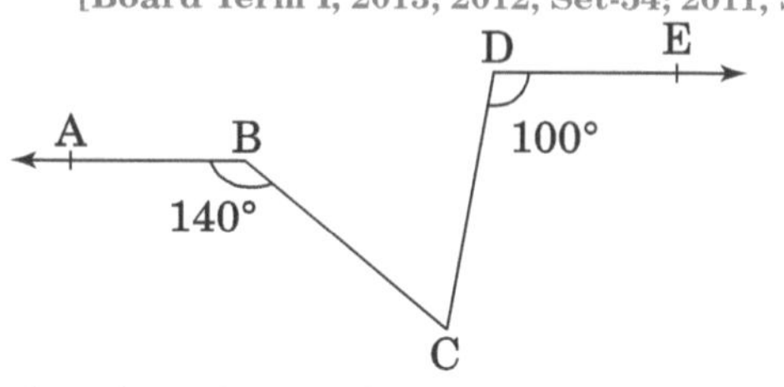

Sol. According to the given figure

$$\angle APR = \angle RPQ = 38°$$

(Angle bisector)

$\therefore \qquad\qquad \angle APQ = 38° + 38° = 76°$

$$\angle FQD = \angle PQC = 104°$$

(Vertically opposite angles)

$$\angle APQ + \angle PQC = 76° + 104° = 180°$$

$\therefore \qquad\qquad$ AB || CD

Hence proved.

6. In the figure AB || CD, find the value of z, $\angle DNM$ and $\angle CNM$.

[Board Term I, 2012, Set-4]

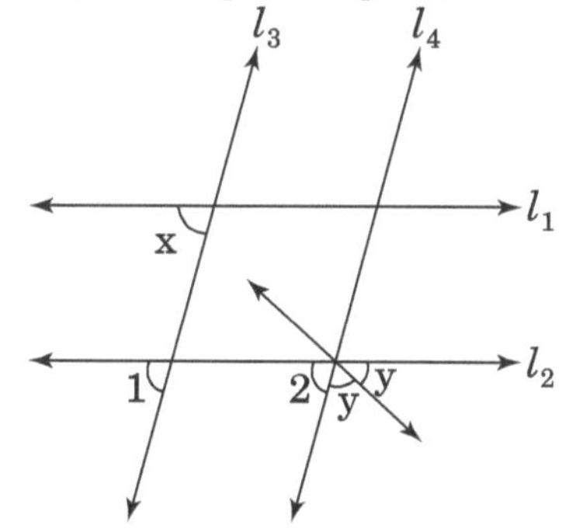

Sol. According to the given figure

$$3z - 42° = 2z + 13°$$

(Alternate interior angles)

$$\Rightarrow \quad 3z - 2z = 13° + 42°$$
$$\therefore \quad z = 55°$$
$$\therefore \quad \angle DNM = 2z + 13° - 110° + 13° = 123°$$

and $\quad \angle CNM = 180° = \angle DNM \quad$ (Linear pair)

$$= 180° - 123° = 57°$$

7. In the given figure if $l_1 || l_2$ and $l_3 || l_4$, what is y in terms of x? [NCERT Examplar]

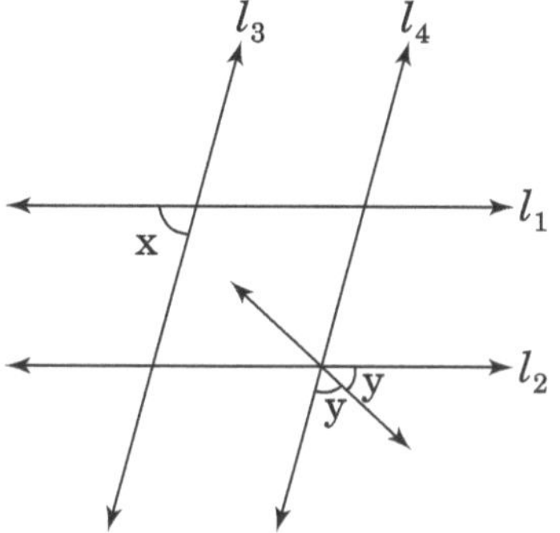

Sol. According to the given figure,

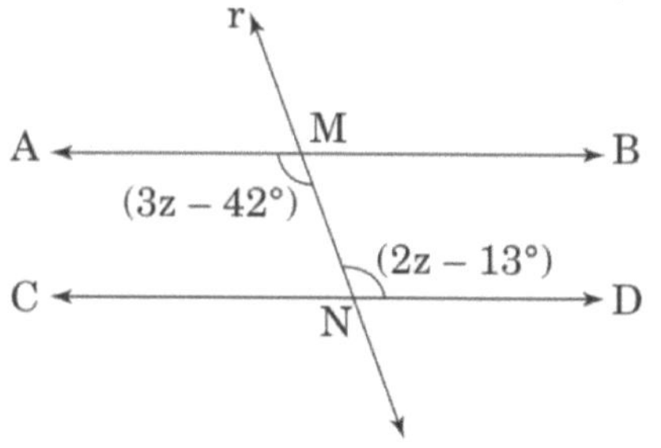

$$x = \angle 1 \qquad \text{(Corresponding angles)}$$
$$\angle 2 = \angle 1 \qquad \text{(Corresponding angles)}$$
$$\therefore \qquad x = \angle 2$$

$$\therefore \quad \angle 2 + 2y = 180°$$
$$\Rightarrow \quad x + 2y = 180°$$
$$\Rightarrow \quad 2y = 180° - x$$
$$\therefore \quad y = \frac{180° - x}{2} = 90° - \frac{x}{2}$$

8. Find the supplement of $\frac{4}{3}$ of a right angle.

[Board Term,I, 2012, Set-41]

Sol. $\frac{4}{3}$ of a right angle $= \frac{4}{3} \times 90° = 120°$

∵ Sum of supplementary angles is 180°

∴ Supplement of $120° = 180° - 120° = 60°$

9. In the figure AB || DC. Determine x.

[Board Term,I, 2012, Set-53]

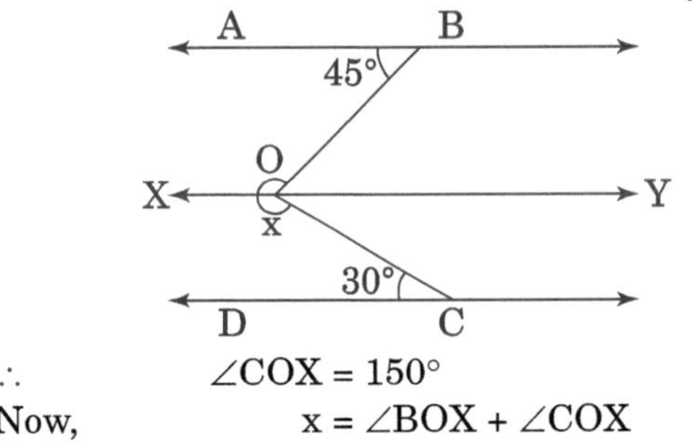

Sol. In the given figure, we draw a line XY parallel to AB, then
$$45° + \angle BOX = 180°$$
(Consecutive Interior Angles)
$$\therefore \quad \angle BOX = 180° - 45° = 135°$$
$$\angle COX + 30° = 180° \text{ (Consecutive Interior}$$
$$\text{Angles)}$$

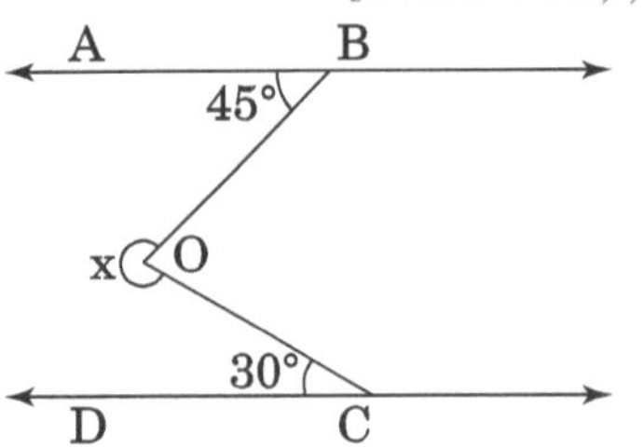

$$\therefore \quad \angle COX = 150°$$
Now, $\qquad x = \angle BOX + \angle COX$
$$= 135° + 150° = 285°$$

10. In the given figure m || n and p || q. If $\angle 1 = 75°$, then prove that $\angle 2 = \angle 1 + \frac{1}{3}$ of right angel.

[Board Term,I, 2012, Set-45]

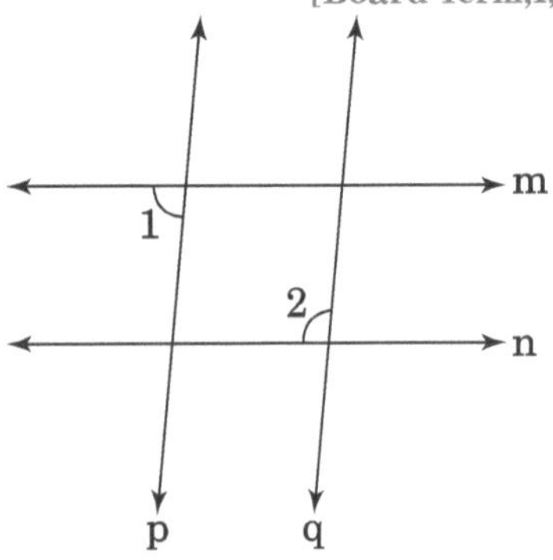

Sol. Given, m || n and p || q and $\angle 1 = 75°$

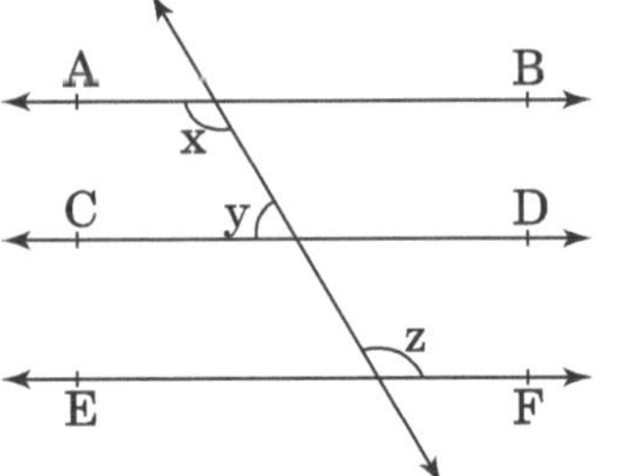

∴ $\qquad \angle 1 = y = 75°$ (Alternate Angles)

and $\qquad \angle 2 = 180° - y = 180° - 75° = 105°$
$$\angle 2 = 105° = 75° + 30°$$
$$= 75° + \frac{1}{3} \times 90°$$

∴ $\qquad \angle 2 = \angle 1 + \frac{1}{3}$ of right angle

Hence proved.

11. In the given figure, state which lines are parallel and why? [Board Term,I, 2012, Set-45]

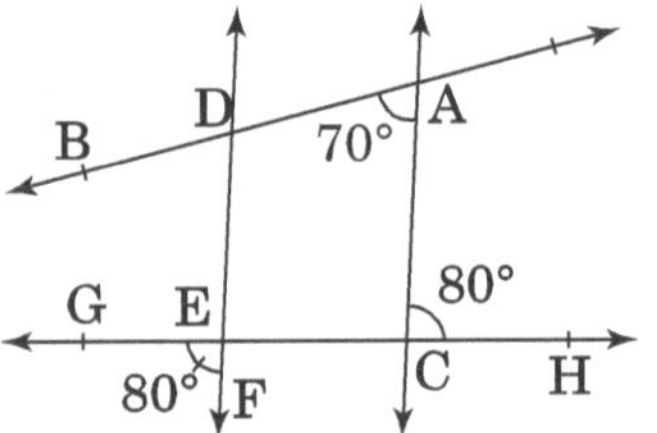

Sol. $\qquad \angle DEC = \angle GEF = 80°$
(Vertically opposite angles)
$$\angle ACH = 80° \qquad\qquad \text{(given)}$$
∴ $\qquad \angle DEC = \angle ACH = 80°$

∵ Corresponding angles $\angle DEC$ and $\angle ACH$ are equal.

Hence, AC || DF

12. In figure if AB || CD || EF and $x : y = 3 : 2$, find z. [Board Term,I, 2012, Set-14]

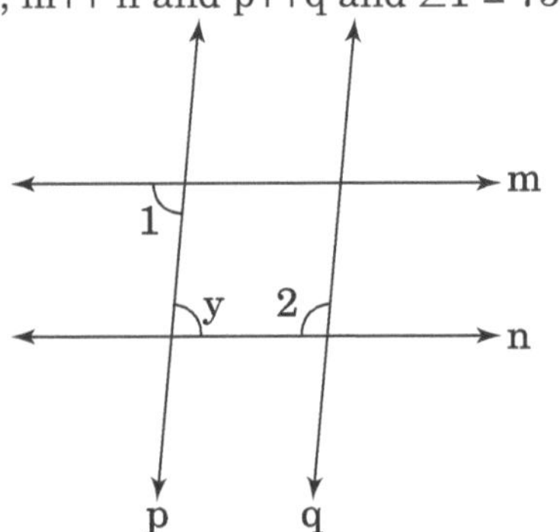

Sol. Let $\qquad x = 3k$ and $y = 2k$

Then, According to the question,
$$x + y = 3k + 2k = 180°$$
(Angles on the same side of transversal)
$$\Rightarrow \qquad 5k = 180°$$

or,
$$k = \frac{180°}{5} = 36°$$

$\therefore$ $x = 3k = 108°$
and $y = 2k = 72°$
Thus, $\angle z = \angle x = 108°$
(Alternate interior angles)

Hence, the value of $z = 108°$

13. In the given figure show that AB || EF.

[Board Term,I, 2012, Set-48]

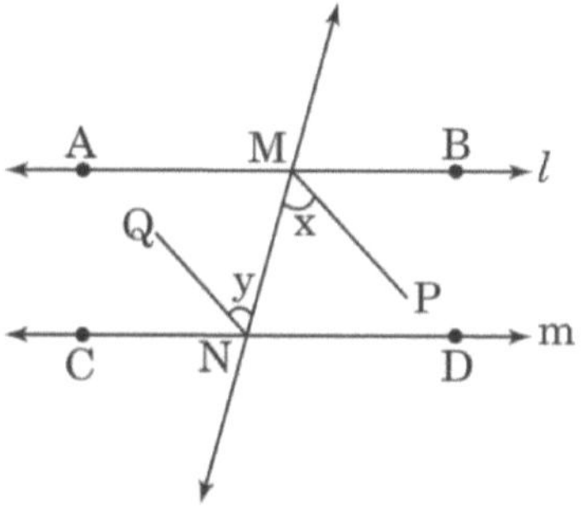

Sol. According to the given figure
$$\angle FEC + \angle DCE = 155° + 25° = 180°$$
(Angles on the same side of transversal)

$\therefore$ EF || CD

$\therefore$ $\angle BCD = \angle BCE + \angle ECD$
$$= 35° + 25°$$
$$= 60° = \angle ABC$$
(Alternate Angles)

$\therefore$ AB || CD
and   AB || CD || EF
$\therefore$ AB || EF

Hence Proved.

14. If a transversal intersects two parallel lines, Then the bisectors of any pair of alternate angles are parallel. Prove it.

[Board Term,I, 2016, 2012, Set-7 AEDLQR, 40]

Sol. According to the question

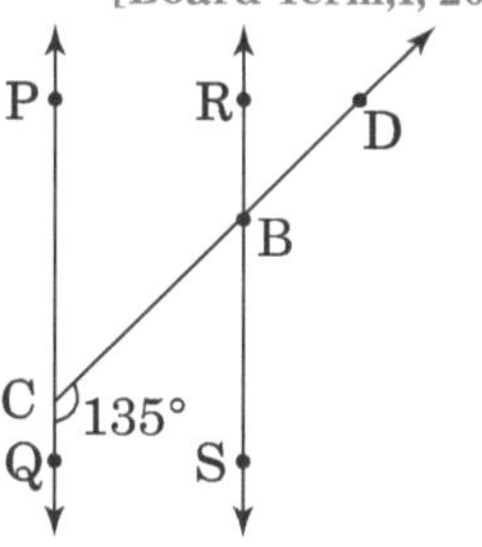

$\angle BMN = \angle CNM$ (Alternate angles)

$\therefore$ $\dfrac{1}{2}\angle BMN = \dfrac{1}{2}\angle CNM$

$\therefore$ $x = y$

(But x and y are alternate angles.)
$\therefore$ MP || NQ
Hence proved.

15. In the figure, l || m and n || p. If $\angle 1 = 60°$, then prove that $\angle 2 = 2\angle 1$.   [Board Term,I, 2015, Set-2]

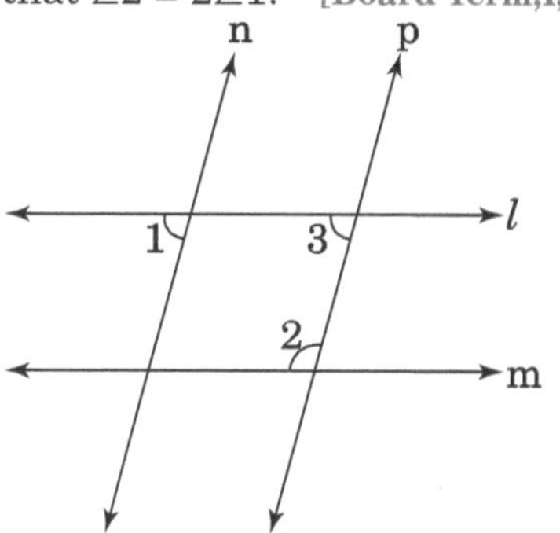

Sol. According to the given figure
$\because$ n || p
$$\angle 3 = \angle 1 = 60°$$
(Corresponding angles)
and $\angle 2 + \angle 3 = 180°$ (Interior angles sum)
$\Rightarrow$ $\angle 2 + 60° = 180°$ ($\because$ $\angle 3 = 60°$)
$\therefore$ $\angle 2 = 120° = 2 \times 60° = 2\angle 1$
Hence, proved.

16. In the figure PQ || RS, CBD is a transversal and $\angle BCQ = 135°$. Find $\angle RBD$.

[Board Term,I, 2016, Set-20CNJE9]

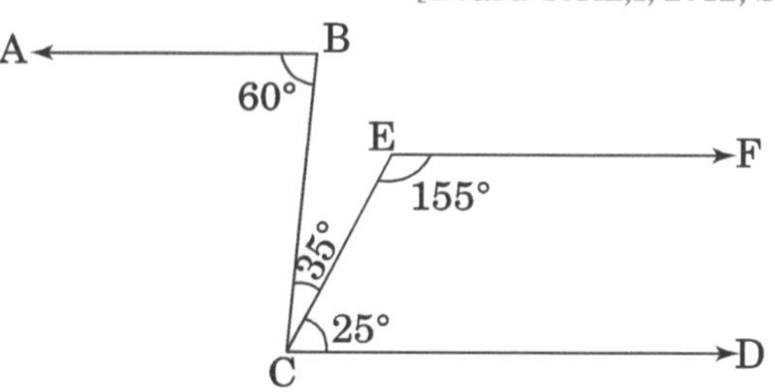

Sol. According to the question,
$\because$ RS || PQ
$\therefore$ $\angle DBS = \angle BCQ = 135°$
[Corresponding angles]
$$\angle RBD = 180° - \angle DBS \text{ (linear pair)}$$
$$= 180° - 135° = 45°$$

Hence, $\angle RBD = 45°$

17. In the figure AB || CD, $\angle ABP = 30°$ and $\angle CDP = 40°$, find x. [Board Term,I, 2016, Set-JQ2215C]

Sol. Draw l | | AB or CD through P

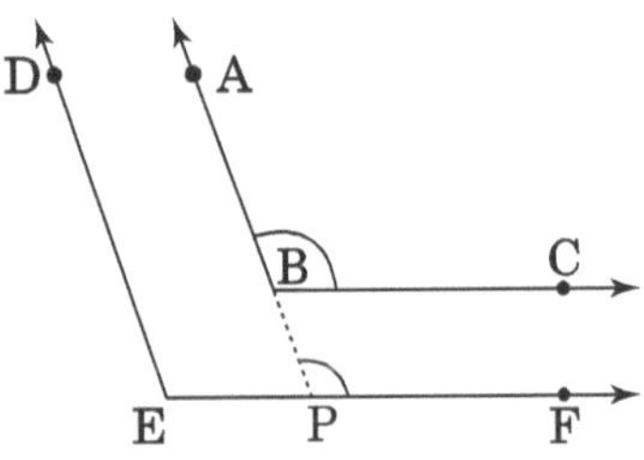

∵   AB | | PQ

∴   ∠ABP = ∠BPQ = 30°

(Alternate interior angles)

∵   PQ | | CD

also   ∠PDC = ∠QPD = 40°

(Alternate interior angles)

∴   x = ∠BPQ + ∠QPD

= 30° + 40°

= 70°

Hence, the value of x = 70°

18. In given figure, BA | | ED and BC | | EF. Show that ∠ABC = ∠DEF.

[Board Term,I, 2016, Set-BQS61ZK]

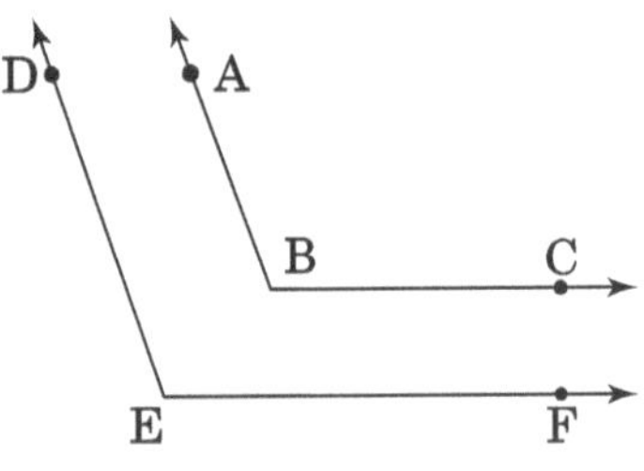

Sol. According to the question

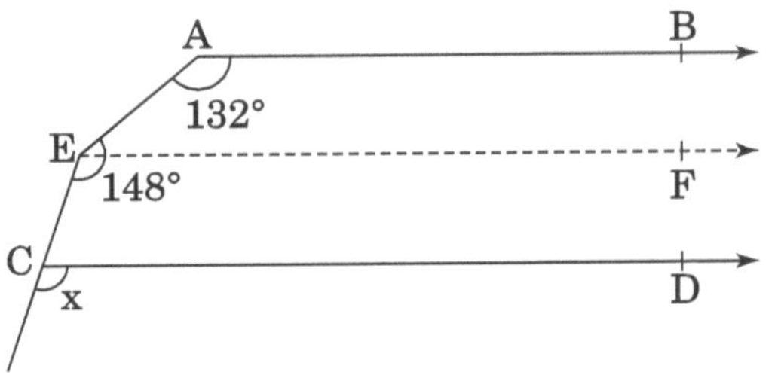

Extend AB to meet EF in P

∠ABC = ∠APE   ...(i)

(Corresponding angles)

Now, ∠DEF = ∠APF   ...(ii)

(Corresponding anlges)

From eq^n (i) and (ii), we get

∠ABC = ∠DEF

Hence proved.

19. In the given figure, find the angles a and b and then show that LM | | XY.

[Board Term,I, 2016, Set-QGL21F5]

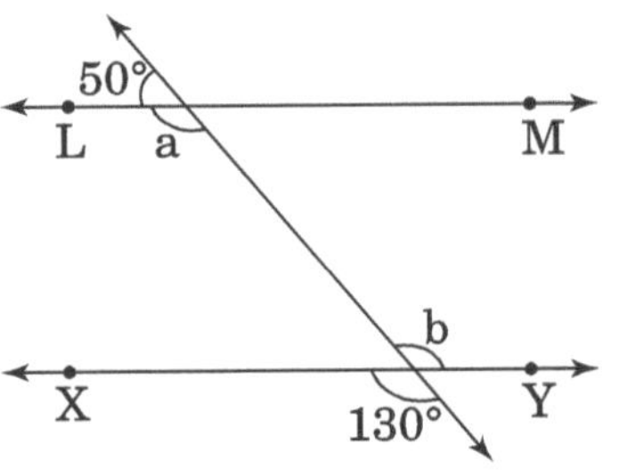

Sol. According to the given figure,

∠a = 180° − 50° = 130°   (Linear pair)

and   ∠b = 130°

Vertically opposite angles

∴   ∠a = ∠b

But they are alternate interior angles,

Hence, LM | | XY

20. In the given figure. If AB | | CD, then find the value of x.

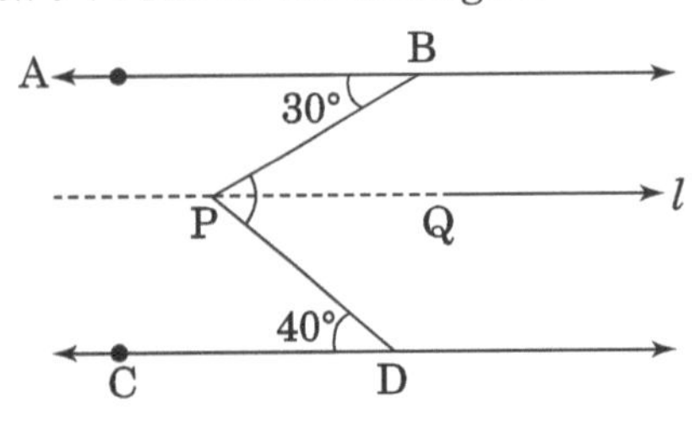

Sol. Draw a line EF | | AB | | CD. Since, AB| | EF and AE is a transversal.

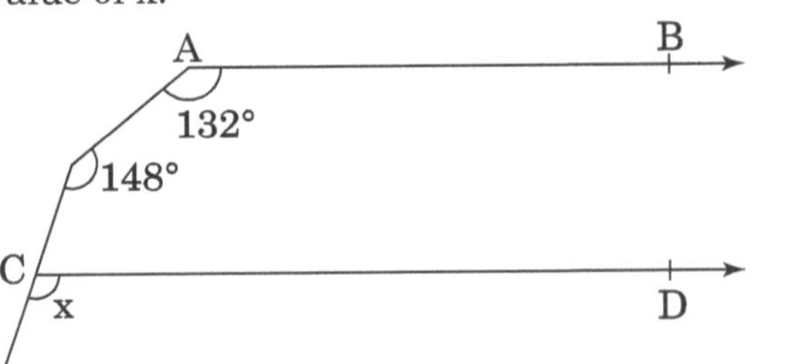

Now, in the given figure,

∴   ∠BAE + ∠AEF = 180°   [co-interior angles]

⇒   132° + ∠AEF = 180°

⇒   ∠AEF = 180° − 132° = 48°

Now,   ∠FEC = ∠AEC − ∠AEF

= 148° − 48°

= 100°

Since, EF | | CD and EC is a transversal.

∴   ∠FEC = ∠x = 100°

[by corresponding angles axiom]

Short Answer Type Questions II

(3 Marks Each)

1. A transversal intersects two parallel lines. Prove that the bisectors of any pair of corresponding angles, so formed are parallel.

   [NCERT Examplar]

Sol. Let Two lines AB and CD are parallel and intersected by transversal t at p and q, respectively. EP and FQ bisect the corresponding angles $\angle$APG and $\angle$CQP, respectively.

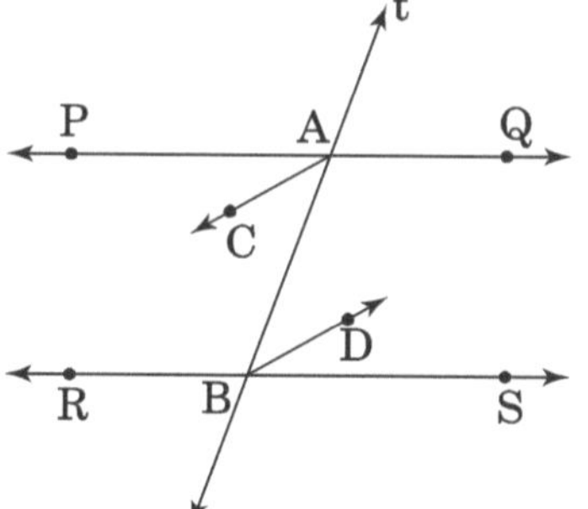

To prove : EP | | FQ

Given AB | | CD

$\therefore$ $\qquad$ $\angle$APG | | $\angle$CQP

$\qquad\qquad$ [corresponding angles]

$\Rightarrow$ $\qquad$ $\dfrac{1}{2}$ ($\angle$APG) = $\dfrac{1}{2}$ ($\angle$CQP)

$\qquad\qquad$ [dividing both sides by 2]

$\Rightarrow$ $\qquad$ $\angle$EPG = $\angle$FQP

But these are corresponding angles.

$\therefore$ $\qquad$ EP | | FQ

$\qquad$ [converse of corresponding angle axiom]

Hence proved.

2. If a transversal intersects two parallel lines, Then prove that bisectors of alternate interior angles are in parallel.

   [Board Term I, 2016, Set-7AEDLQR, NCERT Exemplar]

Sol. Let two lines PQ and RS are parallel and intersected by a transversal t at A and B respectively. AC and BD are the trisector of a pair of alternate interior angles, $\angle$PAB and $\angle$ABS, respectively.

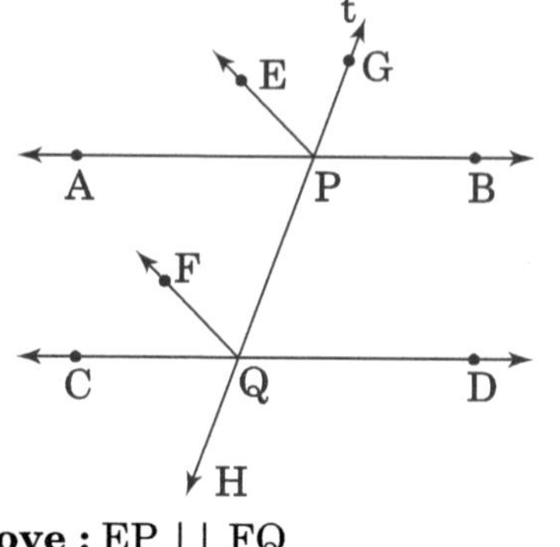

To prove : AC | | BD

Since PQ | | RS and t is transversal we have

$\qquad\qquad$ $\angle$PAB = $\angle$ABS

$\qquad\qquad$ [Alternate interior angles]

$\Rightarrow$ $\qquad$ $\dfrac{1}{2}$ $\angle$PAB = $\dfrac{1}{2}$ $\angle$ABS

$\qquad\qquad$ [on dividing both sides by 2]

$\therefore$ $\qquad$ $\angle$CAB = $\angle$ABD

But these are alternate interior angles.

$\therefore$ $\qquad$ AC | | BD

Hence Proved.

3. In figure., AB | | CD, CD | | EF. EA $\perp$ AB. If $\angle$BEF = 55°, find the value of x, y, and z.

   [Board Term I, 2011, Set-41, Set-16]

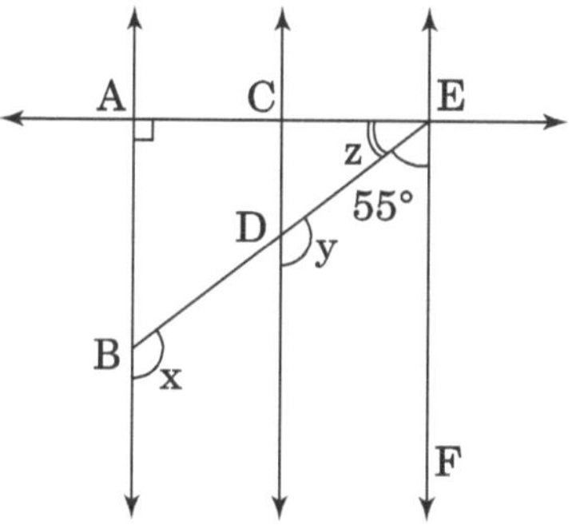

Sol. According to the question,

AB | | CD, CD | | EF, EA $\perp$ AB and $\angle$BEF = 55°

$\qquad$ $\angle$BEF + y = 180°

$\qquad\qquad$ [consecutive interior angles]

$\Rightarrow$ $\qquad$ 55° + y = 180°

$\therefore$ $\qquad$ y = 180° − 55° − 125°

$\therefore$ $\qquad$ x = y = 125°

$\qquad\qquad$ (Correspoinding angles)

$\qquad$ EA $\perp$ AB

Now,

$\because$ $\qquad$ EF $\perp$ EA

$\therefore$ $\qquad$ Z + 55° = 90°

$\therefore$ $\qquad$ Z = 90° − 55° = 35°

4. In the given figure, QP | | ML, find the value of x,

   [Board Term I, 2013; 2012, Set-52; 2011, Set-44]

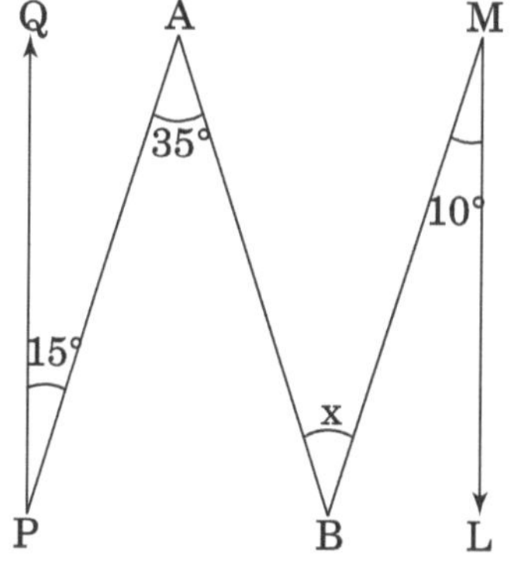

Sol. Extend the lines PQ, AB and ML as given below in the figure,

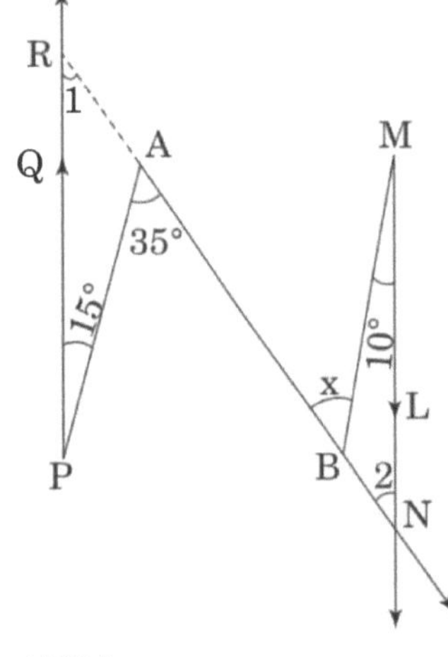

Now In $\triangle$PRA,

$$\angle 1 + 15° = 35°$$
$$\therefore \qquad \angle 1 = 35° - 15° = 20°$$

Similarly, in $\triangle$MNB,

$$\angle 2 + 10° = x$$
$$\therefore \qquad \angle 2 = x - 10° \qquad\qquad …(i)$$

But PR | | MN

$$\therefore \qquad \angle 1 = \angle 2$$
$$\text{and} \qquad \angle 1 = 20°$$
$$\therefore \qquad \angle 2 = 20° \ \text{(Alternate interior angles)}$$

From equation (i),

$$\Rightarrow \qquad x - 10 = 20°$$
$$\therefore \qquad x = 20° + 10 = 30°$$

5. In the figure, AB | | CD, EF | | DQ. Determine $\angle$PDQ, $\angle$AED and $\angle$DEF.

[Board Term I, 2012, Set-50]

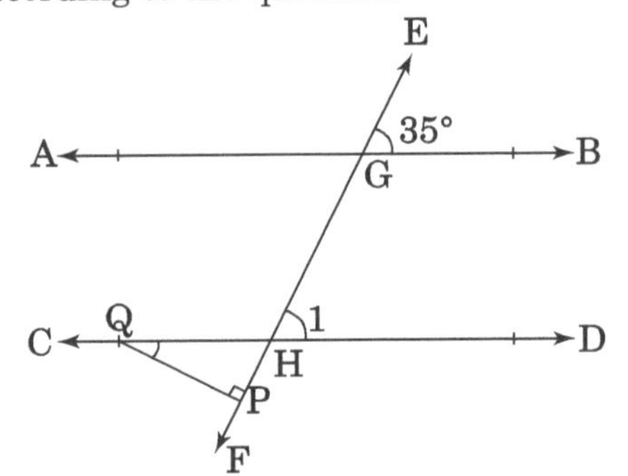

Sol. According to the question,

$$\because \qquad CD \ | | \ AE$$
$$\angle AED = \angle CDP = 43°$$
$$\text{(Corresponding angles)}$$
$$\angle AED + \angle DEF + \angle BEF = 180° \ \text{[Linear pair]}$$
$$\Rightarrow \qquad 43° + \angle DEF + 65° = 180°$$
$$\therefore \qquad \angle DEF = 180° - 108° = 72°$$
$$\because \qquad DQ \ | | \ EF$$
$$\therefore \qquad \angle PDQ = \angle DEF = 72°$$
$$\text{(Corresponding angles)}$$

6. In the given figure., if AB | | CD, $\angle$BPQ = $(5x - 20°)$ and $\angle$PQD = $(2x - 10°)$, find the value of y and z.

[Board Term I, 2012, Set-49]

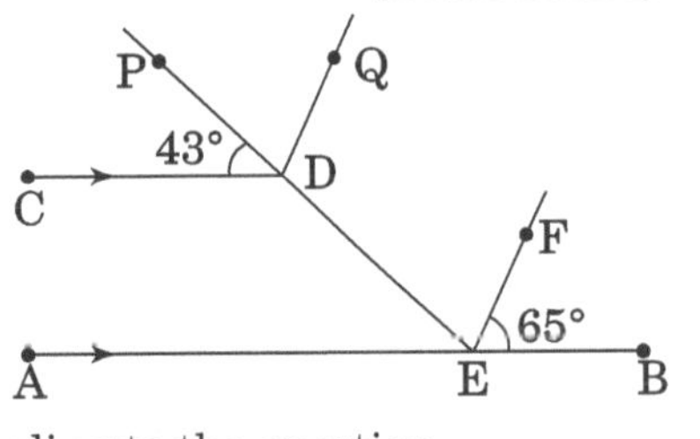

Sol. According to the question,

$$\because \qquad\qquad AB \ | | \ CD$$
$$5x - 20° + 2x - 10° = 180°$$
$$\text{(sum of consecutive interior angles)}$$
$$\Rightarrow \qquad 7x = 180° + 30° = 210°$$
$$\therefore \qquad x = 30°$$
$$5x - 20° + y = 180° \qquad\qquad \text{[Linear pair]}$$
$$\therefore \qquad y = 180° - (5x - 20°)$$
$$= 180° - (5° \times 30° - 20°)$$
$$= 180° - (150° - 20)$$
$$= 180° - 130° = 50$$
$$\text{and} \qquad z = 2x - 10°$$
$$\text{(vertically opposite angles)}$$
$$= 60° - 10° = 50°$$

7. In the given figure, AB | | CD and EF is a transversal intersecting them at G and H respectively. If $\angle$EGB = 35° and QP $\perp$ EF, then find $\angle$PQH.

[Board Term I, 2012, Set-45]

Sol. According to the question.

$$\because \qquad AB \parallel CD$$
$$\therefore \qquad \angle BGE = \angle GHD$$
$$\therefore \qquad \angle 1 = 35°$$
(Corresponding angles)
$$\angle QHP = 35°$$
(Vertically opposite angles)

In $\triangle PQH$,
$$\angle PQH + \angle QHP + \angle HPQ = 180°$$
[Sum of angles of a triangle]
$$\Rightarrow \quad \angle PQH + 35° + 90° = 180°$$
$$\Rightarrow \quad \angle PQH + 125° = 180°$$
$$\therefore \qquad \angle PQH = 180° - 125° = 55°$$

8. In the given figure l $\parallel$ m $\parallel$ n. From the figure, find the ratio of $(x + y) : (y - x)$.

[Board Term I, 2012, Set-51]

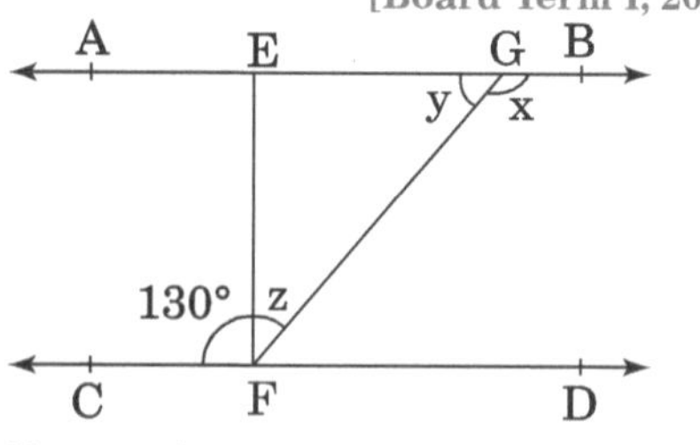

Sol. According the question,
$$30° + y° + 20° = 180° \qquad \text{[Linear Pair]}$$
$$y = 180° - (30° + 20°) = 2300$$
$$\because \qquad l \parallel m$$
$$\therefore \qquad x = 180° - 100° = 80°$$
$$x + y = 210° \text{ and } y - x = 50°$$
Hence $(x + y) : (y - x) = 21 : 5$

9. In the figure, AB $\parallel$ CD, EF $\perp$ CD and $\angle GFC = 130°$. Find x , y, and z.

[Board Term I, 2012, Set-53]

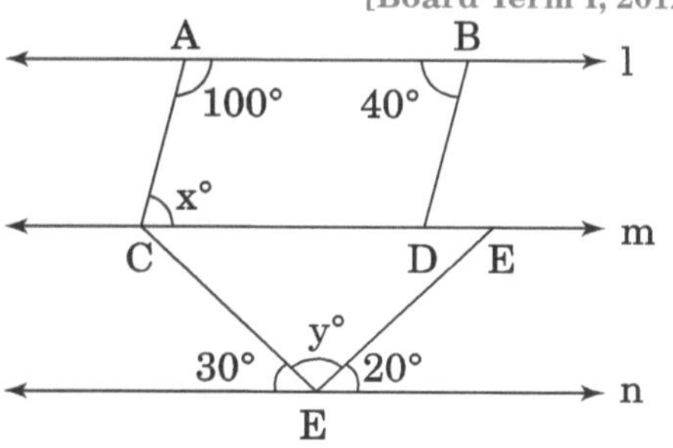

Sol. According to the question,
$$\therefore \qquad EF \perp CD$$
$$\therefore \qquad \angle CFE = 90°$$
$$\text{and} \qquad 90° + z = \angle CFG$$
$$\therefore \qquad z = 130° - 90° = 40°$$
$$x = \angle CFG$$
[Alternate interior angels]
$$= 130°$$
$$\text{Now,} \qquad x + y = 180° \qquad \text{(Linear pair)}$$
$$\Rightarrow \qquad 130° + y = 180°$$
$$\therefore \qquad y = 180° - 130° = 50°$$

10. In figure, a transversal l cuts two lines AB and CD at E and F respectively. EG is the bisector of $\angle AEF$ and FH is the bisector of $\angle EFD$ such that $\angle a = \angle b$. Show that EG $\parallel$ FH and AB $\parallel$ CD.

[Board Term I, 2014]

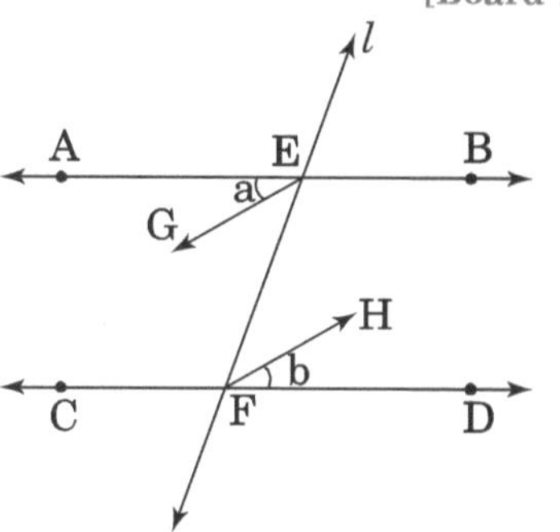

Sol. According to the given figure,
EG is the bisector of $\angle AEF$
$$\therefore \qquad \angle AEG = \angle GEF = a$$
Similarly, $\quad \angle EFH = \angle HFD = b$
$$\therefore \qquad \angle GEF = \angle EFH \qquad (\because \quad a = b)$$
$\because \angle GEF$ and $\angle EFH$ are alternate interior angles.
$$\therefore \qquad EG \parallel FH$$
Again, $\qquad \angle AEF = 2a$
and $\qquad \angle EFD = 2b$
$$\therefore \qquad \angle AEF = \angle EFD = 2a \quad \text{or} \quad 2b$$
$\because \angle AEF$ and $\angle EFD$ are alternate interior angles.
$$\therefore \qquad AB \parallel CD.$$
Hence proved.

11. In figure, AB $\parallel$ CD, then find x.

[Board Term I, 2014, Set-7AEDLQR, 2013]

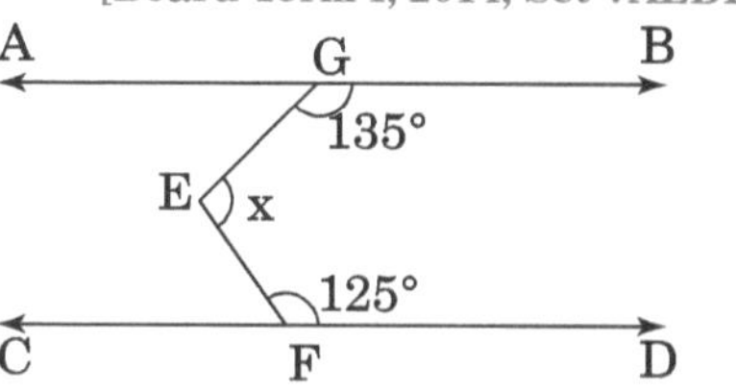

Sol. On drawing a line EH parallel to AB as given below.

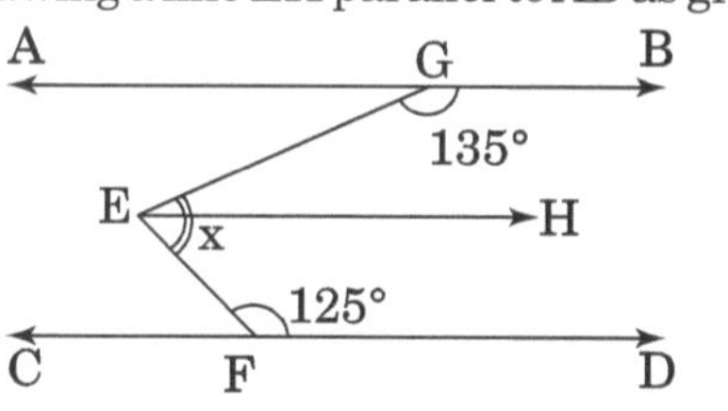

Now, EH $\parallel$ AB and AB $\parallel$ CD.
Therefore, $\qquad$ EH $\parallel$ CD
Now, $\quad \angle BGE + \angle GEH = 180°$
(Sum of consecutive angles)
(AB $\parallel$ EH, Sum of consecutive angles)
$$\Rightarrow \quad 135° + \angle GEH = 180°$$
$$\therefore \qquad \angle GEH = 180° - 135° = 45° \qquad \text{...(i)}$$

Again, $\angle DFE + \angle FEH = 180°$
∴   (CD || EH, Sum of consecutive angles)
⇒ $125° + \angle FEH = 180°$
∴ $\angle FEH = 180° - 125° = 55°$ ...(2)
on adding (1) and (2), we get
        $\angle GEH + \angle FEH = 45° + 55°$
i.e., $x = 100°$
Hence, the value of x = 100°

12. In the figure AB || CD and DE || PF. If $\angle APF$ = 50° and $\angle CDG = 40°$ find
    (i) $\angle AQD$ (iii) $\angle EDG$ and   (iii) $\angle DPF$

[Board Term I, 2016, Set-20 CNJE9]

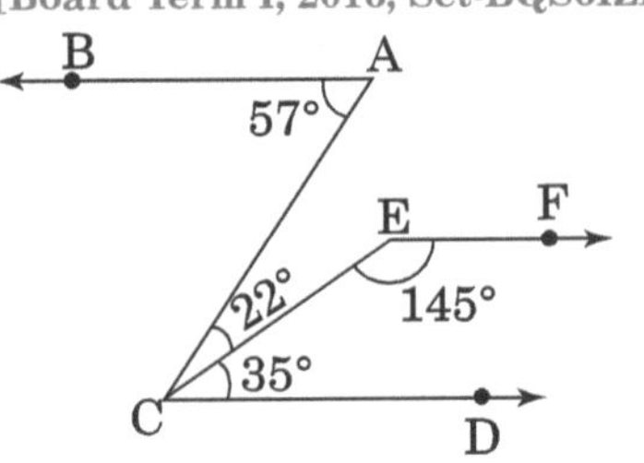

Sol. (i) EQ ||FP and transversal cut them
∴ $\angle AQD = \angle APF$(Corresponding angles)
Hence, $\angle AQD = 50°$
(ii) $\angle DQB = 180° - 50° = 130°$
AB || CD and transversal EQ cuts them
        $\angle EDC = \angle DQB = 130°$
Hence, $\angle EDG = 130° - 40° = 90°$
(iii) FP || EQ and transversal PG cut them
        $\angle DPF = \angle EDG = 90°$

13. In the figure, l || m. prove that
    $\angle 1 + \angle 2 - \angle 3 = 180°$

[Board Term I, 2016, Set-JQ22L5C]

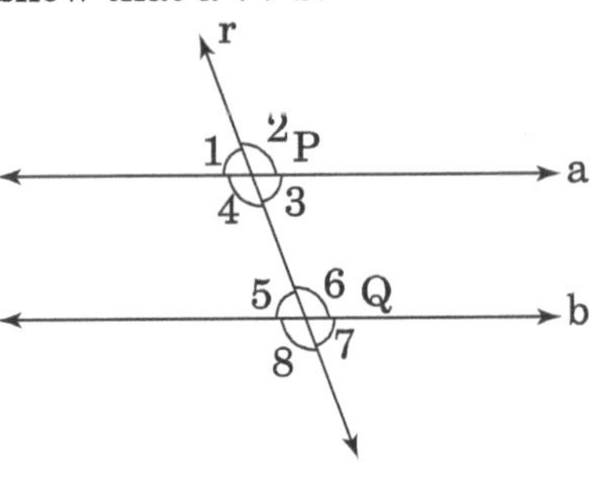

Sol. On drawing a line CF parallel to AB and extend ED to H as given below,

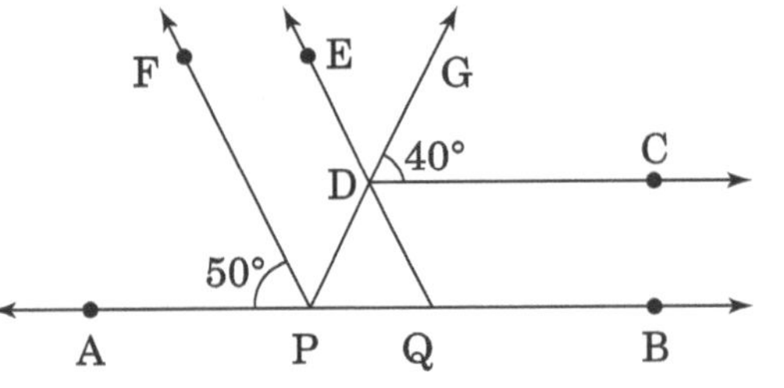

∴   AB || CF || EH
∴ $\angle 1 + \angle BCF = 180°$ ...(i)
        $\angle 3 = 180° - \angle 4$
or, $\angle 4 = 180° - \angle 3$ ...(ii)
Again CF || EH
        $\angle DCF + \angle 4 = 180°$ ...(iii)
On Adding (i) and (iii), we get
    $\angle 1 + \angle 4 + \angle BCF + \angle DCF = 180° + 180°$
⇒ $\angle 1 + \angle BCF + \angle 4 + \angle DCF = 180 + 180° = 360°$
⇒ $\angle 1 + \angle 2 + \angle 4 = 360°$
Using (ii), we get
    $\angle 1 + \angle 2 + 180° - \angle 3 = 360°$
Hence, $\angle 1 + \angle 2 - \angle 3 = 360° - 180° = 180°$

14. In the figure, prove that AB || EF.

[Board Term I, 2016, Set-BQS6IZK, QGL21F5]

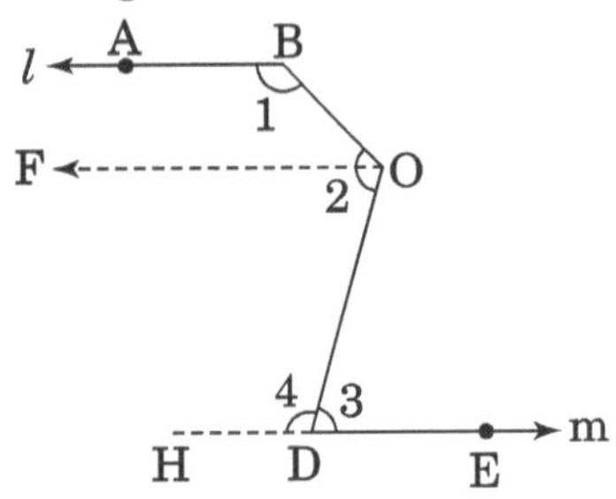

Sol. According to the given figure,
                $\angle A = 57°$
and $\angle ACD = 22° + 35° = 57°$
∴ $\angle A = \angle ACD$
∴ $\angle A$ and $\angle ACD$ are alternate angles
∴   AB || CD
Again, $\angle FEC + \angle ECD = 145° + 35° = 180°$
∵ Sum of consecutive interior angle is 180°
                EF || CD
Now, AB || CD and EF || CD
∴   AB || EF

15. In the given figure, if $\angle 2 = 120°$ and $\angle 5 = 60°$, then show that a || b.

Sol. According to the question,
        $\angle 2 = 120°$ and $\angle 5 = 60°$
Also transversal r intersects two lines a and b at P and Q. respectively
Here, $\angle 2 = \angle 4$ [vertically opposite angles]
∴ $\angle 4 = \angle 2 = 120°$

Now, $\angle 4 + \angle 5 = 120° + 60°$
$\Rightarrow$ $\angle 4 + \angle 5 = 180°$
So, $\angle 4$ and $\angle 5$ are supplementary angles.
Since, a is a straight line.
$\therefore$ $\angle 4 + \angle 3 = 180°$ [by linear pair axiom]
$\Rightarrow$ $120° + \angle 3 = 180°$
$\Rightarrow$ $\angle 3 = 180° - 120° = 60°$
Now, $\angle 7 = \angle 5 = 60°$
                [vertically opposite angles]
        $\angle 7 + \angle 8 = 180°$ [by linear pair axiom]
$\therefore$ $60° + \angle 8 = 180°$
$\Rightarrow$ $\angle 8 = 180° - 60 = 120°$
$\because$ $\angle 6 = \angle 8 = 120°$
                [vertically opposite angles]
$\therefore$ $\angle 3 + \angle 6 = 60° + 120°$
                $= 180°$
$\therefore$ $\angle 3$ and $\angle 6$ are supplementary angles.

Thus, transversal r intersects lines a and b such that pair of interior angles on the same side of the transversal is supplementary.
Hence, line a and b are parallel.
Hence proved

16.   Lines AB and CD are parallel and P is any point between the two lines as shown in figure, prove that $\angle ABP + \angle CDP = \angle DPB$.

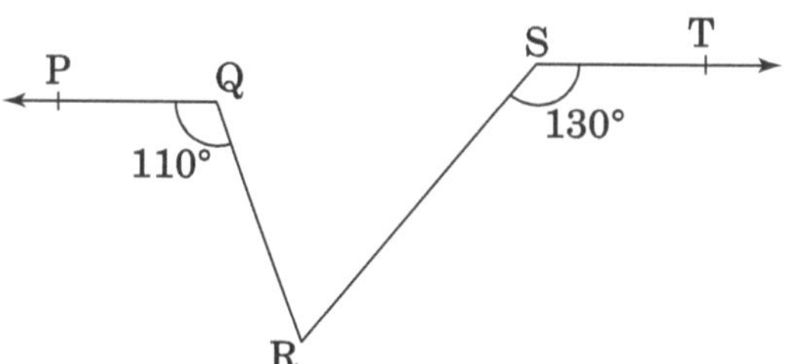

Sol.   According to the question,
                AB | | CD

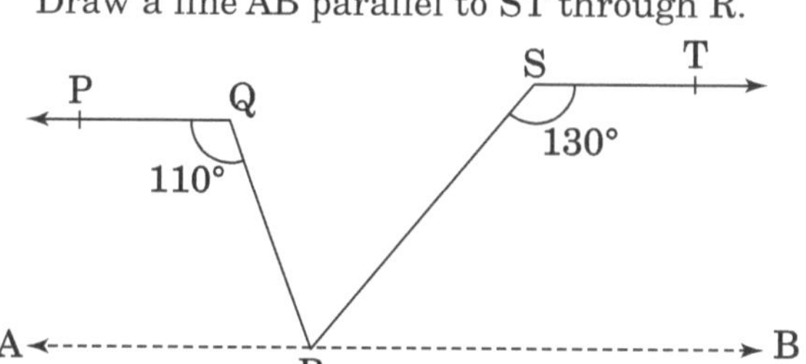

Now, draw a line QM such as
                QM | | AB | | CD
To prove:
        $\angle ABP + \angle CDP = \angle DPB$
Proof:
Now, AB | | QPM and CD | | QPM
$\Rightarrow$ $\angle ABP = \angle BPM$ ...(i)
                [alternate interior angles]
and $\angle CDP = \angle DPM$ ...(ii)
                [alternate interior angles]

On adding eqs. (i) and (ii), we get
        $\angle ABP + \angle CDP = \angle BPM + \angle DPM$
$\therefore$ $\angle ABP + \angle CDP = \angle DPB$
Hence proved.

Long Answer Type Questions
(4 Marks Each)

1.   In the given figure, if PQ | | ST, $\angle PQR = 110°$ and $\angle RST = 130°$, then find $\angle QRS$.   [NCERT]

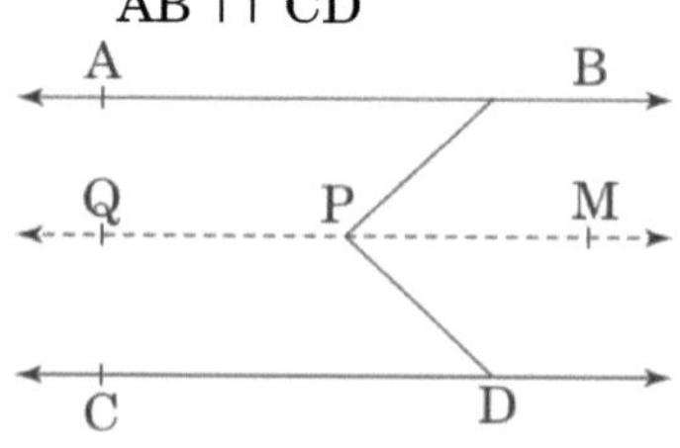

Sol.   According to the question,
        PQ | | ST, $\angle PQR = 110°$ and $\angle RST = 130°$.
        Draw a line AB parallel to ST through R.

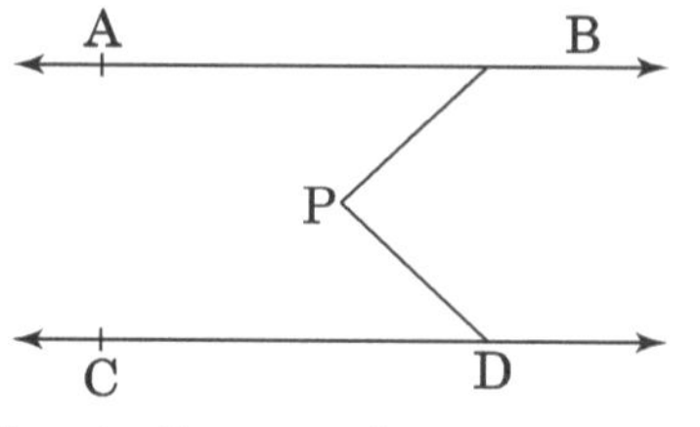

Now, ST | | AB and SR is a transversal.
So, $\angle RST + \angle SRB = 180°$
[$\because$ Sum of the interior angles on the same side
                of the transversal is 180°]
$\Rightarrow$ $130° + \angle SRB = 180°$
$\therefore$ $\angle SRB = 180° - 130°$
                $= 50°$ ...(i)
Since, PQ | | ST and AB | | ST, so PQ | | AB and then QR is a transversal.
So, $\angle PQR + \angle QRA = 180°$
                [since, sum of the interior angles on the
                same side of the transversal is 180°]
$\Rightarrow$ $110° + \angle QRA = 180°$
$\therefore$ $\angle QRA = 180° - 110°$
                $= 70°$ ...(ii)
Now, ARB is a line,
$\therefore$ $\angle QRA + \angle QRS + \angle SRB = 180°$
                [Linear pair]
$\Rightarrow$ $70° + \angle QRS + 50° = 180°$
$\Rightarrow$ $120° + \angle QRS = 180°$
$\therefore$ $\angle QRS = 180° - 120° = 60°$

2. In the given figure, If $AB \parallel CD$, $\angle APQ = 50°$ and $\angle PRD = 127°$, then find the values of x and y.   [NCERT]

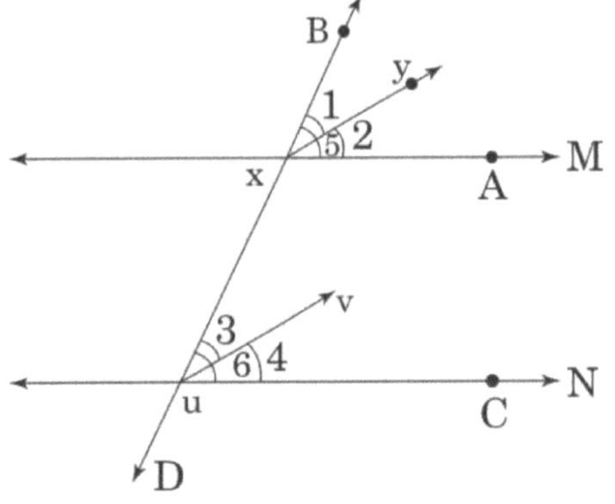

Sol. According to the question,

$\angle APQ = 50°$ and $\angle PRD = 127°$

$AB \parallel CD$ and PQ is a transversal.

$\therefore \angle APQ + \angle PQC = 180°$

[Since, pair of consecutive interior angles on the same side of the transversal is 180°]

$\Rightarrow \quad 50° + \angle PQC = 180°$

$[\because \angle APQ = 50°, \text{given}]$

$\Rightarrow \quad \angle PQC = 180° - 50° = 130°$

Now, CD is a straight line and QP is a ray on it

$\therefore \angle PQC + \angle PQR = 180°$ [by linear pair axiom]

$\Rightarrow \quad 130° + \angle POR = 180°$ $[\because \angle PQC = 130°]$

$\Rightarrow \quad \angle PQR = 180° - 130° = 50°$

$\therefore \qquad x = 50°$ $[\because \angle PQR = x]$

Also, $AB \parallel CD$ and PR is a transversal.

$\therefore \qquad \angle APR = \angle PRD$

[alternate interior angles]

$\Rightarrow \qquad 50° = y = 127°$

$[\because \angle APR = \angle APQ + \angle QPR = 50° \times y]$

$\therefore \qquad y = 127° - 50° = 77°$

Hence, x = 50° and y = 77°.

3. A transversal intersects two parallel lines. Prove that the bisectors of any pair of corresponding angles so formed are parallel.

[Board Term I, 2016, Set-20CNJE9]

[NCERT Examplar]

Sol. According to the question,

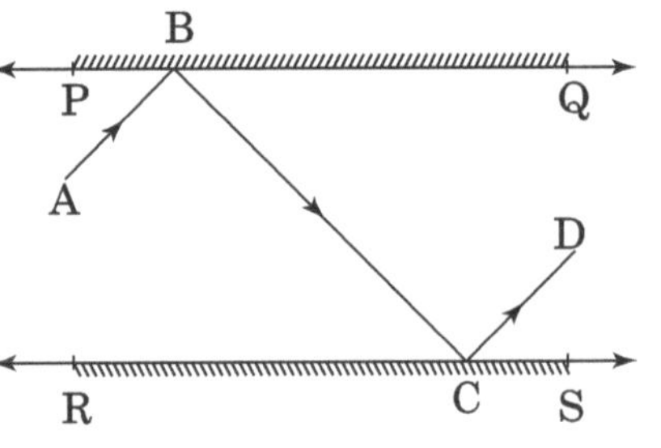

Given $M \parallel N$ line BD is a transversal intersecting them at x and y respectively

To prove: xy $\parallel$ uv

Proof: $\qquad \angle 5 = \angle 6$

(Corresponding angles and $l \parallel m$)

$\because$ Corresponding angles are equal.

$\Rightarrow \qquad \dfrac{1}{2} \angle 5 = \dfrac{1}{2} \angle 6$

$\Rightarrow \qquad \angle 1 = \angle 3$

Hence, xy $\parallel$ uv

4. In the given figure, PQ and RS are two mirrors placed parallel to each other.

An incident ray AB strikes the mirror PQ at B, the reflected ray moves along the path BC and strikes the mirror RS at C and again reflect back along CD. Prove that $AB \parallel CD$.   [NCERT]

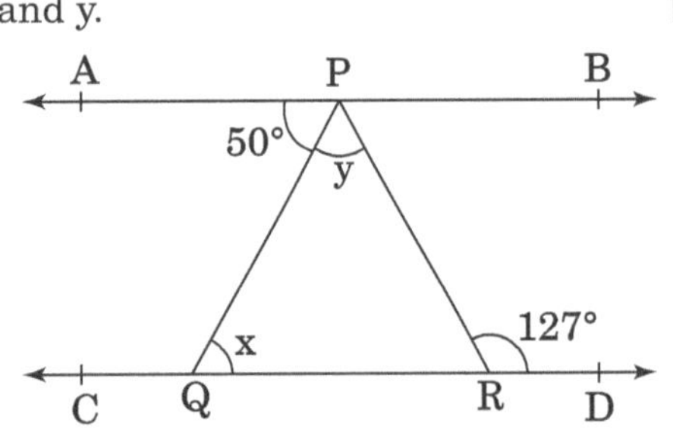

Sol. On drawing a line $BE \perp PQ$ and $CF \perp RS$.

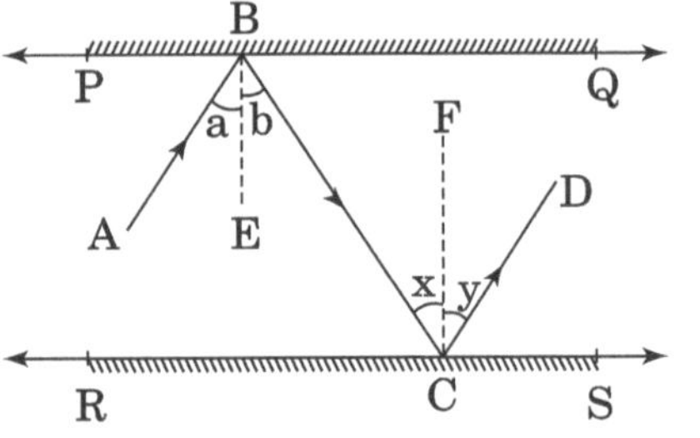

$\Rightarrow \qquad BE \parallel CF$

Also, $\qquad \angle a = \angle b$ $\qquad$ ...(i)

$[\because$ angle of incidence = angles of reflection]

and $\qquad \angle x = \angle y$ $\qquad$ ...(ii)

$[\because$ angle of incidence = angle of reflection]

since, $BE \parallel CF$ and BC is transversal.

$\therefore \qquad \angle b = \angle x$ [alternate interior angles]

$\Rightarrow \qquad 2\angle b = 2\angle x$

[multiplying by 2 on both sides]

$\Rightarrow \quad \angle b + \angle b = \angle x + \angle x$

$\Rightarrow \quad \angle a + \angle b = \angle x + \angle y$ [from eqs. (i) and (ii)]

$\Rightarrow \qquad \angle ABC \parallel \angle DCB$

which are alternate interior angles

Hence, $\qquad AB \parallel BC$

5. In the below figure ABCD is a quadrilateral in
    Which $\angle ABC = 73°$, $\angle C = 97°$ and $\angle D = 110°$. If
    AE || DC and BE || AD and AE intersects BC
    at F, find the measure of $\angle EBF$.

[Board Term I, 2012, Set-48]

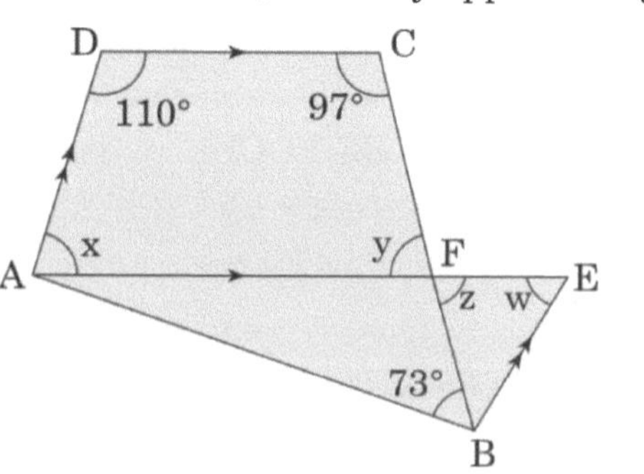

Sol. Let $\qquad \angle DAF = x$

$\qquad\qquad \angle CFA = y$

$\qquad\qquad \angle BFE = z$

and $\qquad\qquad \angle BEF = w$

$\because \qquad\qquad$ AE || DC

$\qquad \angle D + x = 180°$

(Angles on the same side of transversal)

$\qquad x = 180° - 110° = 70°$

$\qquad z = x = 70°$ (Alternate angles)

Again, $\qquad 97° + y = 180°$

(Angle on the same side of transversal)

$\qquad y = 180° - 97° = 83°$

$\qquad y = z = 83°$

(Vertically opposite angles)

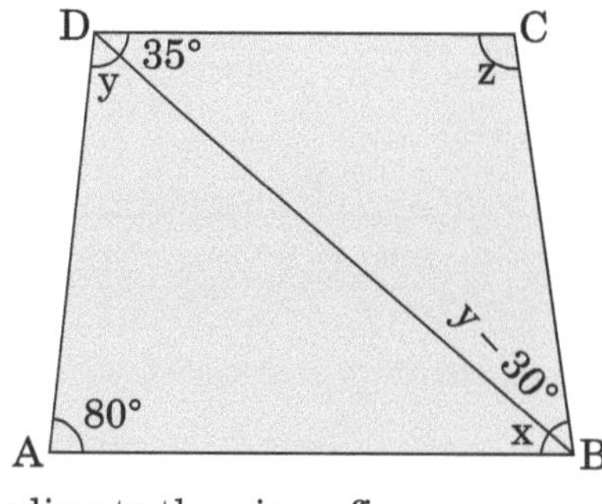

According to the question,

In $\triangle BEF$, $w + z + \angle EBF = 180°$

(Angle sum property)

$\Rightarrow \qquad 83° + 70° + \angle EBF = 180°$

$\therefore \qquad\qquad \angle EBF = 180° - 153° = 27°$

6. In the given figure, AB || DC, $\angle BDC = 35°$ and
    $\angle BAD = 80°$. Find x, y, z.

[Board Term I, 2012, Set-62]

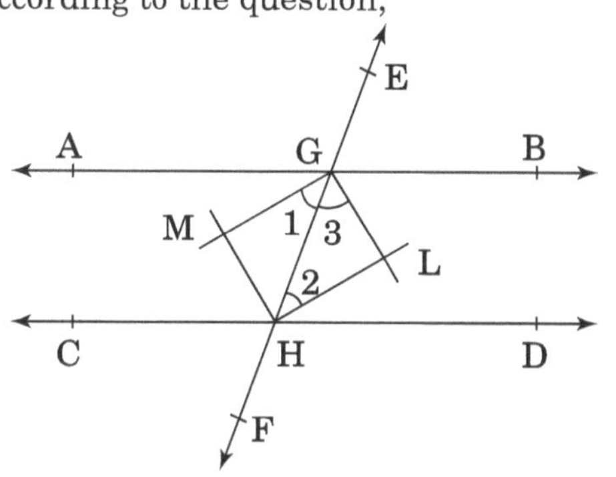

Sol. According to the given figure

$\because \qquad\qquad$ AB || DC

$\therefore \qquad y + 35° + 80° = 180°$

(corresponding interior angels)

$\therefore \qquad\qquad y = 180° - 115° = 65°$

$\qquad \angle ABD = \angle CDB$ [Alternate angles]

$\therefore \qquad\qquad x = 35°$

In $\triangle BCD$,

$\qquad 35° + y - 30° + z = 180°$

[Angle sum of triangle]

$\Rightarrow \qquad 5° + y + z = 180°$

$\Rightarrow \qquad 5° + 65° + z = 180°$

$\therefore \qquad\qquad z = 180° - 70° = 110°$

7. If two parallel lines are intersected by a
    transversal, then prove that bisectors of the
    interior angles form a rectangle.

[Board Term I, 2013; 2012, Set-14]

Sol. According to the question,

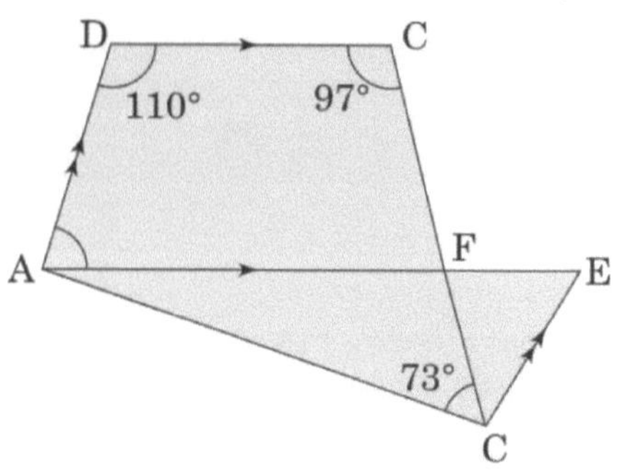

$\qquad \angle AGH = \angle GHD$

$\Rightarrow \qquad \dfrac{1}{2} \angle AGH = \dfrac{1}{2} \angle GHD$

$\Rightarrow \qquad\qquad \angle 1 = \angle 2$

$\because \qquad\qquad$ GM || LH

Similarly, and GL || MH

$\because$ GMHL is a parallelogram

$\therefore \ \angle BGH + \angle GHD = 180°$

$\Rightarrow \qquad \dfrac{1}{2} BGH + \dfrac{1}{2} (\angle GHD) = 90°$

$\Rightarrow \qquad\qquad \angle 3 + \angle 2 = 90° \qquad$ ...(i)

In $\triangle$ GLH $\qquad \angle GLH = 180° - (\angle 2 + \angle 3)$

$\qquad\qquad\qquad\qquad = 180° - 90° = 90°$

$\angle GMH = 90°$

So, $\angle MGL + \angle GLH = 180°$

$\Rightarrow$ $\angle MGL + 90° = 180°$

$\angle MGL = 90°$

$\therefore$ $\angle MHL = 90°$

Hence, bisector of the interior angles from a rectangle

8. In the adjoining figure, AB || CD and l is transversal. Find values of x and y.

[Board Term I, 2016, Set-QGL2F5]

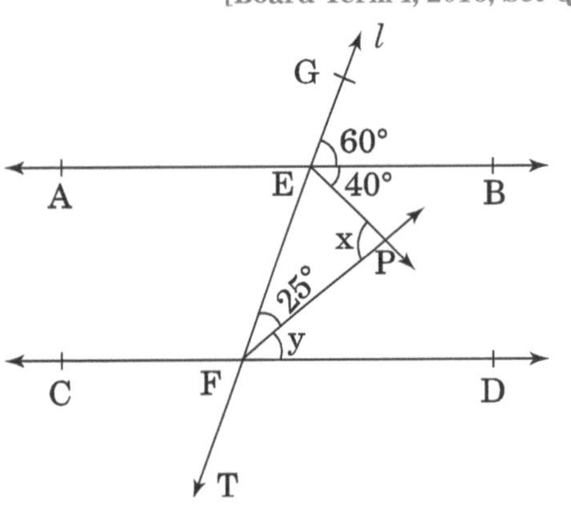

Sol. According to the given figure,

$$\angle EFD = \angle GEP$$

[Corresponding angles]

$\therefore$ $\angle EFD = 60°$

$\Rightarrow$ $25° + y = 60°$

$\therefore$ $y = 60° - 25° = 35°$

Again, $\angle BEF + \angle EFD = 180°$

[Sum of co-interior angles on same side of transversal is supplementary]

$\Rightarrow$ $\angle BEF + 60° = 180°$

$\angle BEF = 180° - 60° = 120°$

$\Rightarrow$ $\angle PEF + 40° = 120°$

$\angle PEF = 120° - 40° = 80°$

Now, in $\triangle PEF$

$$x + 80° + 25° = 180°$$

[Angle sum property]

$\Rightarrow$ $x + 105° = 180°$

$\therefore$ $x = 180° - 105° = 75°$

[Topic 3] Angle Sum property of a Triangle

Points to be Remembered

A closed plane figure formed by three line segments is called a triangle.

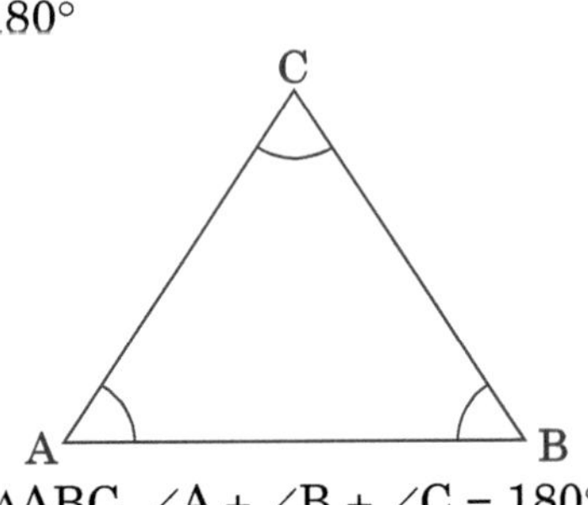

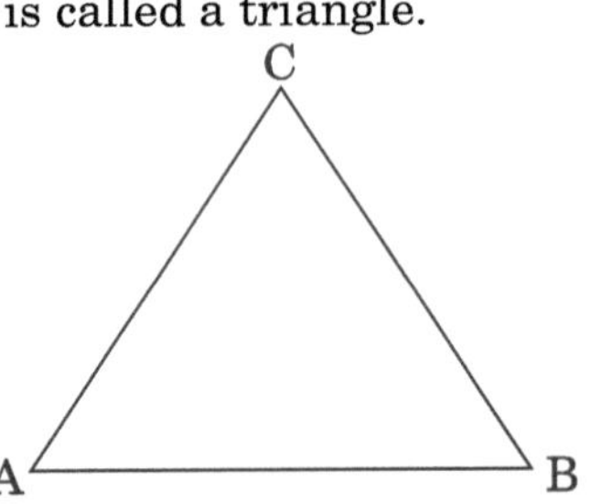

I. **Angle sum property of a Triangle:**

(i) The sum of all interior angles of a triangles is 180°

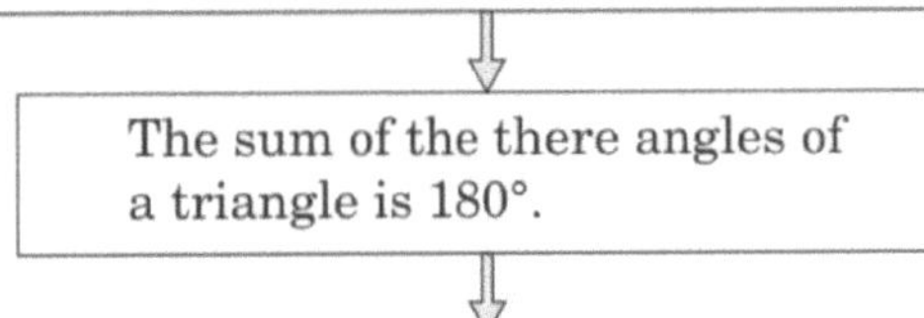

In $\triangle ABC$, $\angle A + \angle B + \angle C = 180°$

(ii) If a side of a triangle is produced, The exterior angle so formed is equal to the sum of the two interior opposite angles.

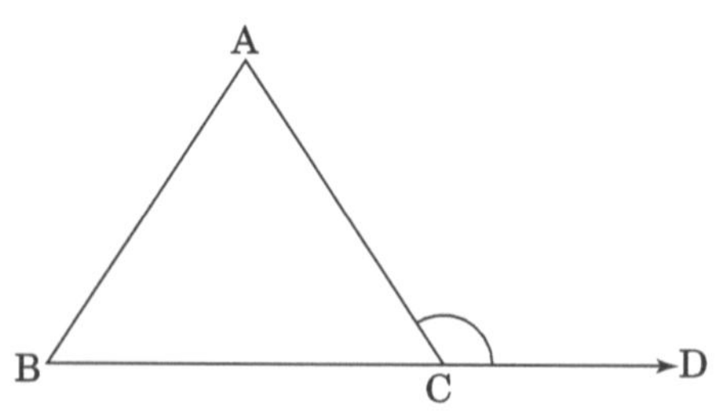

In $\triangle ABC$, $\quad \angle ACD = \angle A + \angle B$

Theorem 1: The sum of the angles of a triangle is $180°$.

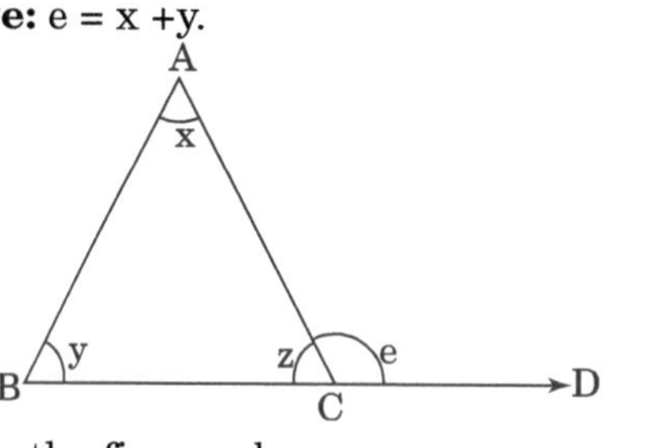

Prove: Sum of all the angles of $\triangle ABC$ is $180°$.

Construction: Draw a line/parallel to BC.

Proof: Since $l \parallel BC$, we have $\angle 2 = \angle y$

$\qquad$ (Alternate angle are equal) $\quad$ ...(i)

Similarly $l \parallel BC$

$$\angle 1 = \angle z$$

$\qquad$ (Alternate angles are equal) ...(ii)

Also, sum of angles at a point A on line l is $180°$.

$\therefore \qquad \angle 2 + \angle x + \angle 1 = 180°$ $\qquad$ (linear pair)

PREVIOUS YEARS'
EXAMINATION QUESTIONS
TOPIC 3

Multiple Choice Questions
(1 Mark Each)

1. Angles of triangle are in the ratio $2 : 4 : 3$. The smallest angle of the triangle is

   (a) $60°$ $\qquad\qquad$ (b) $40°$

   (c) $80°$ $\qquad\qquad$ (d) $20°$ $\quad$ [NCERT Exemp.]

Sol. (b) Let the angles of a triangles are $2x°$, $4x°$ and $3x°$ respectively, Then

According to question

$\Rightarrow 2x + 4x + 3x = 180°$ (Angle sum property)

$\qquad\qquad 9x = 180°$

$\qquad\qquad x = 20°$

Smallest angle of the triangle $= 2 \times 20 = 40°$

2. If one angle of a triangle is equal to the sum of the other two angles, then the triangle is

   (a) an isosceles triangle

   (b) an obtuse triangle

   (c) an equilateral triangle

   (d) a right angle triangle

i.e., $\quad \angle y + \angle x + \angle z = 180°$ $\quad$ (from (i) and (ii))

$\therefore \qquad \angle x + \angle y + \angle z = 180°$

or, $\quad \angle A + \angle B + \angle C = 180°$

Hence, sum of all angles of a triangle is $180°$

Theorem 2: If a side of a triangle is produced, then the exterior angle so formed is equal to the sum of the two interior opposite angles.

Given: A Trianlge ABC with interior angles x, y and z, and exterior angle 'e'.

To Prove: $e = x + y$.

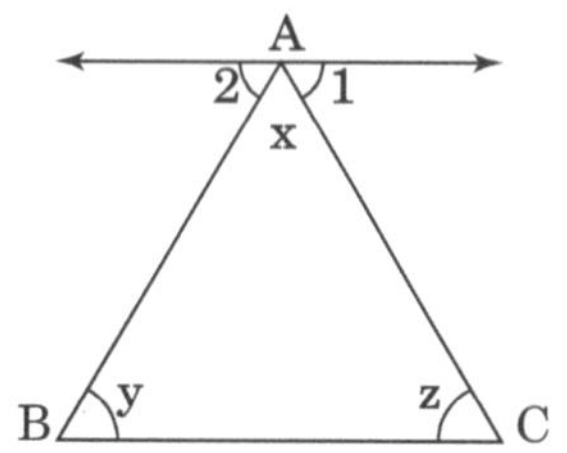

Proof: In the figure above:

$$x + y + z = 180° \qquad\qquad ...(i)$$

$\qquad\qquad$ (Angle Sum Property)

$$e + z = 180° \qquad\qquad ...(ii)$$

$\qquad\qquad$ (Linear Pair)

Comparing equations (i) and (ii),

$$x + y + z = e + z$$

therefore, $x + y = e$,

Hence Proved.

Sol. (d) Let the angles of a triangle are $\angle A$, $\angle B$ and $\angle C$

$$\angle A = \angle B + \angle C \qquad ...(i) \text{ (given)}$$

We know that

$\qquad \angle A + \angle A + \angle C = 180°$ (Angle sum property)

$\Rightarrow \qquad\qquad \angle A + \angle A = 180°$ $\qquad$ [using (i)]

$\Rightarrow \qquad\qquad 2\angle A = 180°$

$\therefore \qquad\qquad \angle A = 90°$

Hence, the triangle is a right-angled triangle.

3. If one of the angles of a triangle is $130°$, then the angle between the bisectors of the other two angles can be.

   (a) $50°$

   (b) $65°$

   (c) $145°$

   (d) $155°$ $\qquad\qquad$ [NCERT Exemp.]

Sol. (d) According to the question,

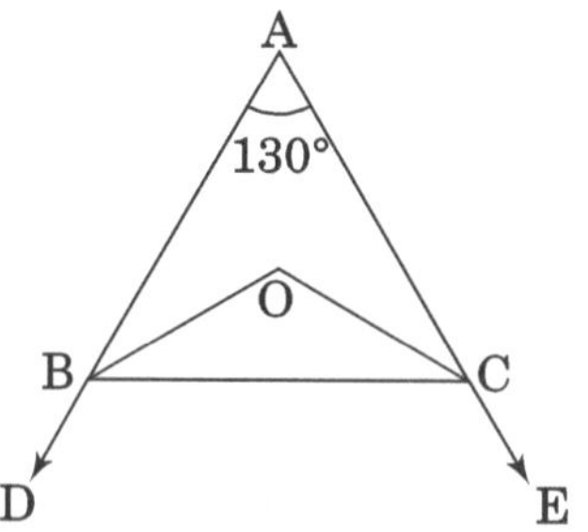

$\angle A + \angle B + \angle C = 180°$ (angle sum property)

On dividing by 2, we have

$$\Rightarrow \quad \frac{1}{2}\angle A + \frac{1}{2}\angle B + \frac{1}{2}\angle C = 90°$$

$$\Rightarrow \quad \frac{1}{2}\angle B + \frac{1}{2}\angle C = 90° - \frac{1}{2}\angle A \ ...(i)$$

Now, In ΔOBC

$\angle OBC + \angle OCB + \angle BOC = 180°$

(angle sum prperty)

$$\Rightarrow \quad \frac{1}{2}\angle B + \frac{1}{2}\angle C + \angle BOC = 180°$$

$$\therefore \quad \angle BOC = 180° - \left(90° - \frac{1}{2}\angle A\right)$$

[By using eqⁿ (i)]

$$= 90° + \frac{1}{2}\angle A$$

$$= 90° + \frac{1}{2} \times 130°$$

$$= 90° + 65° = 155°$$

4. In the given figure ABCD is a rectangle in which $\angle APB = 100°$. The value of x is:

 (a) 40°   (b) 50°

 (c) 60°   (d) 70°

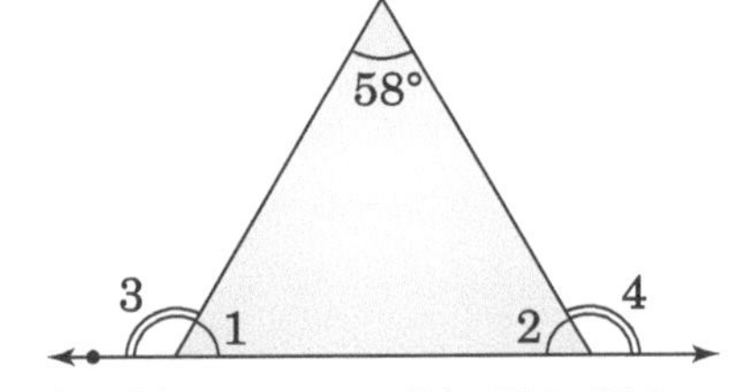

Sol. (b) In ΔAPB,

$\because$ $AP = BP$

$\therefore$ $\angle PAB = \angle ABP$

Now, $\angle PAB + \angle ABP + 100° = 180°$

$\Rightarrow$ $2\angle PAB + 100° = 180°$

$\Rightarrow$ $2\angle PAB = 80°$

$\therefore$ $\angle PAB = \dfrac{80°}{2} = 40°$

Again, in ΔABC,

  $\angle ABC + \angle PAB + \angle ACB = 180°$

$\Rightarrow$ $90° + 40 + x° = 180°$

$\therefore$ $x° = 180° - 130° = 50°$

5. In the given figure, $\angle 1 = \angle 2$ then the measurements of $\angle 3$ and $\angle 4$ are:

 (a) 58°, 61°   (b) 61°, 61°

 (c) 119°, 61°   (d) 119°, 119°

Sol. (b) According to the question :

   $\angle 3 = 58° + \angle 2$ ...(i)

   [$\because$ exterior angle = sum of opposite interior angles]

and $\angle 1 + \angle 2 + 58° = 180°$

   [$\because$ Angle sum property and $\angle 1 = \angle 2$]

$\Rightarrow$ $2\angle 2 = 180° - 58°$

$\therefore$ $\angle 2 = \dfrac{122}{2} = 61°$

Hence, $\angle 3 = 58° + 61° = 119°$

and $\angle 4 = 58° + 61° = 119°$

Very Short Answer Type Questions

(1 Mark Each)

1. can a triangle have all angles less than 60°? Give reason.   **[NCERT Examplar]**

Sol. No, a triangle cannot have all the angles less than 60° because if all the angles will be less than 60°, then their sum will not be equal to 180°. Hence, it will not be a triangle.

2. An exterior angle of a triangle is 105° and its two interior opposite angles are equal. Find each of these equal angles.   **[NCERT Examplar]**

Sol. Let each interior opposite angles of a triangle be x. then,

According to the question, exterior angles of a triangle = 105°

$\therefore$ $x + x = 105°$

   [$\because$ exterior angle = the sum of opposite interior angles]

$\Rightarrow$ $2x = 105°$

$\therefore$ $x = \dfrac{105°}{2} = 52\dfrac{1°}{2}$

3. How many triangles can be drawn having its angles 53°, 64° and 63°? Given reason.

   [NCERT Examplar]

Sol. Here, sum of angles = 53° + 64° + 63° = 180°

Hence, only one triangle can be drawn by the given angles.

4. What is the value of x in the figure given below?

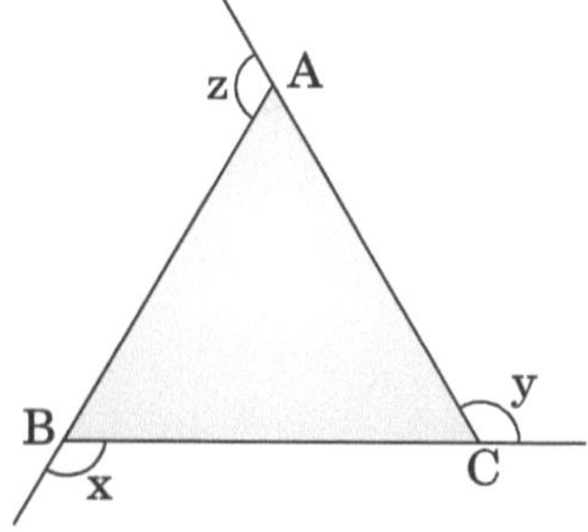

Sol. We know that exterior angle is the sum of the two interior opposite angles of a triangle.

$\therefore \qquad x + 60° = 100°$

$\therefore \qquad x = 100° - 60° = 40°$

5. In the given figure, ABC is an isosceles triangle with AB = AC and $\angle A = 50°$. Calculate $\angle B$

[NCERT Examplar]

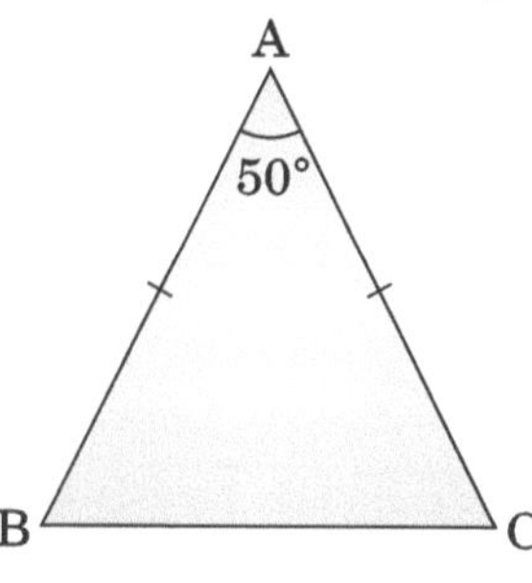

Sol. According to the question,

$\because$ $\triangle ABC$ is an isosceles triangle.

$$AB = AC$$

$\therefore \qquad \angle C = \angle B$

Then,

$$\angle A + \angle B + \angle C = 180°$$

(Prop. of isosceles $\triangle$)

$\Rightarrow \quad 50° + \angle B + \angle B = 180°$

$\Rightarrow \qquad\quad 2\,\angle B = 130°$

$\therefore \qquad\quad \angle B = \dfrac{130°}{2} = 65°$

6. In the figure below, if x, y and z are exterior angles of $\triangle ABC$, then calculate the value of x + y + z.

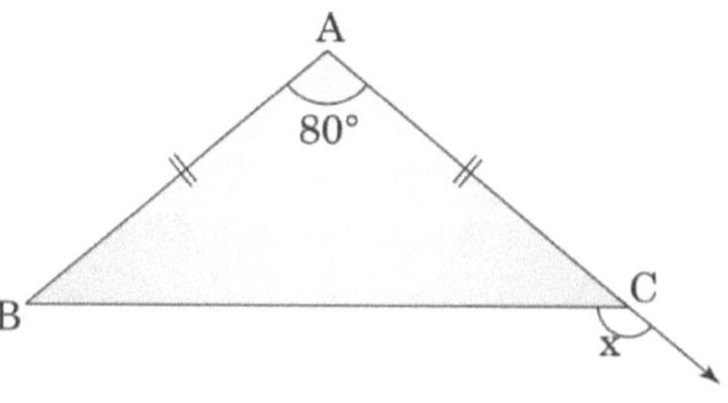

Sol. We know that sum of all the exterior angles formed by producing the sides of a polygon is 360°.

$\therefore \qquad x° + y° + z° = 360°.$

7. An exterior angle of a triangle is 80° and two interior opposite angles are equal. What will be the measure of each?

Sol. Let equal angles are x and x, then

According to the question

$$x + x = 80°$$

$\Rightarrow \qquad\qquad 2x = 80°$

$\therefore \qquad\qquad x = \dfrac{80°}{2} = 40°$

(Exterior angle is the sum of the two opposite interior angles)

8. In the figure below, in $\triangle ABC$, AB = AC, then calculate the value of x.

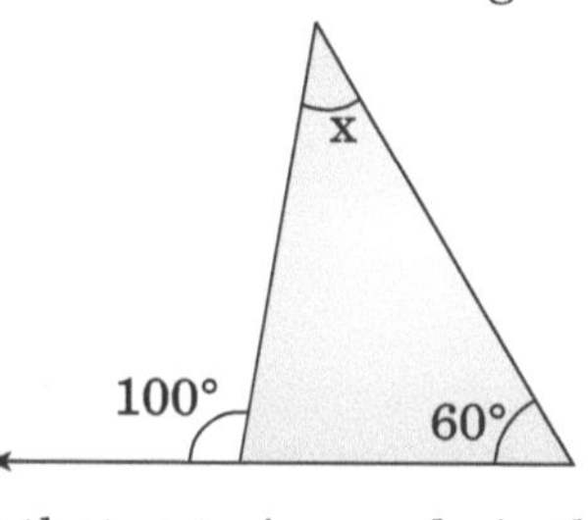

Sol. According to the question,

$$AB = AC$$

$$\angle ACB = \angle B$$

In $\triangle ABC$, $80° + \angle ACB + \angle B = 180°$

(Sum of angles of a triangle)

$\Rightarrow \qquad 2\angle ACB = 100°$

$\therefore \qquad \angle ACB = \dfrac{100°}{2} = 50°$

Again, $\angle ACB + x = 180°$ (Linear Pair)

$\Rightarrow \qquad 50° + x = 180°$

$\therefore \qquad\qquad x = 180° - 50°$

$\qquad\qquad\qquad = 130°$

9. In the figure below, if $\angle A + \angle B + \angle C + \angle D + \angle E + \angle F = k$ right angles, then what is the value of k?

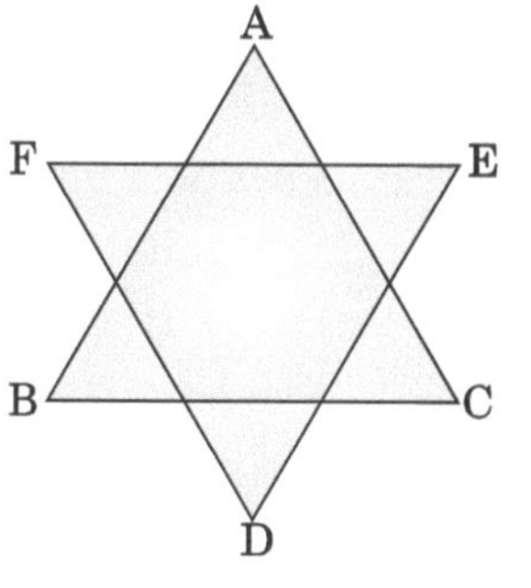

Sol. According to the question, in $\triangle ABC$,

$$\angle A + \angle B + \angle C = 180° \qquad\qquad …(i)$$

Also, in $\triangle DEF$,

$$\angle D + \angle E + \angle F = 180° \qquad\qquad (ii)$$

[angle sum property of a triangle]

On adding equation (i) and (ii), we have

$\therefore \quad \angle A + \angle B + \angle C + \angle D + \angle E + \angle F$

$\qquad\qquad = 360°$

$\qquad\qquad = 4 \times 90°$

Hence, k = 4 right angles

10. In $\triangle ABC$, $\angle A = \angle B/2 = \angle C/6$, then what will be the measure of $\angle A$?

Sol. In $\triangle ABC$, $\angle A + \angle B + \angle C = 180°$

$\qquad$ [Angle sum property of a triangle]

$\Rightarrow \angle A + 2\angle A + 6\angle A = 180°$

$\Rightarrow \qquad\qquad 9\angle A = 180°$

$\qquad\qquad \angle A = \dfrac{180°}{9} = 20°$

Short Answer Type Questions I

(2 Marks Each)

1. In the figure, AD and CE are the angle bisectors of $\angle A$ and $\angle C$ respectively. If $\angle ABC = 90°$, Then find $\angle AOC$. [NCERT Examplar]

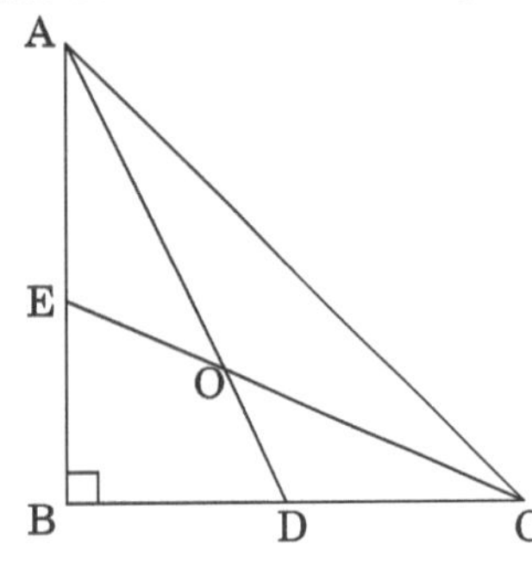

Sol. According to the question, AD and CE are the bisector of $\angle A$ and $\angle C$

$\therefore \qquad \angle OAC = \dfrac{1}{2}\angle A \qquad\qquad …(i)$

and $\qquad \angle OCA = \dfrac{1}{2}\angle C \qquad\qquad …(ii)$

On adding equation (i) and (ii), we have

$\Rightarrow \angle OAC + \angle OCA = \dfrac{1}{2}(\angle A + \angle C)$

$\qquad$ [$\because \angle A + \angle B + \angle C = 180°$ and

$\qquad\qquad \angle B = 90°$

$\therefore \qquad \angle A + \angle C = 180° - 90°$

$\qquad\qquad = \dfrac{1}{2}(180° - 90°)$

$\qquad\qquad = \dfrac{1}{2} \times 90° = 45°$

Now, In $\triangle AOC$,

$\qquad \angle AOC + \angle OAC + \angle OCA = 180°$

$\Rightarrow \qquad\qquad \angle AOC + 45° = 180°$

$\therefore \qquad\qquad \angle AOC = 180° - 45° = 135°.$

2. In figure, if AB $\parallel$ CD, $\angle APQ = 40°$ and $\angle PRD = 118°$, find x and y.

[Board Term I, 2012, Set-14; 2011, Set-42]

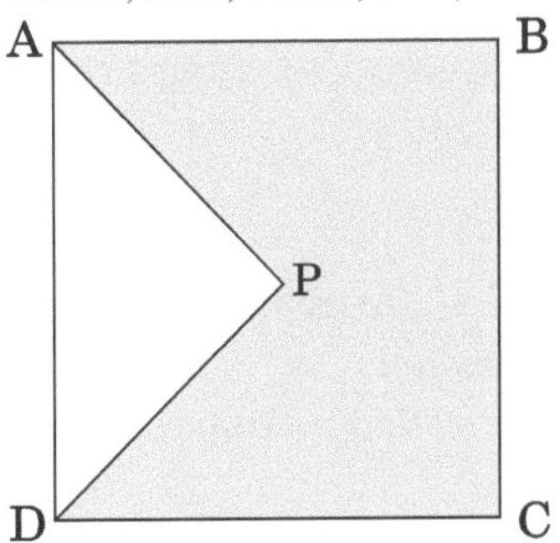

Sol. According to the question

$\because \qquad AB \parallel CD$

$\therefore \qquad \angle APQ = \angle PQR$

$\qquad\qquad x = \angle APQ = 40° \qquad$ (Alternate angles)

$\qquad x + y = 118°$ (Exterior angle is the sum of the two opposite interior angles)

$\Rightarrow 40° + y = 118°$

$\therefore \qquad\qquad y = 118° - 40° = 78°.$

3. In figure, if lines PQ and RS intersect at point T, such that $\angle PRT = 50°$, $\angle TSQ = 60°$ and $\angle RPT = 100°$, find $\angle SQT$.

[Board Term I, 2012, Set-55; 2011, Set-38]

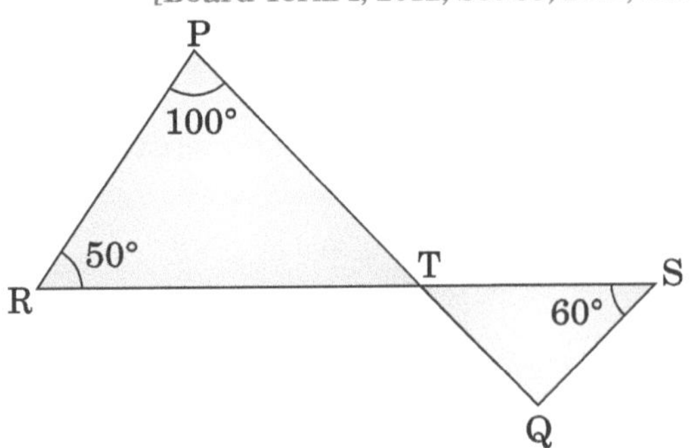

Sol. According to the question, in $\triangle PRT$,

$\qquad \angle PTR = 180° - 50 - 100° = 30°$

and $\qquad \angle STQ = \angle PTR = 30°$

$\qquad\qquad$ (Vertically opposite angles)

In $\triangle SQT$, $\qquad \angle SQT - 180° - 60° - 30° - 90°$

4. In the given figure AP and DP are bisectors of $\angle A$ and $\angle D$. Prove that, $2\angle APD = \angle B + \angle C$.

[Board Term I, 2012, Set 52; 2011, Set-37: 2010, Set-C]

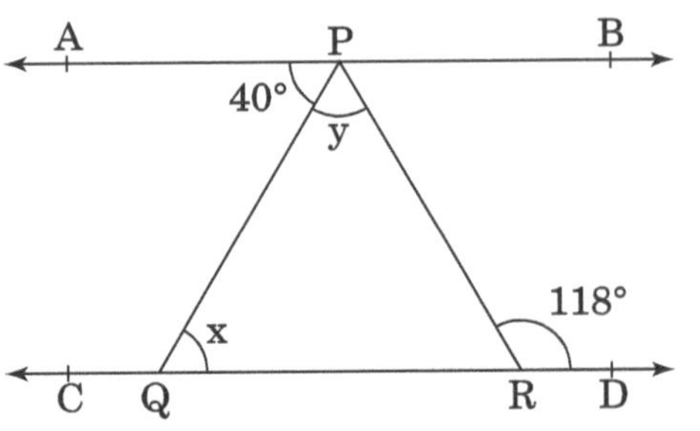

Sol. According to the question,

In $\triangle APD$, $\angle APD + \angle DAP + \angle ADP = 180°$

$\Rightarrow \quad \angle APD + \dfrac{\angle A}{2} + \dfrac{\angle D}{2} = 180°$

Given, $\qquad\qquad \angle DAP = \dfrac{1}{2}\angle A$

and $\qquad\qquad \angle ADP = \dfrac{1}{2}\angle D$

$\qquad$ [$\because$ AP and DP are bisectors of $\angle A$ and $\angle D$]

$\Rightarrow \qquad 2\angle APD = 360° - (\angle A + \angle D) \qquad$ ...(i)

$\qquad \angle B + \angle C = 360° - (\angle A + \angle D) \qquad$ ...(ii)

On comparing (i) and (ii),

$\therefore \qquad\qquad 2\angle APD = \angle B + \angle C.$

5. An exterior angle of a triangle is 110° and one of the interior opposite angles is 30°. Find the measure of another two angles of the triangle.

[Board Term I, 2012, Set-97]

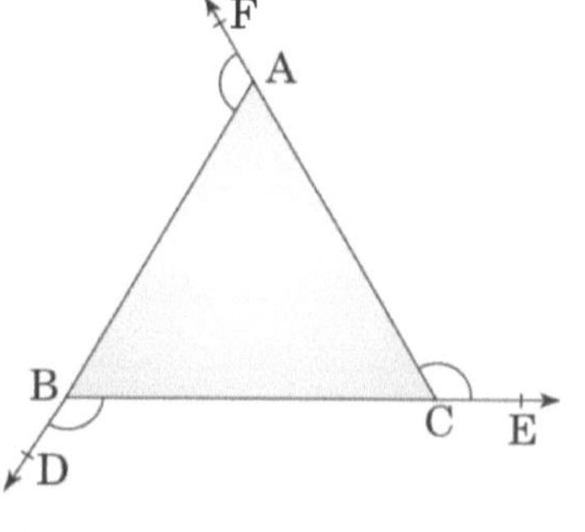

Sol. According to the question,

Exterior angle = Sum of opposite two interior angle

$\qquad\qquad 110° = 30° + x$

$\therefore \qquad\qquad x = 110° - 30°$

$\qquad\qquad\quad = 80°$

Now, $\angle ABC + 110 = 180°$ $\qquad$ [Linear pair]

$\therefore \qquad \angle ABC = 180° - 110° = 70°$

6. Prove that if in a triangle, its sides are produced in order, then the sum of the exterior angles so formed is 360°. [Board Term I, 2012, Set-63]

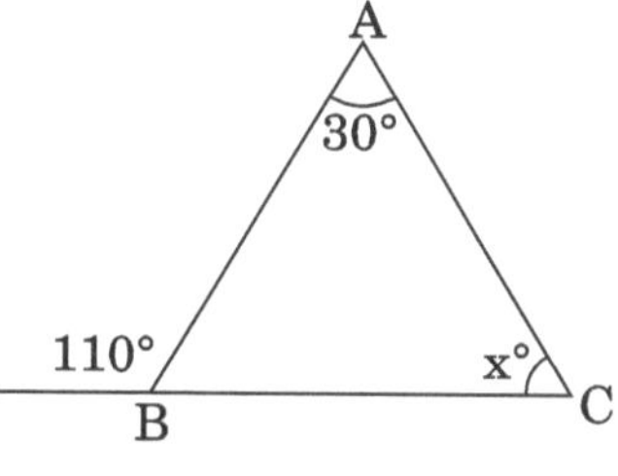

Sol. To prove :

$\qquad \angle BAF + \angle ACE + \angle CBD = 360°$

Proof : Consider,

$\qquad\qquad \angle BAF = 180° - \angle BAC \qquad$ ...(i)

$\qquad\qquad\qquad$ (Linear pair)

$\angle ACE = 180° - \angle ACB \qquad$ ...(ii)

$\qquad\qquad\qquad$ (Linear pair)

and $\qquad \angle CBD = 180° - \angle ABC \qquad$ ...(iii)

$\qquad\qquad\qquad$ (Linear pair)

On adding equation (i), (ii) and (iii), we get

$\angle BAF + \angle ACE + \angle CBD$

$\qquad = 540° - [\angle BAC + \angle ACB + \angle ABC]$

$\qquad = 540° - 180° = 360°$

$\qquad\qquad$ [$\because$ Angle sum property]

Hence proved.

7. In the given figure, $\triangle LMN$ is an isosceles triangle with $\angle M = \angle N$ and LP bisects $\angle NLQ$. Prove that LP | | MN. [Board Term I, 2012, Set-52]

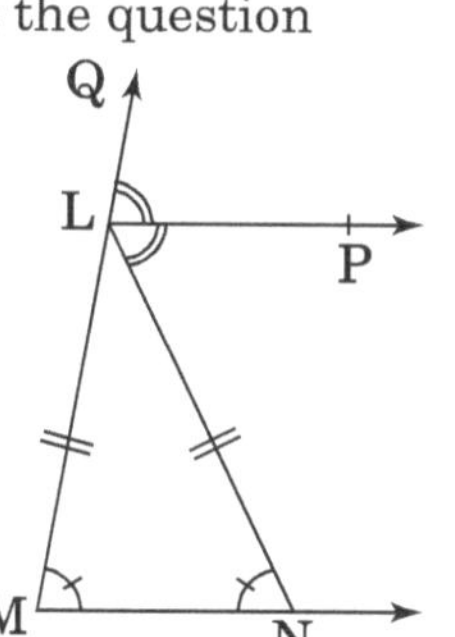

Sol. According to the question

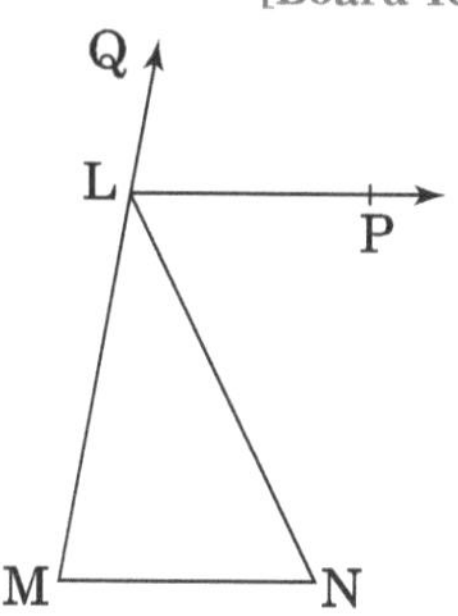

$\qquad \angle M = \angle N \qquad\qquad$ (Given)

$\therefore \qquad \angle NLQ = \angle M + \angle N = 2\angle N$

$\qquad\qquad = 2\,\angle N$

[Exterior angle is equal to the sum of two opposite interior angles]

$\qquad 2\,\angle NLP = 2\,\angle N$

$\qquad \angle NLP = \angle N \quad (\because LP$ bisects $\angle NLQ)$

$\qquad \angle NLP = \angle N$

$\qquad\qquad$ (Alternate interior angles)

$\qquad LP | | MN$

Hence proved.

8. The degree measure of three angles of a triangles are $x°$, $y°$, $z°$. If $z° = \dfrac{x° + y°}{2}$, then find the value of $z°$. [Board TermI, 2012, Set-51]

Sol. Given, $\qquad\qquad z° = \dfrac{x° + y°}{2}$

$\Rightarrow \qquad\qquad 2z° = x° + y° \qquad\qquad$ ...(i)

$\because \qquad x° + y° + z° = 180°$ (Angle sum property)

$\Rightarrow \qquad 2z° + z° = 180°$ [From equation (i)]

$\Rightarrow \qquad 3z° = 180°$

$\therefore \qquad z° = \dfrac{180°}{3} = 60°$

9. In the given figure, AF $\parallel$ BE, AC $\perp$ BE, and AF bisects $\angle$GAD. If $\angle$GAD = 70°, then find the measure of $\angle$ABC and $\angle$ADE.

[Board Term I, 2012, Set-63]

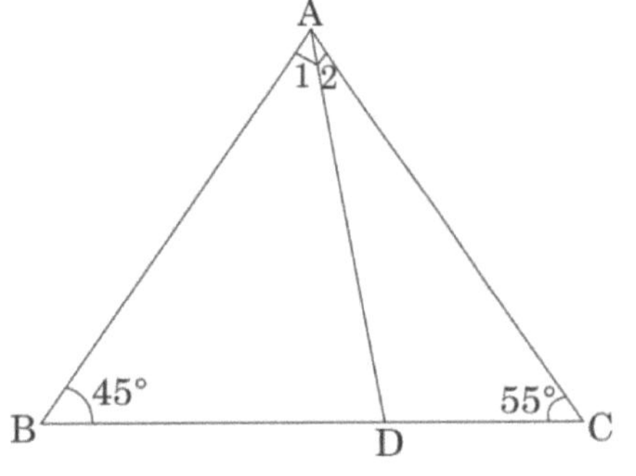

Sol. According to the question AF $\parallel$ BE and AF bisects $\angle$GAD

$\therefore \qquad \angle$GAF = $\angle$DAF = $\dfrac{70°}{2}$ = 35°

and $\qquad \angle$DAF = $\angle$ADB = 35° (Alternate angles)

$\angle$ADE = 180° − 35° = 145° (Linear pair)

Now, $\quad \angle$GAD = $\angle$ABC + $\angle$ADB

(Exterior angle is the sum of the two opposite interior angles)

$\Rightarrow \qquad 70° = \angle$ABC + 35°

$\angle$ABC = 70° − 35° = 35°

10. In $\triangle$ABC, $\angle$B = 45°, $\angle$C = 55°, AD bisects $\angle$A. Find $\angle$ADB and $\angle$ADC.

[Board TErm I, 2012, Set 97]

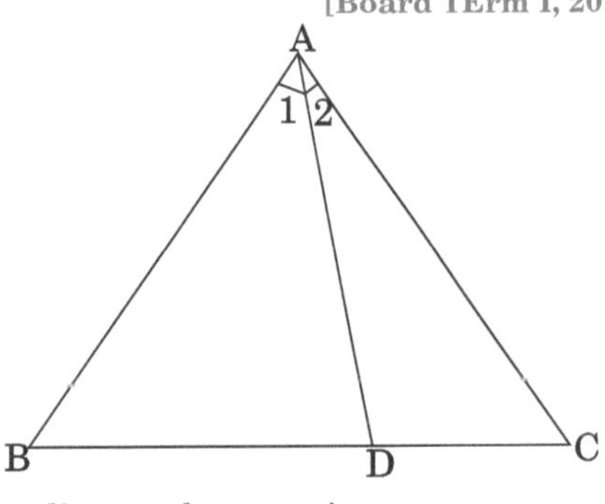

Sol. According to the question,

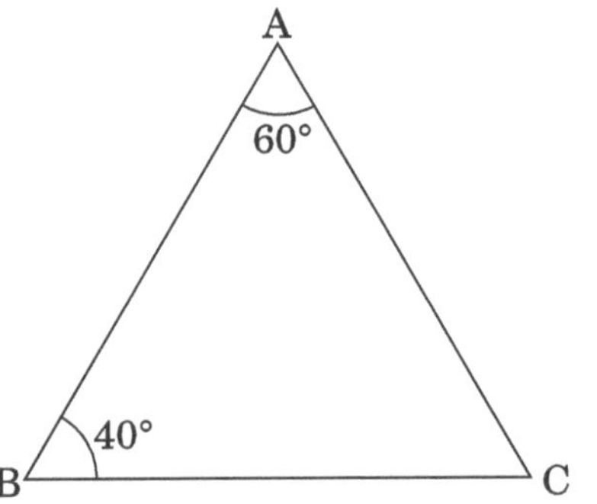

Let $\qquad \angle1 = \angle2 = x,$

$\angle$A + $\angle$B + $\angle$C = 180°, (Angle sum prop. of $\triangle$)

$\Rightarrow \quad 2x + 45° + 55° = 180°$

$\Rightarrow \qquad 2x + 100 = 180°$

$\Rightarrow \qquad 2x = 80°$

$x = 40°$

$\angle$ADB = $\angle2 + \angle$C

(Exterior Angle is the sum of the two interior opposite angles) = 40° + 55° = 95°

Similarly, $\angle$ADC = $\angle1 + \angle$B

(Exterior angle is the sum of the two interior opposite angles)

= 45° + 40° = 85°

11. In $\triangle$ABC, if $\angle$A = (2x − 5°), $\angle$B = (5x + 5°, $\angle$C = (3x + 50°, then find the value of x, $\angle$A, $\angle$B and $\angle$C. [Board Term I, 2012, Set-41]

Sol. According the question, In $\triangle$ABC,

$\angle$A + $\angle$B + $\angle$C = 180°

(Angle sum property of a triangle)

$\Rightarrow \quad 2x − 5° + 5x + 5° + 3x + 50° = 180°$

$\Rightarrow \qquad 10x + 50° = 180°$

$\Rightarrow \qquad 10x = 130°$

$x = 13°$

Hence, $\qquad \angle$A = 2x − 5° = 2 × 13° − 5°

= 26° − 5° = 21°

$\angle$B = 5x + 5° = 5° × 13° +5°

= 65° + 5° = 70°

$\angle$C = 3x + 50° = 3° × 13° + 50°

= 39° + 50° = 89°

12. Prove that if one angle of a triangle is equal to the sum of the other two angles, Then the triangle is right angled triangle. [Board Term I, 2012, Set-49]

Sol. Given, $\qquad \angle$A = $\angle$B + $\angle$C

$\therefore \quad \angle$A + $\angle$B + $\angle$C = 180°

$\Rightarrow \qquad \angle$A + $\angle$A = 180°

$\Rightarrow \qquad 2\angle$A = 180°

$\therefore \qquad \angle$A = 90°

Hence, $\triangle$ABC is a right angled triangle.

13. In $\triangle$ABC, $\angle$A = 60°, $\angle$B = 40°. Which side of this triangle is the smallest? give reason for your answer. [Board Term I, 2012, Set-36]

Sol. According to the question,

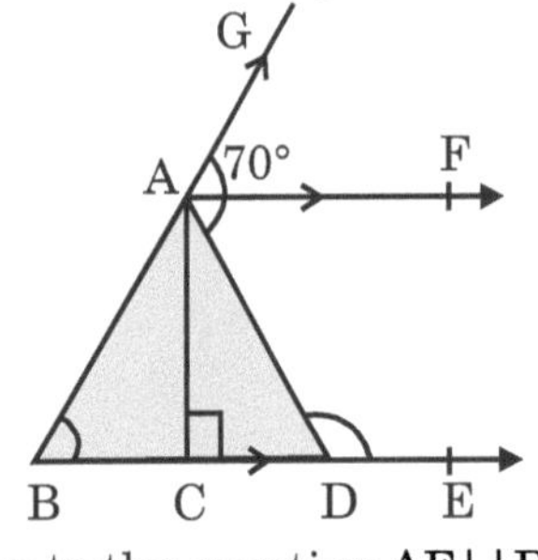

$\therefore$ $\angle A + \angle B + \angle C = 180°$ [Angle sum property]
$$\angle C = 180° - (60° + 40°)$$
$$= 180° - 100° = 80°$$
$\because$ $\angle C > \angle A > \angle B$
$\therefore$ $AB > BC > AC$
Hence, AC is the shortest
Reason: Side opposite to smaller angle is shortest.

14.   In $\triangle ABC$, $\angle A + \angle B = 65°$ and $\angle B + \angle C = 140°$, Find the value of $\angle B$ and $\angle C$.

[Board Term I, 2012, Set-47]

Sol.   Given, $\angle A + \angle B = 65°$
Given, $\angle B + \angle C = 140°$
$$\angle A + \angle B + \angle B + \angle C = 65° + 140° = 205°$$
But $\angle A + \angle B + \angle C = 180°$
(Angle sum property of Δ)
or $180° + \angle B = 205°$
$$\angle B = 25°$$
$$\angle C = 140° - 25° = 115°$$

Alternative Method:
We know that,
$$\angle A + \angle B + \angle C = 180° \qquad ...(i)$$
(Angle sum property of a triangle)
$\Rightarrow$ $65° + \angle C = 180°$
$\therefore$ $\angle C = 180° - 65° = 115°$
Again by (i),
$$\angle A + 140° = 180°$$
$\therefore$ $\angle A = 180° - 140° = 40°$
Again by (i),
$$40° + \angle B + 115° = 180°$$
(Angle sum property of a triangle)
$\therefore$ $\angle B = 180° - 155° = 25°$

15.   In the given figure, if $\angle A = 60°$ and $\angle B = 70°$, then find $\angle ACD$.   [Board Term I, 2014]

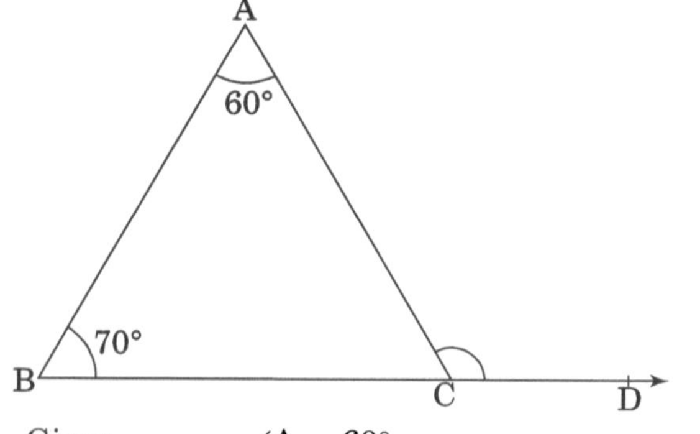

Sol.   Given, $\angle A = 60°$
and $\angle B = 70°$
$$\angle ACD = \angle A + \angle B$$
[Exterior angle is the sum of the two interior opposite angles]
$$= 60° + 70°$$
$\therefore$ $\angle ACD = 130°$

16.   The angles of a triangles are $(x - 40)°$, $(x - 20)°$ and $\left(\dfrac{x}{2} - 10\right)^{\circ}$. Find the value of x and then the angles of the triangle. [Board Term I, 2015, Set-II]

Sol.   According to the question,
$$(x - 40)° + (x - 20)° + \left(\dfrac{x}{2} - 10\right)^{\circ} = 180°$$
$\Rightarrow$ $\left(x + x + \dfrac{x}{2}\right) - (40° + 20° + 10°) = 180°$
$\Rightarrow$ $\dfrac{5x}{2} - 70° = 180°$
$\Rightarrow$ $\dfrac{5x}{2} = 250°$
$\therefore$ $x = 100°$
Hence, angles are
$$(x - 40°) = 100° - 40° = 60°$$
$$(x - 20°) = 100° - 20° = 80°$$
and $(x - 10°) = 50° - 10° = 40°$

17.   In the given figure, AD and CE are the bisectors of $\angle A$ and $\angle C$ respectively. If $\angle ABC = 90°$ find $\angle ADC + \angle AEC$.   [Board Term I, 2015, Set-III]

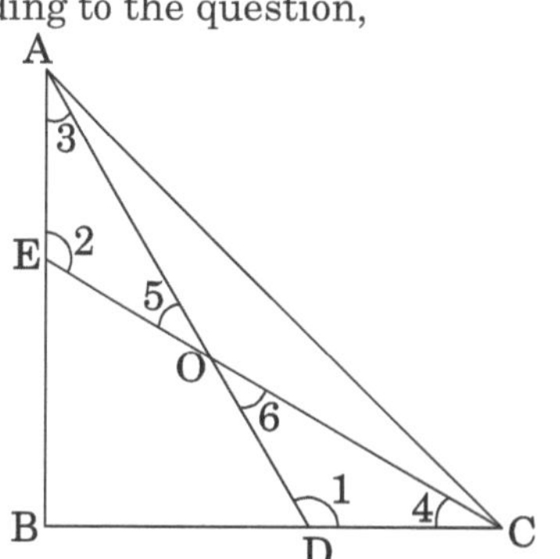

Sol.   According to the question,

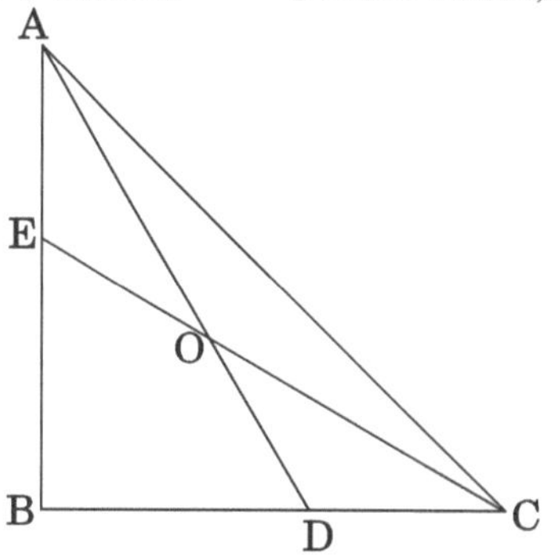

$$2\angle 3 + 2\angle 4 = 180° - \angle ABC = 180° - 90° = 90°$$
$\therefore$ $\angle 3 + \angle 4 = 45°$
$$\angle 1 = 90° + \angle 3 \quad ...(i) \text{ (External angle)}$$
$$\angle 2 = 90° + \angle 3 \quad ...(ii) \text{ (External angle)}$$
On adding equation (i) and (ii), we have
$$\angle 1 + \angle 2 = 180° + \angle 3 + \angle 4$$
$$= 180° + 45° \quad \text{(External angle)}$$
$$= 225°$$

18. In the $\triangle ABC$, $BE \perp AC$, $\angle EBC = 40°$ and $\angle DAC = 30°$. Find the values of x, y, z.

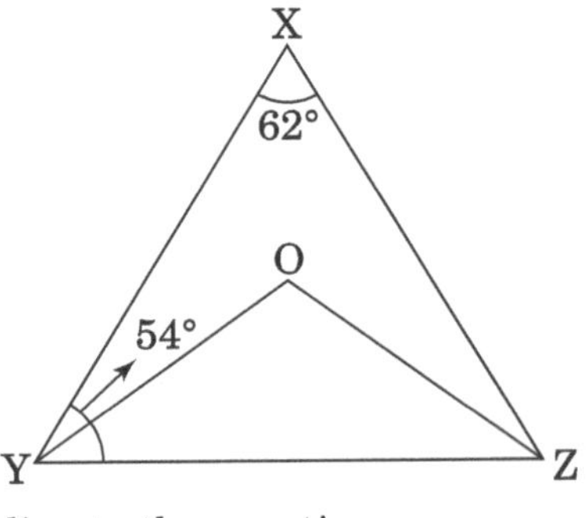

Sol. In $\triangle EBC$, we have
$$\angle EBC + \angle BCE + \angle CEB = 180°$$
$$40° + x + 90° = 180°$$
$$[\because \ BE \perp AC, \therefore \ \ \angle BEC = 90°]$$
$$130° + x + = 180°$$
$$\therefore \qquad x = 50°$$
Further, $\angle ADB$ is exterior angle of $\triangle ADC$.
$$\therefore \qquad \angle ADB = \angle CAD + \angle ACD$$
$$\Rightarrow \qquad y = x + 30°$$
$$\therefore \qquad y = 50° + 30° = 80°$$
Similarly, $\qquad z = 40° + y$
$$= 40° + 80° = 120°$$

19. In the figure, sides QP and RQ of $\triangle PQR$ are produced to points S and T respectively. If $\angle SPR = 135°$ and $\angle PQT = 110°$, find $\angle PRQ$.

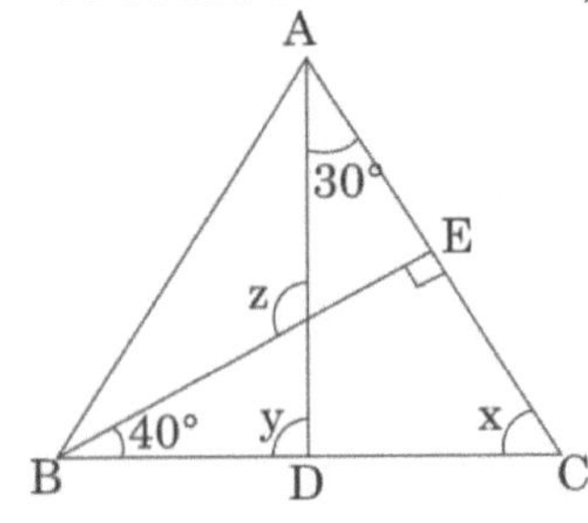

Sol. According to the question,
$$\angle RPS + \angle RPQ = 180° \qquad \text{[linear pair]}$$
$$\Rightarrow \quad 135° + \angle RPQ = 180°$$
$$[\because \ \ \angle RPS = 135° \text{ (given)}]$$
$$\therefore \qquad RPQ = 180° - 135° = 45°$$
Now, $\angle RPQ + \angle PRQ = \angle PQT$
[External angle is the sum of interior opposite angles]
$$\Rightarrow \quad 45° + \angle PRQ = 110°$$
$$\therefore \qquad \angle PRQ = 110° - 45° = 65°$$

Short Answer Type Questions II

(3 Marks Each)

1. In the given figure $\angle X = 62°$, $\angle XYZ = 54°$. If YO and ZO are the bisectors of $\angle XYZ$ and $\angle XZY$ respectively of $\triangle XYZ$, then find $\angle OZY$ and $\angle YOZ$.

[NCERT]

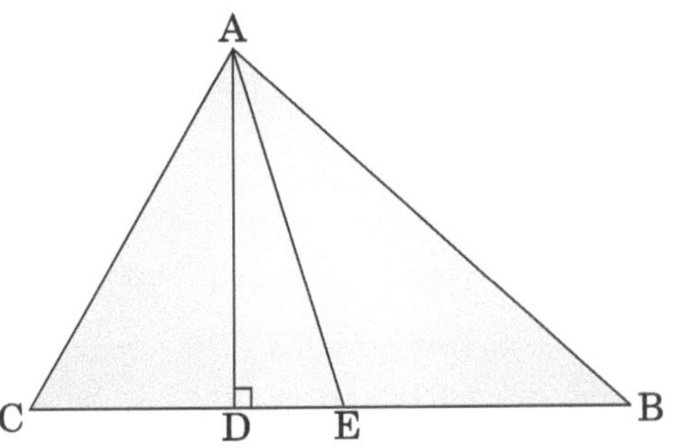

Sol. According to the question,
$$\angle X = 62° \text{ and } \angle XYZ = 54°$$
In $\triangle XYZ$, $\angle XYZ + \angle YXZ + \angle XZY = 180°$
(Angle sum property)
$$\Rightarrow \qquad 54° + 62° + \angle XZY = 180°$$
$$\Rightarrow \qquad 116° + \angle XZY = 180°$$
$$\Rightarrow \qquad XZY = 180° - 116°$$
$$\therefore \qquad \angle XZY = 64°$$
Also, given that YO and ZO are the bisectors of $\angle XYZ$ and $\angle XZY$, respectively.
$$\therefore \qquad \angle OYZ = \frac{1}{2} \angle XYZ$$
$$\Rightarrow \qquad \angle OYZ = \frac{1}{2} \times 54° = 27°$$
and $\qquad \angle OZY = \frac{1}{2} \angle XZY = \frac{1}{2} \times 64° = 32°$
Now, in $\triangle OYZ$,
$$\angle OYZ + \angle OZY + \angle YOZ = 180°$$
[since, sum of all the angles of a triangle is 180°]
$$\Rightarrow \quad 27° + 32° + \angle YOZ = 180°$$
$$59° + \angle YOZ = 180°$$
$$\Rightarrow \qquad \angle YOZ = 180° - 59°$$
$$\therefore \qquad \angle YOZ = 121°$$
Hence, $\qquad \angle OZY = 32°$ and $\angle YOZ = 121°$

2. In the figure of $\triangle ABC$, AE is the bisector of $\angle BAC$ and AD $\perp BC$. Show that $\angle DAE = \frac{1}{2}$ ($\angle C - \angle B$).

[NCERT Examplar, Board Term-1, 2015, Set-1]

Sol. According to the question,

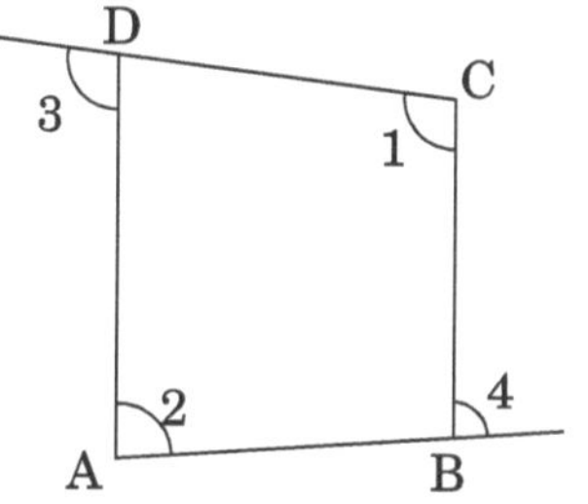

$$\angle CAE = \angle EAB \text{ (given)} \qquad ...(i)$$

Also, $\angle CAD + \angle DAE = \angle CAE = \angle EAB \qquad ...(ii)$

Now, $\angle CAD + \angle C = 90°$

$$= \angle DAE + \angle EAB + \angle B$$

$$\angle CAD + \angle C = \angle DAE + \angle CAD + DAE + \angle B$$

$$[\text{On using equation (ii)}]$$

$$= 2\,\angle DAE + \angle CAD + \angle B$$

$$\therefore \qquad 2\,\angle DAE = \angle C - \angle B$$

$$\therefore \qquad \angle DAE = \frac{1}{2}\,(\angle C - \angle B)$$

3. In the given figure, BO and CO are bisectors of $\angle DBC$ and $\angle ECB$ respectively. If $\angle BAC = 70°$ and $\angle ABC = 40°$, find the measure of $\angle BOC$.

[Board Term I, 2012, Set-54; 2011, Set-79]

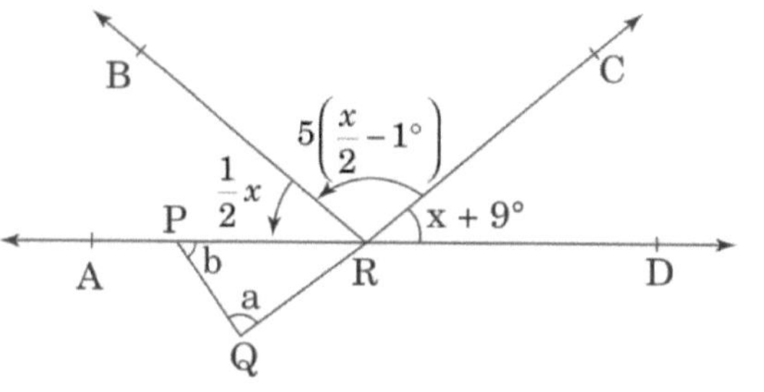

Sol. According to the question,

$$\angle DBC = 180° - 40° = 140° \qquad \text{(Linear pair)}$$

$$\angle CBO = \frac{1}{2}\,\angle DBC = \frac{1}{2} \times 140° = 70°$$

$$\angle ACB = 180° - (70° + 40°) = 70° \text{ (Linear pair)}$$

$$\angle BCE = 180° - 70° = 110°$$

$$\angle BCO = \frac{1}{2} \times 110° = 55° \qquad \text{(Angle bisector)}$$

$$\therefore \quad \angle BOC = 180° - (\angle CBO + \angle BCO)$$

$$= 180° - (70° + 55°)$$

$$= 180° - 125° = 55°$$

4. In the given figure, find a + b.

[Board Term I, 2012, Set-19]

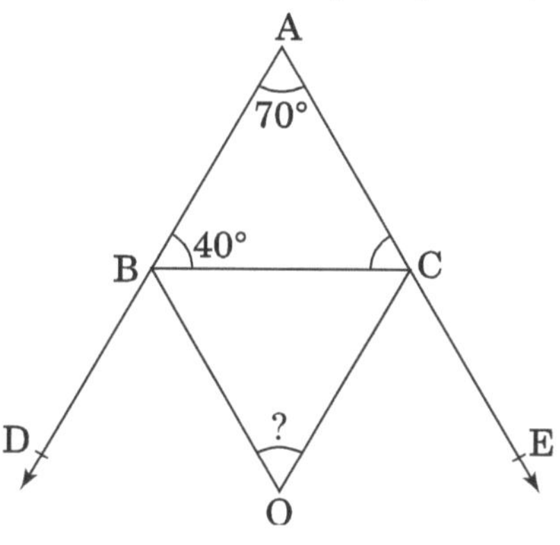

Sol. According to the question,

$$x + 9° + 5\left(\frac{x}{2} - 1°\right) + \frac{1}{2}\,x = 180° \text{ (Linear Pair)}$$

$$x + 9° + \frac{5x}{2} - 5° + \frac{1}{2}x = 180°$$

$$\Rightarrow \qquad \frac{2x + 5x + x}{2} = 180° - 9°$$

$$\Rightarrow \qquad \frac{8x}{2} = 172°$$

$$\Rightarrow \qquad 4x = 172°$$

$$\therefore \qquad x = \frac{172}{4} = 43°$$

Now, In ΔPQR.

$$a + b = \frac{1}{2}x + 5\left(\frac{x}{2} - 1°\right)$$

(Exterior angle)

$$= \frac{1}{2}x + \frac{5x}{2} - 5°$$

$$= 3x - 5°$$

$$= 3 \times 43° - 5°$$

$$= 129° - 5° = 124°$$

5. In the given figure $\angle 3$ and $\angle 4$ are exterior angles of quadrilateral ABCD at point D and B respectively, and $\angle A = \angle 2$, $\angle C = \angle 1$. Prove that $\angle 3 + \angle 4 = \angle 1 + \angle 2$.

[Board Term I, 2012, Set-50]

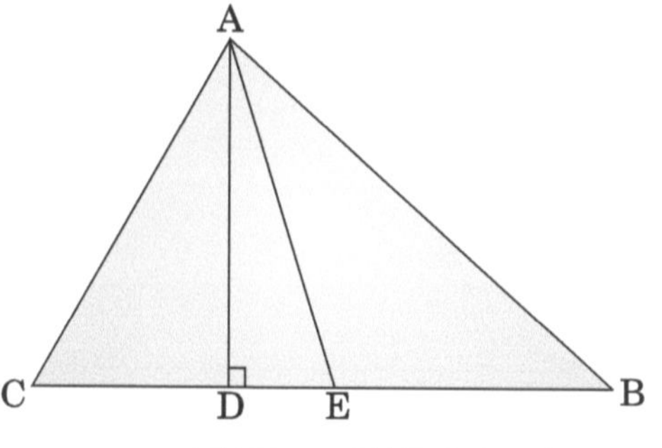

Sol. According to the question, Now draw a line AC as given below,

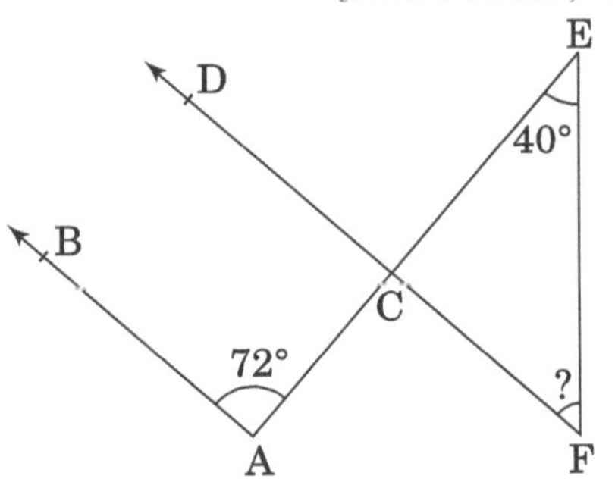

In $\triangle$ABC, [Exterior angle is the sum of two interior opposite angles]

$$\angle 4 = \angle ACB + \angle CAB \qquad …(i)$$

Again in $\triangle$ACD

$$\text{Ext. } \angle 3 = \angle DAC + \angle DCA \qquad …(ii)$$

On adding (i) and (ii), we get

$$\angle 3 + \angle 4 = (\angle ACB + \angle DCA)$$
$$+ (\angle CAB + \angle DAC)$$
$$= \angle 1 + \angle 2$$
$$\angle 3 + \angle 4 = \angle 1 + \angle 2 \qquad \text{Hence Proved}$$

6. In the figure, $\angle BAC = 50°$, $\angle GBD = 70°$ and l and m are parallel lines. Find x, y and z.

[Board Term I, 2012, Set-63]

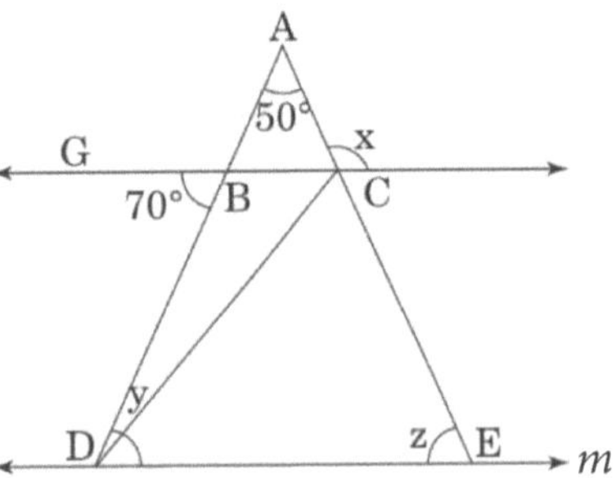

Sol. According to the question,

$$\angle ABC = \angle GBD = 70° \text{ (vertically opp. angles)}$$
$$x = \angle ABC + \angle CAB \text{ [Exterior angle is the}$$
$$\text{sum of interior opposite angle]}$$
$$= 50° + 70° = 120°$$
$$\therefore \qquad l \parallel m$$
$$y = \angle GBD = 70° \qquad \text{(alternate angles)}$$
$$\text{and} \quad z = 180° - \angle EAD \quad y$$
$$\text{(Angle sum property)}$$
$$= 180° - 50° - 70° = 60°$$

7. In the given figure, find the value of x:

[Board Term I, 2016, Set-2 OCNJE9]

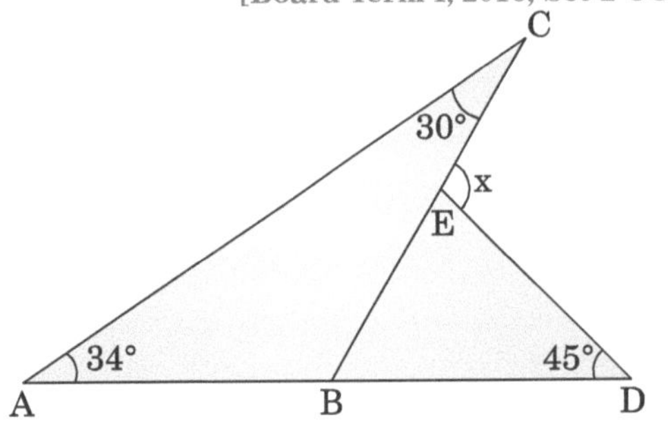

Sol. According to the question,

$$\angle CBD = 34° + 30°$$
$$= 64° \quad \text{(exterior } \angle \text{ of } \triangle ABC)$$
$$x° = \angle EBD + \angle EDB$$
$$= 64° + 45°$$
$$\therefore \qquad x° = 109°$$

8. Prove that the sum of angles of a triangle is 180°.

[Board Term I, 2012, Set-20]

Sol. Through vertex A, draw PAQ $\parallel$ BC

$$\angle PAB = \angle ABC \qquad …(i)$$
$$\text{(Alternate angles)}$$
$$\angle QAC = \angle ACB \qquad …(ii)$$
$$\text{(Alternate angles)}$$

On adding equation (i) and (ii), we have

$$\angle PAB + \angle QAC = \angle ABC + \angle ACB$$

Now, on adding $\angle BAC$ to both sides, we get

$$\angle PAB + \angle QAC + \angle BAC = \angle ABC + \angle ACB + \angle BAC$$
$$180° = \angle ABC + \angle ACB + \angle BAC \text{ (Linear pair)}$$

Hence, the sum of angles of a triangles is 180°

9. In the given figure, AB $\parallel$ CD, $\angle BAC = 72°$ and $\angle CEF = 40°$. Find $\angle CFE$.

[Board Term I, 2012, Set-62]

Sol. Given, AB $\parallel$ CD

$$\angle BAC = \angle DCE = 72°$$
$$\text{(Corresponding angles)}$$
$$\angle DCE = \angle CEF + \angle CFE$$
$$\text{[Exterior angle is the sum of}$$
$$\text{interior opposite angles]}$$
$$\Rightarrow \qquad 72° = 40° + \angle CFE$$
$$\therefore \qquad \angle CFE = 72° - 40° = 32°$$

10. In figure, triangle ABC is right angled at A. AL is drawn perpendicular to BC. Prove that $\angle BAL = \angle ACB$. [Board Term I, 2012, Set-71]

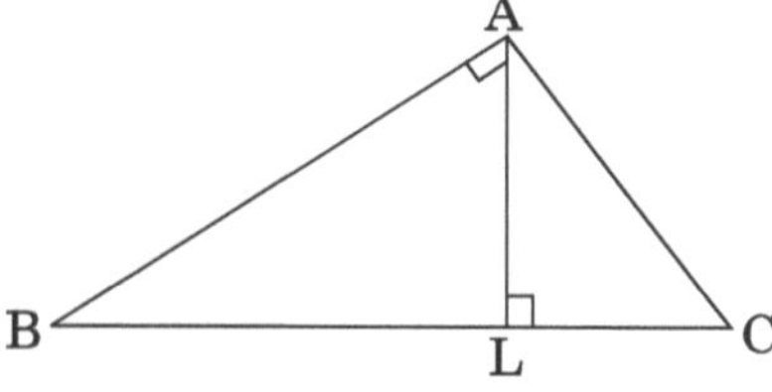

Sol. According to question,

In $\triangle ABC$, $\angle A + \angle B + \angle C = 180°$

(Angle sum property)

$\Rightarrow \quad 90° + \angle B + \angle C = 180°$ ($\angle A = 90°$)

$\Rightarrow \quad \angle B + \angle C = 180° - 90° = 90°$

$\therefore \quad \angle C = \angle ACB = 90° - \angle B$ ...(i)

Also, in $\triangle ALB$,

$\angle ALB + \angle BAL + \angle B = 180°$

(Angle sum property)

or $\quad 90° + \angle BAL + \angle B = 180°$

$\therefore \quad \angle BAL = 90° - \angle B$ ...(ii)

from (i) and (ii), we get

$\angle BAL = \angle ACB$

Hence proved.

11. In $\triangle ABC$, AD and CE are the bisectors of $\angle A$ and $\angle C$ respectively, If $\angle ABC = 90°$, then find $\angle AOC$. [Board Term I, 2012, Set-60]

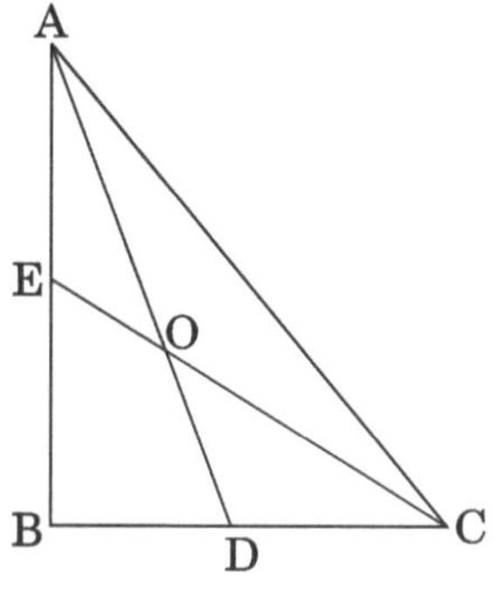

Sol. According to the question

In $\triangle ABC$, $\angle A + \angle B + \angle C = 180°$

(angle sum property of triangle)

$\Rightarrow \quad \angle A + \angle C = 180° - 90° = 90°$

$\Rightarrow \quad \dfrac{1}{2}(\angle A + \angle C) = 45°$ ...(i)

In $\triangle AOC$,

$\dfrac{1}{2}\angle A + \dfrac{1}{2}\angle C + \angle AOC = 180°$

From equation (i), we have

$\therefore \quad \angle AOC = 180° - 45° = 135°$

12. In figure, if AB || CD, then find the measure of x. [Board Term I, 2012, Set-44]

Sol. According to the question,

AB || CD

$\therefore \quad \angle SMU = \angle PST$

$\Rightarrow \quad \angle y = 88°$ [corresponding angles]

$\therefore \quad a = 180° - 88° = 92°$ (Linear Pair)

and $b = 180° - 110° = 70°$ (Linear Pair)

Now, in $\triangle UMQ$,

$\angle UMQ + \angle MUQ + \angle MQU = 180°$

$x = 180° - (92° + 70°)$

(Angle sum property)

$= 180° - 162° = 18°$

Hence, the value of x = 18°

13. In the given figure, find the value of x° [Board Term I, 2012, Set-48]

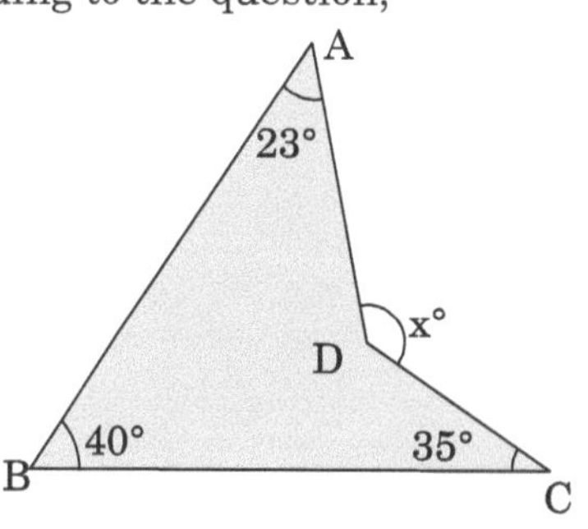

Sol. According to the question,

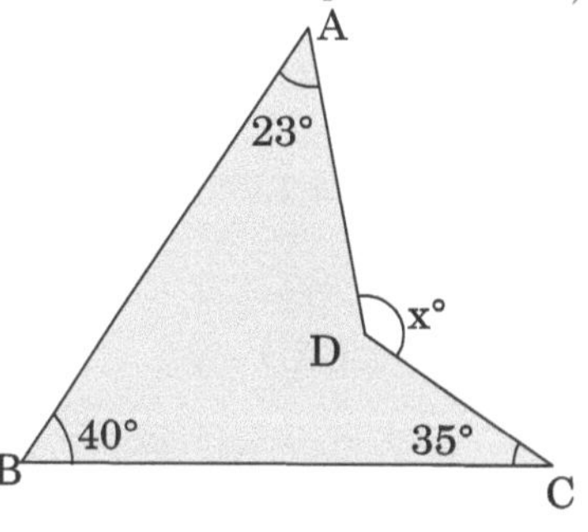

$$\angle A + \angle B + \angle C + \angle D = 360°$$
$$23° + 40° + 35° + \angle D = 360°$$
$$\Rightarrow \quad 98° + \angle D = 360°$$
(Angle sum property of a quadrilateral)
$$\therefore \qquad \angle D = 262°$$
$$x° = \text{Reflex } \angle D$$
$$= 360° - 262° = 98°$$
Hence, the value of x = 98°

14. In the given figure, if $\angle BCD = 25°$, $\angle BAQ = 110°$ and $\angle ACR = 125°$, then find the values of x, y, z.

[Board Term I, 2012, Set -38]

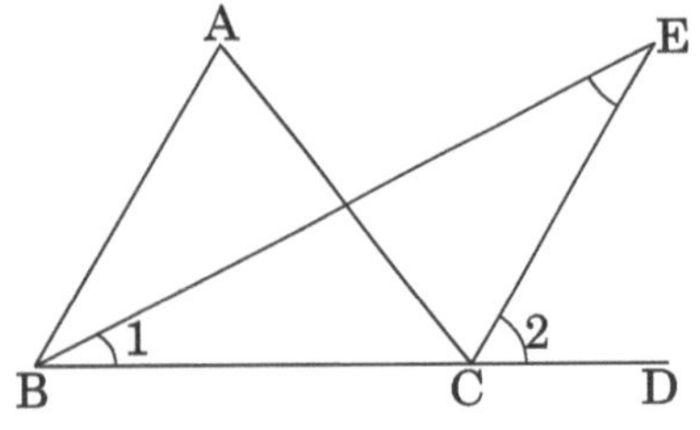

Sol. According to the given figure,
$$y = 180° - (25° + 125°) \quad \text{(Linear pair)}$$
$$= 180° - 150° = 30°$$
$$y + z = 110° \qquad \text{[Exterior angle is the sum of two interior opposite angles]}$$
$$\therefore \qquad z = 110° - 30° = 80°$$
$$x + 25° = z \qquad \text{[Exterior angle is the sum of two interior opposite angles]}$$
$$\therefore \qquad x = 80° - 25° = 55°.$$

15. Prove that the angle between internal bisector of one base angle and the external bisector of the other base angle of a triangle is equal to one-half on the vertical angle.

[Board Term I, 2013; 2012, Set-49]

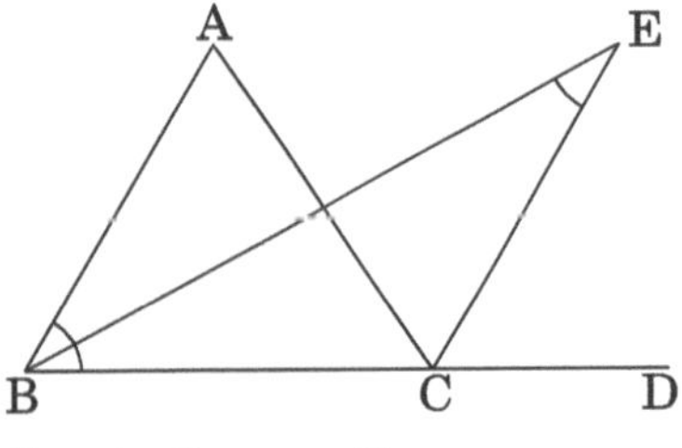

Sol. According to the question,

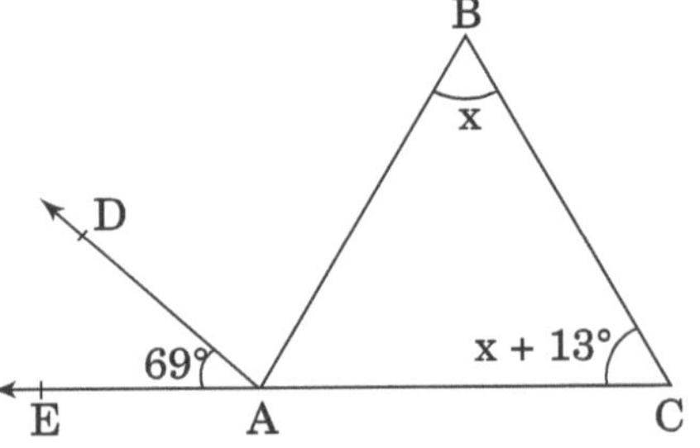

$$\angle ACD = \angle A + \angle B$$
(Exterior angle is the sum of opposite interior angles)
$$\Rightarrow \quad \frac{1}{2} \text{ ext. } \angle ACD = \frac{\angle A}{2} + \frac{\angle B}{2}$$
$$\angle 2 = \angle 1 + \frac{1}{2} \angle A \qquad \text{...(i)}$$
Also,
$$\angle 2 = \angle 1 + \angle E \qquad \text{...(ii)}$$
(Exterior angle is the sum of opposite interior angles)
From eqn. (i) and (ii), we get
$$\angle 1 + \frac{\angle A}{2} = \angle 1 + \angle E$$
$$\therefore \qquad \angle E = \frac{\angle A}{2}$$
Hence proved.

16. In the given figure, $\angle CAB : \angle BAD = 1 : 2$, find all the internal angles of $\triangle ABC$.

[Board Term I, 2014, 2012, Set-20]

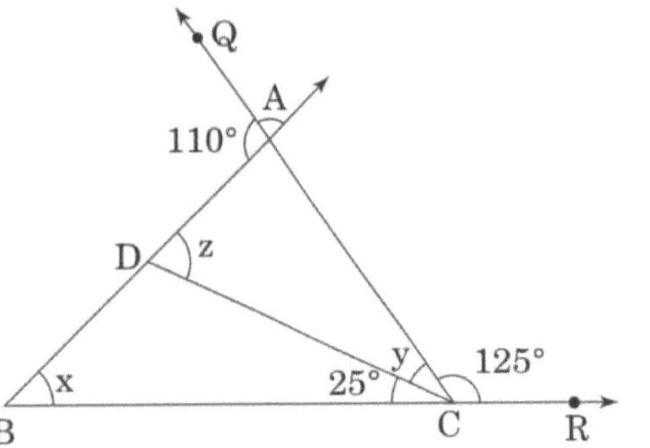

Sol. According to the question,
$$\angle EAD + \angle DAC = 180° \qquad \text{(Linear pair)}$$
$$\Rightarrow \quad 69° + \angle DAC = 180°$$
$$\therefore \qquad \angle DAC = 180° - 69° = 111°$$
Let $\qquad \angle CAB = y$
and $\qquad \angle BAD = 2y$
Then, $y + 2y + 69° = 180°$ (Adjacent angles)
$$\Rightarrow \qquad 3y = 180° - 69° = 111°$$
$$y = 37°$$
$$\angle CAB = y = 37°$$
$$\angle BAD = 2y = 2 \times 37° = 74°$$
$$x + x + 13° = 69° + 74° = 143°$$
[Exterior angle is the sum of two interior opposite angles]
or, $\qquad 2x = 130°$
$$\therefore \qquad x = \frac{130°}{2} = 65°$$
$$\angle C = x + 13°$$
$$= 65° + 13° = 78°$$
$$\angle B = x = 65°$$
Thus, $\qquad \angle BAC = 37°$

17. In figure, PQ $\perp$ PR, QP $||$ RL, $\angle$RQT = 38° and $\angle$QTL = 75°. Find x and y.   [Board Term I. 2014]

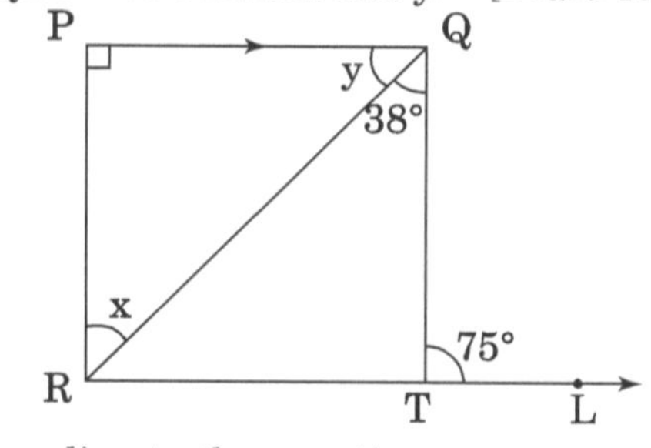

Sol. According to the question

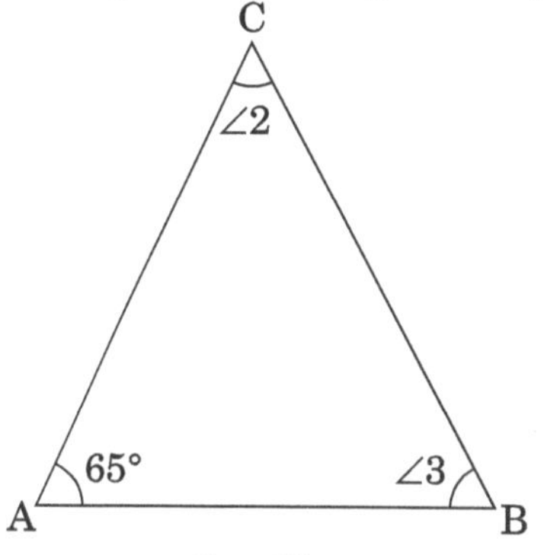

$\therefore$ $\qquad$ PQ $\perp$ PR
and $\qquad$ PQ $||$ RL
$\therefore$ $\qquad$ $\angle$RQT = 38°
and $\qquad$ $\angle$QTL = 75°
To find: x and y
$$\angle 1 = \angle y \qquad \text{...(i)}$$
[alternate interior angles]
Now, in $\triangle$QPR
$$\angle QTL = \angle TQR + \angle QRT$$
[Exterior angle is the sum of two interior opposite angles]
$\Rightarrow$ $\qquad$ $75° = 38° + \angle 1$
$\Rightarrow$ $\qquad$ $\angle 1 = 37°$
$\therefore$ $\qquad$ $\angle y = 37°$ $\qquad$ ...(ii)
[from equation (i)]
Now, in $\triangle$QTR
$$\angle QPR + \angle x + \angle y = 180° \qquad \text{[by ASPT]}$$
$\Rightarrow$ $\quad$ $90° + \angle x + 37° = 180°$
$\Rightarrow$ $\qquad$ $127° + \angle x = 180°$
$\Rightarrow$ $\qquad$ $\angle x = 180° - 127°$
$\therefore$ $\qquad$ $\angle x = 53°$ $\quad$ {from equation (ii)}

18. In given figure DE $\perp$ AB. Find the values of x and y.   [Board Term I, 2014]

Sol. According to the question, In $\triangle$BDE,
$$\angle B + \angle D + \angle DEB = 180°$$
(Angle sum property of a triangle)
$\Rightarrow$ $\qquad$ $40° + x + 90° = 180°$
$\Rightarrow$ $\qquad$ $130° + x = 180°$
$\therefore$ $\qquad$ $x = 180° - 130° = 50°$
In $\triangle$DCF,
$$\angle D + \angle FCD = \angle AFD$$
(Exterior angle is the sum of the two interior opposite angles)
$\qquad$ $50° + y = 110°$
$\therefore$ $\qquad$ $y = 110° - 50° = 60°$

19. One of the angles of a triangle is 65°. If the difference of the remaining angles is 35°, then find remaining angles.

Sol. Let three angles of a triangle be $\angle 1$, $\angle 2$ and $\angle 3$

If, $\qquad$ $\angle 1 = 65°$ $\qquad$ ...(i) [given]
and $\qquad$ $\angle 2 - \angle 3 = 35°$ $\qquad$ ...(ii) [given]
Also, $\angle 1 + \angle 2 + \angle 3 = 180°$
[since, sum of all the angles of a triangle is 180°]
$\Rightarrow$ $\quad$ $65° + \angle 2 + \angle 3 = 180°$ $\quad$ [from equation (i)]
$\Rightarrow$ $\qquad$ $\angle 2 + \angle 3 = 180° - 65°$
$\Rightarrow$ $\qquad$ $\angle 2 + \angle 3 = 115°$ $\qquad$ ...(iii)
Now, on adding equation. (ii) and (iii), we get
$\qquad$ $\angle 2 + \angle 3 = 115°$
$\Rightarrow$ $\qquad$ $\angle 2 - \angle 3 = 35°$
$\qquad$ $2\angle 2 = 150°$
$\therefore$ $\qquad$ $\angle 2 = \dfrac{150°}{2} = 75°$
From equation (iii),
$\qquad$ $\angle 2 + \angle 3 = 115°$
$\therefore$ $\qquad$ $\angle 3 = 115° - 75° = 40°$

Long Answer Type Questions
(4 Marks Each)

1. In $\triangle$ABC, the sides AB and AC of $\triangle$ABC are produced to points E and D, respectively. If bisectors BO and CO of $\angle$CBE and $\angle$BCD, respectively meet at point O, then prove that
$$\angle BOC = 90° - \frac{1}{2} \angle A. \qquad \text{[NCERT Exemplar]}$$

Sol. Given, In $\triangle ABC$, the exterior bisectors of $\angle B$ and $\angle C$ meet at point O.

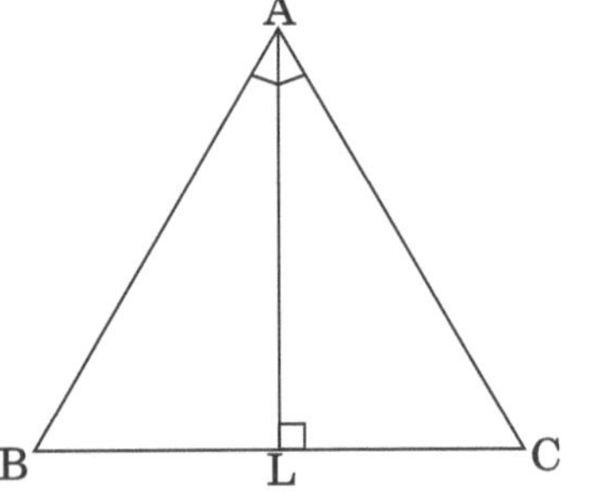

To prove : $\angle BOC = 90° - \dfrac{1}{2} \angle A$

Proof : Since, $\angle ABC$ and $\angle CBE$ from a linear pair.

$\therefore \quad \angle ABC + \angle CBE = 180°$ ...(i)

and BO is the bisector of $\angle CBE$.

$\therefore \qquad \angle CBE = 2\angle 1$

Then, from equation (i), we get

$\qquad \angle ABC + 2\angle 1 = 180°$

$\Rightarrow \qquad 2\angle 1 = 180° - \angle ABC$

$\Rightarrow \qquad \angle 1 = 90° - \dfrac{1}{2} \angle ABD$ ...(ii)

[On dividing both sides by 2].

Again $\angle ACB$ and $\angle BCD$ from a linear pair.

$\therefore \quad \angle ACB + \angle BCD = 180°$ (iii)

and CO is the bisector of $\angle BCD$, therefore

$\qquad \angle BCD = 2 \angle 2$

Then, from equation (iii) we get

$\qquad \angle ACB + 2 \angle 2 = 180°$

$\Rightarrow \qquad 2 \angle 2 = 180° - \angle ACB$

$\Rightarrow \qquad \angle 2 = 90° - \dfrac{1}{2} \angle ACB$ ...(iv)

[On dividing both sides by 2]

In $\triangle OBC$, we have

$\qquad \angle 1 + \angle 2 + \angle BOC = 180°$ ...(v)

[Angle sum property]

From equation (ii), (iv) and (v), we get

$90° - \dfrac{1}{2} \angle BAC + 90° - \dfrac{1}{2} \angle ABC + \angle BOC = 180°$

$\Rightarrow 180° - \dfrac{1}{2} (\angle ABC + \angle ACB) + \angle BOC = 180°$ ...(vi)

Now, in $\triangle ABC$, we have

$\qquad \angle A + \angle B + \angle C = 180°$ [Angle sum property]

$\Rightarrow \qquad \angle B + \angle C = 180° - \angle A$ ...(vii)

From equations (vi) and (vii), we get

$180° - \dfrac{1}{2} (180° - \angle A) + \angle BOC = 180°$

$\Rightarrow \qquad \angle BOC = 180° - 180° + \dfrac{1}{2} (180° - \angle A)$

$\Rightarrow \qquad \angle BOC = \dfrac{1}{2} (180° - \angle A)$

$\therefore \qquad \angle BOC = 90° - \dfrac{1}{2} \angle A$

Hence proved

2. A $\triangle$ ABC is right angled at A. L is at point on BC such that AL $\perp$ BC. Prove that $\angle BAL = \angle ACB$.

[NCERT Examplar]

Sol. Given In $\triangle ABC$,

$\qquad \angle A = 90°$ and AL $\perp$ BC

To Prove: $\angle BAL = \angle ACB$

Proof: In $\angle ABC$ and $\triangle ABL$,

$\qquad \angle BAC = \angle ALB$ [Each 90°] ...(i)

and $\quad \angle ABC = \angle ABL$ [common angles] ...(ii)

On adding equation (i) and (ii), we get

$\qquad \angle BAC + \angle ABC = \angle ALC + \angle ABL$ ...(iii)

$\qquad\qquad [\because \ \angle ALB = \angle ALC = 90°]$

Again, in $\triangle ABC$,

$\qquad \angle BAC + \angle ACB + \angle ABC = 180°$

[Angle sum property]

$\Rightarrow \angle BAC + \angle ABC = 180° - \angle ACB$ ...(iv)

In $\triangle ABL$,

$\qquad \angle ABL + \angle ALB + \angle BAL = 180°$

[Angle sum property]

$\Rightarrow \angle ABL + \angle ALC = 180° - \angle BAL$ ...(v)

$\qquad\qquad [\because \ \angle ALC = \angle ALB = 90°]$

On substituting the values from equation (iv) and (v) in equation (iii), we get

$\qquad 180° - \angle ACB = 180° - \angle BAL$

$\Rightarrow \qquad - \angle ACB = - \angle BAL$

$\therefore \qquad \angle ACB = \angle BAL$

Hence Proved.

3. In the given figure $\angle Q > \angle R$, PA is the bisector of $\angle QPR$ and PM $\perp$ QR. Prove that $\angle APM = \dfrac{1}{2}$ $(\angle Q - \angle R)$.

[NCERT Examplar]

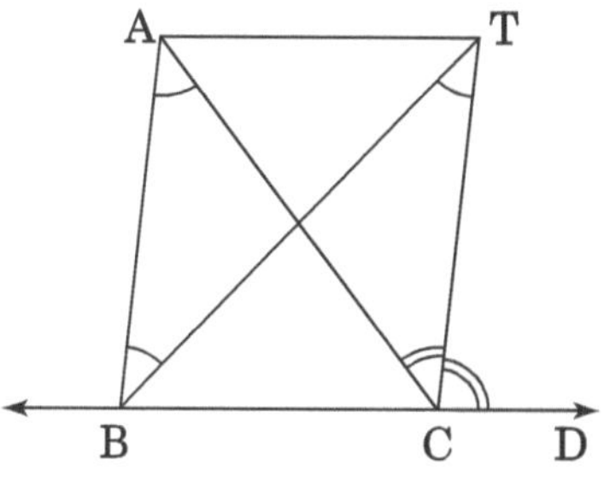

Sol. Given in $\triangle PQR$, $\angle Q > \angle R$, PA is the bisector of $\angle QPR$ and $PM \perp QR$.

To prove $\angle APM = \dfrac{1}{2}(\angle Q - \angle R)$

Proof $\because$ PA is the bisector of $\angle QPR$.

$\therefore \qquad \angle QPA = \angle APR \qquad \qquad \ldots(i)$

In $\ \angle PQM + \angle PMQ + \angle QPM = 180°$

$$[\text{angle sum property}]$$

$\Rightarrow \qquad \angle PQM + 90° + \angle QPM = 180°$

$$[\because PM \perp QR \Rightarrow \angle PMQ = 90°]$$

$\Rightarrow \qquad \angle PQM + \angle QPM = 180° - 90°$

$\Rightarrow \qquad \angle PQM = 90° - \angle QPM \qquad \ldots(ii)$

In $\triangle PMR$,

$\qquad \angle PMR + \angle PRM + \angle RPM = 180°$

$$[\text{by angle sum property of a triangle}]$$

$\Rightarrow \qquad 90° + \angle PRM + \angle RPM = 180°$

$$[\because PM \perp QR \Rightarrow \angle PMR = 90°]$$

$\Rightarrow \qquad \angle PRM = 90° - \angle RPM \qquad (iii)$

On subtracting equation (iii) from equation (ii), we get

$\qquad \angle Q - \angle R = (\angle RPM - \angle QPM) - (90° - \angle RPM)$

$$[\text{where}, \angle PQM = \angle Q \text{ and } \angle PRM = \angle R]$$

$\Rightarrow \ \angle Q - \angle R = \angle RPM - \angle QPM$

$\Rightarrow \ \angle Q - \angle R = \angle RPA + \angle APM - [\angle QPA - \angle APM]$

$$\ldots(iv)$$

$\Rightarrow \ \angle Q - \angle R = \angle QPA + \angle APM - \angle QPA + \angle APM$

$$[\text{from equation (i)}]$$

$\Rightarrow \ \angle Q - \angle R = 2\angle APM$

$\therefore \qquad \angle APM = \dfrac{1}{2}(\angle Q - \angle R)$

Hence proved.

4. Bisectors of interior $\angle B$ and exterior $\angle ACD$ of a $\triangle ABC$ intersect at the point T. Prove that $\angle BTC = \dfrac{1}{2} \angle BAC.$ [NCERT Examplar]

Sol. Given, The bisectors of $\angle ABC$ and $\angle ACD$ meet at point T.

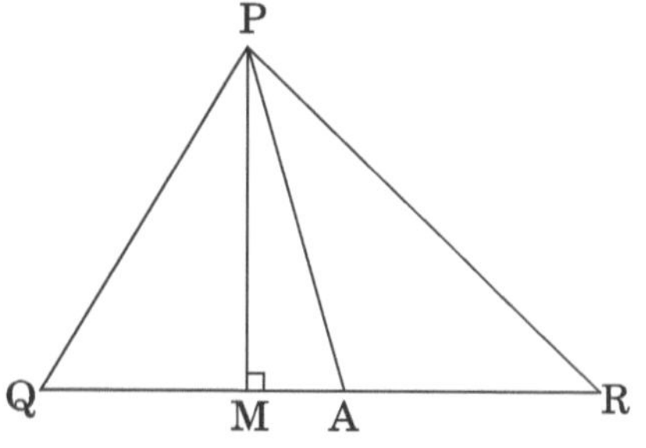

To prove $\angle BTC = \dfrac{1}{2} BAC$

Construction In $\triangle ABC$, produce BC to D.

Proof Proof in $\triangle ABC$ $\angle C$ is an exterior angle

$\therefore \qquad \angle ACD = \angle CAB + \angle ABC$

$$[\because \text{ exterior angle of a triangle is the sum of two opposite interior angles}]$$

$\Rightarrow \qquad \dfrac{1}{2} \angle ACD = \dfrac{1}{2} \angle CAB + \dfrac{1}{2} \angle ABC$

$$[\text{On dividing both sides by 2}]$$

$\Rightarrow \qquad \angle TCD = \dfrac{1}{2} \angle CAB + \dfrac{1}{2} \angle ABC \ \ldots(i)$

$[\because CT \text{ is a bisector of } \angle ACD \ \dfrac{1}{2} \angle ACD = \angle TCD]$

Now, In $\triangle BTC$.

$\qquad \angle TCD = \angle BTC + \angle CBT$

$$[\because \text{ exterior angle of a triangle is the sum of two opposite interior angles}]$$

$\Rightarrow \qquad \angle TCD = \angle BTC + \dfrac{1}{2} \angle ABC \qquad \ldots(ii)$

$[\because BT \text{ bisects } \angle ABC \therefore \angle CBT = \dfrac{1}{2} \angle ABC]$

From Eqs. (i) and (ii),

$\Rightarrow \ \dfrac{1}{2} \angle CAB + \dfrac{1}{2} \angle ABC = \angle BTC + \dfrac{1}{2} \angle ABC$

$\therefore \qquad \angle BTC = \dfrac{1}{2} \angle CAB$

$\Rightarrow \qquad \angle BTC = \dfrac{1}{2} \angle BAC$

Hence proved.

5. In the given figure, $\angle ACD = \angle ABC$ and CP bisects $\angle BCD$. Prove that $\angle APC = \angle ACP$.

[Board Term I, 2012 Set-47]

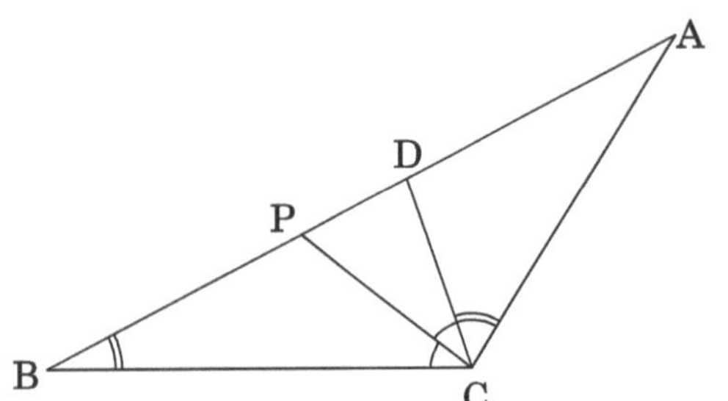

Sol. Given, $\angle ACD = \angle ABC$ and CP is the bisector of $\angle BCD$.

To Prove: $\angle APC = \angle ACP$

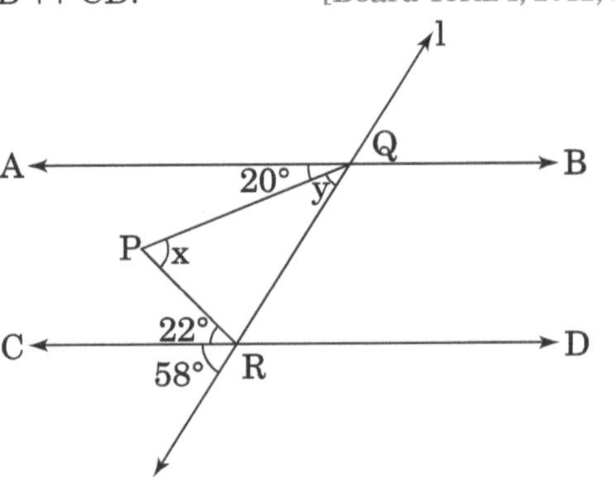

$\angle ACD = \angle ABC = x$ (left)
$\angle BCP = \angle DCP = y$ (left)
$\angle APC = x + y$ ...(i)
[$\because$ Exterior angle is the sum of two opposite interior angles]
and $\angle ACP = x + y$ ...(ii)
From equation (i) and (ii), we get
$$\angle APC = \angle ACP$$

Hence Proved

6. In the given figure, $AM \perp BC$ and AN is the bisector of $\angle A$. If $\angle ABC = 70°$ and $\angle ACB = 20°$, find the value of $\angle MAN$.

[Board Term I, 2012, Set-48]

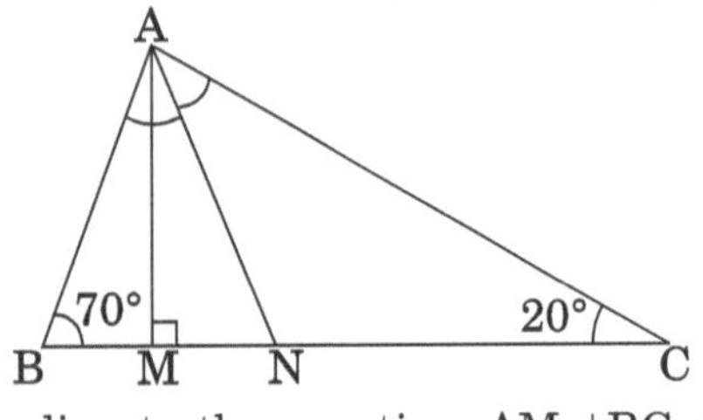

Sol. According to the question, AM $\perp$ BC and AN is the bisector of $\angle A$.

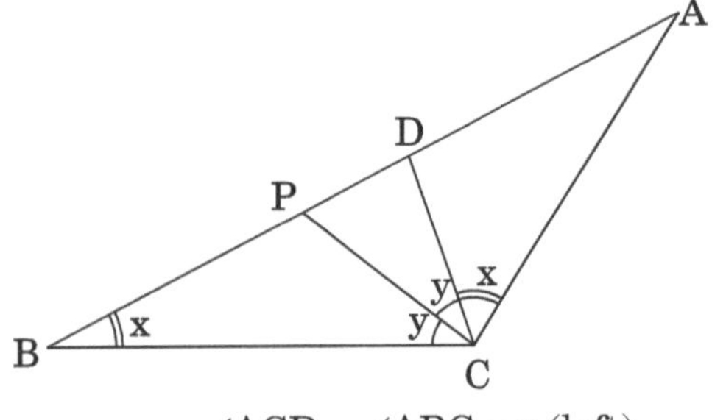

Now, in $\triangle ABM$,
$$\angle M = \angle 1 + 70°$$
[Exterior angle is the sum of two opposite interior angles]
$$90° = \angle 1 + 70°$$

$\angle 1 = 20°$
$\angle 1 + \angle 2 = \angle 3$ (AN is angle bisector)
$20° + \angle 2 = \angle 3$
In $\triangle AMC$, $\angle AMC + \angle ACM + \angle 2 + \angle 3 = 180°$
(Sum of all angles of a $\triangle$ is 180°)
$\Rightarrow$ $90° + 20° + \angle 2 + 20° + \angle 2 = 180°$
$\Rightarrow$ $2\angle 2 + 130° = 180°$
$\Rightarrow$ $2\angle 2 = 180° - 130°$
$2\angle 2 = 50°$
$\angle 2 = 25°$
Hence, the value of $\angle MAN = 25°$

7. In the given figure, find the value of x and y if AB || CD. [Board Term I, 2012, Set-35]

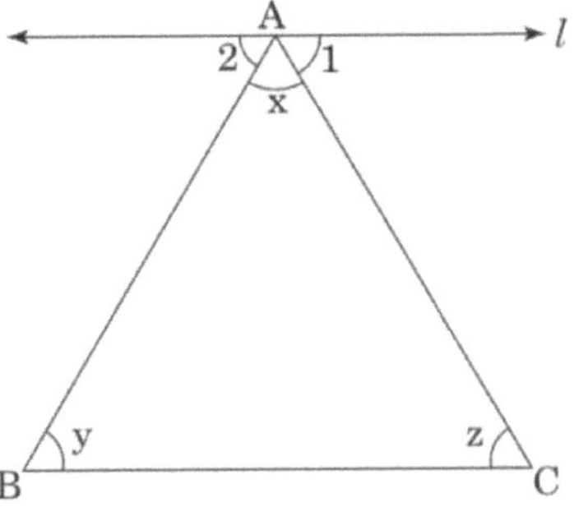

Sol. According to the figure,
$\because$ $\qquad$ AB || CD
$\therefore$ $\qquad y + 20° = 58°$ $\qquad$ (corresponding angle)
$\qquad y = 58° - 20° = 38°$
and $\quad \angle PRQ = 180° - (58° + 22°)$ (Linear pair)
$\qquad\qquad = 180° - 80° = 100°$
Now, In $\triangle PQR$,
$\qquad \angle P + \angle PQR + \angle QRP = 180°$
$\Rightarrow$ $\qquad x + y + \angle QRP = 180$
$\Rightarrow$ $\qquad x + 38° = 180° - 100°$
$x = 180° - (100° + 38°)$ Angle sum property
$\qquad 180° - 138° = 42°$

8. Prove that the sum of all the angles of triangle is 180°. Also find the angle of a triangle if they are in ratio 5 : 6 : 7. [Board Term I, 2012, Set-43]

Sol. Let the angle of a triangle are 5x, 6x and 7x, then

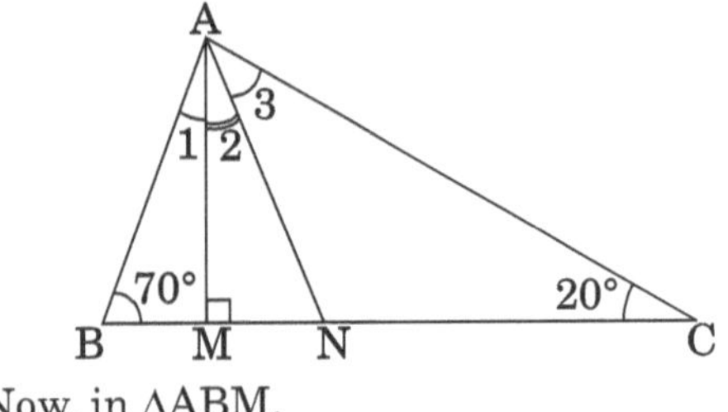

To prove : Sum of all angles of $\triangle ABC$ is $180°$

Construction : Draw a line l parallel to BC.

Proof : Since l | | BC, we have $\angle 2 = \angle y$ ...(i)

(Alternate angles are euqal)

Similarly, l | | BC $\angle 1 = \angle z$ ...(ii)

(Alternate angles are equal)

Also, sum of angles at a point A on line l is $180°$

$\therefore$ $\angle 2 + \angle x + \angle 1 = 180°$ (Line pair)

$\Rightarrow$ $\angle y + \angle x + \angle z = 180°$ (from (i) and (ii))

$\Rightarrow$ $\angle x + \angle y + \angle z = 180°$

$\Rightarrow$ $\angle A + \angle B + \angle C = 180°$

Hence, sum of all angles of a $\triangle$ is $180°$

$$5x + 6x + 7x = 180°$$

$\Rightarrow$ $18x = 180°$

$\therefore$ $x = \dfrac{180}{18} = 10°$

Angles are $50°$, $60°$ and $70°$.

9. Prove that the sum of three angles of a triangle is $180°$. Using this result, find the value of x and all the three angles of the triangle, if the angles are $(2x - 7)$, $(x + 25)°$ and $(3x + 12)°$.

[Board Term I, 2014]

Sol. First prove the theorem

Let A, B and C are the angles of $\triangle$

Then, $\angle A = 2x - 7$ ...(i)

                 $\angle B = x + 25$ ...(ii)

and $\angle C = 3x + 12$ ...(iii)

Then, $\angle A = 2x - 7$ ...(i)

       $\angle A + \angle B + \angle C = 180°$

[Angle sum property]

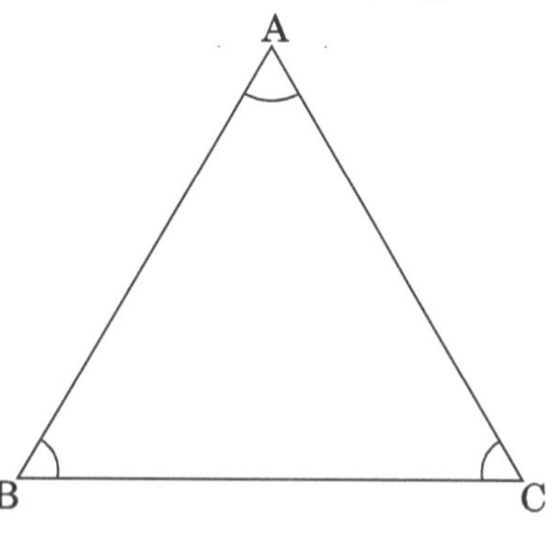

$\Rightarrow$ From equation (i) and (ii) , we get

$$2x - 7 + x + 25 + 3x + 12$$

$$= 180°$$

$\Rightarrow$ $6x - 7 + 37 = 180°$

$\Rightarrow$ $6x = 180° - 30°$

$\Rightarrow$ $6x = 150°$

$\therefore$ $x = \dfrac{150°}{6} = 25°$

10. In the given figure, on a quadrilateral ABCD shaped land is a village. The Panchayat has constructed a school specially for girls. What value are they exhibiting by doing so? How many triangles can be seen in the given figure? Find the measure of $\angle 1$.

[Board Term I, 2016, Set-BQS6IZK]

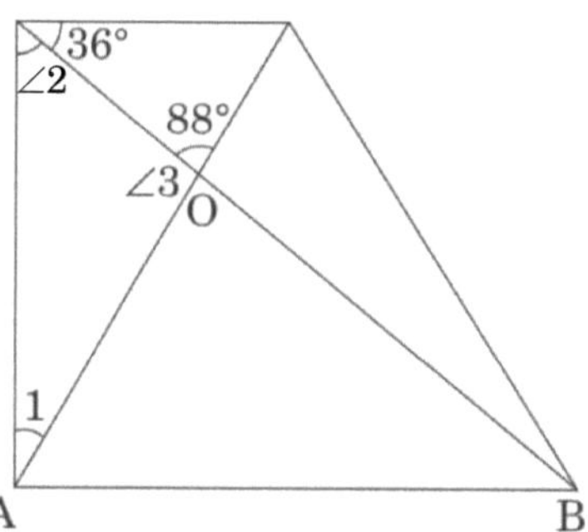

Sol. According to the question,

8 triangles

Now, $\angle 2 = 90° - 36° = 54°$

and $\angle 3 = 180° - 88°$

                 $= 92°$ (Linear pair)

In $\triangle AOD$,

       $\angle 1 + \angle 2 + \angle 3 = 180°$

[Angle sum property of triangle]

$\therefore$ $\angle 1 = 180° - 54° - 92°$

                 $= 34°$

CHAPTER 7

Triangles

- (Motivate) Two triangles are congruent if any two sides and the included angle of one triangle is equal to any two sides and the included angle of the other triangle (SAS Congruence).
- (Prove) Two triangles are congruent if any two angles and the included side of one triangle is equal to any two angles and the included side of the other triangle (ASA congruence).
- (Motivate) Two triangles are congruent if the three sides of one triangle are equal to three sides of the other triangle (SSC Congruence).
- (Motivate) Two right triangles are congruent if the hypotenuse and a side of one triangle are equal (respectively) to the hypotenuse and a side of the other triangle. (RHS Congruence).
- (Prove) the angles opposite to equal sides of a triangle are equal.
- (Motivate) The sides opposite to equal angles of a triangle are equal.
- (Motivate) Triangles inequalities and relation between 'angle and facing side' inequalities in triangles.

A flow chart on basic concepts of Triangles

Triangles

Congruent Figure

- Two figures are congruent, if they are of the same shape and of the same size.
- If two triangles ABC and PQR are congruent under the correspondence $A \leftrightarrow P$, $B \leftrightarrow Q$ and $C \leftrightarrow R$, the symbolically, it is ex.

Rule	Statement	Figure
1. SAS	Two triangles are congruent if two sides and the included angle of one triangle are equal to the two sides and the included angle of the other triangle.	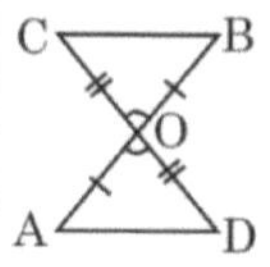 In $\triangle AOD$ and $\triangle COB$ $CO = OD$, $\angle COB = \angle AOD$, $OB = OA$ $\therefore \triangle AOD \cong \triangle COB$
2. ASA	Two triangles are congruent if two angles and the included side of one triangle are equal to two angles and the included side of other triangle.	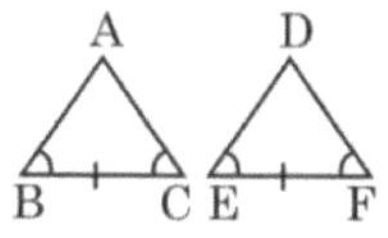 In $\triangle ABC$ and $\triangle DEF$ $\angle B = \angle E$, $BC = EF$ $\angle C = \angle F$ $\therefore \triangle ABC \cong \triangle DEF$
3. AAS	Two triangles are congruent if any two pairs of angles and one pair of corresponding sides are equal.	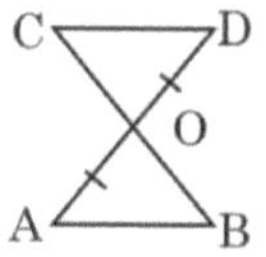 Given $AB \parallel CD$ In $\triangle AOB$ and $\triangle COD$ $\angle ABO = \angle DCO$ $\angle AOB = \angle DOC$, $OA = OD$ $\therefore \triangle AOB \cong \triangle COD$
4. SSS	If three sides of one triangle are equal to the three sides of another triangle, then two triangles are congruent.	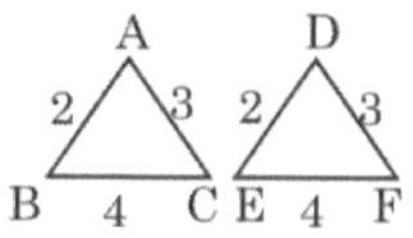 In $\triangle ABC$ and $\triangle DEF$ $AC = DF$, $AB = DE$ $BC = EF$ $\therefore \triangle ABC \cong \triangle DEF$
5.RHS	If in two right triangles the hypotenuse and one side of one triangle are equal to the hypotenuse and one side of the other triangle, then the two triangles are congruent.	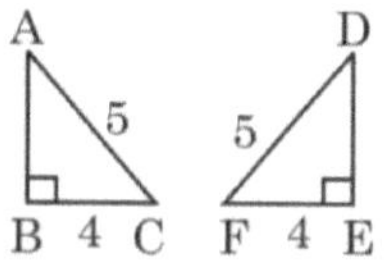 In $\triangle ABC$ and $\triangle DEF$ $AC = DF = 5$ cm $BC = EF = 4$ cm $AB = \sqrt{AC^2 - BC^2} = \sqrt{5^2 - 4^2} = 3$ $DE = \sqrt{DF^2 - EF^2} = \sqrt{5^2 - 4^2} = 3$ $\therefore AB = DE$ Hence $\triangle ABC \cong \triangle DEF$

Some Properties of a Triangle

- Angles opposite to equal sides of a triangle are equal.
- Sides opposite to equal angles of a triangle are equal.
- Each angle of an equilateral triangle is of 60°.
- In an isosceles triangle altitude from the vertex bisects the base. Conversely, if the altitude from one vertex of a triangle bisects the opposite side, then the triangle is isosceles.
- A point equidistant from two given points lies on the perpendicular bisector of the line segment joining the two points.
- A Point equidistant from two intersecting lines lies on the bisectors of the angles formed by the two lines.

Inequalities in a Triangle

- In a triangle, angle opposite to the longer side is larger.
- In a triangle, side opposite to the larger angle is longer.
- Sum of any two sides of a triangle is greater than the third side.
- Of all the line segments that can be drawn on a given line, from a point, not lying on it, the perpendicular line segment is the shortest.

[Topic 1] Criteria for Congruence of Triangles

Points to be Remembered

- The geometrical figures of same shape and size are congruent to each other i.e., two triangles $\triangle ABC$ and $\triangle PQR$ are congruent if and only if their corresponding sides and the corresponding angles are equal.

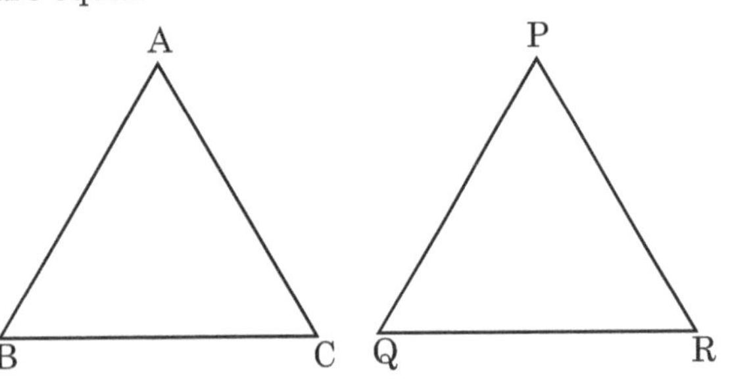

$$\therefore \triangle ABC \cong \triangle PQR$$

- **SAS Congruence Rule:** Two triangles are congruent if two sides and the included angle of one triangle are equal to the sides and the included angle of the other triangle.

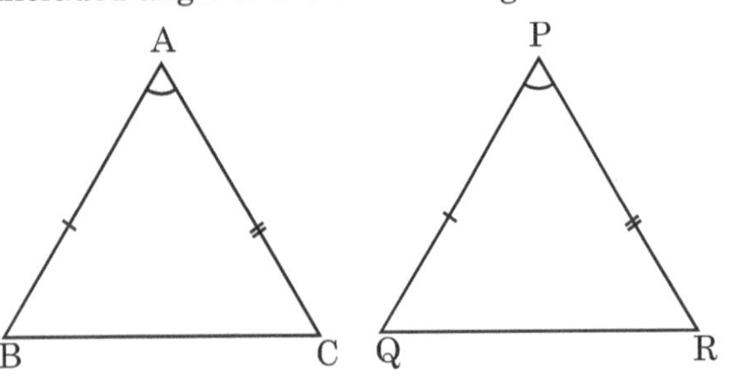

In $\triangle ABC$ and $\triangle PQR$

$$AB = PQ , PR = AC \text{ and } \angle A = \angle P$$
$$\therefore \triangle ABC \cong \triangle PQR$$

- **ASA Congruence Rule:** Two triangles are congruent if two sides and the included angle of one triangle are equal to the sides and the included angle of the other triangle.

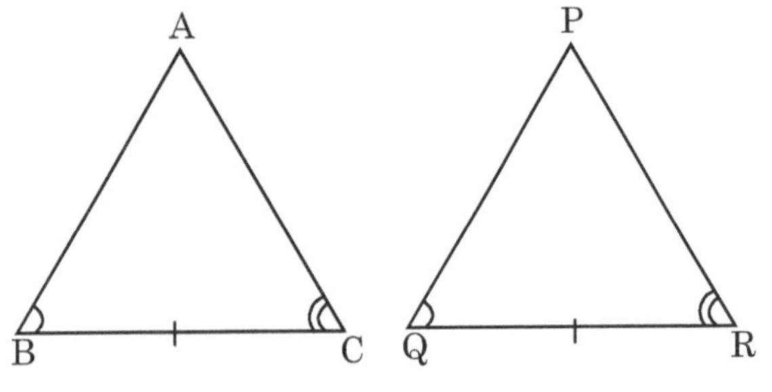

In $\triangle ABC$ and $\triangle PQR$,

$$BC = QR , \angle B = \angle Q \text{ and } \angle C = \angle R$$
$$\therefore \triangle ABC \cong \triangle PQR$$

- **AAS Congruence Rule:** Two triangles are congruent if any two pairs of angles and one pair of corresponding sides are equal.

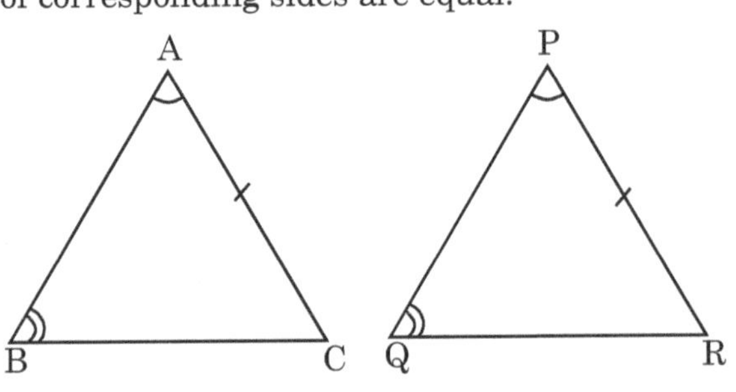

In $\triangle ABC$ and $\triangle PQR$,

$$AC = PR , \angle A = \angle P \text{ and } \angle B = \angle Q$$
$$\therefore \triangle ABC \cong \triangle PQR$$

- **SSS Congruence Rule:** If three sides of a triangle are equal to the three sides of another triangle, then the two triangles are congruent.

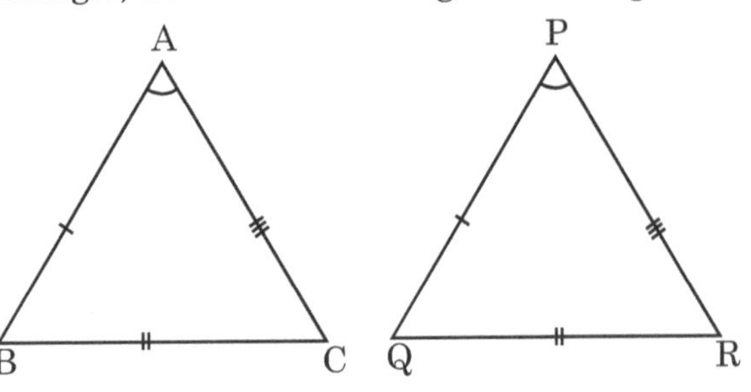

In $\triangle ABC$ and $\triangle PQR$

$$AB = PQ , BC = QR \text{ and } AC = PR$$
$$\therefore \triangle ABC \cong \triangle PQR$$

- **RHS Congruence Rule:** If in two right angled triangles, the hypotenuse and one side of a triangle are equal to the hypotenuse and one side of the other triangle, then the two triangles are Congruent.

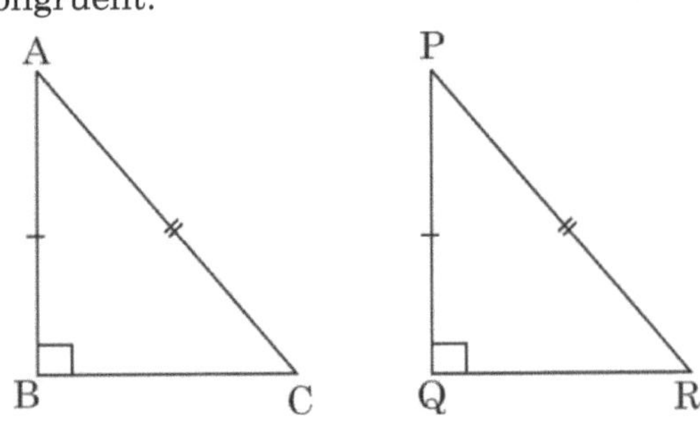

In right angled $\triangle ABC$ and $\triangle PQR$

$$AB = PQ \text{ and } AC = PR$$
$$\therefore \triangle ABC \cong \triangle PQR$$

PREVIOUS YEARS'
EXAMINATION QUESTIONS
TOPIC 1

Multiple Choice Questions
(1 Mark Each)

1. For the given triangles, write the correspondence, if congruent.

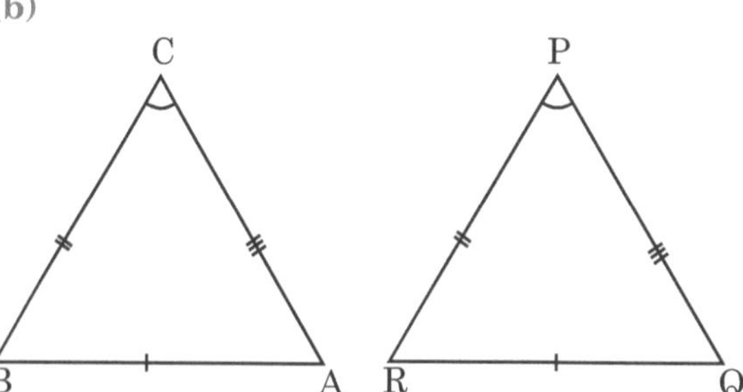

   (a) $\triangle ABC \cong \triangle DEF$

   (b) $\triangle ABC \cong \triangle EFD$

   (c) $\triangle ABC \cong \triangle COD$

   (d) not congruent   **[NCERT Exemp.]**

Sol. **(d)** The given triangles $\triangle ABC$ and $\triangle DEF$ are not congruent.

2. In triangles ABC and PQR, AB = AC, $\angle C = \angle P$ and $\angle B = \angle Q$. The two triangles are

                              [NCERT Exemp.]

   (a) isosceles but not congruent

   (b) isosceles and congruent

   (c) congruent but not isosceles

   (d) neither congruent nor isosceles

Sol. **(a)** According to the question,

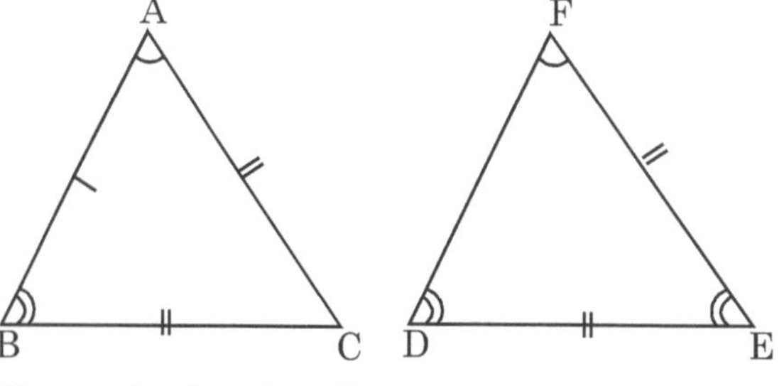

In $\triangle ABC$,

$\therefore$ AB = AC

So, $\triangle ABC$ is an isosceles triangle but it is given that

$\angle B = \angle Q$ and

$\angle C = \angle P$

Therefore, $\angle P = \angle Q$

QR = PR [$\because \angle C = \angle B$]

[Sides opposite to equal angles are equal]

So, $\triangle PQR$ is also an isosceles triangle.

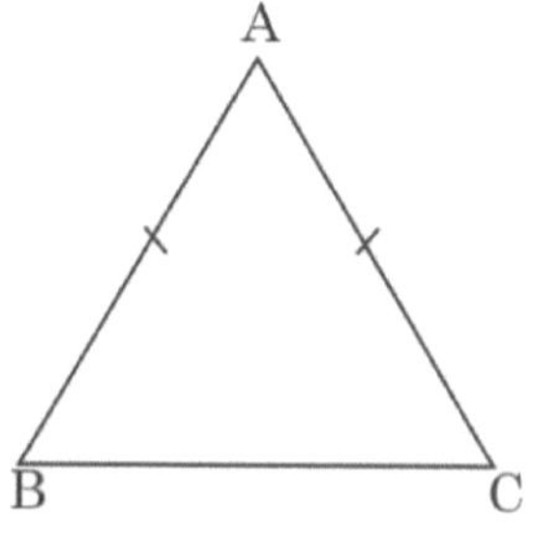

Hence, both triangles are isosceles but not congruent.

3. Which of the following is not a criterion for congruence of triangles?   **[NCERT Exemp.]**

   (a) SAS

   (b) ASA

   (c) SSA

   (d) SSS

Sol. **(c)** We know that

Criterion for congruency are SAS (side angle side), ASA (angle side angle), SSS (side side side), AAS (angle-angle side).

Hence, SSA is not a criterion for congruence of triangle.

4. If AB = QR, BC = PR and CA = PQ, then

                              [NCERT Exemp.]

   (a) $\triangle ABC \cong \triangle PQR$

   (b) $\triangle CBA \cong \triangle PRQ$

   (c) $\triangle BAC \cong \triangle RPQ$

   (d) $\triangle PQR \cong \triangle BCA$

Sol. **(b)**

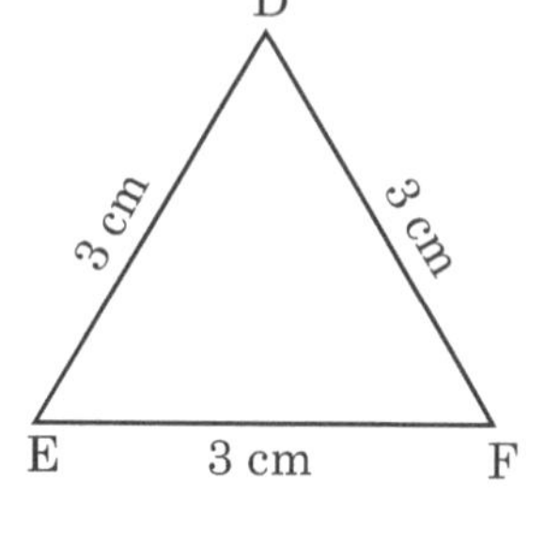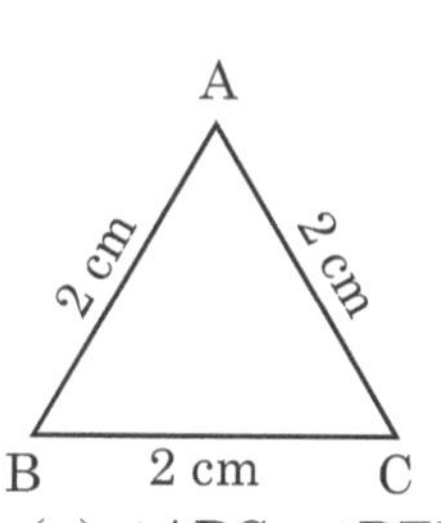

AB = QR & BC = PR

$\Rightarrow \angle B = \angle R$ ...(i)

BC = PR & CA = PQ

$\Rightarrow \angle C = \angle P$ ...(ii)

and CA = PQ & AB = QR

$\Rightarrow \angle A = \angle Q$ ...(iii)

From equations (i), (ii) and (iii), we get

Hence, $\triangle CBA \cong \triangle PRQ$

5. Given two right-angled triangles ABC and PRQ, such that $\angle A = 20°$, $\angle Q = 20°$ and AC = QP. Write the correspondence, if triangles are congruent.

 (a) $\triangle ABC \cong \triangle PQR$ (b) $\triangle ABC \cong \triangle PRQ$

 (c) $\triangle ABC \cong \triangle RQP$ (d) $\triangle ABC \cong \triangle QRP$

Sol. (d) According to the question,

 $\angle A = 20°$, $\angle Q = 20°$ and AC = QP

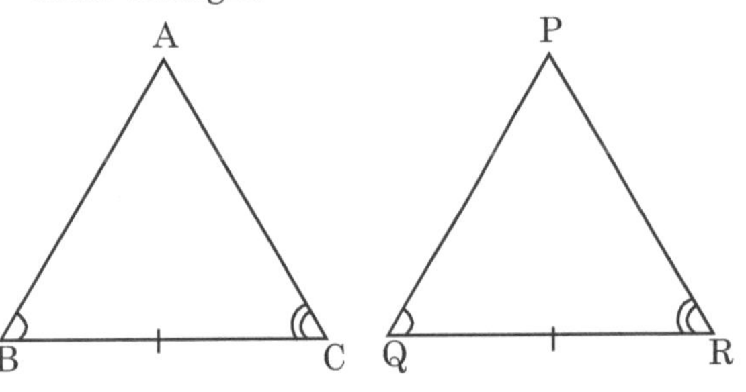

 $\because$ $\angle A = \angle P$, $\angle B = \angle R$ and $\angle C = \angle Q$ and AC = PQ

 $\therefore$ By ASA, both triangles are congruent.

 Hence, $\triangle ABC \cong \triangle QRP$

Very Short Answer Type Questions

(1 Mark Each)

1. If $\triangle ABC \cong \triangle DEF$ by SSS congruence rule, then three equalities of corresponding sides.

 [NCERT Exemp.]

Sol. Since $\triangle ABC \cong \triangle DEF$ by SSS congruence rule, then three equalities of corresponding sides are AB = DE, BC = EF and CA = FD.

2. Write ASA congruence rule for two triangles.

 [BOARD TERM I, 2015, SET-2]

Sol. **ASA congruence :** Two triangles are congruent, if two angles and the included side of one triangle are equal to two angles and the included side of other triangle.

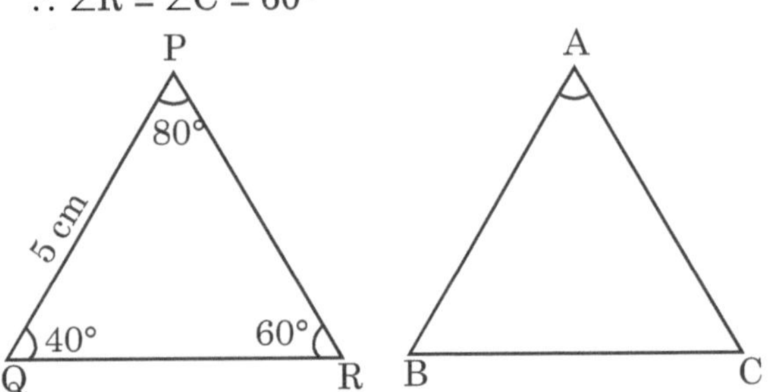

3. $\triangle ABC \cong \triangle PQR$, AB = PQ. Which statement has been followed in this?

Sol. If two triangles are congruent, then one side of a triangle is equal to the corresponding side of the other triangle.

 Hence, AB = PQ

4. In the figure, if AB = DC, $\angle ABD = \angle CDB$, which congruence rule would you apply to prove $\triangle ABD \cong \triangle CDB$?

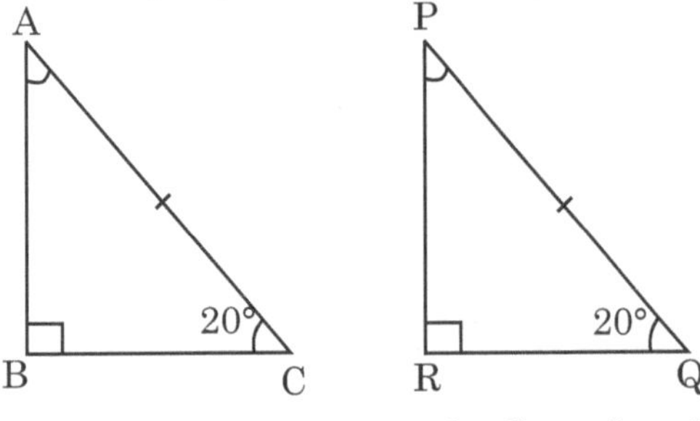

Sol. According to the question,

 $\because$ AB = CD

 $\angle DBA = \angle BDC$,

 and BD = BD (common)

 Hence, by SAS congruence rule.

 $\triangle ABD \cong \triangle CDB$

5. $\triangle PQR \cong \triangle ABC$, if PQ = 5 cm, $\angle Q = 40°$ and $\angle P = 80°$, calculate the value of $\angle C$.

Sol. Given PQ = 5 cm

 $\angle Q = 40°$ and $\angle P = 80°$

 $\therefore$ $\angle R = 180° - 80° - 40° = 60°$

 Since, $\triangle PQR \cong \triangle ABC$

 $\therefore$ $\angle R = \angle C = 60°$

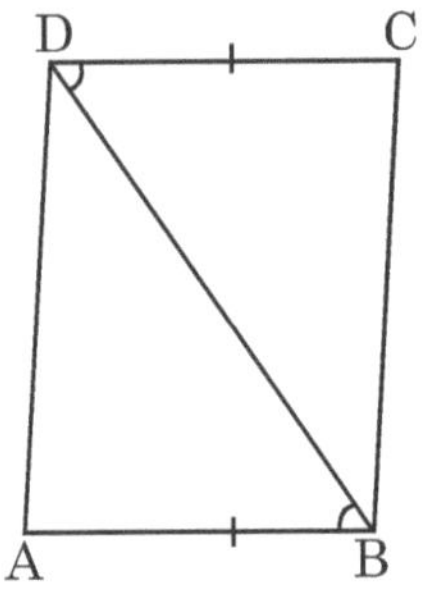

 Hence, the value of $\angle C = 60°$

6. What do we call a triangle if the angles are in the ratio 5 : 3 : 7?

Sol. Let the angles of triangle are 5x, 3x and 7x respectively, then

 According to the question,

 $5x + 3x + 7x = 180°$

 $\Rightarrow 15x = 180°$

 $\therefore x = \dfrac{180°}{15} = 12°$

 Therefore, angles are

 $5x = 5 \times 12 = 60°$

 $3x = 3 \times 12 = 36°$ and $7x = 7 \times 12 = 84°$

 $\because$ Each angle is less than 90°

 Hence, the triangle is an acute angled triangle.

7. In the given figure, find the ratio $\angle ABO : \angle ACO$.

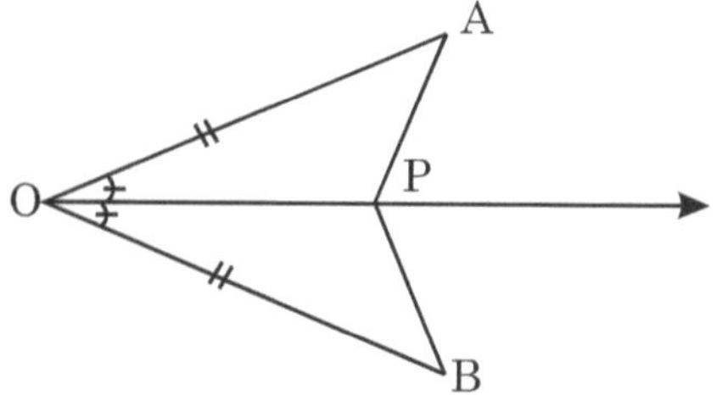

Sol. Here, in $\triangle ABC$, AB = AC $\Rightarrow \angle C = \angle B$

Also, BO = CO

$\Rightarrow \angle OCB = \angle OBC$

$\Rightarrow \angle C - \angle OCB = \angle B - \angle OCB$

$\Rightarrow \angle ACO = \angle ABO$

$\Rightarrow \dfrac{\angle ACO}{\angle ABO} = \dfrac{1}{1}$ or $\dfrac{\angle ABO}{\angle ACO} = \dfrac{1}{1}$

Hence, the required ratio is 1 : 1.

8. In given figure, AD = BC and $\angle BAD = \angle ABC$, then prove that $\angle ACB = \angle BDA$.

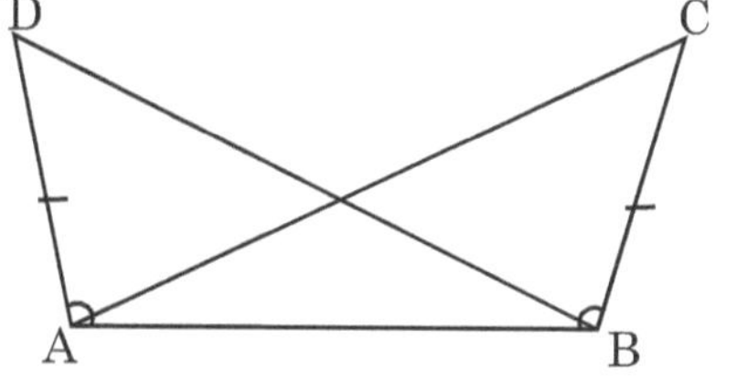

Sol. Given, AD = BC

and $\angle BAD = \angle ABC$

AB = AB (Common)

$\therefore$ By SAS congruence rule.

$\triangle DAB \cong \triangle CBA$

Hence, $\angle BDA = \angle ACB$

9. Given $\triangle OAP \cong \triangle OBP$ in the figure below. Prove the criteria by which the triangles are congruent.

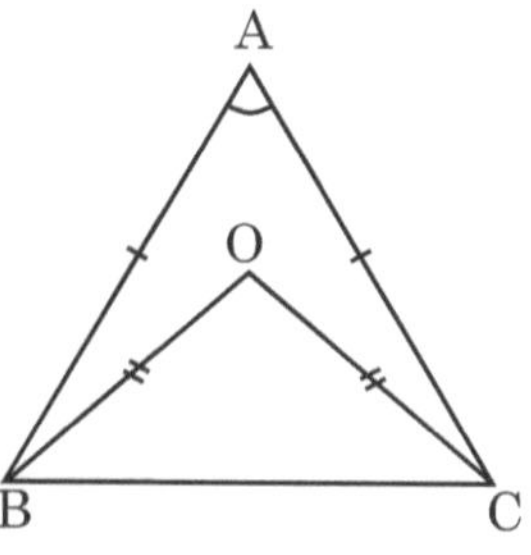

Sol. Given, OA = OB,

OP = OP (Common)

and $\angle AOP = \angle BOP$

Now, by SAS congruence rule,

$\therefore \triangle OAP \cong \triangle OBP$

10. In the given figure given below, if AB = QR, BC = PR and CA = PQ, then ....

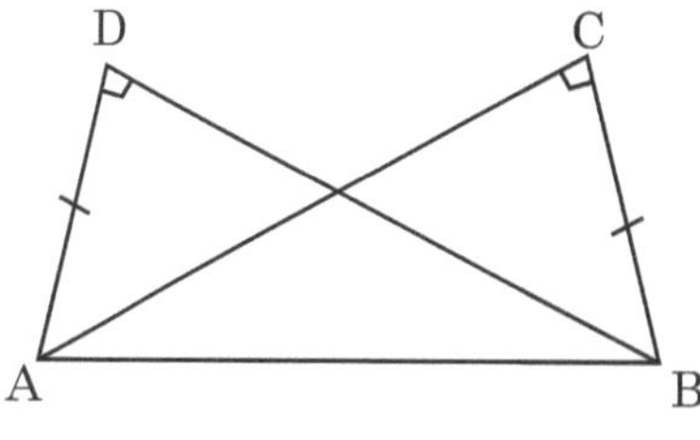

Sol. Given, AB = QR

BC = PR

and CA = PQ

Now, by SSS congruence rule,

$\therefore \triangle CBA \cong \triangle PRQ$

11. In $\triangle ABC$ and $\triangle DEF$, AB = DE, $\angle A = \angle D$. What will be the condition in which the two triangles will be congruent by SAS axiom?

Sol.

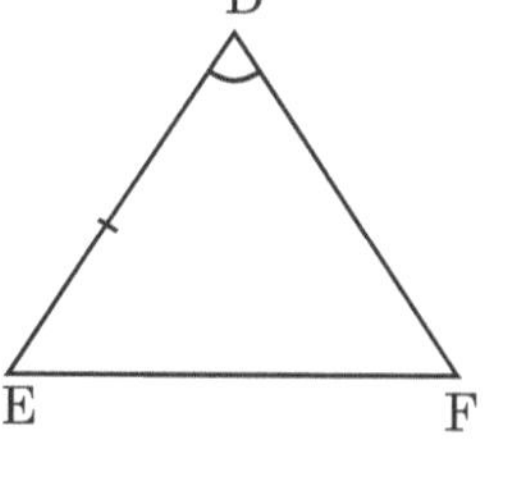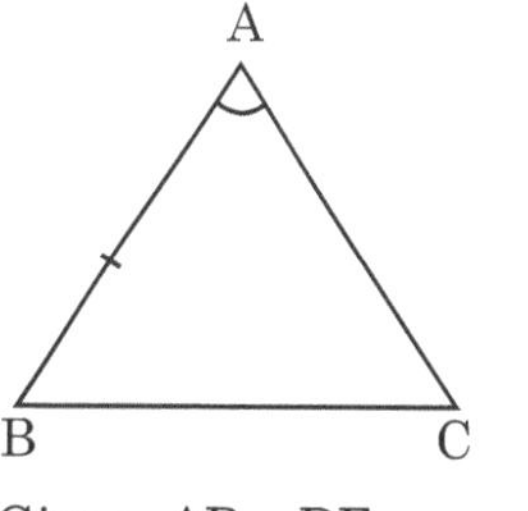

Given, AB = DE

and $\angle A = \angle D$

Therefore, $\triangle ABC$ and $\triangle DEF$ are congruent triangles by SAS,

If AC = DF, then

$\triangle ABC \cong \triangle DEF$

12. In the figure below, it is given that $\triangle ABD \cong \triangle BAC$. What criteria is used to prove that the triangles are congruent?

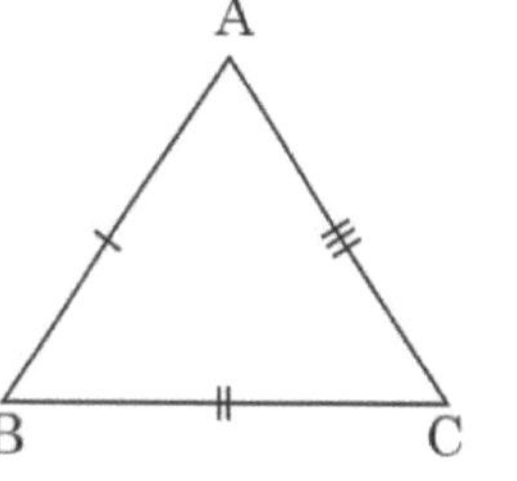

Sol. Given $\angle BDA = \angle ACB = 90°$

and AD = BC

AB = AB (Common)

By RHS congruence rule,

Hence, $\triangle ABD \cong \triangle DEF$

Short Answer Type Questions I
(2 Marks Each)

1. l and m are two parallel lines intersected by another pair of parallel lines p and q (see figure). Show that
$$\Delta ABC \cong \Delta CDA$$

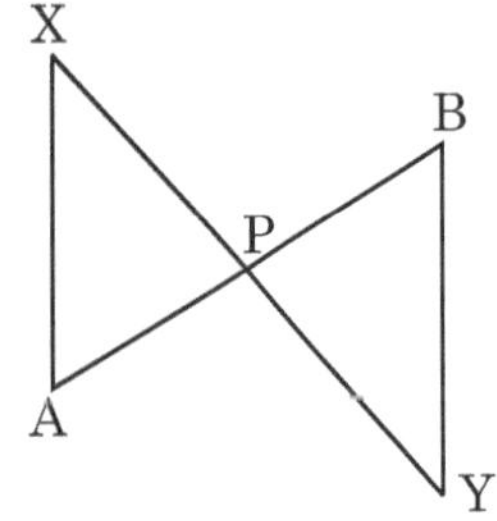

[NCERT]

Sol. Given l ∥ m and p ∥ q

To prove $\Delta ABC \cong \Delta CDA$

Proof In ΔABC and ΔADC,

∵ p ∥ q

∴ ∠BAC = ∠ACD

[alternate interior angles]

Again, ∵ l ∥ m

∴ ∠ACB = ∠DAC [Alternate interior angles]

and AC = AC [common side]

By ASA congruence rule,

∴ $\Delta ABC \cong \Delta CDA$

2. In figure, AX = BY and AX ∥ BY, prove that $\Delta APX \cong \Delta BPY$.

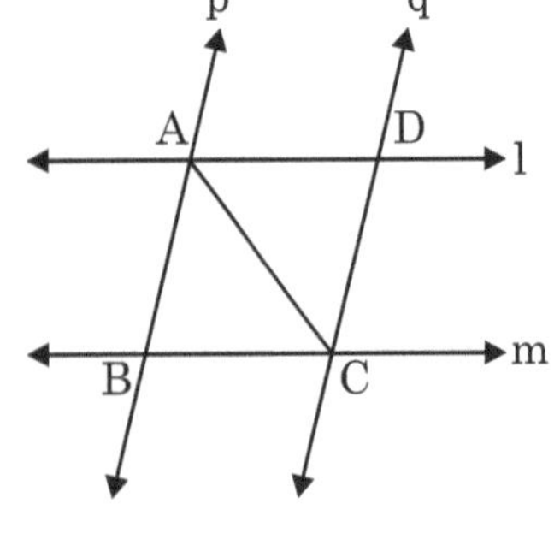

[BOARD TERM I, 2010, SET-C1]

Sol. Given, ∵ AX ∥ BY

∴ ∠BAX = ∠ABY (Alternate angles) ...(i)

and ∠AXY = ∠BYX (Alternate angles) ...(ii)

In ΔAPX and ΔBPY, AX = BY (Given) ...(iii)

From (i), (ii) and (iii), we get

$\Delta APX \cong \Delta BPY$.

[By ASA congruence rule]

Hence proved.

3. In the figure below, O is the mid-point of AB and CD, prove that AC = BD.

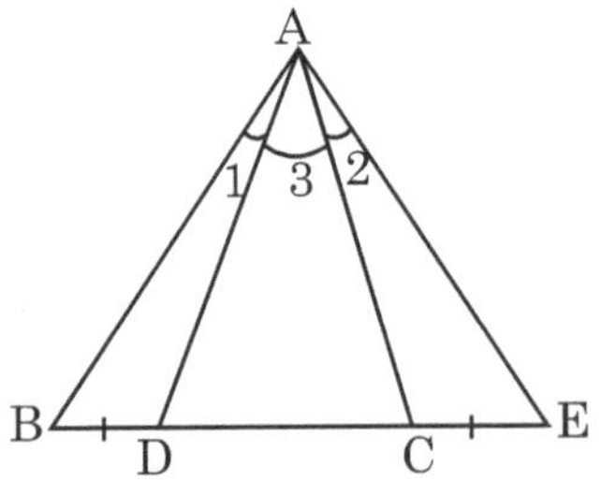

[BOARD TERM I, 2011, SET 14, 19; 2010, SET-A1]

Sol. According to the question,

OA = OB

[O is mid-point of AB]

∴ ∠AOC = ∠BOD

(Vertically opposite angles)

and OC = OD

(O is the mid-point of CD)

By SAS congruence rule,

$\Delta AOC \cong \Delta BOD$

Hence, AC = BD (By c.p.c.t)

4. In the figure below, the diagonal AC of quadrilateral ABCD bisects ∠BAD and ∠BCD. Prove that BC = CD.

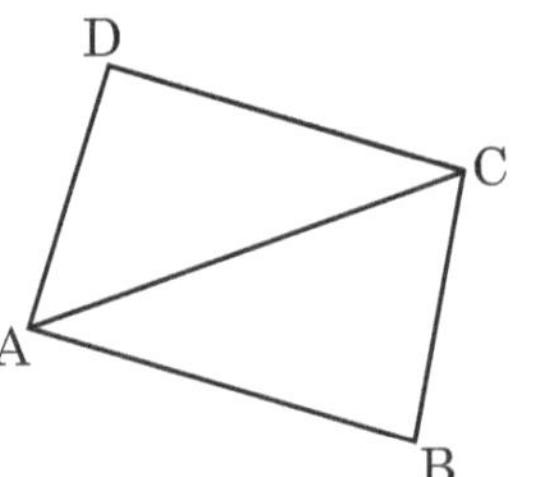

[BOARD TERM I, 2011, SET 20; 2010, SET-C1]

Sol. Given, In ΔADC and ΔABC,

AC = AC [common]

∠DAC = ∠BAC and ∠DCA = ∠BCA

By AAS congruence rule,

∴ $\Delta ADC \cong \Delta ABC$

Hence, CD = BC. (By c.p.c.t.) Proved.

5. In figure ∠B = ∠E, BD = CE and ∠1 = ∠2. Show $\Delta ABC \cong \Delta AED$.

[BOARD TERM I, 2011, SET-12]

Sol. Given, $\angle 1 = \angle 2$

On adding $\angle 3$ both the sides, we get

$\angle 1 + \angle 3 = \angle 2 + \angle 3 \Rightarrow \angle BAC = \angle EAD$ ...(i)

Given that, BD = CE

On adding DC both the sides, we get

$BD + DC = CE + DC \Rightarrow BC = DE$ ...(ii)

and $\angle B = \angle E$ (Given)   ...(iii)

From equation (i), (ii) and (iii),

By AAS congruence rule, we get

$\therefore \triangle ABC \cong \triangle AED$.

6. In the given figure, D is the mid-point of base BC. DE and DF are perpendicular to AB and AC respectively such that DE = DF. Prove that $\angle B = \angle C$.

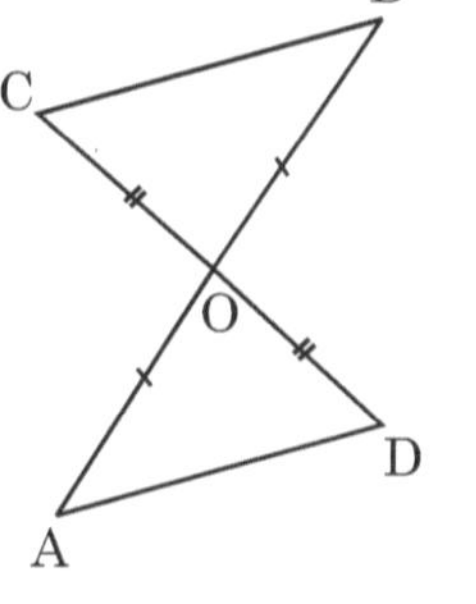

[BOARD TERM I, 2011, SET-17]

Sol. Given,

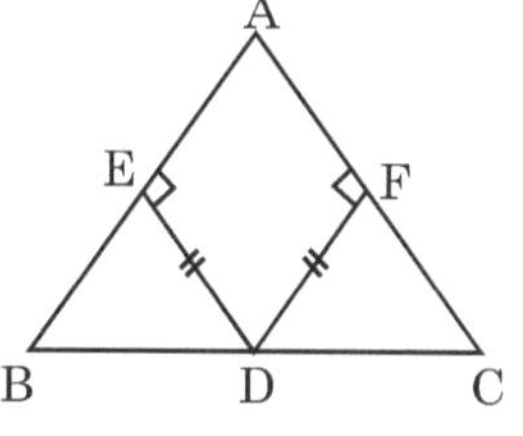

In $\triangle BED$ $\triangle CFD$,

$\angle DEB = \angle DFC = 90°$

$\because$ D is the mid-point.

BD = DC

ED = FD (given)

By RHS congruence rule,

$\triangle BED \cong \triangle CFD$

Hence, $\angle B = \angle C$ (By c.p.c.t.)

7. In the figure, OA = OB and OD = OC. Show that:
(i) $\triangle AOD \cong \triangle BOC$, (ii) AD | | BC.

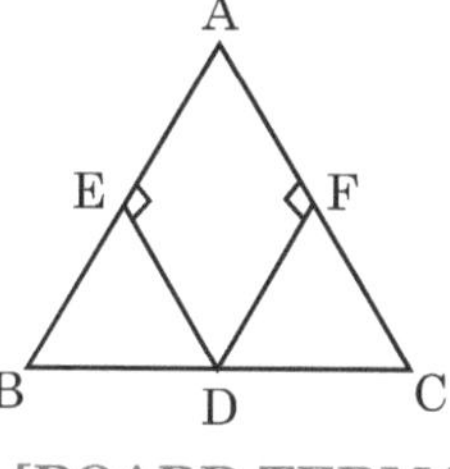

[BOARD TERM I, 2011, SET-19]

Sol. (i) In $\triangle AOD$ and $\triangle BOC$,

OA = OB (Given)

OD = OC (Given)

and $\angle AOD = \angle BOC$

(Vertically opposite angles)

By SAS congruence rule,

$\triangle AOD \cong \triangle BOC$

(ii) $\angle CBA = \angle DAB$ (By c.p.c.t.)

AD and BC are two lines intersected by AB such that $\angle CBA = \angle DAB$ and they form a pair of alternate angles.

Hence, AD ∥ BC.

8. In the figure below, ABCD is a square and P is the mid-point of AD. BP and CP are joined. Prove that $\angle PCB = \angle PBC$.

[BOARD TERM I, 2011, SET-21]

Sol. According to the question,

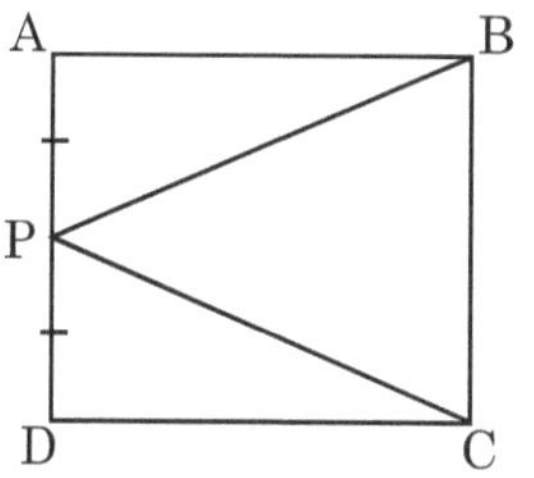

In $\triangle PAB$ and $\triangle PDC$,

PA = PD (P is the mid-point of AD)

AB = CD (Side of square)

and $\angle PAB = \angle PDC = 90°$

[$\because$ ABCD is a square]

By R.H.S, $\triangle PAB \cong \triangle PDC$

$\therefore$ PB = PC (By c.p.c.t)

(Angles opposite to equal sides are equal)

$\therefore$ $\angle PCB = \angle PBC$.   Hence proved.

9. In the figure, $\triangle ABC$ and $\triangle DBC$ are two isosceles triangles on the same base BC. Prove that $\angle ABD = \angle ACD$.

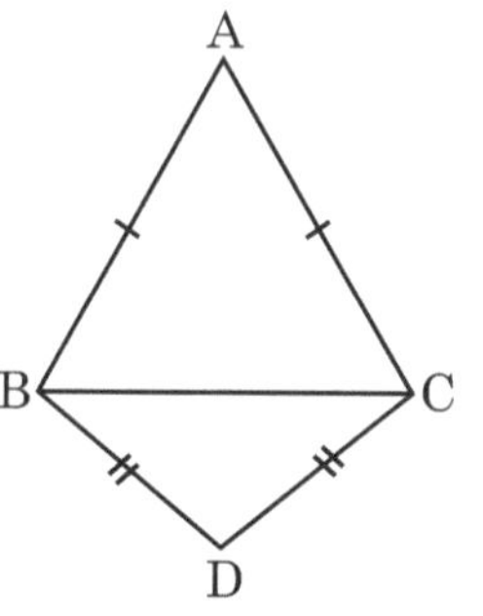

[BOARD TERM I, 2014]

Sol. According to the question,

$\triangle ABC$ and $\triangle DBC$ are two isosceles triangles on the same base BC.

$\therefore$ Now, join the points A and D.

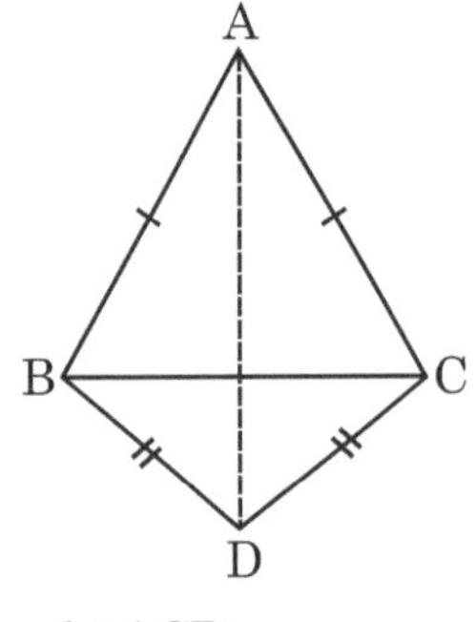

In $\triangle ABD$ and $\triangle ACD$,

AB = AC	(Given)
BD = CD	(Given)
and AD = AD	(Common)

By using SSS Congruency Rule,

$\triangle ABD \cong \triangle ACD$

Hence, $\angle ABD = \angle ACD$ (By c.p.c.t.)

10. AD is an altitude of an isosceles $\triangle ABC$ in which AB = AC. Show that

(i) AD bisects BC.

(ii) AD bisects $\angle A$.

Sol. Given $\triangle ABC$ is an isosceles triangle and AD $\perp$ BC, AB = AC.

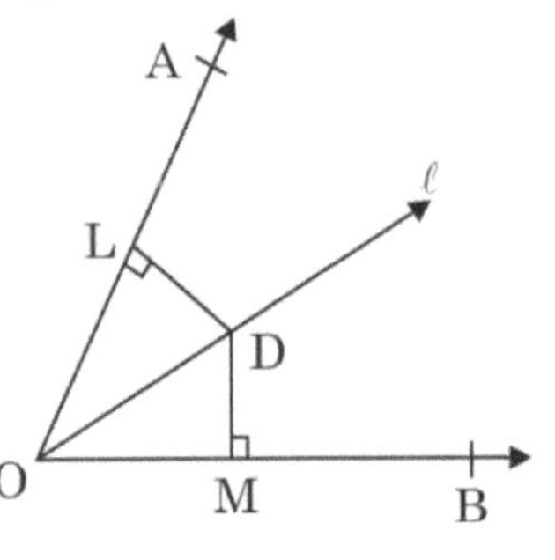

To prove (i) AD bisects BC.

(ii) AD bisects $\angle A$.

Proof (i) In $\triangle ADB$ and $\triangle ADC$.

AB = AC	[given]
$\angle ADB = \angle ADC$	[each 90°]
and AD = AD	[common side]
$\therefore$ $\triangle ADB \cong \triangle ADC$	[by RHS congruence rule]
Then BD = DC	[by CPCT]

Hence, AD bisects BC.

(ii) As AD bisects BC, then $\angle BAD = \angle CAD$

i.e., AD bisects $\angle A$.

Short Answer Type Questions II
(3 Marks Each)

1. BE and CF are two equal altitudes of a $\triangle ABC$. Using RHS congruence rule, prove that the $\triangle ABC$ is an isosceles.

[NCERT]

Sol. Given BE = CF, BE $\perp$ AC

and CF $\perp$ AB

To prove $\triangle ABC$ is an isosceles triangle.

Proof In $\triangle BEC$ and $\triangle CFB$,

$\angle BEC = \angle CFB = 90°$

BE = CF [given]

and BC = BC [common]

By RHS congruence rule,

$\therefore$ $\triangle BEC \cong \triangle CFB$

Then, $\angle BCE = \angle CBF$ [by c.p.c.t.]

$\Rightarrow \angle BCA = \angle CBA \Rightarrow AB = AC$

[$\because$ sides opposite to equal angle of a triangle are equal]

Hence, $\triangle ABC$ is an isosceles triangle.

2. In figure, line l is the bisector of $\angle AOB$. D is a point on l. DL $\perp$ OA and DM $\perp$ OB. Prove that:

(i) $\triangle OMD \cong \triangle OLD$

(ii) DM = DL

[NCERT]

Sol. (i) In $\triangle OMD$ and $\triangle OLD$,

$\angle M = \angle L = 90°$

and $\angle DOM = \angle DOL$

[l is bisector of $\angle O$]

OD = OD (Common)

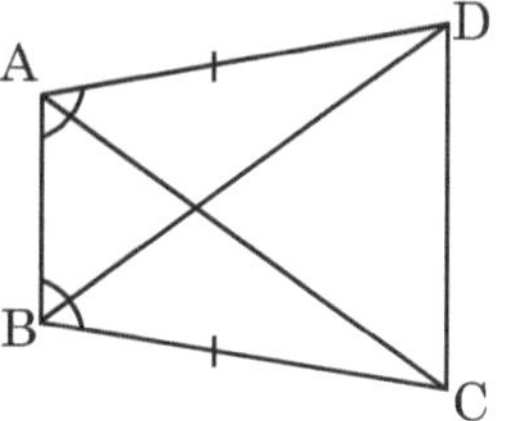

By AAS congruency rule,

∴ ΔOMD ≅ ΔOLD

∴ (ii)   DL = DM   (CPCT)

3. ABCD is a quadrilateral in which AD = BC and ∠DAB = ∠CBA (see figure).

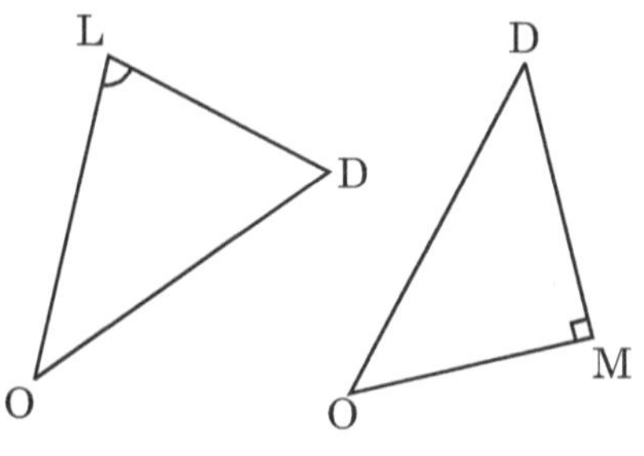

Prove that

(i) ΔABD ≅ ΔBAC

(ii) BD = AC

(iii) ∠ABD = ∠BAC

[NCERT BOARD TERM I, 2012, SET-45]

Sol.   Given in quadrilateral ABCD.

AD = BC

and ∠DAB = ∠CAB

To prove (i) ΔABD ≅ ΔBAC

(ii) BD = AC

(iii) ∠ABD = ∠BAC

Proof (i) in ΔABD and ΔBAC,

AD = BC   [given]

∠DAB = ∠CBA   [given]

and AB = AB   [common side]

By SAS congruence rule, we get

ΔABD ≅ ΔBAC

(ii) From part (i),

ΔABD ≅ ΔBAC

Then, BD = AC   [by CPCT]

(iii) From part (i),

∵ ΔABD ≅ ΔBAC

Then, ∠ABD = ∠BAC   [by CPCT]

Hence proved.

4. In figure, PQRS is a square and SRT is an equilateral triangle. Prove that:

(i) PT = QT

(ii) ∠TQR = 15°

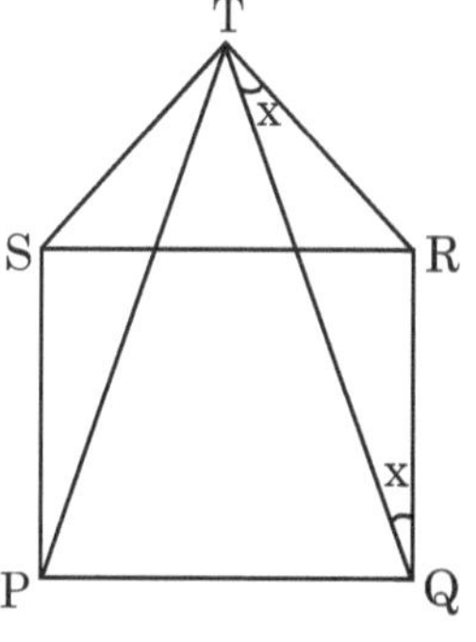

[BOARD TERM I, 2014; 2012, SET 43; 2011, SET-20; 2010, SET-B1]

Sol.   According to the question, PQRS is a square.

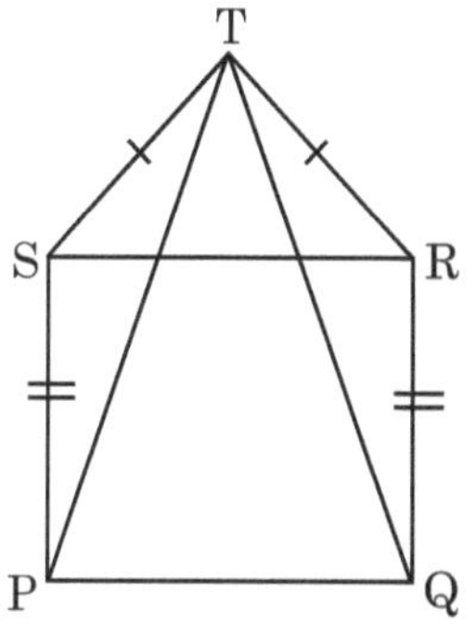

(i) SRT is an equilateral triangle. (given)

∴ ∠PSR = 90° and ∠TSR = 60°

⇒ ∠PSR + ∠TSR = 90° + 60°

Similarly, ∠QRT = 150°

In ΔPST and ΔQRT, we have PS = QR (sides of a square)

∠PST = ∠QRT = 150°

and ST = RT

By SAS congruency rule,

ΔPST ≅ ΔQRT

∴ PT = QT (By c.p.c.t)

Hence proved.

(ii) In ΔTQR, QR = RT

[Square and equilateral triangle on same base]

or, ∠TQR = ∠QTR = x

∴ x + x + ∠QRT = 180° [Angle sum property]

⇒ 2x + 150° = 180° ⇒ 2x = 30°

∴ x = 15°

Hence, ∠LTR = 15°

5. In the given figure, if AB ∥ DC and P is the mid-point of BD, prove that P is also the mid-point of AC

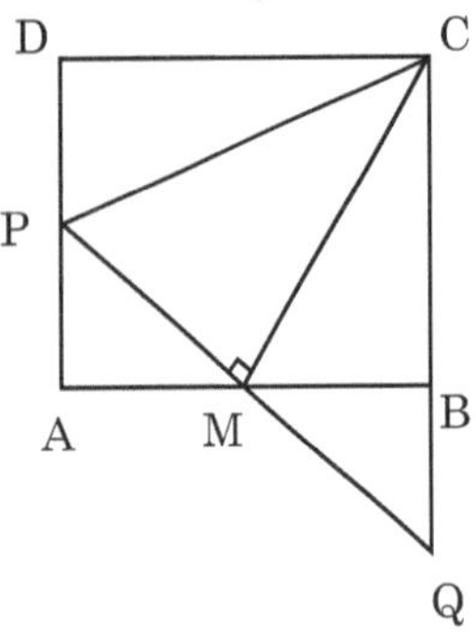

[BOARD TERM I, 2012, SET-52]

Sol. Since AB ∥ DC ∠ABP = ∠CDP

          (Alternate interior angles)

∠APB = ∠CPD   (Vertically opposite angles)

PD = PB   (Given)

∴ ΔAPB ≅ ΔCPD   (By ASA)

or, AP = PC   (By c.p.c.t.)

or, P is also the mid-point of AC.

6. In the given figure, ABCD is a square and M is the mid-point of AB. PQ ⊥ CM meets AD at P and CB produced at Q. Prove that PA = BQ.

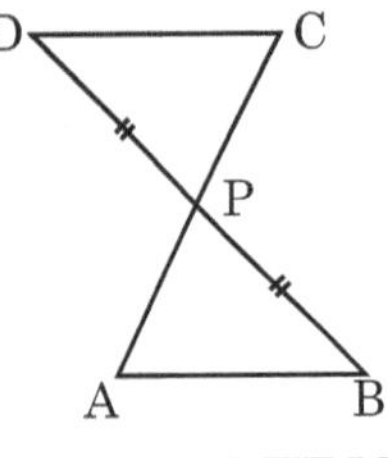

[BOARD TERM I, 2012, SET-45]

Sol.

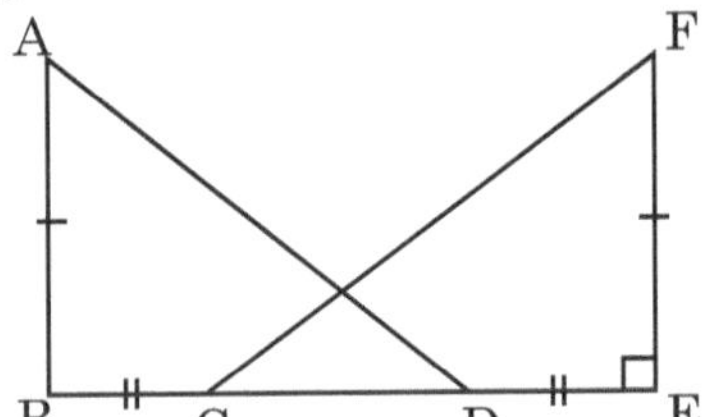

In ΔPAM and ΔQBM,

As M is the mid-point,

or, AM = BM   (Given)

∠1 = ∠2   (Vertically opposite angle)

∠3 = ∠4 = 90°

∴ ΔPAM ≅ ΔQBM   (By ASA Congruance)

∴ PA = BQ. (By c.p.c.t.) Proved.

7. In the given figure AB = CD, ∠ABD = ∠CDB. Prove that AD = CB.

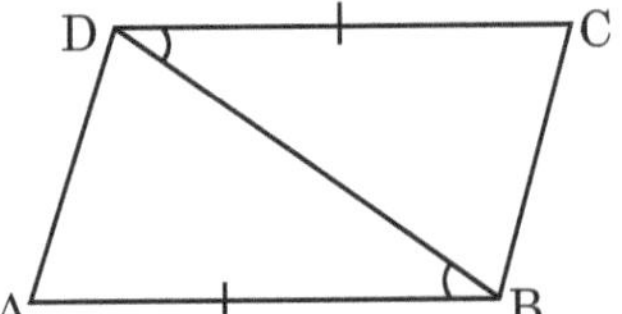

[BOARD TERM I, 2012, SET-35]

Sol. Given, AB = CD and ∠ABD = ∠CDB

In ΔABD and ΔCDB,

BD = BD (Common)

By SAS congruence rule,

∴ ΔABD ≅ ΔCDB

AD = CB. (By c.p.c.t)

8. In the given figure AB ⊥ BE and FE ⊥ BE . If BC = DE and AB = EF, then prove that ΔABD is congruent to ΔFEC.

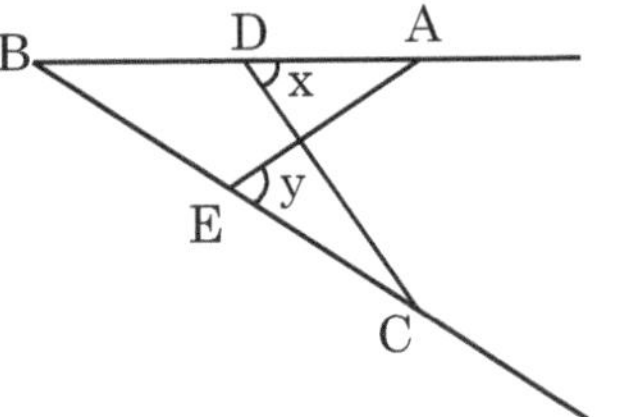

[BOARD TERM I, 2012, SET-44, 48]

Sol. Given in ΔABD and ΔFEC, AB ⊥ BE and FE ⊥ BE in which BC = DE and AB = EF.

To prove ΔABD ≅ ΔFEC

Proof In ΔABD and ΔFEC

AB = FE   [given]

BC = DE   [given]

⇒ BC + CD = DE + CD

              [adding CD on both sides]

⇒ BD = EC

∠ABD = ∠EFC

[each 90°, since AB ⊥ BE and FE ⊥ BE]

∴ ΔABD ≅ ΔFEC   [by SAS congruence rule]

                    Hence proved.

9. In the given figure, if ∠ADC = ∠AEC and AB = BC, then prove that AE = CD.

[BOARD TERM I, 2012, SET-47]

Sol. Given, $\angle ADC = \angle AEC$ and $AB = BC$

$\angle BDC + \angle CDA = 180°$ (Linear pair)

$\Rightarrow \angle BDC + x = 180°$

$\Rightarrow \angle BDC = 180° - x$ ...(i)

Similarly $\angle BEA = 180° - y$ ...(ii)

Since, $\angle ADC = \angle AEC \Rightarrow x = y$

$x = y$ (Given)

In $\triangle BAE$ and $\triangle BCD$,

$\therefore \angle BDC = \angle BEA$

$\angle B = \angle B$ (Common)

and $AB = BC$

By ASA congruency rule,

$\triangle BAE \cong \triangle BCD$

Hence, $AE = CD$ (c.p.c.t)

10. In the given figure, $AB = CD$, $\angle ABC = \angle DCB$. Prove that:

(i) $\triangle ABC \cong \triangle DCB$

(ii) $AC = DB$.

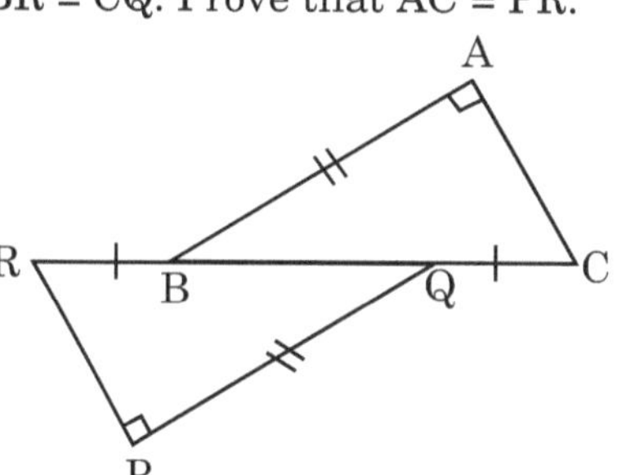

[BOARD TERM I, 2012, SET-39]

Sol. Given,

$AB = DC$

$\angle ABC = \angle DCB$

$BC = CB$ (Common)

$\therefore \triangle ABC \cong \triangle DCB$ (SAS)

$\therefore AC = DB.$ (By c.p.c.t.)

11. In figure $OA \perp OD$, $OC \perp OB$, $OD = OA$ and $OC = OB$. Prove that $AB = CD$.

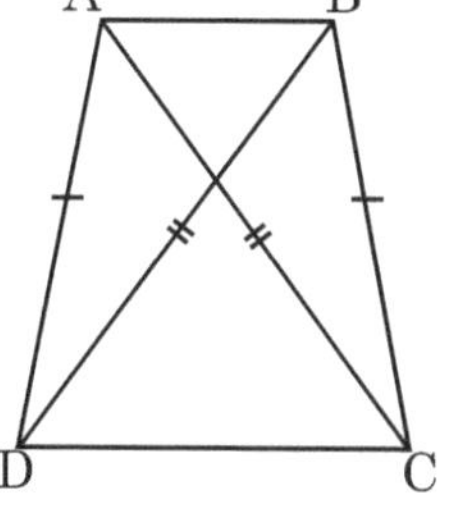

[BOARD TERM I, 2012, SET-58]

Sol. In $\triangle COD$ and $\triangle BOA$,

$OD = OA$ (Given)

$OC = OB$ (Given)

and $\angle DOA = \angle COB = 90°$

On adding $\angle AOC$ on both sides, we have

$\therefore \angle DOA + \angle AOC = \angle COB + \angle AOC$

i.e., $\angle DOC = \angle AOB$

By SAS congruency rule,

$\therefore \triangle COD \cong \triangle BOA$

Hence, $CD = AB$ (By c.p.c.t.)

and $AB = CD$

12. In the given figure, $BA \perp CA$, $RP \perp QP$, $AB = PQ$ and $BR = CQ$. Prove that $AC = PR$.

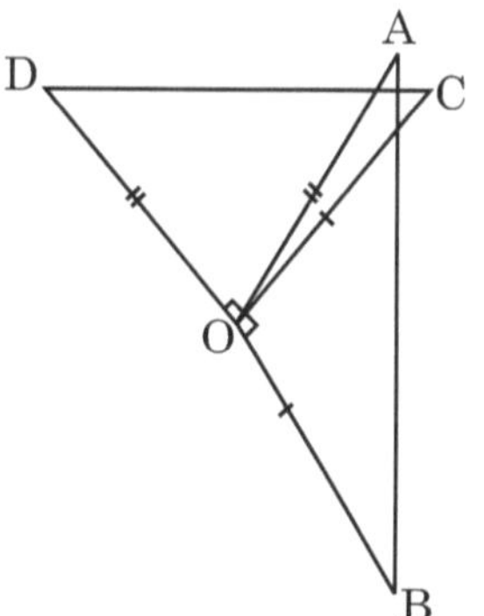

[BOARD TERM I, 2012, SET-51]

Sol. Given $BR = CQ$

On adding BQ in both sides,

$\Rightarrow BR + BQ = CQ + BQ$

$\therefore QR = BC$ ... (i)

In $\triangle ABC$ and $\triangle PQR$,

or, $QR = BC$ [from equation (i)]

$AB = PQ$ (Given)

and $\angle BAC = \angle QPR = 90°$ (Given)

By RHS congruence rule,

$\therefore \triangle ABC \cong \triangle PQR$

Hence, $AC = PR$.   (By c.p.c.t.)

13. In the given figure $AD = BC$ and $BD = AC$. Prove that, $\angle ADB = \angle BCA$ and $\angle DAB = \angle CBA$.

[BOARD TERM I, 2014; 2012, SET-41]

OR

In the figure, $AD = BC$, and $BD = AC$. Prove that $\angle DAB = \angle CBA$.

Sol. **Given,** AD = BC and BD = AC

To prove : $\angle$DAB = $\angle$CBA

Proof: In $\triangle$ABD and $\triangle$BAC,

AD = BC

BD = AC and AB = AB (Common side)

By SSS congruence axiom, $\triangle$ABD $\cong$ $\triangle$BAC

Hence, $\angle$ADB = $\angle$BCA (By c.p.c.t.)

and $\angle$DAB = $\angle$CBA. (By c.p.c.t)

14. In the figure, BM and DN are both perpendicular to AC and BM = DN. Prove that AC bisects BD.

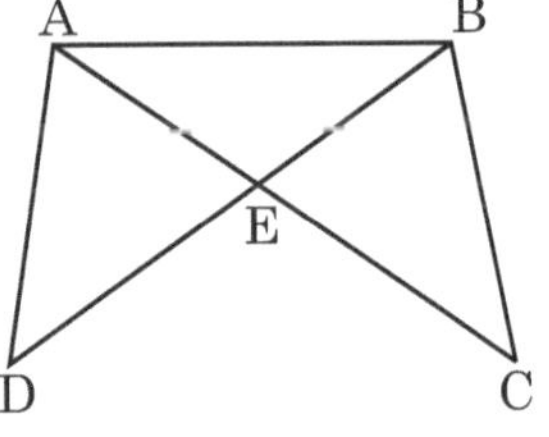

[BOARD TERM I, 2016, SET-BQ56IZK]

Sol. In $\triangle$BMR and $\triangle$DNR.

BM = DN (Given)

$\therefore$ $\angle$N = $\angle$M = 90°

[$\because$ BM and DN are perpendicular to AC]

$\because$ DN $\parallel$ BM

$\angle$NDR = $\angle$MBR (Alternate angle)

By AAS congruency rule,

$\therefore$ $\triangle$BMR $\cong$ $\triangle$DNR

$\therefore$ BR = DR

Therefore, R is mid-point of BD

Hence, AC bisects BD.

15. In a right angled triangle, if one acute angle is double the other, then prove that the hypotenuse is double the smallest side.

[BOARD TERM I, 2016, SET-JQ22L5C]

Sol. Let $\triangle$ABC is right angled at B.

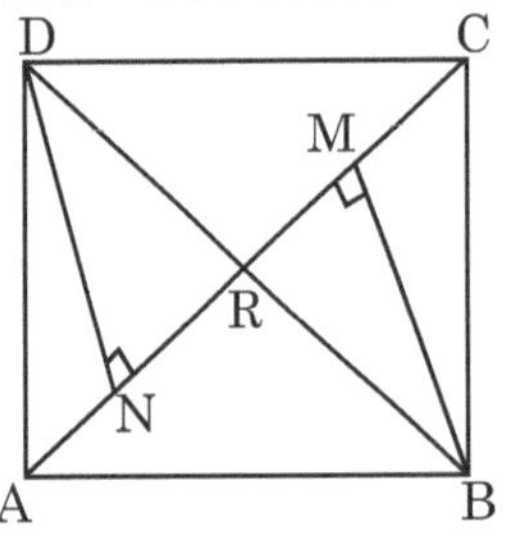

and $\angle$CAB = x° and $\angle$ACB = 2x°

then produce CB to D so that we get BD = BC.

Now In $\triangle$ABC and $\triangle$ABD, we have

AB = AB, [common]

BC = BD [construction]

and $\angle$ABC = $\angle$ABD

By SAS congruence rule,

$\therefore$ $\triangle$ABC $\cong$ $\triangle$ABD

Hence AC = AD and $\angle$CAB = $\angle$DAB (c.p.c.t)

Now, $\angle$CAD = x + x = 2x = $\angle$ACB

Then AD = CD

$\Rightarrow$ AD = 2BC

and AC = 2BC

Hence, hypotenuse AC is double the smallest side BC.

16. In the figure, If AF = CD are $\angle$AFE = $\angle$CDE, prove that EF = ED.

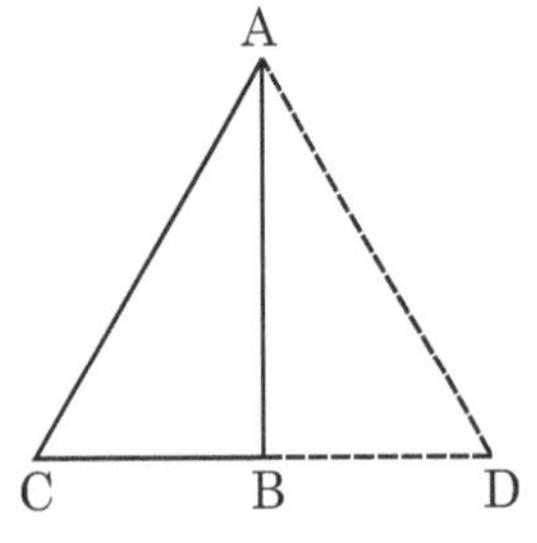

[BOARD TERM I, 2016, SET-QGL21FS]

Sol. According to the question,

In $\triangle$AFE and $\triangle$CDE,

AF = CD (Given)

$\therefore$ $\angle$AFE = $\angle$CDE (Given)

$\angle$E = $\angle$E (Common)

$\therefore$ $\angle$FAE = $\angle$DCE   (Third $\angle$S of triangles)

By ASA congruence rule,

$\therefore$ $\triangle$AFE $\cong$ $\triangle$CDE

Hence, EF = ED

17. In the given figure $\angle$EAB = $\angle$EBA and AC = BD. Prove that AD = BC.

[BOARD TERM I, 2016, SET-7AEDLQR]

Sol. Given $\angle$EAB = $\angle$EBA

$\therefore$ BE = AE

[$\because$ sides opposite to equal angles are equal]

and AC = BD   (Given)

$\therefore$ ED = EC

Now, In $\triangle$ADE and $\triangle$BCE

$\angle AED = \angle BEC$ [Vertically opposite angle]

$AE = BE$

and $ED = EC$

By SAS congruence rule,

$\therefore \triangle ADE \cong \triangle BCE$

Hence, $AD = BC$

18. Line is the bisector of an angle A and B is any point an l. BP and BQ are perpendiculars from B to the arms of $\angle A$ (see figure)

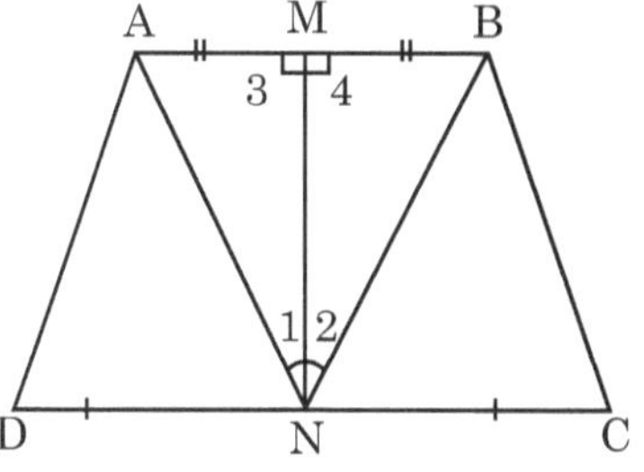

Show that

(i) $\triangle APB \cong \triangle AQB$

(ii) $BP = BQ$ or B is equidistant from the arms of $\angle A$.

Sol. Consider $\triangle APB$ and $\triangle AQB$, we have

$\angle APB = \angle AQB = 90°$

$[\because$ BP and BQ are perpendiculars]

$\angle PAB = \angle QAB$ $[\because$ AB bisects $\angle PAQ]$

and $AB = AB$ [common]

$\therefore$ By AAS congruence axiom, we have

$\triangle APB \cong \triangle AQB$, which proves (i)

$\Rightarrow BP = BQ.$ [by CPCT]

Hence, B is equidistant from the arms of $\angle A$, which proves (ii).

Long Answer Type Questions

(4 Marks Each)

1. In given figure, $PQ \perp QR$, $ST \perp TU$ such that $PQ = UT$ and $PS = RU$. Show that $\triangle PQR \cong \triangle UTS$.

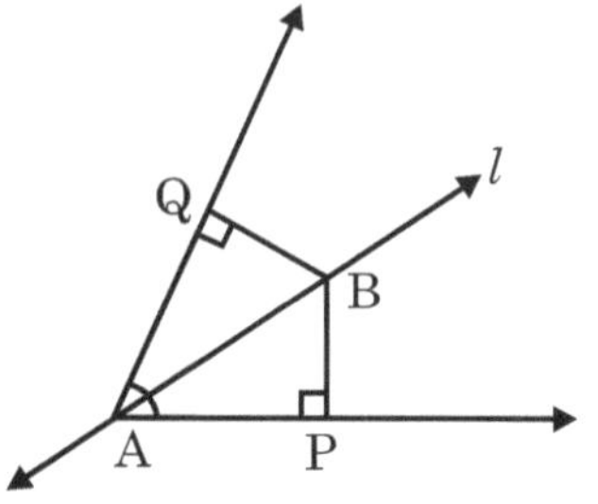

Sol. In figure, $PQ \perp QR$, $ST \perp TU$ such that $PQ = UT$ and $PS = RU$.

Now, we have to show $\triangle PQR \cong \triangle UTS$

Proof We have $PS = RU$ ...(i)

On adding SR in eq^n. (i) we have

$PS + SR = RU + SR \Rightarrow PR = SU$ ... (ii)

In $\triangle PQR$ and $\triangle UTS$; $\angle PQR = \angle STU = 90°$

$[\because$ PQ $\perp$ QR and ST $\perp$ TU]

$PR = SU$ [(hypotenuse) by eq. (ii)]

$PQ = UT$ [side]

$\therefore$ $\triangle PQR \cong \triangle UTS$

[by RHS congruence rule]

2. Line segment joining the mid-points M and N of parallel sides AB and DC, respectively of a trapezium ABCD is perpendicular to both the sides AB and DC. Prove that $AD = BC$

[NCERT EXEMPLAR]

Sol. Given in trapezium ABCD, points M and N are the mid-points of parallel sides AB and DC, respectively and join MN, which is perpendicular to AB and DC.

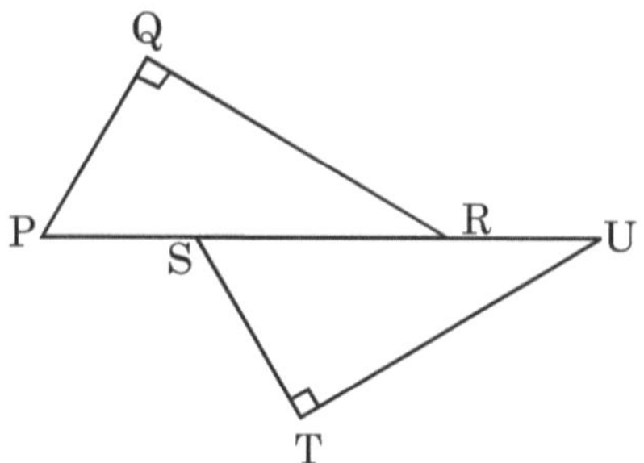

To Prove $AD = BC$

Proof Since, M is the mid-point of AB.

$\therefore AM = MB$

Now, in $\triangle AMN$ and $\triangle BMN$.

$AM = MB$ [proved above]

$\angle 3 = \angle 4$ [each 90°]

and $MN = MN$ [common side]

$\Rightarrow \angle 1 = \angle 2$ [by CPCT] ... (i)

On subtracting both sides of equation (i) from 90°, we have,

$90° - \angle 1 = 90° - \angle 2$

$\Rightarrow \angle AND = \angle BNC$ ...(ii)

Now, in $\triangle ADN$ and $\triangle BCN$,

$\angle AND = \angle BNC$ [from eq. (ii)]

$AN = BN$ $[\because \triangle AMN \cong \triangle BMN]$

and $DN = NC$

[since, N is the mid-point of CD]

By SAS congruence rule, we have

$\therefore \triangle ADN \cong \triangle BCN$

Hence, $AD = BC$ [by CPCT]

3. in given figure, AC = BC, $\angle DCA = \angle ECB$ and $\angle DBC = \angle EAC$. Prove that $\triangle DBC \cong \triangle EAC$ and hence DC = EC and BD = AE.

Sol. Given, $\angle DCA = \angle ECB$

On Adding $\angle DCE$ on both the sides.

$\angle DCA + \angle DCE = \angle DCE + \angle ECB$

$\Rightarrow \angle ACE = \angle BCD$ ...(i)

Now, in $\triangle BDC$ and $\triangle AEC$,

$\angle BCD = \angle ACE$ [From (i)]

BC = AC (Given)

and $\angle DBC = \angle EAC$ (Given)

By ASA criterion of congruence, we have

$\triangle DBC \cong \triangle EAC$

Hence, BD = AE and DC = EC [By cpct]

4. In figure, ABCD is a quadrilateral in which AD = BC and $\angle DAB = \angle CBA$. Prove that :

(i) $\triangle ABD \cong \triangle BAC$

(ii) BD = AC

(iii) $\angle ABD = \angle BAC$

[NCERT, BOARD TERM I, 2012, SET-71]

Sol. Given, ABCD is a quadrilateral and

AD = BC and $\angle DAB = \angle CBA$

In $\triangle ABD$ and $\triangle BAC$,

$\angle DAB = \angle CBA$ (given)

AB = AB (Common)

AD = BC (given)

By SAS congruence rule,

$\therefore$ (i) $\triangle ABD \cong \triangle BAC$

(ii) BD = AC

(iii) $\angle ABD = \angle BAC$ (By c.p.c.t.)

5. In $\triangle ABC$ and $\triangle PQR$, AB = PQ, AC = PR and altitude AM and PN are equal. Show that, $\triangle ABC \cong \triangle PQR$.

[BOARD TERM I, 2012, SET-35]

Sol. According to the question,

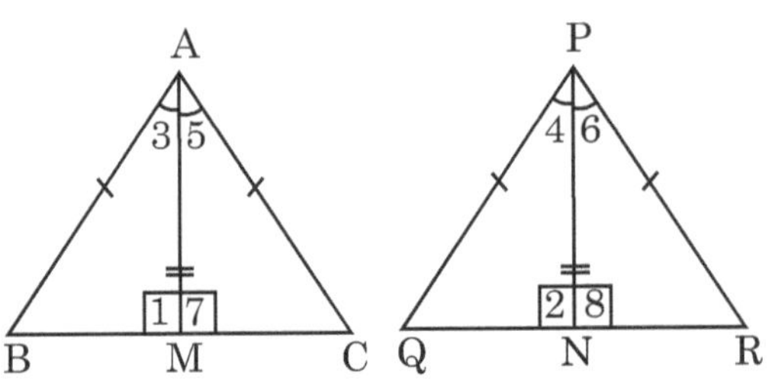

In $\triangle AMB$ and $\triangle PNQ$

AB = PQ (Given)

AM = PN (Given)

$\angle 1 = \angle 2 = 90°$

[$\because$ AM and PN are altitudes on BC and QR]

$\therefore \triangle AMB \cong \triangle PNQ$ [By RHS]

$\Rightarrow \angle 3 = \angle 4$ (By c.p.c.t.)

Similarly, $\triangle AMC \cong \triangle PNR$

$\therefore \angle 5 = \angle 6$

(In congruent triangles, corresponding angles are equal)

Now, In $\triangle ABC$ and $\triangle PQR$,

AB = PQ (Given)

AC = PR (Given)

and $\angle A = \angle P$

[$\because \angle 3 = \angle 4$ and $\angle 5 = \angle 6$]

By SAS congruence rule, we have,

$\therefore \triangle ABC \cong \triangle PQR$

Hence proved.

6. In the given figure, PQRS is a quadrilateral and T and U are points on PS and RS respectively, such that PQ = RQ, $\angle PQT = \angle RQU$ and $\angle TQS = \angle UQS$.

Prove that : QT = QU.

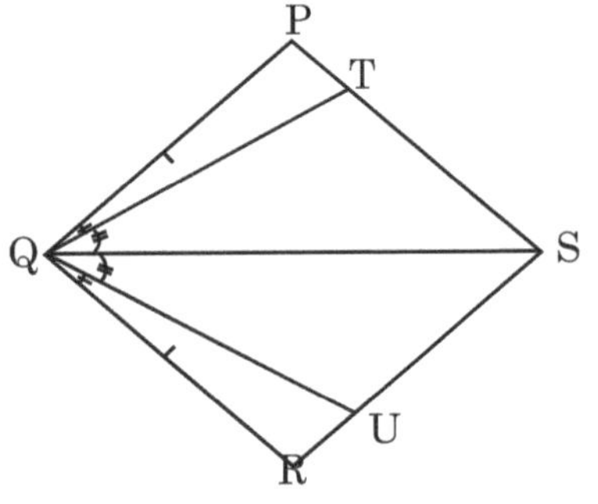

[BOARD TERM I, 2012, SET-20, 37, 67]

Sol. Given, $\angle PQT = \angle RQU$ ...(i)

and $\angle TQS = \angle UQS$ ...(ii)

On adding both the equations we have

$\angle PQT + \angle TQS = \angle RQU + \angle UQS$

$\Rightarrow \angle PQS = \angle RQS$

PQ = RQ, (Given) and

QS = QS (Common)

By SAS congruence rule,

$\therefore \Delta PQS \cong \Delta RQS$

$\therefore \angle P = \angle R$ (By c.p.c.t.)

Again, in ΔPQT and ΔRQU,

$\angle P = \angle R$

$\angle PQT = \angle RQU$

and PQ = QR

By ASA congruence rule,

$\therefore \Delta PQT \cong \Delta RQU$

$\Rightarrow QT = QU.$ (By c.p.c.t.)

Hence proved.

7. In the given figure, AC = AE, AB = AD and $\angle BAD = \angle EAC$. Show that BC = DE.

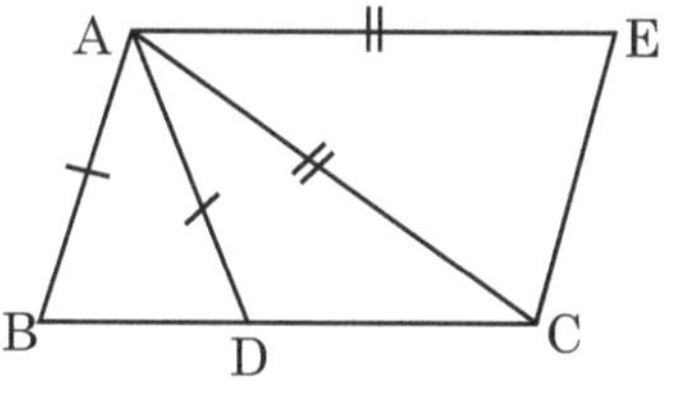

[BOARD TERM I, 2012, SET-14]

Sol.

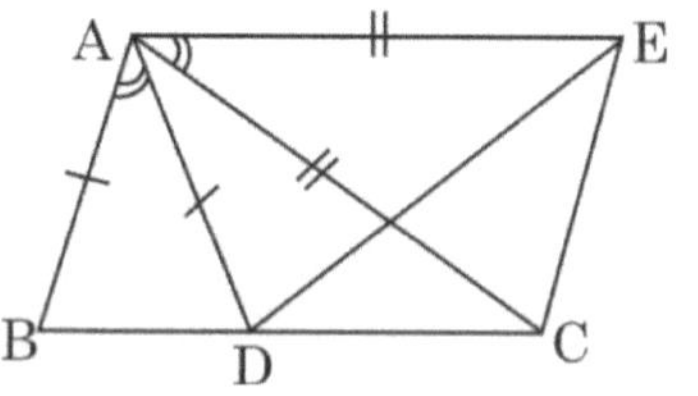

Given $\angle BAD = \angle EAC$

On adding $\angle CAD$ on both sides, we get

$\angle BAD + \angle CAD = \angle EAC + \angle CAD$

$\Rightarrow \angle BAC = \angle DAE$

AC = AE (Given)

and AB = AD (Given)

By SAS congruency rule,

$\therefore \Delta BAC \cong \Delta DAE$

Hence, BC = ED (By c.p.c.t.)

8. In the figure, OA = OB, OC = OD and $\angle AOB = \angle COD$. Prove that AC = BD.

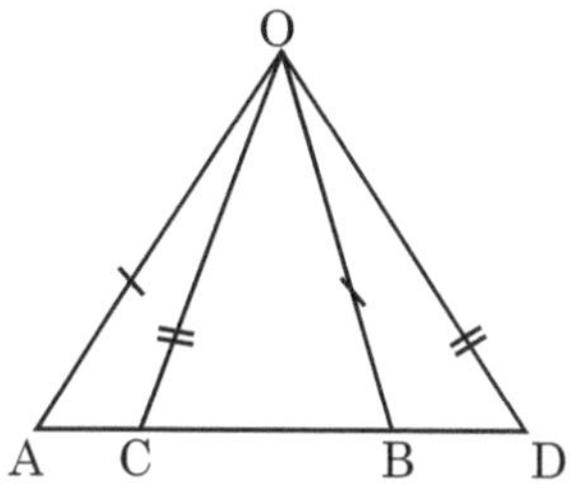

[BOARD TERM I, 2012, SET-19]

Sol. Given, $\angle AOB = \angle COD$

on subtracting $\angle COB$

$\angle AOB - \angle COB = \angle COD - \angle COB$

$\angle AOC = \angle BOD$

In ΔAOC and ΔBOD,

AO = OB (Given)

OC = OD (Given)

$\angle AOC = \angle BOD$ (Proved above)

$\therefore \Delta AOC \cong \Delta BOD$ (SAS Congruence rule)

AC = BD (By c.p.c.t.)

9. In a rhombus ABCD, O is any interior point such that OA = OC. Then prove that D, O and B are collinear.

[BOARD TERM I, 2012, SET-42]

Sol. Given; a rhombus ABCD and O is any interior point such that AO = OC.

To prove : D, O and B are collinear

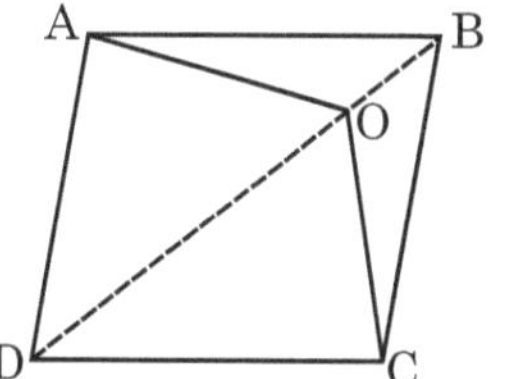

Construction: Join OD and OB.

Proof : In ΔAOB and ΔCOB,

AO = CO (Given)

OB = OB (Common)

and AB = BC ($\because$ ABCD is a rhombus)

By SSS congruence rule,

$\Delta AOB \cong \Delta COB$

$\Rightarrow \angle AOB = \angle COB$ (By c.p.c.t.) ... (i)

Similalry, $\Delta AOD \cong \Delta COD$

$\therefore \angle AOD = \angle COD$ (By c.p.c.t.) ... (ii)

But, $\angle AOD + \angle COD + \angle COB + \angle AOB = 360°$

[Circular angle]

$\Rightarrow 2(\angle AOD + \angle AOB) = 360°$

$\Rightarrow \angle AOD + \angle AOB = 180°$

Hence, D, O and B are collinear.

10. AD, BE and CF, the altitudes of $\triangle$ABC are equal. Prove that $\triangle$ABC is an equilateral triangle.

[BOARD TERM I, 2012]

Sol. According to the question,

AD, BE and CF are equal altitudes.

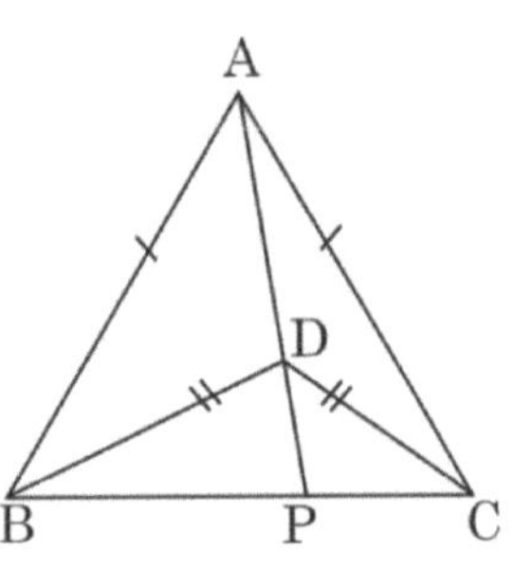

In $\triangle$BCE and $\triangle$CBF,

$\angle$BEC = $\angle$BFC = 90° (Given)

BE = CF (Given)

BC = CB (Common)

By RHS congruence rule,

$\therefore$ $\triangle$BCE $\cong$ $\triangle$CBF

Hence, $\angle$B = $\angle$C

$\therefore$ and AC = AB (By c.p.c.t.)

Similarly, $\triangle$ABD $\cong$ $\triangle$BAE

AC = BC

Therefore, AB = BC = AC

Hence, $\triangle$ABC is an equilateral triangle.

11. $\triangle$ABC and $\triangle$DBC, are two isosceles triangles on the same base BC and vertices A and D are on the same. side of BC. If AD is extended to intersect BC at P, show that:

(i) $\triangle$ABD $\cong$ $\triangle$ACD

(ii) $\triangle$ABP $\cong$ $\triangle$ACP

(iii) AP bisects $\angle$A as well as $\angle$D.

[BOARD TERM I, 2012, SET-52]

Sol.

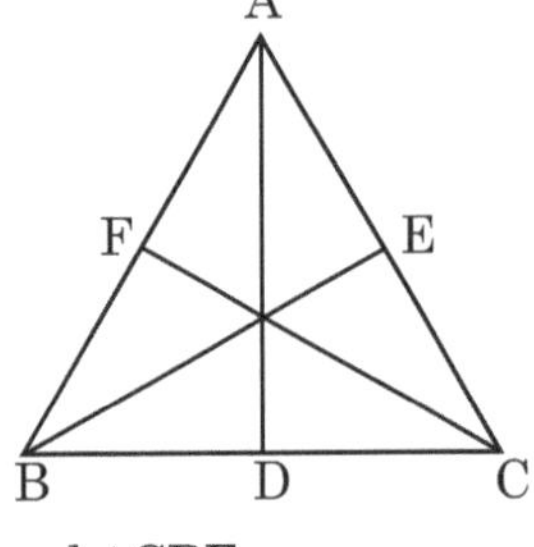

(i) AB = AC, BD = CD and AD = DA

By SSS congruence rule,

$\triangle$ABD $\cong$ $\triangle$ACD ... (i)

$\angle$BAD = $\angle$CAD (By c.p.c.t.)

(ii) AB = AC, $\angle$BAP = $\angle$CAP and AP = AP

By SAS congruence rule,

$\triangle$ABP $\cong$ $\triangle$ACP

BP = CP (By c.p.c.t.)

(iii) From equation (i), $\angle$BAD = $\angle$CAD

Therefore, AP is the bisector of $\angle$A

BD = CD, BP = CP and DP = DP

By SSS congruence rule,

$\triangle$BDP $\cong$ $\triangle$CDP $\therefore$ $\angle$BDP = $\angle$CDP (By c.p.c.t.)

Hence, DP is the bisector of $\angle$D.

12. In the given figure, if AC = BC, $\angle$DCA = $\angle$ECB and $\angle$DBC = $\angle$EAC, then prove that BD = AE.

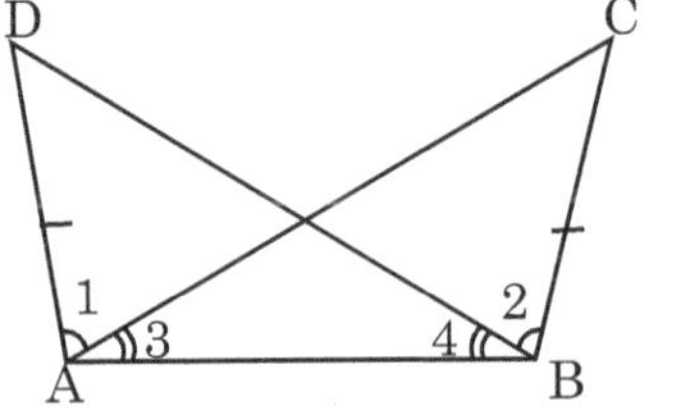

[BOARD TERM I, 2014; 2012, SET-45]

Sol. Given, $\angle$DCA = $\angle$ECB

On Adding $\angle$DCE to both sides, we get

$\Rightarrow$ $\angle$DCA + $\angle$DCE = $\angle$ECB + $\angle$DCE

$\Rightarrow$ $\angle$ECA = $\angle$DCB ... (i)

In $\triangle$ACE and $\triangle$BCD, AC = BC (Given)

$\angle$ECA = $\angle$DCB (From equation (i))

and $\angle$EAC = $\angle$DBC (Given)

By AAS congruency rule,

$\therefore$ $\triangle$ACE $\cong$ $\triangle$BCD

Hence, BD = AE.

13. In figure, $\triangle$ABC and $\triangle$ABD are such that AD = BC, $\angle$1 = $\angle$2 and $\angle$3 = $\angle$4. Prove that BD = AC.

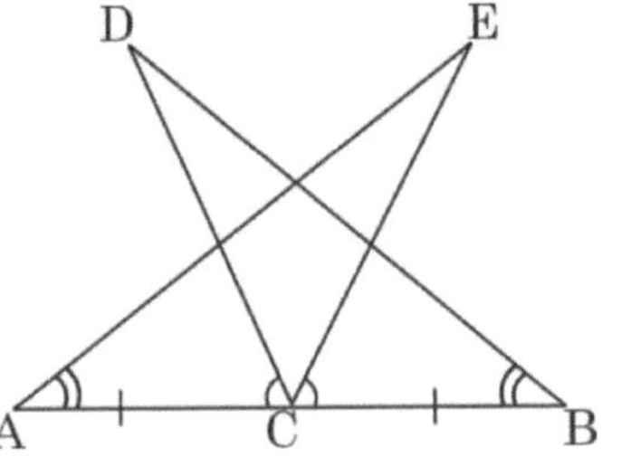

[BOARD TERM I, 2014]

Sol. Given, AD = BC

$\angle$1 = $\angle$2

and $\angle$3 = $\angle$4

Now, In $\triangle$ABC and $\triangle$ABD,

AB = AB (Common side)

$\angle$1 = $\angle$2 ...(i)

$\angle$3 = $\angle$4 ...(ii)

On adding equations (i) and (ii), we get

$\angle 1 + \angle 3 = \angle 2 + \angle 4$

$\Rightarrow \angle DAB = \angle CBA$ and, AD = BC

By SAS congruence rule, we have

$\therefore \triangle ABC \cong \triangle ABD$

Hence, BD = AC

14. In the figure, OA = OB, OC = OD and $\angle AOB = \angle COD$. Prove that AC = BD.

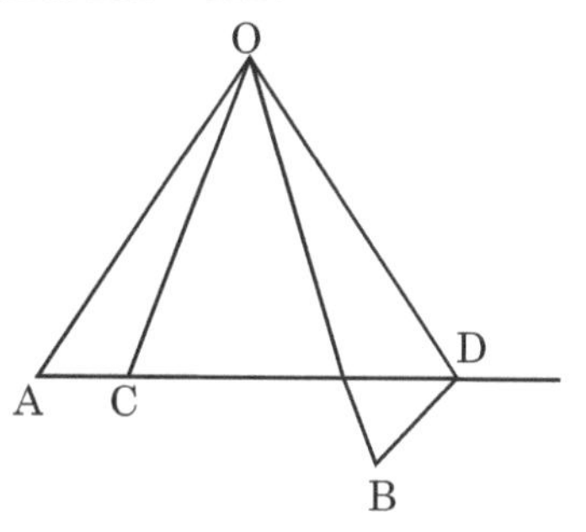

[BOARD TERM I, 2016, SET-7AEDLQR]

Sol. Given, $\angle AOB = \angle COD$

On subtracting $\angle COB$ from both the side,

$\angle AOB - \angle COB = \angle COD - \angle COB$

$\angle AOC = \angle BOD$ ... (i)

In $\triangle AOC$ and $\triangle BOD$

AO = OB   (Given)

OC = OD   (Given)

and $\angle AOC = \angle BOD$ [From equation (i)]

By SAS Congruence rule,

AOC $\cong$ BOD

Hence, AC = BD   (By c.p.c.t)

15. In right triangle ABC, right-angled at C, M is the mid-point of hypotenuse AB. C is joined to M and produced to a point D such that DM = CM. Point D is joined to point B (see fig.).

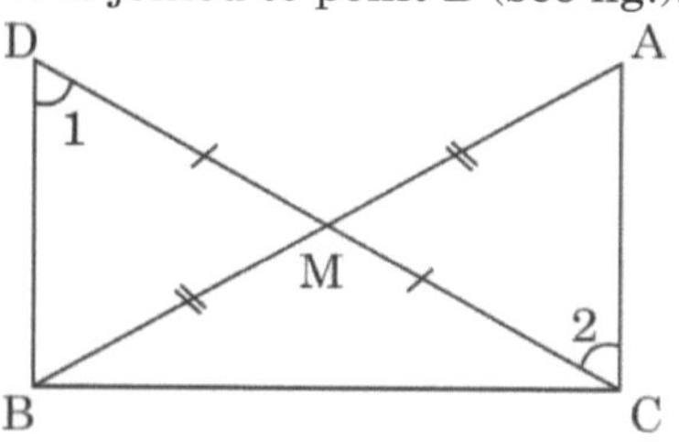

Show that :

(i) $\triangle AMC \cong \triangle BMD$

(ii) $\angle DBC = 90°$

(iii) $\triangle DBC \cong \triangle ACB$

(iv) $CM = \dfrac{1}{2} AB$

[BOARD TERM I, 2016, SET-JQ22L5C]

Sol. Given $\triangle ACB$ in which $\angle C = 90°$ and M is the mid-point of AB.

To Prove

(i) $\triangle AMC \cong \triangle BMD$

(ii) $\angle DBC = 90°$

(iii) $\triangle DBC \cong \triangle ACB$

(iv) $CM = \dfrac{1}{2} AB$

Proof (i) Consider $\triangle AMC$ and $\triangle BMD$, we have

AM = BM [given]

CM = DM [given]

and $\angle AMC = \angle BMD$

[vertically opposite angles]

By SAS congruence rule,

$\triangle AMC \cong \triangle BMD$

$\Rightarrow AC = DB$ ... (i) [by CPCT]

and $\angle 1 = \angle 2$ [by CPCT]

But $\angle 1$ and $\angle 2$ are alternate angles.

Therefore, BD ∥ CA

(ii) Now, BD ∥ CA and BC is transversal.

$\therefore \angle ACB + \angle CBD = 180°$

$\Rightarrow 90° + \angle CBD = 180°$

$\Rightarrow \angle CBD = 90°$

(iii) In $\triangle DBC$ and $\triangle ACB$, we have

CB = BC [common]

DB = AC [using eq. (i)]

and $\angle CBD = \angle BCA$ [each 90°]

By SAS congruence rule,

$\therefore \triangle DBC \cong \triangle ACB$

(iv) $\Rightarrow DC = AB \Rightarrow \dfrac{1}{2} AB = \dfrac{1}{2} DC$

$\Rightarrow \dfrac{1}{2} AB = CM$

$\therefore CM = \dfrac{1}{2} AB$ $\left[\because CM = \dfrac{1}{2} DC\right]$

Hence, proved.

16. If two isosceles triangles have a common base. Prove that the line joining their vertices bisects them at right angles.

OR

ABC and DBC are two isosceles triangle on the same base BC such that A and D lies on the opposite sides of BC. Show that AD is the perpendicular bisector of BC.

[BOARD TERM I, 2016, SET-20CNJE9]

Sol.

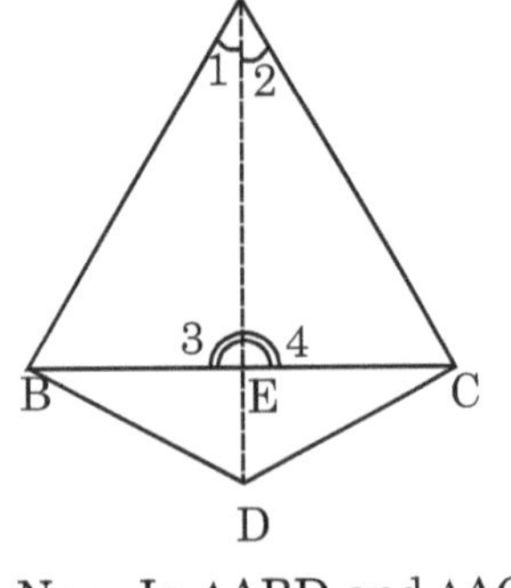

Now, In $\triangle ABD$ and $\triangle ACD$,

AB = AC (Given)

AD = AD (Common)

and BD = CD (Given)

By SSS congruence rule,

∴ $\triangle ABD \cong \triangle ACD$

Again, In $\triangle ABE$ and $\triangle ACE$,

AB = AC

AE = AE

and $\angle 1 = \angle 2$

By SAS congruence rule,

∴ $\triangle ABE \cong \triangle ACE$

or, BE = CE

or, $\angle 3 = \angle 4$

But $\angle 3 + \angle 4 = 180°$ [Linear pair]

$\Rightarrow \angle 3 + \angle 3 = 180°$

$\Rightarrow 2\angle 3 = 180°$

∴ $\angle 3 = 90°$

Therefore, $\angle 3 = \angle 4 = 90°$

Hence AD bisects BC at right angle.

17. In figure, ABC is a triangle in which altitudes BE and CF to sides AC and AB respectively are equal. Show that :

(i) $\triangle ABE \cong \triangle ACF$

(ii) AB = AC.

Sol. (i) Let, BE $\perp$ AC and CF $\perp$ AB

In $\triangle$s ABE and ACF, we have

$\angle AEB = \angle AFC = 90°$ [∵ BE $\perp$ AC and CF $\perp$ AB]

$\angle A = \angle A$ (Common)

and BE = CF (Given)

∴ By AAS criterion of congruence, we have

$\triangle ABE \cong \triangle ACF$

Hence, AB = AC. [By c.p.c.t.]

18. Prove that two triangles are congruent if any two angles and the included side of one triangle is equal to any two angles and the included side of the other triangle.

Sol. Proof : We are given two triangles ABC and PQR in which

$\angle B = \angle Q, \angle C = \angle R$

and BC = QR

We need to prove that $\triangle ABC \cong \triangle PQR$

There are three cases.

From Case I : Let AB = PQ

In $\triangle ABC$ and $\triangle PQR$,

$\angle B = \angle Q$ (Given)

BC = QR (Given)

and AB = PQ (Assumed)

By SAS congruence rule,

∴ $\triangle ABC \cong \triangle PQR$

From Case II : Suppose AB $\neq$ PQ and AB < PQ

Take a point S on PQ such that

QS = AB

Join RS.

In $\triangle ABC$ and $\triangle SQR$,

AB = SQ (By construction)

BC = QR (Given)

and $\angle B = \angle Q$ (Given)

By SAS congruence rule,

$\triangle ABC \cong \triangle SQR$

$\Rightarrow \angle ACB = \angle QRS$ (By c.p.c.t.)

But, $\angle QRP = \angle ACB$

$\Rightarrow \angle QRP = \angle QRS$

Which is impossible unless ray RS coincides with RP.

$\therefore$ AB must be equal to PQ.

Hence $\triangle ABC \cong \triangle PQR$

From Case III : If AB > PQ.

We can choose a point T on AB such that TB = PQ and repeating the arguments as given in Case II, we can conclude that AB = PQ and so,

$\triangle ABC \cong \triangle PQR$

Hence proved.

19. In the figure, if PQ = PS, RQ = RS, then show that $\triangle PQR \cong \triangle PSR$ and $\triangle RQT \cong \triangle RST$.

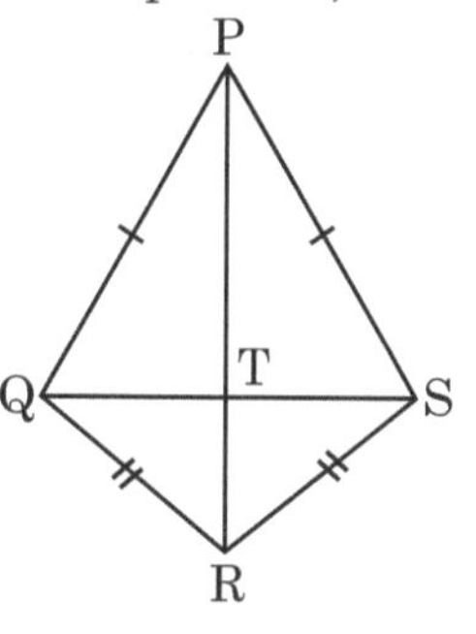

Sol. According to the question,

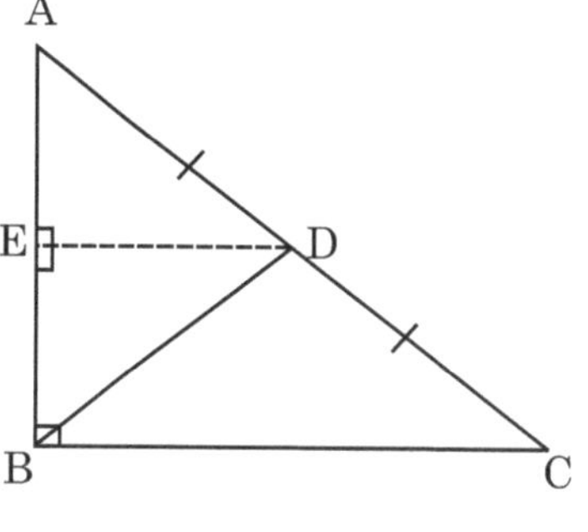

In $\triangle$s PQR and PSR,

PQ = PS (Given)

RQ = RS (Given)

and PR = PR (Common)

By SSS congruence rule, we have

$\triangle PQR \cong \triangle PSR$

$\because$ Corresponding parts of congruent triangles are equal.

$\therefore \angle QRP = \angle SRP$

Again, in $\triangle RQT$ and $\triangle RST$

RQ = RS (Given)

RT = RT (Common)

and $\angle QRT = \angle SRT$ ($\because \angle QRP = \angle SRP$)

By SAS congruence rule, we have

$\therefore \triangle RQT \cong \triangle RST$

Hence proved.

20. If D is the mid-point of the hypotenuse AC of a right triangle ABC, prove that $BD = \dfrac{1}{2} AC$.

Sol. Given, D is the mid-point of hypotenuse AC,

To Prove : $BD = \dfrac{1}{2} AC$

Constant :

On drawing a line DE parallel to line BC.

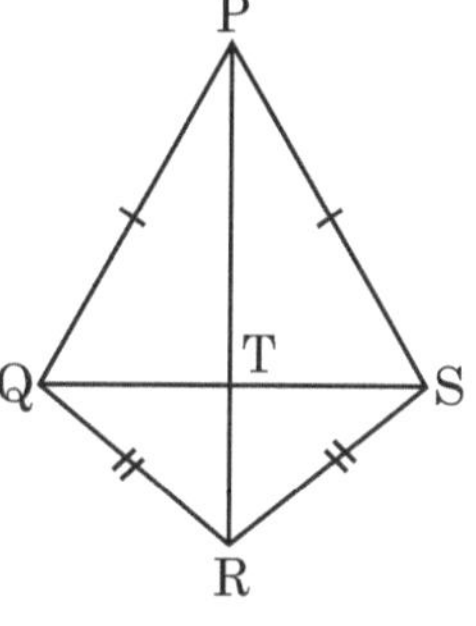

Proof: In $\triangle ABC$

D is the mid-point of AC & ED ∥ BC

$\therefore$ By mid point theorem,

AE = EB   ... (i)

Now, ED | | BC

$\angle AED = \angle ABC$ (Corresponding angles)

$\angle AED = 90°$

$\therefore \angle AED = \angle DEB = 90°$ ... (ii)

Again, in $\triangle ADE$ and $\triangle BDE$,

AE = EB [from eq. (i)]

$\angle AED = \angle DEB$ [from eq. (ii)]

and ED = ED (Common)

By SAS congruence rule,

$\triangle ADE \cong \triangle BDE$

$\therefore$ AD = BD   .... (iii) (By c.p.c.t.)

But $AD = DC = \dfrac{1}{2} AC$ .... (iv)

[D is the mid-point of side AC]

From equation (iii) and (iv) we have

$BD = \dfrac{1}{2} AC$

Hence proved.

[Topic 2] Some Properties of Triangles

Points to be Remembered

- Angles opposite to equal sides of a triangle are equal.

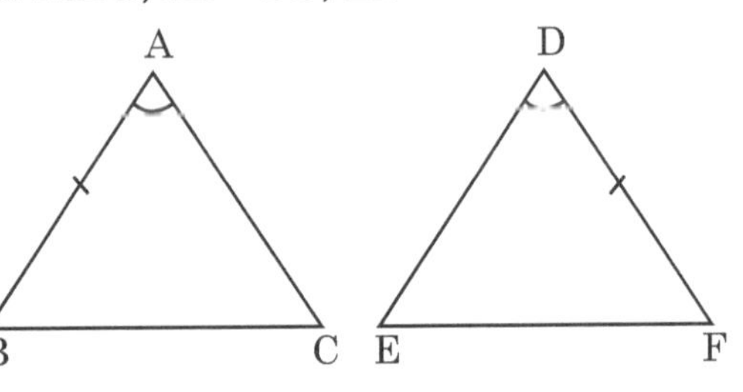

In $\triangle ABC$,

$\because$ AB = AC

$\therefore \angle B = \angle C$

- The sides opposite to equal angles of a triangle are equal.
- Angles opposite to equal side of an isosceles triangle are equal.

PREVIOUS YEARS'
EXAMINATION QUESTIONS
TOPIC 2

Multiple Choice Questions

(1 Mark Each)

1. In $\triangle ABC$, BC = AB and $\angle B = 80°$. Then $\angle A$ is equal to [NCERT Exemp.]
   (a) 80°   (b) 40°
   (c) 50°   (d) 100°

Sol. (c) According to the question,

In $\triangle ABC$, BC = AB and $\angle B = 80°$

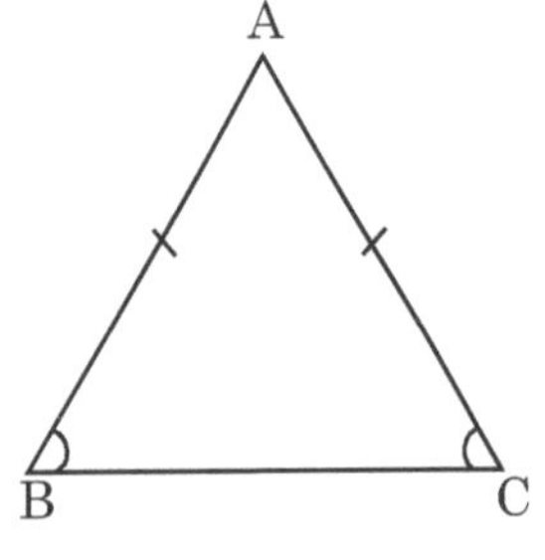

$\therefore \angle C = \angle A$ (angles opposite to equal sides are equal)

Now, $\angle A + \angle B + \angle C = 180°$ (sum of all angles of triangle)

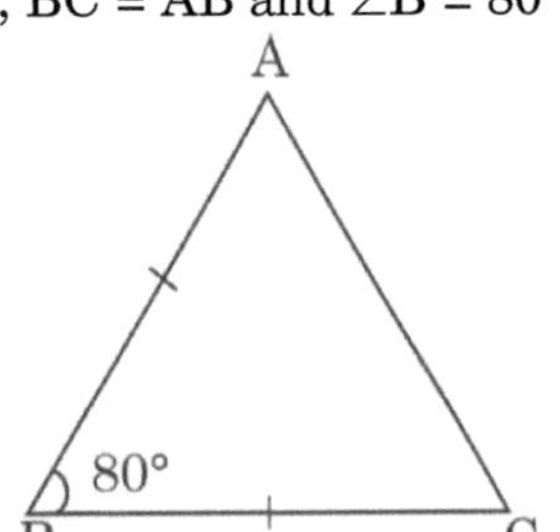

$\because$ AB = AD

$\therefore \angle B = \angle D$

- Each angle of an equilateral triangle is 60°.
- A point equidistant from two given points lies on the perpendicular bisector of the line segment joining the two points.
- A point equidistant from two intersecting lines lies on the bisectors of the angles formed by the two lines.
- In an isosceles triangle altitude from the vertex bisects the base. Conversely, if the altitude from one vertex of a triangle bisects the opposite side, then the triangle is isosceles.

$\Rightarrow \angle A + 80° + \angle A = 180°$

$\Rightarrow 2\angle A = 180° - 80° = 100°$

$\angle A = \dfrac{100°}{2} = 50°$

2. In triangles ABC and DEF, AB = FD and $\angle A = \angle D$. The two triangles will be congruent by SAS axiom if. [NCERT Exemp.]
   (a) BC = EF   (b) AC = DE
   (c) AC = EF   (d) BC = DE

Sol. (b) According to the question,

In $\triangle ABC$, AB = FD, $\angle A = \angle D$

We know that, two triangles will be congruent by SAS axiom if two sides and the included angle between them of one triangle is equal to another triangle.

Therefore, if side AC = DE, then $\triangle ABC \cong \triangle DEF$

3. It is given that $\triangle ABC \cong \triangle FDE$ and AB = 5 cm, $\angle B = 40°$ and $\angle A = 80°$. Then which of the following is true?
   (a) DF = 5 cm, $\angle F = 60°$
   (b) DF = 5 cm $\angle E = 60°$
   (c) DE = 5 cm, $\angle E = 60°$
   (d) DE = 5 cm, $\angle D = 40°$ [NCERT Exemp.]

Sol. (c) According to the question,
   $\triangle ABC \cong \triangle FDE$ and AB = 5 cm, $\angle B = 40°$, $\angle A = 80°$

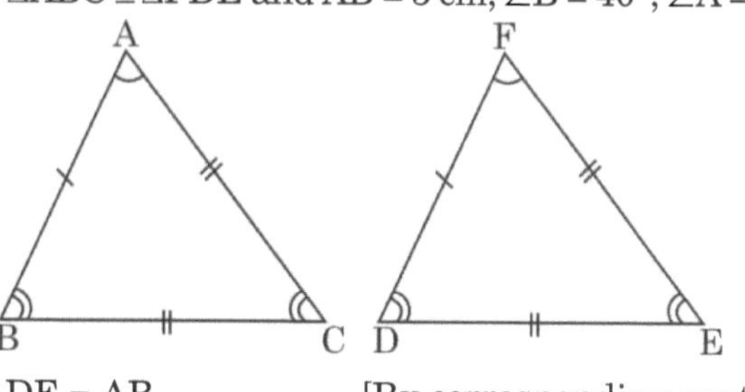

   DF = AB   [By corresponding parts of congruent triangles]
   DF = 5 cm
   and $\angle E = \angle C$ [By corresponding parts of congruent triangles]
   $\angle E = \angle C = 180° - (\angle A + \angle B)$
   [By angle sum property of a $\triangle ABC$]
   $\angle E = 180° - (80° + 40°) = 180° - 120° = 60°$

4. In $\triangle ABC$, AB = AC and $\angle B = 50°$. Then $\angle C$ is equal to   [NCERT Exemp.]
   (a) 40°   (b) 50°
   (c) 80°   (d) 130°

Sol (b) According to the question,
   AB = AC and $\angle B = 50°$

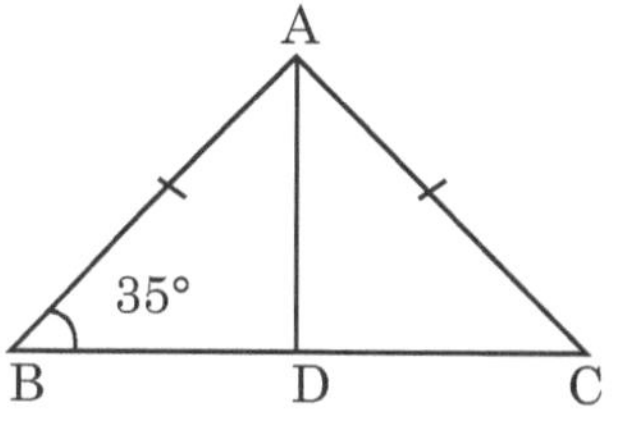

   In $\triangle ABC$, AB = AC (given)
   $\therefore \angle C = \angle B = 50°$ (angles opposites to equal sides are equal)

5. Chose the correct statement :
   (a) a triangle has two right angles
   (b) all the angles of a triangle are more than 60°
   (c) an exterior angle of a triangle is always greater than the opposite interior angles
   (d) all the angles of a triangle are less than 60°

Sol. (c) An exterior angle of a triangle is always greater than the opposite interior angles.

6. In the given figure, AD is the median then $\angle BAD$ is:

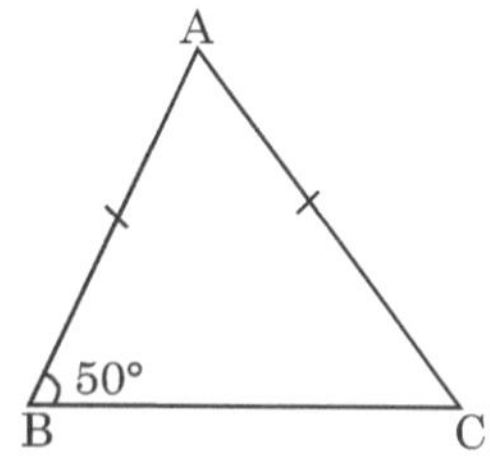

   (a) 35°   (b) 70°
   (c) 110°   (d) 55°

Sol. (d) $\because$ $\triangle ABC$ is an isosceles triangle.
   $\therefore \angle B = \angle C = 35°$
   and AD $\perp$ BC
   $\therefore \angle ADB = 90°$
   Now, in $\triangle ADB$.
   $\angle B + \angle ADB + \angle A = 180°$ [Angle sum property]
   $\Rightarrow 35° + 90° + \angle BAD = 180°$
   $\therefore \angle BAD = 90° - 35° = 55°$

Very Short Answer Type Questions
(1 Mark Each)

1. If in $\triangle ABC$, $\angle A = \angle B + \angle C$, then write the shape of the given triangle.

Sol. Here, $\angle A = \angle B + \angle C$
   And in $\triangle ABC$, by angle sum property, we have
   $\angle A + \angle B + \angle C = 180°$
   $\Rightarrow \angle A + \angle A = 180°$
   $\Rightarrow 2\angle A = 180°$ $\therefore \angle A = 90°$
   Hence, the given triangle is a right triangle.

2. In $\triangle PQR$, $\angle P = 70°$ and $\angle R = 30°$. Which side of this triangle is the longest? Give reason for your answer.

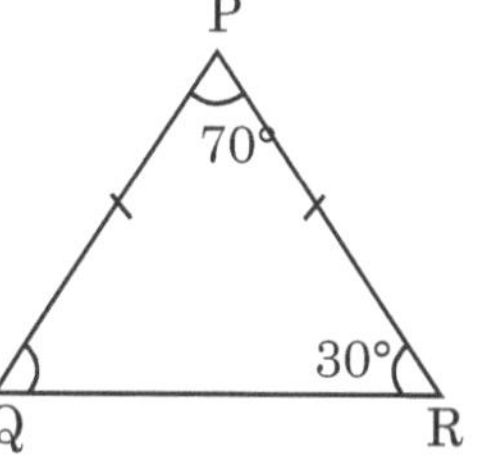

[NCERT EXEMPLAR]

Sol. According to the question,
   In $\triangle PQR$, $\angle P = 70°$ and $\angle R = 30°$
   We know that, sum of angles of a triangle is 180°.
   $\angle P + \angle Q + \angle R = 180°$
   $\Rightarrow 70° + \angle Q + 30° = 180°$
   $\therefore \angle Q = 180° - (70° + 30°) = 80°$
   Here, $\angle Q$ is greatest, so side, PR is longest.
   [since, side opposite to the greatest angle of a triangle is the longest]

3. In $\triangle PQR$, PE is the perpendicular bisector of $\angle QPR$, then prove that PQ = PR.

Sol. According to the question,

In $\triangle PEQ$ and $\triangle PER$,

$\angle PEQ = \angle PER = 90°$

and $\angle QPE = \angle RPE$

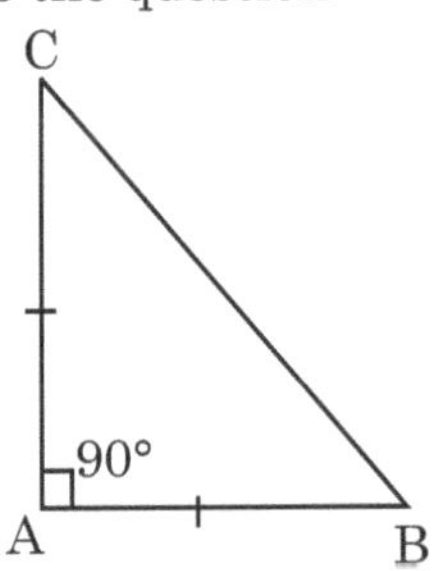

PE = PE   (Common)

$\therefore$ $\triangle PEQ \cong \triangle PER$ (by ASA)

Hence, PQ = PR.

[By corresponding parts of congruent triangles]

4. $\triangle ABC$ is an isosceles right angled triangle in which $\angle A = 90°$. Calculate $\angle B$.

Sol. According to the question,

$\because$ AB = AC

$\therefore$ $\angle C = \angle B$

[Angles opposite to equal sides are equal]

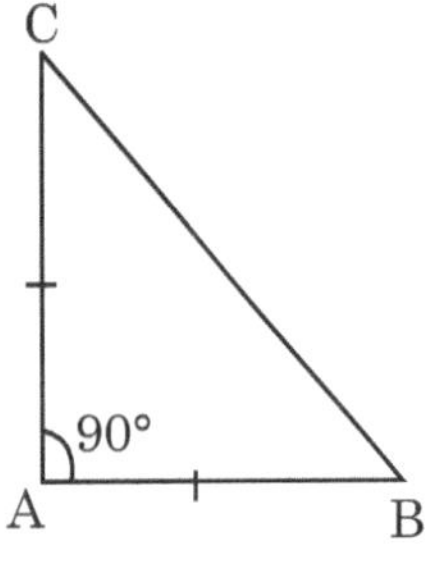

$\angle A + \angle B + \angle C = 180°$ [Angle sum property]

$90° + \angle B + \angle B = 180°$

$2\angle B = 90°$

$\angle B = \dfrac{90°}{2} = 45°$

5. Find the relation between PQ and QR in the given figure.

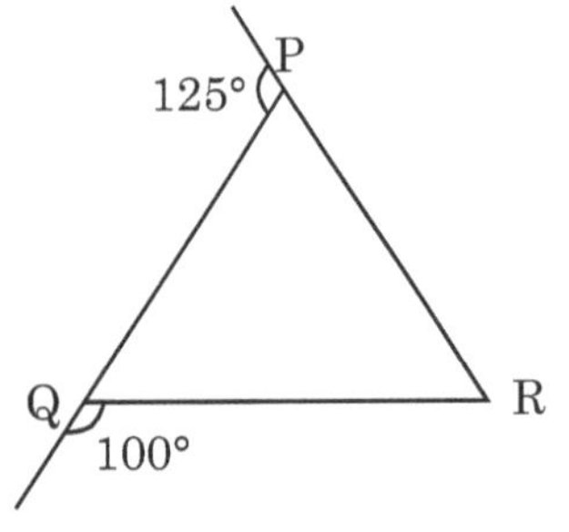

Sol. According to the given figure,

$\angle QPR = 180° - 125° = 55°$

and $\angle PQR = 180° - 100° = 80°$

$\therefore$ $\angle PRQ = 180° - \angle QPR - \angle PQR$

[Angle sum property]

$= 180° - 55° - 80°$

$= 180° - 135° = 45°$

Now, in $\triangle PQR$, $\angle QPR > \angle PRQ$

Hence, QR > PQ or PQ < QR.

Short Answer Type Questions I
(2 Marks Each)

1. Is it possible to construct a triangle with lengths of its sides as 4 cm, 3 cm and 7 cm? Give reason for your answer.

[**NCERT EXEMPLAR**]

Sol. No, it is not possible to construct a triangle with lengths of its sides as 4 cm, 3 cm and 7 cm because here we see that sum of the lengths of two sides is equal to third side, i.e., 4 + 3 = 7.

We know that, the sum of any two sides of a triangle is greater than the third side, so construction of given sides of triangle is not possible.

2. $\triangle ABC$ is a right angled triangle in which $\angle A = 90°$ and AB = AC. Find $\angle B$ and $\angle C$.

[**BOARD TERM I, 2010, SET-C1**]

Sol. According to the question

$\triangle ABC$ is a right angled triangle in which $\angle A = 90°$ and AB = AC.

Then, $\angle C = \angle B$ ...(i)

[$\because$ angles opposite to equal sides of a triangle are equal]

Now, $\angle A + \angle B + \angle C = 180°$

[since, sum of three angles of a triangle is 180°]

$\Rightarrow$ $90° + \angle B + \angle B = 180°$ [from eq. (i)]

$\Rightarrow 2\angle B = 90°$

$\therefore$ $\angle B = 45°$

Hence $\angle B = 45°$ and $\angle C = 45°$ [$\because$ AC = AB]

3. ABC is an isosceles triangle with AB = AC. Draw AP $\perp$ BC. Show that $\angle$B = $\angle$C.

[BOARD TERM I, 2011, SET-15]

Sol. According to the question, on drawing AP $\perp$ BC.

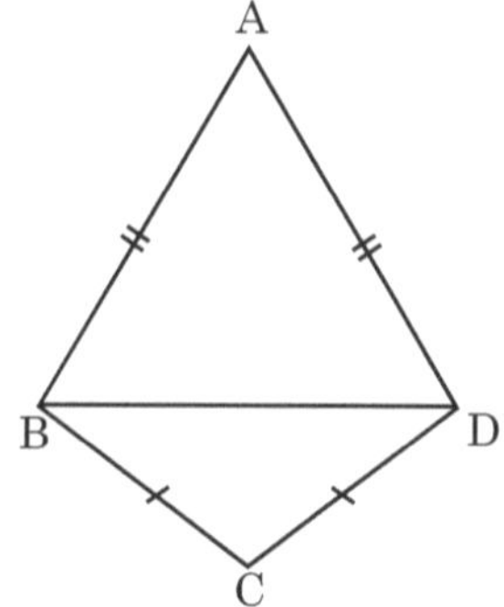

In $\triangle$ABP and $\triangle$ACP,

AB = AC, (Given)

AP = AP (Common)

and $\angle$APB = $\angle$APC = 90°, (AP $\perp$ BC)

By RHS rule, $\triangle$ABP $\cong$ $\triangle$ACP

$\therefore$ $\angle$B = $\angle$C.

[By corresponding parts of congruent triangles]

4. PS is an altitude of an isosceles triangle PQR in which PQ = PR. Show that PS bisects $\angle$P.

[BOARD TERM I, 2011, SET-22]

Sol. Given, in $\triangle$PQS and $\triangle$PRS,

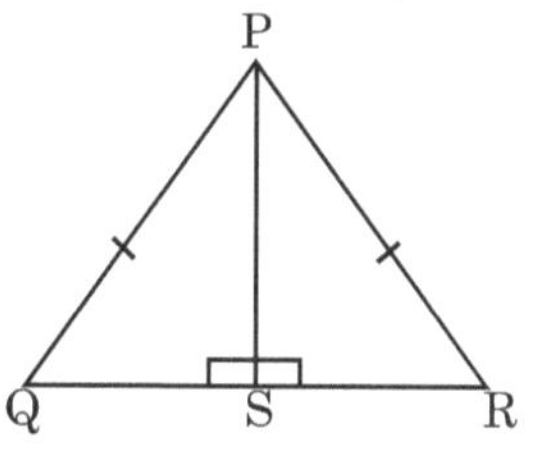

PQ = PR

And PS = PS (Common)

Also $\angle$PSQ = $\angle$PSR = 90° (PS is altitude)

Now, By R.H.S. rule,

$\therefore$ $\triangle$PQS $\cong$ $\triangle$PRS or $\angle$QPS = $\angle$RPS

[By corresponding parts of congruent triangles]

Hence, PS bisects $\angle$P.

5. In the figure below, $\triangle$ABD and $\triangle$BCD are isosceles triangles on the same base BD. Prove that $\angle$ABC = $\angle$ADC.

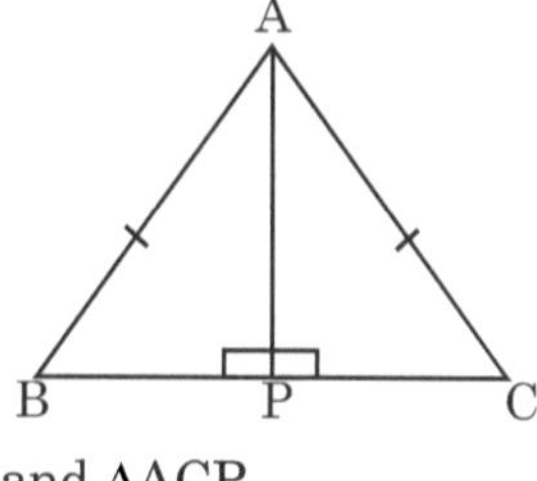

[BOARD TERM I, 2012, SET 67; 2011, SET-19]

Sol. According to the given figure,

AB = AD

[Angles opposite to equal sides are equal]

$\therefore$ $\angle$ABD = $\angle$ADB .....(i)

BC = CD

[Angles opposite to equal sides are equal]

$\therefore$ $\angle$CBD = $\angle$CDB ....(ii)

On adding equations. (i) and (ii), we get

$\angle$ABD + $\angle$CBD = $\angle$ADB + $\angle$CDB

$\therefore$ $\angle$ABC = $\angle$ADC.

Hence proved.

Short Answer Type Questions II

(3 Marks Each)

1. D and E are points on the base BC of $\triangle$ABC, such that BD = CE. If AD = AE, then prove that $\triangle$ABE $\cong$ $\triangle$ACD.

[NCERT]

Sol. Given D and E are the points on the base BC of $\triangle$ABC such that BD = CE and AD = AE.

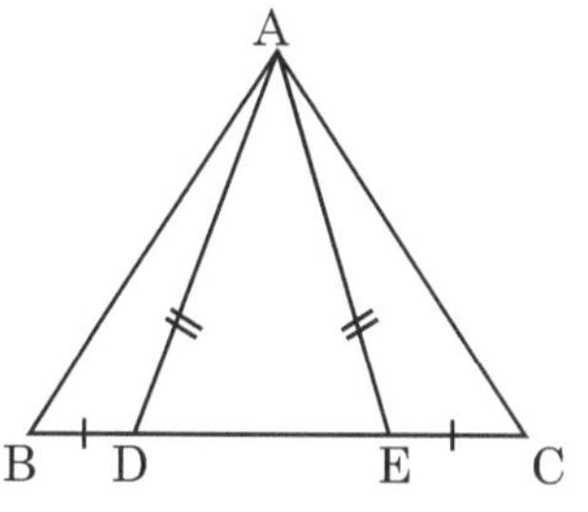

To prove $\triangle$ABE $\cong$ $\triangle$ACD

Proof In $\triangle$ADE,

AD = AE [given]

$\Rightarrow$ $\angle$AED = $\angle$ADE

[$\because$ angle opposite to equal sides of a triangle are equal]

$\Rightarrow$ $\angle$AEB = $\angle$ADC ... (ii)

[$\because$ $\angle$AED = $\angle$AEB and $\angle$ADE = $\angle$ADC]

Now, BD = CE [given]

On adding DE both sides, we get

BD + DE = CE + DE $\therefore$ BE = CD

[$\because$ BE = BD + DE and CD = CE + ED]

In $\triangle$ABE and $\triangle$ACD,

BE = CD [proved above]

$\angle$AEB = $\angle$ADC [from equation (i)]

and AE = AD [given]

$\therefore$ $\triangle$ABE $\cong$ $\triangle$ACD

[by SAS congruence rule]

2. If the bisector of exterior vertical angle of a triangle is parallel to the base, then show that the triangle is isosceles. [NCERT]

Sol.

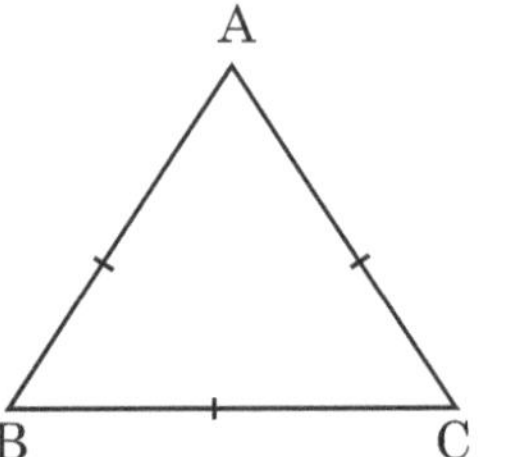

To prove ABC is an isosceles triangle.

Proof In the given figure,

$\angle 1 = \angle 2$ ...(i)

[∵ AE is the bisector of $\angle DAC$]

$\angle 2 = \angle 3$ ...(ii)

[alternate angle as AE || BC]

and $\angle 1 = \angle 4$ ...(iii)

[corresponding angles as AE||BC]

From equations (i), (ii) and (iii), we have

$\angle 3 = \angle 4 \Rightarrow AB = AC$

[∵ sides opposite to equal angles of a triangle are equal]

∴ ΔABC is an isosceles triangle.

Hence, triangle is an isosceles, if the bisector of its exterior vertical angle is parallel to its base.

3. In the given figure, ΔABC is an isosceles triangle with AB = AC. D and E are points on BC such that BE = CD, show that AD = AE.

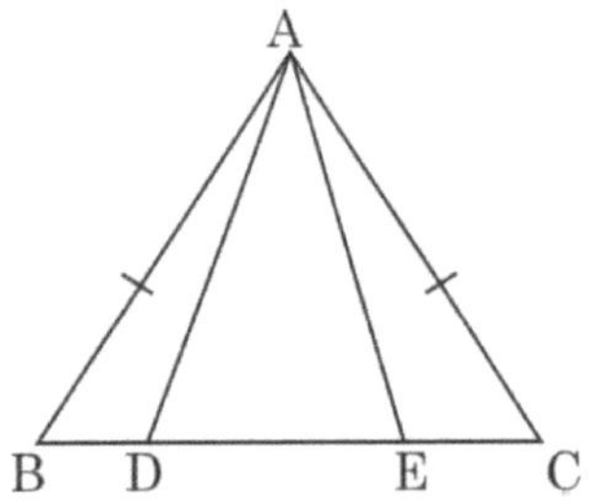

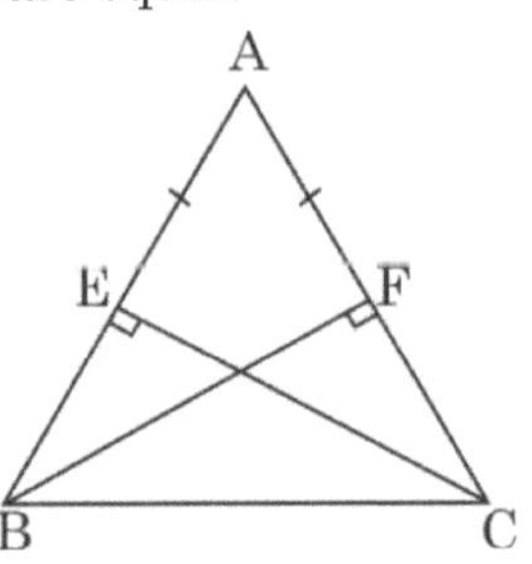

[NCERT BOARD TERM I, 2012, SET-66; 2011, SET-21]

Sol. According to the question,

In ΔABE and ΔACD,

AB = AC

∴ $\angle C = \angle B$

[Angles opposite to equal sides are equal]

BE = CD (Given)

[By SAS congruence rule]

∴ ΔABE ≅ ΔACD

Hence, AD = AE (By c.p.c.t)

4. Prove that each angle of an equilateral triangle is 60°.

[BOARD TERM I, 2012, SET-71, NCERT]

Sol.

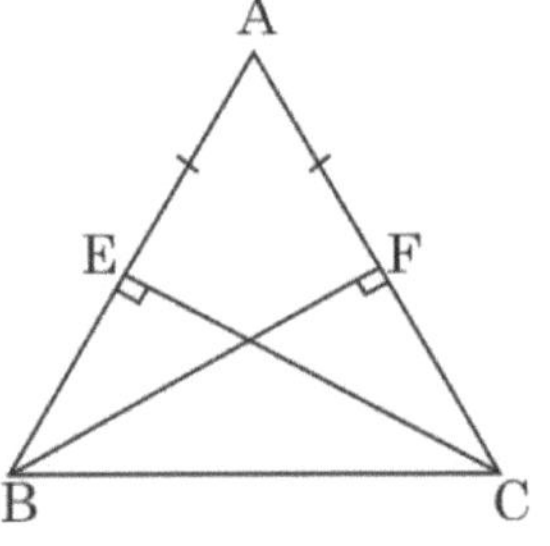

Let ΔABC be an equilateral triangle, so that AB = AC = BC.

Now, AB = AC

or, $\angle B = \angle C$ ... (i)

(∵ Angles opposite to equal sides are equal)

CB = CA or, $\angle A = \angle B$ ...(ii)

(∵ Angles opposite to equal sides are equal)

from equations (i) and (ii), we get

$\angle A = \angle B = \angle C$

Also, $\angle A + \angle B + \angle C = 180°$, (Angle sum property)

∴ $\angle A + \angle A + \angle A = 180°$

$\Rightarrow 3\angle A = 180°$ ∴ $\angle A = 60°$

∴ $\angle A = \angle B = \angle C = 60°$.

Hence, each angle of an equilateral triangle is 60°.

5. E and F are mid-points of equal sides AB and AC of ΔABC respectively. Show that BF = CE.

[BOARD TERM I, 2012, SET-46]

OR

In the given figure, ABC is an isosceles triangle in which altitudes BF and CE are drawn to equal sides AC and AB respectively. Show that these altitudes are equal.

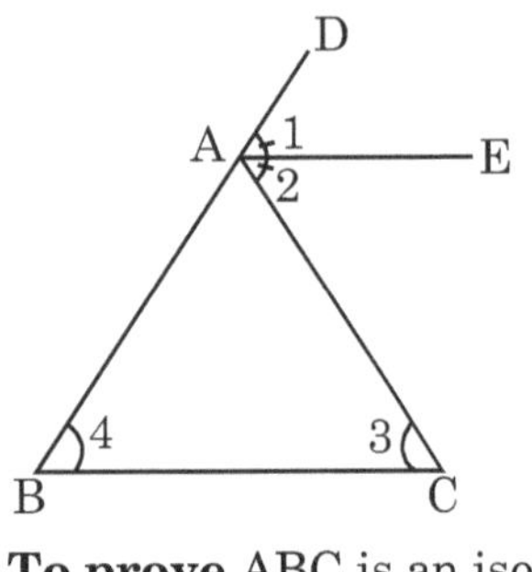

[NCERT]

Sol. According to the question,

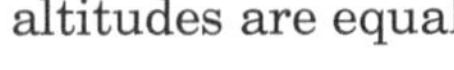

AB = AC

$$\frac{AB}{2} = \frac{AC}{2}$$

$\Rightarrow$ AE = AF,   ... (i)

$\because$ E and F are the mid-points of AB and AC.

Now, In $\triangle$ABF and $\triangle$ACE,

AB = AC (Given)

$\angle$A = $\angle$A   (Common)

and AF = AE [From equation (i)]

By SAS congruence rule,

$\therefore$ $\triangle$ABF $\cong$ $\triangle$ACE

Hence, BF = CE.   (By c.p.c.t)

6. Triangle ABC is an isosceles triangle such that AB = AC. Side BA is produced to D, such that AD = AB. Show that $\angle$BCD is a right angle.

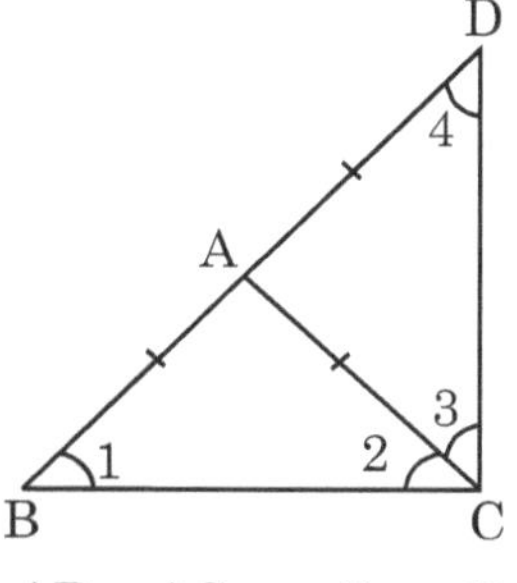

[NCERT BOARD TERM I, 2014; 2012, SET-42]

Sol. Given, AB = AC and AD = AB

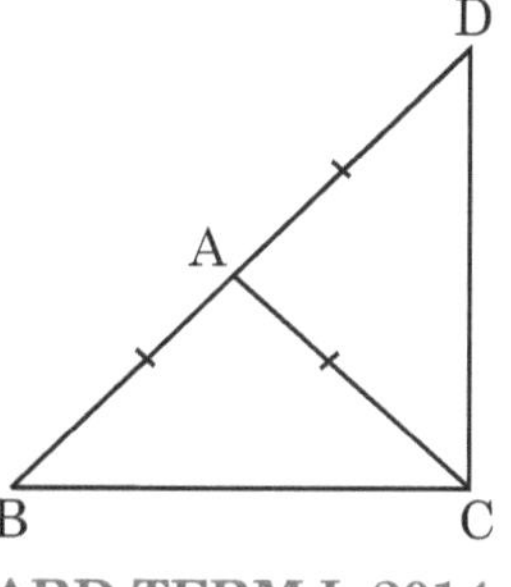

In $\triangle$ABC,   AB = AC $\Rightarrow$ $\angle 1 = \angle 2$ ... (1)

[Angles opposite to equal sides are equal]

In $\triangle$ADC, AB = AD

$\therefore$ AC = AD

$\angle 3 = \angle 4$ ...(2)

[Angles opposite to equal sides are equal]

Now, in $\triangle$BCD,

$\angle 1 + (\angle 2 + \angle 3) + \angle 4 = 180°$

                [By angle sum property]

$\Rightarrow \angle 2 + \angle 2 + \angle 3 + \angle 3 = 180°$

$\Rightarrow 2(\angle 2 + \angle 3) = 180°$

$\Rightarrow \angle 2 + \angle 3 = 90°$

$\therefore \angle$BDC = 90°

Hence, $\angle$BCD is a right angle.

7. In the given figure, AB = AC, D is the point in the interior of $\triangle$ABC such that $\angle$DBC = $\angle$DCB. Prove that AD bisects $\angle$BAC of $\triangle$ABC.

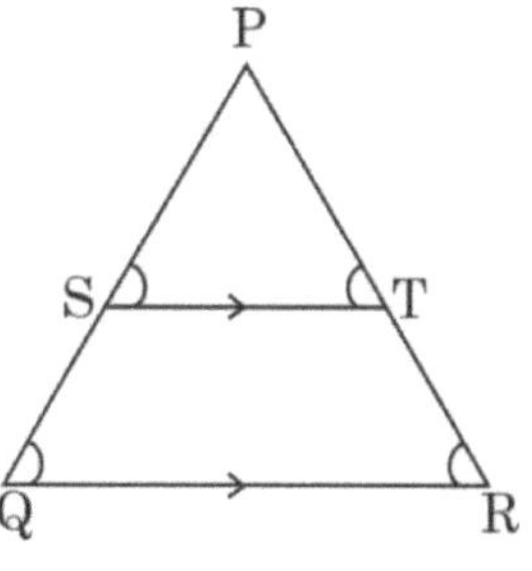

[BOARD TERM I, 2011 SET 11; 2010, SET-B1]

Sol. Given, $\angle$DBC = $\angle$DCB

$\therefore$ DC = DB ... (i)

[Sides opposite to equal angles are equal]

Now, in $\triangle$ABD and $\triangle$ACD,

AB = AC (Given)

BD = CD   [from (i)]

and AD = AD (Common).

By SSS congruence rule,

$\triangle$ABD $\cong$ $\triangle$ACD

$\therefore$ $\angle$BAD = $\angle$CAD   [By c.p.c.t.)

Hence, AD is the bisector of $\angle$BAC.

8. PQR is a triangle in which PQ = PR. S is any point on the side PQ. Through S, a line is drawn parallel to QR intersecting PR at T. Prove that PS = PT.

[BOARD TERM I, 2012, SET-55]

Sol. Given, PQ = PR

and QR || ST

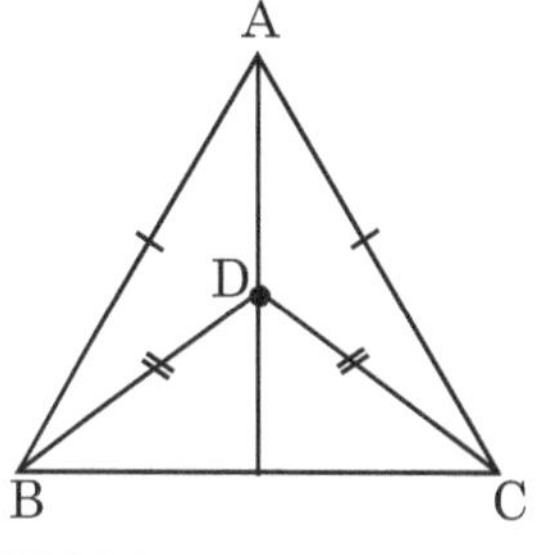

$\angle$PQR = $\angle$PRQ

[Angles opposite to equal sides are equal]

and $\angle$PST = $\angle$PQR

[Corresponding angles]

$\angle$PTS = $\angle$PRQ

(Corresponding angles]

$\therefore$ $\angle$PST = $\angle$PTS   [$\because$ $\angle$PQR = $\angle$PRQ]

Hence, PS = PT.

[Sides opposite to equal angles are equal]

9. In a triangle ABC, X and Y are the points on AB and BC respectively. If BX = $\frac{1}{2}$ AB and BY = $\frac{1}{2}$ BC and AB = BC. Show that BX = BY.

[BOARD TERM I, 2015, SET-20 UI6YH]

Sol. Given, BX = $\frac{1}{2}$ AB,

BY = $\frac{1}{2}$ BC and AB = BC

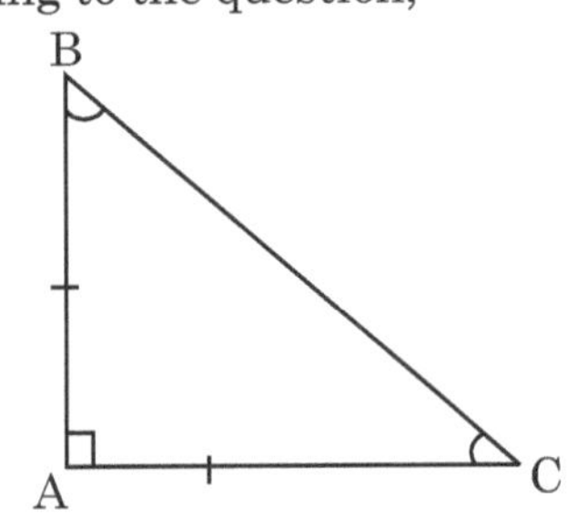

$\Rightarrow$ $\frac{1}{2}$ AB = $\frac{1}{2}$ BC

[$\because$ $\frac{1}{2}$ AB = BX]

$\Rightarrow$ $\frac{1}{2}$ BC = BX   ...(i)

$\because$ $\frac{1}{2}$ BC = BY   .... (ii) [Given]

From equations (i) and (ii), we get

BX = BY

Hence proved.

10. In the given figure, AB = AC and BE and CF are bisectors of $\angle$B and $\angle$C respectively. Prove that $\triangle$EBC $\cong$ $\triangle$FCB

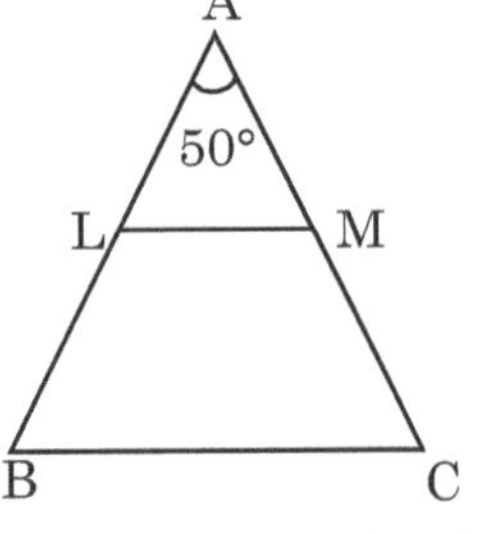

[BOARD TERM I, 2016, SET-JQ22L5C]

Sol. Given, AB = AC

$\therefore$ $\angle$ABC = $\angle$ACB   ...(i)

[Angles opposite to equal sides are equal]

$\because$ BE and CF are the bisector of $\angle$B and $\angle$C

$\therefore$ $\angle$EBC = $\frac{1}{2}$

$\angle$ABC = $\frac{1}{2}$

$\angle$ACB = $\angle$FCB

$\Rightarrow$ $\angle$EBC = $\angle$FCB   ... (ii)

Now, In $\triangle$BEC and $\triangle$CEB

$\angle$ABC = $\angle$ACB   [from equation (i)]

$\angle$EBC = $\angle$FCB [from equation (ii)]

and BC = BC   [Common]

By ASA congruence rule,

Hence, $\triangle$EBC $\cong$ $\triangle$FCB

11. In the figure, ABC is an isosceles triangle in which AB = AC and LM is parallel to BC. If $\angle$A = 50°, find $\angle$LMC.

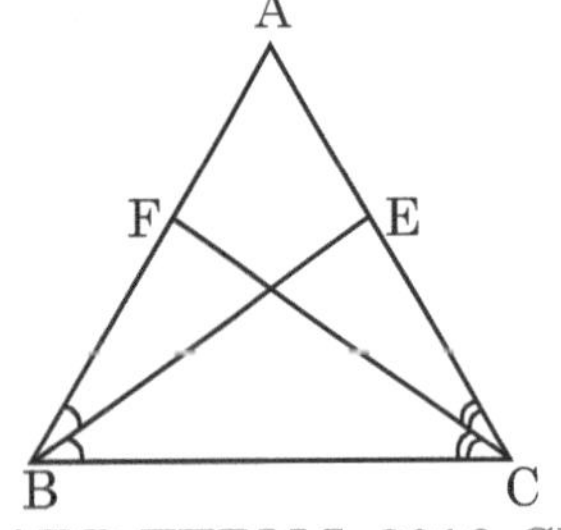

[BOARD TERM I, 2016, SET-7AEDLQR]

Sol. According to the question, $\triangle$ABC is an isosceles triangle.

In $\triangle$ABC

AB = AC

$\therefore$ $\angle$ABC = $\angle$ACB = θ (let)

or, $\angle$B = $\angle$C = θ

$\angle$A + $\angle$B + $\angle$C = 180°

[Angle sum property]

$\Rightarrow$ 50° + θ + θ = 180°

$\Rightarrow$ 2θ = 180° − 50° = 130°

$\therefore$ θ = 65°

$\therefore$ $\angle$B = $\angle$C = 65°

$\because$ LM || BC

$\therefore$ $\angle$LMC + $\angle$BCM = 180°

[consecutive interior angles]

$\Rightarrow$ $\angle$LMC + 65° = 180°

$\therefore$ $\angle$LMC = 180° − 65° = 115°

12. ABC is a right angled triangle in which $\angle$A = 90° and AB = AC. Find $\angle$B and $\angle$C.

Sol. According to the question,

We have, $\angle A = 90°$ and AB = AC

$\angle B = \angle C$

($\because$ Angles opposite to equal sides of a triangle are equal)

Also, in $\triangle ABC$, $\angle A + \angle B + \angle C = 180°$

[Angle sum property]

$\Rightarrow 90° + 2\angle B = 180°$

$\Rightarrow 2\angle B = 180° -90° = 90°$ $\qquad$ ($\because \angle C = \angle B$)

$\therefore \quad \angle B = \dfrac{90°}{2} = 45°$

$\therefore \quad \angle C = \angle B = 45°$

Long Answer Type Questions

(4 Marks Each)

1. ABC and DBC are two isosceles triangle on the same base BC and vertices A and D on the same side of BC. AD is extended to intersect BC at P, show that:

   (i) $\triangle ABD \cong \triangle ACD$

   (ii) AP is perpendicular bisector of BC.

   [BOARD TERM I, 2015, SET- II, NCERT]

Sol.

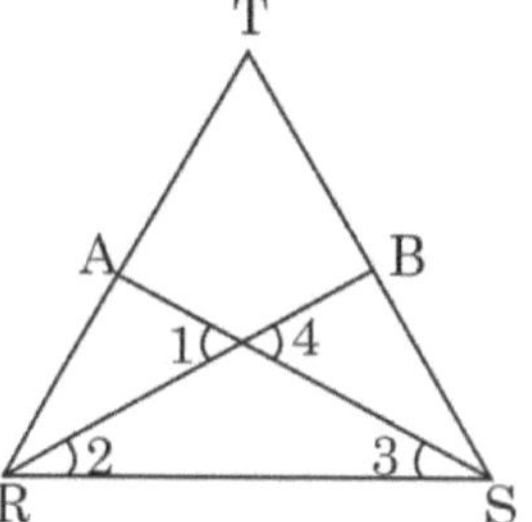

$\because$ AB = AC

$\therefore \quad \angle ABC = \angle ACB$ $\qquad$ ...(i)

[Angles opposite to equal sides are equal]

and $\because$ BD = CD

$\therefore \quad \angle DBC = \angle DCB$ $\qquad$ ...(ii)

[Angles opposite to equal sides are equal]

From equation (i) – (ii), we get

$\angle ABC - \angle DBC = \angle ACB - \angle DCB$

$\Rightarrow \angle ABD = \angle ACD$

By SAS congruence rule,

$\therefore \quad \triangle ABD \cong \triangle ACD$

or $\angle BAP = \angle CAP$

By SAS congruence rule,

$\quad \triangle ABP \cong \triangle ACP$

$\therefore \quad$ BP = PC, $\angle APB = \angle APC$

$\therefore \quad \angle APB = \angle APC = 90°$

Hence, AP is perpendicular bisector of BC

2. In figure, it is given that RT = TS, $\angle 1 = 2\angle 2$ and $\angle 4 = 2\angle 3$. Prove that:

   (i) $\triangle RBT \cong \triangle SAT$

   (ii) RB = AS

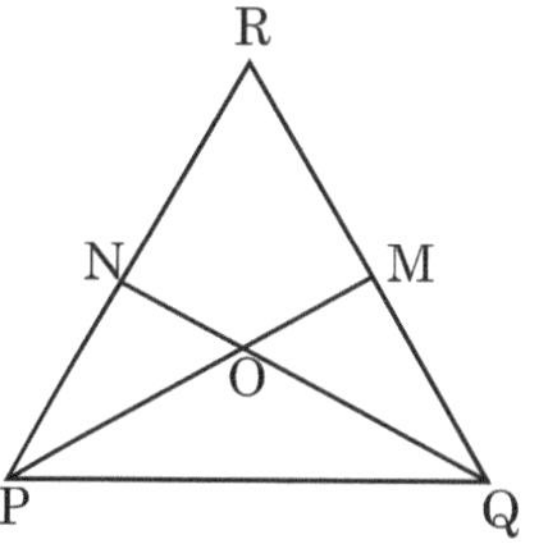

[BOARD TERM I, 2012, SET-44]

Sol. In $\triangle RTS$,

RT = ST

$\angle TSR = \angle TRS$ $\qquad$ ... (i)

(Angles opposite to equal sides are equal)

$\angle 1 = \angle 4$ [Vertically opposite angles]

$\Rightarrow 2\angle 2 = 2\angle 3$

$\Rightarrow \angle 2 = \angle 3$ $\qquad$ ... (ii)

On subtracting equation (ii) from equation (i), we get

$\angle TRS - \angle 2 = \angle TSR - \angle 3$

$\Rightarrow \angle TRB = \angle TSA$ $\qquad$ ...(iii)

In $\triangle RBT$ and $\triangle SAT$,

$\angle RTB = \angle STA$ (Common angles)

RT = ST (Given)

and $\angle TRB = \angle TSA$ [From equation (iii)]

By ASA congruence rule,

$\therefore \quad \triangle RBT \cong \triangle AST$

Hence, RB = AS (By c.p.c.t.)

3. In the given figure, RP = RQ and M and N are respectively points on sides QR and PR of $\triangle PQR$, such that QM = PN. Prove that OP = OQ. where O is the point of intersection of PM and QN.

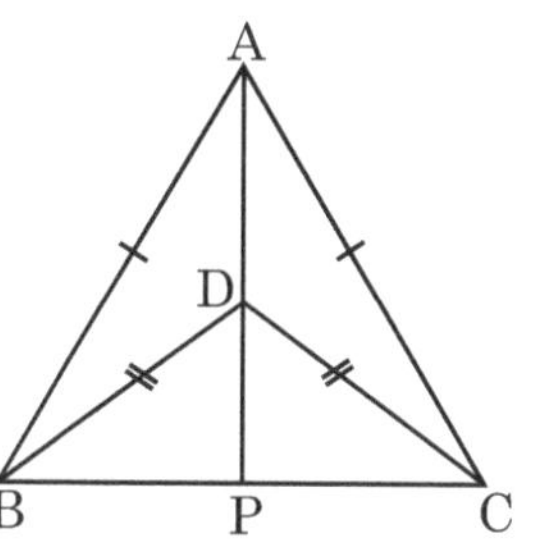

[BOARD TERM I, 2012, SET-35]

Sol. Given, RP = RQ

$\therefore$ $\angle$RQP = $\angle$RPQ

[Angles opposite to equal sides are equal]

$\Rightarrow$ $\angle$NPQ = $\angle$MQP

Now, in ΔPQN and ΔQPM

$\angle$NPQ = $\angle$MQP

PN = QM (Given)

and PQ = PQ (Common)

By SAS congruence rule,

ΔPQN $\cong$ ΔQPM

$\Rightarrow$ $\angle$PQN = $\angle$QPM (By c.p.c.t.)

$\Rightarrow$ $\angle$PQO = $\angle$QPO

Hence, OP = OQ.

($\because$ Sides opposite to equal angles are equal)

4. In figure, ABCD is a square and EF is parallel to diagonal BD and EM = FM. Prove that :

(i) DF = BE

(ii) AM bisects $\angle$BAD.

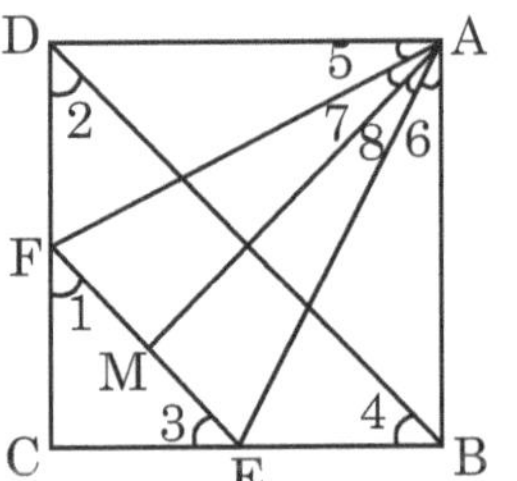

[BOARD TERM I, 2012, SET-53]

Sol.

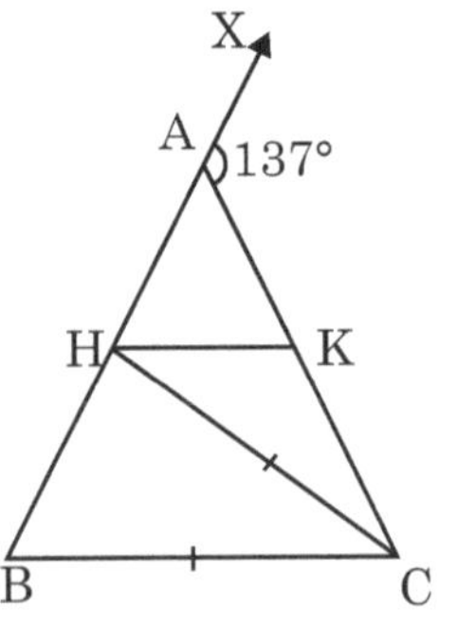

(i) EF || BD or, $\angle$1 = $\angle$2 and $\angle$3 = $\angle$4

(Corresponding angles)

But, $\angle$2 = $\angle$4

$\therefore$ $\angle$3 = $\angle$1

or, FC = FC

(Sides opposite to equal angle)

CD – FC = CB – CE

or DF = BE   Proved.

In ΔABE   AD = AB,

and ΔADF $\angle$D = $\angle$B = 90°

$\therefore$ ΔADF $\cong$ ΔABE (SAS)

or, AF = AE, $\angle$5 = $\angle$6 (By c.p.c.t)

(ii) In ΔAMF and ΔAME,

AF = AE,

AM = AM (Common)

FM = EM (Given)

ΔAMF $\cong$ ΔAME (SSS)

$\therefore$ $\angle$7 = $\angle$8 (By c.p.c.t.)

$\angle$7 + $\angle$5 = $\angle$8 + $\angle$6

or, $\angle$MAD = $\angle$MAB

or, AM bisects $\angle$BAD. Proved.

5. In figure, AB = AC, CH = CB and HK||BC. If $\angle$CAX = 137°, then find $\angle$CHK.

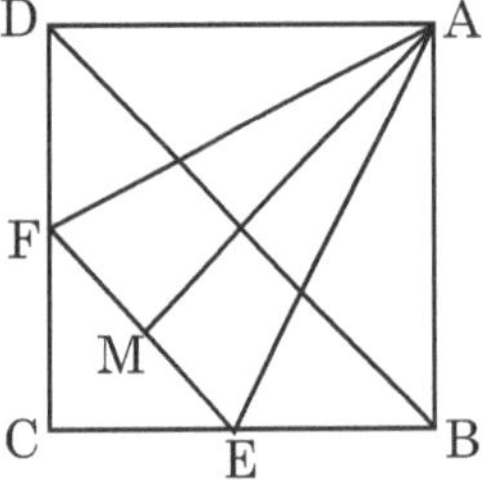

[BOARD TERM I, 2013; 2012, SET-18]

Sol. $\angle$XAK + $\angle$KAH = 180° (Linear pair)

$\angle$KAH = 180° – 137° = 43°

($\because$ $\angle$CAX = $\angle$XAK = 137°, Given)

AB = AC (Given)

$\therefore$ $\angle$ABC = $\angle$ACB

(Angles opposite to equal sides are equal)

$\angle$ABC + $\angle$ACB = 137°, (ext. angle)

$\therefore$ $\angle$ABC = $\angle$ACB = $\dfrac{137°}{2}$ = 68.5°

CH = CB (Given)

or, $\angle$CBA = $\angle$CHB

= 68.5°

$\therefore$ $\angle$HCB = 180° – 137°

= 43°

$\angle$CHK = $\angle$HCB = 43°

(Alternate angles)

6. In figure, OA = OD and $\angle 1 = \angle 2$. Prove that $\triangle OCB$ is an isosceles triangle.

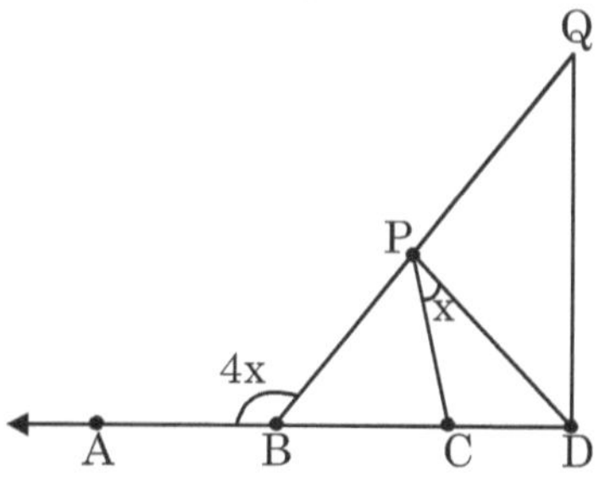

[BOARD TERM I, 2012, SET-18]

[BOARD TERM I, 2016, SET-BQS6IZK]

Sol.

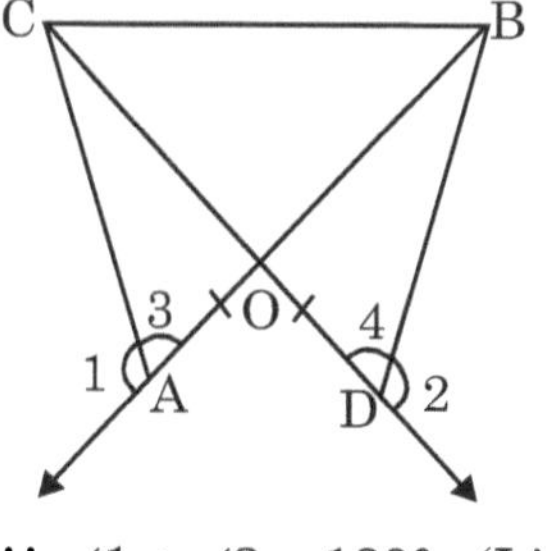

$\because \angle 1 + \angle 3 = 180°$ (Linear pair)

$\because \angle 2 + \angle 4 = 180°$ (Linear pair)

$\therefore \angle 1 + \angle 3 = \angle 2 + \angle 4$

But, $\angle 1 = \angle 2$ (Given)

or, $\angle 3 = \angle 4$

In $\triangle OAC$ and $\triangle ODB$,

$\angle 3 = \angle 4$ (Proved above)

$\angle AOC = \angle DOB$ (Vertically opposite angle)

OA = OD (Given)

$\therefore \triangle OAC \cong \triangle ODB$ (ASA)

or, OC = OB (c.p.c.t.)

or $\triangle OCB$ is an isosceles triangle

7. In the given figure, ABCD and BPQ are straight lines. If BP = BC and DQ is parallel to CP prove that:

(i) CP = CD

(ii) DP bisects $\angle CDQ$

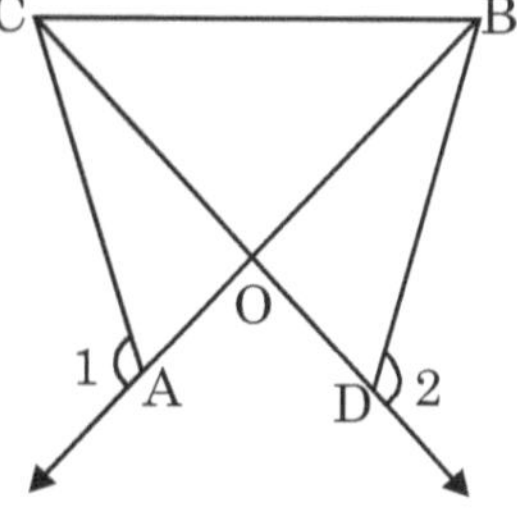

[BOARD TERM I, 2016, SET-JQ22L5C]

Sol. Given, BP = BC

$\therefore \quad \angle BCP = \angle BPC$

[Angles opposite to equal sides are equal]

$= y°$

In $\triangle PCB$,

$\angle ABP = \angle BPC + \angle BCP$

[Exterior angle is the sum of two opposite interior angle]

$4x° = 2y°$

$\because$ DQ $||$ PC, $\therefore \angle 2 = x°$ [Alternate angle]

Again, $y° = x° + \angle 3$

$\therefore x° = \angle 3$ [$\because y° = 2x°$]

CP = CD

Also, we have $\angle 2 = x°$ and $x° = \angle 3$

Hence, DP bisects $\angle CDQ$

8. ABCD is a square and ABE is an equilateral triangle outside the square prove that $\angle ACE = \dfrac{1}{2} \angle ABE$.

[BOARD TERM I, 2016, SET-BQS6IZK]

Sol. $\because \triangle ABE$ is an equilateral triangle

$\therefore \angle ABE = \angle BEA = \angle EAB = 60°$

[Each angle of an equilateral triangle is 60°]

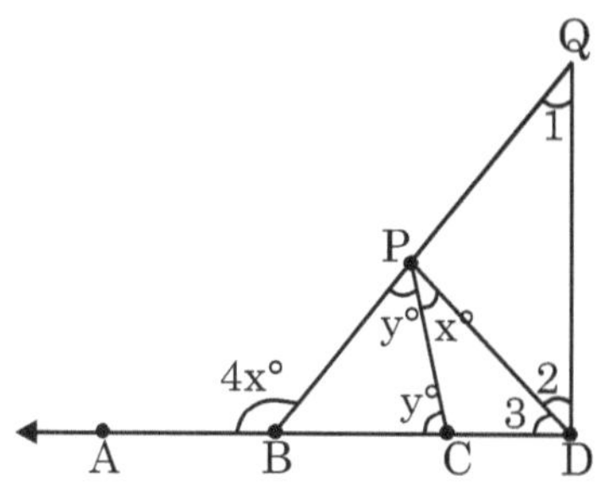

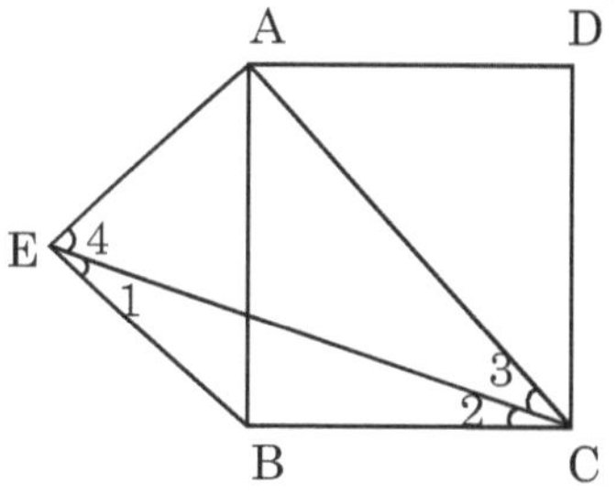

Also $\angle BAC = 45°$

$\because$ BE = BC

$\therefore \angle 1 = \angle 2$

[Angles opposite to equal sides are equal]

In $\triangle BEC$, $\angle 1 + \angle 2 = 180° - (60° + 90°)$

[Angle sum property]

$= 180° - 150° = 30°$

$\Rightarrow 2\angle 1 = 30°$

$\therefore \ \angle 1 = 15°$

and $\angle 3 = 45° - 15°$

$= 30°$

$\therefore \ \angle ACE = 30°,$

$\angle ABE = 60°$

Hence, $\angle ACE = \dfrac{1}{2} \angle ABE$

9. Two sides AB and BC and median AM of one triangle ΔABC are respectively equal to sides PQ and QR and median PN of ΔPQR. Show that

(i) ΔABM ≅ ΔP QN

(ii) ΔABC ≅ ΔPQR

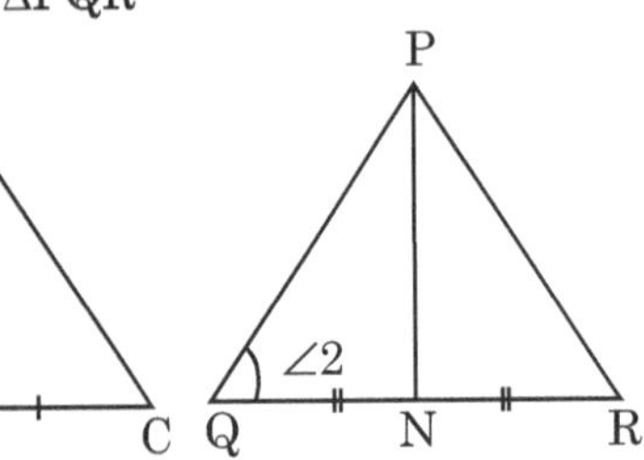

Sol. Given, AB = PQ,

BC = QR

and AM = PN

To prove : (i) ΔABM ≅ ΔPQN

Prove : ∵ BC = QR

$\Rightarrow \ \dfrac{1}{2} BC = \dfrac{1}{2} QR$

$\therefore \ BM = AN$ ...(i)

(∵ M and N are the mid-points of sides BC & QR, respectively)

Now, In ΔABM and ΔPQN,

AB = PQ

and AM = PN

BM = QN [from equation (i)]

By SSS congruence rule,

∴ ΔABM ≅ ΔPQN

∴ ∠1 = ∠2 ... (ii) (By c.p.c.t.)

(ii) Now, In ΔABC & ΔPQR

AB = PQ [Given]

∠1 = ∠2 [From equation (ii)]

and BC = QR (Given)

By SAS congruence rule,

∴ ΔABC ≅ ΔPQR

10. In the given figure, AB = BC, AD = CD. Prove that ∠ADE is a right angle and AE and EC are equal.

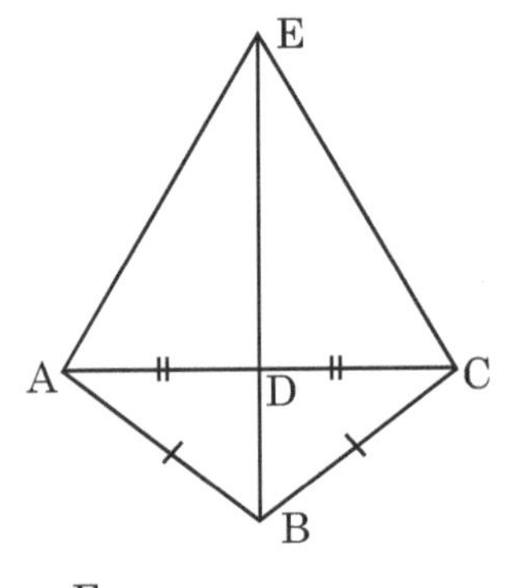

Sol.

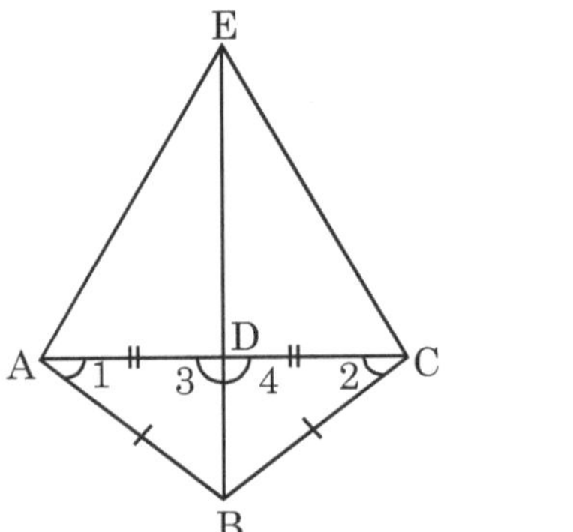

In ΔABC, AB = BC [Given]

∴ ∠1 = ∠2

[Angles opposite to the equal sides are equal]

Again, In ΔABD and ΔCBD,

AB = BC

∠1 = ∠2

and AD = CD

By SAS congruence rule,

∴ ΔABD ≅ ΔCBD

and ∠3 = ∠4 (By. c.p.c.t)

∠3 + ∠4 = 180° [Linear pair]

∴ ∠4 = 90°

∴ ∠ADE = ∠4

[Vertically opposite angle]

∴ ∠ADE = 90°

In ΔEAD and ΔECD,

AD = CD (Given)

∠ADE = ∠CDE = 90°

and DE = DE (Common)

By SAS congruence rule,

So, ΔEAD ≅ ΔECD

Hence, AE = EC. (By c.p.c.t)

[Topic 3] Inequalities of a Triangle

Points to be Remembered

- In any triangle, the angle opposite to the longer side is larger.

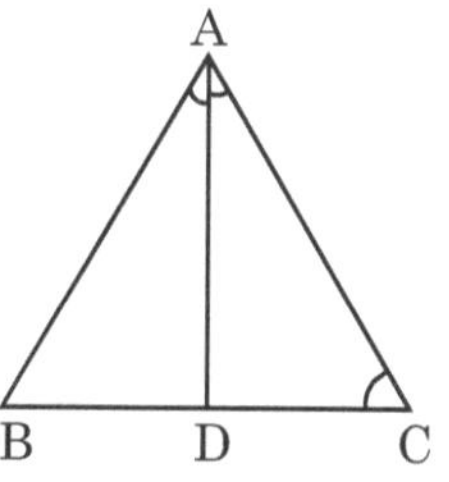

  $\because$ AC is the longest side.

  $\therefore$ $\angle$B is largest.

- In any triangle, the side opposite to the larger (greater) angle is longer.

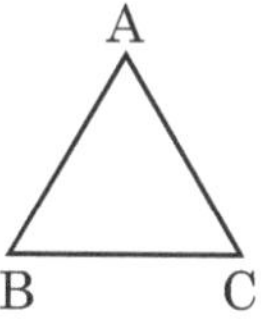

  If $\angle$B is the largest

  $\therefore$ AC is longest

PREVIOUS YEARS'
EXAMINATION QUESTIONS
TOPIC 3

Multiple Choice Questions

(1 Mark Each)

1. Two sides of a triangle are of lengths 5 cm and 1.5 cm. The length of the third side of the triangle cannot be   [NCERT Exemp.]
   (a) 3.6 cm   (b) 4.1 cm
   (c) 3.8 cm   (d) 3.4 cm

Sol. (d) The length of two sides of a triangle are 5 cm and 1.5 cm, respectively.

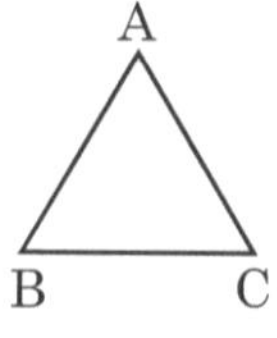

Let sides AB = 5 cm and CA = 1.5 cm, then

- The sum of any two sides of a triangle is greater than the third side.

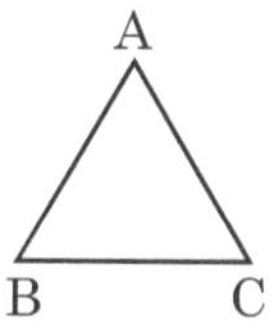

  In $\triangle$ABC

  AB + AC > BC

  AB + BC > AC

  AC + BC > AB

- Difference of any two sides of a triangle is less than the third side.

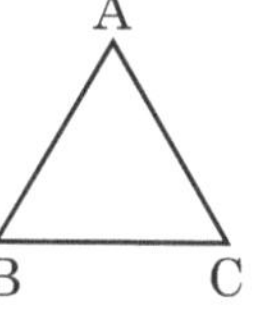

  In $\triangle$ABC

  AB − BC < CA

  AB − AC < BC

  AC − BC < AB

We know that, a closed figure formed by three intersecting lines (or sides) is called a triangle, if difference of two sides < third side and sum of two sides > third side.

$\therefore$ AB − CA = 5 − 1.5 = 3.5 cm

and AB + CA = 5 + 1.5 = 6.5 cm

Therefore, 6.5 > third side > 3.5

2. D is a point on the side BC of a $\triangle$ABC such that AD bisects $\angle$BAC. Then   [NCERT Exemp.]
   (a) BD = CD   (b) BA > BD
   (c) BD > BA   (d) CD > CA

Sol. (b) According to the question,

In $\triangle$ABC, AD bisects $\angle$BAC

$\therefore$ $\angle$BAD = $\angle$CAD

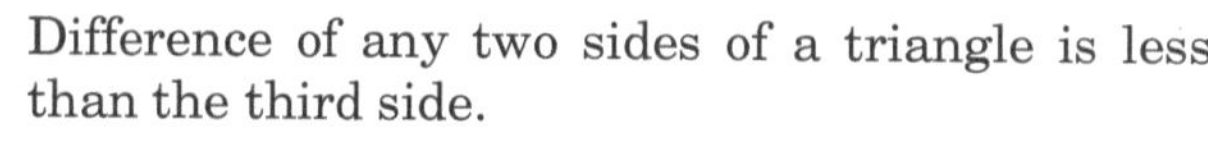

In $\triangle$ACD, $\angle$BDA is an exterior angle.

$\angle$BDA > $\angle$CAD [exterior angle > interior angle]

$\Rightarrow$ $\angle$BDA > $\angle$BAD [$\because$ $\angle$BAD = $\angle$CAD]

$\therefore$ BA > BD [side opposite to greater angle is greater]

3. In ΔPQR, if $\angle R > \angle Q$, then

[NCERT Exemp.]

(a) QR > PR   (b) PQ > PR
(c) PQ < PR   (d) QR < PR

Sol. (b) Given,

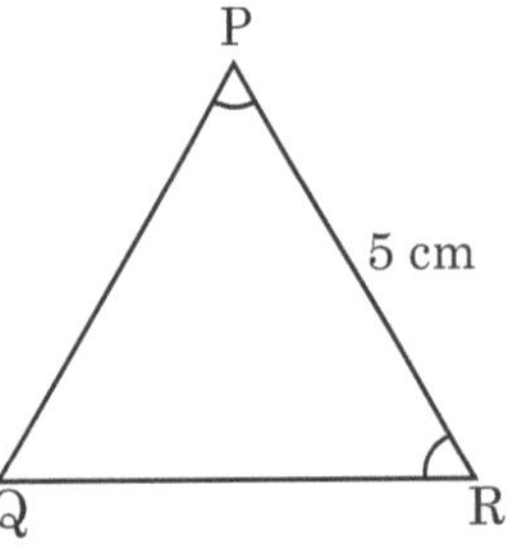

∵ Side opposite to the greatest angle is the largest.

∴ PQ > PR

4. In ΔPQR, $\angle R = \angle P$ and QR = 4 cm and PR = 5 cm. Then the length of PQ is   [NCERT Exemp.]

(a) 4 cm   (b) 5 cm
(c) 2 cm   (d) 2.5 cm

Sol (a) According to the question,

In ΔPQR

$\angle R = \angle P$, QR = 4 cm and PR = 5 cm

∴ PQ = QR [sides opposite to equal angles are equal]

and PQ = 4 cm   [∵ QR = 4 cm]

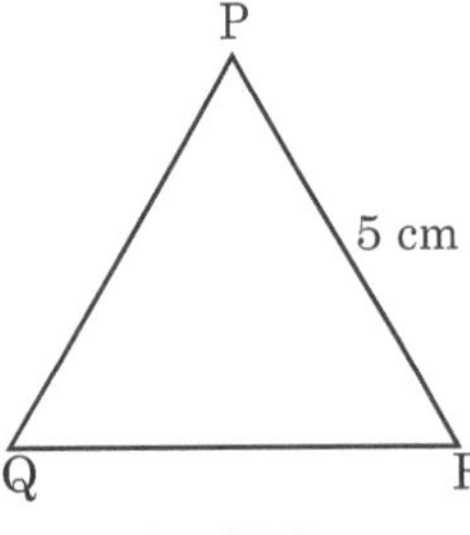

Hence, the length of PQ = 4 cm

5. In the given figure, mark the relation between AB and AD :

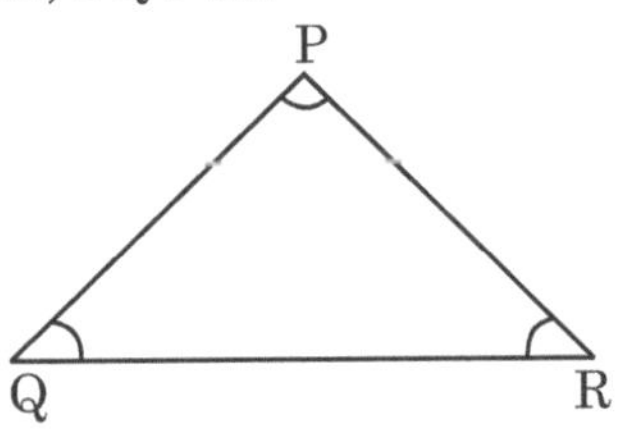

(a) AB = AD   (b) AB < AD
(c) AB > AD   (d) None of these

Sol. (c) According to the given figure,

AC = AD = CD

$\angle CAD = \angle ACD = \angle CDA = 60°$

Now, $\angle ACD > \angle ABC$

[∵ Exterior angle > interior angle]

∴ AB > AD

Very Short Answer Type Questions
(1 Mark Each)

1. Is it possible to draw a triangle with sides of length 2 cm, 3 cm and 7 cm?

Sol. According to the question,

$2 + 3 = 5 \not> 7$

Sum of two sides $\not>$ third side.

We know that triangle can be drawn only when the sum of any two sides is greater than the third sides.

Hence, the triangle cannot be formed.

2. In ΔABC, $\angle B = 30°$, $\angle C = 80°$ and $\angle A = 70°$, then prove that AB > BC > AC.

Sol. According to the question,

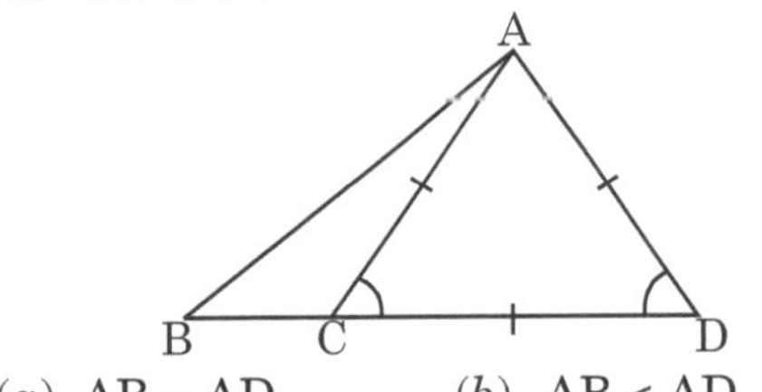

$\angle A = 70°$, $\angle B = 30°$ and $\angle C = 80°$

∴ $\angle C > \angle A > \angle B$

∵ Side opposite to the larger angle is greater.

Hence, AB > BC > AC

3. Is it possible to construct a triangle, when its sides are 5.4 cm, 2.3 cm, 3.1 cm?

Sol. Here, 2.3 + 3.1 = 5.4 cm (third side)

∵ Sum of two sides $\not>$ third side

Hence, the triangle cannot be formed.

4. In ΔPQR, if $\angle R > \angle Q$, then what will be the result?

Sol. Given, $\angle R > \angle Q$

∵ The side opposite to the greatest angle is largest.

Therefore, PQ > RP

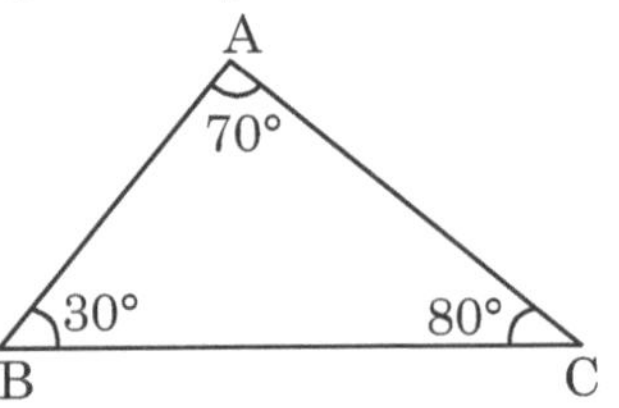

5. In ΔABC, AB = 5 cm, AC = 7 cm and BC = 6 cm. Write the relation among their angles.

Sol. We know that angle opposite to larger side is larger and angle opposite to smaller side is smaller.

∴ AC > BC $\Rightarrow$ $\angle B > \angle A$ ...(i)

Also, BC > AB $\Rightarrow$ $\angle A > \angle C$ ...(ii)

From eq. (i) and (ii), we get $\angle B > \angle A > \angle C$.

Hence the required relation = $\angle B > \angle A > \angle C$.

Short Answer Type Questions I
(2 Marks Each)

1. Show that if two sides of a triangle are of lengths 5 cm and 1.5 cm, then the length of third side of the triangle cannot be 3.4 cm.

   [NCERT EXEMPLAR]

Sol. Given, the length of two sides of a triangle are 5 cm and 1.5 cm, respectively.

Let sides of a $\triangle ABC$ be $AB = 5$ cm and $CA = 1.5$ cm

We know that, difference of two sides < third side and sum of two sides > third side.

$\therefore$ $5 - 1.5 < BC$ and $5 + 1.5 > BC$

$\Rightarrow$ $3.5 < BC$ and $6.5 > BC$

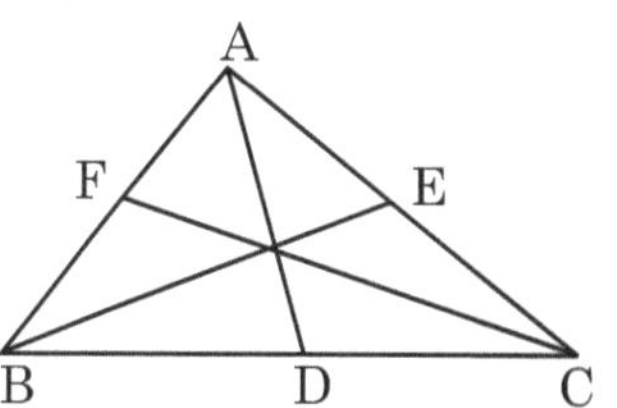

Hence, the length of the third side BC cannot be 3.4 cm.

2. If D is a point on the side BC of a $\triangle ABC$ such that AD bisects $\angle BAC$. Then, show that BA > BD.

   [NCERT EXEMPLAR]

Sol. Given, $\triangle ABC$ such that AD bisects $\angle BAC$.

$\therefore$ $\angle BAD = \angle CAD$ ...(i)

In $\triangle ACD$, $\angle BDA$ is an exterior angle.

$\therefore$ $\angle BDA > \angle CAD$

[Since, exterior angle is greater than each interior angle]

$\Rightarrow$ $\angle BDA > \angle BAD$ [from eq. (i)]

$\because$ Side opposite to the greatest angle is the largest.

$\therefore$ BA > BD

Hence, proved.

3. In the figure, given AC > AB and AD is the bisector of $\angle A$. Show that $\angle ADC > \angle ADB$.

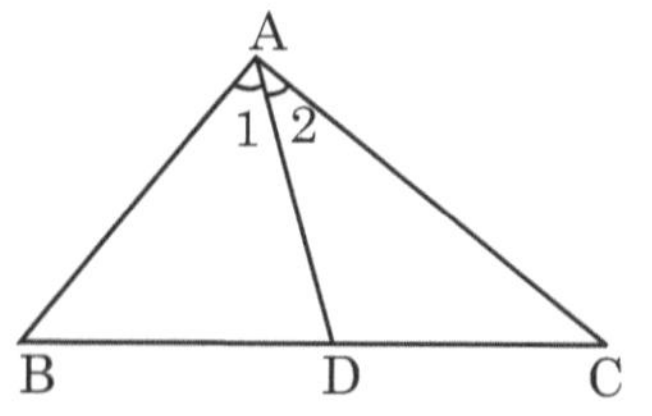

[BOARD TERM I, 2011, SET 12]

Sol. According to the question,

In $\triangle ABC$,

AC > AB

and AD is the bisector of $\angle A$.

$\therefore$ $\angle ABC > \angle ACB$

(Angles opposite to larger side is greater)

On adding $\angle 1$ both the sides, we get

$\Rightarrow$ $\angle ABC + \angle 1 > \angle ACB + \angle 1$

$\Rightarrow$ $\angle ABC + \angle 1 > \angle ACB + \angle 2$

(AD bisects $\angle A$, $\angle 1 = \angle 2$)

$\therefore$ $\angle ADC > \angle ADB$.

(Exterior angle property of triangle)

4. Prove that the perimeter of a triangle is greater than the sum of its three medians.

Sol. Let ABC is a triangle and AD, BE and CF are the medians of $\triangle ABC$.

We know that, the sum of any two sides of a triangle is greater than twice the median drawn to the third side.

$\therefore$ $AB + AC < 2AD$ ...(i)

$AB + BC > 2BE$ ...(ii)

and $BC + AC > 2CF$ ...(iii)

On adding equations (i), (ii) and (iii), we get

$2(AB + BC + AC) > 2(AD + BE + CF)$

$\therefore$ $AB + BC + AC > AD + BE + CF$

Hence, the perimeter of a triangle is greater than the sum of its three medians.

Short Answer Type Questions II
(3 Marks Each)

1. M is a point on side BC of a $\triangle ABC$ such that AM is the bisector of $\angle BAC$. It is true to say that perimeter of the triangle is greater than 2 AM? Give reason for your answer.

   [NCERT EXEMPLAR, BORD TERM I, 2012 SET-48, 49]

Sol. Clearly, in $\triangle ABC$, M is a point of side BC such that AM is the bisector of $\angle BAC$.

In $\triangle ABM$, $AB + BM > AM$ ...(i)

[$\because$ sum of two sides of a triangle is greater than the third side]

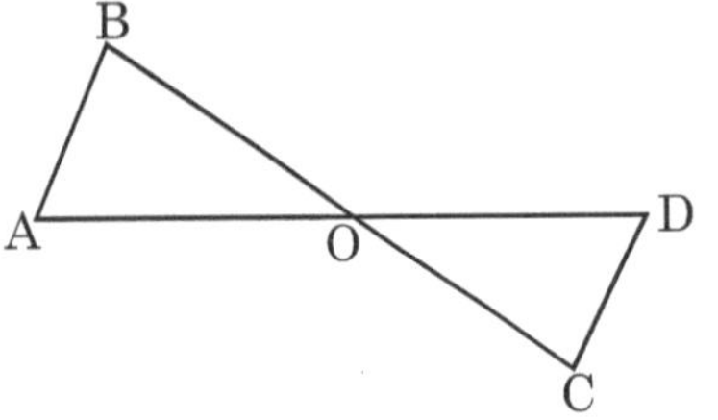

Again, In $\triangle ACM$,

AC + CM > AM ...(ii)

[∵ sum of two sides of a triangle is greater than the third side]

On adding equations (i) and (ii), we get

(AB + BM + AC + CM) > 2 AM

⇒ (AB + BM + MC + AC) > 2 AM

⇒ AB + BC + AC > 2 AM

[∵ BC = BM + MC]

[∵ Perimeter of $\triangle ABC$ = AB + BC + CA]

∴ Perimeter of $\triangle ABC$ > 2 AM

Hence proved.

2. In the given figure $\angle B > \angle A$ and $\angle C > \angle D$. Show that AD > BC.

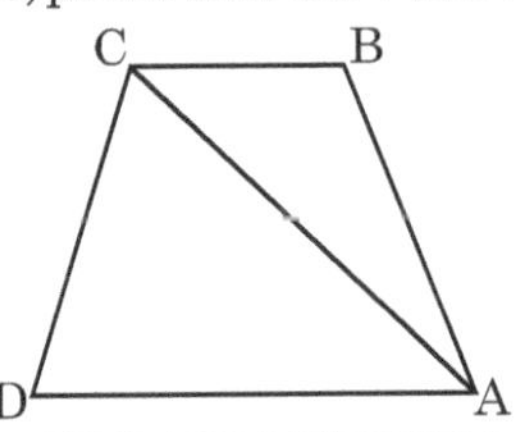

[NCERT, BOARD TERM I, 2012, SET-41, 45]

Sol. Given, $\angle B > \angle A$ and $\angle C > \angle D$

To prove : AD > BC

Proof : In $\triangle AOB$,

$\angle B > \angle A$

$\angle A < \angle B$

OB < OA ...(i)

In $\triangle COD$,

$\angle C > \angle D$

$\angle D < \angle C$

OC < OD ...(ii)

On adding equations (i) and (ii), we get

⇒ OB + OC < OA + OD

∴ BC < AD

or, AD > BC

Hence proved.

3. In the given figure, PR > PQ and PS bisect $\angle QRP$. Prove that $\angle PSR > \angle PSQ$.

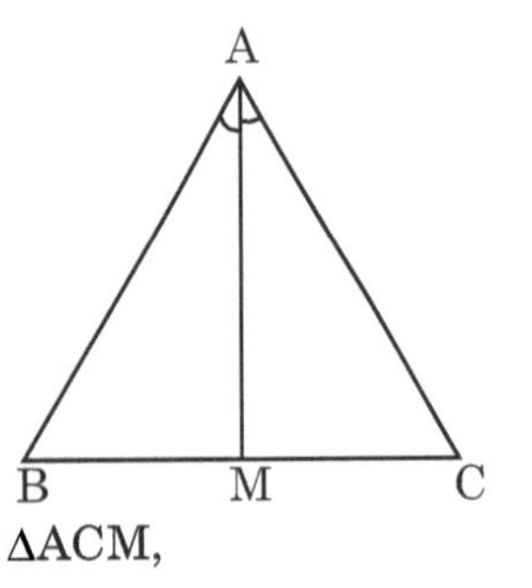

[NCERT]

Sol. Given, In $\triangle PQR$,

PR > PQ (Given)

∴ $\angle PQR > \angle PRQ$

[∵ Angle opposite to the largest side is greatest]

∴ $\angle PQR + \angle 1 > \angle PRQ + \angle 1$

(Adding $\angle 1$ on both sides)

$\angle PQR + \angle 1 > \angle PRQ + \angle 2$ ...(i)

(∵ PS is the bisector at $\angle P$)

∴ $\angle 1 = \angle 2$

Now, in $\triangle PQS$ and $\triangle PSR$, we have

$\angle PQR + \angle 1 + \angle PSQ = 180°$

⇒ $\angle PQR + \angle 1 = 180° - \angle PSQ$ ...(ii)

and $\angle PRQ + \angle 2 + \angle PSR = 180°$

[Angle sum property]

⇒ $\angle PRQ + \angle 2 = 180° - \angle PSR$ ...(iii)

On substitute equations (ii) & (iii) in equation (i), we get

∵ $180° - \angle PSQ > 180° - \angle PSR$

⇒ $-\angle PSQ > - \angle PSR$

⇒ $\angle PSQ < \angle PSR$

∴ $\angle PSR > \angle PSQ$

Hence proved.

4. In the figure, prove that CD + DA + AB + BC > 2AC.

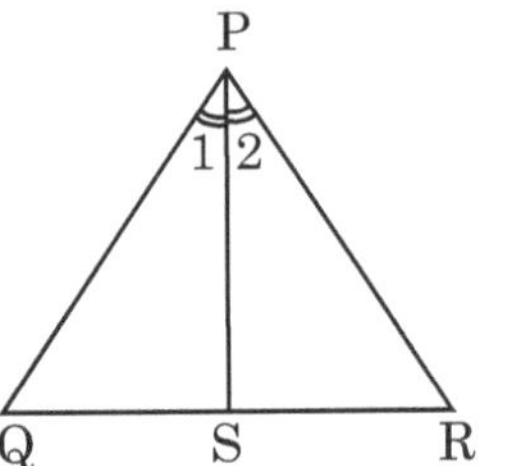

[BOARD TERM I, 2012, SET-62]

Sol. According to the figure,

In $\triangle ABC$, as sum of two sides is greater than the third side,

AB + BC > AC ...(i)

In $\triangle ACD$, as sum of two sides of a triangle is greater than the third side,

CD + DA > AC ... (ii)

On adding (i) and (ii), we get

$AB + BC + CD + DA > AC + AC$

$\therefore$ $CD + DA + AB + BC > 2AC.$

Hence proved.

5. In the given figure, PQR is a triangle and S is any point in its interior. Show that SQ + SR < PQ + PR.

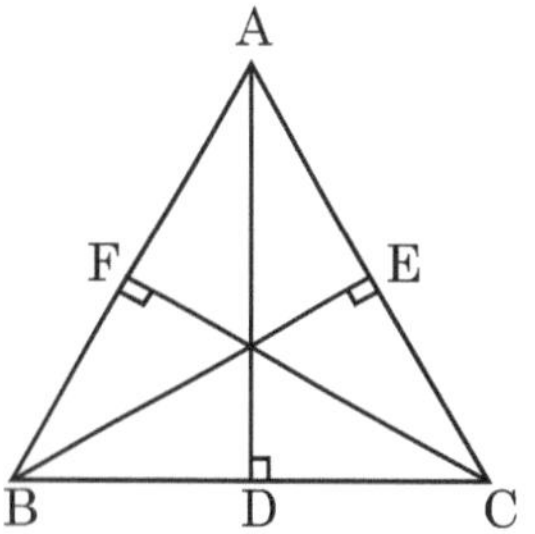

[BOARD TERM I, 2012, SET-51]

Sol. Given, PQR is a triangle and point S is in its interior.

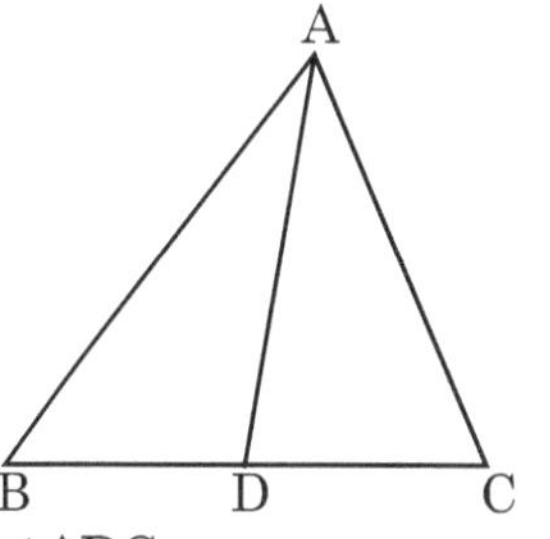

Construction : Produce QS to meet PR on T

In $\triangle$PQT, $PQ + PT > QT$ $\qquad$ [$\because$ $QT = QS + ST$]

$\Rightarrow PQ + PT > QS + ST$ $\qquad$ ...(i)

In $\triangle$SRT, $TR + ST > SR$ $\qquad$ ...(ii)

On adding equations (i) and (ii), we have

$PQ + PT + TR + ST > QS + ST + SR$

$\Rightarrow PQ + PR > QS + SR$

$\therefore$ $QS + SR < PQ + PR$

Hence, proved.

6. Prove that the perimeter of a triangle is greater than the sum of its three altitudes.

[BOARD TERM I, 2012, SET-43]

OR

In a $\triangle$ABC, $AD \perp BC$, $BE \perp AC$ and $CF \perp AB$. Prove that $AD + BE + CF < AB + BC + CA.$

[BOARD TERM I, 2012, SET-47, 14, 54]

OR

Show that sum of the three altitudes of a triangle is less than the sum of three sides of the triangle.

[BOARD TERM I, 2016, SET-QGL21F5]

Sol.

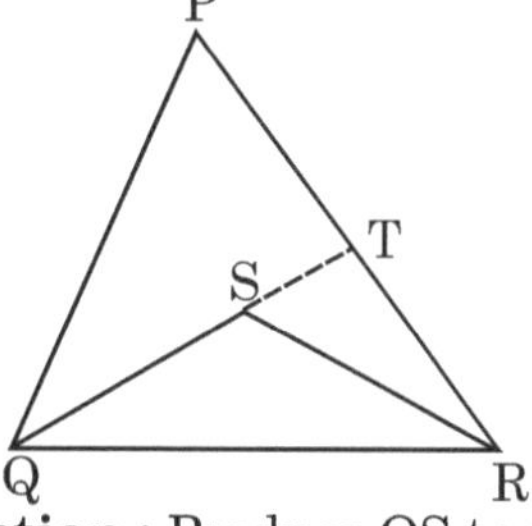

$\because$ The perpendicular line from any vertex is the shortest line.

$CF \perp AB$

$\therefore$ $CF < AC$ and $CF < BC$ $\qquad$ ...(i)

Similarly, BC is a line segment and A does not lie on it. $AD \perp BC$

$\therefore$ $AD < AB$ and $AD < AC$ $\qquad$ ...(ii)

and AC a line segment and B does not lie on it. $BE \perp AC$

$\therefore$ $BE < AB$ and $BE < BC$ $\qquad$ ...(iii)

Now, on adding equations (i), (ii) and (iii), we get

$CF + CF + AD + AD + BE + BE < AC + BC + AB$
$$+ AC + AB + BC$$

$2(AD + BE + CF) < 2 (AB + BC + CA)$

$\therefore$ $AB + BC + CA > AD + BE + CF$

Hence, the sum of the three altitudes of a triangle is less than the sum of three sides of the triangle.

7. D is a point on side BC of $\triangle$ABC (see figure), such that AD = AC. Show that AB > AD.

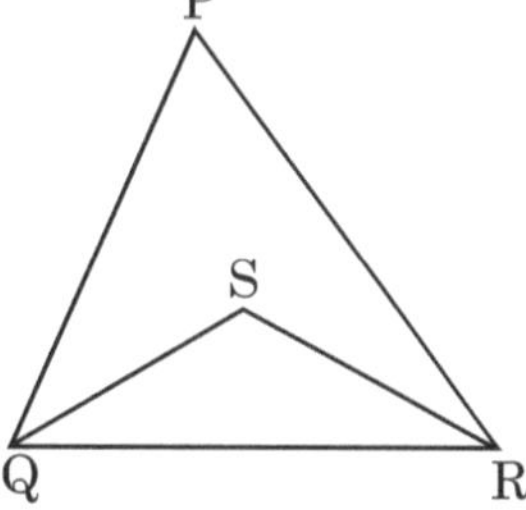

Sol. Given, In, $\triangle$ADC

$AD = AC$

$\angle ACD = \angle ADC$

[$\because$ angle opposite to equal sides are equal] ...(i)

In $\angle$ABD, we have, exterior $\angle ADC > \angle ABD$

[$\because$ exterior angle of a triangle is greater than each of the interior opposite angle]

$\Rightarrow \angle ADC > \angle ABD$ $\qquad$ ....(ii)

From equations (i) and (ii), we have

$\angle ACD > \angle ABC$ [$\because$ $\angle ABD = \angle ABC$]

$\Rightarrow \angle ACB > \angle ABC$ [$\because$ $\angle ACD = \angle ACB$]

$\Rightarrow AB > AC$

[$\because$ sides opposite to greater angle is larger]

$\Rightarrow AB > AD$ [$\because$ $AC > AD$]

Long Answer Type Questions

(4 Marks Each)

1. If AB and CD are the smallest and largest sides of a quadrilateral ABCD, out of $\angle B$ and $\angle D$ decide which is greater?   [NCERT EXEMPLAR]

Sol. Given, In quadrilateral ABCD, AB is the smallest side and CD is the largest side of quadrilateral ABCD.

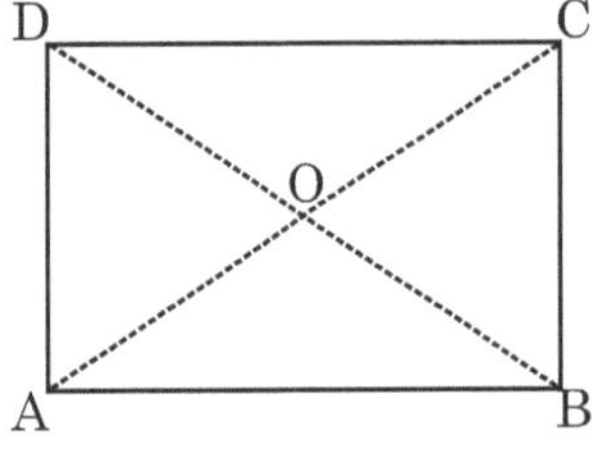

To prove: $\angle B > \angle D$ or $\angle D > \angle B$

Construction Draw the diagonal BD of quadrilateral

Proof Now, in $\triangle ABD$, AD > AB

$[\because$ AB is the smallest side in ABCD]

$\Rightarrow \angle 1 > \angle 3$ ...(i)

$[\because$ angle opposite to largest side is greatest]

In $\triangle BCD$, CD > BC

$[\because$ CD is the largest side in ABCD]

$\Rightarrow \angle 2 > \angle 4$ ...(ii)

$[\because$ angle opposite to the largest side is greatest]

On adding equations (i) and (ii), we get

$\angle 1 + \angle 2 > \angle 3 + \angle 4$

$\Rightarrow \angle B > \angle D$

Hence, $\angle B > \angle D$

2. Show that in a quadrilateral ABCD, AB + BC + CD + DA < 2(BD + AC).

[NCERT EXEMPLAR]

Sol. Given ABCD is quadrilateral and AC and BD are diagonals.

To prove

AB + BC + CD + DA < 2(BD + AC)

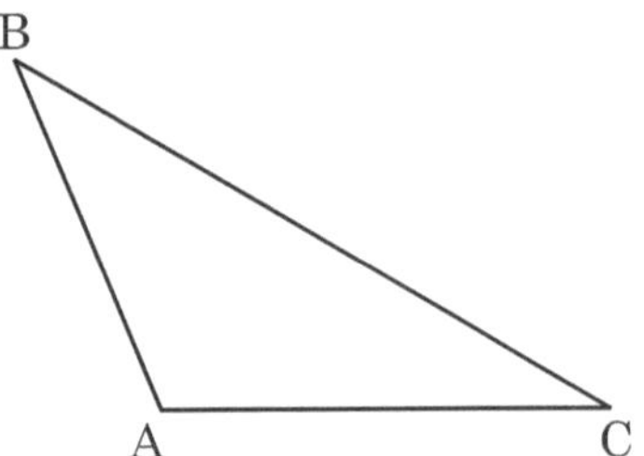

Proof : In $\triangle OAB$,

OA + OB > AB ... (i)

$[\because$ sum of any two sides of a triangle is greater than the third side]

Similarly, in $\triangle OBC$,

OB + OC > BC ... (ii)

In $\triangle OCD$, OC + OD > CD ... (iii)

and in $\triangle ODA$, OD + OA > DA ... (iv)

On adding equations (i), (ii), (iii) and (iv), we have

$2[(OA + OB + OC + OD)] > AB + BC + CD + DA$

$\Rightarrow 2[(OA + OC) + (OB + OD)] > AB + BC + CD + DA$

$\Rightarrow 2(AC + BD) > AB + BC + CD + DA$

$[\because$ OA + OC = AC and OB + OD = BD]

$\therefore$ AB + BC + CD + DA < 2(BD + AC)

Hence proved.

3. Prove that in a triangle other than an equilateral triangle, angle opposite to the longest side is greater than $\frac{2}{3}$ of a right angle.

[NCERT EXEMPLAR]

Sol. Consider, $\triangle ABC$ in which BC is the longest side.

To prove : $\angle A = \frac{2}{3}$ right angle

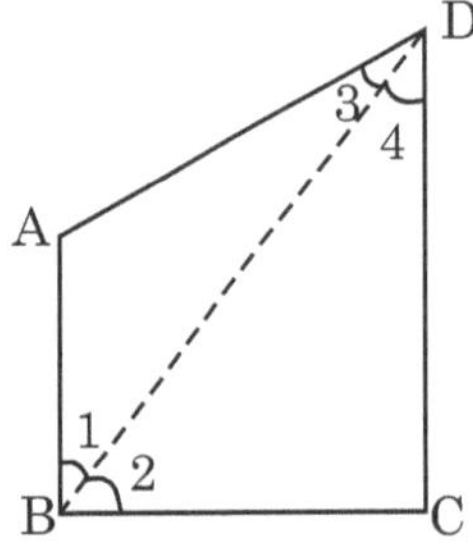

In $\triangle ABC$, BC > AB. $[\because$ BC is the largest side]

$\Rightarrow \angle A > \angle C$ ...(i)

$[\because$ angle opposite to the longer side is greater]

and BC > AC

$\Rightarrow \angle A > \angle B$ ...(ii)

$[\because$ angle opposite to the longer side is greater]

On adding equations (i) and (ii), we get

$2\angle A > \angle B + \angle C$

On adding $\angle A$ on both the sides, we have,

$\Rightarrow 2\angle A + \angle A > \angle A + \angle B + \angle C$

$\Rightarrow 3\angle A > \angle A + \angle B + \angle C$

$\Rightarrow 3\angle A > 180°$

$\therefore \angle A > \frac{2}{3} \times 90°$ $[\because$ Sum of three angles of a triangle is 180°]

$\therefore \angle A > \frac{2}{3}$ of a right angle.

Hence proved.

4. Prove that the sum of two sides of a triangle is greater than twice the median with respect to the third side.   [NCERT EXEMPLAR]

OR

If AD is a medium of $\triangle$ABC. Prove that AB + AC > 2AD.

[BOARD TERM I, 2013, 2012, SET-41]

Sol. Given, $\triangle$ABC and AD is the median.

Now, extend median AD to E such that

AD = DE

and draw a line EC.

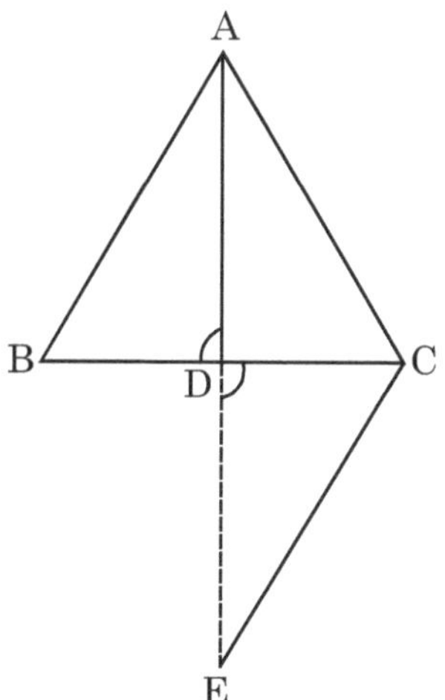

Now, in triangles ADB and EDC,

AD = DE

BD = DC ($\because$ AD is a median)

$\angle$ADB = $\angle$EDC (Vertically opposite angles)

By SAS congruence,

$\therefore$ $\triangle$ADB $\cong$ $\triangle$EDC

and AB = EC

Again, in $\triangle$AEC, AC + EC > AE

[$\because$ Sum of two sides of a triangle is greater than the third side]

$\Rightarrow$ AC + AB > AE ($\because$ EC = AB)

$\Rightarrow$ AC + AB > AD + DE

$\Rightarrow$ AC + AB > AD + AD ($\because$ DE = AD)

$\therefore$ AC + AB > 2AD.

Hence proved.

5. Show that sum of all sides of a quadrilateral is greater than the sum of its diagonals

[BOARD TERM I, 2012, SET-43]

OR

Diagonals AC and BD of a quadrilateral ABCD intersect each other at O. Prove that :

AB + BC + CD + DA > AC + BD.

[NCERT EXEMPLAR, BOARD TERM I, 2013]

Sol. By triangle inequality property, the sum of two sides of a triangle is greater than the third side, then

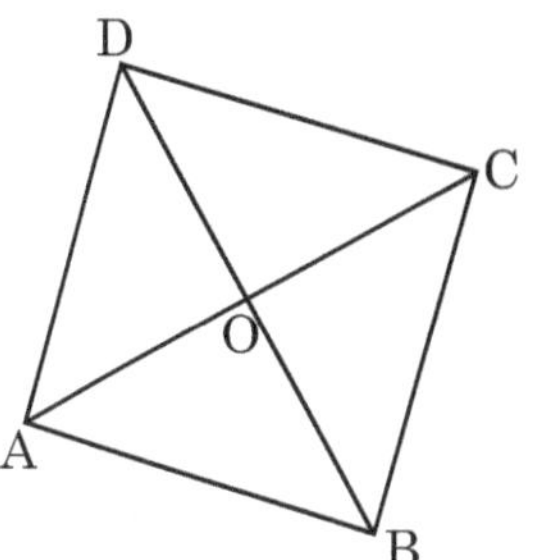

In $\triangle$ABC, AB + BC > AC   ...(i)

In $\triangle$BCD, BC + CD > BD   ...(ii)

In $\triangle$CDA, CD + DA > AC   ...(iii)

In $\triangle$DAB, DA + AB > BD   ...(iv)

Now, on adding (i), (ii), (iii) and (iv), we have

AB+ BC +BC+ CD + CD + DA + DA + AB > AC + BD + AC + BD

$\Rightarrow$ 2(AB + BC +CD + DA) > 2(AC + BD)

$\Rightarrow$ AB + BC + CD + DA > AC + BD

Hence proved.

6. ABCD is a quadrilateral in which AB and CD are smallest and longest sides respectively. Prove that $\angle$A > $\angle$C and $\angle$B > $\angle$D.

[BOARD TERM I, 2012, SET-43]

Sol. According to the question,

ABCD is a quadrilateral given below.

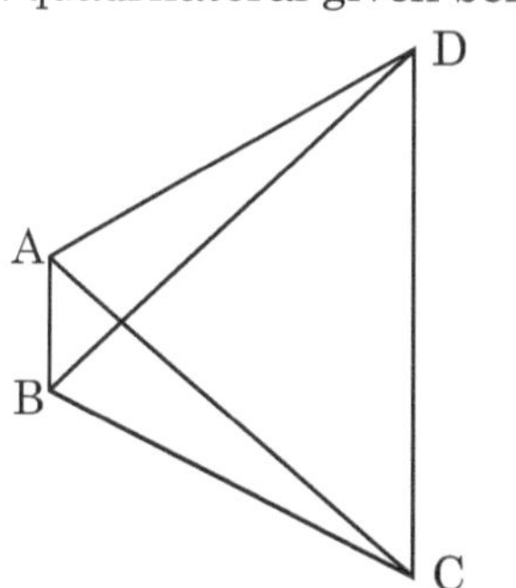

Proof : In $\triangle$ABC

$\because$ Side AB is the smallest side of quadrilateral

BC > AB

$\therefore$ $\angle$BAC > $\angle$BCA   ...(i)

In $\triangle$ACD,

$\because$ Side CD is the greatest side of quadrilateral

CD > AD

$\therefore$ $\angle$CAD > $\angle$ACD   ...(ii)

On adding equations (i) and (ii), we get

$\angle$BAC + $\angle$CAD > $\angle$BCA + $\angle$ACD

$\Rightarrow$ $\angle$BAD > $\angle$BCA

$\therefore \quad \angle A > \angle C$

In $\triangle ABD$, $\because AD > AB$

$\therefore \quad \angle ABD > \angle ADB$ .... (iii)

In $\triangle BCD$, $\because CD > BC$

$\therefore \quad \angle DBC > \angle BDC$ .... (iv)

On adding equations (iii) and (iv), we get

$\angle ABD + \angle DBC > \angle ADB + \angle BDC$

$\Rightarrow \angle ABC > \angle ADC$

$\therefore \quad \angle B > \angle D$

$\angle A > \angle C$ and $\angle B > \angle D$.

Hence proved.

7. In the given figure, AD = BD. Prove that BD < AC.

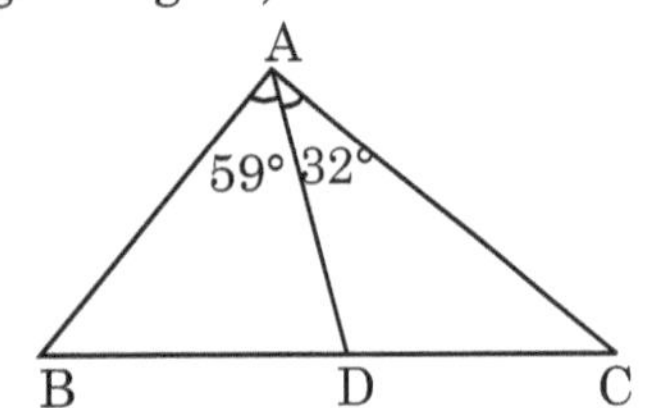

[BOARD TERM I, 2014, 2012, SET-79]

Sol. According to the question,

AD = BD

$\therefore \quad \angle ABD = \angle DAB = 59°$

($\because$ Angles opposite to equal sides are equal)

In $\triangle ABD$,

Sum of the angles of a triangle = 180°

$\Rightarrow 59° + 59° + \angle ADB = 180°$

$\therefore \quad \angle ADB = 180° - 118° = 62°$

and $\angle ADB = \angle DAC + \angle ACD$

$\Rightarrow 62° = 32° + \angle ACD$

$\angle ACD = 62° - 32° = 30°$

(Exterior angle is equal to the sum of interior opposite angles)

Now, In $\triangle ABD$, AB > BD ... (i)

(Side opposite to greatest angle is the longest)

Also in $\triangle ABC$, AB < AC ...(ii)

From equations (i) and (ii), we have

$\therefore \quad BD < AC.$

Hence proved.

CHAPTER 8

Quadrilaterals

- (Prove) The diagonal divides a parallelogram into two congruent triangles.
- (Motivate) In a parallelogram opposite sides are equal and conversely.
- (Motivate) In a parallelogram opposite angles are equal and conversely.
- (Motivate) A quadrilateral is a parallelogram if a pair of its opposite sides is parallel and equal.
- (Motivate) In a parallelogram, the diagonals bisect each other and conversely.
- (Motivate) In a triangle, the line segment joining the mid points of any two sides is parallel to the third side and in half of it and (motivate) its converse.

A flow chart on the basic concepts of Quadrilateral

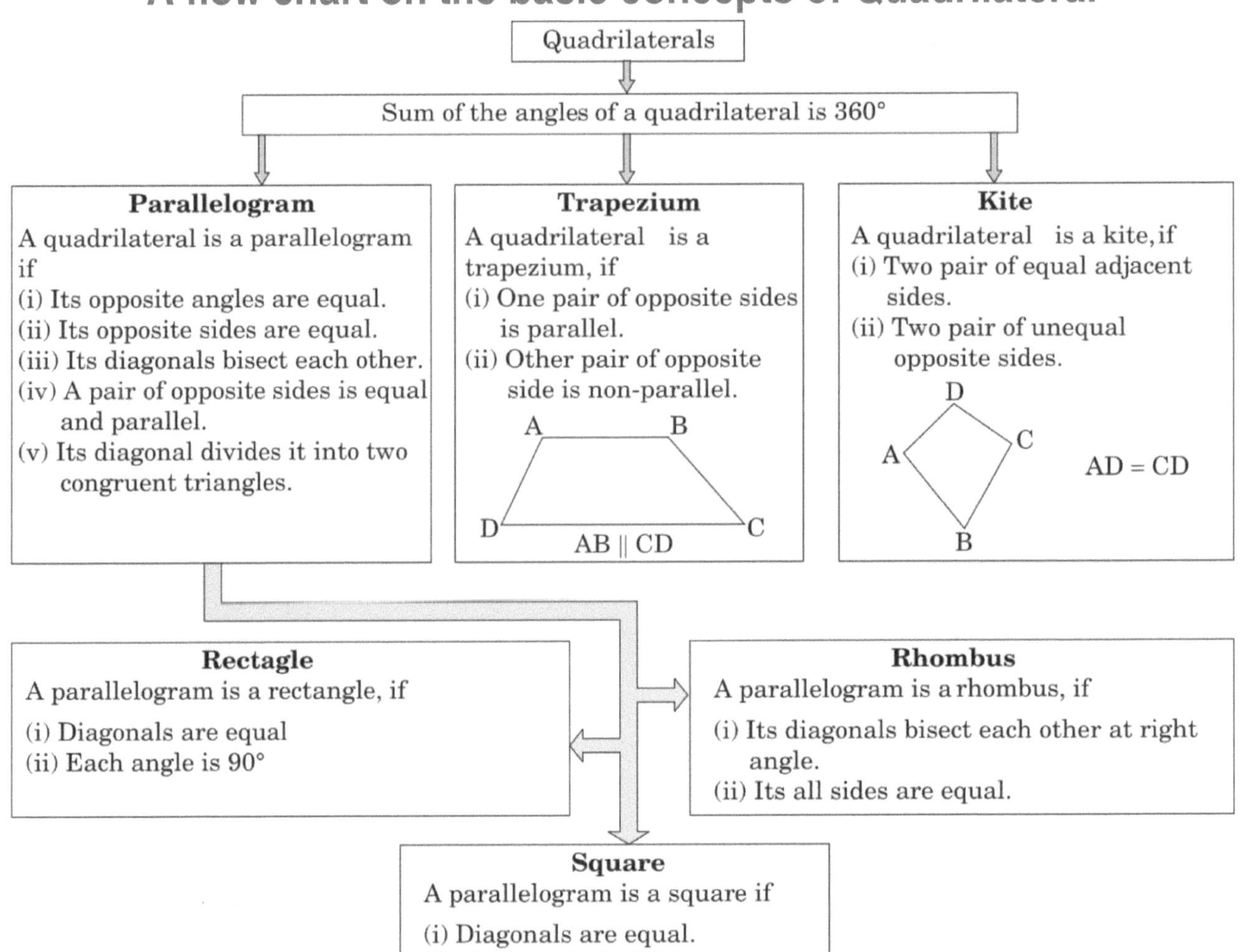

[Topic 1] Types of Quadrilaterals
Points to be Remembered :

S.No.	Name	Diagram	Sides	Angles	Diagonals
1.	Parallelogram		Opposite sides are parallel and equal	Opposite angles are equal and sum of any two adjacent angles is 180°	Diagonals bisect each other.
2.	Rhombus		All sides are equal and opposite sides are parallel	Opposite angles are equal and sum of any two adjacent angles is 180°	Diagonals bisect each other at right angle.
3.	Trapezium		One pair of opposite sides are parallel	The angles at the ends of each non-parallel sides are supplementary	Diagonals need not be equal
4.	Isosceles Trapezium		One pair of opposite sides are parallel and non-parallel sides are equal in length.	The angles at the ends of each parallel sides are equal.	Diagonals are of equal length.
5.	Kite		Two pairs of adjacent sides are equal	One pair of opposite angles are equal	(i) Diagonals intersect at right angle. (ii) Shorter diagonal bisected by longer diagonal (iii) Longer diagonal divides the kite into two congruent triangles

PREVIOUS YEARS'
EXAMINATION QUESTIONS
TOPIC 1

Multiple Choice Questions
(1 Mark Each)

1. Which of the following is not true for a parallelogram ?
   (a) opposite sides are equal
   (b) opposite angles are equal
   (c) opposite angles are bisected by the diagonals
   (d) diagonals bisect each other.

   [NCERT Exemp.]

Sol. (c) For a parallelogram the statement "Opposite angles are bisected by the diagonals" is not true.

2. Three angles of a quadrilateral are 75°, 90°, and 75°. The fourth angle is
   (a) 90°   (b) 95°
   (c) 105°   (d) 120°   [NCERT Exemp.]

Sol. **(d)** We know that

sum of angles in a quadrilateral = 360°.

∴ Fourth angle of the quadrilateral

$$= 360° - (75° + 90° + 75°)$$
$$= 360° - 240°$$
$$= 120°.$$

Hence, the fourth angle is 120°.

3. ABCD is a rhombus such that $\angle ACB = 40°$. Then $\angle ADB$ is

(a) 40° (b) 45°

(c) 50° (d) 60° [NCERT Exemp.]

Sol. **(c)** Given,

ABCD is a rhombus such that $\angle ACB = 40°$

We know that diagonals of a rhombus bisect each other at right angles.

Now, In right triangle BOC, we have

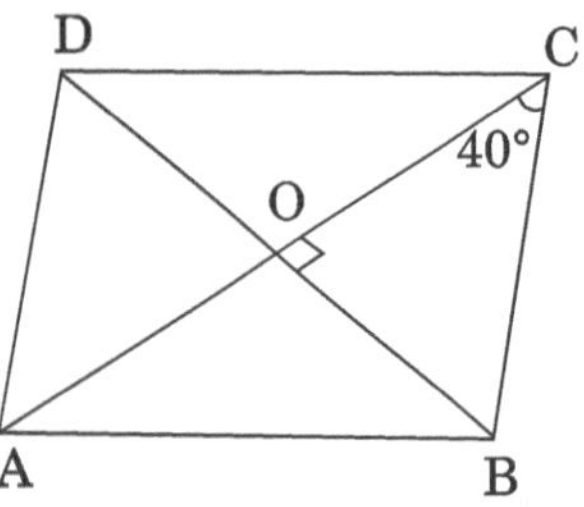

$$\angle OBC + \angle BOC + \angle BCO = 180°$$

(Angle sum property)

∴ $\angle OBC = 180° - (\angle BOC + \angle BCO)$

$$= 180° - (90° + 40°)$$
$$= 180° - 130° = 50°$$

or $\angle DBC = \angle OBC = 50°$

∵ AD ∥ BC

∴ $\angle ADB = \angle DBC$ [Alt. int. angles]

Hence, $\angle ADB = 50°$

4. Given, a quadrilateral ABCD such that $\angle C = 90°$ and diagonal AC and BD bisect each other at O, then the quadrilateral is a :

(a) rhombus (b) trapezium

(c) parallelogram (d) rectangle

Sol. **(d)** Since, in the given options only rectangle has a 90° angle.

∴ 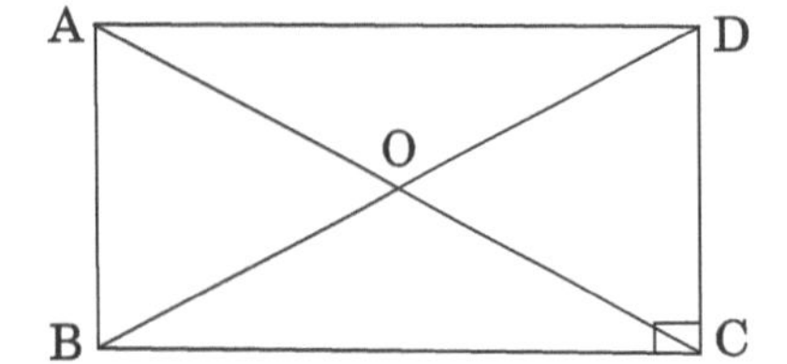

Hence, the quadrilateral is a rectangle.

5. The value of x in the given figure is :

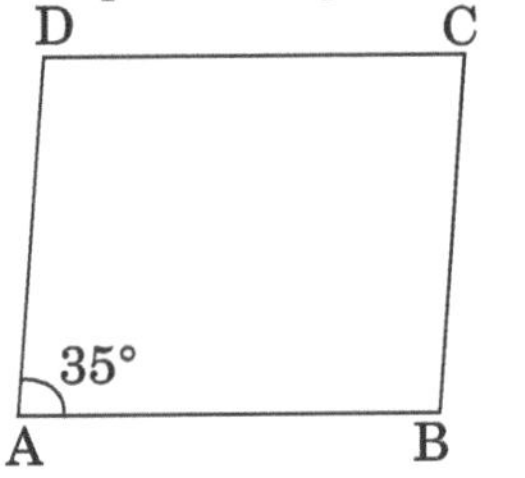

(a) 10° (b) 20°

(c) 30° (d) 40°

Sol. **(b)** We know that,

Sum of the angles of a quadrilateral = 360°.

$$\Rightarrow 5x + 3x + 3x + 7x = 360°$$
$$\Rightarrow 18x = 360°$$
$$\therefore \quad x = \frac{360}{18} = 20°$$

Very Short Answer Type Questions
(1 Mark Each)

1. The angles of quadrilateral are in the ratio 3 : 5 : 9 : 13. Find all the angles of the quadrilateral.

[NCERT Exemplar]

Sol. Let the angles of the quadrilateral are 3x, 5x, 9x and 13x respectively, then

According to the question,

Sum of all the angles of quadrilateral

$$= 360°$$
$$\Rightarrow 3x + 5x + 9x + 13x = 360°$$
$$\Rightarrow 30x = 360°$$
$$\therefore \quad x = \frac{360}{30} = 12°$$

Therefore, $\quad 3x = 3 \times 12° = 36°$

$$5x = 5 \times 12° = 60°$$
$$9x = 9 \times 12° = 108°$$

and $\quad 13x = 13 \times 12° = 156°$

Hence, the required angles of the quadrilateral are 36°, 60°, 108° and 156°.

2. Diagonals of quadrilateral ABCD bisect each other. If $\angle A = 35°$, then find the value of $\angle B$.

[NCERT Exemplar]

Sol. Given, diagonals of a quadrilateral bisect each other, so it is a parallelogram and then

$$\angle A + \angle B = 180°$$

[$\because$ consecutive interior angles of a parallelogram]

$\therefore \qquad \angle B = 180° - \angle A$

$\because \qquad \angle A = 35°$ [Given]

$$\angle B = 180° - 35° = 145°$$

Hence, the value of $\angle B$ is 145°.

3. One angle of a quadrilateral is of 108° and the remaining three angles are equal. Find each of the three equal angles.

[NCERT Exemplar]

Sol. Let one of the three equal angles be x.

Now, according to the question, sum of all the angles of a quadrilateral = 360°

$\Rightarrow 108° + x + x + x = 360°$

$\Rightarrow \qquad 3x = 360° - 108°$

$\Rightarrow \qquad 3x = 252°$

$\therefore \qquad x = \dfrac{252°}{3} = 84°$

Hence, each of the three equal angles is 84°.

4. The angles of a quadrilateral are in the ratio 2 : 3 : 6 : 7 . The largest angle of the quadrilateral is .... [Board Term II, Set A1, 2011]

Sol. Let the angles of the quadrilateral be $2x°$, $3x°$, $6x°$, $7x°$, respectively, now according to the question,

$\therefore 2x° + 3x° + 6x° + 7x° = 360°$

[Angle sum property of quadrilateral]

$\Rightarrow \qquad 18x° = 360°$

$\therefore \qquad x° = 20°$

Largest angle = $7x° = 7 \times 20°$

Hence, the largest angle = 140°

5. The sides BA and DC of a quadrilateral ABCD are produced as shown in figure. Prove that a + b = x + y.

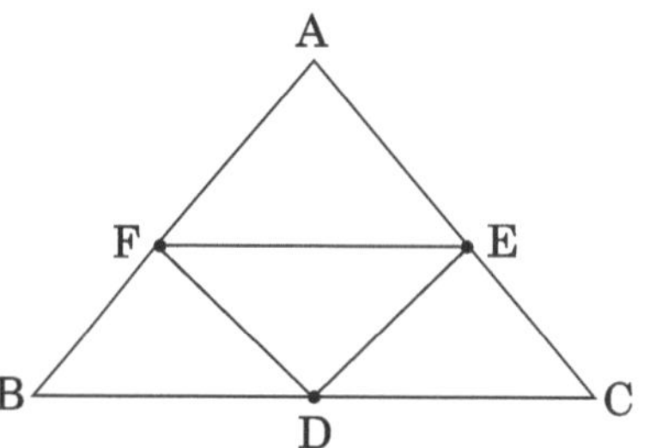

Sol. Given,

$$x = \angle ABD + \angle CBD$$

and $\qquad y = \angle ADB + \angle CDB$

In $\triangle ABD$, we have

$$\angle ABD + \angle ADB = b \qquad\qquad ...(i)$$

[exterior angle of a triangle]

In $\triangle CBD$, we have

$$\angle CBD + \angle CDB = a \qquad\qquad ...(ii)$$

[exterior angle of a triangle]

Now, on adding eqs. (i) and (ii), we get

$(\angle ABD + \angle CBD) + (\angle ADB + \angle CDB)$

$$= a + b$$

$\therefore \qquad x + y = a + b$

Hence proved.

6. If in a quadrilateral ABCD; $\angle A = 90°$ and AB = BC = CD = DA, then ABCD is a square.

Sol. Given, $\angle A = 90°$

and $\qquad\qquad AB = BC = CD = DA$

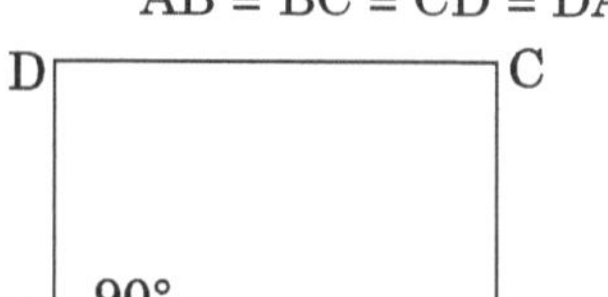

Hence, the given statement is true.

Short Answer Type Questions I

(2 Marks Each)

1. D, E and F are the mid-points of the sides BC, CA and AB, respectively of an equilateral triangle ABC. Show that $\triangle DEF$ is also an equilateral triangle.

[NCERT Exemplar]

Sol. Since the segment joining the mid-points of two sides of a triangle is half of the third side.

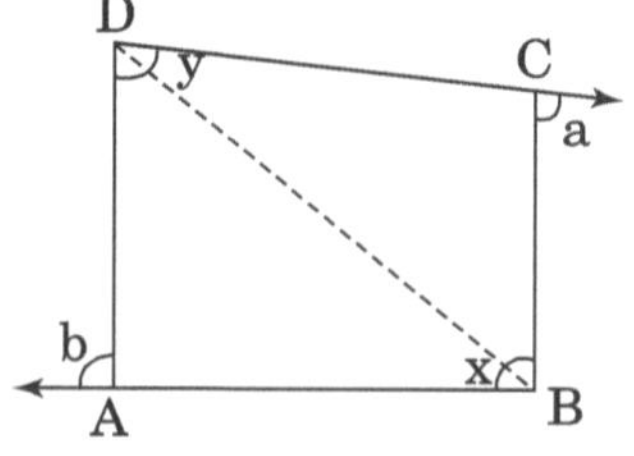

$\therefore$ DE = $\dfrac{1}{2}$AB , EF = $\dfrac{1}{2}$BC and FD = $\dfrac{1}{2}$CA $\qquad$ ...(i)

Now, in equilateral $\triangle ABC$

$\because \qquad\qquad AB = BC = CA$

On dividing by 2.

$\Rightarrow \qquad \dfrac{1}{2}AB = \dfrac{1}{2}BC = \dfrac{1}{2}CA$

$\Rightarrow \qquad DE = EF = FD \qquad$ [From eq. (i)]

Therefore, all the sides of triangle DEF are equal. Hence, triangle DEF is an equilateral triangle.

2. Prove that each angle of a rectangle is a right angle.

[NCERT]

Sol. Let ABCD be a rectangle and $\angle A = 90°$, then

According to the question,

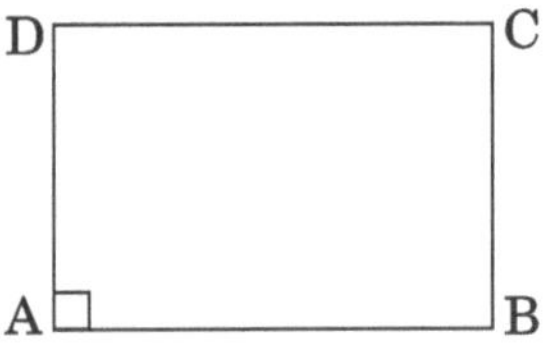

$\Rightarrow$ ABCD is parallelogram also.

$\therefore$ AD $\parallel$ BC

$\Rightarrow \qquad \angle A + \angle B = 180°$ (Co-interior angles)

$\Rightarrow \qquad 90° + \angle B = 180°$

$\therefore \qquad \angle B = 180° - 90° = 90°$

Again $\qquad \angle A = \angle C = 90°$ (Opposite angles of parallelogram)

and $\qquad \angle B = \angle D = 90°$ (Opposite angles of parallelogram)

3. The angles of a quadrilateral are in the ratio $3 : 5 : 9 : 13$. Find all the angles of the quadrilateral.

[NCERT][KVS 2014]

Sol. Let the measure of the angles be $3x°$, $5x°$, $9x°$ and $13x°$ then,

According to the question,

$3x° + 5x° + 9x° + 13x° = 360°$

$\Rightarrow \qquad 30x° = 360°$

[Angle sum property of quadrilateral]

$$x = \frac{360°}{30°} = 12°$$

Hence, required angles are

$3x = 3 \times 12 = 36°$

$5x = 5 \times 12 = 60°$

$9x = 9 \times 12 = 108°$

and $\qquad 13x = 13 \times 12 = 156°$

4. Two parallel lines l and m are intersected by a transversal 't'. Show that the quadrilateral formed by bisectors of interior angles is a rectangle.

[Board Term II, Set-A1, 2011, NCERT]

Sol. $\because$ l $\parallel$ m

$\angle APR = \angle DRP$ (Alternate interior angles)

$\Rightarrow \qquad \angle 1 = \angle 2 \qquad [\because$ PS and QR are bisectors]

But these are alternate interior angles

$\therefore$ SP $\parallel$ RQ and SR $\parallel$ PQ

Therefore, PQRS is a parallelogram

$\angle APR + \angle BPR = 180°$, (linear pair)

$\Rightarrow \dfrac{1}{2}\angle APR + \dfrac{1}{2}\angle BPR = \dfrac{1}{2} \times 180°$

$\Rightarrow \qquad \angle 1 + \angle 3 = 90°$

$\therefore \qquad \angle SPQ = 90°$

Hence, PQRS is a rectangle.

5. If angles of a quadrilateral are in ratio $1 : 2 : 3 : 4$. Find the measure of all the angles of a quadrilateral.

[Board Term II, Set-A1, 2011]

Sol. Let the measure of the angles be $x°$, $2x°$, $3x°$ and $4x°$ then,

According to the question,

$x° + 2x° + 3x° + 4x° = 360°$

$\Rightarrow \qquad 10x° = 360°$

$\therefore \qquad x = 36°$

Hence, angles of quadrilateral are

$x = 36°$

$2x = 2 \times 36° = 72°$

$3x = 3 \times 36° = 108°$

and $\qquad 4x = 4 \times 36° = 144°$

6. Two opposite angles of a parallelogram are $(3x - 2)°$ and $(63 - 2x°)$. Find all the angles of a parallelogram. [Board Term II, Set-A1, 2011]

Sol. Since opposite angles of a parallelogram are equal

$\therefore \qquad 3x - 2 = 63 - 2x$

$\Rightarrow \qquad 3x + 2x = 63 + 2$

$\Rightarrow \qquad 5x = 65$

$\therefore \qquad x = \dfrac{65}{5} = 13$

Hence, angles of parallelogram are

$$(3x - 2) = 3 \times 13 - 2 = 39 - 2 = 37°$$

and $\qquad (63 - 2x) = 63 - 2 \times 13 = 63 - 26 = 37°$

$\because \qquad \angle B + \angle C = 180° \qquad$ [CD ∥ AB]

$\therefore \qquad \angle B = 180° - 37° = 143°$

and $\qquad \angle D = \angle B = 143°$

7. The angles of a quadrilateral are $(4x°)$, $(7x°)$, $(15x°)$ and $(10x°)$. Find the smallest and largest angles of the quadrilateral.

[Board Term II, 2015]

Sol. $\because$ Sum of the angles of a quadrilateral is 360°.

$\therefore 4x° + 7x° + 15x° +10x° = 360°$

[Angle sum property of quadrilateral]

$\Rightarrow \qquad 36x° = 360°$

$\therefore \qquad x° = \dfrac{360°}{36°} = 10°$

Hence, smallest angle $= 4x° = 4 \times 10° = 40°$

and largest angle $= 15x° = 15 \times 10° = 150°$

8. In the figure, ABCD is a rectangle and X and Y are points on sides AD and BC respectively such that AY = BX. Show that $\angle ABX = \angle BAY$.

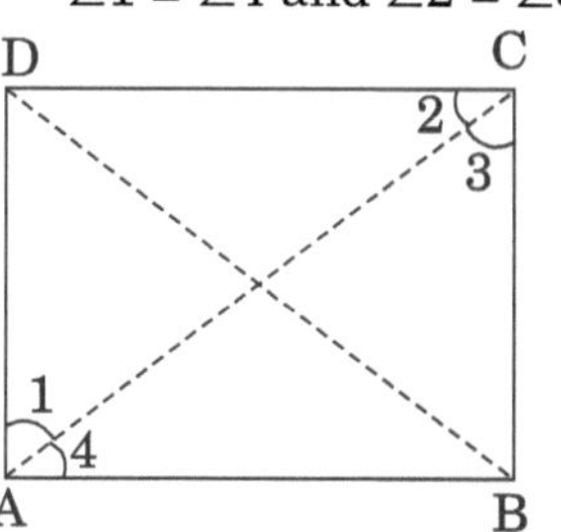

Sol. Given ABCD is a rectangle and X and Y are the points on sides AD and BC, respectively such that AY = BX.

To Prove $\angle ABX = \angle BAY$

Proof In $\triangle BAX$ and $\triangle ABY$, we have

$\qquad AB = BA \qquad$ [common]

$\qquad \angle A = \angle B \qquad$ [each = 90°]

and $\qquad BX = AY \qquad$ [given]

By RHS congruence rule, we have

$\therefore \qquad \triangle BAX \cong \triangle ABY$

Hence, $\qquad \angle ABX = \angle BAY \qquad$ [by CPCT]

Short Answer Type Questions II

(3 Marks Each)

1. Show that if the diagonals of a quadrilateral bisect each other at right angles, then it is a rhombus.

[NCERT]

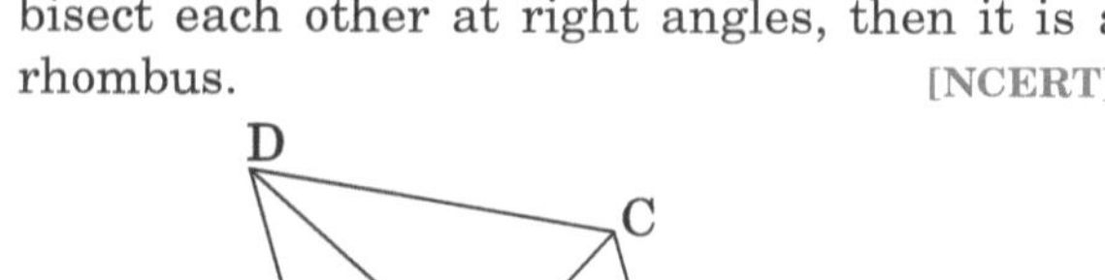
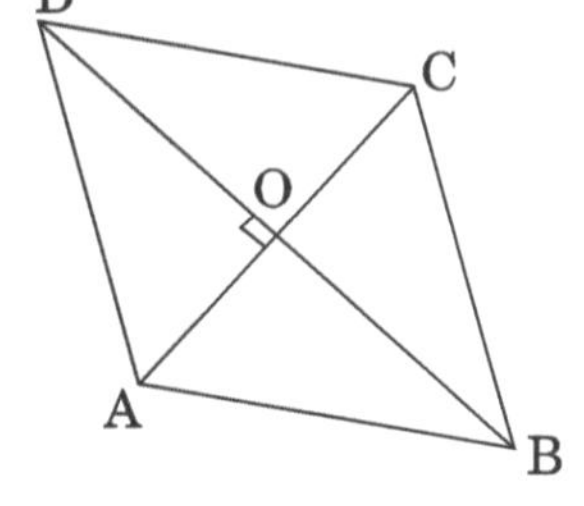

Sol. Given, a quadrilateral ABCD such that the diagonals AC and BD bisect each other at right angles at O.

$\therefore$ In $\triangle AOB$ and $\triangle AOD$, we have

$\qquad AO = AO \qquad$ [common]

$\qquad OB = OD$

$\qquad$ [$\because$ O is the mid-point of BD]

$\qquad \angle AOB = \angle AOD = 90° \qquad$ [Given]

By SAS congruence rule

$\therefore \qquad \triangle AOB \cong \triangle AOD$

$\therefore \qquad AB = AD \qquad$ [by CPCT]...(i)

Similarly, $\qquad AB = BC \qquad$ ...(ii)

$\qquad BC = CD \qquad$ ...(iii)

$\qquad CD = AD \qquad$ ...(iv)

From equations (i), (ii), (iii) and (iv), we have

$$AB = BC = CD = DA$$

Thus, all sides of the given quadrilateral ABCD are equal.

Hence, the quadrilateral ABCD is a rhombus.

2. ABCD is a rectangle in which diagonal AC bisects $\angle A$ as well as $\angle C$. Show that. [NCERT]

(i) ABCD is a square

(ii) diagonal BD bisects $\angle B$ as well as $\angle D$.

Sol. Given, a rectangle ABCD such that AC bisects $\angle A$ as well as $\angle C$.

i.e. $\qquad \angle 1 = \angle 4$ and $\angle 2 = \angle 3 \qquad$ ...(i)

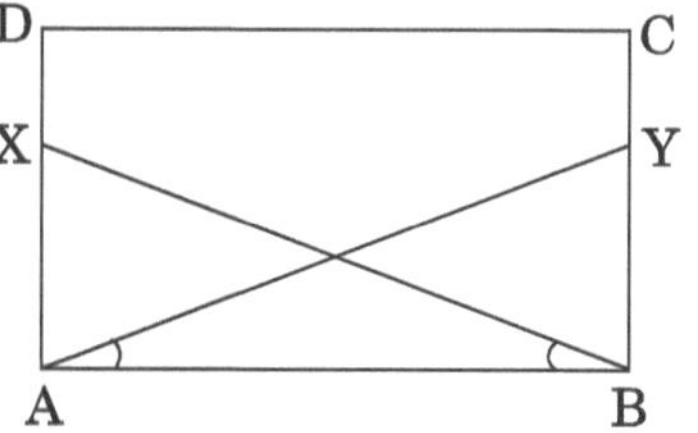

(i) Since, rectangle is a parallelogram.

$\therefore$ ABCD is a parallelogram

$\Rightarrow$ AB ∥ CD and AC is a transversal.

$\therefore \qquad \angle 2 = \angle 4 \qquad$ ...(ii)

$\qquad$ [alternate interior angles]

From equations, (i) and (ii), we have

$\qquad \angle 3 = \angle 4 \Rightarrow AB = BC$

and $\qquad \angle 1 = \angle 2$

$\Rightarrow \qquad AD = CD$

$\qquad$ [$\because$ sides opposite to equal angles are equal]

$\therefore \qquad AB = BC = CD = AD$

Thus, ABCD is a rectangle having all of its sides equal.

Hence, ABCD is a square.

(ii) Since, ABCD is a square, and diagonals of a square bisect the opposite angles.

∴ BD bisects $\angle B$ as well as $\angle D$.

[Hence proved].

3. Prove that the diagonals of a rectangle are equal in length.

[Board Term II, 2014]

Sol.

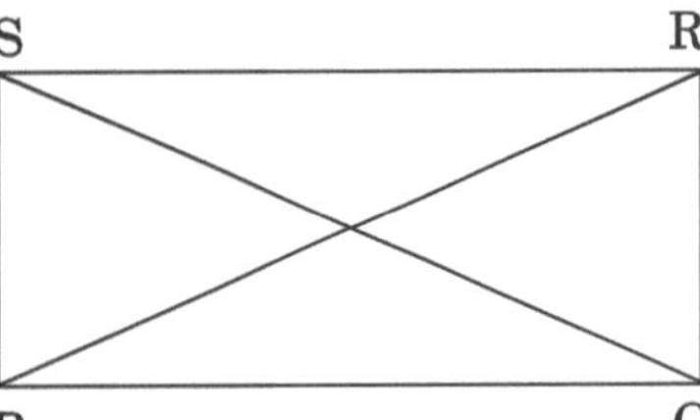

Let PQRS be a rectangle and PR and QS are the diagonals, then

In $\triangle SPQ$ and $\triangle RQP$,

$$SP = RQ$$

(Opp. sides of rectangle are equal)

$$\angle SPQ = \angle RQP = 90°$$

[Each angle of rectangle is right angle]

and $\qquad PQ = QP \qquad$ (Common)

By SAS congruence rule

$$\triangle SPQ \cong \triangle RQP$$

∴ $\qquad QS = PR \qquad$ (by c.p.c.t)

Hence, diagonals of a rectangle are equal in length.

4. ABCD is a rhombus. Show that the diagonal AC bisects $\angle A$ as well as $\angle C$ and diagonal BD bisects $\angle B$ as well as $\angle D$.

[NCERT][KVS 2014]

Sol. Given: ABCD is a rhombus.

⇒ $\qquad AB = BC = CD = AD$

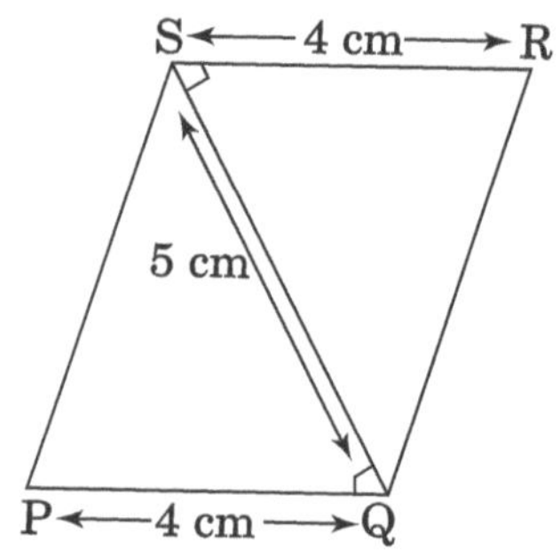

To prove :

$$\angle BAC = \angle DAC \text{ and } \angle DCA = \angle BCA$$

Proof :

In $\triangle ADC$ and $\triangle ABC$,

$$AB = AD \qquad \text{(Given)}$$
$$CD = CB \qquad \text{(Given)}$$

and $\qquad AC = AC \qquad$ (common)

[By SSS congruence rule]

∴ $\qquad \triangle ADC \cong \triangle ABC$

So, $\qquad \angle BAC = \angle DAC$ (c.p.c.t)

and $\qquad \angle DCA = \angle BCA$ (c.p.c.t.)

Hence proved.

5. PQRS is a quadrilateral with SQ as one of its diagonals. If SR = PQ = 4cm, SQ = 5cm and SQ is perpendicular to both SR and PQ, show that ar($\triangle PSQ$) = ar($\triangle SRQ$).

[Board Term II, 2014]

Sol.

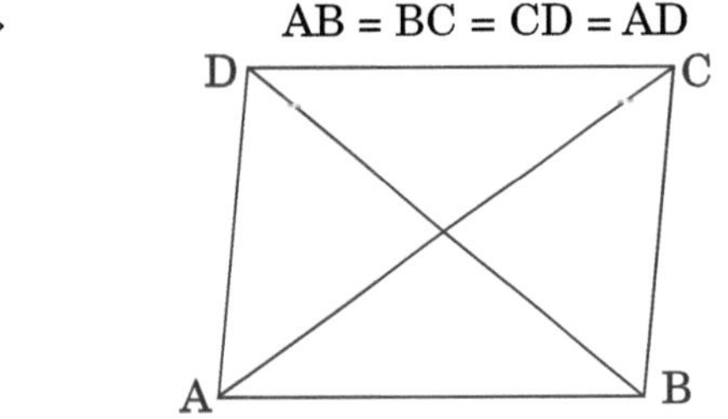

In $\triangle PSQ$ and $\triangle RQS$

$$PQ = SR = 4 \text{ cm} \qquad \text{[Given]}$$
$$SQ = SQ \qquad \text{[common]}$$

and $\qquad \angle SQP = \angle QSR = 90° \qquad$ [∵ SQ is perpendicular to both SR and PQ]

By SAS congruence rule,

$$\triangle PSQ \cong \triangle RQS$$

∴ $\qquad$ Thus, ar($\triangle PSQ$) = ar($\triangle SRQ$)

[∵ Areas of congruent figures are equal].

6. The angles A, B, C and D of a quadrilateral ABCD are in the ratio 2 : 4 : 5 : 7. Find the measures of these angles. What type of quadrilateral is it? Give reasons.

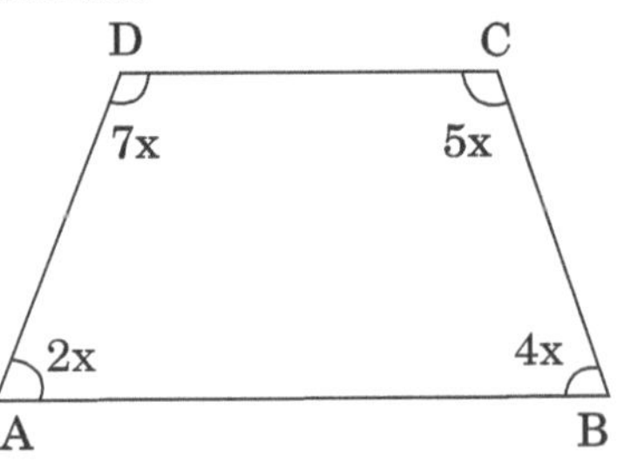

[Board Term II, 2012, Set-15]

Sol. Let the measures of the angles be 2x, 4x, 5x and 7x, then

According to the question,

$$2x + 4x + 5x + 7x = 360°$$

(Angle sum property)

⇒ $\qquad 18x = 360°$

$$\therefore \qquad x = \frac{360°}{18} = 20°$$

Therefore, $\qquad \angle A = 2 \times 20° = 40°$

$\qquad\qquad\qquad \angle B = 4 \times 20° = 80°$

$\qquad\qquad\qquad \angle C = 5 \times 20° = 100°$

and $\qquad\qquad \angle D = 7 \times 20 = 140°$

As $\angle A + \angle D = 180°$ and $\angle B + \angle C = 180°$

$\Rightarrow \qquad\qquad CD \parallel AB$

Hence, ABCD is a trapezium

7. In given figure, ABCD and PQRB are rectangles where Q is the mid-point of BD. If QR = 5 cm, find the measure of AB.

Sol. In ΔBDC, Q is the mid-point of BD.

Now, QR $\parallel$ DC (As ABCD is rectangle and PQRB is a rectangle)

$\Rightarrow$ R is the mid-point of BC (By converse of mid-point theorem)

Again, in ΔBDC, Q and R are the mid-points of BD and BC.

$$\Rightarrow \qquad\qquad QR = \frac{1}{2}DC$$

$$\Rightarrow \qquad\qquad 5 = \frac{1}{2}DC$$

$\therefore \qquad\qquad DC = 10$ cm

Also, $\qquad\qquad DC = AB$

(Opposite sides of rectangle are equal in length)

Hence, DC = AB = 10 cm

8. In given figure, ABCD is a trapezium in which $\angle A = x + 25°$, $\angle B = y°$, $\angle C = 95°$ and CD = $2x + 5°$, then find the values of x and y.

Sol. Given, ABCD is a trapezium.

$\therefore \qquad\qquad CD \parallel AB$

$\angle C + \angle B = 180°$ (Co-interior angles)

$95° + y = 180°$

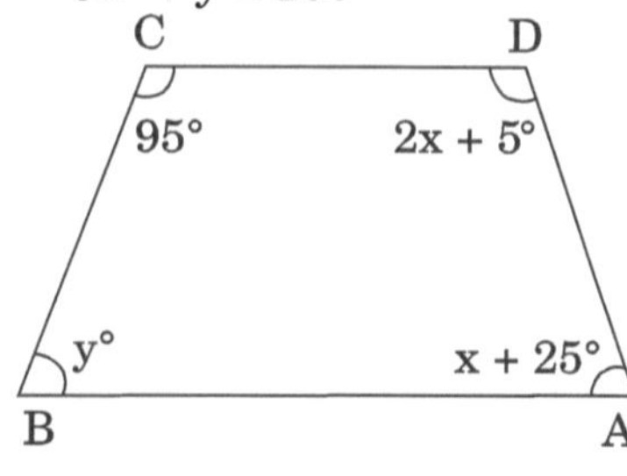

$$\therefore \qquad\qquad y = 180° - 95° = 85°$$

Again $\qquad \angle D + \angle A = 180°$

$(2x + 5) + (x + 25) = 180°$

$\Rightarrow \qquad\qquad 3x + 30° = 180°$

$\Rightarrow \qquad\qquad 3x = 180° - 30°$

$\Rightarrow \qquad\qquad 3x = 150°$

$$\therefore \qquad\qquad x = \frac{150°}{3} = 50°$$

Hence, x = 50° and y = 85°

Long Answer Type Questions
(4 Marks Each)

1. Show that the diagonals of a square are equal and bisect each other at right angles.

[NCERT]

Sol. Given A square PQRS in which diagonals PR and QS intersect each other at O.

To prove PR = SQ, PO = OR,

QO = OS and PR $\perp$ SQ.

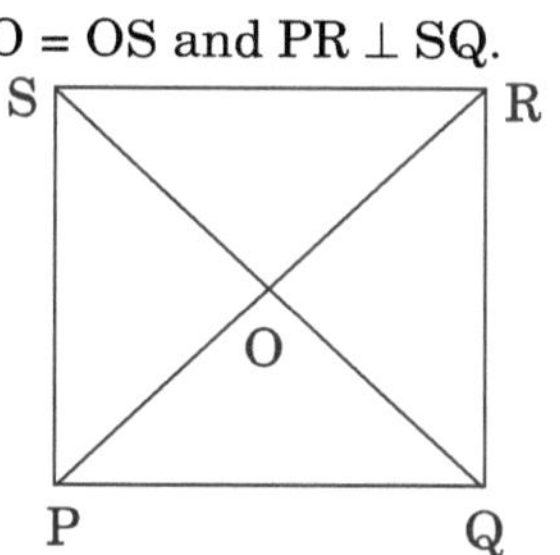

Proof In ΔPOQ and ΔROS

$\qquad\qquad PQ = RS$

[sides of a square are equal]

$\qquad \angle PQO = \angle RSO$ [alternate interior angle]

and $\qquad \angle QPO = \angle SRO$ [alternate interior angle]

By ASA congruence rule

$\Rightarrow \qquad\qquad \Delta POQ \cong \Delta ROS$

$\Rightarrow \qquad\qquad PO = OR \qquad$ ...(i)[by CPCT]

and $\qquad\qquad QO = OS \qquad$ [by CPCT]

Hence, PR and SQ bisect each other at O.

Also, in ΔPOQ and ΔROQ,

$\qquad\qquad PQ = RQ \qquad$ [sides of a square]

$\qquad\qquad PO = OR \qquad$ [From eq^n (i)]

and $\qquad\qquad OQ = OQ \qquad$ [common]

By SSS congruence rule

$\Rightarrow \qquad\qquad \Delta POQ \cong \Delta ROQ$

$\therefore \qquad\qquad \angle POQ = \angle ROQ \qquad$ [by CPCT]

Also, $\angle POQ + \angle ROQ = 180°$ [linear pair]...(ii)

$\Rightarrow \angle POQ + \angle POQ = 180°$ [From eq^n (ii)]

$\Rightarrow \qquad\qquad 2\angle POQ = 180°$

$$\therefore \qquad \angle POQ = \frac{1}{2} \times 180° = 90°$$

Thus, diagonals PR and SQ are perpendicular to each other.

Again, in $\triangle PQS$ and $\triangle QPR$

$$PQ = PQ \qquad \text{[common]}$$
$$PS = QR \qquad \text{[sides of a square]}$$
and $\qquad \angle QPS = \angle PQR \qquad$ [each 90°]

By SAS congruence rule,

$\Rightarrow \qquad \triangle PQS \cong \triangle QPR$

$\Rightarrow \qquad SQ = PR \qquad$ [by CPCT]

Hence, diagonals of a square are equal and bisect each other at right angles.

2. If $\triangle ABC$ and $\triangle DEF$ are two triangles such that AB, BC are respectively equal and parallel to DE, EF then show that:

(i) quadrilateral ABED is a parallelogram.

(ii) quadrilateral BCFE is a parallelogram.

(iii) AC = DF.

(iv) $\triangle ABC \cong \triangle DEF$.

[Board Term II, 2012; Set (20)] [NCERT]

Sol. Given : Two triangles ABC and DEF, such that

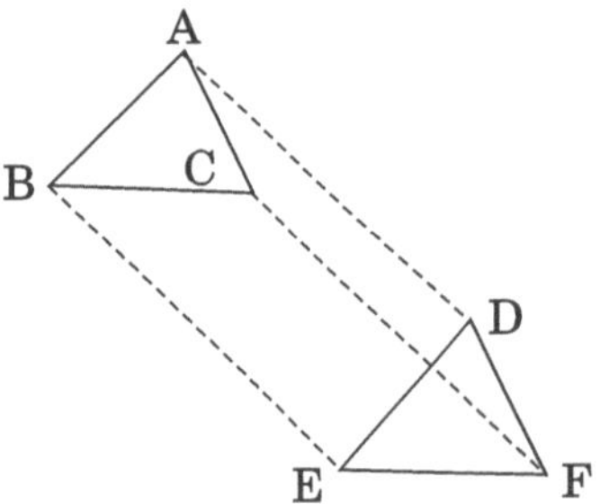

$$AB = DE \text{ and } AB \parallel DE$$
and $\qquad BC = EF$ and $BC \parallel EF$

Proof : (i) In a quadrilateral ABED,

$$AB = DE \text{ and } AB \parallel DE$$

∴ One pair of opposite sides are equal and parallel.

Hence, ABED is a parallelogram

or, $\qquad AD = BE$ and $AD \parallel BE$. ...(i)

(ii) In quadrilateral BCFE,

$$BC = EF \text{ and } BC \parallel EF$$

∴ One pair of opposite sides are equal and parallel.

Hence, BCFE is a parallelogram

or, $\qquad CF = BE$ and $CF \parallel BE$. ...(ii)

(iii) From equations (i) and (ii),we get

$$AD = CF \text{ and } AD \parallel CF$$

∴ ACFD is a parallelogram

Hence, $\qquad AC = DF$ and $AC \parallel DF$ ...(iii)

(iv) In $\triangle ABC$ and $\triangle DEF$,

$$AB = DE \qquad \text{(Given)}$$
$$BC = EF \qquad \text{(Given)}$$
and $\qquad AC = DF \qquad$ [from eqⁿ (iii)]

By SSS congruence rule,

$$\triangle ABC \cong \triangle DEF.$$

Hence proved.

3. ABCD is a trapezium in which AB ∥ CD and AD = BC, show that :

(i) $\angle A = \angle B$

(ii) $\angle C = \angle D$

(iii) $\triangle ABC \cong \triangle BAD$

[Board Term II, 2012; Set (01)] [NCERT]

Sol. Given : ABCD is a trapezium.

Here, AB ∥ CD and AD = BC

(i) Through C draw CE ∥ AD

∴ AECD is a parallelogram

or $\qquad \angle A + \angle 2 = 180°$ ...(i)

(Consecutive interior Angles)

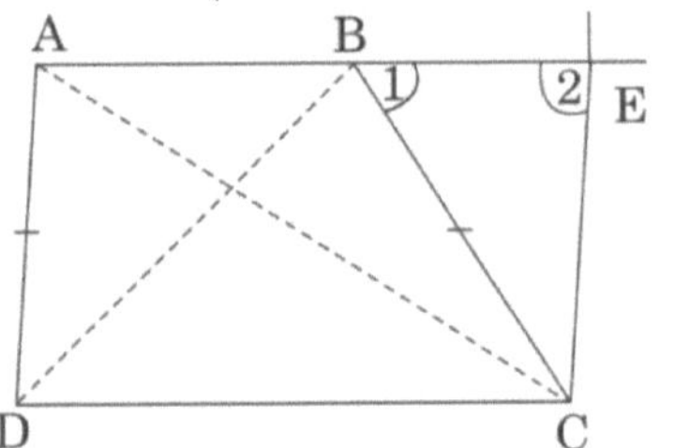

In $\triangle BCE$, BC = CE

or, $\qquad \angle 1 = \angle 2$

Also, $\qquad \angle B + \angle 1 = 180°$ ...(ii) (Linear Pair)

from eqⁿ (i) and (ii),

$$\angle A = \angle B$$
$$\angle A + \angle B = 180° \qquad \text{...(iii)}$$
and $\qquad \angle B + \angle C = 180° \qquad$ ...(iv)

(Consecutive interior Angles)

(ii) Again,

$$\angle A + \angle D = \angle B + \angle C = 180°$$

On comparing eqⁿ (iii) and (iv), we get

$$\angle A + \angle D = \angle B + \angle C$$

$\Rightarrow \qquad \angle C = \angle D \qquad [\because \angle A = \angle B]$

(iii) In $\triangle$'s ABC and BAD

$$AB = BA \qquad \text{(Common)}$$
$$\angle B = \angle A \qquad \text{(Proved above)}$$
and $\qquad BC = AD \qquad \text{(Given)}$

By SAS congruence rule,

Hence, $\qquad \triangle ABC = \triangle BAD$

4. Prove that the opposite angles of an isosceles trapezium are supplementary.

[Board Term II, 2012; Set-12]

Sol. In trapezium ABCD,

AB ∥ DC and AD = BC.

Through C, draw CE parallel to DA.

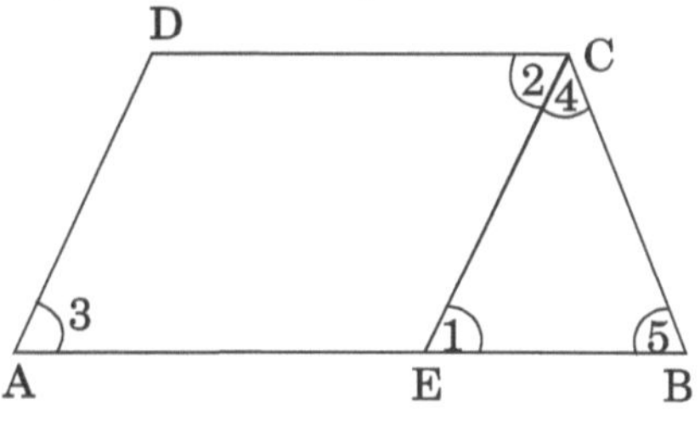

∵ DC ∥ AE and CE is a transversal line.

∴ $\angle 1 = \angle 2$ (Alternate angles)

Also $\angle 3 = \angle 1$ ...(i)(Corresponding angles)

∴ $\angle 2 = \angle 3 = \angle 1$ ...(ii)

On adding eqⁿ (i) and (ii), we have

∴ $\angle 2 + \angle 3 = 2\angle 1$

∴ $\angle A + \angle C = \angle 3 + \angle 2 + \angle 4$

  $= 2\angle 1 + \angle 4$ ...(iii)

Also, In ΔBEC,

  CE = BC

∴ $\angle 1 = \angle 5$

(Angles opposite to equal sides are equal).

$\angle A + \angle C = \angle 1 + \angle 4 + \angle 5 = 180°$

Similarly, we can show that $\angle B + \angle D = 180°$

Hence, the opposite angles of an isosceles trapezium are supplementary.

5. ABCD is a square and on the side DC, an equilateral triangle is constructed. prove that :

(i) AE = BE

(ii) $\angle DAE = 15°$

[Board Term II, 2012; Set -38]

Sol. (i) Since ABCD is a square and ΔDCE is an equilateral triangle.

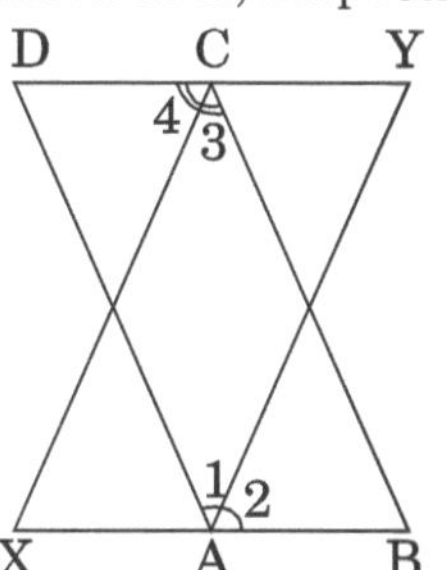

∴ $\angle ADC = 90°$ ...(i)

and $\angle EDC = 60°$ ...(ii)

On adding eqⁿ (i) and (ii)

or, $\angle ADC + \angle EDC = 90° + 60°$

⇒ $\angle ADE = 150°$

Similarly, we have

  $\angle BCE = 150°$

Thus, in ΔADE and ΔBCE, we have

  AD = BC   [Sides of a square]

  $\angle ADE = \angle BCE = 150°$

and   DE = CE

By SAS congruence rule, we get

  ΔADE ≅ ΔBCE

∴   AE = BE   (c.p.c.t.)

(ii) In ΔEAD, we have

  AD = DE   (sides of a square)

and $\angle EAD = \angle AED = x$ (let)

Now, $\angle ADE + \angle AED + \angle DAE = 180°$

⇒ $150° + x + x = 180°$

⇒ $2x = 180° - 150° = 30°$

∴ $x = \angle DAE = 15°$

Hence proved.

6. ABCD is a quadrilateral in which the bisectors of $\angle A$ and $\angle C$ meet DC produced at Y and BA produced at X respectively. Prove that,

$$\angle X + \angle Y = \frac{1}{2}(\angle A + \angle C).$$

[Board Term II, 2014]

Sol. Given ABCD is a quadrilateral in which the bisectors of $\angle A$ and $\angle C$ meet DC produced at Y and BA produced at X, respectively.

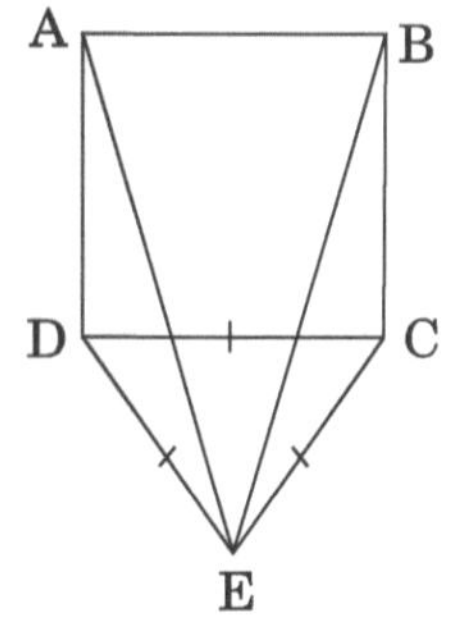

To prove : $\angle X + \angle Y = \dfrac{1}{2}(\angle A + \angle C)$

Proof : $\angle 1 = \angle 2 = \dfrac{1}{2}\angle A$

[∵ AY is the bisector of $\angle A$]

and $\angle 3 = \angle 4 = \dfrac{1}{2}\angle C$

[∵ CX is the bisector of $\angle C$]

In ΔCXB, $\angle 3 + \angle X + \angle B = 180°$ ...(i)

[by angle sum property of a triangle]

In $\triangle DAY, \angle 1 + \angle Y + \angle D = 180°$ ...(ii)

On adding equations (i) and (ii), we get

$\angle 3 + \angle X + \angle B + \angle 1 + \angle Y + \angle D = 360°$

$\Rightarrow \angle X + \angle Y + \angle 3 + \angle 1 + \angle B + \angle D = 360°$

$\Rightarrow \angle X + \angle Y + \dfrac{1}{2}\angle C + \dfrac{1}{2}\angle A + \angle B + \angle D = 360°$ ...(iii)

But $\angle A + \angle B + \angle C + \angle D = 360°$ ...(iv)

[angle sum property of a quadrilateral]

From equations (iii) and (iv), we have

$$\angle X + \angle Y + \dfrac{1}{2}\angle C + \dfrac{1}{2}\angle A + \angle B + \angle D$$
$$= \angle A + \angle B + \angle C + \angle D$$

$\Rightarrow \qquad \angle X + \angle Y = \dfrac{1}{2}\angle A + \dfrac{1}{2}\angle C$

$\therefore \qquad \angle X + \angle Y = \dfrac{1}{2}(\angle A + \angle C)$

Hence proved.

[Topic 2] Properties of Parallelogram

Points to be Remembered:

- A quadrilateral PQRS is a parallelogram, if a pair of opposite sides is parallel and equal.

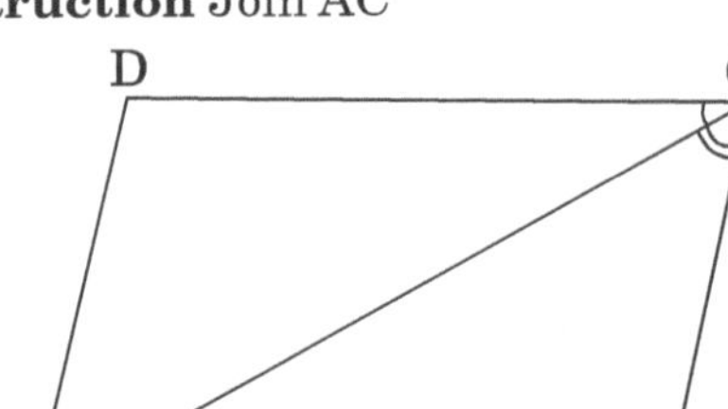

Here, PQ ∥ RS and PS ∥ QR

- Opposite angles of a parallelogram are equal i.e., $\angle P = \angle R$ and $\angle Q = \angle S$.
- Opposite sides of a parallelogram are equal i.e., PQ = RS and PS = QR.
- Diagonals of a parallelogram bisect each other i.e., PO = OR and SO = OQ
- A rectangle is an equiangular parallelogram.
- A rhombus is an equilateral parallelogram.
- A square is an equilateral parallelogram.
- Consecutive angles of a parallelogram are supplementary.
- Parallelograms on the same base and between the same parallel lines are equal in area.
- The angle bisectors of a parallelogram form a rectangle.

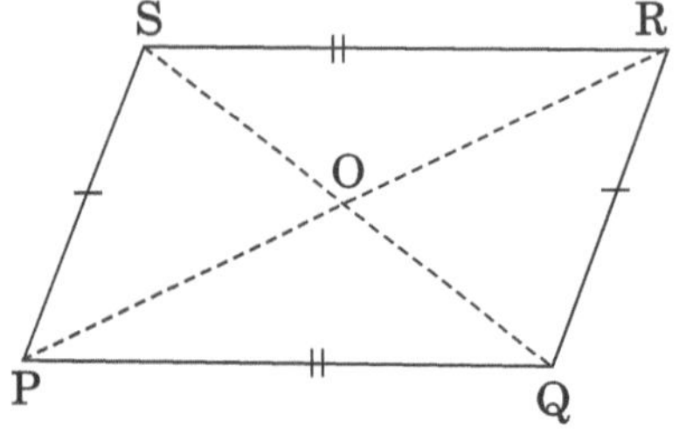

Here, PQRS is a rectangle.

Theorem 1

In a parallelogram, opposite sides are equal

Given ABCD is a parallelogram

To Prove AB = CD and DA = BC

Construction Join AC

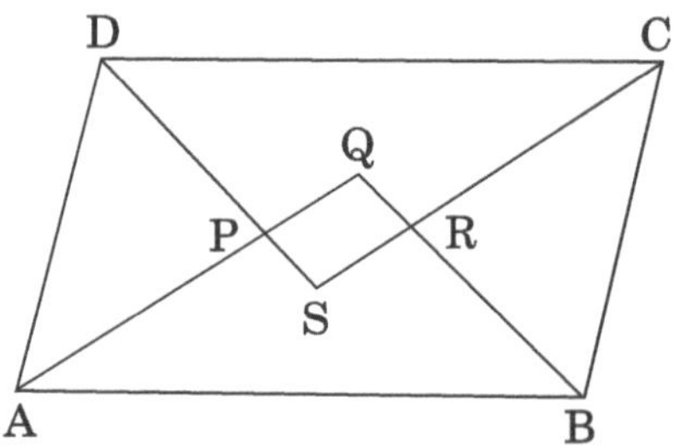

Proof

Since ABCD is a parallelogram

AD ∥ BC and AC is the transversal

$\qquad \angle DAC = \angle BCA$ ...(i) (alternate angles are equal)

AB ∥ DC and AC is the transversal

$\qquad \angle BAC = \angle DCA$ ...(ii) (alternate angles are equal)

In $\triangle ADC$ and $\triangle CBA$,

$\qquad \angle DAC = \angle BCA$ [from (i)]

and AC is common.

$\qquad \angle DCA = \angle BAC$ [from (ii)]

$\qquad \triangle ADC \cong \triangle CBA$ (By ASA)

Hence,

$\qquad AD = CB$ and $DC = BA$
(Corresponding sides are equal)

PREVIOUS YEARS'
EXAMINATION QUESTIONS
TOPIC 2

Multiple Choice Questions
(1 Mark Each)

1. If bisectors of $\angle A$ and $\angle B$ of a quadrilateral ABCD intersect each other at P, of $\angle B$ and $\angle C$ at Q, of $\angle C$ and $\angle D$ at R and of $\angle D$ and $\angle A$ at S, then PQRS is a:

    (a) rectangle.

    (b) rhombus.

    (c) parallelogram

    (d) quadrilateral whose opposite angles are supplementary.   [NCERT Exemp.]

Sol. (d) According to the question,

PQRS is a quadrilateral whose opposite angles are supplementary.

2. A diagonal of a rectangle is inclined to one side of the rectangle at 25°. The acute angle between the diagonals is

    (a) 55°   (b) 50°

    (c) 40°   (d) 25°   [NCERT Exemp.]

Sol. (b) According to the question,

ABCD is a rectangle in which diagonal AC is inclined to one side, AB of the rectangle at an angle of 25°.

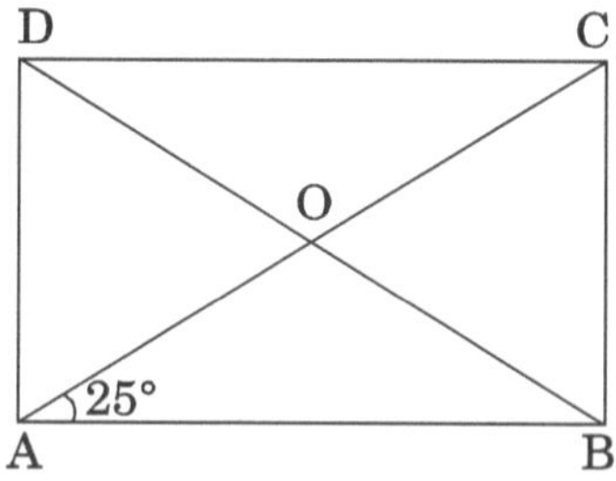

Now, AC = BD [Diagonals of a rectangle are equal]

$\Rightarrow \qquad \dfrac{1}{2}AC = \dfrac{1}{2}BD$

$\Rightarrow \qquad OA = OB$

In triangle AOB, we have

$$OA = OB$$

$\therefore \qquad \angle OBA = \angle BAO = 25°$

[Angles opposite to the equal sides are equal]

Now, By angle sum property, we have

$$\angle OBA + \angle AOB + \angle BAO = 180°$$

$\Rightarrow 25° + 25° + \angle AOB = 180°$

$\therefore \qquad \angle AOB = 180° - 50° = 130°$

We know that $\angle AOB$ and $\angle AOD$ from linear pair.

$\therefore \quad \angle AOB + \angle AOD = 180°$

$\Rightarrow \quad 130° + \angle AOD = 180°$

$\therefore \qquad \angle AOD = 180° - 130° = 50°$

Therefore, the acute angle between the diagonals is 50°.

3. If angles A,B,C and D of the quadrilateral ABCD, taken in order, are in the ratio 3:7:6:4, then ABCD is a

    (a) rhombus.

    (b) parallelogram.

    (c) trapezium.

    (d) kite.   [NCERT Exemp.]

Sol. (c) Let the angles A, B, C and D be 3x, 7x, 6x, and 4x.

We know that the sum of the angles of a quadrilateral is 360°.

then,

According to the question

$3x + 7x + 6x + 4x = 360°$

$\Rightarrow \qquad 20x = 360°$

$\therefore \qquad x = \dfrac{360°}{20} = 18°$

Thus, required angles are

$$A = 3 \times 18° = 54°$$
$$B = 7 \times 18° = 126°$$
$$C = 6 \times 18° = 108°$$

and $\qquad D = 4 \times 18° = 72°.$

Now, AD and BC are two lines which are cut by a transversal line CD such that the sum of angles $\angle C$ and $\angle D$ on the same side of transversal:

Therefore, AD ∥ BC

So, ABCD is a quadrilateral in which one pair of opposite sides are parallel.

Hence, ABCD is a trapezium.

4. In the given figure, ABCD is a parallelogram. If $\angle A = 65°$ then ($\angle B + \angle D$) is equal to :

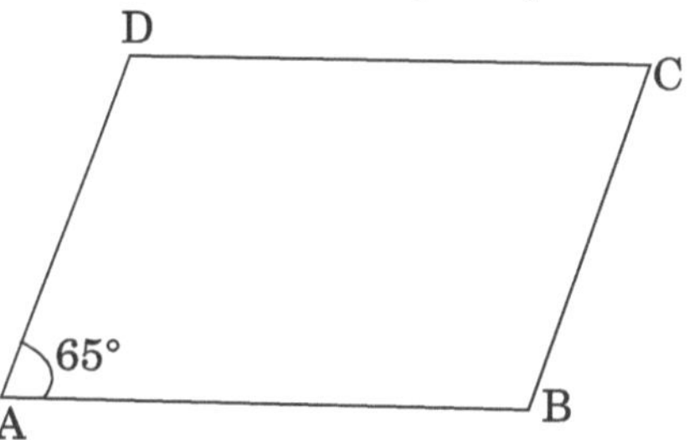

(a) $180°$

(b) $115°$

(c) $155°$

(d) $230°$

Sol. (d) We know that opposite angles of a parallelogram are equal.

$$\therefore \qquad \angle A = \angle C = 65°$$

Now,

$$\angle A + \angle B + \angle C + \angle D = 360°$$

[Angle sum property]

$$\Rightarrow \qquad \angle B + \angle D = 360° - (65° + 65°)$$

$$= 360° - 130° = 230°$$

5. Which of the following is not a parallelogram ?

(a) Trapezium

(b) Square

(c) Rectangle

(d) Rhombus

Sol. (a) We know that square, rectangle and rhombus are parallelogram. Therefore, trapezium is not a parallelogram.

Very Short Answer Type Questions
(1 Mark Each)

1. In adjoining figure, ABCD and AEFG are two parallelograms. If $\angle C = 55°$, determine $\angle F$.

[NCERT Exemplar]

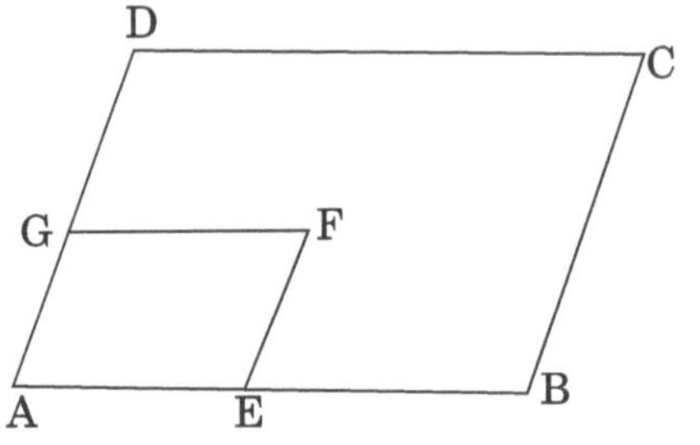

Sol. According to the question,

ABCD is a parallelogram and $\angle C = 55°$

$$\therefore \qquad \angle A = \angle C = 55°$$

[in a parallelogram, opposite angles are equal]

Also, AEFG is a parallelogram.

$$\therefore \qquad \angle A = \angle F = 55°$$

2. ABCD is a trapezium, In which AB ∥ CD and $\angle A = \angle B = 45°$. Then, find $\angle C$ and $\angle D$ of a trapezium.

[NCERT Exemplar]

Sol. According to the question,

$$\angle A = \angle B = 45°$$

Given, AB ∥ CD and BC is transversal.

$$\therefore \qquad \angle B + \angle C = 180°$$

[consecutive interior angles]

$$\Rightarrow \qquad \angle C = 180° - \angle B = 180° - 45°$$

$[\because \angle B = 45°,$ given$]$

$$\therefore \qquad \angle C = 135°$$

Similarly, $\angle A + \angle D = 180°$

[consecutive interior angles]

$$\therefore \qquad \angle D = 180° - 45°$$

$[\because \angle A = 45°,$ given$]$

$$= 135°$$

3. Two consecutive angles of a parallelogram are in the ratio 1 : 3, then what will be the smaller angle? [Board Term II, Set A1, 2011]

Sol. Let the consecutive angles be $x°$ and $(3x)°$, then

According to the question,

$$\therefore \qquad x° + 3x° = 180°$$

$$\Rightarrow \qquad 4x° = 180°$$

$$\therefore \qquad x° = \frac{180°}{4} = 45°$$

Hence, the smaller angle $= 45°$

4. In a parallelogram LMNO, If $\angle M = (3x + 23)°$ and $\angle N = (4x - 11)°$, then find the angles of the parallelogram LMNO.

Sol. Given, LMNO is parallelogram in which $\angle M = (3x + 23)°$ and $\angle N = (4x - 11)°$

Since, $\angle M$ and $\angle N$ are consecutive interior angles on the same side of transversal.

$$\therefore \qquad \angle M + \angle N = 180°$$

$$\Rightarrow 3x + 23 + 4x - 11 = 180°$$

$$\Rightarrow \qquad 7x = 180° - 12° = 168°$$

$$\therefore \qquad x = \frac{168}{7} = 24°$$

Hence, $\qquad \angle L = \angle N = (4 \times 24 - 11)° = 85°$

and $\qquad \angle M = \angle O = (3 \times 24 + 23)° = 95°$

5. In the given figure, ABCD is a parallelogram. If $\angle B = 105°$, then find the value of $\angle A + \angle C$.

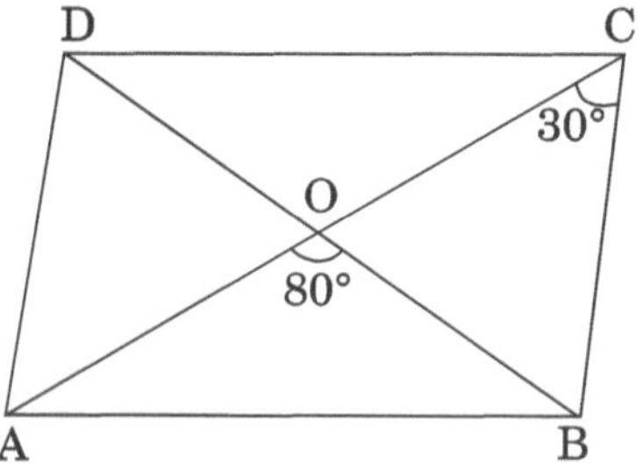

Sol. Here, ABCD is a parallelogram

$\because$ AD || BC

$\therefore \qquad \angle A + \angle B = 180°$ [adjacent angles]

$\Rightarrow \qquad \angle A + 105° = 180°$

$\therefore \qquad \angle A = 180° - 105°$

$$= 75°$$

Also, opposite angles of a parallelogram are equal

$\therefore \qquad \angle A = \angle C = 75°$

Now, $\quad \angle A + \angle C = 75° + 75° = 150°$

Hence, the value of $(\angle A + \angle C)$ is 150°.

6. The diagonals of a parallelogram ABCD intersect at O. If $\angle AOB = 80°$ and $\angle ACB = 30°$, then find $\angle OBC$.

Sol. According to the question,

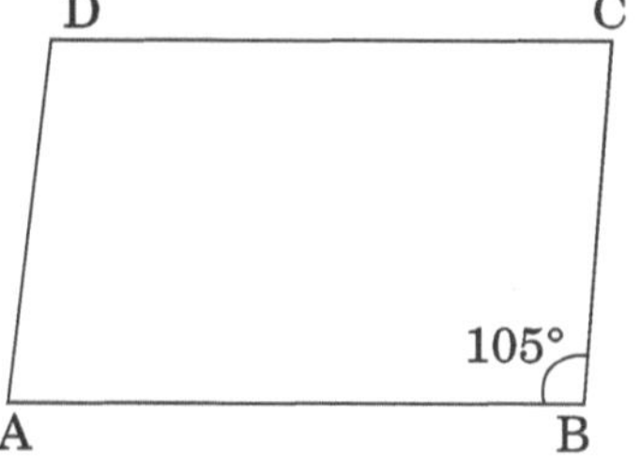

$\angle AOB$ is an exterior angle of $\triangle BOC$

$\therefore \ \angle OBC + \angle OCB = 80°$

[Exterior angle is the sum of two opposite angles]

$\Rightarrow \qquad \angle OBC + 30° = 80°$

$\therefore \qquad \angle OBC = 50°$

Hence, the measure of $\angle OBC$ is 50°.

Short Answer Type Questions- I
(1 Mark Each)

1. ABCD is a rhombus. Show that diagonal AC bisects $\angle A$ as well as $\angle C$ and diagonal BD bisects $\angle B$ as well as $\angle D$.

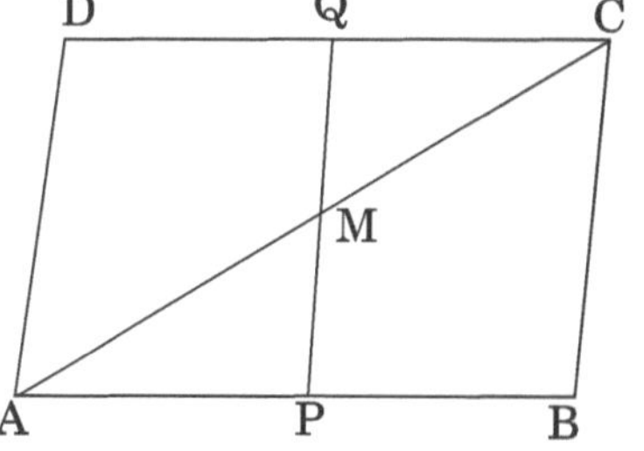

[NCERT.]

Sol. Given: ABCD is a rhombus in which

$$AB = BC = CD = AD.$$

To prove :

(i) Diagonal AC bisects $\angle A$ as well as $\angle C$.

(ii) Diagonal BD bisects $\angle B$ as well as $\angle D$.

Construction : Join diagonals AC and BD.

Proof : ABCD is a rhombus.

$\therefore \qquad AB = BC = CD = AD$

Also, AB || CD and AD || BC

Now, $\qquad AD = CD \Rightarrow \angle 1 = \angle 2$ ...(i)

[angles opposite to equal sides are equal]

Also, $\qquad CD \ || \ AB$

[opposite sides of the parallelogram and AC is transversal].

$\therefore \qquad \angle 1 = \angle 3$ ...(ii)

[alternate interior angles]

From eqs. (i) and (ii), we have

$\therefore \qquad \angle 2 = \angle 3$ and $\angle 1 = \angle 4$

Hence, AC bisects $\angle C$ as well as $\angle A$.

Similarly, we prove that BD bisects $\angle B$ as well as $\angle D$.

2. Points P and Q have been taken on opposite sides AB and CD, respectively of a parallelogram ABCD such that AP = CQ (see figure). Show that AC and PQ bisect each other.

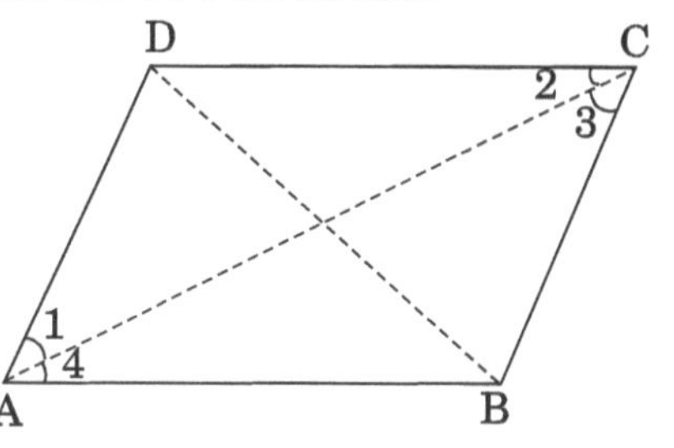

[NCERT Exemp.]

Sol. Given : ABCD is a parallelogram and AP = CQ.

To prove : AC and PQ bisect each other.

Proof : In $\triangle$AMP and $\triangle$CMQ,

$$\angle MAP = \angle MCQ$$

[alternate interior angles]

$$AP = CQ \qquad \text{[given]}$$

and $\qquad \angle APM = \angle CQM$

[alternate interior angles]

By ASA congruence rule,

$\therefore \qquad \triangle AMP \cong \triangle CMQ$

Then, $\qquad$ AM = CM $\qquad$ [by CPCT]

and $\qquad$ PM = QM $\qquad$ [by CPCT]

Hence, AC and PQ bisect each other.

3. PQRS is a parallelogram ad PL and RM are perpendiculars drawn from the vertices P and R of the parallelogram on diagonal SQ. Show that

(i) $\triangle$PQL $\cong$ $\triangle$RMS.

(ii) PL = RM.

[KVS 2014; Board Term II, 2012, NCERT]

Sol. (i), In $\triangle$RSM and $\triangle$PQL,

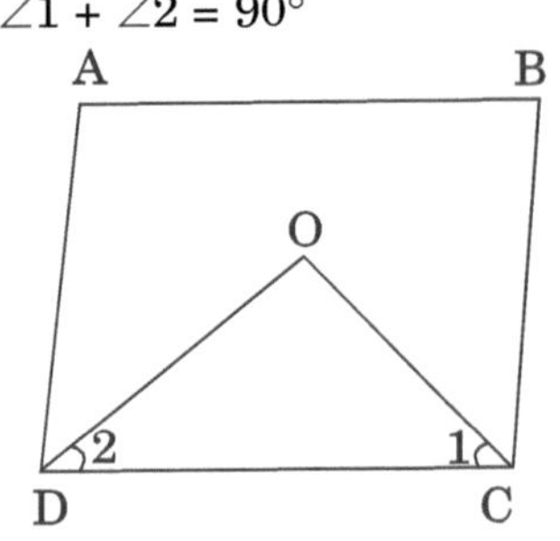

$\because$ SR $\parallel$ PQ

$$\angle RSM = \angle PQL \quad \text{[Alternate angle]}$$
$$\angle M = \angle L = 90°$$
$$SR = PQ$$

By AAS congruence rule,

$\therefore \qquad \triangle RSM \cong \triangle PQL.$

(ii) $\qquad$ PL = RM $\qquad$ (c.p.c.t)

4. The angle between the two altitudes of a parallelogram through the vertex of a obtuse angle is 50°. Find the angles of a parallelogram.

[Board Term II, Set A1, 2011]

Sol. Given, AM $\perp$ DC, AN $\perp$ BC

In quadrilateral AMCN,

$$\angle A + \angle M + \angle C + \angle N = 360° \text{ [Angle sum property]}$$
$$\Rightarrow \angle A + 90° + \angle C + 90° = 360°$$
$$\Rightarrow \qquad \angle A + \angle C = 360° - (90° + 90°) = 180°$$
$$\Rightarrow \qquad 50° + \angle C = 180°$$
$$\therefore \qquad \angle C = 180° - 50° = 130°$$

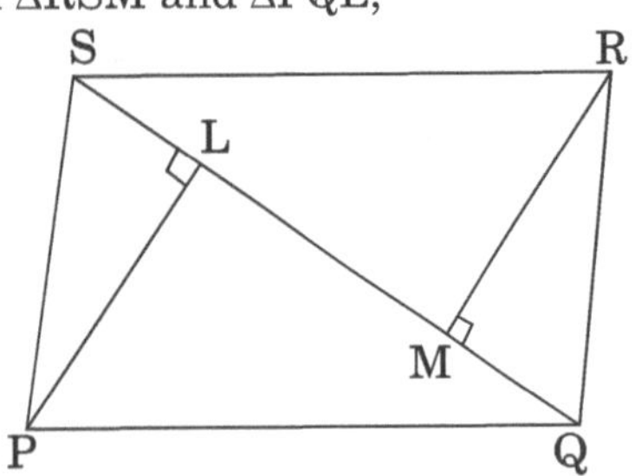

In parallelogram,

$$\angle A = \angle C = 130°$$

and $\qquad \angle B = \angle D = 180° - 130°$

$$= 50°.$$

5. In a parallelogram, show that the angle bisectors of two adjacent angles intersect at right angle.

[Board Term II, Set A1, 2011]

Sol. Given, a parallelogram ABCD.

To prove: $\angle$DOC = 90°

Proof: $\angle ADC + \angle BCD = 180°$[Adjacent angles]

$$\Rightarrow \frac{1}{2}\angle ADC + \frac{1}{2}\angle BCD = 90°$$

$$\Rightarrow \qquad \angle 1 + \angle 2 = 90°$$

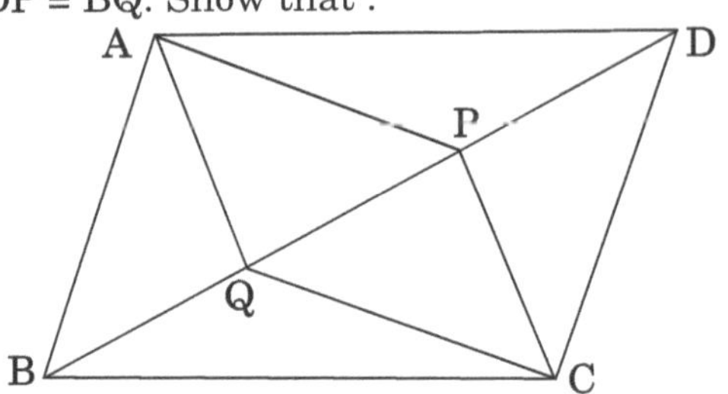

Now, In $\triangle$ODC,

$$\angle 1 + \angle 2 + \angle DOC = 180° \text{[Angle sum property]}$$
$$\Rightarrow \quad 90° + \angle DOC = 180° \Rightarrow \angle DOC = 180° - 90°$$

Hence, $\qquad \angle DOC = 90°.$

6. In the given parallelogram ABCD, two points P and Q are taken on the diagonal BD such that DP = BQ. Show that :

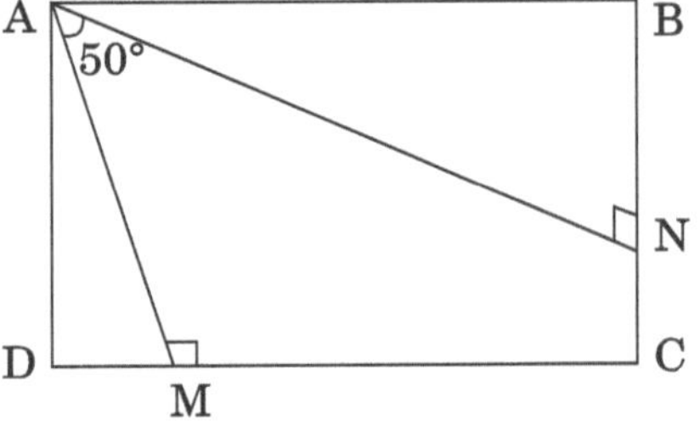

(i) $\triangle$APD $\cong$ $\triangle$CQB

(ii) $\triangle$AQB $\cong$ $\triangle$CPD

(iii) APCQ is a parallelogram.

[Board Term II, 2012 Set (01), 2012 (01), NCERT]

Sol. (i) In $\triangle$APD and $\triangle$CQB

$$AD = BC \qquad \text{[opposite sides of a}$$
$$\text{parallelogram]}$$

$$PD = BQ \qquad \text{(Given)}$$
and $\qquad \angle ADP = \angle QBC$ [Alternate angles]
By SAS congruence rule,
$\therefore \qquad \triangle APD \cong \triangle CQB$
$\Rightarrow \qquad AP = CQ \qquad$ (c.p.c.t)
(ii) In $\triangle AQB$ and $\triangle CPD$
$$AB = DC, \; BQ = DP$$
and $\qquad \angle ABQ = \angle PDC$ [Alternate angles]
By SAS congruence rule,
$\therefore \qquad \triangle AQB \cong \triangle CPD$
$\Rightarrow \qquad AQ = CP$
(iii) In quad. APCQ,
$$AP = CQ \text{ and } AQ = CP$$
Hence, APCQ is a parallelogram.

7. PQRS is a square. Diagonals PR and QS intersect each other at O. If ar($\triangle$POQ) is 4 cm², find ar(PQRS).

[Board Term II 2017, Set-UAH4DQ7, Z6K408K]

Sol. Given, PQRS is a square and diagonals PR and QS intersect each other at right angle

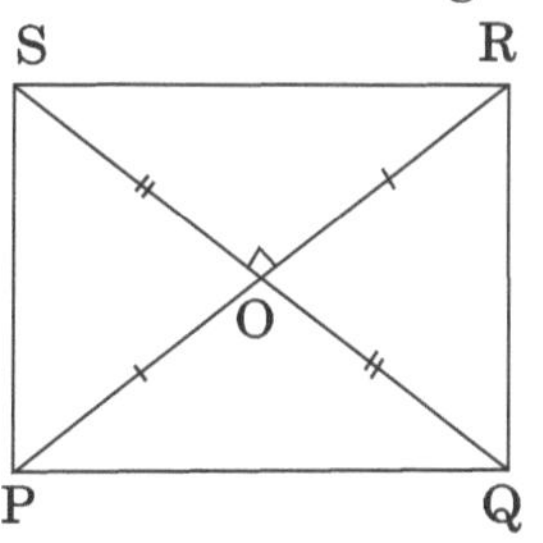

$\therefore \qquad \triangle POQ \cong \triangle ROQ$ and $\triangle ROQ \cong \triangle ROS$
Now, Area of $\triangle POQ$ = Area of $\triangle ROQ$
$$= \text{Area of } \triangle ROS = \text{Area of } \triangle POS$$
and Area of PQRS= 4 Area of $\triangle POQ$
$$= 4 \times 4 \text{ cm}^2$$
$$= 16 \text{ cm}^2$$

8. PQRS is a parallelogram and $\angle SPQ = 60°$. If the bisectors of $\angle P$ and $\angle Q$ meet at point A on RS, prove that A is the mid-point of RS.

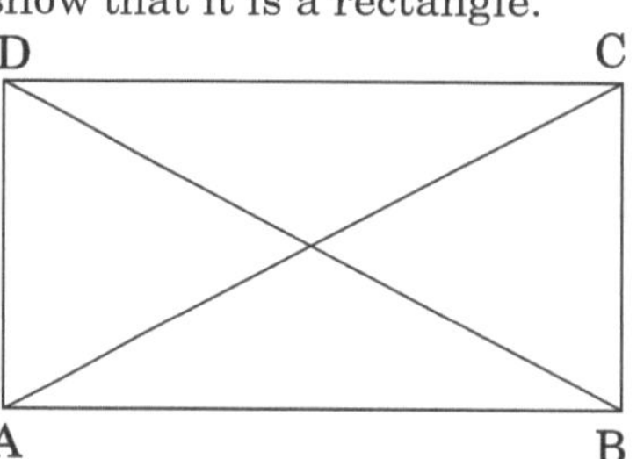

Sol. Given, PQRS is a parallelogram
and $\qquad \angle SPQ = 60°$
$$\angle P + \angle Q = 180°$$
[adjacent angles of a parallelogram]
$\Rightarrow \qquad 60° + \angle Q = 180°$

$\Rightarrow \qquad \angle Q = 180° - 60°$
$$= 120°$$
$\because$ SR $\parallel$ PQ
$\therefore \qquad \angle SAP = \angle APQ$
[alternate interior angles]
$\Rightarrow \qquad \angle SAP = 30°$
In $\triangle ASP$, we have
$$\angle SAP = \angle APS$$
$\Rightarrow \qquad SP = AS \qquad$ ...(i)
[sides opposite to equal angles are equal]
Similarly, we can prove
$$QR = AR$$
But $\qquad QR = SP$
$\Rightarrow \qquad SP = AR \qquad$ ...(ii)
From eqs. (i) and (ii), we have
$$AS = AR$$
Hence, A is the mid-point of SR.

Short Answer Type Questions-II
(1 Mark Each)

1. If the diagonals of a parallelogram are equal, then show that it is a rectangle.

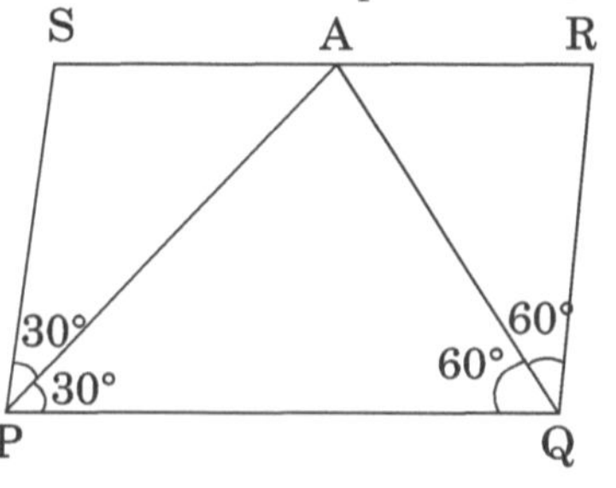

[NCERT]

Sol. Given: A parallelogram ABCD such that AC = BD
To prove: ABCD is a rectangle.
Proof : In $\triangle ABC$ and $\triangle DCB$
$$AC = DB \qquad \text{[given]}$$
$$AB = DC$$
[opposite sides of a parallelogram]
and $\qquad BC = CB \qquad$ [common]
By SSS congruence rule,
$$\triangle ABC \cong \triangle DCB$$
$\Rightarrow \qquad \angle ABC = \angle DBC \qquad$ ...(i)
$\because$ AB $\parallel$ DC and BC is a transversal.
[$\because$ ABCD is parallelogram]
$\therefore \quad \angle ABC + \angle DCB = 180° \qquad$ ...(ii)
[interior opposite angles are supplementary]
From equations (i) and (ii), we have
$$\angle ABC = \angle DCB = 90°$$
$\therefore$ ABCD is a parallelogram having an angle equal to 90°.
Hence, ABCD is a rectangle.

2. The angle between two altitudes of a parallelogram through the vertex of an obtuse angle of the parallelogram is 60°. Find the angles of the parallelogram.

[NCERT Exemplar]

Sol. Given, parallelogram ABCD, in which $\angle$ADC and $\angle$ABC are obtuse angles. Now, DE and DF are two altitudes of parallelogram and angle between them is 60°.

Now, BEDF is a quadrilateral, in which

$$\angle BED = \angle BFD = 90°$$

$\therefore$ $\angle FBE = 360° -(\angle FDE + \angle BED + \angle BFD)$

[angle sum property of a quadrilateral]

$$= 360° - (60° + 90° + 90°)$$
$$= 360° - 240° = 120°$$

Since, ABCD is a parallelogram.

$\therefore$ $\angle ADC = 120°$ $[\because \angle ADC = \angle FBE]$

$\Rightarrow$ $\angle A = 60°$

Also, $\angle C = \angle A = 60°$

$[\because$ opposite angles of a parallelogram are equal]

Now, $\angle A + \angle B = 180°$

[co-interior angles of a parallelogram]

$\therefore$ $\angle A = 180° - \angle B = 180° - 120°$
$$= 60°$$

Hence, angles of the parallelogram are 60°, 120°, 60° and 120°, respectively.

3. Diagonal AC of a parallelogram ABCD bisects $\angle$A. Show that:
   (i) it bisects $\angle$C also
   (ii) ABCD is a rhombus

[Board Term II, 2012, Set-20, NCERT]

Sol. Given, ABCD is a parallelogram and diagonal AC bisects $\angle$A.

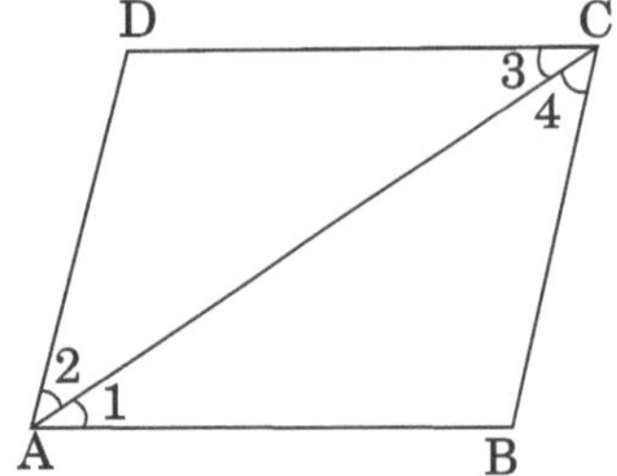

AB = CD, AD || BC

$$\angle 2 = \angle 3 \qquad \text{...(i)}$$
$$\angle 1 = \angle 4$$

(Alternate interior angles)

But $\angle 1 = \angle 2$ ...(ii)

(Given, Diagonal AC bisects $\angle$A)

On comparing eqⁿ (i) and (ii), we get

$$\angle 3 = \angle 4$$

Hence, AC bisects $\angle$C

$$\angle 1 = \angle 4 \text{ But } \angle 1 = \angle 2$$
$$\angle 2 = \angle 4$$
$$AB = BC$$

[sides opposite to equal angles are equal].

Hence, ABCD is a rhombus (in a parallelogram if one pair of adjacent are equal then it is a rhombus)

4. In the given figure, PQRS is a parallelogram in which PT and QT are angle bisectors of $\angle$P and $\angle$Q respectively. Find the value of $\angle$PTQ.

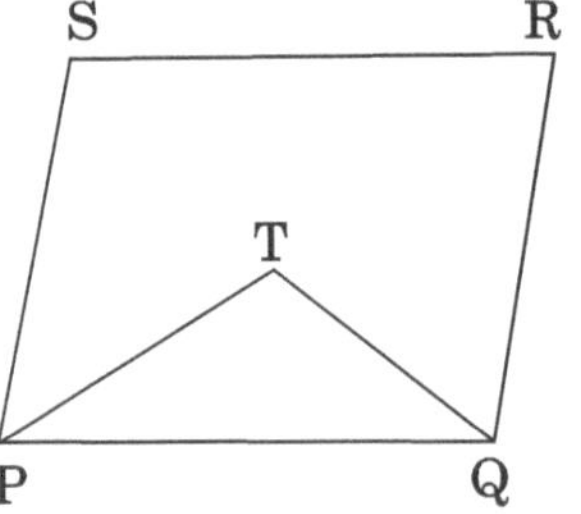

[Board Term II, 2013, Set-261C]

Sol. Given, PQRS is a parallelogram

$\therefore$ $\angle P + \angle Q = 180°$ (adjacent angles)

On dividing by 2, we get

$$\Rightarrow \quad \frac{1}{2}\angle P + \frac{1}{2}\angle Q = \frac{180°}{2} = 90° \qquad \text{...(i)}$$

Hence, $\angle PTQ = 180° - \left\{\frac{1}{2}(\angle P + \angle Q)\right\}$

[Angle sum property]

$$= 180° - 90° \quad \text{[from eqⁿ (i)]}$$
$$= 90°.$$

5. Two parallel lines l and m are intersected by a transversal p. Show that the quadrilateral formed by the bisectors of interior angles is a parallelogram.

[Board Term II, 2012, Set-24]

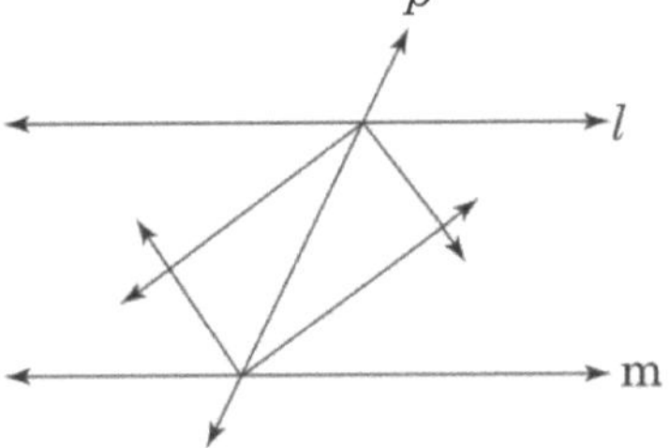

Sol. $\because l \parallel m$

$\therefore$ $\qquad$ $\angle XCA = \angle YAC$ $\qquad$ ...(i)

[Alternate interior angles]

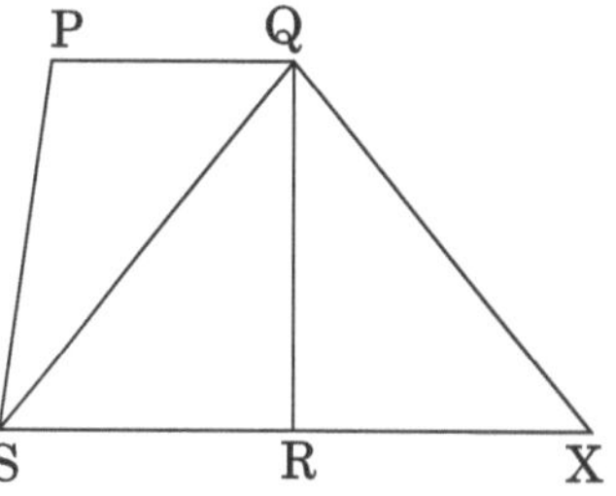

On dividing by 2, we get

$$\frac{1}{2}\angle XCA = \frac{1}{2}\angle YAC$$

$\Rightarrow$ $\qquad$ $\angle 1 = \angle 2$

$\therefore$ $\qquad$ $CB \parallel DA$

Similarly, $\qquad$ $AB \parallel DC$

Therefore, ABCD is a parallelogram.

6.

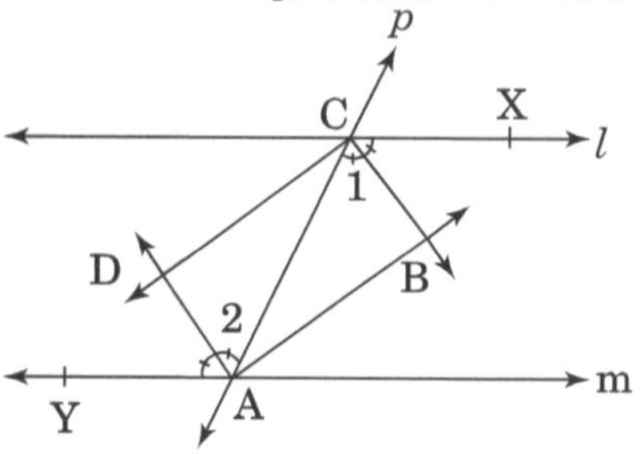

In a parallelogram PQRS of the given figure, the bisectors of $\angle P$ and $\angle Q$ meet SR at O. Show that $\angle POQ = 90°$. **[Board Term II, 2015]**

Sol. Given: A parallelogram PQRS in which the bisectors of $\angle P$ and $\angle Q$ meet SR at O.

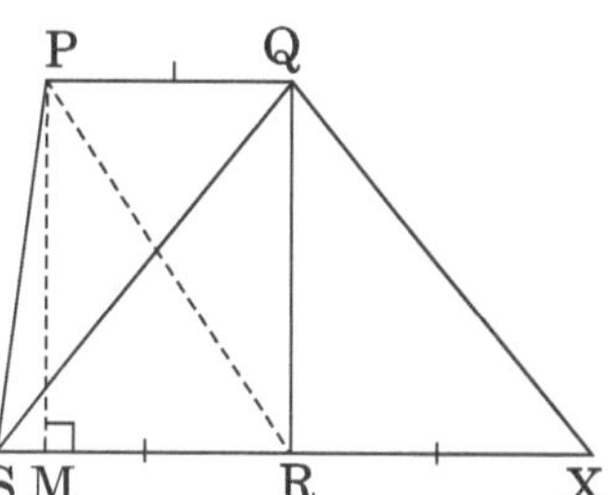

To Prove : $\angle POQ = 90°$

Proof : Now, since PQRS is a parallelogram,

$\therefore$ $\qquad$ $PS \parallel QR$

Now, PS $\parallel$ QR and transversal PQ intersects them.

$\therefore$ $\qquad$ $\angle P + \angle Q = 180°$

($\because$ sum of consecutive interior angles is supplementary)

$\therefore$ $\qquad$ $\frac{1}{2}\angle P + \frac{1}{2}\angle Q = 90°$

$\angle 1 + \angle 2 = 90°$ $\qquad$ ...(i)

($\because$ OP is bisector of $\angle P$ and OQ is bisector of $\angle Q$)

$\left(\because \angle 1 = \frac{1}{2}\angle P \text{ and } \angle 2 = \frac{1}{2}\angle Q\right)$

Now, in ΔPOQ

$\angle 1 + \angle POQ + \angle 2 = 180°$ [Angle sum property]

$\Rightarrow$ $\qquad$ $90° + \angle POQ = 180°$

$\therefore$ $\qquad$ $\angle POQ = 180° - 90° = 90°$

Hence Proved.

7. PQRS is a trapezium with PQ $\parallel$ SR. Side SR is produced to X such that RX = PQ. Prove that ar(ΔPSQ) = ar(ΔQRX).

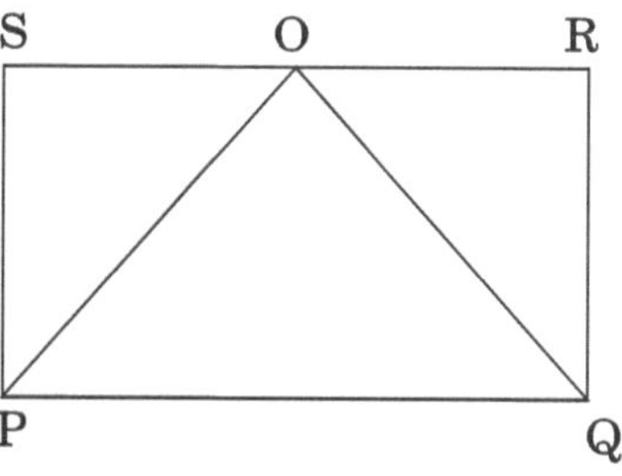

[Board Term II, 2017, Set-Z6K408K]

Sol. Given: PQRS is a trapezium with PQ $\parallel$ SR.

Draw PM $\perp$ SR

$$\text{ar}(\Delta PSQ) = \frac{1}{2}\times b \times h = \frac{1}{2}\times PQ \times PM \qquad ...(i)$$

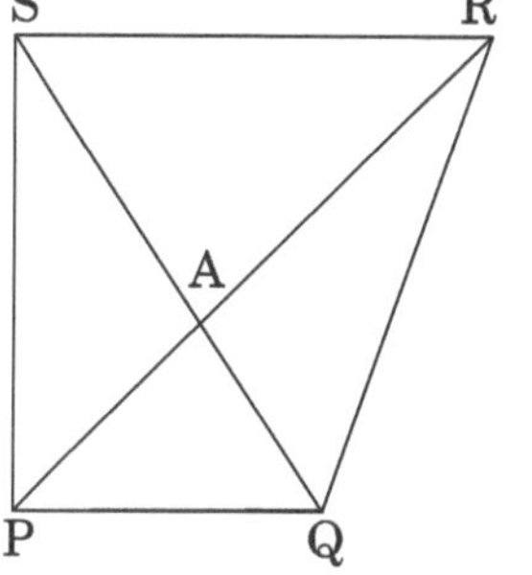

Also, $\qquad$ $\text{ar}(\Delta QRX) = \frac{1}{2}\times PM \times RX$

But $\qquad$ $PQ = RX$ $\qquad$ (given)

$\therefore$ $\qquad$ $\text{ar}(\Delta QRX) = \frac{1}{2}\times PM \times PQ$ $\qquad$ ...(ii)

Using (i) and (ii), we get

$$\text{ar}(\Delta PSQ) = \text{ar}(\Delta QRX)$$

8. Diagonals PR and QS of quadrilateral PQRS intersect each other at A. Show that

$$\text{ar}(\Delta PSA) \times \text{ar}(\Delta QAR) = \text{ar}(\Delta PAQ) \times \text{ar}(\Delta SAR)$$

[Board Term II, 2017, Set-UAM4DQ7]

Sol. Given, Diagonals PR and QS of quadrilateral PQRS intersect each other at A.

To Prove: $ar(\Delta PSA) \times ar(\Delta QAR)$
$$= ar(\Delta PAQ) \times ar(\Delta SAR)$$

Draw PM $\perp$ QS ad RN $\perp$ QS

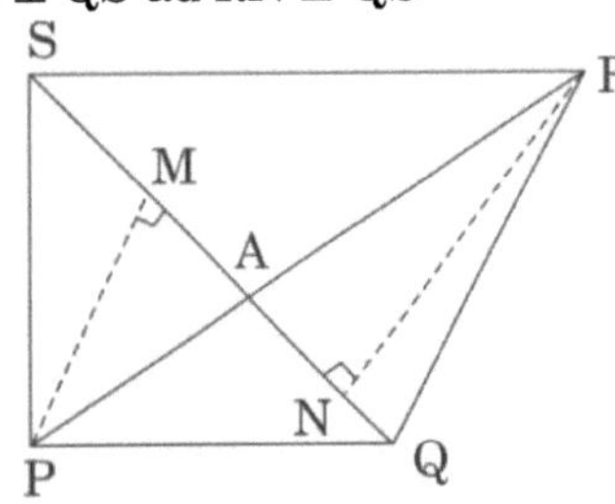

$ar(\Delta PSA) \times ar(\Delta QAR)$

$$= \left(\frac{1}{2} \times AS \times PM\right) \times \left(\frac{1}{2} \times AQ \times RN\right)$$

$$= \left(\frac{1}{2} \times RN \times AS\right) \times \left(\frac{1}{2} \times PM \times AQ\right)$$

$$= ar(\Delta SAR) \times ar(\Delta PAQ)$$
$$= ar(\Delta PAQ) \times ar(\Delta SAR)$$

Long Answer Type Questions

(4 Marks Each)

1. In the given figure, ABC is an isosceles triangle in which AB = AC, AD

   bisects the exterior angle PAC and CD ∥ AB. Show that :

   (i) $\angle DAC = \angle BCA$, and

   (ii) ABCD is a parallelogram.

   [Board Term II, 2012, Set (24)][NCERT]

Sol.

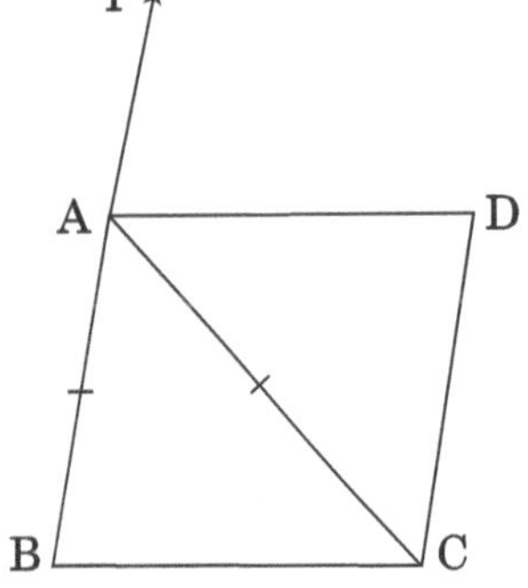

∵ ΔABC is an isosceles triangle

and $\qquad\qquad$ AB = AC

∴ $\qquad\qquad \angle ABC = \angle BCA$

$\qquad$ [Angles opposite to equal sides are equal]

and $\qquad \angle PAC = \angle ABC + \angle BCA$

⇒ $\qquad \angle PAC = 2\angle BCA \qquad$ ...(i)

∵ AD bisects $\angle PAC$ or, $\angle PAC = 2\angle DAC \qquad$ ...(ii)

From (i) and (ii), $\angle BCA = \angle DAC$

These are alternative angles when lines BC and AD are intersected by AC

or, $\qquad\qquad$ BC ∥ AD,

Also, $\qquad\qquad$ BA ∥ CD $\qquad\qquad$ (Given)

Hence, ABCD is a parallelogram.

2. Show that the bisectors of angles of a parallelogram enclose a rectangle.

   [Board Term II, 2012, Set-(8)]

   OR

   Show that the bisectors of angles of a parallelogram from a rectangle $\qquad$ [NCERT]

Sol. Let ABCD is a parallelogram.

To show LMNO is a rectangle,

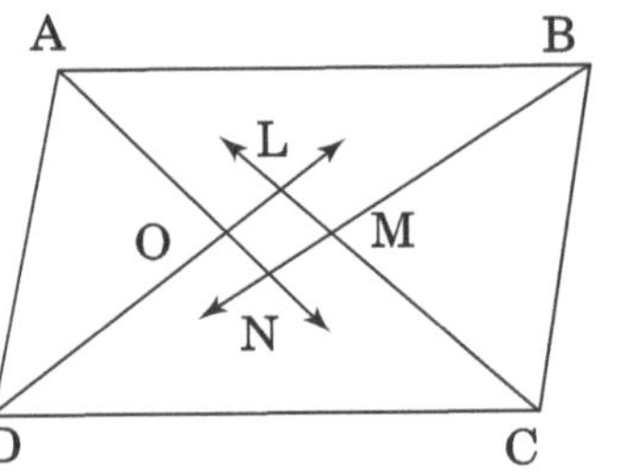

$\qquad\qquad \angle A + \angle D = 180° \qquad$ [Adjacent angles]

On dividing by 2, we get

$$\Rightarrow \frac{1}{2}\angle A + \frac{1}{2}\angle D = 90° = 90°$$

$\Rightarrow \angle OAD + \angle ODA = 90° \qquad\qquad$ ...(i)

In ΔAOD,

$\angle OAD + \angle ODA + \angle DOA = 180°$

$\qquad\qquad$ [Angle sum property]

⇒ $\qquad 90° + \angle DOA = 180°$

⇒ $\qquad\qquad \angle DOA = 180° - 90° = 90°$

Now, $\qquad \angle DOA = \angle LON = 90°$

$\qquad\qquad$ [Vertically opposite angles]

Similarly, $\quad \angle OLM = \angle LMN = \angle MNO = 90°$

Hence, A quadrilateral with all angles 90° is a rectangle. Also opposite angles are equal. It is rectangle.

3. In figure, PQRS is a parallelogram, PO and QO are respectively the angle bisectors to $\angle P$ and $\angle Q$. Line LOM is drawn parallel to PQ. Prove that (i) PL = QM, (ii) LO = OM

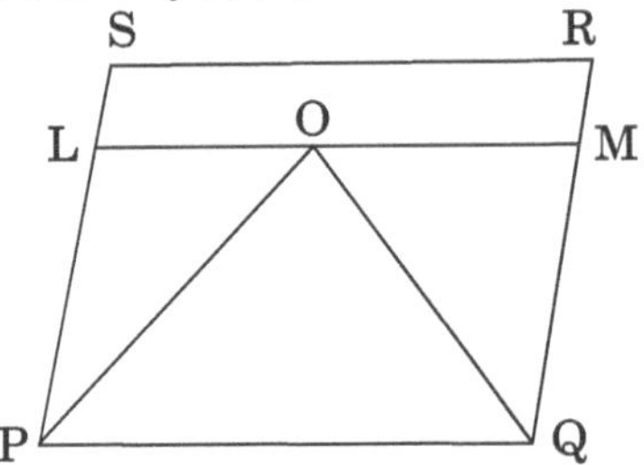

Sol. Given : a parallelogram PQRS, in which PO and QO are angle bisectors of $\angle P$ and $\angle Q$. A line LOM is drawn parallel to PQ.

To prove : (i) PL = QM (ii) LO = OM

Proof : (i) Since PQRS is a parallelogram.

$\Rightarrow$ PS $\parallel$ QR

$\Rightarrow$ PL $\parallel$ QM   ...(i)

[$\because$ opposite sides of a parallelogram are parallel]

Also,   LOM $\parallel$ PQ   ...(ii)

From eqs. (i) and (ii), we get

$\therefore$ PQML is a parallelogram.

$\therefore$ PL = QM   ...(iii)

(ii) Now $\angle 1 = \angle 2$

[$\because$ OP is the bisector of $\angle P$ (given)]

and $\angle 1 = \angle 3$

[alternate interior angles]

$\Rightarrow$ $\angle 2 = \angle 3$

$\Rightarrow$ PL = LO   ...(iv)

[opposite sides of equal angles of a triangle]

Similarly,   QM = OM   ...(v)

From eqs, (iii), (iv) and (v), we have

LO = OM

Hence, (i) PL = QM (ii) LO = OM

4. In parallelogram ABCD, two points P and Q are taken on diagonal BD such that DP = BQ (see the figure).

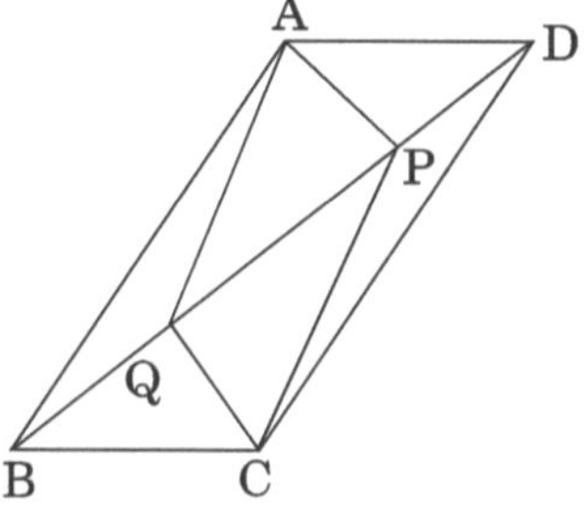

Show that

(i) $\triangle APD \cong \triangle CQB$

(ii) AP = CQ

(iii) $\triangle AQB \cong \triangle CPD$

(iv) AQ = CP

(v) APCQ is a parallelogram.

Sol. Given, ABCD is a parallelogram and P and Q are points on BD such thats

DP = BQ   ...(i)

(i) Now, in $\triangle APD$ and $\triangle CQB$

DP = BQ   [given]

AD = BC

[opposite sides are equal in parallelogram so alternate interior and angles are equal]

$\angle ADP = \angle CBQ$

[$\because$ AD $\parallel$ BC and BD is a transversal]

$\therefore$ $\triangle APD \cong \triangle CQB$ ...(i)

[By SAS congruence rule]

(ii) Since, $\triangle APD \cong \triangle CQB$ [from eq^n (i)]

$\Rightarrow$ AP = CQ   [by CPCT]

(iii) Now, in $\triangle AQB$ and $\triangle CPD$

BQ = DP   [given]

AB = CD

[opposite sides of parallelogram]

$\angle ABQ = \angle CDP$

[$\because$ AB $\parallel$ CD and BD is a transversal, so alternate interior angles]

Hence, $\triangle AQB \cong \triangle CPD$

[by SAS congruence rule]

(iv) Since,

$\triangle AQB \cong \triangle CPD$

$\therefore$ AQ = CP   [by CPCT]

(v) Now, in $\triangle APQ$ and $\triangle CQP$, we have

AQ = CP   [from part (iv)]

AP = CQ   [from part (ii)]

and   PQ = QP   [common]

By SSS congruence rule, we get

$\therefore$ $\triangle APQ \cong \triangle CQP$

Then, $\angle APQ = \angle CQP$ [by CPCT]

and $\angle AQP = \angle CPQ$ [by CPCT]

Now, these equal angles form a pair of alternate angles, when line segments AP and QC are intersected by a transversal PQ.

$\therefore$ AP $\parallel$ QC and AQ $\parallel$ PC

Now, both pairs of opposite sides of quadrilateral APCQ are parallel and equal.

Hence, APCQ is a parallelogram.

[Topic 3] Mid-point Theorem

Points to be Remembered:

- **Mid-point Theorem:** The line segment joining the mid-points of any two sides of a triangle is parallel to the third side and equal to half of it.

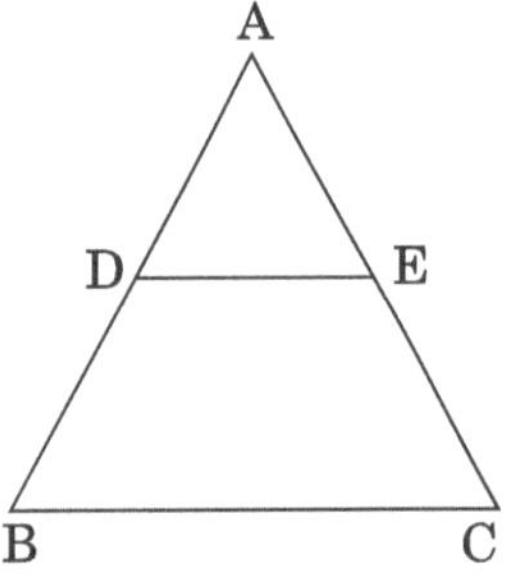

Here, DE $= \dfrac{1}{2}$BC and DE $\parallel$ BC

- **Converse of mid-point theorem:** A line through the mid-point of a side of a triangle parallel to another side bisects the third side.

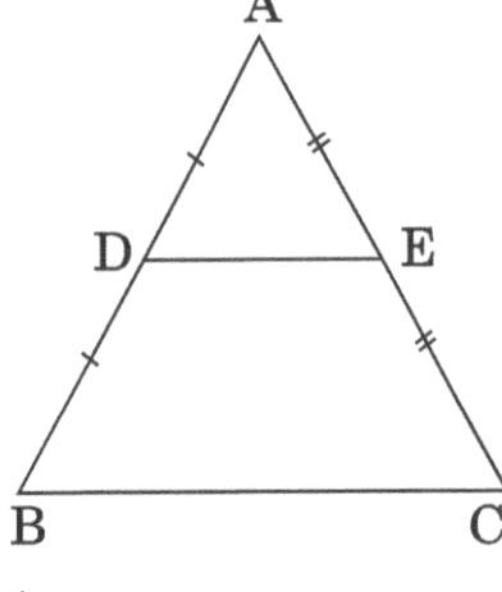

Here, D is the mid-point of AB and E is the mid-point of AC.

PREVIOUS YEARS'
EXAMINATION QUESTIONS
TOPIC 3

Multiple Choice Questions
(1 Mark Each)

1. D and E are the mid-points of the sides AB and AC, respectively of ABC, DE is produced to F. To prove that CF is equal and parallel to DA, we need additional information which is
   - (a) $\angle$DAE = $\angle$EFC
   - (b) AE = EF
   - (c) DE = EF
   - (d) $\angle$ADE = $\angle$ECF.   [NCERT Exemp.]

Sol. (c) To prove that CF is equal and parallel to DA. We need DE = EF.

2. The figure formed by joining the mid-points of the sides of a quadrilateral ABCD, taken in order, is a square only if,
   - (a) ABCD is a rhombus.
   - (b) diagonals of ABCD are equal.
   - (c) diagonals of ABCD are equal and perpendicular.
   - (d) diagonals of ABCD are perpendicular.   [NCERT Exemp.]

Sol. (c) The quadrilateral ABCD is a square, if diagonals of ABCD are equal and perpendicular.

3. The figure obtained by joining the mid-points of the sides of a rhombus, taken in order, is
   - (a) a rhombus.
   - (b) a rectangle.
   - (c) a square.
   - (d) any parallelogram.   [NCERT Exemp.]

Sol. (b) The figure obtained by joining the mid-points of the sides of a rhombus is a rectangle.

4. The quadrilateral formed by joining the midpoints of the sides of a quadrilateral PQRS, taken in order, is a rhombus, if
   - (a) PQRS is a rhombus.
   - (b) PQRS is a parallelogram.
   - (c) diagonals of PQRS are perpendicular
   - (d) diagonals of PQRS are equal.   [NCERT Exemp.]

Sol. (d) The quadrilateral PQRS is a rhombus, if the diagonals of PQRS are equal.

5. The quadrilateral formed by joining the midpoints of the sides of a quadrilateral PQRS, taken in order is a rectangle, if ?
   - (a) PQRS is a rectangle.
   - (b) PQRS is a parallelogram.
   - (c) diagonals of PQRS are perpendicular.
   - (d) diagonals of PQRS are equal.   [NCERT Exemp.]

Sol. (c) The quadrilateral PQRS is a rectangle, if the diagonals of PQRS should be perpendicular to each other.

6. The diagonals AC and BD of a parallelogram ABCD intersect each other at the point O. If $\angle$DAC = 32° and $\angle$AOB = 70°, then $\angle$DBC is equal to
   - (a) 24°
   - (b) 86°
   - (c) 38°
   - (d) 32°   [NCERT Exemp.]

Sol. (c) According to the question,

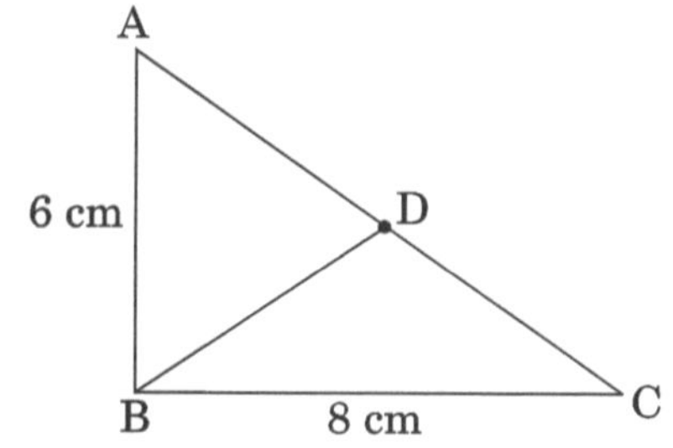

∵ AD is a parallel to BC and AC cuts them,
∴   ∠DAC = ∠ACB   [Alternate interior angle]
⇒   ∠DAC = 32°

In triangle BOC, CO is produced to A
Therefore,

∠BOA = ∠OCB + ∠OBC   [Exterior angle is the sum of two opposite interior angles]
⇒ $70° = 32° + ∠OBC$
∴ $∠OBC = 70° - 32° = 38°$
Hence,   ∠DBC = ∠OBC = 38°.

7. D and E are the midpoints of the sides AB and AC of triangle ABC and O is any point on side BC. O is joined to A. If P and Q are the midpoints of OB and OC, respectively, then DEQP is
(a) a square.   (b) a rectangle.
(c) a rhombus.   (d) a parallelogram.

[NCERT Exemp.]

Sol. (d) According to the question, the line segment joining the midpoints of any two sides of a triangle is parallel to the third side and is half of it, so, DE ∥ BC
Similarly,   DP ∥ AO
And   EQ ∥ AO
And   DP ∥ EQ

[DP ∥ AO and EQ ∥ AO]

Now, DEQP is quadrilateral in which one pair of its opposite sides is equal and parallel.
Therefore, quadrilateral DEQP is a parallelogram.

8. A triangle ABC, right angled at B. Side AB = 6 cm and side BC = 8 cm. D is midpoint of AC. Then length of BD is :
(a) 10 cm   (b) 4 cm
(c) 3 cm   (d) 5 cm

Sol. (d) According to the question,

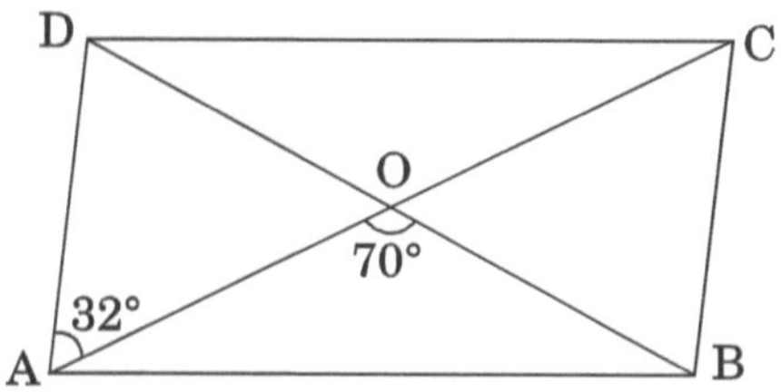

∴ $AC = \sqrt{AB^2 + BC^2}$

$= \sqrt{(6)^2 + (8)^2}$

$= \sqrt{36 + 64}$

$= \sqrt{100} = 10cm$

∴ $BD^2 = AD \times DC$

$= 5 \times 5 = 25$

Hence, $BD = \sqrt{25} = 5cm$

9. Given an equilateral triangle ABC, D, E and F are the midpoints of AB, BC and AC respectively, then the quadrilateral BEFD is exactly a
(a) square   (b) rectangle
(c) parallelogram   (d) rhombus

Sol. (d) According to the question,

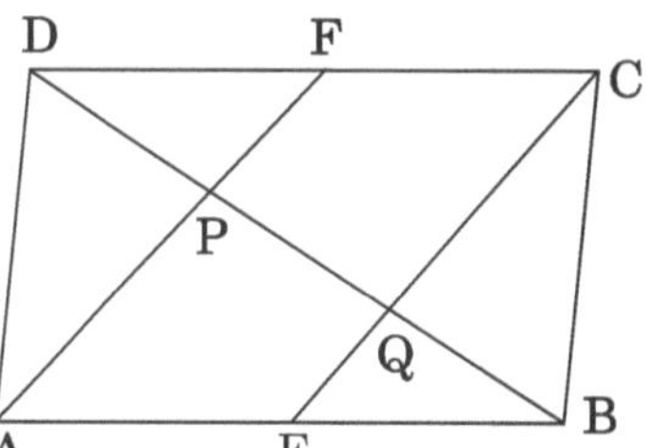

∴ $BE = EF = DF = BD$

Hence, quadrilateral BEFD is exactly a rhombus.

10. In a parallelogram ABCD, E and F are the midpoints of sides AB and CD respectively. AF and CE meet the diagonal BD of length 12 cm at P and Q. Then length of PQ is :
(a) 6 cm   (b) 4 cm
(c) 3 cm   (d) 5 cm

Sol. (d) According to the question,

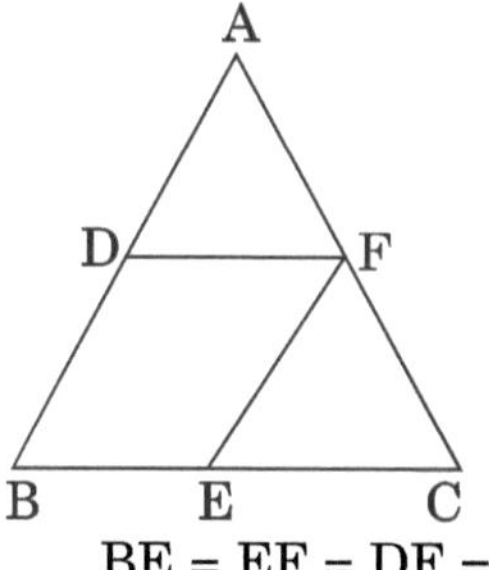

We know that all three segments

DP = PQ = BQ

∴ $PQ = \dfrac{12}{3} = 4cm$.

Very Short Answer Type Questions
(1 Mark Each)

1. D, E, F are the mid-points of sides BC, CA and AB of $\triangle$ABC. If perimeter of $\triangle$ABC is 12.8 cm, then perimeter of $\triangle$DEF is: ....?

[Board Term II Set A1, 2011]

Sol. $\because$ Points D, E and F are the mid-points of sides BC, CA and AB.

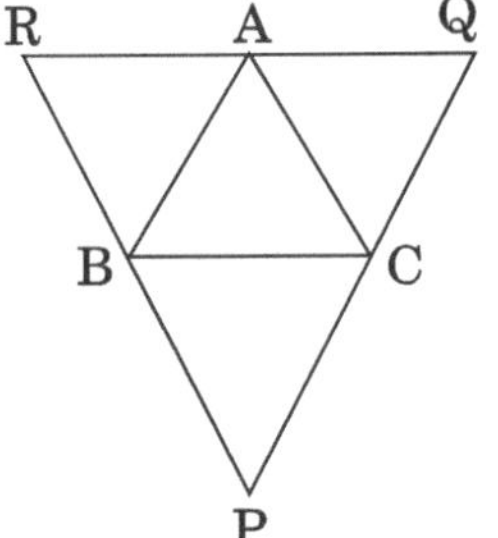

Given, perimeter of $\triangle$ABC = 12.8 cm

Hence, perimeter of $\triangle$DEF = $\dfrac{12.8}{2}$ = 6.4cm.

2. In an equilateral triangle ABC, D and E are the mid-points of sides AB and AC respectively, then length of DE is ....

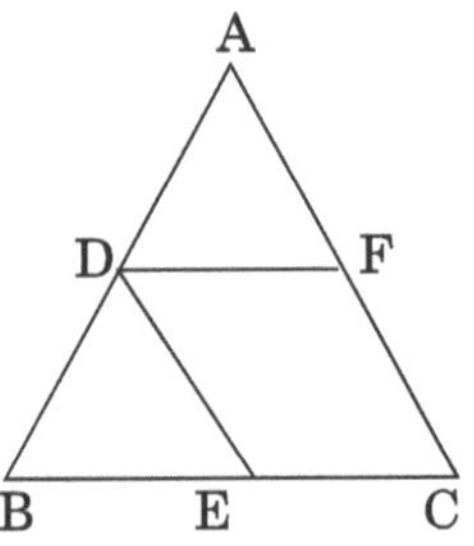

[Board Term II Set A1, 2011, NCERT]

Sol. Given, D and E are mid-points of sides AB and AC respectively,

By mid-point theorem,

Hence, DE = $\dfrac{1}{2}$BC.

3. In the given figure, p $\parallel$ q $\parallel$ r, l and m are two transversals, such that AB = 2.8 cm, BC − 4.2 cm, EF = 6 cm, then find the value of DE.

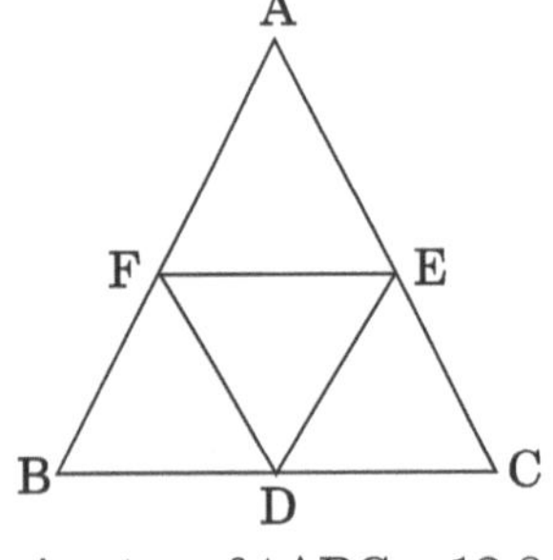

Sol. Given, p $\parallel$ q $\parallel$ r and l, m are two transversals

$\therefore$ $\qquad \dfrac{AB}{BC} = \dfrac{DE}{EF}$

$\Rightarrow \qquad \dfrac{2.8}{4.2} = \dfrac{DE}{6}$

$\therefore \qquad DE = \dfrac{28 \times 6}{42} = 4cm$

Hence, the value of DE is 4 cm.

4. In $\triangle$ABC, D, E and F are the mid-points of the sides AB, BC and AC, respectively. Then, prove that quadrilateral DECF is a parallelogram.

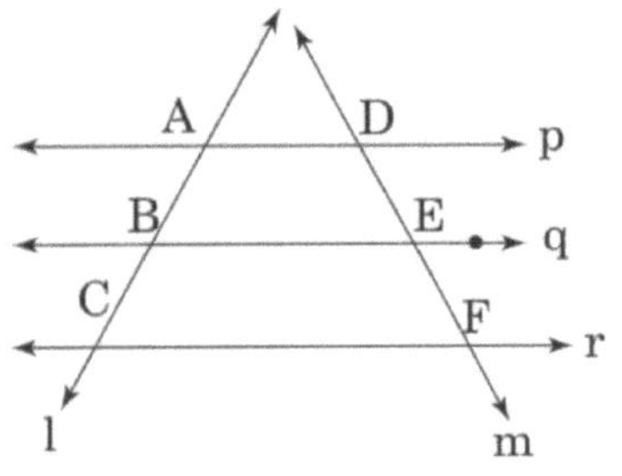

Sol. **Given :** In $\triangle$ABC, D and F are the mid-points of the sides AB and AC, respectively.

To prove : Quadrilateral DECF is a parallelogram.

Proof: By mid-point theorem,

$\qquad$ DF $\parallel$ BC $\qquad\qquad\qquad$ ...(i)

$\Rightarrow \qquad$ DF $\parallel$ EC $\qquad\qquad\qquad$ ...(ii)

and $\qquad$ DF = $\dfrac{1}{2}$BC

$\Rightarrow \qquad$ DF = EC $\qquad$ [$\because$ E is mid-point of BC]

From eqs. (i) and (ii), we have

$\qquad\qquad$ DF $\parallel$ EC

and $\qquad\qquad$ DF = EC

Since, a pair of opposite sides of a quadrilateral DECF are equal and parallel.

Hence, DECF is a parallelogram.

Short Answer Type Questions-I
(1 Mark Each)

1. Through A, B and C, lines RQ, PR and QP has been drawn respectively parallel to sides BC, CA and AB of a $\triangle$ABC as shown in figure. Show that BC = $\dfrac{1}{2}$QR.

[NCERT Exemplar]

Sol. Given PQ || AB and PR || AC and RQ || BC.

To prove : $BC = \dfrac{1}{2}QR$

Proof : In quadrilateral BCAR,

BR || CA and BC || RA

So, BCAR is a parallelogram.

$\therefore$ $\qquad\qquad$ BC = RA $\qquad\qquad$ ...(i)

Now, in quadrilateral BCQA

$\therefore$ $\qquad\qquad$ BC || AQ

and $\qquad\qquad$ AB || QC

So, BCQA is a parallelogram.

$\therefore$ $\qquad\qquad$ BC = AQ $\qquad\qquad$ ...(ii)

On adding eqs. (i) and (ii), we get

$\qquad\qquad$ 2BC = AR + AQ

$\Rightarrow$ $\qquad\qquad$ 2BC = RQ

$\therefore$ $\qquad\qquad$ $BC = \dfrac{1}{2}QR$

$\qquad\qquad\qquad\qquad$ Hence proved.

2. In $\triangle$ABD, AB = 5 cm, BC = 8 cm and CA = 7 cm. If D and E are respectively the mid-point of AB and BC, determine the length of DE.

$\qquad\qquad\qquad\qquad$ [NCERT Exemplar]

Sol. According to the question,

In $\triangle$ABC, we have AB = 5 cm, BC = 8 cm and CA = 7 cm. Since, D and E are the mid-points of AB and BC, respectively.

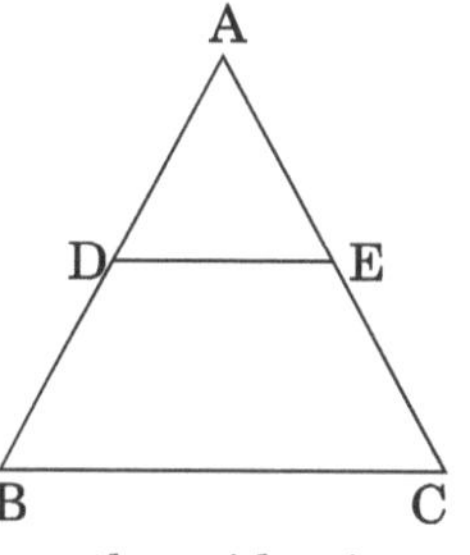

By mid-point theorem.

$\qquad\qquad$ DE || AC

and $\qquad\qquad$ $DE = \dfrac{1}{2}AC = \dfrac{7}{2} = 3.5cm$

Hence, the length of DE is 3.5 cm.

3. $\triangle$ABC is an isosceles triangle in which AB = AC. D and E are the mid-points of sides AB and AC and DE = 3.5 cm. Find the perimeter of $\triangle$ABC, when AD = 4.5 cm.

Sol. According to the question,

$\qquad$ $\triangle$ABC in which AB = AC

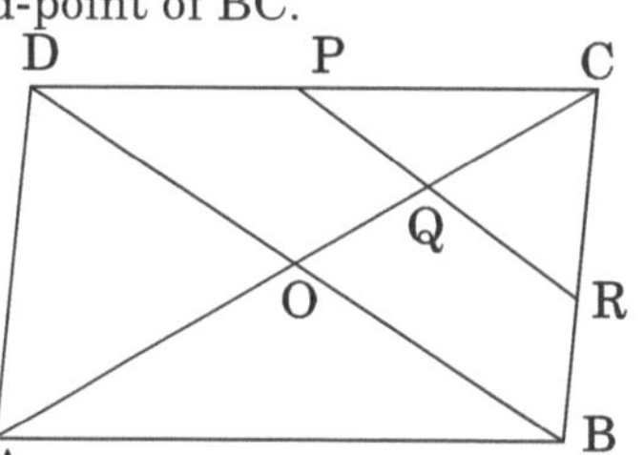

$\because$ D and E are the mid-points of AB and AC.

$\qquad\qquad$ AD = DB = 4.5 cm

Then, $\qquad\qquad$ AB = 2 × 4.5 = 9 cm

So, $\qquad\qquad$ AB = AC = 9 cm $\qquad$ [Given]

Since, D and E are the mid-points of AB and AC respectively.

By mid-point theorem, we have

$\qquad\qquad$ DE || BC

and $\qquad\qquad$ $DE = \dfrac{1}{2}BC$

Then, $\qquad\qquad$ BC = 2DE = 2 × 3.5 = 7 cm

$\qquad\qquad\qquad\qquad$ [DE = 3.5 cm, given]

Now, perimeter of $\triangle$ABC

$\qquad\qquad$ = AB + BC + CA

$\qquad\qquad$ = 9 + 7 + 9 = 25 cm

Hence, the perimeter of $\triangle$ABC is 25 cm.

4. In the adjoining figure, ABCD is a parallelogram in which P is the mid-point of DC and Q is a point on AC, such that $CQ = \dfrac{1}{4}AC$. Also, PQ when produced meets BC at R. Prove that R is the mid-point of BC.

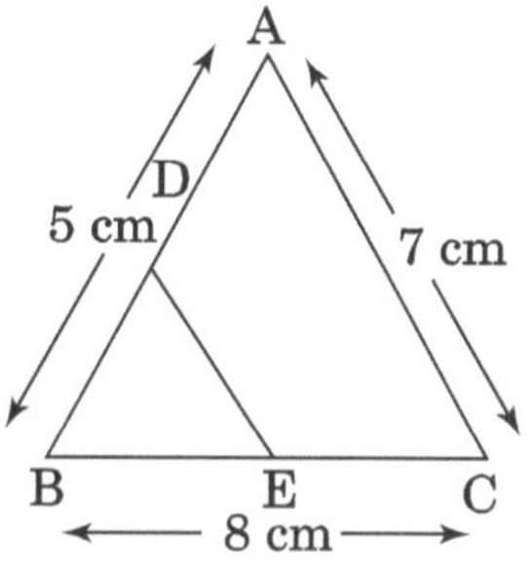

Sol. Given, a parallelogram ABCD, AO = OC

$\qquad$ [$\because$ diagonals of a parallelogram bisect each other]

$\qquad\qquad$ AC = AO + OC $\Rightarrow$ AC = OC + OC

$\qquad\qquad$ = 2OC

and $\qquad\qquad$ $CQ = \dfrac{1}{4}AC = \dfrac{1}{4}\times(2OC) = \dfrac{1}{2}OC$

Thus, Q is the mid-point of OC.

Now, ion $\triangle$CDO, P and Q are the mid-points of CD and CO, respectively.

$\therefore$ PQ || DO and therefore, QR || OB

$\qquad\qquad\qquad\qquad$ [by mid-point theorem]

$\qquad\qquad$ [$\because$ PQ || DO $\Rightarrow$ PQR || DOB]

Now, in $\triangle COB$, Q is the mid-point of CO and QR $\parallel$ OB.   [by converse of mid-point]

Hence, R must be the mid-point of BC.

5. D and E are the mid-points of sides AB and AC respectively of triangle ABC. If the perimeter of $\triangle ABC = 35$ cm, find the perimeter of $\triangle ADE$.

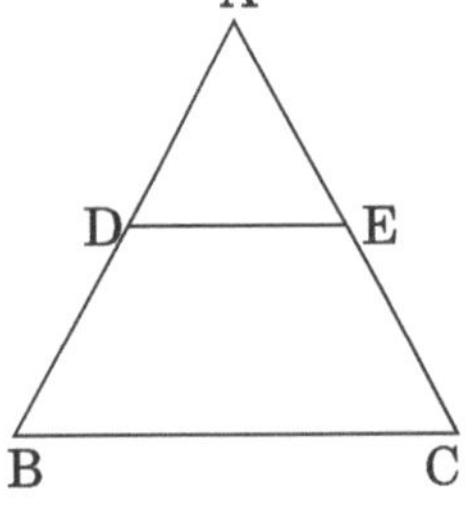

Sol. According to the question, D and E are the mid-point of sides AB and AC respectively.

$$\therefore \qquad AD = \frac{1}{2}AB \text{ and } AE = \frac{1}{2}AC$$

By mid-point theorem, $DE = \frac{1}{2}BC$

$$\therefore AD + AE + DE = \frac{1}{2}(AB + AC + BC)$$

$$\Rightarrow \text{Perimeter of } \triangle ADE = \frac{1}{2} \times \text{perimeter of } \triangle ABC$$

$$= \frac{1}{2} \times 35 cm = 17.5 cm$$

Hence, the perimeter of $\triangle ADE$ is 17.5 cm.

Short Answer Type Questions-II
(1 Mark Each)

1. Prove that the line joining mid-points of the diagonals of a trapezium is parallel to the parallel sides of the trapezium..
                                                    [NCERT Exemplar]

Sol. Given : ABCD is a trapezium in which AB $\parallel$ DC and M and N are the mid-points of the diagonals AC and BD, respectively.

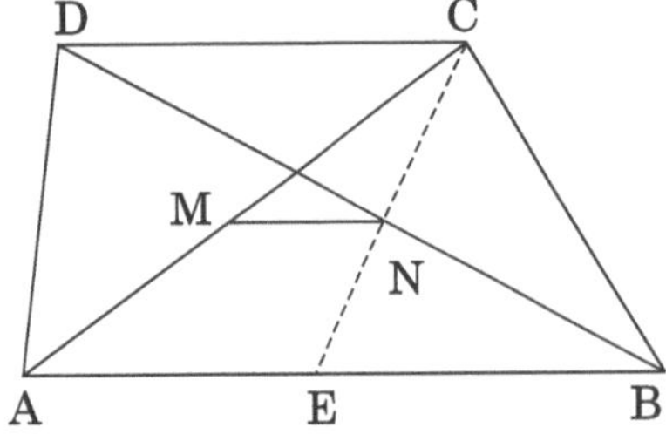

To prove : MN $\parallel$ AB $\parallel$ CD

Construction : Join CN and produce it to meet AB at E.

Proof : In $\triangle CDN$ and $\triangle EBN$, we have

$$DN = BN$$
                    [$\because$ N is mid-point of BD]

$$\angle DCN = \angle BEN$$
                    [alternate interior angles]

and $\qquad \angle CDN = \angle EBN$
                    [alternate interior angles]

By AAS congruence rule, we get

$\therefore \qquad\qquad \triangle CDN \cong \triangle EBN$

So, $\qquad\qquad DC = BE$ and $CN = NE$
                    [by CPCT]

$\therefore$ N is the mid-point of CE.

Thus, in $\triangle CAE$, the points M and N are the mid-points of AC and CE, respectively.

$\therefore \qquad\qquad$ MN $\parallel$ AE [by mid-point theorem]

$\Rightarrow \qquad\qquad$ MN $\parallel$ AB $\parallel$ CD

                                        Hence proved.

2. In given figure, ABCD is a parallelogram P, Q are the mid-points of AB and DC. Show that :
    (i) APCQ is a parallelogram.
    (ii) DPBQ is a parallelogram.
    (iii) PSQR is a parallelogram.

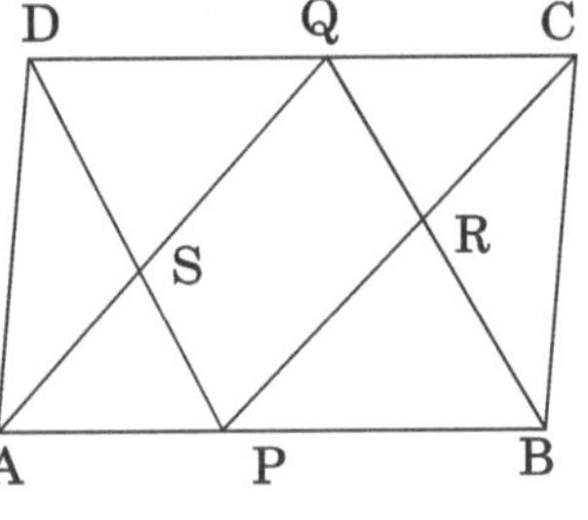

                                                    [NCERT]

Sol. Given: ABCD is a parallelogram and P, Q are the mid-points of AB and DC.

(i) Since, ABCD is a parallelogram

$$AB = CD \text{ and } AB \parallel CD$$

On dividing by 2, we get

$\Rightarrow \qquad\qquad \frac{1}{2}AB = \frac{1}{2}CD$

$\therefore \qquad\qquad AP = CQ$ and $AP \parallel CQ$

Hence, APCQ is a parallelogram.

(ii) Again,

$$\frac{1}{2}AB = \frac{1}{2}CD$$

                    [$\because$ P and Q are the mid-points]

$\therefore \qquad\qquad PB = DQ$ and $PB \parallel DQ$

Hence, DPBQ is a parallelogram

(iii) $\because$ QS $\parallel$ PR and SP $\parallel$ QR

Hence, PSQR is a parallelogram.   Proved.

3. E and F are respectively the mid-points of non-parallel sides AD and BC of a trapezium ABCD.

   Prove that EF ∥ AB and $EF = \frac{1}{2}(AB + CD)$.

   [NCERT Exemplar]

Sol. Given : E and F are respectively the mid-points of non-parallel sides AD and BC of trapezium ABCD.

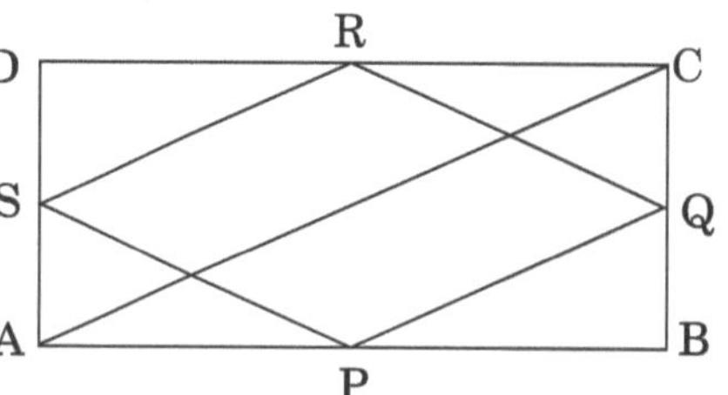

To prove : EF ∥ AB

and $\qquad EF = \frac{1}{2}(AB + CD)$

Construction : Join CE and produce it to meet BA at P.

Proof : In ΔDEC and ΔAEP, we have

$$\angle DEC = \angle AEP$$

[vertically opposite angles]

$$\angle DCE = \angle APE$$

[∵ DC ∥ PB and PC is transversal, so alternate angles are equal]

and $\qquad DE = AE$

[∵ E is the mid-point of AD]

By AAS congruence rule, we get

∴ $\qquad \Delta DEC \cong \Delta AEP$

then, $\qquad CE = PE \qquad$ [by CPCT]

and $\qquad CD = PA \qquad$ [by CPCT]

Now, in ΔCPB, E is the mid-point of CP.

[since, CE = PE]

and F is the mid-point of BC. [given]

Now, by mid-point theorem

$$EF \parallel PB \text{ and } EF = \frac{1}{2}PB$$

⇒ $\qquad EF \parallel AB \text{ and } EF = \frac{1}{2}(PA + AB)$

$$= \frac{1}{2}(CD + AB) \quad [\because PA = CD]$$

Hence, $EF \parallel AB$ and $EF = \frac{1}{2}(AB + CD)$

4. ABC is a triangle right-angled at C. A line through the mid point M of hypotenuse AB and parallel to BC intersect AC at D. Show that:
   (i) D is the mid-point of AC
   (ii) MD ⊥ AC.

   [Board Term II, Set A1, 2010,11 NCERT]

Sol.

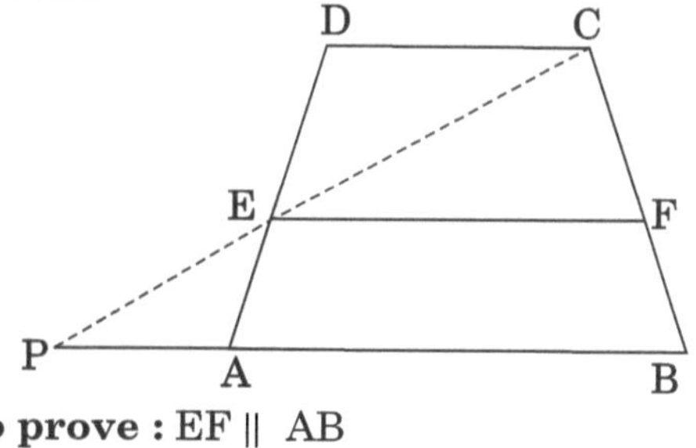

We know that, if a line is draw parallel to one side of a triangle through the mid-point of the second side, then it bisects the third side.

Now, according to the question,

∴ D is the mid-point of AC.

Since, $\qquad$ MD ∥ BC

∴ $\qquad \angle ADM = \angle ACB$

(Corresponding angles)

$$= 90°$$

[∵ ΔACB is right angled triangle at C]

Hence, $\qquad$ MD ⊥ AC.

5. Prove that the quadrilateral formed by joining the mid-points of the consecutive sides of a rectangle is a rhombus..

   [Board Term II, 2012, Set-10]

OR

ABCD is a rectangle and P,Q,R and S are mid point of the sides AB, BC, CD and DA respectively Show that the quadrilateral PQRS in rhombus.

[NCERT]

Sol. Given, ABCD is a rectangle and P, Q, R and S are the mid-points of side AB, BC, CD and DA respectively,

Now, In ΔABC, P and Q are mid points of AB and BC respectively

∴ $\qquad PQ = \frac{1}{2} AC \text{ and } PQ \parallel AC \quad$ ...(i)

[By mid-point theorem]

Similarly, $\qquad RS = \frac{1}{2} AC \text{ and } RS \parallel AC \quad$ ...(ii)

∴ PQRS is a parallelogram

Also $\qquad$ AD = BC or, AS = BQ

In ΔAPS and ΔBPQ,

$$AP = BP, AS = BQ$$

and $\qquad \angle A = \angle B = 90°$

By SAS congruence rule, we get

$\therefore$ $\quad\quad\quad\quad\quad \triangle APS \cong \triangle BPQ$

or, $\quad\quad\quad\quad\quad PS = PQ \quad\quad\quad$ (c.p.c.t)...(iii)

From eq^n (i) and (iii), PQRS is a parallelogram with PQ = PS

Hence, PQRS is a rhombus. $\quad\quad$ Hence proved.

6. ABC is an equilateral triangle and L, M and N are the mid-points of the sides AB, BC and CA, respectively. prove that $\triangle$LMN is an equilateral triangle.

[NCERT] [Board Term II, 2012, Set-30]

Sol. Given : $\triangle$ABC is an equilateral triangle and L, M, N are the mid-points of the sides AB, BC and CA respectively.

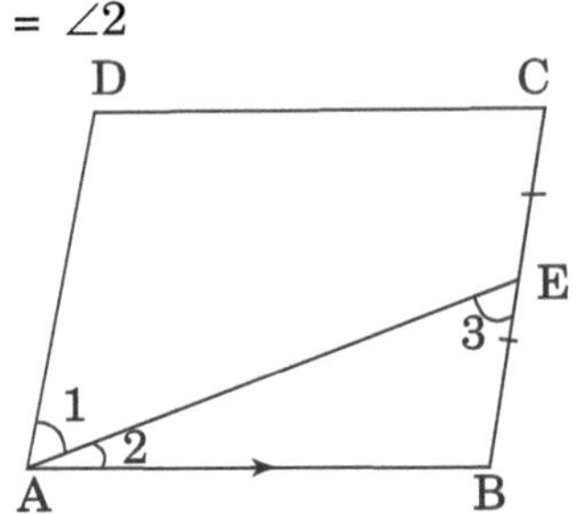

To Prove : $\triangle$LMN is an equilateral triangle.

Proof : Since, L and N are the mid-points of AB and AC, respectively.

$\therefore$ $\quad\quad\quad\quad LN = \dfrac{1}{2}BC$

[by mid-point theorem]

Similarly, $\quad LM = \dfrac{1}{2}AC$ and $MN = \dfrac{1}{2}AB$

Now, $\triangle$ABC is an equilateral triangle.

$\therefore$ $\quad\quad\quad\quad AB = BC = CA$

On dividing by 2, we get

$\Rightarrow$ $\quad\quad\quad \dfrac{1}{2}AB = \dfrac{1}{2}BC = \dfrac{1}{2}CA$

$\therefore$ $\quad\quad\quad\quad MN = LN = LM$

Hence, $\triangle$LMN is an equilateral triangle.

7. ABCD is a quadrilateral in which P, Q, R and S are the mid-points of the sides AB, BC, CD and DA respectively. Show that PQRS is a parallelogram.

[NCERT][Board Term II, 2012, Set-30]

Sol. Given ABCD is a quadrilateral and P, Q, R and S are the mid-points of side AB, BC, CD and DA respectively.

Now, Join diagonal AC,

In $\triangle$ADC,

S is the mid-point of AD.

and R is the mid-point of DC.

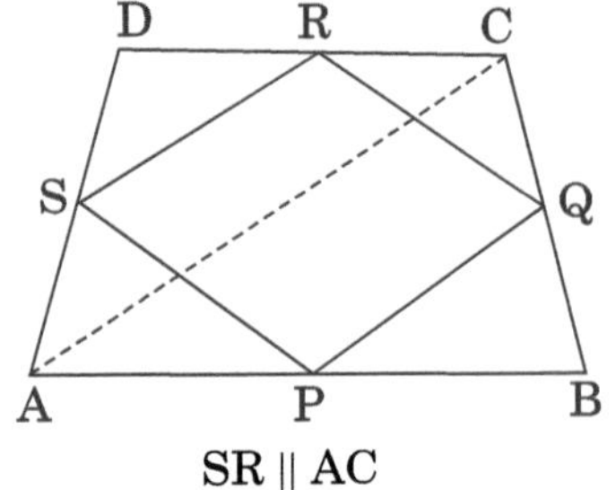

$\therefore$ $\quad\quad\quad\quad SR \parallel AC$

and $\quad\quad\quad\quad SR = \dfrac{1}{2}AC$ $\quad\quad\quad$ ...(i)

(By mid-point theorem)

Similarly in $\triangle$BAC,

$\quad\quad\quad\quad PQ \parallel AC$

and $\quad\quad\quad\quad PQ = \dfrac{1}{2}AC$ $\quad\quad\quad$ ...(ii)

From (i) and (ii),

$\quad\quad\quad\quad SR \parallel PQ$

and $\quad\quad\quad\quad SR = PQ$

Hence, PQRS is a parallelogram.

8. ABCD is a parallelogram. If E is mid-point of BC and AE is the bisector of $\angle$A, prove that $AB = \dfrac{1}{2}AD$.

[Board Term II, 2012, Set-12]

Sol. Given,

$\quad\quad\quad\quad \angle 1 = \angle 2$

(AE is the angle bisector)

But $\quad \angle 1 = \angle 3$ $\quad$ (alternate angles as AD $\parallel$ BC)

$\Rightarrow$ $\quad \angle 3 = \angle 2$

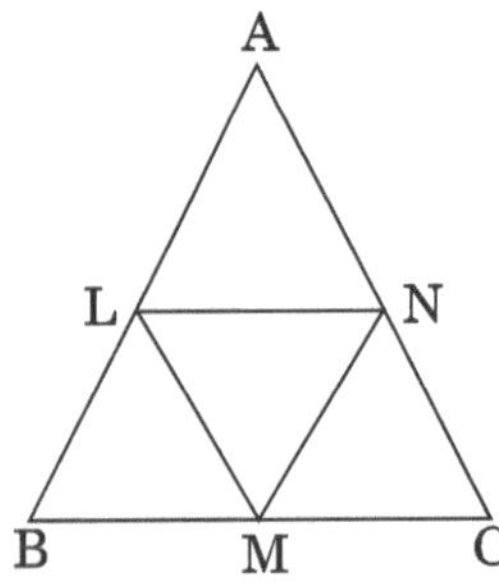

Therefore, $\quad\quad BE = AB$

(sides opposite to equal angles are equal)

But $\quad\quad\quad\quad BE = \dfrac{1}{2}BC$, (E is the mid-point of BC)

$\therefore$ $\quad\quad\quad\quad AB = \dfrac{1}{2}BC$ $\quad\quad\quad$ ...(i)

and $\quad\quad\quad\quad BC = AD$ $\quad\quad\quad$ ...(ii)

(opposite sides of a parallelogram)

from eq^n (i) and (ii), we get

$\therefore$ $\quad\quad\quad\quad AB = \dfrac{1}{2}AD$.

Hence proved.

9. In the figure, ABCD is a parallelogram and E is the mid-point of side BC. DE and AB on producing meet at F. Prove that AF = 2AB.

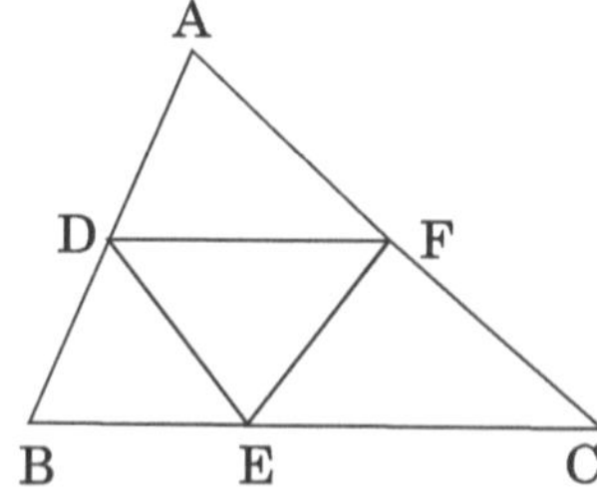

[Board Term II, 2012, Set-6]

Sol. Given, CE = BE

In $\triangle$DCE and $\triangle$FBE,

$\angle$DCE = $\angle$FBE

(alternate interior angles)

CE = BE   (given)

and $\angle$DEC = $\angle$BEF

(Vertically opposite angle)

By ASA congruence rule, we get

$\triangle$DCE $\cong$ $\triangle$FBE

$\therefore$ DC = FB   (c.p.c.t)

AF = AB + BF = AB + AB = 2AB

Hence proved.

10. In ABC, D, E and F are the mid-points of sides AB, BC and CA. If AB = 6 cm, BC = 7.2 cm and AC = 7.8 cm, find the perimeter of $\triangle$DEF.

[Board Term II, 2012, (20)]

Sol. According to the question, AB = 6 cm, BC = 7.2 cm and AC = 7.8 cm.

Now, by mid-point theorem,

$$DE = \frac{1}{2}AC$$

$$EF = \frac{1}{2}AB$$

and $$DF = \frac{1}{2}BC$$

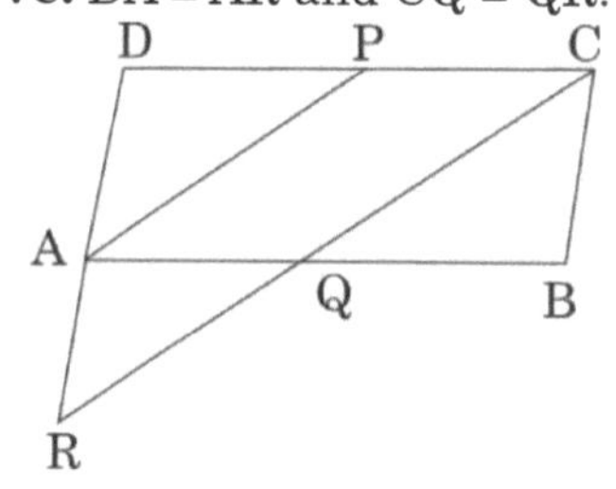

Hence, Perimeter of DEF = DE + EF + DF

$$= \frac{1}{2}(AC + AB + BC)$$

$$= \frac{1}{2}(7.8 + 6 + 7.2) = \frac{21}{2}$$

$$= 10.5 \text{ cm.}$$

Long Answer Type Questions
(4 Marks Each)

1. P is the mid-point of the side CD of a parallelogram ABCD. A line through C parallel to PA intersects AB at Q and DA produced at R. Prove that DA = AR and CQ = QR.

[NCERT Exemplar]

Sol. **Given:** ABCD is a parallelogram in which P is the mid-point of side CD.

To prove: DA = AR and CQ = QR.

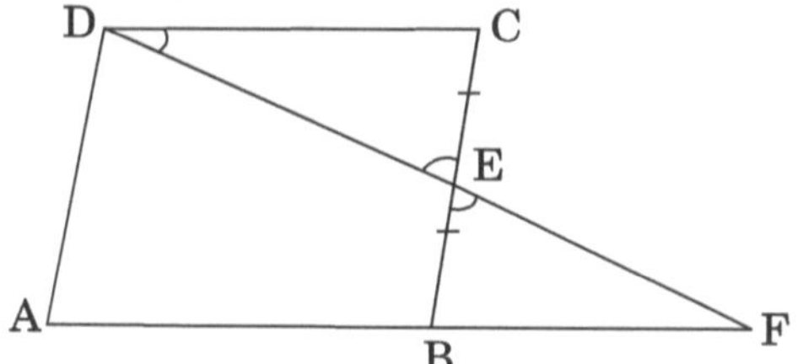

(i) In $\triangle$DRC

P is the mid-point of DC and PA $\parallel$ CR   [given]

$\therefore$ A is the mid-point of DR

[by converse of mid-point theorem]

Hence, DA = AR

(ii) Since, ABCD is a parallelogram

$\Rightarrow$ AB $\parallel$ DC

$\Rightarrow$ AQ $\parallel$ DC

In $\triangle$DRC, A is the mid-point of DR and

AQ $\parallel$ DC

$\therefore$ Q is the mid-point of RC.

[by converse of mid-point theorem]

CQ = QR   Hence proved.

2. ABC is a triangle. D is a point on AB such that $AD = \frac{1}{4}AB$ and E is a point on AC such that $AE = \frac{1}{4}AC$. Prove that $DE = \frac{1}{4}BC$.

[NCERT Exemplar]

Sol. **Given :** In $\triangle$ABC, $AD = \frac{1}{4}AB$ and $AE = \frac{1}{4}AC$

To prove : $DE = \frac{1}{4}BC$

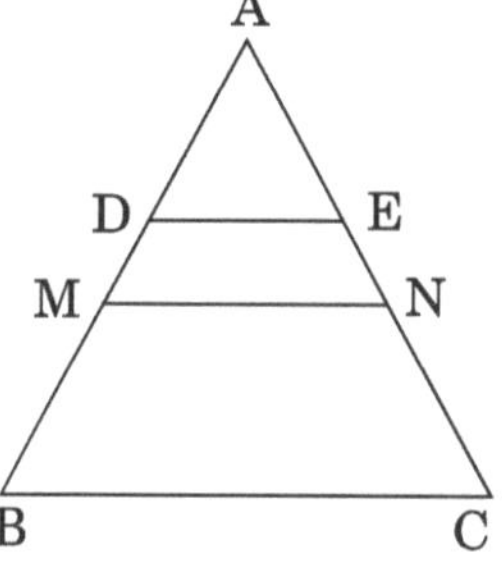

Proof : Let M and N be the mid-points of sides AB and AC, respectively.

By mid-point theorem,

$$MN \parallel BC$$

and $\qquad MN = \dfrac{1}{2}BC \qquad\qquad$ ...(i)

We have, $\qquad AM = \dfrac{1}{2}AB$

$$[\because \text{M is mid-point of AB}]$$

$\Rightarrow \qquad \dfrac{1}{2}AM = \dfrac{1}{4}AB$

$\Rightarrow \qquad \dfrac{1}{2}AM = AD \qquad [\because AD = \dfrac{1}{4}AB\,]$

So, D is mid-point of AM.

Similarly, $AN = \dfrac{1}{2}AC \quad [\because \text{N is mid-point of AC}]$

$\Rightarrow \qquad \dfrac{1}{2}AN = \dfrac{1}{4}AC$

$\Rightarrow \qquad \dfrac{1}{2}AN = AE \qquad [\because AE = \dfrac{1}{4}AC\,]$

Therefore, E is mid-point of AN.

In $\triangle$AMN, D and E are the mid-points of AM and AN, respectively.

By mid-point theorem.

$$DE \parallel MN \text{ and } DE = \dfrac{1}{2}MN$$

$\Rightarrow \qquad DE = \dfrac{1}{2}\left(\dfrac{1}{2}BC\right) \qquad [\text{using eq. (i)}]$

$\therefore \qquad DE = \dfrac{1}{4}BC$

Hence proved.

3. Show that the quadrilateral formed by joining the mid-points of the consecutive sides of a square is also a square. **[NCERT Exemplar]**

Sol. Given: ABCD is a quadrilateral and P, Q, R and S are the mid-points of the sides AB, BC, CD and DA, respectively.

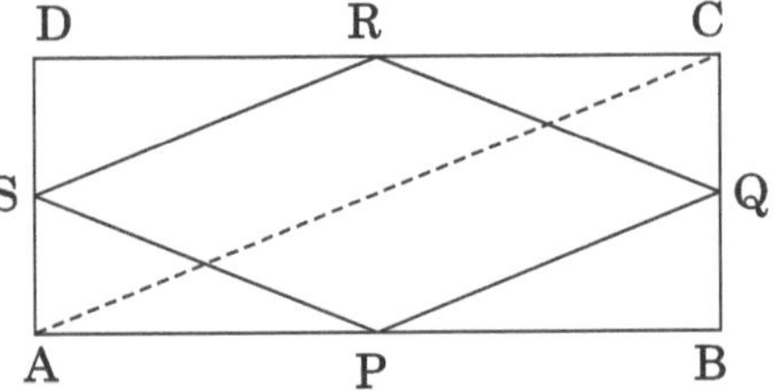

$$AC = BD \text{ and } AC \perp BD$$

To prove : PQRS is a square.

Proof : Now, in $\triangle$ADC, S and R are mid-point of AD and CD respectively, by mid-point theorem.

$$SR \parallel AC \text{ and } SR = \dfrac{1}{2}AC \quad ...(i)$$

In $\triangle$ABC, P and Q are mid-points of AB ad BC respectively, by mid-points theorem.

$$PQ \parallel AC \text{ and } PQ = \dfrac{1}{2}AC \quad ...(ii)$$

From eqs. (i) and (ii), we get

$$PQ \parallel SR \text{ and } PQ = SR = \dfrac{1}{2}AC \qquad ...(iii)$$

Now, in $\triangle$ABD, P and S are mid-points of AB and AD respectively, by mid-point theorem.

$$PS \parallel BD \text{ and } PS = \dfrac{1}{2}BD = \dfrac{1}{2}AC \qquad ...(iv)$$

$$[\because BD = AC, \text{ given}]$$

In $\triangle$BCD, S and R are the mid-points of BC and CD respectively, by mid-point theorem,

$$QR \parallel BD$$

and $\qquad QR = \dfrac{1}{2}BD = \dfrac{1}{2}AC \qquad ...(v)$

From eqs. (iv) and (v), we get

$$PS \parallel QR \text{ and } PS = QR = \dfrac{1}{2}AC \qquad ...(vi)$$

Now, from eqs. (iii) and (vi), we get

$$PQ = SR = PS = QR$$

Thus, PQRS is a rhombus.

Now, in quadrilateral OERF,

OE $\parallel$ FR and OF $\parallel$ ER

So, OERF is a parallelogram.

$\therefore \qquad\qquad \angle ERF = \angle EOF = 90° \ [\because AC \perp BD]$

[opposite angles of a parallelogram are equal]

$\therefore \qquad\qquad \angle QRS = 90°$

Hence, PQRS is a square.

4. ABCD is rectangle and P, Q, R and S are the mid-points of the sides AB, BC, CD and DA respectively. Show that the quadrilateral PQRS is a rhombus.

[NCERT Exemplar][Board Term II, 2012, Set(10)]

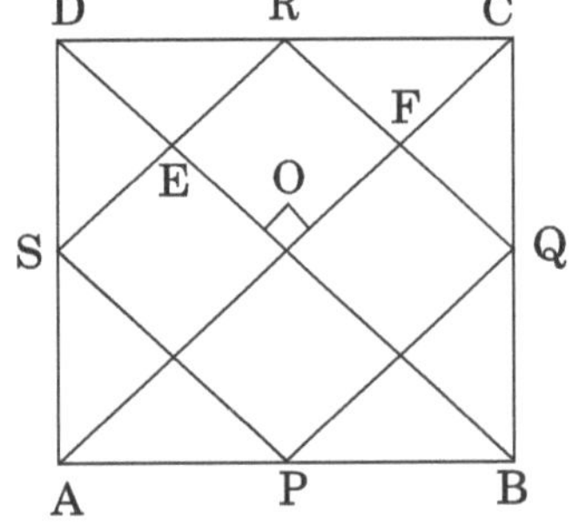

Sol. Given, In a rectangle ABCD, P is the mid-point of AB, Q is the mid-point of BC, R is the mid-point of CD, S is the mid-point of DA, AC is the diagonal.

Now, in $\triangle ABC$,

$$PQ = \frac{1}{2}AC \text{ and } PQ \parallel AC$$

[by mid-point theorem]

Similarly, in $\triangle ACD$,

$$SR = \frac{1}{2}AC \text{ and } SR \parallel AC \quad ...(ii)$$

From eqs, (i) and (ii), we get

$$PQ = SR \text{ and } PQ \parallel SR$$

Similarly, by joining BD, we get

$$PS = QR \text{ and } PS \parallel QR$$

i.e., Both pairs of opposite sides of quadrilateral PQRS are equal and parallel.

Therefore, PQRS is a parallelogram.

Now, in $\triangle PAS$ and $\triangle PBQ$,

$$\angle A = \angle B = 90°$$

$$AP = BP = \frac{1}{2}AB$$

and $\qquad\qquad AS = BQ$

$$\left[\text{each} = \frac{1}{2} \text{ of opposite sides of a rectangle}\right]$$

By SAS congruence rule, we get

$\therefore \qquad\qquad \triangle PAS \cong \triangle PBQ$

$\Rightarrow \qquad\qquad PS = PQ \qquad$ [by CPCT]

Also $\qquad\qquad PS = QR \qquad$ [proved]

and $\qquad\qquad PQ = SR \qquad$ [proved]

$\therefore \qquad\qquad PQ = QR = RS = SP$

$\therefore$ PQRS is a parallelogram having all of its sides equal.

Hence, PQRS is a rhombus.

5. ABCD is a rhombus and P, Q, R and S are the mid-points of AB, BC, CD and DA respectively. prove that the quadrilateral PQRS is a rectangle.

[Board Term II, 2012, Set-01, NCERT]

Sol. Given : ABCD is a rhombus and P, Q, R and S are the mid-points of AB, BC, CD and DA respectively.

To prove: PQRS is a rectangle

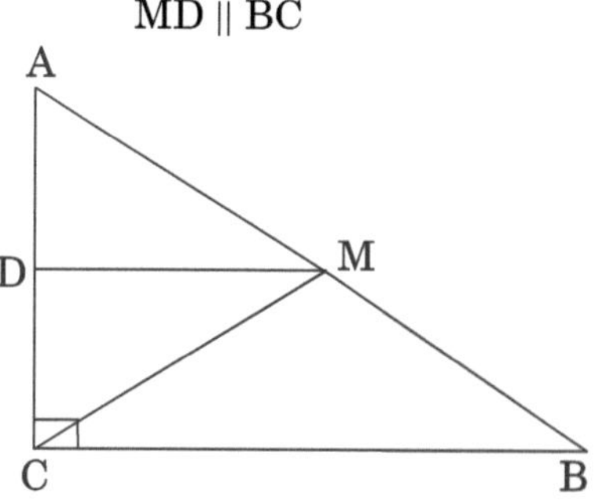

Construction: Join AC and BD.

Proof : In $\triangle DAC$, S and R are the mid-points of AD and DC.

$\therefore \qquad\qquad SR = \frac{1}{2} AC \text{ and } SR \parallel AC \quad ...(i)$

Also, In $\triangle BAC$, P and Q are the mid-points of AB and BC.

$\therefore \qquad\qquad PQ = \frac{1}{2} AC \text{ and } PQ \parallel AC \quad ...(ii)$

From eqⁿ (i) and (ii), we get PQRS is a parallelogram.

From eqⁿ (i), we get SM $\parallel$ NO $\qquad\qquad$ ...(iii)

and $\qquad\qquad SP \parallel BD$

or, $\qquad\qquad SN \parallel MO \qquad\qquad$ ...(iv)

From, eqⁿ (iii) and (iv), we get MSNO, is a parallelogram.

Since, ABCD is a rhombus, so

$$\angle DOA = 90°$$

and $\qquad\qquad \angle MSN = 90°$

Hence, PQRS is a rectangle.

6. ABC is a triangle right angled at C. A line through the mid-point M of hypotenuse AB and parallel to BC intersects AC at D.

Show that

(i) D is the mid-point of AC

(ii) MD $\perp$ AC

(iii) $CM = MA = \frac{1}{2}AB$

[NCERT][Board Term II, 2012, Set-69]

Sol. Given : ABC is a right angled triangle, in which $\angle C = 90°$ and M is the mid-point of AB.

Also, a line through the mid-point M of hypotenuse AB and parallel to BC intersects AC at D such that

$$MD \parallel BC$$

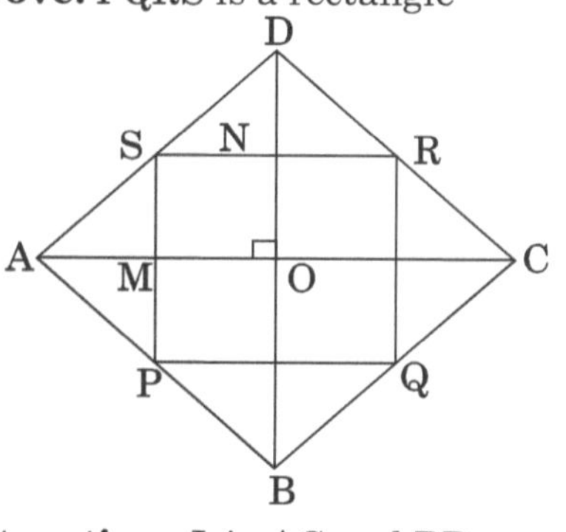

To prove:

(i) D is the mid-point of AC.

(ii) MD $\perp$ AC

(iii) $CM = MA = \frac{1}{2}AB$

Proof:

(i) In $\triangle ABC$, BC $\parallel$ MD and M is mid-point of AB.

Hence, D is the mid-point of AC.

[by converse of mid-point theorem]

(ii) Given, MD $\parallel$ BC and CD is a transversal.

$\therefore \qquad\qquad \angle ADM = \angle ACB$

[corresponding angles]

But $\qquad \angle ACB = 90°$ $\qquad$ [given]

$\therefore \qquad \angle ADM = 90°$

Hence, $\qquad MD \perp AC$

(iii) Now, in $\triangle ADM$ and $\triangle CDM$, we have

$\qquad DM = MD$ $\qquad$ [common]

$\qquad AD = CD$

$\qquad\qquad$ [$\because$ D is the mid-point of AC]

and $\qquad \angle ADM = \angle MDC$ $\qquad$ [each 90°]

By SAS congruence rule, we get

$\therefore \qquad \triangle ADM \cong \triangle CDM$

Then, $\qquad CM = AM$ $\qquad$ [by CPCT]...(i)

Also, given M is the mid-point of AB.

$\therefore \qquad AM = BM = \dfrac{1}{2}AB$ $\qquad$ ...(ii)

From eqs. (i) and (ii), we get

$\therefore \qquad CM = AM = \dfrac{1}{2}AB$

$\qquad\qquad\qquad$ Hence proved.

7. D, E and F are respectively the mid-points of the sides AB, BC and CA of a $\triangle ABC$. Prove that by joining these mid-points D, E and F, the $\triangle ABC$ is divided into four congruent triangles.

[NCERT][Board Term II, 2012, Set-05]

Sol. **Given :** ABC is a triangle and D, E and F are mid-points of sides AB, BC ands CA respectively.

To prove : $\triangle ABC$ is divided into four congruent triangles.

Construction : Join DE, EF and FD.

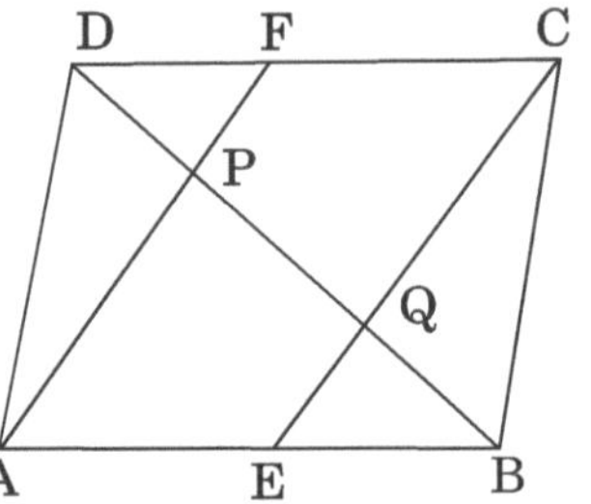

Proof Given, D, E, and F arc thc mid-points of sides AB, BC and CA respectively.

Then, $\qquad AD = BD = \dfrac{1}{2}AB$

$\qquad BE = EC = \dfrac{1}{2}BC$ and

$\qquad AF= CF = \dfrac{1}{2}AC$

Now, by mid-point theorem,

$\qquad EF \parallel BA$ and

$\qquad EF = \dfrac{1}{2}AB = AD = BD$

$\Rightarrow \qquad EF \parallel DA$ and $EF = DA$

$\therefore$ ADEF is a parallelogram.

$\qquad ED \parallel CA$ and

$\qquad ED = \dfrac{1}{2}AC = AF = CF$

$\Rightarrow \qquad ED \parallel CF$ and $ED = CF$

$\therefore$ EDFC is a parallelogram.

and DF $\parallel$ BC and DF $= \dfrac{1}{2}BC = BE = CE$

$\Rightarrow$ DF $\parallel$ BE and DF $=$ BE

$\therefore$ DFEB is a parallelogram.

Now, is $\triangle ADF$ and $\triangle EFD$, AD $=$ EF

[$\because$ opposite sides of a parallelogram are equal]

$\qquad AF = DE$

[$\because$ opposite sides of a parallelogram are equal]

and $\qquad DF = FD$ $\qquad$ [common side]

By SSS congruence rule, we get

$\therefore \qquad \triangle ADF \cong \triangle EFD$

Similarly, $\quad \triangle DEF \cong \triangle DEB$

and $\qquad \triangle DEF \cong \triangle CFE$

Therefore, $\triangle ABC$ is divided into four congruent triangles. $\qquad$ **Hence proved.**

8. In a parallelogram ABCD, E and F are the mid-points of sides AB an CD respectively (see fig.) Show that the line segments AF and EC trisect the diagonal BD.

[Board Term II, 2013; 2012, Set(30)]

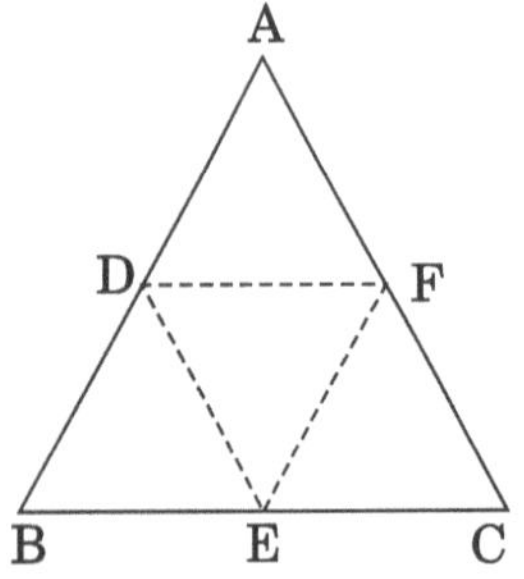

Sol. Given ABCD is a parallelogram and E, F are the mid-points of sides AB and CD, respectively.

To prove Line segments AF and EC trisect the diagonal BD.

Proof Since, ABCD is a parallelogram.

$\therefore \qquad AB \parallel DC$ and $AB = DC$

$\qquad$ [opposite sides of a parallelogram]

$\Rightarrow \qquad AE \parallel FC$ and $\dfrac{1}{2}AB = \dfrac{1}{2}DC$

$\Rightarrow \qquad AE \parallel FC$ and $AE = FC$

[$\because$ E and F are the mid-points of AB and CD]

Since, a pair of opposite sides of a quadrilateral AECF is equal and parallel.

Therefore, AECF is a parallelogram.

Then, $\qquad$ AF || EC

$\Rightarrow$ $\qquad$ AP || EQ and FP || CQ

Since, opposite sides of a parallelogram are parallel.

In ΔBAP, E is the mid-point of AB and EQ || AP, so Q is the mid-point of BP.

[by converse of mid-point theorem]

$\therefore$ $\qquad$ BQ = PQ $\qquad$ ...(i)

Again, in ΔDQC, F is the mid-point of DC and FP || CQ.

Thus, P is the mid-point of DQ.

[by converse of mid-points theorem]

$\therefore$ $\qquad$ QP = DP $\qquad$ ...(ii)

From eqs. (i) and (ii), we get BQ = PQ = PD

Hence, CE and AF trisect the diagonal BD.

Hence proved.

9. ABCD and PQRC are rectangles and Q is the mid-point of AC. Show that P is the mid-point of DC and R is the mid-point of BC. Also, find the ratio of ar(ABCD) and ar(PQRC)

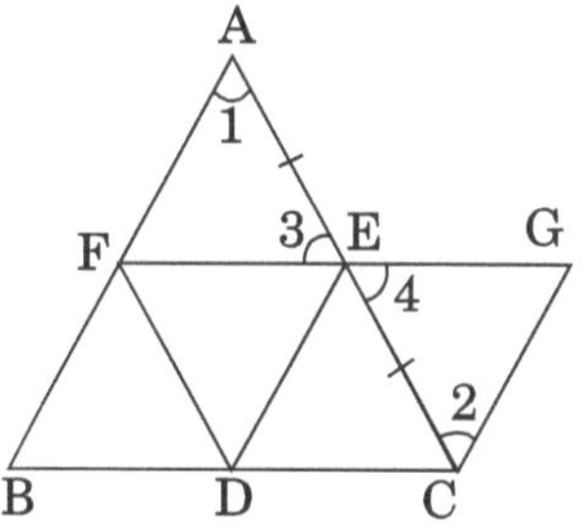

[Board Term II, 2017, Set-UAH4DQ7]

Sol. According to the question, ABCD and PQRC are rectangles

$\therefore$ AD || PQ and QR || AB

Now, in ΔDCA

$\because$ PQ || AD and Q is the mid-point of AC,

[By the converse of mid-point theorem]

$\therefore$ R is the mid-point of BC

$$\text{ar(PQRC)} = PQ \times QR = CR \times PC$$

$$[\because PQ = CR \text{ and } QR = PC]$$

$$= \frac{1}{2}(BC) \times \frac{1}{2}(CD)$$

$$\left[\because CR = \frac{BC}{2} \text{ and } CP = \frac{CD}{2}\right]$$

$$= \frac{1}{4}(BC \times CD) = \frac{1}{4}\text{ar(ABCD)}$$

Hence, required ratio

$$= \frac{\text{ar(ABCD)}}{\text{ar(PQRC)}} = \frac{4}{1} \text{ or } 4 : 1$$

10. In ABC; D, E and F are mid-points of sides BC, AC and AB respectively. A line through C drawn parallel to DE meets FE produced to G. Show that ar(ΔFDE) = ar(ΔEGC).

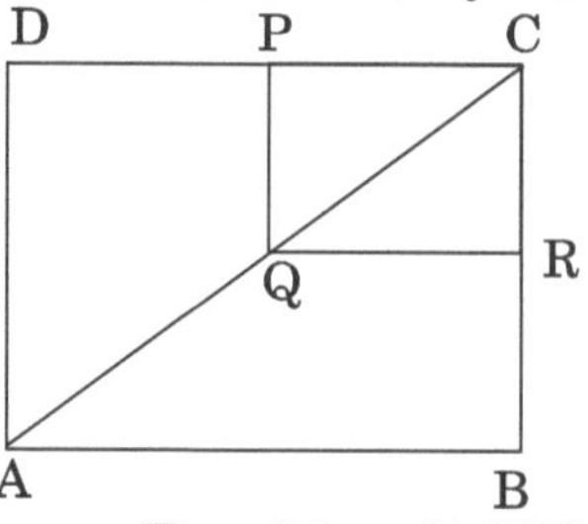

[Board Term II, 2017, Set-UAH4DQ7, Z6K408K]

Sol. Given: In ΔABC, points D, E and F are the mid-points of sides BC, AC and AB, respectively.

$\because$ D and F are mid-points of BC and AB respectively, using mid-point theorem in ΔABC

$$FD \parallel AC \text{ and } FD = \frac{1}{2}AC$$

$\therefore$ $\qquad$ FD = AE and FD || AE

Thus, AFDE is parallelogram

$\therefore$ $\qquad$ ar(ΔFAE) = ar(ΔFDE) $\qquad$ ...(i)

Here, FE is the diagonal of parallelogram AFDE and it divides it into two congruent triangles.

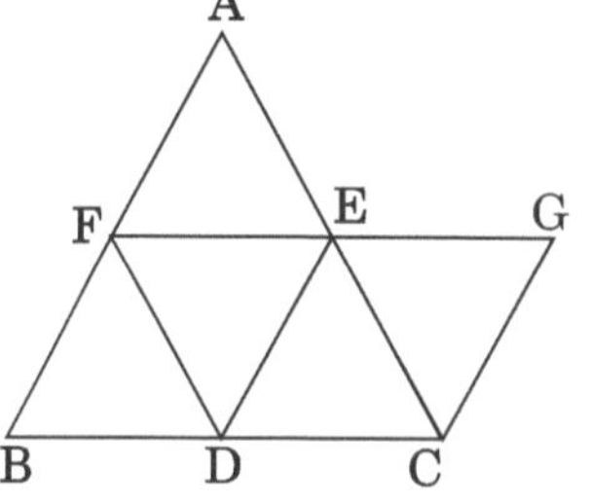

Now, In ΔFAE and ΔGCE

$\qquad$ $\angle 1 = \angle 2$

$\qquad$ (alternate interior angles)

$\qquad$ AE = EC $\qquad$ (given)

and $\qquad$ $\angle 3 = \angle 4$

$\qquad$ (vertically opposite angles)

By ASA congruence rule, we get

$\therefore$ $\qquad$ ΔFAE $\cong$ ΔGCE

so $\qquad$ ar(ΔFAE) = ar(ΔGCE)

i.e., $\qquad$ ar(ΔFAE) = ar(ΔEGC) $\qquad$ ...(ii)

Using (i) and (ii), we have

$\qquad$ ar(FDE) = ar(EGC)

Hence proved.

CHAPTER 9

Area of Parallelograms and Triangles

Review concept of area, recall area of a rectangle.

- (Prove) Parallelogram on the same base and between the same parallels have the equal area.
- (Motivate) Triangles on the same base (or equal base) and between the same parallels are equal in area.

A flow chart on the basic concepts of Areas of parallelogram and triangles

Area of Parallelograms and Triangle

Area of parallelogram is the product of its base and the corresponding altitude.

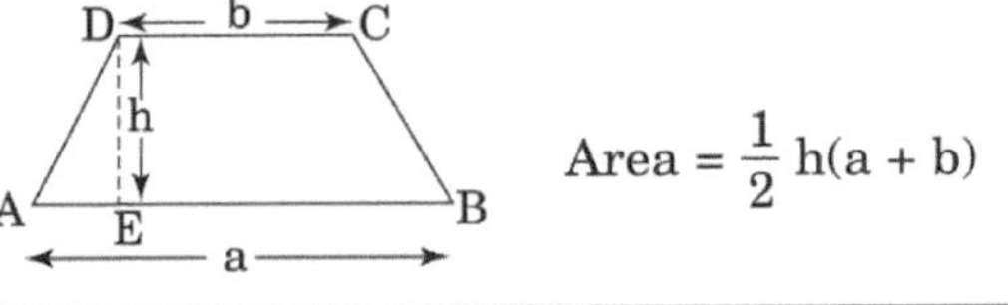

Area of a triangle is half of the product of its base and the corresponding altitude.

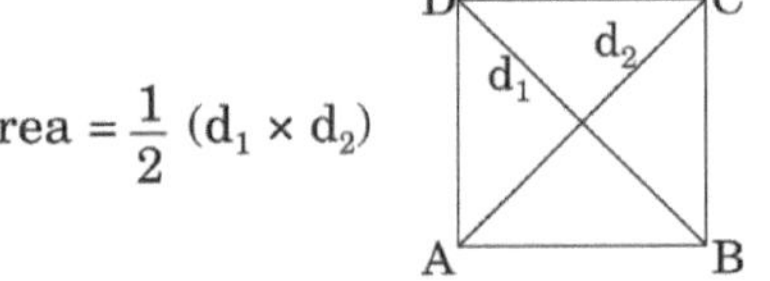

Area of rhombus is half of the product of the length of its diagonals.

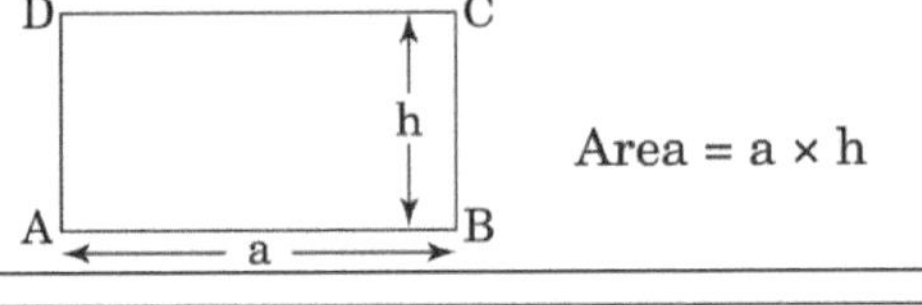

Area of a trapezium is half of the product of the length of its height and the sum of its parallel sides.

Some Important Points

- A diagonal of a parallelogram divides the parallelogram in two triangles of equal area.
- A median of a triangle divides it into two triangle of equal area.
- Diagonals of a parallelogram divide it into four triangles of equal area.
- Parallelograms on the same base and between the same parallel lines are equal in area.
- A parallelogram and a rectangle on the same base and between the same parallels are equal in area.
- Triangles on the same base and between the same parallel are equal in area.
- Triangles on the same base and having equal areas lie between the same parallels.
- Triangles with equal bases and equal areas have equal corresponding altitude

[Topic 1] Area of Parallelograms

Points to be Remembered

- Area of a parallelogram is the product of its base and the corresponding altitude.

  Area of a parallelogram = Base × Corresponding altitude

- Parallelograms on the same base and between the same parallels are equal in areas.

- A diagonal of a parallelogram divides it into two triangles of equal area.

- Parallelograms on the same base and having equal area lies between the same parallels.

PREVIOUS YEARS'
EXAMINATION QUESTIONS
TOPIC 1

Multiple Choice Questions
(1 Mark Each)

1. Two parallelograms are on equal bases and between the same parallels. The ratio of their areas is
   - (a) 1 : 2
   - (b) 1 : 1
   - (c) 2 : 1
   - (d) 3 : 1

   [NCERT Exemplar]

Sol. (b) We know that parallelogram on the same or equal bases and between the same parallels are equal in area.

Hence, the ratio of their area is 1 : 1.

2. In which of the following figures, you find two polygons on the same base and between the same parallels?

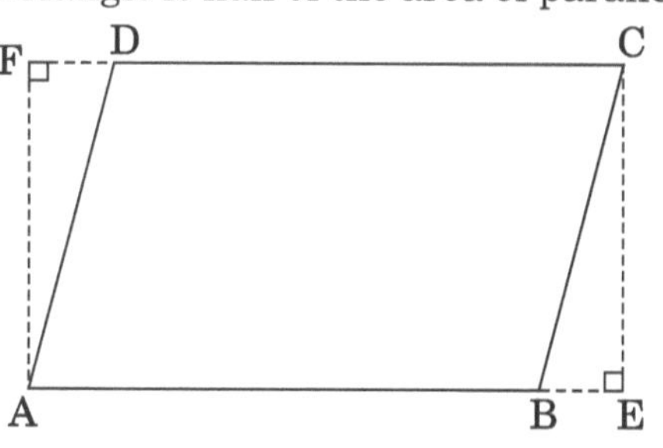

- If a parallelogram and a triangle are on the same base and between the same parallels, then the area of the triangle is half of the area of parallelogram.

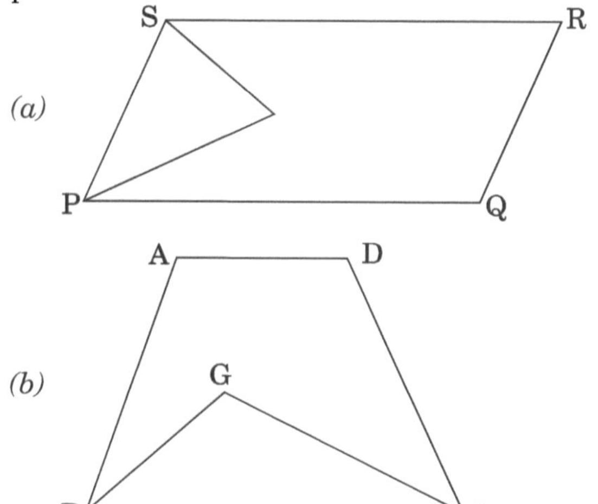

Here, *ABCD* is a parallelogram.

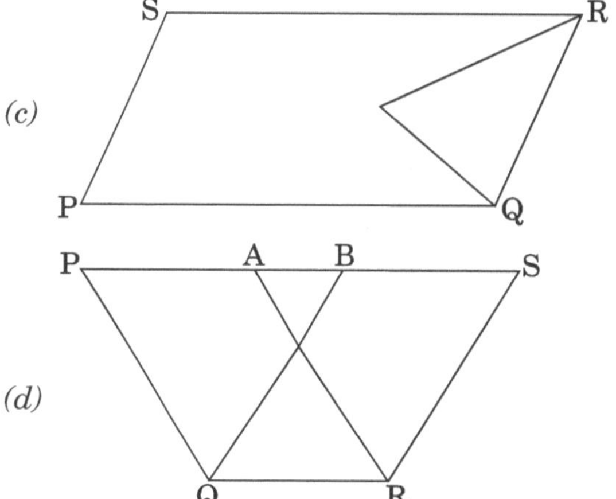

[NCERT Exemplar]

Sol. (d) We find two polygons (parallelograms) on the same base and between the same parallels in figure (d).

3. ABCD is a quadrilateral whose diagonal AC divides it in two parts, equal in area, then ABCD
   - (a) is a rectangle
   - (b) is always a rhombus
   - (c) is a parallelogram
   - (d) need not be any of (A), (B) or (C)

   [NCERT Exemplar]

Sol. (d) We know that the diagonal of a parallelogram divides it into two triangles of equal area. The rectangle and a rhombus are also parallelograms. It may be a kite as diagonal of a kite divides it into two triangles of equal areas.

4. In the given Figure, the area of parallelogram ABCD is:
   - (a) AB × BM
   - (b) BC × BN
   - (c) DC × DL
   - (d) AD × DL

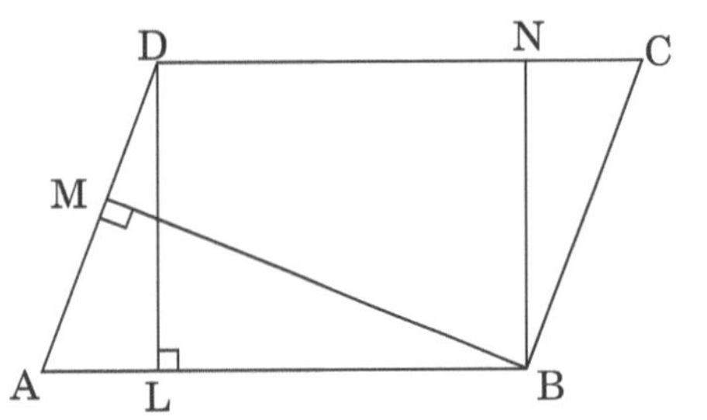

[NCERT Exemplar]

Sol. (c) According to the question,

Area of parallelogram = Base × Corresponding altitude

$$= AB \times DL = DC \times DL \qquad [\because AB = DC]$$

(Opposite sides of a parallelogram are equal)

5. ABCD is a trapezium with parallel sides AB = a cm and DC = b cm (as shown in the Figure). E and F are the midpoints of the non-parallel sides. The ratio ar(ABFE) and ar(EFCD) is

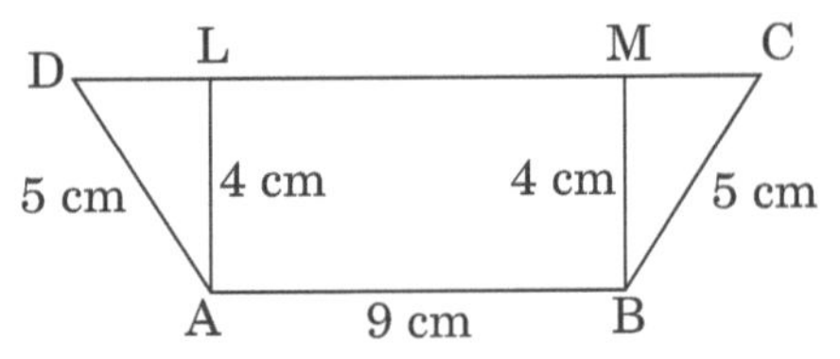

(a) a : b

(b) (3a + b) : (a + 3b)

(c) (a + 3b) : (3a + b)

(d) (2a + b) : (3a + b) [NCERT Exemplar]

Sol. (b) According to the question,

ABCD is a trapezium in which AB ∥ DC. E and F are the midpoints of AD and BC

∴   ABEF and EFCD are also trapeziums.

$$ar(ABEF) = \frac{1}{2}\left[\frac{1}{2}(a+b)+a\right]\times h$$

$$= \frac{h}{4}(3a+b)$$

and

$$ar(EFCD) = \frac{1}{2}\left[b+\frac{1}{2}(a+b)\right]\times h$$

$$= \frac{h}{4}(a+3b)$$

Hence, the required ratio

$$= \frac{ar\,(ABEF)}{ar\,(EFCD)} = \frac{\dfrac{h}{4}(3a+b)}{\dfrac{h}{4}(a+3b)} = \frac{3a+b}{a+3b}$$

or (3a + b) : (a + 3b).

6. In the given Figure, if parallelogram ABCD and rectangle ABEM are of equal area, then:

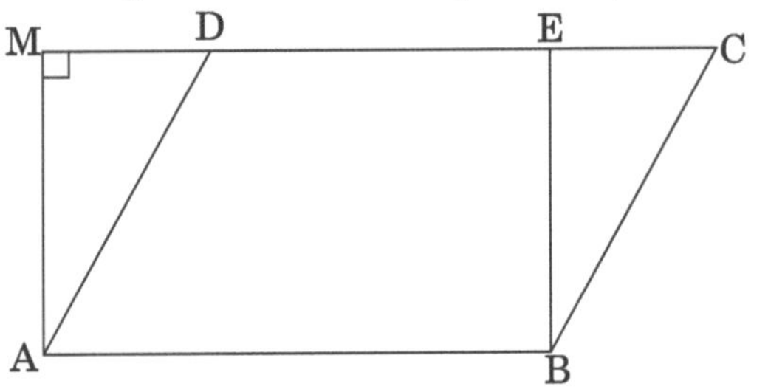

(a) Perimeter ABCD = Perimeter of ABEM.

(b) Perimeter of ABCD < Perimeter of ABEM.

(c) Perimeter of ABCD > Perimeter of ABEM.

(d) Perimeter of ABCD = $\dfrac{1}{2}$

(Perimeter of ABEM).

[NCERT Exemplar]

Sol. (c) According to the question, parallelogram ABCD and rectangle ABEM are of equal, then perimeter of ABCD > Perimeter of ABEM, because the perpendicular distance between two parallel sides of a parallelogram is always less than the length of the other parallel sides.

7. In the given figure, the area of trapezium ABCD is:

(a) 36 cm² (b) 20 cm²

(c) 48 cm² (d) 60 cm²

[NCERT Exemplar]

Sol. (c) We know that

$$\text{Area of trapezium} = \frac{1}{2}\times(AB+DC)\times BM$$

In ΔALD,

$$DL = \sqrt{(5)^2-(4)^2}$$

$$= \sqrt{25-16} = \sqrt{9} = 3\text{ cm}$$

Similarly,

$$MC = 3\text{ cm}$$

∴

$$DC = 9+3+3 = 15\text{ cm.}$$

∴   required area $= \dfrac{1}{2}\times(9+15)\times4$

$$= \frac{1}{2}\times24\times4 = 48\text{ cm}^2.$$

Very Short Answer Type Questions
(1 Mark Each)

1. Two parallelogram are on same base and between the same parallels. What is the ratio of their areas?   [NCERT Exemplar]

Sol. We know that the areas of two parallelograms on same base and between the same parallels are equal.

Hence, required ratio of Area of two parallelogram = 1 : 1.

2. In the given figure, PQ ∥ RS, ABCD is a parallelogram and AEB is a triangle. Area of the parallelogram ABCD is twice the area of ....

[Board Term II, 2012, Set-23]

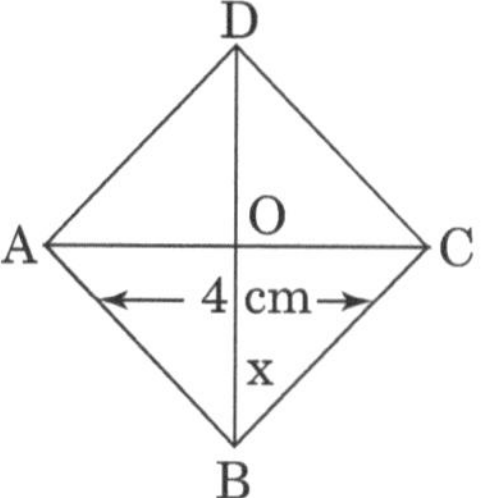

Sol. According to the given figure, Parallelogram ABCD and ∆AEB are on the same base (AB) and between same parallels, (PQ ∥ RS) therefore

$$\text{ar}(\Delta AEB) = \frac{1}{2}\ (\text{ar} \parallel {}^{gm}\ ABCD)$$

$\Rightarrow$ ar ($\parallel {}^{gm}$ ABCD) = 2 ar(AEB)

Hence, area of parallelogram ABCD is twice the area of ∆AEB.

3. If a triangle and a parallelogram are on same base and between same parallels, then the ratio of the area of the triangle to the area of a parallelogram is .... .   [Board Term II, 2012, Set-6]

Sol. Since, a triangle and a parallelogram are on same base and between same parallels, then the ratio of area of the triangle to the area of parallelogram is 1 : 2.

4. In the given figure, ABCD is a parallelogram, AE ⊥ DC and CF ⊥ AD. If AB = 16 cm, AE = 8 cm and CF = 10 cm, find AD.

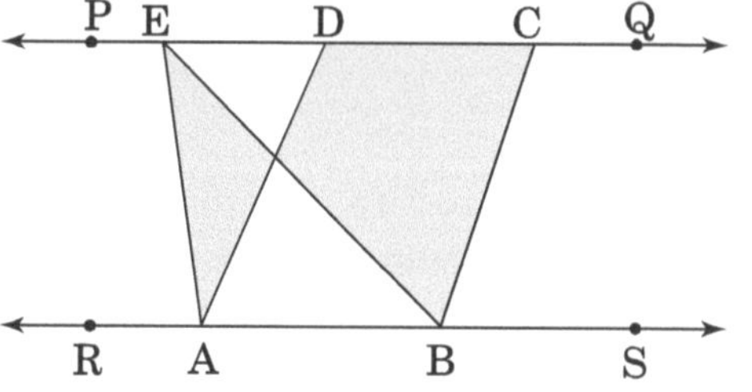

Sol. According to the question, we have

$$AB = 16 \text{ cm, } AE = 8 \text{ cm}$$

and $CF = 10$ cm,

We know that

Areas of a parallelogram = Base × Height

$$= DC \times AE$$

[∵ opposite sides of a parallelogram are equal i.e., AB = DC = 16 cm]

$$= 16 \times 8 = 128 \text{ cm}^2 \qquad ...(i)$$

Also, Area of a parallelogram

$$= AD \times CF = AD \times 10 \quad ...(ii)$$

From Eqs. (i) and (ii), we have

$$AD \times 10 = 128$$

∴ $AD = \dfrac{128}{10} = 12.8$ cm.

Hence, the value of AD is 12.8 cm.

5. In the given figure, find x, if ABCD is a rhombus, AC = 4 cm and ar (rhombus ABCD) = 20 cm².

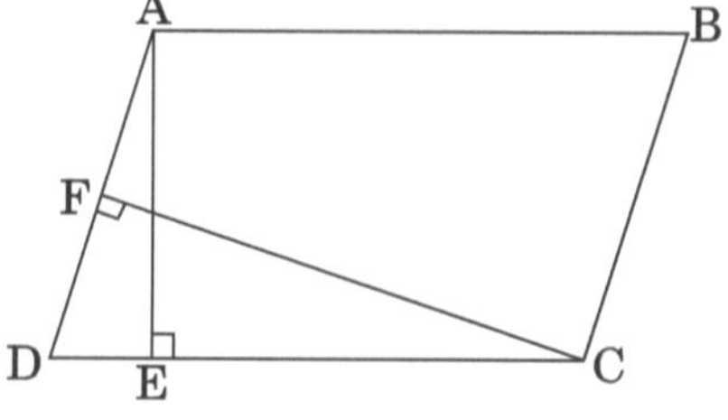

Sol. Given, diagonal of a rhombus, AC = 4 cm

diagonal of a rhombus BD = 2 × OB = 2x cm

and ar (rhombus ABCD) = 20 cm²

According to the question,

$$\text{Area of rhombus} = \frac{1}{2} \times \text{Product of diagonals}$$

$$20 = \frac{1}{2} \times 4 \times 2x$$

$\Rightarrow$ $4x = 20$

∴ $x = \dfrac{20}{4} = 5$

Hence, the value of x is 5 cm.

6. PQRS is a parallelogram whose area is 180 cm² and A is any point on the diagonal QS. The area of ASR = 90 cm².   [NCERT Exemplar]

Sol. The given statement is false.

PQRS is a parallelogram.

We know that diagonal (QS) of a parallelogram divides parallelogram into two triangles of equal area,

Therefore, ar (QRS) = $\dfrac{1}{2}$ ar (PQRS)

$$= \frac{1}{2} \times 180$$

$$= 90 \text{ cm}^2$$

∴   A is any point on SQ

Hence, ar (ASR) < 90 cm².

7. ABCD is a parallelogram and X is the midpoint of AB. If ar (AXCD) = 24 cm², then ar (ABC) = 24 cm².

[NCERT Exemplar]

Sol. The given statement is false.

We have given that ABCD is a parallelogram and X is the midpoint of AB.

Now,   ar (ABCD) = ar (AXCD) + ar (XBC) ...(i)

Diagonal AC of a parallelogram divides it into two triangles of equal area.

$$ar\ (ABCD) = 2ar\ (ABC) \qquad \text{...(ii)}$$

Again, X is the mid-point of AB, So

$$ar\ (CXB) = \frac{1}{2}\ ar\ (ABC) \qquad \text{...(iii)}$$

[Median divides the triangle in two triangles of equal area]

Now, from eqⁿ (i),

Therefore, $2ar\ (ABC) = 24 + \frac{1}{2}\ ar\ (ABC)$

$\Rightarrow 2ar\ (ABC) - \frac{1}{2}\ ar\ (ABC) = 24$

$\Rightarrow \qquad \frac{3}{2}\ ar\ (ABC) = 24$

$\therefore \qquad ar\ (ABC) = \frac{24 \times 2}{3} = 16$ cm².

8. PQRS is a rectangle inscribed in a quadrant of a circle of radius 13 cm. A is any point on PQ. If PS = 5 cm, then ar (PAS) = 30 cm².

[NCERT Exemplar]

Sol. The given statement is false.

It is given that A is any point on PQ, therefore,   PA > PQ.

It is given that A is any on PQ, therefore,   PA < PQ.

Now, we know that

$$ar\ (PQR) = \frac{1}{2} \times \text{base} \times \text{height}$$

Now, $PQ = \sqrt{13^2 - 5^2} = 12$ cm

Now, $ar\ (PQR) = \frac{1}{2} \times PQ \times QR$

$$= \frac{1}{2} \times 12 \times 5 = 30 \text{ cm}^2$$

[PQRS is a rectangle RQ = SP = 5 cm]

As,   PA < PQ (= 12 cm)

∴   ar (PAS) < ar (PQR)

⇒   ar (PAS) < 30 cm²

[∵ ar (PQR) = 30 cm²].

Short Answer Type Questions I
(2 Marks Each)

1. ABCD is a parallelogram AE ⊥ DC and CF ⊥ AD. If AB = 16 cm, AE = 8 cm, CF = 10, find AD.

[Board Term II, 2012, Set-(02), KVS 2014]

Sol. According to the question,

AB = 16 cm, AE = 8 cm and CF = 10 cm

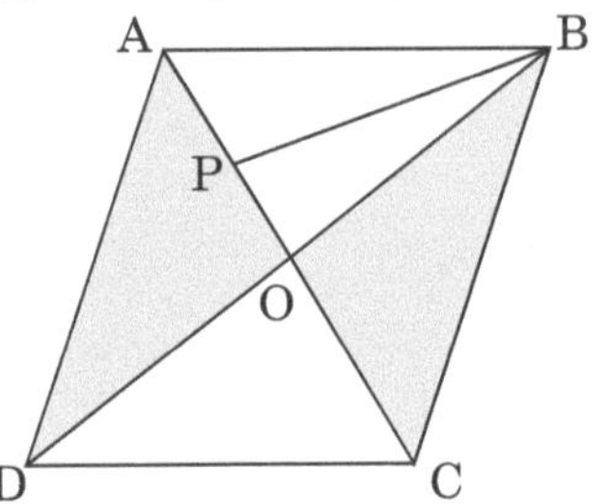

Now, Area of parallelogram

$$= AD \times CF = CD \times AE$$

[∵ CF = perpendicular at AD]

$$= AD \times 10$$

$\Rightarrow \qquad AD \times 10 = 16 \times 8 \qquad [\because CD = AB]$

$\Rightarrow \qquad AD = \dfrac{16 \times 8}{10}$

$\therefore \qquad AD = 12.8$ cm

Hence, the length of AD is 12.8 cm.

2. ABCD ia a parallelogram with area 80 sq. cm. The diagonals AC and BD intersect at O. P is the mid-point of OA. Calculate ar (ΔBOP).

[Board Term II, 2012, Set-12]

Sol. According to the question,

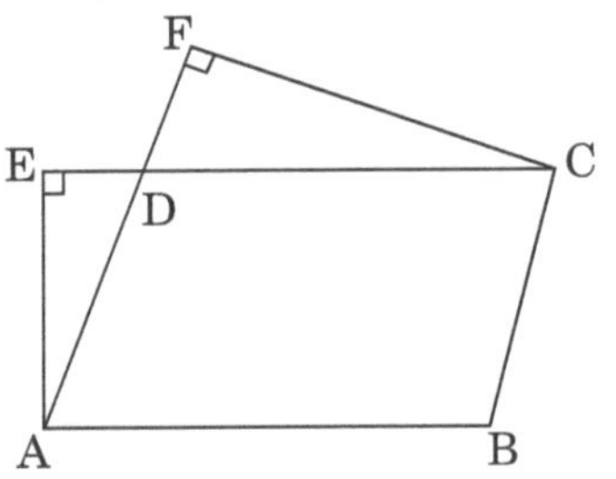

∵ Area of a parallelogram is divided into four equal Parts by the diogonals

Therefore, $ar\ (AOB) = \frac{1}{4}\ ar\ (ABCD) \qquad \text{...(i)}$

and $ar\ (\Delta BOP) = \frac{1}{2}\ ar\ (AOB)$

$$= \frac{1}{8}\ ar\ (ABCD)$$

[From eqⁿ (i)]

$$= \frac{1}{8} \times 80 = 10 \text{ cm}^2$$

[∵ or (ABCD) = 80 cm²]

Hence, the area of ΔBOP = 10 cm².

3. P and Q are any two points lying on the sides DC and AD respectively of a parallelogram ABCD. Show that ar ($\triangle$APB) = ar ($\triangle$BQC).

[Board Term II, 2012, Set-8]

Sol. Given, a parallelogram ABCD and two points P and Q lying on the sides DC and AD respectively.

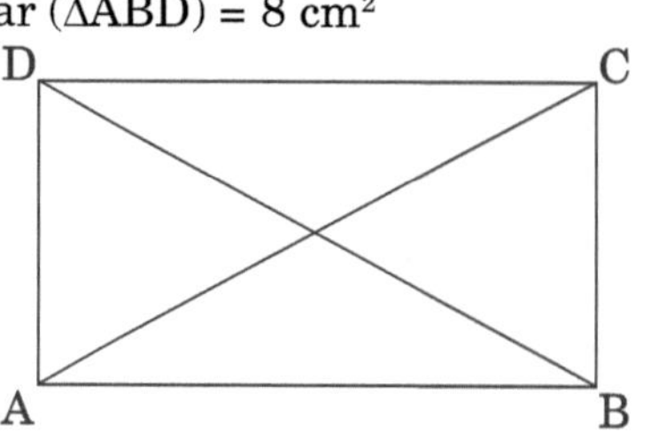

∵ $\triangle$APB and parallelogram ABCD are on same base AB and between same parallel line AB and DC.

∴   ar (APB) = $\dfrac{1}{2}$ ar (ABCD)   ...(i)

Similarly,   ar (BQC) = $\dfrac{1}{2}$ ar (ABCD)   ...(ii)

Now, on comparing eq^n. (i) and eq^n. (ii), we get

ar ($\triangle$APB) = ar ($\triangle$BQC)

Hence proved.

4. ABCD is a quadrilateral and BD is one of its diagonals as shown in figure. Show that ABCD is a parallelogram and find its area.

[Board Term II, 2012, Set-01]

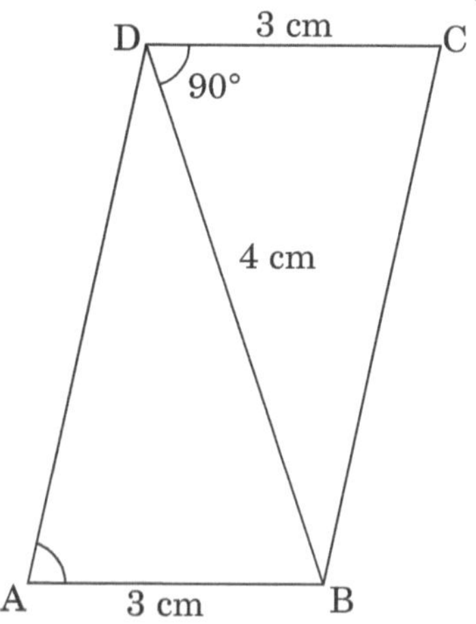

Sol. According to the given figure.

AB = CD = 3cm

BD = 4 cm

and $\angle$CDB = $\angle$ABD = 90°

But they are alternate angles.

∴   AB ∥ DC

Also,   DC = AB = 3 cm.

Therefore, A quadrilateral with a pair of equal and parallel sides is a parallelogram.

∴   Area of parallelogram = b × h

= (3 × 4) cm^2

= 12 cm^2.

5. ABCD is a rectangle and BD is one of its diagonals. If ar ($\triangle$ABD) = 8 cm^2, find ar ($\triangle$BCD).

[Board Term II, 2015]

Sol. According to the question

ar ($\triangle$ABD) = 8 cm^2

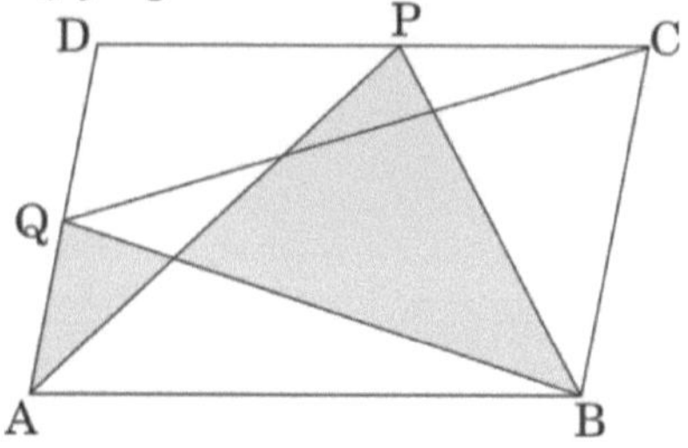

We know that

A diagonal of a parallelogram divides it into two triangles of equal area

∴   ar ($\triangle$ABD) = ar ($\triangle$BCD)

Since, given,   ar ($\triangle$ABD) = 8 cm^2

Hence,   ar ($\triangle$BCD) = 8 cm^2.

6. In the given figure, PQRS is parallelogram with PQ = 8 cm and ar ($\triangle$PXQ) = 32 cm^2. Find the altitude of PQRS and hence its area.

[Board Term II, Set RQTZFBW, 2016]

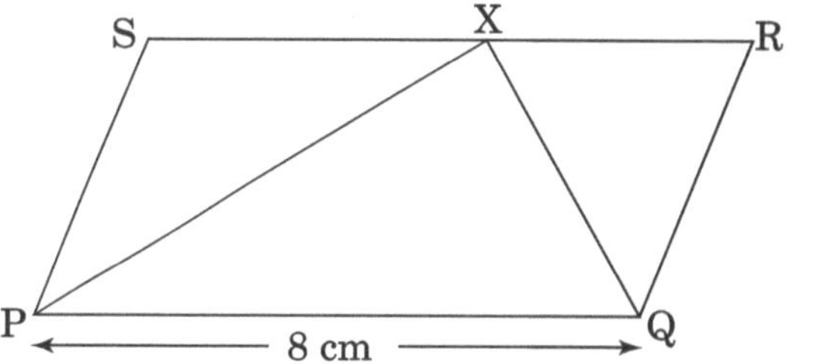

Sol. According to the given figure, we have

PQ = 8 cm and

ar ($\triangle$PXQ) = 32 cm^2

Now, Area of ($\triangle$PXQ) = $\dfrac{1}{2}$ × b × h

(b = base, h = height)

⇒   32 = $\dfrac{1}{2}$ × PQ × h

⇒   32 = $\dfrac{1}{2}$ × 8 × h

∴   h = $\dfrac{32 \times 2}{8}$ = 8

Now, area of ∥^{gm} PQRS = b × h

= 8 × 8 = 64 cm^2

Hence, altitude of PQRS = 8 cm and area of parallelogram PQRS = 64 cm^2.

7. ABCD is a parallelogram in which CD = 10 cm, DF = EB = 2 cm and AD = 4 cm. Find ar (AECF).

Sol. According to the question,

ABCD is a parallelogram where

AB = CD = 10 cm AD = BC = 4 cm.

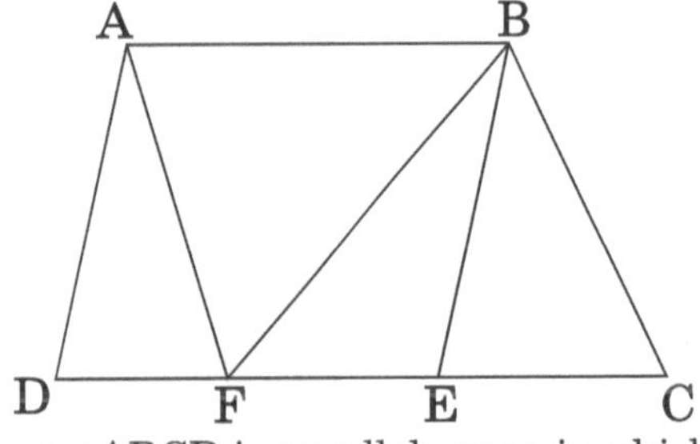

Also, in $\triangle ADF$,

$$\angle AFD = 90$$

$\therefore \qquad AF^2 + DF^2 = AD^2$

[By Pythagoras theorem]

$\Rightarrow \qquad AF^2 = AD^2 - DF^2$

$$= (4)^2 - (2)^2 \quad [\because \ DF = 2 \text{ cm}]$$

$$= 16 - 4 = 12$$

$\therefore \qquad AF = \sqrt{12} = 2\sqrt{3} \text{ cm}$

Now, $\qquad AE = AB - BE = 10 - 2 = 8 \text{ cm}$

and $\qquad FC = DC - DF = 10 - 2 = 8 \text{ cm}$

$\Rightarrow \qquad AE = FC \ \text{ and } \ AE \parallel FC$

$$[\because \ AB \parallel CD]$$

Therefore, AECF is a parallelogram,

$\therefore \qquad$ ar (AECF) = Base × Height

$$= AE \times AF$$

$$= 8 \times 2\sqrt{3} = 16\sqrt{3} \text{ cm}^2$$

Hence, the area of parallelogram

$$AECF = 16\sqrt{3} \text{ cm}^2.$$

8. In the given figure, ABED is a parallelogram in which DE = EC. Show that ar (ABF) = ar (BEC).

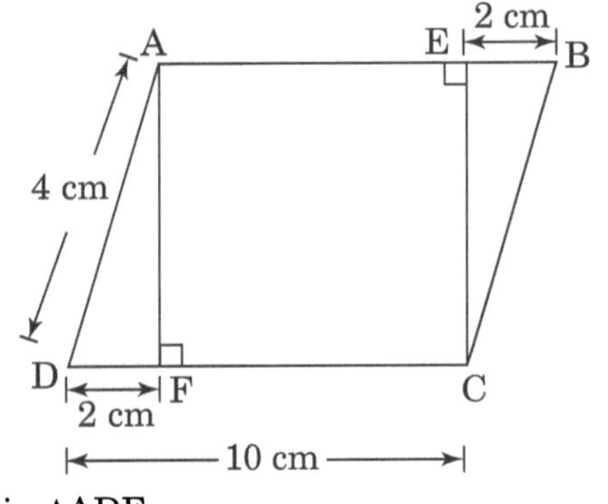

Sol. Given : ABCD is parallelogram is which

$$DE = EC$$

We know that triangle and parallelogram on same base and between same parallels have areas in ratio 1 : 2.

$\therefore \qquad$ ar (ABF) $= \dfrac{1}{2}$ ar (ABED)

and $\quad$ ar (BEC) $= \dfrac{1}{2}$ ar (ABED)

[Triangle and parallelogram on same base and between same parallels]

$\therefore \qquad$ ar (ABF) = ar (BEC) $\qquad$ **Hence proved**

Short Answer Type Questions II

(3 Marks Each)

1. Diagonals AC and BD of a quadrilateral ABCD intersect at O in such a way that ar ($\triangle$AOD) = ar ($\triangle$BOC). Prove that ABCD is a trapezium.

[NCERT]

Sol. Given : ABCD is a quadrilateral and diagonals AC and BD intersect at O such that ar ($\triangle$AOD) = ar ($\triangle$BOC).

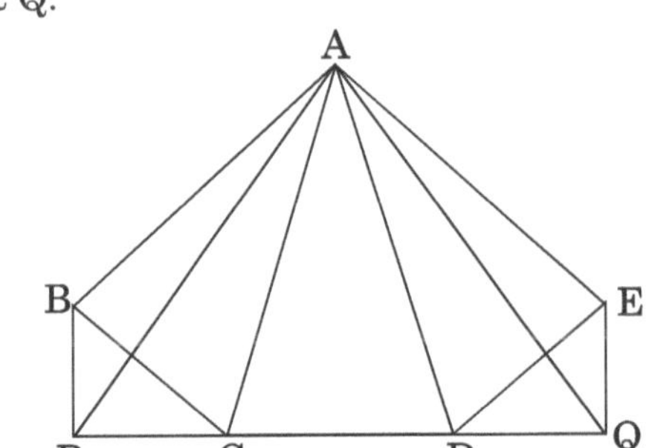

To prove : ABCD is a trapezium

Proof : $\therefore$ ar ($\triangle$AOD) + ar ($\triangle$AOB) $\qquad$ [Given]

On adding ar ($\triangle$AOB) both sides, we get

$\Rightarrow \quad$ ar ($\triangle$AOD) + ar ($\triangle$AOB)

$$= \text{ar } (\triangle \text{BOC}) + \text{ar } (\triangle \text{AOB})$$

$\therefore \qquad$ ar ($\triangle$ADB) = ar ($\triangle$ACB)

Now, $\triangle$ADB and $\triangle$ACB lie on same base AB

Also, $\quad$ ar ($\triangle$ADB) = ar ($\triangle$ACB)

Therefore, $\triangle$ADB and $\triangle$ACB will lie between same parallel lines.

$\therefore \qquad\qquad$ AB $\parallel$ DC

Hence, ABCD is a trapezium. $\qquad$ **Hecne proved**

2. In the adjoining figure, ABCDE is any pentagon. BP drawn parallel to AC meets DC produced at P and EQ drawn parallel to AD meets CD produced at Q.

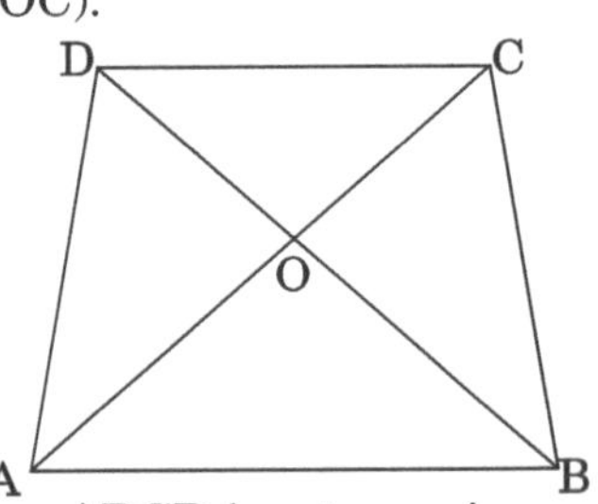

Prove that

$$\text{ar (ABCDE)} = \text{ar } (\triangle \text{APQ}).$$

[NCERT Exemplar]

Sol. **Given :** ABCDE is a pentagon, in which BP $\parallel$ AC and EQ $\parallel$ AD.

To prove : ar (ABCDE) = ar ($\triangle$APQ)

Proof : We know that triangles on the same base and between the same parallels are equal in area.

Now, $\qquad$ ar ($\triangle$ADE) = ar ($\triangle$ADQ) $\qquad$ ...(i)

[$\because$ $\triangle$ADQ and $\triangle$ADE lie on the same base AD and between the same parallels AD and EQ]

Similarly,   ar (ΔCAB) = ar (ΔCAP) ...(ii)

[$\because$ same base is AC and same parallels are AC and BP]

On adding eqs. (i) and (ii), we get

ar (ΔADE) + ar (ΔCAB) = ar (ΔADQ) + ar (ΔCAP)

On adding ar (ΔCDA) both sides, we get

ar (ΔADE) + ar (ΔCAB) + ar (ΔCDA)

= ar (ΔADQ) + ar (ΔCAP) + ar (ΔCDA)

$\therefore$ ar (ABCDE) = ar (ΔPAQ) **Hence Proved.**

3. In the following figure, PQRS and ABRS are parallelograms and X is any point on side BR.

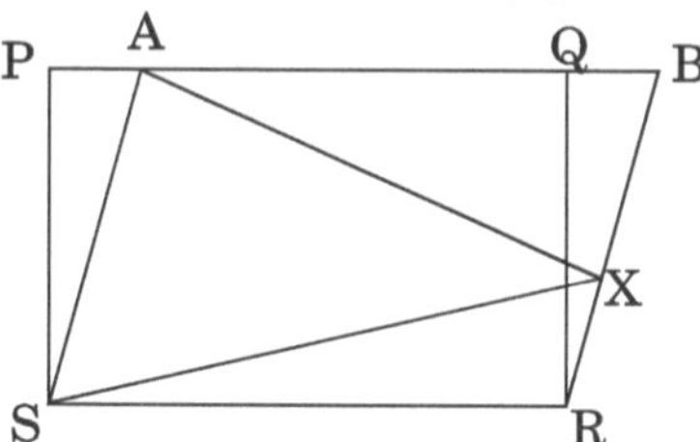

Show that

(i) ar ($\|^{gm}$ PQRS) = ar ($\|^{gm}$ ABRS)

(ii) ar (ΔAXS) = $\dfrac{1}{2}$ ar ($\|^{gm}$ PQRS)   [NCERT]

Sol. **Given :** PQRS and ABRS both are parallelograms and X is any point on BR.

To prove :

(i) ar ($\|^{gm}$ PQRS) = ar ($\|^{gm}$ ABRS)

(ii) ar (ΔAXS) = $\dfrac{1}{2}$ ar ($\|^{gm}$ PQRS)

Proof :

(i) Here, in the given question Parallelograms PQRS and ABRS lie on the same base SR and between the same parallel lines SR and PB.

$\therefore$ ar ($\|^{gm}$ PQRS) = ar ($\|^{gm}$ ABRS)   ...(i)

(ii) Again, ΔAXS and parallelogram ABRS lie on the same base AS and between the same parallel lines AS and BR.

$\therefore$ ar (ΔAXS) = $\dfrac{1}{2}$ ar ($\|^{gm}$ ABRS)   ...(ii)

From eqs. (i) and (ii), we get

$\therefore$ ar (ΔAXS) = $\dfrac{1}{2}$ ar ($\|^{gm}$ PQRS)

Hecen Proved.

4. Show that the diagonals of a parallelogram divide it into four triangles of equal area.

[NCERT][Board Term II, 2012, Set-10]

Sol. **Given :** ABCD is a $\|^{gm}$

To prove :

ar (ΔABO) = ar (ΔBCO)

= ar (ΔCDO)

= ar (ΔDAO)

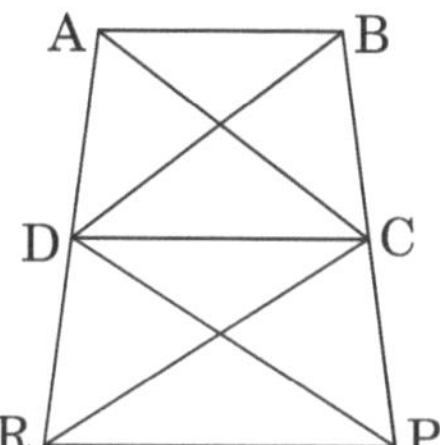

In parallelogram ABCD.

Diagonals AC and BD of bisect each other.

$\therefore$ OA = OC and OB = OD

(O is the mid-point of diagonals AC and BD)

Now, in ΔABC,

$\therefore$ OA = OC and BO is the Median of ΔABC.

Therefore, ar (ΔABO) = ar (BCO)   ...(i)

[$\because$ Median of a triangle divides it into two triangles of equal area]

Similarly,

ar (ΔADO) = ar (ΔCDO) ...(ii)

ar (ΔADO) = ar (ΔABO) ...(iii)

and   ar (ΔBCO) = ar (ΔCDO) ...(iv)

Now, from eqⁿ (i), (ii), (iii) and (iv), we have

ar (ΔABO) = ar (ΔBCO)

= ar (ΔCDO = ar (ΔDAO)

Hence Proved.

5. In the figure, ar (ΔDRC) = ar (ΔDPC) and ar (ΔBDP) = ar (ΔARC). Show that both the quadrilaterals ABCD and DCPR are trapezium.

[NCERT Board Term II, 2012, (13, 20); Set-A1, 2011]

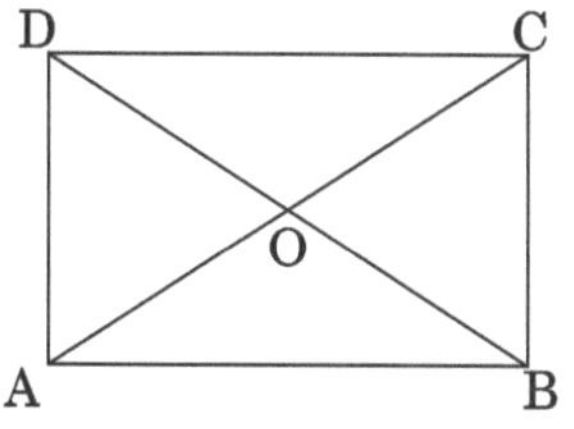

Sol. **Given :** ar (ΔDRC) = ar (ΔDPC),

and   ar (ΔBDP) = ar (ΔARC)

But they are on the same base DC.

Therefore, ΔDRC and ΔDPC must lie between the same parallels.

$\therefore$ DC $\|$ RP

Therefore, one pair of opposite sides of quadrilateral DCPR is parallel.

Hence, DCPR is trapezium.

Also,   ar (ΔBDP) = ar (ΔARC) ...(i)

(Given)

and   ar (ΔDPC) = ar (ΔDRC) ...(ii)

(Given)

On subtracting eqⁿ (ii) from (i), we get

ar (ΔBDP) − ar (ΔDPC) = ar (ΔARC) − ar (ΔDRC)

$\Rightarrow$ ar (ΔBDC) = ar (ΔADC)

But they are on the same base DC.

Therefore, ΔBDC and ΔADC must lie between the same parallels.

$\therefore$ $\qquad$ AB $\parallel$ DC

Therefore, one pair of opposite side of quadrilateral ABCD is parallel.

Hence, ABCD is a trapezium.

6. If a parallelogram and a triangle are on the same base and between the same parallels, then prove that area of a triangle is equal to half the area of a parallelogram.

[Board Term II, 2012, Set-01, NCERT]

Sol. **Given :** ΔABQ and parallelogram ABCD are on the same base AB and between the same parallels DC and AB.

To prove :

$$\text{Area } (\Delta ABQ) = \frac{1}{2} \text{ Area (Parallelogram ABCD)}$$

Construction : Extend DC to R so that BR $\parallel$ AQ

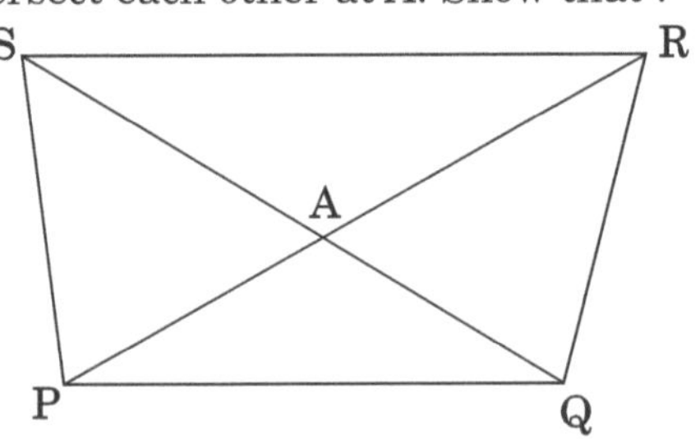

Proof : Parallelogram's DCBA and QRBA are on the same base and between same parallels.

$$\text{ar (DCBA)} = \text{ar (QRBA)} \qquad ...(i)$$

$\because$ A diagonal divides a parallelogram into two congruent triangles with equal area.

$\therefore$ $\qquad$ $\text{ar } (\Delta QAB) = \dfrac{1}{2} \text{ ar (QRBA)}$ $\qquad ...(ii)$

From (i) and (ii), we get

$$\text{ar } (\Delta QAB) = \frac{1}{2} \text{ ar (DCBA)}$$

Hence proved.

7. MNOP is a parallelogram and PN is one of its diagonals show that ar (ΔPMN) = ar (ΔPON).

[Board Term II, 2015]

Sol. **Given :** A parallelogram MNOP in which one of the diagonals is PN

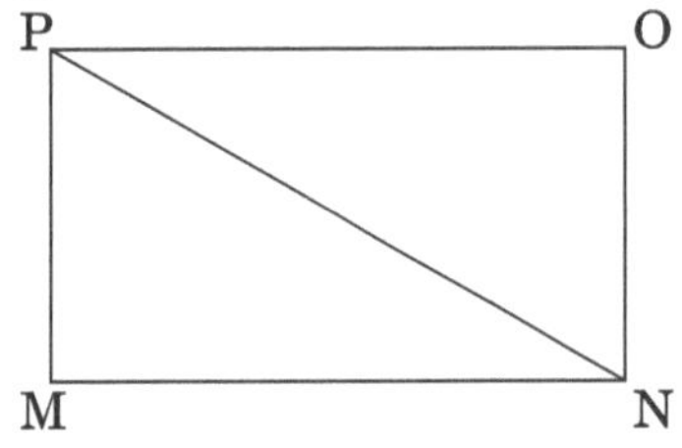

To prove : ar (ΔPMN) = ar (ΔPON)

Proof : Since two congruent figures are equal in area, so we will show that

$$\Delta \text{PMN} \cong \Delta \text{PON}$$

$\therefore$ in Δ's PMN and PON,

$$\text{MN} = \text{PO}$$

$\qquad$ [$\because$ In a parallelogram opposite sides are equal]

$$\text{PM} = \text{ON}$$

and, $\qquad$ PN = NP $\qquad$ [Common]

$\therefore$ By SSS congruence criterion, we get

$\therefore$ $\qquad$ $\Delta \text{PMN} \cong \Delta \text{PON}$

Therefore, ar (ΔPMN) = ar (ΔPON)

Hence proved.

8. Diagonals PR and QS of quadrilateral PQRS intersect each other at A. Show that :

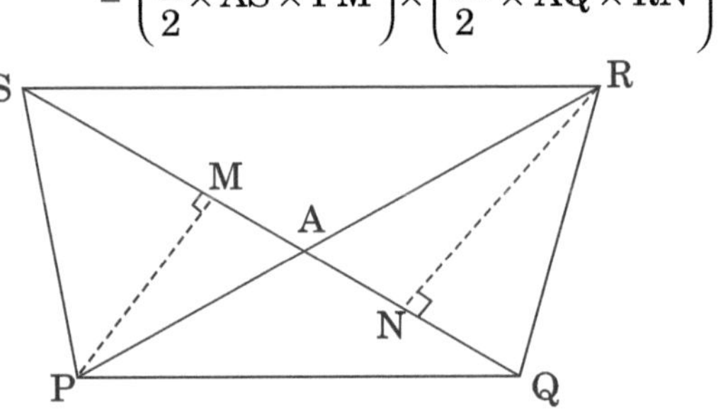

$$\text{ar } (\Delta \text{PSA}) \times \text{ar } (\Delta \text{QAR}) = \text{ar } (\Delta \text{PAQ}) \times \text{ar } (\Delta \text{SAR})$$

[Board Term II, Set RQTZFBW, 2016]

Sol. **Given :** Diagonals PR and QS of quadrilateral PQRS intersect each other at A.

To prove : ar $(\Delta \text{PSA}) \times \text{ar } (\Delta \text{QAR})$

$\qquad$ = ar $(\Delta \text{PAQ}) \times \text{ar } (\Delta \text{SAR})$

Construction : Draw PM $\perp$ QS and RN $\perp$ QS

$$= \left(\frac{1}{2} \times \text{AS} \times \text{PM}\right) \times \left(\frac{1}{2} \times \text{AQ} \times \text{RN}\right)$$

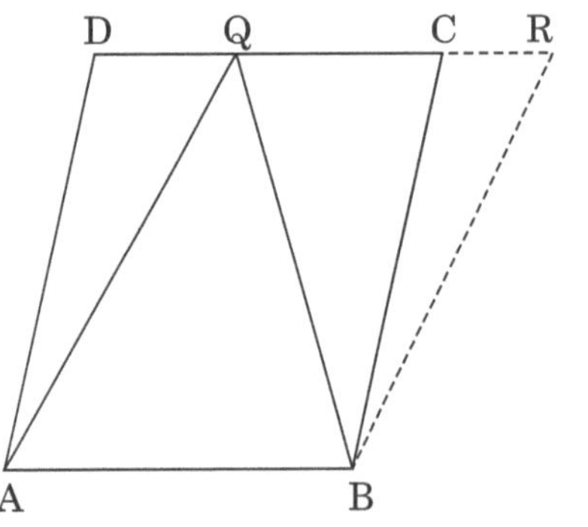

Proof : ar $(\Delta \text{PSA}) \times \text{ar } (\Delta \text{QAR})$

$$\left(\frac{1}{2} \times \text{AS} \times \text{PM}\right) \times \left(\frac{1}{2} \times \text{AQ} \times \text{RN}\right)$$

$$= \left(\frac{1}{2} \times \text{RN} \times \text{AS}\right) \times \left(\frac{1}{2} \times \text{PM} \times \text{AQ}\right)$$

$$= \text{ar } (\Delta \text{SAR}) \times \text{ar } (\Delta \text{PAQ})$$

Hence proved.

Long Answer Type Questions

(4 Marks Each)

1. In the mid-points of the sides of a quadrilateral are joined in order, then prove that the area of the parallelogram so formed will be half of the area of the given quadrilateral (see figure.)

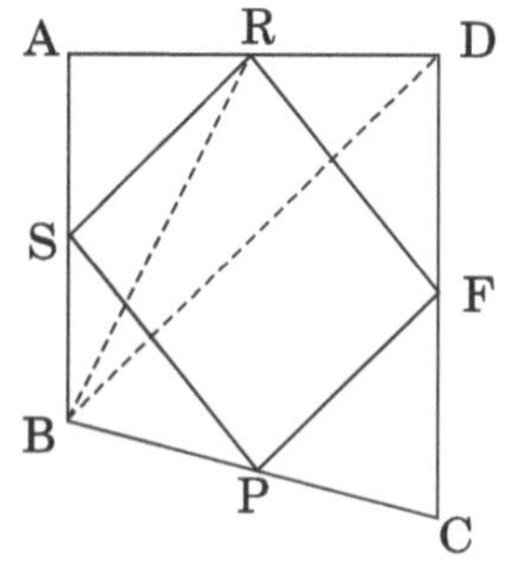

[NCERT Exemplar]

Sol. **Given :** ABCD is a quadrilateral and P, F, R, S are mid-points of the sides BC, CD, AD, AB respectively and PFRS is a parallelogram.

To prove : Area of parallelogram PFRS

$$= \frac{1}{2} \text{ ar (quadrilateral ABCD)}$$

Construction : Join BD and BR

Proof : $\because$ Median BR divides ΔBDA into two triangles of equal area.

$$\therefore \qquad \text{ar } (\Delta \text{BRA}) = \frac{1}{2} \text{ ar } (\Delta \text{BDA}) \qquad \text{...(i)}$$

Similarly, median RS divides ΔBRA into two triangles of equal area.

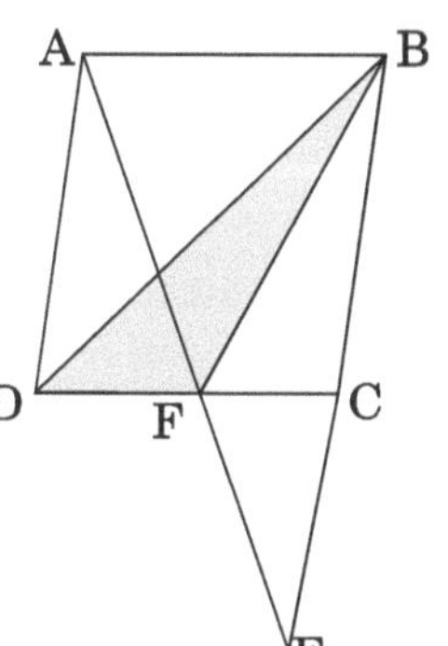

$$\therefore \qquad \text{ar } (\Delta \text{ASR}) = \frac{1}{2} \text{ ar } (\Delta \text{BRA}) \qquad \text{...(ii)}$$

From eqs. (i) and (ii), we get

$$\text{ar } (\Delta \text{ASR}) = \frac{1}{4} \text{ ar } (\Delta \text{BDA}) \qquad \text{...(iii)}$$

Similarly,

$$\text{ar } (\Delta \text{CFP}) = \frac{1}{4} \text{ ar } (\Delta \text{BCD}) \qquad \text{...(iv)}$$

On adding eqs. (iii) and (iv), we get

ar (ΔASR) + ar (ΔCFP)

$$= \frac{1}{4} [\text{ar } (\Delta \text{BDA}) + \text{ar } (\Delta \text{BCD})]$$

$\Rightarrow$ ar (ΔASR) + ar (ΔCFP)

$$= \frac{1}{4} \text{ ar (quadrilateral ABCD)} \qquad \text{...(v)}$$

similarly, ar (ΔDRF) + ar (ΔBSP)

$$= \frac{1}{4} \text{ ar (quadrilateral ABCD)} \qquad \text{...(vi)}$$

On adding eqs. (v) and (vi), we get

ar (ΔASR) + ar (ΔCFP) + ar (ΔDRF) ar + (ΔBSP)

$$= \frac{1}{4} \text{ ar (quadrilateral ABCD)} \qquad \text{...(vii)}$$

But ar (ΔASR) + ar (ΔCFP) + ar (ΔDRF) + ar (ΔBSP) + ar $(\|^{\text{gm}} \text{PFRS})$

$$= \frac{1}{2} \text{ ar (quadrilateral ABCD)...(viii)}$$

On subtracting eq. (vii) from eq. (viii), we get

$$\therefore \quad \text{ar } (\|^{\text{gm}} \text{PFRS}) = \frac{1}{2} \text{ ar (quadrilateral ABCD)}$$

Hence proved.

2. In the figure, ABCD is a parallelogram in which BC is produced to E such that CE = BC. AE intersects CD at F. Show that ar $(\Delta \text{BDF}) = \frac{1}{4}$ ar (ABCD).

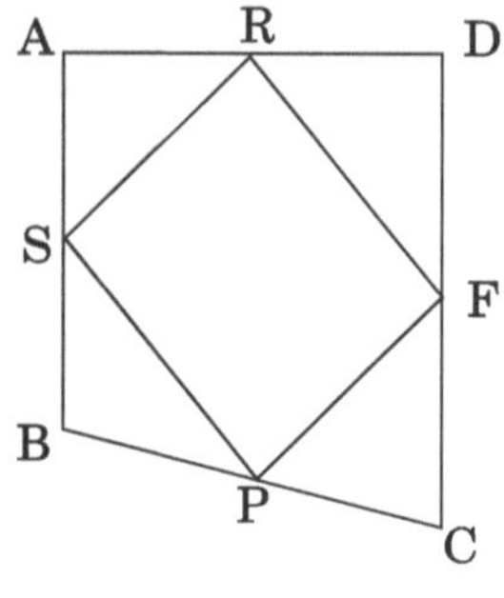

[Board Term II, 2012, Set-(06), 11, 33; Set A1, 2011; 2010]

Sol. **Given :** ABCD is a parallelogram and CE = BC

To prove : ar $(\Delta \text{BDF}) = \frac{1}{4}$ ar (ABCD)

Proof : $\because$ $\angle$AFD = $\angle$EFC   [vertically

       CE = AD   opposite angles]

and $\angle$DAF = $\angle$CEF   [$\because$ AD $\|$ CE]

       $\angle$ADF = $\angle$ECF

by AAS congruence rule,

       ΔADF $\cong$ ΔECF

$$\therefore \qquad\qquad \text{DF = FC} \qquad \text{(By c.p.c.t)}$$

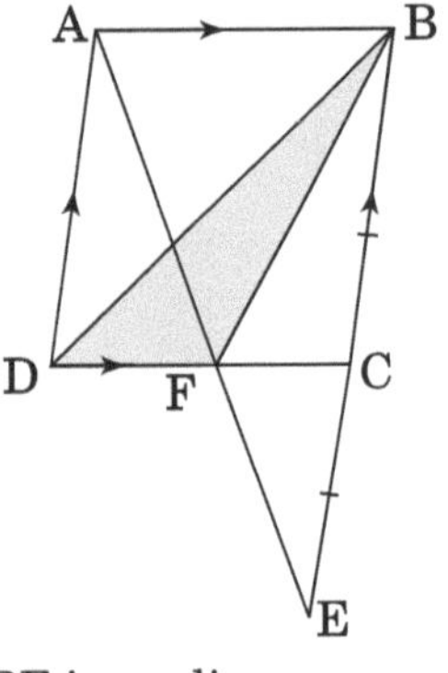

In $\triangle DBC$, BF is median.

$\therefore \qquad \text{ar}(\triangle BDF) = \dfrac{1}{2}\,\text{ar}(\triangle BDC)$

and $\qquad \text{ar}(\triangle BDC) = \text{ar}(\triangle BDA)$

$\qquad\qquad\qquad = \dfrac{1}{2}\,\text{ar}(\|^{gm} ABCD)$

(BD is a diagonal which divides a parallelogram into two congruent triangles)

$\therefore \qquad \text{ar}(\triangle BDF) = \dfrac{1}{2}\left(\dfrac{1}{2}\text{ar}(\|^{gm} ABCD)\right)$

$\qquad\qquad\qquad = \dfrac{1}{4}\,\text{ar}(\|^{gm} ABCD)$

Hence proved.

3. PQRS is a parallelogram and O is a point in the interior of the parallelogram. Show that ar (POS) + ar (QOR) = ar (PQRS).

[Board Term II, 2012, Set-8]

Sol. Given, PQRS is a parallelogram

Construction through O, draw AB ∥ PS.

Also, $\qquad\qquad\qquad$ PA ∥ BS

Thus, quadrilateral PABS is a parallelogram.

$$\text{ar}(POS) = \dfrac{1}{2}\,\text{ar}(PABS) \qquad\qquad ...(i)$$

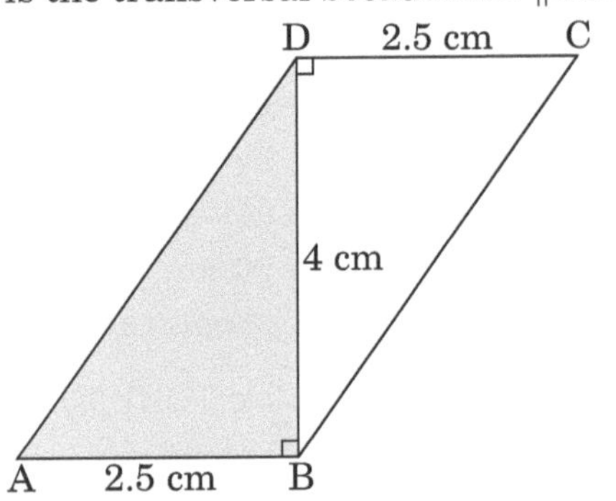

(Triangle and a parallelogram are on the same base and between the same parallels)

Similarly, ar (QOR) $= \dfrac{1}{2}$ ar (QABR) $\qquad$ ...(ii)

Now, on adding eq^n, (i) and (ii), we get

$\therefore$ ar (POS) + ar (QOR)

$\qquad = \dfrac{1}{2}$ [ar (PABS) + ar (QABR)]

$\qquad = \dfrac{1}{2}$ ar (PQRS) $\qquad$ **Hence proved**

4. ABCD is a quadrilateral with BD as one of its diagonals and AB = CD = 2.5 cm, $\angle$ABD = $\angle$CDB = 90° and DB = 4 cm. Show that quad. ABCD is a parallelogram and find its area.

[Board Term II, 2013]

Sol. According to the question,

$\qquad$ AB = CD = 2.5 cm

$\qquad \angle$ABD =$\angle$CDB = 90°

$\qquad$ and DB = 4 cm

$\qquad$ DB is the transversal because DC ∥ AB

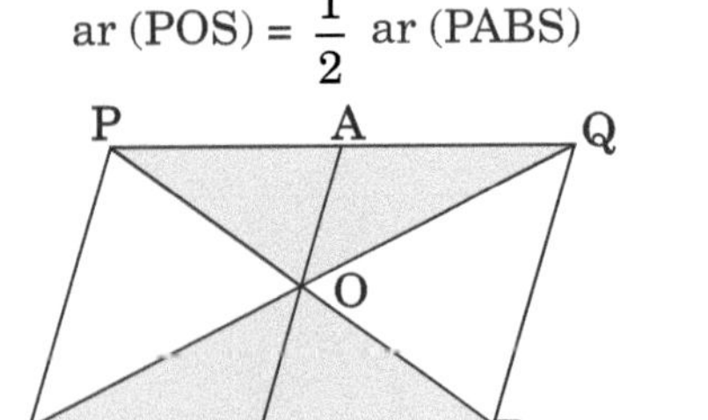

$\because \qquad\qquad \angle$CDB = $\angle$ABD = 90°

$\qquad$ (form a pair of alternate angles)

$\qquad$ DC ∥ AB $\quad$ and $\quad$ DC = AB

Thus, quadrilateral ABCD is a parallelogram,

$\therefore \qquad \text{ar}(ABCD) = b \times h$

$\qquad\qquad\qquad = 2.5 \times 4 = 10 \text{ cm}^2.$

Hence, area of parallelogram ABCD = 10 cm^2.

5. PQRS is a square. N and M are the mid-points of sides SR and QR respectively. O is a point on diagonal PR such that OP = OR. Show that ONRM is a square. Also find the ratio of ar ($\triangle$ORM) and ar (PQRS). [Board Term II, 2014]

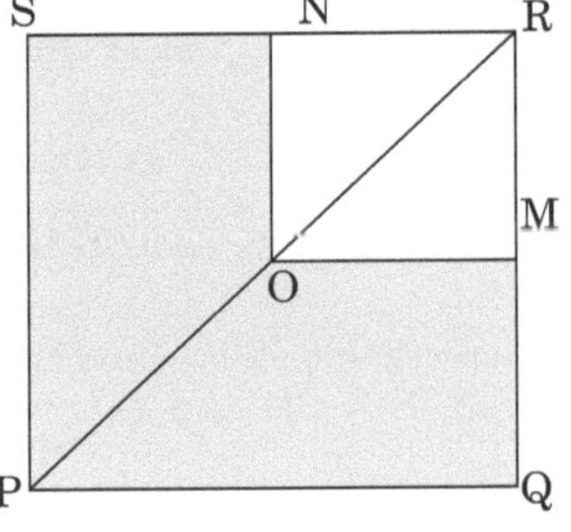

Sol. According to the question,

$\qquad$ since $\qquad\qquad$ OP = OR

$\qquad \therefore$ O is the mid-point of PR.

$\qquad$ Now, in $\triangle$SRP,

$\qquad \because$ O and N are mid-pionts of sides PR and SR respectively

∴   by mid-point theorem,

$$ON = \frac{1}{2} SP \text{ and } ON \parallel SP \qquad ..(i)$$

Similarly, $OM \parallel PQ$ ...(ii)

From eq^n. (i) and (ii), we get

∴ ONRM is a parallelogram.

Now, $ON = \frac{1}{2} SP$

$$= \frac{1}{2} SR \qquad (\because SP = SR)$$

$$= NR$$

In $\parallel^{gm}$ ONRM, a pair of adjacent sides ON and NR are equal and $\angle S = \angle N = 90°$.

(corresponding angles as ON $\parallel$ PS)

Therefore, ONRM is a square

Since, OR is diagonal of square

$$ar\,(ORM) = \frac{1}{2}\,ar\,(ONRM) \qquad ...(iii)$$

($\because$ diagonal of a parallelogram divides it into two congruent triangles)

and $ar\,(ONRM) = NR \times RM$

$$= \frac{1}{2} SR \times \frac{1}{2} RQ$$

$$= \frac{1}{4}(SR \times RQ)$$

$$= \frac{1}{4}(SR)^2$$

$$= \frac{1}{4}\,ar\,(PQRS) \qquad ...(iv)$$

Form equations (iii) and (vi), we get

Hence, required ratio $= \dfrac{ar\,(ONRM)}{ar\,(PQRS)}$

$$= \frac{\frac{1}{2}\,ar\,(ONRM)}{4\,ar\,(PQRS)} = \frac{1}{8}$$

or   1 : 8.

6. ABCD is a rectangle. E, F, G and H are mid–point of sides AB, BC, CD and DA, respectively. If ar (EFGH) = 16 cm², find ar (ABCD).

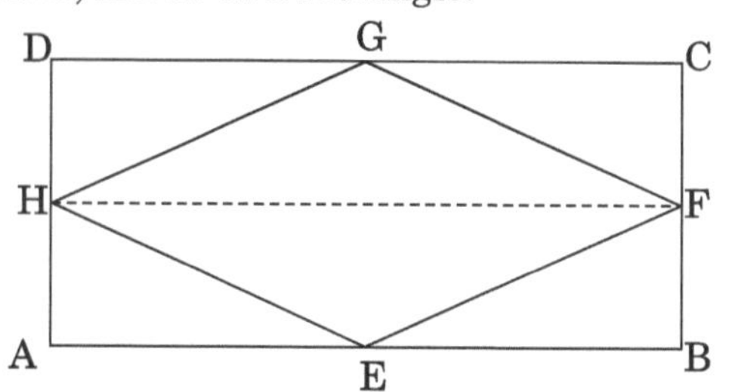

[Board Term II, Set-LF0MCQ2, 2016]

Sol. According to the question,

$$ar\,(EFGH) = 16 \text{ cm}^2$$

H and F are the mid-points of AD and BC, respectively

or, $HD = FC$ [AD $\parallel$ BC]

∴ $HD \parallel FC$

Thus, HDCF is a rectangle.

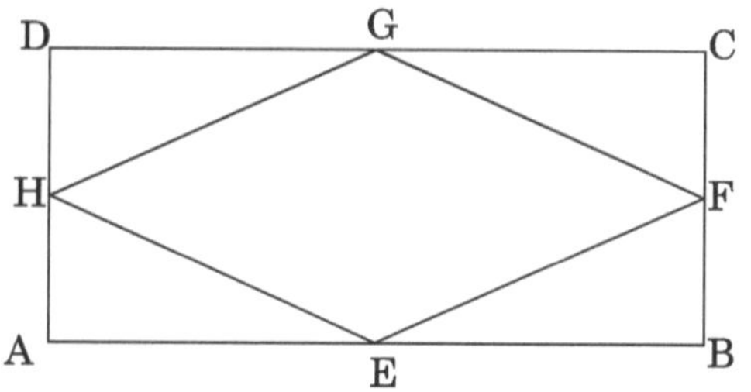

Now, ΔHFG and rectangle HFCD are on the same base HF and lie between the same parallels HF and DC. Therefore,

$$\therefore \qquad ar\,(\Delta HFG) = \frac{1}{2}\,ar\,(\square HFCD) \quad ...(i)$$

Similarly, $ar\,(\Delta EHF) = \dfrac{1}{2}\,ar\,(\square ABFH)$ ...(ii)

On adding eq^n (i) and (ii), we get

$ar\,(\Delta HFG) + ar\,(\Delta EHF)$

$$= \frac{1}{2}\,ar\,(\square HFCD) + ar\,(\square ABFH)$$

$$\Rightarrow ar\,(\Delta EFGH) = \frac{1}{2}\,ar\,(\square ABCD)$$

$$\Rightarrow \qquad 16 = \frac{1}{2}\,ar\,(\square ABCD)$$

Hence, ar $(\square ABCD) = 32$ cm².

7. In the figure, ABCD and AGFE are parallelogram with equal areas. Show that DG $\parallel$ FC.

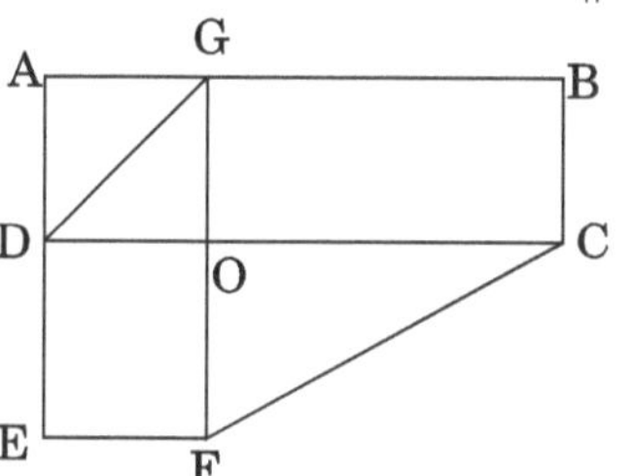

[Board Term II, 2017, Set-Z6K408K]

Sol. **Given :** ABCD and AGFE are parallelogram.

Join DF and GC

$$ar\,(ABCD) = ar\,(AGFE)$$

On subtracting ar (AGOD) from both sides, we have

$$\Rightarrow \quad ar\,(ABCD) - ar\,(AGOD)$$

$$= ar\,(AGFE) - ar\,(AGOD)$$

$$\Rightarrow \qquad ar\,(GOCB) = ar\,(DOFE)$$

Clearly GOCB and DOFE are parallelograms and $ar\,(GOCG) = ar\,(DOFE)$

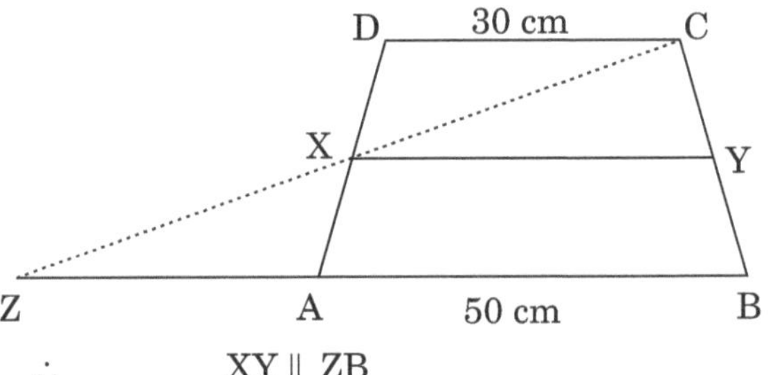

($\because$ diagonal divides a parallelogram into two congruent triangles)

$\therefore$ ar ($\triangle$GOC) = ar ($\triangle$DOF)

On adding ar ($\triangle$DGO) on both sides we have

$\Rightarrow$ ar ($\triangle$GCO) + ar ($\triangle$DGO)

$\qquad$ = ar ($\triangle$DOF) + ar ($\triangle$DGO)

$\Rightarrow$ ar ($\triangle$DGC) = ar ($\triangle$DGF)

Now, $\triangle$DGC and $\triangle$DGF are triangles on same base DG and have equal areas

$\therefore$ They must lie between same parallels

Hence, $\qquad$ DG $\parallel$ FC.

8. ABCD is a trapezium is which AB $\parallel$ DC, DC = 30 cm and AB = 50 cm. If X and Y are respectively the mid-points of AD and BC. prove that ar (quad. DCYX = $\dfrac{7}{9}$ ar (XYBA).

Sol. **Given :** ABCD is a trapezium in which AB $\parallel$ DC, DC = 30 cm and AB = 50 cm. X and Y are the mid-points of AD and BC, respectively.

To prove : ar (DCYX) = $\dfrac{7}{9}$ ar (XYBA)

Construction : Join CX and produce it to meet BA produced at Z.

Proof : In $\triangle$AZX and $\triangle$DCX, we have

$\qquad$ $\angle$AZX = $\angle$DCX

$\qquad\qquad$ [alternate interior angles]

$\qquad$ $\angle$AXZ = $\angle$DXC

$\qquad\qquad$ [vertically opposite angles]

and $\qquad$ AX = DX

$\qquad\qquad$ [$\because$ X is mid-point of AD]

$\therefore$ By AAS congruence rule, we have

$\qquad\qquad$ $\triangle$AZX $\cong$ $\triangle$DCX

$\Rightarrow$ $\qquad\qquad$ CX = XZ

and $\qquad\qquad$ DC = AZ $\qquad$ ...[by CPCT]

Thus, X is the mid-point of CZ, also Y is the mid-point of CB.

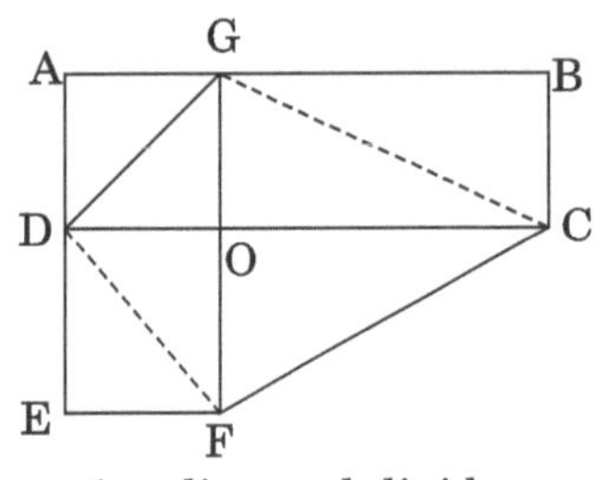

$\therefore$ $\qquad$ XY $\parallel$ ZB

and $\qquad$ XY = $\dfrac{1}{2}$ ZB

$\Rightarrow$ $\qquad$ XY = $\dfrac{1}{2}$ (ZA + AB)

$\qquad\qquad$ = $\dfrac{1}{2}$ (DC + AB) $\qquad$ [$\because$ ZA = DC]

$\qquad\qquad$ = $\dfrac{1}{2}$ (30 + 50) = 40 cm $\qquad$ ...(i)

Now, $\dfrac{\text{ar (trapezium DCYX)}}{\text{ar (trapezium XYBA)}} = \dfrac{\frac{1}{2}(30 + 40)h}{\frac{1}{2}(40 + 50)h}$

[$\because$ X and Y are the mid-points of AD and BC.

$\therefore$ trapaezium DCXY and trapaezium XYBA are of same height (h).]

$\qquad\qquad$ = $\dfrac{70}{90} = \dfrac{7}{9}$

$\therefore$ ar (trapaezium DCYX) = $\dfrac{7}{9}$ ar (trapaezium XYBA).

Hence proved.

[Topic 2] Area of Triangles

Points to be Remembered

- Area of a triangle is half the product of its base and the corresponding altitude.

$$\boxed{\text{Area of a triangle} = \frac{1}{2} \times \text{Base} \times \text{corresponding altitude}}$$

- Two triangles on the same base and between the same parallels are equal in area.

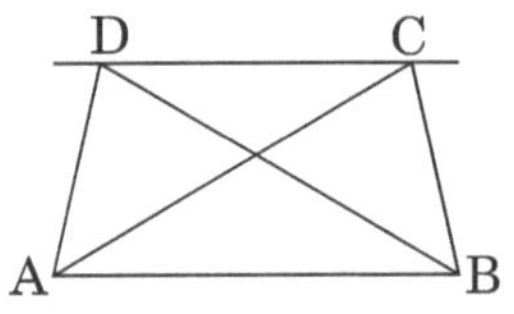

Here, CD $\parallel$ AB and Base = AB

$\therefore$ Area of $\triangle$ABC = Area of $\triangle$ABD

- A median of a triangle divides it into two triangle of equal area.

PREVIOUS YEARS' EXAMINATION QUESTIONS
TOPIC 2

Multiple Choice Questions
(1 Mark Each)

1. If a triangle and a parallelogram are on the same base and between same parallels, then the ratio of the area of the triangle to the area of parallelogram is

   (a) $1:3$ (b) $1:2$

   (c) $3:1$ (d) $1:4$

   [NCERT Exemplar]

Sol. (b) We know that a triangle and a parallelogram are on the same base and between the same parallels then the area of the triangle is equal to half the area of the parallelogram.

Hence, required area = $1:2$.

2. The figure obtained by joining the midpoints of the adjacent sides of a rectangle of sides 8 cm and 6 cm is :

   (a) a rectangle of area 24 cm².

   (b) a square of area 25 cm².

   (c) a trapezium of area 24 cm².

   (d) a rhombus of area 24 cm².

   [NCERT Exemplar]

Sol. (d) Suppose, ABCD is a rectangle and E, F, G and H are the midpoints of the sides AB, BC, CD and DA, respectively. The figure obtained is rhombus whose are $= \dfrac{1}{2} \times EG \times FH = \dfrac{1}{2} \times 6 \times 8$ = 24 cm².

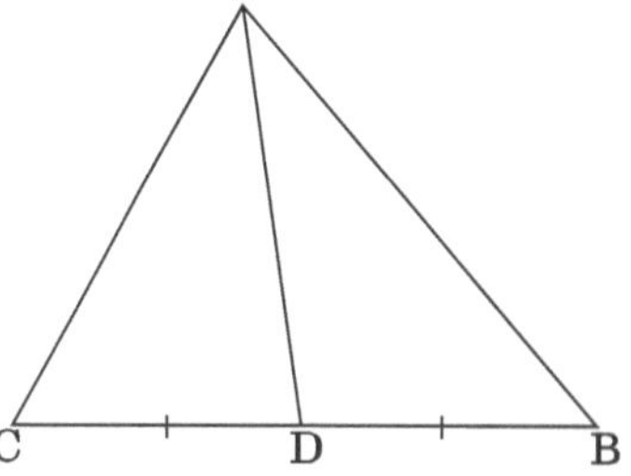

3. The median of a triangle divides it into two

   (a) triangles of equal area.

   (b) congruent triangles.

   (c) right triangles.

   (d) isosceles triangles.   [NCERT Exemplar]

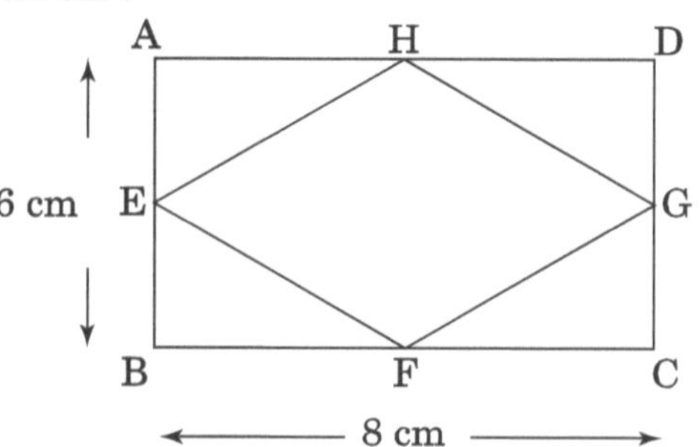

Sol. (a) The median of a triangle divides it into two triangles of equal area.

∴   Area of $\triangle$ADC = Area of $\triangle$BDC

4. The midpoint of the sides of a triangle along with any of the vertices as the fourth point make a parallelogram of area equal to

   (a) $\dfrac{1}{2}$ ar (ABC)   (b) $\dfrac{1}{3}$ ar (ABC)

   (c) $\dfrac{1}{4}$ ar (ABC)   (d) ar (ABC)

   [NCERT Exemplar]

Sol. (a) Median of a triangle divides it into two triangles of equal area

$$ar (ADE) = ar (BDE) \qquad \text{...(i)}$$

and $\quad$ ar (AEF) = ar (EFC) $\qquad$ ...(ii)

Since, AE is the diagonal of a parallelogram ADEF. It divides it into two triangles of equal area.

$$ar (ADE) = ar (AFE) \qquad \text{...(iii)}$$

From (i), (ii) and (iii) we get

$$ar (ADE) = ar (BDE)$$
$$= ar (AFE) = ar (EFC)$$

∴ $\qquad$ ar (ADE) $= \dfrac{1}{2}$ ar (ABC).

Hence proved.

Very Short Answer Type Questions
(1 Mark Each)

1. If a triangle and parallelogram are on the same base and between same parallels, then find the ratio of the area of the triangle to the area of parallelogram.   [NCERT Exemplar]

Sol. We know that if a triangle and a parallelogram are on the same base and between the same parallels, then the area of the triangle is half of the area of parallelogram.

i.e., Area of triangle

$$= \dfrac{1}{2} \times \text{Area of parallelogram}$$

$$\Rightarrow \quad \dfrac{\text{Area of triangle}}{\text{Area of parallelogram}} = \dfrac{1}{2}$$

Hence, Area of triangle : Area of parallelogram $= 1:2$.

2. In the figure, parallelogram ABCD and $\triangle$BCP are on the same base BC and between the same parallels. If ar (BCP) = 15 cm^2, then ar (ABCD) is equal to .... [Board Term II, 2012, Set-5]

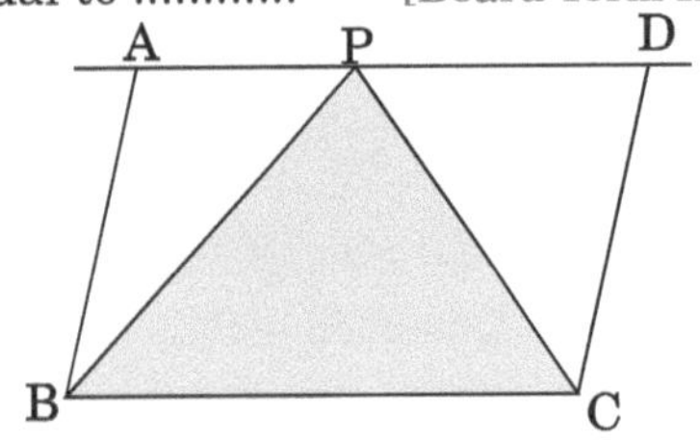

Sol. We know that if parallelogram ABCD and $\triangle$BCP are on the same base BC and between the same parallels the area of parallelogram is twice the area of triangle.

$$ar\ (BCP) = 15\ cm^2 \qquad \text{(given)}$$

Hence, ar (ABCD) = 2 × ar (BCP)

$$= 2 \times 15 = 30\ cm^2.$$

3. In the figure, BE = 2 EC and ar ($\triangle$ABC) = 60 cm^2, then find ar ($\triangle$AEC). [Board Term II, 2012, Set-(12)]

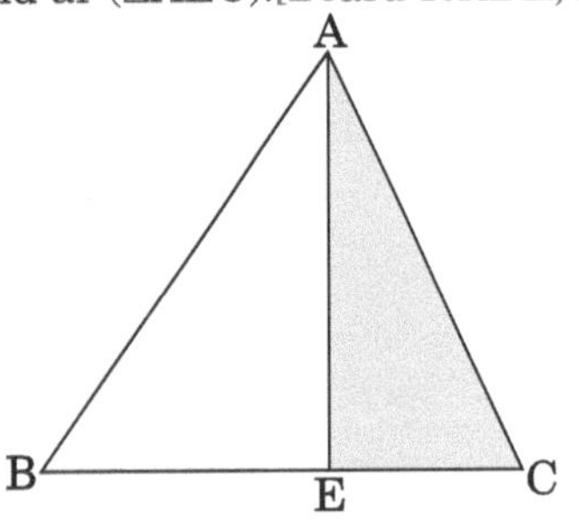

Sol. Given, $\qquad\qquad$ BE = 2 EC

$\Rightarrow \qquad\qquad\qquad$ BC = 3 EC $\qquad\qquad$ ...(i)

and $\qquad$ ar ($\triangle$ABC) = 60 cm^2

$\Rightarrow \qquad \dfrac{1}{2} \times BC \times h = 60$

$\qquad\qquad$ [let h = perpendicular distance]

$\Rightarrow \qquad \dfrac{1}{2} \times 3 \times EC \times h = 60 \qquad$ [From eq^n(i)]

$\Rightarrow \qquad \dfrac{1}{2} \times EC \times h = \dfrac{60}{3} = 20\ cm^2$

Hence, $\quad$ ar ($\triangle$AEC) = 20 cm^2.

4. In $\triangle$ABC, E is the mid-point of median AD, then the ratio of area of $\triangle$BED to the area $\triangle$ABC is .... [Board Term II, 2012, Set-01]

Sol. Since median of a triangle divides it into two triangles of equal area.

$\therefore \qquad$ ar ($\triangle$ACD) = ar ($\triangle$ABD)

$\Rightarrow \qquad$ ar ($\triangle$ABD) = $\dfrac{1}{2}$ ar ($\triangle$ABC) $\qquad$ ...(i)

Now, in $\triangle$ABD, BE is a median

$\therefore \qquad$ ar ($\triangle$BED) = $\dfrac{1}{2}$ ar ($\triangle$ABD)

$$= \dfrac{1}{2} \times \dfrac{1}{2} \times ar\ (\triangle ABC)$$

$$\text{[from eq}^n\text{(i)]}$$

$$= \dfrac{1}{4} ar\ (\triangle ABC)$$

Hence, required ratio = 1 : 4.

5. Why we cannot construct a triangle of given sides as 5 cm, 5 cm and 10 cm ?

[Board Term II, Set-RQTZFBW, 2016]

Sol. Since, 5 + 5 = 10 is not greater than the third side of a triangle.

Hence construction of triangle is not possible.

Short Answer Type Questions

(2 Marks Each)

1. In the given figure, ABCD and EFGD are two parallelograms and G is the mid-point of CD.

Then ar (DPC) = $\dfrac{1}{2}$ ar (EFGD)

[NCERT Exemplar]

Sol. Given, ABCD and EFGD are two parallelograms and G is the mid-point of CD.

Now, construct PG.

Thus, PG is a median of $\triangle$DPC and it divides the triangle into two parts of equal areas.

Then, $\quad$ ar ($\triangle$DPG) = ar ($\triangle$GPC)

$$= \dfrac{1}{2} ar\ (DPC) \qquad \text{...(i)}$$

Also we know that, if a parallelogram and a triangle lie on the same base between the same parallels, then area of triangle is equal to half of the area of parallelogram.

Here, parallelogram EFGD and ($\triangle$DPG) lie on the same base DG and between the same parallels DE and GF.

So, $\text{ar}(\Delta DPG) = \dfrac{1}{2} \text{ar}(EFGD)$ ...(ii)

From eq. (i) and (ii), we get

$$= \dfrac{1}{2}\text{ar}(\Delta DPC) = \dfrac{1}{2}\text{ar}(EFGD)$$

$\Rightarrow$ $\text{ar}(\Delta DPC) = \text{ar}(EFGD)$

Hence, the given statement is false.

2. ABC and BDE are two equilateral triangles such that D is the mid-point of BC. Then ar (BDE) = $\dfrac{1}{4}$ ar (ABC)   **[NCERT Exemplar]**

Sol. Given, triangles ABC and BDE are two equilateral triangles.

Let each sides of triangles ABC be x, then

According to the question,

$\because$ D is the mid-point of BC, so each side of triangle BDE is $\dfrac{x}{2}$,

Now, $\dfrac{\text{ar}(BDE)}{\text{ar}(ABC)} = \dfrac{\dfrac{\sqrt{3}}{4}\left(\dfrac{x}{2}\right)^2}{\dfrac{\sqrt{3}}{4}x^2} = \dfrac{x^2}{4x^2} = \dfrac{1}{4}$

$\therefore$ $\text{ar}(BDE) = \dfrac{1}{4}\text{ar}(ABC)$

Hence, the given statement is true.

Short Answer Type Questions I

(3 Marks Each)

1. ABCD is a parallelogram and X is the mid-point of AB. If ar $(\Delta ADC) = 24$ cm^2, then find ar (AXCD).   **[NCERT Exemplar]**

Sol. According to the question,

$$\text{ar}(\Delta ADC) = 24 \text{ cm}^2$$

and, ABCD is a parallelogram and X is the mid-point of AB. Draw the diagonal AC.

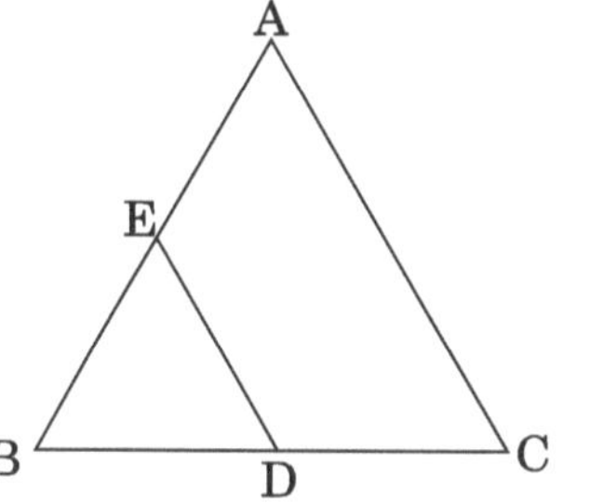

We know that diagonal of a parallelogram divides it into two triangles of equal areas.

$\therefore$ $\text{ar}(\|^{gm} ABCD) = \text{ar}(\Delta ADC) \times 2$

$$= 2 \times 24 = 48 \text{ cm}^2$$

Since, CX is the median of ΔABC.

$\therefore$ $\text{ar}(\Delta BCX) = \dfrac{1}{2}\text{ar}(\Delta ABC)$

$$= \dfrac{1}{2} \times 24 = 12 \text{ cm}^2$$

$[\because \text{ar}(\Delta ABC) = \text{ar}(\Delta ADC)]$

Hence, $\text{ar}(AXCD) = \text{ar}(\|^{gm} ABCD) - \text{ar}(\Delta BXC)$

$$= 48 - 12$$

$$= 36 \text{ cm}^2.$$

2. ΔABC and ΔBDE are two equilateral triangles such that D is the mid-point of BC. Then, prove that ar $(\Delta BDE) = \dfrac{1}{4}$ ar (ΔABC).

   [NCERT Exemplar]

Sol. Given : ΔABC and ΔBDE are two equilateral triangles.

$\therefore$ Area of $\Delta ABC = \dfrac{\sqrt{3}}{4} \times (BC)^2$ ...(i)

$$\left[\because \text{ area of an equilateral triangle} = \dfrac{\sqrt{3}}{4} \times (\text{side})^2\right]$$

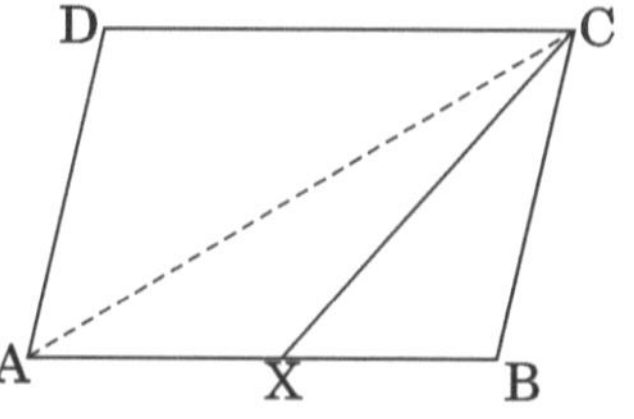

and D is the mid-point of BC.

To prove : ar $(\Delta BDE) = \dfrac{1}{4}$ ar (ΔABC)

Proof : $\therefore$ $BD = CD = \dfrac{1}{2}BC$

$[\because$ D is the mid-point of BC$]$

$\therefore$ Area of $\Delta BDE = \dfrac{\sqrt{3}}{4}(BD)^2$

$$= \dfrac{\sqrt{3}}{4}\left(\dfrac{BC}{2}\right)^2$$

$$= \dfrac{\sqrt{3}}{4} \times \dfrac{(BC)^2}{2}$$ ...(ii)

From eqs. (i) and (ii), we get

$\therefore$ $\text{ar}(\Delta BDE) = \dfrac{1}{4}\text{ar}(\Delta ABC)$

Hence proved

3. $\triangle ABC$ and $\triangle ABD$ are two triangles on the same base AB. If the line segment CD is bisected by AB at O. Show that ar (ABC) = ar (ABD).

[NCERT] [Board Term II, 2012, Set-1]

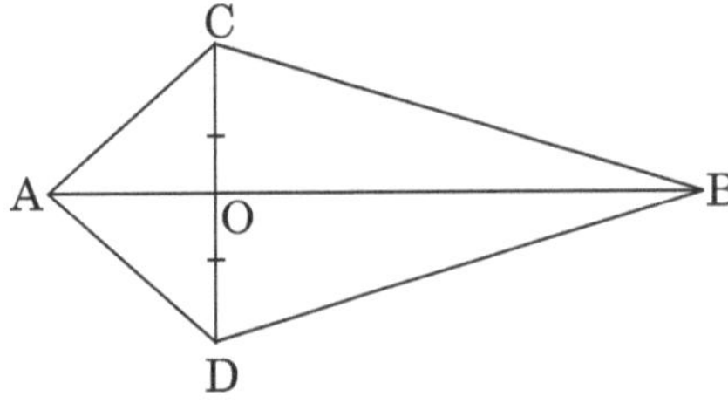

Sol. Given, $\triangle ABC$ and $\triangle ABD$ are two triangles on the same base AB.

CD is bisected by AB at O.

$\therefore$ $\quad\quad\quad\quad$ CO = OD

In $\triangle ADC$, AO is the median.

$\therefore$ $\quad\quad$ ar ($\triangle AOC$) = ar (AOD) $\quad\quad$ ...(i)

[$\because$ Median of a triangle divides it into two triangles of equal area.]

In $\triangle CDB$, BO is the median.

$\quad\quad$ ar (BOC) = ar (BOD) $\quad\quad$ ...(ii)

[$\because$ Median of a triangle divides it into two triangles of equal area.]

On adding (i) and (ii), we get

ar (AOC) + ar (BOC) = ar (AOD) + ar (BOD)

$\therefore$ $\quad\quad$ ar (ABC) = ar (ABD).

Hence proved.

4. Diagonals AC and BD of a trapezium ABCD with AB ∥ DC intersect each other at O. Prove that ar (AOD) = ar (BOC).

[NCERT] [Board Term II, 2012, Set-(20)]

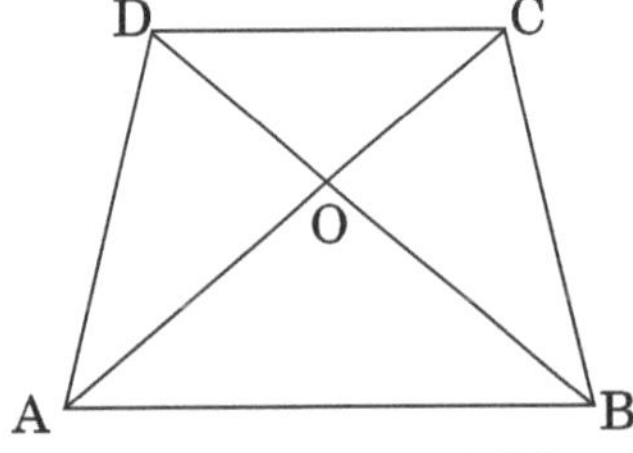

Sol. **Given :** Diagonals AC and BD of a trapezium ABCD with AB ∥ DC intersect each other at O.

To prove : ar ($\triangle AOD$) = ar ($\triangle BOC$)

Proof : Given AB ∥ DC.

$\quad\quad$ ar ($\triangle ABD$) = ar ($\triangle ABC$)

On subtracting ($\triangle ABO$) both sides, we get

ar ($\triangle ABD$) – ar ($\triangle ABO$) = ar ($\triangle ABC$) – ar ($\triangle ABO$)

$\therefore$ $\quad$ ar ($\triangle AOD$) = ar ($\triangle BOC$)

Hence Proved.

5. E is any point on the median AD of a $\triangle ABC$. Prove that ar ($\triangle ABE$) = ar ($\triangle ACE$).

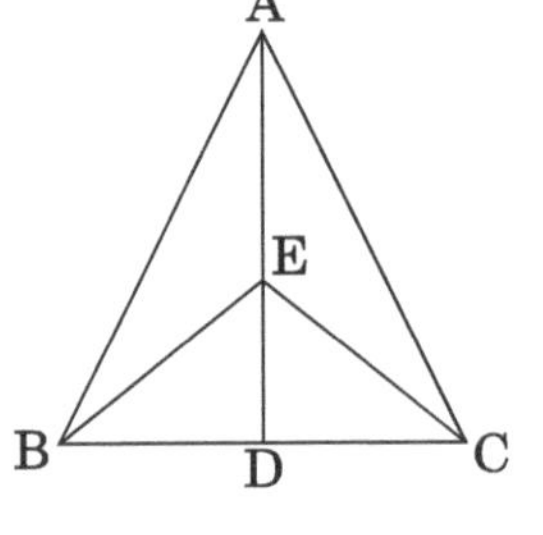

[NCERT] [Board Term II, 2012, Set-23]

Sol. **Given :** E is any point on the median AD of a $\triangle ABC$.

To prove : ar ($\triangle ABE$) = ar ($\triangle ACE$)

Proof : Since, median of a triangle divides it into two triangles of equal area.

In $\triangle ABC$, AD is median.

$\quad\quad$ ar ($\triangle ABD$) = ar ($\triangle ACD$) $\quad\quad$ ...(i)

In $\triangle BEC$, ED is a median.

$\quad\quad$ ar ($\triangle BDE$) = ar ($\triangle CDE$) $\quad\quad$ ...(ii)

On subtraction equation (ii) from equation (i), we get

ar ($\triangle ABD$) – ar ($\triangle BDE$)

$\quad\quad\quad\quad$ = ar ($\triangle ACD$) – ar ($\triangle CDE$)

$\therefore$ $\quad\quad$ ar ($\triangle ABE$) = ar ($\triangle ACE$).

6. Show that a median divides a triangle into two triangles equal areas.

[Board Term II, 2012, Set-(30), KVS 2016, NCERT]

Sol. **Given :** A triangle ABC and a median AD.

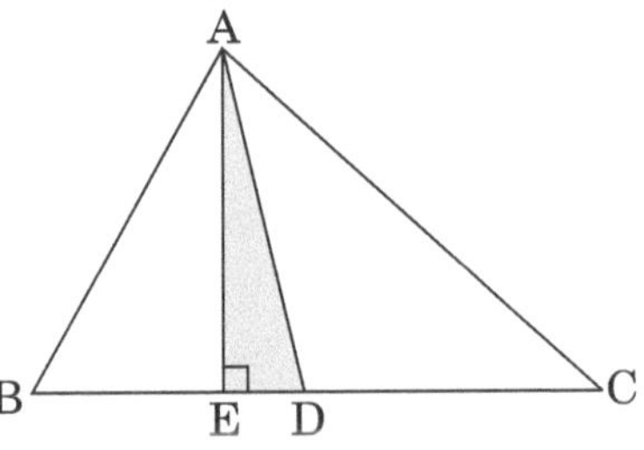

To prove : ar ($\triangle ABD$) = ar ($\triangle ADC$).

Construction : Draw a perpendicular AE on side BC.

Proof : $\quad\because$ $\quad$ AD is a median and AE $\perp$ BC

$\therefore$ $\quad$ Area of $\triangle ABD = \dfrac{1}{2} \times BD \times AE$

and Area of $\triangle ADC = \dfrac{1}{2} \times DC \times AE$

But $\quad\quad\quad\quad$ BD = DC, $\quad$ ($\because$ AD is a median)

$\therefore$ $\quad\quad$ ar ($\triangle ABD$) = ar ($\triangle ADC$)

Hence proved.

7. In the given figure, PS ∥ QR. Show that:
ar (ΔROS) = ar (ΔPOQ).

[Board Term II, 2012, Set-25]

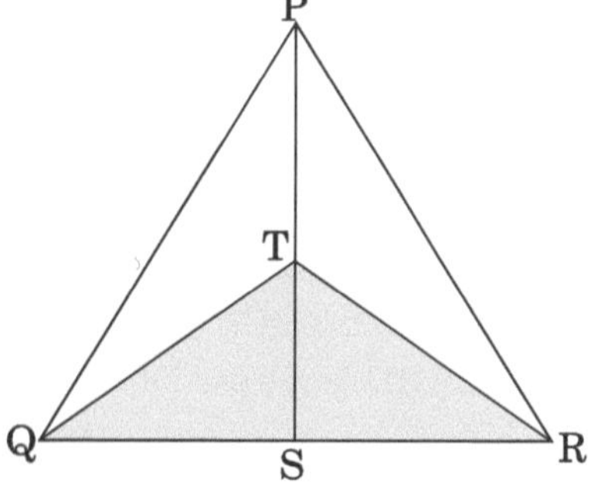

Sol. **Given :** PS ∥ QR

To prove : ar (ΔROS) = ar (ΔPOQ)

Proof : Since ΔPSR and ΔPSQ are on the same base PS and between the same parallels PS and QR.

∴   ar (ΔPSR) = ar (ΔPSQ)

On subtracting the ar (ΔPSO) from both sides, we get

⇒   ar (ΔPSR) – ar (ΔPSO)

        = ar (ΔPSQ) – ar (ΔPSO)

∴   ar (ΔROS) = ar (ΔPOQ).   **Hence proved.**

8. In the given figure, ABCD is a parallelogram and BE ⊥ AD. If BE = 14 cm and AD = 8 cm, find the area of ΔDBC.   [Board Term II, 2012, Set-24]

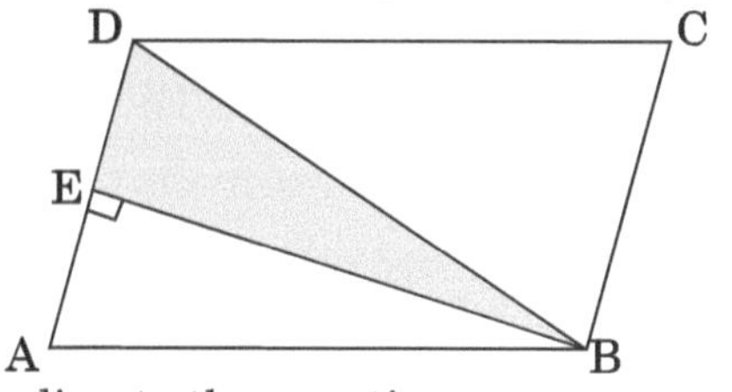

Sol. According to the question.

BE = 14 cm, AD = 8 cm

∴   Area $(\triangle ADB) = \dfrac{1}{2} \times 8 \times 14 = 56 \text{ cm}^2$

∵   ABCD is a parallelogram.

∴   ar $(\triangle DBC) = $ ar $(\triangle ADB) = 56 \text{ cm}^2$

        [∵ Diagonal of a parallelogram divides it into two triangles of equal area]

Hence, the area of ΔDBC is 56 cm².

9. In the given figure T is mid-point of PS. Find ar (QTR).   [Board Term II, 2013]

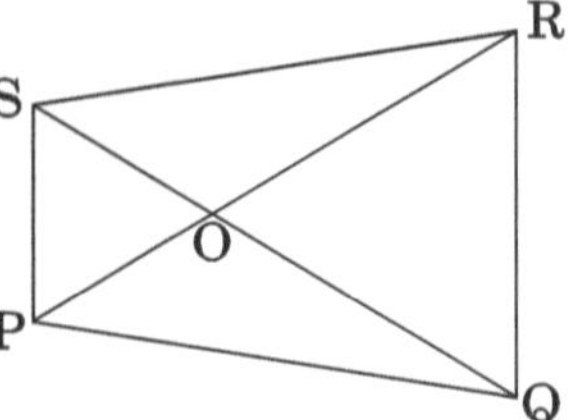

Sol. Since, median QT and RT divide ΔPQS and ΔPRS in two triangles of equal areas.

$$\text{ar } (\triangle QTS) = \dfrac{1}{2} \text{ ar } (\triangle PQS) \qquad …(i)$$

and $\text{ar } (\triangle RTS) = \dfrac{1}{2} \text{ ar } (\triangle RPS) \qquad …(ii)$

On adding eqⁿ (i) and (ii), we get

$$\text{ar } (\triangle QTS + \triangle RTS) = \dfrac{1}{2} [\text{ar } (\triangle PQS) + \text{ar } (\triangle PRS)]$$

∴ $\text{ar } (\triangle QTR) = \dfrac{1}{2} \text{ ar } (\triangle PQR)$

Hence, the area of $\triangle QTR = \dfrac{1}{2} \text{ ar } (\triangle PQR)$.

10. ΔPQR is an equilateral triangle with PM ⊥ QR. Show that ar (ΔPQM) = ar (ΔPRM).

[Board Term II, 2015]

Sol. **Given :** ΔPQR is equilateral and PM ⊥ QR.

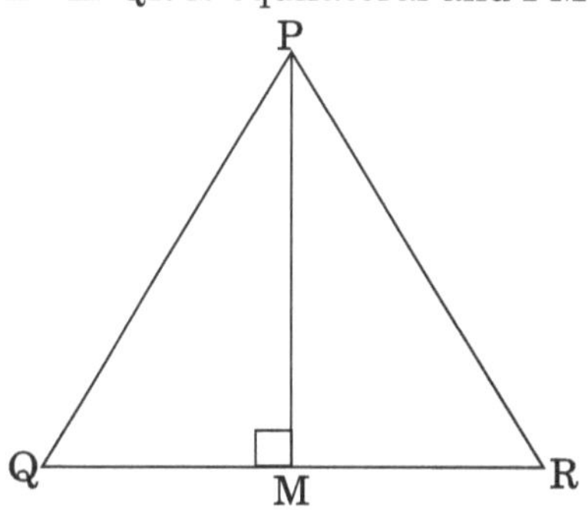

To prove : ar (ΔPQM) = ar (ΔPRM)

Proof : In triangles PQM and PRM, we have

        PQ = PR   (∵ ΔPQR is equilateral)

        PMQ = PMR = 90   [∵ PM ⊥ QR]

and,   PM = PM   (Common side)

∴   By RHS criterion of congruency, we get

        ΔPQM = ΔPRM

Now, since two congruent regions have equal area,

∴   ar (ΔPQM) = ar (ΔPRM)   **Hence proved.**

Short Answer Type Questions II

(3 Marks Each)

1. In the following figure, CD ∥ AE and CY ∥ BA. Prove that ar (ΔCBX) = ar (ΔAXY)

[NCERT Exemplar]

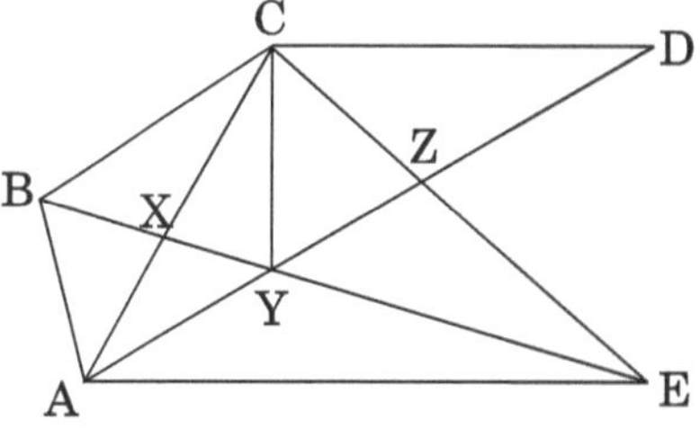

Sol. **Given :** $CD \parallel AE$ and $CY \parallel BA$

To prove : ar $(\triangle CBX) = $ ar $(\triangle AXY)$

Proof : Since, $\triangle ABC$ and $\triangle BAY$ both lie on the same base AB and between the same parallel AB and CY.

$\therefore$ ar $(\triangle ABC) = $ ar $(\triangle BAY)$

$\Rightarrow$ ar $(\triangle ABX) + $ ar $(\triangle CBX)$

$\qquad\qquad = $ ar $(\triangle BAX) + $ ar $(\triangle AXY)$

$\therefore$ ar $(\triangle CBX) = $ ar $(\triangle AXY)$

[eliminating ar $(\triangle ABX)$ from both sides]

Hence proved.

2. O is any point on the diagonal PR of a parallelogram PQRS (figure).

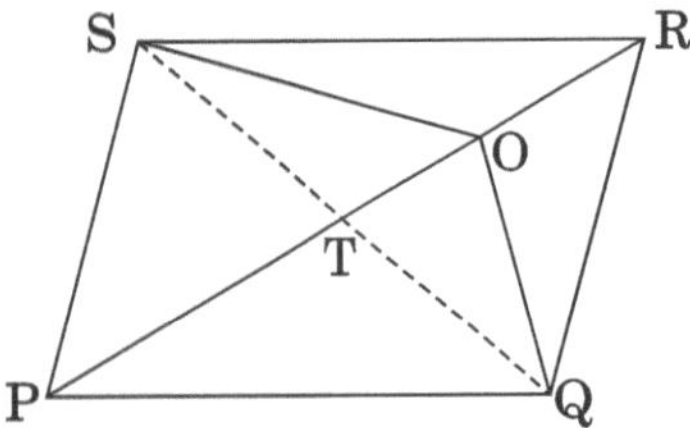

Prove that : ar $(\triangle PSO) = $ ar $(\triangle PQO)$

[NCERT Exemplar]

Sol. **Given :** PQRS is a parallelogram and O is any point on the diagonal PR.

To prove : ar $(\triangle PSO) = $ ar $(\triangle PQO)$.

Construction : Join SQ, which intersect PR at T.

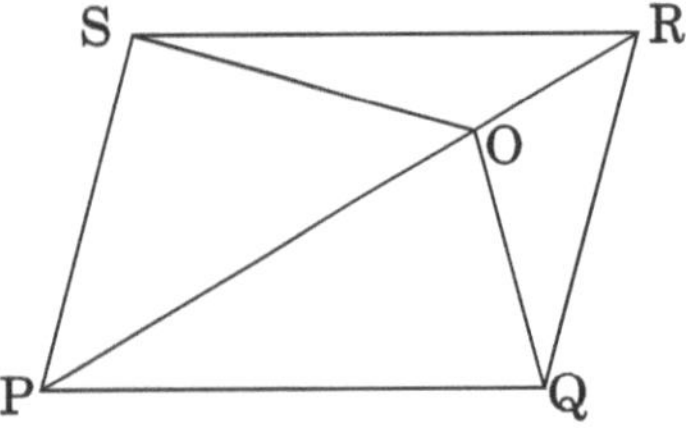

Proof : We know, that diagonals of a parallelogram bisect each other.

$\therefore$ T is the mid-point of QS

Since, a median of a triangle divides it into two triangles of equal area.

PT is its median of $\triangle PQS$.

$\Rightarrow$ ar $(\triangle PTS) = $ ar $(\triangle PQT)$ ...(i)

Also, OT is a median of $\triangle SQO$.

$\Rightarrow$ ar $(\triangle STO) = (\triangle QTO)$ ...(ii)

On adding, Eqs. (i) and (ii), we have

ar $(\triangle PTS) + $ ar $(\triangle STO)$

$\qquad\qquad = $ ar $(\triangle PQT) + $ ar $(\triangle QTO)$

$\therefore$ ar $(\triangle PSO) = $ ar $(\triangle PQO)$ **Hence proved.**

3. A point E is taken of the side BC of a parallelogram ABCD. AE and DC are produced to meet at F. Prove that ar $(\triangle ADF) = $ ar (quadrilateral ABFC).

[NCERT Exemplar]

Sol. **Given :** ABCD is a parallelogram.

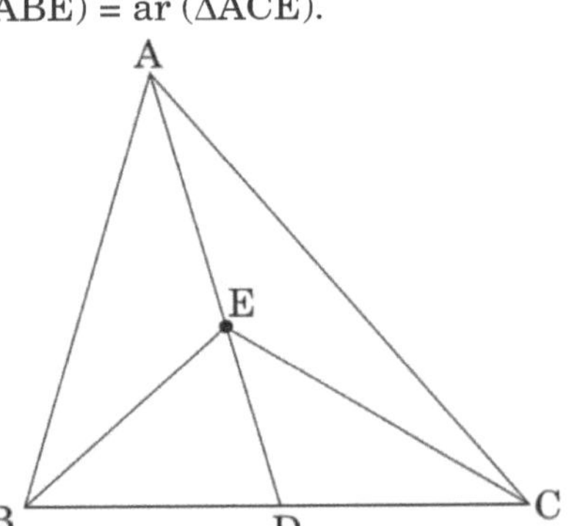

To prove : ar $(\triangle ADF) = $ ar (quadrilateral ABFC)

Proof : Since, $\triangle ACB$ and $\triangle AFB$ are on the same base AB and between same parallels AB and DF.

$\therefore$ ar $(\triangle ACB) = $ ar $(\triangle AFB)$ ...(i)

Also, ar $(\triangle ACB) = $ ar $(\triangle ADC)$ ...(ii)

[$\because$ diagonal of parallelogram divides it into two triangles of equal area]

From eqs. (i) and (ii), we get

ar $(\triangle ADC) = $ ar $(\triangle AFB)$

On adding ar $(\triangle ACF)$ both sides, we get

ar $(\triangle ADC) + $ ar $(\triangle ACF) = $ ar $(\triangle AFB) + $ ar $(\triangle ACF)$

$\therefore$ ar $(\triangle ADF) = $ ar (quadrilateral ABFC).

Hence proved.

4. In the given figure E is any point on median AD of a $\triangle ABC$. Show that

ar $(\triangle ABE) = $ ar $(\triangle ACE)$. [NCERT]

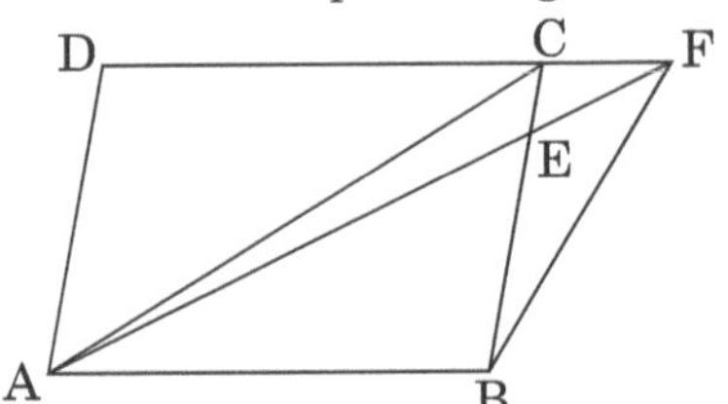

Sol. **Given :** AD is a median of $\triangle ABC$ and E any point on AD.

To prove : ar $(\triangle ABE) = $ ar $(\triangle ACE)$

Proof : Since, AD is the median of $\triangle ABC$.

$\therefore$ ar $(\triangle ABD) = $ ar $(\triangle ACD)$ ...(i)

[since, a median of a triangle divides it into two triangles of equal areas]

Also, ED is the median of $\triangle EBC$.

$\therefore$ ar $(\triangle BED) = $ ar $(\triangle CED)$ ...(ii)

[since, a median of a triangles divides it into two triangles of equal areas

On subtracting eq. (ii) from eq. (i), we get

ar $(\triangle ABD) - $ ar $(\triangle BED)$

$\qquad\qquad = $ ar $(\triangle ACD) - $ ar $(\triangle CED)$

$\therefore$ ar $(\triangle ABE) = $ ar $(\triangle ACE)$ **Hence proved.**

5. In the following figure, AP ∥ BQ ∥ CR. Prove that ar (ΔAQC) = ar (ΔPBR).   [NCERT]

[Board Term II, KVS, 2014; 2012, Set-33, 65]

Sol. **Given :** AP ∥ BQ ∥ CR

To prove : ar (ΔAQC) = ar (ΔPBR)

According to the given figure we have

ar (ΔPBR) = ar (ΔPBQ) + ar (ΔQBR)   ...(i)

and ar (ΔAQC) = ar (ΔAQB) + ar (ΔBQC)   ...(ii)

Clearly, ar (ΔBQC) = ar (ΔQBR)   ...(iii)

[∵ ΔBQC and ΔQBR lie on same base BQ between the same parallel lines BQ and CR]

Similarly, ar (ΔAQB) = (ΔQBR)   ...(iv)

[∵ ΔAQB and ΔPBQ lie on same base BQ between the same parallel lines BQ and AP]

On adding eqs. (iii) and (iv), we get

ar (ΔBQC) + ar (ΔAQB)

= ar (ΔQBR) + ar (ΔPBQ)

On putting the values from eqs. (i) and (ii), we get

∴   ar (ΔAQC) = ar (ΔPBR)   **Hence proved.**

6. D is the mid-point of side BC of ΔABC and E is the mid-point of BD. If O is the mid-point of AE, then prove that ar (ΔBOE) = $\frac{1}{8}$ ar (ΔABC).

[Board Term II, 2012, Set-15]

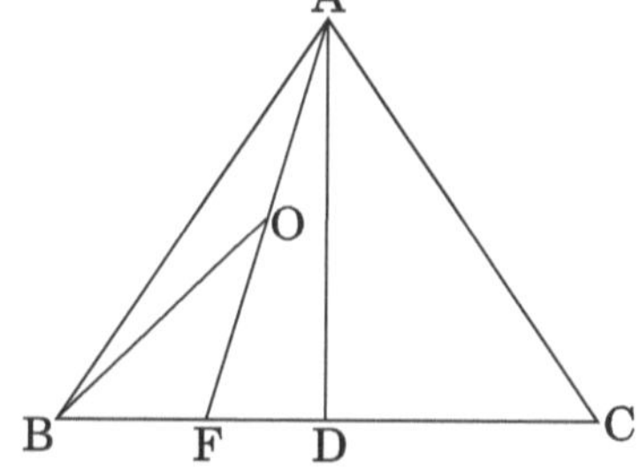

Sol. **Given :** In ΔABC, D is the mid-point of side BC and E is the mid-point of side BD.

To prove : ar (ΔBOE) = $\frac{1}{8}$ ar (ΔABC)

Proof : A median divides a triangle into two triangles of equal areas.

$$ar\ (\Delta BOE) = \frac{1}{2}\ AR\ (\Delta ABE),$$

[∵ BO is a median]

$$= \frac{1}{2} \times \frac{1}{2}\ ar\ (\Delta ABD),$$

[∵ AE is a median]

$$= \frac{1}{2} \times \frac{1}{2} \times \frac{1}{2}\ ar\ (\Delta ABC),$$

[∵ AD is a median]

∴   ar (ΔBOE) = $\frac{1}{8}$ ar (ΔABC).

Hence proved.

7. In ΔGHK; D, E and F are the mid-points of sides HK, KG and GH respectively. Show that EFHK is trapezium and ar (EFHK) = $\frac{3}{4}$ ar (ΔGHK).

[Board Term II, 2014]

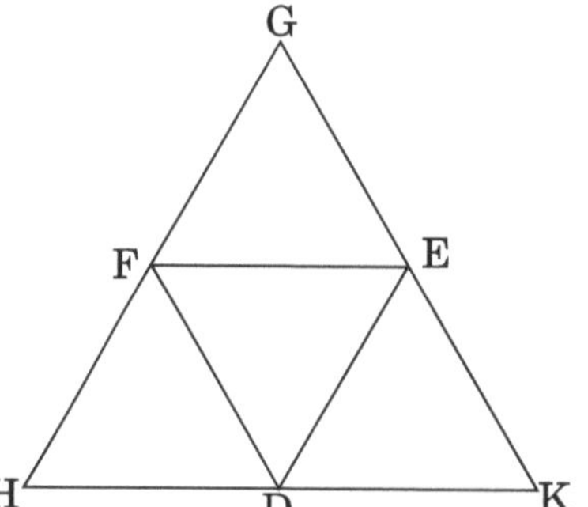

Sol. **Given :** In ΔGHK, points D, E and F are mid-points of sides HK, KG and GH respectively.

To prove : EFHK is a trapezium and ar (EFHK) = $\frac{3}{4}$ ar (ΔGHK).

Proof : ∵ By mid-point theorem,

$$FE = \frac{1}{2}\ KH\quad and\quad FE \parallel KH\quad ...(i)$$

In quadrilateral EFHK,

EF ∥ HK   ...(by (i))

Hence, EFHK is a trapezium.

Also, ar (EFHK) = ar (ΔFHD) + ar (ΔDEF) + ar (ΔDEK)   ...(ii)

We have,   FE ∥ HD   and   FE = HD

Hence, FEDH is a parallelogram.

So, ar (ΔFHD) = ar (ΔDEF)   ...(iii)

Similarly, DFGE is a parallelogram.

∴   ar (ΔDEF) = ar (ΔGEF)   ...(iv)

Also, DFEK is a parallelogram.

∴   ar (ΔDEF) = ar (ΔDEK)   ...(v)

From eq^n (iii), (iv) and (v) we get,

ar (ΔGEF) = ar (ΔFHD)

$\qquad$ = ar (ΔDEK) = ar (ΔDEF)

$\qquad = \dfrac{1}{4}$ ar (ΔGHK)   ...(vi)

From eq^n (vi) and (ii), we get

∴   ar (EFHK) = $\dfrac{3}{4}$ ar (ΔGHK)

Hence proved.

8. In ΔPQR, A and B are points on sides QR such that they trisect QR. Prove that :

ar (ΔPQB) = 2ar (ΔPBR)

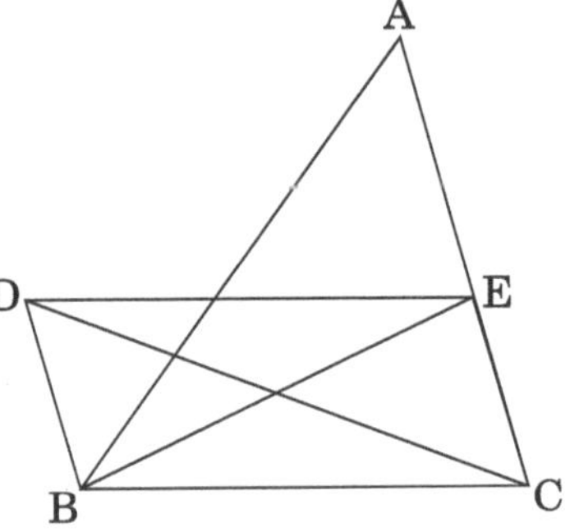

[Board Term II, Set LF0MCQ 2, 2016]

Sol. **Given :** PQR is a triangle and A and B are points on QR such that QA = AB = BR

To prove : ar (ΔPQB) = 2ar (ΔPBR)

Proof : Let h be the height of triangle PQR.

Now, According to the question,

$$ar\ (\Delta PQA) = \frac{1}{2} \times QA \times h$$

$$= \frac{1}{2} \times \frac{1}{3} \times QR \times h$$

$$= \frac{1}{6} \times QR \times h \qquad ...(i)$$

$$[\because\ QR = 3QA]$$

$$ar\ (\Delta PAB) = \frac{1}{2} \times AB \times h$$

$$= \frac{1}{2} \times \frac{1}{3} \times QR \times h$$

$$= \frac{1}{6} \times QR \times h \qquad ...(ii)$$

$$[\because\ QR = 3AB]$$

$$ar\ (\Delta PBR) = \frac{1}{2} \times BR \times h$$

$$= \frac{1}{2} \times \frac{1}{3} \times QR \times h$$

$$= \frac{1}{6} \times QR \times h \qquad ...(iii)$$

$$[\because\ QR = 3BR]$$

$$and \quad ar\ (\Delta PQB) = \frac{1}{2} \times QB \times h$$

$$= \frac{1}{2} \times \frac{2}{3} QR \times h$$

$$= \frac{1}{3} \times QR \times h \qquad ...(iv)$$

$$\left[\because\ QR = \frac{3}{2} QB\right]$$

From (i), (ii) and (iii), we get

$\qquad$ ar (ΔPQA) = ar (ΔPAB) = ar (ΔPBR) ...(v)

Now, ar (ΔPQB) = ar (ΔPQA) + ar (ΔPAB)

∴   ar (ΔPQB) = ar (ΔPBR) + ar (ΔPBR)

$\qquad\qquad$ [From (iv)]

∴   ar (ΔPQB) = 2ar (ΔPBR)

Hence proved.

Long Answer Type Questions
(4 Marks Each)

1. In the given figure, BD ∥ CA, E is mid-point of CA and BD = $\dfrac{1}{2}$ CA.

Prove that: ar (ΔABC) = 2ar (ΔDBC)

[NCERT Exemplar]

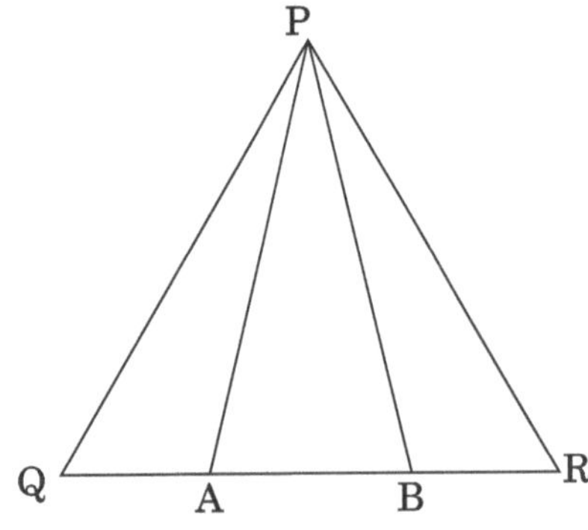

Sol. **Given :** BD ∥ CA, E is mid-point of CA. i.e., BE is median of ΔABC, also BD = $\dfrac{1}{2}$ CA.

To prove : ar (ΔABC) = 2ar (ΔDBC)

Proof : Since, median of a triangle divides it into two triangles of equal area.

$$\therefore \qquad \text{ar}(\triangle ABE) = \text{ar}(\triangle EBC)$$

$$\Rightarrow \qquad \text{ar}(\triangle EBC) = \frac{1}{2}\,\text{ar}(\triangle ABC) \qquad \text{...(i)}$$

and $\qquad \text{ar}(\triangle DBC) = \text{ar}(\triangle EBC) \qquad \text{...(ii)}$

[∵ triangles on same base and between same parallel lines are equal in area]

From eqs. (i) and (ii), we get

$$\text{ar}(\triangle DBC) = \frac{1}{2}\,\text{ar}(\triangle ABC)$$

$$\Rightarrow \qquad \text{ar}(\triangle ABC) = 2\text{ar}(\triangle DBC)$$

Hence proved.

2. P and Q are any two points lying on the sides DC and AD respectively of a parallelogram ABCD. Show that

ar ($\triangle$APB) = ar ($\triangle$BQC)   [NCERT]

Sol. **Given :** In parallelogram ABCD, P and Q are any two points lying on the sides DC and AD, respectively.

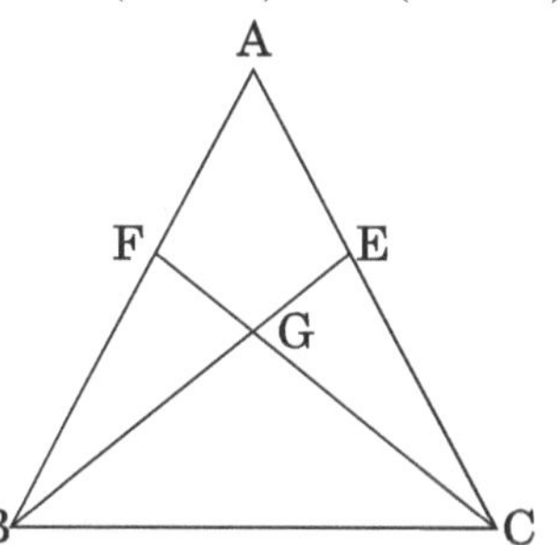

To prove : ar ($\triangle$APB) = ar ($\triangle$BQC)

Proof : Since, parallelogram ABCD and $\triangle$BQC stand on the same base BC and lie between the same parallel BC and AD.

$$\therefore \quad \text{ar}(\triangle BQC) = \frac{1}{2}\,\text{ar}(ABCD) \qquad \text{...(i)}$$

Similarly, $\triangle$APB and parallelogram ABCD stand on the same base AB and lie between the same parallel AB and CD.

$$\therefore \quad \text{ar}(\triangle APB) = \frac{1}{2}\,\text{ar}(ABCD) \qquad \text{..(ii)}$$

From eqs. (i) and (ii), we get

$\therefore \quad$ ar ($\triangle$APB) = ar ($\triangle$BQC)   **Hence proved.**

3. XY is a line parallel to side BC of a $\triangle$ABC. BE ∥ AC and CF ∥ AB meets XY at E and F respectively. Show that ar ($\triangle$ABE) = ar ($\triangle$ACF).

[NCERT] [Board Term II, 2012, Set-(26)]

Sol. **Given :** XY is a line parallel to side BC of a $\triangle$ABC. BE ∥ AC and CF ∥ AB meets XY at E and F respectively.

To prove : ar ($\triangle$ABE) = ar ($\triangle$ACE)

Construction : Join AE and AF.

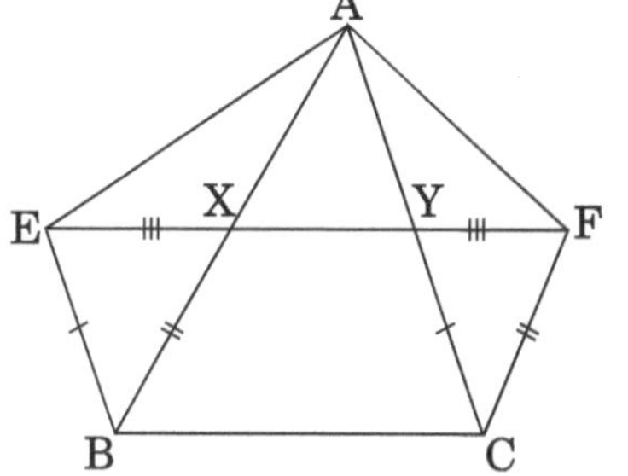

Proof : Since, CFXB is a parallelogram.

$$\Rightarrow \qquad XF = BC$$

Similarly, $\qquad$ EY = BC $\quad \Rightarrow \quad$ EX = YF

[Since, opposite sides of a parallelogram are equal]

In $\triangle$XBE and $\triangle$CFY,

$$BE = CY$$
$$BX = CF$$

and $\qquad EX = YF$

By SSS congruence rule, we get

$$\triangle XBE \cong \triangle CFY$$
$$\text{ar}(\triangle AXE) = \text{ar}(\triangle AYF)$$
$$\therefore \qquad \text{ar}(\triangle AEB) = \text{ar}(\triangle ACF).$$

Hence proved.

4. The medians BE and CF of a $\triangle$ABC intersect at G. Prove that

ar ($\triangle$GBC) = ar (quadrilateral AFGE).

[NCERT Exemplar]

Sol. **Given :** BE and CF are medians of a $\triangle$ABC.

To prove : ar ($\triangle$GBC) = ar (AFGE)

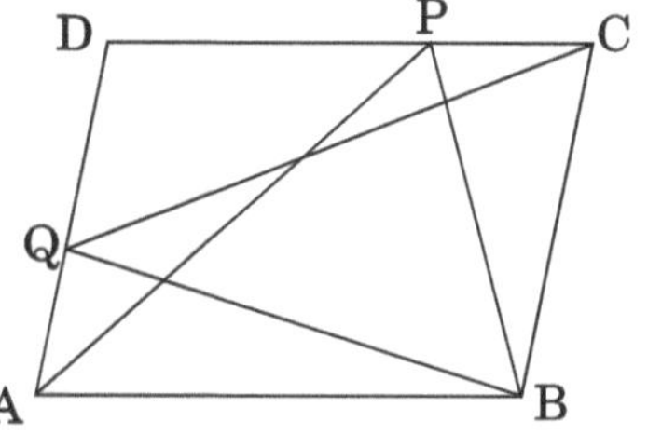

Proof : Since, median of a triangle divides it into two parts of equal area.

$$\therefore \qquad \text{ar}(\triangle FBC) = \text{ar}(\triangle AFC)$$

$$\Rightarrow \qquad \text{ar}(\triangle FBC) = \frac{1}{2}\,\text{ar}(\triangle ABC) \qquad \text{..(i)}$$

Similarly, ar ($\triangle$AEB) $= \frac{1}{2}\,\text{ar}(\triangle ABC) \qquad \text{..(ii)}$

From equations (i) and (ii), we get

$$\text{ar}(\triangle FBC) = \text{ar}(\triangle AEB)$$

On subtracting ar ($\triangle$GBF) from both sides, we get

ar ($\triangle$FBC) – ar ($\triangle$GBF)

$$= \text{ar}(\triangle AEB) - \text{ar}(\triangle GBF)$$

$$\Rightarrow \qquad \text{ar}(\triangle GBC) = \text{ar}(\text{quadrilateral AFGE})$$

Hence proved.

5. In a $\triangle ABC$, E is the mid-point of median AD. Show that

$$\text{ar }(\triangle BED) = \frac{1}{4}\text{ ar }(\triangle ABC).$$ [NCERT]

[Board Term II, KVS 2016, 2012]

Sol. Given : ABC is a triangle and E is the mid-point of the median AD.

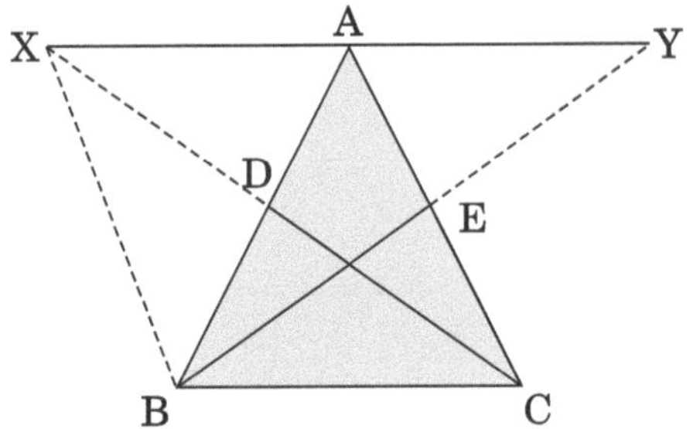

To prove : ar $(\triangle BED) = \frac{1}{4}$ ar $(\triangle ABC)$

Proof : We know that the median divides a triangle into two triangles of equal areas.

$\therefore \qquad$ ar $(\triangle ABD) = $ ar $(\triangle ADC)$

$\Rightarrow \qquad$ ar $(\triangle ABD) = \frac{1}{2}$ ar $(\triangle ABC)$ $\qquad$ ...(i)

In $\triangle ABD$, BE is the median.

$\therefore \quad$ ar $(\triangle BED) = $ ar $(\triangle BAE)$

$\qquad$ [$\because$ median divides a triangle into two triangles of equal areas.]

$\Rightarrow \qquad$ ar $(\triangle BED) = \frac{1}{2}$ ar $(\triangle ABD)$

$\Rightarrow \qquad$ ar $(\triangle BED) = \frac{1}{2} \times \frac{1}{2}$ ar $(\triangle ABC)$

$\qquad\qquad\qquad$ [from eq. (i)]

$\therefore \quad$ ar $(\triangle BED) = \frac{1}{4}$ ar $(\triangle ABC)$ **Hence proved.**

6. In the given figure, ABC and DBC are triangles on the same base and between the parallel lines l and m. If AB = 3 cm, BC = 5 cm, $\angle A = 90°$, find the area of $\triangle DBC$.

[Board Term II, 2012, Set-12]

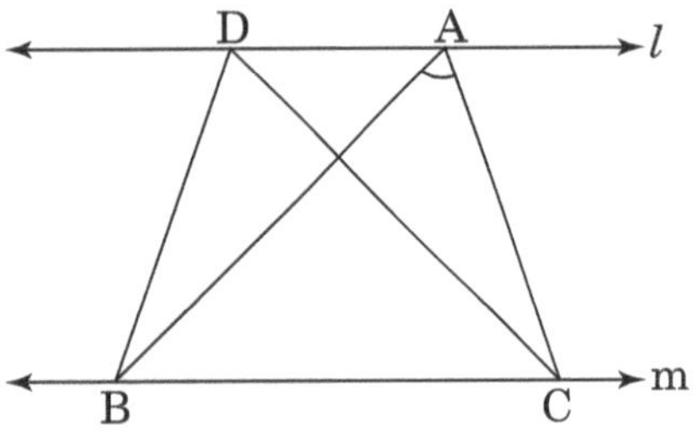

Sol. According to the question,

In $\triangle ABC$,

By Pythagoras theorem,

$$AC = \sqrt{BC^2 - AB^2} = \sqrt{5^2 - 3^2} = 4 \text{ cm}$$

Now, $\qquad$ ar $(\triangle ABC) = \frac{1}{2} \times AB \times AC$

$\qquad\qquad\qquad = \frac{1}{2} \times 3 \times 4 = 6 \text{ cm}^2$

$\therefore \qquad$ ar $(\triangle DBC) = $ ar $(\triangle ABC) = 6 \text{ cm}^2$

$\qquad$ [$\because$ $\triangle ABC$ and $\triangle DBC$ on the same base and between the same parallels]

Hence, the area of $\triangle DBC$.

7. In $\triangle ABC$, medians CD and BE are produced respectively to points X and Y such that CD = DX and BE = EY as shown in figure. Show the points X, A and Y are collinear. Also, show that A is the mid-point of XY.

[Board Term II, Set-LF0MCQ 2, 2016]

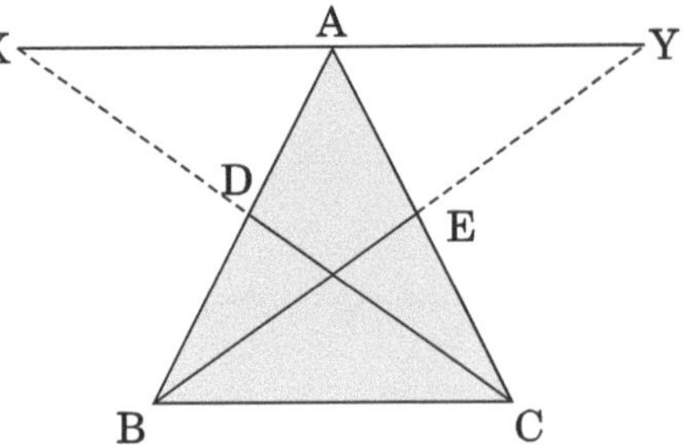

Sol. Given : In $\triangle ABC$, medians CD and BE are produced respectively to point X and Y such that

$$CD = DX \quad \text{and} \quad BE = EY$$

To prove : Points X, A and Y are collinear and A is the mid-point of XY.

Construction : Join BX.

In $\triangle XDB$ and $\triangle ADC$,

$\qquad\qquad XD = CD \qquad\qquad$ (given)

$\qquad\qquad \angle XDB = \angle ADC$

$\qquad\qquad\qquad$ (vertically opposite angles)

and BD = DA $\quad$ (CD is median of triangle ABC)

By SAS congruent rule, we have

$\qquad\qquad \triangle XDB \cong \triangle ADC$

$\therefore \qquad\qquad XB = AC \qquad\qquad$ (By c.p.c.t.)

$\qquad\qquad \triangle(XDB) = \triangle(ADC)$

Now, add XDA to both sides, we get

$\triangle(XDB) + \triangle(XDA) = \triangle(ADC) + \triangle(XDA)$

$\therefore \qquad\qquad \triangle(XBA) = \triangle(XAC)$

$\qquad\qquad\qquad$ (since the two triangles are on the same base and have equal areas, they lie between same parallels XA and BC)

Similarly, we can prove Δs BAY and CAY are equal and then AY $\parallel$ BC.

Hence, XACB and BCYA are parallelograms, where XA = BC and AY = BC. Thus, XA = AY.

Therefore, A is the mid-points of XY.

Now, since XA = AY and points XAY lie on the same line, therefore they are collinear.

Hence proved.

8. In the following figure, ABCD is a parallelogram and BC is produced to a point Q such that AD = CQ. If AQ intersect DC at P, then show that

ar (ΔBPC) = ar (ΔDPQ)

[**NCERT Exemplar Board Term II, 2012, Set-20**]

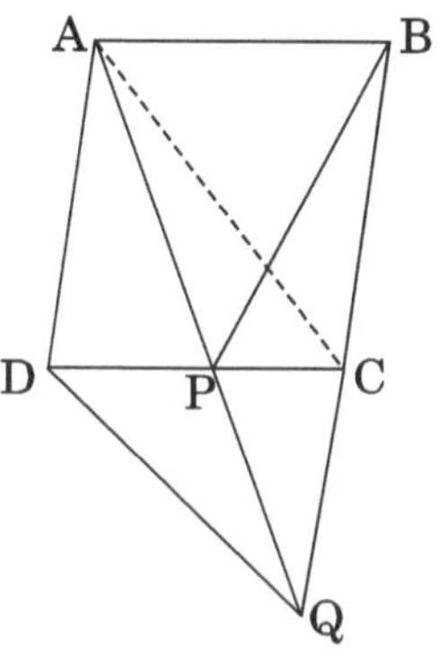

Sol. **Given :** ABCD is a parallelogram and AD = CQ.

To prove : ar (ΔBPC) = ar (ΔDPQ)

Construction : Join the line segment AC.

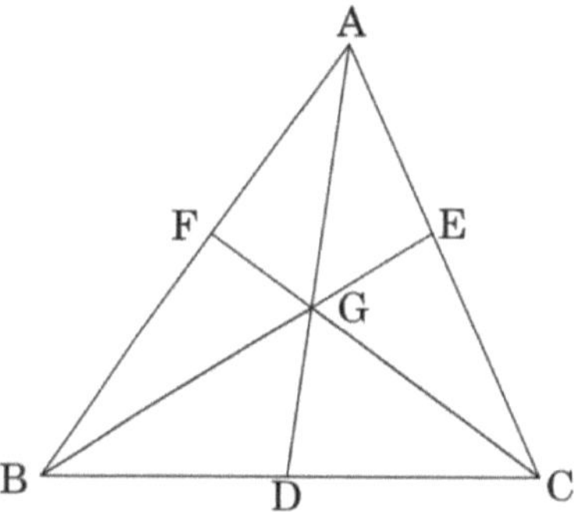

Proof : Since, ΔAPC and ΔBPC lie on the same base PC and between the same parallels PC and AB, therefore,

ar (ΔAPC) = ar (ΔBPC)   ...(i)

Also, AD = CQ   and   AD $\parallel$ CQ   [given]

Thus, in quadrilateral ACQD, one pair of opposite sides is equal and parallel.

Therefore, ADQC is a parallelogram.

Now, as ΔADQ and ΔADC lie on the same base AD and between the same parallels AD and CQ.

$\therefore$ ar (ΔADQ) = ar (ΔADC)

On subtracting ar (ΔADC) from both sides, we have

$\Rightarrow$ ar (ΔADQ) – ar (ΔADP)

$\qquad$ = ar (ΔADC) – ar (ΔADP)

$\therefore$ ar (ΔDPQ) = ar (ΔAPC)   ...(ii)

From Eqs. (i) and (ii), we get

$\therefore$ ar (ΔBPC) = ar (ΔDPQ)   **Hence proved.**

9. If the medians of a ΔABC intersect at G, show that

ar (ΔAGB) = ar (ΔAGC) = ar (ΔBGC)

$$= \frac{1}{3} \text{ ar } (\Delta ABC).$$

Sol. **Given :** In ΔABC, all median intersect at G.

To prove : ar (ΔAGB) = ar (ΔAGC)

$$= \text{ar } (\Delta BGC) = \frac{1}{3} \text{ ar } (\Delta ABC)$$

Proof : Since, the median of a triangle divides the triangles of equal area.

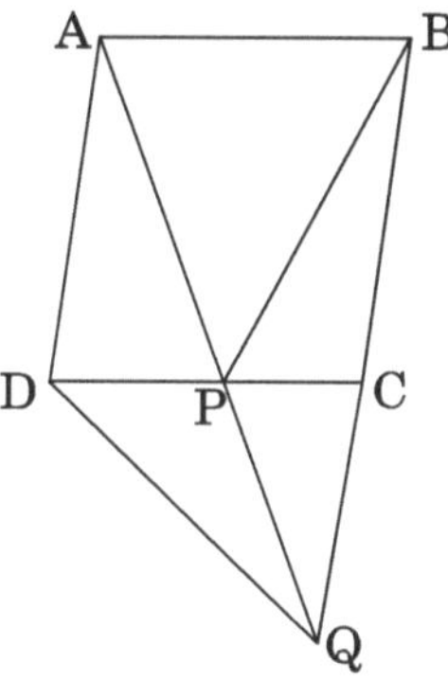

In ΔABC, AD is the median.

$\Rightarrow$ ar (ΔABD) = ar (ΔACD)   ...(i)

In ΔGBC, GD is the median.

$\Rightarrow$ ar (ΔGBD) = ar (ΔGCD)   ...(ii)

On subtracting eq. (ii) from eq. (i), we obtain

ar (ΔABD) – ar (ΔGBD)

$\qquad$ = ar (ΔACD) – ar (ΔGCD)

$\Rightarrow$ ar (ΔAGB) = ar (ΔAGC)   ...(iii)

Similarly, ar (ΔAGB) = ar (ΔBGC)   ...(iv)

From eqs. (iii) and (iv), we have

$\qquad$ ar (ΔAGB) = ar (ΔAGC) = ar (ΔBGC)

Also,

ar (ΔAGB) + ar (ΔAGC) + ar (ΔBGC) = ar (ΔABC)

$\therefore$ 3 ar (ΔAGB) = ar (ΔABC)

$\Rightarrow$ ar (ΔAGB) = $\frac{1}{3}$ ar (ΔABC)   ...(v)

From eq^n (iii), (iv) and (v), we get

$\therefore$ ar (ΔAGB) = ar (ΔAGC) = ar (ΔBGC)

$$= \frac{1}{3} \text{ ar } (\Delta ABC).$$

Hence proved.

CHAPTER 10

Circles

- Through examples, arrive at definition of circle and related concepts- radius, circumference, diameter, chord, arc, secant sector, segment, subtended angle.
- (Prove) Equal chords of a circle subtend equal angles at the center and (motivate) its converse.
- (Motivate) The perpendicular from the center of a circle to a chord bisects the chord and conversely, the line draw through the center of a circle to bisect a chord is perpendicular to the chord.
- (Motivate) There is one and only one circle passing through three given non-collinear points.
- (Motivate) Equal chords of a circle (or of congruent circles) are equidistant from the center (or their respective centers) and conversely.
- (Prove) The angle subtended by an arc at the center is double the angle subtended by it at any point on the remaining part of the circle.
- (Motivate) Angles in the same segment of a circle are equal.
- (Motivate) If a line segment joining two points subtends equal angle at two other points lying on the same side of the line containing the segment, the four points lie on a circle.
- (Motivate) The sum of either of the pair of the opposite angles of a cyclic quadrilateral is 180° and its converse.

A flow chart on basic concepts of circle

Circle

A circle is the collection of all those points in a plane, which are equidistant from a fixed point in the plane. There is one and only circle passing through three non-collinear points.

Important Results

- Equal chords of a circle subtend equal angles at the centre
- If the angles subtended by two chords of a circle at the centre are equal then the chords are equal.
- The perpendicular drawn from the centre of the circle to a chord bisects the chord.
- The line drawn through the centre of a circle to bisect a chord is perpendicular to the chord.
- Equal chords of a circle are equidistant from the centre
- Choreds equidistant rom the centre of a circle are equal in length.
- The angle subtended by an are at the centre is double the angle subtended by it at any other point on the remaining part of the circle.
- Angle in the same segment of a circle are equal.
- The angle in a semicircle is right angle.
- If two circles intersect in two points, then the line through the centres is perpendicular to the common chord.
- Congruent arcs of a circle subtend equal angle at the centre.

Cyclic Quadrilateral

If all vertices of a quadrilateral lie on a circle, it is called a cyclic quadrilateral.

- The sum of either pair of opposite angles of a cyclic quadrilateral is 180°.
- If sum of a pair of opposite angles of a quadrilateral is 180°, the quadrilatoral is cyclic.
- If a line segment joining two points subtends equal angles at two other points lying on the same side of the line, the four points are concyclic.

[Topic 1] [Basic Properties of Circles]

Points to be Remembered:

- The collection of all the points in a plane which are at a fixed distance from a fixed point in the plane is called a circle.
- The fixed point is called the centre and the constant distance is called the radius of the circle.

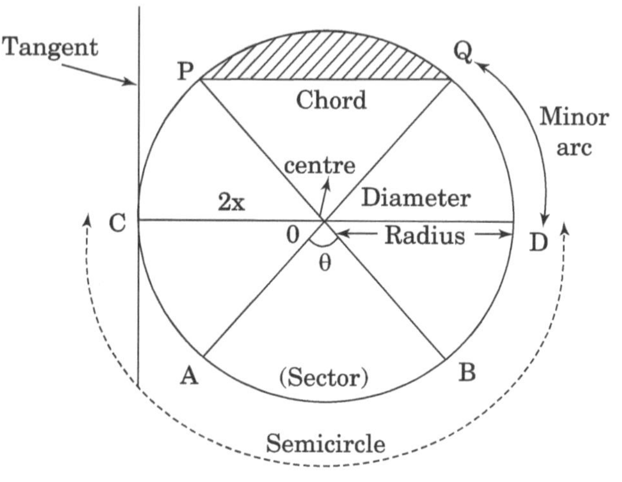

- The length of the complete circle is called its circumference.
- A piece of a circle between two points is called an arc.
- Angles in the same segment of a circle are equal.
- The angle subtended by an arc at the centre is double the angle subtend by it at any point on the remaining part of the circle.
- The angles subtended by two chords of a circle (or of congruent circles) at the centre (of corresponding centres) are equal, the chords are equal.
- Circles having same centre are said to be concentric circle.
- Angle in a semi-circle is a right angle. Conversely, the arc of a circle subtending a right angle at any point of the circle in its alternate segment is a semi-circle.

PREVIOUS YEARS'
EXAMINATION QUESTIONS
TOPIC 1

Multiple Choice Questions
(1 Mark Each)

1. In the given figure, if OA = 5 cm, AB = 8 cm and OD is perpendicular to AB, then CD is equal to

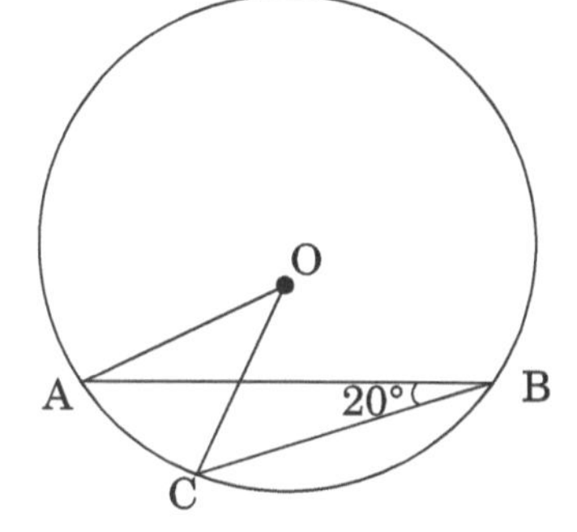

   (a) 2 cm   (b) 3 cm

   (c) 4 cm   (d) 5 cm [NCERT Exemp.]

Sol. (a) According to the question,

The perpendicular drawn from the centre of a chord bisect the chord,

$$AC = \frac{1}{2} \times AB = \frac{1}{2} \times 8 = 4 \text{ cm}$$

In $\triangle AOC$, by pythagoras theorem,

$$OC = \sqrt{OA^2 - AC^2} = \sqrt{5^2 - 4^2}$$
$$= \sqrt{25 - 16} = \sqrt{9} = 3\text{cm}$$

Hence,   CD = OD – OC

$$= 5\text{cm} - 3\text{cm} = 2 \text{ cm}.$$

2. In the given figure, if $\angle ABC = 20°$, then $\angle AOC$ is equal to :

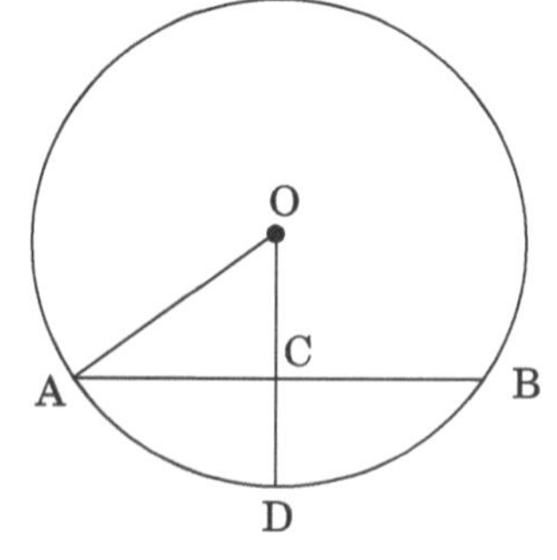

   (a) 20°   (b) 40°

   (c) 60°   (d) 10°

[NCERT Exemp.]

Sol. (b) According to the question figure,

$$\angle ABC = 20°$$

Arc AC of a circle subtends AOC at the centre O and ABC at a point B on the remaining part of the circle.

Since, the angle subtended by an arc of a circle at the centre is double the angle subtended by it at any point on the remaining part of the circle.

$$\angle AOC = 2\angle ABC$$

Hence, $\angle AOC = 2 \times 20° = 40°$

3. In the given figure, if $\angle DAB = 60°$, $\angle ABD = 50°$, then $\angle ACB$ is equal to

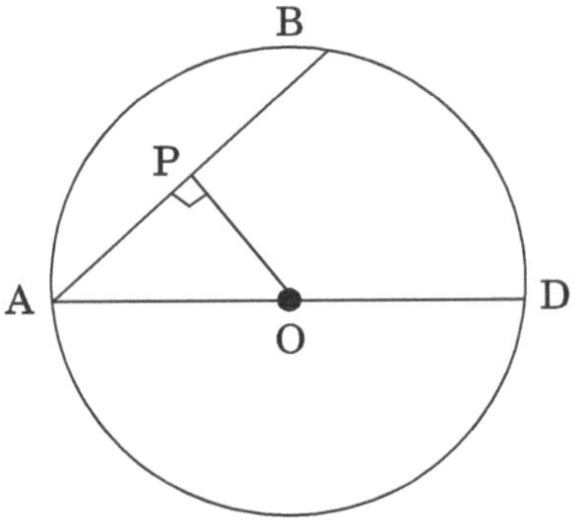

(a) 60°   (b) 50°

(c) 70°   (d) 80°   [NCERT Exemp.]

Sol. (c) According to the question,

In $\triangle ADB$ we have

$$\angle A + \angle B + \angle D = 180°$$

[Sum of all interior angles of a triangle]

$\Rightarrow$ $60° + 50° + \angle D = 180°$

$\therefore$ $\angle D = 180° - 110° = 70°$

So, $\angle ADB = 70°$

Hence, $\angle ADB = \angle ACB = 70°$

[Angles in the same segment of a circle are equal].

4. In the given figure, if $\angle OAB = 40°$, then $\angle ACB$ is equal to :

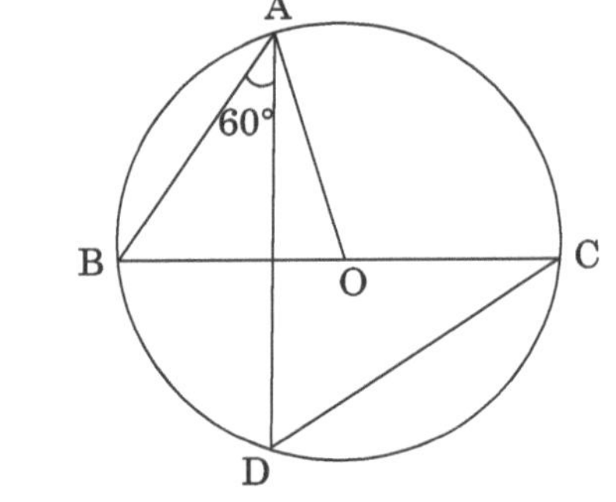

(a) 50°   (b) 40°

(c) 60°   (d) 70°   [NCERT Exemp.]

Sol. (a) According to the given figure,

In $\triangle OAB$, OA = OB   [Radii of circle]

Since, [angles opposite to equal sides of a triangle are equal] Therefore,

$\therefore$ $\angle OAB = 180° - (40° + 40°) = 100°$ ...(i)

Since, the angle subtended by an arc of a circle at the centre is double the angle subtended by it at any point on the remaining part of the circle.

Hence, $\angle ACB = \dfrac{1}{2}\angle AOB = \dfrac{1}{2}\times 100°$

                    $= 50°$ [From eqⁿ (i)]

5. AD is a diameter of a circle and AB is a chord. If AD = 34 cm, AB = 30 cm, the distance of AB from the centre of the circle is

(a) 17 cm   (b) 15 cm

(c) 4 cm   (d) 8 cm

Sol. (d) According to the question,

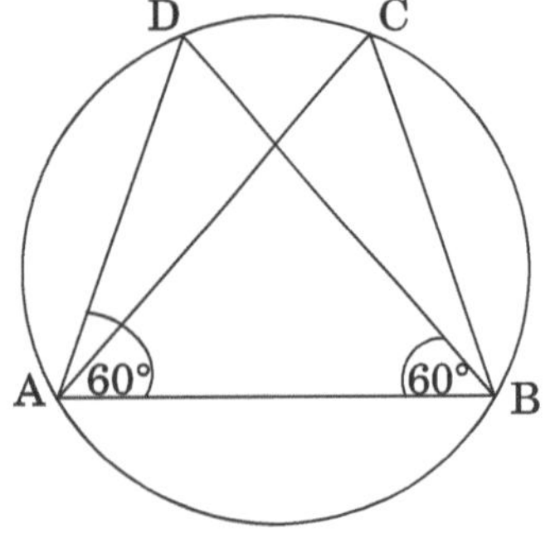

Construction : Draw OP $\perp$ AB

We know that the perpendicular from the centre of the circle bisects the chord.

Therefore, $AP = \dfrac{1}{2}\times AB = \dfrac{1}{2}\times 30 = 15$ cm

and radius $= OA = \dfrac{1}{2}\times 34 = 17$ cm

In right $\triangle OPA$, by pythagoras theorem, we have

$\therefore$ $OP = \sqrt{OA^2 - AP^2}$

              $= \sqrt{17^2 - 15^2}$

              $= \sqrt{289 - 225}$

              $= \sqrt{64} = 8cm$

Hence, the distance of AB from the centre of circle is 8cm.

6. In the given figure, BC is a diameter of the circle and $\angle BAO = 60°$. Then $\angle ADC$ is equal to :

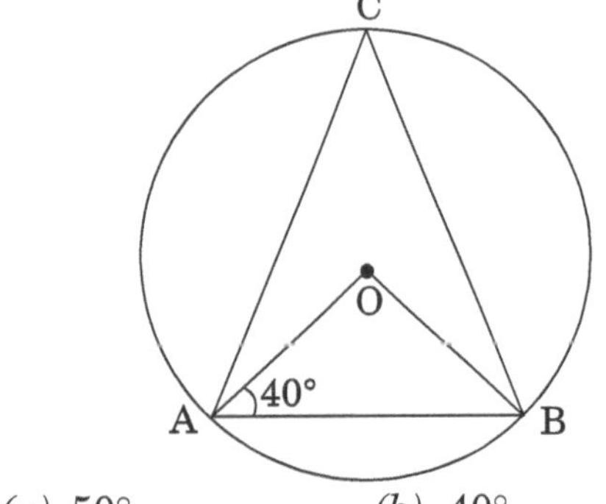

(a) 30°   (b) 45°

(c) 60°   (d) 120°   [NCERT Exemp.]

Sol. **(c)** According to the given figure,

In ΔOAB,   OA = OB [Radii of the same circle]

$\therefore$ $\angle$ABO = $\angle$BAO

[Angles opposite to equal sides are equal]

$\angle$ABO = $\angle$BAO = 60°   [Given]

Now, $\angle$ADC = $\angle$ABC = 60°

[Angles in the same segment of a circle are equal]

Hence, required angle $\angle$ADC = 60°.

7.   If AB = 12 cm, BC = 16 cm and AB is perpendicular to BC, then the radius of the circle passing through the points A, B, and C is :

(a) 6 cm   (b) 8 cm

(c) 10 cm   (d) 12 cm

[NCERT Exemp.]

Sol. **(c)** According to the question,

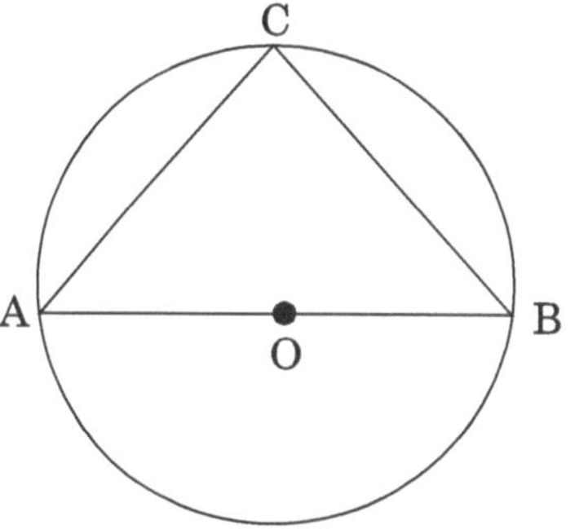

Since, AB is perpendicular to BC, therefore, ABC is right angled triangle.

In right triangle ABC, by pythagoras theorem, we have

$$AC = \sqrt{AB^2 + BC^2} = \sqrt{12^2 + 16^2}$$

$$= \sqrt{144 + 256} = \sqrt{400} = 20 \text{ cm}$$

Hence, radius $= \dfrac{1}{2} \times 20 = 10$ cm

[$\because$ AC is the diameter of circle]

8.   In the given figure, $\angle$AOB = 90° and $\angle$ABC = 30°, then $\angle$CAO is equal to

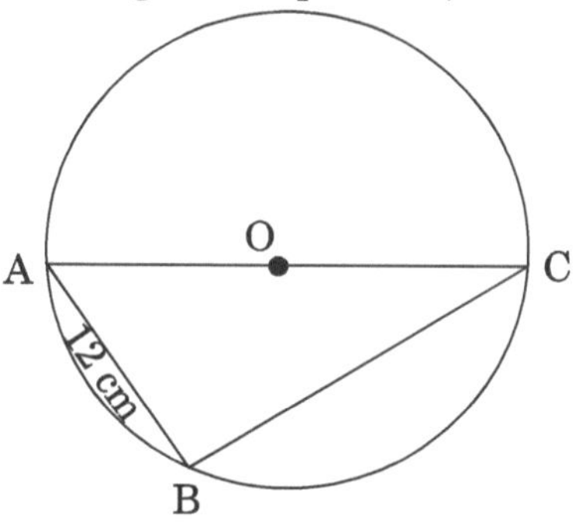

(a) 30°

(b) 45°

(c) 90°

(d) 60°   [NCERT Exemp.]

Sol. **(d)** According to the given figure,

In ΔOAB, we have

OA = OB   [Radii of the same circle]

$\therefore$ $\angle$OAB = $\angle$OBA

[$\because$ Angles opposite to equal sides are equal]

In triangle OAB, we have

$\angle$OAB + $\angle$OBA + $\angle$AOB = 180°

[Sum of angles of a triangle is 180°]

$\Rightarrow$ 2OAB = 180° −AOB = 180° − 90°

$\therefore$ $\angle$OAB $= \dfrac{1}{2} \times 90° = 45°$

Also, $\angle$ACB $= \dfrac{1}{2}\angle$AOB $= \dfrac{1}{2} \times 90° = 45°$

[$\because$ $\angle$AOB = 90°]

Now, in ΔCAB, we have

$\angle$CAB = 180° − ($\angle$ABC + $\angle$ACB)

$= 180° − (30° + 45°) = 105°$

Now, $\angle$CAO = $\angle$CAB − $\angle$OAB

$= 105° − 45° = 60°$

Hence, required angle = 60°

9.   In the given figure, if AOB is a diameter of the circle and AC = BC, then $\angle$CAB is equal to :

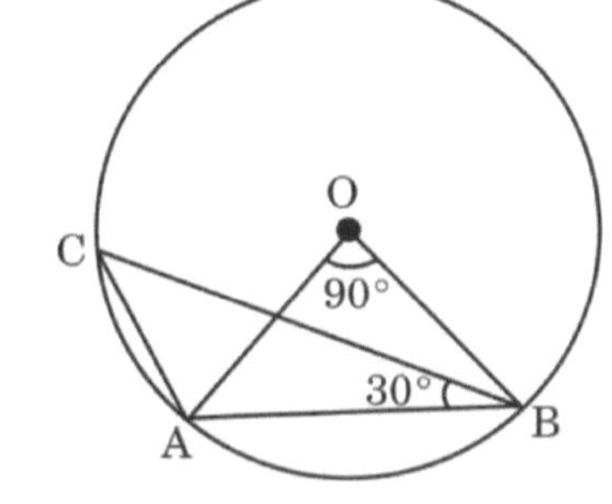

(a) 30°   (b) 60°

(c) 90°   (d) 45°   [NCERT Exemp.]

Sol. **(d)** Given: AC = BC

$\because$ AOB is a diameter of the circle,

$\angle$C = 90°

[Angles in a semi-circle is 90°]

Now,   AC = BC

$\angle$A = $\angle$B   [Angles opposite to equal sides of triangle are equal]

Using angle-sum property of a triangle, we have

$\angle$A + $\angle$B + $\angle$C = 180°

$\Rightarrow$ $\angle$A + $\angle$A +90° = 180°

$\Rightarrow$ 2$\angle$A = 180° − 90°

$\therefore$ $\angle$A $= \dfrac{90°}{2} = 45°$

Hence, $\angle$CAB = 45°.

10. The region between a chord and either of the arcs is called :

(a) an arc   (b) a sector

(c) a segment   (d) a semi-circle

Sol. (c) The region between a chord and either of the arc is called as segment.

11. Given a circle of radius 5 cm and centre O. OL is drawn perpendicular to the chord AB. If OL = 3 cm, then length of chord AB is :

(a) 4 cm   (b) 6 cm

(c) 8 cm   (d) 10 cm

Sol. (c) According to the question,

In $\triangle$AMO,

By pythagoras theorem,

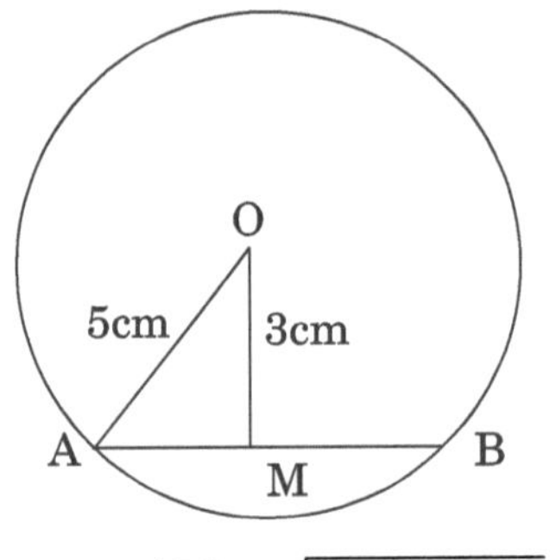

$$AM = \sqrt{OA^2 - OM^2}$$

$$= \sqrt{(5)^2 - (3)^2}$$

$$= \sqrt{25 - 9} = \sqrt{16} = 4 \text{ cm}$$

Hence, chord AB = 4 × 2 = 8 cm.

Write whether the statement are true or false. Justify your answer.

1. Two chords AB and AC of a circle with centre O are on the opposite sides of OA. Then $\angle$OAB = $\angle$OAC   [NCERT Exemp.]

Sol. Here, two chords AB and AC are not given equal, because the angles will be equal if AB = AC.

Hence, the given statement is false.

2. Line segment joining the centre to any point on the circle is a radius of the circle.

[NCERT Exemp.]

Sol. Since, all the points on the circle are at equal distance from the centre of the circle, this equal distance is called the radius of the circle.

Therefore, the given statement is true.

3. A circle is a plane figure.   [NCERT Exemp.]

Sol. Since, it is a two-dimensional figure and it can also be referred to as a plane figure.

Therefore, the given statement is true.

4. A circle of radius 3 cm can be drawn through two points A, B such that AB = 6 cm.

[NCERT Exemp.]

Sol. Since, radius of circle = 3 cm

Diameter of circle = 2 × r = 2 × 3cm = 6 cm

Therefore, the given statement is true.

5. A chord of a circle, which is twice as long as its radius, is a diameter of the circle.

[NCERT Exemp.]

Sol. If a chord is passing through the centre of the circle and is twice as long as its radius, so it is called the diameter of the circle.

Therefore, the given statement is true.

6. Through three collinear points a circle can be drawn.   [NCERT Exemp.]

Sol. Since, a circle that passes through two points cannot passes through a point which is collinear to these two points. A circle can be drawn through three non-collinear points only.

Therefore, the given statement is false.

7. A circle has only finite number of equal chords.

[NCERT Exemp.]

Sol. Since, there are infinite points on a circle. Hence, a circle has infinite number of equal chords.

Therefore, the given statement is false.

8. If AOB is a diameter of a circle and C is a point on the circle, then $AC^2 + BC^2 = AB^2$.

[NCERT Exemp.]

Sol. Since, AOB is a diameter of a circle and C is a point on the circle.

Therefore $\angle$ACB = 90°

[Angle in a semi-circle is a right angle]

In right triangle ABC, we have

$AC^2 + BC^2 = AB^2$ [By pythagoras therem]

Therefore, the given statement is true.

9. If a circle is divided into three equal arcs, each is a major arc.   [NCERT Exemp.]

Sol. Because a major arc is always bigger than a minor arc, and they cannot be equal.

Therefore, the given statement is false.

10. Two chords AB and CD of a circle are each at distances 4 cm from the centre. Then AB = CD.

[NCERT Exemp.]

Sol. Since, we know that chords equidistant from the centre of a circle are equal.

Here, we are given that two chords AB and CD of a circle are each at distance 4 cm (equidistant) from the centre of a circle. So, chords are equal, that is, AB = CD.

Therefore, the given statement is true.

11. Two congruent circles with centres O and O′ intersect at two points A and B. Then $\angle AOB = \angle AO'B$. **[NCERT Exemp.]**

Sol. Since, equal chords of congruent circles subtend equal angles at the respective centres.

Therefore, the given statement is true.

12. Sector is the region between the chord and its corresponding arc. **[NCERT Exemp.]**

Sol. Since, it is the region between an arc and two radii joining the centre to the end points of the arc.

Therefore, the given statement is false.

Very Short Answer Type Questions
(1 Mark Each)

1. In figure A, B and C are three points on a circle with centre O such that $\angle BOC = 30°$ and $\angle AOB = 60°$. If D is a point on the circle other than the arc ABC, then find $\angle ADC$. **[NCERT]**

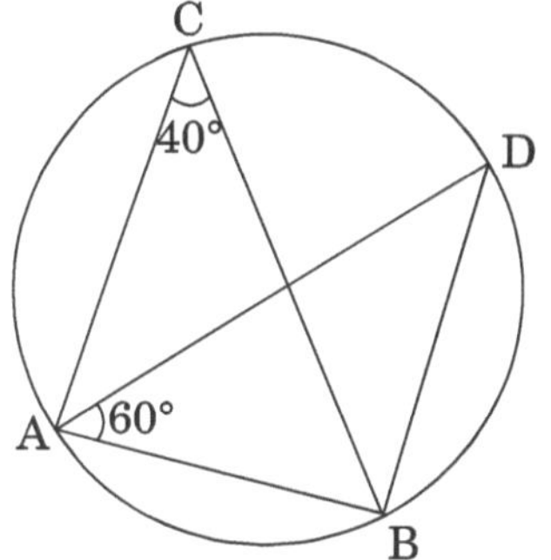

Sol. According to the question,
$$\angle AOC = \angle AOB + \angle BOC$$
$$= 60° + 30° = 90°$$

Since, arc ABC makes an angle of 90° at the centre of the circle.

∴
$$\angle ADC = \frac{1}{2}\angle AOC$$

[since, the angle subtended by an arc at the centre is double the angle subtended by it at any point on the remaining part if the circle]

$$= \frac{1}{2}\times 90° = 45°$$

Hence, required angle $\angle ADC = 45°$

2. In figure, $\angle ABC = 69°$ and $\angle ACB = 31°$. Find $\angle BDC$. **[NCERT]**

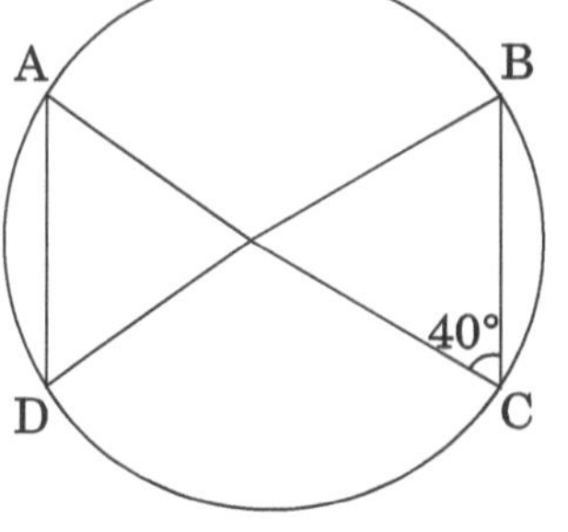

Sol. According to the question,
$$\angle BDC = \angle BAC \qquad ...(i)$$
[since, the angles in the same segment are equal]
Now, in $\triangle ABC$, we get
$$\angle BAC + \angle ABC + \angle ACB = 180°$$
[angle sum property of triangle]
$$\Rightarrow \angle BAC + 69° + 31° = 180°$$
$$\Rightarrow \angle BAC + 100° = 180°$$
$$\Rightarrow \angle BAC = 180° - 100° = 80°$$
$$\Rightarrow \angle BAC = 80°$$
$$\angle BAC = \angle BDC = 80° \quad \text{[from eq}^n\text{(i)]}$$
Hence, $\angle BDC = 80°$

3. In the given figure A, B, C and D are the points on a circle such that $\angle ACB = 40°$ and $\angle DAB = 60°$, the measure of $\angle DBA$ is ....
[Board Term II, 2012, Set-01]

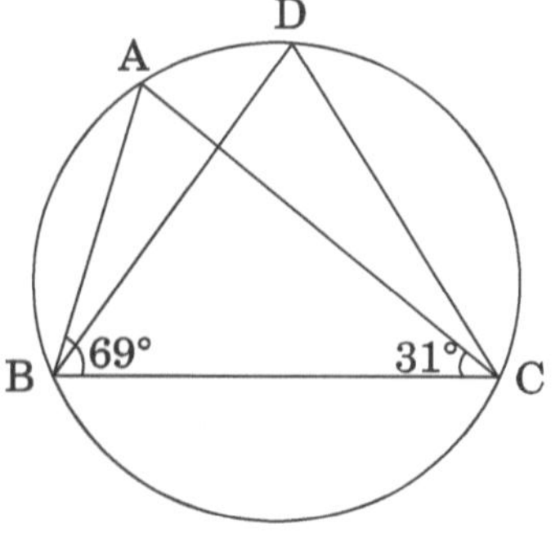

Sol. According to the question,
$$\angle ACB = \angle ADB$$
[Angles in the same segment]
∴
$$\angle ADB = 40°$$
Now, in $\triangle ADB$,
$$\angle ADB + \angle DBA + \angle BAD = 180°$$
[Angle sum property]
$$\Rightarrow 40° + \angle DBA + 60° = 180°$$
Hence, $\angle DBA = 80°$

4. In the given figure, AD ∥ BC and $\angle BCA = 40°$. The measure of $\angle DBC$ is equal to ....
[Board Term II, 2012, Set -10]

Sol. According to the given figure,
$$\angle BDA = \angle BCA = 40°$$
[Angles in the same segment]

Now, since AD ∥ BC

$$\angle DBC = \angle BDA$$

[Alternate interior angles]

Hence, $\angle DBC = 40°$

5. In the given figure, O is the centre of the circle and PA = PB. Find $\angle OPA$..

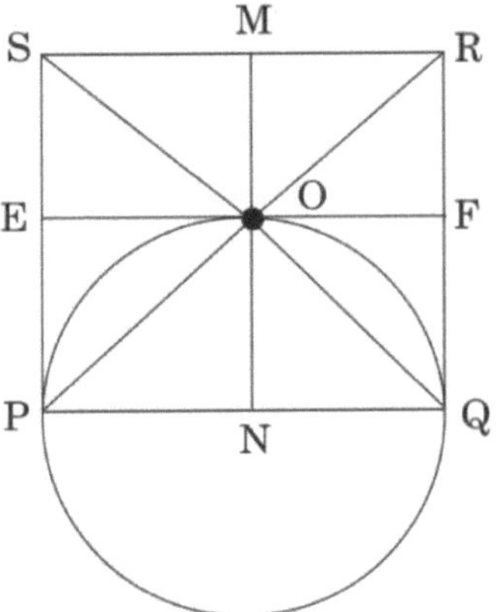

Sol. According to the question,

Since,   PA = PB

⇒   OP ⊥ AB

Hence, $\angle OPA = 90°$

Short Answer Type Questions I

(2 Marks Each)

1. Prove that the line of centres of two intersecting circles subtends equal angles at the two points of intersection.   [NCERT]

Sol. Given Two circles with centres O and O′ which intersect each other at C and D.

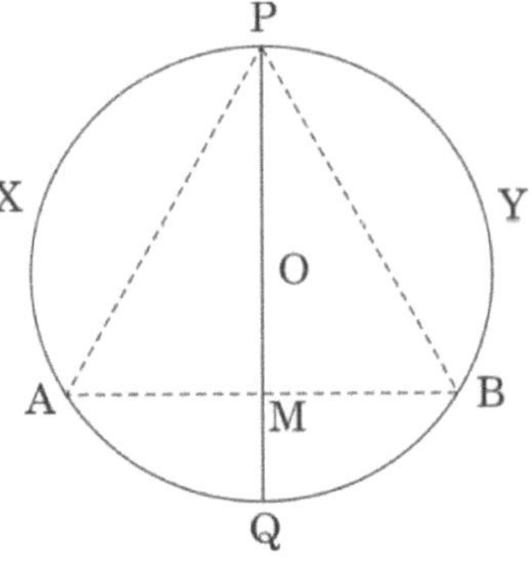

To prove : $\angle OCO' = \angle ODO'$

Construction : Join OC, OD, O′C and O′D.

Proof : In ΔOCO′ an ΔODO′, we have

OC = OD   [radii of the same circle]

O′C = O′D   [radii of the same circle]

and   OO′ = OO′   [common sides]

∴   ΔOCO′ ≅ ΔODO′ [by SSS congruence rule]

Then, $\angle OCO' = \angle ODO'$ [by CPCT]

Hence proved.

2. Prove that the circle drawn with any side of a rhombus as diameter, passes through the point of intersection of its diagonals.   [NCERT]

Sol. Given Let PQRS be a rhombus and PR and SQ are its two diagonals which bisect each other at right angles at O.

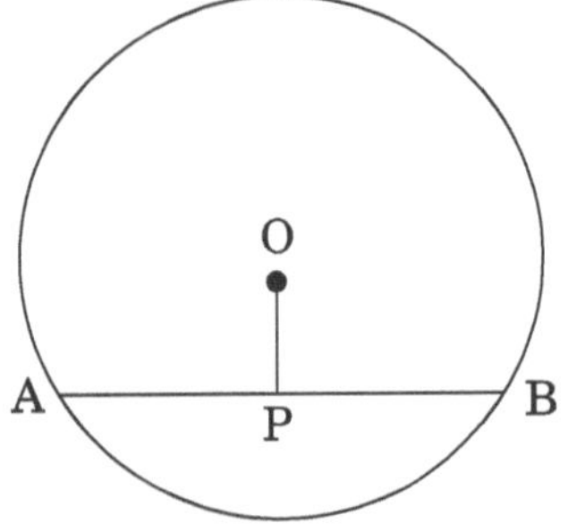

To prove : A circle drawn on PQ as diameter will pass through O.

Construction : Through O, draw MN ∥ PS and EF ∥ PQ.

Proof : Here, PQ = SR

⇒ $\dfrac{1}{2}PQ = \dfrac{1}{2}SR$

⇒   PN = NQ = SM = MR

Similarly,   PE = SE = ON

So,   PN = ON = NQ

[∵ all sides of a rhombus are equal]

Therefore, a circle drawn with N as centre and radius PN passes through P, O and Q.

Hence proved.

3. If the perpendicular bisector of a chord AB of a circle PXAQBY intersects the circle at P and Q, then prove that arc PXA ≅ arc PYB.

[NCERT Exemplar]

Sol. Given AB is a chord of a circle having O. PQ be the perpendicular bisector of the chord AB, which intersects at M and it always passing through O.

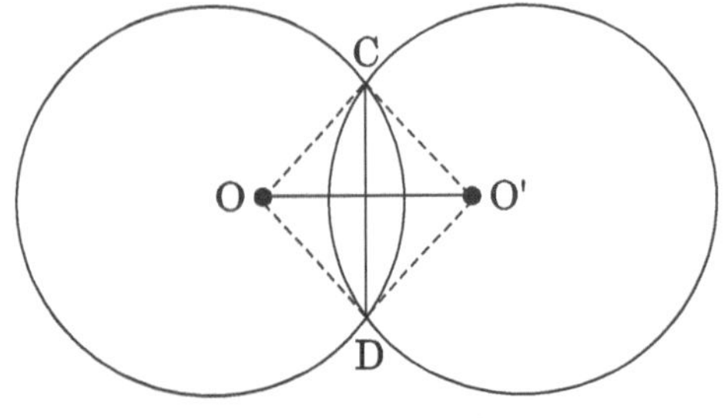

To prove : Arc PXA ≅ Arc PYB.

Construction : Join AP and BP.

Proof : In ΔPMA and ΔPMB,

AM = MB   [∵ PM bisects AB]

$\angle PMA = \angle PMB$ [each 90°]

and $\quad$ PM = PM $\qquad$ [common sides]

$\therefore \qquad \Delta$PMA $\cong \Delta$PMB

$\qquad$ [by SAS congruence rule]

Then, $\qquad$ PA = PB $\qquad$ [by CPCT]

$\Rightarrow \qquad$ arc PXA $\cong$ arc PYB $\quad$ Hence proved.

4. The circumcentre of the ΔABC is O. Prove that $\angle$OBC + $\angle$BAC = 90°. $\qquad$ [NCERT Exemplar]

Sol. **Given :** A circle is circumscribed on a ΔABC having centre O.

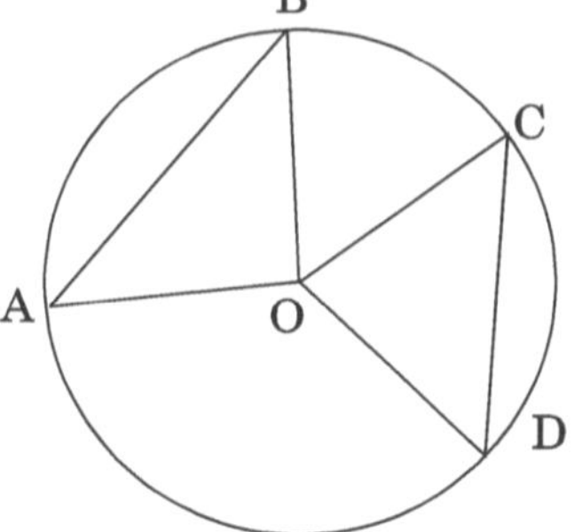

Let $\qquad \angle$OBC = $\angle$OCB = θ

In ΔOBC,

$\angle$BOC + $\angle$OCB + $\angle$CBO = 180°

$\qquad$ [by angle sum property of a triangle]

$\Rightarrow \quad \angle$BOC + θ + θ = 180°

$\Rightarrow \qquad \angle$BOC = 180° − 2$\theta$ $\qquad$ ...(i)

$\because \qquad \angle$BAC = $\dfrac{\angle BOC}{2}$

[since, angle subtended at the arc is half of the angle subtended at the centre]

$$\angle BAC = \frac{180° - 2\theta}{2} = 90° - \theta$$

$\qquad$ [From eq^n (i)]

$\qquad = 90° - \angle$OBC

$\qquad$ [$\because \angle$OBC = θ]

$\therefore \quad \angle$BAC + $\angle$OBC = 90° $\qquad$ Hence proved.

5. Prove that "equal chords of a circle subtend equal angles at the centres".

[Board Term II, KVS 2016, 2012 Set-15, NCERT]

Sol. Given: AB and CD are the chords of a circle with centre at O such that AB = CD

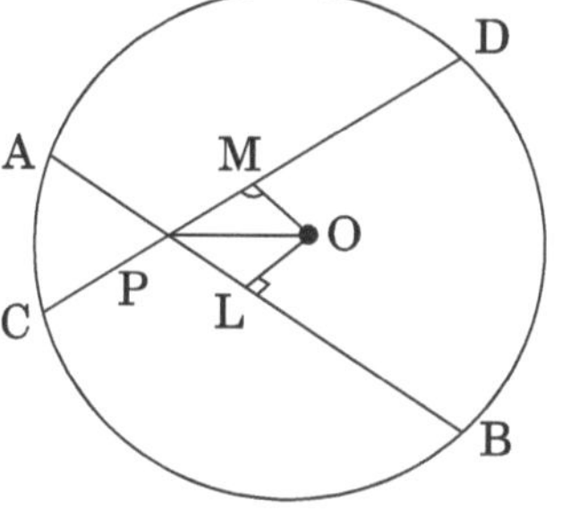

To prove: $\angle$AOB = $\angle$COD

Proof: In ΔAOB and ΔCOD

$\qquad$ AO = CO $\quad$ (radii of same circle)

$\qquad$ AB = CD $\qquad$ (given)

and $\qquad$ BO = DO $\quad$ (radii of same circle)

By SSS $\:$ congruence rule,

$\qquad \Delta$AOB $\cong \Delta$COD

$\therefore \qquad \angle$AOB = $\angle$COD $\qquad$ (c.p.c.t.)

$\qquad$ Hence Proved.

6. If two equal chords of a circle intersect within the circle, prove that the segments of one chord are equal to corresponding segments of the other chord. $\qquad$ [Board Term II, 2012, Set-06, NCERT]

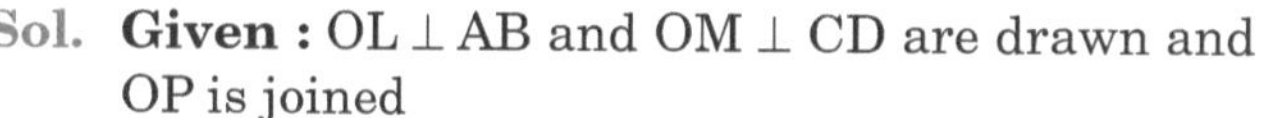

Sol. **Given :** OL $\perp$ AB and OM $\perp$ CD are drawn and OP is joined

To prove : BP = DP

Proof : In ΔOPL and ΔOPM

$\qquad$ OP = OP $\qquad$ (common)

$\qquad \angle$OLP = $\angle$OMP $\qquad$ [each 90°]

and $\qquad$ OL = OM

(Equal chords are equidistant from the centre)

By SAS congruence rule, we get

$\qquad \Delta$OPL $\cong \Delta$OPM $\qquad$ (RHS)

$\therefore \qquad$ PM = PL $\qquad$ (c.p.c.t.)

$\qquad$ AL = CM $\qquad \left(\because \dfrac{1}{2}AB = \dfrac{1}{2}CD\right)$

or, $\qquad$ AL − PL = CM −PM

or, $\qquad$ AP = CP

Also, $\qquad$ AB − AP = CD − CP

$\qquad$ BP = DP $\qquad$ Hence proved.

7. Prove that the perpendicular from the centre of a circle to a chord, bisects the chord.

[Board Term II, 2012 Set-05, NCERT]

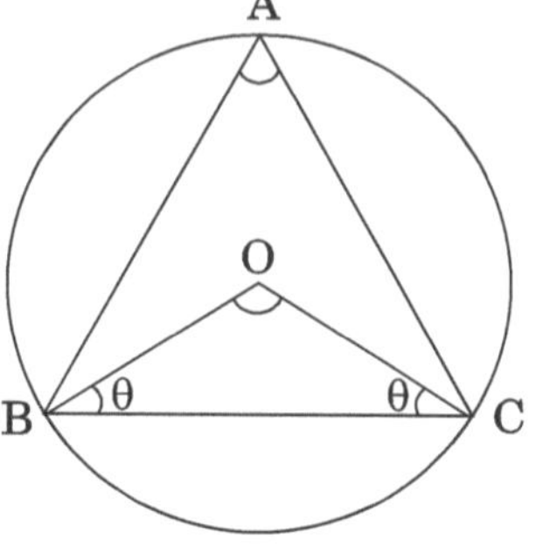

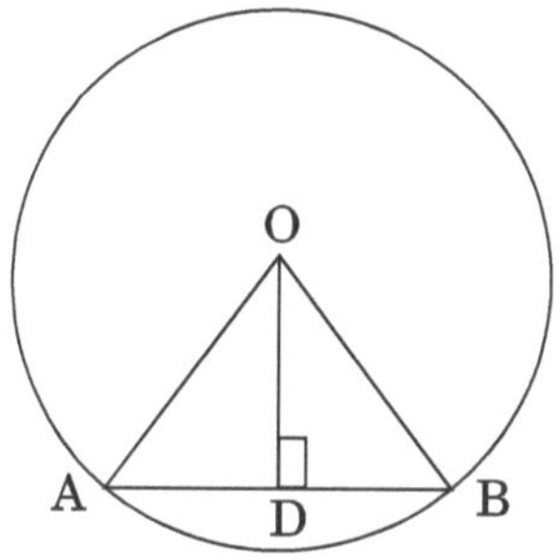

Sol. **Given :** AB is the chord of a circle with centre O and OD $\perp$ AB.

To prove : AD = DB

Proof : In triangles ODA and ODB, OA = OB

(radii of circle)

$$OD = OD \qquad \text{(common)}$$

and $\qquad \angle ODA = \angle ODB = 90° \; [\because OD \perp AB]$

By RHS congruence rule, we get

$\therefore \qquad \Delta ODA \cong \Delta ODB$

$\therefore \qquad AD = DB \qquad \text{(c.p.c.t.)}$

Hence proved.

8. In the given figure, A, B, C and D are four points on a circle. AC and BD intersect at E such that $\angle BEC = 130°$ and $\angle ECD = 20°$. Find $\angle BAC$.

[Board Term II, 2012 Set-08, KVS 2014, NCERT]

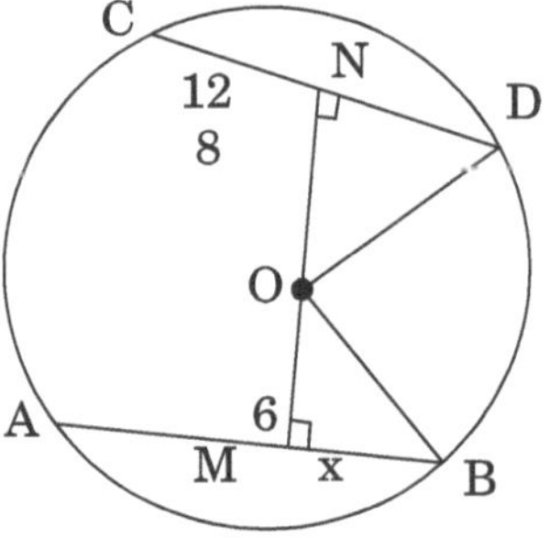

Sol. According to the question,

In ΔEDC, $\angle EDC + \angle ECD = \angle BEC$ (exterior angle of a Δ is equal to sum of two opposite angles)

$\Rightarrow \qquad \angle EDC + 20° = 130°$

$\therefore \qquad \angle EDC = 110°$

$\Rightarrow \qquad \angle BDC = 110°$

Hence, $\qquad \angle BAC = \angle BDC = 110°$

(Angle in the same segment)

9. If a line intersects two concentric circles with common centre O, at A, B, C, and D. Prove that AB = CD.

[NCERT][Board Term II, Set IA21924, 2016; KVS 2014; 2012, Set-10]

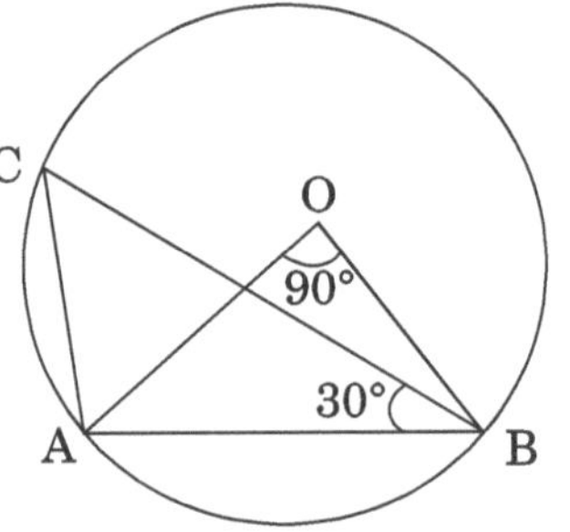

Sol. **Given :** A line intersects two concentric circles with centre O at point A, B, C, and D.

To prove : $\qquad$ AB = CD

Construction : Draw OP perpendicular to xy from the centre to a chord bisecting it.

Proof : Since OP $\perp$ to chord BC.

$\therefore \qquad BP = PC \qquad \qquad \text{...(i)}$

Similarly, $\qquad AP = PD \qquad \qquad \text{...(ii)}$

On subtracting eqn (i) from eqn. (ii), we get

$$AP - BP = PD - PC$$

Hence, $\qquad AB = CD$

10. In the given figure, $\angle AOB = 90°$ and $\angle ABC = 30°$, then find the measure of $\angle CAO$.

[Board Term II, 2012 Set-06,]

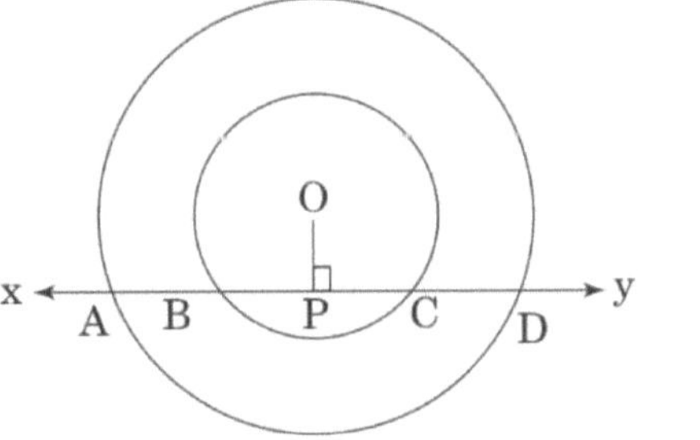

Sol. According to the question,

[Since, angle subtended at the arc is half of the angle subtended at the centre.]

$$\angle ACB = \frac{1}{2} \times \angle AOB$$

$$= \frac{1}{2} \times 90° = 45°$$

Now, In $\Delta ACB, \angle CAB = 180° - (30° + 45°) = 105°$

and $\qquad \angle OAB = \angle OBA = 45°$

(Angles opposite to equal sides of triangle are equal as OA = OB radius of same circle)

Hence, $\qquad \angle CAO = 105° - \angle OAB$

$$= 105° - 45° = 60°$$

11. A chord 12 cm long is 8 cm away from the centre of the circle. What is the length of a chord which is 6 cm away from the centre?

[Board Term II, 2012 Set-12]

Sol. Perpendicular from the centre bisects the chord.

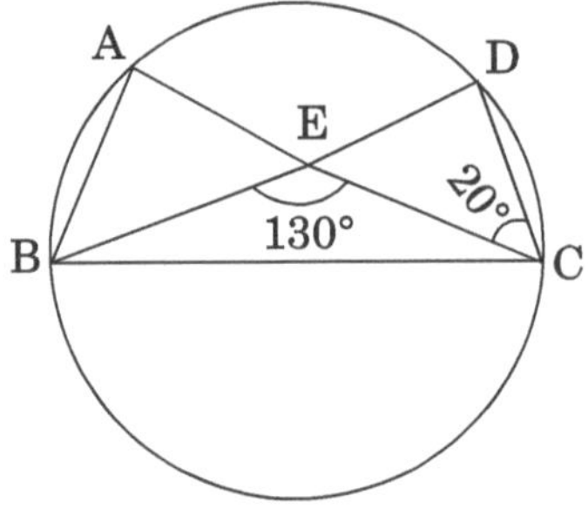

or, $\qquad DN = \frac{1}{2} CD = 6cm$

and $\qquad BM = x, \qquad \qquad \text{(Let)}$

$$OD = OB$$

(Radius of the same circle)

$$OD^2 = OB^2$$

By pythagoras theorem, we have

$\Rightarrow \qquad ON^2 + ND^2 = OM^2 + MB^2$

$\Rightarrow \qquad 8^2 + 6^2 = 6^2 + x^2$

$\qquad 64 + 36 = 36 + x^2 \Rightarrow x^2 = 64$

$\therefore \qquad x = 8$ cm

Therefore, $\qquad BM = 8$

and $\qquad AB = 2BM$

$\qquad = 2 \times 8$

$\qquad = 16$ cm.

12. In the given figure, O is the centre of the circle. If $\angle AOB = 80°$, then find the measure of $\angle ADB$ and $\angle ACB$.

[Board Term II, 2012 Set-24]

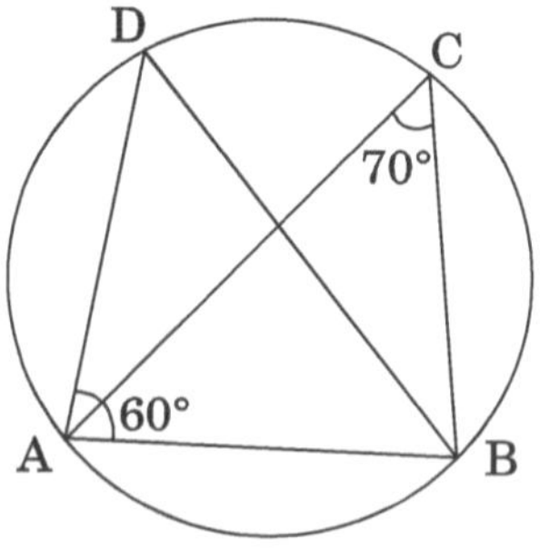

Sol. According to the given figure,

$\qquad \angle AOB = 80°$

or, $\qquad \angle ADB = 40° \quad (\because \angle AOB = 2 \angle ADB)$

Since, angles in the same segment are equal.

$\therefore \qquad \angle ACB = \angle ADB = 40°$

Hence, required angles $\angle ADB = \angle ACB = 40°$

13. In the adjoining figure if $\angle DAB = 60°$ and $\angle ACB = 70°$, find the measures of $\angle DBA$.

[Board Term II, 2012 Set-05,]

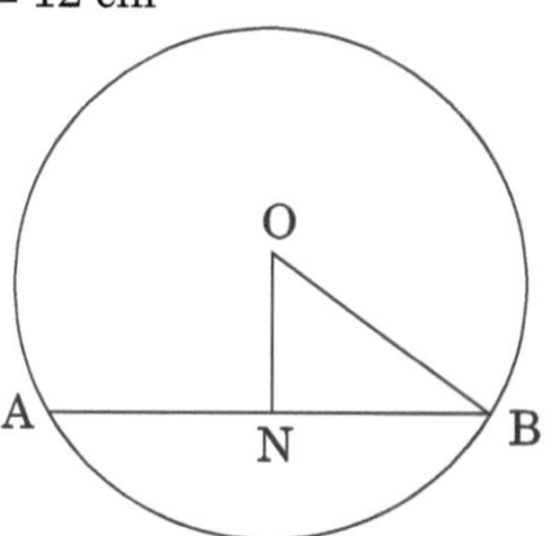

Sol. According to the given figure,

$\qquad \angle ACB = 70°$

$\qquad \angle ADB = \angle ACB = 70°$

(Angles in the same segment of a circle)

In ΔDAB,

$\angle DAB + \angle ADB + \angle DBA = 180°$

(Angles sum property of triangle)

$\Rightarrow \ 60° + 70° + \angle DBA = 180°$

$\therefore \qquad \angle DBA = 180° - 130° = 50°$

14. In the given figure, O is the centre of the circle and chord AC and BD intersect at P such that $\angle APB = 120°$ and $\angle PBC = 15°$, find the value of $\angle ADB$.

[Board Term II, KVS 2014]

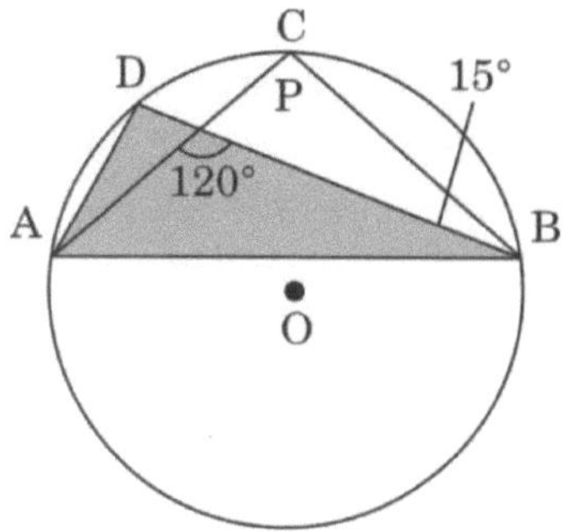

Sol. According to the question,

In ΔPCB,

$\angle PCB + \angle PBC = \angle APB$ \qquad (exterior angle of a triangle is equal to the sum of two opposite angles)

$\qquad \angle PCB = 15° = 120°$

$\Rightarrow \qquad \angle PCB = 120° - 15°$

$\therefore \qquad \angle PCB = 105°$

$\Rightarrow \qquad \angle ACB = 105°$

Hence, $\qquad \angle ADB = \angle ACB$

$\qquad = 150°$

[Angle in same segment]

15. A chord of length 10 cm is at a distance of 12 cm from the centre of a circle. Find the radius of the circle. [Board Term II, Set-LF0MCQ2, 2016]

Sol. Given, AB = 10 cm

and   ON = 12 cm

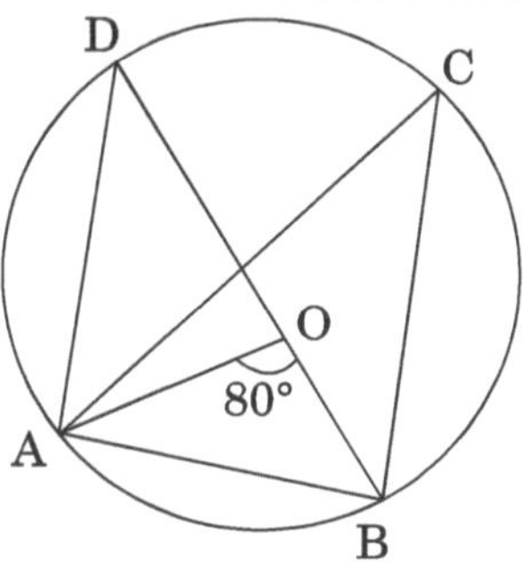

Also, $\qquad ON \perp AB$

and $\qquad AN = BN$

($\because$ perpendicular drawn from the centre of the circle bisects the chord)

In ΔONB, $\qquad OB^2 = ON^2 + NB^2$

(By pythagoras theorem)

$\qquad = 12^2 + 5^2 \quad (\because BN = 5$ cm$)$

$\qquad = 144 + 25$

$\qquad = 169$

$\therefore \qquad OB = 13$ cm

Hence, the radius of the circle is 13 cm.

16. In the figure, if $\angle DAB = 60°$, $\angle ABD = 50°$, then find $\angle ACB$.   [Board Term II, KVS 2016]

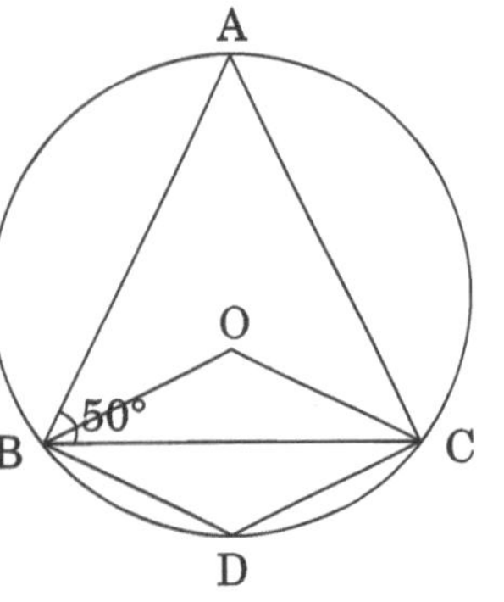

Sol. According to the given figure,

In $\triangle ADB$,

By angle sum property

$\angle ABD + \angle ADB + \angle BAD = 180°$

$\Rightarrow 50° + \angle ADB + 60° = 180°$

$\therefore \qquad \angle ADB = 180° - (50° + 60°)$

$\qquad\qquad = 70°$

$\therefore \ \angle ACB = \angle ADB = 70°$

($\because$ angles in the same segment of a circle are equal)

Hence, required angle $\angle ACB = 70°$

17. In the given figure, O is the centre of the circle and BA = AC. If $\angle ABC = 50°$, find $\angle BOC$ and $\angle BDC$.

[Board Term II, 2017, Set Z6K408K]

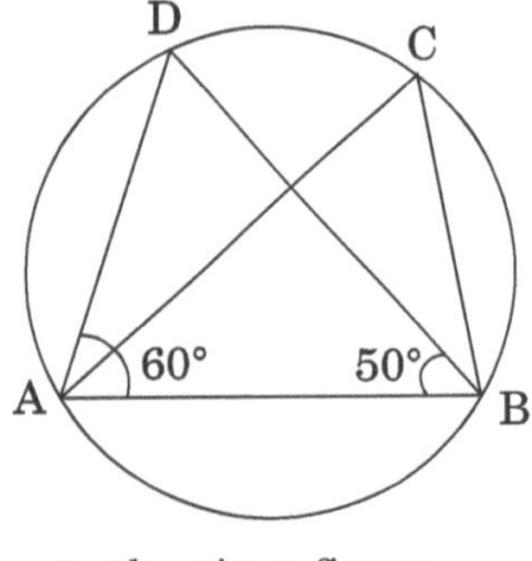

Sol. According to the question,

$\qquad\qquad AB = AC$

$\therefore \qquad \angle ABC = \angle ACB = 50°$

By angle sum property of a triangle

$\qquad \angle BAC = 180° - \angle ABC - \angle ACB$

$\qquad\qquad = 180° - 50° - 50° = 80°$

$\therefore \qquad \angle BOC = 2\angle BAC$

(angle at the centre is twice the angle at the circumference)

Hence, $\qquad \angle BOC = 2 \times 80° = 160°$

Now, $\angle BDC + \angle BAC = 180°$

(opposite angles of cyclic quadrilateral)

Hence, $\qquad \angle BDC = 180° - 80° = 100°$

Short Answer Type Questions II

(3 Marks Each)

1. In figure, $\angle PQR = 100°$, where P, Q and R are points on a circle with centre O. Find $\angle OPR$.

[NCERT]

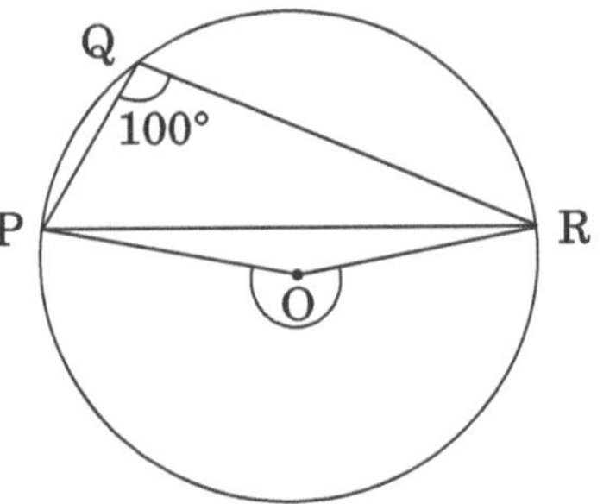

Sol. According to the given figure,

$\therefore \ \angle POR = 2\angle PQR = 2 \times 100° = 200°$

[since, the angle subtended by an arc at the centre is double the angle subtended by it at any point on the remaining part of the circle]

In $\triangle OPR$, $\qquad \angle POR = 360° - 200° = 160°$ ...(i)

Again, in $\triangle OPR$, $\quad OP = OR$

[radii of the same circle]

$\therefore \qquad\qquad \angle ORP = \angle OPR$ ...(ii)

[$\because$ angles opposite to equal sides of a triangle are also equal]

Also, $\angle OPR + \angle ORP + \angle POR = 180°$

[by angle sum property of triangle]

On putting the values from eqs. (i) and (ii), we get

$\angle OPR + \angle OPR + 160° = 180°$

$\Rightarrow \qquad\qquad 2\angle OPR = 180° - 160° = 20°$

Hence, $\qquad \angle OPR = \dfrac{20°}{2} = 10°$

2. If a line segment joining mid-points of two chords of a circle passes through the centre of the circle. prove that the two chords are parallel.

[NCERT Exemplar]

Sol. Given, AB and CD are two chords of a circle, whose centre is O and PQ is a diameter bisecting the chords AB and CD at L and M, respectively and the diameter PQ passes through the centre O of the circle.

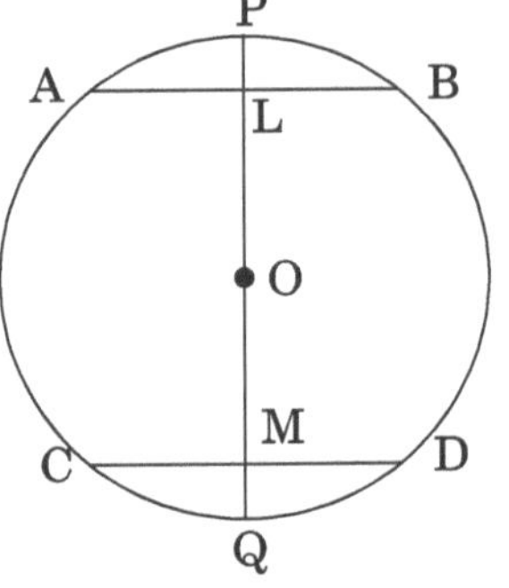

To prove : AB ∥ CD
Proof : Since, L is the mid-point of AB.
∴   OL ⊥ AB
[since, the line joining the centre of a circle to the mid-point of a chord is perpendicular to the chord]
∴ $\angle ALO = 90°$ ...(i)
Similarly,   OM ⊥ CD
∴ $\angle OMD = 90°$ ...(ii)
From eqs. (i) and (ii), we get
                    $\angle ALO = \angle OMD$ [each 90°]
But these are alternate angles.
∴   AB ∥ CD   [Hence proved]

3. If BM and CN are the perpendiculars drawn on the sides AC and AB of the ΔABC, then prove that the points B, C, M and N are concyclic.
[NCERT Exemplar]

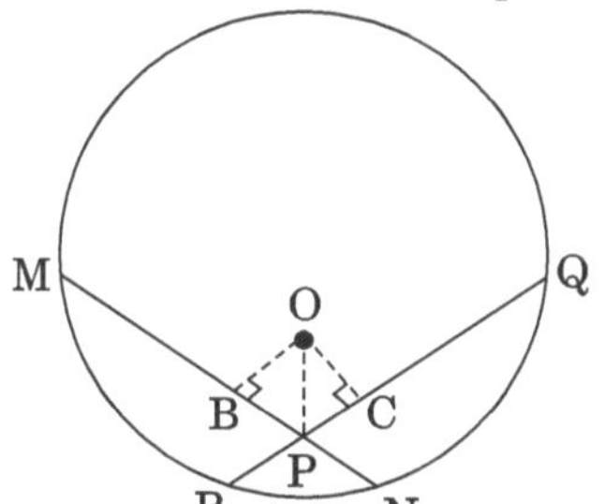

Sol. **Given :** In ΔABC, BM ⊥ AC and CN ⊥ AB.

To prove : Points B, C, M and N are concyclic.

Construction : Draw a circle passing through the points B, C, M and N.

Proof : Suppose, we consider BC as a diameter of the circle. Also, we know that, BC subtends an angle of 90° to the circle.

So, the points M and N should be on a circle.

Hence, points B, C, M and N are concyclic.

4. AD is a diameter of a circle and AB is a chord. If AD = 34 cm and AB = 30 cm, then find the distance of AB from the centre of the circle.
[NCERT Exemplar]

Sol. According to the question,
AD is a diameter of circle, AB is a chord.
                    AD = 34 cm
and   AB = 30 cm
From O, draw OL ⊥ AB.

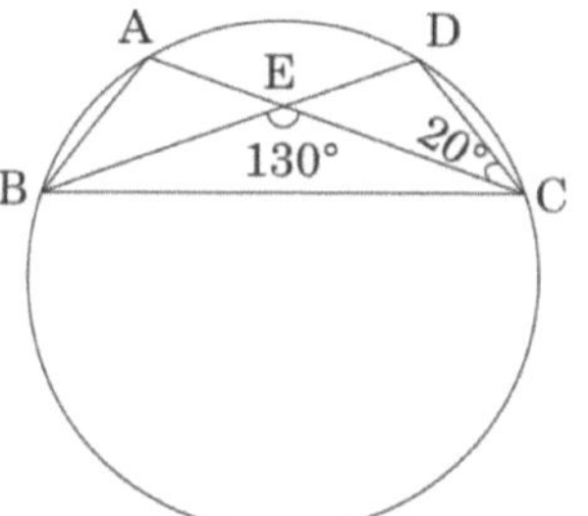

Since, the perpendicular from the centre of a circle to a chord bisects the chord.

∴ $AL = LB = \dfrac{1}{2}AB = 15\text{cm}$

In right angled OLA,

$$OA^2 = OL^2 + AL^2$$
                    [by pythagoras theorem]
⇒ $(17)^2 = OL^2 + (15)^2$
⇒ $289 = OL^2 + 225$
⇒ $OL^2 = 289 - 225 = 64$
∴   OL = 8 cm

Hence, the distance of the chord from the centre is 8 cm.

5. If two equal chords of a circle intersect within the circle, then prove that the line joining the point of intersection to the center makes equal angles with the chords.   [NCERT]

Sol. Let RQ and MN be two equal chords of circles with centre O. MN and RQ intersect at P and MN = RQ.

To prove : $\angle OPM = \angle OPQ$

Construction : draw OC ⊥ RQ and OB ⊥ MN. Join OP.

Proof : In right angled ΔOCP and ΔOBP, we have
                    $\angle OCP = \angle OBP$ [each 90°]
                    OP = OP   [common sides]

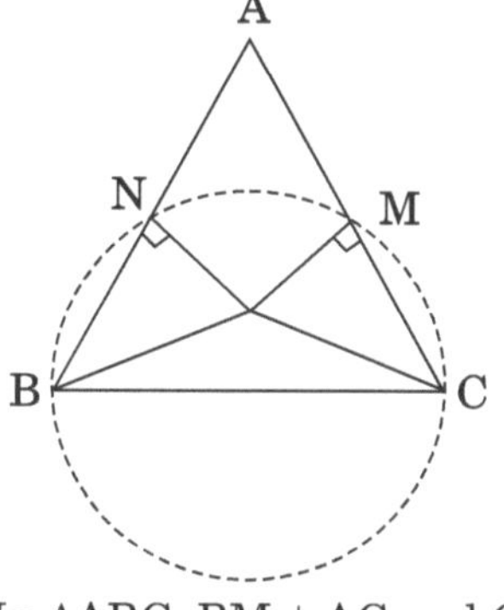

and   OC = OB
[∵ equal chords of a circle are equidistant from the centre]

By RHS congruence rule, we get
∴   ΔOCP ≅ ΔOBP
Then, $\angle OPC = \angle OPB$ [by CPCT]
∴ $\angle OPQ = \angle OPM$ Hence proved.

6. In figure, A, B, C and D are four points on a circle. AC and BD intersect at a point E such that $\angle BEC = 130°$ and $\angle ECD = 20°$. Find $\angle BAC$.   [NCERT]

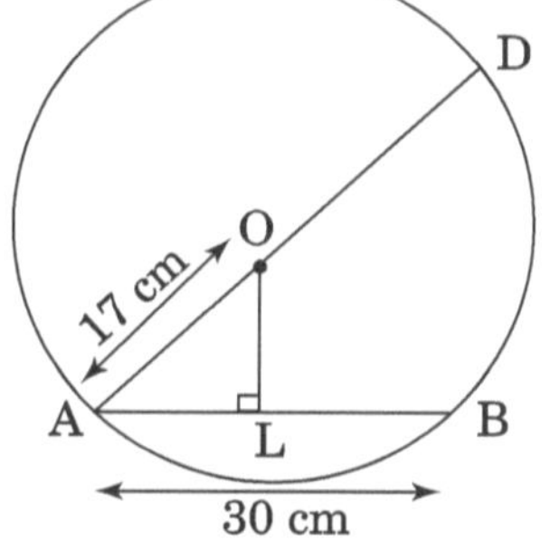

Sol. According to the given figure,

$\angle BEC = 130°$ and $\angle ECD = 20°$

$\because$ AC is a straight line.

So, $\angle AEB + \angle BEC = 180°$ [linear pair]

$\Rightarrow$ $\angle AEB = 180° - 130° = 50°$

$[\because \angle BEC = 130°]$

$\therefore$ $\angle CED = \angle AEB = 50°$

[vertically opposite angles]

Now, in ΔEDC, $\angle CED + \angle EDC + \angle DCE = 180°$

[angle sum property of triangle]

$\Rightarrow$ $\angle EDC = 180° - 20° - 50° = 110°$ ...(i)

Also, $\angle BAC = \angle BDC$

[since, the angle in the same segment are equal]

$\Rightarrow$ $\angle BAC = \angle EDC = 110°$ [using eq. (i)]

Hence, $\angle BAC = 110°$

7. Two circles intersect at two points B and C. Through B, two line segments ABD and PBQ are drawn to intersect the circles at A, D, P and Q respectively (see figure). Prove that $\angle ACP = \angle QCD$.   [NCERT][Board Term II, Set C1, 2011]

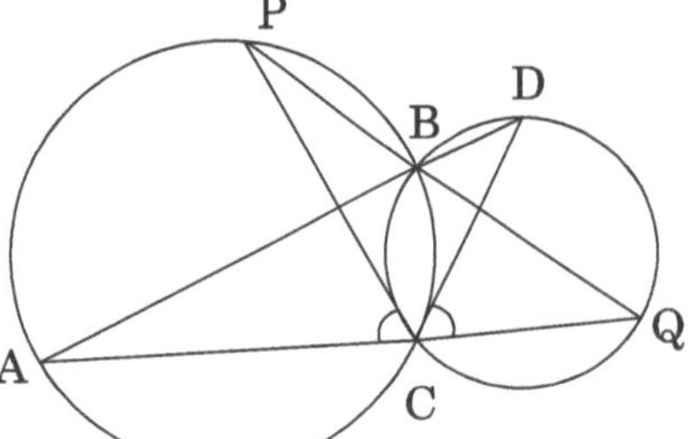

Sol. **Given :** Two circles intersect at two points B and C. Through B, two line segments ABD and PBQ are drawn which intersect the circles at A, D, P and Q respectively.

To prove : $\angle ACP = \angle QCD$

Proof : In circle I,

$\angle ACP = \angle ABP$ ...(i)

$[\because$ angles in the same segment are equal]

In circle II,

$\angle QCD = \angle QBD$ ...(ii)

$[\because$ angles in the same segment are equal]

Also, $\angle ABP = \angle QBD$ ...(iii)

[vertically opposite angles]

From eqs. (i), (ii) and (iii), we get

$\therefore$ $\angle ACP = \angle QCD$ Hence proved.

8. Two circles whose centres are O and O' intersect at P. Through P, a line parallel to OO', intersecting the circles at C and D is drawn as shown, Prove that CD = 2OO'.

[Board Term II, 2015, 2014 NCERT Exemplar]

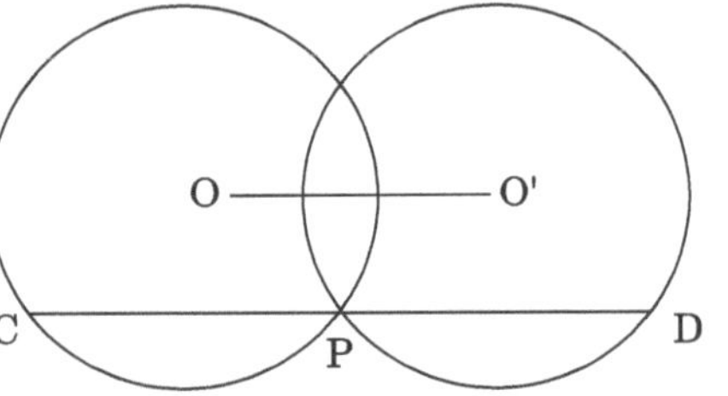

Sol. **Given:** Two circles whose centres are O and O intersect at P and CD ∥ OO'.

To prove: CD = 2OO'

Construction: Draw OA and O'B perpendicular to CD from O and O' respectively,

Proof: OA ⊥ CD

$\therefore$ OA bisects the chord CP (perpendicular from the centre to the chord bisects the chord)

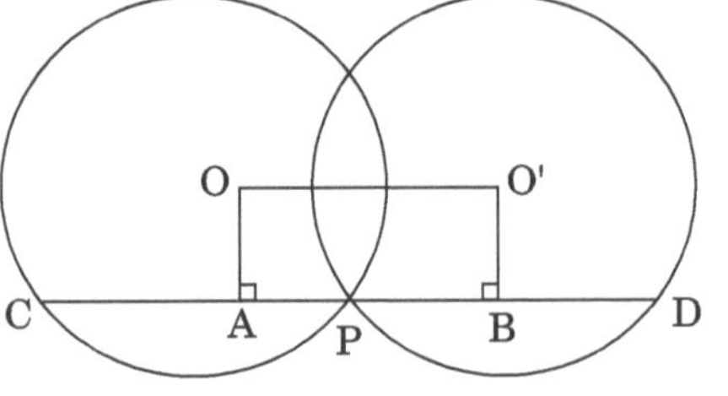

$\therefore$ $AP = \dfrac{1}{2}CP$

or $CP = 2AP$ ...(i)

Similarly O'B ⊥ PD

$\therefore$ $BP = \dfrac{1}{2}PD$

or, $PD = 2BP$ ...(ii)

$CD = CP + DP = 2AP + 2BP$

[from (i) and (ii)]

$= 2(AB)$ ...(iii)

Now, in quadrilateral ABO'O

$OA = O'B$

(two lines ⊥ to same line CD)

and $AB \parallel OO'$ (given)

ABO'O is parallelogram and AB ∥ OO'

(opposite sides of parallelogram are equal)

$CD = 2AB = 2OO'$

$\Rightarrow$ $CD = 2OO'$ Hence proved.

9. In ΔABE, AE = BE. Circle through A and B intersects AE and BE at D and C. prove that DC ∥ AB.   [Board Term II, 2012, 48 Set A1, 2011]

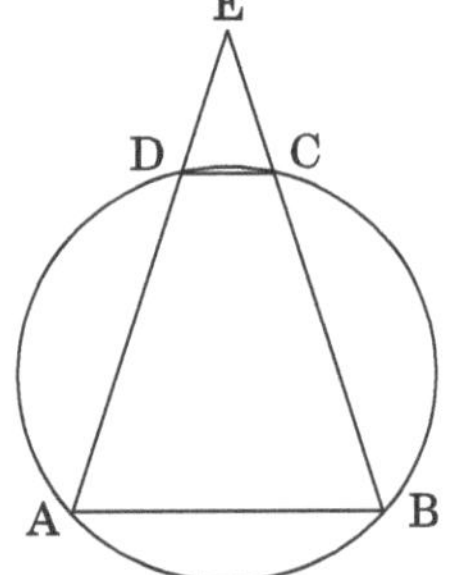

Sol. **Given :** In ΔABE, $AE = BE$ and circle through A and B intersects AE and BE at D and C.

To prove : DC || AB

Proof : $\because$ AE = BE

$\therefore$ $\qquad \angle A = \angle B$

(angle opposite to equal sides of a triangle are equal)

$\angle EDC = \angle B;$

$\angle ECD = \angle A$

(exterior angle of cyclic quadrilateral)

$\therefore$ $\angle EDC = \angle A$ (Corresponding Angles)

$\therefore$ $\qquad$ AB || DC $\qquad$ Hence proved

10. AB and CD are two parallel chords on the same side of the circle. AB = 6 cm, CD = 8 cm. The small chord is at a distance of 4 cm from the centre. At what distance from the centre is the other chord ?

[Board Term II, 2012, Set-08]

Sol. According to the question,

In ΔOMB, OM = 4 cm, MB = 3 cm

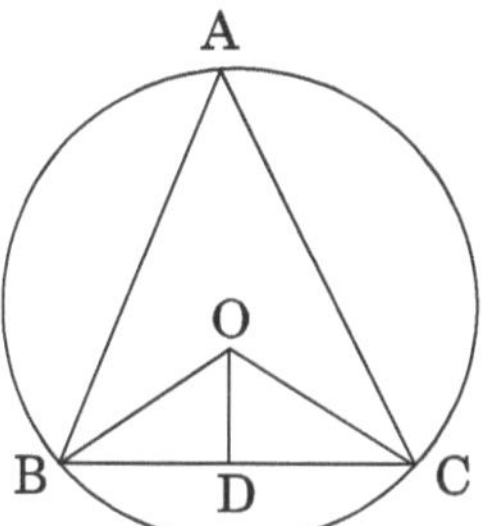

By using pythagoras theorem,

$$OB^2 = OM^2 + MB^2$$
$$= 16 + 9 = 25$$

$\therefore \qquad OB = \sqrt{25} = 5$ cm

Again, In ΔOND,

By pythagoras theorem,

$$ON^2 = OD^2 - DN^2$$
$$DN = 4 \text{ cm,}$$

and $\qquad OD = OB = 5$ cm $\qquad$ (Radii)

$\Rightarrow \qquad ON^2 = 5^2 - 4^2 = 25 - 16 = 9$

$\therefore \qquad ON = 3$ cm.

Hence, The other chord is at a distance of 3 cm from the centre.

11. In the given figure, AB and AC are two chords of circle whose centre is O. If OD $\perp$ AB, OE $\perp$ AC and AO bisects $\angle DAE$, prove that ΔADE is an isosceles triangle and $\angle ABC = \angle ACB$..

[Board Term II, Set LF0MCQ, 2016, 2012, Set-10]

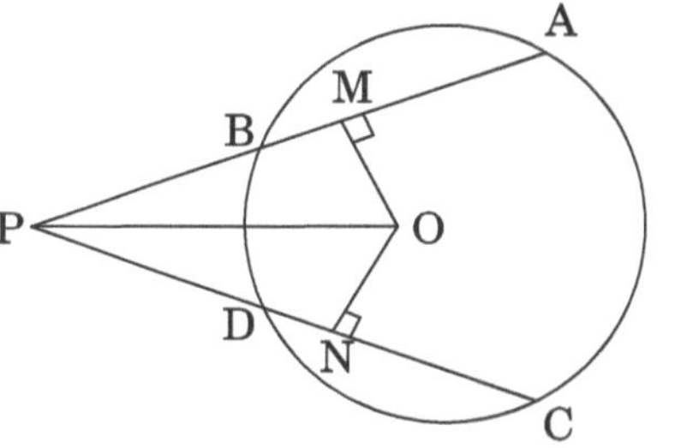

Sol. **Given:** OD $\perp$ AB, OE $\perp$ AC and AO bisects $\angle DAE$

To prove: ΔADE is isosceles triangle

and $\qquad \angle ABC = \angle ACB$

Proof: In ΔAOD and ΔAOE

$\angle OAD = \angle OAE$ $\qquad$ (AO is bisector)

$\angle ADO = \angle AEO = 90°$ $\qquad$ (Given)

$AO = AO$ $\qquad$ (Common)

$\therefore$ $\qquad \Delta ADO \cong \Delta AEO$ $\qquad$ (AAS)

$\therefore$ $\qquad AD = AE$ $\qquad$ (c.p.c.t)

Therefore, ΔADE is an isosceles Δ,

Also, $\qquad OD = OE$ $\qquad$ (c.p.c.t.)

$\therefore$ $\qquad AB = AC$

(chords equidistant from centre are equal)

$\angle ABC = \angle ACB$

(isosceles Δ prop. for ΔABC)

Hence proved

12. If O is the circumcentre of a ΔABC and OD $\perp$ BC, then prove that $\angle BOD = \angle BAC$.

[Board Term II, Set 261C-2013]

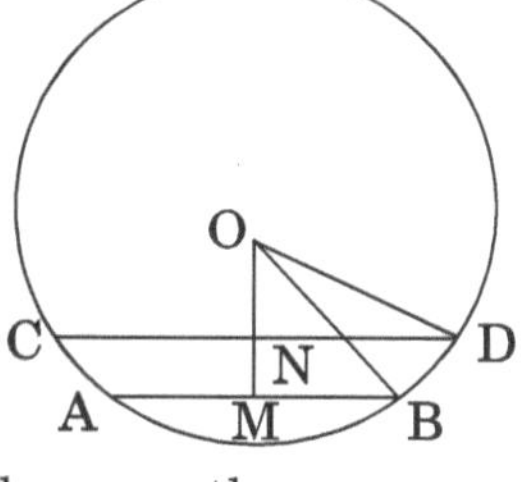

Sol. **Given:** OD $\perp$ BC

To prove: $\angle BOD = \angle BAC$

Proof: In ΔOBD and ΔOCD

$OB = OC$ $\qquad$ (radii)

$OD = OD$ $\qquad$ (Common)

and $\qquad \angle ODB = \angle ODC = 90°$ $[\because$ OD $\perp$ BC]

By RHS congruence rule,

$\Delta OBD \cong \Delta OCD$ $\qquad$ (RHS rule)

$\Rightarrow \qquad \angle BOD = \angle COD$ $\qquad$ (c.p.c.t.)

But $\qquad \angle BOC = 2\angle BOD = 2\angle BAC$

$\therefore \qquad \angle BOD = \angle BAC$ $\qquad$ Hence proved.

13. In the given figure, AB and CD are two chords of a circle with centre O such that MP = NP. If OM $\perp$ AB and ON $\perp$ DC, show that AB = CD.

[Board Term II, 2014]

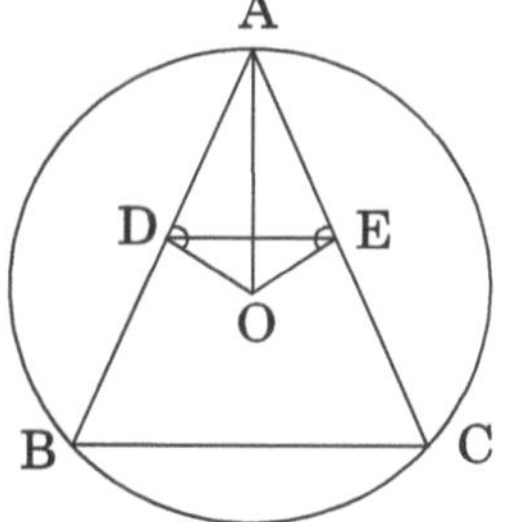

Sol. **Given:** MP = NP

and OM $\perp$ AB, ON $\perp$ DC

To prove: AB = CD

Construction: Join OP

Proof: In ΔOMP and ΔONP,

$$\angle OMP = \angle ONP = 90° \quad \text{(given)}$$
$$OP = OP \quad \text{(common)}$$

and $\qquad MP = NP \qquad$ (given)

By RHS congruence rule,

$\therefore \qquad \Delta OMP \cong \Delta ONP \qquad$ (RHS)

$\Rightarrow \qquad OM = ON \qquad$ (c.p.c.t.)

$\therefore \qquad AB = CD$

(chords equidistant from the centre are equal)

Hence proved.

14. In the given figure, AB and CD are two chords of a circle with centre O at a distance of 6 cm and 8 cm from O. If the radius of the circle is 10 cm, find the length of chords.   [Board Term II, 2014]

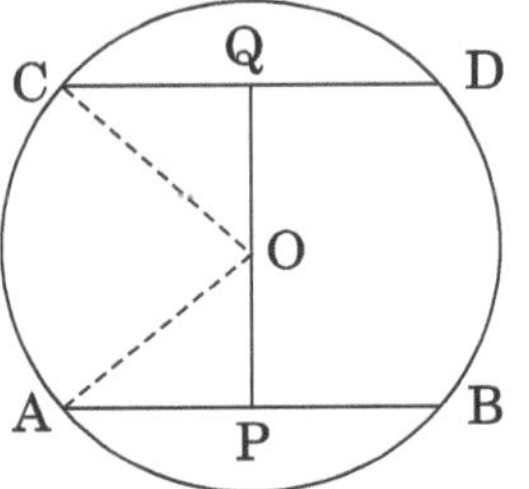

Sol. According to the question,

Since, perpendicular from centre bisects the chord,

$$\therefore \qquad AP = BP = \frac{1}{2}AB$$

and $\qquad CQ = QD = \dfrac{1}{2}CD$

In ΔOAP, By Pythagoras theorem,

$$AP^2 = OA^2 - OP^2 = 10^2 - 6^2 = 64$$

$\therefore \qquad AP = 8$ cm

and $\qquad AB = 2AP = 2 \times 8 = 16$ cm

Again, In ΔOQC,

By pythagoras theorem,

$$CQ^2 = OC^2 - OQ^2 = 10^2 - 8^2$$

$\therefore \qquad CQ = 6$ cm,

and $\qquad CD = 2CQ = 2 \times 6 = 12$ cm.

15. In the given figure, a diameter PQ of a circle bisects the chord RS at the point O. If PS is parallel to RQ, prove that RS is also a diameter of the circle.   [Board Term II, Set IA 21924, 2016]

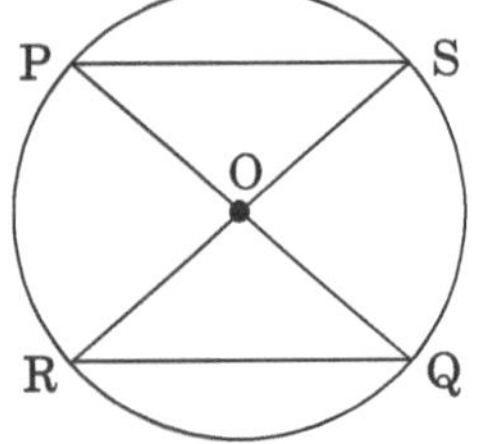

Sol. **Given:** PS $\parallel$ RQ

To prove : RS is the diameter of circle.

Proof: since, PS $\parallel$ RQ

$\therefore \qquad \angle PSO = \angle QRO$

and $\qquad \angle OPS = \angle OQR \quad$ (alternate angles)

Also, $\qquad \angle POS = \angle QOR$

(vertically opposite angles)

Thus, $\qquad \Delta OQR \sim \Delta OPS$

$$\therefore \qquad \frac{OQ}{OR} = \frac{OP}{OS} = \frac{OP}{OR}$$

[from ΔOQR and ΔOPS]

[$\because$ OR = OS as it is given that O bisects RS]

$\Rightarrow \qquad OQ = OP$

Therefore, O is the mid-point of PQ

$\therefore$ O is the centre of the circle.

Now, since RS passes through O, it means that RS passes through the centre of the circle.

$\therefore$ RS is a diameter of the circle. Hence proved.

16. In the given figure, AB and CD are two parallel chords of a circle with centre O and radius 5 cm such that AB = 8 cm and CD = 6 cm. If OP is perpendicular to AB and OQ is perpendicular to CD, determine the length of PQ.

[Board Term II, Set RQTZFBW, 2016]

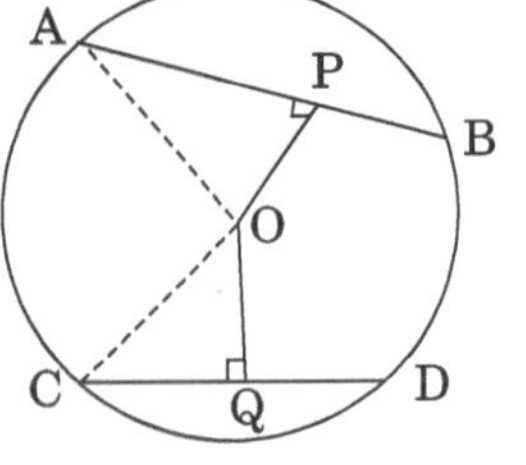

Sol. According to the question,

Construction: Join OA and OC

Since perpendicular from centre of the circle to the chord bisects the chord

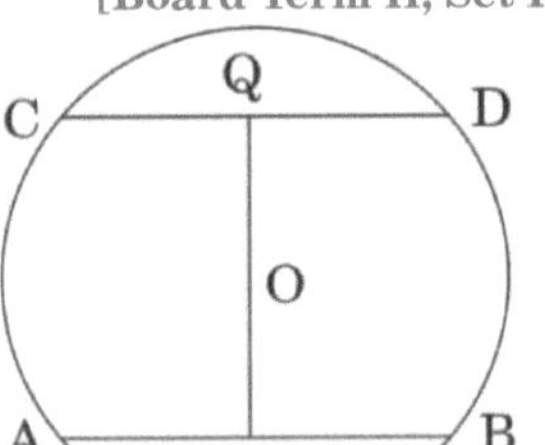

$$AP = PB = \frac{1}{2}AB = 4 \text{ cm}$$

and $\qquad CQ = QD = \dfrac{1}{2}CD = 3$ cm

Now, In ΔOAP,

By pythagoras theorem,

$$OP^2 = OA^2 - AP^2$$

$\Rightarrow \qquad OP^2 = 5^2 - 4^2 = 25 - 16 = 9$

$\therefore$ $\qquad$ OP = 3 cm

Again, In $\triangle OCQ$,

By Pythagoras theorem,

$\qquad$ $OQ^2 = OC^2 - CQ^2 = 5^2 - 3^2$

$\qquad$ $= 25 - 9 = 16$

$\qquad$ OQ = 4 cm

$\therefore$ $\qquad$ PQ = OP + OQ

$\qquad$ = 3 + 4 = 7 cm.

Hence, the length of PQ = 7 cm.

17. Prove that the circle drawn on any one of the equal sides of an isosceles as diameter, bisects the third side. [Board Term II, Set LF0MCQ 2, 2016]

Sol. Given: $\triangle ABC$ is an isosceles triangle with AB = AC. A circle is drawn taking AB as the diameter which intersects the side BC at D.

To prove: BD = DC

Construction: Join AD

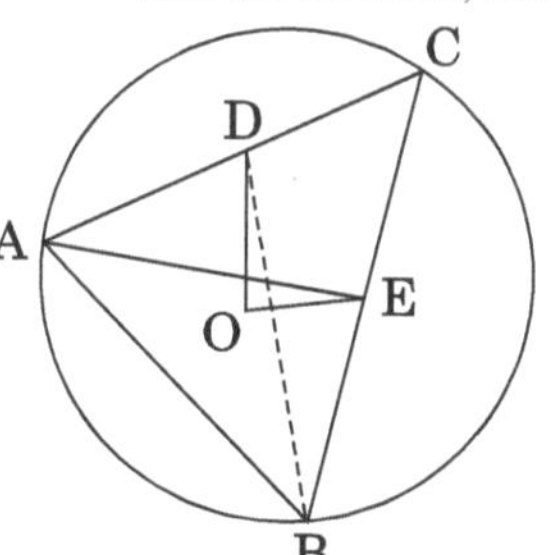

Proof: $\qquad$ $\angle ADB = 90°$

$\qquad$ (angle in semi-circle is 90°)

$\angle ADB + \angle ADC = 180°$ $\qquad$ [Linear angles]

$\therefore$ $\qquad$ $\angle ADC = 180° - 90° = 90°$

In $\triangle ABD$ and $\triangle ACD$,

$\qquad$ AB = AC $\qquad$ (given)

$\qquad$ $\angle ADB = \angle ADC$ $\qquad$ (proved)

and $\qquad$ AD = AD $\qquad$ (common)

By ASS congruence rule,

$\therefore$ $\qquad$ $\triangle ABD \cong \triangle ACD$

$\therefore$ $\qquad$ BD = DC $\qquad$ (c.p.c.t.)

$\qquad$ Hence proved.

18. In the given figure, O is the centre of the circle and L and M are the mid-points of AB and CB respectively. If $\angle OAB = \angle OCB$, prove that BL = BM.

[Board Term II, 2017, Set-Z6K408K]

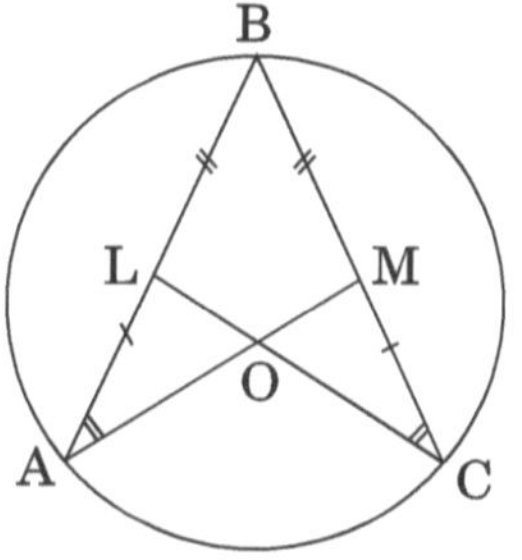

Sol. Given: L and M are the mid-points of AB and CB respectively.

and $\qquad$ $\angle OAB = \angle OCB$

To prove: $\qquad$ BL = BM

OL is a line from the centre to the mid-point of chord AB.

$\therefore$ OL is perpendicular to AB

i.e, $\qquad$ $\angle ALO = 90°$

OM is a line from the centre of the mid-point of chord BC.

i.e, $\qquad$ CMO = 90°

In $\triangle ALO$ and $\triangle CMO$

$\qquad$ $\angle ALO = \angle CMO = 90°$ $\qquad$ (proved above)

$\qquad$ $\angle LAO = \angle MCO$ $\qquad$ (given)

and $\qquad$ AO = CO $\qquad$ (radius)

By AAS congruence rule,

$\therefore$ $\qquad$ $\triangle ALO \cong \triangle CMO$

$\Rightarrow$ $\qquad$ AL = CM $\qquad$ (c.p.c.t.)

$\therefore$ $\qquad$ BL = BM

(L and M are mid-point of AB and CB respectively.)

$\qquad$ Hence proved.

19. In the given figure, O is the centre of the circle, OD $\perp$ AC, OE $\perp$ BC and OD = OE. Show that $\triangle DBA \cong \triangle EAB$.

[Board Term II, 2017, Set-UAH4Q7]

Sol. Given: OD $\perp$ AC, OE $\perp$ BC

and $\qquad$ OD = OE

To prove: $\qquad$ $\triangle DBA \cong \triangle EAB$

Since, $\qquad$ OD = OE

$\therefore$ $\qquad$ AC = BC

(chords equidistant from the centre are equal)

In $\triangle ACE$ and $\triangle BCD$

$\qquad$ AC = BC $\qquad$ (prove above)

$\qquad$ CE = CD $\qquad$ $\left(\dfrac{1}{2}BC = \dfrac{1}{2}AC\right)$

and $\qquad$ $\angle C = \angle C$ $\qquad$ (Common angle)

By SAS congruence rule, we get

$\therefore$ $\qquad$ $\triangle ACE \cong \triangle BCD$

$\Rightarrow$ $\qquad$ AE = BD $\qquad$ (c.p.c.t.)...(i)

In $\triangle DBA$ and $\triangle EAB$

$\qquad$ BD = AE $\qquad$ (from eq^n (i)

$\qquad$ DA = EB $\qquad$ $\left(\because \dfrac{1}{2}AC = \dfrac{1}{2}BC\right)$

and $\qquad$ AB = AB $\qquad$ (Common)

By SSS congruence rule,

$\therefore$ $\qquad$ $\triangle DBA \cong \triangle EAB$

Long Answer Type Questions

(4 Marks Each)

1. A circular park of radius 20 m is situated in a village. Three girls Rita, Sita and Gita are sitting at equal distance on its boundary each having a toy telephone in their hands to talk to each other. Find the length of the string of each phone. (There is no slack in the string.)

OR

A circular park of radius 20 m is situated in a colony. Three boys Ankur, Syed and Dayd are sitting at equal distance on its boundary each having a toy telephone in his hands to talk each other. Find the length of the string of each phone. **[NCERT]**

Sol. According to the question,

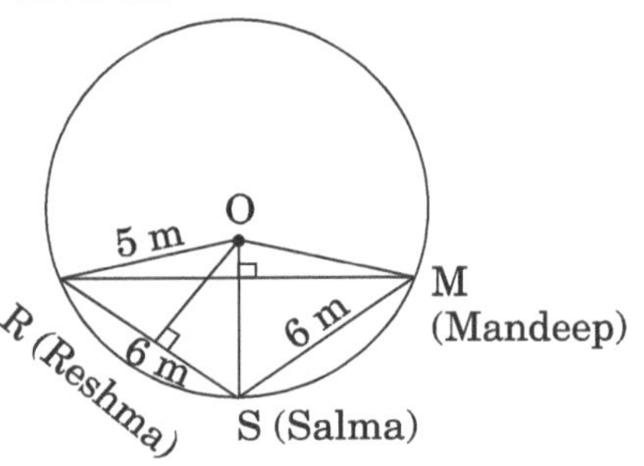

Here A, B, C are the three points where three girls are sitting.

∴ $\triangle ABC$ is an equilateral triangle.

In an equilateral triangle, the circumcentre is the point of intersection of median.

∴ O divides AD in the ratio 2 : 1.

Hence, if $\qquad$ AO = 20 m

then, $\qquad$ OD = 10 m

Also median is same as the altitude for an equilateral triangle.

Now, In $\triangle ODC$,

By pythagoras theorem,

$$OC^2 = OD^2 + DC^2$$
$$\Rightarrow \qquad 20^2 = 10^2 + DC^2$$
$$\Rightarrow \qquad DC^2 = 400 - 100 = 300$$
$$\therefore \qquad DC = 10\sqrt{3}\,m$$

and $\qquad$ BC = 2DC

$$= 20\sqrt{3}\,m$$

Hence, Length of the string of each phone

$$= 20\sqrt{3}\,m.$$

2. Two circles of radii 5cm and 3 cm interest at two points and the distance between their centres is 4 cm. Find the length of the common chord. **[NCERT]**

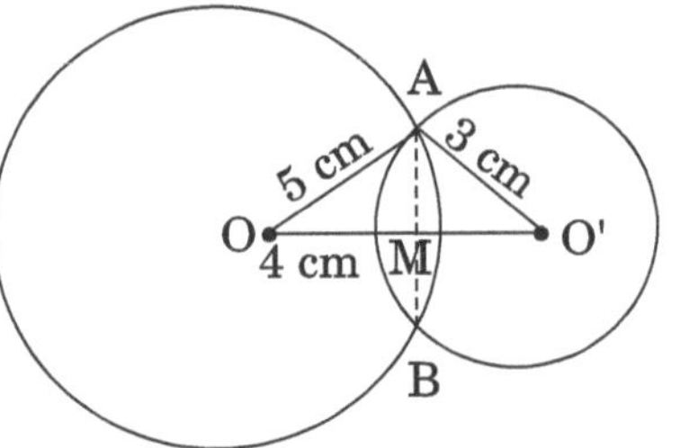

Sol. Let O and O′ be the centres of the circles of radii 5 cm and 3 cm, respectively. let AB be their common chord.

Given, OA = 5 cm, O′A = 3 cm

and $\qquad$ OO′ = 4 cm

Then, $\;$ AO′² + OO′² = 3² + 4²

$$= 9 + 16 = 25 = OA^2$$

So OO′ A is a right angled triangle and right angled at O′.

∴ Area of $\triangle OO'A = \dfrac{1}{2} \times O'A \times OO'$

$$= \dfrac{1}{2} \times 3 \times 4 = 6 \text{ cm}^2 \qquad ...(i)$$

Also, we know that when two circles intersect at two points, then their centres lie on the perpendicular bisector of the common chord.

∴ Area of $\triangle OO'A = \dfrac{1}{2} \times OO' \times AM$

$$= \dfrac{1}{2} \times 4 \times AM = 2AM \qquad ...(ii)$$

From eqs. (i) and (ii), we get

$$2AM = 6 - AM = 3 \text{ cm}$$
$$\therefore \qquad AM = 2 \times AM = 2 \times 3 = 6 \text{ cm}$$

Hence, the length of the common chord = 6 cm.

3. Three girls Reshma, Salma and Mandeep are playing a game by standing on a circle of radius 5 cm drawn in a park. Reshma throws a ball to Salma, Salma to Mandeep, Mandeep to Reshma. If the distance between Reshma and Salma and between Salma and Mandeep is 6 cm each, then what is the distance between Reshma and Mandeep? **[NCERT]**

Sol. Let O be the centre of the circle and Reshma, Salma and Mandeep are represented by the points R, S and M respectively. Draw OP ⊥ RM and ON ⊥ RS.

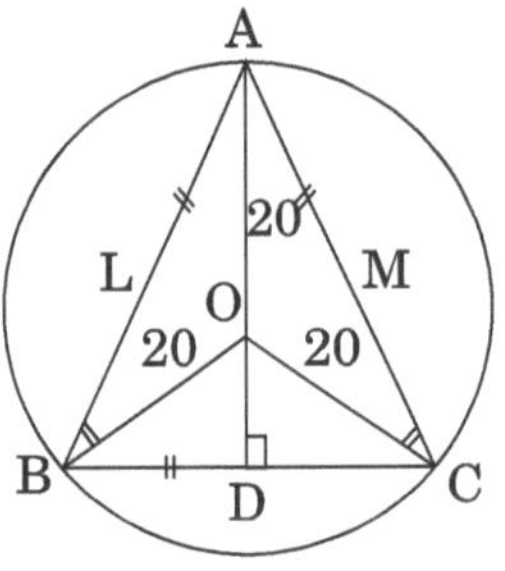

Let $\qquad$ RP = x m, then

According to the question,

$$\text{Area of } \Delta ORS = \frac{1}{2} \times RP \times OS$$

$$\left[\because \text{ area of triangle} = \frac{1}{2} \times \text{base} \times \text{height}\right]$$

$$\Rightarrow \text{Area of } \Delta ORS = \frac{1}{2} \times x \times 5 = \frac{5x}{2} \, m^2 \qquad ...(i)$$

In right angled ΔRNO,

$$OR^2 = RN^2 + NO^2$$

$$[\text{by pythagoras theorem}]$$

$$\Rightarrow \qquad 5^2 = 3^2 + NO^2$$

$$\left[\because ON \perp RS, \text{ therefore } RN = SN = \frac{6}{2} = 3m\right]$$

$$\Rightarrow \qquad NO^2 = 25 - 9 = 16$$

$$\therefore \qquad NO = 4 \, m$$

$$[\text{on taking positive square root}]$$

Again,

$$\text{area of } \Delta ORS = \frac{1}{2} \times RS \times ON$$

$$= \frac{1}{2} \times 6 \times 4 = 12m^2 \qquad ...(ii)$$

From eqs. (i) and (ii), we get

$$\frac{5x}{2} = 12 \Rightarrow x = \frac{24}{5} = RP$$

Here, P is the mid-point of RM.

$$[\because \text{ perpendicular from the centre the chord bisects the chord}]$$

$$\therefore \qquad RM = 2RP = 2 \times \frac{24}{5}$$

$$= \frac{48}{5} = 9.6 \, m$$

Hence, the distance between Reshma and Mandeep is 9.6 m.

4. Bisectors of $\angle A$, $\angle B$ and $\angle C$ of a ΔABC intersect its circumcircle at D, E and F, respectively. Prove that the angles of the ΔDEF are $90° - \frac{1}{2}A$, $90° - \frac{1}{2}B$ and $90° - \frac{1}{2}C$. $\qquad$ [NCERT]

Sol. **Given:** Bisectors of $\angle A$, $\angle B$, and $\angle C$ of a ΔABC intersect its circumcircle at D, E and F.

To prove: $\qquad \angle D = 90° - \dfrac{\angle A}{2}$

$$\angle E = 90° - \frac{\angle B}{2}$$

and $\qquad \angle F = 90° - \dfrac{\angle C}{2}$

Proof: $\qquad \angle EDF = \angle EDA + \angle ADF \qquad ...(i)$

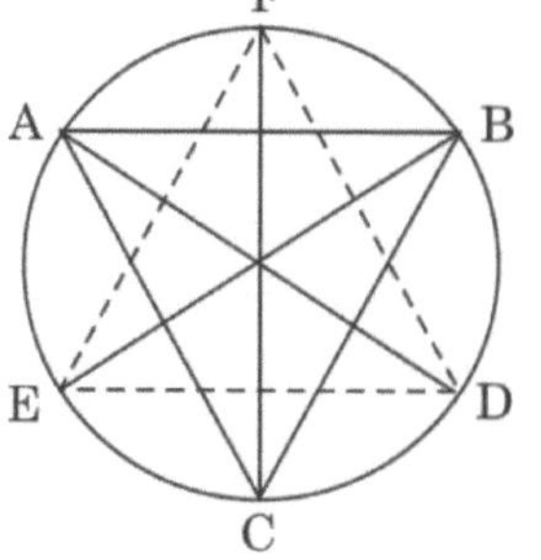

Since, $\angle EDA$ and $\angle EBA$ are the angles in the same segment of the circle.

$$\therefore \qquad \angle EDA = \angle EBA = \frac{1}{2}\angle B \qquad ...(ii)$$

$$[\because EB \text{ bisects } \angle ABC]$$

Similarly, $\angle ADF$ and $\angle FCA$ are the angles in the same segment.

$$\therefore \qquad \angle ADF = \angle FCA = \frac{1}{2}\angle C$$

$$[\because FC \text{ bisector } C]...(iii)$$

From eq. (i) $\angle EDF = \dfrac{1}{2}\angle B + \dfrac{1}{2}\angle C$

$$[\text{using eqs. (ii) and (iii)}]$$

$$\Rightarrow \qquad \angle D = \frac{\angle B + \angle C}{2}$$

Similarly, $\qquad \angle F = \dfrac{\angle A + \angle B}{2}$

and $\qquad \angle E = \dfrac{\angle C + \angle A}{2}$

Now, $\qquad \angle D = \dfrac{\angle B + \angle C}{2} = \dfrac{180° - \angle A}{2}$

$$= 90° - \frac{\angle A}{2}$$

$$[\because \angle A + \angle B + \angle C = 180°]$$

Similarly, $\qquad \angle E = \dfrac{180° - \angle B}{2} = 90° - \dfrac{\angle B}{2}$

$$[\because \angle A + \angle B + \angle C = 180°]$$

and $\qquad \angle F = \dfrac{180° - \angle C}{2} = 90° - \dfrac{\angle C}{2}$

$$[\because \angle A + \angle B + \angle C = 180°]$$

Hence proved.

5. A circle has radius $\sqrt{2}$ cm. It is divided into two segments by a chord of length 2 cm. Prove that the angle subtended by the chord at a point in major segment is 45°. $\qquad$ [NCERT Exemplar]

Sol. **Given:** A circle having centre O.

Construction : A chord of a circle. AB = 2cm, which is divided by the line OM in two equal segments.

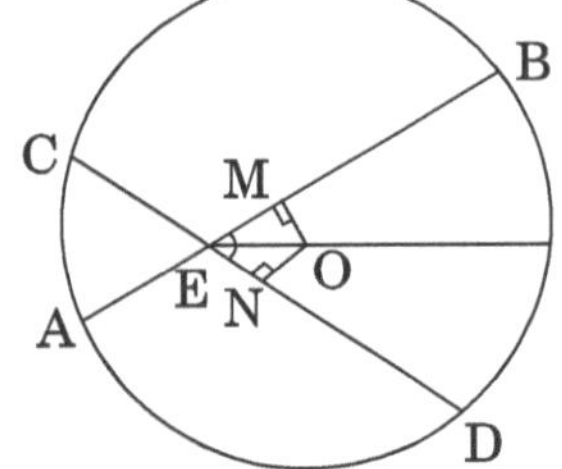

To prove : $\angle APB = 45°$

Proof : $\qquad$ AN = NB = 1 cm $\quad [\because AB = 2\ cm]$

and $\qquad\qquad$ OA = OB = $\sqrt{2}$cm

In $\triangle ONB$, by Pythagoras theorem,

$$OB^2 = ON^2 + NB^2$$

$\Rightarrow \qquad\qquad \left(\sqrt{2}\right)^2 = ON^2 + (1)^2$

$\Rightarrow \qquad\qquad ON^2 = 2 - 1 = 1 \therefore ON = 1$

Therefore, $\triangle ONB$ is an isosceles triangle.

$\because \qquad\qquad \angle ONB = 90°$

[since, ON is the perpendicular bisector of the chord AB]

$\therefore \qquad\qquad \angle NOB = \angle NBO = 45°$

Similarly, $\quad \angle AON = 45°$

Now, $\qquad\qquad \angle AOB = \angle AON + \angle NOB$

$\qquad\qquad\qquad\qquad = 45° + 45° = 90°$

$\therefore \qquad\qquad \angle APB = \dfrac{1}{2}\angle AOB$

[since, the angle subtended by an arc at the centre is twice the angle subtended by it at any point on the remaining part of the circle]

$\therefore \qquad\qquad \angle APB = \dfrac{90°}{2} = 45°$ $\quad$ Hence proved.

6. If two intersecting chords of a circle make equal angles with the diameter passing through their point of intersection, prove that the chords are equal.

[Board Term II, 2012, Set-65; Set A1, B1, C1, 2011, NCERT]

Sol. **Given :** $\angle OEM = \angle OEN$

Draw : OM $\perp$ AB and ON $\perp$ CD.

To Prove : $\quad$ AB = CD

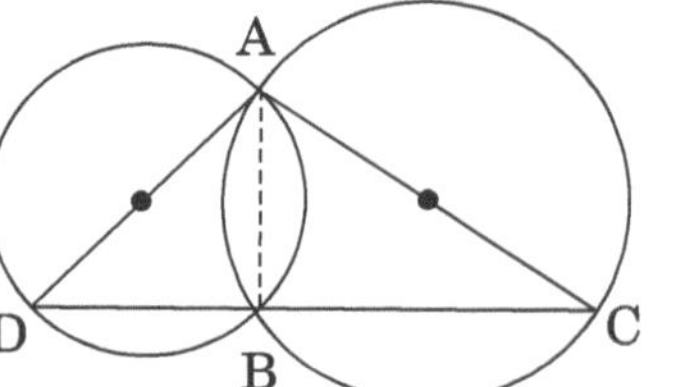

Proof : In $\triangle OME$ and $\triangle ONE$,

$\qquad\qquad \angle OEM = \angle OEN \qquad\qquad$ (given)

$\qquad\qquad \angle OME = \angle ONE \qquad\qquad$ (each 90°)

$\qquad\qquad\qquad OE = OE \qquad\qquad$ (common)

$\therefore$ By A.A.S congruence rule

$\qquad\qquad \triangle OME \cong \triangle ONE$

$\Rightarrow \qquad\qquad OM = ON \qquad\qquad$ (c.p.c.t.)

$\therefore \qquad\qquad AB = CD \quad$ (Chords equidistant from the centre are equal) Hence proved.

7. Two circles intersect at two points A and B. AD and AC are the diameters of the two circles. Prove that D, B and C are collinear.

[Board Term II, 2012, Set-08 KVS 2016]

OR

Two circles intersect at two points A and B. AD and AC are diameters of the two circles. Prove that B lies on the line segment DC. $\quad$ [NCERT]

Sol. **Given:** Two circles intersect at two points A and B.

To prove: points D, B and C are collinear

Construction: Join AB

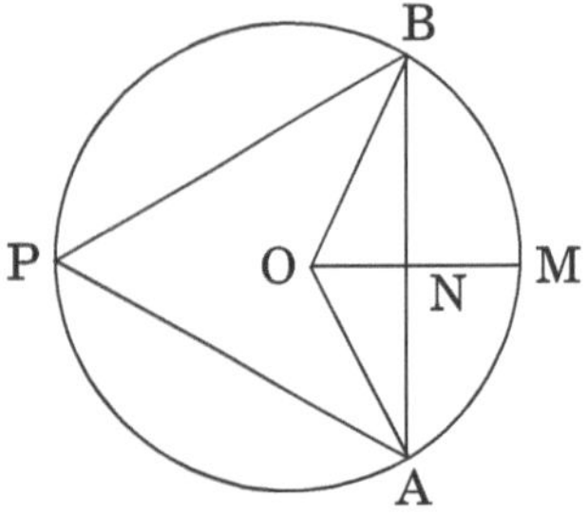

$\qquad\qquad \angle ABD = 90°$ (angle in a semi-circle)

$\therefore \qquad\qquad \angle ABC = 90°$ (angle in a semi-circle)

$\qquad \angle ABD + \angle ABC = 180°$

$\therefore$ DBC is a line

Hence, D, B and C are collinear.

8. Prove that "The angle subtended by an arc at the centre is double the angle subtended by it at any point on the remaining part of the circle".

[Board Term II, KVS 2016, NCERT]

OR

In the given figure, O is the centre of the circle. Prove that $\angle BOC = 2 \angle BAC$.

[Board Term II, 2012, Set-08]

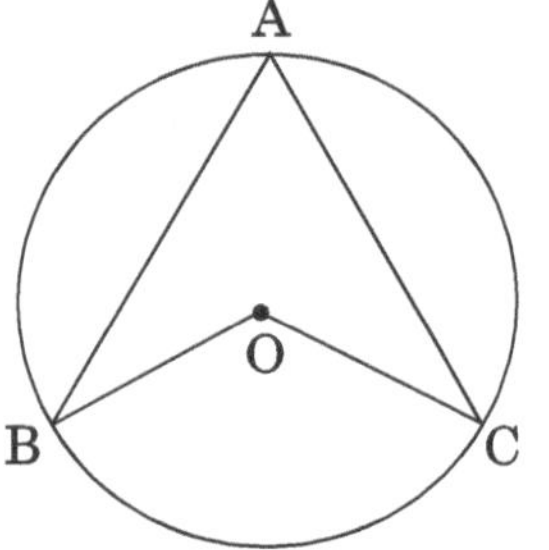

Sol. **Given:** O is the centre of the circle.

To prove: $\angle BOC = 2\angle BAC$

Construction : Join O to A.

Proof: In $\triangle AOB$, OA = OB (radii of same circle)

or, $\angle 1 = \angle 2$

(opposite angles to equal sides are always equal)

Similarly, in $\triangle AOC$

$$\angle 3 = \angle 4$$

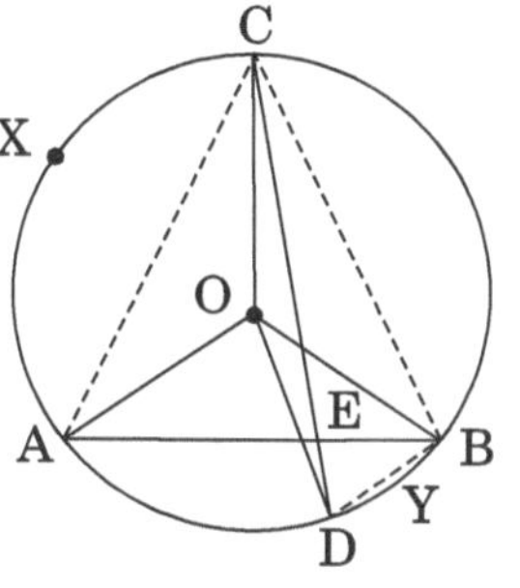

Now, by exterior angle property,

$$\angle 5 = \angle 1 + \angle 2 \qquad \text{...(i)}$$

and $\qquad \angle 6 = \angle 3 + \angle 4 \qquad \text{...(ii)}$

On adding eqn. (i) and eqn. (ii)

or, $\qquad \angle 5 + \angle 6 = \angle 1 + \angle 2 + \angle 3 + \angle 4$

$\Rightarrow \qquad \angle 5 + \angle 6 = \angle 2 + \angle 2 + \angle 3 + \angle 3$

$\qquad (\angle 1 = \angle 2, \angle 3 = \angle 4,$ proved above)

$\Rightarrow \qquad \angle 5 + \angle 6 = 2\angle 2 + 2\angle 3$

$\Rightarrow \qquad \angle 5 + \angle 6 = 2(\angle 2 + \angle 3)$

$\therefore \qquad \angle BOC = 2\angle BAC$

Hence proved.

9. In the given figure, AB and CD are two chords of a circle, with centre O, intersecting each other at point E, prove that $\angle AEC$ to $\dfrac{1}{2}$ (angle subtended by arc CXA at the centre + angle subtended by arc DYB at centre).

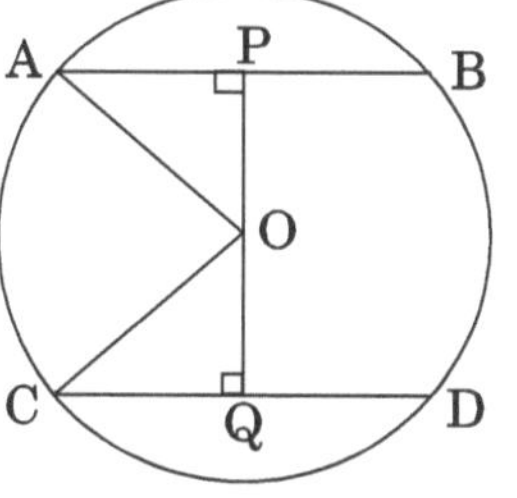

[Board Term II, Set LF0MCQ2, 2016, NCERT Exemplar]

Sol. **Given:** AB and CD are two chords of circle with centre O, which intersects at E.

To prove: $\angle AEC = \dfrac{1}{2}(\angle COA + \angle DOB)$

Construction: Join AC, BC and BD

Proof : AC is a chord.

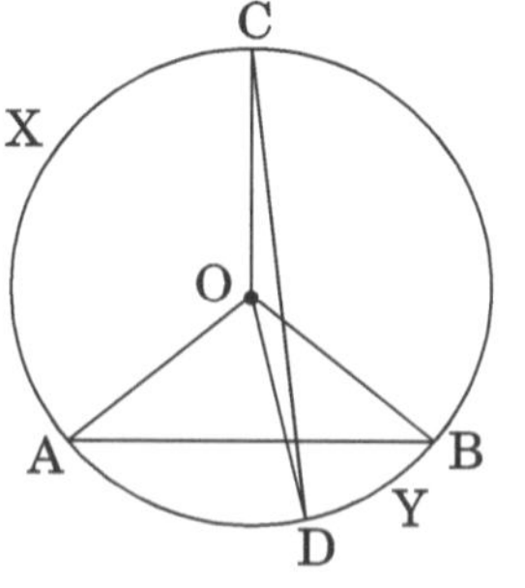

$\therefore \qquad \angle AOC = 2\angle ABC \qquad \text{...(i)}$

(angle subtended at centre is double the angle subtended at circumference)

Similarly, $\quad \angle DOB = 2\angle DCB \qquad \text{...(ii)}$

(angle subtended by the chord BD)

On adding (i) and (ii), we get

$\qquad \angle AOC + \angle DOB = 2(\angle ABC + \angle DCB) \quad \text{...(iii)}$

In $\triangle CEB$, $\quad \angle AEC = \angle ECB + \angle CBE$

(exterior angle is sum of two opposite interior angles)

$\Rightarrow \qquad \angle AEC = \angle DCB + \angle ABC \qquad \text{...(iv)}$

from eq^{n} (iii) and (iv), we get

$\therefore \ \angle AOC + \angle DOB = 2\angle AEC$

$\therefore \qquad \angle AEC = \dfrac{1}{2}(\angle AOC + \angle DOB)$

Hence proved.

10. In figure, O is the centre of the cirlce of radius 5 cm. OP $\perp$ AB, OQ $\perp$ CD, AB $\parallel$ CD. AB = 6cm CD = 8 cm. Determine PQ.

[Board Term II, 2012, Set A1, B1, C1, 2011]

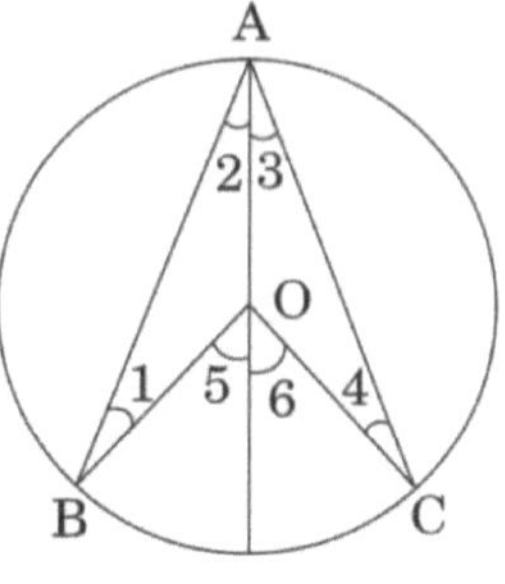

Sol. Since, perpendicular from the centre of the circle to a chord bisects the chord.

$\therefore$ P and Q are the mid-points of AB and CD

$$AP = \dfrac{1}{2}AB = 3\,cm$$

and $\qquad CQ = \dfrac{1}{2}CD = 4\,cm$

In right angled $\triangle OAP$,

By pythagoras theorem,

$$OA^2 = OP^2 + AP^2$$

$\Rightarrow \qquad (5)^2 = OP^2 + (3)^2$

$\Rightarrow \qquad OP^2 = 25 - 9 = 16$

$\therefore \qquad OP = 4\ cm$

Again, in right angled ΔOCQ,

By pythagoras theorem,

$$OC^2 = OQ^2 + CQ^2$$
$$\Rightarrow \qquad (5)^2 = OQ^2 + (4)^2$$
$$\Rightarrow \qquad OQ^2 = 25 - 16 = 9$$
$$\therefore \qquad OQ = 3 \text{ cm}$$

Hence, $\qquad PQ = OP + OQ = 4 + 3 = 7 \text{ cm}$

11. In a circle with centre O, chord SR = chord SM. Radius OS intersects the chord RM at P. Prove that RP = PM. [Board Term II, 2012, Set (25)]

Sol. **Construction:** Join RO and OM.

Proof: Since, SR = SM

$$\angle ROS = \angle SOM$$

(equal chord subtend equal angles at the centre)

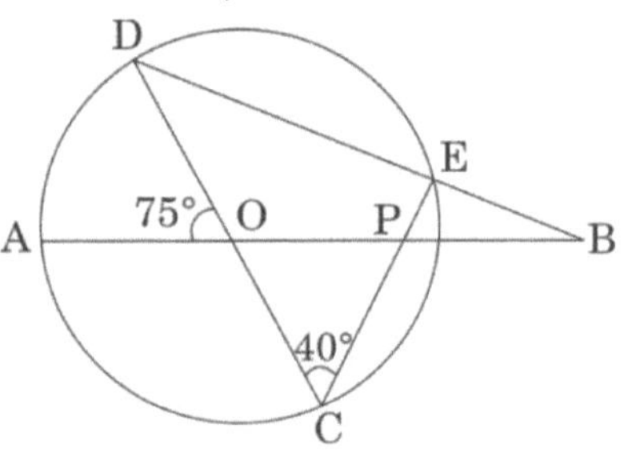

In ΔROP and ΔMOP, OR = OM (radius)

$$\angle ROS = \angle SOM \qquad \text{(proved above)}$$
$$OP = OP \qquad \text{(common)}$$

By SAS congruence rule, we get

$$\therefore \qquad \Delta ROP \cong \Delta MOP$$
$$\therefore \qquad RP = PM \qquad \text{(c.p.c.t.)}$$

Hence proved.

12. Three boys Rohit, Samir and Tarun are sitting at equal distances from each other on the boundary of a circular garden. The radius of the circular garden is 40 m. Find their distance from each other.

[Board Term II, 2012, Set-10]

Sol. Rohit, Samir and Tarun from an equilateral triangle. In an equilateral triangle the median and perpendicular bisector of a side are on same line.

Hence, O is circumcentre and centroid.

Centroid divides the median in the ratio 2 : 1

$$SO : OM = 2 : 1$$

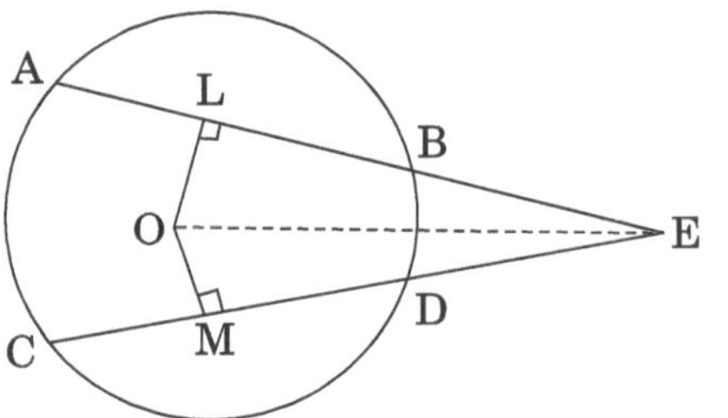

Hence, $\qquad SM = \dfrac{\sqrt{3}}{2}a$

(a = side of the triangle)

According to the question,

$$SO = \frac{2}{3} \times SM$$

$$\Rightarrow \qquad 40 = \frac{2}{3} \times \frac{\sqrt{3}}{2} \times a$$

$$\therefore \qquad a = \frac{40 \times 3}{\sqrt{3}} = 40\sqrt{3} \text{ m}$$

Hence, Required distance = $40\sqrt{3}$ m ·

13. In the given figure, straight lines AB and CD pass through the centre O of the circle. If $\angle OCE = 40°$. and $\angle AOD = 75°$, find $\angle CDE$ and $\angle OBE$.

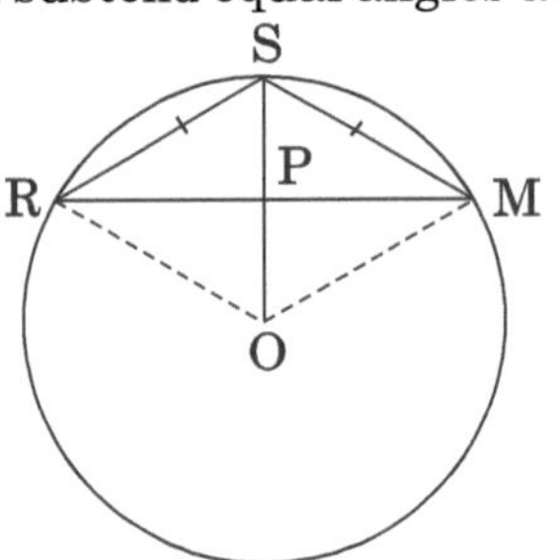

[Board Term II, 2012, Set 30]

Sol. According to the question,

$$\angle AOD + \angle BOD = 180° \qquad \text{(linear pair)}$$
$$\Rightarrow \qquad \angle BOD = 180° - \angle AOD$$
$$= 180° - 75° = 105°$$
$$\angle CED = 90° \quad \text{(angle in semi-circle)}$$
$$\angle CDE = 90° - \angle OCE = 90° - 40° = 50°$$

In ΔOBD, $\quad \angle OBD = 180° - (105° + 50°)$
$$= 180° - 155° = 25°$$

(In ΔDBO, Angle sum property of a triangle)

Hence, $\qquad \angle OBE = \angle OBD = 25°$.

14. Two equal chords AB and CD of a circle with centre O, are produced to meet at a point E as shown in figure. Prove that BE = DE and AE = CE.

[Board Term II, 2012, Set-69]

Sol. **Construction:** Join OE,

Draw : OL $\perp$ AB and OM $\perp$ CD

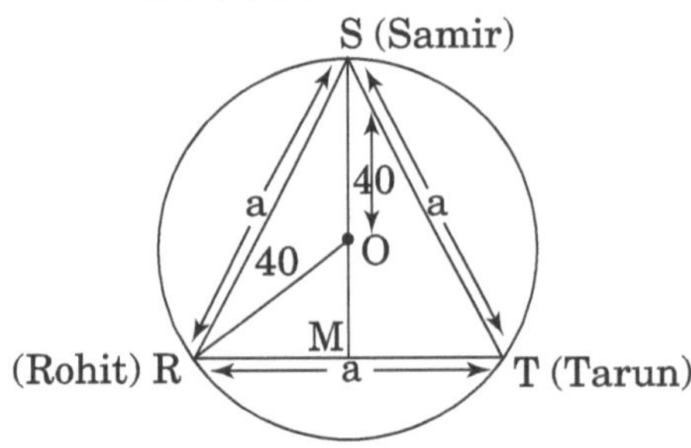

Given: AB = CD

or,   OL = OM

In $\triangle$OLE and $\triangle$OME

OE = OE   (Common)

OL = OM

(Equal chords are equidistant from the centre)

and $\angle$OLE = $\angle$OME   (each 90°)

By R.H.S congruence rule, we have

$\triangle$OLE $\cong$ $\triangle$OME

or,   LE = ME   (c.p.c.t.)...(i)

Since   AB = CD   (given)

On dividing by 2 both sides,

$\Rightarrow$ $\dfrac{1}{2}$AB $=$ $\dfrac{1}{2}$CD

$\Rightarrow$ BL = DM   ...(ii)

On subtracting (ii) from (i)

LE –BL = ME – DM

$\therefore$ BE = DE.

Again,   BE = DE   ...(iii)

and   AB = CD   (Given)... (iv)

On adding eq^n (iii) and eqn. (iv)

AB + BE = CD + DE

$\therefore$ AE = CE   Hence proved.

15. Find the angles ABC, ADE, BCD in the given figure, where 'O' is the centre of the circle.

[Board Term II, 2012, Set-23]

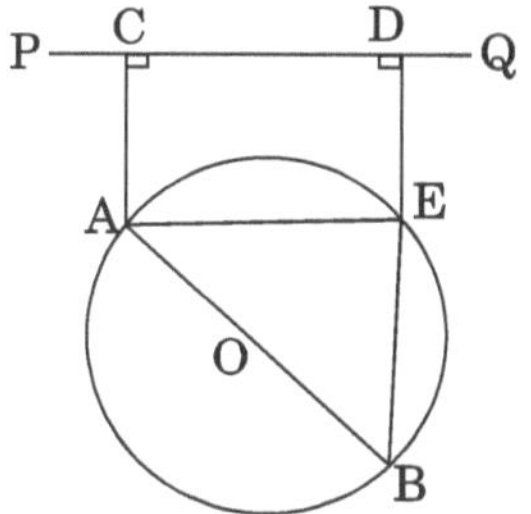

Sol.   According to the given figure,

$\angle$ACD = 90° and $\angle$AED = 90°

(angle in semi-circle)

In $\triangle$ADE,

$\angle$ADE = 180° − (60° + 90°)

= 30°   (angle sum property)

and $\angle$ABC = 180° − $\angle$CDA

= 180° − 70° = 110°

(ADCB is a cyclic quadrilateral)

In $\triangle$ABC,

$\angle$BCA = 180 − (110° + 30°) = 40°

(Angle sum property)

$\angle$BCD = $\angle$BCA + $\angle$ACD

Hence, $\angle$BCD = 40° + 90° = 130°.

16. If two circles intersect at two points, prove that their centres lie on the perpendicular bisector of the common chord.   [Board Term II, 2012, Set-01]

Sol.   **Given:** Two circles intersecting at two points.

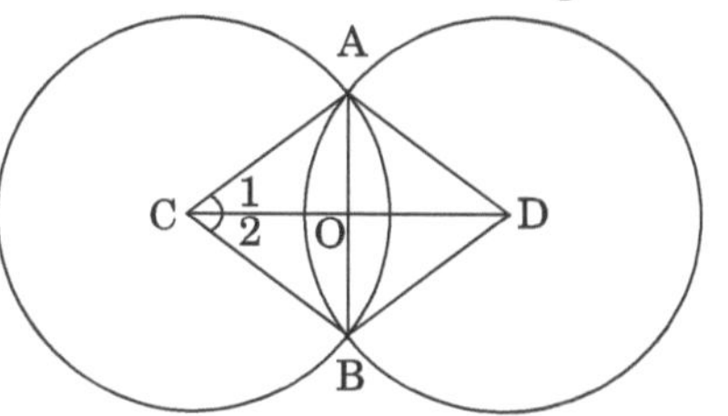

To prove: CD is the perpendicular bisector of AB.

Proof: In $\triangle$ACD and $\triangle$BCD,

AC = BC

AD = BD, CD is common

(radii of same circle)

or, $\triangle$ACD $\cong$ $\triangle$BCD   (by S.S.S)

$\therefore$ $\angle$1 = $\angle$2   (by c.p.c.t.)

In ACO and BCO,

AC = BC

and $\angle$1 = $\angle$2   (OC is common)

By SAS congruence rule, we get

$\triangle$ACO $\cong$ $\triangle$BCO

$\Rightarrow$ AO = OB   (c.p.c.t.)

$\angle$AOC = $\angle$BOC = 90°

but $\angle$AOC + $\angle$BOC = 180°

$\therefore$ CD $\perp$ AB.   Hence proved.

17. In the given figure, AB is a diameter of the circle with centre O. If AC and BD are perpendicular on a line PQ and BD meets the circle at E, then prove that AC = ED.

[Board Term II, 2013]

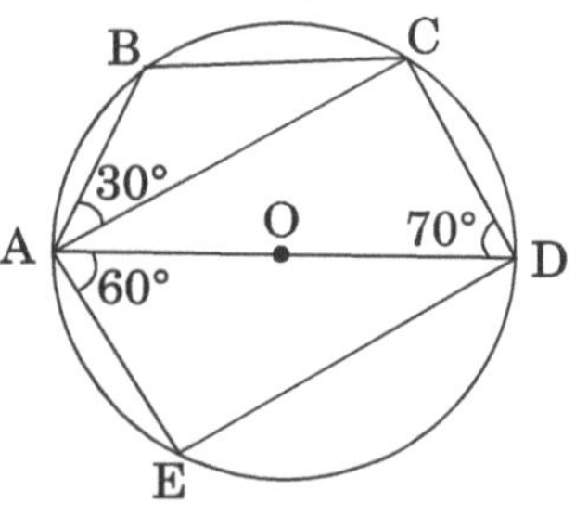

Sol.   **Given:** AC $\perp$ PQ, BD $\perp$ PQ

To prove: AC = ED

Proof: $\angle$AEB = 90° = $\angle$AED   (semi-circle)

$\angle$EAC + $\angle$ACD + $\angle$CDE +$\angle$AED = 360°

(sum of angles of a quadrilateral)

$\Rightarrow$$\angle$EAC + 90° + 90° + 90° = 360°

$\therefore$ $\angle$EAC = 360° − 270°

= 90°

Therefore, each angle = 90°

Thus, EACD is a rectangle

AC = ED.

Hence proved.

[Topic 2] Cyclic Quadrilaterals

Points to be Remembered:

- If all vertices of a quadrilateral lie on a circle, it is called a cyclic quadrilateral.
- The sum of either pair of opposite angles of a cyclic quadrilateral is $180°$. Conversely, if the sum of any pair of opposite angles of a quadrilateral is $180°$, then the quadrilateral is cyclic.
- If the side of a cyclic quadrilateral be produced then the exterior angle so formed is equal to the opposite interior angle.
- Any exterior angle of a cyclic quadrilateral is equal to the interior opposite angle.
- Circles with a common centre are called concentric circles.
- The degree measure of a semi-circle is $180°$.
- The degree measure of a circle is $360°$.
- Area of a circle $= \pi r^2$ sq. units.

PREVIOUS YEARS' EXAMINATION QUESTIONS

TOPIC 2

Multiple Choice Questions

(1 Mark Each)

1. ABCD is a cyclic quadrilateral such that AB is a diameter of the circle circumscribing it and $\angle ADC = 140°$, then $\angle BAC$ is equal to:

    (a) $80°$ (b) $50°$

    (c) $40°$ (d) $30°$ [NCERT Exemp.]

    Sol. (b) According to the question,

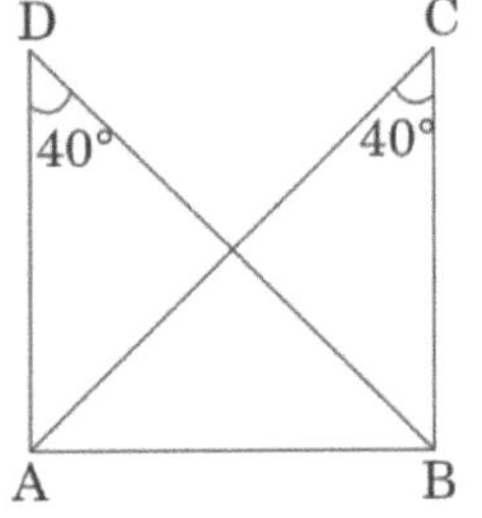

$$\angle ADC + \angle ABC = 180° \quad \text{[opposite angles of a cyclic quadrilateral]}$$
$$\Rightarrow \quad 140° + \angle ABC = 180°$$
$$\therefore \quad \angle ABC = 180° - 40° = 40°$$

∵ ABCD is a cyclic quadrilateral such that AB is the diameter of the circle circumscribing it.

Now, Join AC $\angle ACB = 90°$ [Angles in a semi-circle is a right angle]

In $\triangle ABC$, we have

$$\therefore \quad \angle BAC = 180° - (90° + 40°) = 50°$$

[Angle sum property]

2. In the given figure, the value of $\angle OPR$ is :

    (a) $65°$ (b) $40°$

    (c) $20°$ (d) $50°$

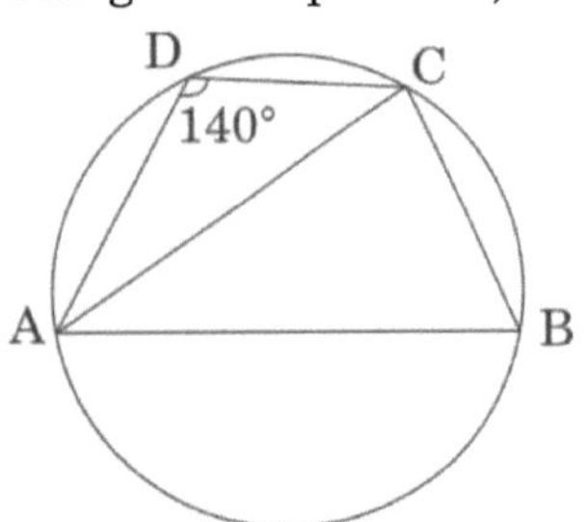

Sol. (b) According to the question,

$$\because \quad OP = OR \quad \text{[Radii]}$$
$$\angle OPR = \angle ORP$$

[Angles opposite to equal sides are equal]

Now, $\angle PQR + \angle POR = 180°$

$$\therefore \quad \angle POR = 180° - 100° = 80°$$

In $\triangle OPR$, $\angle OPR + \angle ORP + \angle POR = 180°$

[Angle sum property]

$$\Rightarrow \quad 2\angle OPR = 180° - 100°$$
$$\therefore \quad \angle OPR = 40°$$

3. Diagonals of a cyclic quadrilateral are the diameters of that circle, then quadrilateral is a:

    (a) parallelogram   (b) Square

    (c) rectangle   (d) trapezium

    Sol. (c) If diagonals of a cyclic quadrilateral are the diameters of that circle, then quadrilateral is a rectangle.

4. In the given figure, $\angle C = \angle D = 40°$, then the four points A, B, C, D:

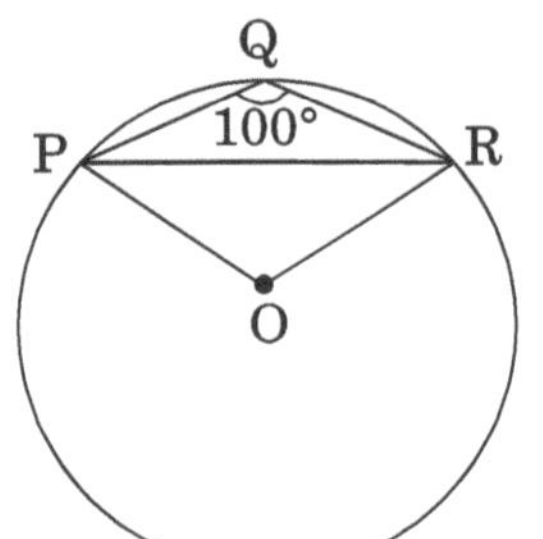

(a) are concyclic

(b) lie on the same circle

(c) are collinear

(d) A, B, D and A, B, C lie on the different circles

Sol. *(a)* Four points A, B, C and D are concyclic, *(b)* lie on the same.

Write whether the statements are true or false. Justify your answer.

1. In figure, if AOB is a diameter and ADC = 120°, then CAB = 30°

[NCERT Exemp.]

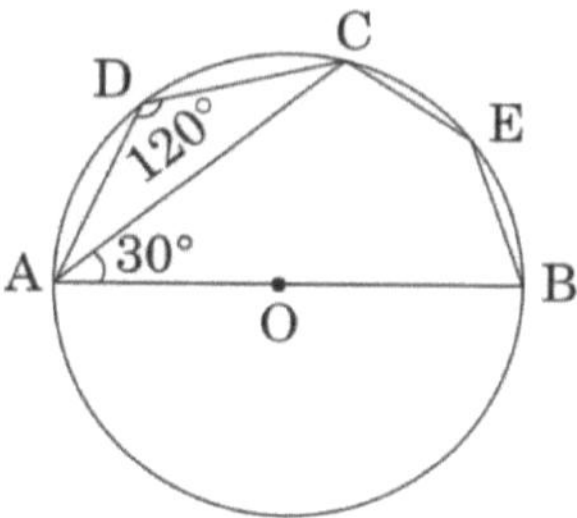

Sol. Since, AOB is a diameter of circle with centre O.

$$\angle ADC + \angle ABC = 180° \quad [ABCD \text{ is a cyclic quadrilateral}]$$

$$\Rightarrow \quad 120° + \angle ABC = 180°$$

$$\therefore \quad \angle ABC = 180° - 120° = 60°$$

In triangle ABC, we have

$$\angle ACB = 90° \quad [\text{Since, proved above}]$$

Therefore, $\angle CAB = 180° - (90° + 60°) = 30°$

Hence, the given statement is true.

2. ABCD is a cyclic quadrilateral such that $\angle A = 90°$, $\angle B = 70°$, $\angle C = 95°$ and $\angle D = 105°$

[NCERT Exemp.]

Sol. We know that opposite angles of a cyclic quadrilateral are supplementary.

Here, sum of opposite angles is not equal to 180°

$$\angle A + \angle C = 90° + 95° = 185°$$

And $\qquad \angle B + \angle D = 70° + 105° = 175°$

Hence, ABCD is not a cyclic quadrilateral.

Therefore, the given statement is false.

3. If A, B, C, D are four points such that $\angle BAC = 30°$ and $\angle BDC = 60°$, then D is the centre of the circle through A, B and C. [NCERT Exemp.]

Sol. Since, there can be many points D such that $\angle BDC = 60°$ and each such point cannot be centre of the circle through A, B and C.

Therefore, the given statement is false.

4. If A, B, C and D are four points such that $\angle BAC = 45°$ and $\angle BDC = 45°$, then A, B, C, D are concyclic. [NCERT Exemp.]

Sol. Since, the two angles $\angle BAC = 45°$ and $\angle BDC = 45°$ are in the same segment of a circle.

Therefore, the given statement is true.

Very Short Answer Type Questions (1 Mark Each)

1. In the given figure, quadrilateral PQRS is cyclic. If $\angle P = 80°$ then $\angle R$ is equal to ....

[Board Term I Set A1, 2011]

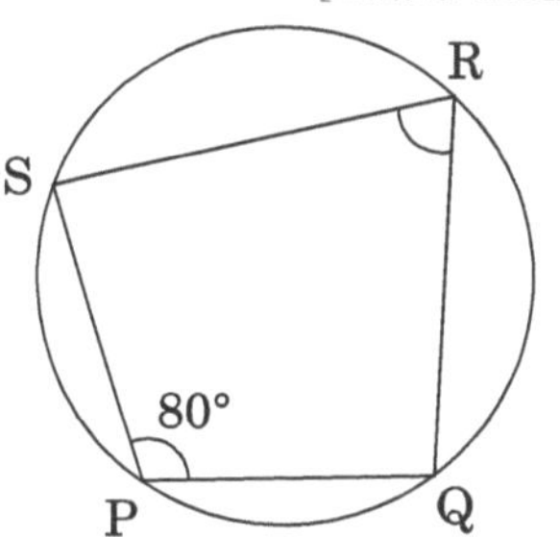

Sol. Since, quadrilateral PQRS is cyclic

$$\therefore \quad \angle P + \angle R = 180°$$

[opposite angles are supplementary]

$$\Rightarrow \quad 80° + \angle R = 180°$$

$$\therefore \quad \angle R = 100°$$

2. The sum of the opposite angles of a cyclic quadrilateral is :......... .

[Board Term II Set A1, 2011]

Sol. The sum of opposite angles of a cyclic quadrilateral is 180°.

3. In the given figure $\angle ACP = 40°$ and $\angle BPD = 120°$, then $\angle CBD = $ ....

[Board Term II, 2012, Set 01]

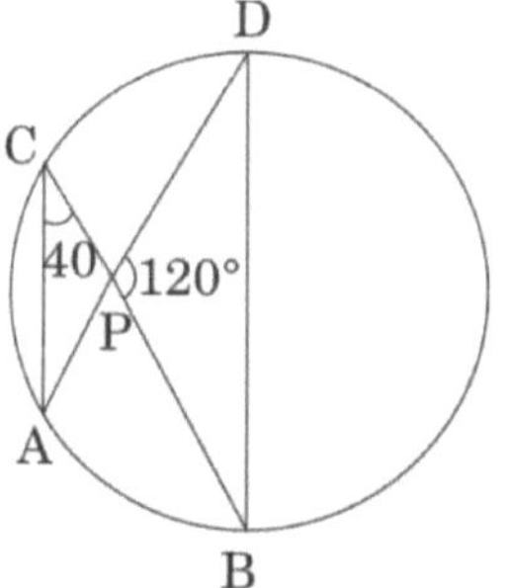

Sol. According to the question,

$$\angle ADB = \angle ACB = 40°$$

[∵ Angles in the same segment are equal]

Now, in $\triangle DPB$, $\angle DPB + \angle DBP + \angle PDB = 180°$

[Angle sum property]

$$\Rightarrow 120° + \angle DBP + 40° = 180°$$

$$\Rightarrow \quad \angle DBP = 180 - (120° + 40°)$$

$$= 180° - 160° = 20°$$

$$\therefore \quad \angle CBD = \angle PBD = 20°$$

Hence, the value of $\angle CBD = 20°$

4. In the given figure, if $\angle POR$ is 110° then find the value of $\angle PQR$.   [Board Term II, 2012 Set 06,]

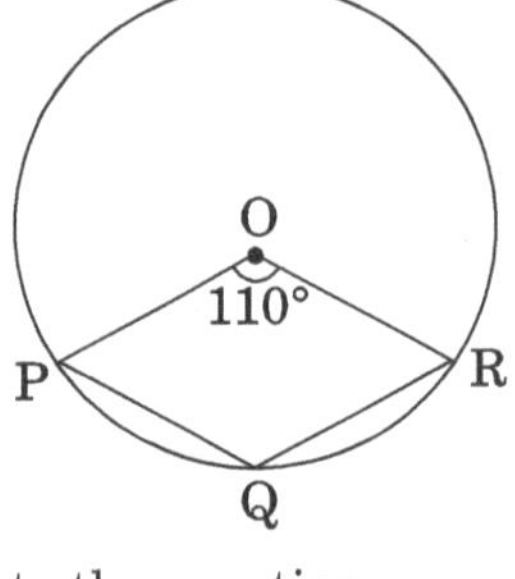

Sol. According to the question,

Reflex angle POR = 360° − 110° = 250°

∴ By degree measure theorem,

Hence, $\angle PQR = \dfrac{1}{2}$ (reflex angle POR)

$$= \dfrac{1}{2}(250°) = 125°.$$

5. In the given figure, $\angle M$ is 75°, then find $\angle O$.

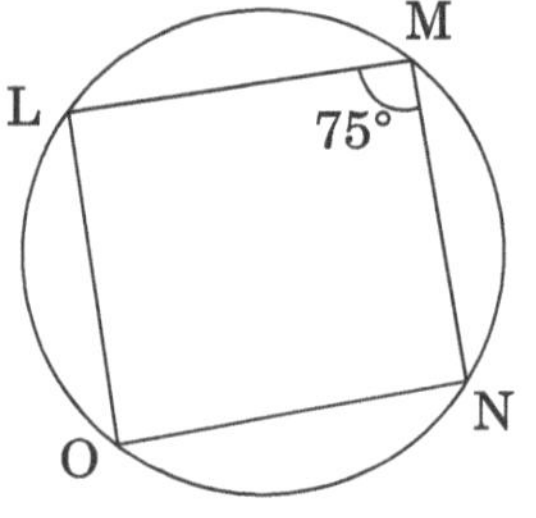

Sol. We know that sum of opposite angles of a cyclic quadrilateral is 180°.

∴ $\angle O + \angle M = 180°$

⇒ $\angle O + 75° = 180°$

∴ $\angle O = 105°$

Hence, the measure of $\angle O$ is 105°.

6. In the figure, PQRS is a cyclic quadrilateral. Find the value of x.

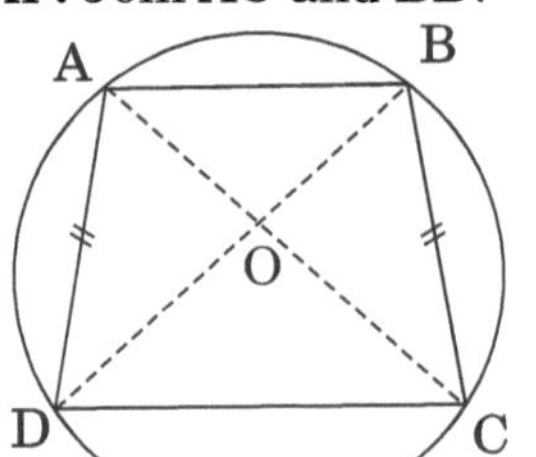

Sol. According to the question,

In $\triangle$PRS, by using angle sum property of a triangle we have

$\angle PSR + \angle SRP + \angle RPS = 180°$

⇒$\angle PSR + 50° + 35° = 180°$

∴ $\angle PSR = 180° − 85° = 95°$

Since, PQRS is a cyclic quadrilateral.

∴ $\angle PSR + \angle PQR = 180°$

[∵ opposite angles of a cyclic quadrilateral are supplementary]

⇒ $95° + x = 180°$

∴ $x = 180° − 95° = 85°$

Hence, the value of x is 85°.

Short Answer Type Questions-I
(2 Marks Each)

1. If a pair of opposite sides of a cyclic quadrilateral is equal, then prove that its diagonals are also equal.   [NCERT Exemplar]

Sol. Given : Let ABCD be a cyclic quadrilateral.

To prove :   AC = BD

Construction : Join AC and BD.

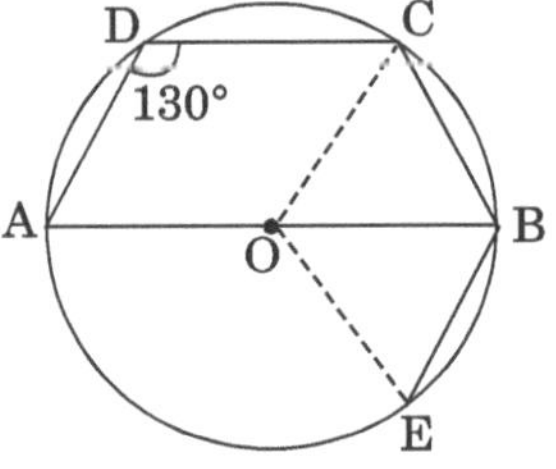

Proof : In $\triangle$AOD and $\triangle$BOC, we have

$\angle DAO = \angle CBO$

[angle is same segment]

and   AD = BC   [given]

By ASA congruence rule, we get

∴ $\triangle AOD \cong \triangle BOC$

∴ $OA = OB$ ...(i)

$OC = OD$ ...(ii) [by CPCT]

Adding eqs. (i) and (ii), we get

$OA + OC = OB + OD$

⇒   AC = BD   Hence proved.

2. In the given figure, $\angle ADC$ = 130° and chord BC = chord BE. Find $\angle CBE$.

[NCERT Exemplar]

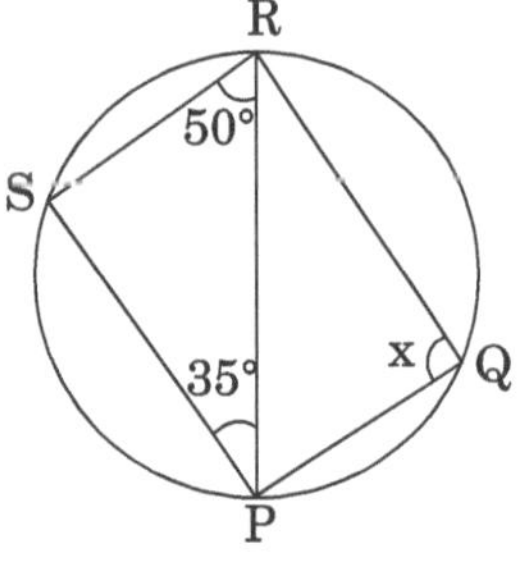

Sol. Let we consider the points A, B, C and D formed a cyclic quadrilateral. Then, according to the question, sum of opposite angles of a quadrilateral is 180°.

∴ $\angle ADC + \angle OBC = 180°$

⇒ $130° + \angle OBC = 180°$

∴ $\angle OBC = 180° − 130° = 50°$

Now, in $\triangle BOC$ and $\triangle BOE$,

$$BC = BE \qquad \text{[given]}$$
$$OC = OE \quad \text{[radii of the same circle]}$$
and $\qquad OB = OB \qquad$ [common sides]

By SSS congruence rule, we get

$$\therefore \qquad \triangle BOC \cong \triangle BOE$$
[by SSS congruence rule]

Then, $\quad \angle OBC = \angle OBE \qquad$ [by CPCT]

$$\angle OBE = \angle OBC = 50° \qquad \text{[from eq. (i)]}$$
$$\therefore \qquad \angle CBE = \angle OBC + \angle OBE$$
$$= 50° + 50° = 100°$$

3. Prove that a cyclic parallelogram is a rectangle.

[NCERT [KVS-2014; Board Term II Set A2, 2011]]

Sol. Given : PQRS is a parallelogram inscribed in a circle.

To prove : PQRS is a rectangle.

Proof : Since, PQRS is a cyclic quadrilateral.

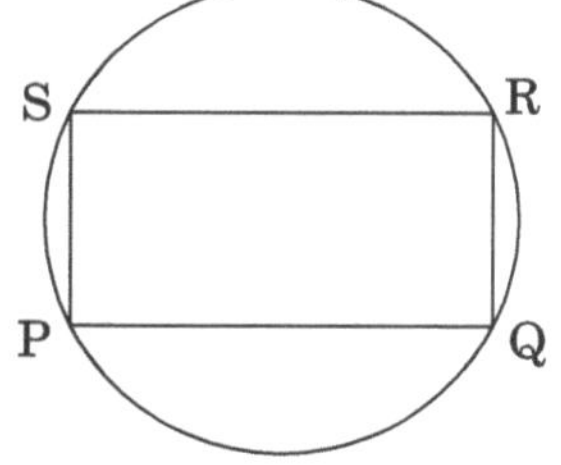

$$\angle P + \angle R = 180° \qquad \text{...(i)}$$

[since, sum of pair of opposite angles in a cyclic quadrilateral is 180°]

But $\qquad \angle P = \angle R \qquad$ ...(ii)

[since, in a parallelogram, opposite angles are equal]

From eqs. (i) and (ii), we get

$$\angle P + \angle P = 180°$$
$$\Rightarrow \qquad 2\angle P = 180°$$
$$\angle P = 90°$$
$$\therefore \qquad \angle P = \angle R = 90°$$

Similarly, $\qquad \angle Q = \angle S = 90°$

Thus, each angle of PQRS is 90°.

Hence, PQRS is a rectangle. Hence proved.

4. If non-parallel sides of a trapezium are equal. prove that the trapezium is cyclic.

[Board Term I Set A1, 2011, NCERT]

Sol. Draw CE ∥ AD.

Therefore, AECD is a parallelogram

$$CE = DA = CB$$
$$\therefore \qquad \angle 1 = \angle 2$$

[Angles opposite to equal sides are equal]

$$\angle 4 + \angle 5 = 180°$$

[Adjacent interior angles]

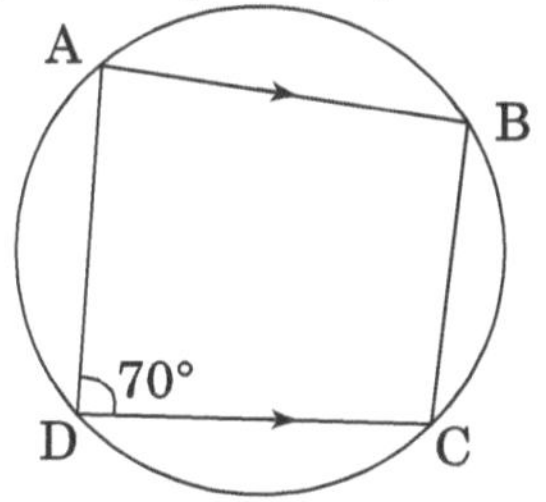

But, $\qquad \angle 5 = \angle 1 = \angle 2$

[Corresponding angles]

$$\therefore \qquad \angle 4 + \angle 2 = 180°$$

Hence, ABCD is a cyclic trapezium.

5. In the given figure, find the value of x.

[Board Term II, 2012, Set -09]

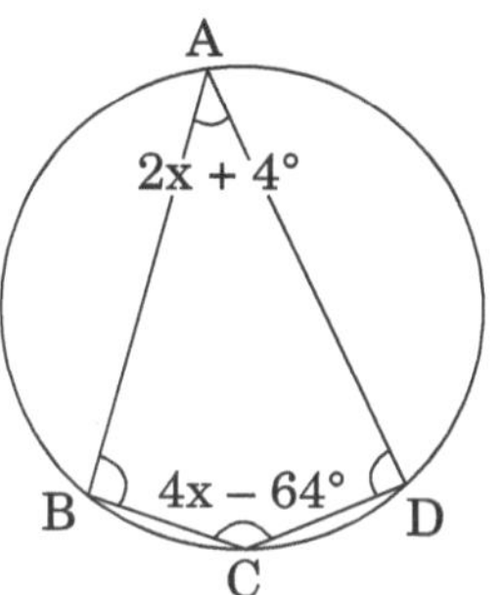

Sol. According to the given figure,

In a cyclic quadrilateral,

$$\angle A + \angle C = 180°$$

(opposite angles of cyclic quadrilateral are supplementary)

$$\Rightarrow 2x + 4° + 4x - 64° = 180°$$
$$\Rightarrow \qquad 6x - 60° = 180°$$
$$\Rightarrow \qquad 6x = 180° + 60° = 240°$$
$$\therefore \qquad x = \frac{240°}{6}$$
$$\therefore \qquad = 40°.$$

6. ABCD is a cyclic quadrilateral in which AB ∥ CD. If $\angle D = 70°$, find all the remaining angles.

[Board Term II, 2012, Set-15]

Sol. According to the question,

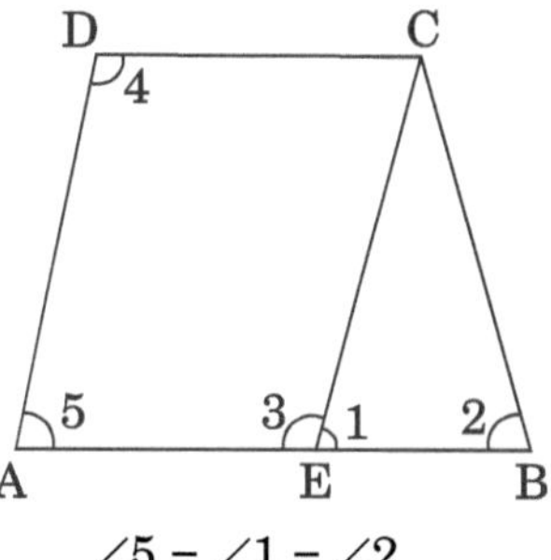

Since, sum of the opposite pairs of angles in a cyclic quadrilateral is 180°.

Hence, $\quad \angle B + \angle D = 180°$
$$\Rightarrow \qquad \angle B + 70° = 180°$$
$$\therefore \qquad \angle B = 180° - 70° = 110°$$

Again, AB ∥ CD and AD is its transversal, so

$$\angle A + \angle D = 180°$$

(Consecutive interior angles)

$\Rightarrow \qquad \angle A + 70° = 180°$

$\therefore \qquad \angle A = 180° - 70° = 110°$

and $\qquad \angle A + \angle C = 180°$

[Consecutive interior angles]

$\Rightarrow \qquad 110° + \angle C = 180°$

$\therefore \qquad \angle C = 180° - 110 = 70°$

7. ABCD is a cyclic quadrilateral in which AC and BD are its diagonals. If $\angle DBC = 55°$ and $\angle BAC = 45°$, find $\angle BCD$.

[Board Term II, 2012, Set-01, 05]

Sol. According to the question,

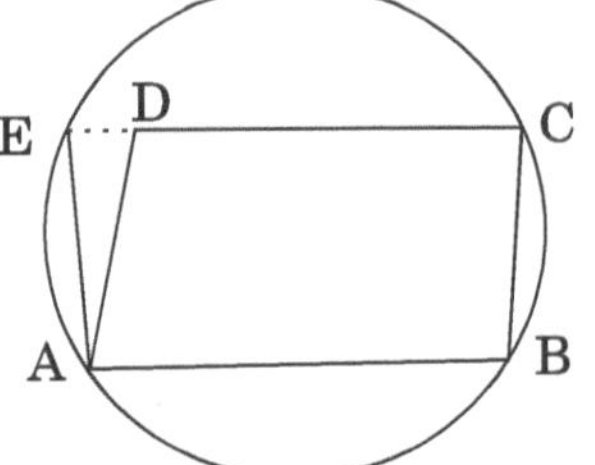

$\therefore \qquad \angle BAC = \angle BDC = 45°,$

(angles in the same segment)

In ΔDBC, $\angle DBC + \angle BCD + \angle CDB = 180°$

[Angle sum property]

$\Rightarrow 55° + \angle BCD + 45° = 180°$

$\therefore \qquad \angle BCD = 180° - 100° = 80°$

8. If diagonals of a cyclic quadrilateral are diameters of the circle through the opposite vertices of the quadrilateral, prove that the quadrilateral is a rectangle.

[Board Term II 2017, Set-UAH4DQ7J]

Sol. According to the question,

ABCD is a cyclic quadrilateral in which AC and BD are diameters

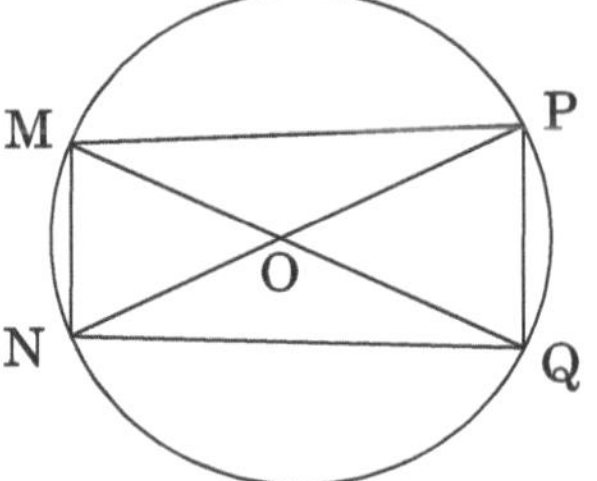

Since, AC is diameter

$\therefore \qquad \angle ABC = \angle ADC = 90°$

(angle of semicircle)

and BD is the diameter

$\therefore \qquad \angle BAD = \angle BCD = 90°$

(angle of semicircle)

Since, all angles of quadrilateral ABCD are 90° each

Therefore, ABCD is a rectangle.

Short Answer Type Questions-II

(3 Marks Each)

1. ABCD is a parallelogram. The circle through A, B and C intersects CD (produced, if necessary) at E. Prove that AE = AD. [NCERT]

Sol. Since, ABCE is a cyclic quadrilateral, therefore

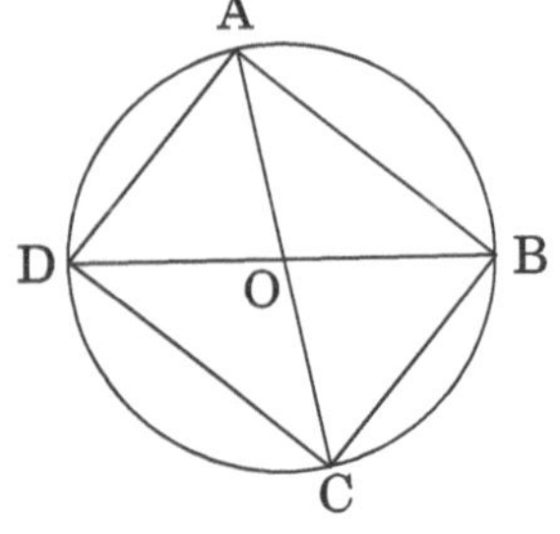

$$\angle AED + \angle ABC = 180° \qquad \qquad ...(i)$$

[∵ sum of pair of opposite angles of a cyclic quadrilateral is 180°]

$\therefore \quad \angle ADE + \angle ADC = 180° \qquad ...(ii)$

[∵ EDC is a straight line]

$\Rightarrow \angle ADE + \angle ABC = 180°$

[∵ $\angle ADC = \angle ABC$, opposite angles of a parallelogram]

From eqs. (i) and (ii), we get

$\angle AED + \angle ABC = \angle ADE + \angle ABC$

$\Rightarrow \qquad \angle AED = \angle ADE$

In ΔAED, $\quad \angle AED = \angle ADE$

So, $\qquad \qquad AD = AE$

[since, sides opposite to equal angles of a triangle are equal]

Hence proved.

2. If diagonals of a cyclic quadrilateral are diameters of the circle through the vertices of the quadrilateral, then prove that it is a rectangle. [NCERT]

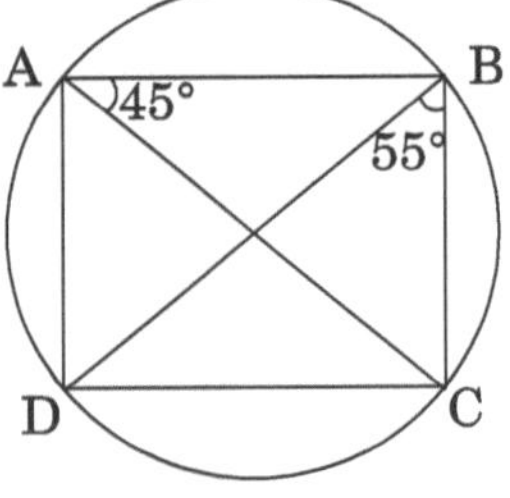

Sol. Given: Diagonals NP and QM of a cyclic quadrilateral NQPM are diameters of the circle passing through the vertices M, P, Q and N.

To prove : Quadrilateral NQPM is a rectangle.

Proof : Here, ON = OP = OQ = OM

[radii of same circle]

Then, $ON = OP = \dfrac{1}{2}NP$

and $OM = OQ = \dfrac{1}{2}MQ$

$\therefore$ $NP = MQ$

Therefore, the diagonals of the quadrilateral NQPM are equal and bisect each other. So, quadrilateral NQPM is a rectangle.

Hence proved.

3. If bisectors of opposite angles of a cyclic quadrilateral ABCD intersect the circle circumscribing it at the points P and Q, then prove that PQ is a diameter of the circle.

HOTS

[NCERT Exemplar]

Sol. Given : ABCD is a cyclic quadrilateral.

DP and QB are the bisectors of $\angle$D and $\angle$B, respectively.

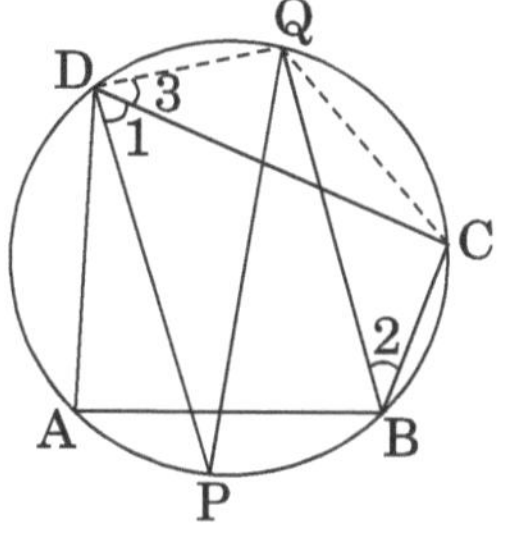

To prove : PQ is the diameter of the circle.

Construction : Join QD and QC.

Proof : Since, ABCD is a cyclic quadrilateral.

$\therefore$ $\angle CDA + \angle CBA = 180°$

[opposite angles of cyclic quadrilateral]

$\Rightarrow \dfrac{1}{2}\angle CDA + \dfrac{1}{2}\angle CBA = \dfrac{1}{2}\times 180° = 90°$

[dividing by 2]

$\Rightarrow$ $\angle 1 + \angle 2 = 90°$

$$\left[\because \angle 1 = \frac{1}{2}\angle CDA \text{ and } \angle 2 = \frac{1}{2}\angle CBA\right]$$

But $\angle 2 = \angle 3$

[angles in the same segment]

$\therefore$ $\angle 1 + \angle 3 = 90° \Rightarrow \angle PDQ = 90°$

Hence, PQ is a diameter.

[since, diameter subtends angle 90° in semi-circle.]

Hence proved.

4. If a line is drawn parallel to the base of an isosceles triangle to intersect its equal sides, prove that the quadrilateral so formed is cyclic.

[Board Term II, 2012, Set-30, NCERT Exemplar]

Sol.

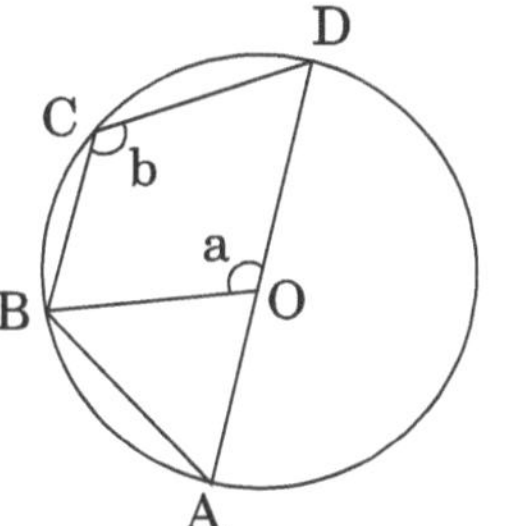

Given, ED $\parallel$ BC

     $AB = AC$

$\therefore$ $\angle 2 = \angle 3$ ...(i)

(Angles opposite to equal sides are always equal)

Since, sum of two adjacent interior angles is 180°.

     $\angle 1 + \angle 2 = 180°$ ...(ii)

and $\angle 3 + \angle 4 = 180°$

from eqⁿ (i) and (ii),

$\therefore$ $\angle 1 + \angle 3 = 180°$

     $\angle 2 + \angle 4 = 180°$

but these are opposite angles of a quadrilateral .

Hence, BCDE is a cyclic quadrilateral.

5. In the given figure, AB is a chord equal to the radius of the given circle with centre O. Find the values of a and b.   [Board Term II, 2014]

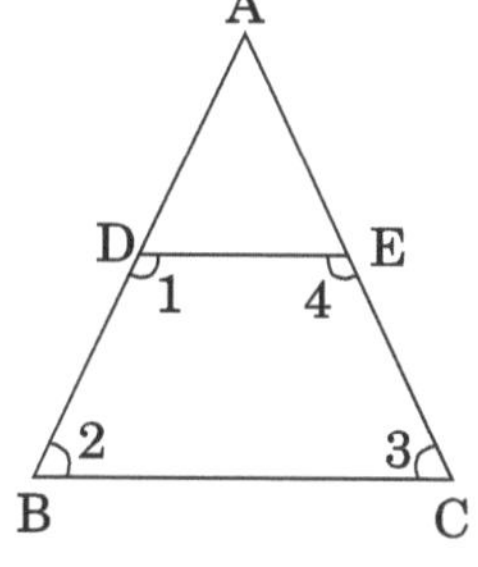

Sol. According to the question,

     $OB = OA$ (radius)

     $OA = OB = AB$ (given)

Therefore, ΔOAB is an equilateral triangle

$\therefore$ $\angle AOB = 60°$

(angles of equilateral triangle are 60° each)

$\therefore$ $a + \angle AOB = 180°$ (linear pair)

$\Rightarrow$ $a + 60° = 180°$

     $a = 180° - 60°$

     $= 120°$

Reflex angle BOD $= 2\angle BCD$

(angle subtended by an arc at the centre is twice at the circumference)

$\Rightarrow$ $360° - a = 2b$

$\Rightarrow$ $360° - 120° = 2b$

$\Rightarrow$ $2b = 240°$

$\therefore$ $b = 120°$

Hence, the value of a = 120° and b = 120°

6. In the given figure, PQ = QR = RS and $\angle$PQR = 128°. Find $\angle$PTQ, $\angle$PTS and $\angle$ROS.

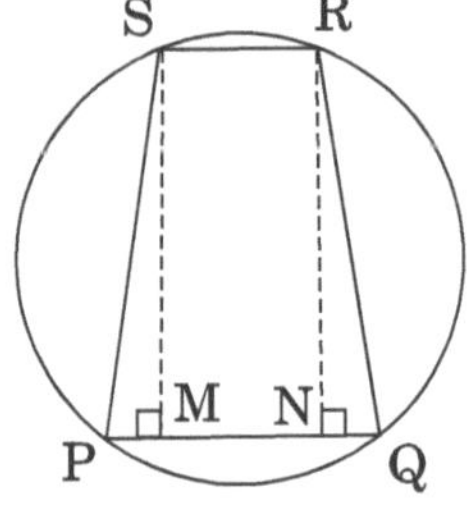

Sol. According to the question,

In ΔPQR,   PQ = QR = RS, $\angle$PQR = 128°

$\therefore$ $\angle 1 = \angle 2 = \dfrac{(180° - 128°)}{2}$

[Angles opposite to equal sides are equal]

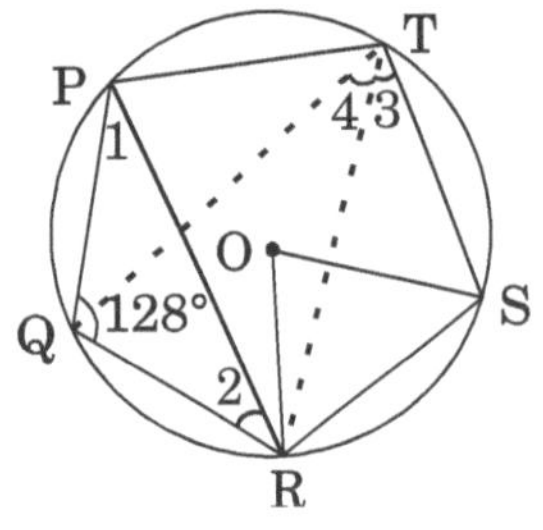

$$= \dfrac{52°}{2} = 26°$$

$\therefore$ $\angle$PTQ = $\angle$QRP = 26°

[Angles of same segment]

$\angle$PTS = 26° + $\angle 4$ + $\angle 3$

$= 26° + 26° + 26° = 78°$

$\angle$ROS = 2$\angle$RTS

$= 2 \times 26° = 52°$

Long Answer Type Questions-I
(4 Marks Each)

1. If the non-parallel sides of a trapezium are equal, then prove that it is cyclic.   [NCERT]

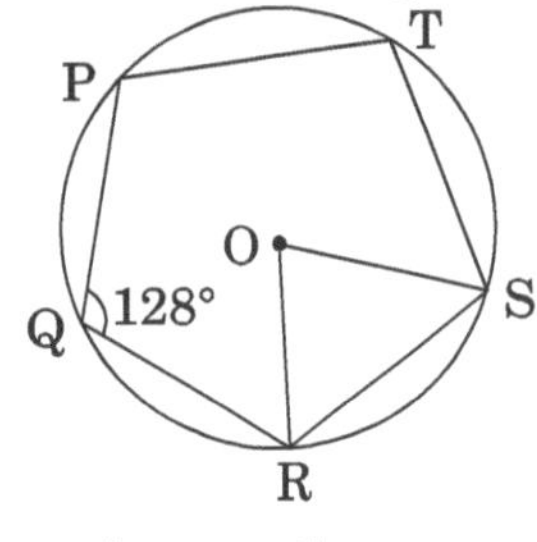

Sol. Given : Non-parallel sides PS and QR of a trapezium PQRS are equal.

To prove : PQRS is a cyclic trapezium.

Construction : Draw SM $\perp$ PQ and RN $\perp$ PQ.

Proof : In ΔSMP and ΔRNQ, we have

SP = RQ   [given]

$\angle$SMP = $\angle$RNQ   [each 90°]

and   SM = RN

[since, distance between two parallel lines is always equal]

$\therefore$ ΔSMP $\cong$ ΔRNQ

[by RHS congruence rule]

Then, $\angle$P = $\angle$Q and $\angle$PSM = $\angle$QRN [by CPCT]

Now, $\angle$PSM = $\angle$QRN

$\Rightarrow$ 90° + $\angle$PSM = 90° + $\angle$QRN

[adding 90° both sides]

$\Rightarrow$$\angle$MSR + $\angle$PSM = $\angle$NRS + $\angle$QRN

[$\because$ $\angle$MSR = $\angle$NRS = 90°]

$\Rightarrow$ $\angle$PSR = $\angle$QRS, i.e, $\angle$S = $\angle$R

Thus, $\angle$P = $\angle$Q and $\angle$R = $\angle$S   ...(i)

Now, $\angle$P + $\angle$Q + $\angle$R + $\angle$S = 360°

[$\because$ sum of the angles of a quadrilateral is 360°]

$\Rightarrow$ 2$\angle$S + 2$\angle$Q = 360°   [from eq. (i)]

$\Rightarrow$ $\angle$S + $\angle$Q = 180°

Hence, PQRS is a cyclic trapezium.

Hence proved.

2. If ΔABC and ΔADC are two right angled triangles with common hypotenuse AC, then prove that $\angle$CAD = $\angle$CBD.   [NCERT]

Sol. Given : ΔADC and ΔABC are right angled triangles with common hypotenuse.

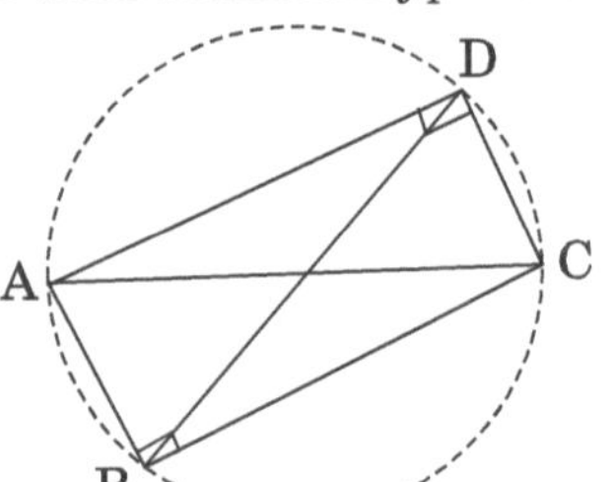

To prove : $\angle$CAD = $\angle$CBD

Proof : In ΔABC, we have

$\angle$ABC + $\angle$BCA + $\angle$CAB = 180°

[by angle sum property of a triangle]

$\Rightarrow$ 90 + $\angle$BCA + $\angle$CAB = 180°

$\Rightarrow$ $\angle$BCA + $\angle$CAB = 90°   ...(i)

In ΔADC, we have

$\angle$ADC + $\angle$CAD + $\angle$ACD = 180°

$\Rightarrow$ 90° + $\angle$CAD + $\angle$ACD = 180°

$\Rightarrow$ $\angle$CAD + $\angle$ACD = 90°   ...(ii)

On adding eqs. (i) and (ii), we get

$\angle$BCA + $\angle$CAB + $\angle$CAD + $\angle$ACD = 180°

$\Rightarrow$ ($\angle$BCA + $\angle$ACD) + ($\angle$CAD + $\angle$CAB) = 180°

$\Rightarrow$ $\angle$BCD + $\angle$BAD = 180°

i.e. $\angle$A + $\angle$C = 180°   ...(iii)

However, it is given that

$\angle$B + $\angle$D = 180°   ...(iv)

Thus, from Eqs. (iii) and (iv), it can be observed that the sum of the measures of opposite angles of quadrilateral ABCD is 180°. Therefore, ABCD is a cyclic quadrilateral.

We know that, angles in the same segment are equal.

$\therefore$ $\angle CAD = \angle CBD$ Hence proved.

3. In the given figure, AB is a diameter of the circle; CD is a chord equal to the radius of the circle. AC and BD when extended intersect at a point E. Prove that $\angle AEB = 60°$.

[NCERT] [Board Term II, Set B1, 2011; 2012, 01, 10]

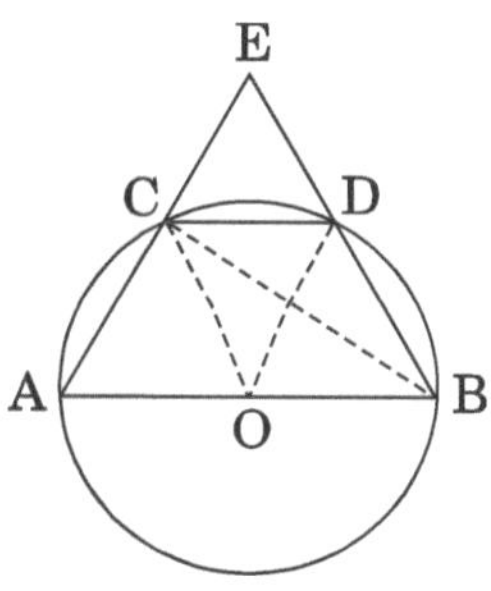

Sol. According to the question,

Join OC, OD and BC.

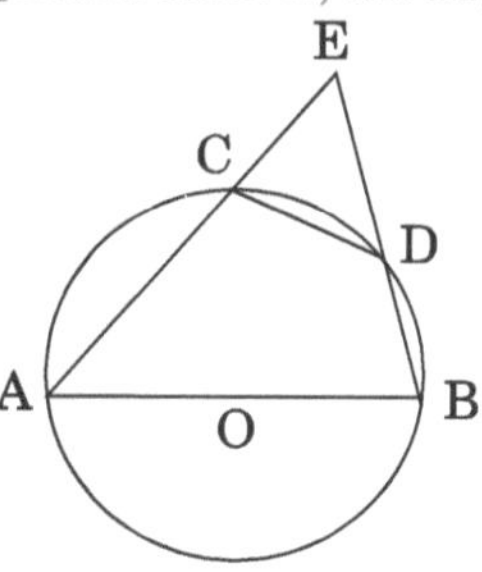

CD = Radius of the circle   (Given)

$\therefore$ CD = OD = OC

Therefore, $\triangle ODC$ is an equilateral triangle.

$\therefore$ $\angle COD = 60°$

Now, $\angle CBD = \dfrac{1}{2}\angle COD = \dfrac{1}{2}\times 60° = 30°$

Also, $\angle ACB = 90°$ (angle in a semi-circle is 90°)

$\therefore$ $\angle BCE = 180° - \angle ACB$

$= 180° - 90° = 90°$

Now, in $\triangle BCE$,

$\angle CBE + \angle BCE + \angle CEB = 180°$

[Angle sum property]

$\Rightarrow 30° + 90° + \angle CEB = 180°$

$\Rightarrow$ $120° + \angle CEB = 180°$

$\Rightarrow$ $\angle CEB = 180° - 120° = 60°$

Hence, $\angle AEB = 60°$

4. Prove that the quadrilateral formed by internal angle bisectors of any quadrilateral is cyclic.

[Board Term II, 2012, Set-01][NCERT]

Sol. Given : ABCD is a quadrilateral.

$$\angle DAE = \frac{1}{2}\angle A$$

$$\angle ADE = \frac{1}{2}\angle D$$

$$\angle GBC = \frac{1}{2}\angle B$$

and $$\angle GCB = \frac{1}{2}\angle C$$

To prove: EFGH is a cyclic quadrilateral.

$$\angle FEH = \angle AED$$

$$= 180° -\left(\frac{1}{2}\angle A + \frac{1}{2}\angle D\right) \;...(i)$$

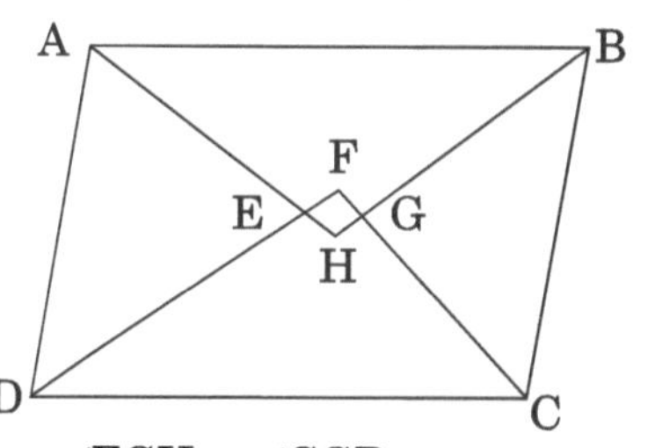

Similarly, $\angle FGH = \angle CGB$

$$= 180° -\left(\frac{1}{2}\angle C + \frac{1}{2}\angle B\right)...(ii)$$

On adding, (i) and (ii), we get

$\angle FEH + \angle FGH = 180°$

$\therefore$ EFGH is a cyclic quadrilateral.

Hence proved.

5. ABCD is a cyclic quadrilateral whose diagonals intersect at a point E. If $\angle DBC = 70°$ and $\angle BAC = 30°$, then find $\angle BCD$. Further, if AB = BC, find $\angle ECD$.

[Board Term II, 2012, Set-02][NCERT]

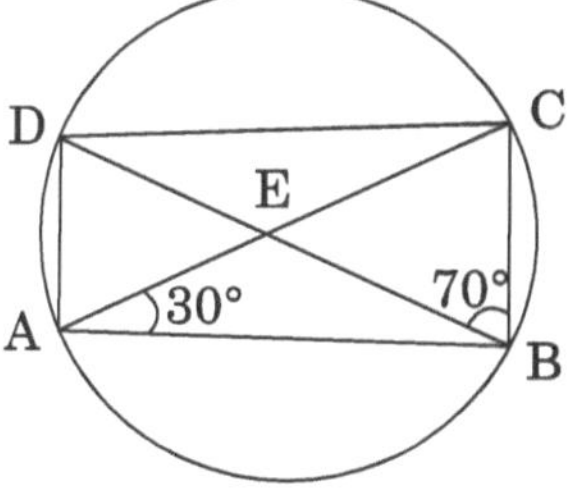

Sol. We know that, angles in the same segment are equal.

$\therefore$ $\angle BDC = \angle BAC$

$\Rightarrow$ $\angle BDC = 30°$

In △BCD, we have

$$\angle BDC + \angle DBC + \angle BCD = 180°$$
[angle sum property of triangle]
$$\Rightarrow 30° + 70° + \angle BCD = 180°$$
[∵ ∠DBC = 70° and ∠BDC = 30°]
$$\Rightarrow \angle BCD = 180° - 30° - 70° = 80°$$

If AB = BC, then
$$\angle BCA = \angle BAC = 30°$$
[since, angles opposite to equal sides in a triangle are equal]

Now,
$$\angle ECD = \angle BCD - \angle BCA$$
$$= 80° - 30° = 50°$$
[∵ ∠BCD = 80° and ∠BCA = 30°]

Hence, $\angle BCD = 80°$ and $\angle ECD = 50°$

6. In the given figure, PQ is the diameter of the circle. If ∠PQR = 65°, ∠QPT = 60°, then find the measure of :

(i) ∠QRP, (ii) ∠PRS, (iii) ∠PSR, (iv) ∠PQT.

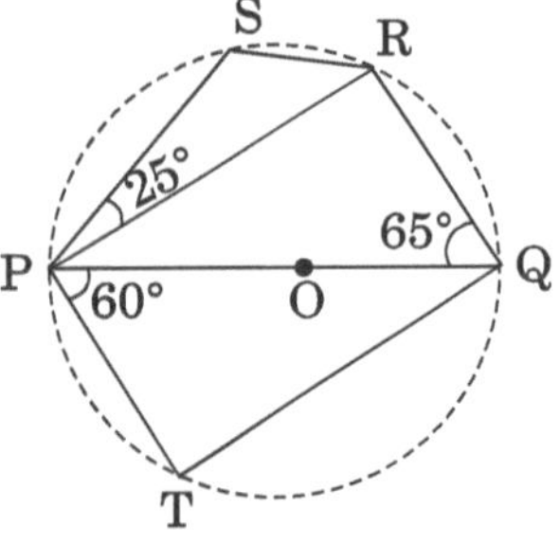

Sol. According to the given figure,

(i) $\angle QRP = 90°$ (angle in the semi-circle)

(ii) In △PRQ,
$$65° + 90° + \angle RPQ = 180°$$
$$\Rightarrow 155° + \angle RPQ = 180°$$
$$\therefore \angle QPR = 25°$$ (angle sum property)
$$\angle QPS = \angle QPR + \angle RPS = 50°$$
and
$$\angle QRS = 180° - 50° = 130°$$
(PQRS is a cyclic quad.)

Hence, $\angle PRS = 130° - \angle QRP$
$$= 130° - 90° = 40°$$

(iii) $\angle PSR + \angle PQR = 180°$
[∵ PQRS is a cyclic quadrilateral]
$$\Rightarrow \angle PSR + 65° = 180°$$
$$\therefore \angle PSR = 180° - 65°$$
$$= 115°$$

(iv) $\angle PTQ = 90°$ [Angle in semi-circle]
$$\therefore \angle PQT = 90° - 60° = 30°$$

7. In the given figure, B and E are points on line segments AC and DF respectively. prove that AD ∥ CF.

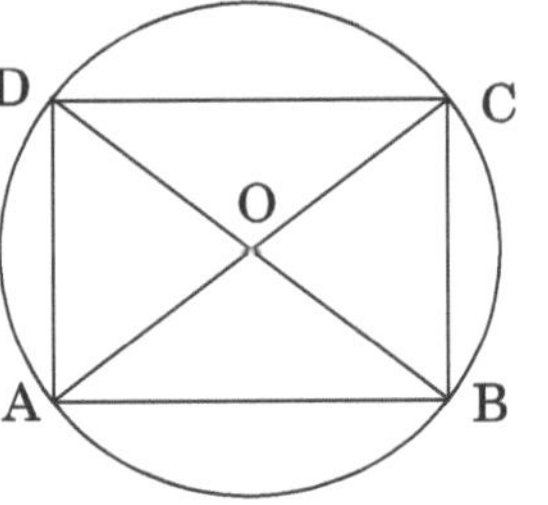

Sol. Given: B and E are the points on line segments AC and DF respectively.

To prove: AD ∥ CF

Construction: Join B and E.

Proof : ADEB is a cyclic quadrilateral
$$\therefore \angle ADE = \angle EBC,$$
(exterior angle of a cyclic quad. = interior opp. angle)   ...(i)

Similarly FEBC is a cyclic quadrilateral,
$$\therefore \angle EBC + \angle CFE = 180°$$ ...(ii)
(opp. angles are supp.)

From (i) and (ii)
$$\angle ADE + \angle CFE = 180°$$

But these are interior angles for the lines AD and CF.

Interior angles are supplementary.
$$\therefore AD \parallel CF.$$ Hence proved.

8. AC and BD are chords of a circle which bisect each other. Prove that:

(i) AC and BD are diameters

(ii) ABCD is a rectangle.

Sol. Given, AC and BD bisect each other.

Therefore, AC and BD are diagonals of the parallelogram.

Therefore, ABCD is a parallelogram.
$$\therefore \angle A = \angle C \text{ and } \angle B = \angle D$$
[opposite angles of parallelogram are equal]

But, ABCD is a cyclic quadrilateral
$$\therefore \angle A + \angle C = 180° \text{ and } \angle B + \angle D = 180°$$
[sum of opposite angles of a cyclic quadrilateral]

$\Rightarrow \qquad\qquad 2\angle A = 180° \text{ and } 2\angle B = 180°$

$\Rightarrow \qquad\qquad \angle A = 90° \text{ and } \angle B = 90°$

$\therefore \qquad\qquad \angle A = \angle B = \angle C = \angle D = 90°$

Hence, ABCD is a rectangle and diagonals AC and BD are diameters.

9. PQRS is a trapezium with PQ || SR and PS = QR. Prove that the trapezium is cyclic.

[Board Term II, 2012, Set-15]

Sol. Given: PQRS is a trapezium with PQ || RS and PS = QR

To prove: Trapezium PQRS is cyclic.

Construction: Draw RM || SP meeting PQ in M.

Proof: PQ || SR (Given)

PS || MR (Construction)

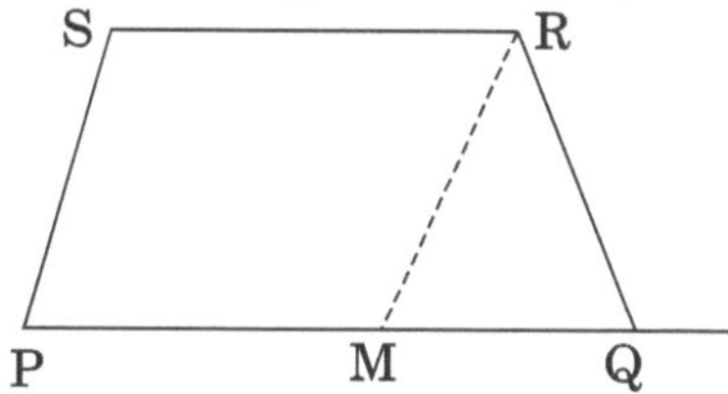

Thus, PMRS is a parallelogram

$\therefore \qquad\qquad \angle S = \angle PMR$

In $\triangle$RMQ, RM = RQ (as RM = SP, opposite sides of a parallelogram and PS = QR)

$\therefore \qquad\qquad \angle RMQ = \angle Q$

But $\qquad\qquad \angle RMQ = 180° - \angle PMR$ (linear pair)

$= 180° - \angle S.$ (proved)

$\therefore \qquad\qquad \angle Q = 180° - \angle S$

Hence $\quad \angle Q + \angle S = 180°$

Since one pair of opposite angles is supplementary, Therefore, PQRS is cyclic quadrilateral.

Hence proved.

10. A chord of a circle is equal to the radius of the circle. Find the angle subtended by the chord at a point on the minor arc and also at a point on the major arc. [Board Term II, 2012, Set-05]

Sol. According to the question,

$$OA = AB = OB$$

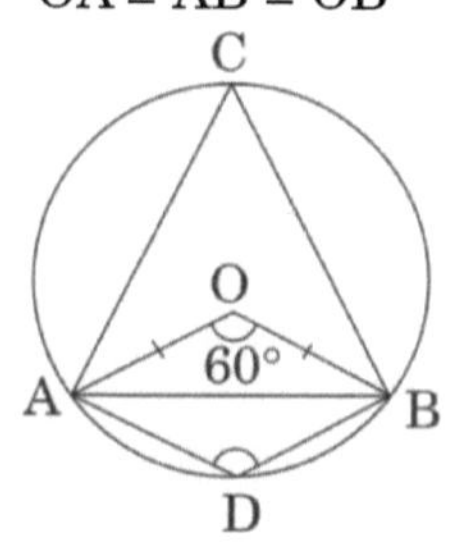

Therefore, $\triangle$OAB is an equilateral triangle

$\therefore \qquad\qquad \angle AOB = 60°$

Now, $\qquad \angle ACB = \dfrac{1}{2}\angle AOB$

(angle subtended by an arc at the centre is twice the angle at the remaining circle)

$\Rightarrow \qquad\qquad \angle ACB = \dfrac{1}{2}\times 60°$

$\therefore \qquad\qquad \angle ACB = 30°$

In $\square$ABCD,

$\angle ACB + \angle ADB = 180°$ (opposite angles of cyclic quadrilateral are supplementary)

Hence, $\qquad \angle ADB = 180° - \angle ACB$

$= 180° - 30° = 150°.$

11. In the given figure, find the values of a, b, c and d. Given that $\angle BCD = 43°$ and $\angle BAE = 62°$.

[Board Term II, 2012, Set-23]

Sol. According to the question,

In $\triangle$ACE, $43° + 62° + d = 180°$

[Angle sum property]

$\therefore \qquad\qquad d = 180° - (43° + 62°)$

$= 180° - 105° = 75°$

Now, $\qquad a + d = 180°$

(Opposite angles of cyclic quadrilateral are supplementary)

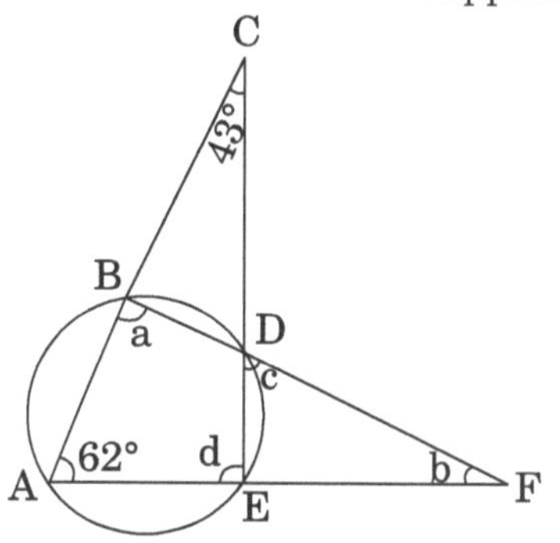

$\Rightarrow \qquad\qquad a + 75° = 180°$

$\therefore \qquad\qquad a = 180° - 75° = 105°$

Again, In $\triangle$ABF,

$62° + 105° + b = 180°$ [Angle sum property]

$\therefore \qquad\qquad b = 180° - (62° + 105°)$

$= 180° - 167° = 13°$

Hence, $\qquad \angle DEF = 180° - 75° = 105°$

[Linear pair]

In $\triangle$DEF, $105° + 13° + c = 180°$

[Angle sum property]

$\Rightarrow \qquad\qquad 118° + c = 180°$

$\therefore \qquad\qquad c = 180° - 118° = 62°$

Hence, $\qquad a = 105°, b = 13°, c = 62°$ and

$d = 75°.$

12. In figure, equal chords AB and CD intersect each other at Q at right angle. P and R are the mid-points of AB and CD respectively. Show that OPQR is a square.

[Board Term II, 2012, Set-26, 56]

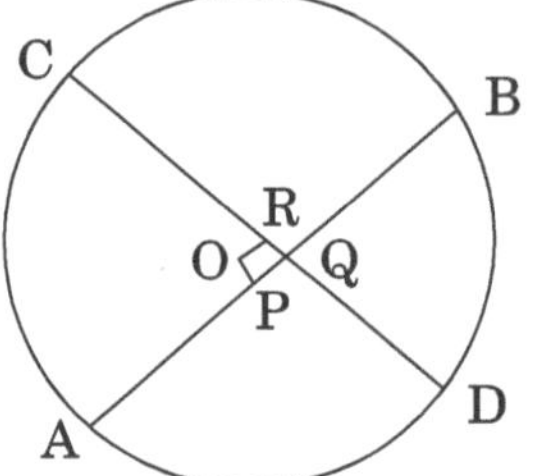

Sol. Given: AB and CD are equal chords intersecting at 90°.

To prove: OPQR is a square.

Construction: Join OQ

Proof: Since P and R are the mid-points of AB and CD respectively

$\therefore$ $\angle OPB = \angle ORD = 90°$

or, $\angle OPQ = \angle ORQ = 90°$

Since equal chords on a circle are equidistant from the centre.

$\therefore$ $OP = OR$

Thus in ΔOPQ and ΔORQ, we have

          $OP = OR$

          $\angle OPQ = \angle ORQ$

and $OQ = OQ$

By SAS congruence rule, we get

$\therefore$ $\Delta OPQ \cong \Delta ORQ$

Thus in quadrilateral OPQR,

We have $OP = OR$ and $PQ = RQ$

and $\angle OPQ = \angle ORQ = 90°$

Hence, OPQR is a square.

13. In the given figure, ABDC is a cyclic quadrilateral in which AC ∥ BD.

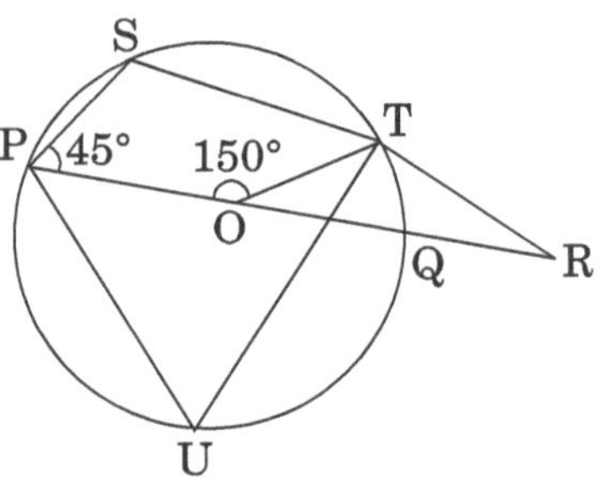

(i) If $\angle BAD = 52°$, $\angle BCA = 35°$. Find $\angle ACX$.

(ii) Prove that, $\angle CBD = \angle ADB$. Also prove that, $DY = BY$.

(iii) Prove that, ΔXBD is an isosceles triangle

(iv) Prove that, $XA = XC$

[Board Term II, 2014]

Sol. (i) $\angle BCD = \angle BAD = 52°$

          (angles in the same segment)

$\angle BCD + \angle BCA + \angle ACX = 180°$

          (angle on the straight line)

$\Rightarrow 52° + 35° + \angle ACX = 180°$

$\therefore$ $\angle ACX = 180° - 87 = 93°$

Hence, $\angle ACX = 93°$

(ii) $\angle CBD = \angle DAC$

          (angles in the same segment)...(i)

          $\angle DAC = \angle ADB$

          (alternate angle)...(ii)

From (i) and (ii),

          $\angle CBD = \angle ADB$.   ...(iii)

In ΔYBD,

$\therefore$ $\angle YBD = \angle YDB$ [from (iii)]

          $DY = BY$

          (sides opposite to equal in a Δ are equal)

(iii) $\angle ABD = \angle ACX$ ...(iv)

          (exterior angle of a cyclic quadrilateral is equal to interior opp. angles)

          $\angle BDC = \angle ACX$ ...(v)

          (corresponding angles)

From (iv) and (v),

          $ABD = BDC$ ...(vi)

$\therefore$ $XB = XD$ [sides opposite to equal angles are equal]

Hence, ΔXBD is an isosceles triangle

(iv) $\angle BDC = \angle ACX$

          [corresponding angles]

          $\angle ABD = \angle XAC$

          [corresponding angles]

$\therefore$ $\angle ACX = \angle XAC$ [from (vi)]

Hence, $XA = XC$

[since, sides opposite to equal angles are equal]

14. In the given figure $\angle SPQ = 45°$, $\angle POT = 150°$ and O is the centre of circle. Find the measures of $\angle RQT$, $\angle RTQ$ and $\angle PUT$.

[Board Term II, 2015]

Sol. According to the given figure,

$$\angle POT + \text{reflex } \angle POT = 360°$$
$$\Rightarrow 150° + \text{reflex } \angle POT = 360°$$
$$\Rightarrow \quad \text{reflex } \angle POT = 210°$$
$$\Rightarrow \quad \text{reflex } \angle POT = 2\angle PST$$
$$\Rightarrow \quad\quad 210° = 2\angle PST$$
$$\therefore \quad\quad \angle PST = \frac{210°}{2} = 105°$$

In □ PQTS

$$\angle PQT + \angle PST = 180°$$

(opposite angles of cyclic quadrilateral are supplementary)

$$\therefore \quad \angle PQT = 180° - 105° = 75°$$

Now, $\angle RQT + \angle PQT = 180°$ (linear pair)

$$\therefore \quad \angle RQT = 180° - 75° = 105°$$

and $\quad \angle RTQ = \angle SPQ = 45°$

(Exterior angle of a cyclic quadrilateral is equal to interior opposite angle)

Now, $\quad \angle PUT = \dfrac{1}{2}\angle POT$

(angle subtended by an arc at the centre is twice the angle at the remaining circle)

$$= \frac{1}{2} \times 150°$$
$$= 75°$$

15. D and E are points on equal sides AB and AC of isosceles $\triangle ABC$ such that AD = AE. Prove that the points B, C, E and D are concyclic.

Sol. Given: D and E are points on equal sides AB and AC of isosceles $\triangle ABC$ and **AB = AC**

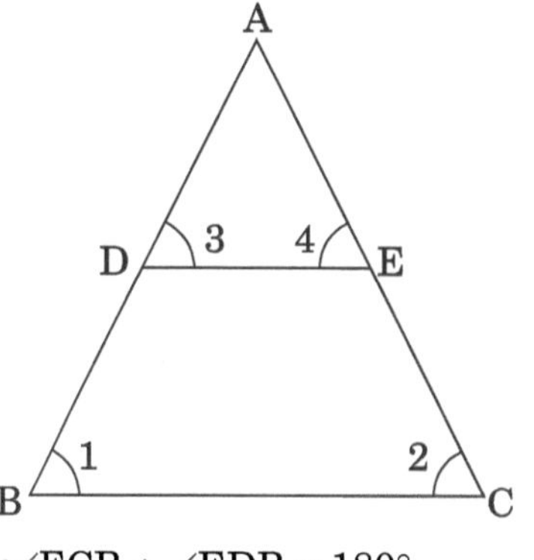

To prove: $\angle ECB + \angle EDB = 180°$

Proof: AB = AC or, $\angle 1 = \angle 2$

         AD = AE or, $\angle 3 = \angle 4$ ...(i)

In $\triangle ABC$,

$$\angle A + \angle 1 + \angle 2 = 180° = \angle A + \angle 3 + \angle 4 \text{ [DE } \| \text{BC]}$$

[Angle sum property]

$$\Rightarrow \quad\quad 2\angle 1 = 2\angle 3 \quad\quad ....\text{(ii)}$$

By eqⁿ. (i) and (ii)

$$\therefore \quad\quad \angle 1 = \angle 3 = \angle 2 = \angle 4$$

or, $\quad\quad$ DE $\|$ BC

$$\therefore \quad \angle 1 + \angle BDE = 180°$$

(Corresponding angle)

($\angle BDE = \angle CED$, as $\angle 3 = \angle 4$)

Similarly, $\angle 1 + \angle CED = 180°$

Hence, Points B, C, E and D are concyclic.

CHAPTER 11

Geometric Constructions

- Construction of bisectors of line segments and angles of measure 60°, 90°, 45° etc., equilateral triangles.
- Construction of a triangle given its base, sum/difference of the other two sides and one base angle.
- Construction of a triangle of given perimeter and base angles.

A flow chart on the basic concepts of constructions :

Construction

Geometrical construction is the process of drawing a geometrical figure mainly using only two instruments a ruler and a pair of compasses.

Triangles

- If base, angles and difference of two sides.
(i) Draw AB = base and make given angles.
(ii) Cut AC = difference of sides, join BC
(iii) Draw perpendicular bisector BC and let it intersect AX. Name it as D.

(iv) Join AD, ABD is the required triangle.

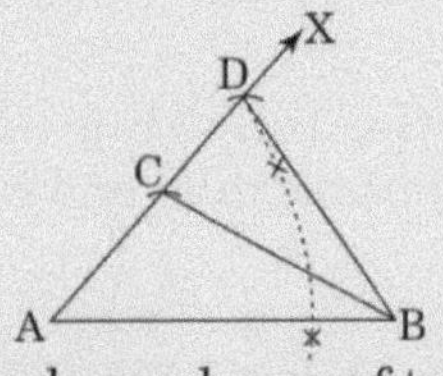

- If base, angles and sum of two sides.
(i) Draw AB = base and make given angle.
(ii) Cut AC = equal to sum of sides join BC
(iii) Draw perpendicular bisector of BC and let it intersect AD.
Name it as D.
(iv) Join AD, ABD is the required triangle.

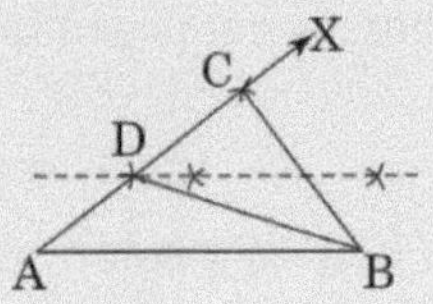

Perpendicular Bisector

(i) With A and B as and radius
> ½ AB, draw intersecting arc on both sides.
(ii) Join PQ
(iii) PQ intersect AB at a point M to from perpendicular bisector

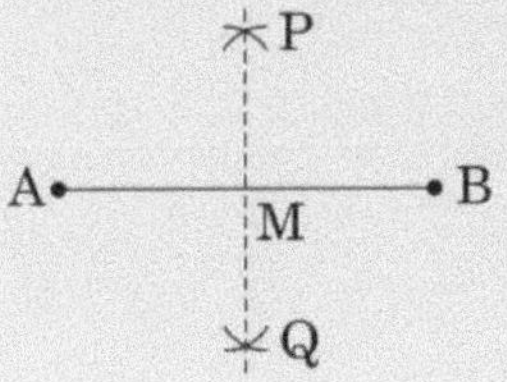

Angle Bisector

(i) Take B as centre, draw arcs intersecting AB and BC (of any radius)
(ii) D and E as centres and radius > DE, draw two arcs and join B to it.
(iii) BF is the required angle bisector.

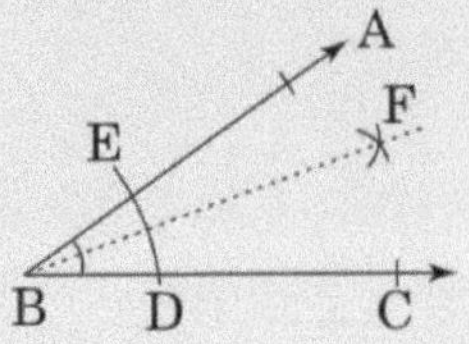

[Topic 1] Constructions of Bisectors of Line Segment and Angles

Points to be Remembered

I. Construction of an angle of 60°:

Step 1. Draw any line OP.

Step 2. With O as center and any suitable radius, draw an arc to meet OP at R.

Step 3. With R as center and same radius (as in step 2), draw an arc to meet the previous arc at S.

Step 4. Join OS and produce it to Q, then at $\angle POQ = 60°$.

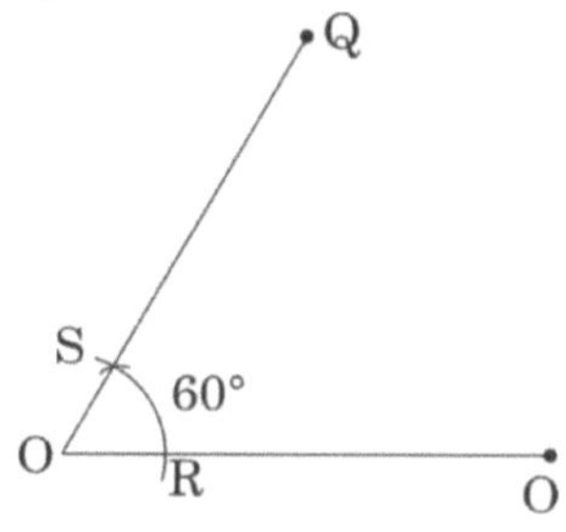

II. Construction of angle bisector:

Step 1. With O as centre and any radius, draw an arc to meet OP at R and OQ at S.

Step 2. With R as centre and any suitable radius (not necessarily) equal to radius of step 1 (but is greater than $\dfrac{1}{2}$ RS), draw an arc. Also, with S as centre and same radius draw another arc to meet the previous arc at T.

Step 3. Join OT and produce it, then OT is the required bisector of $\angle POQ$. Join ST and RT.

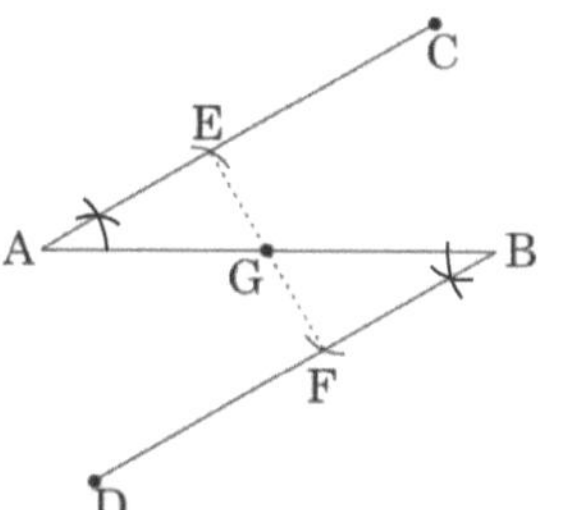

III. Construction of bisector of a line segment:

Step 1. At point A, construct any suitable angle BAC.

Step 2. At point B, construct $\angle ABD = \angle BAC$ on the other side of the line AB.

Step 3. With A as centre and any suitable radius, draw an arc to meet AC at E.

Step 4. With B as centre, draw an arc BF which is equal to AE on line BD.

Step 5. Join EF to meet AB at G, then EG is a bisector of the line segment AB and G is the mid-point of AB.

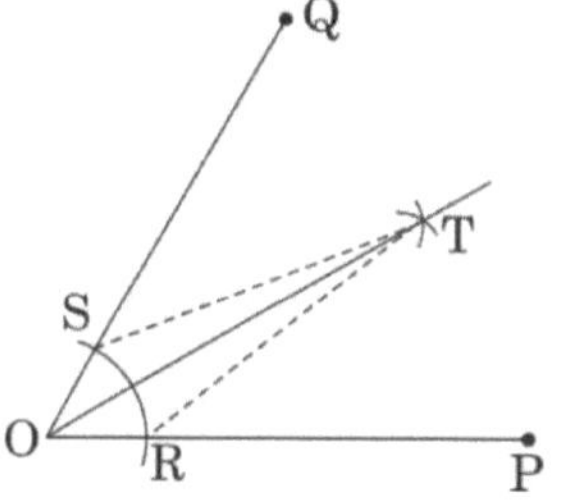

PREVIOUS YEARS'
EXAMINATION QUESTIONS
TOPIC 1

Multiple Choice Questions
(1 Mark Each)

1. With the help of a ruler and compasses, which of the following is not possible to construct?
   (a) 120°
   (b) 135°
   (c) 140°
   (d) None of the above

Sol. (c) With the help of a ruler and compasses, the angle of 140°, is not possible to construct.

2. Which of the following angles cannot be constructed using ruler and compass only?
   (a) $22\dfrac{1}{2}°$
   (b) 15°
   (c) $52\dfrac{1}{2}°$
   (d) $32\dfrac{1}{2}°$

Sol. (d) Angle $32\dfrac{1}{2}°$ cannot be constructed using ruler and compass only.

3. With the help of a ruler and compasses, which of the following is not possible to construct?
   (a) 70°
   (b) 60°
   (c) 135°
   (d) None of the above

Sol. (a) With the help of a ruler and compasses, the angle of 70°, is not possible to construct.

4. With the help of a ruler and a compass it is not possible to construct an angle of:

   (a) 37.5°   (b) 40°

   (c) 22.5°   (d) 67.5°

[NCERT Exemp.]

Sol. (b) With the help of ruler and compasses, the angle of 40°, is not possible to construct.

5. Which of the following angles can be constructed using ruler and compass only?

   (a) 65°   (b) 72°

   (c) 80°   (d) 67.5°

Sol. (d) The angle of 67.5° can be constructed using ruler and compass only.

6. Which of the following angle can be constructed with the help of a ruler and a pair of compasses?

   (a) 35°   (b) 40°

   (c) 37.5°   (d) 47.5°

Sol. (c) The angle of 37.5° can be constructed with the help of a ruler and a pair of compasses.

Very Short Answer Type Questions
(1 Mark Each)

1. Can an angle of 67.5° be constructed?

[NCERT Exemplar]

Sol. Because $67.5° = \dfrac{135°}{2} = \dfrac{1}{2}(90° + 45°)$

   Hence, an angle of 67.5° can be constructed.

2. Construct an obtuse angle and draw bisector of its supplement.

[Board Term II, 2017, Set-Z6K408K]

Sol. An obtuse angle $\angle AOB$ is constructed and its supplement angle is $\angle BOC$.

   Therefore, angle bisectors are

   $$\angle BOP = \angle COP$$

   [$\because$ OP is the angle bisector]

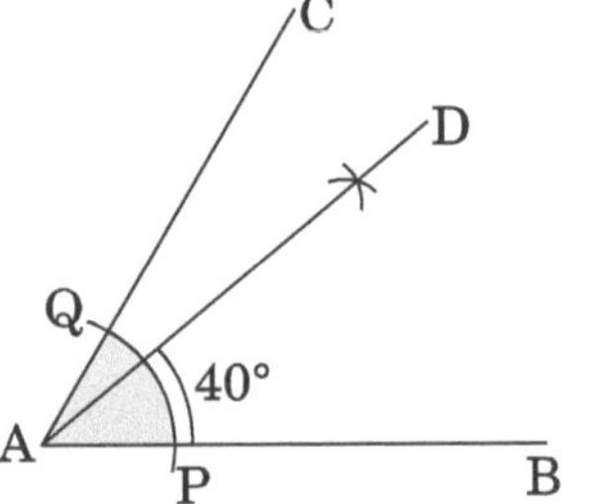

3. Construct an acute angle and draw its bisector.

[Board Term II 2017, Set-UAH4DQ7]

Sol. Here we are taking an acute angle of 80°

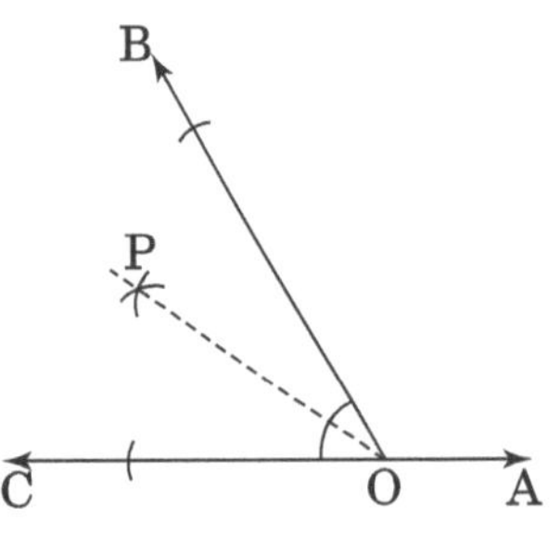

   $\therefore$ AD is bisector of acute angle

   Hence, angle bisectors are

   $$\angle BAD = \angle CAD = 40°$$

4. If a 60° angle is bisected twice, what will be measure of each angle that is constructed?

Sol. Since bisector of an angle divides it in two equal parts, so, which it is bisected twice, measure of each angle is 15°.

5. Is it possible to construct an angle of $32\dfrac{1}{2}°$ using ruler and compass only?

Sol. No, it is not possible to construct an angle of $32\dfrac{1}{2}°$ using ruler and compass only because $32.5° = \dfrac{1}{2} \times 65°$ and 65° cannot be constructed with the help of a ruler and compass. We can construct the angles 60°, 90°, 75°, 37.5°, 45°, 22.5°, 30°, 15°, etc. and compass generate only the bisector of an angle.

6. In the given figure, PR is the perpendicular bisector of a line segment AB = 16 cm. Is PA = PB true?

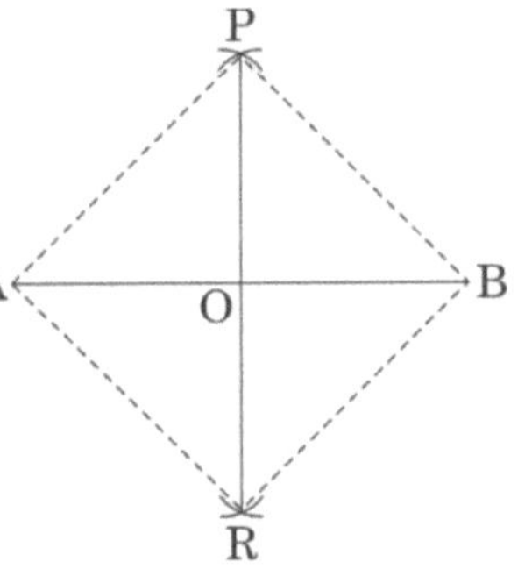

Sol. $\because$ PR is the perpendicular bisector of line AB = 16 cm

   $\therefore$ $\qquad AO = OB$

   $\qquad\qquad = \dfrac{1}{2}\,AB = 8$ cm.   ...(i)

   and $\angle POA = \angle POB = 90°$ ...(ii)

Now, In $\triangle POA$ and $\triangle POB$

$$AO = BO \qquad \text{[From equation (i)]}$$
$$\angle POA = \angle POB \text{ [From equation (ii)]}$$
and $\qquad PO = PO \qquad$ [Common]

By SAS congruence rule, we get

$$\triangle POA \cong \triangle POB$$
$\therefore \qquad PA = PB \qquad$ [by c.p.c.t.]

Hence, PA = PB is true.

Short Answer Type Questions-I

(2 Marks Each)

1. Construct an equilateral triangle, given its side and justify the construction.

   [NCERT] [Board Term-II, Set-LFOMCQ2, 2016]

Sol. Steps of construction :

Step (i) Fist we draw a line AX with initial point A.

Step (ii) Taking A as centre and same radius (say 4 cm), draw and arc of a circle, which intersects AX at point B.

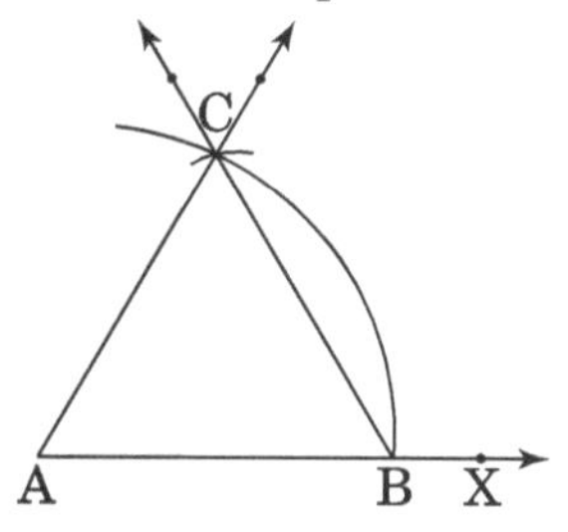

Step (iii) Taking B as centre and with the same radius as before, draw an arc intersecting the previously drawn arc, say at a point C.

Step (iv) Join AC and BC.

Thus, $\triangle ABC$ is an equilateral triangle.

Justification

In $\triangle ABC$,

$$AB = BC \qquad \text{[radii of same circle]}$$
$$AB = AC \qquad \text{[radii of same circle]}$$
$\therefore \qquad AB = BC = CA$

Therefore, $\triangle ABC$ is an equilateral triangle.

Hence, the construction is justified.

2. Construct an angle of 15°.

   [NCERT] [Board Term II, KVS 2014]

Sol. Steps of construction :

Step (i) Draw a line OL using a ruler.

Step (ii) Taking O as centre, with any radius draw an arc cutting the ray at point M using compass.

Step (iii) Taking M as centre, draw arc to meet at previous arc at P.

Step (iv) With P and M as centres and equal radius draw arcs intersecting at R. Join OR and extend to Q.

Step (v) Now, we get $\angle LOQ = 30°$

Step (vi) With R and M as centre, draw arcs with same radius or more than half of RM, meeting at point S.

Step (vii) Join OS, which makes an angle, $\angle LOS = 15°$.

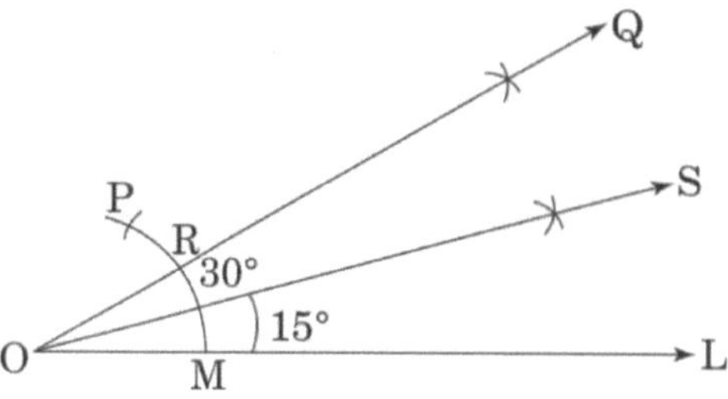

3. Construct $\angle POY = 30°$, using compass and ruler.

   [Board Term-II, Set IA21924, 2016] [NCERT]

Sol. Steps of construction :

Step (i) Draw any line OP with initial point O.

Step (ii) With O as centre and any suitable radius, draw an arc to meet OP at R.

Step (iii) With R as center and same radius (as in step 2), draw an arc to meet the previous arc at S.

Step (iv) Join OS and produce it to Q then we get $\angle POQ = 60°$

Step (v) With R as centre and any suitable radius (not necessarily) equal to radius of step 1 (but $> \dfrac{1}{2}$ RS), draw an arc. Also, with S as centre and same radius draw another arc to meet the previous arc at Y.

Step (vi) Join OY, which makes an angle of 30° i.e., $\angle POY = 30°$.

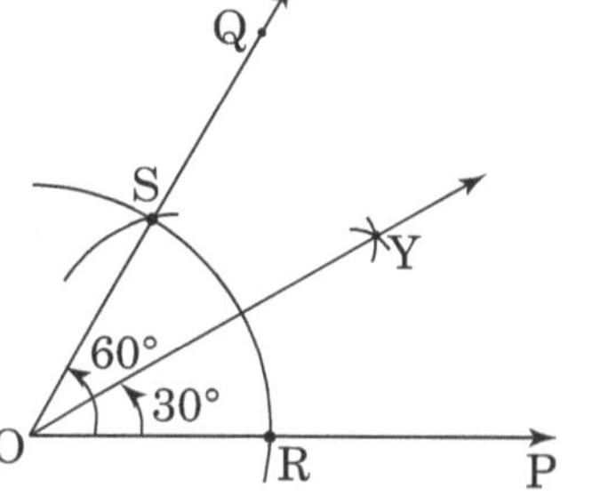

4. Construct an equilateral triangle PQR, when PQ = 5.5 cm.   [Board Term II, 2013]

Sol. Steps of construction :

Step   (i) Draw any line segment PQ = 5.5 cm

Step   (ii) With P as centre and radius 5.5 cm draw an arc.

Step (iii) Again with Q as cetnre and radius 5.5 cm draw an arc to cut the previous arc at R.

Step (iv) Join PR and QR, then PQR is the required triangle.

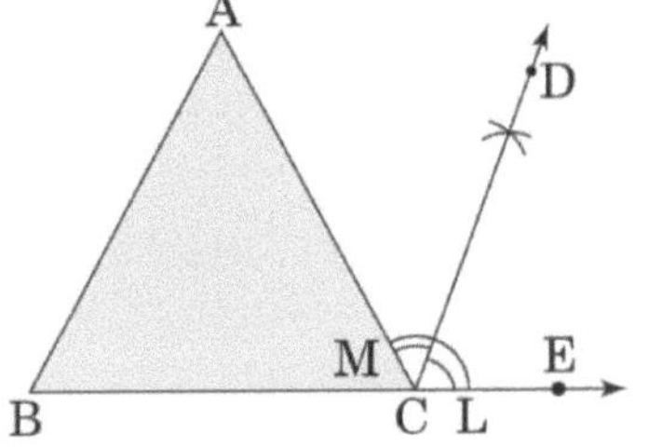

Hence, the above constructed triangle is the required equilateral triangle.

5. Draw $\angle DEF = 72°$. Construct $\frac{3}{4}$ $\angle DEF$ using a compass.

[Board Term II, 2014]

Sol. We have to construct

$$\frac{3}{4} \times 72° = 54°$$

Steps of construction :

Step   (i) Draw $\angle DEF = 72°$ on a line EF by using protractor.

Step   (ii) Now, bisect the $\angle DEF$ by using compass.

Step (iii) Let the bisected angle be $\angle DEK$.

Step (iv) Again bisect $\angle DEK$ by using compass.

Step   (v) Now, $\angle GEF = \frac{3}{4} \angle DEF$.

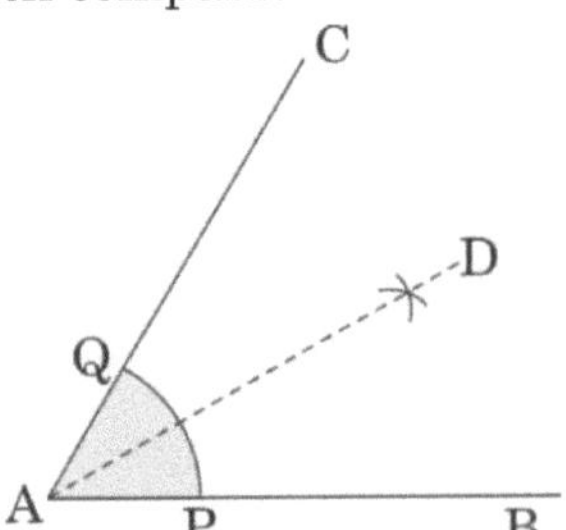

Thus, required angle $\angle GEF = 36° + 18° = 54°$

6. Draw any exterior angle of a triangle using compass, bisect it.   [Board Term II, 2014]

Sol. Steps of construction:

Step   (i) Construct a triangle ABC.

Step   (ii) Mark an exterior angle outside the triangle ABC, and name the point as E.

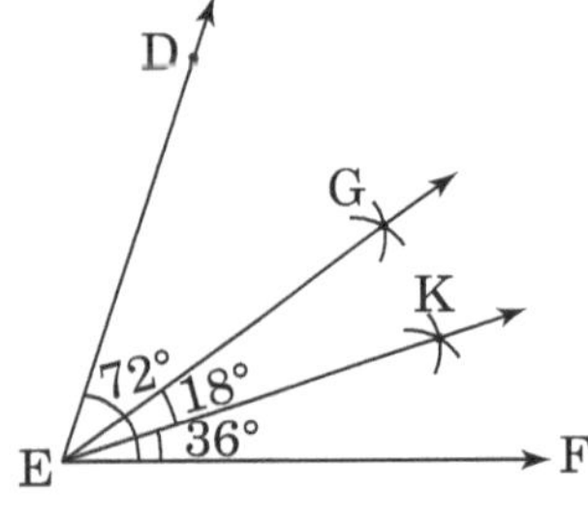

Step (iii) Now, ACE is the exterior angle.

Step (iv) Draw an arc with center C of same radius.

Step   (v) This arc cut the line AC at M and line CE at L.

Step (vi) With centre L draw an arc and again with centre M draw an arc which intersect at point D.

Step (vii) Join CD and $\angle DCE$ is the bisector of $\angle ACE$.

7. Using protractor, draw an angle of 52°. Using compass, divide this angle into two equal parts.

[Board Term II, 2012, Set-UAH4DQ7]

Sol. Draw an angle of 52° i.e., $\angle CAB$. Now, bisect the $\angle CAB$ with compass.

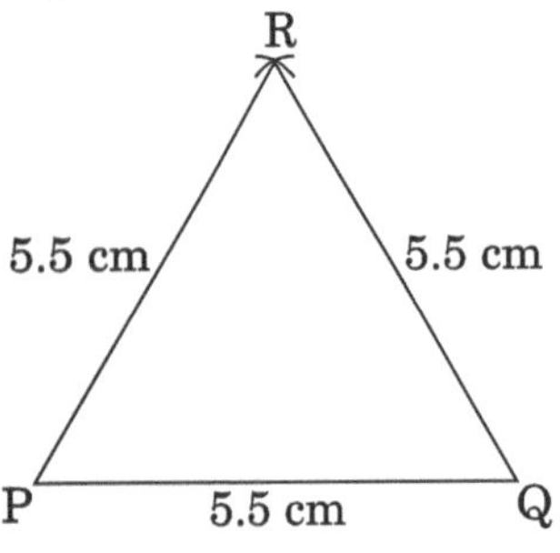

Hence, AD is the bisector of acute angle

8. Construct an angle of $22\frac{1}{2}°$ at the initial point of a given ray.

Sol. **Given** A ray AB (say) with initial point A.

Required To construct an angle of $22\frac{1}{2}°$.

Steps of construction :

Step   (i) Draw any ray AB with initial point A.

Step (ii) Construct an $\angle BAS = 90°$

Step (iii) Bisect $\angle BAS$ and let AT be the bisector of $\angle BAS$, then $\angle BAT = 45°$

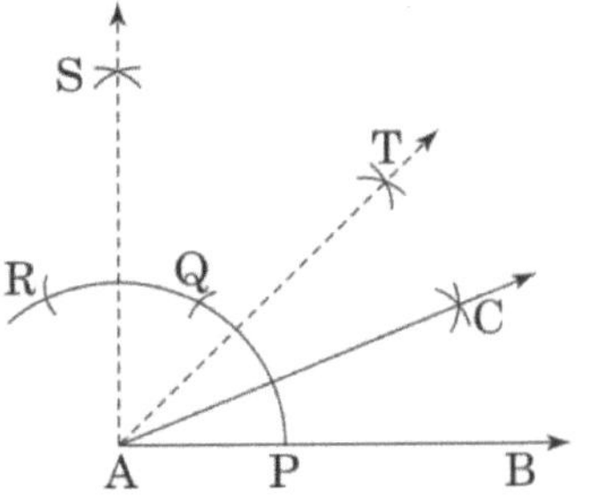

Step (iv) Once again bisect angle BAT and let AC be the bisector of $\angle$BAT.

Hence, $\angle$BAC is the bisector of $\angle$BAT (= 45°) or

$\angle$BAC = $22\dfrac{1}{2}°$.

Short Answer Type Questions-II

(3 Marks Each)

1. Construct $\triangle$ABC in which BC = 6.8 cm, $\angle$B = 45° and $\angle$C = 45°. Construct angle bisector of $\angle$B and $\angle$C and let them intersect at point O. Measure $\angle$BOC. [NCERT]

Sol. Given: In $\triangle$ABC, BC = 6.8 cm, $\angle$B = 45° and $\angle$C = 45°.

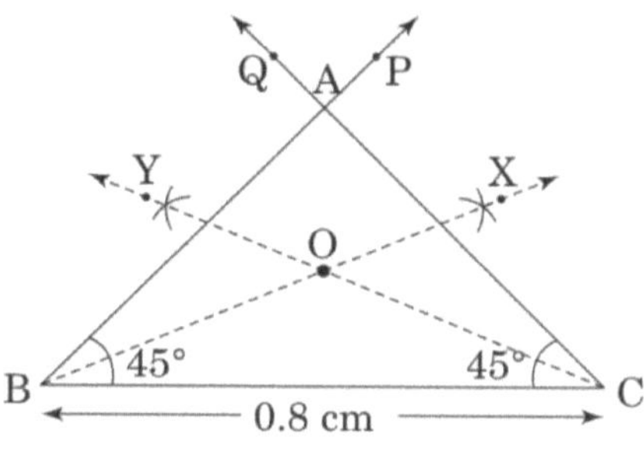

Steps of construction :

Step (i) Draw a line segment BC = 6.8 cm.

Step (ii) Draw $\angle$PBC = 45° at point B and draw $\angle$QCB = 45° at point C.

Step (iii) Mark the point of intersection of ray BP and ray CQ at A.

Step (iv) Now, draw the angle bisector of $\angle$ABC and $\angle$ACB, let them to intersect each other at point O. On measuring the $\angle$BOC, we get the value 135°.

2. Construct an angle of 75° at the initial point of a given ray and justify the construction. [NCERT]

Sol. Steps of construction :

Step (i) Draw a line segment AB with initial point B.

Step (ii) At B, draw an arc of any radius and let it intersect BA is S.

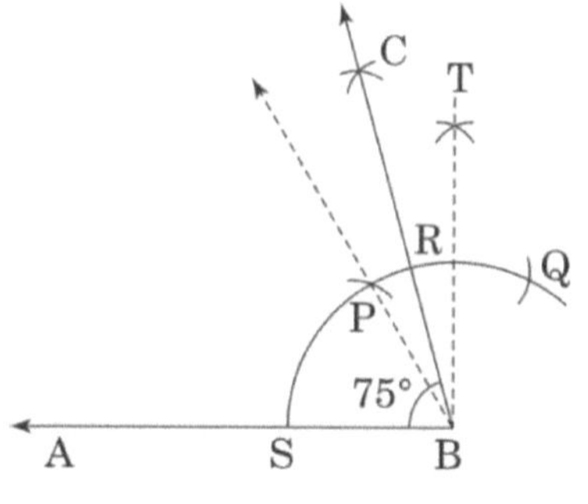

Step (iii) With S as centre and same radius as in step (ii), draw arc P and then with same radius from P draw arc Q.

Step (iv) With P and Q as centres, draw two arcs of same radius as in step (iii). Let they intersect each other in T. Join BT and let it intersect previous arc at R.

Step (v) With centres P and R, draw two arcs of same radii and let they intersect each other in C.

Step (vi) Join BC and produce.

Thus, $\angle$ABC is the required angle of 75°.

Justification

We have, $\angle$ABP = 60° and $\angle$PBQ = 60°

Now, $\angle$PBT = $\dfrac{1}{2} \times \angle$PBQ = $\dfrac{1}{2} \times 60° = 30°$.

Since, BC is the bisector of $\angle$PBT

$$\angle PBC = \dfrac{1}{2} \times 30° = 15°$$

Now, $\qquad \angle$ABC = $\angle$ABP + $\angle$PBC

$\Rightarrow \qquad \angle$ABC = 60° + 15° = 75°

Hence, it will justify the construction.

3. Draw a line segment SR of length 10 cm. Divide it into 4 equal parts using compasses. [Board Term II, 2014]

Sol. Steps of construction :

Step (i) Draw a line of length SR = 10 cm.

Step (ii) Then divided it into half and taken arc of more than half length of the line and place point at S and make two arcs on both sides of the line. Now, repeat the same for point R.

Step (iii) This gives, AE = EB.

Step (iv) Now, divide SE and ER into two equal parts to get for equal parts of the line, SR = 10 cm.

Step (v) By repeating step (ii) for line segment SE and ER, we get, FG and HI.

Hence, the length of four sections,

$$\textbf{SJ = JE = EK = KR = 2.5 cm}$$

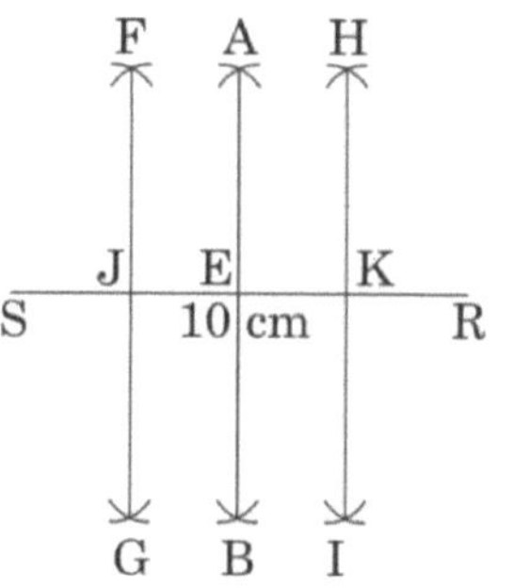

4. Draw lines PQ and RS intersecting at point O. Measure a pair of vertically opposite angles. Bisect them. Are the bisecting rays forming a straight line?

[Board Term II, Set-RQTZFBW, 2016]

Sol. Steps of construction :

Step (i) Draw a line a segment PQ of any size (let be 8 cm)

Step (ii) Draw another line segment RS intersecting PQ at point O (length of RS = 10 cm)

Step (iii) Measure pair of vertically opposite angles (Both are equal)

Step (iv) Bisect both the angles (OX is bisector of $\angle$QOS and OY is bisector of $\angle$POR).

Step (v) From the construction it is clear that the bisecting rays from a straight line.

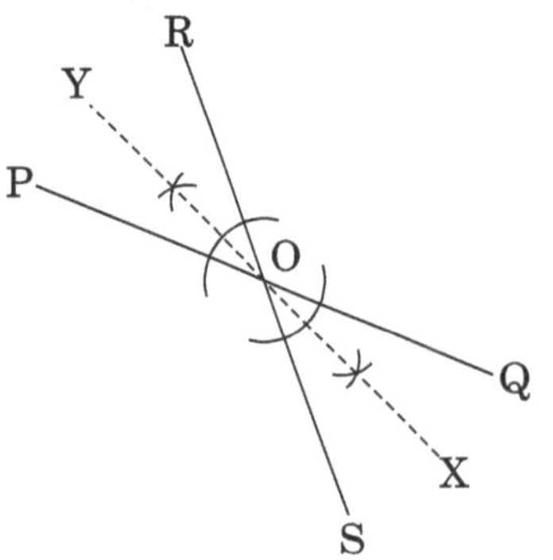

5. Construct angle of $52\frac{1}{2}^{\circ}$, using compasses and ruler.

[Board Term II, Set-LF0MCQ2, 2016]

Sol. Steps of construction :

Step0 (i) Draw a line with end points A and B using ruler.

Step (ii) With A as centre and any radius, draw an arc cutting the ray at point C Using compass.

Step (iii) With C as centre and same radius draw an arc cutting the arc drawn at D.

Step (iv) With D as centre and the same radius, draw an arc intersecting the previously drawn arc at E.

Step (v) Now, take any radius and draw two arcs with D and E as centres. Let these two arcs intersect at a point F.

Step (vi) Join AF, $\angle$FAB obtained is the angle of measure of 90°.

Step (vii) The line AF intersect the arc at the point named as G.

Step(viii) With G and E as center, draw an arc with same radius the arc intersect at point P.

Step (ix) Join the point P and A. $\angle$PAB obtained is the angle of measurement 105° with reference to line AB.

Step (x) Now, bisecting the angle will give angle

$$\frac{105°}{2} = 52\frac{1}{2}^{\circ} \text{ angle.}$$

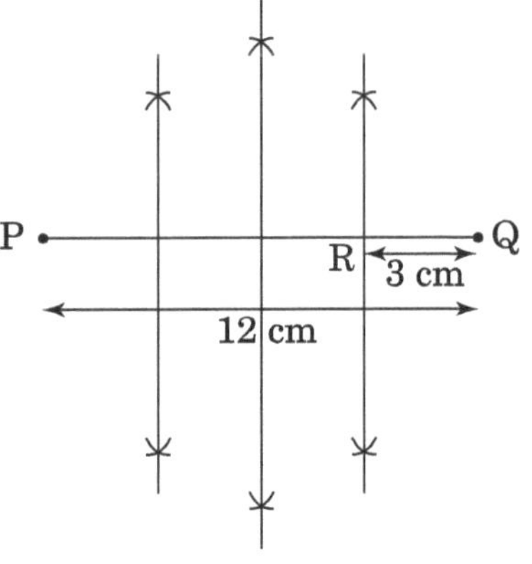

Thus, $\angle$RAB = $52\frac{1}{2}^{\circ}$ is the required angle.

6. Draw a line segment PQ = 12 cm and by ruler and compass, obtain a point R on it such that RQ = 3 cm. Write steps of construction.

[Board Term II, 2017, Set-Z6K408K]

Sol. Steps of construction :

Step (i) Construct a line segment PQ = 12 cm construct perpendicular bisector to divide it into two equal parts.

Step (ii) Divide each equal part into two equal parts again by the construction of perpendicular bisector to obtain four equal parts of the line segment.

Step (iii) Mark the point near Q as R such that QR = 3 cm

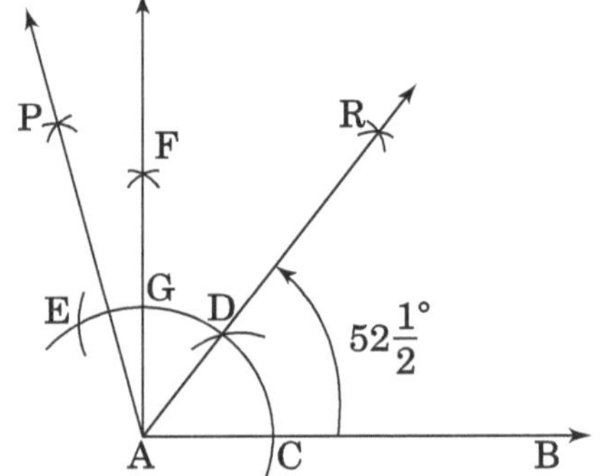

Long Answer Type Questions

(4 Marks Each)

1. Construct an angle of 90° at the initial point of a given ray and justify the construction.

[NCERT]

Sol. Steps of construction :

Step (i) First, draw a ray OA with initial point O.

Step (ii) Taking O as centre and some radius, draw an arc of a circle which intersects OA at a point B (say).

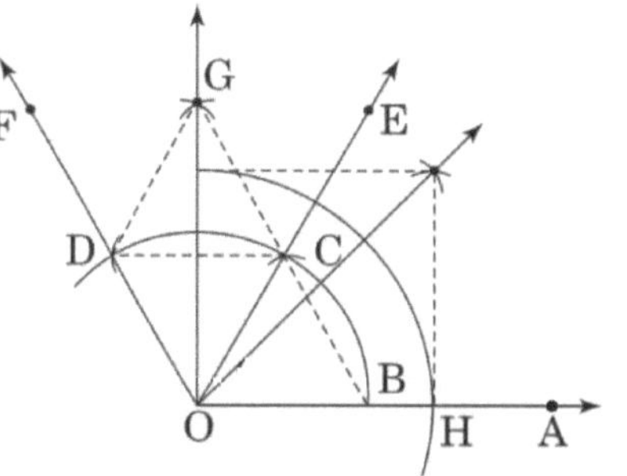

Step (iii) Taking B as centre and with the same radius as before, draw an arc intersecting the previous arc at a point C (say).

Step (iv) Taking C as centre and with the same radius as before , draw an arc intersecting the arc drawn in step (ii) at D (say).

Step (v) Draw the ray OE passing through C, then $\angle EOA = 60°$ and the ray of passing through D, then $\angle FOE = 60°$.

Step (vi) Next taking C and D as centres and with the radius more than $\frac{1}{2}$ CD, draw arcs to intersect each other at a point G (say).

Step (vii) Draw the ray OG, which is the angle bisector of the $\angle FOE$.

i.e., $\qquad \angle FOG = \angle GOE = \frac{1}{2}\ \angle FOE$

$\qquad\qquad = \frac{1}{2}\ (60°) = 30°$

Thus, $\qquad \angle GOA = \angle GOE + \angle EOA$

$\qquad\qquad = 30° + 60° = 90°$

Hence, $\angle GOA$ is the required angle of 90°.

Justification

(i) Join BC.

Then,

$\qquad\qquad OC = OB = BC$ [by construction]

So, ΔCOB is an equilateral triangle.

$\therefore \qquad\qquad \angle COB = 60° = \angle EOA \qquad\qquad …(i)$

(ii) Join CD.

Then,

$\qquad\qquad OD = OC = CD$ [by construction]

So, ΔDOC is an equilateral triangle.

$\therefore \qquad\qquad \angle DOC = 60° = \angle FOE$

(iii) Join CG and DG.

In ΔODG and ΔOCG,

$\qquad\qquad OD = OC$ [radii of the same arc]

$\qquad\qquad DG = CG \qquad$ [arc of equal radii]

$\qquad\qquad OG = OG \qquad\qquad$ [common sides]

$\therefore \qquad\qquad \Delta ODG \cong \Delta OCG$

$\qquad\qquad\qquad$ [by SSS congruence rule]

Then,

$\qquad\qquad \angle DOG = \angle COG \qquad\qquad$ [by CPCT]

$\therefore \qquad\qquad \angle FOG = \angle EOG = \frac{1}{2}\ \angle FOE$

$\qquad\qquad\qquad = \frac{1}{2}(60)° = 30°$

Thus,

$\qquad\qquad \angle GOA = \angle GOE + \angle EOA$

$\qquad\qquad\qquad = 30° + 60 = 90°$

$\qquad\qquad\qquad$ [from eq. (i)]

2. Construct an angle of 45° at the initial point of a given ray and justify the construction.

[NCERT]

Sol. Steps of construction :

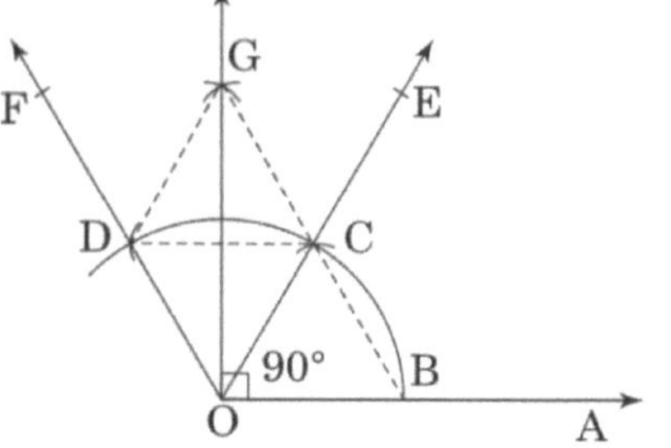

Step (i) First draw a ray OA with initial point O.

Step (ii) Talking O as centre and some radius, draw an arc of a circle which intersects OA, say at a point B.

Step (iii) Taking B as centre and with the same radius as before, draw an arc intersecting the previously drawn arc , say at a point C.

Step (iv) Taking C as centre draw an arc intersecting the arc drawn in step (ii) say at D.

Step (v) Draw the ray OE passing through C. Then, $\angle EOA = 60°$.

Step (vi) Draw the ray OF passing through D. then, $\angle FOE = 60°$.

Step (vii) Next taking C and D as centres and with radius more than $\frac{1}{2}$ CD, draw arcs to intersect each other, say at G.

Step(viii) Draw the ray OG, which is the angle bisector of the $\angle$FOE

i.e., $\angle$FOG = $\angle$EOG = $\frac{1}{2}$ $\angle$FOE

$$= \frac{1}{2}\ (60°) = 30°$$

Thus,

$$\angle GOA = \angle GOE + \angle EOA$$
$$= 30° + 60° = 90°$$

Step (ix) Now, taking O as centre and any radius more than OB, draw an arc to intersect the rays OA and OG, say at H and I, respectively.

Step (x) Next, taking H and I as centres and with the radius more than $\frac{1}{2}$ HI, draw arcs to intersect each other say at J.

Step (xi) Draw the ray OJ. This ray OJ is the required angle bisector of the $\angle$GOA.

Thus, $\angle$GOJ = $\angle$AOJ = $\frac{1}{2}$ $\angle$GOA

$$= \frac{1}{2}\ (90°) = 45°$$

Justification

(i) Join BC.

Then,

OC = OB = BC [by construction]

∴ ΔCOB is an equilateral triangle.

∴ $\angle$COB = 60° $\Rightarrow$ $\angle$EOA = 60°

(ii) Join CD.

Then,

OD = OC = CD [by construction]

∴ ΔDOC is an equilateral triangle.

∴ $\angle$DOC = 60° $\Rightarrow$ $\angle$FOE = 60°

(iii) Join CG and DG.

In ΔODG and ΔOCG,

OD = OC [radii of the same arc]

DG = CG   [arc of equal radii]

OG = OG

[common congruence rule]

∴ ΔODG $\cong$ ΔOCG

[SSS congruence rule]

∴ $\angle$DOG = $\angle$COG   [by CPCT]

∴ $\angle$FOG = $\angle$EOG = $\frac{1}{2}$ $\angle$FOE

$$= \frac{1}{2}\ (60°) = 30°$$

Thus, $\angle$GOA = $\angle$GOE + $\angle$EOA
$$= 30° + 60° = 90°$$

(iv) Join HJ and IJ.

In ΔOIJ and ΔOHJ,

OI = OH [radii of the same arc]

IJ = HJ   [arc of equal radii]

OJ = OJ   [common side]

∴ ΔIOJ $\cong$ ΔOHJ

[by SSS congruence rule]

∴ $\angle$IOJ = $\angle$HOJ   [by CPCT]

∴ $\angle$AOJ = $\angle$GOJ = $\frac{1}{2}$ $\angle$GOA

$$= \frac{1}{2}\ (90°) = 45°$$

Topic 2 [Construction of a Triangle, Given its Base, Sum or Difference of Other Two Sides and One Base Angle]

Points to be Remembered

I. Construction of a triangle, when its base, difference of the other two sides and one base angle.

Step 1. Draw BC = base and make given angle.

Step 2. Cut an arc BD = Difference of sides join DC.

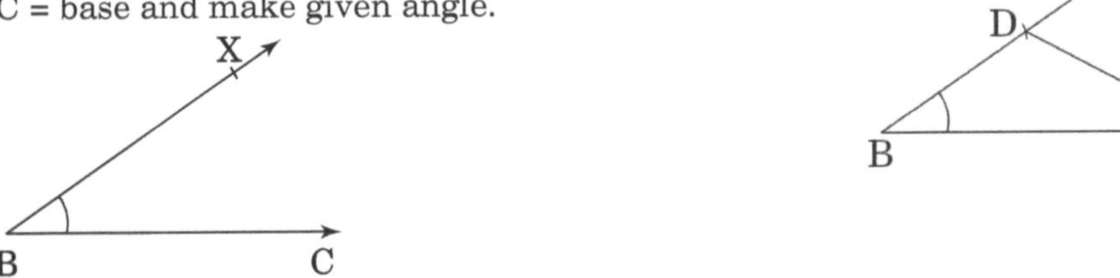

Step 3. Draw perpendicular bisector DC and let it intersect BX name it as A.

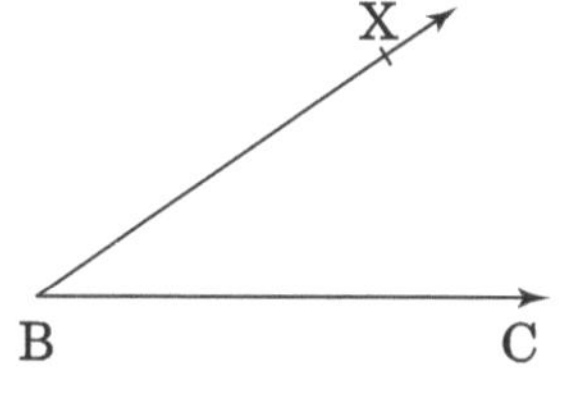

Step 4. Join AC, ABC is the required triangle.

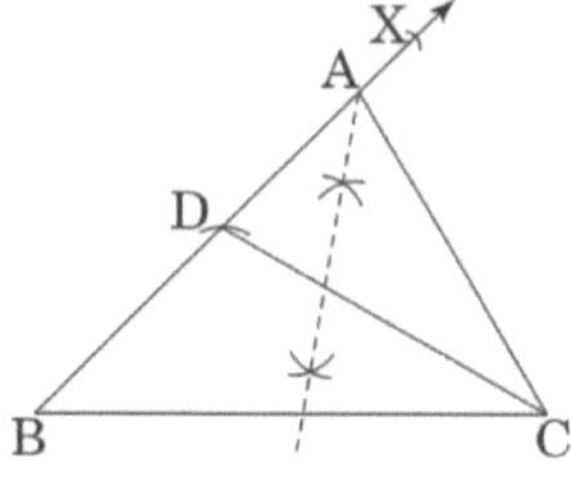

II. Construction of triangle, when its base, sum of the other two sides and one base angle.

Step 1. Draw BC = base and make given angle.

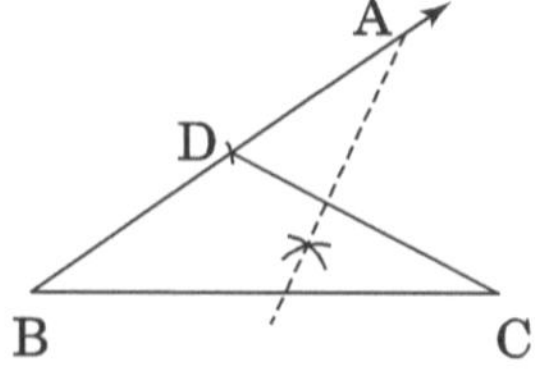

PREVIOUS YEARS'
EXAMINATION QUESTIONS
TOPIC 2

Multiple Choice Questions
(1 Mark Each)

1. The construction of a triangle PQR in which QR = 5.4 cm and $\angle Q = 60°$ is not possible when (PQ + QR) is:

   (a) 6 cm (b) 6.5 cm

   (c) 5 cm (d) 7 cm

Sol. (c) The value of (PQ + QR) must be less than 5.4 cm because the sum of any two sides of a triangle is always greater than the third side. If the value of (PQ + QR) = 5, the construction of a triangle PQR.

2. Which of the following sets of angles can be the angles of a triangle?

   (a) 30°, 60°, 80° (b) 40°, 60°, 70°

   (c) 50°, 30°, 100° (d) None of the above

Sol. (c) In any triangle, the sum of all interior angles is 180°. Hence, required set of angles is 50°, 30°, 100°.

Step 2. Cut an arc BD equal to sum of sides, join DC

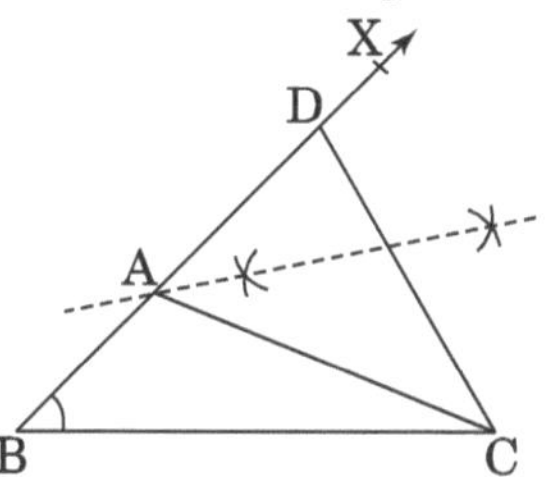

Step 3. Draw perpendicular bisector of DC and let it intersect BD. Name it as A.

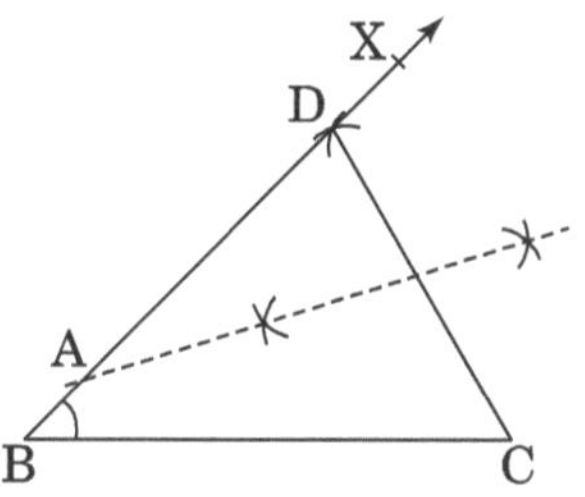

Step 4. Join AC, ABC is the required triangle

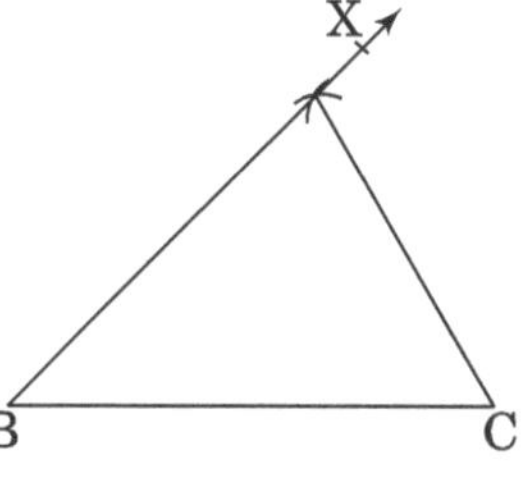

3. The construction of a triangle ABC, given that BC = 3 cm, $\angle C = 60°$ is possible when difference of AB and AC is equal to:

   (a) 3.2 cm (b) 3.1 cm

   (c) 3 cm (d) 2.8 cm

   [NCERT Exemp.]

Sol. (d) The value of difference of AB and AC is 2.8 cm which is less than the third side. Hence, the triangle ABC can be constructed.

4. The construction of a triangle ABC in which AB = 7 cm, $\angle A = 75°$ is possible when (BC − AC) is equal to:

   (a) 7.5 cm (b) 7 cm

   (c) 8 cm (d) 6.5 cm

Sol. (d) The value of difference of BC and AC is 6.5 cm which is less than the third side AB. Hence, the triangle ABC can be constructed.

5. The construction of a triangle ABC , given that BC = 6 cm, $\angle B = 45°$ is not possible when difference of AB and AC is equal to:

   (a) 6.9 cm (b) 5.2 cm

   (c) 5.0 cm (d) 4.0 cm

   [NCERT Exemp.]

Sol. (a) Since, (AB − AC) = 6.9 cm which is greater than the third side BC = 6 cm. Hence, the construction of a triangle ABC can not be possible.

6. Which of the following set of lengths can be the sides of a triangle?
   (a) 2 cm, 4 cm, 1.9 cm
   (b) 5.5 cm, 6.5 cm, 8.9 cm
   (c) 1.6 cm, 3.7 cm, 5.3 cm
   (d) None of the above

Sol. (b) From option (b),
$$(5.5 + 6.5) > 8.9$$
$$\Rightarrow \qquad 12 > 8.9$$
Hence, 5.5 cm, 6.5 cm and 8.9 cm are the sides of a triangle.

7. If the construction of a triangle ABC in which AB = 6 cm, $\angle A = 70°$ and $\angle B = 40°$ is possible then find the measure of $\angle C$.
   (a) 40° (b) 70°
   (c) 80° (d) None of the above

Sol. (b) ∵ Sum of all interior angles of a triangles
$$= 180°$$
$$\therefore \quad \angle A + \angle B + \angle C = 180°$$
$$\Rightarrow \quad 70° + 40° + \angle C = 180°$$
$$\therefore \qquad \angle C = 180° - 110° = 70°$$

8. Which of the following can be the length of BC required to construct the triangle ABC such that AC = 7.4 cm and AB = 5 cm?
   (a) 3.5 cm (b) 2.1 cm
   (c) 4.7 cm (d) None of the above

Sol. (b) The required length of side BC can be 2.1 cm.

Very Short Answer Type Questions
(1 Mark Each)

1. Can a $\triangle ABC$ be constructed, in which BC = 6 cm, $\angle C = 30°$ and AC − AB = 4 cm?

   [NCERT Exemplar]

Sol. Because the difference of any two sides of a triangle is less than the third side.

Hence, the $\triangle ABC$ can be constructed.

2. For what value of (BC + AC), the construction of a $\triangle ABC$ is possible, if AB = 6 cm and $\angle A = 45°$?

Sol. The value of (BC + AC) must be greater than 6 cm, because the sum of any two sides of a triangle is always greater than the third side.

3. Can you construct a right angled triangle, whose base is 4 cm and sum of its hypotenuse and other side is 8 cm?

Sol. Yes, here, in right angled $\triangle ABC$,

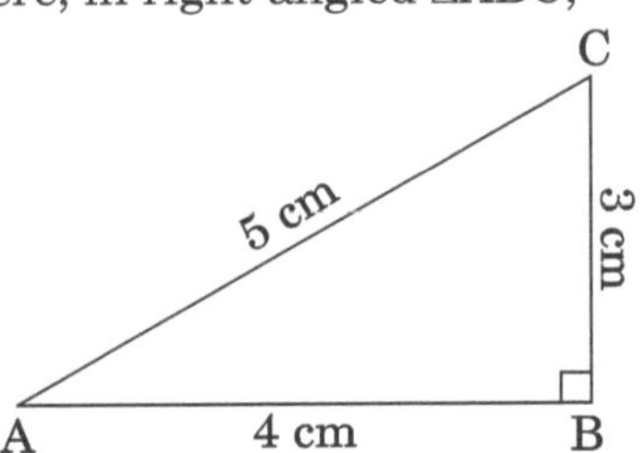

base AB = 4 cm, $\angle B = 90°$ and sum of hypotenuse and other side is 8 cm.
i.e., BC + AC = 8 cm
Let BC = 3 cm and AC = 5 cm
$$\therefore \qquad AB^2 + BC^2 = AC^2$$
$$\Rightarrow \qquad 4^2 + 3^2 = 5^2$$
$$\Rightarrow \qquad 25 = 25, \text{ which is true.}$$

Short Answer Type Questions-I
(2 Marks Each)

1. Construct a right angled triangle, whose base is 12 cm and sum of its hypotenuse and other side is 18 cm. [NCERT]

Sol. Given, in $\triangle ABC$, base BC = 12 cm, $\angle B = 90°$ and AB + BC = 18 cm

Steps of construction :

Step (i) Draw the base BC = 12 cm.

Step (ii) At the point B, draw a ray BX making $\angle XBC = 90°$

Step (iii) Cut a line segment BD = AB + AC = 18 cm from the ray BX.

Step (iv) Join DC.

Step (v) Now, draw the perpendicular bisector PQ of CD, which intersects BD at a point A.

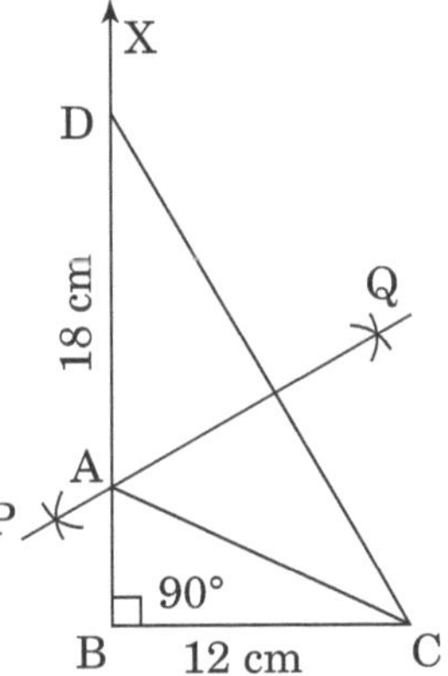

Step (vi) Join AC, Thus, ABC is the required right angled triangle.

2. Construct a triangle ABC, such that AB = 5 cm, BC = 4 cm and median AD = 5 cm.

   [Board Term II, 2013]

Sol. Steps of construction:

Step   (i) Draw a line segment BC = 4 cm.

Step   (ii) Bisect BC at D.

Step   (iii) From B and D, draw arcs at distances 5 cm each on the same side of BC, cutting each other at A.

Step   (iv) Join AB and AC.

Thus, $\triangle$ABC is the required triangle.

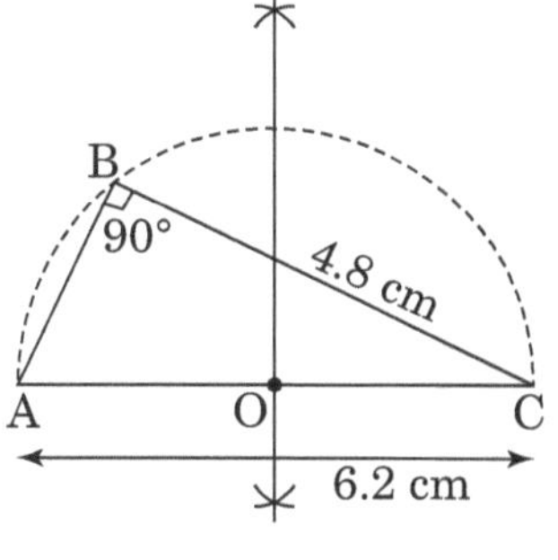

3.   Construct a triangle XYZ in which
$\angle Y = 90°$, XY = 8 cm and XY – ZY = 4 cm.

[Board Term II, 2014]

Sol. Steps of construction:

Step   (i) Draw a line segment XY = 8 cm.

Step   (ii) At the point Y, construct an angle 90°.

Step   (iii) Cut a line segment equal to XY – ZY = 4 cm from the line segment YP.

Step   (iv) XY – ZY = 4 cm, XY = 8 cm and ZY = 4 cm. At join ZX.

Thus, $\triangle$XYZ is the required triangle.

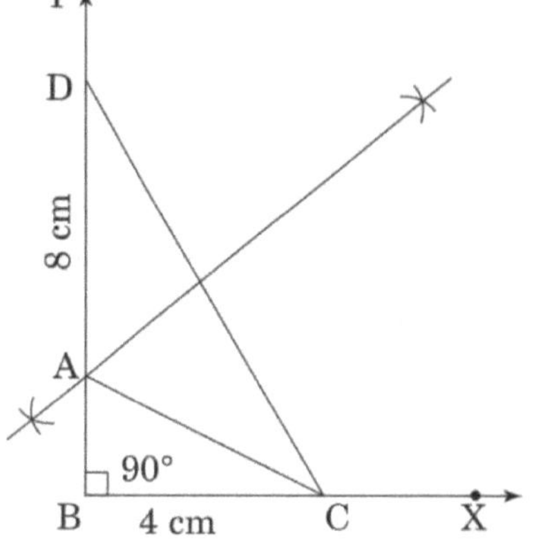

4.   Construct a right triangle whose base is 4 cm and sum of its hypotenuse and other side is 8 cm.

[Board Term II, 2014]

Sol. Steps of construction:

Step   (i) Draw a ray BX and cut off line segment BC = 4 cm.

Step   (ii) Construct $\angle XBY = 90°$.

Step   (iii) From BY cut off line segment BD = 8 cm.

Step   (iv) Join CD.

Step   (v) Draw the $\perp$ bisector of CD, intersecting BD at A.

Step   (vi) Join AC, thus ABC is the required triangle.

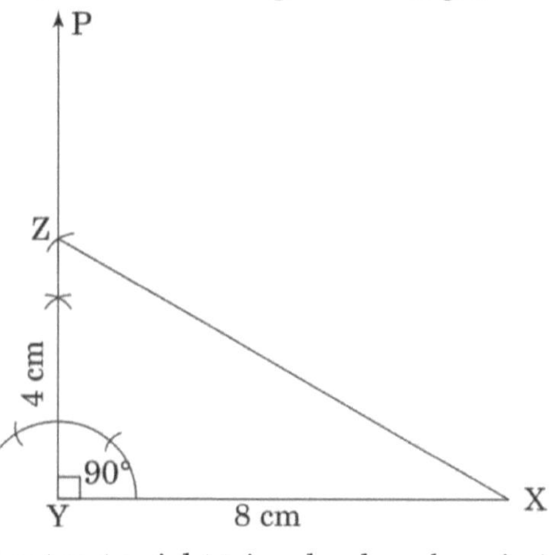

5.   Construct a right angled $\triangle$ABC, in which BC = 4.8 cm, AC = 6.2 cm and $\angle B = 90°$.

Sol. Steps of construction:

Step   (i) Draw a line segment AC = 6.2 cm.

Step   (ii) Draw the perpendicular bisector of line segment AC, which cuts AC at O.

Step   (iii) Taking O as centre and radius OA, draw a semi-circle on AC.

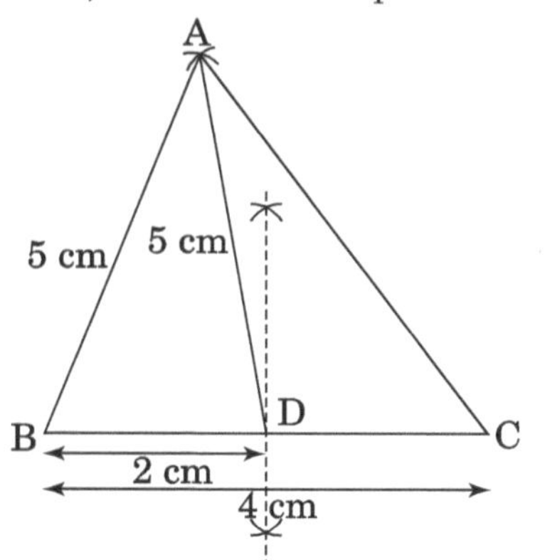

Step   (iv) Taking C as center and radius equal to 4.8 cm, draw an arc cutting the semi-circle at B.

Step   (v) Join BA and BC

Thus, ABC is the required right angled triangle.

6. Construct a $\triangle ABC$ such that BC = 3.2 cm, $\angle B = 45°$ and AC – AB = 2.1 cm.

Sol. Steps of construction:

Step (i) Draw a line segment BC = 3.2 cm.

Step (ii) At B, construct an angle $\angle CBX = 45°$ and produce it to point X'.

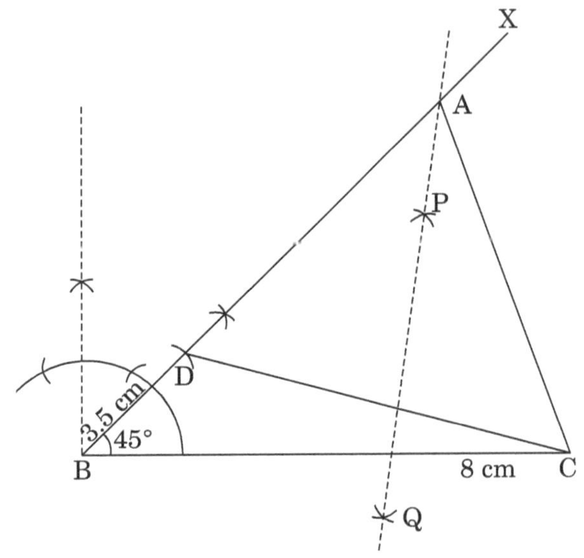

Step (iii) Cut-off BD = 2.1 cm and join CD.

Step (iv) Draw the perpendicular bisector of CD and let it intersect X' BX in A.

Step (v) Join AC.

Thus, $\triangle ABC$ is the required triangle.

Short Answer Type Questions-II

(3 Marks Each)

1. Construct a right triangle whose base is 12 cm and sum of its hypotenuse and other is 18 cm.

[NCERT]

Sol. Steps of construction:

Step (i) Draw a line segment AB = 12 cm. Draw a ray AX making an angle of 90° with AB.

Step (ii) Cut a line segment AD of 18 cm. (As sum of other two sides is 18 cm) from ray AX.

Step (iii) Join DB and make an angle DBY equal to ADB.

Step (iv) Let BY intersects AX at C.

Step (v) Join BC $\triangle ABC$ is the required triangle.

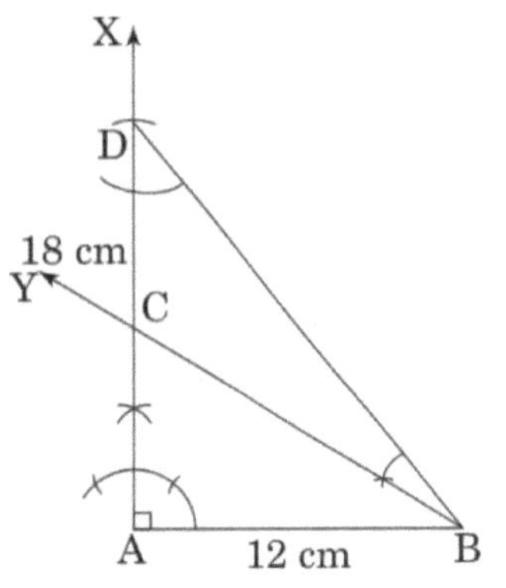

2. Construct a triangle PQR in which QR = 6 cm, $\angle Q = 60°$ and PR – PQ = 2 cm.

[Board Term II, 2012, Set-01, 06, NCERT]

Sol. Steps of construction:

Step (i) Draw a line segment QR = 6 cm.

Step (ii) At point Q construct an angle = 60°, i.e., $\angle XQR = 60°$.

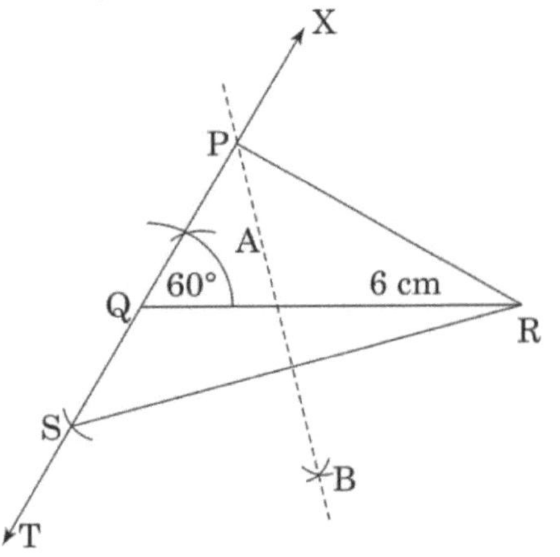

Step (iii) Cut a line segment QS = 2 cm from the line segment QT extended on opposite side of line segment XQ. (As PR > PQ and PR – PQ = 2 cm). Join SR.

Step (iv) Draw perpendicular bisector AB of line segment SR, Which intersect QX at point P.

Step (v) Join PQ and PR. $\triangle PQR$ is the required triangle.

3. Construct a triangle ABC in which BC = 8 cm, $\angle B = 45°$ and AB – AC = 3.5 cm.

[NCERT] [Board Term II, 2012, Set (36, 40)]

Sol.

Steps of construction:

Step (i) Draw the line segment BC = 8 cm and at point B construct an angle 45°, i.e., $\angle XBC = 45°$.

Step (ii) Cut the line segment BD = 3.5 cm (equal to AB − AC) on ray BX.

Step (iii) Join DC and draw the perpendicular bisector PQ of DC.

Step (iv) The perpendicular bisector intersects BX at point A.

Step (v) Join AC, thus ∆ABC is the required triangle.

4. Construct a triangle ABC in which BC = 7 cm, ∠B = 75° and AB + AC = 13 cm.   [NCERT]

Sol. Steps of construction:

Step (i) Draw a line segment BC = 7 cm, At point B draw ∠XBC = 75°.

Step (ii) Cut a line segment BD = 13 cm (i.e., equal to AB + AC) from BX.

Step (iii) Join DC and make an angle DCY equal to ∠BDC.

Step (iv) Line CY intersects BX at A. ∆ABC is the required triangle.

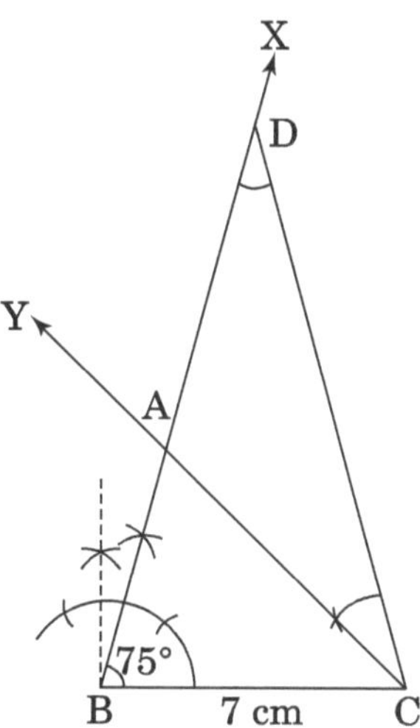

5. Construct a triangle with base of length 7.5 cm, the difference of the other two sides 2.5 cm and one base angle of 45°. Justify the construction.

[Board Term II, 2012, Set-(67, 70)]

Sol. Given : Base BC = 7.5 cm, the difference of the other two sides AB − AC or AC − AB = 2.5 cm and one base angle 45°.

Let AB > AC

AB − AC = 2.5 cm

Steps of construction:

Step (i) Draw a ray BX and cut off a line segment BC = 7.5 cm from it.

Step (ii) Construct YBC = 45°

Step (iii) Cut off a line segment BD = 2.5 cm from BY.

Step (iv) Join CD

Step (v) Draw the perpendicular bisector RS of CD intersecting BY at a point A.

Step (vi) Join AC, then ABC is the required triangle.

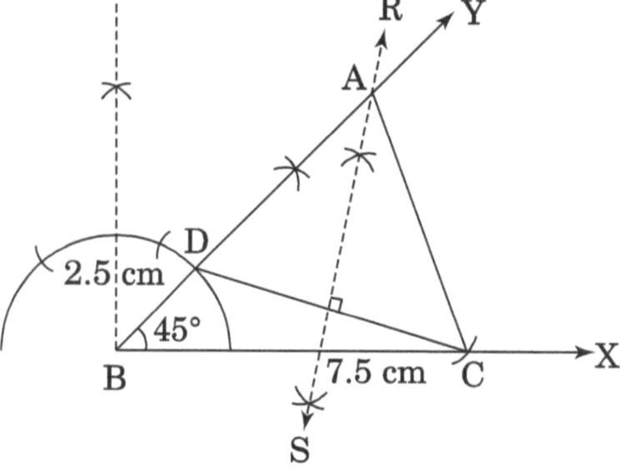

Justification of Construction:

RS is the perpendicular bisector of DC.

So,   AD = AC

and   BD = AB − AD = AB − AC.

Hence, the above construction is justified

6. Construct an isosceles triangle whose base = 7.5 cm and the vertical angle is twice each of its base angles.

[Board Term II, 2012, 65]

Sol. Let each of the base angles = $x°$.

and the vertical angle = $2x°$.

According to the question,

$$\therefore \qquad x° + x° + 2x° = 180°$$
$$\Rightarrow \qquad 4x° = 180°$$
$$\therefore \qquad x° = \frac{180}{4} = 45°$$

Therefore, each of the base angle is 45° and the vertical angle is 90°.

Steps of construction:

Step (i) Draw BC = 7.5 cm.

Step (ii) At point B, construct ∠CBA = 45° and at point C, construct ∠BCA = 45° so that CA intersect at A.

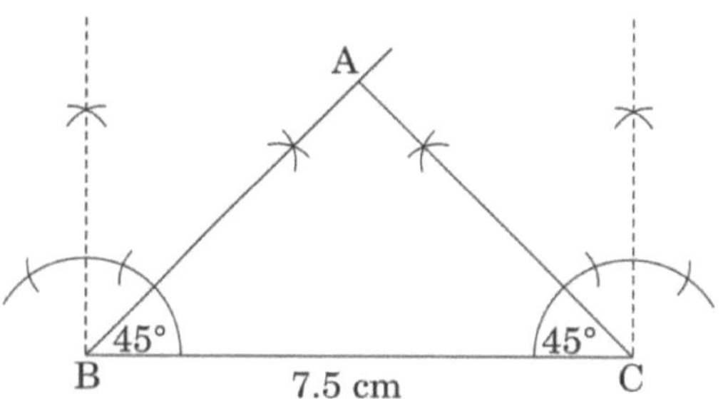

Thus, ∆ABC is the required triangle.

7. Construct a triangle whose angles are in the ratio 1 : 3 : 5 and length of sides included by first and last angles is 6 cm.

[Board Term II, Set-IA21924-2016]

Sol. Let angles be x, $3x$, and $5x$

According to the question,

$\therefore \qquad x + 3x + 5x = 180°$ (angle sum property)

$\Rightarrow \qquad\qquad 9x = 180°$

$\therefore \qquad\qquad x = 20°$

First angle = 20°

Second = 60°

and   third angle = 100°

Steps of construction:

Step (i) Draw a line segment BC = 6 cm.

Step (ii) At point A draw $\angle XAB = 20°$. and

Step (iii) At point B draw $\angle YBA = 100°$.

Step (iv) XA and YB intersect at point C.

Thus, ABC is the required triangle.

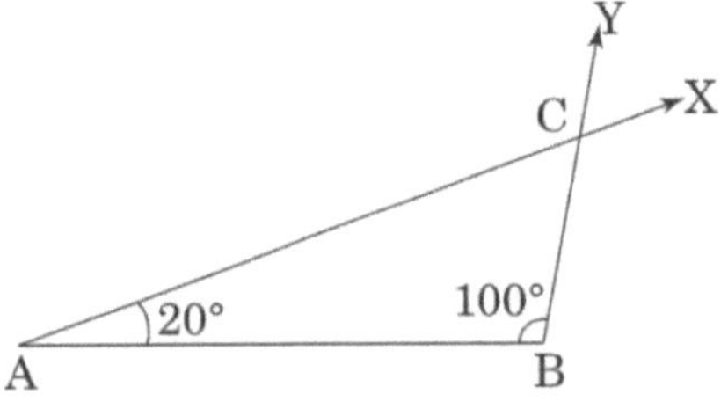

8. Construct a triangle ABC such that BC = 6 cm, AB = 3 cm and median AD = 4.5 cm. Write steps of construction.   [Board Term II, IA21924, 2016]

Sol. **Steps of construction:**

Step (i) Draw line segment BC = 6 cm.

Step (ii) Draw the perpendicular bisector of BC which intersect BC at D.

Step (iii) Now with D as the centre and radius = 4.5 cm draw an arc.

Step (iv) With B as the centre and radius = 3 cm, draw an arc cutting the previous arc at A.

Step (v) Join the point B and D to A.

Step (vi) Now Join A to C.

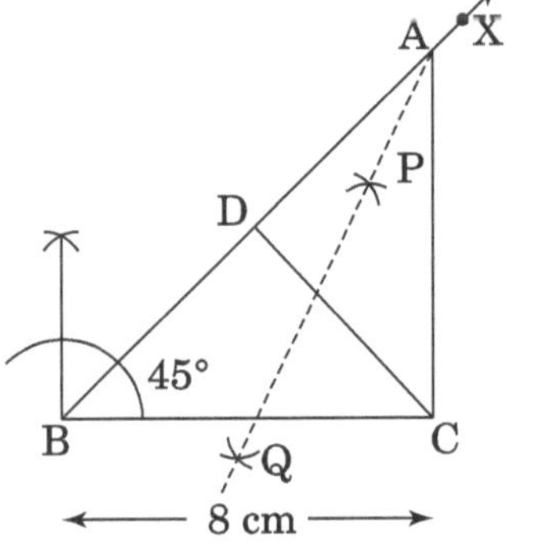

Thus, ABC is the required triangle.

Long Answer Type Questions
(4 Marks Each)

1. Construct a $\triangle PQR$, in which QR = 6 cm, $\angle Q = 60°$ and PR – PQ = 2 cm.   [NCERT]

Sol. Given, In $\triangle PQR$, QR = 6 cm, $\angle Q = 60°$ and PR – PQ = 2 cm

Here, PR > PQ i.e., the side containing base angle is less than third side.

Sol.

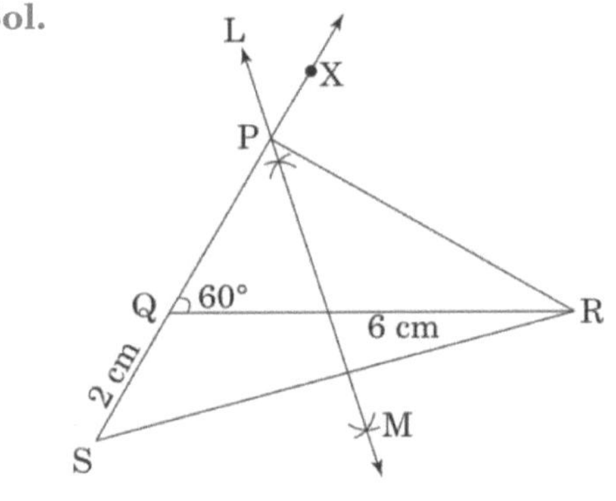

Steps of construction:

Step (i) Draw the base QR = 6 cm.

Step (ii) At the point Q, make an $\angle XQR = 60°$

Step (iii) Cut line segment QS = PR – PQ = 2 cm from the line QX extended on opposite side of line segment QR.

Step (iv) Join SR.

Step (v) Draw the perpendicular bisector LM of SR.

Step (vi) Let LM intersects QX at P.

Step (vii) Join PR. Thus, PQR is the required triangle.

2. Construct as $\triangle ABC$, in which BC = 8 cm, $\angle B = 45°$ and AB – AC = 3.5 cm.   [NCERT]

Sol. Given, in $\triangle ABC$, BC = 8 cm, $\angle B = 45°$

and   AB – AC = 3.5 cm

Here, AB > AC, i.e., the side containing base angle is greater than third side.

Steps of construction:

Step (i) First, draw the base BC = 8 cm.

Step (ii) At the point B, make an $\angle XBC = 45°$.

Step (iii) Cut the line segment BD is equal to AB − AC = 3.5 cm form the ray BX.

Step (iv) Join DC.

Step (v) Draw the perpendicular bisector, say PQ of DC.

Step (vi) Let PQ intersects BX at a point A.

Step (vii) Join AC.

Thus, ABC is the required triangle.

3. Construct a $\triangle$ABC, in which BC = 7 cm, $\angle$B = 75° and AB + AC = 13 cm.

Given : In $\triangle$ABC, BC = 7 cm, $\angle$B = 75° and AB + AC = 13 cm.   [NCERT]

Sol.

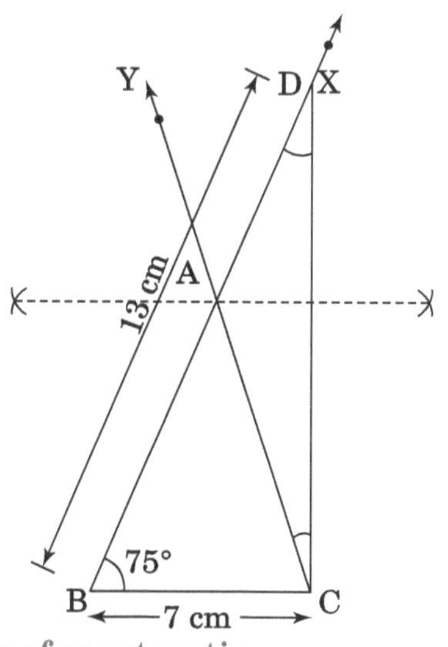

Steps of construction:

Step (i) First, draw the base BC = 7 cm.

Step (ii) At the point B, make an $\angle$XBC = 75°

Step (iii) Cut a line segment BD equal to AB + AC = 13 cm from the ray BX.

Step (iv) Now, join DC.

Step (v) Make an $\angle$DCY at C is equal to $\angle$BDC.

Step (vi) Let CY intersects BX at A. Then join AC. Thus, ABC is the required triangle.

4. Construct a $\triangle$ABC in which BC = 4.7 cm, $\angle$B = 45° and AB − AC = 2 cm.

[Board Term II, RQTZFBW, 2016, IA21924, 2016]

Sol. Steps of construction:

Step (i) Draw a line segment BC = 4.7 cm and at point B construct an angle i.e., $\angle$XBC = 45°

Step (ii) Cut the line segment BD = 2 cm (equal to AB − AC) on ray BX.

Step (iii) Join DC and draw the perpendicular bisector PQ of DC.

Step (iv) The perpendicular bisector intersects BX at point A. Join AC.

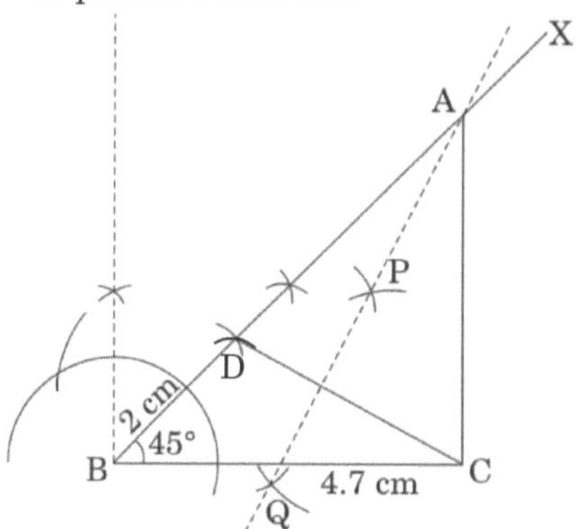

Thus, $\triangle$ABC is the required triangle.

Topic 3 [Construction of a Triangle of Given Perimeter and Base Angle]

Points to be Remembered

I. Construction of a triangle of given perimeter and base angles.

Step 1. Draw line equal to the sum of sides DE.

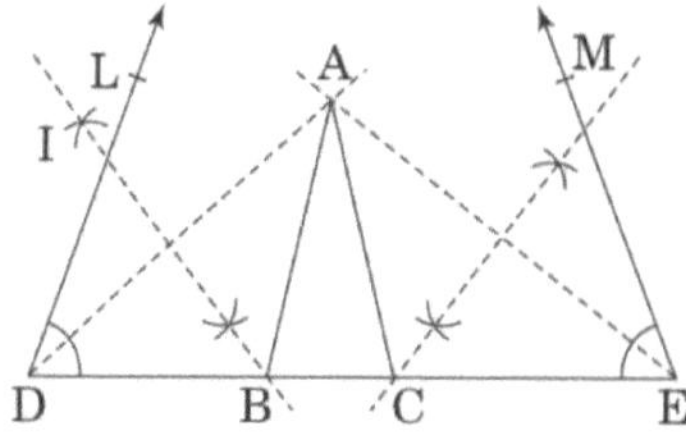

Step 2. Draw given two angles at D and E.

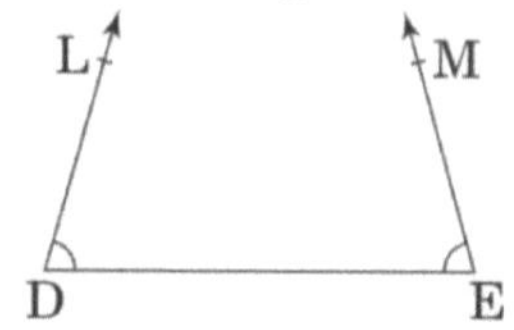

Step 3. Bisect $\angle$LDE and $\angle$MED, let the bisectors meet at A.

Step 4. Draw perpendicular bisectors of AD and AE. Extend them to intersect DE. ABC is the required triangle.

PREVIOUS YEARS'
EXAMINATION QUESTIONS
TOPIC 3

Multiple Choice Questions
(1 Mark Each)

1. If a, b and c are the lengths of the three sides of a triangle, then which of the following is true?

   (a) $a + b < c$ (b) $a - b - c$

   (c) $a + b = c$ (d) None of the above

   Sol. (b) If a, b and c are the lengths of three sides of a triangle.

   ∴ Difference of two sides is always less than the third side.

   Hence, $(a - b) < c$

2. The construction of a triangle ABC in which BC = 6 cm, $\angle A = 50°$ is not possible, when difference of BC and AC is equal to :

   (a) 4.6 cm   (b) 6.4 cm

   (c) 5.1 cm   (d) None of the above

   Sol. (b) When difference of BC and AC is less than the third sides. The construction of $\triangle$ABC is not possible.

   ∴ Difference = 6.4 cm > 6 cm

3. The construction of the triangle ABC is not possible if it is given that BC = 4 cm, $\angle C = 60°$ and the difference of AB and AC is:

   (a) 3.5 cm   (b) 4.5 cm

   (c) 3 cm   (d) 2.5 cm

   Sol. (b) The construction of $\triangle$ABC is possible if (AB − AC) < BC

   Hence, required difference = 4.5 cm.

Very Short Answer Type Questions
(1 Mark Each)

1. Can a $\triangle$ABC can be constructed in which $\angle B = 105°$, $\angle C = 90°$ and AB + BC + CA = 10 cm?

   [NCERT Exemplar]

   Sol. Given,

   $$AB + BC + CA = 10 \text{ cm}$$
   $$\angle B = 105° \quad \text{and} \quad \angle C = 90°$$

   ∵ $\angle A + \angle B + \angle C = 180°$

   (∵ Sum of three angles of a triangle is 180°)

   Here, $\angle B + \angle C = 105° + 90°$

⇒ 195° > 180°, which is not true,

Thus, $\triangle$ABC cannot be constructed.

2. The construction of a $\triangle$ABC, Given that BC = 5 cm, $\angle B = 45°$ is not possible when difference of AB and AC is equal to 5.2 cm. Why?

   Sol. Since, one side of the triangle is less than the difference of two sides. Therefore, the $\triangle$ABC cannot be constructed.

3. Can we construct an angle of 52.5°? Justify for your answer.

   Sol. Because $52.5° = \dfrac{1}{4} \times 210°$ and $210° = 180° + 30°$.

   Hence, we can construct an angle of 52.5°.

4. An angle of 42.5° can be constructed. State true or false and give reason for your answer.

   Sol. Because $42.5° = \dfrac{1}{2} \times 85°$ and 85° cannot be constructed. Hence the given statement is false.

5. Cans we construct an angle of 67.5°? Justify for your answer.

   Sol. Because $67.5° = \dfrac{135°}{2} = \dfrac{1}{2}(90° + 45°)$. Hence, we can construct an angle of 67.5°

Short Answer Type Questions-I
(2 Marks Each)

1. Construct an isosceles right triangle with perimeter 11 cm.   [Board Term II, 2012, Set-(30)]

   Sol. Given : Isosceles right triangle with perimeter 11 cm. Its two angle will be 45° each.

   Steps of construction:

   Step (i) Draw a line segment PQ = 11 cm.

   Step (ii) At P, construct $\angle LPQ = 45°$ and at Q, $\angle PQM = 45°$.

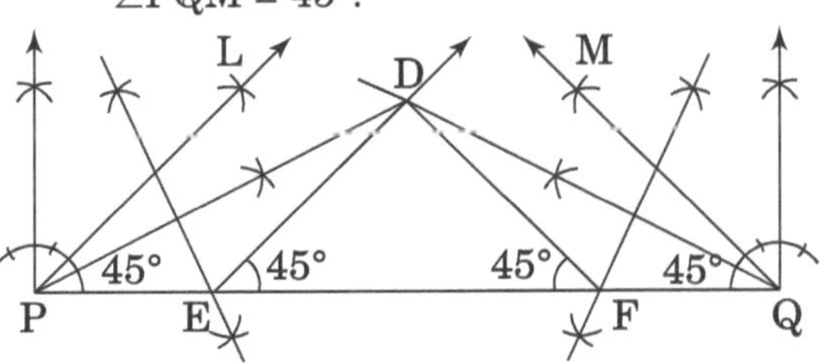

   Step (iii) Draw bisectors of these angles and mark their point of intersection as D.

   Step (iv) Draw perpendicular bisector of PD and QD which intersect PQ at point E and F respectively.

   Step (v) Join DE and DF.

   Thus, $\triangle$DEF is the required triangle.

2. Construct a triangle whose base is 6 cm and the sum of the other two sides is 10 cm and one base angle is 30°.   [Board Term II, 2012, Set (9, 13)]

Sol. Steps of construction:

Step   (i) Draw a line segment BC = 6 cm.

Step   (ii) Draw ray BX such that $\angle$CBX = 30°.

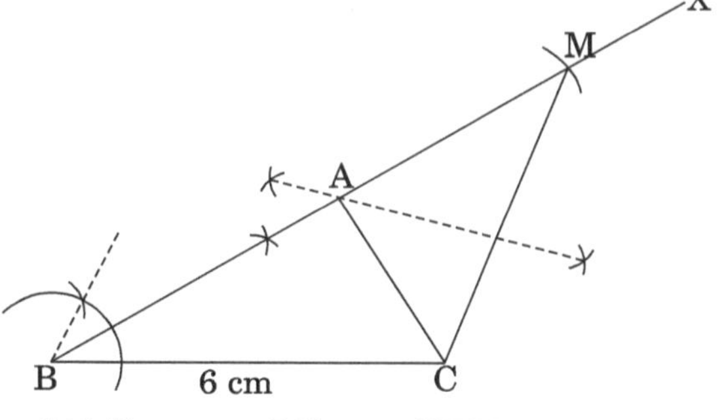

Step (iii) From ray BX, cut off BM = 10 cm.

Step (iv) Join MC.

Step   (v) Draw the perpendicular bisector of MC, intersecting BM at A.

Step (vi) Join AC, Thus, ABC is the required triangle.

3. Construct an isosceles triangle whose perimeter is 10 cm and altitude is 3 cm.

Sol. Steps of construction:

Step   (i) Draw a line segment XY = 10 cm.

Step   (ii) Draw a perpendicular bisector PQ of XY, which intersect XY at M.

Step (iii) Cut AM = 3 cm from PQ.

Step (iv) Join AX and AY.

Step   (v) Draw the perpendicular bisector of XA and YA, which cut XY at B and C, respectively.

Step (vi) Join AB and AC.

Thus, ABC is the required triangle.

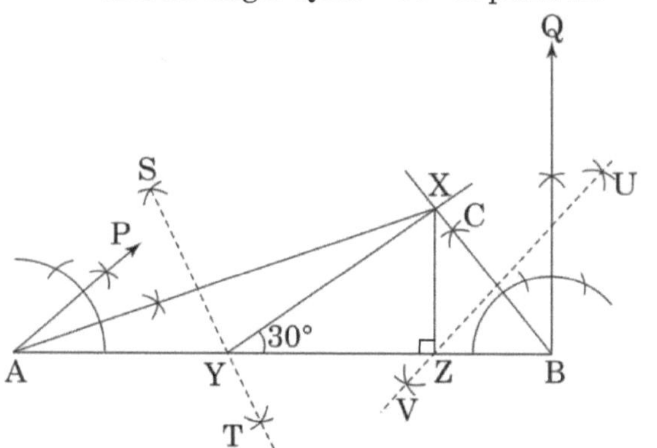

Short Answer Type Questions-II

(3 Marks Each)

1. Construct a triangle XYZ in which $\angle$Y = 30°, $\angle$Z = 90° and XY + YZ + ZX = 11 cm.   [NCERT]

[Board Term-II, KVS2014; 2012 (01, 10, 15)]

Sol. Steps of construction:

Step   (i) Draw a line segment AB = 11 cm (As XY + YZ + ZX = 11 cm).

Step   (ii) Construct an angle PAB of 30° at point A and an angle QBA = 90° at point B.

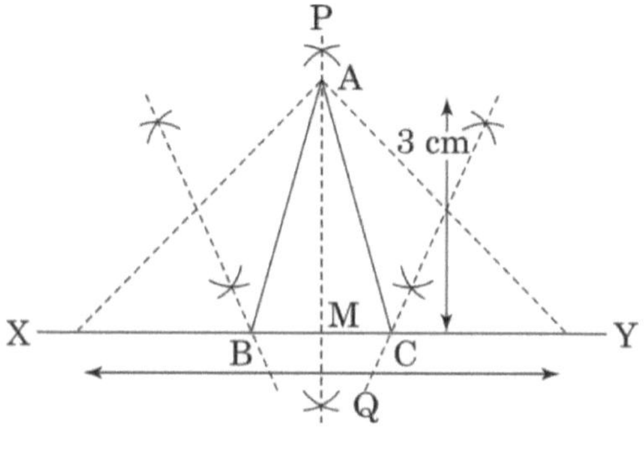

Step (iii) Bisect $\angle$PAB and $\angle$QBA. These bisectors intersect each other at point X.

Step (iv) Draw perpendicular bisectors ST of AX and UV of BX.

Step   (v) $\perp$ bisector ST intersects AB at Y and UV intersects AB at Z. Join XY, XZ.

ΔXYZ is the required triangle.

2. Construct a right triangle with base 4.5 cm and the perimeter = 11.7 cm

[Board Term II 2012, Set-24]

Given : In right ΔABC, base BC = 4.5 cm and perimeter as 11.7 cm

i.e., AB + AC + BC = 11.7 cm or AB + AC = 7.2 cm, ΔABC = 90°.

Sol. Steps of construction:

Step   (i) Draw BC = 4.5 cm.

Step   (ii) Draw BY such that $\angle$CBY = 90°.

Step (iii) From BY cut off BD = 7.2 cm.

Step (iv) Join DC.

Step   (v) Draw the perpendicular bisector of DC intersecting BD at A.

Step (vi) Join AC, Thus ABC is the required triangle.

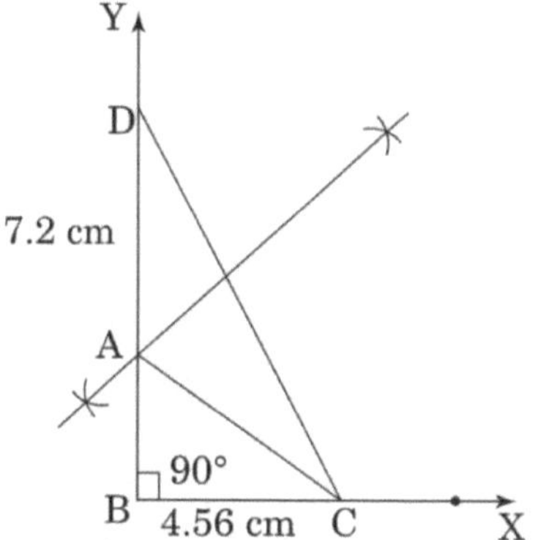

3. Construct an equilateral triangle with perimeter 12 cm and justify the construction.

[Board Term II, 2012, Set-6, 12]

Sol. Let a be the length of each side. Since perimeter, $3a = 12$ cm so each side of triangle is, $a = 4$ cm.

Steps of Construction:

Step   (i) Draw AB = 4 cm.

Step   (ii) At A and B, draw angles of 60°

Step (iii) Mark the point of intersection of two angles as C.

Step (iv) Join AC and BC.

Thus, ΔABC is the required triangle.

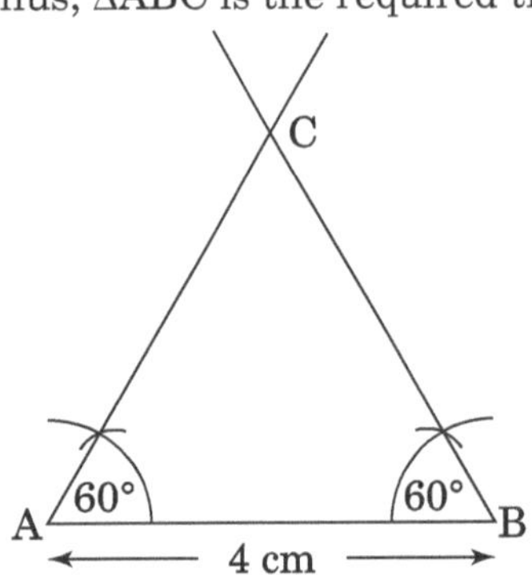

Justification of Construction:

AS $\angle CAB = \angle CBA = 60°$

So, $\angle CAB + \angle CBA + \angle ACB = 180°$

So, $\angle ACB = 60°$

Also,   AC = BC   (as $\angle CAB = \angle CBA$)

                AB = AC   (as $\angle CAB = \angle ACB$)

Hence,   AB = BC = AC = 4 cm

4. Construct a triangle having its perimeter 12.5 cm and the ratio of the angles 3 : 4 : 5.

[Board Term II, 2012, Set 18, 20]

Sol. Let the angles are $3x°$, $4x°$ and $5x°$, respectively, According to ΔABC,

$$3x° + 4x° + 5x° = 180°$$
$$\Rightarrow \qquad 12x° = 180°$$
$$\therefore \qquad x° = \frac{180°}{12} = 15°$$
$$\angle A = 3 \times 15° = 45°$$
$$\angle B = 4 \times 15° = 60°$$
$$\angle C = 5 \times 15° = 75°$$

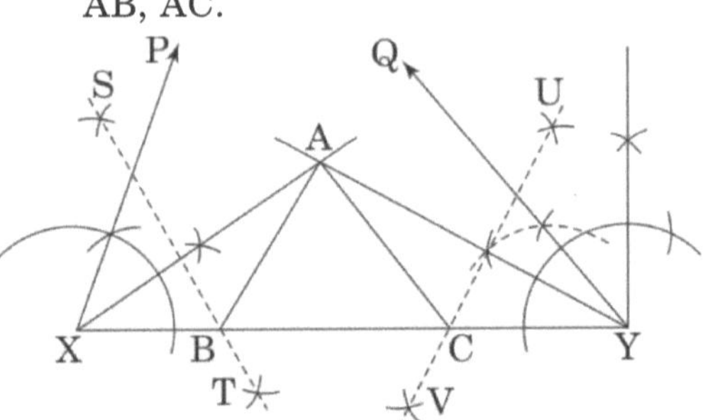

Steps of construction:

Step   (i) Draw a line PQ = 12.5 cm.

Step   (ii) At P, construct $\angle SPQ = 60°$ and at Q, construct $\angle RQP = 75°$.

Step (iii) Draw the bisectors of $\angle SPQ$ and $\angle RQP$, intersecting at A.

Step (iv) Draw the perpendicular bisectors of AP and AQ intersecting PQ at B and C respectively.

Step   (v) Join A to B and A to C.

Hence, ABC is the required triangle.

Long Answer Type Questions
(4 Marks Each)

1. Construct a triangle ABC, in which $\angle B = 60°$, $\angle C = 45°$ and AB + BC + CA = 11 cm.

[NCERT] [Board Term II, KVS 2016]

Sol. Steps of construction:

Step   (i) Draw a line segment XY = 11 cm (As AB + BC + CA = 11 cm).

Step   (ii) Construct an angle PXY of 60° at point X and an angle QYX of 45° at point Y.

Step (iii) Bisect $\angle PXY$ and $\angle QYX$. These bisectors intersect each other at point A.

Step (iv) Draw perpendicular bisectors ST of XA and UV of YA.

Step   (v) Perpendicular bisectors ST intersects XY at B and UV intersects XY at C. Join AB, AC.

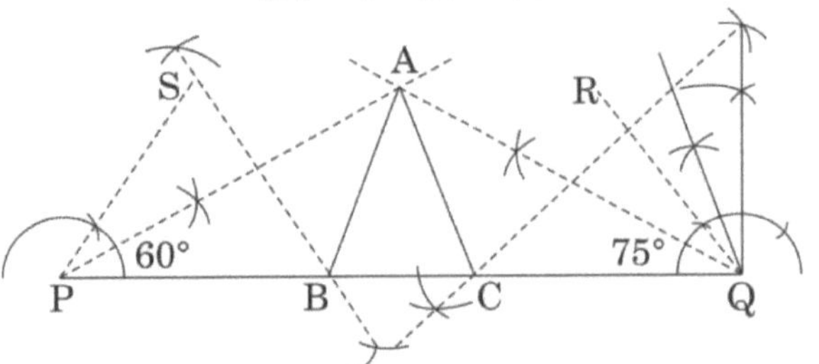

Thus, ABC is the required triangle.

2. **Give Reasons:**

   (i) Construction of an angle of 22.5° is possible with the help of ruler and compass.

   (ii) It is not possible to construct a ΔABC, given that BC = 7 cm, $\angle B = 45°$ and AB − AC = 10 cm.

   (iii) It is possible to construct an angle of 67.5° using ruler and compass.

   (iv) Construction of Δ DEF, if EF = 5.5 cm, $\angle E = 75°$ and DE − DF = 2 cm is possible.

[Board Term II, 2015]

Sol. Steps of construction:

Step (i) Construction of an angle of 22.5° is possible with the help of ruler and compass. Since, 22.5° is the bisector angle of 45° first we will construct 45° using ruler and compass and then draw its bisector.

Step (ii) Given that BC = 7 cm, $\angle$B = 45° and AB – AC = 10 cm.

We know that, construction of a triangle is possible only if difference of two sides is less than the third side i.e., AB – AC < BC

Therefore, $\triangle$ABC is not constructed.

Step (iii) With the help of ruler and compass, we can construct an angle of 67.5° since,

$$67.5° = \frac{135°}{2} = \frac{1}{2}\left(90° + 45°\right).$$

Step (iv) Given that, EF = 5.5 cm, $\angle$E = 75° and DE – DF = 2 cm,

We know that construction of a triangle is only possible if difference of two sides is less than the third side i.e., DE – DF < EF.

Therefore, $\triangle$DEF is not constructed.

3. Construct A $\triangle$XYZ, which $\angle$Y = 30°, $\angle$Z = 90° and XY + YZ + ZX = 11 cm.

Sol. Given, in $\triangle$XYZ, $\angle$Y = 30°, $\angle$Z = 90° and XY + YZ + ZX = 11 cm

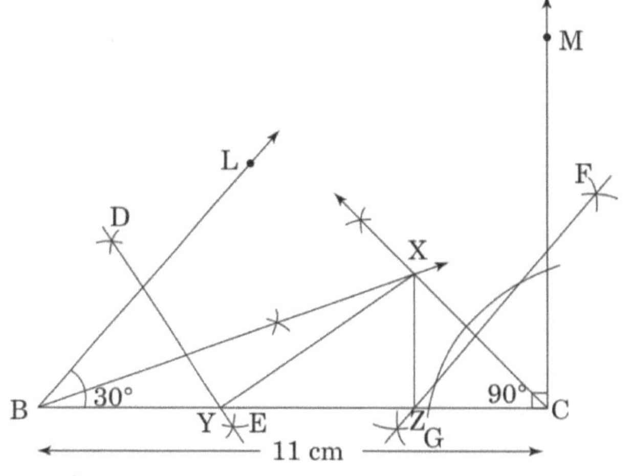

Steps of construction:

Step (i) Draw a line segment BC = XY + YZ + ZX = 11 cm.

Step (ii) Draw a ray LB making an $\angle$LBC = 30° at B and a ray MC making an $\angle$MCB = 90° at C.

Step (iii) Draw the angle bisector of $\angle$LBC and $\angle$MCB. Let these bisectors meet at a point X.

Step (iv) Draw perpendicular bisectors DE of XB and FG of XC.

Step (v) Let DE intersects BC at Y and FG intersects BC at Z.

Step (vi) Join XY and XZ.

Thus, XYZ is the required triangle.

UNIT V
Mensuration

CHAPTER 12

Areas

- Area of a triangle using Heron's formula (without proof) and its application in finding the area of a quadrilateral.

A flow chart on the basis of basic concepts of area

Area

Area of plane figure is measure of region enclosed by it

Area of Quadrilateral

Rectangle : If the length (l) and breadth (b), then
$$\text{Area} = l \times b$$
$$\text{Perimeter} = 2(l + b) \; ; \; \text{Diagonal} = \sqrt{l^2 + b^2}$$

Square : If the side of a square is (a), then
$$\text{Area} = a^2; \; \text{Perimeter} = 4a \; ; \; \text{Diagonal} = \sqrt{2}a$$

Rhombus : If the diagonals are d_1 and d_2, then
$$\text{Area} = \tfrac{1}{2} d_1 \times d_2;$$
$$\text{Perimeter} = 2\sqrt{d_1^2 + d_2^2}$$

Trapezium : If the parallel sides are a and b, the distance between parallel lines as h
$$\therefore \;\; \text{Area} = \tfrac{1}{2}(a + b)h$$

Regular Hexagon : If the side of a hexagon is (a), then
Area = $6 \times$ Area of an equilateral triangle
$$= 6 \times \tfrac{\sqrt{3}}{4} a^2 = \tfrac{3\sqrt{3}}{2} a^2$$

Area of Triangle

If the base (b) and altitude (h) then
$$\text{Area} = \frac{1}{2} \times b \times h$$

Heron's formula : Triangle with sides as a, b, c, then
$$\text{Semi-perimeter (s)} = \frac{a + b + c}{2}$$
$$\text{Area} = \sqrt{s(s - a)(s - b)(s - c)}$$

Equilateral Triangle : If the side of triangle is a, then
$$\text{Altitude} = \frac{\sqrt{3}}{2} a$$
$$\text{Area} = \frac{\sqrt{3}}{4} a^2$$

Isosceles Triangle : If the base of a triangle is 'a' and equal sides b, then
$$\text{Area} = \frac{a}{4}\sqrt{4b^2 - a^2}$$

[Topic 1] Area of Triangle

Points to be Remembered

- An $\triangle ABC$, there are three vertices namely A, B and C and three sides are AB, BC and CA and CD is the corresponding height.

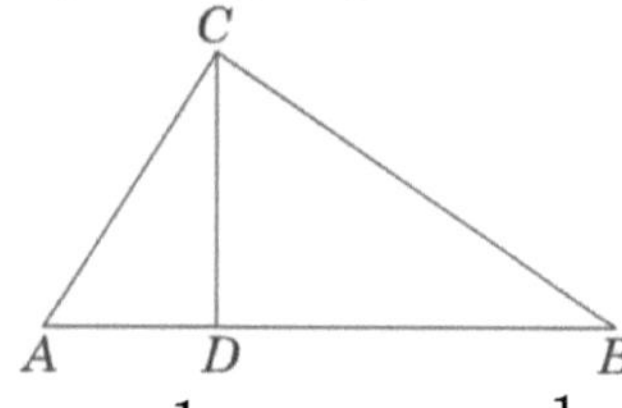

- Area of $\triangle ABC = \dfrac{1}{2} \times AB \times CD = \dfrac{1}{2} \times$ base $\times$ height
- If $\triangle ABC$ is an equilateral triangle with side 'a', then

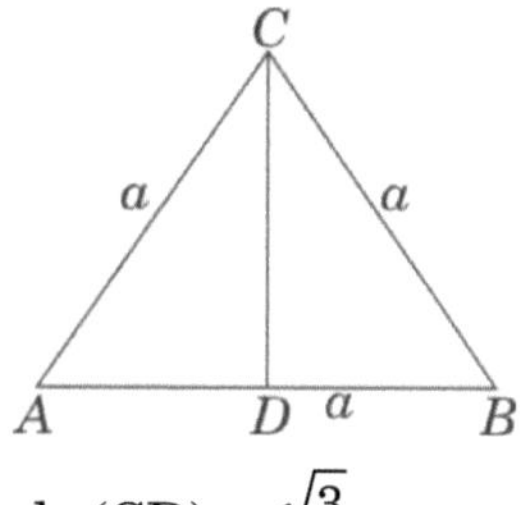

$$\text{Altitude (CD)} = \frac{\sqrt{3}}{2}a \; ;$$
$$\text{Perimeter} = 3a$$
$$\text{Area of } \triangle ABC = \frac{\sqrt{3}}{4}a^2$$

PREVIOUS YEARS'
EXAMINATION QUESTIONS
TOPIC 1

Multiple Choice Questions
(1 Mark Each)

1. If the area of an equilateral triangle is $16\sqrt{3}$ cm^2, then the perimeter of the triangle is
   - (a) 48 cm
   - (b) 24 cm
   - (c) 12 cm
   - (d) 36 cm

   [NCERT Exemp.]

Sol. (b) According to the question,

Area of equilateral $\triangle = 16\sqrt{3}$ cm^2

$$\Rightarrow \qquad \frac{\sqrt{3}}{4}a^2 = 16\sqrt{3}$$
$$\Rightarrow \qquad a^2 = \frac{16\sqrt{3} \times 4}{\sqrt{3}} = 64$$
$$\therefore \qquad a = \sqrt{64} = 8 \text{ cm}$$

Hence, perimeter of the triangle

$$= 3 \times a = 3 \times 8 = 24 \text{ cm}$$

- If $\triangle ABC$ is an isosceles triangle with equal sides 'b' and base 'a', then

$$\text{Altitude (CD)} = \frac{1}{2}\sqrt{4b^2 - a^2}$$

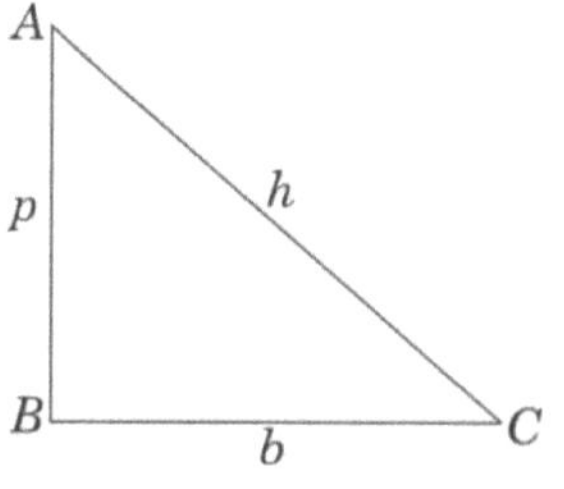

$$\text{Perimeter} = (2b + a)$$
$$\text{Area of } \triangle ABC = \frac{a}{4}\sqrt{4b^2 - a^2}$$

- If $\triangle ABC$ is a right angled triangle with base 'b', perpendicular 'p' and hypotenuse 'h', then

$$\text{Area of } \triangle ABC = \frac{1}{2} \times b \times p$$

2. The area of an equilateral triangle with side $2\sqrt{3}$ cm is

   [NCERT Exemp.]
   - (a) 5.196 cm^2
   - (b) 0.866 cm^2
   - (c) 3.496 cm^2
   - (d) 1.732 cm^2

Sol. (a) According to the question,

Area of equilateral triangle

$$= \frac{\sqrt{3}}{4} \times (2\sqrt{3})^2$$
$$= \frac{\sqrt{3}}{4} \times 4 \times 3 = 3\sqrt{3}$$
$$= 3 \times 1.732 = 5.196 \text{ cm}^2$$

3. The perimeter of an equilateral triangle is 60 m. The area is

   [NCERT Exemp.]
   - (a) $10\sqrt{3}$m^2
   - (b) $15\sqrt{3}$ m^2
   - (c) $20\sqrt{3}$ m^2
   - (d) $100\sqrt{3}$ m^2

Sol. (d) Perimeter of equilateral triangle = 60 m

$$\Rightarrow \qquad 3a = 60 \text{ m}$$
$$\therefore \qquad a = \frac{60}{3} = 20 \text{ m}$$

Hence, area of equilateral triangle

$$= \frac{\sqrt{3}}{4}a^2 = \frac{\sqrt{3}}{4} \times 20 \times 20 = 100\sqrt{3} \text{ m}^2$$

4. An isosceles right triangle has area 8 cm². The length of its hypotenuse is

(a) $\sqrt{32}$ cm

(b) $\sqrt{16}$ cm

(c) $\sqrt{48}$ cm

(d) $\sqrt{24}$ cm

[NCERT Exemp.]

Sol. (a) According to the question,

$\therefore$ Area of isosceles triangle $= \dfrac{1}{2} \times$ Base $\times$ Height

$\Rightarrow \qquad \dfrac{1}{2} \times (B)^2 = 8$

$\Rightarrow \qquad (B)^2 = 16$

$\therefore \qquad B = \sqrt{16}$

Now, In $\triangle ABC$, $= 4$ cm

By Pythagoras theorem

$(B)^2 + (P)^2 = (H)^2$

$\Rightarrow \qquad (H)^2 = (4)^2 + (4)^2 = 16 + 16$

$\therefore \qquad H = \sqrt{32}$ cm

Hence, the length of its hypotenuse

$= \sqrt{32}$ cm

5. The length of each side of an equilateral triangle having an area of $9\sqrt{3}$ cm² is

(a) 8 cm

(b) 36 cm

(c) 4 cm

(d) 6 cm

[NCERT Exemp.]

Sol. (d) According to the question,

Area of equilateral triangle $= 9\sqrt{3}$ cm²

$\Rightarrow \qquad \dfrac{\sqrt{3}}{4}a^2 = 9\sqrt{3}$

$\Rightarrow \qquad a^2 = \dfrac{9\sqrt{3} \times 4}{\sqrt{3}} = 36$

$\therefore \qquad a = \sqrt{36} = 6$ cm

Hence, the length of each side = 6 cm

6. Area of a triangle whose base is 24 cm and the corresponding height is 10 cm is:

(a) 135 cm²

(b) 120 cm²

(c) 130 cm²

(d) 240 cm²

[NCERT Exemp.]

Sol. (b) According to the question,

$\therefore$ Area of triangle $= \dfrac{1}{2} \times$ base $\times$ height

$= \dfrac{1}{2} \times 24 \times 10$

$= 120$ cm²

Very Short Answer Type Questions
(1 Mark Each)

1. The perimeter of an equilateral triangle is 60 m. What will be its area? [NCERT Exemplar]

Sol. According to the question,

Perimeter of an equilateral triangle

$= 3a = 60$ m (a is one side)

$\therefore \qquad a = 20$ m

Hence, area of equilateral triangle

$= \dfrac{\sqrt{3}}{4}a^2$

$= \dfrac{\sqrt{3}}{4} \times 20 \times 20$

$= 100\sqrt{3}$ m²

2. If the perimeter of an equilateral triangle is 60 m, then find its area. [NCERT Exemplar]

Sol. Let each side of an equilateral triangle be a m, then

According to the question,

Perimeter of an equilateral triangle = 60 m

$\therefore \qquad a + a + a = 60$

$\Rightarrow \qquad 3a = 60$

$\therefore \qquad a = \dfrac{60}{3} = 20$ m

Now, area of an equilateral triangle

$= \dfrac{\sqrt{3}}{4}(\text{side})^2$

$= \dfrac{\sqrt{3}}{4} \times 20 \times 20$

$= 100\sqrt{3}$ m²

Hence, the area of an equilateral triangle is $100\sqrt{3}$ m².

3. The base of a right triangle is 6 cm and hypotenuse is 10 cm. What will be its area? [NCERT Exemplar]

Sol. According to the question, In $\triangle ABC$,

By Pythagoras theorem,

$AB = \sqrt{AC^2 - BC^2} = \sqrt{10^2 - 6^2}$

$= \sqrt{100 - 36} = \sqrt{64}$

$= 8$ cm

$\therefore$ Area of right triangle

$$= \frac{1}{2} \times \text{base} \times \text{height}$$

$$= \frac{1}{2} \times 6 \times 8$$

$$= \frac{48}{2} = 24 \text{ cm}^2$$

4. Find the area of regular hexagon of side a cm.

[NCERT Exemplar]

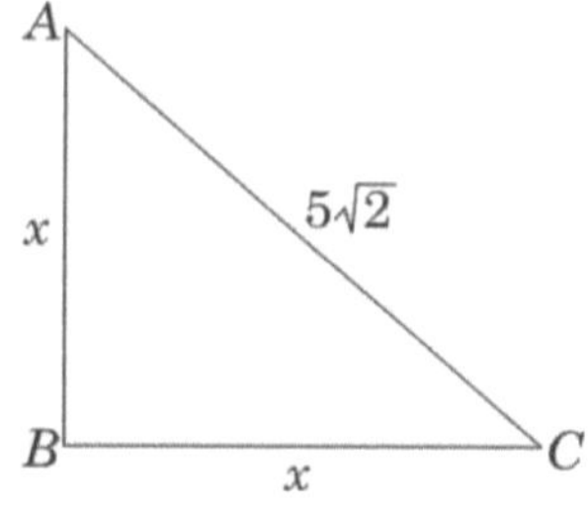

Sol. We know that, regular hexagon is divided into six equilateral triangles.

$\therefore$ Area of regular hexagon of side a

= sum of the areas of six equilateral triangles

$$= 6 \times \frac{\sqrt{3}}{4} \times a^2$$

$\left[\because \text{ area of equilateral triangle} = \frac{\sqrt{3}}{4} \ (\text{side})^2 \right]$

$$= \frac{3\sqrt{3}}{2} a^2 \text{ cm}^2$$

5. The area of a parallelogram of altitude 12 cm is 108 cm². Find the base of the parallelogram.

[Board Term I, 2016, Set-JQ22L5C]

Sol. According to the question,

Area of parallelogram = base × height

$$108 = \text{base} \times 12$$

$\therefore$ $\qquad \text{base} = \dfrac{108}{12} = 9 \text{ cm}$

Hence, the base of the parallelogram = 9 cm.

6. Write the formula used to calculate the area of an equilateral triangle of side 'a' units.

Sol. $\qquad \text{Area} = \dfrac{\sqrt{3}}{4} \ a^2 \ \text{unit}^2$

7. Calculate the side of an isosceles right triangle of hypotenuse $5\sqrt{2}$ cm.

Sol.

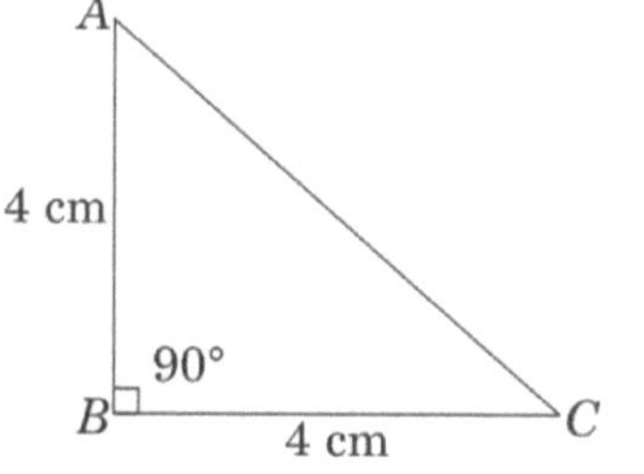

In $\triangle ABC$, by Pythagoras theorem,

$$AB^2 + BC^2 = AC^2$$

$\Rightarrow \qquad x^2 + x^2 = \left(5\sqrt{2}\right)^2$

$\Rightarrow \qquad 2x^2 = 25 \times 2$

$\Rightarrow \qquad x^2 = 25$

$\therefore \qquad x = 5 \text{ cm}$

8. The perimeter of a triangle is 36 cm and its sides are in the ratio a : b : c = 3 : 4 : 5, then find the value of a, b, c respectively.

Sol. Let the sides of a triangle are 3x, 4x and 5x, then

According to the question,

$\Rightarrow \qquad 3x + 4x + 5x = 36$

$\Rightarrow \qquad 12x = 36$

$\therefore \qquad x = 3$

Hence, the sides a, b, c are 9 cm, 12 cm, 15 cm.

9. What is the area of $\triangle ABC$ in which AB = BC = 4 cm and $\angle B = 90°$?

Sol. According to the question,

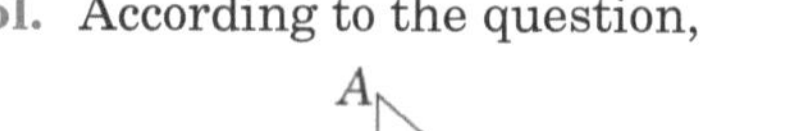

$\therefore$ Area of $\triangle ABC = \dfrac{1}{2} \times AB \times BC$

$$= \frac{1}{2} \times 4 \times 4 = 8 \text{ cm}^2$$

10. The sides of a triangular plot are in the ratio 4 : 5 : 6 and its perimeter is 150 cm, then find its sides.

Sol. Let the sides of a triangle are 4x, 5x and 6x, then

According to the question,

$\Rightarrow \qquad \text{Perimeter} = 4x + 5x + 6x$

$$= 150$$

$\Rightarrow \qquad 15x = 150$

$\therefore \qquad x = \dfrac{150}{10} = 15 \text{ cm}$

Hence, the sides are 40 cm 50 cm and 60 cm.

11. The area of an equilateral triangle is $16\sqrt{3}$ cm². Find its perimeter.

Sol. Let a be the side of an equilateral triangle, then

According to the question,

$\therefore \qquad \dfrac{\sqrt{3}}{4} \times a^2 = 16\sqrt{3}$

$\Rightarrow \qquad a^2 = 64$

$\Rightarrow \qquad a = 8 \text{ cm}$

Hence, perimeter of the triangle

$$= 3 \times a = 3 \times 8 = 24 \text{ cm}$$

12. Find out the area of an isosceles triangle whose base is 'a' and equal sides are of length 'b'.

Sol. Let 'b' be the equal sides length and 'a' be the base.

According to the question,

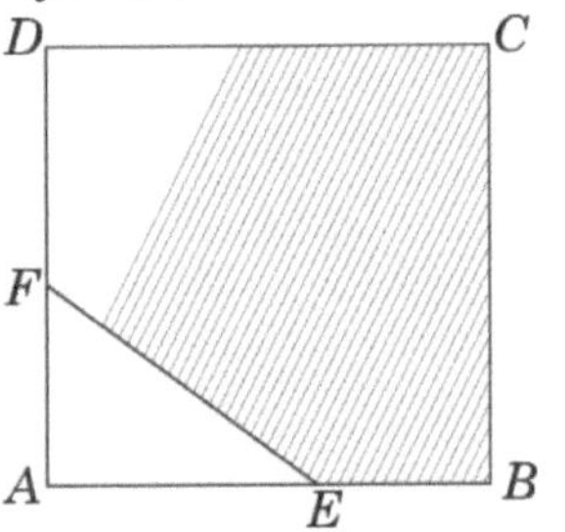

$$x = \sqrt{b^2 - \left(\frac{a}{2}\right)^2} = \frac{\sqrt{4b^2 - a^2}}{2}$$

$\therefore$ Area of triangle $= \dfrac{1}{2} \times$ base $\times$ height

$$= \frac{1}{2} \times a \times x$$

$$= \frac{1}{2} \times a \times \frac{\sqrt{4b^2 - a^2}}{2}$$

$$= \frac{a}{4}\sqrt{4b^2 - a^2} \ \text{units}^2$$

Write whether the statements are true or false. Justify your answer.

1. The area of a regular hexagon of side 'a' is the sum of the areas of the five equilateral triangles with side a. [NCERT Exemplar]

Sol. Since, area of regular hexagon of side a = sum of area of the six equilateral triangles.

Therefore, the given statement is false.

2. The base and the corresponding altitude of a parallelogram are 10 cm and 3.5 cm, respectively. The area of the parallelogram is 30 cm^2. Is this statement true? [NCERT Exemplar]

Sol. Since, area of parallelogram $= B \times H$

$$= 10 \times 3.5 = 35 \text{ cm}^2$$

Therefore, the given statement is false.

Short Answer Type Questions I
(2 Marks Each)

1. An isosceles right angled triangle has area 8 cm^2. Find the length of its hypotenuse. [NCERT Exemplar]

Sol. Given, area of an isosceles right angled triangle = 8 cm^2

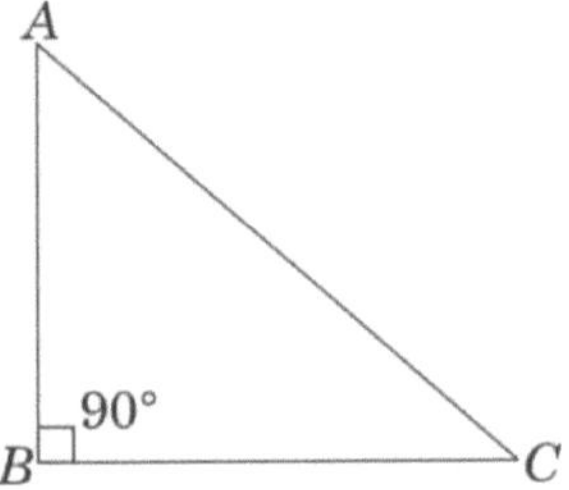

$\because$ Area of an isosceles triangle

$$= \frac{1}{2}(\text{Base} \times \text{Height})$$

$\therefore$ $\qquad 8 = \dfrac{1}{2}(\text{Base} \times \text{Base})$

[$\because$ base = height, as triangle is an isosceles triangle]

$\Rightarrow \qquad (\text{Base})^2 = 16$

$\therefore \qquad \text{Base} = 4 \text{ cm}$

In $\triangle ABC$, we have

$$AC^2 = AB^2 + BC^2$$

[By Pythagoras theorem]

$\Rightarrow \qquad AC^2 = 4^2 + 4^2$

$$= 16 + 16 = 32$$

$\therefore \qquad AC = \sqrt{32} \text{ cm} = 4\sqrt{2} \text{ cm}$

[Taking positive square root because length is always positive]

Hence, the length of its hypotenuse is $4\sqrt{2}$ cm.

2. If the area of an equilateral triangle is $81\sqrt{3}$ cm^2. Find its perimeter. [Board Term I, 2012, Set-41]

Sol. According to the question,

Area of an equilateral triangle $= \dfrac{\sqrt{3}}{4}a^2$

$\Rightarrow \qquad \dfrac{\sqrt{3}}{4}a^2 = 81\sqrt{3}$

$\Rightarrow \qquad a^2 = 81 \times 4$

$\therefore \qquad a = 9 \times 2 = 18 \text{ cm}$

Hence, Perimeter of equilateral triangle

$$= 3a = 3 \times 18 = 54 \text{ cm}$$

3. In the given figure, ABCD is a square of side 4 cm. E and F are the mid-points of AB and AD, respectively. Find the area of the shaded region.

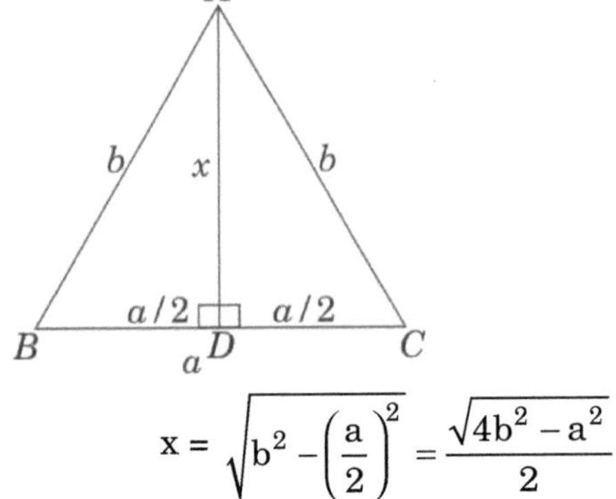

Sol. Given, sides of a square are
$$AB = BC = CD = AD = 4 \text{ cm}$$
∴ Area of square = $(\text{side})^2 = (4)^2 = 16 \text{ cm}^2$

Also, given E and F are the mid-points of AB and AD.

∴
$$AE = \frac{AB}{2} = \frac{4}{2} = 2 \text{ cm}$$

and
$$AF = \frac{AD}{2} = \frac{4}{2} = 2 \text{ cm}$$

∴ Area of $\triangle AEF = \frac{1}{2} \times AE \times AF$

$\left[\because \text{Area of right angled triangle} = \frac{1}{2} \times \text{base} \times \text{height} \right]$

$$= \frac{1}{2} \times 2 \times 2 = 2 \text{ cm}^2$$

Now, area of shaded region
= Area of square ABCD − Area of $\triangle AEF$
= $16 − 2 = 14 \text{ cm}^2$

Short Answer Type Questions II

(3 Marks Each)

1. An isosceles triangle has perimeter 30 cm and each of the equal sides is 12 cm. Find the area of the triangle.　　　**[NCERT Exemplar]**

Sol. According to the question,

Each equal side of an isosceles triangle is 12 cm.
And perimeter of the given triangle is 30 cm

∴ Third side of the triangle
$$= 30 − 12 − 12 = 6 \text{ cm}$$

Now,
$$s = \frac{12 + 12 + 6}{2} = \frac{30}{2} = 15 \text{ cm}$$

Hence, Area of the triangle by using Heron's formula
$$= \sqrt{s(s-a)(s-b)(s-c)}$$
$$= \sqrt{15(15-12)(15-12)(15-6)}$$
$$= \sqrt{15 \times 3 \times 3 \times 9} = 9\sqrt{15} \text{ cm}^2$$

2. Find the area of an isosceles triangle having base 2 cm and the length of one of the equal sides is 4 cm.　　　**[NCERT Exemplar]**

Sol. Let ABC be an isosceles triangle in which
AB = AC = 4 cm and BC = 2 cm

According to the question,

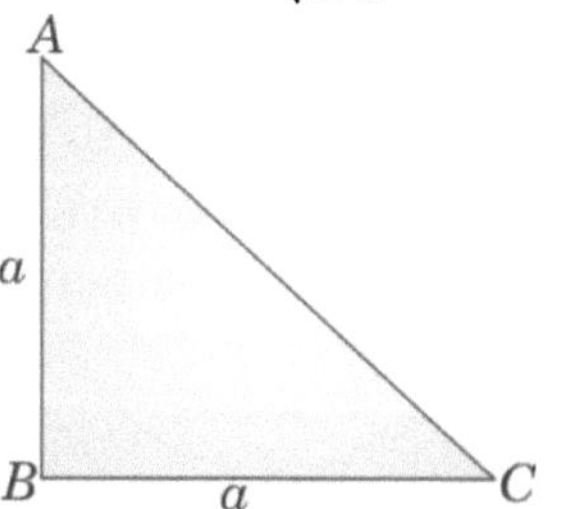

In right angled $\triangle ADB$,
$$(AB)^2 = (AD)^2 + (BD)^2$$
$$[\text{by Pythagoras theorem}]$$
$$\Rightarrow \qquad (4)^2 = AD^2 + 1$$
$$\Rightarrow \qquad AD^2 = 16 − 1$$
$$\Rightarrow \qquad AD^2 = 15$$
∴
$$AD = \sqrt{15} \text{ cm}$$
[taking positive square root, length is always positive]

∴ Area of an isosceles $\triangle ABC$
$$= \frac{1}{2} \times \text{Base} \times \text{Height}$$
$$= \frac{1}{2} \times BC \times AD$$
$$= \frac{1}{2} \times 2 \times \sqrt{15} = \sqrt{15} \text{ cm}^2$$

3. For an isosceles right angled triangle having each of equal sides a, find the perimeter.

Sol. In right angled $\triangle ABC$,
By Pythagoras theorem,
$$AC^2 = AB^2 + BC^2$$
$$= a^2 + a^2 = 2a^2$$
∴
$$AC = \sqrt{2} \text{ a units}$$

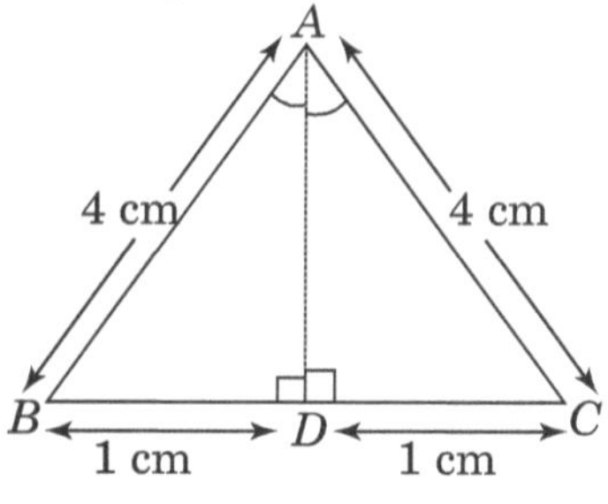

Hence, Perimeter of triangle ABC
$$= AB + BC + CA$$
$$= a + a + \sqrt{2} \text{ a}$$
$$= 2a + \sqrt{2} \text{ a}$$
$$= a\left(2 + \sqrt{2}\right) \text{ units}$$

Long Answer Type Questions

(4 Marks Each)

1. Sides of a triangle are in the ratio of 12 : 17 : 25 and its perimeter is 540 cm. Find its area.　　　**[NCERT]**

Sol. Given, sides of a triangle are in the ratio 12 : 17 : 25 and perimeter = 540 cm

Let the sides of a triangle be a = 12x, b = 17x and c = 25x.

According to the question,

Perimeter of triangle = a + b + c

$$540 = 12x + 17x + 25x$$

$$\Rightarrow \quad 540 = 54x$$

$$\Rightarrow \quad x = \frac{540}{54}$$

$$\therefore \quad x = 10$$

Then, $a = 12x = 12 \times 10 = 120$ cm;

$b = 17x = 17 \times 10 = 170$ cm

and $c = 25x = 25 \times 10 = 250$ cm

Now, semi-perimeter of a triangle

$$s = \frac{a+b+c}{2} = \frac{120+170+250}{2}$$

$$= \frac{540}{2} = 270 \text{ cm}$$

$$\therefore \quad \text{Area of triangle} = \sqrt{s(s-a)(s-b)(s-c)}$$

[by Heron's formula]

$$= \sqrt{270(270-120)(270-170)(270-250)}$$

$$= \sqrt{270 \times 150 \times 100 \times 20}$$

$$= \sqrt{\begin{array}{l}(2 \times 3 \times 3 \times 3 \times 5 \times 2 \times 3 \times 5 \times 5 \times 2 \\ \times 2 \times 5 \times 5 \times 2 \times 2 \times 5)\end{array}}$$

$$= \sqrt{2^6 \times 3^4 \times 5^6} = 2^3 \times 3^2 \times 5^3$$

$$= 2 \times 2 \times 2 \times 3 \times 3 \times 5 \times 5 \times 5 = 9000 \text{ cm}^2$$

Hence, the area of a triangle is 9000 cm².

2. From a point in the interior of an equilateral triangle, perpendiculars are drawn on three sides. The lengths of the perpendiculars are 14 cm, 10 cm and 6 cm. Find the area of the triangle

[NCERT Exemplar]

Sol. Let ΔABC be an equilateral triangle and OP, OQ and OR be the perpendiculars from an interior point O. Then join OA, OB and OC.

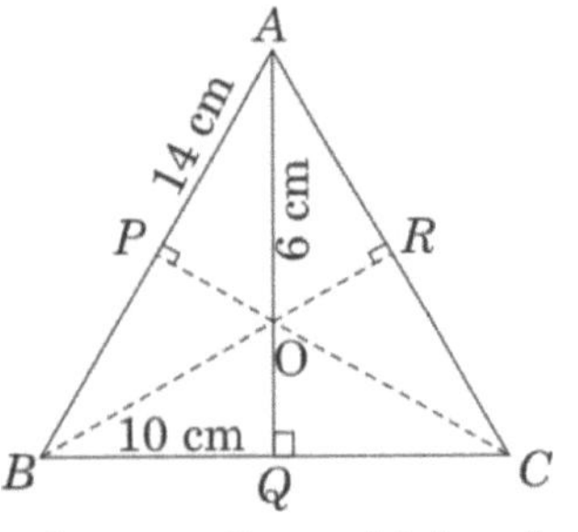

Let sides of an equilateral triangle be a cm.

Then, according to the question

$$\text{Area of } \Delta OAB = \frac{1}{2} \times AB \times OP$$

$$= \frac{1}{2} \times a \times 14$$

$$= 7a \text{ cm}^2 \qquad ...(i)$$

$$\text{Area of } \Delta OBC = \frac{1}{2} \times BC \times OQ$$

$$= \frac{1}{2} \times a \times 10$$

$$= 5a \text{ cm}^2 \qquad ...(ii)$$

and $\text{Area of } \Delta OAC = \dfrac{1}{2} \times AC \times OR$

$$= \frac{1}{2} \times a \times 6$$

$$= 3a \text{ cm}^2 \qquad ...(iii)$$

Now, area of an equilateral ΔABC

$$= \text{Area of } (\Delta OAB + \Delta OBC + \Delta OAC)$$

$$= (7a + 5a + 3a) \text{ cm}^2$$

$$= 15a \text{ cm}^2 \qquad ...(iv)$$

But area of equilateral triangle is $\dfrac{\sqrt{3}}{4}a^2$

$$\therefore \quad \frac{\sqrt{3}}{4}a^2 = 15a$$

$$\Rightarrow \quad a = \frac{15 \times 4}{\sqrt{3}} \times \frac{\sqrt{3}}{\sqrt{3}}$$

[by rationalising]

$$= \frac{60\sqrt{3}}{3}$$

$$= 20\sqrt{3} \text{ cm}$$

On putting a = $20\sqrt{3}$ in eqn. (iv), we get

$\therefore$ Area of an equilateral

$$\Delta ABC = 15 \times 20\sqrt{3}$$

$$= 300\sqrt{3} \text{ cm}^2$$

Hence, the required area of an equilateral ΔABC is $300\sqrt{3}$ cm².

[Topic 2] Heron's Formula

Points to be Remembered

- **Heron's formula:** If a, b and c are the sides of a triangle, then the area of a triangle is as follows:

$$\Delta = \sqrt{s(s-a)(s-b)(s-c)}$$

where $s = \dfrac{a+b+c}{2}$, is the semi-perimeter (that is half of the perimeter) of the triangle.

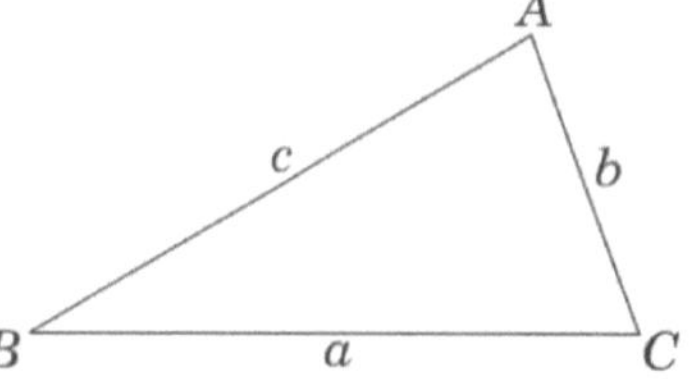

PREVIOUS YEARS'

EXAMINATION QUESTIONS
TOPIC 2

Multiple Choice Questions
(1 Mark Each)

1. The sides of a triangle are 35 cm, 54 cm and 61 cm, respectively. The length of its longest altitude is

   (a) $16\sqrt{5}$ cm 　　(b) $10\sqrt{5}$ cm

   (c) $24\sqrt{5}$ cm 　　(d) 28 cm

   [NCERT Exemp.]

Sol. (c) Semi perimeter (s) = $\dfrac{35+54+61}{2}$ = 75 cm

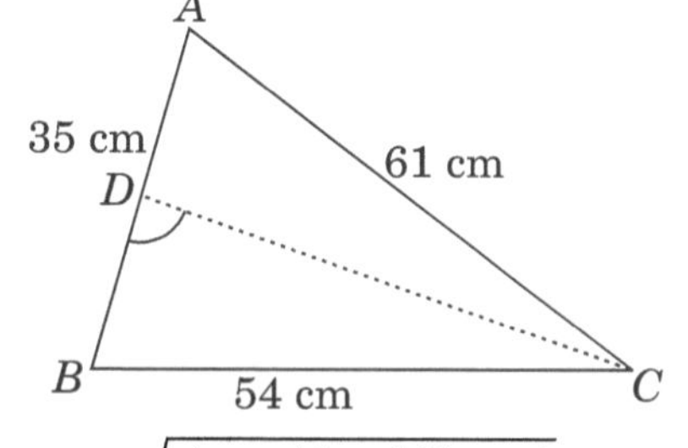

$$\therefore \text{ Area} = \sqrt{s(s-a)(s-b)(s-c)}$$
$$= \sqrt{75(75-35)(75-54)(75-61)}$$
$$= \sqrt{75 \times 40 \times 21 \times 14} = 420\sqrt{5} \text{ cm}^2$$

According to the question,

$$\Rightarrow \quad \frac{1}{2} \times 35 \times h = 420\sqrt{5}$$
$$\therefore \quad\quad h = 24\sqrt{5} \text{ cm}$$

2. The edges of a triangular board are 6 cm, 8 cm and 10 cm. The cost of painting it at the rate of 9 paise per cm^2 is

   (a) ₹ 2.00 　　(b) ₹ 2.16

   (c) ₹ 2.48 　　(d) ₹ 3.00

   [NCERT Exemp.]

Sol. (b) According to the question,

$$a = 6 \text{ cm}, b = 8 \text{ cm}$$
$$c = 10 \text{ cm}$$
$$s = \frac{a+b+c}{2}$$
$$= \frac{6+8+10}{2} = \frac{24}{2} = 12 \text{ cm}$$

$\therefore$　Area of triangle

$$= \sqrt{s(s-a)(s-b)(s-c)}$$
$$= \sqrt{12(12-6)(12-8)(12-10)}$$
$$= \sqrt{12 \times 6 \times 4 \times 2}$$
$$= 24 \text{ cm}^2$$

Hence, required cost of painting
$$= 0.09 \times 24 = ₹ 2.16$$

3. The area of an isosceles triangle having base 2 cm and the length of one of the equal sides 4 cm, is

   (a) $\sqrt{15}\text{cm}^2$ 　　(b) $\sqrt{\dfrac{15}{2}} \text{ cm}^2$

   (c) $2\sqrt{15} \text{ cm}^2$ 　　(d) $4\sqrt{15} \text{ cm}^2$

   [NCERT Exemp.]

Sol. (a) According to the question,

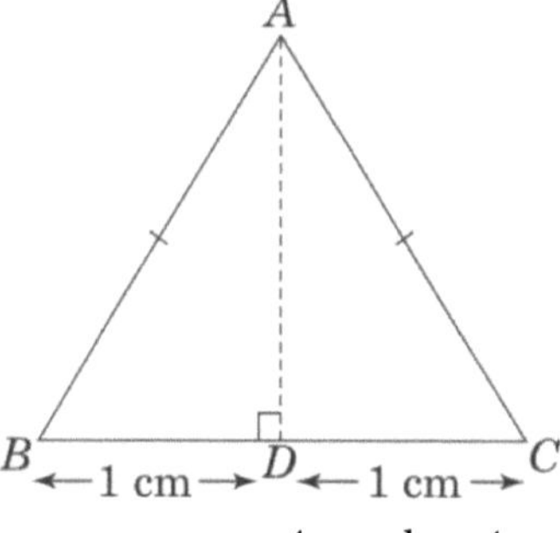

$$a = 4 \text{ cm}, b = 4 \text{ cm}, c = 2 \text{ cm}$$
$$s = \frac{a+b+c}{2} = \frac{4+4+2}{2} = 5$$

Hence, required area

$$= \sqrt{s(s-a)(s-b)(s-c)}$$
$$= \sqrt{5(5-4)(5-4)(5-2)}$$
$$= \sqrt{5\times1\times1\times3}$$
$$= \sqrt{15}\ \text{cm}^2$$

4. The sides of a triangle are 56 cm, 60 cm and 52 cm long. Then the area of the triangle is
   (a) 1322 cm² (b) 1311 cm²
   (c) 1344 cm² (d) 1392 cm²

   [NCERT Exemp.]

Ans. (c)

Sol. According to the question,

$$\text{Semi-perimeter (s)} = \frac{56+60+52}{2} = \frac{168}{2} = 84\ \text{cm}$$
$$\Rightarrow \text{Area} = \sqrt{84(84-56)(84-60)(84-52)}$$
$$= \sqrt{84\times28\times24\times32}$$
$$= 1344\ \text{cm}^2$$

Hence, the area of the triangle = 1344 cm²

5. Area of a triangle whose sides are 9 cm, 12 cm and 15 cm is:
   (a) 52 cm² (b) 54 cm²
   (c) 50 cm² (d) 56 cm²

   [NCERT Exemp.]

Ans. (b)

Sol. Semi-perimeter (s)

$$= \frac{9+12+15}{2}$$
$$= \frac{36}{2} = 18\ \text{cm}$$
$$\therefore \quad \text{Area} = \sqrt{18(18-9)(18-12)(18-15)}$$
$$= \sqrt{18\times9\times6\times3}$$
$$= 54\ \text{cm}^2$$

Hence, required area = 54 cm²

Very Short Answer Type Questions
(1 Mark Each)

1. The sides of $\triangle ABC$ are 8 cm, 7 cm and 5 cm respectively. Find out its semi-perimeter.

Sol. $\text{Semi-perimeter (s)} = \dfrac{a+b+c}{2} = \dfrac{8+7+5}{2} = 10\ \text{cm}$

2. Write the name of formula for finding the area of a triangle when sides are given.

   [Board term I, 2014]

Sol. Heron's formula.

$$\text{Area} = \sqrt{s(s-a)(s-b)(s-c)}$$

where s is the semi-perimeter.

3. Write Heron's formula.

Sol. $\text{Area }(\Delta) = \sqrt{s(s-a)(s-b)(s-c)}\ \text{unit}^2$

where, $s = \dfrac{a+b+c}{2}\ \text{unit}$

4. The edges of a triangular board are 6 cm, 8 cm and 10 cm. Calculate the cost of painting it at the rate of 9 paise per cm². [NCERT Exemplar]

Sol. Semi-perimeter

$$(s) = \frac{6+8+10}{2} = 12\ \text{cm}$$
$$\therefore \text{ Area of triangle} = \sqrt{12(12-6)(12-8)(12-10)}$$
$$= \sqrt{12\times6\times4\times2} = 24\ \text{cm}^2$$

Hence, cost of painting

$$= \frac{24\times9}{100} = ₹\ 2.16$$

5. The sides of a triangle are 7 cm, 24 cm and 25 cm. What will be its area?

Sol. Semi-perimeter

$$s = \frac{7+24+25}{2} = 28\ \text{cm}$$
$$\therefore \text{Area of triangle}$$
$$= \sqrt{28(28-7)(28-24)(28-25)}$$
$$= \sqrt{28\times21\times4\times3} = 84\ \text{cm}^2$$

6. Two sides of a triangle are 13 cm and 14 cm and its semi-perimeter is 18 cm, then what will be the third side of the triangle.

Sol. According to the question,

$$\text{Semi-perimeter (s)} = \frac{a+b+c}{2}$$
$$\Rightarrow \quad 18 = \frac{13+14+c}{2}$$
$$\Rightarrow \quad 36 = 27 + c$$
$$\therefore \quad c = 36 - 27 = 9\ \text{cm}$$

7. If a, b and c are the sides of a triangle, and s = semi-perimeter, then calculate the area of triangle.

Sol. Area of a triangle $(\Delta)\ \sqrt{s(s-a)(s-b)(s-c)}\ \text{unit}^2$

8. Using Heron's formula, find the area of an equilateral triangle with side 16 cm.

Sol. According to the question,

Sides of triangle are 16 cm, 16 cm and 16 cm

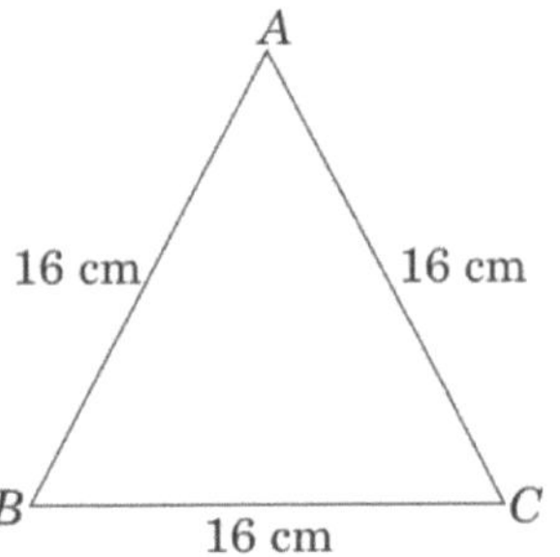

Semi-perimeter $(s) = \dfrac{a+b+c}{2} = \dfrac{16+16+16}{2}$

$$= \dfrac{48}{2} = 24 \text{ cm}$$

$\therefore$ Area of triangle

$$(\Delta) = \sqrt{s(s-a)(s-b)(s-c)}$$

$$= \sqrt{24(24-16)(24-16)(24-16)}$$

$$= \sqrt{24 \times 8 \times 8 \times 8}$$

$$= \sqrt{3 \times 8 \times 8 \times 8 \times 8}$$

$$= 64\sqrt{3} \text{ cm}^2$$

Short Answer Type Questions I
(2 Marks Each)

1. Find the area of a triangle whose two sides are 8 cm and 11 cm and the perimeter is 32 cm.

[Board Term I, 2015, Set-2 NCERT]

Sol.   According to the question,

$$a = 8 \text{ cm}, b = 11 \text{ cm},$$

$$= 2 \text{ Perimeter} = 32 \text{ cm}$$

$\therefore$

$$c = 32 - (8 + 11)$$

$$= 13 \text{ cm}$$

$\therefore$

$$s = \dfrac{32}{2} = 16 \text{ cm}$$

$\therefore$ Area of triangle (Δ)

$$= \sqrt{16(16-8)(16-11)(16-13)}$$

$$= \sqrt{16 \times 8 \times 5 \times 3}$$

$$= 8\sqrt{30} \text{ cm}^2$$

2. The sides of a triangle are in the ratio $3 : 5 : 7$ and its perimeter is 300 m. Find its area.

[Board Term I, 2016, Set-1 JQ22L5C] [NCERT]

Sol.   Let the sides of a triangle are

$$a = 3x, b = 5x \text{ and } c = 7x$$

then According to the question,

$$a + b + c = 300$$

$\Rightarrow \qquad 3x + 5x + 7x = 300$

$\Rightarrow \qquad 15x = 300$

$\therefore \qquad x = 20 \text{ cm}$

$\therefore \qquad a = 60, b = 100 \text{ and } c = 140$

Semi-perimeter $s = \dfrac{a+b+c}{2} = \dfrac{300}{2} = 150$

Area of triangle $= \sqrt{s(s-a)(s-b)(s-c)}$

$$= \sqrt{150(150-60)(150-100)(150-140)}$$

$$= \sqrt{150 \times 90 \times 50 \times 10}$$

$$= 1500\sqrt{3} \text{ m}^2$$

3. Find the area of an isosceles triangle whose equal sides are of length 15 cm each and third side is 12 cm.   [Board Term I, 2012, Set-43]

Sol.   According to the question,

$$a = 15 \text{ cm}, b = 15 \text{ cm}$$

and $c = 12 \text{ cm}$

$$s = \dfrac{a+b+c}{2} = \dfrac{15+15+12}{2} = 21 \text{ cm}$$

$\therefore$ Area $= \sqrt{s(s-a)(s-b)(s-c)}$

$$= \sqrt{21(21-15)(21-15)(21-12)}$$

$$= \sqrt{21 \times 6 \times 6 \times 9} = 18\sqrt{21} \text{ cm}^2$$

Hence, the area of an isosceles triangle

$$= 18\sqrt{21} \text{ cm}^2$$

4. Using Heron's formula, find the area of a triangle whose sides measure are 20 cm, 30 cm and 40 cm.   [Board Term I, 2012, Set-48, 44, 45, 49, 50]

Sol.   Let $a = 20 \text{ cm}, b = 30 \text{ cm}$

and $c = 40 \text{ cm}$

Then according to the question,

$$s = \dfrac{a+b+c}{2}$$

$$= \dfrac{20+30+40}{2} = 45 \text{ cm}$$

Now, using Heron's formula,

$\therefore$ Area of $\Delta = \sqrt{s(s-a)(s-b)(s-c)}$

$$= \sqrt{45(45-20)(45-30)(45-40)} \text{ cm}^2$$

$$= \sqrt{45 \times 25 \times 15 \times 5} \text{ cm}^2$$

$$= \sqrt{3 \times 3 \times 5 \times 5 \times 5 \times 3 \times 5 \times 5} \text{ cm}^2$$

$$= 3 \times 5 \times 5 \times \sqrt{15} \text{ cm}^2$$

$$= 75\sqrt{15} \text{ cm}^2 = 290.48 \text{ cm}^2$$

Hence, the area of a triangle $= 290.48 \text{ cm}^2$

5. Sides of a triangle are 70 cm, 80 cm and 90 cm. Find its area. (Use $= \sqrt{5} = 2.23$)

[Board Term I, 2014]

Sol.   Semi-perimeter $(s) = \dfrac{a+b+c}{2}$

$$= \dfrac{70+80+90}{2} = \dfrac{240}{2}$$

$$= 120 \text{ cm}$$

$\therefore$ Now, by using Heron's formula,

$\therefore \qquad$ Area $= \sqrt{s(s-a)(s-b)(s-c)}$

$$= \sqrt{120(120-70)(120-80)(120-90)}$$

$$= \sqrt{120 \times 50 \times 40 \times 30}$$

$$= \sqrt{40 \times 3 \times 5 \times 10 \times 4 \times 10 \times 3 \times 10}$$

$$= 40 \times 10 \times 3 \times \sqrt{5}$$

$$= 1200 \times 2.23 = 2676 \text{ cm}^2$$

Hence, the area of triangle $= 2676 \text{ cm}^2$

6. The longest side of a right angled triangle is 125 m and one of the remaining two sides is 100 m. Find its area using Heron's formula.

[Board Term I, 2015, Set-20 UI6YH]

Sol. According to the question,

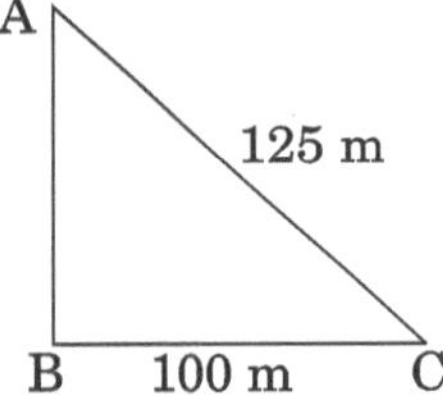

By Pythagoras theorem

$$AB = \sqrt{(125)^2 - (100)^2} = 75$$

$$\text{Semi-perimeter (s)} = 150 \left[s = \frac{100 + 75 + 125}{2} \right]$$

$$= \sqrt{150 \times (150 - 125)}$$

$$= (150 - 100) \times (150 - 75)$$

Hence, area of triangle

$$= \sqrt{150 \times 25 \times 50 \times 75}$$

$$= 3750 \text{ m}^2$$

7. If the sides of a triangle are 26 cm, 28 cm and 30 cm. Find the area of triangle.

[Board Term I, 2016, Set-QGL21F5]

Sol. According to the question,

$$a = 26 \text{ cm}, b = 28 \text{ cm},$$

and $\qquad c = 30 \text{ cm}$

$$\text{Semi-perimeter (s)} = \frac{a + b + c}{2}$$

$$= \frac{26 + 28 + 30}{2} = \frac{84}{2} = 42$$

Area of triangle (Δ)

$$= \sqrt{s(s - a)(s - b)(s - c)}$$

$$= \sqrt{42(42 - 26)(42 - 28)(42 - 30)}$$

$$= \sqrt{42 \times 16 \times 14 \times 12}$$

$$= 336 \text{ cm}^2$$

8. The base (in unequal side) of an isosceles triangle is 4 cm and its perimeter is 20 cm. Find its area.

[Board Term I, 2016, Set-BQS6IZK]

Sol. Let $\qquad AC = BC = x$

then, according to the question,

$$\text{Perimeter} = 20 \text{ m}$$

$$\Rightarrow \qquad x + x + 4 = 20$$

$$\Rightarrow \qquad 2x = 16$$

$$\therefore \qquad x = 8 \text{ cm}$$

$$\therefore \quad \text{Area of triangle} = \sqrt{s(s - a)(s - b)(s - c)}$$

$$= \sqrt{10(10 - 8)(10 - 8)(10 - 4)}$$

$$= \sqrt{10 \times 2 \times 2 \times 6}$$

$$= 4\sqrt{15} \text{ cm}^2$$

Hence, the area of an isosceles triangle

$$= 4\sqrt{15} \text{ cm}^2.$$

9. The semi-perimeter of a triangle is 132 cm and the product of the differences of semi-perimeter and its respective sides (in cm) is 13200. Find the area of triangle.

[Board Term I, 2016, Set-20 CNJE9]

Sol. According to the question,

$$s = 132 \text{ cm}$$

and $\quad (s - a)(s - b)(s - c) = 13200$

$$\therefore \quad \text{Area of triangle} = \sqrt{s(s - a)(s - b)(s - c)}$$

$$= \sqrt{132 \times 13200}$$

$$= 132 \times 10$$

$$= 1320 \text{ cm}^2$$

Hence, the area of triangle = 1320 cm^2

10. The sides of a triangular field are 51 m, 37 m and 20 m. Find the number of flower beds that can be prepared, if each bed is to occupy 9 m^2 of spaces.

Sol. Let the given sides of a triangular field be a

$$= 51 \text{ m}, b = 37 \text{ m}$$

and $\qquad c = 20 \text{ m}$

Then, according to the question,

Semi-perimeter (s)

$$= \frac{a + b + c}{2} = \frac{51 + 37 + 20}{2}$$

$$= \frac{108}{2} = 54 \text{ m}$$

$$\therefore \quad \text{Area of triangular field}$$

$$= \sqrt{s(s - a)(s - b)(s - c)}$$

[by Heron's formula]

$$= \sqrt{54(54 - 51)(54 - 37)(54 - 20)}$$

$$= \sqrt{54 \times 3 \times 17 \times 34}$$

$$= \sqrt{2 \times 3 \times 3 \times 3 \times 3 \times 17 \times 17 \times 2}$$

$$= (17 \times 2 \times 3 \times 3) \text{m}^2$$

Now, number of flower beds

$$= \frac{\text{Area of triangular field}}{\text{Space occupied by each flower bed}}$$

$$= \frac{2 \times 3 \times 3 \times 17}{9} = \frac{306}{9} = 34$$

Hence, 34 flower beds can be prepared.

Short Answer Type Questions II

(3 Marks Each)

1. The triangular side walls of a flyover have been used for advertisements. The sides of the walls are 13 m, 14 m and 15 m, The advertisements yield and earning of ₹ 2000 per m^2 per year. A company hired one of its walls for 6 months. How much rent did it pay?

[NCERT Exemplar]

Sol. Let the given sides of a triangular walls be a = 13 m, b = 14 m and c = 15 m.

Then, according to the question,

∴ Semi-perimeter of triangular side wall,

$$s = \frac{a+b+c}{2} = \frac{13+14+15}{2}$$

$$= \frac{42}{2} = 21 \text{ m}$$

∴ Area of triangular side wall

$$= \sqrt{s(s-a)(s-b)(s-c)}$$

[by Heron's formula]

$$= \sqrt{21(21-13)(21-14)(21-15)}$$

$$= \sqrt{21 \times 8 \times 7 \times 6}$$

$$= \sqrt{21 \times 4 \times 2 \times 7 \times 3 \times 2}$$

$$= \sqrt{(21)^2 \times (4)^2} = 21 \times 4 = 84 \text{ m}^2$$

Given, the advertisement yield earning per year for 1 m^2 = ₹ 2000

∴ Advertisement yield earning per year for

$$84 \text{ m}^2 = 2000 \times 84 = ₹ 168000$$

As the company hired one of its walls for 6 months therefore company paid the rent

$$= \frac{1}{2}(168000) = ₹ 84000$$

Hence, the company paid rent of ₹ 84000.

2. The sides of a triangular field are 51 m, 37 m and 20 m. Find the number of rose beds that can be prepared in the field if each rose bed occupies a space of 6 sq. m.

[Board Term I, 2012, Set-39]

Sol. Semi perimeter (s)

$$= \frac{51+37+20}{2} = \frac{108}{2} = 54 \text{ cm}$$

∴ Area $= \sqrt{s(s-a)(s-b)(s-c)}$

$$= \sqrt{54(54-51)(54-37)(54-20)}$$

$$= \sqrt{54 \times 3 \times 17 \times 34}$$

$$= 306 \text{ m}^2$$

∴ Number of rose beds

$$= \frac{\text{Total area of triangular field}}{\text{Area occupied by each rose bed}}$$

$$= \frac{306}{6} = 51$$

3. Find the area of an isosceles triangle whose one side is 10 cm greater than its equal side and its perimeter is 100 cm (Take $\sqrt{5}$ = 2.23).

[Board Term I, 2012, Set-51]

Sol. Let each equal side = x cm

and   third side = x + 10

According to the question,

Perimeter = 100

$\Rightarrow$ x + x + x + 10 = 100

$\Rightarrow$ 3x + 10 = 100

$\Rightarrow$ 3x = 90

∴   x = 30

Equal sides = 30 cm third side = 40 cm, s = 50

$$s = \frac{30+30+40}{2}$$

∴ Area $= \sqrt{50(50-30)(50-30)(50-40)}$

$$= \sqrt{5(20)(20)(10)} = 200\sqrt{5}$$

$$= 200 \times 2.23$$

$$= 446 \text{ cm}^2$$

Hence, the area of triangle = 446 cm^2

4. The sides of a triangle are x, x + 1, 2x − 1 and its area is $x\sqrt{10}$. What is the value of x?

[Board Term I, 2012, Set-19]

Sol. Semi-perimeter (s) $= \dfrac{x+x+1+2x-1}{2}$

$$= \frac{4x}{2} = 2x$$

According to the question,

∴ Area of triangle $= \sqrt{s(s-a)(s-b)(s-c)}$

$\Rightarrow$ $x\sqrt{10} = \sqrt{2x(2x-x)[2x-(x+1)][2x-(2x-1)]}$

$\Rightarrow$ $10x^2 = 2x(x)(x-1)(1)$

$\Rightarrow$ $10x^2 = 2x^3 - 2x^2$

$\Rightarrow$ $2x^3 - 2x^2 - 10x^2 = 0$

$\Rightarrow$ $2x^2(x-6) = 0$

∴   x = 0   or   x = 6

        x = 0   [Invalid]

we get,   x = 6 units

5. The sides of a triangle are 120 m, 170 m and 250 m. Find its area and height of the triangle if base is 250 m.

[Board Term I, 2012, Set-41]

Sol. According to the question,

$$a = 120 \text{ m}, b = 170 \text{ m}$$

and $$c = 250 \text{ m}$$

$$\text{Semi-perimeter (s)} = \frac{a+b+c}{2}$$

$$= \frac{120+170+250}{2} = \frac{540}{2} = 270$$

$$\text{Area of triangle} = \sqrt{s(s-a)(s-b)(s-c)}$$

$$= \sqrt{270\times(270-120)(270-170)(270-250)}$$

$$= \sqrt{270\times150\times100\times20}$$

$$= \sqrt{81000000}$$

$$= 9000 \text{ m}^2$$

Now, $$\text{Area} = \frac{1}{2} \times \text{base} \times \text{height}$$

$$\Rightarrow \quad 9000 = \frac{1}{2} \times 250 \times h$$

$$\Rightarrow \quad \frac{18000}{250} = h$$

$$h = 72 \text{ m}$$

Hence, the height of triangle = 72 m

6. An umbrella is made by stitching ten triangular pieces of cloth, each measuring 60 cm, 60 cm and 20 cm. Find the area of the cloth required for the umbrella. [Board Term I, 2014]

Sol. According to the question,

Area of one piece of cloth is made by sides 60 cm, 60 cm and 20 cm is,

$$\text{Semi-perimeter (s)} = \frac{60+60+20}{2}$$

$$= \frac{140}{2} = 70 \text{ cm}$$

$$\therefore \quad \text{Area} = \sqrt{70(70-60)(70-60)(70-20)}$$

$$= \sqrt{70\times10\times10\times50}$$

$$= \sqrt{7\times10\times10\times10\times5\times10}$$

$$= 10 \times 10 \times \sqrt{35}$$

$$= 100\sqrt{35} \text{ cm}^2$$

Area of cloth required = 10 × Area of cloth for one piece

Area of cloth required

$$= 10 \times 100 \times \sqrt{35}$$

$$= 1000\sqrt{35} \text{ cm}^2$$

7. The sides of a quadrilateral ABCD are AB = 13 cm, BC = 16 cm, CD = 20 cm and DA = 5 cm. If BD = 12 cm, find the area of the quadrilateral, using Heron's formula.

[Board Term I, 2015, Set-2]

Sol. According to the question,

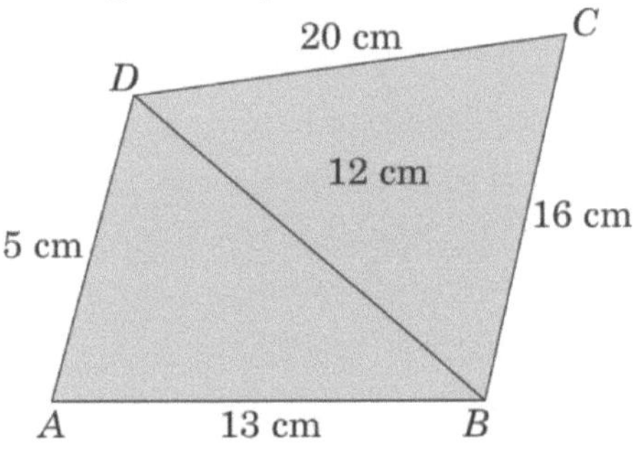

For ΔABD,

$$\text{Semi-perimeter (s)} = \frac{13+5+12}{2}$$

$$= \frac{30}{2} = 15 \text{ cm}$$

$$\therefore \quad \text{Area of } \Delta ABD = \sqrt{15(15-13)(15-12)(15-5)}$$

$$= \sqrt{15\times2\times3\times10} = 30 \text{ cm}^2$$

For ΔBCD,

$$\text{Semi-perimeter (s)} = \frac{16+20+12}{2}$$

$$= \frac{48}{2} = 24 \text{ cm}$$

and Area of ΔBCD

$$= \sqrt{24(24-16)(24-20)(24-12)}$$

$$= \sqrt{24\times4\times12\times8}$$

$$= 96 \text{ cm}^2$$

Hence, Area of quadrilateral = 30 + 96 = 126 cm²

8. Find the area of a triangular field of sides 18 m, 24 m and 30 m. Also find the altitude corresponding to the shortest side.

[Board Term I, 2016, Set-20 CNJE9]

Sol. According to the question,

$$\text{Semi-perimeter (s)} = \frac{18+24+30}{2} = 36$$

$$\therefore \quad \text{Area} = \sqrt{s(s-a)(s-b)(s-c)}$$

$$= \sqrt{36(36-18)(36-24)(36-30)}$$

$$= \sqrt{36\times18\times12\times6}$$

$$= 216 \text{ m}^2$$

$$\therefore \quad \text{Altitude (height)} = \frac{2\times\text{Area}}{\text{Base}}$$

$$= \frac{2\times216}{18} = 24 \text{ m}$$

Hence, the altitude corresponding to the shortest side = 24 m.

9. Find the percentage increase in the area of a triangle, if its each side is doubled.

Sol. Let a, b, c be the given sides, then

According to the question,

Semi-perimeter of original

$$s = \frac{a+b+c}{2}$$

$\therefore$ Area of original triangle

$$= \sqrt{s(s-a)(s-b)(s-c)}$$

Again, 2a, 2b, 2c be the new sides, then

According to the question,

Semi-perimeter of new triangle,

$$s = \frac{2a+2b+2c}{2}$$

$$= \frac{2(a+b+c)}{2} = 2s$$

$\therefore$ New area

$$= \sqrt{2a(2s-2a)(2s-2b)(2s-2c)}$$

$$= \sqrt{2\times s\times 2(s-a)\times 2(s-b)\times 2(s-c)}$$

$$= 4\sqrt{s(s-a)(s-b)(s-c)}$$

$$= 4 \times \text{original area}$$

$\therefore$ Increase in area

$$= 4 \times \text{original area} - \text{original area}$$

$$= 3 \times \text{original area}$$

% Increase in area

$$= \frac{3\times \text{original area}\times 100}{\text{original area}} = 300\%$$

Long Answer Type Questions
(4 Marks Each)

1. An umbrella is made by stitching 10 triangular pieces of cloth of two different colours, each piece measuring 20 cm, 50 cm and 50 cm. How much cloth of each colour is required for the umbrella?

[NCERT]

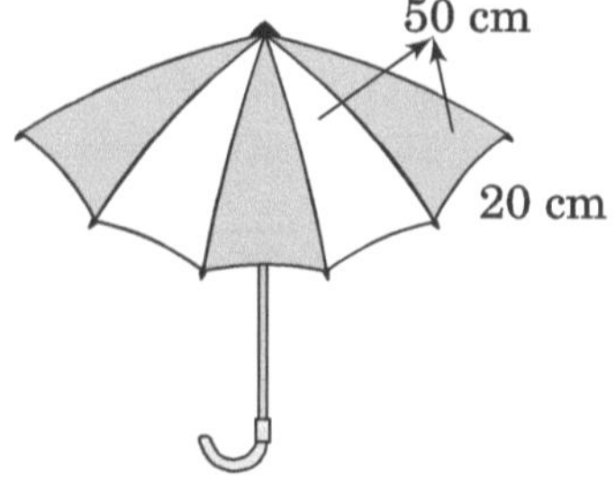

Sol. Let given sides of one triangular piece of cloth be a = 20 cm, b = 50 cm and c = 50 cm.

Then, according to the question,

Semi-perimeter of one triangular piece.

$$s = \frac{a+b+c}{2} = \frac{20+50+50}{2} = 60 \text{ cm}$$

$\therefore$ Area of one triangular piece of cloth

$$= \sqrt{s(s-a)(s-b)(s-c)}$$

[by Heron's formula]

$$= \sqrt{60(60-20)(60-50)(60-50)}$$

$$= \sqrt{60\times 40\times 10\times 10} = 200\sqrt{6} \text{ cm}^2$$

Now, there are 10 pieces of two colours, so number of pieces of one colour is 5, then area of cloth of each colour

$$= 5\times 200\sqrt{6} \text{ cm}^2 = 1000\sqrt{6} \text{ cm}^2$$

Hence, the area of cloth of each colour, required for the umbrella is $1000\sqrt{6}$ cm^2 .

2. A triangular park ABC has sides 120 m, 80 m and 50 m (See the fig.) A gardener Dhania has to put a fence all around it and also plant grass inside. How much area does she need to plant? Find the cost of fencing it with barbed wire at the rate of ₹ 20 per metre leaving a space 3 m wide for a gate on one side.

[NCERT Exmplar]

Sol. According to the question,

For finding area of the park, we have

$$2s = 50 \text{ m} + 80 \text{ m} + 120 \text{ m}$$

$$= 250 \text{ m}$$

$\therefore \qquad s = \frac{250}{2} = 125 \text{ m}$

Now $\qquad (s-a) = (125-120) = 5$ m

$\qquad\qquad (s-b) = (125-80) = 45$ m

and $\qquad (s-c) = (125-50) = 75$ m

Therefore, area of the park

$$= \sqrt{s(s-a)(s-b)(s-c)}$$

$$= \sqrt{125\times 5\times 45\times 75} \text{ m}^2$$

$$= 375\sqrt{15} \text{ m}^2$$

Also perimeter of the park

$$= AB + BC + CA = 250 \text{ m}$$

Therefore, length of the wire needed for fencing

= 250 m − 3 m (to be left for gate)

$$= 247 \text{ m}$$

Hence, the cost of fencing

$$= ₹ 20 \times 247 = ₹ 4940$$

3. The sides of a triangle are in the ratio of 13 : 14 : 15 and its perimeter is 84 cm. Find the area of the triangle.   [NCERT]

Sol. Let the sides of a triangle 13x, 14x and 15x, then
According to the question,
Perimeter of triangle = 84
$\Rightarrow$ 13x + 14x + 15x = 84
$\Rightarrow$ 42x = 84
$\therefore$ $x = \dfrac{84}{42} = 2$ cm
$\therefore$ Sides are   a = 13 × 2 = 26 cm
b = 14 × 2 = 28 cm
c = 15 × 2 = 30 cm

Semi-perimeter (s) $= \dfrac{26+28+30}{2}$
$= \dfrac{84}{2} = 42$ cm

By Heron's formula
$\therefore$ Area of triangle
$= \sqrt{s(s-a)(s-b)(s-c)}$
$= \sqrt{42(42-26)(42-28)(42-30)}$ cm^2
$= \sqrt{42 \times 16 \times 14 \times 12}$ cm^2
$= \sqrt{2 \times 3 \times 7 \times 16 \times 2 \times 7 \times 3 \times 4}$ cm^2
$= 2 \times 3 \times 7 \times 4 \times 2$ cm^2
$= 336$ cm^2

4. The triangular side walls of a flyover have been used for advertisements. The side of the walls are 122 m, 22 m and 120 m (see Fig.). The advertisements yield an earning of ₹ 5000 per m^2 per year. A company hired one of its walls for 3 months. How much rent did it pay?   [NCERT]

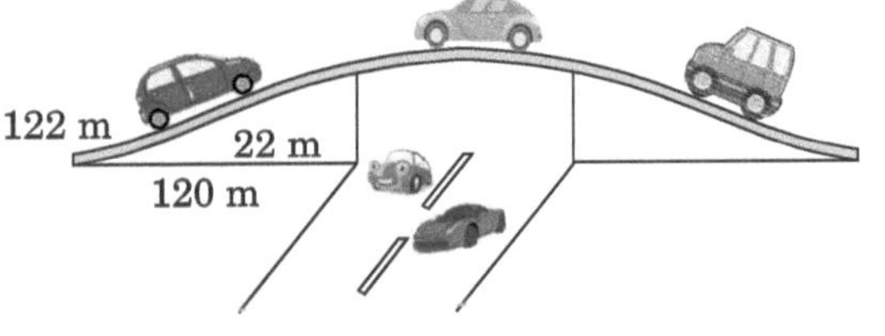

Sol. The lengths of the sides of the triangular walls are 122 m, 22 m and 120 m.
According to the question,
$\therefore$ Perimeter $s = \dfrac{122+22+120}{2}$
$= \dfrac{264}{2} = 132$ m

Area of one triangular wall
$= \sqrt{s(s-a)(s-b)(s-c)}$ [by Heron's formula]
$= \sqrt{132(132-122)(132-22)(132-120)}$
$= \sqrt{132 \times 10 \times 110 \times 12} = 1320$ m^2

Now, yearly rent = ₹ 5000 per m^2
$\therefore$ Monthly rent = ₹ $5000 \times \dfrac{1}{12}$ per m^2

Company hired one of its walls for 3 months.
Thus, rent paid by the company for 3 months
$= ₹\ 1320 \times \dfrac{5000}{12} \times 3 = ₹\ 1650000$

5. A floral design on a floor is made up of 16 tiles, which are triangular, the sides of the triangle being 28 cm, 9 cm and 35 cm, Find the cost of polishing the tiles at the rate of 50 paise per cm^2 [NCERT]

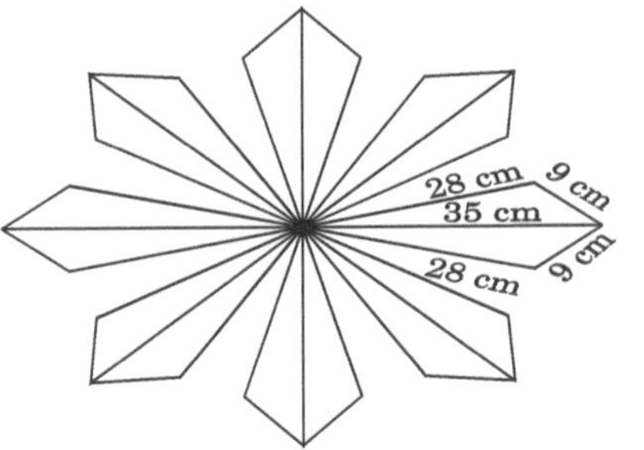

Sol. Given, length of the side of the triangular tile are 28 cm, 9 cm and 35 cm.
Let   a = 28 cm, b = 9 cm
and   c = 35 cm
Then, According to the question,
Semi-perimeter of one triangular tile.
$s = \dfrac{a+b+c}{2}$
$= \dfrac{28+9+35}{2} = \dfrac{72}{2} = 36$ cm

$\therefore$ Area of triangular tiles
$= \sqrt{s(s-a)(s-b)(s-c)}$ [by Heron's formula]
$= \sqrt{36(36-28)(36-9)(36-35)}$
$= \sqrt{36 \times 8 \times 27 \times 1}$
$= \sqrt{36 \times 2 \times 4 \times 9 \times 3} = 36\sqrt{6}$ cm^2

Now, are of 16 triangular tiles
$= 16 \times 36\sqrt{6}$ cm^2
$= 576\sqrt{6}$
$= 576 \times 2.45$
$= 1411.2$ cm^2

Hence, cost of polishing the tiles at the rate of 50 paise per m^2, *i.e.*, ₹ $\dfrac{1}{2}$ per cm^2
$= 1411.2 \times \dfrac{1}{2} = ₹\ 705.60$

6. Two identical circles with same inside design as shown in the figure are to be made at the entrance. The identical triangular leaves are to be painted red and the remaining are to be painted green. Find the total area to be painted red.

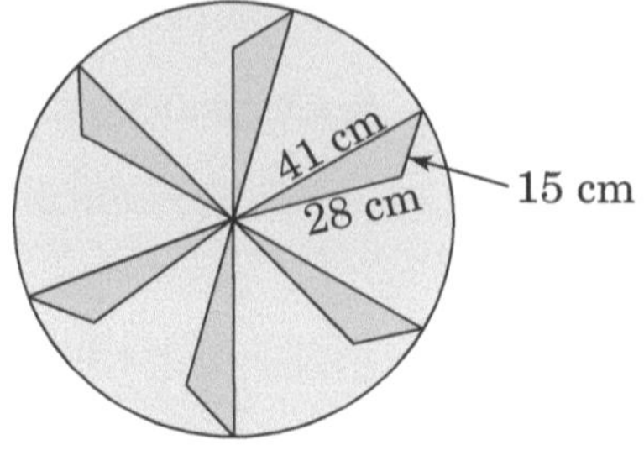

Sol. For one identical triangular leaf, let
$a = 28$ cm, $b = 15$ cm and $c = 41$ cm
According to the question,

$$\text{Semi-perimeter (s)} = \frac{a+b+c}{2} = \frac{28+15+41}{2}$$
$$= \frac{84}{2} = 42 \text{ cm}$$

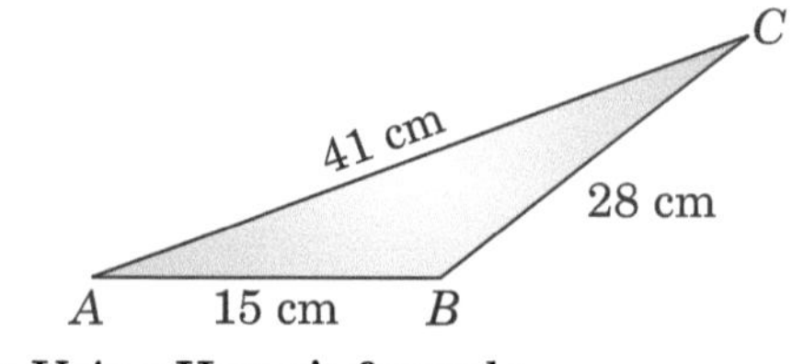

By Using Heron's formula,

$\therefore$ Area of one triangular leaf

$$= \sqrt{s(s-a)(s-b)(s-c)}$$
$$= \sqrt{42(42-28)(42-15)(42-41)}$$
$$= \sqrt{42\times14\times27\times1}$$
$$= \sqrt{3\times14\times14\times3\times9}$$
$$= 9 \times 14 = 126 \text{ cm}^2$$

There are 6 leaves in a circle.
So, total number of leaves in 2 circles
$$= 2 \times 6 = 12$$
$\therefore$ Area of 12 leaves $= (12 \times 126)$ cm$^2 = 1512$ cm^2
Hence, total area to be painted red $= 1512$ cm^2

[Topic 3] Application of Heron's Formula in Finding Area of Quadrilaterals

Points to be Remembered

- To find the area of a quadrilateral by Heron's formula we need to divide the quadrilateral into two triangles.
  Area of quadrilateral PQRS = Area of ΔPRS + Area of ΔPQR

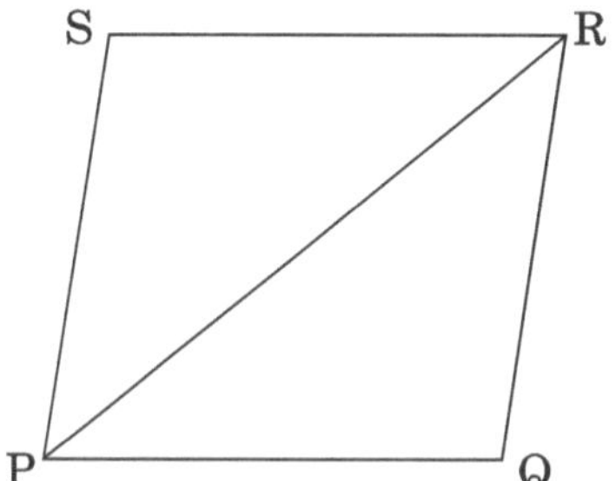

PREVIOUS YEARS'

EXAMINATION QUESTIONS

TOPIC 3

Multiple Choice Questions
(1 Mark Each)

1. If the perimeter of an equilateral triangle is 60 cm, then what is its area?
   (a) $200\sqrt{2}$ cm^2 (b) $100\sqrt{2}$ cm^2
   (c) $100\sqrt{3}$ cm^2 (d) $200\sqrt{3}$ cm^2

Sol. (c) According to the question, perimeter of equilateral triangle = 3a

$$\Rightarrow \qquad 3a = 60$$
$$\therefore \qquad a = \frac{60}{3} = 20 \text{ cm}$$
$$\therefore \quad \text{Required area} = \frac{\sqrt{3}}{4}\times a^2$$
$$= \frac{\sqrt{3}}{4}\times 20\times 20 = 100\sqrt{3} \text{ cm}^2$$

2. The area of a triangle is 150 cm^2 and its sides are in the ratio 3 : 4 : 5. What is its perimeter?
   (a) 10 cm   (b) 30 cm
   (c) 45 cm   (d) 60 cm

Sol. (d) Let the sides are 3x, 4x and 5x, then According to the question,

$$\text{Semi-perimeter (s)} = \frac{3x+4x+5x}{2} = \frac{12x}{2} = 6x$$

$$\therefore \text{Area} = \sqrt{6x(6x-3x)(6x-4x)(6x-5x)}$$

$$\Rightarrow \qquad 150 = \sqrt{6x \times 3x \times 2x \times x}$$
$$\Rightarrow \qquad 6x^2 = 150$$
$$\Rightarrow \qquad x^2 = \frac{150}{6} = 25$$
$$\therefore \qquad x = 5 \text{ cm}$$

Hence, perimeter $= 3x + 4x + 5x$

$$= 12 \times 5 = 60 \text{ cm}$$

3. Length of one of the equal sides of an isosceles triangle is 4 cm. If its base is 2 cm then what is its area?

(a) $\sqrt{15}$ cm^2 (b) $\sqrt{13}$ cm^2

(c) $\sqrt{12}$ cm^2 (d) $\sqrt{14}$ cm^2

Sol. (a) Let sides of a triangles are

$$a = 2 \text{ cm}, b = 4 \text{ cm}$$

and $\qquad\qquad c = 4$ cm

$$\text{Semi-perimeter (s)} = \frac{2+4+4}{2} = \frac{10}{2} = 5 \text{ cm}$$

Hence, required area

$$= \sqrt{5(5-2)(5-4)(5-4)}$$

$$= \sqrt{5 \times 3 \times 1 \times 1} = \sqrt{15} \text{ cm}^2$$

4. What is the length of each side of an equilateral triangle having an area of $4\sqrt{3}$ cm^2?

(a) 4 cm   (b) 5 cm

(c) 5 cm   (d) 6 cm

Sol. (a) According to the question,

$$\text{Area of equilateral triangle} = \frac{\sqrt{3}}{4}a^2$$

$$\Rightarrow \qquad 4\sqrt{3} = \frac{\sqrt{3}}{4}a^2$$
$$\Rightarrow \qquad a^2 = 16$$
$$\therefore \qquad a = 4 \text{ cm}$$

5. The sides of a triangle are in the ratio of 3 : 4 : 5. If its perimeter is 36 cm, then what is its area?

(a) 32 cm^2 (b) 54 cm^2

(c) 67 cm^2 (d) 72 cm^2

Sol. (b) According to the question,

Perimeter = 36

$$\therefore \qquad a = \frac{36}{12} \times 3 = 9 \text{ cm}$$

$$b = \frac{36}{12} \times 4 = 12 \text{ cm}$$

and $\qquad\qquad c = \dfrac{36}{12} \times 5 = 15$ cm

$$s = \frac{36}{2} = 18 \text{ cm}$$

$$\therefore \qquad \text{Area} = \sqrt{18(18-15)(18-12)(18-9)}$$

$$= \sqrt{18 \times 3 \times 6 \times 9} = 54 \text{ cm}^2$$

6. The sides of a triangle are 3 cm, 5 cm and 6 cm. What is its area?

(a) $2\sqrt{3}$ cm^2 (b) $2\sqrt{14}$ cm^2

(c) $5\sqrt{12}$ cm^2 (d) $2\sqrt{5}$ cm^2

Sol. (b) Semi-perimeter(s) $= \dfrac{3+5+6}{2} = \dfrac{14}{2} = 7$ cm

$$\therefore \qquad \text{Area} = \sqrt{7(7-3)(7-5)(7-6)}$$

$$= \sqrt{7 \times 4 \times 2 \times 1}$$

$$= 2\sqrt{14} \text{ cm}^2$$

7. An umbrella is made by stitching 8 triangular pieces of cloth of two different colours. Each piece measuring 20 cm, 50 cm and 50 cm. How much cloth of each colour is required?

(a) $800\sqrt{6}$ cm^2 (b) $1000\sqrt{6}$ cm^2

(c) $1600\sqrt{6}$ cm^2 (d) $500\sqrt{6}$ cm^2

Sol. (a) According to the question,

$$\text{Semi-perimeter (s)} = \frac{20+50+50}{2}$$

$$= \frac{120}{2} = 60 \text{ cm}$$

$$\therefore \quad \text{Area} = \sqrt{60(60-20)(60-50)(60-50)}$$

$$= \sqrt{60 \times 40 \times 10 \times 10}$$

$$= 200\sqrt{6} \text{ cm}^2$$

Hence, required cloth $= 4 \times 200\sqrt{6} = 800\sqrt{6}$ cm^2

Very Short Answer Type Questions
(1 Mark Each)

1. The area of a rhombus is 96 cm^2. If one of its diagonals is 16 cm, then find out the length of its sides.

Sol. According to the question,

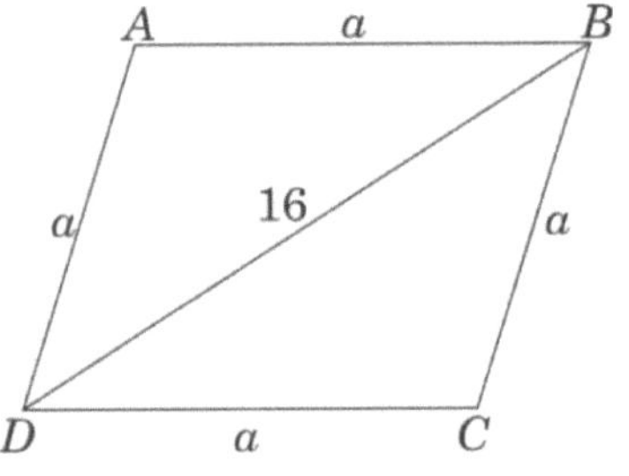

In $\triangle BCD$, semi-perimeter

$$s = \frac{16 + a + a}{2} = (a + 8)$$

$\therefore$ Area of $\triangle BCD$

$$= \sqrt{(a+8)(a+8-16)(a+8-a)(a+8-a)}$$

$$= \sqrt{(a+8)(a-8)(8)(8)}$$

$$= 8\sqrt{a^2 - 64} \text{ unit}^2$$

$\therefore$ Area of rhombus

$$= 2 \times \text{Area of } \triangle BCD$$

$\Rightarrow \qquad 96 = 2 \times 8\sqrt{a^2 - 64}$

$\Rightarrow \qquad 6 = \sqrt{a^2 - 64}$

$\Rightarrow \qquad 36 = a^2 - 64$

$\Rightarrow \qquad a^2 = 64 + 36 = 100$

$\therefore \qquad a = 10 \text{ cm}$

2. What will be the area of a triangle whose sides are 13 cm, 14 cm and 15 cm?

Sol. According to the question,

$$\text{Semi-perimeter (s)} = \frac{a+b+c}{2}$$

$$= \frac{13+14+15}{2} = 21 \text{ cm}$$

$\therefore \quad \text{Area} = \sqrt{s(s-a)(s-b)(s-c)}$

$$= \sqrt{21(21-13)(21-14)(21-15)}$$

$$= \sqrt{21 \times 8 \times 7 \times 6} = 21 \times 4 = 84 \text{ cm}^2$$

Short Answer Type Questions I

(2 Marks Each)

1. Find the area of parallelogram given in the figure. Also, find the length of the altitude from vertex A on the side DC. [NCERT Exmplar]

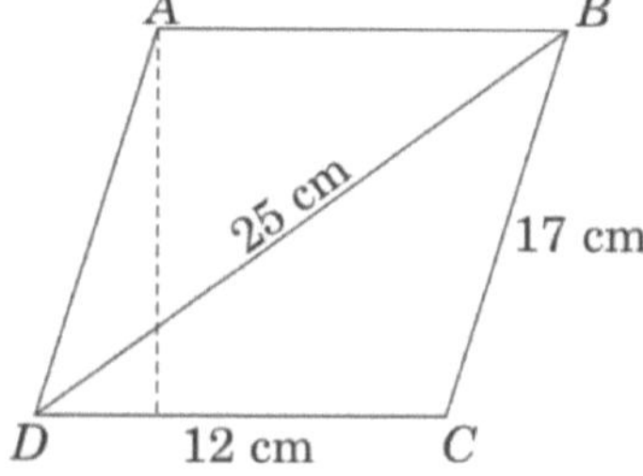

Sol. Area of parallelogram

$$\text{ABCD} = 2(\text{Area of } \triangle BCD) \qquad ...(i)$$

Now, let the sides of a $\triangle BCD$ be a = 12 cm, b = 17 cm and c = 25 cm.

Then, according to the question, semi-perimeter of $\triangle BCD$,

$$s = \frac{a+b+c}{2} = \frac{12+17+25}{2} = \frac{54}{2} = 27 \text{ cm}$$

$\therefore$ Area of $\triangle BCD$

$$= \sqrt{s(s-a)(s-b)(s-c)}$$

[by Heron's formula]

$$= \sqrt{27(27-12)(27-17)(27-25)}$$

$$= \sqrt{27 \times 15 \times 10 \times 2}$$

$$= \sqrt{3 \times 3 \times 3 \times 3 \times 5 \times 5 \times 2 \times 2}$$

$$= 3 \times 3 \times 5 \times 2 = 90 \text{ cm}^2$$

From eqn. (i),

Area of parallelogram ABCD

$$= 2 \times \text{Area of } \triangle BCD$$

$$= 2 \times 90 = 180 \text{ cm}^2 \qquad ...(ii)$$

Let altitude of the parallelogram be h.

Also, area of parallelogram ABCD

$$= \text{Base} \times \text{Altitude}$$

$\Rightarrow \qquad 180 = DC \times h$

$\Rightarrow \qquad 180 = 12 \times h$

$\therefore \qquad h = \frac{180}{12} = 15 \text{ cm}$

Hence, the area of a parallelogram is 180 cm² and the length of altitude is 15 cm.

2. A rectangular plot is given for constructing a house having a measurement of 40 m long and 15 m in the front. According to the laws, a minimum of 3 m wide space should be left in the front and back each and 2 m wide space on each of other sides. Find the largest area, where house can be constructed. [NCERT Exmplar]

Sol. Let ABCD be a rectangular plot having a measurement of 40 m long and 15 m front. then

According to the question,

$\therefore$ Length of inner rectangle,

$$EF = 40 - 3 - 3 = 34 \text{ m}$$

and breadth of inner rectangle,

$$FG = 15 - 2 - 2 = 11 \text{ m}$$

Another rectangle EFGH will be formed inside the rectangle ABCD.

$\therefore$ Area of inner rectangle,

$$EFGH = EF \times FG = 34 \times 11 = 374 \text{ m}^2$$

[$\because$ area of a rectangle = length × breadth]

Hence, the largest area, where the house can be constructed, is 374 m².

3. In the given figure, ABCD is a rectangle, where AB = 8 cm, BC = 6 cm and the diagonals bisect each other at O. Find the area of the shaded region by Heron's formula.

[Board Term I, 2012, Set-66]

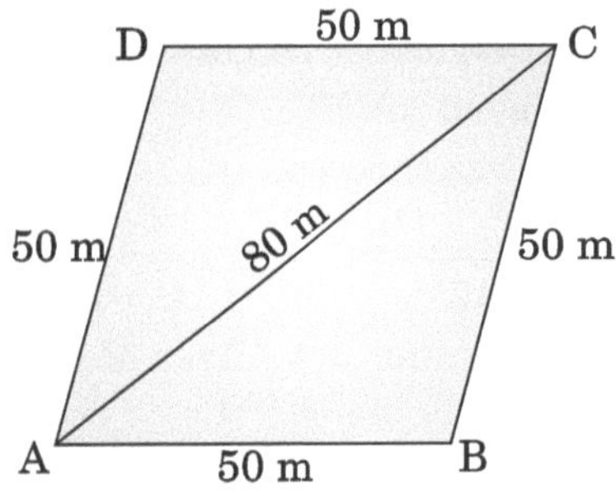

Sol. According to the question,

Diagonals bisect each other at O

Draw, LOM$\perp$ AB and CD

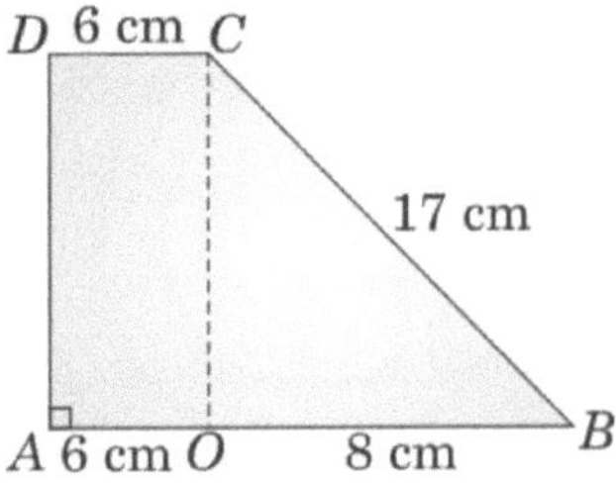

$$OL = OM = 3 \text{ cm}$$

In $\triangle OMB$, $\quad OM = 3$ cm

and $\quad MB = 4$ cm

By Pythagoras theorem

$$OB^2 = OM^2 + MB^2$$

$\Rightarrow \quad OB = 5$ cm

and $\quad OB = OA = 5$ cm

In $\triangle AOB$, semi-perimeter

$$(s) = \frac{8+5+5}{2} = 9 \text{ cm}$$

$\therefore \quad \text{Area} = \sqrt{s(s-a)(s-b)(s-c)}$

$$= \sqrt{9(9-8)(9-5)(9-5)}$$

$$= 12 \text{ cm}^2$$

Hence, area of shaded region = 12 cm^2.

4. Find the area of a rhombus whose perimeter is 200 m and one of the diagonal is 80 m.

[Board Term I, 2012, Set-36]

Sol. According to the question,

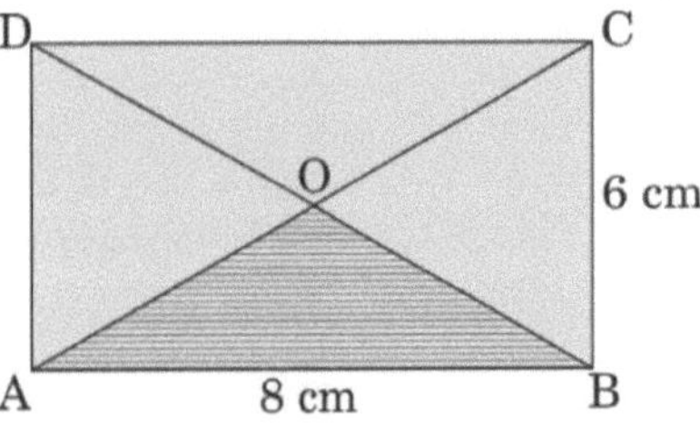

Perimeter of rhombus = 4 × sides = 200

or, $\quad$ side = 50 m

For $\triangle ABC$, semi-perimeter

$$(s) = \frac{50+50+80}{2} = 90 \text{ m}$$

$\therefore$ Area of $\triangle ABC = \sqrt{s(s-a)(s-b)(s-c)}$

$$= \sqrt{90\times(90-50)(90-50)(90-80)}$$

$$= \sqrt{90\times40\times40\times10}$$

$$= 1200 \text{ m}^2 \qquad ...(i)$$

Hence, Area of rhombus = 2 × Area of $\triangle ABC$

$$= 2 \times 1200 = 2400 \text{ m}^2$$

5. Compute the area of the trapezium shown in the figure:

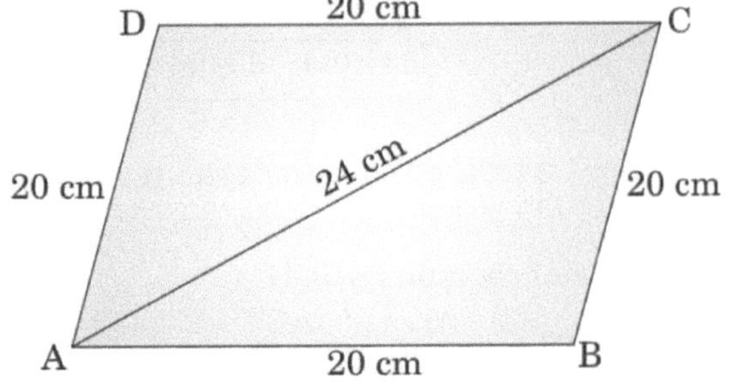

Sol. According to the given figure,

Area of trapezium ABCD

$\quad$ = Area of rectangle AOCD + Area of $\triangle OBC$

In $\triangle OBC$, by Pythagoras theorem

$$BC^2 = OC^2 + OB^2$$

or $\quad 17^2 = OC^2 + 8^2$

or $\quad OC^2 = 289 - 64 = 225$

$\therefore \quad OC = 15$ cm

So, Area of rectangle AOCD = 6 × 15 = 90 cm^2

and $\,$ Area of $\triangle OBC = \dfrac{1}{2} \times 8 \times 15 = 60$ cm^2

Hence, Area of Trapezium ABCD

$$= 90 + 60 = 150 \text{ cm}^2$$

6. Find the area of a rhombus whose side is 20 cm and one of its diagonal is 24 cm.

Sol. According to the question,

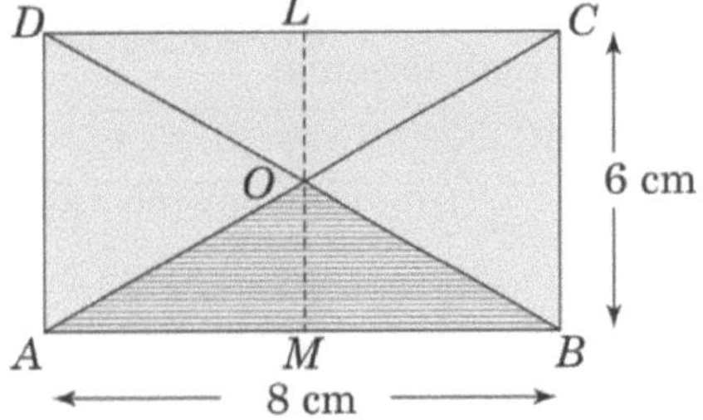

Semi-perimeter of triangle ABC

$$s = \frac{a+b+c}{2} = \frac{20+20+24}{2} = \frac{64}{2} = 32 \text{ cm}$$

$$\therefore \text{Area of } \triangle ABC = \sqrt{s(s-a)(s-b)(s-c)}$$
$$= \sqrt{32(32-24)(32-20)(32-20)}$$
$$= \sqrt{32\times8\times12\times12}$$
$$= \sqrt{8\times4\times8\times12\times12}$$
$$= 8 \times 2 \times 12 = 192 \text{ cm}^2$$

Hence, area of rhombus ABCD
$$= 2 \times \text{Area of } \triangle ABC$$
$$= 2 \times 192 = 384 \text{ cm}^2.$$

Short Answer Type Questions II

(3 Marks Each)

1. A rhombus shaped field has green grass for 18 cows to graze. If each side of the rhombus is 30 m and its longer diagonal is 48 m, then how much area of grass field will each cow be getting? [NCERT]

Sol. According to the question, ABCD is a rhombus shaped field whose each side is 30 m and longer diagonal AC is 48 m.

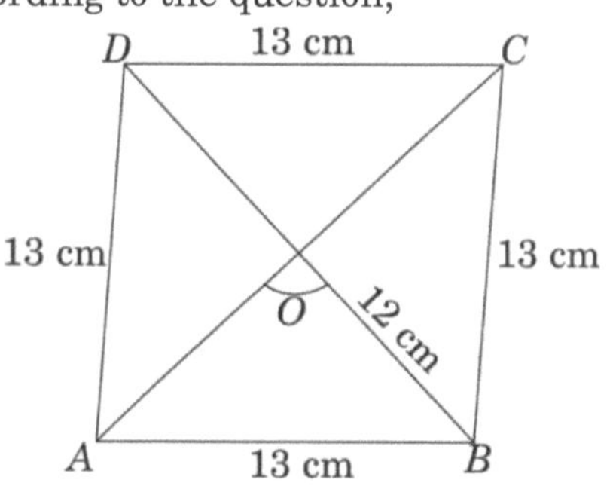

Clearly, the diagonal AC divides the rhombus into two triangles, $\triangle ABC$ and $\triangle ADC$ which are congruent.

$\therefore$ Area of $\triangle ABC$ = Area of $\triangle ADC$

Also, $\triangle ABC$ and $\triangle ADC$ have equal perimeters.

Now, semi-perimeter of $\triangle ABC$
$$= \frac{a+b+c}{2}$$
$$= \frac{30+30+48}{2} = \frac{108}{2} = 54 \text{ m}$$

$\therefore$ Area of $\triangle ABCs = \sqrt{s(s-a)(s-b)(s-c)}$

[by Heron's formula]
$$= \sqrt{54\times(54-30)(54-30)(54-48)}$$
$$= \sqrt{54\times24\times24\times6}$$
$$= \sqrt{18\times3\times24\times24\times6}$$
$$= 18 \times 24 = 432 \text{ m}^2$$

$\therefore$ Area of rhombus ABCD
$$= 2 \times \text{Area of } \triangle ABC = 2 \times 432 = 864 \text{ m}^2$$

Now, area of grass field each cow will get
$$= \frac{864}{18} = 48 \text{ m}^2$$

Hence, each cow will get grass field of 48 m² area.

2. A rhombus field has green grass for 20 cows to graze. If each side of the rhombus is 52 m and longer diagonal is 96 m, how much area of the grass field will each cow be getting?

[Board Term I, 2012, Set-47]

Sol. According to the question,

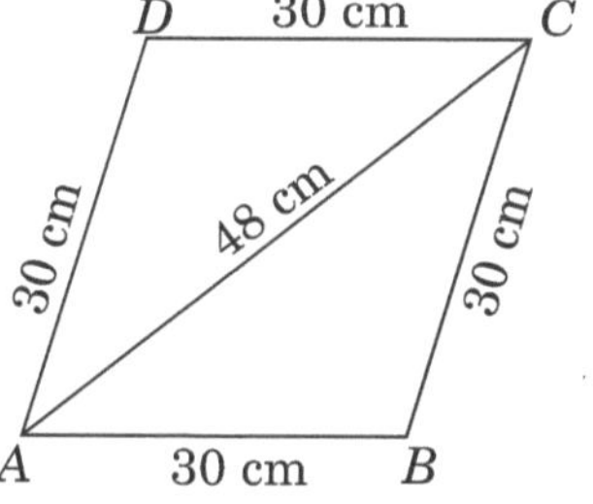

For $\triangle ABC$, semi-perimeter
$$(s) = \frac{96+52+52}{2} = \frac{200}{2} = 100 \text{ m}$$

By using heron's formula,

Area of $\triangle ABC = \sqrt{s(s-a)(s-b)(s-c)}$
$$= \sqrt{100(100-96)(100-52)(100-52)}$$
$$= \sqrt{100\times4\times48\times48}$$
$$= 10 \times 2 \times 48 = 960 \text{ m}^2$$

Area of rhombus = $960 \times 2 = 1920 \text{ m}^2$

Thus, area to be grazed by 20 cows = 1920 m²

Hence, area to be grazed by one cow
$$= \frac{1920}{20} = 96 \text{ m}^2$$

3. The perimeter of a rhombus is 52 cm. One of the diagonals is 24 cm. Find the area of the rhombus.

[Board Term I, 2012, Set-43]

Sol. According to the question,

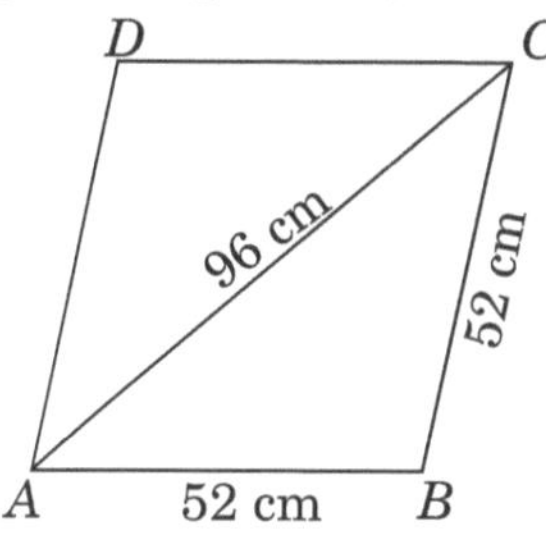

Perimeter = 52 cm
$$\text{Side} = \frac{52}{4} = 13 \text{ cm}$$

Diagonal = 24 cm

In right angled $\triangle AOB$,

By Pythagoras theorem,
$$OB = OD = 12 \text{ cm}$$
$$OA = \sqrt{13^2 - 12^2} = \sqrt{169-144} = \sqrt{25} = 5$$

$\therefore$ Area of rhombus = $4 \times$ Area of $\triangle AOB$
$$= 4 \times \frac{1}{2} \times 5 \times 12 = 120 \text{ cm}^2$$

4. A triangle and a parallelogram have the same base and the same area. If the sides of the triangle are 26 cm, 28 cm and 30 cm and the parallelogram stands on the base 28 cm. Find the height of the parallelogram.

[Board Term I, 2012, Set-46, 54, 37]

Sol.

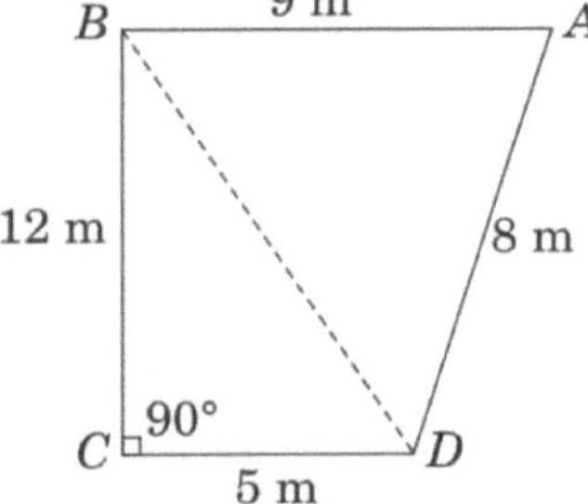

For triangle,

Semi-perimeter (s) $= \dfrac{26+28+30}{2} = \dfrac{84}{2} = 42$

$\therefore$ Area of $\triangle ABC = \sqrt{s(s-a)(s-b)(s-c)}$

$\qquad = \sqrt{42 \times 16 \times 14 \times 12}$

$\qquad = \sqrt{14 \times 3 \times 16 \times 14 \times 4 \times 3}$

$\qquad = 14 \times 4 \times 2 \times 3 = 336 \ cm^2$

According to the question,

Area of parallelogram = Area of triangle (given)

$\Rightarrow \qquad b \times h = 336$

$\Rightarrow \qquad 28 \times h = 336$

$\therefore \qquad h = 12 \ cm$

Hence, the height of the parallelogram = 12 cm

5. The adjacent sides of a parallelogram are 34 cm, 20 cm and a diagonal is 42 cm. Find the area of the parallelogram.

[Board Term I, 2012, Set-45]

Sol. According to the question,

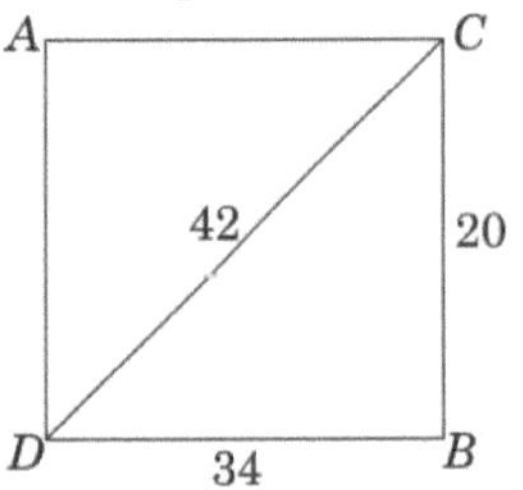

Semi-perimeter of $\triangle ABC$,

$\qquad s = \dfrac{34+20+42}{2} = \dfrac{96}{2} = 48 \ cm$

$\therefore$ Area of $\triangle DBC = \sqrt{s(s-a)(s-b)(s-c)}$

$\qquad = \sqrt{48 \times 14 \times 28 \times 6}$

$\qquad = 6 \times 8 \times 7 = 336 \ cm^2$

Hence, Area of parallelogram

$\qquad = 2 \times$ Area of $\triangle DBC$

$\qquad = 2 \times 336 = 672 \ cm^2$

Long Answer Type Questions
(4 Marks Each)

1. A park in the shape of a quadrilateral ABCD has $\angle C = 90°$, AB = 9 m, BC = 12 m, CD = 5 m and AD = 8 m. How much area does it occupy?

[NCERT]

Sol. Given quadrilateral ABCD in which AB = 9 m, BC = 12 m. CD = 5 m, AD = 8 m and $\angle C = 90°$. Now, join the diagonal BD which divides quadrilateral ABCD into two triangles.

In $\triangle BCD$, we have

$\qquad (BD)^2 = (BC)^2 + (CD)^2 = (12)^2 + (5)^2$

[by Pythagoras theorem]

$\Rightarrow \qquad (BD)^2 = 144 + 25 = 169$

$\Rightarrow \qquad BD = \sqrt{169} = 13 \ m$

For $\triangle BCD$, let a = 12 m, b = 5 m and c = 13 m. Then, According to the question, semi-perimeter of $\triangle BCD$,

$\qquad s = \dfrac{a+b+c}{2}$

$\qquad = \dfrac{12+5+13}{2} = \dfrac{30}{2} = 15 \ m$

$\therefore$ Area of $\triangle BCD = \sqrt{s(s-a)(s-b)(s-c)}$

[by Heron's formula]

$\qquad = \sqrt{15(15-12)(15-5)(15-13)}$

$\qquad = \sqrt{15 \times 3 \times 10 \times 2} = \sqrt{900}$

$\qquad = 30 m^2$

For $\triangle ABD$, let d = 9 m, e = 8 m and f = 13 m. Then, semi-perimeter of $\triangle ABD$.

$\qquad s = \dfrac{d+e+f}{2}$

$\qquad = \dfrac{9+8+13}{2} = \dfrac{30}{2} = 15 \ m$

$\therefore$ Area of $\triangle ABD = \sqrt{s(s-d)(s-e)(s-f)}$

[by Heron's formula]

$\qquad = \sqrt{15(15-9)(15-8)(15-13)}$

$\qquad = \sqrt{15 \times 6 \times 7 \times 2}$

$\qquad = \sqrt{3 \times 5 \times 3 \times 2 \times 7 \times 2}$

$\qquad = 2 \times 3 \times \sqrt{35} = 6\sqrt{35} \ m^2$

Now, area of quadrilateral ABCD

= Area of $\triangle$BCD + Area of $\triangle$ABD

= 30 + $6\sqrt{35}$ = 30 + 6 × 5.92

= 30 + 35.52 = 65.52 m² (approx).

Hence, area of the park in the shape of quadrilateral ABCD is 65.5 m².

2. How much paper of each shade is needed to make a kite given in the figure, in which ABCD is square with diagonal 44 cm?

[NCERT Exemplar]

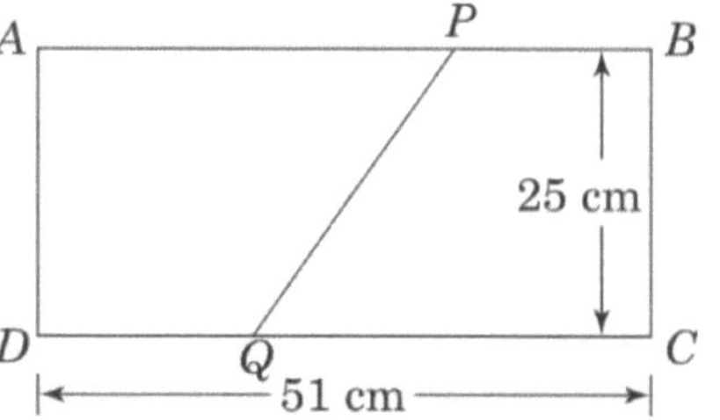

Sol. We know that, all sides of a square equal, so

$$AB = BC = CD = DA \qquad ...(i)$$

In $\triangle$ADC, we have

AC = 44 cm   [∵ diagonal = 44 cm, given]

and $\angle D = 90°$

[Since, angle between two adjacent sides of a square is 90°]

∴ $AC^2 = AD^2 + DC^2$

[by Pythagoras theorem]

$\Rightarrow$ $44^2 = AD^2 + AD^2$ [∵ DC = AD]

$\Rightarrow$ $2AD^2 = 44 \times 44$

$\Rightarrow$ $AD = \sqrt{22 \times 44}$

∴ $AD = \sqrt{2 \times 11 \times 4 \times 11} = \sqrt{22 \times 22 \times 2}$

$= 22\sqrt{2}$ cm

So, $AB = BC = CD = DA = 22\sqrt{2}$ cm

Then, area of square ABCD = Side × Side

$= 22\sqrt{2} \times 22\sqrt{2} = 484 \times 2$

$= 968$ cm²

∴   Area of red portion (IV) in square

$= \dfrac{968}{4} = 242$ cm²

[Since, area of square is divided into four quadrants]

Area of green portion (III) in square

$= \dfrac{968}{4} = 242$ cm²

Now, in $\triangle$PCQ, we have

PC = a = 20 cm

CQ = b = 20 cm

and   PQ = c = 14 cm

Then, semi-perimeter of $\triangle$PCQ,

$$s = \dfrac{20 + 20 + 14}{2}$$

$$= \dfrac{54}{2} = 27 \text{ cm} \qquad (1/2)$$

∴   Area of $\triangle$PCQ = $\sqrt{s(s-a)(s-b)(s-c)}$

[by Heron's formula]

$= \sqrt{27(27-20)(27-20)(27-14)}$

$= \sqrt{27 \times 7 \times 7 \times 13}$

$= \sqrt{3 \times 3 \times 3 \times 7 \times 7 \times 13} = 21\sqrt{39}$

$= 21 \times 6.24 = 131.04$ cm²

Hence, total area of green portion

[part of square + Area of $\triangle$PCQ]

= (242 + 131.04) = 373.04 cm²

Hence, quantity of yellow, red and green shade papers require to make a kite are 484 cm², 242 cm² and 373.04 cm² respectively.

3. The dimensions of a rectangle ABCD are 51 cm × 25 cm. A trapezium PBCQ with its parallel sides QC and PB in the ratio 9 : 8, is cut-off from the rectangle as shown in figure. If the area of the trapezium PBCQ is 5/6ᵗʰ part of the area of the rectangle, then find the lengths of QC and PB.

[NCERT Exemplar]

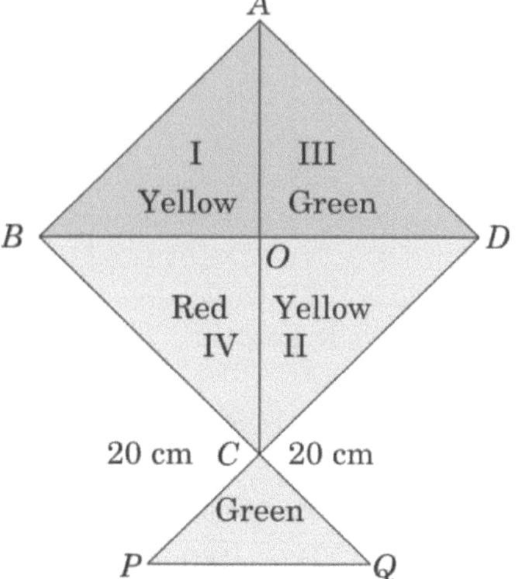

Sol. Given, dimensions of a rectangle ABCD are 51 cm × 25 cm.

Area of rectangle ABCD = AB × BC

$= 51 \times 25 = 1275$ cm²

According to the question,

Area of trapezium PBCQ

$= \dfrac{5}{6} \times$ Area of rectangle ABCD

$= \dfrac{5}{6} \times 1275 = \dfrac{6375}{6}$ cm²   ...(i)

Let the sides of trapezium PBCQ be

QC = 9x cm

and   PB = 8x cm

Then, area of trapezium PBCQ

$$= \frac{1}{2}\,(QC + PB) \times BC$$

$\left[\because\ \text{Area of trapezium} = \dfrac{1}{2}\ \text{(sum of the length}\right.$

of two parallel side $\times$ distance between two

parallel sides)]

$$\Rightarrow \qquad \frac{6375}{6} = \frac{1}{2}\,(9x + 8x) \times 25$$
$$\text{[From eqn. (i)]}$$

$$\Rightarrow \qquad \frac{17x \times 25}{2} = \frac{6375}{6}$$

$$\Rightarrow \qquad x = \frac{6375}{6} \times \frac{2}{17 \times 25}$$

$$\therefore \qquad x = 5$$

Then, length of sides of the trapezium PBCQ,

$$QC = 9x = 9 \times 5 = 45 \text{ cm}$$

and $\qquad PB = 8x = 8 \times 5 = 40$ cm

Hence, the length side QC and PB of trapezium PBCQ are 45 cm and 40 cm, respectively.

4. A field is in the shape of a trapezium, whose parallel sides are 25 m and 10 m and the non-parallel sides are 14 m and 13 m. Find the area of the field. **[NCERT]**

Sol. Let ABCD be the given field in the form of a trapezium in which AB = 25 m and CD = 10 m, BC = 13 m, AD = 14 m and DC ∥ AB.

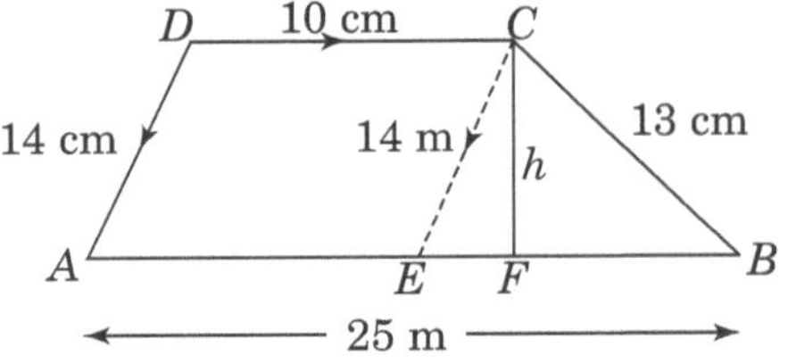

Through C. draw CE ∥ DA and let it meets AB at E.

Let CP h m be the height of the trapezium.

Now, $\qquad$ DC ∥ AE $\qquad$ [∵ DC ∥ AB given]

and $\qquad$ CE ∥ DA $\qquad$ [by construction]

Thus, AECD is a parallelogram.

$\Rightarrow \qquad$ AE = DC = 10 cm

and $\qquad$ CE = DA = 14 cm

In ΔCEB, we have,

$\qquad$ CB = 13 m, CE = 14 cm

and $\qquad$ BE = AB − AE = 25 − 10 = 15 cm

Let $\qquad$ a = 14 m, b = 13 m

and $\qquad$ c = 15 m

Then, semi-perimeter of ΔCEB,

$$s = \frac{a+b+c}{2}$$

$$= \frac{14+13+15}{2} = \frac{42}{2} = 21 \text{ m}$$

∴ $\quad$ Area of ΔCEB

$= \sqrt{s(s-a)(s-b)(s-c)}$ $\qquad$ [by Heron's formula]

$= \sqrt{21(21-14)(21-13)(21-15)}$

$= \sqrt{21 \times 7 \times 8 \times 6}$

$= \sqrt{3 \times 7 \times 7 \times 2 \times 2 \times 2 \times 3}$

$= \sqrt{3^2 \times 7^2 \times 2^2 \times 2^2} = 2 \times 2 \times 3 \times 7 = 84 \text{ m}^2$ $\quad$ ...(i)

Also, area of ΔCEB $= \dfrac{1}{2} \times$ Base $\times$ Altitude

$$= \frac{1}{2} \times BE \times h = \frac{1}{2} \times 15 \times h \ \text{...(ii)}$$

From equations (i) and (ii),

$$\frac{1}{2} \times 15 \times h = 84$$

$$\Rightarrow \qquad h = \frac{84 \times 2}{15} = \frac{28 \times 2}{5}$$

$$\Rightarrow \qquad h = \frac{56}{5} \text{ m}$$

∴ $\quad$ Area of a trapezium ABCD

$$= \frac{1}{2}\,(DC + AB) \times h$$

$\left[\because\ \text{Area of a trapezium} = \dfrac{1}{2} \times \text{(sum of two}\right.$

parallel sides) $\times$ height]

$$= \frac{1}{2}(10 + 25) \times \frac{56}{5}$$

$$= \frac{1}{2} \times 35 \times \frac{56}{5}$$

$$= 7 \times 28 = 196 \text{ m}^2$$

Hence, the area of field is 196 m²

5. A field is in the shape of a trapezium whose parallel sides are 35 m and 10 m. The non-parallel sides are 14 m and 13 m. Find the area of the field. **[Board Term I, 2014]**

Sol. Let ABCD be the given field in the form of trapezium in which AB = 35 m, CD = 10 m, BC = 13 m, AD = 14 m and DC ∥ AB.

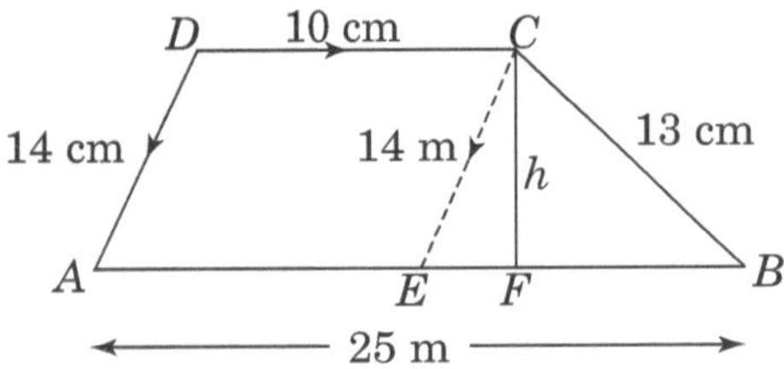

Through C, draw CE ∥ DA and let in meet AB at E.

Let h metres (CF) be the height of the trapezium.

According to the question,

$\qquad$ DC ∥ AE

and $\qquad$ CE ∥ DA

Therefore, AECD is a parallelogram.

$$AE = DC = 10 \text{ m}$$

and $\quad CE = DA = 14 \text{ m}$

In $\triangle CEB$, $\quad CB = 13 \text{ m}, CE = 14 \text{ m}$

and $\quad BE = AB - AE = 35 - 10 = 25 \text{ m}$

Let $a = 14$ m, $b = 13$ m and $c = 25$ m

Then, semi-perimeter

$$(s) = \frac{a+b+c}{2}$$
$$= \frac{14+13+25}{2} = 26 \text{ m}$$

$\therefore$ Area of $\triangle CEB = \sqrt{s(s-a)(s-b)(s-c)}$

$$= \sqrt{26(26-14)(26-13)(26-25)}$$
$$= \sqrt{26 \times 12 \times 13 \times 1}$$
$$= \sqrt{13 \times 2 \times 2 \times 6 \times 13} = 26\sqrt{6} \text{ m}^2$$

Also, Area of $\triangle CEB$

$$= \frac{1}{2} \times \text{base} \times \text{height} = \frac{1}{2} \times BE \times h$$

$\Rightarrow \quad \frac{1}{2} \times 25 \times h = 26\sqrt{6} \text{ m}^2$

$\therefore \quad\quad h = \frac{52}{25}\sqrt{6} \text{ m}$

Hence, Area of trapezium

$$= \frac{1}{2}(DC+AB) \times h$$
$$= \frac{1}{2}(10+35) \times \frac{52}{25}\sqrt{6}$$
$$= \frac{1}{2} \times 45 \times \frac{52}{25}\sqrt{6}$$
$$= \frac{9}{5} \times 26\sqrt{6} = 114.66 \text{ m}^2 \text{ (approx.)}$$

6. A triangular park has sides 60 m, 40 m and 26 m. Gardener has to put a fence all around its boundary and also plant grass inside.

   Find the area in which grass will be planted. Also calculate the cost of fencing it with barbed wire at the rate of ₹ 30 per meter, leaving a spare 2 m wide for a gate on one side.

   [Board Term I, 2016, Set-BQ56IZK]

Sol. Semi-perimeter (s) $= \dfrac{60+40+26}{2} = \dfrac{126}{2} = 63$ m

$\therefore \quad$ Area of $\Delta = \sqrt{s(s-a)(s-b)(s-c)}$

$$= \sqrt{63 \times 3 \times 23 \times 37}$$
$$= 401 \text{ m}^2 \text{ opp.}$$

Therefore, length of wire needed for fencing

$$= 60 + 40 + 26 - 2 = 124 \text{ m}$$

Hence, cost of fencing

$$= 124 \times 30 = ₹ 3720$$

7. In a rectangular field of dimensions 50 m × 30 m, a triangular park is constructed. If the dimensions of the park are 14 m, 15 m and 13 m, find the area of remaining field.

   [Board Term I, 2016, Set-7AEDLQR]

Sol. Area of rectangular field $= 50 \times 30 = 1500$ m^2

Sides of triangular park are 14 m, 15 m and 13 m.

So, $\quad\quad a = 14$ m, $b = 15$ m, $c = 13$ m

Semi-perimeter (s) $= \dfrac{a+b+c}{2}$

$$= \frac{14+15+13}{2} = \frac{42}{2} = 21 \text{ m}$$

$\therefore$ Area of triangular park $= \sqrt{s(s-a)(s-b)(s-c)}$

$$= \sqrt{21(21-14)(21-15)(21-13)}$$
$$= \sqrt{21 \times 7 \times 6 \times 8} = 84 \text{ m}^2$$

Hence, Area of remaining field

= Area of rectangular field

$\quad\quad\quad\quad$ − Area of triangular park

$$= 1500 - 84 = 1416 \text{ m}^2$$

8. In a four-sided field, the length of the longer diagonal is 120 m. The length of the perpendiculars from the opposite sides vertices upon this diagonal are 12.7 m and 7.3 m. Find the area of the field.

   [Board Term I, 2016, Set-7AEDLQR]

Sol. According to the question,

$$\text{Diagonal (AC)} = 120 \text{ m}$$
$$h_1 = 7.3 \text{ m}$$

and $\quad\quad\quad h_2 = 12.7 \text{ m}$

$\therefore \quad$ Area of quadrilateral ABCD

$$= \left[\frac{1}{2} \times AC \times (h_1 + h_2)\right]$$
$$= \frac{1}{2} \times 120 \times (7 \cdot 3 + 12 \cdot 7)$$
$$= \frac{1}{2} \times 120 \times 20 = 1200 \text{ m}^2$$

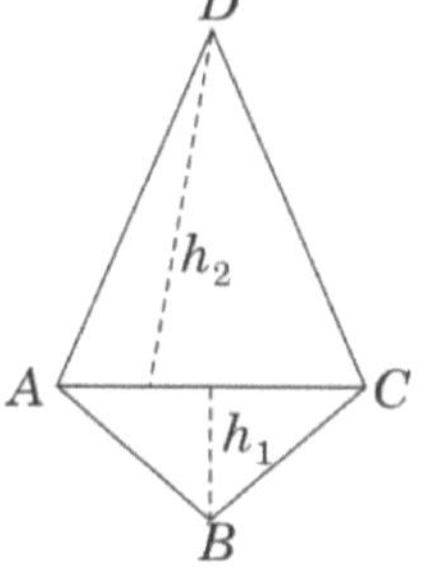

CHAPTER 13

Surface Areas and Volumes

- Surface areas and volumes of cubes, cuboids, spheres (including hemispheres) and right circular cylinders/ cones.

A flow chart on basic concepts of Surface Areas and Volumes :

Solid

Polyhedrons

Cube : The edge of a cube is a 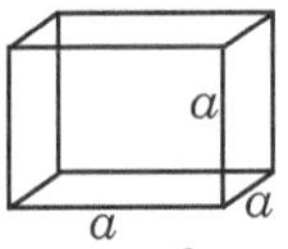
(i) Diagonal $= \sqrt{3}a$
(ii) Lateral surface area of cube $= 4a^2$
(iii) Total surface area of cube $= 6a^2$
(iv) Volume of cube $= a^3$

Cuboid : The length of cuboid $= l$, breadth $= b$ and height $= h$ 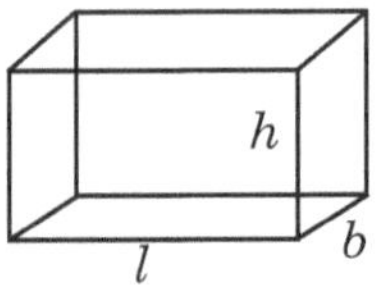
(i) Diagonal $= \sqrt{l^2 + b^2 + h^2}$
(ii) Lateral surface area of cuboid $= 2(l + b)h$
(iii) Total surface area of cuboid $= 2(lb + bh + hl)$
(iv) Volume of cuboid $= lbh$

Non - Polyhedrons

Cylinder : Radius $= r$ and height $= h$ 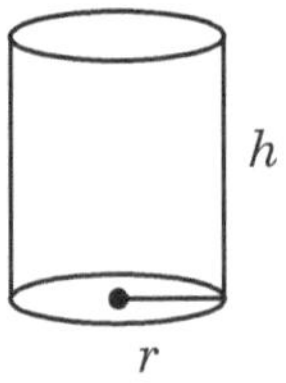
(i) Curved surface area of cylinder $= 2\pi rh$
(ii) Total surface area $= 2\pi r(r + h)$
(iii) Volume of cylinder $= \pi r^2 h$

Cone : Height $= h$ and Radius $= r$ 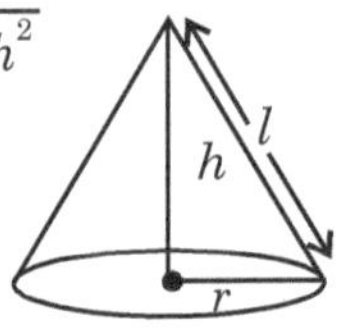
(i) Slant height $(l) = \sqrt{r^2 + h^2}$
(ii) Curved surface area of cone $= \pi rl$
(iii) Total surface area of cone $= \pi r(r + l)$
(iv) Volume of cone $= \dfrac{1}{3}\pi r^2 h$

Sphere : Radius $= r$ 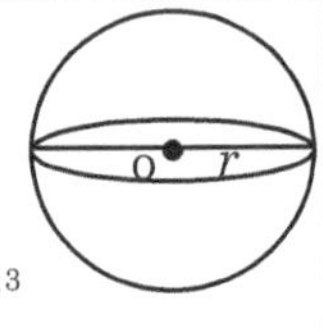
(i) Surface area of sphere $= 4\pi r^2$
(ii) Volume of sphere $= \dfrac{4}{3}\pi r^3$

Hemisphere : Radius $= r$ 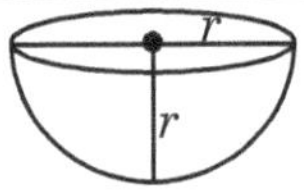
(i) Curved surface area of hemisphere $= 2\pi r^2$
(ii) Total surface area of hemisphere $= 3\pi r^2$
(iii) Volume of Hemisphere $= \dfrac{2}{3}\pi r^3$

[Topic 1] Surface Areas and Volumes of Cube, Cuboid and Sphere (Including Hemisphere)

Points to be Remembered

- **Cuboid :** A cuboid is a closed solid figure bounded by six rectangular plane regions.

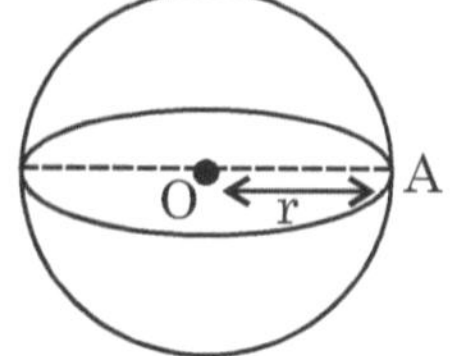

- A line segment where any two adjacent faces of a cuboid meet, is called an edge.
- The point of intersection of three edges of a cuboid, is called vertex.
- A cuboid has 6 faces, 12 edges and 8 vertices.
- If the length, breadth and height of a cuboid are l, b and h respectively, then
  (i)   Total surface area of cuboid = $2(lb + bh + hl)$ sq. units
  (ii) Lateral surface area of cuboid = $2(l + b)$ h sq. units.
  (iii) Volume of cuboid = lbh cubic units.
  (iv) Diagonal of cuboid = $\sqrt{l^2 + b^2 + h^2}$ units.
- **Cube:** A cuboid whose length, breadth and height are equal is called a cube. A cube has six square faces.
- If the side of a cube is 'a', then

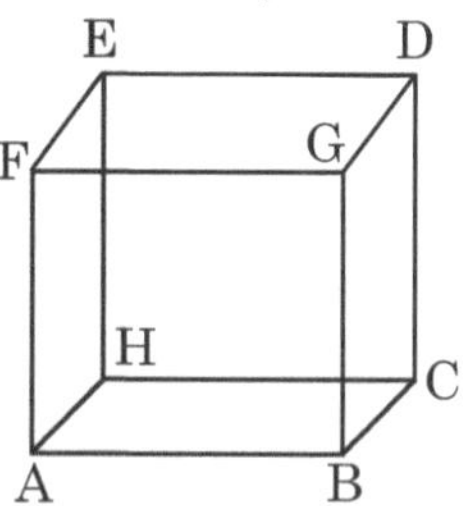

  (i)   The total surface area = $6a^2$ sq. units
  (ii) The lateral surface area = $4a^2$ sq. units
  (iii) Volume of a cubic = a^3 cu. units
  (iv) Diagonal of a cube = $\sqrt{3}a$ units
- **Sphere:** A sphere is a perfectly round geometrical object in three - dimensional space, such as the shape of a round ball.

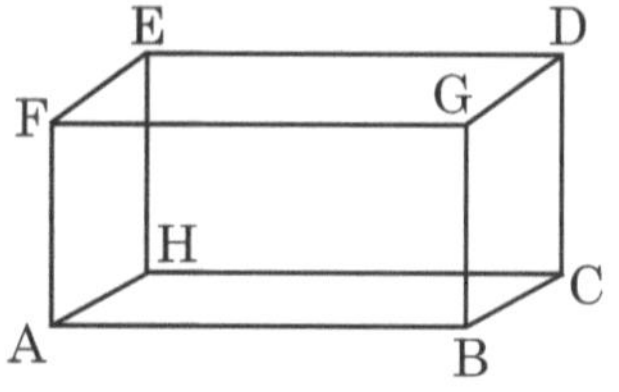

- If the radius of a sphere is 'r' units, then
  (i)   Total surface area = $4\pi r^2$ sq. units
  (ii) Volume of sphere = $\dfrac{4}{3}\pi r^3$ cu. units
- **Hemisphere :** A hemisphere is half of a sphere.
- If the radius of a hemisphere is 'r' units, then

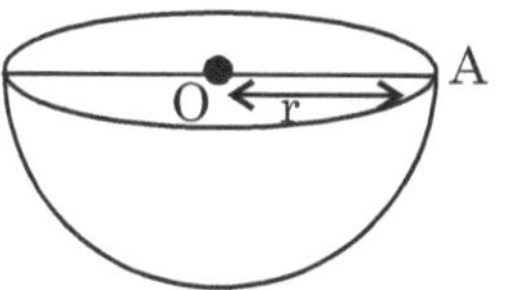

  (i)   Curved surface area of hemisphere
        $= 2\pi r^2$ sq. units
  (ii) Total surface area of hemisphere
        $= 3\pi r^2$ sq.units
  (iii) Volume of hemisphere = $\dfrac{2}{3}\pi r^3$ cu. units.

PREVIOUS YEARS'
EXAMINATION QUESTIONS
TOPIC 1

Multiple Choice Questions
(1 Mark Each)

1. The radius of a sphere is 2r, then its volume will be **[NCERT Exemp.]**

   (a) $\dfrac{4\pi r^3}{3}$

   (b) $4\pi r^3$

   (c) $\dfrac{8\pi r^3}{3}$

   (d) $\dfrac{32}{3}\pi r^3$

Sol. (d) According to the question

Volume of the sphere = $\dfrac{4}{3}\pi r^3$

But radius r = 2r

Hence, volume of the sphere $= \dfrac{4}{3}\pi(2r)^3 = \dfrac{32}{3}\pi r^3$

2. The total surface area of a cube is 96 cm². The volume of the cube is:

   [NCERT Exemp.]

   (a) 8 cm³
   (b) 512 cm³
   (c) 64 cm³
   (d) 27 cm³

Sol. (c) According to the question,

Total surface area = 96 sq. cm

$\Rightarrow \quad 6a^2 = 96$

$\Rightarrow \quad a^2 = \dfrac{96}{6}$

$\Rightarrow \quad a^2 = 16$

$\therefore \quad a = 4$

Hence, volume of cube = $a^3 = 4^3 = 64$ cu. cm.

3. The number of planks of dimensions (4 m × 50 cm × 20 cm) that can be stored in a pit which is 16 m long, 12 m wide, and 4 m deep is

[NCERT Exemp.]

(a) 1900   (b) 1920

(c) 1800   (d) 1840

Sol. (b) Number of planks $= \dfrac{\text{Volume of a pit}}{\text{Volume of a plank}}$

$= \dfrac{(16 \times 12 \times 4)}{4 \times 0.5 \times 0.2} = 1{,}920$

4. The length of the longest pole that can be put in a room of dimensions (10 m × 10 m × 5 m) is

[NCERT Exemp.]

(a) 15 m   (b) 16 m

(c) 10 m   (d) 12 m

Sol. (a) According to the question,

Length of the pole = Diagonal of the room

$= \sqrt{x^2 + y^2 + z^2} = \sqrt{10^2 + 10^2 + 5^2}$

$= \sqrt{225} = 15$

5. The radius of a hemispherical balloon increases from 6 cm to 12 cm as air is being pumped into it. The ratios of the surface areas of the balloon in the two cases is

[NCERT Exemp.]

(a) 1 : 4   (b) 1 : 3

(c) 2 : 3   (d) 2 : 1

Sol. (a) According to the question,

Radius r = 6 cm

$\therefore$ Surface area $= 3\pi r^2 = 3(6)^2 = 3\pi \times 6 \times 6$

When radius R = 12 cm

Surface area $= 3\pi(R)^2 = 3\pi (12)^2 = 3\pi \times 12 \times 12$

Hence, required ratio $= 3\pi \times 6 \times 6 : 3\pi \times 12 \times 12$

$= 1 : 4$

6. The lateral surface area of a cube is 256 m². The volume of the cube is

[NCERT Exemp.]

(a) 512 m³   (b) 64 m³

(c) 216 m³   (d) 256 m³

Sol. (a) According to the question,

Lateral surface area of cube = 256 sq.m.

$\Rightarrow \quad 4a^2 = 256$

$\Rightarrow \quad a^2 = \dfrac{256}{4}$

$\Rightarrow \quad a^2 = 64$

$\therefore a = 8$

Hence, volume of cube = $a^3 = 8^3 = 512$ cu.m

7. The edge of a cube whose total surface area is 1176 cm² is :

(a) 14 cm   (b) 16 cm

(c) 17 cm   (d) 18 cm

Sol. (a) According to the question,

Total surface area of cube = 1176

$\Rightarrow \quad 6a^2 = 1176$

$\Rightarrow \quad a^2 = \dfrac{1176}{6} = 196$

$\therefore \quad a = 14$ cm

Hence, required edge of cube = 14 cm

8. Given a cuboid of dimensions $l = 5$ cm, b = 4 cm h = 2 cm. How many cubes of 2 cm side can be cut out of it?

[NCERT Exemp.]

(a) 18   (b) 20

(c) 10   (d) none of these

Sol. (d) Number of cubes $= \dfrac{\text{Volume of cuboid}}{\text{Volume of small cube}}$

$= \dfrac{5 \times 4 \times 2}{2 \times 2 \times 2} = 5$

9. Total surface area of the hemisphere is given by:

[NCERT Exemp.]

(a) πr^2 sq. units   (b) $2\pi r^2$ sq. units

(c) $3\pi r^2$ sq. units   (d) $4\pi r^2$ sq. units

Sol. (c) Total surface area of hemisphere = $3\pi r^2$ sq. units

10. Diameter of the earth is four times (approximately) the diameter of the moon then the ratio of their surface area is :

(a) 4 : 1   (b) 8 : 1

(c) 16 : 1   (d) 2 : 1

Sol. (c) Let the radius of moon = r, then

Required ratio $= \dfrac{\text{Surface area of earth}}{\text{Surface area of moon}}$

$= \dfrac{4\pi(4r)^2}{4\pi r^2}$

$= \dfrac{16}{1} = 16 : 1$

Very Short Answer Type Questions
(1 Mark Each)

1. A cuboidal water tank is 6 m long, 5 m wide 4.5 m deep. How many litres of water can it hold? $(1m^3 = 1000L)$ **[NCERT]**

Sol. According to the question,

length $(l) = 6$m, breadth $(b) = 5$ m and depth or height $(h) = 4.5$ m

Volume of cuboidal water tank
$$= 6 \text{ m} \times 5 \text{ m} \times 4.5 \text{ m}$$
$$[\because \text{ Volume of cuboid (V)} = lbh]$$
$$\Rightarrow 30 \times 4.5 \text{ m}^3 = 135 \text{ m}^3$$
$$\Rightarrow 135 \times 1000 \text{ L} = 135000 \text{ L} \quad [\because 1 \text{ m}^3 = 1000 \text{ L}]$$

Hence, tank can hold 135000 L of water.

2. Find the cost of digging a cuboidal pit of 8 m long, 6 m broad and 3 m deep at the rate of ₹30 per m³. **[NCERT]**

Sol. $\because$ Volume of a cuboidal pit
$$= l \times b \times h = (8 \times 6 \times 3) = 144 \text{ m}^3$$
$$[\because l = 8 \text{ m}, b = 6 \text{ m and } h = 3, \text{ given}]$$

$\because$ Cost of digging 1 m³ = ₹30

Hence, Cost of digging 144 m³ cuboidal pit
$$= 30 \times 144 = ₹4320.$$

3. Find the total surface area of a hemisphere of radius 10 cm (take, $\pi = 3.14$). **[NCERT]**

Sol. According to the question,

Radius of a hemisphere (r) = 10 cm

$\therefore$ Total surface area of hemisphere = $3\pi r^2$
$$= 3 \times 3.14 \times (10)^2$$
$$= 9.42 \times 100 = 942 \text{ cm}^2.$$

4. A cuboidal vessel is 10 m long and 8 m wide. How high must it be made to hold 380 m³ of a liquid? **[NCERT]**

Sol. Let h be the height of vessel,

Given, length $(l) = 10$ m

and breadth $(b) = 8$ m

According to the question,

Volume of cuboidal vessel = Liquid to be hold

$\therefore l \times b \times h = 380$ (given)
$$\Rightarrow 10 \times 8 \times h = 380$$
$$\therefore h = \frac{380}{80} = 4.75 \text{ m}$$

Hence. the cuboidal vessel must be made 4.75 m high.

5. Compute the curved surface area of a hemisphere whose diameter is 14 cm.

[BOARD TERM II, 2015, NCERT]

Sol. According to the question,

$\therefore$ Radius = 7 cm

$\therefore$ Curved surface area of hemisphere
$$= 2\pi r^2$$
$$= 2 \times \frac{22}{7} \times 7 \times 7$$
$$= 308 \text{ cm}^2.$$

6. The diameter of a football is five times the diameter of a cricket ball. Ratio of surface areas of football and cricket ball is ....

[BOARD TERM II, 2013]

Sol. According to the question,

Diameter of football = 5 × diameter of cricket ball

If r denotes radius of a football and r′ that of a cricket ball, then we have
$$\Rightarrow 2r = 5 \times (2 \, r')$$
$$\Rightarrow \frac{2r}{2r'} = 5$$
$$\therefore \frac{r}{r'} = 5$$

Hence, ratio of surface areas,
$$= \frac{4\pi r^2}{4\pi (r')^2} = \left(\frac{r}{r'}\right)^2 = \frac{25}{1}$$
$$= 25 : 1$$

7. Calculate the volume of cuboid whose dimensions are 3.6 cm, 8.2 cm and 11 cm.

[BOARD TERM II, 2014]

Sol. According to the question,

Volume of cuboid = length × breadth × height
$$= 3.6 \times 8.2 \times 11$$
$$= 324.72 \text{ cm}^3.$$

8. If the number of square centimetres in the surface area of a sphere is equal to the number of cubic cm in its volume. Find the diameter of the sphere.

[BOARD TERM II, 2014]

Sol. According to the question,

Area of sphere = Volume of sphere
$$\Rightarrow 4\pi r^2 = \frac{4}{3}\pi r^3$$
$$\Rightarrow r^2 = \frac{r^3}{3}$$

where r is the radius of sphere

$\therefore$ r = 3 cm   [On solving]

Hence, diameter = 2r = 6 cm.

9. Find the capacity of a tank of dimensions 8 cm × 6 cm × 2.5 cm.

[BOARD TERM II, 2015]

Sol. According to the question,

Volume of tank = length × breadth × height

$$= 8 \text{ cm} \times 6 \text{ cm} \times 2.5 \text{ cm}$$

$$= 120 \text{ cm}^3.$$

Hence, capacity of the tank = 120 cm³.

10. Find the amount of water displaced by a solid spherical ball of diameter 4.2 cm, when it is completely immersed in water.

[BOARD TERM II, KVS 2016]

Sol. According to the question,

Amount of water displaced

$$= \text{Volume of solid spherical ball}$$

$\therefore$ Volume of solid spherical ball $= \dfrac{4}{3}\pi r^3$

$\therefore$ $r = \dfrac{4.2}{2} = 2.1 \text{ cm}$ (given)

$\therefore$ Volume of solid spherical ball $= \dfrac{4}{3}\pi(2.1)^3$

$$= \dfrac{4}{3} \times \dfrac{22}{7} \times (2.1)^3 \text{ cm}^3$$

$$= 38.808 \text{ cm}^3$$

Hence, amount of water displaced = 38.808 ml

11. The total surface area of a cube is 726 cm². Find the length of its edge.

[BOARD TERM II, 2017, SET-Z6K408K]

Sol. Total surface area of a cube $= 6a^2$

$\Rightarrow 6a^2 = 726$ [a is the length of a cube]

$\Rightarrow a^2 = 121$

$\therefore a = \sqrt{121} = 11 \text{ cm}$

Hence, the length of its edge = 11 cm.

12. Calculate the edge of the cube, if its volume is 1331 cm³.

[BOARD TERM II, 2017, SET-UAH47DQ7]

Sol. Let the edge of cube a, then

According to the question,

Volume of cube $= a^3$.

$\Rightarrow 1331 = a^3$

$\therefore a = \sqrt[3]{1331} = 11 \text{ cm}$

Hence, the edge of a cube = 11 cm.

Write whether the statement are true or false. Justify your answer.

1. If a sphere is inscribed in a cube, then the ratio of the volume of the cube to the volume of the sphere will be 6 : π.

[NCERT Exemp.]

Sol. Volume of cube $= a^3$

and volume of sphere $= \dfrac{4}{3}\pi r^3$

Since $a = 2r$

We get volume of cube $= 8r^3$

$\therefore$ Required Ratio $= 8r^3 : \dfrac{4}{3}\pi r^3 = 6 : \pi$

Hence, the given statement is true.

2. If the length of the diagonal of a cube is $6\sqrt{3}$ cm, then the length of the edge of the cube is 3 cm.

[NCERT Exemp.]

Sol. False

$$\text{Diagonal} = \sqrt{3^2 + 3^2 + 3^2} = \sqrt{27} = \sqrt{9 \times 3}$$

$$= 3\sqrt{3} \neq 6$$

Short Answer Type Questions I
(2 Marks Each)

1. A capsule of medicine is in the shape of a sphere of diameter 3.5 mm. How much medicine (in mm³) is needed to fill this capsule? **[NCERT]**

Sol. Given, diameter of capsule = 3.5 mm

$\therefore$ Radius $(r) = \dfrac{3.5}{2} \text{ mm} \left[\because \text{radius} = \dfrac{\text{diameter}}{2} \right]$

Now, volume of capsule

$$= \dfrac{4}{3}\pi r^3 = \dfrac{4}{3} \times \dfrac{22}{7} \times \dfrac{3.5}{2} \times \dfrac{3.5}{2} \times \dfrac{3.5}{2}$$

$$= \dfrac{11 \times 0.5 \times 3.5 \times 3.5}{3}$$

$$= 22.45833$$

$$= 22.46 \text{ mm}^3$$

Hence, 22.46 mm³ medicine is needed to fill this capsule.

2. A river 3 m deep and 40 m wide is flowing at the rate of 2 kmph. How much water will fall into the sea in a minute? **[NCERT]**

Sol. According to the question,

Breadth of the river = 40 m

Depth of the river = 3 m

and length per hour of the river = 2 km

$\Rightarrow$ Length per minute of the flowing water

$$= \dfrac{2000}{60} \text{ m}$$

$\therefore$ Water flowing per minute $= \dfrac{2000}{60} \times 40 \times 3$

$$= 4000 \text{ m}^3.$$

3. The diameter of a metallic ball is 4.2 cm. What is the mass of the ball, if the density of the metal is 8.99 per cm^3?   [NCERT]

Sol. According to the question,

Diameter (d) = 4.2 cm

$\therefore$ Radius (r) $= \dfrac{4.2}{2} = 2.1$ cm

Volume of metallic ball $= \dfrac{4}{3}\pi r^3$

$= \dfrac{4}{3} \times \dfrac{22}{7} \times (2.1)^3$

$= \dfrac{4}{3} \times \dfrac{22}{7} \times 2.1 \times 2.1 \times 2.1$

$= 88 \times 0.3 \times 0.7 \times 2.1$

$= 38.808$ cm^3

Given, the density of the metal per cm^3 = 8.9 g

$\therefore$ The mass of the ball = 38.808 × 8.9 = 345.39 g.

Hence, the mass of the ball is 345.39 g.

4. The diameter of the Moon is approximately one-fourth of the diameter of the Earth. Find the ratio of their surface area.   [NCERT]

Sol. Let diameter of the Earth = d_1

Then, according to the question,

Diameter of the Moon $= \dfrac{1}{4}d_1$

$\therefore$ Radius of the Earth $(r_1) = \dfrac{d_1}{2}$

and radius the Moon $(r_2) = \dfrac{d_1}{2 \times 4} = \dfrac{d_1}{8}$

Surface area of the Earth $(S_1) = 4\pi r_1^{\,2}$

$= 4\pi\left(\dfrac{d_1}{2}\right)^2 = \pi d_1^2$

and Surface area of the Moon

$S_2 = 4\pi\left(\dfrac{d_1}{8}\right)^2 = 4\pi\dfrac{d_1^2}{64}$

$\therefore \;\; S_2 = \dfrac{\pi d_1^2}{16}$

Hence, required ratio,

$S_1 : S_2 = \dfrac{\pi d_1^2}{1} : \dfrac{\pi d_1^2}{16} = 16 : 1$

5. A solid shotput is a metallic sphere of radius 4.9 cm. Find the volume of the shotput.
    [BOARD TERM I, 2012, SET 02]

Sol. According to the question,

Radius of sphere, r = 4.9 cm

Volume of sphere, $V = \dfrac{4}{3}\pi r^3$

$= \dfrac{4}{3} \times \dfrac{22}{7} \times 4.9 \times 4.9 \times 4.9$

$= 493$ cm^3 (approx.)

6. A match box measures 4 cm × 2.5 cm × 1.5 cm. What will be the volume of a packet containing 12 such boxes?

    [BOARD TERM II, 20121, SET 30, NCERT]

Sol. Given, $l = 4$ cm

b = 2.5 cm

and h = 1.5 cm

Volume of one match box = 4 × 2.5 × 1.5 cm^3

$= 15$ cm^3

$\therefore$ Volume of 12 such boxes = 15 × 12 = 180 cm^3.

7. A shopkeeper has one spherical laddoo of radius 5 cm. With the same amount of material, how many laddoos of radius 2.5 cm can be made?
    [NCERT EXEMPLAR]

Sol. Given, radius of the spherical laddoo (r) = 5 cm

$\therefore$ Volume of the spherical laddoo

$= $ Volume of sphere

$= \dfrac{4}{3} \times \pi r^3 = \dfrac{4}{3}\pi(5)^3$

$= \dfrac{4}{3} \times 125\pi = \dfrac{500}{3}\pi$ cm^3

Now, radius of small laddoo = 2.5 cm

So, volume of a small laddoo

$= \dfrac{4}{3}\pi \times (2.5)^3$

$= \dfrac{62.5}{3}\pi$ cm^3

$\therefore$ Number of laddoos

$= \dfrac{\text{Volume of the spherical laddoo}}{\text{Volume of a small laddoo}}$

$= \dfrac{\dfrac{500\pi}{3}}{\dfrac{62.5\pi}{3}} = \dfrac{500}{62.5} = 8$

Hence, 8 laddoos can be made of radius 2.5 cm.

8. If the length of the diagonal of a cube is $6\sqrt{3}$ cm, find the edge of the cube.
    [NCERT EXEMPLAR][BOARD TERM II, 2012 SET 01]

Sol. Diagonal of a cube $\sqrt{x^2 + x^2 + x^2} = 6\sqrt{3}\dfrac{1}{2}$

Let the edge of the cube is x cm, then

According to the question,

$\Rightarrow \sqrt{3 \times x^2} = 6\sqrt{3}$

$\Rightarrow \sqrt{3}x = \left(6\sqrt{3}\right)$

$\therefore x = 6$ cm

Hence, edge of the cube = 6 cm.

9. The surface area of a cuboid is 1372 cm². If its dimensions are in the ratio 4 : 2 : 1, find its length.   [BOARD TERM II, 2012, SET 25]

Sol. According to the question,

Surface Area of cuboid = 1372

$\Rightarrow 2(lb + bh + hl) = 1372$

$[\because l = 4x, b = 2x, h = x]$

$\Rightarrow 2(4x \times 2x + 2x \times x + 4x \times x) = 1372$

$\Rightarrow 2(8x^2 + 2x^2 + 4x^2) = 1372$

$\Rightarrow 28x^2 = 1372$

$\Rightarrow x^2 = 49$

$\therefore x = 7$ cm

Hence, the length of cuboid = 4 × 7 = 28 cm.

10. The total surface area of a solid hemisphere is 5940 cm². Find the diameter of the hemisphere.

[BOARD TERM II, 2012, SET 23]

Sol. Let the radius of hemisphere be r, then

According to the question,

Total surface area of hemisphere = 5940

$$\Rightarrow 3\pi r^2 = 5940$$

$$r^2 = \frac{5940 \times 7}{3 \times 22} = 630$$

$$\therefore r = \sqrt{630} = 3\sqrt{70} \text{ cm.}$$

$$d = 2r = 6\sqrt{70} \text{ cm.}$$

Hence, diameter of the hemisphere is $6\sqrt{70}$ cm.

11. If the volume of the cuboid is 880 cm³ and the area of its base is 88 cm². Find the height of the cuboid.   [BOARD TERM II, 2013]

Sol. According to the question,

Volume = 880 cm³,

Area of its base = 88 cm².

Volume of cuboid = $l \times$ b $\times$ h = 880 cm³.   ...(i)

and area = $l \times$ b = 88 cm²   ...(ii)

From (i) and (ii),

88 × h = 880

$$\therefore \quad h = \frac{880}{88} = 10 \text{ cm}$$

Hence, the height of cuboid is 10 cm.

12. A cuboidal block of wood is of dimensions 5 m × 2 m × 1 m. Find the number of cubes of dimensions 1 m × 1 m × 1 m which can be cut from it.   [BOARD TERM II, 2013]

Sol. Number of cubes $(n) = \dfrac{V_{cuboid}}{V_{cube}}$

$$= \frac{5 \times 2 \times 1}{1 \times 1 \times 1} = 10 \text{ cubes}$$

13. Find the volume of a sphere whose surface area is 154 cm².

[BOARD TERM II, 2015, NCERT]

Sol. We know that, volume of sphere = $\dfrac{4}{3}\pi r^3$

But, given that, surface area of sphere = 154 cm².

$$4\pi r^2 = 154$$

$$\Rightarrow 4 \times \frac{22}{7} \times r^2 = 154$$

$$\Rightarrow r^2 = \frac{154 \times 7}{4 \times 22} = \frac{49}{4}$$

$$\therefore r = \frac{7}{2}$$

Hence, volume of sphere

$$= \frac{4}{3} \times \frac{22}{7} \times \frac{7}{2} \times \frac{7}{2} \times \frac{7}{2}$$

$$= \frac{539}{3} \text{ cm}^3$$

$$= 179.67 \text{ cm}^3.$$

14. Find the radius of a sphere whose surface area is 616 cm².

[BOARD TERM II, SET-LF0MCQ2, 2016]

Sol. According to the question,

Surface area of sphere = $4\pi r^2$

$$\Rightarrow 4\pi r^2 = 616$$

$$\Rightarrow \pi r^2 = = 154$$

$$\Rightarrow r^2 = \frac{154 \times 7}{22} \quad \left(\because \pi = \frac{22}{7}\right)$$

$$\Rightarrow r^2 = 49$$

$$\therefore r = 7$$

Hence, the radius of sphere is 7 cm.

Short Answer Type Questions II
(3 Marks Each)

1. A hemispherical bowl is made of steel, 0.25 cm thick. The inner radius of the bowl is 5 cm. Find the outer curved surface area of the bowl.

[NCERT]

Sol. According to the question,

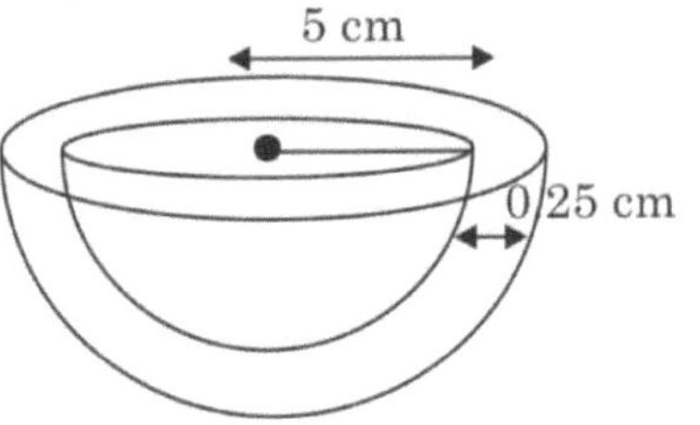

The inner radius of the hemispherical bowl = 5 cm

Thickness of the hemispherical bowl = 0.25 cm

We know that, outer radius of the bowl

$= $ Inner radius + Thickness

$= (5 + 0.25) = 5.25$ cm

Outer curved surface area of the bowl

$= 2\pi r^2 = 2 \times \dfrac{22}{7} \times 5.25 \times 5.25$

$= 173.25$ cm^2.

2. A small indoor greenhouse (herbarium) is made entirely of glass panes (including base) held together with tape. It is 30 cm long, 25 cm wide and 25 cm high. **[NCERT]**

(i)   What is the area of the glass?

(ii) How much of tape is needed for all the 12 edges?

Sol. Dimensions of herbarium are $l = 30$ cm, $b = 25$ cm and $h = 25$ cm

(i) Area of the glass

$= $ Total surface area of herbarium

$= 2\,(l \times b + b \times h + h \times l)$

$= 2\,(30 \times 25 + 25 \times 25 + 25 \times 30)$

$= 2\,(750 + 625 + 750)$

$= 2(2125)$

$= 4250$ cm^2

(ii) Herbarium is a shape of cuboid.

So, length of required tape will be equal to total length of edges of cuboid.

$\therefore$ Length of the tape $= 4(l + b + h)$

$= 4(30 + 25 + 25)$

$= 4 \times 80$

$= 320$ cm

3. How many litres of milk can a hemispherical of diameter 10.5 cm hold? **[NCERT]**

Sol. According to the question,

Diameter $= 10.5$ cm

$\therefore$ Radius $(r) = \dfrac{10.5}{2} = 5.25$ cm

Volume of hemisphere $= \dfrac{2}{3}\pi r^3$

$= \dfrac{2}{3} \times \dfrac{22}{7} \times 5.25 \times 5.25 \times 5.25$

$= 303.1875$ cm^3.

Quantity of milk that hemispherical bowl can hold

$= \dfrac{303.1875}{1000}$ L $= 0.303$ L (approx)

$\left[\because 1 \text{ cm}^3 = \dfrac{1}{1000} \text{L} \right]$

4. A village, having a population of 4000, requires 150 L of water per head per day. It has a tank measuring 20 m $\times$ 15 m $\times$ 6 m. For how many days, will the water of this tank last? **[NCERT]**

Sol. According to the question,

length $(l) = 20$ m, breadth $(b) = 15$ m and height $(h) = 6$ m

$\therefore$ Capacity of the tank $= $ Volume of the tank

$= lbh = (20 \times 15 \times 6) = 1800$ m^3.

$\because$ Water required for one person per day $= 150$L

$\therefore$ Water required for 4000 persons per day

$= (4000 \times 150)$ L

$= \left(\dfrac{4000 \times 150}{1000} \right) \quad \left[\because 1 \text{ L} = \dfrac{1}{1000} \text{m}^3 \right]$

$= 600$ m^3

Now, number of days the water will last

$= \dfrac{\text{Capacity of tank}}{\text{Total water required per day}}$

$= \dfrac{1800}{600} = 3$

Hence, the water will last for 3 days.

5. A plastic box 1.5 m long, 1.25 m wide and 65 cm deep is to be made. It is opened at the top. Ignoring the thickness of the plastic sheet, determine.

(i)   the area of the sheet required for making the box.

(ii) the cost of sheet for it, if a sheet measuring 1 m^2 costs ₹20. **[NCERT]**

Sol. We have, a plastic box whose length (l) 1.5 m, width $(b) = 1.25$ m

and depth $(h) = 65$ cm

$= \dfrac{65}{100} = 0.65$ m $\qquad \left[\because 1 \text{ cm} = \dfrac{1}{100} \text{m} \right]$

Surface area of the box $= 2(lb + bh + hl)$

$= 2(1.5 \times 1.25 + 1.25 \times 0.65 + 0.65 \times 1.5)$

$= 2(1.875 + 0.8125 + 0.975)$

$= 2(3.6625) = 7.325$ m^2

(i) Area of sheet required for making the box

$= $ Surface area of the box

$- $ Area of opened the top $= 7.325 - 1 \times b$

[since, box is opened at the top]

$= 7.325 - 1.875 = 5.45$ m^2

(ii) Given, cost of 1 m^2 sheet $= $ ₹20

$\therefore$ Cost of 5.45 m^2 sheet $= 20 \times 5.45 = $ ₹109

6. A shot-put is a metallic sphere of radius 4.9 cm. If the density of the metal is 7.5 g per cm^3, find the mass of the shot-put.

[BOARD TERM II, 2012, SET 30 NCERT]

Sol. According to the question,

Mass = density × volume

$$\text{Volume of sphere} = \frac{4}{3}\pi r^3$$

$$= \frac{4}{3} \times \frac{22}{7} \times 4.9 \times 4.9 \times 4.9$$

∴ Mass of the shot-put

$$= \frac{4}{3} \times \frac{22}{7} \times \frac{49 \times 49 \times 49 \times 75}{10^4}\,g$$

$$= \frac{22 \times 7 \times 49 \times 49}{100}\,g = 3697.54\ g$$

7. The length, breadth and height of a room are 5 m, 4 m and 3 m, respectively. Find the cost of white washing the walls of the room and the ceiling at the rate of ₹7.50 per m^2.

[BOARD TERM II, KVS, 2014, NCERT]

Sol. Given, dimensions of room are $l = 5$ m, $b = 4$ m and $h = 3$ m.

Required area for white washing

$$= \text{Area of the four walls} + \text{Area of ceiling}$$
$$= 2(l + b) \times h + (l \times b)$$
$$= 2(5 + 4) \times 3 + (5 \times 4)$$
$$= 54 + 20 = 74\ m^2.$$

Given, cost of white washing 1 m^2 = ₹ 7.50

Hence, cost of white washing of 74 m^2 wall

$$= 7.50 \times 74 = ₹555$$

8. The floor of a rectangular hall has a perimeter 250 m. If the cost of painting the four walls at the rate of ₹10 per m^2 is ₹15000, then find the height of the hall

[BOARD TERM II, KVS 2016, NCERT]

Sol. Let l, b and h be the length, breadth and height of rectangular hall respectively.

Now, area of four walls

$$= \frac{\text{Cost of painting the four walls}}{\text{Cost of painting per m}^2}$$

$$= \frac{15000}{10} = 1500\ m^2$$

Given, perimeter of base of the hall

$$= 2(l + b) = 250\ m \qquad \ldots(i)$$

and we have area of four walls = 1500 m^2

$$\Rightarrow 2(l + b) \times h = 1500$$

$$[\because \text{Area of four walls} = 2(l + b) \times h]$$

$$\Rightarrow \quad 250 \times h = 1500 \quad \text{[from eq. (i)]}$$

$$\therefore \quad h = \frac{1500}{250} = 6\ m$$

Hence, the height of the hall is 6 m

9. The external and internal diameters of a hollow hemi-spherical vessel are 16 cm and 12 cm respectively. The cost of painting 1 sq. cm of surface is ₹2. Find the cost of painting the vessel all over $\left(\pi = \dfrac{22}{7}\right)$

[BOARD TERM II, 2012, SET 15]

Sol. According to the question,

Total surface area = $2\pi R^2 + 2\pi r^2 + (\pi R^2 - \pi r^2)$

Where R is external radius and r^2 is the internal radius

$$= 3\pi r^2 + \pi r^2$$
$$= \pi(3R^2 + r^2)$$
$$= \pi[3(8)^2 + 6^2]$$
$$= \frac{22}{7} \times [228]\,cm^2$$
$$= 716.57\ cm^2$$

∵ The cost of painting 1 sq. cm of surface is ₹2.

Hence, cost of painting the vessel all over

$$= ₹(716.57 \times 2)$$
$$= ₹1433.14$$

10. A shot-put is a metallic sphere of radius 3.5 cm. If the density of the metal is 7.8 g per cm^3, find the mass of the shot-put. (Take $\pi = \dfrac{22}{7}$)

[BOARD TERM II, 2012, SET 24]

Sol. Volume of the shot-put $= \dfrac{4}{3}\pi r^3$

$$= \frac{4}{3} \times \frac{22}{7} \times \frac{35}{10} \times \frac{35}{10} \times \frac{35}{10}$$

$$= \frac{11 \times 49}{3}\ cm^3$$

∵ The density of the metal is 7.8 gm per cm^3.

Hence, mass of the shot-put

$$= \frac{11}{3} \times 49 \times \frac{78}{10}$$
$$= 1401.40\ gm.$$

11. A box with lid is made out of 2 cm thick wood. Its inner dimensions are 21 cm, 14 cm and 11 cm. Its external length, breadth and height are 25 cm, 18 cm, and 15 cm respectively. Find the capacity of the box and volume of the wood used. **[BOARD TERM II, 2012, SET 24]**

Sol. According to the question,

Inner dimensions of the box are 21 cm, 14 cm and 11 cm

∴ Inner volume or capacity of the box

$$= 21 \times 14 \times 11\ cm^3$$
$$= 3234\ cm^3.$$

and outer volume of the box = $25 \times 18 \times 15$ cm^3.

$$= 6750 \text{ cm}^3.$$

Hence, volume of the wood used $= 6750 - 3234$

$$= 3516 \text{ cm}^3.$$

12. The total cost of making a solid spherical ball is ₹33,957 at the rate of ₹7 per cubic metre. Find the radius of this ball.

[BOARD TERM II, 2012, SET 08]

Sol. According to the question,

$$\frac{\text{Total cost}}{\text{Cost}/\text{m}^3} = \text{Volume of sphere}$$

$$\Rightarrow \frac{33957}{7} = \frac{4}{3}\pi r^3$$

$$\Rightarrow \frac{33957}{7} = \frac{4}{3} \times \frac{22}{7} \times r^3$$

$$\Rightarrow \frac{101871}{88} = r^3$$

$$\Rightarrow 1157.625 = r^3.$$

$$\therefore \ r = 10.5 \text{ cm}$$

Hence, the radius of the ball (r) = 10.5 cm

13. The volumes of two spheres are in the ratio of $64 : 27$. Find their radii if the sum of their radii is 21 cm.   [BOARD TERM II, 2012, SET 01]

Sol. Let the radii of two spheres be r_1, r_2

$$r_1 + r_2 = 21$$

$$\Rightarrow r_1 = 21 - r_2.$$

Volume of I sphere $= \dfrac{4}{3}\pi r_1^3$ cm^3

Volume of II sphere $= \dfrac{4}{3}\pi r_2^3$ cm^3

According to the question,

$$\frac{\text{Volume of I sphere}}{\text{Volume of II sphere}} = \frac{\frac{4}{3}\pi(21 - r_2)^3}{\frac{4}{3}\pi r_2^3}$$

$$= \frac{64}{27}$$

$$\Rightarrow \frac{(21 - r_2)^3}{r_2^3} = \frac{64}{27}$$

$$\Rightarrow \frac{21 - r_2}{r_2} = \frac{4}{3}$$

$$\Rightarrow 63 - 3r_2 = 4r_2$$

$$\Rightarrow 63 = 7r_2$$

$$\therefore r_2 = 9 \text{ cm}$$

and $r_1 = 21 - r_2 = 21 - 9 = 12$ cm.

14. Find the volume of metal used to construct a hollow sphere of internal and external diameters as 10 cm and 13 cm respectively. (use $\pi = 3.14$)

[BOARD TERM II, 2012, SET 15]

Sol. According to the question,

Internal radius r = 5 cm

and external radius $R = \dfrac{13}{2}$ cm

$$\therefore \ \text{Volume} = \frac{4}{3}\pi\left(R^3 - r^3\right)$$

$$\frac{4}{3} \times 3.14\left[\left(\frac{13}{2}\right)^3 - 5^3\right] = \frac{4}{3} \times 3.14\left[\frac{2197 - 1000}{8}\right]$$

$$= \frac{1}{3} \times 3.14 \times \frac{1197}{2}$$

$$= 626.43 \text{ cm}^3.$$

Hence, volume of metal = 626.43 cm^3.

15. The floor of a rectangular hall has a perimeter 110 m. If the cost of painting the four walls at the rate of ₹10 per m^2 is ₹13200, find the height of the hall.

[BOARD TERM II, 2012, SET12]

Sol. According to the question,

Cost of painting at ₹10/m^2 = ₹13200

$$\therefore \ \text{Area painted} = \frac{13200}{10} = 1320 \text{ m}^2.$$

and perimeter of base = 110 m.

$$\therefore \ \text{Area of 4 walls} = \text{Perimeter} \times \text{Height}$$

$$\Rightarrow 1320 = 110 \text{ h}$$

$$\therefore \ \text{h} = \frac{1320}{110} = 12 \text{ m}.$$

Hence, the height of the hall = 12 m

16. The length, breadth and height of a rectangular box are $1 : 2 : 3$. Find the volume of the box, when its surface area is 1078 sq. m.

[BOARD TERM II, 2012, SET 01]

Sol. According to the question,

Surface area = 1078

$$\Rightarrow 2(lb + bh + hl) = 1078.$$

$$\Rightarrow lb + bh + hl = 539$$

Let dimensions be x, $2x$, $3x$, then

$$2x^2 + 6x^2 + 3x^2 = 539$$

$$11x^2 = 539$$

$$x^2 = 49$$

$$\therefore x = 7 \text{ m}$$

$l = 7$ m, $b = 14$ m and $h = 21$

$$= 2058 \text{ m}^3.$$

Hence volume of the box $= lbh = 7 \times 14 \times 21$

17. To construct a wall 25 m long, 0.3 m thick and 6 m high, bricks of dimensions 50 cm × 15 cm × 10 cm, are used. If the mortor occupies $\dfrac{1}{10}^{\text{th}}$ of the volume of the wall, find the number of bricks used.
[BOARD TERM II, 2012, SET 15]

Sol. According to the question,

Length = 25 m = 2500 cm

Thickness = 0.3 m = 600 cm

and Height = 5m = 600 cm

Volume of wall = $l \times b \times h$

Volume of wall = 2500 × 30 × 600 cm^3

Volume of 1 brick = 50 × 15 × 10 cm^3.

Number of bricks × Volume of one brick

$$= \text{Volume of the wall}$$

$$\Rightarrow \text{Number of bricks} = \frac{2500 \times 30 \times 600}{50 \times 15 \times 10} = 6000$$

But, mortor occupies = $\dfrac{1}{10}^{\text{th}}$ of volume

Hence, number of bricks used

$$= 6000 - \frac{6000}{10} = 5400$$

18. The internal and external diameters of a hollow hemispherical vessel are 24 cm and 25 cm respectively. If the cost of painting 1 cm^2 of the surface area is ₹ 0.05, find the total cost of painting the vessel all over.
[BOARD TERM II, 2013]

Sol. Internal radius (r) = 12 cm

and external radius (R) = 12.5 cm

$\therefore$ Surface area $= 2\pi r^2 + 2\pi R^2 + \pi(R^2 - r^2)$

$$= 2\pi(r^2 + R^2) + \pi(R - r)\,R + r)$$

$$= 2\pi[(12)^2 + (12.5)^2] + \pi(12.5 - 12)(12.5 + 12)$$

$$= 2\pi\,(144 + 156.25) + \pi(12.5 + 12)(12.5 - 12)$$

$$= (600.50 + 12.25) \times \frac{22}{7}$$

$$= \frac{22}{7} \times 612.75$$

$$= 1925.79 \text{ cm}^2.$$

Hence, Cost of painting 1925.79 cm^2 at the rate of 0.05/cm^2.

$$= 1925.79 \times 0.05$$

$$= ₹96.29.$$

19. A dome of a building is in the form of a hemisphere From inside, it was white washed at the cost of ₹ 997.92. If the cost of white washing is 400 paisa per square meter, find the volume of air inside the dome. (Take $\pi = \dfrac{22}{7}$)

[BOARD TERM II, 2013, 2015]

Sol. Let r be the inner radius of the hemispherical dome.

Then, according to the question,

Inside surface area $= 2\pi r^2$

$\therefore$ Cost of white washing at the rate of 400 paisa i.e., ₹4 per sq. meter $= 2\pi r^2 \times 4 = 8\pi r^2$.

It is given that the cost of white washing is ₹ 997.92

$$\Rightarrow 8\pi r^2 = 997.92$$

$$\Rightarrow 8 \times \frac{22}{7} \times r^2 = 997.92$$

$$\Rightarrow r^2 = \frac{997.92 \times 7}{8 \times 22}$$

$$\Rightarrow r^2 = = 39.69$$

$$\therefore r = 6.3$$

$\therefore$ Volume of the dome $= \dfrac{2}{3}\pi r^3$

$$= \frac{2}{3} \times \frac{22}{7} \times (6.3)^3$$

$$= 523.90 \text{ m}^3.$$

20. A solid piece of metal, cuboidal in shape, with dimensions 24 cm, 18 cm and 4 cm is recast into a cube. Calculate the lateral surface area of the cube.
[BOARD TERM II, 2014]

Sol. Let x be the edge of cube.

According to the question, we have

Volume of cube = Volume of cuboid

$$\Rightarrow x^3 = 24 \times 18 \times 4$$

$$\Rightarrow x^3 = 1728$$

$$\therefore \quad x = 12$$

$\therefore$ Edge of the cube = 12 cm

Hence, Lateral surface area of cube

$$= 4x^2 = 4(12)^2$$

$$= 576 \text{ cm}^2.$$

21. The length, breadth and height of a room are 6 m, 4 m and 3 m respectively. Find the cost of white washing the four walls of the room at the rate of ₹12 per m^2. The room has an entrance door measuring 2.5 × 1 m which is not be white washed.
[BOARD TERM II, 2015]

Sol. According to the question.

$l = 6$ m, $b = 4$ and $h = 3$m.

and area of 4 walls $= 2(l + b)h$

$$= 2(6 + 4)3 = 60 \text{ m}^2$$

and area of door $= 2.5 \times 1 = 2.5 \text{ m}^2$

$\therefore$ Net area to be white washed

$$= \text{Area of four walls} - \text{Area of door.}$$

$$= 60 - 2.5 = 57.5 \text{ m}^2$$

Hence, cost of white washing $= 57.5 \times 12 = ₹690$

22. A cuboidal water tank is 6 m long, 10 m wide and 4.5 m deep. How many litres of water it can hold?

[BOARD TERM II, SET RQTZFBW, 2016]

Sol. According to the question,

Length of cuboidal tank = 6 m

Width of cuboidal tank = 10 m

and depth of cuboidal tank = 4.5 m

Volume of water tank = $l \times b \times h$

$= 6 \times 10 \times 4.5 = 270$ m^3 $\because$ 1 m^3 = 1000 litres

Hence, capacity of water tank in litre

$= 270 \times 1000 = 270000$ litres.

23. How many litres of milk can a hemispherical bowl of diameter 10.5 cm hold?

[BOARD TERM II, KVS, 2016]

Sol. According to the question.

Diameter of hemispherical bowl = 10.5 cm

$\therefore$ Radius of hemispherical bowl

$r = \dfrac{10.5}{2} = 5.25$ cm

Now, volume of hemispherical bowl

$$= \frac{2}{3}\pi r^3 = \frac{2}{3} \times 3.14 \times (5.25)^3$$

$= 302.91 = 303$ cm^3

Hence, amount of milk that the hemispherical bowl can hold = 0.303 litres

24. Metallic spheres of radii 6 m, 8 m and 10 m, respectively are melted to form a single solid sphere. Find the radius of the resulting sphere.

[BOARD TERM II, 2017, SET Z6K408K]

Sol. Let $r_1 = 6$ m, $r_2 = 8$ m and $r_3 = 10$ m and the radius of resulting sphere be R.

According to the question,

Volume of resulting sphere = Sum of volume of small spheres.

$$\Rightarrow \frac{4}{3}\pi R^3 = \frac{4}{3}\pi r_1^3 + \frac{4}{3}\pi r_2^3 + \frac{4}{3}\pi r_3^3$$

$$\Rightarrow \frac{4}{3}\pi R^3 = \frac{4}{3}\pi\left(r_1^3 + r_2^3 + r_3^3\right)$$

$$\Rightarrow \frac{4}{3}\pi R^3 = \frac{4}{3}\pi\left(6^3 + 8^3 + 10^3\right)$$

$$\Rightarrow \frac{4}{3}\pi R^3 = \frac{4}{3}\pi(216 + 512 + 1000)$$

$$\Rightarrow \frac{4}{3}\pi R^3 = \frac{4}{3}\pi(1728)$$

$$\Rightarrow R^3 = 1728$$

$$\therefore \quad R = \sqrt[3]{1728} = 12 \text{ m}$$

25. A hemispherical bowl made of brass has . diameter 10.5 cm. Find the cost of tin plating on the inside at the rate of ₹16 per 100 cm^2.

[BOARD TERM II, 2017, SET-UAH4DQ7]

Sol. We have, inner diameter = 10.5 cm

$\therefore$ Inner radius (r) $= \dfrac{10.5}{2} = 5.25$ cm

Curved surface area of hemispherical bowl of inner side

$$= 2\pi r^2 = 2 \times \frac{22}{7} \times (5.25)^2.$$

$$= 2 \times \frac{22}{7} \times 5.25 \times 5.25$$

$$= 173.25 \text{ cm}^2$$

$\because$ Cost of tin plating on inside for 100 cm^2 = ₹16

$\therefore$ Cost of tin plating on the inside for 173.25 cm^2

$$= \frac{16 \times 173.25}{100} = ₹27.72$$

Long Answer Type Questions
(4 Marks Each)

1. Twenty seven solid iron spheres, each of radius r and surface area S are melted to form a sphere with surface area S′. Find the

(i) radius r′ of the new sphere.

(ii) ratio of S and S′. HOTS   [NCERT]

Sol. (i) Given, r be the radius of each solid iron sphere and r′ be the radius of new solid iron sphere, then

Volume of new sphere $\dfrac{4}{3}\pi r'^3$ and volume of old

sphere $= \dfrac{4}{3}\pi r^3$

Then, volume of 27 solid iron spheres

$= 27 \times$ volume of old sphere

$= 27 \times \dfrac{4}{3}\pi r^3 = 36\,\pi r^3$

$\because$ Twenty seven solid iron spheres are melted to new sphere with radius r′.

$$\Rightarrow \frac{4}{3}\pi r'^3 = 36\,\pi r^3$$

$$\Rightarrow r'^3 = \frac{36 \times 3r^3}{4}$$

$$\Rightarrow (r')^3 = 27r^3 = (3r)^3$$

$$r' = 3r \qquad \qquad ...(i)$$

Radius (r′) of the new sphere = 3r

(ii) Surface area (S) of solid iron sphere = $4\pi r^2$

Surface area (S′) of new sphere = $4\pi(r')^2$

$4\pi\,(3r)^2 = 36\,\pi r^2$ [From eq. (i)]

$\therefore$ Required ratio = S : S′ = $4\pi r^2 : 36\,\pi r^2 = 1 : 9$

2. A godown measures 40 m × 25 m × 15 m. Find the maximum number of wooden crates each measuring 1.5 m × 1.25 m × 0.5 m that can be stored in the godown. **[NCERT]**

Sol. Given, dimensions for godown are as

length (l) = 40 m, breadth (b) = 25 m and height (h) = 15 m

∴ Volume of the godown = $l \times b \times h$

$$= 40 \text{ m} \times 25 \text{ m} \times 15 \text{ m}$$

Dimensions for each wooden crates are as length (l_1) = 1.5 m, breadth (b_1) = 1.25 m and height (h_1) = 0.5 m

∴ Volume of each wooden crate = $l_1 \times b_1 \times h_1$

$$= 1.5 \text{ m} \times 1.25 \text{ m} \times 0.5 \text{ m}$$

Number of wooden crates

$$= \frac{\text{Volume of the godown}}{\text{Volume of one wooden crate}}$$

$$= \frac{40\text{m} \times 25\text{m} \times 15\text{m}}{1.5\text{m} \times 1.25\text{m} \times 0.5\text{m}}$$

$$= \frac{15000}{0.9375} = 16000$$

3. A cubical box has each edge 10 cm and another cuboidal box is 12.5 cm long, 10 cm wide and 8 cm high.

   (i) Which box has the greater lateral surface area and by how much?

   (ii) Which box has the smaller total surface area and by how much? **[NCERT]**

Sol. Given, length of the cubical box (l) = 10 cm

For cuboidal box, length (l) = 12.5 cm, breadth (b) = 10 cm and height (h) = 8 cm,

(i) Lateral surface area of cubical box

$$= 4l^2 = 4(10)^2 = 4 \times 100 = 400 \text{ cm}^2$$

Lateral surface area of cuboidal box

$$= 2(l + b) \times h = 2 (12.5 + 10) \times 8$$
$$= 2 (22.5) \times 8 = 45 \times 8 = 360 \text{ cm}^2$$

(Lateral surface area of cubical box) > (Lateral surface area of cuboidal box)

$$[\because 400 > 360]$$

∴ Required difference = $400 - 360 = 40 \text{ cm}^2$

Hence, cubical box has 40 cm² more lateral surface area.

(ii) Total surface area of cubical box

$$= 6l^2 = 6(10)^2 = 6 \times 100 = 600 \text{ cm}^2$$

Total surface area of cuboidal box

$$= 2(l \times b + b \times h + h \times l)$$
$$= 2 (12.5 \times 10 + 10 \times 8 + 8 \times 12.5)$$
$$= 2(125 + 80 + 100)$$
$$= 2 \times 305 = 610 \text{ cm}$$

(Total surface area of cuboid box) > (Total surface area of cubical box) $[\because 610 > 600]$

∴ Required difference = $610 - 600 = 10 \text{ cm}^2$

Hence, cubical box has 10 cm² less total surface area.

4. Shanti Sweets Stall was placing an order for making cardboard boxes for packing their sweets. Two sizes of boxes were required. The bigger of dimensions 25 cm × 20 cm × 5 cm and the smaller of dimensions 15 cm × 12 cm × 5 cm. For all the overlaps, 5% of the total surface area is required extra. If the cost of the cardboard is ₹4 for 1000 cm², then find the cost of cardboard required for supplying 250 boxes of each kind.

[NCERT]

Sol. Dimensions of bigger box are l = 25 cm, b = 20 cm and h = 5 cm

∴ Total surface area of the bigger box

$$= 2(l \times b + b \times h + h \times l)$$
$$= 2(25 \times 20 + 20 \times 5 + 5 \times 25)$$
$$= 2(500 + 100 + 125)$$
$$= 2(725) = 1450 \text{ cm}^2$$

Dimensions of smaller box are l = 15 cm, b = 12 cm and h = 5 cm

∴ Total surface area of the smaller box

$$= 2(15 \times 12 + 12 \times 5 + 5 \times 15)$$
$$= 2(180 + 60 + 75)$$
$$= 2(315) = 630 \text{ cm}^2$$

Total surface area of both boxes

$$= 1450 + 630 = 2080 \text{ cm}^2$$

Area for all the overlaps

$$= 5\% \text{ total surface area}$$
$$= 5\% \times 2080$$
$$= \frac{5}{100} \times 2080 = 104 \text{ cm}^2$$

Total surface area of both boxes with area of overlaps $- 2080 + 104 = 2184 \text{ cm}^2$.

∴ Total surface area for such 250 boxes

$$= 2184 \times 250 \text{ cm}^2$$

Now, cost of the cardboard for 1000 cm² = ₹4

Then, cost of the cardboard for 1 cm² = ₹ $\dfrac{4}{1000}$

∴ Cost of the cardboard for (2184 × 250) cm²

$$= \frac{4 \times 2184 \times 250}{1000} = ₹2184$$

Hence, required cost of cardboard is ₹2184.

5. The paint in a certain container is sufficient to paint an area equal to 9.375 m². How many bricks of dimensions 22.5 cm × 10 cm × 7.5 cm can be painted out of this container?

[BOARD TERM I, 2012, SET-36, NCERT]

Sol. Given, dimensions of a brick are l = 22.5 cm, b = 10 cm and h = 7.5 cm

and total surface area of container = 9.375 m²

Total surface area of brick

$$= 2(l \times b + b \times h + h \times l)$$
$$= 2(22.5 \times 10 + 10 \times 7.5 + 7.5 \times 22.5)$$
$$= 2(225 + 75 + 168.75)$$
$$= 2 \times 468.75 = 937.5 \text{ cm}^2$$
$$= \frac{937.5}{100 \times 100} \text{ m}^2$$

$$\left[\because (1 \text{ cm})^2 = \left(\frac{1}{100} \text{ m} \right)^2 \right.$$
$$\left. \Rightarrow 1 \text{ cm}^2 = \frac{1}{100 \times 100} \text{ m}^2 \right]$$

Number of bricks that painted out of this container

$$= \frac{\text{Total area painted by container's paint}}{\text{Total surface area of a brick}}$$

$$\Rightarrow \frac{9.375}{\dfrac{937.5}{100 \times 100}} = \frac{9.375 \times 100 \times 100}{937.5}$$

$$= \frac{937500}{9375} = 100$$

Hence, 100 bricks can be painted out.

6. A solid cube of side 12 cm is cut into eight cubes of equal volume. What will be the side of the new cube? Also, find the ratio between their surface areas [surface area of 8 new cubes and the original cube]

[BOARD TERM II, 2012, SET-26, 30, NCERT]

Sol. Let, side of new cube = x, then

According to the question,

Volume of cube = x^3

$(12)^3 = 8x^3$

$$\Rightarrow \frac{(12)^3}{8} = x^3$$

$$\Rightarrow \left(\frac{12}{2} \right)^3 = x^3$$

$$\therefore \ x = 6 \text{ cm}$$

Therefore, side of new cube = 6 cm.

$\therefore$ Ratio of surface areas of 8 new cubes to original cube

$$\Rightarrow \frac{8 \times 6x^2}{6(12)^2} = \frac{8 \times 6(6)^2}{6 \times 12 \times 12}$$

$$= \frac{8 \times 6 \times 6 \times 6}{6 \times 12 \times 12} = \frac{2}{1}$$

Hence, required ratio = 2 : 1

7. A dome of a building is in the form of hemisphere. From inside, it was white-washed at the cost of ₹ 498.96. If the cost of white washing is ₹ 2.00 per sq m, then find the

(i) inside surface area of the dome.

(ii) volume of the air inside the dome.

[BOARD TERM II, 2014, 2012, SET-69, 2013, NCERT]

Sol. Given, cost of white-washed = ₹498.96

and cost of white-washing per sq m = ₹2.00

(i) Inside surface area of the dome

$$= \frac{\text{Cost of white – washed}}{\text{Cost of white – washing per sq m}}$$

$$= \frac{₹498.96}{₹2.00} = 249.48 \text{ sq. m}$$

(ii) Let r be the radius of the dome.

$\therefore$ Inside surface area = 249.48 sq m

$$\Rightarrow 2\pi r^2 = 249.48$$

$$[\because \text{ Surface area of hemisphere} = 2\pi r^2]$$

$$= 2 \times \frac{22}{7} \times r^2 = 249.48$$

$$\Rightarrow r^2 = \frac{249.48 \times 7}{44}$$

$$\Rightarrow r^2 = 36.69 \Rightarrow \ r = 6.3 \text{ m}$$

$\therefore$ Volume of the air inside the dome $= \dfrac{2}{3}\pi r^3$

$$= \frac{2}{3} \times \frac{22}{7} \times (6.3)^3$$

$$= 523.908 \text{ m}^3 \text{ (approx)}$$

8. The radius of a spherical balloon increases from 7 cm to 14 cm as air is pumped into it. Find the ratio of surface area of the balloon in two cases.

[BOARD TERM I, 2012, SET-23 NCERT]

Sol. According to the question,

Original surface area $S_1 = 4\pi r_1^2$
$$= 4\pi \times 7 \times 7 \text{ cm}^2$$

and new surface area $S_2 = 4\pi r_2^2$
$$= 4\pi \times 14 \times 14 \text{ cm}^2$$

Hence, required ratio

$$\left(S_1 : S_2 \right) = \frac{4\pi \times 7 \times 7}{4\pi \times 14 \times 14} = \frac{1}{2} \times \frac{1}{2} = \frac{1}{4} = 1 : 4$$

9. The capacity of a cuboidal tank is 50,000 litres of water. Find the breadth of the tank, if its length and depth are respectively 2.5 m and 10 m.

[BOARD TERM II, 2012, SET-06. KVS, 2016, NCERT]

Sol. Given, volume of cuboidal tank = 50000 litres

$$= 5 \times 10^4 \text{ litres}$$
$$= 5 \times 10^4 \times 10^3 \text{ cm}^3 \quad [\because 1 \text{ litre} = 1000 \text{ cm}^3]$$

and Length of cuboidal tank = 2.5 m = 250 cm

Depth of cuboidal tank = 10 m = 1000 cm

According to the question,

$\because$ Volume of tank = Length × Breadth × Depth

$\Rightarrow 5 \times 10^4 \times 10^3 = 250 \times$ Breadth $\times 1000$

$$\therefore \text{ Breadth} = \frac{5 \times 10^4 \times 10^3}{250 \times 1000} = 200 \text{cm} = 2 \text{ m}.$$

10. The diameter of the Moon is approximately one-fourth of the diameter of the Earth. What fraction of the volume of the Earth is the volume of the Moon?   [KVS 2014, NCERT]

Sol. Let diameter of the Earth be d_2.

According to the question,

Diameter of Moon $(d_1) = \dfrac{1}{4} \times$ Diameter of the Earth

$$\Rightarrow d_1 = \frac{1}{4} d_2.$$

Hence, the radius of the Moon $= \dfrac{d_1}{2} = \dfrac{d_2}{8}$ and

Radius of the Earth $= \dfrac{d_2}{2}$

$\therefore$ Volume of the Earth (V_1)

$$= \frac{4}{3}\pi\left(\frac{d_2}{2}\right) = \frac{4}{3}\pi \times \frac{d_2^3}{8}$$

and volume of the Moon (V_2)

$$= \frac{4}{3}\pi\left(\frac{d_2}{8}\right)^3 = \frac{4}{3}\pi \times \frac{d_2^3}{512}$$

Now, required fraction $= \dfrac{V_1}{V_2} = \dfrac{\dfrac{4}{3}\pi\left(\dfrac{d_2^3}{8}\right)}{\dfrac{4}{3}\pi\left(\dfrac{d_2^3}{512}\right)}$

$$\Rightarrow \frac{V_1}{V_2} = \frac{512}{8}$$

$$\Rightarrow \frac{V_1}{V_2} = \frac{64}{1} \Rightarrow V_2 = \frac{1}{64}V_1$$

Hence, volume of the Moon is $\dfrac{1}{64}$ of the volume of Earth

11. A river 3 m deep and 40 m wide is flowing at the rate of 2 km/hr. How much water will fall into the sea in a minute?

[BOARD TERM II, KVS 2014, NCERT]

Sol. According to the question,

Rate of flow of water = 2 km/h

$$= \frac{2000}{60}\text{m}\,/\,\text{min}$$

$$= \frac{100}{3}\text{m}\,/\,\text{min}$$

Height of river = 3 m

and Width of river = 40 m.

$\therefore$ Volume of the water flowed in 1 min

$$= \left(\frac{100}{3} \times 40 \times 3\right)\text{m}^3$$

$$= 4000 \text{ m}^3 = 4000000 \text{ litres}$$

$$[1 \text{ m}^3 = 1000 \text{ litres}]$$

Hence, in 1 minute, 4000 m³ water will fall into the sea.

12. How many bricks each measuring 18 cm × 12 cm × 10 cm will be required to build a wall 12 m long, 6 dm wide and 4.5 m high when $\dfrac{1}{10}$ of its volume is occupied by mortor? Also find the cost of bricks at ₹ 225 per 100 bricks.

[BOARD TERM I, 2012, SET-12]

Sol. Given, Length of wall = 12 m

Width of wall = 6 dm and height of wall = 4.5 m

$$\text{Volume of wall } = 12 \times \frac{6}{10} \times 4.5 \text{ m}^3$$

$$\text{Volume of wall for bricks } = \frac{9}{10} \times 12 \times \frac{6}{10} \times 4.5 \text{ m}^3$$

$$\text{Volume of 1 brick } = \frac{18}{100} \times \frac{12}{100} \times \frac{10}{100}\text{m}^3$$

$\therefore$ Number of bricks

$$= \frac{\text{Volume of wall for bricks}}{\text{Volume of 1 brick}}$$

$$= \frac{\dfrac{9}{10} \times 12 \times \dfrac{6}{10} \times 4.5}{\dfrac{18}{100} \times \dfrac{12}{100} \times \dfrac{10}{100}}$$

$$= \frac{9}{10} \times 12 \times \frac{6}{10} \times \frac{45}{10} \times \frac{100}{18} \times \frac{100}{12} \times \frac{100}{10}$$

$$= 13500$$

Hence, cost of bricks @ ₹225 per 100 bricks

$$= \frac{13500 \times 225}{100} = ₹30,375$$

13. An open box is made of wood 3 cm thick. Its external dimensions are 1.4 m, 1.1 m and 0.8 m. Find the cost of painting the outer surface of box at 75 paise per 100 cm². **[BOARD TERM II, 2014]**

Sol. According to the question,

Length = 1.4 m = 140 cm

Breadth = 1.1 m = 110 cm

and Height = 0.8 m = 80 cm

$\therefore$ Surface area of open box = lb + 2(bh + hl)

$$= [154 + 2(88 + 112)] \times 100$$
$$= [154 + 2 \times 200] \times 100$$
$$= [154 + 400] \times 100 = 55400$$

Hence, cost of painting the outer surface of box

$$= \frac{75}{100 \times 100} \times 55400 = ₹415.50$$

14. A hemispherical dome, open at base is made from sheet of fibre. If the diameter of hemispherical dome is 80 cm and $\frac{13}{170}$ of sheet actually used was wasted in making the dome, then find the cost of dome at the rate of $\frac{35}{100}$ cm² .

[BOARD TERM II, 2014]

Sol. Given, Diameter = 80 cm

and Radius (r) $= \dfrac{80}{2} = 40$ cm

Curved surface area of the dome $= 2\pi r^2$

$$2 \times \frac{22}{7} \times 40 \times 40 = \frac{70400}{7} \text{ cm}^2$$

Since, $\dfrac{13}{170}$ of sheet was wasted

$\therefore$ Area of sheet wasted $= \dfrac{13}{170} \times \dfrac{70400}{7}$

$$= \frac{915200}{1190} \text{ cm}^2$$

$\therefore$ Total area $= \dfrac{70400}{7} + \dfrac{915200}{1190}$

$$= 10826.21 \text{ cm}^2.$$

Since, cost of sheet per square metre $= ₹ \dfrac{35}{100}$

$\therefore$ Total cost of sheet $= \dfrac{35}{100} \times 10826.21 = ₹\,3789.14$

Hence, total cost of dome is ₹3789.14.

15. The length and breadth of a hall are in the ratio 4 : 3 and its height is 550 cm. The cost of decorating its walls on Diwali (including doors and windows) at ₹ 6.60 per square metres is ₹ 5082. Find the length and breadth of the room.

[BOARD TERM II, 2015]

Sol. Let length and breadth of the hall be 4x and 3x respectively. Also, length, h = 550 cm = 5.5 m

According to the question,

Now, total cost of decorating walls

$$= \text{L.S.A.} \times \text{Rate per sq. metre}$$
$$\Rightarrow \qquad 5082 = 2h(l + b) \times 6.60$$
$$\Rightarrow \qquad 2 \times 5.5(4x + 3x) \times 6.60 = 5082$$
$$\Rightarrow \qquad 14x \times 5.5 \times 6.60 = 5082$$
$$\therefore x = \frac{5082}{5.5 \times 6.60 \times 14} = 10$$

Hence, length of the room $(l) = 4x = 4 \times 10 = 40$m

and breadth of the room $(b) = 3x = 3 \times 10 = 30$m

16. A teak wood log is in the form of cuboid of length 2.3 m, width 75 cm and of certain thickness. Its volume is 1.104 cu. m. How many rectangular planks of size 2.3 m × 75 cm × 4 cm can be cut from the cuboid? **[BOARD TERM II, 2015]**

Sol. We know that,

Volume of cuboid = Length × Width × Thickness

$\Rightarrow$ Thickness $= \dfrac{\text{Volume}}{\text{Length} \times \text{Width}}$

$\Rightarrow \dfrac{1.104}{2.3 \times 0.75} = 0.64$ m

Also, volume of rectangular planks

$$= 2.3 \text{ m} \times 0.75 \text{ m} \times 0.04 \text{ m}$$

Hence, Required number of planks

$$= \frac{\text{Volume of teak wood}}{\text{Volume of rectangular plank}}$$

$$= \frac{1.104}{2.3 \times 0.75 \times 0.04} = 16$$

17. The ratio of dimensions of a cuboidal box is 2 : 3 : 4. The difference between the cost of wrapping the box at the rate of ₹4 per square metre and ₹4.50 per square meter is ₹416. Find the dimensions of the cuboidal box.

[BOARD TERM II, SET-RQTZFBW, 2016]

Sol. Let length = 2x, breadth = 3x and height = 4x, then

$\therefore$ Total surface area of the box

$$= 2(lb + bh + hl)$$
$$= 2(2x \times 3x + 3x \times 4x + 4x \times 2x)$$
$$= 2(6x^2 + 12x^2 + 8x^2) = 52x^2$$

$\therefore$ Cost of wrapping at the rate of ₹4 per m²

$$= ₹4 \times 52x^2 = ₹208x^2.$$

and Cost of wrapping at the rate of ₹4.50 per m²

$$= ₹4.50 \times 52x^2 = ₹234x^2.$$

According to question,

$$234x^2 - 208x^2 = 416$$
$$\Rightarrow 26x^2 = 416 \Rightarrow x^2 = 16$$
$$\therefore x = 4 \text{ m}$$

Hence, the dimensions of the cuboidal box are

Length = 2x = 2 × 4 = 8 m

Breadth = 3x = 3 × 4 = 12 m

and Height = 4x = 4 × 4 = 16 m

18. The water for a industry is stored in a hemispherical tank of internal diameter 14 m. The tank contains 40 kilolitres of water. Water is pumped into the tank to fill it to full capacity. Calculate the volume of water pumped into the tank.

[BOARD TERM II, SET-RQTZFBW, 2016]

Sol. According to the question,

Volume of hemispherical tank $= \dfrac{2}{3}\pi r^3$

$$= \dfrac{2}{3} \times \dfrac{22}{7} \times 7 \times 7 \times 7 = \dfrac{44}{3} \times 49$$

$$= \dfrac{2156}{3}\,m^3 = 718.67\ m^3$$

$$= 718.67\ kl.$$

and volume of water already present
$$= 40\ Kilolitres$$

Hence, volume of water to be pumped
$$= 718.67 - 40 = 678.67\ m^3.$$

19. A closed cubical box of edge 20 cm is made up of wood of thickness 2 cm. Find the:
(i) Volume of the wood used to make it.
(ii) Volume of air trapped in it.

[BOARD TERM II, SET-LF0MCQ2, 2016]

Sol. (i) Given edge of cubical box (a) = 20 cm
Thickness of wood = 2 cm
We know that,
Volume of cubical box $= a^3 - (20)^3$
$\therefore$ Volume of the wood $= (22)^3 - (20)^3$.
$$= (22 \times 22 \times 22) - (20 \times 20 \times 20)$$
$$= 2648\ cm^3$$
(ii) Volume of air trapped in it
$$= \text{volume of cubical box}$$
$$= 20 \times 20 \times 20 = 8000\ cm^3.$$

20. A hemispherical bowl is made of 0.2 cm thick steel. The inner diameter of the bowl is 8 cm. Find outer curved surface area of the bowl. Also, find the cost of polishing its outer surface at the rate of ₹2 per cm³.

$$\left(\text{Take } \pi = \dfrac{22}{7}\right)$$

[BOARD TERM II, SET-LF0MCQ2, 2016]

Sol. According to the question,
The inner diameter of hemispherical bowl = 8 cm
Then its inner radius (r) = 4 cm
and thickness of steel = 0.2 cm
Therefore, outer radius of bowl (R) = 4 + 0.2
$$= 4.2\ cm$$
So, the outer curved surface area of the bowl
$$= 2\pi R^2 = 2 \times \dfrac{22}{7} \times (4.2)^2$$
$$= \dfrac{44}{7} \times \dfrac{42}{10} \times \dfrac{42}{10} = 110.88\ cm^2$$

Hence, the cost of polishing its outer surface area
$$= 2 \times 110.88 = ₹221.76.$$

21. A village has a population of 4000 people 60 litres of water is required per person per day. The village tanker of water is cuboidal in shape with dimensions 48 m × 27 m × 5 m which is completely filled with water. For how many days the water of this is sufficient?

[BOARD TERM II, SET-IA21924, 2016]

Sol. The given tanks is cuboidal in shape having its length (l) as 48 m, breadth (b) as 27 m, and height (h) as 5 m, then
According to the question,
$\therefore$ Volume of tank $= l \times b \times h = 48 \times 27 \times 5$
$$= 6480\ m^3 = 6480000\ litres$$
Total water consumption in village per day
$$= 4000 \times 60 = 240000\ litres$$
Hence, number of days for which water is sufficient
$$= \dfrac{6480000}{240000} = 27\ days.$$

22. The cost of papering the walls of the room 12 m long at the rate of ₹1.35 per m² is ₹340.20 and the cost of matting the floor at the rate of 85 paisa per m² is ₹91.80 find the height of the room.

[BOARD TERM II, 2015] [BOARD TERM II 2017, SET-UAH4DQ7]

Sol. According to the question,
Total cost of papering the walls of the room 12 m long at rate ₹1.35 per m² = ₹340.20
We know that,
Area of four walls $= 2(l + b)h$

$$\Rightarrow \text{Area of four walls } = \dfrac{\text{Total Cost}}{\text{Cost Per } m^2}$$

$$\Rightarrow 2(l + b)h = \dfrac{340.20}{1.35} = 252\ sq.m.$$

$\Rightarrow 2(l + b)h = 252$ ....(i)
Also, area of the floor $= l \times b$

$$\Rightarrow l \times b = \dfrac{91.80}{0.85}$$

$\Rightarrow l \times b = 108$ sq. m
$\Rightarrow l \times b = 108$
$\Rightarrow 12 \times b = 108$
$\therefore b = 9$ m ...(ii)
and $l \times 9 = 108$

$$\therefore l = \dfrac{108}{9} = 12\ m$$

On putting $l = 12$ m and $b = 9$ m in (i), we get
$2(12 + 9)h = 252$
$\Rightarrow 42h = 252$

$$\therefore h = \dfrac{252}{42} = 6\ m$$

Hence, height of the room = 6 m.

[Topic 2] Surface Areas and Volumes of Right Circular Cylinder and Cone

Points to be Remembered

- **Right circular cylinder :** A right circular is a cylinder whose base is a circle and whose elements are perpendicular to its base.
- If radius and height of a right circular cylinder are 'r' and 'h' units, respectively, then

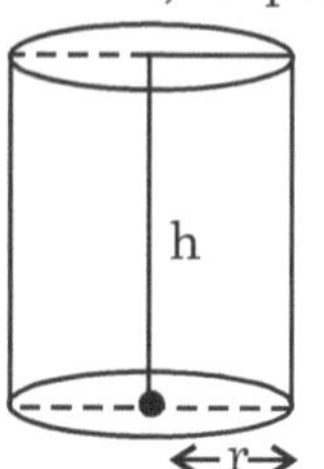

(i)   Curved surface area of cylinder = $2\pi rh$ sq. units

(ii) Total surface area = $2\pi rh\,(r + h)$ sq. units

(iii) Volume of a right circular cylinder = $\pi r^2 h$ cu. units

- **Right circular cone :** A right circular cone is a circular cone whose axis is perpendicular to its

base. The slant height of a right circular cone is the length $= \sqrt{(\text{Height})^2 + (\text{Radius})^2}$

- If the height and radius of a right circular cone are 'h' and 'r' units respectively, then

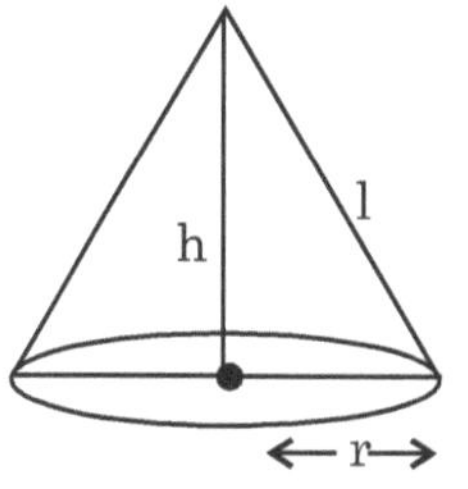

(i)   Slant height $(l) = \sqrt{r^2 + h^2}$ units

(ii) Curved surface area of a right circular cone = πrl sq. units

(iii) Total surface area of a right circular cone = $\pi r\,(r + l)$ sq. units

(iv) Volume of a right circular cone = $\dfrac{1}{3}\pi r^2 h$ cu. units

PREVIOUS YEARS'
EXAMINATION QUESTIONS
TOPIC 2

Multiple Choice Questions

1. The radii of two cylinders are in the ratio of 2:3 and their heights are in the ratio of 5:3. The ratio of their volumes is :
   (a) 10:17
   (b) 20:27
   (c) 17:27
   (d) 20:37   [NCERT Exemp.]

Sol. (b) Let the radii of two cylinders are $2x$ and $3x$ and their heights are $5y$ and $3y$ respectively

Hence, ratio of their volumes

$= \pi R^2 H : \pi r^2 h = \pi(2x)^2 5y : \pi (3x)^2 (3y)$

$= \dfrac{4 \times 5}{9 \times 3} = \dfrac{20}{27}$ or 20:27

2. In a cylinder, radius is doubled and height is halved, curved surface area will be
   (a) halved
   (b) doubled
   (c) same
   (d) four times.   [NCERT Exemp.]

Sol. (c) Radius of cylinder = 2r

Height of cylinder = $\dfrac{h}{2}$

∴ Curved surface area = $2\pi rh$

$\Rightarrow \qquad 2 \times \pi \times 2r \times \dfrac{h}{2} = 2\pi rh.$

Hence, curved surface area will be same.

3. The total surface area of a cone whose radius is $2r$ and slant height $2l$ is   [NCERT Exemp.]
   (a) $2\pi r\,(l + r)$
   (b) $\pi r\,(l + 4r)$
   (c) $\pi r\,(l + r)$
   (d) $2\pi rl$

Sol (a) Radius of a cone = 2r
   and Slant height of a cone = 2l
   Total surface area = $\pi r(l + r)$

$\qquad\qquad = \pi r(2l + 2r)$

$\qquad\qquad = 2\pi r(l + r).$

4. A conical tent is 60 m high and its base radius is 11 m. The slant height of the tent is:

(a) 57m (b) 61m (c) 71m (d) 49m

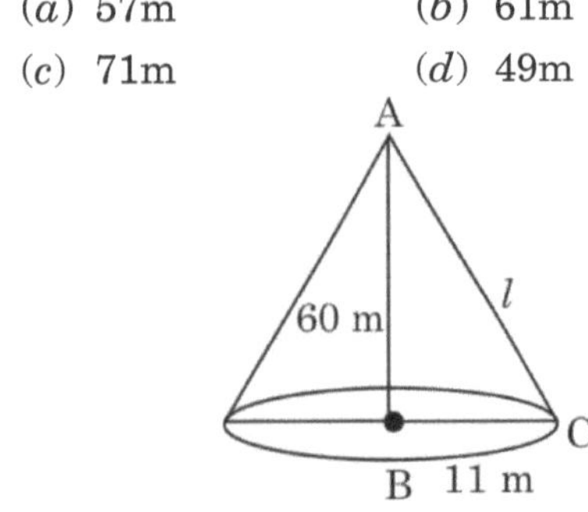

Sol. (b) Let slant height of the tent is l, then

According to the question,

$AC^2 = AB^2 + BC^2 = (60)^2 + (11)^2 = 3600 + 121$

$\therefore AC = l = \sqrt{3721} = 61m$

Very Short Answer Type Questions
(1 Mark Each)

1. Find the volume of a right circular cone with radius 6 cm and height 7 cm

[BOARD TERM II, 2012, NCERT]

Sol. According to the question,

Volume of right circular cone $= \dfrac{1}{3}\pi r^2 h$

$= \dfrac{1}{3} \times \dfrac{22}{7} \times (6)^2 \times 7$

$= \dfrac{1}{3} \times \dfrac{22}{7} \times 36 \times 7 = 22 \times 12 = 264 \text{ cm}^3$

2. The radii of two right circular cylinders are in the ratio 2:3 and their heights are in the ratio 5:3, then the ratio of their volumes will be----------

[BOARD TERM II, 2012, SET-69]

Sol. Let radii of cylinders be $2x$ and $3x$ and heights be $5y$ and $3y$ respectively, then

According to the question

Ratio of volumes $= \dfrac{\pi(2x)^2 \times 5y}{\pi(3x)^2 \times 3y}$

$= \dfrac{4x^2 \times 5}{9x^2 \times 3} = 20 : 27$

3. Two cylinders have bases of same size. The diameter of each is 7 cm. If one of the cylinder is 10 cm high and the other is 20 cm high, then the ratio of their volumes is........

[BOARD TERM II, 2013,]

Sol. Let r denotes the radius of both cylinders and h and h' be their heights respectively, then

According to the questions,

Ratio of their volumes $= \dfrac{\pi r^2 h}{\pi r^2 h'} = \dfrac{h}{h'} = \dfrac{10}{20} = 1{:}2$

4. How many faces does a right circular cylinder have?

[BOARD TERM II, SET-RQTZFBW,2016]

Sol. A right circular cylinder has three faces.

5. If the height and the radius of cone is tripled, then find ratio of volume of new cone and that of original.

[BOARD TERM II, SET-1A21924, 2016]

Sol. Let h and r be the height and radius of original cone and h' and r' be the height and radius of new cone.

h' = 3h and r' = 3r

According to the question,

Volume of original cone $V = \dfrac{1}{3}\pi r^2 h$

and volume of new cone $V' = \dfrac{1}{3}\pi (r')^2 h'$

$\therefore \dfrac{\text{Volume of new cone}}{\text{Volume of original cone}} = \dfrac{\dfrac{1}{3}\pi (r')^2 h'}{\dfrac{1}{3}\pi r^2 h}$

$= \dfrac{(r')^2 h'}{r^2 h}$

$= \dfrac{(3r)^2 \, 3h}{r^2 h} = \dfrac{27}{1}$

Hence, required ratio = 27:1

6. Curved surface area of a right circular cylinder is 4.4m². If the radius of the base of the cylinder is 0.7 m, then find its height.   **[NCERT]**

Sol. Let height of cylinder be h m.

Given, radius of base (r) = 0.7m

According to the question,

Curved surface area of a right circular

Cylinder = 4.4 m²

$2\pi rh = 4.4$

$\Rightarrow 2 \times \dfrac{22}{7} \times 0.7 \times h = 4.4$

$h = \dfrac{44}{44} = 1 \text{ m}$

Hence, the height of the right circular cylinder is 1 m.

7. Diameter of the base of a cone is 10.5 cm and its slant height is 10 cm. Find its curved surface area.   **[NCERT]**

Sol. We have, diameter = 10.5 cm

$\therefore$ Radius (r) $= \dfrac{10.5}{2} = 5.25$ cm

and slant height (l) = 10 cm

Now, curved surface area of the cone $= \pi r l$

$\Rightarrow \dfrac{22}{7} \times 5.25 \times 10 = 165 \text{ cm}^2$

8. A conical pit of top diameter 3.5 m is 12 m deep. What is its capacity (in litre)?   [NCERT]

Sol. Given, diameter of the top of conical pit = 3.5 m

$\therefore$ Radius (r) $= \dfrac{3.5}{2}$ m and height of conical pit (h) = 12 m

$\therefore$ Capacity of a conical pit = Volume of a cone

$$= \frac{1}{3}\, \pi r^2 h$$

$$= \frac{1}{3} \times \frac{22}{7} \times \left(\frac{3.5}{2}\right)^2 \times 12$$

$$= \frac{1}{3} \times \frac{22}{7} \times \frac{3.5}{2} \times \frac{3.5}{2} \times 12$$

$$= 22 \times 0.5 \times 3.5 = 38.5 \text{ m}^3$$

$$= 38.5 \text{ kL} \quad [\because 1 \text{ m}^3 = 1 \text{ kL}]$$

9. It is required to make a closed cylindrical tank of height 1 m and base diameter 140 cm from a metal sheet. How many square meters of the sheet are required for the same?   [NCERT]

Sol. Let r be the radius and h be the height of the cylinder.

Given, diameter of the base = 140 cm

$\therefore$ Radius (r) $= \dfrac{140}{2}$ = 70 cm = 0.70 m

and h = 1 m

So, metal sheet required to make a closed cylinder tank

= Total surface area of right circular cylinder

$$= 2\pi r\,(h + r) = 2 \times \frac{22}{7} \times 0.7(1 + 0.7)$$

$$= 2 \times 22 \times 0.1 \times 1.7 = 7.48 \text{ m}^2$$

Hence, the sheet required to make a closed cylindrical tank is 7.48 m².

10. In a hot water heating system, there is a cylindrical pipe of length 28 m and diameter 5 cm. Find the total radiating surface in the system.   [NCERT]

Sol. Given, length or height of the pipe (h) = 28 m and diameter = 5 cm

$\therefore$ Radius (r) $= \dfrac{5}{2}$ = 2.5 cm

$$= \frac{2.5}{100} \text{ m} = 0.025 \text{ m} \quad \left[\because 1\text{cm} = \frac{1}{100}\text{ m}\right]$$

Total radiating surface in the system

= Curved surface area of the cylindrical pipe

$$= 2\pi rh = 2 \times \frac{22}{7} \times 0025 \times 28$$

$$= 4.4 \text{ m}^2$$

Write whether the statements are true or false. Justify your answer.

1. If the length of the diagonal of a cube is $6\sqrt{3}$ cm, then the length of the edge of the cube is 3 cm.   [NCERT Exemp.]

Sol. Diagonal of a cube $= \sqrt{l^2 + b^2 + h^2}$

$$= \sqrt{3^2 + 3^2 + 3^3} = \sqrt{27} = \sqrt{9 \times 3}$$

$$= 3\sqrt{3} \neq 6$$

Hence, the given statement is false.

2. The volume of a sphere is equal to two-third of the volume of a cylinder whose height and diameter is equal to the diameter of the sphere.   [NCERT Exemp.]

Sol. Given,

H = 2r and R = r

Volume of sphere $= \dfrac{2}{3}$rd volume of cylinder

$$\Rightarrow \frac{4}{3}\pi r^3 = \frac{2}{3}\pi R^2 H$$

$$\Rightarrow \frac{4}{3}\pi r^3 = \frac{4}{3}\pi r^3 \text{ which is equal.}$$

Hence, the given statement is true.

3. A cylinder and a right circular cone are having the same base and same height.

The volume of the cylinder is three times the volume of the cone.   [NCERT Exemp.]

Sol. Volume of cylinder = $\pi r^2 h$

Volume of cone $= \dfrac{1}{3}\,\pi r^2 h$

$\therefore$ Volume of cylinder = 3 × volume of cone.

Hence, the given statement is true.

4. If the radius of a right circular cone is halved and height is doubled, the volume will remain unchanged.   [NCERT Exemp.]

Sol. Radius of a right circular cone $= \dfrac{r}{2}$

and Height of a right circular cone = 2h

$\therefore$ Volume $= \dfrac{1}{3}\,\pi r^2 h$

$$= \frac{1}{3}\pi\left(\frac{r}{2}\right)^2 2h$$

$$= \frac{1}{2} \times \frac{1}{3} \times \pi r^2 h$$

Hence, the given statement is false.

5. A cone, a hemisphere and a cylinder stand on equal bases and have the same height. The ratio of their volumes is $1 : 2 : 3$. [NCERT Exemp.]

Sol. Volume of cone $= \dfrac{1}{3}\pi r^2 \times r = \dfrac{1}{3}\pi r^3$

Volume of hemisphere $= \dfrac{2}{3}\pi r^3$

and Volume of cylinder $= \pi r^2 r = \pi r^3$

$\therefore$ Required ratio $= \dfrac{1}{3}\pi r^3 : \dfrac{2}{3}\pi r^3 : \pi r^3$

$= \dfrac{1}{3} : \dfrac{2}{3} : 1$

$= 1 : 2 : 3$

Hence, the given statement is true.

6. The volume of the largest right circular cone that can be fitted in a cube whose edge is 2r equals to the volume of a hemisphere of radius r.
[NCERT Exemp.]

Sol. $\therefore$ Volume of cone $= \dfrac{1}{3}\pi r^2 2r = \dfrac{2}{3}\pi r^3$

$=$ Volume of hemisphere.

Therefore, the given statement is true.

Short Answer Type Questions I

(2 Mark Each)

1. The diameter of a roller is 84 cm and its length is 120 cm. It takes 500 complete revolutions to move once over to level a playground. Find the area (in sq m) of the playground.   [NCERT]

Sol. According to the question,

Diameter of a roller = 84 cm

$\therefore$ r = Radius of a roller $= \dfrac{84}{2} = 42$ cm

and height (h) = 120 cm

Area covered in 1 revolution

$\qquad\qquad$ = Curved surface area of roller

$\Rightarrow 2\pi rh = 2 \times \dfrac{22}{7} \times 42 \times 120$

$\Rightarrow 44 \times 720 = 31680$ cm^2

$\Rightarrow \left(\dfrac{31680}{100 \times 100}\right)$ m^2 = 3.168 m^2

$$\left[\because (1\text{cm})^2 = \left(\dfrac{1}{100}\text{m}\right)^2 \\ \Rightarrow 1\,\text{cm}^2 = \dfrac{1}{100 \times 100}\text{m}^2 \right]$$

Now, area of the playground

$\qquad$ = Area covered in 500 complete revolutions

$\qquad$ = $500 \times 3.168 = 1584$ m^2

2. A cylindrical pillar is 50 cm in diameter and 3.5 m in height. Find the cost of painting the curved surface of the pillar at the rate of ₹ 12.50 per m^2.
[NCERT]

Sol. Given, diameter of a cylindrical pillar

$\therefore$ Radius (r) $= \dfrac{50}{2 \times 100} = 0.25$ m

$$\left[\because 1\text{cm} = \dfrac{1}{100}\text{m} \right]$$

and height (h) = 3.5 m

$\therefore$ Curved surface area of the cylindrical pillar

$\qquad\qquad = 2\pi rh$

$\qquad\qquad = 2 \times \dfrac{22}{7} \times 0.25 \times 3.5$

$\qquad\qquad = 2 \times 22 \times 0.25 \times 0.5$

$\qquad\qquad = 5.5$ m^2

$\because$ Cost of painting per m^2 = ₹ 12.50

$\therefore$ Cost of painting 5.5 m^2 = $12.50 \times 5.5 =$ ₹ 68.75

3. The curved surface area of a right circular cylinder of height 14 cm is 88 cm^2. Find the diameter of the base of the cylinder. $\left[\text{Take } \pi = \dfrac{22}{7}\right]$
[BOARD TERM II, KVS 2014, NCERT]

Sol. Let radius of the base be r cm.

Given, height (h) = 14 cm

and curved surface area of a right circular cylinder = 88 cm^2

$\therefore 2\pi rh = 88$

$\qquad$ [$\because$ Curved surface area of cylinder $= 2\pi rh$]

$\Rightarrow 2 \times \dfrac{22}{7} \times r \times 14 = 88$

$\therefore r = \dfrac{88 \times 7}{2 \times 22 \times 14} = 1$ cm

Hence, diameter $= 2 \times$ radius $= 2 \times 1 = 2$ cm

4. A cone is 8.4 cm high and the radius of its base is 2.1 cm. It is melted and recast into a sphere. Then, what is the radius of the sphere?
[NCERT Exemp.] [BOARD TERM II, SET-IA21929, 2016]

Sol. Given, height of a cone (h) = 8.4 cm

and radius of its base (r) = 2.1 cm

According to the question,

Volume of a cone = Volume of a sphere

$\Rightarrow \dfrac{1}{3}\pi r^2 h = \dfrac{4}{3}\pi R^3$ [Let radius of sphere be R]

$\Rightarrow 4R^3 = r^2 h$

$\Rightarrow 4R^3 = (2.1)^2 \times (8.4)$

$$\Rightarrow R^3 = \frac{2.1 \times 2.1 \times 8.4}{4} = \frac{21 \times 21 \times 21}{10 \times 10 \times 10}$$

$$\therefore R = \frac{21}{10} = 2.1 \qquad \text{[On taking cube root]}$$

Hence, the radius of the sphere is 2.1 cm.

5. A right circular cylinder is 3 m high and the circumference of its base is 22 m. Find its curved surface area.

[BOARD TERM II, 2012, SET 05]

Sol.- Circumference, $2\pi r = 22$ m and h = 3 m

$\therefore$ Curved surface area = $2\pi r \times h = 22 \times 3 = 66$ m^2.

6. A square piece of paper of side 22 cm is rolled to form a cylinder. Find the volume of the cylinder.

$$\left(\text{Take } \pi = \frac{22}{7} \right)$$

[BOARD TERM II, 2012, SET 24]

Sol. Height of the cylinder formed, h = 22 cm

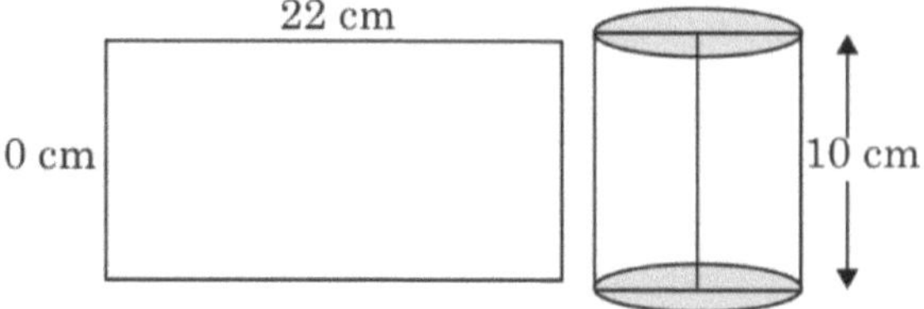

According to the question,

Circumference of the base, $2\pi r = 22$ cm

$$\therefore r = \frac{11}{\pi} = \frac{11 \times 7}{22} = \frac{7}{2} \text{cm}$$

$\therefore$ Volume of the cylinder = $\pi r^2 h$

$$\Rightarrow \frac{22}{7} \times \frac{7}{2} \times \frac{7}{2} \times 22 = 847 \text{ cm}^3.$$

7. What is the radius and curved surface area of a cone made from a quadrant of a circle of radius 28 cm?

[BOARD TERM II, 2012, SET 20]

Sol. According to the question,

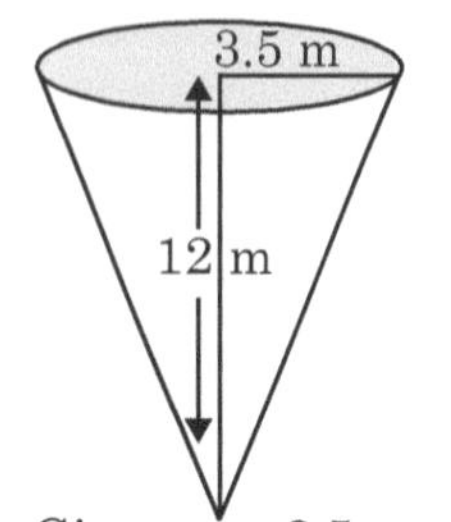

l = Radius of quadrant of circle = R

l = 28 cm

Area of quadrant = Curved surface area of cone

$$\Rightarrow \frac{1}{4}\pi R^2 = \pi r l$$

$$\Rightarrow \frac{1}{4} \times \pi \times (28)^2 = \pi r l$$

$$\Rightarrow \frac{28 \times 28}{4} = r \times 28$$

r = 7 cm

Hence, curved surface area of cone = $\pi r l$

$$\frac{22}{7} \times 7 \times 28 = 22 \times 28 = 616 \text{ cm}^2.$$

8. A conical pit of top diameter 7 m is 12 m deep. What is its capacity in litre ?

[BOARD TERM II, 2012, SET 01]

Sol.

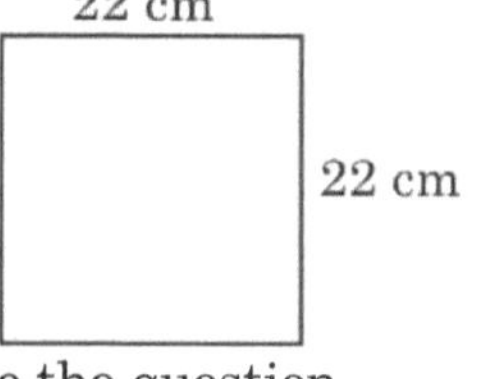

Given, r = 3.5 m and h = 12 m

$$\therefore V = \frac{1}{3}\pi r^2 h$$

$$= \frac{1}{3} \times \frac{22}{7} \times 3.5 \times 3.5 \times 12$$

$$= 154 \text{ m}^3 \ [1 \text{ m}^3 = 1000 \text{ litre}]$$

Hence, required capacity = 154000 litres.

9. A rectangular piece of paper is 22 cm long and 10 cm wide. A cylinder is formed by rolling the paper along its length. Find the volume of the cylinder.   [BOARD TERM II, 2013]

Sol. When the rectangular piece of paper is rolled along its length, then the length of the sheet forms the circumference of its base and breadth becomes the height of cylinder.

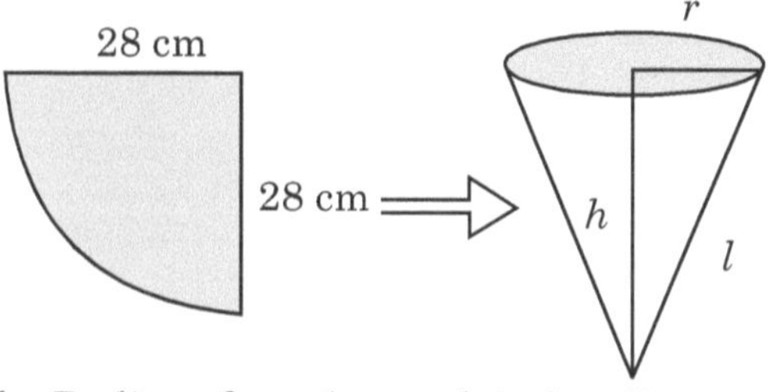

Let r denotes the radius of the base and h be the height. Then, h = 10 cm

Now, according to the question,

Circumference of base = Length of sheet

$$\Rightarrow 2\pi r = 22$$

$$\Rightarrow 2 \times \frac{22}{7} \times r = 22$$

$$\therefore r = \frac{7}{2} \text{cm}$$

$\therefore$ Volume of cylinder = $\pi r^2 h$

$$= \frac{22}{7} \times \frac{7}{2} \times \frac{7}{2} \times 10$$

$$= 385 \text{ cm}^3.$$

10. If the curved surface area of a cylinder is 94.2 cm^2 and height is 5 cm, then find radius of its base and volume of the cylinder (use $\pi = 3.14$). ?

[BOARD TERM II, 2013, NCERT]

Sol. Let, radius of base = r

According to the question, curved surface area of cylinder = $2\pi rh$

$$2\pi rh = 94.2 \text{ cm}^2$$

$$\Rightarrow 2 \times 3.14 \times r \times 5 = 94.2$$

$$\therefore r = \frac{94.2}{10 \times 3.14} = 3 \text{ cm}$$

Now, volume = $\pi r^2 h$

$$= 3.14 \times 3 \times 3 \times 5$$

$$= 141.3 \text{ cm}^3.$$

11. What is the volume of a right circular cylinder whose base area is 606 cm^2 and height is 2 m?

[BOARD TERM II, 2014]

Sol. Given, area = $\pi r^2 = 606$ cm^2

and h = 2 m = 200 cm

$\therefore$ Volume = $\pi r^2 h$

$$= (\text{Area}) \, h$$

$$= 606 \times 200$$

$$= 121200 \text{ cm}^3.$$

Hence, the volume of a right circular cylinder

$$= 121200 \text{ cm}^3$$

Alternative Method

According to the question,

Base area of cylinder = 606 cm^2

$$\Rightarrow \pi r^2 = 606$$

$$\therefore r^2 = \frac{606 \times 7}{22}$$

Also, given height (h) of cylinder = 2 m = 200 cm

Now, volume of right circular cylinder

$$= \pi r^2 h$$

$$= \frac{22}{7} \times \frac{600 \times 7}{22} \times 200 \quad \left[\because r^2 = \frac{606 \times 7}{22} \right]$$

$$= 121200 \text{ cm}^3.$$

12. Find the radius of the base of a right circular cylinder whose curved surface area is $\frac{2}{3}$ of the sum of the surface areas of two circular faces. The height of the cylinder is given to be 15 cm.

[BOARD TERM II, 2015]

Sol. Given, h = 15

According to the question,

Curved surface area of cylinder $= \frac{2}{3}$ (sum of circular faces)

$$\Rightarrow 2\pi rh = \frac{2}{3}\left(2\pi r^2\right)$$

$$\Rightarrow 15 = \frac{2}{3} r$$

$$\therefore r = \frac{45}{2} = 22.5 \text{ cm}$$

Hence, the radius of a right circular cylinder

$$= 22.5 \text{ cm}.$$

13. The total surface area of a solid right circular cylinder is 1540 cm^2. If the height is four times the radius of the base, then find the height of the cylinder.

[BOARD TERM II, 2016 SET RQTZFBW]

Sol. According to the question,

Total surface area = 1540 cm^2

$$\Rightarrow 2\pi r(h + r) = 1540 \text{ cm}^2 \qquad (\because \text{ h = 4r})$$

$$\therefore 2\pi r \, (4r + r) = 1540$$

$$\Rightarrow 2\pi \times 5r^2 = 1540$$

$$\Rightarrow r^2 = \frac{1540 \times 7}{2 \times 5 \times 22}$$

$$\Rightarrow r^2 = 49$$

$$\therefore r = 7 \text{ cm}$$

Now, h = 4r = 4 × 7 = 28 cm.

Hence, the height of the cylinder = 28 cm.

14. The radius and slant height of a cone are in the ratio 4 : 7. If its curved surface area is 792 cm^2, find its radius.

[BOARD TERM II, 2017 SET Z6K408K]

Sol. Let the radius of a cone

$$r = 4x$$

and in slant height $(l) = 7x$

Curved surface area of cone = 792 cm^2

$$\Rightarrow \pi r l = 792$$

$$\Rightarrow \frac{22}{7} \times 4x \times 7x = 792$$

$$\Rightarrow x^2 = \frac{792 \times 7}{22 \times 4 \times 7}$$

$$\Rightarrow x^2 = 9$$

$$\therefore x = 3 \text{ cm}$$

Hence, radius of the cone = 4 × 3 = 12 cm.

15. How much ice-cream can be put into a cone with base radius 3.5 cm and height 12 cm?.

[BOARD TERM II, 2017, SET UAH4DQ7]

Sol. Given, r = 3.5 cm and h = 12 cm

$$\therefore \text{ Amount of ice-cream } = \frac{1}{3}\pi r^2 h$$

$$= \frac{1}{3} \times \frac{22}{7} \times 3.5 \times 3.5 \times 12 = 154 \text{ cm}^3$$

Short Answer Type Questions II

(3 Marks Each)

1. The inner diameter of a cylindrical wooden pipe is 24 cm and its outer diameter is 28 cm. The length of the pipe is 35 cm. Find the mass of the pipe, if 1 cm³ of wood has a mass of 0.6 g.

[NCERT]

Sol. According to the question,

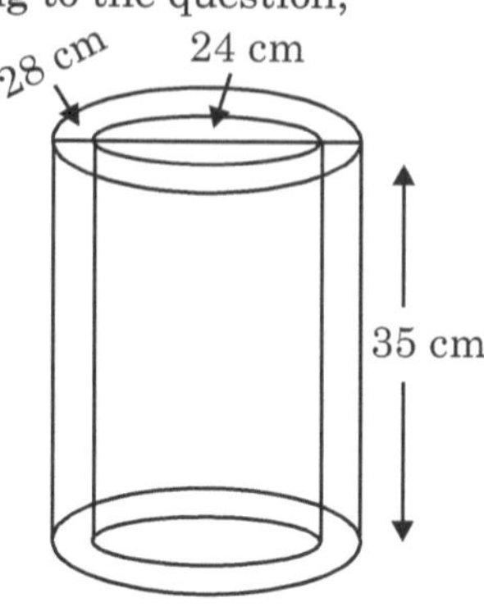

Given, inner diameter = 24 cm

$\therefore$ Inner radius $(r_1) = \dfrac{24}{2} = 12$ cm

and outer diameter = 28 cm

$\therefore$ Outer radius $(r_2) = \dfrac{28}{2} = 14$ cm

and height (h) = 35 cm

So, volume of cylindrical wooden pipe

= Outer volume − Inner volume

$= \pi\left(r_2^2 - r_1^2\right)h = \dfrac{22}{7}(14^2 - 12^2) \times 35$

$= \dfrac{22}{7}(14 + 12)(14 - 12) \times 35 = \dfrac{22}{7} \times 26 \times 2 \times 35$

$= 22 \times 26 \times 2 \times 5 = 5720$ cm³

$\because$ Mass of 1 cm³ of wood = 0.6 g

Hence, mass of 5720 cm³ of wood = 0.6 × 5720

$= 3432$ gm $= \left(\dfrac{3432}{1000}\right)$ kg

$= 3.432$ kg $\qquad [\because\ 1$ kg = 1000 gm$]$

2. If the lateral surface area of a cylinder is 94.2 cm² and its height is 5 cm, then find
   (i)   radius of its base.
   (ii) its volume. (take, π = 3.14)   [NCERT]

Sol. Let r be the radius of the base.

We have, height (h) = 5 cm

Now, according to the question,

Lateral surface area of a cylinder = 94.2 cm²

$\Rightarrow 2\pi rh = 94.2$

$\Rightarrow 2 \times 3.14 \times r \times 5 = 94.2\ \ r = \dfrac{94.2}{31.4} = 3$ cm

(i) Hence, radius of base (r) = 3 cm

(ii) Volume of a cylinder = $\pi r^2 h = 3.14 \times (3)^2 \times 5$

$\qquad = 3.14 \times 9 \times 5 = 141.3$ cm³

3. A conical tent is 10 m high and the radius of its base is 24 m. Find
   (i) slant height of the tent.
   (ii) cost of the canvas required to make the tent, if the cost of 1 m² canvas is ₹ 70.   [NCERT]

Sol. We have, height (h) = 10 m and radius (r) = 24 m

(i)

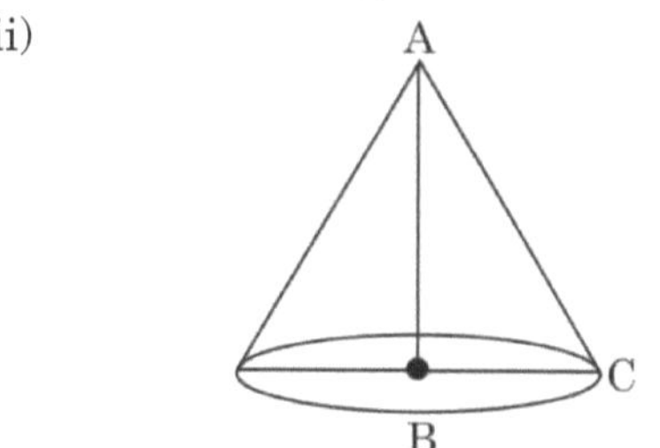

We known that,

$l^2 = h^2 + r^2 \Rightarrow l = \sqrt{r^2 + h^2}$

[On taking positive square root]

$\therefore l = \sqrt{(24)^2 + \left(10^2\right)} = \sqrt{576 + 100}$

$\qquad = \sqrt{676} = 26$ m

Hence, the slant hight of the canvas tent is 26 m.

(ii)

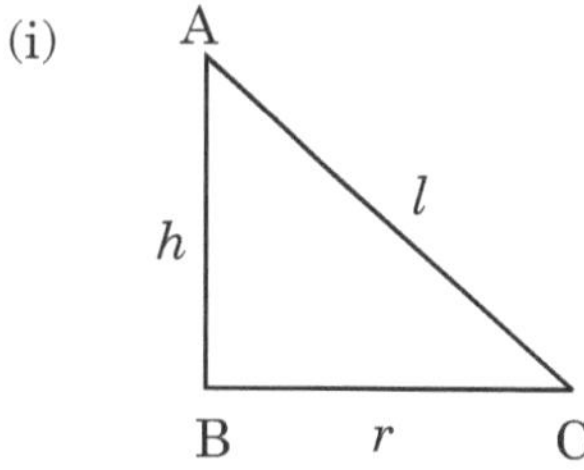

Canvas required to make the tent

= Curved surface area of tent

$= \pi rl = \pi \times 24 \times 26 = 624\ \pi$ m²

$\because$ Cost of 1 m² canvas = ₹ 70

$\therefore$ Cost of 624 π m² curved = 70 × 624 π

$\qquad = 70 \times 624 \times \dfrac{22}{7}$

$\qquad = 10 \times 624 \times 22$

$\qquad = ₹ 137280$

Hence, required cost of the canvas is ₹ 137280.

4. A cylindrical tube opened at both the ends is made of iron sheet which is 2 cm thick. If the outer diameter is 16 cm and its length is 100 cm, then find how many cubic centimetres of iron has been used in making the tube?

[NCERT Exemplar]

Sol.

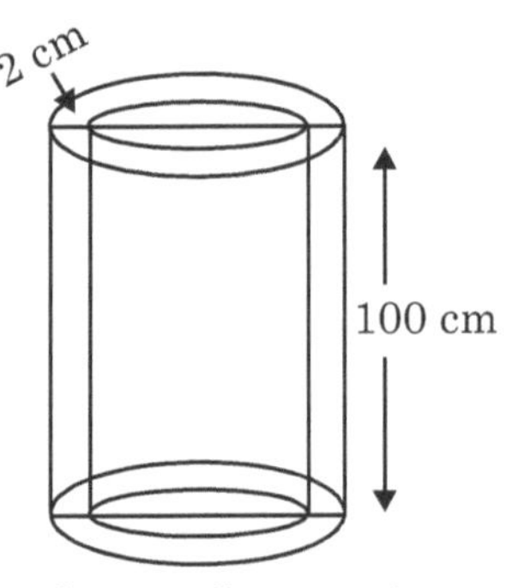

According to the question,

Given, outer diameter of cylindrical tube

$$(d) = 16 \text{ cm}$$

$\therefore$ Outer radius (r_1) of a cylindrical tube

$$= \frac{16}{2} = 8 \text{cm}$$

and inner radius (r_2) of a cylindrical tube

$$= (r_1 - \text{thickness of the sheet})$$
$$= (8 - 2) = 6 \text{ cm}$$

Height of a cylindrical tube (h) = 100 cm

Volume of metal used in making cylindrical tube

$$= \text{Outer volume of a cylindrical tube}$$
$$- \text{Inner volume of a cylindrical tube}$$
$$= \pi r_1^2 h - \pi r_2^2 h = \pi h\left(r_1^2 - r_2^2\right)$$

$$= \frac{22}{7} \times 100\left(8^2 - 6^2\right)$$

$$\frac{22}{7} \times 100\,(8 + 6)\,(8 - 6)$$
$$[\because\ a^2 - b^2 = (a + b)\,(a - b)]$$

$$\frac{22}{7} \times 100 \times 14 \times 2$$

$$= 2200 \times 4 = 8800 \text{ cm}^3$$

Hence, 8800 cm³ of iron has been used in making a cylindrical tube.

5. In given figure, you see the frame of a lampshade. It is to be covered with a decorative cloth. The frame has a base diameter of 20 cm and height of 30 cm. A margin of 2.5 cm is to be given for folding it over the top and bottom of the frame. Find how much cloth is required for covering the lampshade?

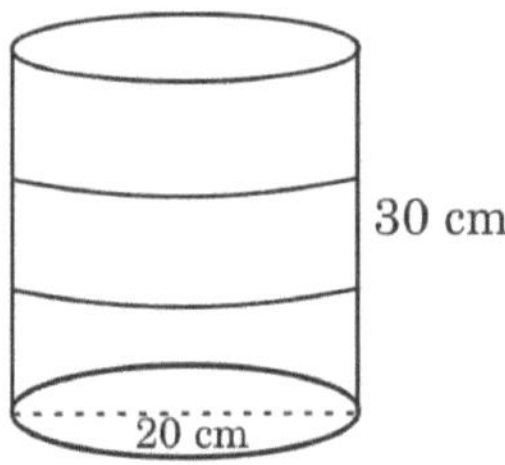

[NCERT]

Sol. Given, diameter of the base = 20 cm

$$\therefore \text{ Radius (r)} = \frac{20}{2} = 10 \text{ cm}$$

and height (h) = 30 cm

Since, a margin of 2.5 cm is used for folding it over the top and bottom.

So, the total height of frame (h_1)

$$= 30 + 2.5 + 2.5 = 35 \text{ cm}$$

$\therefore$ Cloth required for covering the lampshade

$$= \text{Curved surface area of lampshade}$$

$$= 2\pi r(h_1) = 2 \times \frac{22}{7} \times 10 \times (35)$$

$$= \frac{440}{7} \times 35$$

$$= 440 \times 5 = 2200 \text{ cm}^2$$

Hence, 2200 cm² cloth is required for covering the lampshade.

6. The slant height and base diameter of a conical tomb are 25 m and 14 m, respectively. Find the cost of white-washing its curved surface at the rate of ₹ 210 per 100 m².

[NCERT][BOARD TERM II, 2012 SET 15]

Sol.

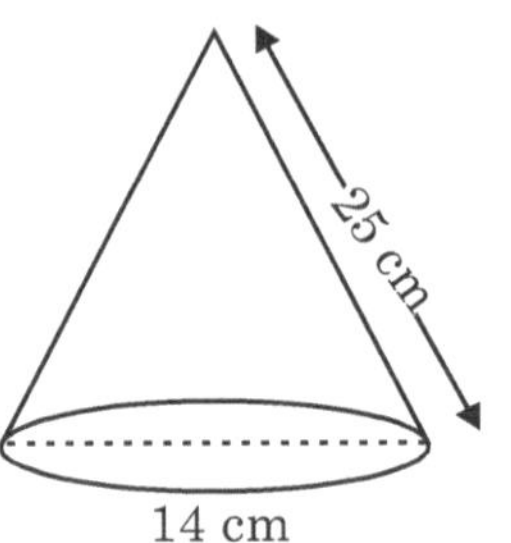

We have, slant height $(l) = 25$ m and

$$\text{Diameter} = 14 \text{ m}$$

$$\therefore \text{ Radius (r)} = \frac{14}{2} = 7 \text{ m}$$

Curved surface area of the conical tomb

$$= \text{Curved surface area of a cone}$$

$$= \pi r l$$

$$= \frac{22}{7} \times 7 \times 25 = 22 \times 25 = 550 \text{ m}^2$$

Given, cost of the white-washing per 100 m²

$$= ₹\ 210$$

$\therefore$ Cost of white-washing per 1 m² $= ₹\ \dfrac{210}{100}$

Then, cost of white-washing 550 m²

$$= \frac{210 \times 550}{100} = ₹\ 1155$$

7. A joker's cap is in the form of right circular cone of base radius 7 cm and slant height 25 cm. Find the area of sheet required for 10 such caps.

[NCERT] [BOARD TERM II, KVS 2014]

Sol.

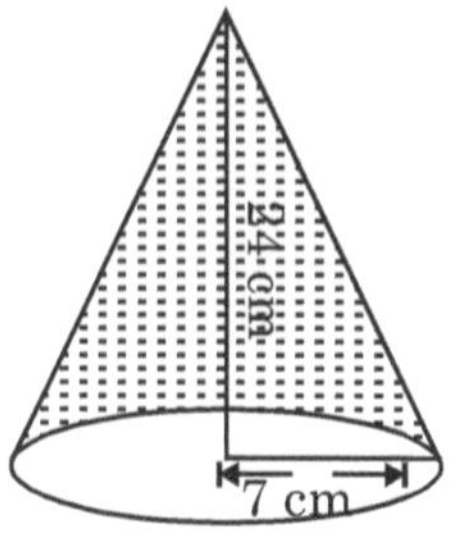

We have, radius (r) = 7cm
and height (h) = 24 cm
We know that, $l^2 = h^2 + r^2$

$\Rightarrow l = \sqrt{h^2 + r^2}$

[On taking positive square root]

$\Rightarrow l = \sqrt{(24)^2 + 7^2} = \sqrt{576 + 49} = \sqrt{625}$

$\therefore l$ = 25 cm

Curved surface area of a joker's cap

$\quad$ = Curved surface area of a cone = πrl

$\quad = \dfrac{22}{7} \times 7 \times 25 = 22 \times 25 = 550$ cm^2

$\because$ The sheet required to make 1 cap = 550 cm^2

Hence, the sheet required to make 10 such caps

$\quad$ = 550 × 10 = 5500 cm^2

8. The height of a cone is 16 cm and its base radius is 12 cm. Find the total surface area of the cone. (use π = 3.14)

[NCERT] [BOARD TERM II, KVS, 2016]

Sol. Total surface area of cone $\pi r(l + r)$

Given, r = 12 cm and h = 16 cm

$\therefore$ Slant height $(l) = \sqrt{r^2 + h^2}$

$\quad = \sqrt{(12)^2 + (16)^2}$

$\quad = \sqrt{144 + 256}$

$\quad = \sqrt{400} = 20$cm

$\therefore$ Total surface area = $2\pi h(l + r)$

$\quad$ = 3.14 × 12 (20 + 12)

$\quad$ = 3.14 ×12 × 32

$\quad$ = 1205.76 cm^2.

9. The circumference of the base of a cylindrical vessel is 132 cm and its height is 25 cm. How many litres of water can it hold? (1000 cm^3 = 1L)

[BOARD TERM II, KVS 2014, 2012, SET 15]

Sol. Let r be the radius of cylindrical vessel.

According to the question,

Circumference of the base = 132 cm

$\therefore 2\pi r$ = 132

$\Rightarrow 2 \times \dfrac{22}{7} \times r = 132$

$\therefore r = \dfrac{132 \times 7}{22 \times 2} = 21$ cm

Given, height (h) = 25 cm

Now, volume of cylinder = $\pi r^2 h$

$\quad = \dfrac{22}{7} \times 21 \times 21 \times 25 = 34650$ cm^3

$\therefore$ Volume (in litres) $= \dfrac{34650}{1000}$ L = 34.65 L

$\left[\because 1000\,\text{cm}^3 = 1\,\text{L} \Rightarrow 1\text{cm}^3 = \dfrac{1}{1000}\text{L} \right]$

10. The circumference of the base of a 24 m high solid wooden cone is 44 m. Find its curved surface area. **[BOARD TERM II, 2012, SET 12]**

Sol. Height of cone = 24 m

and circumference = 44 cm

According to the question,

Circumference of the base = $2\pi r$ = 44

$\therefore r = \dfrac{44 \times 7}{2 \times 22} = 7$m

Slant height $(l) = \sqrt{h^2 + r^2}$

$\quad = \sqrt{576 + 49} = \sqrt{625} = 25$m

Hence, curved surface area = πrl

$\quad = \dfrac{22}{7} \times 7 \times 25$

$\quad$ = 550 m^2.

11. The radius and height of a right circular cone are in the ratio 4 : 3. If the area of the base of the cone is 154 cm^2, find its curved surface. [Use $\pi = \dfrac{22}{7}$]

[BOARD TERM II, 2012, SET 08]

Sol. Let $4x$ and $3x$ respectively be the radius and height of cone, then

According to the question,

Area of base = $\pi r^2 = \pi(4x)^2 = 154$ cm^2

$\Rightarrow = \dfrac{22}{7} (4x)^2 = 154$

$\Rightarrow (4x)^2 = 49$

$\Rightarrow (4x)^2 = 7^2 \Rightarrow (4x) = 7$

$\therefore x = \dfrac{7}{4}$ cm

$\therefore$ Radius = $4x = \dfrac{4 \times 7}{4} = 7$ cm.

and Height $= 3x = 3 \times \dfrac{7}{4} = \dfrac{21}{4}$ cm

$\therefore$ Slant height, $l = \sqrt{r^2 + h^2}$

$$= \sqrt{7^2 + \left(\dfrac{21}{4}\right)^2}$$

$$= \sqrt{\dfrac{1225}{16}} = \dfrac{35}{4}\text{cm}$$

Hence, curved surface of cone $= \pi rl$

$$= \dfrac{22}{7} \times 7 \times \dfrac{35}{4} = \dfrac{385}{2}\text{cm}^3$$

$$= 192\dfrac{1}{2}\text{cm}^2.$$

$$= 192.5 \text{ cm}^2.$$

12. The radius and height of a right circular cone are in the ratio 5 : 12. If its volume is 314 cm³, find its slant height and curved surface area (use $\pi = 3.14$).

[BOARD TERM II, 2012, SET 24]

Sol. Given, $\dfrac{r}{h} = \dfrac{5}{12} \Rightarrow h = \dfrac{12}{5}r$

According to the question,

$\therefore \dfrac{1}{3}\pi r^2 h = 314$ cm³

$\Rightarrow \dfrac{1}{3} \times 3.14 \times r^2 \times \dfrac{12}{5}\, r = 314$

$\Rightarrow \dfrac{1}{3} \times \dfrac{314}{100} \times r^3 \times \dfrac{12}{5} = 314$

$\Rightarrow r^3 = \dfrac{314 \times 3 \times 100 \times 5}{314 \times 12}$

$\Rightarrow r^3 = 25 \times 5 = (5)^3$

$\therefore\ r = 5$ cm

and $h = 12$ cm

Slant height, $l = \sqrt{r^2 + h^2} = \sqrt{5^2 + 12^2} = 13$ cm

Hence, curved surface area $= \pi rl$

$$= 3.14 \times 5 \times 13$$

$$= 15.70 \times 13$$

$$= 204.10 \text{ cm}^2.$$

13. How many metres of cloth $1\dfrac{4}{7}$ m wide will be required to make a conical tent whose base diameter is 10 m and vertical height is 12 m?

[BOARD TERM II, 2012, SET 12]

Sol. According to the question,

$r = 5$ m and $h = 12$ m.

Slant height; $l = \sqrt{5^2 + 12^2} = 13$ m

Curved surface area of tent $= \pi rl$

$$= \dfrac{22}{7} \times 5 \times 13 \text{ m}^2$$

$$= \dfrac{1430}{7}\text{ m}^2$$

$\therefore$ Area of cloth required $= \dfrac{1430}{7}\text{m}^2$

Hence, width of cloth $= 1\dfrac{4}{7}\text{m} = \dfrac{11}{7}\text{m}$

and length of cloth $= \dfrac{1430}{7} \div \dfrac{11}{7} = 130$ m.

14. The curved surface area of a right circular cone is twice that of another right circular cone. If the slant height of the second cone is twice that of the first cone, find the ratio of the radius of first cone to that of second cone.

[BOARD TERM II, 2012, SET 8]

Sol.

I cone	II cone
r = radius	r′ = radius
l = slant height	l′ = slant height
h = height	h′ = height
Curved surface area = πrl	Curved surface area = πr′l′

Given, as per question,

Curved surface area of first cone

$\qquad = 2 \times$ Curved surface area of second cone

$\Rightarrow \pi rl = 2\pi r'l'$

$\Rightarrow \pi rl = 2\pi r'2l$ $\qquad [l' = 2l,\ \text{Given}]$

$\therefore\ \dfrac{r}{r'} = \dfrac{2\pi \times 2l}{\pi l} = \dfrac{4}{1}$

Hence, $r : r' = 4 : 1$

15. The difference between the outside and inside surface of a cylindrical metallic pipe 14 cm long is 44 cm². If the pipe is made of 99 cm³ of the Metal, find the outer and inner radii of the pipe.

[BOARD TERM II, 2012, SET 12]

Sol. Let the outer radius be R and inner radius be r, then according to the question,

Outer surface area $-$ Inner surface area $= 44$ cm²

$\Rightarrow 2\pi Rh - 2\pi rh = 44$

$\Rightarrow 2\pi \times 14\,(R - r) = 44$

$\Rightarrow R - r = \dfrac{44 \times 7}{2 \times 22 \times 14} = \dfrac{1}{2}\,cm$ ...(i)

Again, volume of metal = 99 cm³

$\Rightarrow \pi R^2 h - \pi r^2 h = 99$

$\Rightarrow 14\pi(R^2 - r^2) = 99$

$\Rightarrow R^2 - r^2 = \dfrac{99 \times 7}{22 \times 14} = \dfrac{9}{4}\,cm^2$

$\Rightarrow (R + r)(R - r) = \dfrac{9}{4}$

$\Rightarrow R + r = \dfrac{9}{4} \times 2 = \dfrac{9}{2}$ ...(ii)

On adding (i) and (ii), we get

$2R = \dfrac{10}{2}$

$\therefore R = \dfrac{5}{2} = 2.5\,cm$

From equation (ii),

$\therefore r = \dfrac{9}{2} - \dfrac{5}{2} = \dfrac{9-5}{2} = \dfrac{4}{2} = 2\,cm.$

Hence, outer radius = 2.5 cm and

inner radius = 2 cm.

16. Bhavya has a piece of canvas whose area is 552 m². She uses it to make a conical tent with a base radius of 7 m. Assuming that all the stitching margins and the wastage incurred while cutting amounts to approximately 2 m². Find the volume of the tent that can be made with it.

(Take $\pi = \dfrac{22}{7}$)

[BOARD TERM II, 2014, 2012, SET 24]

Sol. According to the question,

Curved surface area of the tent = 552 − 2

$= 550\ m^2$

and Radius (r) = 7 m

$\therefore \pi \times 7 \times l = 550$

or, $l = 25$ m

$\because h = \sqrt{l^2 - r^2} = \sqrt{25^2 - 7^2} = 24$ m

Hence, volume of the tent $= \dfrac{1}{3} \times \dfrac{22}{7} \times 7 \times 7 \times 24$

$= 1232\ m^3.$

17. The radius and height of a right circular cone are in the ratio 4 : 3 and its volume is 2156 cm³. Find the curved surface area of the cone.

[BOARD TERM II, 2013]

Sol. Let the radius of the cone = $4x$

and the height of the cone = $3x$

According to the question,

Volume of the cone = 2156 cm³

$\Rightarrow \dfrac{1}{3}\pi r^2 h = 2156$

$\Rightarrow \dfrac{1}{3} \times \dfrac{22}{7} \times 4x \times 4x \times 3x = 2156$

$\Rightarrow \dfrac{22}{7} \times 16x^3 = 2156$

$\Rightarrow x^3 = \dfrac{7 \times 7 \times 7}{2 \times 2 \times 2} = \left(\dfrac{7}{2}\right)^3$

$\therefore x = \dfrac{7}{2} = 3.5\,cm$

$\therefore$ Radius of the cone r = $4x$ = 4 × 3.5 = 14 cm

and height of the cone h = $3x$ = 3 × 3.5 = 10.5 cm

Slant height of the cone,

$l = \sqrt{h^2 + r^2} = \sqrt{10.5^2 + 14^2}$

$l = 17.5$ cm

Curved surface area of the cone = $\pi r l$

$= \dfrac{22}{7} \times 14 \times 17.5\ cm^2$

$= 44 \times 17.5\ cm^2 = 770\ cm^2$

Hence, curved surface area of the cone = 770 cm².

18. A rectangular sheet of metal foil with dimension 66 cm by 12 cm is rolled to form a cylinder of height 12 cm. Find the volume of the cylinder.

[BOARD TERM II, 2016, SET IA21924]

Sol. Let r be the base radius and h be the height of the cylinder.

$\therefore h = 12$ cm

According to the question,

$2\pi r = 66$

$\Rightarrow 2 \times \dfrac{22}{7} \times r = 66$

$\therefore r = \dfrac{66 \times 7}{22 \times 2} = \dfrac{21}{2}\,cm.$

$\therefore$ Volume of cylinder = $\pi r^2 h$

$= \dfrac{22}{7} \times \left(\dfrac{21}{2}\right)^2 \times 12$

$= \dfrac{22}{7} \times \dfrac{21}{2} \times \dfrac{21}{2} \times 12$

$= 4158\ cm^3.$

Hence, the volume of the cylinder = 4158 cm³

19. The radius and height of a cylinder are in the ratio 5 : 7. If its volume is 4400 cm³, find radius of the cylinder.

[BOARD TERM II, 2016, SET F0MCQ2]

Sol. Let r and h be the radius and height of the cylinder

∴ The radius of the cylinder $(r) = 5x$

and the height of the cylinder $(h) = 7x$, then

According to the question,

Volume of the cylinder $= \pi r^2 h$

$$\Rightarrow 4400 = \frac{22}{7} \times (5x^2) \times 7x \qquad \left(\because \pi = \frac{22}{7} \right)$$

$$\Rightarrow 4400 = \frac{22}{7} \times 5x \times 5x \times 7x$$

$$\Rightarrow x^3 = \frac{4400 \times 7}{22 \times 5 \times 5 \times 7}$$

$$\Rightarrow x^3 = 8 = 2^3$$

$$\therefore x = 2$$

Hence, the radius of the cylinder $= 5x = 5 \times 2$
$$= 10 \text{ cm.}$$

Long Answer Type Questions

(4 Marks Each)

1. What length of tarpaulin 3 m wide will be required to make conical tent of height 8 m and base radius 6 m? Assume that the extra length of material that will be required for stitching margins and wastage in cutting is approximately 20 cm. (take, $\pi = 3.14$) [NCERT]

So Let r, h and l be the radius, height and slant height of the tent, respectively.

Given, $r = 6$ m and $h = 8$ m

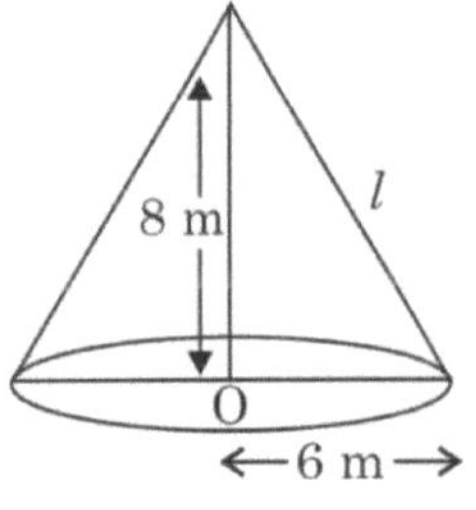

We known that, $l^2 = h^2 = r^2$.

$$\Rightarrow l = \sqrt{r^2 + h^2}$$

[On taking positive square root]

$$\Rightarrow l = \sqrt{(6)^2 + (8)^2}$$

$$\Rightarrow l = \sqrt{36 + 64}$$

$$\therefore l = \sqrt{100} = 10 \text{ m}$$

Area of the canvas used for the tent
$$= \text{Curved surface area of the cone}$$
$$= \pi rl = 3.14 \times 6 \times 10 = 188.4 \text{ m}^2$$

∴ Length of tarpaulin required

$$= \frac{\text{Area of tarpaulin required}}{\text{Width of tarpaulin}} = \frac{188.4}{3}$$
$$= 62.8 \text{ m}$$

[∵ Width of tarpaulin = 3 m, given]

The extra material required for stitching margins and cutting

$$= 20 \text{ cm} = 0.2 \text{ m} \left[\because 1 \text{ cm} = \frac{1}{100} \text{ m} \right]$$

Hence, the total length of tarpaulin required
$$= 62.8 + 0.2 = 63 \text{ m}$$

2. A lead pencil consists of a cylinder of wood with a solid cylinder or graphite filled in the interior. The diameter of the pencil is 7 mm and the diameter of the graphite is 1 mm. If the length of the pencil is 14 cm, then find the volume of the wood and that of the graphite. [NCERT]

Sol. Given, diameter of the graphite cylinder

$$= 1 \text{ mm} = \frac{1}{10} \text{ cm} \qquad \left[\because 1 \text{ mm} = \frac{1}{10} \text{ cm} \right]$$

∴ Radius of graphite cylinder $(r) = \frac{1}{20}$ cm

$$\left[\because \text{ radius} = \frac{\text{diameter}}{2} \right]$$

and length of the graphite (h) = 14 cm

∴ Volume of the graphite cylinder

$$= \pi r^2 h = \left(\frac{22}{7} \times \frac{1}{20} \times \frac{1}{20} \times 14 \right) = 0.11 \text{ cm}^3$$

Also, diameter of the pencil $= 7 \text{ mm} = \frac{7}{10}$ cm

∴ Radius of the pencil $(r_1) = \frac{7}{20}$ cm

and length of the pencil $(h_1) = 14$ cm

∴ Volume of the pencil $= \pi r_1^2 h_1 = \frac{22}{7} \times \frac{7}{20} \times \frac{7}{20} \times 14$
$$= 5.39 \text{ cm}^3$$

Now, volume of wood
$$= \text{Volume of the pencil} - \text{Volume of the graphite}$$
$$= 5.39 - 0.11 = 5.28 \text{ cm}^3$$

3. A metal pipe is 77 cm long. The inner diameter of a cross-section is 4 cm, the outer diameter being 4.4 cm (see figure). Find its

(i) inner curved surface area.

(ii) outer curved surface area.

(iii) total surface area. [Use $\pi = \frac{22}{7}$]

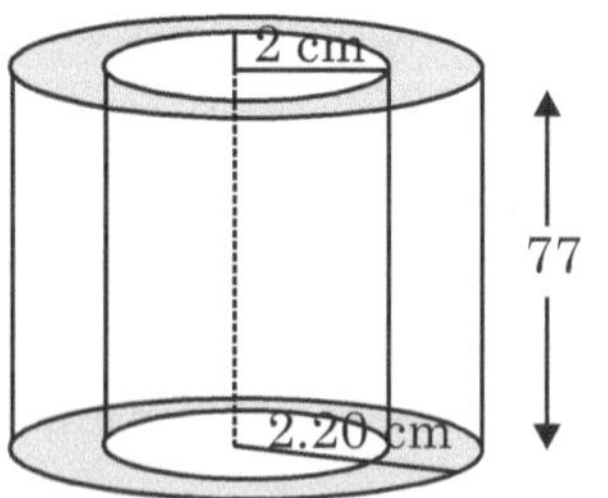

[BOARD TERM II, 2012, SET-02, 15, NCERT]

Sol. Given, height of pipe (h) = 77 cm

Outer diameter (d_1) = 4.4 cm

and inner diameter (d_2) = 4 cm

$\therefore$ Outer radius (r_1) = 2.2 cm $\left[\because \text{radius} = \dfrac{\text{diameter}}{2}\right]$

Inner radius (r_2) = 2 cm

(i) Inner curved surface area = $2\pi r_2 h$

$[\because$ Curved surface area of a right circular cylinder

$= 2\pi rh]$

$= 2 \times \dfrac{22}{7} \times 2 \times 77 = 88 \times 11 = 968 \text{ cm}^2$

(ii) Outer curved surface area = $2\pi r_1 h$

$= 2 \times \dfrac{22}{7} \times 2.2 \times 77 = 44 \times 2.2 \times 11 = 1064.8 \text{ cm}^2$

(iii) Total surface area

= Inner curved surface area + Outer curved surface area + Area of two bases

$= 968 + 1064.8 + 2\pi \left(r_1^2 - r_2^2\right)$

$= 968 + 1064.8 + 2 \times \dfrac{22}{7} \,[(2.2)^2 - 2^2]$

$= 2032.8 + 2 \times \dfrac{22}{7} \,(4.84 - 4)$

$= 2032.8 + \dfrac{44}{7} \times 0.84$

$= 2032.8 + 44 \times 0.12$

$= 2032.8 + 5.28 = 2038.08 \text{ cm}^2$

4. The capacity of a closed cylindrical vessel of height 1 m is 15.4 L. How many square metres of metal sheet would be needed to make it?

[BOARD TERM II, 2012, SET-6, NCERT]

Sol. Let r be the radius of the vessel, then

According to the question,

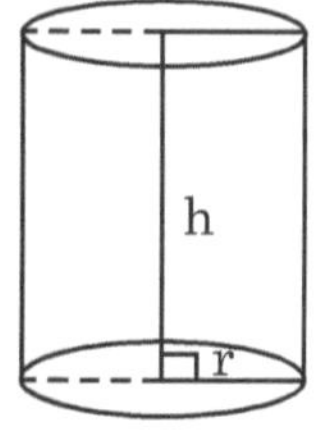

Capacity of a closed cylindrical vessel

$= 15.4 \text{ L}$

$= 15.4 \times 1000 \text{ cm}^3 \quad [\because 1 \text{ L} = 1000 \text{ cm}^3]$

$\therefore \pi r^2 h = 15400$

$\Rightarrow \pi r^2 \times 100 = 15400 \quad [h = 1 \text{ m} = 100 \text{ cm}]$

$\Rightarrow r^2 = 154 \times \dfrac{7}{22}$

$\Rightarrow r^2 = 7 \times 7 \therefore r = 7 \text{ cm}$

Total surface area of the closed cylindrical vessel

$= 2\pi r\,(r + h) = 2 \times \dfrac{22}{7} \times 7(7 + 100)$

$= 44 \times 107 = 4708 \text{ cm}^2$

$= \left(\dfrac{4708}{100 \times 100}\right)\text{m}^2 \quad \left[\because 1 \text{ cm} = \dfrac{1}{100}\text{m}\right]$

$= 0.4708 \text{ m}^2$

Hence, the required metal sheet is 0.4708 m².

5. A corn cob shaped some what like a cone, has the radius of its broadest end as 2.1 cm and length (height) as 20 cm. If each 1 cm² of the curved surface carries an average of four grains, find how many grains you would find on the entire corn cob.

[NCERT][BOARD TERM II, 2012, SET-06]

Sol. According to the question,

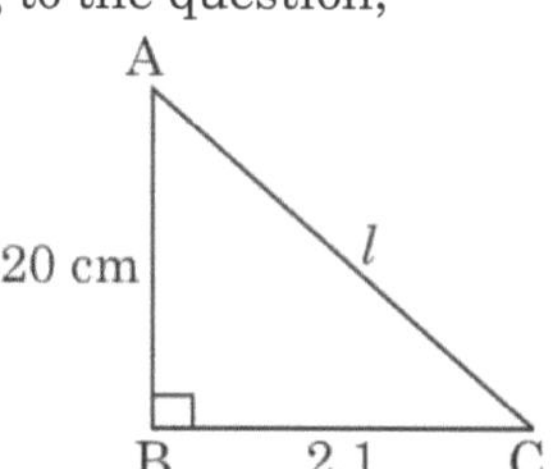

Slant height $l = \sqrt{h^2 + r^2}$, $h = 20$ cm, and $r = 2.1$ cm

$= \sqrt{20^2 + (2.1)^2}\ = \sqrt{404.41} \text{ cm}$

$\therefore l = 20.11$ cm

Therefore, the curved surface area of corn cob = πrl

$= \dfrac{22}{7} \times 2.1 \times 20.11 \text{ cm}^2$

$= 132.726 \text{ cm}^2$

$= 132.73 \text{ cm}^2 \text{ (approx.)}$

and number of corn cobs on 1 cm² of the surface of the corn cob = 4

Therefore, number of grains on the entire curved surface of the corn cob

$= 132.73 \times 4$

$= 530.92 \approx 531. \text{ (Approx.)}$

6. The pillars of a temple are cylindrically shaped. If each pillar has a circular base of radius 20 cm and height 10 m, how much concrete mixture would be required to build 14 such pillars?

[BOARD TERM II, 2012, SET-23, NCERT]

Sol.

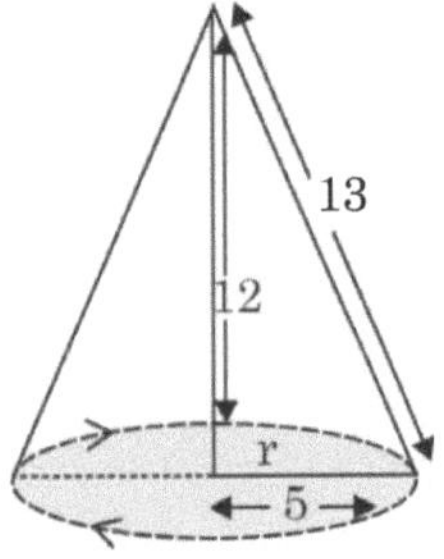

According to the question,

Radius of each pillar = 20 cm $= \dfrac{20}{100}$ m

and height of each pillar = 10 m

So, volume of each pillar = $\pi r^2 h$

$$= \dfrac{22}{7} \times \dfrac{20}{100} \times \dfrac{20}{100} \times 10 \text{ m}^3 = \dfrac{8.8}{7} \text{m}^3$$

∴ Volume of 14 pillars = Volume of one pillar × 14

$$\Rightarrow \quad \dfrac{8.8}{7} \times 14 \text{m}^3 = 17.6 \text{ m}^3$$

Hence, 14 pillars would need 17.6 m³ of concrete mixture.

7. A right triangle ABC with sides 5 cm, 12 cm and 13 cm is revolved about the side 5 cm. Find the volume of the solid so obtained. If, it is revolved about the side 12 cm, what would be the ratio of volumes of two solids obtained in two cases?

[BOARD TERM II, 2014, NCERT]

Sol. Case I : When revolved about the side 5 cm.

Here, r = 12 cm and h = 5 cm

∴ Volume of the solid

$$= \dfrac{1}{3} \pi r^2 h$$

$$= \dfrac{1}{3} \pi \times (12)^2 \times 5.$$

$$= \dfrac{5\pi}{3} \times 144 = 5 \times 48\pi$$

$$= 240\pi \text{ cm}^3$$

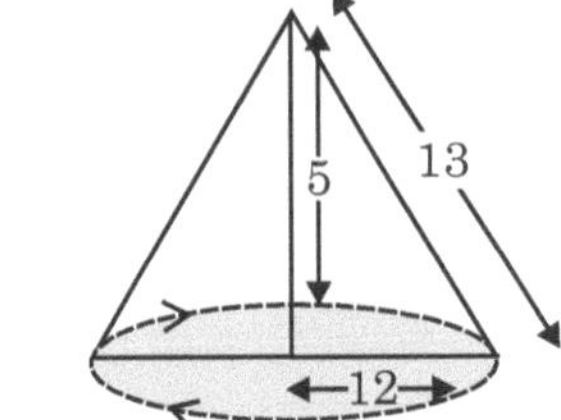

Hence, the cone is formed with radius 12 cm and height 5 cm.

Case II : When revolved about 12 cm, r = 5 cm and h = 12 cm

∴ Volume of solid $= \dfrac{1}{3} \pi r^2 h$

$$\Rightarrow \dfrac{1}{3} \times \pi \times (5)^2 \times 12 = \dfrac{\pi}{3} \times 25 \times 12 = 100 \, \pi \text{ cm}^3$$

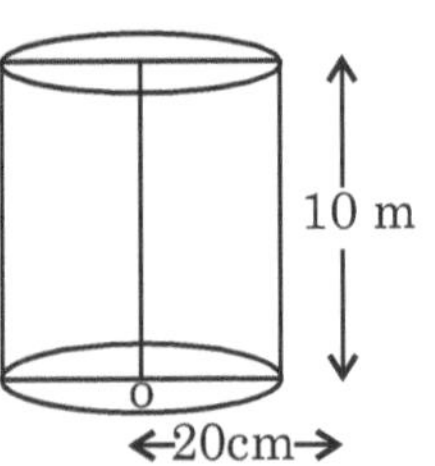

Hence, the cone is formed with radius 5 cm and height 12 cm.

Hence, required ratio $= \dfrac{240\pi}{100\pi} = \dfrac{24}{10} = 12 : 5$

8. What is the mass of a metallic hollow cylindrical pipe 24 cm long with internal diameter 10 cm and made up of metal 5 mm thick. Density of the metal is 7 g per cm³.

[BOARD TERM II, 2012, SET-10]

Sol.

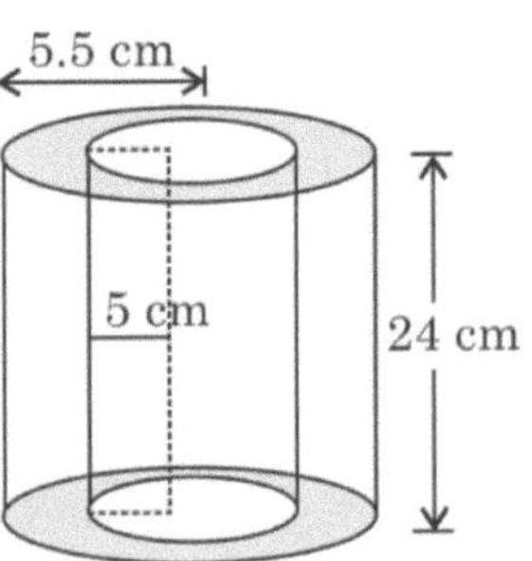

Given, diameter = 10 cm

∴ Radius (r) = $\dfrac{10}{2}$ = 5 cm.

h = 24 cm, R = 5 + 0.5 = 5.5 cm

Volume of hollow pipe = π [R² − r²]h

$$= \dfrac{22}{7} \, [(5.5)^2 − 5^2] \, 24$$

$$= \dfrac{22}{7} \times 5.25 \times 24 \text{ cm}^3$$

∴ Mass = Volume × Density

$$= \dfrac{22}{7} \times 5.25 \times 24 \times 7$$

$$= 2772 \text{ g} = 2.772 \text{ kg}$$

Hence, the mass of a metallic hollow cylindrical pipe is 2.772 kg.

9. Lead spheres of diameter 6 cm each are dropped into a cylindrical beaker containing some water and are fully submerged. If the diameter of the beaker is 18 cm and water level rises by 40 cm, find the number of lead spheres dropped in the water.

[BOARD TERM II, 2012, SET-8]

Sol. According to the question,

Volume of water = $\pi r^2 h$

$$= \pi \times 9 \times 9 \times 40 = 3240 \, \pi$$

and volume of sphere = $\dfrac{4}{3} \, \pi r^3$

$$= \dfrac{4}{3} \, \pi \times 3 \times 3 \times 3$$

$$= 4 \, \pi \times 9 = 36 \, \pi$$

Hence, number of spheres = $\dfrac{3240\pi}{36\pi} = 90$

10. A cylindrical container of base radius 6 cm, has water upto a height of 5 cm. Find:

   (a) Volume of water

   (b) A metal sphere of radius 2 cm is totally submerged in the water. Find rise in the water level.

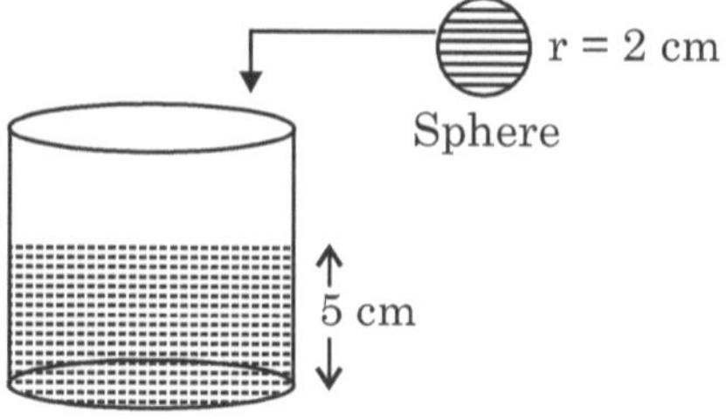

[BOARD TERM II, 2012, SET-12]

Sol. For cylinder : Given, H = 5 cm and R = 6 cm.

For sphere : r = 2 cm

Volume of water in cylinder = $\pi R^2 H$

$$= \frac{22}{7} \times 6 \times 6 \times 5 = \frac{110 \times 36}{7} = 565.71 \text{ cm}^3$$

Let rise in water level in cylinder be 'h' units, then according to the question,

Volume of sphere = Volume of water displaced in cylinder

$$\Rightarrow \frac{4}{3}\pi r^3 = \pi R^2 h$$

$$\therefore \ h = \frac{4r^3}{3R^2} = \frac{4 \times 2 \times 2 \times 2}{3 \times 6 \times 6} = \frac{8}{27} = 0.29 \text{ cm.}$$

Hence, the rise in the water level is 0.29 cm.

11. A hemispherical bowl of internal diameter 36 cm contains a liquid. This liquid is to be filled in cylindrical bottles of radius 3 cm and height 6 cm. How many bottles are required to empty the bowl ? [use $\pi = \frac{22}{7}$]

[BOARD TERM II, 2012, SET-69]

Sol. Volume of hemispherical bowl $= \frac{2}{3}\pi r^3$

$$= \frac{2}{3}\pi \left(\frac{36}{2}\right)^3 \text{ cm}^3$$

Volume of cylindrical bottle = $\pi r^2 h$

$$= \pi(3)^2 \times 6 \text{ cm}^3$$

Let required number of bottles are x, then

According to the question,

$$x = \frac{\text{Volume of hemispherical bowl}}{\text{Volume of cylindrical bottle}}$$

$$= \frac{\frac{2}{3}\pi(18)^3}{\pi(3)^3 \times 6} = \frac{2 \times 18 \times 18 \times 18}{3 \times 3 \times 3 \times 6 \times 3} = 24$$

12. The height, curved surface area and volume of a cone are h, c... and V respectively. Prove that $3\pi Vh^3 - c^2h^2 + 9V^2 = 0$

[BOARD TERM II, 2012, SET-01]

Sol. Let r be the radius of cone, then slant height

$$l = \sqrt{h^2 + r^2}$$

According to the question,

$$\therefore \ c = \pi r l$$

and $V = \frac{1}{3}\pi r^2 h$ [Given]

To prove: $3\pi Vh^3 - c^2h^2 + 9V^2 = 0$

Proof: L.H.S. $= 3\pi Vh^3 - c^2h^2 + 9V^2$

$$= 3\pi\left(\frac{1}{3}\pi r^2 h\right)h^3 - (\pi r l)^2 h^2 + 9\left(\frac{1}{3}\pi r^2 h\right)^2$$

$$= \pi^2 r^2 h^2 - \pi^2 r^2 \, l^2 \, h^2 + \pi^2 r^4 h^2$$

$$= \pi^2 r^2 h^4 - \pi^2 r^2 (h^2 + r^2)h^2 + \pi^2 r^4 h^2$$

$$= 0$$

Hence proved.

13. A cylindrical tent has a conical top with dimensions as shown in the figure. Calculate the total cost of the canvas required to make the tent, if the cost of canvas is ₹ 50/ per sq. m.

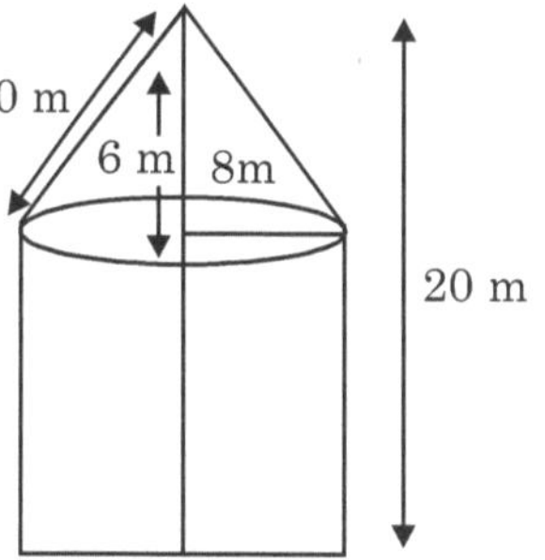

[BOARD TERM II, 2012, SET-20]

Sol. According to the question,

Total height of tent = 20 m and Radius = 8 m

Height of cylindrical portion of tent h = 20 − 6

$$= 14 \text{ m}$$

Height of conical portion = 6 m

Slant height of cone, $l = \sqrt{r^2 + h^2} = \sqrt{8^2 + 6^2}$

$$= \sqrt{100} = 10 \text{ m}$$

∴ Total surface area of tent

$$= \text{Curved surface area of cone}$$
$$+ \text{ Curved surface area of cylinder}$$
$$= \pi r l + 2\pi r h$$

$$= \frac{22}{7} \times 8 \times 10 + 2 \times \frac{22}{7} \times 8 \times 14$$

$$= \frac{1760}{7} + 704$$

$$= 251.42 + 704 = 955.42 \text{ m}^2$$

Hence, total cost of canvas = ₹ 955.42 × 50

$$= ₹ 47,771.$$

14. A cylindrical bowl of internal diameter 18 cm and height 15 cm is full of liquid. The whole of the liquid is to be filled in small cylindrical bottles of diameter 3 cm and height 4 cm. Each bottle is sold for ₹ 5, then find the amount earned.

[BOARD TERM II, 2014, SET-LFOMCQ2, 2016]

Sol. Given, diameter = 18 cm

∴ Radius (r) = $\dfrac{18}{2}$ = 9 cm.

Volume of liquid = $\dfrac{1}{3}\pi r^2 h$

$$= \dfrac{1}{3}\,\pi(9)^2\,15 = \dfrac{1}{3} \times \pi \times 81 \times 15$$

$$= 405\,\pi\ cm^3$$

Also, radius of small bottle $(r') = \dfrac{3}{2} = 1.5\,cm$

and height of small bottle (h′) = 4 cm

∴ Volume of small bottle = $\dfrac{1}{3}\,\pi(r')^2 h'$

$$= \dfrac{1}{3}\,\pi(1.5)^2 4$$

$$= \dfrac{1}{3} \times \pi \times 2.25 \times 4$$

$$= \dfrac{9\pi}{3} = 3\,\pi$$

Thus, number of bottles = $\dfrac{405\pi}{3\pi} = 135$

Hence, amount earned = 135 × 5 = ₹ 675

15. A hemispherical bowl of internal and external diameters 6 cm and 10 cm is melted and formed into a cylinder of diameter 14 cm. Find the height of the cylinder.

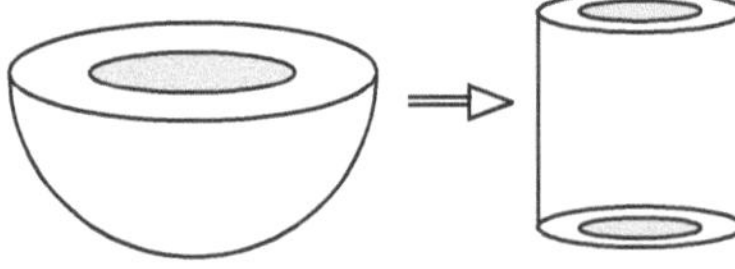

[BOARD TERM II, 2012, SET-20]

Sol. Outer radius of hemispherical bowl

$$R = \dfrac{10}{2}\ cm = 5\ cm$$

Inner radius, r = $\dfrac{6}{2}$ cm = 3 cm

and Radius of cylinder = $\dfrac{14}{2}$ = 7 cm

Let H be the height of the cylinder, then

According to the question,

∴ Volume of hemispherical bowl = Volume of cylinder

$$\Rightarrow \dfrac{2}{3}\,\pi(R^3 - r^3) = \pi(7)^2\,H$$

$$\Rightarrow \dfrac{2}{3}\,(5^3 - 3^3) = 49\,H$$

$$\therefore H = \dfrac{2}{3} \times 98 \times \dfrac{1}{49} = \dfrac{4}{3}\,cm = 1\dfrac{1}{3}\,cm$$

Hence, the height of the cylinder = 1.33 cm.

16. Calculate the curved surface area of a cone whose radius of base and height are in the ratio 5 : 12 and its volume is 2512 cu. cm.

[BOARD TERM II, 2014]

Sol. Let the radius of cone and height of cone are $5x$ and $12x$, respectively, then

According to the question,

Volume of cone = 2512

$$\Rightarrow \dfrac{1}{3}\,\pi r^2 h = 2512\ cu.\ cm$$

$$\Rightarrow \dfrac{1}{3} \times \dfrac{22}{7}\,(5x)^2 \times 12x = 2512$$

$$\Rightarrow x^3 = \dfrac{2512 \times 3 \times 100}{5 \times 5 \times 12 \times 314} = 8$$

∴ $x = 2$

∴ r = 10, h = 24, l = 26

∴ Curved surface area of cone = $\pi r l = \dfrac{5720}{7}$

$$= 817.14\ cm^2.$$

17. A pen stand is cylindrical in shape with the base radius 3.5 cm and height 10.5 cm. How much card board will be required to make 25 such pen stand? Also, find volume of 1 pen stand.

[BOARD TERM II, SET-IA21924,2016]

Sol. Given, base radius of cylinder r = 3.5 cm

and Height of cylinder h = 10.5 cm

∵ Amount of card board required to make 1 pen stand = Total surface area of cylinder

According to the question,

∴ Total surface area = 2πr (h + r)

$$= 2 \times \dfrac{22}{7} \times 3.5(10.5 + 3.5)$$

$$= 2 \times \dfrac{22}{7} \times 3.5 \times 14$$

$$= 44 \times 3.5 \times 2$$

$$= 44 \times 7 = 308\ cm^2$$

∴ 308 cm² is the amount of card board needed for 1 pen stand, then for 25 stands

$$= 25 \times 308 = 7700\ cm^2$$

Hence, volume of 1 pen stand = $\pi r^2 h$

$$= \dfrac{22}{7} \times 3.5 \times 3.5 \times 10.5$$

$$= 404.25\ cm^3.$$

18. A cone, a hemisphere and a cylinder stand on the same base and have equal height. Find the ratio of their :

(i) Volumes

(ii) Curved Surface Areas.

[BOARD TERM II, SET-IA21924, 2016]

Sol. Let r and h be the radius of base and height of the cylinder, cone and hemisphere, then

According to the question,

Height = Radius of hemisphere.

$\therefore$ h = r ...(i)

(i) Volume of cylinder = $\pi r^2 h = \pi r^2 \times r = \pi r^3$

Volume of cone $= \dfrac{1}{3}\pi r^2 h = \dfrac{1}{3}\pi r^2 \times r = \dfrac{1}{3}\pi r^3$

and volume of hemisphere $= \dfrac{2}{3}\pi r^3$

Now, volume of cone : Volume of hemisphere : Volume of cylinder

$= \dfrac{1}{3}\pi r^3 : \dfrac{2}{3}\pi r^3 : \pi r^3 = \dfrac{1}{3} : \dfrac{2}{3} : 1 = 1 : 2 : 3$

Hence, required ratio = 1 : 2 : 3.

(ii) Curved surface area of cone = $\pi r l$

$= \pi r\left(\sqrt{r^2 + h^2}\right) = \pi r\left(\sqrt{r^2 + r^2}\right)$ $(\because r = h)$

$= \pi r\left(\sqrt{2r^2}\right) = \pi r . r\sqrt{2} = \sqrt{2}\pi r^2$

Curved surface area of hemisphere = $2\pi r^2$

and Curved surface area of cylinder

$= 2\pi r h = 2\pi . r . r$ $(\because r = h)$

$= 2\pi r^2$

Again, curved surface area of cone : Curved surface area of hemisphere : Curved surface area of cylinder

$= \sqrt{2}\pi r^2 : 2\pi r^2 : 2\pi r^2 = \sqrt{2} : 2 : 2$

Hence, required ratio : $= \sqrt{2} : 2 : 2$

19. A solid cylinder has total surface area 462 cm². Its curved surface area is one third of its total surface area. Find :

(i) Its radius   (ii) Its height   (iii) Its volume

[BOARD TERM II, 2017 SET-Z6K408K]

Sol. According to the question,

Total surface area of cylinder = 462 cm²

$\therefore$ $2\pi r(r + h) = 462$ ...(i)

Since, curved surface area of cylinder

$= \dfrac{1}{3} \times$ Total surface area of cylinder

$\therefore$ $2\pi r h = \dfrac{1}{3} \times 462$ ...(ii)

On dividing equation (i) by (ii), we get

$\dfrac{2\pi r(r + h)}{2\pi r h} = \dfrac{462}{\dfrac{1}{3} \times 462}$

$\Rightarrow \dfrac{r + h}{h} = 3 \Rightarrow r + h = 3h$

$\therefore$ r = 2h

From equation (ii),

$2 \times \dfrac{22}{7} \times 2h \times h = \dfrac{1}{3} \times 462$

$h^2 = \dfrac{154 \times 7}{2 \times 22 \times 2}$

$\therefore$ $h = \dfrac{7}{2}$ cm

and r = 7 cm

$\therefore$ Volume = $\pi r^2 h = \dfrac{22}{7} \times 7 \times 7 \times \dfrac{7}{2} = 539$ cm³

Hence, the volume of cylinder = 539 cm³

20. The frame of a lampshade is cylindrical in shape. It has base diameter 28 cm and height 17 cm. It is to be covered with a decorative cloth. A margin of 2 cm is to be given for folding it over top and bottom of the frame. If $\dfrac{1}{12}$ of cloth is wasted in cutting and pasting, find how much cloth is required to be purchased for covering the frame.

[BOARD TERM II, 2017 SET-UAH4DQ7]

Sol. According to the question,

In a lampshade of cylindrical shape,

Base diameter = 28 m

and base radius $= \dfrac{28}{2} = 14$ cm

$\therefore$ Height of cloth required = 17 + 2 + 2 = 21 cm

Now, area of cloth required = Curved surface area of cylinder of radius 14 cm and height 21 cm

$= 2\pi r h = 2 \times \dfrac{22}{7} \times 14 \times 21$

$= 44 \times 2 \times 21 = 1848$ cm²

Let A sq. cm of cloth be purchased.

So, wastage of cloth for cutting and pasting

$= \dfrac{A}{12}$ cm²

$\therefore$ Area of cloth actually used $= A - \dfrac{A}{12} = \dfrac{11}{12} A$ cm²

Again, area of cloth actually used = Area of cloth required

$\Rightarrow \dfrac{11}{12} A = 1848$

$\therefore$ $A = \dfrac{1848 \times 12}{11} = 2016$ cm²

UNIT VI
Statistics & Probability

CHAPTER 14

Statistics

- **Introduction to Statistics:** Collection of data, presentation of data-tabular form, ungrouped/grouped, bar graphs, histograms (with varying base lengths), frequency polygons.
- Mean, Median and Mode of ungrouped data.

Statistics

Graphical representation of data

Bar graphs

Histograms of uniform width and of varying width

Frequency polygons

Measure of central tendency

Mode

The mode is the most frequently occurring observation. Mode of the ungrouped data can be determined by observation/inspection

Mean

Raw Data

$$\text{Mean} = \bar{x} = \frac{x_1 + x_2 + \dots + x_n}{n} = \frac{\Sigma f_i x_i}{n}$$

Where $x_1, x_2, x_3, \dots x_n$ are n Observations

Ungrouped Data

Mean of ungrouped data

$$\bar{x} = \frac{\Sigma f_i x_i}{\Sigma f_i}$$

Where f_i are frequencies of x_i

Median

Mean is the value of the middle-most observation (s)

If n is an odd number,

$$\text{Median} = \text{value of the} \left(\frac{n+1}{2}\right) \text{observation}$$

If n is an even number,

$$\text{Median} = \text{Average of the} \left(\frac{n+1}{2}\right)^{th} \text{and} \left(\frac{n}{2}+1\right)^{th} \text{observations.}$$

[Topic 1] Frequency Distribution, Bar Graphs, Histogram and Frequency Polygon

Points to be Remembered

- The facts or figures (i.e., observations/information collected) which are numerical or otherwise, collected with a definite purpose, are called data.
  - (i) The data collected by the investigator himself for a definite plan or purpose, is known as primary data.
  - (ii) The data which are not collected directly but obtained from some other sources (published or unpublished), is known as secondary data.

- Class-size or class-width of a class is a measure of the range of the data that can fit in that class. It is defined by

  Class width = Upper limit of the class
  $$\qquad\qquad - \text{Lower limit of the class}$$

- Class mark of a class is the mid-value of the two limits of that class.

$$\text{Class mark} = \frac{\text{Lower class limit} + \text{Upper class limit}}{2}$$

- Data can be represented graphically in following ways:

  (i) **Bar Graph:** It is a pictorial representation of data in which rectangular bars of uniform width are drawn with equal spacing between them on one axis, usually the x-axis. The value of the variable is shown on the other axis that is y-axis.

  (ii) **Histogram:** A histogram is one of the most commonly used graphs. A histogram is vertical bar-graph with no spacing between the bars.

  (iii) **Frequency Polygon:** The frequency polygon of a frequency distribution is a line-graph drawn by plotting the class marks on the x-axis against the frequencies on the y-axis.

  In case of grouped data, where the classes are of equal width, the frequency polygon is obtained by joining the mid-points of the top edges of the rectangles in the histogram. Two extra lines are drawn by introducing two extra classes (or values).

- The cumulative frequency of a class-interval is the sum of frequencies of that class and the classes which precede it.

$$\text{Class size} = \frac{\text{Range}}{\text{Number of Classes}}$$

$$\text{Class size} = \text{Upper limit} - \text{Lower limit}$$

PREVIOUS YEARS'
EXAMINATION QUESTIONS
TOPIC 1

Multiple Choice Questions
(1 Mark Each)

1. For drawing a frequency polygon of a continuous frequency distribution, we plot the points whose ordinates are the frequencies of the respective classes and abscissae are respectively
   - (a) upper limits of the classes
   - (b) lower limits of the classes
   - (c) class marks of the classes
   - (d) upper limits of preceding classes.

   [NCERT Exemplar]

   Sol. (c) For drawing a frequency polygon of a continuous frequency distribution, we have to take only class marks.

2. The sum of the upper limit and lower limit of a class and divide it by 2 is called:
   - (a) class mark
   - (b) mean
   - (c) class size
   - (d) range

   Sol. (a) The sum of the upper limit and lower limit of a class and divide it by 2 is called class mark.

3. The range of the given data is:

   184, 130, 195, 132, 134, 114, 174, 188, 210, 202, 211, 110, 166, 178, 115, 111, 209
   - (a) 98
   - (b) 99
   - (c) 100
   - (d) 101

   Sol. (d) The range of given data = $211 - 110 = 101$

4. Which of the following is not the methods of graphical representation of data?
   - (a) Bar graph
   - (b) Frequency graph
   - (c) Histogram
   - (d) Frequency polygon

   Sol. (b) Frequency graph is not the methods of graphical representation of data.

5. The values of x and y in the given distribution are:

Class Intervals	Frequency	Cumulative Frequency
10-20	5	5
20-30	3	x
30-40	5	13
40-50	6	y

(a) 8, 18   (b) 8, 19

(c) 7, 18   (d) 7, 19

Sol. (b) $x = 5 + 3 = 8$

and $y = 13 + 6 = 19$

Very Short Answer Type Questions (1 Mark Each)

1. Is it correct to say that in a histogram, the area of each rectangle is proportional to the class size of the corresponding class interval? If not, correct the statement.   [NCERT Exemplar]

Sol. It is not correct because in a histogram the area of each rectangle is proportional to the frequency of its class.

2. Two consecutive class marks of a distribution are 52, and 57, then the class size is:

[Board Term II, 2012, Set-12]

Sol. Class size = $57 - 52 = 5$

3. Let m be the mid value and l be the upper limit of a class in a frequency distribution. The lower limit of the class is: [Board Term II, 2012, Set-8]

Sol.   Mid value $= \dfrac{\text{Lower} + \text{Upper}}{2}$

$\Rightarrow$ $m = \dfrac{\text{Lower Limit} + 1}{2}$

$\Rightarrow$ Lower limit $= 2m - 1$

4. The class-mark of the class 130-150 is:

[Board Term II, 2012, Set-02]

Sol. Class-mark $= \dfrac{130 + 150}{2} = 140$

5. The class marks of frequency distribution are 10, 20, 30, 40, ... The class representing the class mark 30 is: [Board Term II, 2012, Set-23]

Sol. The class 25-35 representing the class mark 30.

6. Facts or information collected with a definite purpose are called: [Board Term II, 2012, Set-24]

Sol. Facts or information collected with a definite purpose are called data

7. The range of the data is :

25, 18, 20, 22, 16, 6, 17, 12, 30, 32, 10, 19, 8, 11, 20 is: [Board Term II, Set-261C 2013]

Sol. Range of the data = highest value – low of value

$= 32 - 6 = 26$

8. Find the range of the data :

22, 25, 20, 32, 36, 28, 40, 45, 35, 38

[Board Term II, Set-LF0MCQ2, 2016]

Sol. Range of the data = highest value – lowest value

$= 45 - 20 = 25$

9. The points scored by a basketball team in a series of matches are as follows:

17, 2, 7, 27, 25, 5, 14, 18, 10 Find range.

[Board Term II, Set-ROTZFBW, 2016]

Sol. Range of the data = highest point – lowest point

$= 27 - 2 = 25$

10. In a grouped frequency distribution, the class intervals are 1-10, 11-20, 21-30... . Find the class width.

Sol. This is a discontinuous class interval, so both 1 and 10 are included in the interval.

Hence, the class width is 10.

11. The class marks of a frequency distribution are 15, 20, 25, ... Find the class corresponding to the class mark 20.

Sol. Since, the difference between mid values is 5. So the corresponding class to the class mark 20 must have difference 5.

$\therefore \quad \dfrac{17.5 + 22.5}{2} = \dfrac{40}{2} = 20$

Hence, the required class is $17.5 - 22.5$.

12. The mid value of a class interval is 42 and the class size is 10. What are the lower and upper limits?

Sol. Let the lower limit be x,

Then upper limit is $(x + 10)$

According to the question,

$\dfrac{x + (x + 10)}{2} = 42$

$\Rightarrow$ $2x + 10 = 84$

$\Rightarrow$ $2x = 84 - 10$

$\Rightarrow$ $2x = 74$

$\Rightarrow$ $x = 37$

Hence, the lower limit is 37 and upper limit is 47.

Short Answer Type Questions–I

(2 Marks Each)

1. In a frequency distribution the mid value of a class is 10 and the width of the class is 6. Find the lower limit of the class.   [NCERT Exemplar]

Sol. Let x and y be the upper and lower class limits in a frequency distribution, then
According to the question,

Now, mid value of a class $= \dfrac{x + y}{2} = 10$ [given]
$\Rightarrow \qquad x + y = 20$ ...(i)
Also given that width of class $= 6$
$\Rightarrow \qquad x - y = 6$ ...(ii)
On solving equation (i) and (ii), we get
$$x + y = 20$$
$$x - y = 6$$
$$2x = 26$$
$\Rightarrow \qquad x = \dfrac{26}{2} = 13$

Now, putting $x = 13$ in equation (i), we get
$$13 + y = 20$$
$\therefore \qquad y = 20 - 13 = 7$
Hence, the lower class limit is 7.

2. A company manufactures car batteries of a particular type. The lives (in years) of 40 such batteries were recorded as follows

2.6	3.0	3.7	3.2	2.2	4.1	3.5	4.5
3.5	2.3	3.2	3.4	3.8	3.2	4.6	3.7
2.5	4.4	3.4	3.3	2.9	3.0	4.3	2.8
3.5	3.2	3.9	3.2	3.2	3.1	3.7	3.4
4.6	3.8	3.2	2.6	3.5	4.2	2.9	3.6

Construct a grouped frequency distribution table for this data, using class intervals of size 0.5 starting from the interval 2-2.5.   [NCERT]

Sol. We condense the given data into groups like 2.0-2.5, 2.5-3.0, ...-4.5-5.0 (Since, our data is from 2.2 to 4.6). The class width in this case is 0.5. Now, the given data can be condensed in tabular form as follows

Life of Batteries(in year)	Tally marks	Frequency
2.0-2.5	||	2
2.5-3.0	𝍸|	6
3.0-3.5	𝍸 𝍸 ||||	14
3.5-4.0	𝍸 𝍸|	11
4.0-4.5	||||	4
4.5-5.0	|||	3
Total		40

3. Thirty children were asked about the number of hours they watched TV programmes in the previous week. The results were found as follows

1	6	2	3	5	12	5	8	4	8
10	3	4	12	2	8	15	1	17	6
3	2	8	5	9	6	8	7	14	12

(i) Make a grouped frequency distribution table for this data, taking class width 5 and one of the class intervals as 5-10

(ii) How many children watched television for 15 or more hours a week?   [NCERT]

Sol. (i) We condense the given data into groups like 0-5, 5-10, ..., 15-20 (Since, our data is from 1 to 17). The class width in this case is 5. Now, required grouped frequency distribution table is

Number of hours	Frequency
0-5	10
5-10	13
10-15	5
15-20	2
Total	30

(ii) From the table, we observe that the number of children is 2, who watched television for 15 or more hours a week.

4. From the following observations:
0.03, 0.05, 1.04, 0.08, 0.05, 1.03, 0.03, 0.04, 0.07, 0.05, 0.02, 1.00, 0.08
(i) Calculate the Mode
(ii) Calculate the Range.

[Board Term II, 2012, Set-08]

Sol. Arranging the data in ascending order
0.02, 0.03, 0.03, 0.04, 0.05, 0.05, 0.05, 0.07, 0.08, 0.08, 1.00, 1.03, 1.04

$\because$ Number of terms (n) = 13(odd)

$\therefore \qquad \text{Mode} = \dfrac{n + 1}{2} = \dfrac{13 + 1}{2} = 7^{\text{th}} \text{ term}$

Mode = 0.05

and Range of the given data $= 1.04 - 0.02 = 1.02$.

5. The class marks of a distribution are 37, 42, 47, 52, 57. Determine the class size and the class limits of one last class mark.

[Board Term II, 2012, Set-20]

Sol. According to the question, Class size $= 42 - 37 = 5$

Lower limit of last class mark $= 57 - \dfrac{5}{2} = 54.5$

and upper limit of last class mark $= 57 + \dfrac{5}{2} = 59.5$

6. The relative humidity (in%) of a certain city of month of 30 days was as follows:

98	98	99	90	86	95	92	96	94	95
89	92	97	93	92	95	97	93	95	97
96	92	84	90	95	98	97	96	92	89

Construct a grouped frequency distribution table with classes 84-88, 88-92 etc.

[Board Term II, 2012, Set-16]

Sol.

Class Interval	Tally Marks	Frequency
84-88	||	2
88-92	||||	4
92-96	ℕℕ ℕℕ |||	13
96-100	ℕℕ ℕℕ |	11

7. Read the bar graph. Find the percentage of excess expenditure on wheat than pulses and ghee taken together.

Sol. Expenditure on pulses and ghee

$$= 10\% + 20\% = 30\%$$

Expenditure on wheat = 35%

∴   Excess expenditure on wheat

$$= 35\% - 30\% = 5\%$$

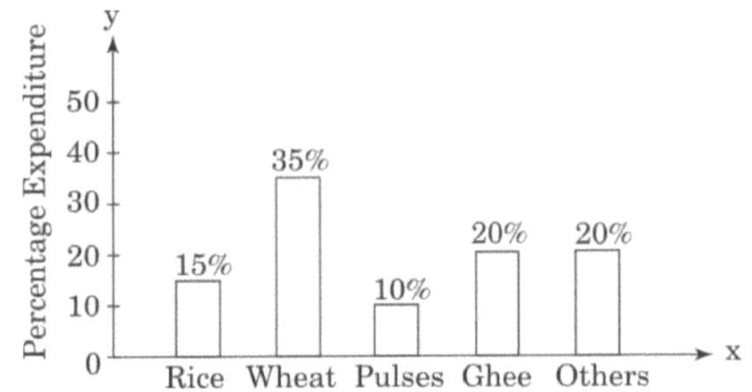

8. The class marks of a frequency distribution are 47, 52, 57, 62, 67, 72, 77, 82, 87, 92, 97 and 102. Find the class size and class limits.

Sol.   Class size = 52 − 47 = 5

∴   Lower limit = $47 - \dfrac{5}{2}$

$$= 47 - 2.5 = 44.5$$

and   upper limits = $47 + \dfrac{5}{2}$

$$= 47 + 2.5 = 49.5$$

So, the first class is 44.5 − 49.5.

The other class limits are 49.5-54.5, 54.5-59.5, 59.5-64.5, 64.5-69.5, 69.5-74.5, 74.5-79.5, 79.5-84.5, 84.5-89.5, 89.5-94.5, 94.5-99.5, 99.5-104.5.

Short Answer Type Questions–II

(3 Marks Each)

1. The relative humidity (in%) of a certain city for a month of 30 days was as follows :

98.1	98.6	99.2	90.3	86.5	95.3
92.9	96.3	94.2	95.1	89.2	92.3
97.1	93.5	92.7	95.1	97.2	93.3
95.2	97.3	96.2	92.1	84.9	90.2
95.7	98.3	97.3	96.1	96.1	89.0

(i) Construct a grouped frequency distribution table with classes 84-86, 86-88 etc.

(ii) Which month or season do you think this data is about?

(ii) What is the range of this data?   [NCERT]

Sol. (i) We condense the given data into groups, like 84-86, 86-88, …, 98-100 (since, our data is from 84.9 to 99.2). So, the class width in this case is 2.

Now the given data can be condensed in tabular from as follows :

Relative Humidity	Tally Marks	Frequency
84-86	|	1
86-88	|	1
88-90	||	2
90-92	||	2
92-94	ℕℕ ||	7
94-96	ℕℕ |	6
96-98	ℕℕ ||	7
98-100	||||	4
Total		**30**

(ii) From the table, we observe that the data appears to be taken in the rainy season as the relative humidity is high.

(iii) We know that,

Range of the data = Upper limit of data

− Lower limit of data

2. The blood groups of 30 students of class VIII are recorded as follows

A, B, O, O, AB, O, A, O, B, A, O, B, A, O, O, A, AB, O, A, A, O, O, AB, B, A, O, B, A, B, O

Represents this data in the from of a frequency distribution table. Which is the most common and which is the rarest blood group among these students?   [NCERT]

Sol. The number of students who have a certain type of blood group is called the frequency of those blood groups. To make data more easily understandable, we write it in a table, as given ahead

Blood Group	Number of Students
A	9
B	6
O	12
AB	3
Total	30

From table, we observe that the higher frequency blood group i.e., most common blood group is O and the lowest frequency blood group i.e., rarest blood group is AB.

3. The height of 50 students, measured to the nearest centimetres have been found to be as follows :

161	150	154	165	168	161	154	162	150	151
162	164	171	165	158	154	156	172	160	170
153	159	161	170	162	165	166	168	165	164
154	152	153	156	158	162	160	161	173	166
161	159	162	167	168	159	158	153	154	159

(i) Represent the data given above by a grouped frequency distribution table, taking class intervals as 160-165, 165-170 etc.

(ii) What can you conclude about their heights from the table?　　　[NCERT]

Sol. (i) We condense the given data into groups like 150-155, 155-160 …170-175 (since, our data is from 150 to 172). The class width in this case is 5.

Now the given data can be condensed in tabular form as follows

Heights (in cm)	Tally Marks	Frequency
150-155	卌 卌 II	12
155-160	卌 IIII	9
160-165	卌 卌 IIII	14
165-170	卌 卌	10
170-175	卌	5
Total		50

(ii) From the table, our conclusion is that more than 50% of students (i.e., 12 + 9 + 14 = 35) are shorter than 165 cm height.

4. The blood group of 30 students of class IX are recorded as follows:

A, B, O, O, AB, O, A, O, B, A, O, B, A, O, O, A, AB, O, A, A, O, O, AB, B, A, O, B, A, B, O.

(i) Represent this data in the form of a frequency distribution table.

(ii) Which is the most common and which is the rarest blood group among these students? [NCERT] [Bord Term II, 2012, Set-23]

Sol. (i) Frequency distribution Table:

Blood Group	Tally Marks	No. of students (frequency)
A	卌 IIII	9
B	卌 I	6
O	卌 卌 II	12
AB	III	3
Total		30

(ii) Blood group 'O' is most common as it has highest frequency i.e., 12. Blood group AB is rarest.

5. Draw a histogram of the following data:

Class	10-20	20-30	30-40	40-50	50-60	60-70
Frequency	5	10	13	9	6	2

[Board Term II, 2012, Set-6]

Sol. The histogram is as follows :

6. Draw a bar graph of the following data:

Product	Number of Consumers
A	152
B	136
C	180
D	165
E	126
F	152

[Board Term II, 2012, Set-30]

Sol. The bar graph of the given data is as follows:

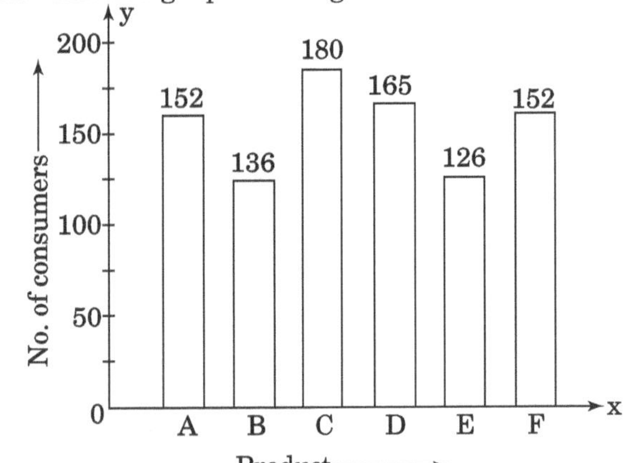

7. A family with a monthly income of ₹ 20,000 had planned the following expenditure per month under various heads. [Board Term II, 2012, Set-6]

Heads	Expenditure (in thousands Rupees)
Grocery	04
Rent	05
Education	05
Medicine	02
Fuel	02
Entertainment	01
Miscellaneous	01

Draw a bar graph for the data above.

Sol. The bar graph of the given data is as follows:

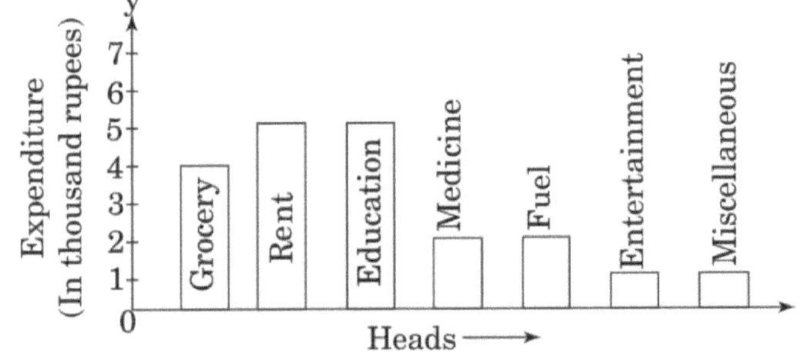

8. The marks obtained by 40 students of class IX in an examination are given below:

12, 8, 18, 8, 6, 16, 12, 5, 23, 2, 10, 20, 12, 9, 7, 6, 5, 3, 5, 13, 21, 13, 15, 20, 24, 1,7, 16, 21, 13, 23, 18, 7, 3, 18, 17, 16, 16, 23, 12.

Represent the data in the form of a frequency distribution using 15-20(20 not included) as one of the class intervals. [Board Term II, 2012, Set-20]

Sol. Frequency distribution table of the given data is as follows:

C.I.	Tally Marks	Frequency
0-5	IIII	4
5-10	₪₪ I	11
10-15	₪ III	8
15-20	₪ IIII	9
20-25	₪ III	8
Total		40

9. Thirty children spent about the number of hours they watched TV programs in the previous week. The result was as follow:

1	2	10	10	8	4
10	2	5	8	9	8
3	4	5	6	1	4
6	8	2	5	8	6
3	3	9	10	4	8

(i) Prepare a frequency table for the data given.

(ii) Find the mode of the data.

[Board Term II, 2012, Set-12]

Sol. (i) Frequency Table of the data is as follows:

Number of Hours	Tally Marks	Noumber of Students
1	II	2
2	III	3
3	III	3
4	IIII	4
5	III	3
6	III	3
8	₪ I	6
9	II	2
10	IIII	4
Total		30

(ii) Mode = 8, as 8 occurs maximum number of times i.e. (6 times)

10. For a particular year, following is the distribution of the ages (in years) of primary school teachers in a particular state:

Age (in years)	Number of Teachers
Less than 20	11
21-25	32
26-30	51
31-35	49
36-40	27
41-45	6
46-50	4

(*i*) Determine the class limits of the fourth class.

(ii) What is the class size?

(iii) Construct a cumulative frequency table.

[Board Term II, 2012, Set-12]

Sol. (i) Class limits of 4th class

Lower limit 31 and Upper limit 35

(ii) Class size = 25 − 21 + 1 = 5

(iii) Cumulative frequency table of the given data is as follows:

Age (in years)	Number of Teachers	Cumulative Frequency
Less than 20	11	11
21-25	32	43
26-30	51	94
31-35	49	143
36-40	27	170
41-45	6	176
46-50	4	180
Total	180	

11. Two coins were tossed 20 times simultaneously. Each time the number of "Heads" occurring was noted down as follows:

0, 1, 1, 2, 0, 1, 2, 0, 0, 1, 2, 2, 0, 2, 1, 0, 1, 1, 0, 2.

Prepare as frequency distribution table for the data. [Board Term II, 2017, Set-Z6K408K]

Sol. Frequency distribution table of the given data is as follows:

Observation	Tally Marks	Frequency
0									7
1									7
2								6
Total		20

12. A company manufactures car tyres of a particular type. The lives (in years) of 40 such tyres are as follows:

26, 3.0, 3.7, 3.2, 2.2, 4.1, 3.5, 4.5, 3.5, 2.3, 3.2, 3.4, 3.8, 3.2, 4.6, 3.7, 2.5, 4.4, 3.4, 3.3, 2.9, 3.0, 4.3, 2.8, 3.5, 3.2, 3.9, 3.2, 3.2, 3.1, 3.7, 3.4, 4.6, 3.8, 3.2, 2.6, 2.5, 4.2, 2.9, 3.6.

Construct a continuous grouped frequency distribution for the above data of equal class size and with first class interval as 2–2.5, (2.5 is not included) [Board Term II, Set RQTZFBW, 2016]

Sol. Frequency distribution table is as follows:

Class Intervals	Tally Marks	Number of Tyres
2.0-2.5	||	2
2.5-3.0	||||| ||	7
3.0-3.5	||||| ||||| ||||	14
3.5-4.0	||||| |||||	10
4.0-4.5	||||	4
4.5-5.0	|||	3
Total		40

13. The electricity bills of twenty households in a locality are as follows:

375, 415, 525, 275, 815, 720, 1085, 717, 807, 780, 315, 380, 417, 425, 375, 223, 245, 255, 615, 575.

Construct a frequency distribution table with class size 100. [Board Term II, 2017, Set-UAH4DQ7]

Sol. The frequency distribution table may be presented as shown below:

Class Intervals(in ₹)	Tally Marks	Frequency
200-300	||||	4
300-400	||||	4
400-500	|||	3
500-600	||	2
600-700			1
700-800	|||	3
800-900	||	2
900-1000		0
1000-1100			1
Total		20

14. Represent the following frequency distribution by means of a histogram.

Marks	10-20	20-30	30-40	40-50	50-60	60-70
Number of students	7	11	9	13	16	4

Sol. A histogram is as follows:

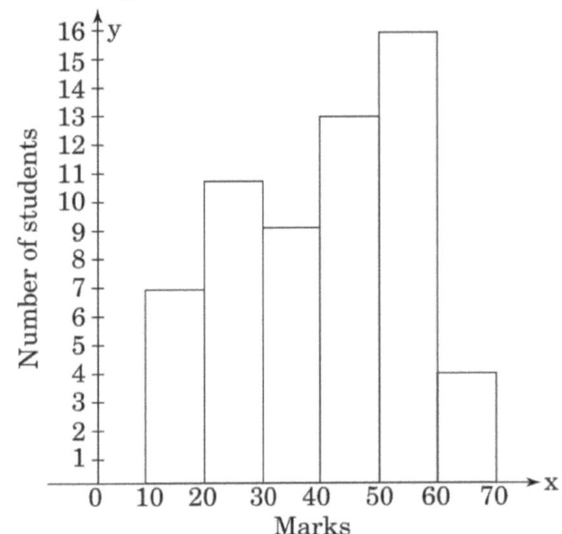

15. An insurance company selected 1600 drivers at random in a particular city to find a relationship between age and number of accidents. The data obtained are given in the following table:

Age of Drivers (in years)	Number of accidents (in one year)				
	0	1	2	3	More than 3
18-25	320	125	75	45	30
25-40	400	45	50	15	10
40-55	150	85	13	8	10
Above 55	150	25	17	20	7

Find the number of drivers:

(i) In the age of 25-40 years and has more than 2 accidents in the year.

(ii) The age is above 40 years and has accidents more than 1 but less then 3.

Sol. (i) Number of drivers in the age of 25-40 years and has more than 2 accidents in the year

$$= 15 + 10$$

$$= 25$$

(ii) Number of drivers in the age above 40 years and has accidents more than 1 but less than 3.

$$= 13 + 17$$

$$= 30$$

Long Answer Type Questions

(4 Marks Each)

1. The runs scored by two teams A and B on the first 60 balls in a cricket match are given below

Number of Balls	Team A	Team B
1-6	2	5
7-12	1	6
13-18	8	2
19-24	9	10
25-30	4	5
31-36	5	6
37-42	6	3
43-48	10	4
49-54	6	8
55-60	2	10

Represent the data of both the teams on the same graph by frequency polygons. [NCERT]

Sol. First, we make the class intervals continuous then modified table of given data is as shown below:

Number of Balls	Class Marks	Team A	Team B
0.5-6.5	3.5	2	5
6.5-12.5	9.5	1	6
12.5-18.5	15.5	8	2
18.5-24.5	21.5	9	10
24.5-30.5	27.5	4	5
30.5-36.5	33.5	5	6
36.5-42.5	39.5	6	3
42.5-48.5	45.5	10	4
48.5-54.5	51.5	6	8
54.5-60.5	57.5	2	10

Now, frequency polygon for both teams are given below:

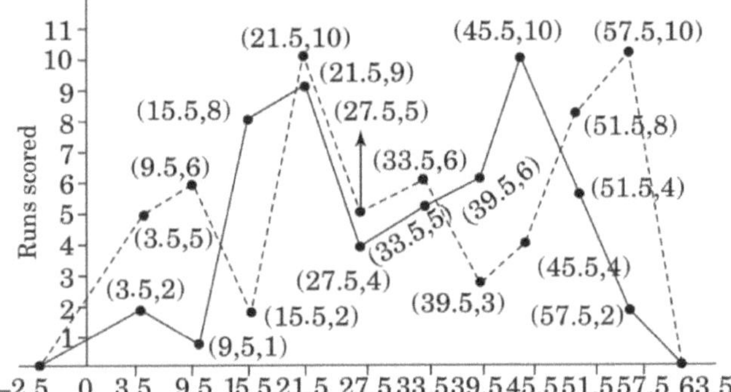

2.   The runs scored by two teams A and B on the first 60 balls in a cricket match are given below:

Number or Balls	1-6	7-12	13-18	19-24	25-30	31-36	37-42	45-48	49-54	55-60
Team A	3	2	9	5	6	10	6	12	3	1
Team B	6	7	3	11	6	7	4	5	9	11

Represent the data of both the teams on the same graph by frequency polygon.   [NCERT]

Sol.

Number of Balls	Team A	Team B	Continuous Number of Balls	Class Mark
1-6	3	6	0.5-6.5	3.5
7-12	2	7	6.5-12.5	9.5
13-18	9	3	12.5-18.5	15.5
19-24	5	11	18.5-24.5	21.5
25-30	6	6	24.5-30.5	27.5
31-36	10	7	30.5-36.5	33.5
37-42	6	4	36.5-42.5	39.5
43-48	12	5	42.5-48.5	45.5
49-54	3	9	48.5-54.5	51.5
55-60	1	11	54.5-60.5	57.5

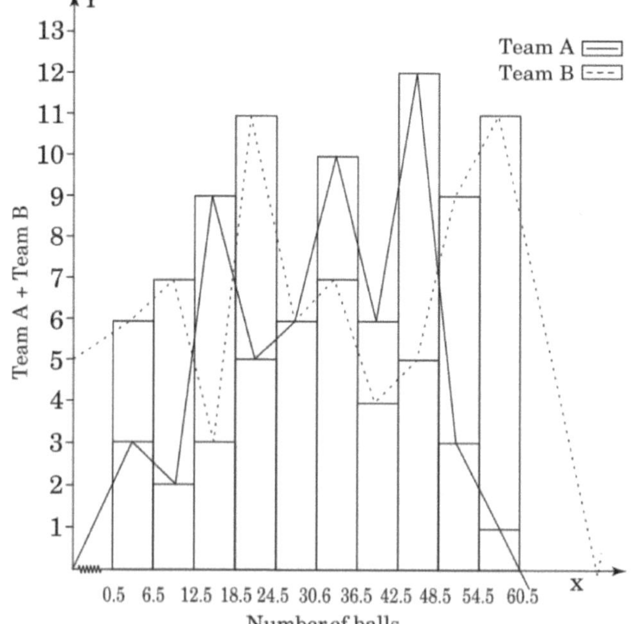

3.   The following table gives the distribution of students of two sections according to the marks obtained by them

Section A		Section B	
Marks	Frequency	Marks	Frequency
0-10	3	0-10	5
10-20	9	10-20	19
20-30	17	20-30	15
30-40	12	30-40	10
40-50	9	40-50	1

Represent the marks of the students of both the sections on the same graph by two frequency polygons. From the two polygons compare the performance of the two sections.   [NCERT]

Sol.   We make modified table by given data as shown below

Classes	Class Marks	Frequency (Section A)	Frequency (Section B)
0-10	5	3	5
10-20	15	9	19
20-30	25	17	15
30-40	35	12	10
40-50	45	9	1

Now, the required frequency polygons are as follows

It is clear that from the polygon that the performance of section A is better in comparison of section B.

4. The length of 40 leaves of a plant measured correct to one millimetre and the obtained data is represented in the following table.

Length (in mm)	Number of Leaves
118-126	3
127-135	5
136-144	9
145-153	12
154-162	5
163-171	4
172-180	2

(i) Draw a histogram to represent the given data.
(ii) is there any other suitable graphical representation for the same data?
(iii) Is it correct to conclude that the maximum number of leaves are 153 mm long and why? [NCERT]

Sol. (i) We know that the areas of the rectangles are proportional to the frequencies in a histogram. Here, the given frequency distribution, we get first interval as $(118-0.5)-(126+0.5) = 117.5 - 126.5$. The class width in this case is 9.

$$\left[\because \ \frac{127-126}{2} = 0.5\right]$$

So, we get the following modified table of given data

Length (in mm)	Frequency	Width of the Class
117.5-126.5	3	9
126.5-135.5	5	9
135.5-144.5	9	9
144.5-153.5	12	9
153.5-162.5	5	9
162.5-171.5	4	9
171.5-180.5	2	9

Now, we can draw the histogram for given data

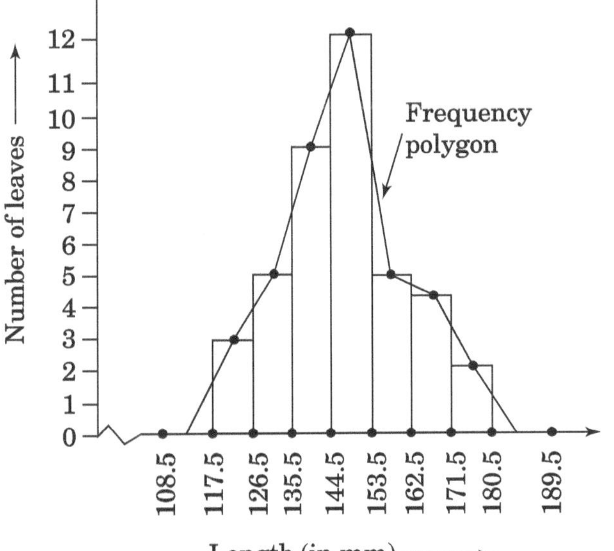

(ii) Yes, other suitable graphical representation for the same data is frequency polygon.
(iii) No, because the maximum number of leaves have their lengths lying in the interval 145-153.

5. A random survey of the number of children of various age groups playing in park was found as follows

Age (in years)	Number of Children
1-2	5
2-3	3
3-5	6
5-7	12
7-10	9
10-15	10
15-17	4

Draw a histogram to represent the data above.
[NCERT]

Sol. Here, the widths of the rectangles are varying . So, we need to make certain modifications in the lengths of the rectangles, so that the areas are became proportional to the frequencies. The minimum class size is 1.

Length of rectangle (Adjusted frequency)

$$= \frac{\text{Minimum class size}}{\text{Class of this class}} \times \text{frequency}$$

Then modified table of given data is shown below

Age (In years)	Number of Children	Width of the Class	Length of the Rectangle
1-2	5	1	$1/1 \times 5 = 5$
2-3	3	1	$1/1 \times 3 = 3$
3-2	6	2	$1/2 \times 6 = 3$
5-7	12	2	$1/2 \times 12 = 6$
7-10	9	3	$1/3 \times 9 = 3$
10-15	10	5	$1/5 \times 10 = 2$
15-17	4	2	$1/2 \times 4 = 2$

So, the histogram with varying width is given below

6. The following table gives the life time of 400 neon lamps:

Life Time (in hours)	Number of Lamps
300-400	14
400-500	56
500-600	60
600-700	86
700-800	74
800-900	62
900-1000	48

(i) Represent the given information with help of histogram.

(ii) How many lamps have life time of more than 700 hours?   [NCERT] [Board Term II, KVS, 2016]

Sol. (i) The histogram of the given data is as follows:

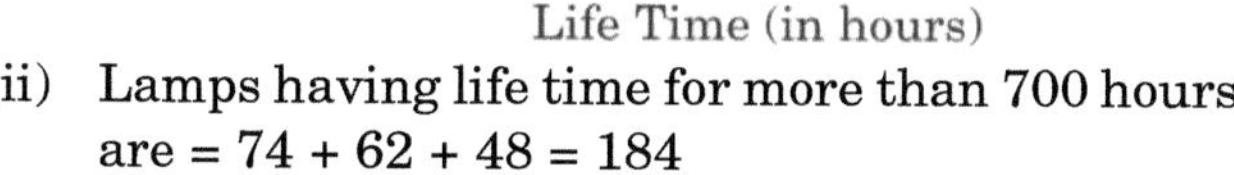

(ii) Lamps having life time for more than 700 hours are = 74 + 62 + 48 = 184

7. For the following data, draw a histogram.

Classes	Frequency
1-4	6
4-6	30
6-8	44
8-12	16
12-20	4

OR

100 surnames were randomly picked up from a loocal telephone directory and a frequency distribution of the number of letter in the English alphabets in the surname was found as follows:

Draw a Histogram to depict the given information.

[Board Term II, 2012, Set-15] [NCERT]

Sol.

Classes	Frequency	Width of Class	Length of the rectangle
1-4	6	3	$\frac{6}{3} \times 2 = 4$
4-6	30	2	$\frac{30}{2} \times 2 = 30$
6-8	44	2	$\frac{44}{2} \times 2 = 44$
8-12	16	4	$\frac{16}{4} \times 2 = 8$
12-20	4	8	$\frac{4}{8} \times 2 = 1$

The histogram of the given data is as follows:

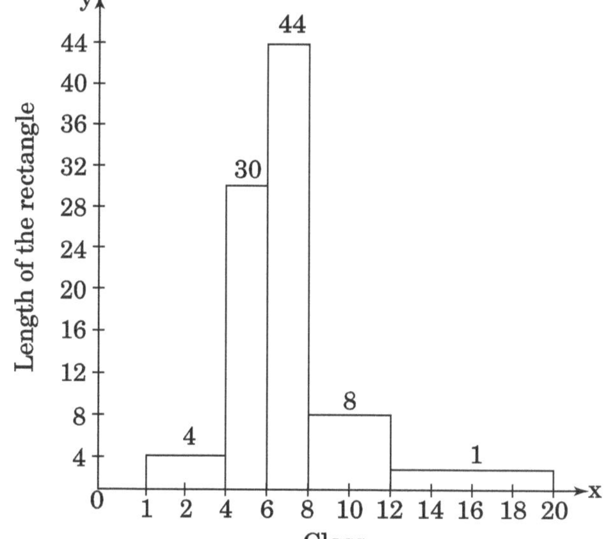

8. The number of literate females in the group (10-57 years) in a village are given below:

Age Group (in years)	Number of Females
10-17	300
18-25	980
26-33	740
34-41	580
42-49	260
50-57	140
Total	**3000**

Draw a histogram to represent the data above.

[Board Term II, 2012, Set-23]

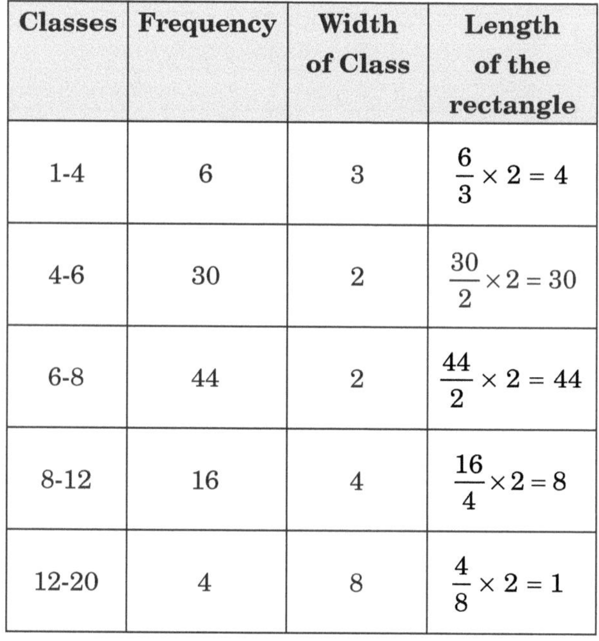

Sol. Consider the classes 10-17 and 18-25.

The lower limit of 18-25 = 18

Th upper limit of 10-17 = 17

The difference = 18-17 = 1

∴   Half the difference = $\dfrac{1}{2}$ = 0.5

Age Group (in years)	Frequency
9.5-17.5	300
17.5-25.5	980
25.5-33.5	740
33.5-41-.5	580
41.5-49.5	260
49.5-57.5	140
Total	**3000**

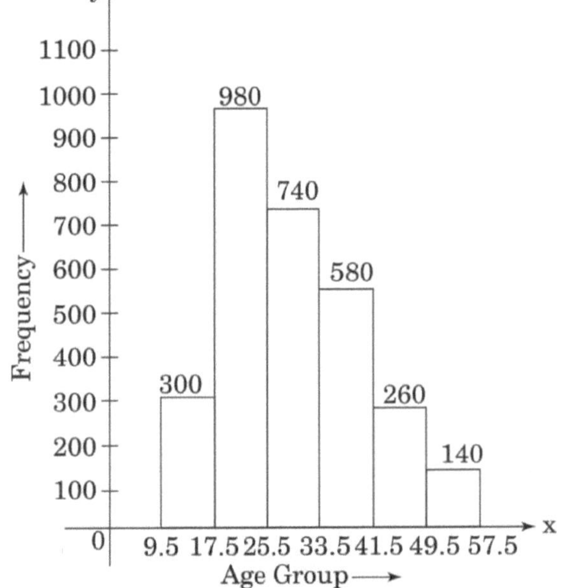

9. The runs scored by two teams A and B on the first 42 balls in a cricket match are given below. Draw the frequency polygon on the same graph paper.   [Board Term II, 2012, Set-08]

Number of Balls	Team A	Team B
0-6	2	5
6-12	1	6
12-18	8	2
18-24	9	10
24-30	4	5
30-36	5	6
36-42	6	3

Sol. The frequency polygon of the given data is as follows:

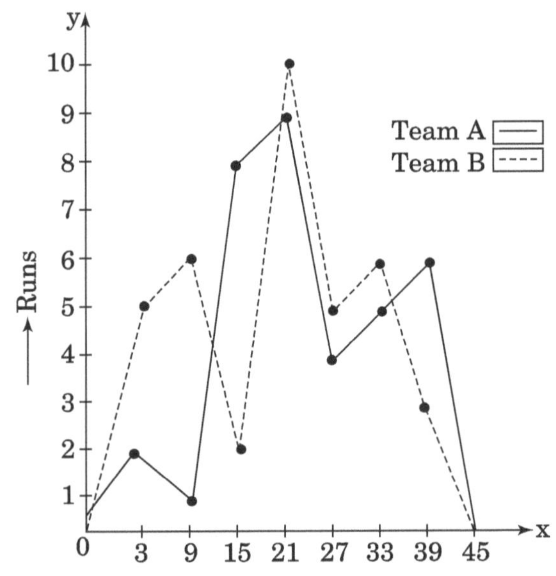

10. For the following data, draw a histogram.   [Board Term II, 2012, Set-24]

Age (in years)	Number of Persons
0-6	8
6-12	12
12-18	15
18-24	18
24-30	12
30-36	4

Sol. The histogram of the given data is as follows:

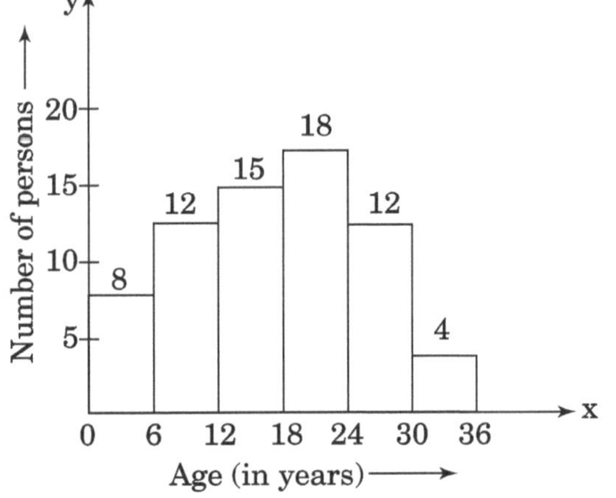

11. Consider the marks out of 100, obtained by 50 students of a class in a test, given as below.

Marks	0-20	20-40	40-60	60-80	80-100
Number of Students	15	10	10	11	4

Draw a frequency polygon representing the data.

[Board Term II, Set-TFX 2013]

Sol.

Marks	Number of Students
0-20	15
20-40	10
40-60	10
60-80	11
80-100	4

∴   Frequency polygon graph is ABCDEFG.

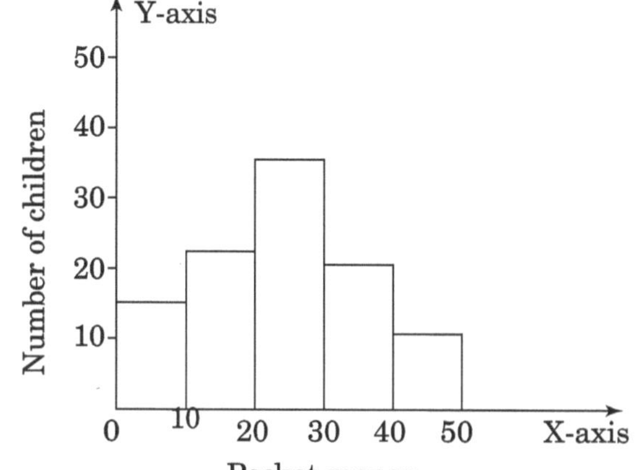

12. The following table gives the pocket money (in ₹) given to children per day by their parents:

Pocket Money	0-10	10-20	20-30	30-40	40-50
Number of Children	12	23	35	20	10

Represent the data in the from of a histogram.

[Board Term II, Set-IA21924, 2016]

Sol. The histogram of the given data is as follows:

Pocket Money	Number of Children
0-10	12
10-20	23
20-30	35
30-40	20
40-50	10

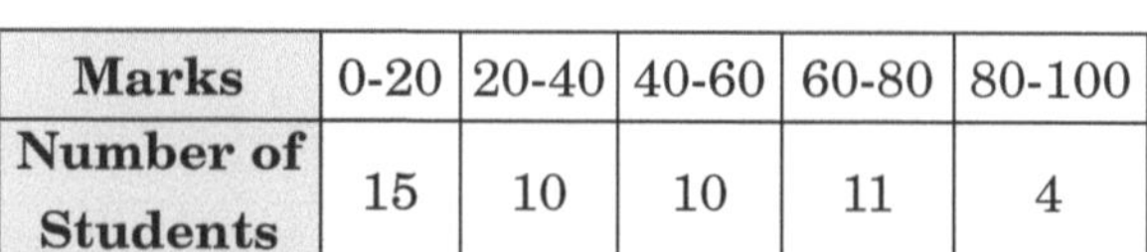

13. Draw a histogram to represent the following grouped frequency.

Age (in years)	5-9	10-14	15-19	20-24	25-29	30-34	35-39
Number of Persons	10	28	32	48	50	35	12

Also draw frequency polygon.

[Board Term-II, Set-RQTZFBW, 2016]

Sol.

Age (in years)	Number of Persons	Continuous Age (in years)	Class Marks
5-9	10	4.5-9.5	7
10-14	28	9.5-14.5	12
15-19	32	14.5-19.5	17
20-24	48	19.5-24.5	22
25-29	50	24.5-29.5	27
30-34	35	29.5-34.5	32
35-39	12	34.5-39.5	37

Draw a histogram and frequency polygon of the given data:

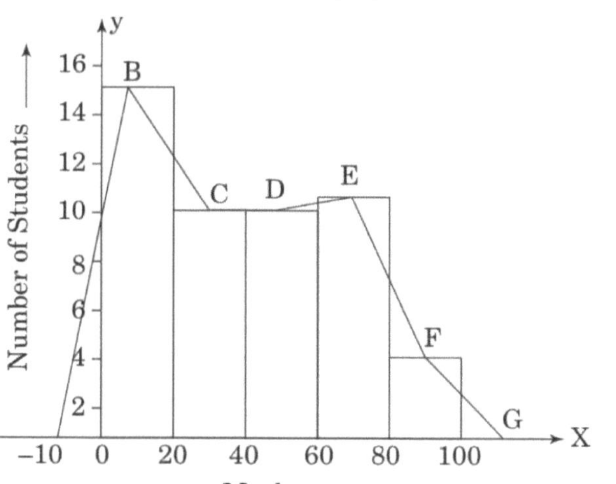

14. Draw a histogram and frequency polygon for the following data: [Board Term II, 2012, Set-01)]

Age (in years)	Number of Persons
0-4	3
4-8	6
8-12	8
12-16	10
16-20	8
20-24	6
24-28	3

Sol. A histogram and frequency polygon of the given data is as follows,

∴   y-axis = one square = 2 persons

and   x-axis = one square = 4 years

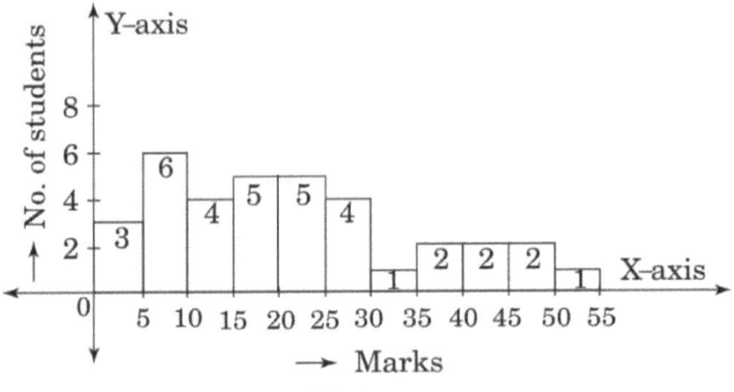

15. Construct a grouped frequency distribution table with class intervals 0-5, 5-10 and so on for the following marks obtained in Biology (Out of 50) by a group of 35 students in an examination:

0, 5, 6, 7, 10, 12, 14, 15, 20, 22, 25, 26, 27, 8, 11, 17, 3, 6, 9, 17, 19, 21,22, 29, 31, 35, 37, 40, 42, 45, 49, 4, 50, 16, 20

Also, draw a histogram to represent the above data.

[Board term II, 2017, Set-UAH4DQ7]

Sol.

Marks	0-5	5-10	10-15	15-20	20-25	25-30	30-35	35-40	40-45	45-50	50-55
Number of Students	3	6	4	5	5	4	1	2	2	2	1

The histogram to represent the above data is as follow:

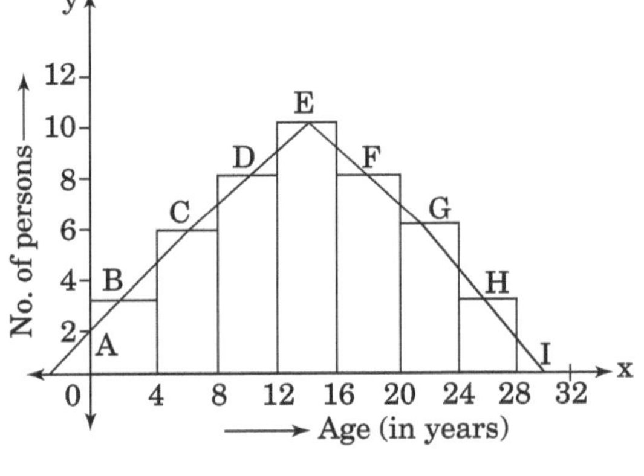

Histogram

16. The following two tables gives the distribution of students of two sections according to the marks obtained by them :   [Board Term II, 2017, Set-Z6K408K]

Section A		Section B	
0-10	4	0-10	6
10-20	10	10-20	20
20-30	18	20-30	16
30-40	13	30-40	11
40-50	10	40-50	2

Represent the marks of the students of both the sections on the same graph by two frequency polygons.

Sol.

Class Marks	Section A	Section B
5	4	6
15	10	20
25	18	16
35	13	11
45	10	2

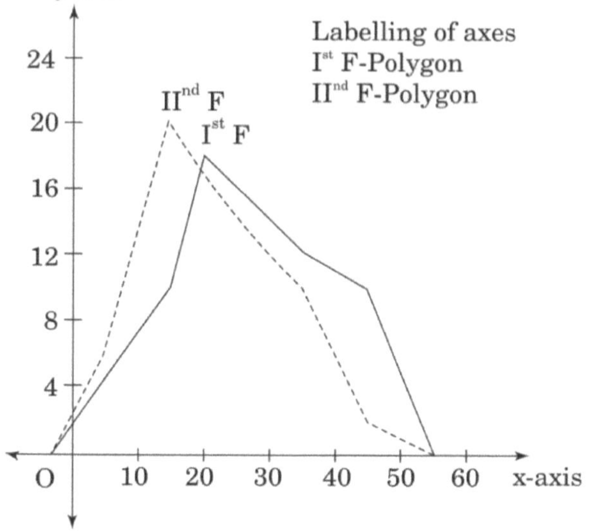

Here, marks scored by section A has been plotted in line and that of marks scored by section B has been drawn in dotted line.

Topic 2 [Mean, Median and Mode]

Points to be Remembered

- The mean of a number of observations is the sum of the values of all the observations divided by the total number of observations.

$$\text{Mean } \bar{x} = \frac{\text{Sum of all observations}}{\text{Number of observations}}$$

$$\therefore \qquad \bar{x} = \frac{\sum\limits_{i=1}^{n} X_i}{n}$$

For an ungrouped frequency distribution,

$$\bar{x} = \frac{\sum\limits_{i=1}^{n} f_i X_i}{\sum\limits_{i=1}^{n} f_i}$$

- Median is that value of the given observation, which divides it into exactly two parts. Suppose, there are observations. Firstly arrange the given observations in ascending or descending order. Then,

(i) If n is odd, then Median = value of $\left(\dfrac{n+1}{2}\right)^{th}$ observation

(ii) If n is even, then

$$\text{Median} = \frac{1}{2}\left[\text{value of } \left(\frac{n}{2}\right)^{th} \text{ and } \left(\frac{n}{2}+1\right)^{th} \text{ Observations} \right]$$

- Mode is that value of the given observations, which occurs most frequently i.e., an observation with the maximum frequency.

PREVIOUS YEARS'

EXAMINATION QUESTIONS
TOPIC 2

Multiple Choice Questions
(1 Mark Each)

1. If each observation of the data is increased by 5, then their mean
   (a) remains the same.
   (b) becomes 5 times the original mean.
   (c) is decreased by 5.
   (d) is increased by 5. [NCERT Exemp.]

Sol. (d) If every observation is increased by 5, then their mean is also increased by 5

2. If $\bar{x}$ represents the mean of n observations x_1, $x_2, \ldots, x_n$, then value of $\sum\limits_{i=1}^{n} x_i - \bar{x}$
   (a) -1
   (b) 0
   (c) 1
   (d) $n-1$ [NCERT Exemp.]

Sol. (b) Since, $\bar{x} = \dfrac{x_1 + x_2 + x_3 + \ldots + x_n}{n}$

$$\therefore \qquad \sum\limits_{i=1}^{n} x_i - \bar{x} = 0$$

3. Mode of the data 15, 14, 19, 20, 14, 15, 16, 14, 15, 18, 14, 19, 15, 17, 15 is
   (a) 14
   (b) 15
   (c) 16
   (d) 17 [NCERT Exemp.]

Sol. **(b)** Here, the most frequently repeated value is 15. Hence, the mode of the given data is 15

4. The mean of five numbers is 30. If one number is excluded, their mean becomes 28. The excluded number is

(a) 28   (b) 30

(c) 35   (d) 38   [NCERT Exemp.]

Sol. **(d)** According to the question,

Mean of 5 numbers = 30

Sum of 5 numbers = 30 × 5 = 150

Again, Mean of 4 numbers = 28

Sum of 4 numbers = 28 × 4 = 112

Hence, excluded number = 150 − 112 = 38

5. The median of the data 78, 56, 22, 34, 45, 54, 39, 68, 54, 84 is

(a) 45   (b) 49.5

(c) 54   (d) 56   [NCERT Exemp.]

Sol. **(c)** Given data is,

78, 56, 22, 34, 45, 54, 39, 68, 54, 84

Ascending order of the data is 22, 34, 39, 45, 54, 54, 56, 68, 78 and 84.

Number of observations = 10 which is even

Therefore median = Mean of 5th observation and 6th observation

$$= \frac{(54 + 54)}{2} = \frac{108}{2} = 54$$

6. The mean of 100 observations is 50. If one of the observations which were 50 is replaced by 150, the resulting mean will be

(a) 50.5   (b) 51

(c) 51.5   (d) 52   [NCERT Exemp.]

Sol. **(b)** According to the question,

$\because$ Mean of 100 observations = 50

$\therefore$ Sum of 100 observations = 50 × 100

$$- 5,000$$

$\therefore$ New sum of observations

$$= 5,000 - 50 + 150$$
$$= 5150 - 50$$
$$= 5,100$$

Hence, new mean of observations $= \dfrac{5,100}{100} = 51$

7. Median of the following numbers : 4, 4, 5, 7, 6, 7, 7, 12, 3 is

(a) 4   (b) 5

(c) 6   (d) 7   [NCERT Exemp.]

Sol. **(c)** Given data is 4, 4, 5, 7, 6, 7, 7, 12, 3

Ascending order of the data = 3, 4, 4, 5, 6, 7, 7, 7 and 12.

Number of observation = 9 which is odd

Therefore, median $= \left(\dfrac{9+1}{2}\right)^{\text{th}}$, observation

$$= \frac{10^{\text{th}}}{2} = \text{5th observation} = 6$$

Hence, the required median = 6

8. Let $\bar{x}$ be the mean of $x_1, x_2, ..., x_n$ and $\bar{y}$ the mean of $y_1, y_2, ..., y_n$. If $\bar{z}$ is the mean of $x_1, x_2, ..., x_n, y_n, y_1, y_2, ..., y_n$ then $\bar{z}$ is equal to

(a) $\bar{x} + \bar{y}$ (b) $\dfrac{(\bar{x} + \bar{y})}{2}$

(c) $\dfrac{(\bar{x} + \bar{y})}{n}$ (d) $\dfrac{(\bar{x} + \bar{y})}{2n}$

[NCERT Exemp.]

Sol. **(b)** Given, $\bar{x} = \dfrac{x_1 + x_2 + x_3 + ... + x_n}{n}$

and $\bar{x} = \dfrac{y_1 + y_2 + y_3 + ... + y_n}{n}$

$\because$ $\bar{z} = \dfrac{x_1 + x_2 + ... + x_n + y_1 + y_2 + ... + y_n}{2n}$

$\bar{z}$ is mean of $\bar{x}$ and $\bar{y}$

Therefore, $\bar{z} = \dfrac{(\bar{x} + \bar{y})}{2}$

9. The mean of 25 observations is 36. Out of these observations if the mean of first 13 observations is 32 and that of the last 13 observations is 40, the 13th observation is

(a) 23   (b) 36

(c) 38   (d) 40

Sol. **(b)** According to the question,

Mean of 25 observations = 36

$\therefore$ Sum of 25 observations = 36 × 25

$$= 900$$

$\because$ Mean of first 13 observations = 32

$\therefore$ Sum of first 13 observations = 13 × 32

$$= 416$$

$\because$ Mean of last 13 observations = 40

$\therefore$ Sum of last 13 observations = 13 × 40 = 520

Therefore, The 13th observation = 512 + 416 − 900

$$= 928 - 900 = 28$$

10. There are 50 numbers. Each number is subtracted from 53 and the mean of the numbers so obtained is found to be –3.5. The mean of the given number is

(a) 46.5 (b) 49.5

(c) 53.5 (d) 56.5   [NCERT Exemp.]

Sol. (d) According to the problem:

$$\Rightarrow \quad \frac{(53 - x_1) - (53 - x_2) + \dots + (53 - x_{50})}{50} = -3.5$$

$$\Rightarrow \quad 53 \times 50 - (x_1 + x_2 + \dots + x_{50}) = 3.5 \times 50$$

$$\Rightarrow \quad 2{,}350 - (x_1 + x_2 + \dots + x_{50}) = -175$$

$$\Rightarrow \quad (x_1 + x_2 + \dots + x_{50}) = 2{,}350 + 175$$

$$\Rightarrow \quad (x_1 + x_2 + \dots + x_{50}) = 2{,}825$$

Hence, required mean

$$= \frac{(x_1 + x_2 + \dots + x_{50})}{50}$$

$$= \frac{2{,}825}{50} = 56.5$$

11. If the mean of the observations:

$x, x + 3, x + 5, x + 7, x + 10$ is 9, the mean of the last three observations is   [NCERT Exemp.]

(a) $\dfrac{31}{3}$ (b) $\dfrac{32}{3}$

(c) $\dfrac{34}{3}$ (d) $\dfrac{35}{3}$.

Sol. (c) According to the question,

$$\frac{(x + x + 3 + x + 5 + x + 7 + x + 10)}{5} = 9$$

$$\Rightarrow \quad x + x + 3 + x + 5 + x + 7 + x + 10 = 9 \times 5$$

$$\Rightarrow \quad x + x + 3 + x + 5 + x + 7 + x + 10 = 45$$

$$\Rightarrow \quad 5x + 25 = 45$$

$$\Rightarrow \quad 5x = 45 - 25$$

$$\Rightarrow \quad 5x = 20$$

$$\therefore \quad x = \frac{20}{5} = 4$$

By substituting x value for 3 observations, we get

Last 3 observations = 9, 11, 14

Hence, require mean $= \dfrac{(9 + 11 + 14)}{3} = \dfrac{34}{3}$

12. If x is the mean of $x_1, x_2, \dots, x_n$, then for $a \ne 0$, the mean of $ax_1, ax_2, \dots, ax_n, \dfrac{x_1}{a}, \dfrac{x_2}{a}, \dots, \dfrac{x_n}{a}$ is

(a) $\left(a + \dfrac{1}{a}\right)\overline{x}$ (b) $\left(a + \dfrac{1}{a}\right)\dfrac{\overline{x}}{2}$

(c) $\left(a + \dfrac{1}{a}\right)\dfrac{\overline{x}}{n}$ (d) $\left(a + \dfrac{1}{a}\right)\dfrac{\overline{x}}{2n}$

[NCERT Exemplar]

Sol. (c) According to the question,

$$\text{Mean} = \left[\frac{\dfrac{(ax_1 + ax_2 + \dots + ax_n)}{n} + \dfrac{\left(\dfrac{x_1}{a} + \dfrac{x_2}{a} + \dots + \dfrac{x_n}{a}\right)}{n}}{2} \right]$$

$$= \frac{\left[\dfrac{a(x_1 + x_2 + \dots + x_n)}{n} + \dfrac{\dfrac{1}{a}(x_1 + x_2 + x_n)}{n} \right]}{2}$$

$$= \frac{\left[ax + \dfrac{1}{ax} \right]}{2}$$

$$= \left(a + \frac{1}{a}\right)\frac{\overline{x}}{2}$$

13. If $x_1, x_2, x_3, \dots, x_n$ are the means of n groups with $n_1, n_2, \dots, n_n$ number of observations respectively, then the mean $\overline{x}$ of all the groups taken together is given by :

(a) $\displaystyle\sum_{i=1}^{n} n_i \overline{x}_i$ (b) $\dfrac{\displaystyle\sum_{i=1}^{n} n_i \overline{x}_i}{n^2}$

(c) $\dfrac{\displaystyle\sum_{i=1}^{n} n_i \overline{x}_i}{\displaystyle\sum_{i=1}^{n} n_i}$ (d) $\dfrac{\displaystyle\sum_{i=1}^{n} n_i \overline{x}_i}{2n}$

[NCERT Exemplar]

Sol. (c) To find the mean of the group we have to multiply the means with their respective groups and then we have to divide with total number of groups.

Hence, the mean $\overline{x} = \dfrac{\displaystyle\sum_{i=1}^{n} n_i x_i}{\displaystyle\sum_{i=1}^{n} n_i}$

14. The mean of five numbers $x + 1$, $x + 3$, $x + 5$, $x + 7$, $x + 9$ is 8, then the value of x is :

    (a) 5
    (b) 4
    (c) 3
    (d) 2

Sol. (c) According to the question,

$$\text{Mean} = \frac{(x+1)+(x+3)+(x+5)+(x+7)+(x+9)}{5}$$

$$\Rightarrow \quad 8 = \frac{5x+25}{5}$$

$$5x = 40 - 25 = 15$$

$$\therefore \quad x = \frac{15}{5} = 3$$

15. The sum of the values of all the observations divided by the total number of observations is called :

    (a) mean
    (b) summation
    (c) median
    (d) mode

Sol. (a) We know that

$$\text{Mean} = \frac{\text{Sum of all the observations}}{\text{Total number of observations}}$$

16. The mean of 10 numbers 4, 2, 3, 0, 2, 3, 5, 6, 1, 4 is

    (a) 4
    (b) 2
    (c) 3
    (d) 5

Sol. (c) We know that

$$\text{Mean} = \frac{4+2+3+0+2+3+5+6+1+4}{10}$$

$$= \frac{30}{10} = 3$$

Very Short Answer Type Questions
(1 Mark Each)

1. Find the mode of 14, 25, 14, 28, 18, 17, 18, 14, 23, 22, 14 and 18.

Sol. The given data is, 14, 25, 14, 28, 18, 17, 18, 14, 23, 14, 18

Arranging the data in ascending order, we have

14, 14, 14, 14, 17, 18, 18, 18, 22, 23, 25 28

Here, 14 occurs most frequently (4 times)
Mode = 14.

2. The mean of perimeters of two squares having sides x units and y units is:

    [NCERT Exemplar]

Sol. According to the question,

$$\text{Mean} = \frac{4x + 4y}{2} \quad (x, y \text{ sides of two squares})$$

$$= \frac{2(2x + 2y)}{2}$$

$$= 2x + 2y = 2(x + y)$$

3. Mean of first five prime numbers is:

    [Board Term II, 2012, Set-25]

Sol. We know that the first five prime numbers be 2, 3, 5, 7, 11

$$\text{Mean} = \frac{2 + 3 + 5 + 7 + 11}{5}$$

$$= \frac{28}{5} = 5.6$$

4. The mean of x_1, x_2 is 6 and mean of x_1, x_2, x_3 is 7. The value of x_3 is :   [Board Term II, 2012, Set-25]

Sol. According to the question,

$$\frac{x_1 + x_2}{2} = 6$$

$$\Rightarrow \quad x_1 + x_2 = 12 \qquad \ldots(i)$$

Again,

$$\Rightarrow \quad \frac{x_1 + x_2 + x_3}{3} = 7$$

$$\Rightarrow \quad x_1 + x_2 + x_3 = 21 \qquad (ii)$$

By using (i) and (ii), we get

$$12 + x_3 = 21$$

$$\Rightarrow \quad x_3 = 21 - 12 = 9$$

5. Median of first 8 prime numbers is:

    [Board Term II, 2012, Set-15]

Sol. We know that the first 8 prime numbers are 2, 3, 5, 7, 11, 13, 17, 19

Total number of terms = 8 (Even)

$$\text{Median} = \frac{1}{2}\left[\left(\frac{n}{2}\right)^{th} + \left(\frac{n}{2} + 1\right)^{th} \text{term}\right]$$

$$\text{Median} = \frac{7+11}{2} = \frac{18}{2} = 9$$

6. Median of the given data is

    144, 145, 147, 148, 149, 150, 152, 155, 160

    [Board Term II, Set-261C 2013]

Sol. Given data is, 144, 145, 147, 148, 149, 150, 152, 155, 160

Total number of terms = 9 (odd)

$$\therefore \quad \text{Required median} = \left(\frac{n+1}{2}\right)^{th} \text{term}$$

$$= \left(\frac{9+1}{2}\right)^{th} \text{ term}$$

$$= \frac{10}{2} = 5^{th} \text{ term}$$

So, Median = 149

7. Mean of first 10 natural numbers is :

[Board Term II, 2013]

Sol. We know that the first 10 natural numbers be 1, 2, 3, 4, 5, 6, 7, 8, 9, 10

$$\text{Mean} = \frac{1+2+3+4+5+6+7+8+9+10}{10}$$

$$= \frac{55}{10} = 5.5$$

8. Following observations have been written in ascending order. In median of the data is 22, then value of x will be   [Board Term II, 2013]

11, 12, 14, 16, 18, x + 2, x + 4, 30, 32, 35, 41

Sol. In the given series, Total numbers are 11

$$\therefore \qquad \text{Median} = \left(\frac{11+1}{2}\right)^{th} \text{ term}$$

$$\Rightarrow \qquad 22 = 6^{th} \text{ term}$$

$$\Rightarrow \qquad x + 2 = 22 - 2$$

$$x = 22 - 2 = 20$$

9. For the given data : 11, 15, 17, y + 1, 19, y − 2, 3; if the mean is 14, find the value of y.

[Board Term II, Set-IA21924, 2016]

Sol. According to the question,

$$\text{Mean} = \frac{\text{Sum of all observation}}{\text{Total number of term}}$$

$$\Rightarrow \qquad 14 = \frac{11+15+17+y+1+19+y-2+3}{7}$$

$$\Rightarrow \qquad 98 = 64 + 2y$$

$$\Rightarrow \qquad 2y = 34$$

$$\therefore \qquad y = \frac{34}{2} = 17$$

10. Find the mode of the numbers:

14, 14, 15, 27, 26, 27, 27, 22, 13

[Board Term II, Set-IA21924, 2016]

Sol. In the given data,

27 occurs most frequently (3 times).

Hence, mode = 27

11. The number of children in 10 families of a locality are : 2, 4, 3, 4, 2, 0, 3, 5, 1, 6. Find the mean number of children per family.

[Board Term II, KVS, 2016]

Sol. According to the question,

Mean number of children per family

$$= \frac{2+4+3+4+2+0+3+5+1+6}{10} = \frac{30}{10} = 3$$

12. Mean of 15 observations is 23. If each observation is multiplied by 2, find new mean.

[Board Term II, Set-LF0MCQ2, 2016]

Sol. If each observation under consideration is multiplied by 2, then new mean is obtained by multiplying same quantity (i.e., 2) in old mean

$$\therefore \qquad \text{New mean} = 2 \times \text{old mean}$$

$$= 2 \times 23 = 46.$$

13. Find the mean of first six odd numbers.

[Board Term II, Set-RQTZFBW, 2016]

Sol. We know that the first six odd numbers be 1, 3, 5, 7, 9, 11

$$\therefore \quad \text{Mean} = \frac{1+3+5+7+9+11}{6} = \frac{36}{6} = 6$$

14. The mean of five numbers is 30. If one number is excluded, their mean becomes 28. What is the excluded number?   [NCERT Exemplar]

Sol. We known that

$$\text{Mean} = \frac{\text{Sum of all observations}}{\text{Number of observations}}$$

$$\Rightarrow \qquad 30 = \frac{\text{Sum of five numbers}}{5}$$

$$\Rightarrow \quad \text{Sum of five numbers}$$

$$= 30 \times 5$$

$$= 150$$

$$\text{Also, new mean} = \frac{\text{Sum of all observations}}{\text{Number of observations}}$$

$$\Rightarrow \qquad 28 = \frac{\text{Sum of four observations}}{5}$$

$$\Rightarrow \quad \text{Sum of four observations} = 28 \times 4$$

$$= 112$$

Hence, excluded number = 150 − 112

$$= 38.$$

15. What is median of the numbers 4, 4, 5, 7, 6, 7, 7, 12 and 3?

Sol. Firstly, arrange the data in ascending order, we have

3, 4, 4, 5, 6, 7, 7, 7, 12

Here, n = 9, which is odd.

$$\therefore \qquad \text{Median} = \left(\frac{n+1}{2}\right)^{th} \text{ observation}$$

$$= \frac{1}{2}(9+1)^{th} \text{ observation}$$

$$= \frac{1}{2} \times (10)^{th} \text{ observation}$$

$$= 5^{th} \text{ observations}$$

$$= 6$$

Hence, the median is 6.

Short Answer Type Questions–I

(2 Marks Each)

1. In a diagnostic test of Mathematics given to students, the following marks (out of 100) are recorded :

   46, 52, 48, 11, 41, 62, 54, 53, 96, 40, 98, 44

   Which average will be a good representative of the above data and why?   [NCERT Exemplar]

Sol. Median will be a good representation of the data because.

   (i) Each value occurs once.

   (ii) The data is influenced by extreme values

   Arranging the given data in ascending order,

   11, 40, 41, 44, 46, 48, 52, 53, 54, 62, 96, 98

   Here $n = 12$

$$\text{Median} = \frac{\left(\frac{n}{2}\right)^{th} + \left(\frac{n}{2}+1\right)^{th} \text{ term}}{2}$$

$$= \frac{6^{th} + 7^{th} \text{ term}}{2}$$

$$= \frac{48 + 52}{2} = \frac{100}{2} = 50$$

2. Find the median of ascending order 34, 32, x, x − 1, 19, 15, 11, where x is the mean of 10, 20, 30, 40, 50.

Sol. Given, x be the mean of 10, 20, 30, 40, 50.

$$\therefore \qquad x = \frac{10 + 20 + 30 + 40 + 50}{5}$$

$$= \frac{150}{5} = 30$$

and median of $34, 32, x, x - 1, 19, 15, 11$

$$= \left(\frac{7+1}{2}\right)^{th} \text{ term}$$

$$= 4^{th} \text{ term} = x - 1$$

$$= 30 - 1 = 29 \qquad [\because \quad x = 30]$$

3. Find the median of the following data 15, 28, 72, 56, 44, 32, 31, 43 and 51. If 32 is replaced by 23, find the new median.

   [Board Term II, 2012, Set-23, Set-30]

Sol. According to the question,

   Arranging the data in ascending order,

   15, 28, 31, 32, 43, 44, 51, 56, 72.

$$n = 9, \text{ which is odd}$$

$$\text{Median} = \left[\left(\frac{9+1}{2}\right)\right]^{th} \text{ term} = 5^{th} \text{ term} = 43$$

   If 32 is replaced by 23, then the new order is

   15, 23, 28, 31, 43, 44, 51, 56, 72.

   Here $n = 9$

$$\therefore \quad \text{New median} = \left(\frac{9+1}{2}\right)^{th} \text{ term} = 5^{th} \text{ term} = 43.$$

4. The median of observations 11, 12, 14, 18, x + 2, x + 4, 30, 32, 35 and 41 arranged in ascending order is 24. Find x.

   [Board Term II, 2012, Set-25]

Sol. Given data is,

   11, 12, 14, 18, x + 2, x + 4, 30, 32, 35, 41

   Here, $n = 10$

   $\therefore$ Median = average of 5th and 6th observations

$$\Rightarrow \qquad 24 = \frac{(x + 2) + (x + 4)}{2}$$

$$\Rightarrow \qquad 24 = \frac{2x + 6}{2}$$

$$\Rightarrow \qquad 48 = 2x + 6 \quad \Rightarrow \quad 2x = 42$$

$$\therefore \qquad x = 21$$

5. Find the mode of the observations 17, 23, 25, 18, 17, 23, 19, 23, 17, 26, 23. If 4 is subtracted from each observation, what will be the mode of the new observations?

   [Board Term II, 2012, Set-01]

Sol. According to the question,

   Arranging the data in ascending order:

   17, 17, 17, 18, 19, 23, 23, 23, 25, 26

   Here, the occurance of 23 is maximum (4 times)

   $\therefore$ Mode = 23

   Hence, new mode = 23 − 4 = 19.

6. Arithmetic mean of terms 21, 16, 24, x, 29, 15 is 23. Find the value of x.

   [Board Term II, 2012, Set-24]

Sol. According to the question,

$$\text{A.M.} = \frac{21 + 16 + 24 + x + 29 + 15}{6}$$

$$\Rightarrow \qquad 23 = \frac{105 + x}{6}$$

$$\Rightarrow \qquad 105 + x = 138 \quad \Rightarrow \quad x = 138 - 105 = 33$$

7. The mean of 40 observations of a data was calculated as 16.5. Later it was noticed that a value 20.4 was wrongly read as 16.4. Find the correct mean.   [Board Term II, 2012, Set-12]

Sol. According to the question,

The mean of 40 observations = 16.5

Total of 40 observations = $16.5 \times 40 = 660$

$\because$ 20.4 was wrongly read as 16.4

$\therefore$ Corrected total = $660 - 16.4 + 20.4 = 664.0$

Hence, Corrected mean = $\dfrac{664.0}{40} = 16.6$

8. The mean of 100 observations is 60. If one observation of 50 is replaced by 110, then what will be the new mean?

[Board Term II, 2012, Set-69]

Sol. According to the question,

The mean of 100 observations = 60

Sum of 100 observations = $60 \times 100 = 6000$

After replacement, sum of new observations.

$= 6000 - 50 + 110 = 6060$

Hence, new mean = $\dfrac{6060}{100} = 60.6$

9. Calculate mean of prime numbers lying between 6 and 20.   [Board Term II, 2012, Set-41]

Sol. We know that, prime numbers lying between 6 and 20 are 7, 11, 13, 17, 19

Hence,

$$\text{Mean} = \frac{7 + 11 + 13 + 17 + 19}{5} = \frac{67}{5}$$

$$= 13.4$$

10. The mean of 40 observations was 160. It was detected on rechecking that the value 165 was wrongly copied as 125. Find the correct mean.

[Board Term II, 2012, Set-01]

Sol. According to the question,

Mean of 40 observations = 160

Sum of 40 observations = 160×40

$= 6400$

$\because$ 165 was wrongly copied as 125.

$\therefore$ New sum = $6400 + 165 - 125$

$= 6400 + 40 = 6440$

Hence, new mean = $\dfrac{6440}{40} = 161$

11. The mean of 5 observations was calculated as 145, but it was later on detected that one observation was misread as 45 in place of 25. Find the correct mean of the observations.

[Board Term II, 2012, Set-01]

Sol. According to the question,

$$\text{Mean} = \frac{\text{Sum of observations}}{\text{Number of observations}}$$

Total of all observations = $145 \times 5 = 725$

$\because$ One observation was misread as 45 in place of 25.

$\therefore$ Correct total of all observations

$= 725 - 45 + 25 = 705$

Hence, correct mean = $\dfrac{705}{5} = 141$

12. If the mean of five observations x, x + 2, x + 4, x + 6, x + 8 is 13, then find the value of x.

[Board Term II, 2012, Set-08]

Sol. According to the question,

$$\text{Mean} = \frac{\begin{array}{c}x + x + 2 + x + 4 \\ + x + 6 + x + 8\end{array}}{5}$$

$\Rightarrow$ $13 = \dfrac{5x + 20}{5}$

$\Rightarrow$ $13 = x + 4$

$\therefore$ $x = 13 - 4 = 9$

13. A class consists of 50 students out of which 30 are girls. The mean of marks scored by girls in a test is 73 and that of the boys is 71. Find the mean score of whole class.

[Board Term II, 2012, Set-12]

Sol. According to the question,

Sum of marks obtained by 30 girls

$= 30 \times 73 = 2190$

Sum of marks obtained by 20 boys

$= 20 \times 71 = 1420$

Sum of marks of 50 students of class

$= 2190 + 1420 = 3610$

Hence, mean for class = $\dfrac{3610}{50} = 72.2$ marks

14. Find the median of the squares of the first 8 natural numbers.   [Board Term II, 2012, Set-12]

Sol. According to the question,

Ascending order of terms :

1, 4, 9, 16, 25, 36, 49, 64

Number of terms = 8 (even)

$\therefore$ Median = Mean of 4th and 5th terms

$$= \frac{\left(\dfrac{n}{2}\right)^{th} + \left(\dfrac{n}{2}+1\right)^{th}}{2} = \frac{4^{th} + 5^{th}}{2}$$

$$= \frac{16 + 25}{2} = \frac{41}{2} = 20.5$$

15. Ten observations 6, 14, 15, 17, x + 1, 2x − 13, 30, 32, 34, 43 are written in ascending order. The median of data is 24. Find the value of x.

[Board Term II, 2012, Set-20]

Sol. Given data is, 6, 14, 15, 17, x + 1, 2x − 13, 30, 32, 34, 43

Median = mean of 5th and 6th observations

$\Rightarrow \quad 24 = \dfrac{x + 1 + 2x - 13}{2}$

$\Rightarrow \quad 48 = 3x - 12$

$\Rightarrow \quad 60 = 3x$

$\therefore \quad x = \dfrac{60}{3} = 20.$

16. Find the mode of the following data:

4, 6, 5, 9, 3, 2, 7, 7, 6, 5, 4, 9, 10, 10, 3, 4, 7, 6, 9, 9.

[Board Term II, 2012, Set-05]

Sol. According to the question,

Arranging the data in the following form, we get

2, 3, 3, 4, 4, 4, 5, 5, 6, 6, 6, 7, 7, 7, 9, 9, 9, 9, 10, 10

In the data 9 occurs most frequently (four times)

Hence, mode of data is 9.

17. Find the median of the following data:

95, 65, 75, 70, 75, 100, 50, 40.

[Board Term II, 2012, Set-01]

Sol. According to the question,

Arranging the data in increasing order,

40, 50, 65, 70, 75, 75, 95, 100

Number of terms (n) = 8 (even)

$\therefore \quad$ Median $= \dfrac{\left(\dfrac{n}{2}\right)^{th} \text{Obs.} + \left(\dfrac{n}{2} + 1\right)^{th} \text{obs.}}{2}$

$= \dfrac{4^{th}\,\text{obs.} + 5^{th}\,\text{obs.}}{2}$

$= \dfrac{70 + 75}{2}$

$= \dfrac{145}{2} = 72.5$

Hence, required median = 72.5

18. Find the value of 3x + 1, if median of 2, 3, x, x + 2 , 11, 17 is 9. (The observations are arranged in ascending order of magnitude).

[Board Term II, 2012, Set-05]

Sol. Given data is,

2, 3, x, x + 2, 11, 17

According to the question,

Median of the observations = Means of 3rd and 4th observations

$\Rightarrow \quad \dfrac{x + (x + 2)}{2} = 9$

$\Rightarrow \quad 2x + 2 = 9 \times 2$

$\Rightarrow \quad 2x = 16$

$\therefore \quad x = \dfrac{16}{2} = 8$

Hence, required value = 3x + 1

$= 3 \times 8 + 1$

$= 25.$

19. Find the mode and median of the following data:

15, 3, 7, 27, 17, 5, 14, 8, 9, 12, 24, 27, 7, 27, 30

[Board Term II, 2012, Set-30]

Sol. According to the question,

Arranging the data in ascending order:

3, 5, 7, 7, 8, 9, 12, 14, 15, 17, 24, 27, 27, 27, 30,

Total number of observations = 15 (odd)

$\therefore \quad$ Median $= \left(\dfrac{15 + 1}{2}\right)^{th}$ i.e., 8th observation = 14

In the data 27 occurs most frequently (three times)

Hence, mode = 27

20. Find the median of the following data:

2, 12, 32, 17, 26, 39, 42, 12, 18, 32, 15

[Board Term II, 2013]

Sol. According to the question,

Arrange the data in increasing order:

2, 12, 12, 15, 17, 18, 26, 32, 39, 42

Number of terms = 11(odd)

$\therefore \quad$ Median $= \left(\dfrac{n + 1}{2}\right)^{th}$ observation

$= \left(\dfrac{11 + 1}{2}\right)^{th} = 6^{th}$ observation

$= 18$

21. A set of data consists of six numbers 7, 8, 8, 9, 9 and 'x'. Find the difference between the modes when x = 9 and x = 8.

[Board Term II, 2013]

Sol. According to the question,

The numbers are 7, 8, 8, 9, 9, x

When $\qquad$ x = 9, mode = 9

When $\qquad$ x = 8, mode = 8

$\therefore$ Difference between the modes

$= 9 - 8 = 1.$

Hence, required difference = 1

22. There are 100 students in a class. 40 of them are girls. The average marks of the boys in science is 75% and that of the girls is 65%. Find the average marks of the class in science.

[Board Term II, 2013]

Sol. According to the question,

$$\text{Total marks of boys} = 60 \times 75$$
$$= 4500$$

and Total marks of girls $= 40 \times 65$
$$= 2600$$

$$\therefore \quad \text{Sum for class} = 4500 + 2600$$
$$= 7100$$

Hence, mean marks of the class $= \dfrac{7100}{100} = 71$

23. The following observations have been arranged in ascending order. If the median of the data is 63, find x:

29, 32, 48, 50, x, x + 2, 72, 78, 84, 95.

[Board Term II, KVS 2016, Set-LF0MCQ 2, 2016, 2012, 02]

Sol. Given data in ascending order is 29, 32, 48, 50, x, x + 2, 72, 78, 84, 95.

Number of terms (n) = 10(even)

According to the question,

$$\therefore \quad \text{Median} = \text{Mean of} \left\{ \left(\frac{n}{2}\right)^{th} + \left(\frac{n}{2} + 1\right)^{th} \right\} \text{obs.}$$

$$\Rightarrow \quad 63 = \text{mean of } 5^{th} \text{ and } 6^{th} \text{ obs.}$$

$$\Rightarrow \quad 63 = \frac{x + x + 2}{2}$$

$$\Rightarrow \quad 63 = x + 1$$

$$\therefore \quad x = 63 - 1$$
$$= 62$$

Hence, the value of x = 62

24. Find the mean of the following distribution

x	4	6	9	10	15
f	5	10	10	7	8

[Board Term II, 2013]

Sol. According to the question,

$$\text{Mean} = \frac{\Sigma f_i x_i}{\Sigma f_i}$$

$$= \frac{\begin{array}{c} 4 \times 5 + 6 \times 10 + 9 \times 10 \\ + 10 \times 7 + 15 \times 8 \end{array}}{5 + 10 + 10 + 7 + 8}$$

$$= \frac{20 + 60 + 90 + 70 + 120}{40}$$

$$= \frac{360}{40} = 9$$

Short Answer Type Questions–II

(3 Marks Each)

1. For mathematics test given to 15 students, the following marks (out of 100) are recorded:

41, 39, 48, 52, 46, 62, 54, 40, 96, 52, 98, 40, 52, 52, 60.

Find the mean and mode of the above data.

[NCERT][Board Term II, 2012, Set-6; 261, C-2013]

Sol. Given data is

41, 39, 48, 52, 46, 62, 54, 40, 96, 52, 98, 40, 52, 52, 60.

Mean of the data

$$= \frac{\begin{array}{c} 41 + 39 + 48 + 52 + 46 + 62 + 54 + 40 \\ + 96 + 52 + 98 + 40 + 52 + 52 + 60 \end{array}}{15}$$

$$= \frac{832}{15} = 55.5$$

Arranging the data in ascending order

39, 40, 40, 41, 46, 48, 52, 52, 52, 52, 54, 60, 62, 96, 98

Here, 52 occurs at most frequently (4 times)

$$\therefore \text{Mode} = 52$$

2. The score of 15 students in a examination out of 10 marks is as below:

3, 9, 7, 5, 6, 3, 7, 6, 7, 4, 7, 7, 4, 8, 2

Find the mean, mode and median.

[Board Term II, 2012, 10]

Sol. Arranging the given data in ascending order:

2, 3, 3, 4, 4, 5, 6, 6, 7, 7, 7, 7, 7, 8, 9

Number of terms (n) = 15, Mean $= \dfrac{\Sigma x}{n}$

$$= \frac{85}{15} = 5.7$$

$\because$ 7 occurs at most frequently (5 times)

$\therefore \qquad \text{Mode} = 7$

and $\qquad$ Median $= \left(\dfrac{15 + 1}{2}\right)^{th}$ term

$$= 8^{th} \text{ term} = 6.$$

3. The average height of 230 students is 150 cm. It was later detected that one observation 165 cm was wrongly copied as 135 cm. Find the correct mean height. [NCERT Exemplar]

Sol. According to the question,

$$\text{Mean} = \frac{\text{Sum of observations}}{\text{Number of observations}}$$

$$\therefore \quad \text{Sum of observations} = 150 \times 30$$
$$= 4500$$

∵   165 cm was wrongly copied as 135 cm.

∴   Correct sum of observations

$$= 4500 - 135 + 165$$
$$= 4530$$

Hence, correct mean height $= \dfrac{4530}{30} = 151$ cm

4. Find the mean for the weekly pocket money (in ₹) using the following data:

[Board Term II, 2012, Set- 20]

Pocket money (in ₹) (x)	55	50	49	81	48	57	65
Number of Students (f)	8	3	10	7	3	7	2

Sol.

x	f	fx
55	8	440
50	3	150
49	10	490
81	7	567
48	3	144
57	7	399
65	2	130
Total	$\Sigma f = 40$	$\Sigma fx = 2320$

$$\text{Mean } (\overline{x}) = \dfrac{\Sigma fx}{\Sigma f} = \dfrac{2320}{40} = 58$$

Hence, mean pocket money per week = ₹ 58.

5. Find mean, median and mode of the following data:

15, 17, 16, 14, 17, 16, 11, 15, 17, 14.

[Board Term II, 2012, Set-24]

Sol. According to the question,

Arranging data in ascending order:

11, 14, 14, 15, 15, 16, 16, 17, 17, 17

∴ $\text{Mean} = \dfrac{\Sigma x}{n} = \dfrac{152}{10} = 15.2$

Here, number of terms n = 10(even),

∴ $\text{Median} = \left[\dfrac{n^{th}}{2} + \left(\dfrac{n}{2} + 1 \right)^{th} \right]^{term}$

$$= \dfrac{5^{th}\text{ term} + 6^{th}\text{ term}}{2}$$

$$= \dfrac{15 + 16}{2} = 15.5$$

∵   17 occurs at most in the given data (3 times)

∴   Mode = 17.

6. Find the median and mode of the following data:

38, 40, 39, 40, 46, 41, 42, 52, 54, 52, 60, 62, 52, 98, 96.

[Board Term II, 2012, Set-15]

Sol. According to the question,

Arranging the given data in increasing order,

38, 39, 40, 40, 41, 42, 46, 52, 52, 52, 54, 60, 62, 96, 98

Here, number of terms (n) = 15 (odd)

∴ $\text{Median} = \left(\dfrac{n + 1}{2} \right) = \left(\dfrac{15 + 1}{2} \right)^{th}$ term

$$= \left(\dfrac{16}{2} \right)^{th} \text{ term } = 8^{th} \text{ term}$$

$$= 52$$

and Mode = observation with maximum frequency

$$= 52.$$

7. Find the mean for the following data:

[Board Term II, 2012, Set-10]

x	4	6	8	10	12
f	4	8	14	11	3

Sol.

x	f	fx
4	4	16
6	8	48
8	14	112
10	11	110
12	3	36
Total	$\Sigma f = 40$	$\Sigma fx = 322$

∴ $\text{Mean} = \dfrac{\Sigma fx}{\Sigma f}$

$$= \dfrac{322}{40} = 8.05$$

8. If the mean of the following distribution is 6, find the value of m.

[Board Term II, 2012, SEt-15]

x	2	4	6	10	m+5
f	3	2	3	1	2

Sol. According to the question,

$$\text{Mean} = \dfrac{2 \times 3 + 4 \times 2 + 6 \times 3 + 10 \times 1 + (m + 5) \times 2}{3 + 2 + 3 + 1 + 2}$$

$\Rightarrow$ $6 = \dfrac{6 + 8 + 18 + 10 + 2m + 10}{11}$

$\Rightarrow$ $66 = 52 + 2m$

$\Rightarrow$ $2m = 66 - 52 = 14$

∴ $m = \dfrac{14}{2} = 7$

9. Find the mean, median, mode of the following data:

41, 39, 48, 52, 41, 48, 36, 41, 37, 35

[Board Term II, 2012, Set-01]

Sol. According to the question,

$$\text{Mean} = \frac{\Sigma x_i}{N} = \frac{418}{10} = 41.8$$

Arranging the data in increasing order, we get

35, 36, 37, 39, 41, 41, 41, 48, 48, 52

There are 10 observations.

∴ Median = Mean of 5th and 6th observation

$$= \frac{41 + 41}{2} = 41$$

∵ The frequency of 41 is the most (3 times)

and   Mode = 41.

10. A cricketer has a mean score of 58 runs in nine innings. Find out how many runs are to be scored in the tenth innings to raise his mean score to 61.   [Board Term II, 2012, Set-01]

Sol. According to the question,

Total score of 8 innings

$$= 58 \times 9 = 522$$

and for mean score of 61, the total needed

$$= 61 \times 10 = 610$$

Hence, score to be added in the 10th inning

$$= 610 - 522 = 88.$$

11. Determine the median of the observations 24, 23, a, a − 1, 12, 16, where a is the mean of 10, 20, 30, 40, 50.   [Board Term II, 2012, Set-8]

Sol. According to the question,

$$\text{Mean} = \frac{10 + 20 + 30 + 40 + 50}{5}$$

$$= \frac{150}{5} = 30 = a$$

Arranging in ascending order, we get 12, 16, 23, 24, 29, 30.   [∵   a = 30 (Mean)

∴ a − 1 = 30 − 1 = 29]

Hence, number of terms (n) = 6

$$\therefore \quad \text{Median} = \left[\frac{1}{2}\left(\frac{6}{2}\right)^{th} \text{term} + \left(\frac{6}{2} + 1\right)^{th} \text{term}\right]$$

$$= \frac{1}{2}[3^{rd} \text{term} + 4^{th} \text{term}]$$

$$= \frac{23 + 24}{2} = \frac{47}{2} = 23.5$$

12. Find the mean of the following distribution:

Variable (x)	5	15	25	35	45
Frequency(f)	6	4	9	6	5

[Board Term II, 2012, Set-24]

Sol.

x	f	fx
5	6	30
15	4	60
25	9	225
35	6	210
45	5	225
Total	Σf = 30	Σfx = 750

$$\therefore \quad \text{Mean } (\overline{x}) = \frac{\Sigma fx}{\Sigma f} = \frac{750}{30} = 25.$$

13. The mean of monthly salary of 12 employees of a firm is ₹ 14,500. If one more person joins the firm who gets ₹ 18,400 per month, then what will the mean monthly salary now.

[Board Term II, Set-IA21924, 2016]

Sol. According to the question,

Mean monthly salary of 12 employees = ₹ 14,500

Sum of monthly salary of 12 employees

$$= 14,500 \times 12$$

$$= 1,74,000$$

∴ Sum of monthly salary of 13 employees

$$= 1,74,000 + 18,400$$

$$= ₹ 1,92,400$$

Hence, mean of monthly salary of 13 employees

$$= \frac{1,92,400}{13}$$

$$= ₹14,800$$

14. The mean of 10 numbers is 55. If one number is included, their mean becomes 60. Find the included number.

[Board Term II, Set-RQTZFBW, 2016]

Sol. According to the question,

N = 10, x = 55

$$\because \quad \overline{x} = \frac{\Sigma x_i}{N}$$

∴ Sum of 10 observations = 10 × 55 = 550 ...(i)

When N = 11, $\overline{x}$ = 60

⇒ Sum of 11 observations = 11 × 60 = 660...(ii)

∴ 11th observation = 660 − 550

$$= 110$$

Hence, the included number = 110

15. The mean of 9 numbers is 50, If one number is included, their mean becomes 55. Find the included number.

[Board Term II, 2017, Set-UAH4DQ7]

Sol. According to the question,

N = 9

and $\overline{x}$ = 50

$$\therefore \qquad \overline{x} = \frac{\Sigma x_i}{N}$$

$\therefore$ Sum of 9 observations $= 9 \times 50 = 450$

when $\qquad N = 10, \overline{x} = 55$

$\Rightarrow$ Sum of 10 observations $= 10 \times 55 = 550$

Hence, included number $= 550 - 450 = 100$

16. Find median and mode of following data.

6, 9, 12, 15, 9, 3, 6, 9, 12, 6, 10, 3, 6, 15, 6

Sol. Firstly, arrange the given data in ascending order

i.e., 3, 3, 6, 6, 6, 6, 6, 9, 9, 9, 10, 12, 12, 15, 15

Number of terms (n) = 15 (odd)

$$\therefore \qquad \text{Median} = \left(\frac{n+1}{2}\right)^{th} \text{term}$$

$$= \frac{15+1}{2}$$

$$= 8^{th} \text{ term} = 9$$

From the data we see that 6 occurs maximum five times.

$$\therefore \qquad \text{Mode} = 6$$

17. The mean height of 6 girls is 148 cm. If the individual heights of five of them are 142 cm, 154 cm, 146 cm, 145 cm and 150 cm, then find height of the sixth girl.

Sol. According to the question,

Mean height of 6 girls = 148 cm

$\therefore$ Sum of the heights of 6 girls $= 148 \times 6$

$$= 888 \text{ cm}$$

Now, sum of the heights of 5 girls

$$= 142 + 154 + 146 + 145 + 150$$

$$= 737 \text{ cm}$$

Height of the sixth girl = sum of the heights of 6 girls – sum of the heights of 5 girls

$$= 888 - 737$$

$$= 151 \text{ cm.}$$

Hence, the height of the sixth girl is 151 cm.

Long Answer Type Questions

(4 Marks Each)

1. In mathematics test given to 15 students, the following marks (out of 90) are recorded.

41, 39, 48, 52, 46, 62, 54, 40, 88, 52, 86, 40, 42, 52, 60.

Find the mean, median and mode of this data.

[NCERT][Board Term II, 2017, Set-Z6K408K]

Sol. According to the question,

$$\text{Mean } (\overline{x}) = \frac{\text{Sum of observations}}{\text{Total number of observations}}$$

$$= \frac{\Sigma x_i}{N}$$

$$= \frac{\begin{array}{c} 41 + 39 + 48 + 52 + 46 + 62 \\ + 54 + 40 + 88 + 52 + 86 \\ + 40 + 42 + 52 + 60 \end{array}}{15}$$

$$= \frac{802}{15} = 53.47 \text{ marks}$$

Now, arranging the marks in ascending order

39, 40, 40, 41, 42, 46, 48, 52, 52, 52, 54, 60, 62, 86, 88

Number of terms (N) = 15(odd)

$$\therefore \qquad \text{Median} = \left(\frac{N+1}{2}\right)^{th} \text{observation}$$

$$= \left(\frac{15+1}{2}\right)^{th} \text{observation}$$

$$= 8^{th} \text{ observation}$$

$$= 52 \text{ marks}$$

Here, 52 occurs at most frequently (3 times)

Hence, mode = 52

2. The mean of the following distribution is 50:

x_i	10	30	50	70	90
y_i	17	5p + 3	32	7p – 11	19

Find the value of p.   [Board Term II, 2012, Set-25]

Sol.

x	**f**	**fx**
10	17	170
30	5p + 3	150p + 90
50	32	1600
70	7p – 11	490p – 770
90	19	1710
Total	60 + 12p	2800 + 640p

$$\therefore \qquad \text{Mean} = \frac{\Sigma f_i x_i}{\Sigma f_i}$$

$$\Rightarrow \qquad 50 = \frac{2800 + 640p}{60 + 12p}$$

$$\Rightarrow \qquad 3000 + 600p = 2800 + 640p$$

$$\Rightarrow \qquad 3000 - 2800 = 640p - 600p$$

$$\Rightarrow \qquad 200 = 40p$$

$$\therefore \qquad p = \frac{200}{40} = 5$$

3. Find the mean $(\overline{x})$ of first ten prime numbers

and, show that $\displaystyle\sum_{i=1}^{10} (x_1 - \overline{x}) = 0$

[Board Term II, 2012, Set-23]

Sol. We know that, first ten prime numbers are 2, 3, 5, 7, 11, 13, 17, 19, 23, 29;

$$\text{Mean} = \frac{2 + 3 + 5 + 7 + 11 + 13 + 17 + 19 + 23 + 29}{10}$$

$$= \frac{129}{10} = 12.9$$

To prove: $\sum_{i=1}^{10} (x_i - \overline{x}) = 0$

Proof: Now,

$$\sum_{i=1}^{10} (x_i - \overline{x}) = (2 - 12.9) + (3 - 12.9)$$

$$+ (5 - 12.9) + (7 - 12.9) + (11 - 12.9)$$
$$+ (13 - 12.9) + (17 - 12.9) + (19 - 12.9)$$
$$+ (23 - 12.9) + (29 - 12.9)$$
$$= -10.9 - 9.9 - 7.9 - 5.9 - 1.9$$
$$+ 0.1 + 4.1 + 6.1$$
$$+ 10.1 + 16.1$$
$$= -36.5 + 36.5 = 0.$$

$$\sum_{i=1}^{10} (x_i - \overline{x}) = 0.$$

Hence proved.

4. The mean of a-observations is $(\overline{x})$. If constant "a" is subtracted from each observation, then show that the new mean is "$(\overline{x}) - a$".

[Board Term II, Set-LF0MCQ2, 2016]

Sol. According to the question,

Mean of n observations = $\overline{x}$

Let observations are $x_1, x_2, x_3, ..., x_n$

$$\therefore \quad \text{Mean} = \frac{\text{Sum of observations}}{\text{Number of observations}}$$

$$\therefore \quad \overline{x} = \frac{x_1 + x_2 + x_3 + ... + x_n}{n}$$

$$\Rightarrow \quad x_1 + x_2 + x_3 + ... + x_n = n^{\overline{x}}$$

If each observation is reduced by a, the observation will be $x_1 - a, x_2 - a, x_3 - a, ..., x_n - a$

Let the new mean be k

$$\therefore \quad \text{Mean} = \frac{x_1 - a + x_2 - a + x_3 - a + ... + x_n - a}{n}$$

$$\Rightarrow \quad nk = x_1 - a + x_2 - a + x_3 - a + ... + x_n - a$$

$$\Rightarrow \quad nk = n\overline{x} - na$$

$$(\because x_1 + x_2 + x_3 + ... + x_n = n\overline{x})$$

$$\therefore \quad k = \overline{x} - a$$

Hence, the new mean is $\overline{x} - a$.

5. Find median and mode of the following data:

24, 17, 13, 24, 26, 20, 26, 30, 8, 41, 24

If one 24 is replaced by 26, find new median and new mode. [Board Term II, Set-IA21924,2016]

Sol. According the question,

Arranging data in ascending order :

8, 13, 17, 20, 24, 24, 24, 26, 26, 30, 41

Number of terms (n) =11 (odd)

$$\therefore \quad \text{Median} = \left(\frac{n + 1}{2}\right)^{th} \text{term}$$

$$= \left(\frac{11 + 1}{2}\right)^{th} \text{term}$$

$$= 6^{th} \text{term}$$

$$\therefore \quad \text{Median} = 24$$

$\because$ 24 occurs at most frequently (3 times)

$$\therefore \quad \text{Mode} = 24$$

If we replace one 24 by 26, the given data will be (in ascending order):

8, 13, 17, 20, 24, 24, 26, 26, 30, 41

Number of terms (n) = 11 (odd)

$$\therefore \quad \text{Median} = \frac{n + 1}{2} = \frac{11 + 1}{2}$$

$$= \frac{12}{2} = 6^{th} \text{term}$$

$$= 24$$

$\because$ 26 occurs at most (3 times)

$$\therefore \quad \text{Mode} = 26$$

CHAPTER 15

Probability

- History, repeated experiments and observed frequency approach to probability.
- Focus is on empirical probability. A large amount of time to be devoted to group and to individual activities to motivate the concept.
- The experiments to be drawn from real-life situations and from examples used in the chapter on statistics.

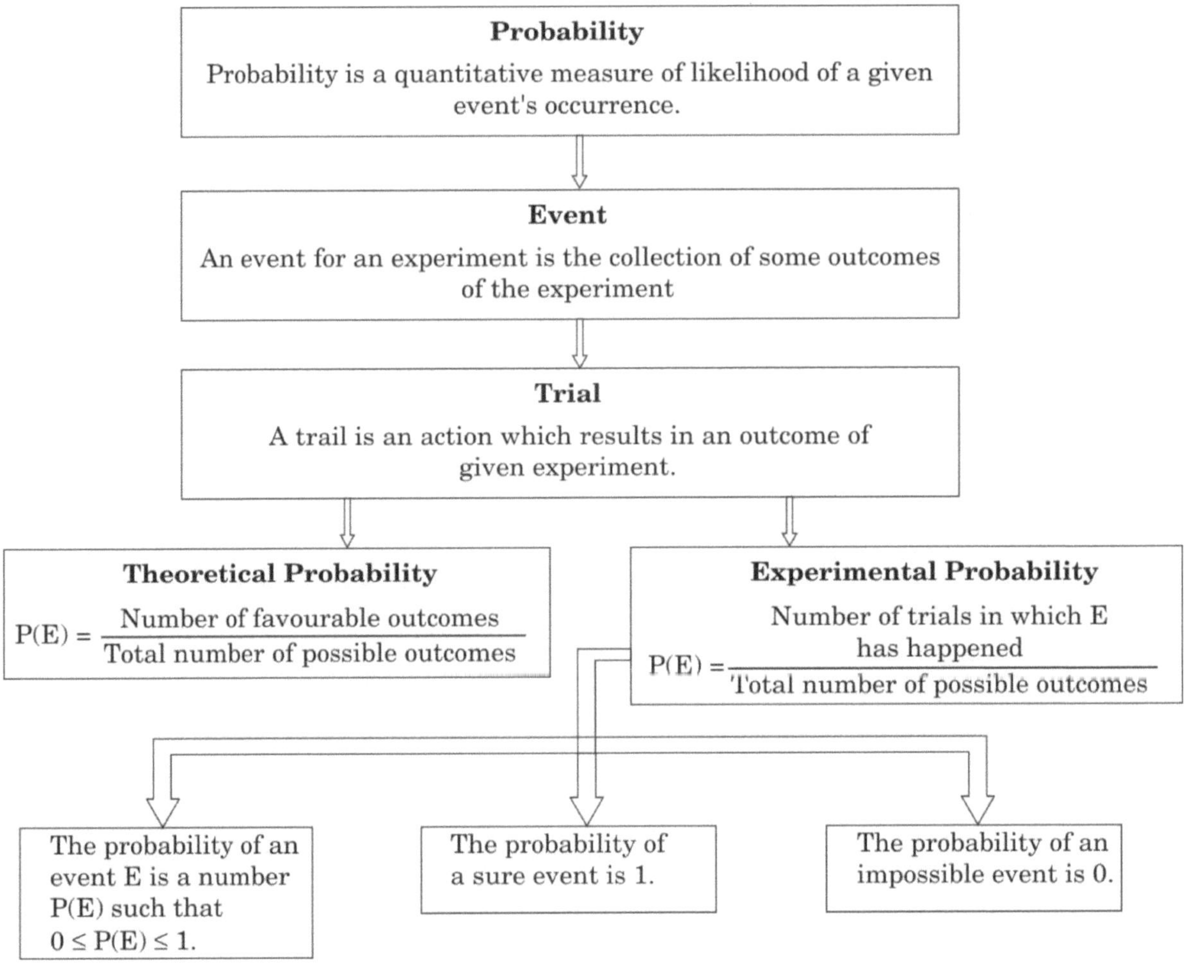

Probability

Probability is a quantitative measure of likelihood of a given event's occurrence.

Event

An event for an experiment is the collection of some outcomes of the experiment

Trial

A trail is an action which results in an outcome of given experiment.

Theoretical Probability

$$P(E) = \frac{\text{Number of favourable outcomes}}{\text{Total number of possible outcomes}}$$

Experimental Probability

$$P(E) = \frac{\text{Number of trials in which E has happened}}{\text{Total number of possible outcomes}}$$

The probability of an event E is a number P(E) such that $0 \leq P(E) \leq 1$.

The probability of a sure event is 1.

The probability of an impossible event is 0.

[Topic 1] Experimental Approach

Points to be Remembered

- An operation which can produce some well-defined outcomes is called an experiment.
- Probability is a quantitative measure of certainty.
- A trial is an action which will result in one or several outcomes.
- An event for an experiment is the collection of some outcomes of the experiment.
  - (i) getting a head on tossing a coin.
  - (ii) getting a face card when a card is drawn from a pack of 52 cards.
- An experiment which, when repeated under identical condition, produce the same result or outcomes, is known as deterministic experiment.

PREVIOUS YEARS'
EXAMINATION QUESTIONS
TOPIC 1

Multiple Choice Questions
(1 Mark Each)

1. Two coins are tossed 1,000 times and the outcomes are recorded as below:

Numbers of heads	2	1	0
Frequency	200	550	250

Based on this information, the probability for at most one head is

(a) $\dfrac{1}{5}$ (b) $\dfrac{1}{4}$

(c) $\dfrac{4}{5}$ (d) $\dfrac{3}{4}$ [NCERT Exemp.]

Sol. (c) According to the question,

Total number of outcomes = 1,000

Number of times getting at most one head
$$= 250 + 550 = 800$$

$\therefore$ P(getting at most one head) $= \dfrac{(550 + 250)}{1000} = \dfrac{4}{5}$

Hence, required probability $= \dfrac{4}{5}$

2. In a sample study of 642 people, it was found that 514 people have a high school certificate. If a person is selected at random, the probability that the person has a high school certificate is

(a) 0.5   (b) 0.6

(c) 0.7   (d) 0.8   [NCERT Exemp.]

Sol. (d) According to the question,

Total number of people in a sample study = 642

Number of people with high school certificate = 514

$\therefore$ P(person with high school certificate) $= \dfrac{514}{642} = 0.8$

Hence, required probability = 0.8

3. Two coins are tossed 1000 times of a class, the following blood groups are recorded:

Blood group	A	AB	B	O
Numbers of students	10	13	12	5

A student is selected at random from the class. The probability that he/she has blood group B, is

(a) $\dfrac{1}{4}$ (b) $\dfrac{13}{40}$

(c) $\dfrac{3}{10}$ (d) $\dfrac{1}{8}$ [NCERT Exemp.]

Sol. (c) According to the question,

Total number of students
$$= 10 + 13 + 12 + 5 = 40$$

Total number of students with blood group B = 12

$\therefore$ P(students with blood group B) $= \dfrac{12}{40} = \dfrac{3}{10}$

Hence, required probability $= \dfrac{3}{10}$

4. A coin is tossed 100 times and head appears 64 times. The probability of getting a tail is

(a) $\dfrac{18}{25}$ (b) $\dfrac{9}{25}$

(c) 0   (d) 1   [NCERT Exemp.]

Sol. (b) According to the question,

Total number of outcomes = 100

Since, number of times head appears = 64

$\therefore$ Number of times tail appears $= 100 - 64 = 36$

$\therefore$ P(getting a tail) $= \dfrac{36}{100} = \dfrac{9}{25}$

Hence, required probability $= \dfrac{9}{25}$

5. Emperical probability of an event is also known as:

    (a) an experimental probability

    (b) a theoretical probability

    (c) theoretical expectation of a chance

    (d) none of these

Sol. (a) Emperical probability of an event is also known as an experimental probability.

6. A die is thrown 225 times and the results were as follows:

Outcomes	1	2	3	4	5	6
Frequencies	34	50	16	71	24	30

The probability of getting a prime number is

    (a) $\dfrac{8}{45}$ (b) $\dfrac{2}{5}$

    (c) $\dfrac{24}{225}$ (d) $\dfrac{124}{225}$

Sol. (b) According to the question,

Total number of outcomes = 225

Number of favourable outcomes of getting prime number = 50 + 16 + 24 = 90

∴   P(getting prime number)

$$= \dfrac{90}{225} = \dfrac{2}{5}$$

Hence, required probability = $\dfrac{2}{5}$

7. A coin is tossed 500 times and head appeared 300 times. Then sum of the probability of getting a head and the probability of getting a tail is

    (a) 35   (b) 25

    (c) 15   (d) 1

Sol. (d) P(H) + P(T) = 1

Since the sum of all probabilities of an experiments is 1.

8. In an experiment a coin is tossed 500 times. If the head turns up 280 times, the experimental probability of getting a head is

    (a) $\dfrac{14}{25}$ (b) $\dfrac{11}{25}$

    (c) $\dfrac{13}{25}$ (d) $\dfrac{19}{25}$ [NCERT Exemp.]

Sol. (a) According to the question,

Total number of outcomes = 500

Number of times head turns up = 280

∴   P(getting a head) = $\dfrac{280}{500} = \dfrac{14}{25}$

Hence, required probability = $\dfrac{14}{25}$

9. A die is tossed 200 times simultaneously, and the frequencies of various outcomes are given below:

Outcomes	1	2	3	4	5	6
Frequencies	15	40	25	50	65	5

The probability of getting 5 is

    (a) $\dfrac{1}{40}$ (b) $\dfrac{13}{40}$

    (c) $\dfrac{11}{40}$ (d) $\dfrac{1}{5}$

Sol. (b) According to the question,

Total number of outcomes = 200

Number of favourable outcomes getting 5 = 65

∴   P(getting 5) = $\dfrac{65}{200} = \dfrac{13}{40}$

Hence, required probability = $\dfrac{13}{40}$

10. Three coins are tossed simultaneously 200 times with following outcomes :

Outcomes	3 heads	2 heads	1 head	No head
Frequency	23	72	77	28

The probability of getting two heads is

    (a) $\dfrac{23}{25}$ (b) $\dfrac{9}{25}$

    (c) $\dfrac{18}{25}$ (d) $\dfrac{4}{5}$

Sol. (b) According to the question,

Total number of outcomes = 200

Number of favourable outcomes = 72

∴   P(getting at least 2 heads) = $\dfrac{72}{200} = \dfrac{9}{25}$

Hence, required probability = $\dfrac{9}{25}$

11. A coin is tossed 100 times with the following frequencies:

Head : 64, Tail : 36

The ratio of probabilities for each event is

    (a) 16 : 9   (b) 9 : 16

    (c) 1 : 1   (d) 3 : 4

Sol. (a) Total number of outcomes = 100

∴   Number of times getting head = 64

∴   P(getting head) = $\dfrac{64}{100}$

∴   Number of times getting tail = 36

$\therefore$ P(getting tail) = $\dfrac{36}{100}$

Hence, required ratio = $\left(\dfrac{64}{100}\right):\left(\dfrac{36}{100}\right)$

$= 64 : 36 = 16 : 9$

12. Which of the following words does not show the probability?

(a) Chances　　　(b) Probably

(c) Definitely　　(d) Doubt

Sol. (a) The word 'chances' does not show the probability.

13. A die is tossed 270 times and the results were as follows :

Outcomes	1	2	3	4	5	6
Frequencies	40	65	60	32	55	18

The probability of getting either 1 or 3 is

(a) $\dfrac{4}{27}$　　　(b) $\dfrac{2}{9}$

(c) $\dfrac{1}{25}$　　　(d) $\dfrac{10}{27}$

Sol. (d) According to the question,

Total number of outcomes = 270

Number of outcomes getting either 1 or 3

$= 40 + 60 = 100$

$\therefore$ P(getting either 1 or 3) = $\dfrac{100}{270}=\dfrac{10}{27}$

Hence, required probability = $\dfrac{10}{27}$

Very Short Answer Type Questions

(1 Mark Each)

1. Three coins are tossed simultaneously 200 times with the following frequencies at different outcomes.

Outcomes	3 heads	2 heads	1 head	No head
Frequency	23	72	77	28

If the three coins are simultaneously tossed again, compute the probability of 2 heads coming up. [NCERT]

Sol. In tossing of three coins, getting two heads comes out 72 times.

i.e.,　　　　n(E) = 72

The total number of tossed three coins

n(S) = 200

Hence, probability of 2 heads coming up

$= \dfrac{n(E)}{n(S)}=\dfrac{72}{200}=\dfrac{9}{25}$

2. Can the experimental probability of an event be a negative number? If not, why?

[NCERT Exemplar]

Sol. The experimental probability of an event can not be negative because the value of probability always lies from 0 to 1.

3. Can experimental probability of an event be greater than 1? Justify your answer.

[NCERT Exemplar]

Sol. The experimental probability of an event can never be greater than 1, because it always lies from 0 to 1.

4. When a coin is tossed 500 times, the following outcomes were recorded :

Head : 270 times, Tail : 230 times

If a coins is tossed, what is the probability of getting a head?

[Board Term II, 2012, Set-01]

Sol. Total number of outcomes = 500

and total possible outcomes = 270

Required probability = $\dfrac{270}{500}=\dfrac{27}{50}=0.54$

5. A coin is tossed 500 times with the following observations :

Head : 245 times, Tail : 255 times

The coin is tossed again. The probability of getting a head is ....

[Board Term II, 2012, Set-08]

Sol. Total number of outcomes = 500

and total number of heads = 245

Probability of getting a head = $\dfrac{245}{500}=0.49$

6. Some families with 2 children were selected randomly and the following data recorded

Number of girls in a family	0	1	2
Number of families	111	714	375

If a family is chosen at random, then compute the probability that it has 1 girl.

Sol. Total number of families = 111 + 714 + 375 = 1200

Number of families having 1 girl = 714

Hence, required probability = $\dfrac{714}{1200}=0.595$

Short Answer Type Questions-I
(2 Marks Each)

1. A teacher wanted to analyse the performance of two sections of students in a mathematics test of 100 marks. Looking at their few got 70 marks or above. So she decided to group them into intervals of varying sizes as follows:

   0–20, 20–30, ..., 60–70, 70–100. Then she formed the following table.

Marks	Number of students
0–20	7
20–30	10
30–40	10
40–50	20
50–60	20
60–70	15
70-above	8
Total	90

   (i) Find the probability that a student obtained less than 20% in the mathematics test.

   (ii) Find the probability that a student obtained marks 60 or above.   [NCERT]

Sol. According to the question,

Total number of students in a class, $n(S) = 90$

(i) The number of students less than 20% lies in the interval 0–20. *i.e.,*
$$n(E) = 7$$
Hence, the probability, that a student obtained less than 20% in the Mathematics test
$$= \frac{n(E)}{n(S)} = \frac{7}{90}$$

(ii) The number of students obtained marks 60 or above lies in the marks interval 60–70 and 70–above *i.e.,*
$$n(F) = 15 + 8 = 23$$
Hence, the probability that a student obtained marks 60 or above
$$= \frac{n(F)}{n(S)} = \frac{23}{90}$$

2. To know the opinion of the students about the subject statistics, a survey of 200 students was conducted. The data is recorded in the following table:

Opinion	Number of students
Like	135
Dislike	65

Find the probability that a student chosen at random

(i) likes statistics, (ii) does not like it
[NCERT]

Sol. According to the question,

Total number of students in a survey
$$n(S) = 200$$

(i) The number of students who like statistics
$$n(E) = 135$$
∴ The probability, that the student like Statistics
$$= \frac{n(E)}{n(S)} = \frac{135}{200} = \frac{27}{40}$$

(ii) The number of students who does not like statistics, $n(F) = 65$

∴ The probability, that the student does not like Statistics
$$= \frac{n(F)}{n(S)} = \frac{65}{200} = \frac{13}{40}$$

3. On a particular day, the number of vehicles passing through a crossing is given below:

Vehicle	2 wheeler	3 wheeler	4 wheeler
Frequency	57	33	30

   A particular vehicle is chosen at random. What is the probability that it is not a four wheeler?
   [Board Term II, 2012, Set-24]

Sol. According to the question,

Total number of vehicles $= 57 + 33 + 30 = 120$

Vehicles which are not four wheelers
$$= 57 + 33 = 90$$
∴ P(chosen vehicle is not four wheeler)
$$= \frac{90}{120} = \frac{3}{4}$$

Hence, required probability $= \dfrac{3}{4}$

4. Three coins are tossed simultaneously 200 times with the following frequencies of different outcomes:

Outcomes	3 heads	2 heads	1 head	No head
Frequency	28	72	72	28

   Find the probability of getting 2 or more heads.
   [Board Term II, 2012, Set-05]

Sol. According to the question,

Total outcomes $= 200$

Number of times 2 or more heads occur
$$= 28 + 72 = 100$$

Hence, required probability $= \dfrac{100}{200} = \dfrac{1}{2}$

5. A dice is rolled 300 times and following outcomes are recorded:

Outcomes	1	2	3	4	5	6
Frequencies	42	60	55	53	60	30

Find the probability of getting a number more than 4. [Board Term II, 2012, Set-30]

Sol. Total number of times a dice is rolled = 300

Frequency of outcomes of number more than 4
$$= 60 + 30 = 90$$

∴ P(getting a number more than 4)
$$= \frac{90}{300} = \frac{3}{10}$$

Hence, required probability = $\frac{3}{10}$

6. A die is tossed 100 times and the data are recorded as below:

Outcomes	1	2	3	4	5	6
Frequencies	20	15	20	15	20	10

The die is tossed again. Find the probability of getting:

(i) an odd number (ii) a prime number

[Board Term II, 2012, Set-06]

Sol. According to the question,

Total number of cases = 100

(i) Number of cases favourable to an odd number
$(1, 3, 5) = 20 + 20 + 20 = 60$

∴ P(odd number) $= \frac{60}{100} = \frac{3}{5}$

Hence, required probability = $\frac{3}{5}$

(ii) Number of cases favourable to the event a prime number $(2, 3, 5) = 15 + 20 + 20 = 55$

∴ P(Prime number) $= \frac{55}{100} = \frac{11}{20}$

Hence, required probability = $\frac{11}{20}$

7. The table given below shows the marks obtained by 80 students of a class in a test with maximum marks 100 :

Marks	Number of students
0–20	8
20–40	16
40–60	40
60–80	10
Above 80	6

A student is chosen at random. Find the probability that he gets.

(i) less than 40 marks.

(ii) 60% or more marks.

[Board Term II, 2012, Set-10]

Sol. According to the question,

Total number of students = 80

(i) Number of students getting less than 40 marks
$$= 8 + 16 = 24$$

∴ P(less than 40 marks) $= \frac{24}{80} = \frac{3}{10}$

Hence, required probability = $\frac{3}{10}$

(ii) Number of students getting 60 or more than 60 marks = 10 + 6 = 16

∴ P(60 or more than 60 marks) $= \frac{16}{80} = \frac{1}{5}$

Hence, required probability = $\frac{1}{5}$

8. A die is thrown 1000 times with the frequencies of outcomes 1, 2, 3, 4, 5 and 6 as given below:

Outcomes	1	2	3	4	5	6
Frequencies	179	150	157	149	175	190

A die is thrown once again. Find the probability of outcome "greater than 3".

[Board Term II, 2012, Set-01]

Sol. According to the question,

Total number of outcomes = 1000 and Number of outcomes greater than 3
$$= (149 + 175 + 190) = 514$$

Hence, required probability
$$= \frac{514}{1000} = 0.514$$

9. Two coins are tossed 100 times with the following frequencies of different outcomes :

Outcomes	2 heads	1 head	No heads
Frequency	30	48	22

Find the probability of getting less than 2 heads.

[Board Term II, 2013]

Sol. According to the question,

Total number of outcomes = 100

Probability of getting less than 2 heads
= Number of times 0 or 1 head appeared
$$= 48 + 22 = 70$$

∴   P(E) $= \frac{70}{100} = 0.7$

Hence, the required probability = 0.7

10. Three coins are tossed simultaneously 150 times with the following frequencies of different outcomes.

Number of tails	0	1	2	3
Frequency	25	30	32	63

Compute the probability of getting.
(i) At least 2 tails (ii) Exactly one tail

[Board Term II, 2015]

Sol. According to the question,

Total number of outcomes = 150

(i) At least 2 tails = [Frequency of number of 2 tails + number of 3 tails]

$$\therefore \quad P(E) = \frac{32+63}{150} = \frac{95}{150} = \frac{19}{30}$$

Hence, required probability $= \dfrac{19}{30}$

(ii) $P(E) = \dfrac{30}{150} = \dfrac{1}{5}$

Hence, the probability of getting exactly one tail

$$= \frac{1}{5}$$

11. In an experiment, a coin is tossed 600 times. If the tail turns up 380 times, find the experimental probability of getting.
(i) A head   (ii) A tail

[Board Term II, 2015]

Sol. According to the question,

Total number of times, the coin is tossed = 600

Number of times a tail comes up = 380

$\therefore$ Number of times, a head comes up

$$= 600 - 380 = 220$$

$$\therefore \quad P(\text{getting a head}) = \frac{220}{600} = \frac{11}{30}$$

$$\text{and} \quad P(\text{getting a tail}) = \frac{380}{600} = \frac{19}{30}$$

Hence the probabilities of getting a head $= \dfrac{11}{30}$

and of getting a tail $= \dfrac{19}{30}$

12. 1000 families with 2 children were selected randomly and following data was recorded :

Number of girls in a family	0	1	2
Number of families	198	527	275

If a family member is chosen at random, compute the probability that it has:
(i) 0 boys   (ii) 2 boys

[Board Term II, 2015]

Sol. According to the question,

Total number of families = 198 + 527 + 275 = 1000

(i) Probability of family having 0 boys

$$\therefore \quad P(E) = \frac{275}{1000} = \frac{11}{40}$$

(ii) Probability of family having 2 boys

$$P(E) = \frac{198}{1000} = \frac{99}{500}$$

13. The probability of guessing the correct answer to a certain question is $\dfrac{x}{3}$. If the probability of not guessing the correct answer is $\dfrac{5x}{3}$, then find the value of x.

[Board Term II, 2015]

Sol. We know that

$$P(E) + P(E') = 1$$

According to the question,

$$\Rightarrow \qquad \frac{x}{3} + \frac{5x}{3} = 1$$

$$\Rightarrow \qquad \frac{x+5x}{3} = 1$$

$$\Rightarrow \qquad \frac{6x}{3} = 1$$

$$\Rightarrow \qquad 2x = 1$$

$$\therefore \qquad x = \frac{1}{2}$$

14. Teachers and students are selected at random to make two teams of 20 members each on sports day to participate in the event of "tug of war". The number of volunteers are as follows:

Teachers		Students	
Male	Female	Male	Female
12	18	20	10

Find the probability that the person chosen at random.
(i) is a male   (ii) is a female student

[Board Term II, 2015]

Sol. According to the question,

Total number of volunteers = 12 + 18 + 20 + 10 = 60

(i) Total number of males = 12 + 20 = 32

$$\therefore \quad P(\text{person is male}) = \frac{32}{60} = \frac{8}{15}$$

Hence, the probability that the person chosen at random is a male $= \dfrac{8}{15}$

(ii) P(person is female student) $= \dfrac{10}{60} = \dfrac{1}{6}$

Hence, the probability that the person chosen at random is a female student $= \dfrac{1}{6}$

15. A coin is tossed 1000 times with the following frequencies :

Head : 455, Tail : 545

Compute the probability for each event.

[Board Term II, KVS 2016]

Sol. According to the question,

Total number of outcomes = 1000

Total number of heads occur = 455

Probability of getting head $= \dfrac{455}{1000} = \dfrac{91}{200}$

Total number of tails occur = 545

∴   Probability of getting tail

$$= \dfrac{545}{1000} = \dfrac{109}{200}$$

16. Some families with 2 children were surveyed and the following data was recorded :

Number of girls in a family	0	1	2
Number of families	184	714	425

If a family is chosen at random, compute the probability that it has

(i)   exactly 1 girl

(ii) exactly 2 boys

[Board Term II, Set-IA 21924, 2016]

Sol. According to the question,

Total number of families = 184 + 714 + 425 = 1323

(i) Probability that chosen family has exactly one

$$girl = \dfrac{714}{1323} = \dfrac{34}{63}$$

(ii) Probability that chosen family has exactly

$$2 \text{ boys} = \dfrac{184}{1323}$$

17. The probability of winning a game is $\dfrac{1}{3}$ less than the twice of losing the game. Find probability of winning the game.

[Board Term II, 2016, Set-IA21924]

Sol. Let the probability of winning a game = p

and probability of losing a game = q

According to the question,

We know that p + q = 1   ...(i)

and $p = 2q - \dfrac{1}{3}$

$6q - 3p = 1$ ...(ii)

On solving equations (i) and (ii), we get

$$q = \dfrac{4}{9} \quad \text{and} \quad p = \dfrac{5}{9}$$

Hence, probability of winning a game $= \dfrac{5}{9}$

18. A coin is tossed 1200 times with the following outcomes :

Head : 455, Tail : 745

Compute the probability for each case

[Board Term II, Set-LF0MCQ2, 2016]

Sol. According to the question,

Total number of outcomes = 1200

Probability of getting head $= \dfrac{455}{1200} = \dfrac{91}{240}$

and probability of getting tail $= \dfrac{745}{1200} = \dfrac{149}{240}$

19. A die is rolled 200 times and its outcomes are recorded as below:

Outcomes	1	2	3	4	5	6
Frequencies	25	35	40	28	42	30

Find probability of getting:

(i)   An even prime

(ii) A multiple of 3.

[Board Term II, Set-RQTZFBW 2016]

Sol. (i) An even prime number *i.e.,* 2'.

∴   P(getting an even prime number) $= \dfrac{35}{200} = \dfrac{7}{40}$

(ii) Multiple of 3 *i.e.,* 3 and 6

∴   P(getting multiple of 3) $= \dfrac{40 + 30}{200} = \dfrac{70}{200} = \dfrac{7}{20}$

20. Two coins are tossed simultaneously 500 times, following are the outcomes

No head = 100 times

One head = 200 times

Two heads = 200 times

If the two coins are simultaneously tossed again, compute the probability of obtaining :

(i)   One head

(ii) Two heads

[Board Term II, Set-RQTZFBW 2016]

Sol. According to the question,

Total number of outcomes = 500

Let E_1 and E_2 be the events of one head and two heads respectively

The probability of getting one head

$$P(E_1) = \dfrac{200}{500} = \dfrac{2}{5}$$

and The probability of getting two heads

$$P(E_2) = \dfrac{200}{500} = \dfrac{2}{5}$$

21. A dice is thrown 100 times and the outcomes are recorded as follows:

Outcome	1	2	3	4	5	6
Frequency	25	20	12	18	15	10

If the dice is thrown once again, what is the probability of getting:

(i) even number   (ii) prime number

[Board Term II, Set-Z6K408K 2017]

Sol. According to the question,

Total number of outcomes

$$= 25 + 20 + 12 + 18 + 15 + 10 = 100$$

(i) P(Even number in a trial) $= \dfrac{20 + 18 + 10}{100}$

$$= \dfrac{48}{100} = \dfrac{12}{25} \text{ or } 0.48$$

(ii) P(Prime number in a trial) $= \dfrac{20 + 12 + 15}{100}$

$$= \dfrac{47}{100} \text{ or } 0.47$$

22. Three coins are tossed simultaneously 200 times with the following frequencies of different outcomes :

Number of tails	0	1	2	3
Frequency	35	45	42	78

Compute the probability of getting :

(i) at least 2 heads (ii) all heads

[Board Term II, 2017, Set-UAH4DQ7]

Sol. According to the question,

Total number of outcomes

$$= 35 + 45 + 42 + 78 = 200$$

(i) Probability of getting at least 2 heads

$$P(E) = \dfrac{200 - (42 + 78)}{200}$$

$$= \dfrac{80}{200} = \dfrac{4}{5}$$

(ii) Probability of getting all heads

$$P(E) = \dfrac{35}{200} = \dfrac{7}{40}$$

23. Following table shows the marks obtained by 30 students in a class test :

Marks obtained	70	58	60	52	65	75	68
Number of students	3	5	4	7	6	2	3

Find the probability that a student scores :

(i) 60 marks   (ii) less than 60 marks

Sol. According to the question,

Total number of students = 30

(i) Students getting 60 marks = 4

∴   Probability of getting 60 marks $= \dfrac{4}{30} = \dfrac{2}{15}$

(ii) Students getting less than 60 marks

$$= (5 + 7) = 72$$

∴   Probability of getting less than 60 marks

$$= \dfrac{12}{30} = \dfrac{2}{5}$$

Short Answer Type Questions-II
(3 Marks Each)

1. 1500 families with 2 children were selected randomly, and following data were recorded.

Number of girls	2	1	0
Number of families	475	814	211

Find the probability that a family chosen at random, having

(i) 2 girls   (ii) 1 girl

(iii) no girl

[NCERT Board Term II, 2014, KVS 2016]

Sol. Total number of families

$$= 475 + 814 + 211 = 1500$$

(i) Probability of choosing two girls

$$P(2 \text{ girls}) = \dfrac{475}{1500}$$

(ii) Probability of choosing one girl

$$P(1 \text{ girl}) = \dfrac{814}{1500}$$

(iii) Probability of choosing no girl

$$P(\text{no girl}) = \dfrac{211}{1500}$$

2. Two dice are thrown 400 times. Each time sum of two numbers appearing on the top is noted as given in the following table:

Sum	Frequency
2	14
3	20
4	32
5	45
6	62
7	65
8	60
9	43
10	36
11	18
12	5

What is the probability of getting a sum
(i)   5   (ii) more than 10
(iii) between 5 and 10

[Board Term II, 2012, (43, 45), Set-A1,2011]

Sol. According to the question,

Total number of outcomes $= 14 + 20 + 32 + 45$
$+ 62 + 65 + 60 + 43 + 36 + 18 + 5 = 400$

(i) $\qquad P(5) = \dfrac{45}{400} = \dfrac{9}{80}$

(ii) P(more than 10) $= \dfrac{18+5}{400} = \dfrac{23}{400}$

(iii) P(between 5 and 10) $= \dfrac{62+65+60+43}{400}$

$$= \dfrac{230}{400} = \dfrac{23}{40}$$

3. Following distribution gives the weight of 38 students of a class:

Weight in kg.	Number of students
31–35	9
36–40	5
41–45	14
46–50	3
51–55	1
56–60	2
61–65	2
66–70	1
71–85	1

Find the probability that weight of a student in the class is:
(i) at most 60 kg
(ii) at least 36 kg
(iii) not more than 50 kg.

[Board Term II, 2012, (28, 36) Set-B1, 2011]

Sol. According to the question,

Total number of students

$= 9 + 5 + 14 + 3 + 1 + 2 + 2 + 1 + 1 = 38$

(i) Number of students whose weight is at most
60 kg $= 9 + 5 + 14 + 3 + 1 + 2 = 34$

$\therefore$ Probability that weight of a student is at

most 60 kg $= \dfrac{34}{38} = \dfrac{17}{19}$

(ii) Number of students whose weight is at least
36 kg $= 5 + 14 + 3 + 1 + 2 + 2 + 1 + 1 = 29$

$\therefore$ Probability that weight is at least 36 kg $= \dfrac{29}{38}$

(iii) Number of students whose weight is not more
than 50 kg $= 9 + 5 + 14 + 3 = 31$

$\therefore$ Probability that the weight of a student is not

more than 50 kg $= \dfrac{31}{38}$

4. The given table shows the month of birth of 40 students.

[Board Term II, Set-LF0MCQ2, 2016, 2012, Set-08]

Month	Number of students
January	3
February	4
March	2
April	2
May	5
June	1
July	2
August	6
September	3
October	4
November	4
December	4

(i) Find the probability that a student was born in the month with 31 days.
(ii) Find the probability that a student was born in the month of February.

[Board Term II, 2012, Set-25]

Sol. According to the question,

Total number of students

$= 3 + 4 + 2 + 2 + 5 + 1 + 2 + 6 + 3 + 4 + 4 + 4 = 40$

(i) P(a student born in a month with 31 days)

$$= \dfrac{3+2+5+2+6+4+4}{40} = \dfrac{26}{40} = 0.65$$

(ii) P(student born in February) $= \dfrac{4}{40} = 0.1$

5. Fifty seeds were selected at random from each of 5 bags of seeds and were kept under standardised conditions favourable to germination. After 20 days, the number of seeds which had germinated in each collection were counted and recorded at follows:

Bag	1	2	3	4	5
Number of seeds germinated	40	48	42	39	36

What is the probability of germination of:
(i) more than 40 seeds in a bag?
(ii) less than 41 seeds in a bag?
(iii) 49 seeds in a bag?

[Board Term II, 2012, Set-20]

Sol. According to the question,

Total number of bags = 5

(i) P(more than 40 seeds in a bag) = $\dfrac{2}{5}$

(ii) P(less than 41 seeds in a bag) = $\dfrac{3}{5}$

(iii) P(49 seeds in a bag) = 0

6. On a busy road, following data was observed about cars passing through it and number of occupants:

Number of occupants	1	2	3	4	5
Number of cars	29	26	23	17	5

Find the chance that it has :
(i) exactly 5 occupants
(ii) more than 2 occupants.
(iii) less than 5 occupants.

[Board Term II, 2012, Set-12]

Sol. According to the question,

Total numbers of cars = 29 + 26 + 23 + 17 + 5

= 100

(i) P(exactly 5 occupants)

$= \dfrac{5}{100} = \dfrac{1}{20}$

(ii) P(more than 2 occupants)

$= \dfrac{23+17+5}{100} = \dfrac{45}{100} = \dfrac{9}{20}$

(iii) P(less than 5 occupants)

$= \dfrac{29+26+23+17}{100} = \dfrac{95}{100} = \dfrac{19}{20}$

7. In a Mathematics test, 90 students obtained (out of 100) the marks given in the following table:

Marks	Number of students
1–20	08
21–40	12
41–50	15
51–60	20
61–70	13
71–80	17
81–90	05

Find the probability:
(i) a student obtained less than 41.
(ii) a student obtained more than 50.
(iii) a student obtained between 41 and 80.

[Board Term II, 2012, Set-25]

Sol. According to the question,

Total number of students

= 8 + 12 + 15 + 20 + 13 + 17 + 5 = 90

(i) Probability of less than 41

$= \dfrac{8+12}{90} = \dfrac{20}{90} = \dfrac{2}{9}$

(ii) Probability of more than 50

$= \dfrac{20+13+17+5}{90} = \dfrac{55}{90} = \dfrac{11}{18}$

(iii) Probability of marks between 41 and 80

$= \dfrac{15+20+13+17}{90} = \dfrac{65}{90} = \dfrac{13}{18}$

8. Fifty seeds were selected at random from each of 5 bags of seeds and were kept under standardised conditions favourable to germination. After 20 days, the number of seeds germinated were counted and recorded as follows :

Bag	1	2	3	4	5
No. of seeds germinated	42	45	48	41	38

What is the probability of germination of:
(i) more than 40 seeds in a bag?
(ii) 49 seeds in a bag?
(iii) less than 40 seeds in a bag?

[Board Term II, 2012]

Sol. According to the question,

Total number of bags = 5

(i) There are 4 bags in which seeds are more than 40.

P(more than 40 seeds in a bag) = $\dfrac{4}{5}$

(ii) There is no bag of 49 seeds.

P(49 seeds in a bag) = 0

(iii) There is only one bag out of 5 in which seeds are less than 40.

P(Less than 40 seeds in a bag) = $\dfrac{1}{5}$

9. Marks obtained by 90 students in a particular subject out of a total of 100 are given below, find the probability that a selected student obtained marks 60 or above and a selected student obtained less than 40.

Marks out of 100	Number of students
0–20	7
20–30	10
30–40	10
40–50	20
50–60	20
60–70	15
70 and above	8

[Board Term II, 2012, Set-20]

Sol. Total number of students
$$= 7 + 10 + 10 + 20 + 20 + 15 + 8 = 90$$
Number of students obtained marks 60 or above
$$= 15 + 8 = 23$$
$$\therefore \quad P(\text{marks 60 or above}) = \frac{23}{90}$$
$\therefore$ Students who obtained marks less than 40
$$= 7 + 10 + 10 = 27$$
$$\therefore \quad P(\text{marks less than 40}) = \frac{27}{90} = \frac{3}{10}$$

10. Following is the data about the months of birth of 40 students in class IX:

Feb, Jan, July, June, March, Feb, Feb, Feb, Nov, Jan, Jan, Dec, May, June, June, July, June, Nov, Dec, June, July, June, Aug, Dec, June, Mar, July, July, June, Dec, Sep, Mar, Jan, Dec, June, Dec, Sep, March, Jan, Nov.

One student is chosen at random. Find the probability that the student chosen :

(i) was born in June.

(ii) was not born in the month of June.

[Board Term II, 2014]

Sol. According to the question,
Total number of students born
$$= 5 + 4 + 4 + 1 + 9 + 5 + 1 + 2 + 3 + 6 = 40$$

Month	Students born
January	5
February	4
March	4
May	1
June	9
July	5
August	1
September	2
November	3
December	6

(i) Let E_1 be the event of student born in June
$$\therefore \quad P(E_1) = \frac{9}{40}$$

(ii) Let E_2 be the event of student not born in June
Favourable outcomes $= (40 - 9) = 31$
$$\therefore \quad P(E_2) = \frac{31}{40}$$

11. A survey of 200 people was conducted about their preference of visiting various pavilions.

Pavilion	Good living	Delhi Pavilion	Toy Pavilion	Defence
Number of people	95	45	40	20

Find the probability that selected person visited :

(i) both Good living and Delhi pavilion.

(ii) only Defence pavilion

(iii) only Toy pavilion

(iv) both Toy and Defence pavilion

[Board Term II, 2014]

Sol. According to the question,
Total number of people $= 95 + 45 + 40 + 20 = 200$
(i) P(both good living and Delhi pavilion)
$$= \frac{95 + 45}{200}$$
$$= \frac{140}{200} = \frac{7}{10}$$

(ii) P(only defence pavilion) $= \frac{20}{200} = \frac{1}{10}$

(iii) P(only toy pavilion) $= \frac{40}{200} = \frac{1}{5}$

(iv) P(both toy and defence pavilion)
$$= \frac{40 + 20}{200}$$
$$= \frac{3}{10}$$

12. The weights of 60 persons in a group are given below:

Weight (in kg)	60	61	62	63	64	65
Number of persons	5	18	4	16	5	12

Find the probability that a person selected at random has:

(i) weight less than 65 kg

(ii) weight between 61 and 64 kg

(iii) weight equal to or more than 64 kg

[Board Term II, 2014, Set-20]

Sol. According to the question,
Total number of persons
$$= 5 + 18 + 4 + 16 + 5 + 12 = 60$$
(i) P(weight less than 65 kg) $= \dfrac{5 + 18 + 4 + 16 + 5}{60}$
$$= \frac{48}{60} = \frac{4}{5}$$

(ii) P(weight between 61 and 64 kg)
$$= \frac{4 + 16}{60} = \frac{20}{60} = \frac{1}{3}$$

(iii) P(weight equal to or more than 64 kg)
$$= \frac{5 + 12}{60} = \frac{17}{60}$$

13. A die is thrown 500 times. The frequency of numbers (1, 2, 3, 4, 5, 6) appearing on the uppermost face are given :

Outcomes	1	2	3	4	5	6
Frequency	89	75	78	73	88	97

Find the probability of having an outcome
(i) Number 3 on uppermost face
(ii) Number greater than 4
(iii) Number < 4
(iv) Number between 1 and 3

[Board Term II, KVS 2014]

Sol. According to the question,

(i) $P(\text{Number } 3) = \dfrac{78}{500}$

(ii) $P(\text{Number} > 4) = \dfrac{88 + 97}{500} = \dfrac{185}{500}$

(iii) $P(\text{Number} < 4) = \dfrac{89 + 75 + 78}{500} = \dfrac{242}{500}$

(iv) $P(\text{Number between 1 and 3}) = \dfrac{75}{500}$

14. Given below is the frequency distribution of salary (in rupees) of 80 workers in a factory.

Salary (in ₹)	1000–2000	2000–3000	3000–4000	4000–5000
Number of workers	12	18	22	28

If a worker is selected at random, find the probability that his salary is
(i) Less than ₹ 3000
(ii) More than or equal to ₹ 1000
(iii) More than or equal to ₹ 2000 but less than ₹ 4000. [KVS 2016]

Sol. According to the question,
Total number of workers = 12 + 18 + 22 + 28 = 80
(i)   Probability of getting salary less than ₹ 3000

$$= \frac{12 + 18}{80} = \frac{30}{80} = \frac{3}{8}$$

(ii) Probability of getting salary more than or equal to ₹ 1000

$$= \frac{12 + 18 + 22 + 28}{80}$$

$$= \frac{80}{80} = 1$$

(iii) Probability of getting salary more or equal to ₹ 2000 but less than ₹ 4000.

$$= \frac{18 + 22}{80} = \frac{40}{80} = \frac{1}{2}$$

15. Three coins were tossed 30 times simultaneously. Each time the number of heads occurring was noted down as follows :

0	1	2	2	1	2	3	1	3	0
1	3	1	1	2	2	0	1	2	1
3	0	0	1	1	2	3	2	2	0

Prepare frequency distribution table for the data given above. [Board Term II, KVS 2016]

Sol. Frequency distribution table for the given data as follows:

Outcomes	0 heads	1 head	2 heads	3 heads
Frequency	6	10	9	5

16. The following table show the daily earnings of 25 shops.

Daily Earnings (in ₹)	20–40	40–60	60–80	80–100	100–120
Frequency	5	13	2	3	2

What the probability that a shop earns :
(i) ₹ 100 and more
(ii) at least ₹ 60 but less than ₹ 80
(iii) less than ₹ 40

Sol. According to the question,
Total number of outcomes = 5 + 13 + 2 + 3 + 2 = 25

(i) $P(\text{Earning } ₹ \, 100 \text{ and more}) = \dfrac{2}{25}$

(ii) $P(\text{at least } ₹ \, 60 \text{ but} < 80) = \dfrac{2}{25}$

(iii) $P(\text{less than } ₹ \, 40) = \dfrac{5}{25} = \dfrac{1}{5}$

Long Answer Type Questions
(4 Marks Each)

1. A study was conducted to find out the concentration of sulphur dioxide in the air in parts per million (ppm) of a certain city. The data obtained for 30 days is as follows :

0.03	0.08	0.08	0.09	0.04	0.17
0.16	0.05	0.02	0.06	0.18	0.20
0.11	0.08	0.12	0.13	0.22	0.07
0.08	0.01	0.10	0.06	0.09	0.18
0.11	0.07	0.05	0.07	0.01	0.04

You were asked to prepare a frequency distribution table, regarding the concentration of sulphur dioxide in the air in parts per million of a certain city for 30 days. Using this table, find the probability of the concentration of sulphur dioxide in the interval 0.12–0.16 on any of these days. [NCERT]

Sol. Now, we prepare a frequency distribution table

Interval	Frequency
0.01–0.04	5
0.04–0.08	11
0.08–0.12	7
0.12–0.16	2
0.16–0.20	4
0.20–0.24	1
Total	**30**

The total number of days for data, to prepare sulphur dioxide

$$n(S) = 30$$

The frequency of the sulphur dioxide in the interval 0.12–0.16,

$$n(E) = 2$$

Hence, required probability

$$= \frac{n(E)}{n(S)} = \frac{2}{30} = \frac{1}{15}$$

2. A company selected 4000 households at random and surveyed them to find out a relationship between income level and the number of television sets in a home. The information, so obtained is listed in the following table :

Monthly income (in ₹)	Number of television/ households			
	0	1	2	above 2
Less than 10000	20	80	10	0
10000–14999	10	240	60	0
15000–19999	0	380	120	30
20000–24999	0	520	370	80
25000 and above	0	1100	760	220

Find the probability

(i) of a household earning ₹ 10000–14999 per month and having exactly one television.

(ii) of a household earning ₹ 25000 and above per month and owning 2 televisions.

(iii) of a household not having any television.

[NCERT Exemplar]

Sol. According to the question,

The total number of the households selected by the company = 4000

(i) The number of households earning ₹ 10000–14999 per month and having exactly one television = 240

$$\therefore \quad \text{Required probability} = \frac{240}{4000} = \frac{6}{100}$$

$$= \frac{3}{50} = 0.06$$

Hence, the probability of a household earning ₹ 10000–14999 per month and having exactly one television is 0.06.

(ii) The number of households earning ₹ 25000 and above per month and owning 2 televisions = 760

$$\text{Hence, required probability} = \frac{760}{4000} = 0.19$$

Hence, the probability of a household earning ₹ 25000 and more per month owning 2 televisions is 0.19.

(iii) The number of households not having any television = 20 + 10 = 30

$$\therefore \quad \text{Required probability} = \frac{30}{4000} = \frac{3}{400}$$

Hence, the probability of a households not having any television is $\frac{3}{400}$

3. Two sections of class IX having 27 students in each section appeared for mathematics olympiad. The marks obtained by them are shown below.

46, 31, 74, 68, 42, 54, 14, 61, 48, 37, 26, 8, 64, 57, 93, 72, 53, 59, 38, 16, 88, 56, 46, 66, 45, 61, 54, 27, 27, 44, 63, 58, 43, 81, 64, 36, 49, 50, 76, 38, 47, 77, 62, 53, 40, 71, 60, 45, 42, 34, 46, 40, 59, 42

One student is selected at random. Find the probability that selected student is :

(i) Having marks more than 49.

(ii) Having marks between 39 and 99.

[Board Term II, 2015]

Sol. According to the question,

Total number of students appeared in mathematics olympiad = 27 + 27 = 54

Class Marks	Tally Marks	Frequency
0–9	|	1
10–19	||	2
20–29	|||	3
30–39	ⅢⅡ	6
40–49	Ⅲ Ⅲ Ⅲ	15
50–59	Ⅲ Ⅲ	10
60–69	Ⅲ ||||	9
70–79	Ⅲ	5
80–89	||	2
90–99	|	1
Total		**54**

(i) P(Student having marks more than 49)

$$= \frac{10+9+5+2+1}{54} = \frac{27}{54} = \frac{1}{2}$$

(ii) P(student having marks between 39 and 99)

$$= \frac{15+10+9+5+2+1}{54}$$

$$= \frac{42}{54} = \frac{7}{9}$$

4. Following table shows the marks scored by a group of 90 students in a mathematics test of 100 marks:

Marks	Number of students
0–20	7
20–30	10
30–40	10
40–50	20
50–60	20
60–70	15
70–80	8

A student is selected at random. Find the probability that student has obtained :

(i) less than 30

(ii) 60 or more marks

(iii) between 40 and 70 marks

(iv) 70 or more marks.

[Board Term II, Set-LF0MCQ2, 2016]

Sol. Total number of student = 90

(i) Probability of less than 30 marks

$$= \frac{7+10}{90} = \frac{17}{90}$$

(ii) Number of students has obtained marks 60 or more marks = 15 + 8 = 23

Probability of marks 60 or more marks

$$= \frac{15+8}{90} = \frac{23}{90}$$

(iii) Number of students has obtained marks between 40 and 70

Probability of marks between 40 and 70

$$= 20 + 20 + 15 = 55 = \frac{20+20+15}{90} = \frac{55}{90}$$

(iv) Number of students has obtained 70 or more marks = 8

Probability of marks 70 or more $= \dfrac{8}{90} = \dfrac{4}{45}$

5. In class IX of 50 students second language opted by the students is as follows :

Sanskrit–14

Japanese–8

French–12

Urdu–6

Rest of than opted for German.

A student is selected at random. Find the probability that the student.

(i) opts for French

(ii) does not opts for Japanese

(iii) Either opts for Sanskrit or for German

[Board Term II, Set-I A21924, 2016]

Sol. (i) Total number of students = 50

Number of students who opted French = 12

Probability that a student selected opts

French language $= \dfrac{12}{50} = \dfrac{6}{25}$

(ii) Probability that a student selected does not opt for Japanese = 1 – selected student opts Japanese

$$= 1 - \frac{8}{50} = \frac{42}{50} = \frac{21}{25}$$

(iii) Probability that selected student either opts for Sanskrit or for German = Probability of student opts Sanskrit + Probability of student opts German

∵ Number of student who opted German

$$= 50 - (14 + 08 + 12 + 6)$$
$$= 50 - 40$$
$$= 10$$

∴ Probability that selected student either opt for sanskrit or for German

$$= \frac{14}{50} + \frac{10}{50} = \frac{24}{50} = \frac{12}{25}$$

6. The heights of the students of a class is measured and recorded as given below:

Height (in cm)	Number of students
120–125	7
125–130	7
130–135	11
135–140	3
140–145	5
145–150	9
150–155	8

A student is selected at random. Find the probability that height of the student is:

(i) more than 135 cm

(ii) at least 145 cm

(iii) less than 130 cm

(iv) 125 cm or more but less than 140 cm

[Board Term II, Set-RQTZFBW, 2016]

Sol. Total number of students

$$= 7 + 7 + 11 + 3 + 5 + 9 + 8 = 50$$

(i) Number of students whose height is more than 135 cm $= 3 + 5 + 9 + 8 = 25$

P(height of student is more than 135 cm)

$$= \frac{25}{50} = \frac{1}{2}$$

(ii) Number of students whose height is at least 145 cm $= 9 + 8 = 17$

P(height of student is at least 145 cm) $= \dfrac{17}{50}$

(iii) Number of students whose height is less than 130 cm $= 7 + 7 = 14$

P(height of student is less than 130 cm)

$$= \frac{14}{50} = \frac{7}{25}$$

(iv) Number of students whose height is 125 cm or more but less than 140 cm $= 7 + 11 + 3 = 21$

P(height of student is 125 or more but less than 140 $= \dfrac{21}{50}$

[Topic 2] Probability of an Event

Points to be Remembered

- A possible outcome or combination of outcomes is called an event.

- If probability of an event say A is 1 i.e., P(A) = 1, then even A is called a certain event or sure event.

$$P(E) = \frac{\text{Number of trials in which the event has happened}}{\text{Total number of trials}}$$

- The probability of an event lies between 0 and 1.

- The probability can never be negative.

- The sum of all the probabilities of all possible outcomes of an experiment is 1.

- P(E) + P(E') = 1

PREVIOUS YEARS'
EXAMINATION QUESTIONS
TOPIC 2

Multiple Choice Questions

(1 Mark Each)

1. In a survey of 364 children aged 19–36 months, it was found that 91 liked to eat potato chips. If a child is selected at random, the probability that he/she does not like to eat potato chips is

(a) 0.25 (b) 0.50

(c) 0.75 (d) 0.80 [NCERT Exemp.]

Sol. (c) Total number of children in a survey = 364

Number of children who eat potato chips = 91

Number of children who don't eat potato chips

$$= 364 - 91 = 273$$

∴   P(children don't like potato chips)

$$= \frac{273}{364} = 0.75$$

Hence, required probability = 0.75

2. Probability of an event E of an experiment is:

(a) $\dfrac{\text{Number of trials in which event E has not happened}}{\text{Total number of trials}}$

(b) Ratio of the number of trials in which event E has not happened to the total number of trials.

(c) $\dfrac{\text{Number of trials in which event E has happened}}{\text{Total number of trials}}$

(d) None of the above

Sol. (c) Required probability

$$= \frac{\text{Number of trials in which event E has happened}}{\text{Total number of trials}}$$

3. In a cricket match, a batsman hits a boundary 4 times out of 25 balls he plays. The probability that he hits a boundary is

(a) $\dfrac{4}{25}$ (b) $\dfrac{21}{25}$

(c) $\dfrac{25}{4}$ (d) $\dfrac{25}{21}$

Sol. **(a)** Total number of balls he plays = 25

Number of times he hits boundary = 4

$\therefore$ P(he hits boundary) = $\dfrac{4}{25}$

Hence, required probability = $\dfrac{4}{25}$

4. The probability of happening of an event is 37%. Then probability of the event is:
(a) 37　　　　　(b) 0.037
(c) 3.7　　　　　(d) 0.37

Sol. **(d)** Required probability = $\dfrac{37}{100}$ = 0.37

5. In a cricket match, a batsman hits a boundary 6 times out of 36 balls he plays. The probability that he did not hit a boundary is

(a) $\dfrac{1}{6}$　　　　　(b) $\dfrac{5}{6}$

(c) $\dfrac{6}{5}$　　　　　(d) 1

Sol. **(b)** Total number of balls he plays = 36

Number of boundary hits = 6
Number of times he did not hit boundary
$= 36 - 6 = 30$

$\therefore$ P(he did not hit boundary) = $\dfrac{30}{36} = \dfrac{5}{6}$

Hence, required probability = $\dfrac{5}{6}$

6. If E and F are the two possible outcomes of an event, then:
(a) P(E) = P(F)　　　(b) P(E) + P(F) < 1
(c) P(E) + P(F) = 1　(d) P(E) + P(F) $\leq$ 1

Sol. **(c)** P(E) + P(F) = 1

7. A machine generated these 10 codes:
{0A1, AAA, ABC, 2B1, 3B7, BB2, 1AC, 111, 222, 333}.

A code is drawn at random to allot an employee. The probability that the code have at least two digits is

(a) $\dfrac{2}{5}$　　　　　(b) $\dfrac{3}{5}$

(c) $\dfrac{4}{5}$　　　　　(d) None of these

Sol. **(b)** Total number of outcomes machine generated = 10

Number of favourable outcomes with at least two digits = 6

$\therefore$ P(at least with two digits) = $\dfrac{6}{10} = \dfrac{3}{5}$

Hence, required probability = $\dfrac{3}{5}$

8. In a One-Day cricket match, a batsman played 40 balls.

The runs scored were as follows :

Runs scored	No. of balls
0	13
1	15
2	5
3	1
4	4
5	2

The probability that the batsman scored no run is

(a) 0　　　　　(b) $\dfrac{1}{13}$

(c) $\dfrac{13}{40}$　　　　　(d) $\dfrac{2}{11}$

Sol. **(c)** Total number of balls a batsman played = 40

Number of runs not scored = 13

$\therefore$ P(batsman scored no run) = $\dfrac{13}{40}$

Hence, required probability = $\dfrac{13}{40}$

9. Packets of salt, each marked 2 kg, actually contained the following weights (in kg) of salt: 1.980, 2.000, 2.025, 1.850, 1.990, 2.040, 1.950, 2.050, 2.060, 1.980, 2.030, 1.970

Out of these packets one packet is chosen at random.

The probability that the chosen packet contains less than 2 kg of salt is

(a) $\dfrac{1}{12}$　　　　　(b) $\dfrac{1}{4}$

(c) $\dfrac{1}{3}$　　　　　(d) $\dfrac{1}{2}$

Sol. **(d)** Total number of salt packets = 12

Number of salt packets less than 2 kg = 6

$\therefore$ P(packet contains less than 2 kg) = $\dfrac{6}{12} = \dfrac{1}{2}$

Hence, required probability = $\dfrac{1}{2}$

10. In a class of 50 students there are 20% boys, then the number of boys in class are:

(a) 120 (b) 60

(c) 1.2 (d) none of the above

Sol. (d) Total number of boys $= 50 \times \dfrac{20}{100} = 10$

11. The following table shows the blood groups of 60 students of a class:

Blood groups	A	B	O	AB
Number of students	16	12	23	9

One student of the class is chosen at random. What is the probability that the chosen student has either blood group A or B?

(a) $\dfrac{1}{5}$ (b) $\dfrac{1}{30}$

(c) $\dfrac{7}{15}$ (d) $\dfrac{17}{30}$

Sol. (c) Total number of students in the class = 60

Number of students has either blood group A or B

$$= 16 + 12$$
$$= 28$$

$\therefore$ P(students has either blood group A or B)

$$= \dfrac{28}{60} = \dfrac{7}{15}$$

Hence, required probability $= \dfrac{7}{15}$

12. The salaries of 150 employees in an office are given below:

Salary (in ₹)	Number of employees
3000–6000	52
6000–9000	35
9000–12000	29
12000–15000	26
15000 and above	8

An employee is selected at random. The probability that his salary is ₹ 6,000 or more but less than ₹ 12,000 is

(a) $\dfrac{7}{30}$ (b) $\dfrac{32}{75}$

(c) $\dfrac{29}{150}$ (d) $\dfrac{58}{75}$

Sol. (b) Total number of employees in an office = 150

Number of employees whose salary is between ₹ 6000 and ₹ 12000 = 35 + 29 = 64

$\therefore$ P(employees whose salary is between

₹ 6,000 and ₹ 12,000) $= \dfrac{64}{150} = \dfrac{32}{75}$

Hence, required probability $= \dfrac{32}{75}$

Very Short Answer Type Questions

(1 Mark Each)

1. In a cricket match, a batswoman hits a boundary 6 times out of 30 balls she plays. Find the probability that she did not hit a boundary.

[NCERT]

Sol. Given, a batswoman plays 30 balls, therefore total number of trials = 30 and number of events of hitting the boundary = 6

Now, number of balls in which she is not hitting the boundary = 30 − 6 = 24

$\therefore$ The probability that she did not hit a boundary $= \dfrac{24}{30} = \dfrac{4}{5}$

2. A dice is thrown, what will be the probability of getting an even number?

[Board Term II, 2012, Set-20]

Sol. Total number of even numbers when a dice is thrown = 3(2, 4, 6)

Total number of outcomes in a dice = 6

Hence, required probability $= \dfrac{3}{6} = \dfrac{1}{2}$

3. If the probability of an event is represented by p, then $0 \leq p \leq 1$ is True/False?

[Board Term II, 2012, Set-24]

Sol. We know that the probability of an event associated with a random experiment lies between 0 and 1 (both included).

Hence, the given statement is true.

4. When a coin is tossed, the probability of getting a head is?   [Board Term II, KVS 2014]

Sol. When a coin is tossed, total number of outcomes = 2(Head or Tail)

$\therefore$ P(getting a head) $= \dfrac{1}{2}$

Hence, the probability of getting a head is $\dfrac{1}{2}$

5. A Mathematics book contains 250 pages. A page is selected at random. What is the probability that the number on the page selected is a perfect square?

Sol. Total number of pages, n(S) = 250 [given]

Now, numbers on the pages which are perfect square, are 1, 4, 9, 16, 25, 36, 49, 64, 81, 100, 121, 144, 169, 196, 225.

So, the total numbers on pages which are perfect square = 15

Hence, required probability

$$= \frac{\text{Numbers on pages which are perfect square}}{\text{Total number of pages}}$$

$$= \frac{15}{250} = \frac{3}{50}$$

Short Answer Type Questions-I

(2 Marks Each)

1. Eleven bags of wheat flour, each marked 5 kg, actually contained the following weight of flour (in kg) : 4.97, 5.05, 5.08, 5.03, 5.00, 4.86, 5.08, 4.98, 5.04, 5.07, 5.00

Find the probability of a bag chosen at random which contains more than 5 kg of flour.

[NCERT Board Term II, 2012, Set-06, 25]

Sol. Total number of wheat flour bags = 11

Number of bags more than 5 kg of flour bags = 6

Hence, probability of more than 5 kg of flour

$$\text{bags} = \frac{6}{11}$$

2. A and B are the only two outcomes of an event. Probability of (A) = 0.72, then what will be the probability of (B) and why?

[Board Term II, 2012, Set-01]

Sol. We know that

$$P(A) + P(B) = 1$$
$$P(B) = 1 - 0.72 \quad [\because \quad P(A) = 0.72]$$
$$= 0.28$$

Hence, the probability of B is 0.28 because sum of probability is 1.

3. In a group of 70 persons there are 15 boys, 20 girls, 30 men and rest women. Find the probability that a selected person is a woman.

[Board Term II, 2012, Set-69]

Sol. Total number of persons = 70

Number of women = 70 − (15 + 20 + 30) = 5

$$\therefore \qquad P(\text{women}) = \frac{5}{70} = \frac{1}{14}$$

Hence, required probability = $\frac{1}{14}$

4. A survey of 500 families was conducted to know their opinion about a particular detergent powder. If 375 families liked the detergent powder and the remaining families disliked, it, find the probability that a family chosen at random.

(i) likes the detergent powder.

(ii) does not like it.   [Board Term II, 2012, Set-01]

Sol. Total number of families = 500 and families liked detergent powder = 375

(i) P(likes the detergent) = $\dfrac{375}{500}$ = $\dfrac{3}{4}$

(ii) P(does not like the detergent)

$$= 1 - P(\text{likes the detergent})$$
$$= 1 - \frac{3}{4} = \frac{1}{4}$$

5. In a cricket match, a batsman hits boundary in 20% of the balls he played. Find the probability that he did not hit a boundary.

[Board Term II, 2012, Set-15]

Sol. Let a batsman played 100 balls.

Hits boundary = 20% of balls = 20

Balls does not hit boundary = 80% of balls = 80

$$\therefore \quad P(\text{not hitting boundary}) = \frac{80}{100} = \frac{4}{5}$$

Hence, required probability = $\dfrac{4}{5}$

6. There are 13 girls and 15 boys in a line. If one student is chosen at random, then find the probability that he is a boy.

[Board Term II, 2013, 2014]

Sol. Number of boys in a line = 15

Number of girls in a line = 13

$$\therefore \quad \text{Total number of students} = 15 + 13 = 28$$

Hence, probability of selecting a boy = $\dfrac{15}{28}$

7. Some bags of rice containing the following weights of rice (in kg):

4.97, 3.999, 5.05, 5.08, 5.03, 5.00, 4.35, 5.06, 5.00, 5.07, 5.04, 5.00, 4.098, 4.098, 5.001.

Find the probability that any one of these bag chosen at random contains less than 5 kg of rice.

[Board Term II, 2017, Set-Z6K408K]

Sol. Total number of rice bags = 15

Number of rice bags containing rice < 5 kg = 5

$$\therefore \quad P(\text{less than 5 kg}) = \frac{5}{15} = \frac{1}{13}$$

Hence, required probability = $\dfrac{1}{3}$

8. A box contains 50 bolts and 150 nuts. On checking the box, it was found that half of the bolts and half of the nuts are rusted. If one item is chosen at random, find the probability that it is rusted.   [Board Term II, 2017, Set-UAH4DQ7]

Sol. Number of bolts a box contains = 50

and Number of nuts a box contains = 150

Total number of bolts and nuts = 50 + 150 = 200

$$\text{Rusted bolts} = \frac{50}{2} = 25 \text{ bolts}$$

$$\text{Rusted nuts} = \frac{150}{2} = 75 \text{ nuts}$$

Therefore, total of rusted bolts and nuts

$$= 25 + 75 = 100$$

Let E be the event of selecting one out of them which is rusted.

$\therefore$ Number of favourable outcomes = 75 + 25 = 100

$$\therefore \qquad P(E) = \frac{100}{200} = \frac{1}{2}$$

Hence, required probability $= \dfrac{1}{2}$

9. A state government organised a survey related to family planning and its impact. In 1000 families, 650 families have 1 child, 250 families have 2 children and rest of families have more than two children. Find the probability of having

(i)   1 child

(ii) 2 children

(iii) More than 2 children

(iv) What value represents from this data?

Sol. According to the question,

Total number of families = 1000

(i) Number of families have 1 child = 650

$$\therefore \quad p(\text{having 1 child}) = \frac{650}{1000} = \frac{13}{20}$$

(ii) Number of families having 2 children = 250

$$\therefore \quad p(\text{having 2 children}) = \frac{250}{1000} = \frac{1}{4}$$

(iii) Number of families having more than 2 children

$$= 1000 - (650 + 250)$$

$$= 1000 - 900 = 100$$

$\therefore$ p(having more than 2 children)

$$= \frac{100}{1000} = \frac{1}{10}$$

(iv) This data represents that population should be control and small family is a happy family.

10. Three coins are tossed simultaneously 400 times and following frequencies of the outcomes were recorded

Outcomes	Frequencies
3 heads	103
2 heads	124
1 head	98
No head	x

(i) Find the probability of getting no head.

(ii) Find the probability of getting 1 head.

(iii) Find the probability of getting exactly 2 heads.

Sol. According to the question,

Total number of outcomes = 400

Now, outcomes for getting no head.

$$\therefore \qquad x = 400 - (103 + 124 + 98) = 75$$

(i) Probability of getting no head $= \dfrac{75}{400} = \dfrac{3}{16}$

(ii) Probability of getting 1 head $= \dfrac{98}{400} = \dfrac{49}{200}$

(iii) Probability of getting exactly 2 heads.

$$= \frac{124}{400} = \frac{31}{100}$$

Short Answer Type Questions-II

(3 Marks Each)

1. The distance (in km) of 40 engineers from their residence to their place of work were found as follows:

5	3	10	20	25	11	13	7	12	31
19	10	12	17	18	11	32	17	16	2
7	9	7	8	3	5	12	15	18	3
12	14	2	9	6	15	15	5	6	12

What is the empirical probability that an engineer lives

(i) less than 7 km from her place of work?

(ii) more than or equal to 7 km from her place of work?

(iii) within $\dfrac{1}{2}$ km from her place of work?   [NCERT]

Sol. Total number of engineers lives, n(S) = 40

(i) The number of engineers whose residence is less than 7 km from their place,

$$n(E) = 9$$

$\therefore$ The probability, than an engineer lives less than 7 km from their place of work

$$= \frac{n(E)}{n(S)} = \frac{9}{40}$$

(ii) The number of engineers whose residence is more than or equal to 7 km from their place of work, $n(F) = 40 - 9 = 31$

$\therefore$ The probability, that an engineer lives more than or equal to 7 km from their place of

$$\text{work} = \frac{n(F)}{n(S)} = \frac{31}{40}$$

(iii) The number of engineers whose residence within $\frac{1}{2}$ km from their place of work i.e.,

$$n(G) = 0$$

$\therefore$ The probability, than an engineer lives within $\frac{1}{2}$ km from their place

$$= \frac{n(G)}{n(S)} = \frac{0}{40} = 0$$

2. In a one-day cricket Match, Sachin played 40 balls and hit 12 sixes and Saurav played 30 balls and hit 9 fours. Find the probability that Sachin will hit a six in the next ball and also find the probability that Saurav will not hit a four in the next ball.

[Board Term II, 2014]

Sol. Total number of balls played by Sachin = 40

Number of balls on which he hit a six = 12

Let E_1 be the event of hitting a six.

$\therefore$ Number of balls on which Sachin hits a six = 12

$$\therefore \qquad P(E_1) = \frac{12}{40} = \frac{3}{10}$$

Now, total number of balls faced by Saurav = 30

Let E_2 be the event of Saurav did not hit the boundary

Number of balls on which Sachin did not hits a boundary

$$= 30 - 9 = 21$$

$$\therefore \qquad P(E_2) = \frac{21}{30} = \frac{7}{10}$$

3. A coin is tossed for a certain number of times. If the probability of getting a head is 0.4 and head appears for 24 times, find the number of times, the coin was tossed. Hence, find probability of getting a tail and verify that $P(H) + P(T) = 1$.

[Board Term II, 2014]

Sol. Let x be the number of times a coin is tossed.

$$\therefore \qquad P(H) = 0.4$$

and Number of favourable outcomes = 24

or, $\qquad P(H) = 0.4$

$$\Rightarrow \qquad \frac{24}{x} = 0.4$$

$$\therefore \qquad x = \frac{24}{4} \times 10 = 60 = 60$$

$\therefore$ The coin was tossed 60 times

Hence, number of times getting a tail

$$= 60 - 24 = 36$$

$$\therefore \qquad P(T) = \frac{36}{60} = 0.6$$

$$\therefore \qquad P(H) + P(T) = 0.4 + 0.6 = 1$$

Hence proved.

4. On the occassion of independence Day celebration out of 1200 students, 900 students took part in this celebration.

(i) Evaluate the probability that the students participated in celebration.

(ii) Evaluate the probability that the students not participated in celebration.

(iii) Which value is represented through this activity?

Sol. According to the question,

Total number of students = 1200

So, we can say that total number of trials = 1200

(i) Number of students took part in celebration = 900

$\therefore$ P(students participated in celebration)

$$= \frac{900}{1200} = \frac{3}{4}$$

(ii) Now, P(students not participated in celebration)

$= 1 - P$ (Students participated in celebration)

$$= 1 - \frac{3}{4} = \frac{1}{4}$$

(iii) This activity represents student's love for nation.

Long Answer Type Questions
(4 Marks Each)

1. Over the past 200 working days, the number of defective parts produced by a machine is given in the following table

Number of defective parts	Days
0	50
1	32
2	22
3	18
4	12
5	12
6	10
7	10
8	10
9	8
10	6
11	6
12	2
13	2

Determine the probability that tomorrow's output will have

(i) no defective part.

(ii) atleast 1 defective part.

(iii)not more than 5 defective parts.

(iv)more than 13 defective parts.

[NCERT Exemplar]

Sol. Total number of working days = 200

(i) Number of days in which no defective part produced = 50

∴ The probability that tomorrow's output will have no defective part

$$= \frac{50}{200} = \frac{1}{4} = 0.25$$

Hence, the probability that tomorrow's output will have no defective part is 0.25.

(ii) Number of days in which atleast one defective part produced

$$= 32 + 22 + 18 + 12 + 12 + 10 + 10 + 10 + 8 + 6 + 6 + 2 + 2$$

$$= 150$$

∴ Probability that tomorrow's output will have atleast one defective part

$$= \frac{150}{200} = \frac{3}{4} = 0.75$$

Hence, the probability that tomorrow's output will have atleast 1 defective part is 0.75.

(iii)Number of days in which not more than 5 defective parts produced

$$= 50 + 32 + 22 + 18 + 12 + 12$$

$$= 146$$

∴ Probability that tomorrow's output will not have more than 5 defective parts

$$= \frac{146}{200} = 0.73$$

Hence, the probability that tomorrow's output will not have more than 5 defective parts is 0.73.

(iv)Number of days in which more than 13 defective parts produced = 0

∴ Probability that tomorrow's output will have more than 13 defective parts

$$= \frac{0}{200} = 0$$

Hence, the probability that tomorrow's output will have more than 13 defective parts is 0.

2. Two dice are thrown simultaneously 500 times. Each time the sum of two numbers appearing on their top is noted and recorded as given in the following table:

Sum of numbers	Frequency
2	19
3	30
4	22
5	55
6	52
7	75
8	70
9	53
10	26
11	28
12	70
Total	**500**

If the dice are thrown once more, find the probability of getting a sum

(i) of 7

(ii) more than 11

(iii)less than or equal to 6

(iv)between 5 and 10   [Board Term II, 2015]

Sol. (i) Probability of getting a sum of 7 $= \dfrac{75}{500} = \dfrac{3}{20}$

(ii) Probability of getting a sum of more than 11

$$= \frac{70}{500} = \frac{7}{50}$$

(iii) Probability of getting a sum less than or equal to 6

$$= \frac{19 + 30 + 22 + 55 + 52}{500} = \frac{178}{500} = \frac{89}{250}$$

(iv)Probability of getting a sum between 5 and 10

$$= \frac{52 + 75 + 70 + 53}{500} = \frac{250}{500} = \frac{1}{2}$$

3. The marks obtained by 30 students in a competitive exam are given below:

Marks	70	58	61	52	65	75	68
Number of Students	3	5	4	7	6	2	3

One student is chosen at random. Find the probability :

(i) that the student scored more than 65 marks.

(ii) that the marks scored by the students is an odd number.

[Board Term II, 2017, Set-UAH4DQ7]

Sol. Total number of students in a competitive exam

$$= 3 + 5 + 4 + 7 + 6 + 2 + 3 = 30$$

(i) Let E_1 be the event of getting more than 65 marks

∴ Number of favourable outcomes

$$= 3 + 2 + 3 = 8$$

Hence probability of the event, $P(E_1) = \dfrac{8}{30} = \dfrac{4}{15}$

(ii) Let E_2 be the event of selecting a child having marks as odd number.

∴ Number of favourable outcomes

$$= 4 + 6 + 2 = 12$$

Hence, probability of an event i.e., $P(E_2)$

$$= \dfrac{12}{30} = \dfrac{2}{5}$$

4. A school organised an adventure camp for students to Kanatal. The following table shows the participation of students in different types of adventure activities:

Type I   → trekking

Type II   → trekking and mountain climbing

Type III   → trekking, mountain climbing and rappellings

Type IV   → trekking, rappelling and rafting.

Type of activities	Number of students
Type I	75
Type II	62
Type III	55
Type IV	36
All	22

Find the probability that the student chosen at random participated in:

(i) Type III activities.

(ii) All the activities.

(iii) Type I activity.

(iv) Type II and Type IV activities

[Board Term II, 2017, Set-Z6K408K]

Sol. (i) Let E_1 be an event of selecting a student doing type III actiivity

Total number of students = 250

Number of students participated in Type III activities = 55

Hence probability of the event,

$$P(E_1) = \dfrac{55}{250} = \dfrac{11}{50}$$

(ii) Let E_2 be an event of selecting a student doing all activities

Number of students participated in all activities = 22

Hence, probability of the event,

$$(E_2) = \dfrac{22}{250} = \dfrac{11}{125}$$

(iii) Let E_3 be an event of selecting a student doing type I activity.

Number of students participated in Type I activities = 75

Hence, probability of an event,

$$P(E_3) = \dfrac{75}{250} = \dfrac{3}{10}$$

(iv) Let E_4 be an event of selecting student participated in II and IV activities.

Number of students participated in Type II and Type IV activities = 62 + 36 = 98

Hence, probability of event,

$$P(E_4) = \dfrac{98}{250} = \dfrac{49}{125}$$

5. Cards marked with the numbers 2 to 101 are placed in a box and mixed thoroughly. One card is drawn from this box. Find the probability that the number on the card is

(i) an even number

(ii) a number less than 14.

(iii) a number which is a perfect square.

Sol. According to the question, the cards are marked from 2 to 101.

Therefore, total number of cards = 100

(i) There are 50 cards marked with even numbers from 2 to 101.

∴ $P(\text{getting an even number}) = \dfrac{50}{100} = \dfrac{1}{2}$

Hence, the probability of getting even number card is $\dfrac{1}{2}$

(ii) There are 12 cards on which marked number are less than 14.

∴ $P(\text{getting a number less than 14})$

$$= \dfrac{12}{100} = \dfrac{3}{25}$$

Hence, the probability that the number on card is less than 14, is $\dfrac{3}{25}$.

(iii) The numbers from 2 to 101 which are perfect square are 4, 9, 16, 25, 36, 49, 64, 81, 100. i.e., Squares of 2, 3, 4, 5, 6, 7, 8, 9 and 10 respectively.

Total number of cards having a number which is a perfect square = 9

∴   P(getting a number which is a perfect square) = $\dfrac{9}{100}$

Hence, the probability that the number market on the card which is a perfect square,

is $\dfrac{9}{100}$.

6. Given below is the frequency distribution of daily wages (in ₹) of 30 workers in a certain factory

Daily wages (in ₹)	Number of workers
110–130	3
130–150	4
150–170	5
170–190	6
190–210	5
210–230	4
230–250	3

A worker is selected at random. Find the probability that his wage is

(i) less than ₹ 150.

(ii) at least ₹ 210

(iii) more than or equal to ₹ 150 but less than ₹ 210.

(iv) in the interval ₹ 190 – ₹ 250.

Sol.   According to the question,

Total number of workers = 30

(i) Number of workers whose wage is less than ₹ 150 = 3 + 4 = 7

∴   Probability that a worker gets wage less than ₹ 150 = $\dfrac{7}{30}$

(ii) Number of workers whose wage is at least ₹ 210 = 4 + 3 = 7

Probability that a worker gets wage of at least ₹ 210 = $\dfrac{7}{30}$

(iii) Number of workers whose wage is more than or equal to ₹ 150 but less than ₹ 210

= 5 + 6 + 5 = 16

∴   Probability that a worker gets wage is more than or equal to ₹ 150 but less than ₹ 210

$= \dfrac{16}{30} = \dfrac{8}{15}$

(iv) Number of workers whose wage lies in the interval (₹ 190 – ₹ 250)

= 5 + 4 + 3 = 12

∴   Probability that a worker gets wage lies in the interval (₹ 190 – ₹ 250)

$= \dfrac{12}{30} = \dfrac{2}{5}$

Printed by Libri Plureos GmbH in Hamburg,
Germany